Eisenhower: At War
1943–1945

Eisenhower: At War
1943–1945

David Eisenhower

COLLINS
8 Grafton Street, London W1
1986

c ᶜ

312552

William Collins Sons & Co. Ltd
London · Glasgow · Sydney · Auckland
Toronto · Johannesburg

British Library Cataloguing in Publication Data

Eisenhower, David
Eisenhower at war 1943–45.
I. Eisenhower, Dwight D. 2. Presidents—United States—Biography
I. Title
973.921′092′4   E836
ISBN 0–00–217769–2

Made and printed in the United States of America
Book design by Bernard Klein

To Julie

Contents

Maps

Introduction

THIS book is the first of three volumes on the Eisenhower years. In 1974, when I first thought of undertaking this project, my idea was to do one book, shorter than this one, which would focus on my grandfather's second term. This was the year of Watergate, a turbulent year in politics and for our family especially. I was drawn to such a book because it seemed to offer a kind of refuge. More important, it seemed to offer perspective. Dwight Eisenhower's second term was a time of developments in civil rights, arms control, space and economics, and it featured a significant debate of America's national purpose which was a prelude to the upheavals of the sixties and early seventies.

But when I began to work on that smaller book in 1976, my research led me steadily back from the years when I knew my grandfather to years that I knew little about. I found that a book focusing on the second Eisenhower Administration could have an ending but not a beginning; that to understand the second Eisenhower Administration, the first had to be explored, and that if I were to describe the first term I would probably have to delve extensively into what my grandfather called his "war background"—specifically, the eighteen months covered herein. These are the months when Dwight Eisenhower shouldered perhaps the greatest responsibility of his career, a period when decisions were made and implemented by him and others which continue to shape the world. As I perused the record of the war years, their formative significance became manifest; so did the reasons Dwight Eisenhower chose to run for President, and the reasons his presidency took the course it did.

Though perhaps it was inevitable that I begin my grandfather's biography with the war, I reached the decision gradually and through trial and error. As I studied his second term I found that the real story of the 1956 elections, for instance, is interwoven with the Suez crisis. But I could not tell the story

of Suez without explaining the problems in NATO earlier that year stemming from U.S.-British-French differences over Third World questions,
East-West relations, control of the atom bomb and the related question of
newly sovereign West Germany's place in the alliance. All of this was in
turn related to the recently ended McCarthy period in American politics,
the Korean War, the fall of Nationalist China, Soviet development of the
A-bomb, and the Cold War that had emerged in the late forties. None of
these developments—all crucial—could I condense, and eventually I saw
that many important issues facing Eisenhower the President traced back to
his role as Supreme Commander, a role that I was forced to conclude had
not been fully understood by historians and not fully revealed by the memoirs of the major participants, including Eisenhower's own memoirs.

The most important omission in the accounts of Eisenhower's role in
World War II was the crucial bearing on his thinking and actions of the
German-Russian war on the eastern front. The omission is a key one. For
to underestimate the interdependence of the eastern and western fronts is
to overlook the fact that without a resurgent Russian front an Allied invasion of Europe would have been impossible, and that without the pledge
of Soviet cooperation in the form of a major simultaneous offensive on the
eastern front, the Allied landings in northwest France could not have
been undertaken when they were. To overlook this interdependence—and
Eisenhower's sensitivity to it—entails the risk of misunderstanding the
nature of Allied-Soviet wartime cooperation, and the evolution of the
postwar settlement. The ensuing Cold War is often explained as an unforeseen tragedy attributable to Soviet deceit or Allied blunders or a lack
of foresight on the part of America's wartime leadership, but the reality is
more complex.

It is apparent that the Cold War had all along been deeply rooted in
national and ideological differences with the Soviet Union that had been
well defined before the war and that almost, but not quite, made wartime
cooperation impossible between the Allies and the Russians. Indeed, the
prospect that U.S. intervention against Germany would contribute to a
Russian victory in Europe was perhaps the strongest element of the isolationist case against intervention before Pearl Harbor, and anti-Communism
was to remain a major constraint on Roosevelt's war policy thereafter,
making it exceedingly difficult for the President to adhere to his Europe
First policy. Tension between the Allies and Russians was constant from
1941 on, growing, it seems, even as—perhaps especially as—the goal of
wartime cooperation became a reality. But the important point is that the
eventual East-West split, whether inevitable or the result of misunderstanding, did not occur when it might really have mattered in the struggle against
Germany. Hand in hand with the story of Allied-Soviet tensions is the
unfolding story of grudging but effective Allied and Soviet cooperation in
World War II, and of argument between the two sides on the crucial points

of the evolving postwar settlement on which Eisenhower had effect as both Supreme Commander and President. In my opinion, any portrayal of Eisenhower as Supreme Commander that does not focus on the Russian problem and the various Allied responses to it is incomplete, for it was the complex Allied-Soviet relationship that forced Eisenhower to think as a politician and ultimately to assume political responsibilities by such actions as his decision to cede Berlin and Prague to the Russians.

Naturally, Eisenhower's wartime role had prewar antecedents as well. Conceivably, for the sake of a fuller account, I could have kept going back to Eisenhower's interwar military career set in the politics of the Depression era, to his early Army career and such formative episodes as his relationship with his mentor General Fox Conner, his commanding general in Panama. I considered beginning this book as biographies usually begin—with Eisenhower's birth. But my purpose was a book that was not strictly biographical. I was interested mainly in my grandfather's political career and the events that had a direct bearing on it. I concluded that while the war years are essential to illuminate Eisenhower's presidency, a detailed treatment of his earlier years is not. Dwight Eisenhower's early life is nonetheless fascinating to me. The town of Abilene, Kansas, provides a colorful backdrop for the saga of my grandfather's career. From stories I heard as a boy, I know that the Eisenhowers' sudden descent into poverty at about the time of Dwight's birth meant the end of a settled way for the family and was a strong motivating factor in the careers of the Eisenhower brothers. Tempered by hardships, Dwight Eisenhower matured from his rough-and-tumble boyhood into the man of determination and tenacity shown in these pages. But by his own reckoning, he was the beneficiary of circumstances in a larger sense. It was the war that propelled him from relative obscurity and deeply marked him, thrusting him into positions of great responsibility and pointing the way to future responsibilities—which are the subject of my next volumes.

Thus, I decided not only that it was important to cover the war in detail, but also that I would try to imagine how my grandfather experienced it daily: to study the reports and messages he read; to visualize or actually visit the places he visited; to chart the progress of his armies; to try to speculate, as he did, about German intentions, Russian intentions, and the deliberations of the Combined Chiefs of Staff—the American-British committee in Washington which acted as Eisenhower's supervising authority. Viewing the war this way, one can begin to gauge its full impact and to define the unfinished business: the problem of restoring devastated Europe and of defusing the dangerous tensions built up between the Western Allies and the Russians that threatened the peace and prolonged the climate of postwar disillusionment in Europe and America. Likewise, chronicling these events day by day, one can see what historian Robert Abzug meant when he observed that, at least from the American point of view, the war in

Europe was unimaginable, an experience often causing denial and disbelief, but awareness as well of "the fragility of life in a world where the possibility of evil had been irrevocably widened."

In a detailed study of World War II the political and military obstacles to Allied success also emerge. The more closely one looks at them, however, the less remarkable they seem. Why, after all, should we have intervened in Europe? The answer to this question, however clear-cut in retrospect, was not self-evident at the time. Was America menaced by German aggression? Even interventionists were hard put to argue that Nazi Germany, incapable of invading England in 1940–41, was capable of direct aggression against America and the Western Hemisphere, and even more hard put to argue so after the Germans became embroiled in war with Russia in June 1941. Thereafter, the millions who insisted that America had a clear-cut moral duty to aid England against the Nazis had to reckon with a new element: that U.S. intervention on behalf of England would have the further effect of saving Communist Russia and, indeed, that depending on the degree of its effectiveness, American intervention meant the triumph of Russia and the spread of Communism over vast stretches of Europe. On the other hand, it had been apparent for some time that the actual threat to liberty in Europe was not an expansionist Russia but Nazi Germany, which by late 1941 had conquered practically all of Europe by force or subversion, culminating in the fall of France and the evacuation of the British Expeditionary Force at Dunkirk in June 1940.

In the course of these disasters, it came to be seen that American vacillation and abstention had also been a factor in the Nazi triumphs. Thus, sooner or later, for obvious moral and political reasons, the Americans found that they could not stand by and permit even the temporary Nazi domination of Europe; that they had to assume a direct role in the defeat of Hitler. But recognizing and then backing this decision with "more than mere words" was a painstaking process. American intervention would neither come soon nor be large enough to permit the Allies to wage military operations or to frame a European peace independently of the Russians. One can see in retrospect that by late 1942 the triumph of the democracies over Hitler had probably become inseparable from the triumph of Russian Communism, an anomaly that was to be a major complicating factor in the conduct of the war and a source of endless troubles to come.

That this was so was never more apparent than on the eve of the momentous Allied decision to mount OVERLORD, code name for the Allied invasion of France in 1944. As late as the end of 1943, only months before the scheduled invasion, the bulk of American military resources were, in the main, still uncommitted to overseas destinations, and it was entirely possible that they would be sent to the Pacific at the expense of Europe. Simultaneously, it was evident after the pivotal Soviet victories at Stalingrad and later at Kursk in the summer of 1943 that Germany had been irrevocably checked by the

Russians on the eastern front, though not yet defeated. Moreover, for the Allies to invade France, Russian cooperation was essential, since the Allies still lacked the forces to invade France successfully without a concurrent Russian offensive, one that would prevent the Germans from reinforcing France while the Allied forces struggled to establish and expand a lodgement. Well-timed Russian operations thereafter would also be necessary to prevent the Germans from concentrating their forces for one all-out bid for victory in the west, wherein lay Germany's one hope for stalemate.

Would the Soviets cooperate with OVERLORD? This was an urgent question to be explored by Roosevelt and Churchill when they met with Stalin at the Teheran conference, called in late November 1943, by which time all parties recognized that the Russians had gained the upper hand in the east. But the real question at that conference—posed by Stalin—involved the central issue facing the Allies: whether in fact Roosevelt and Churchill considered the aim of defeating Germany quickly and unconditionally to be so important as to justify making common cause with Russia.

The long-range political ramifications of an Allied invasion of northwest France were now so obvious that they needed little elaboration at Teheran. For a time, OVERLORD would involve maximum military risks for the Allies. Success would therefore require the Allies to commit the bulk of their resources in France, a commitment that stood to benefit the Russians in two ways. First, OVERLORD, should it succeed, would eventually divert significant German forces from the eastern front, and thus enhance Russia's relative position. Second, OVERLORD, in requiring the Allies to commit forces drawn from their front in Italy, meant in all probability the Soviet conquest of southeastern Europe, the Balkans, Czechoslovakia and Austria, a probability greatly enhanced by the commitment made to Stalin at Teheran to secondary Allied landings at Marseilles—the so-called ANVIL landings. ANVIL was in effect a commitment to the Russians that the Allies, in sparing no effort to establish themselves in France, would not attempt to reinforce their Italian front with the aim of pushing it eastward. But the Allies would achieve their primary aim—that of assuming a major role in bringing about the defeat of Hitler, something that Roosevelt and Churchill deemed essential to redeem the French and British setbacks of 1938–41 and with it the prestige and self-confidence of the Western democracies.

Thus, Roosevelt and Churchill pledged OVERLORD accompanied by ANVIL, but not without misgivings. Churchill, for his part, had doubts about downgrading the Italian front on military and especially on political grounds, lest Stalin construe the Allied commitment to France to be a blank check and be encouraged to overreach. Roosevelt exhibited similar doubts, and the tension surrounding that conference leaves no doubt that it was a decisive moment. In the aftermath of Teheran, upon Stalin's demand that the Allies prove their determination by naming a commander, Eisenhower was elevated to Supreme Commander of OVERLORD. In reviewing the events of that conference and the weeks preceding it, I concluded that it was important to focus on the circumstances surrounding Eisenhower's appointment, to understand Eisenhower's role both as Supreme Commander and, by extension, as President. Accordingly, it was with the weeks preceding this conference that I decided to start this volume.

As my work proceeded, I drew up a very detailed chronology, juxtaposing the messages Eisenhower received and sent; the published and unpublished versions of the diary kept by his aide, Harry C. Butcher; Churchill's memoir, which includes hundreds of primary documents; the spare but valuable Summersby diary, the First Army diary; the available minutes of Eisenhower's conferences; the Brooke diary; the Patton diary; the weekly intelligence summary and daily reports; Eisenhower's letters home; and the weekly periodicals and the various memoirs and secondary sources. This was done in an effort to connect all parts of the story as they occurred, to observe the interplay of command, strategy and politics and to get as close as possible to Eisenhower and the personalities he dealt with. This account is based primarily on that material, though I rely as well on personal impressions, including memories of my grandfather.

I should add that in the years when I knew him, my grandfather rarely discussed the war in my presence. No doubt he had other things on his mind or perhaps I was too young, but I gathered that another reason was the intensity of his feelings on the subject. My grandfather looked back on the war with great pride. Indeed, one of my favorite rooms in the White House was the second-floor oval room adjoining his bedroom in which he displayed his wartime decorations and swords. Curious about the war, I had ample opportunity as a boy to explore his library of books on the subject and to spend Saturday afternoons viewing wartime documentary films. But somewhere along the line, I learned that nothing aroused Granddad's impatience—even anger—more readily than casual or ill-informed talk about the war. Perhaps it was impossible for anyone to grasp the true meaning of that event entirely to my grandfather's satisfaction, or perhaps Granddad was simply determined not to dwell on the past. In any event, my curiosity about the subject grew as time went on, a curiosity whetted by talks with my father and my fleeting but memorable exposure to some of the illustrious figures portrayed in this book.

To name a few, I can remember Field Marshal Bernard Montgomery's visits to America in 1954 and 1957. I vividly recall also the day in the spring of 1959 when I was excused from my fifth-grade class to spend an afternoon and dine with Sir Winston Churchill. In April 1960, President Charles de Gaulle visited our home on the corner of Granddad's Gettysburg farm. Two years later on a trip I took to Europe with Granddad, I was permitted to attend a luncheon he hosted at the Elysée Palace, at which I met General

James Gavin. James Gault, an occasional visitor at Gettysburg, was our host in Scotland on that same trip. From Scotland we journeyed on to London, where I was introduced to a number of my grandfather's wartime commanders, including Field Marshal Sir Harold Alexander and Air Marshal Sir Arthur Tedder. Others, including Generals Mark Clark, Elwood Quesada, Lyman Lemnitzer and Omar Bradley, were occasional visitors in Gettysburg in the next few years.

My interviews in connection with this volume included talks with General Clark. Though Clark does not figure prominently in *Eisenhower: At War,* he provided insights about the Eisenhower he had known well before the war and in North Africa. I had the opportunity of spending an afternoon with General Bradley, who conversed freely on subjects ranging from the African campaign to OVERLORD to Berlin. Twice I was a weekend guest in Santa Barbara, California, at the home of Harry Butcher, who described his long association with my family and his wartime friendship with Granddad. My grandfather's wartime valet, Sergeant Mickey McKeogh, gave me a day-long interview in which he discussed life in Algiers, at Telegraph Cottage and in Paris. Governor Averell Harriman granted me an interview in which he described his friendship with Eisenhower, which survived the vicissitudes of partisan politics. General Lucius Clay described his relationship with Eisenhower in their service together in Manila, in France during the war and during the German occupation. Clay also described his role as an informal political counselor during the 1952 campaign and particularly in the White House years. I spent time with Ambassador Robert Murphy, who was involved in the Darlan episode described in Chapter 1. In addition, I spent time with General Craig Cannon, who joined the Eisenhower staff in Bad Homburg shortly after the war and stayed on. I had many opportunities to visit Kevin McCann, who served Granddad as a speech writer and adviser beginning in 1945 and had innumerable insights on politics, on the war and the personalities of the era. General Lawton Collins granted me an interview on the subject of Normandy. And I interviewed General Alfred Gruenther, a fixture during the White House years who also served closely with Eisenhower in North Africa and Italy.

One could readily see why these strong individuals did not always agree and why in some cases their paths diverged after the war. But I sensed deep mutual respect and a bond based on their wartime service, which they could recall in detail thirty years after the fact. It was enough simply to meet some of the British and French figures of the war to see why the Americans held them in such esteem. And in interviewing my grandfather's American colleagues, I could sense their sureness as members of the generation who went to war and returned home, in the words of an American foreign correspondent, with "new notions about the earth, about people who were not American, not rich, not powerful, who represented a different race or faith . . . who left behind some of their own ideas and a great many dead comrades and . . . if [they] had not made the world safe for democracy, had at least helped rid it of an inhuman despotism."

But time did not stop in May 1945 and more was required of the war generation than ridding the world of an inhuman despotism. Despite differences, the victorious powers emerged from World War II resolved that such a war must never happen again. The last eighteen months of the war exposed sharp differences over how to accomplish this end. But again, a close reading of the Teheran conference and subsequent events suggests that the Americans, British and Russians were united on the basic objective— the unconditional surrender of Germany—and accepted the short- and long-range consequences of that policy.

What did unconditional surrender mean? As a practical matter, it was apparent all along that at a certain stage it would be advantageous to allow a German authority to step forward and agree to implement peace terms on behalf of the victors, which could hardly happen without negotiations. But negotiations with whom and over what? As it developed, unconditional surrender, which had all along been the basis for Allied-Soviet military cooperation, meant that the Americans, British and Russians would fight on until they could find a German—not Hitler—who would carry out the minimal terms completely agreed upon by themselves.

Inevitably, the only terms the Americans, British and Russians could agree upon were harsh ones, including stiff reparations, removal and trial of all Nazi officials, and the partition of Germany into military occupation zones that was likely to evolve into permanent partition. Logically, the Germans would fight long and hard to avoid these terms, and so unconditional surrender, then and later, was criticized for prolonging the war. From the Allied point of view, it was foreseeable that a prolonged war would not only magnify the destruction but invite a Russian invasion of Germany, making the partition of that country into zones—the key point—automatic and something that could not be bargained over. At Teheran, however, the Allied leadership had reaffirmed that decisive Allied action to bring about the defeat of Nazi Germany was clearly worth these consequences, which also included a greatly diminished role for a postwar Germany as a counterweight to Soviet power in Europe. In short, a formula for peace in Europe was implicit in unconditional surrender, as was a long-range accommodation between the Allies and the Soviet Communists, an accommodation that Roosevelt and Churchill had judged to be impossible between the Allies and Nazi Germany.

Such a course was bound to be controversial and hard to carry out. Perhaps it is a truism to say that Eisenhower's mission as an Allied commander was a political as well as a military challenge in that the political and military aspects of any conflict are interrelated. It is nonetheless the thesis of this book that the political and military challenges Eisenhower faced were exceptional, and that he met these challenges in ways that have not yet been fully understood, if understood at all. At no point did Eisenhower's forces enjoy the kind of local superiority that could have made his task an easy one. In the overall picture, it is essential to emphasize that Eisenhower's Allied army, though backed by tremendous air superiority, was vastly outnumbered by the German army as a whole and necessarily dependent on Russian action on the eastern front. This latter factor increased Eisenhower's political burdens at each step, burdens that were extraordinarily complex, to begin with. In nationalistic terms, Eisenhower had to reckon with the American and British concern for the safety of their respective forces. American and British political needs were distinct, and the long-range aims of the two nations were not identical. Simultaneously, Eisenhower had to contend with divided counsels in both camps about issues ranging from unconditional surrender to particular Allied objectives in both France and Italy. My grandfather's reticence, which was typical of the American and British military leaders, about any aspect of his job that could be considered "political," as distinguished from "military," makes it perilous at times to generalize. But the loyalty he felt toward his civilian superiors cannot alter the nature of his job, that in Eisenhower, as Catton wrote of Lincoln, "war and politics walked together . . . not merely hand in hand but in one body."

Thus, I have focused on the political aspects of Eisenhower's job. I have also focused on the related and long-standing controversies about Eisenhower's personal form of leadership, and his responsibility for the decisions that set the course of the war. I should say at the outset that Dwight Eisenhower poses problems for a historian because his actions do not clearly flow from well-defined positions toward day-to-day policy choices, a characteristic usually associated with great leadership. During the war, however, it is also plain that a man exerting visible and decisive leadership as advocated by the British—Brooke and Montgomery—could not have functioned. Such a style of leadership would have required complete unity within the Alliance, the unqualified control of all the military resources in the West and, probably, control of the preponderant Russian force facing Germany—none of which Eisenhower could have had. And yet, measured in terms of the mission assigned him in his directive from the Combined Chiefs of Staff (CCS) calling on him to seize a lodgement in France and, in conjunction with the Russians, to wage operations "aimed at the heart of Germany," it is clear that Eisenhower's leadership was successful.

I conceived this narrative in three parts. The first, consisting roughly of Chapters 1 through 5, covers Eisenhower's effort to consolidate his command: the preparations for the invasion, the landings and the battle of Normandy, a period in which Eisenhower sought to establish and expand his personal authority and to gain the initial successes necessary to establish northwest France as the main Allied theater. Possibly, OVERLORD could

have succeeded without the kind of integrated command Eisenhower tried
to achieve at SHAEF (Supreme Allied Headquarters). But OVERLORD was
hazardous, and forming an integrated command was inseparable, in his
opinion, from the problem of dispelling both American and British misgivings about an undertaking that many still felt was unnecessary or undesirable. His earliest test was his effort to persuade the CCS to grant him
temporary authority over the strategic air forces. It is apparent that Eisenhower was asking for unprecedented authority—probably more than was
strictly necessary. He did so, evidently, believing that he had to convince
all echelons of command in OVERLORD that the CCS was determined to
see OVERLORD through to success—indeed, that the CCS saw no alternative to OVERLORD. At the time, a program of strategic bombardment was
widely seen as a far less expensive, quicker and equally effective alternative
to a land invasion of western Europe. It was important to Eisenhower that
the CCS reject this theory, lest the Allied command, anticipating a change
of heart, fail to press land operations aggressively enough or risk the casualties inherent in the frontal strategy underlying OVERLORD. In the end,
Eisenhower prevailed in this debate, partly because of his positive outlook
and his habit of invariably assuming that his needs would be met. But it was
also soon apparent that every step toward consolidating an effective command brought with it new challenges.

Phase one of this book ends with the Normandy breakout, when the
all-out Allied commitment to northwest France became irreversible. This
victory also produced the first real cracks in Allied unity: the intense
controversy over the British proposal to abandon the commitment, made
to Stalin at Teheran, to bolster the landings in Normandy with ANVIL, the
secondary landings in the south of France. The British proposal to abandon
ANVIL at the risk of jeopardizing military cooperation with the Soviets was
one of the great controversies of the war, though it appears in retrospect
that there was never much question that ANVIL would be carried out. Also,
in retrospect, the British proposal to advance eastward instead from Italy
into Yugoslavia and Austria was idle from a military point of view, since
the Allies, committed as they were in Normandy, hardly had the resources
for such an undertaking. Thus, the British proposal to abandon ANVIL in
favor of a campaign into southeastern Europe seems to have been made
mainly for political reasons—to alert Roosevelt to the postwar consequences of ANVIL and perhaps to fix responsibility for the "loss" of Eastern
Europe on the Americans. For this reason, I have chosen to relate the
ANVIL controversy in considerable detail.

It is significant that Eisenhower, who had as great a stake in compromise
as anyone, saw no basis for one in the case of ANVIL. Eisenhower's crucial
decision to back ANVIL rested on military factors: that opening a secondary
front in France would ensure that victory in France would follow on the
heels of victory in Normandy; that a front in the Marseilles area would

strengthen the vulnerable Allied southern flank along the German frontier and open Marseilles as a port of entry for the American forces still in the United States, as well as for additional reinforcements drawn from Italy if necessary. Perhaps most important, ANVIL conformed to Soviet expectations, which meant that by not carrying it out, the Allies would jeopardize essential military cooperation with the Soviets later that year. Churchill opposed ANVIL almost to the end, and embraced it only several days before the actual landings, whereupon the ANVIL controversy faded. But the underlying problems—waning British influence within Allied councils and the long-range implications of the Allied course for Eastern Europe—remained. What would also remain and deeply affect Eisenhower's subsequent actions as Supreme Commander and later as President was his sense of personal responsibility for the political and diplomatic consequences of ANVIL.

The second phase covering Chapters 6, 7 and most of 8 concerns this new question: not whether the Allies would commit resources to France but how the Allied resources committed there would be used and who would control them. Once again, Eisenhower was building up his command in the belief that its unity and strength were essential to overall Allied success. Nor is it surprising that Eisenhower confronted an enervating challenge in Montgomery's effort to retain overall command of the Allied ground forces—American and British—which, in effect, would have elevated Eisenhower to a kind of figurehead, and reduced Bradley to be Montgomery's subordinate.

Having invested enormously in France, both the British and the Americans were concerned about the security of their respective forces and determined to assert their influence over the theater that would inevitably be the springboard for the final pursuit operations in the European campaign. The looming hazards of a fall campaign, following the frustrations of the six-week Normandy battle, contributed to the intensity of this debate. So did the sudden hope—which I think did not represent Montgomery's actual belief—that a Rhine crossing in Holland (Operation MARKET-GARDEN) to be followed up by a single massive Allied offensive toward Berlin in September 1944 would end the war, thereby avoiding a long campaign and preempting a Russian advance into Eastern Europe. Once again, as in the case of ANVIL, it appears that the British were posing the issues of Russia and Eastern Europe in the guise of a strategic choice, and once again forcing Eisenhower to confront the political consequences of his military actions—specifically, his decision to follow up the victory in Normandy with a broad-front offensive, rather than a single thrust as proposed by the British, that would clear the Germans out of France and establish the Allies in defensible positions along the length of the German frontier in anticipation of an eventual German counteroffensive.

Were the Germans on the verge of surrender in September 1944? Countless histories have documented the German conspiracy against Hitler, which was prompted by the hope that Germany might be spared a Russian invasion and partition if she came to terms quickly with the Allies. On the other hand, the Allies, committed to unconditional surrender, were doing nothing to encourage these hopes. Thus, barring a complete change of heart by the Allies, it was unclear what the conspirators hoped to gain, at least politically. Montgomery's assertion that in the weeks after Normandy the Allies had a passing chance to defeat Germany militarily seems similarly disingenuous. A close reading of the battle reports after Normandy available to Montgomery indicates that no general enemy surrender was in process, which was the only practical basis for his proposed thrust across the Rhine into Germany. It is also apparent from British accounts of those crucial weeks that Churchill and the British Chiefs of Staff quarreled over the wisdom of basing their strategic proposals and mobilization plans on the assumption of a quick victory. Significantly, Churchill opposed such an assumption as unrealistic. Presumably, he had misgivings about picking a quarrel over a strictly military question in a theater where the Americans, by September, were contributing the bulk of the forces and were necessarily committed to Eisenhower's more prudent course. Furthermore, Montgomery's cautious actions throughout those weeks contrast sharply with the boldness of his proposals. His apparent satisfaction with the token support Eisenhower offered him in late August in an attempt to resolve the dispute before it reached an impasse suggests that he was probably serving as a conduit for a high-level political initiative rather than as a military strategist. Finally, Eisenhower's undeviating view of Montgomery's "single thrust" concept for a dash to Berlin was negative. At no point did he see the possibility of success: on the contrary, he considered the idea "fantastic," and said as much to Montgomery, who nonetheless pressed on.

However fantastic it may have been, Montgomery's advocacy of a "single thrust" strategy was troublesome, as troublesome as Churchill's not dissimilar campaign against ANVIL, if not more so. It presented Eisenhower with several unattractive choices. One course was for him to approve the "single thrust" concept as a whole, which at no point did Eisenhower so much as consider. A second course—and the one Montgomery evidently hoped Eisenhower would take—would have been to refuse Montgomery's ideas flatly, which made sense on military grounds but was, in Eisenhower's opinion, impossible politically. For had Eisenhower refused Montgomery's proposals outright, Montgomery would have been free to maintain a steady drumfire of accusations, claiming that Eisenhower and the Americans had needlessly prolonged the war because of timidity, inflexibility, election-year politics, or indifference to the consequences of a long war. Churchill, of course, had made similar charges in the ANVIL dispute—but with one vital difference. Whereas ANVIL was a high-level contest over the allocation of forces between France and Italy, Montgomery's proposal involved the unity and discipline of American and British forces fighting side by side in France. Thus, in Eisenhower's opinion, to permit such recriminations would be an unacceptable burden on his command, and would hamper if not cripple essential unity by provoking wasteful and premature competition over the wrong objective—Berlin—at the expense of vital military action then and later that fall, and at the long-range expense of careful preparations for the eventual invasion of Germany, which Eisenhower felt must be closely coordinated with the Russians. Thus, Eisenhower, unable to say yes or no categorically, was left with a third course: calling Montgomery's bluff by authorizing MARKET-GARDEN, the preliminary phase of the "single thrust" concept, but doing so within carefully prescribed limits. Eisenhower's recourse was to allow—indeed, order—Montgomery to proceed with a doomed operation that would test the validity of his idea that the Germans were incapable of further resistance. This, in turn, would confront Montgomery with a choice: either to rescind his "single thrust" proposals entirely or to risk a severe if local setback in Holland. Either way, Montgomery would be effectively silenced.

Plainly, the MARKET-GARDEN affair, which involved a conflict between military expediency and the unity of Eisenhower's Allied force, could have no painless or completely satisfactory outcome. In the end, MARKET-GARDEN went forward and had the redeeming and intended effect of settling the issues of ground command and the broad front versus "single thrust" and of alerting Eisenhower's armies to the hard task ahead. But unity achieved at the seemingly needless expense of ten thousand casualties could not last, and the MARKET-GARDEN affair emphasized a definite time limit on inter-Allied cooperation once the crisis of the German winter offensive had passed.

The German Ardennes counteroffensives—the battle of the Bulge—stands midway between the second and third phases of the war. In one sense, the size of the German assault and its initial successes vindicated Eisenhower's earlier caution, for the battle made it clear that the Germans had been far from defeated and would have resisted an Allied attempt to take Berlin in September 1944. On the other hand, once the Americans had recovered from the initial setbacks, it became apparent that the Germans lacked the strength to sustain an all-out offensive in the west, rekindling the idea that the Germans might not have resisted a Berlin offensive effectively. The Allied check of the German offensive marked the beginning of the final phase of the war, one in which the Allies emerged with large armies on the border of Germany poised at last to gain any objective—perhaps many objectives—of their choosing.

How should the Allies exploit their freedom of action? It is apparent that Eisenhower's authority, which reached its zenith after the Ardennes, rested on two interrelated factors. First, the CCS was unable to unite on an alternative to his plans. Second, Eisenhower perceived that Allied indecision at this hour was in effect a decision by his political superiors to proceed with the policy of confining the Allied pursuit to "military" objectives—or, in other words, objectives calculated to produce unconditional surrender by the Germans rather than objectives that held out long-range advantages over the Russians such as Prague and Berlin.

But by March 1945 time was running out on Allied-Soviet cooperation and American attitudes toward Russia had definitely shifted, though attitudes at this stage were not yet policy. Churchill, for instance, emerged as a proponent of an Allied move on Berlin, ostensibly designed as before to preempt the Soviet occupation of eastern Germany and to gain decisive say over the crucial issue of partitioning Germany into occupation zones. Plainly, by March 1945, Churchill was concerned about the Russians and anxious for the Americans to adopt a new hardheaded negotiating posture. But under close analysis, renewed British pressure for a British-led thrust toward the German capital undermined what turned out to be Bradley's actual chance of reaching Berlin from the Ruhr. One must therefore assume that despite Churchill's urgings, the British were in fact lukewarm if not opposed to a Berlin campaign, or at least to a Berlin campaign under American auspices—an assumption borne out by Montgomery's cautious advance to the Elbe, which denied Bradley flank support for a move on Berlin, and by Churchill's private acceptance on April 19 of Eisenhower's fateful decision to halt Simpson's Ninth U.S. Army short of Berlin at the Elbe in mid-April, thereby ceding the city to the Russians. This, and Churchill's acquiescence on the same date, as well as Eisenhower's effort to barter Russian access to western Czechoslovakia and Prague for British access to Denmark, suggest that the real British concern in April 1945 was less far-reaching than generally understood or than Churchill later appeared to claim: evidently, the British aim was to ensure American support for British operations and attainment of minimum British objectives, including the occupation of northwest Germany and Denmark, rather to challenge the Russians for control of east Germany.

Throughout this phase, the American position was also ambiguous. Long before April 1945, it had become evident that the American Chief of Staff, General George C. Marshall, impatient to wrap up the war and alert to difficulties with the Soviets, was thinking along the same lines as the British, insofar as they were both interested in a speedy end to the fighting and in gaining diplomatic leverage over the European situation. In the end, however, while closely questioning Eisenhower's strategy, Marshall endorsed the operations Eisenhower set in motion in late March, operations away from Berlin and toward Denmark and Austria in the hope of avoiding a collision with the Russians, who were massing forces in the vicinity of Berlin. This suggests that the debates in the CCS over

Berlin and Eisenhower's freedom to deal with Stalin directly were probably not symptomatic of actual disagreement but reflected doubts about the
practicality of Eisenhower's plans and reluctance on the part of the CCS
to take formal responsibility for Eisenhower's strategy. Indeed, it is possible to view Eisenhower's role in this period as resembling one alluded to
at the beginning of this book when he accepted the support of the pro-
Vichy Admiral Darlan at the time of the Allied landings in North Africa
in November 1942, for here too Eisenhower implemented a policy agreed
upon by his superiors in a manner that did not directly commit them and
compromise their ability to disavow bad results. But the parallel is inexact. Eisenhower's relationship with the CCS in the Darlan affair cannot
be compared with that relationship in April 1945 when the Allied and
Soviet armies overran Germany. In the course of two and a half years,
Eisenhower's stature had grown, and by then he was acting in the void
left by Roosevelt's illness and death.

In any event, the final advance into Germany proceeded smoothly in
cooperation with the Russians, which is testimony to Eisenhower's military
judgment, his leadership, his skill in anticipating the wishes of his superiors
and, above all, to his loyalty to the basic aims of the CCS, all of which he
perhaps demonstrated most dramatically by his decision to halt his armies
short of Berlin. For it is apparent that by then Eisenhower enjoyed far
greater latitude than at any time before and was in a position to find
"military" reasons for taking Berlin, or, at a minimum, to absolve himself
of responsibility for its loss to the Russians by mounting a serious attempt
to take the city. By not doing so, Eisenhower exhibited more than skill in
serving his superiors. He assumed personal responsibility for the consequences and, with Roosevelt's death, responsibility as well for the consequences of unconditional surrender and the policy of cooperating with the
Soviets toward this end. In this way, Eisenhower assumed a political burden, as events in the years ahead would show.

The purpose of this detailed narrative of my grandfather's role as Supreme Commander is to provide the setting for his years in the White
House. I have tried to convey the essence of the research material: the
incredible complexity of the war in Europe, the complexity of my grandfather's role in it, and the grimness of that war relieved by the heroism and
high purpose exhibited by the soldiers and statesmen who successfully
fulfilled their appointed tasks. Specifically, my purpose has been to give a
sense of my grandfather's perspective—what he did and why, and the
responsibilities he assumed along the way which led him to seek the presidency.

It is significant that the fifteen-year interval separating the end of the
Eisenhower Administration and the events recounted in this book is
roughly the same interval separating the end of the Vietnam war and today.
One can now see that Eisenhower's task as President was to manage the

aftereffects of the war in Europe: to promote the reconstruction of Europe, to bring about an end to the wartime debates, to defuse the Cold War and to respond to the "sharp and apparent need" for a genuine world community backed by a sustained American commitment to world betterment of the kind that he discussed with Brooke and Churchill in the dark days of mid-December 1944. It was on the eve of the German winter offensive that Eisenhower for the first time expressed his resolve to remain active after the war and described his commitment to the cause of Anglo-American relations, which he saw as a responsible postwar position for America, and as a precedent for efforts to draw the Russians out of their dangerous isolation and for wider international cooperation.

As President, Eisenhower pursued these goals steadily. That he left office sixteen years later without ending the Cold War caused him to warn his countrymen in his farewell address to be alert to the implications for American democracy of what had evolved into an apparently permanent struggle. In later years his farewell would be recalled because of his warnings about the military industrial complex and the dangers of overreacting to foreign crises. But in the same speech, as he reflected upon his career, Eisenhower emphasized the inescapable obligations America had assumed in his lifetime: how the record of decades stood as proof, as he put it, that America's supreme goals as a free society could not be pursued in isolation but had become inseparable from America's need "to enhance liberty, dignity and integrity among peoples and among nations."

It is this latter theme of Eisenhower's farewell reflections that matters in these pages. *Eisenhower: At War* is an account of Eisenhower's striving during the mightiest and most complex military intervention across oceans ever attempted. In writing about it, I have tried to present the controversies in full, mindful that they persist but mindful also that the intervention served its purpose, and that it summoned "the emotional and transitory sacrifices of crisis," the energies needed to rebuild and the high purpose necessary to set the world on a course toward an era of progress and reconciliation.

In writing *Eisenhower: At War,* I received help and encouragement from many people. Kate Kernan spent a year doing research, which included several productive months at the Eisenhower Library in Abilene, Kansas, gathering key documents not only for this volume but also for future ones. I am grateful to David Haight of the Eisenhower Library for his assistance during my five trips to Abilene, and to Hugh Hewitt and Brian Gleason for undertaking specific research projects during the writing of this book. Colonel Harry Summers of the Army War College and Drew Middleton of the *New York Times* read the manuscript to check its accuracy, and contributed suggestions.

Dr. Karl von Vorys, professor of political science at the University of

Pennsylvania, spent many hours with me discussing the issues raised in this book.

My father-in-law, former President Richard Nixon, was enthusiastic about this project from its inception and was a strong source of encouragement and ideas as each year I delved further into research and rewriting.

My parents lent time and encouragement throughout. My father's unique perception of his father, and his military and political insights into this era, are crucial to this book.

There are two people without whose help and belief in this project there would be no book: first, my wife, Julie, whose assistance ranged from doing assorted research tasks to editing my numerous drafts while making our home a happy and productive environment; and, second, my editor, Jason Epstein, who has guided and prodded me at every step along this journey. Their encouragement and help have been indispensable in the writing of *Eisenhower: At War.*

Eisenhower: At War
1943–1945

1

"What Is His Name?"

I N the autumn of 1943 Allied Forces Headquarters, Algiers, was a magnet for prominent visitors. October brought the last stretch of good weather along the famed Turquoise Coast of Algeria before the onset of the gray, raw, rainy winter. The rapid-fire events of recent weeks—Mussolini's overthrow, the Italian armistice, and the Allied landings at Taranto and Salerno had receded, and the war on the central Italian front had settled into a slow struggle over hard mountainous terrain laced with rivers and marshes.

At his spacious offices in the luxurious St. Georges Hotel in the center of the city, General Dwight D. Eisenhower played host. Congressional delegations arrived at theater headquarters for briefings. Members of the American and British press passed through, as did businessmen on assignment for wartime agencies, and an unusual number of diplomats and Cabinet officials from Washington and London. The comings and goings of high-level officials indicated far-reaching decisions in the wind.

The war was entering a new phase. In late October the foreign ministers of the United States, Britain and the Soviet Union were to gather in Moscow. Rumor had it that arrangements would be made for a long-overdue first meeting of Stalin, Churchill and Roosevelt to iron out Allied-Soviet difficulties and to coordinate the actions of the Russian and Allied armies. Hand in hand with the advances on all fronts that summer, Allied-Soviet relations had sunk to a wartime low amid Soviet recriminations over the inability of the Western Allies to land in northwest France and open the long-promised "second front," and looming disputes over the future of Poland and the German satellites. Eisenhower's visitors told of the dismay in Washington and London over how arrogantly assertive the Soviets had become since the Russian victories that summer, an attitude fed by comparisons between the powerful Red Army drive then under way toward Kiev and the Allied halt south of Rome.

The St. Georges Hotel was a heavily guarded compound near the Boulevard de Telemny in the modern city center. Visitors entered through large wrought-iron gates and drove along a pebbled driveway that led to a long terrace overlooking lush gardens of palms and bougainvillaea, which bloomed year-round. The first floor and lobby of the hotel had been converted into rows of cramped offices. At the head of a grand staircase, in a second-floor suite tucked behind an anteroom, Eisenhower punctually kept his daily appointments. Next to a small file cabinet, he sat at a clean desk, its only adornment a framed picture of his wife, Mamie Doud Eisenhower. On the facing wall hung a map of Italy, a photograph of President Franklin D. Roosevelt, and a print of French soldiers marching arm in arm beneath the motto *"Tous Ensemble Nous Vaincrons."*

Eisenhower, fifty-three years old, made a strong first impression, one that combined informality with reserve and dignity. His trim battle dress of khaki breeches, sharply creased, and a short plain tunic, the so-called Eisenhower jacket, accentuated a powerful, athletic build. He had striking bright blue eyes, a firm jaw, thinning blond hair and unusually large and expressive hands, which he used to emphasize his points in conversation. "Accustomed to command," he spoke with frankness, earnestness and goodwill, but rarely with humor. And in his twelve months at AFHQ, Eisenhower had gained a reputation as a first-class military organizer and skilled diplomat.

Speculation now centered on the forthcoming Allied invasion of France. Shortly after the Salerno landings in September, Norman Davis, president of the American Red Cross, had visited with news about the recent talks in Quebec, where Churchill and Roosevelt had reaffirmed plans for a cross-Channel invasion of France, code-named OVERLORD, by May 1944 with simultaneous landings in southern France (ANVIL). Davis had alluded to Anglo-American differences at Quebec, however, and the controversy in Washington over the proper approach to be adopted toward the Russians, now that diplomatic-military discussions were inevitable.

British misgivings about the Quebec decisions were evident. On October 1 the venerable South African Field Marshal Jan Smuts visited Eisenhower midway on a journey to London to assume full membership in the British War Cabinet. Skeptical of the cross-Channel project, Smuts solicited Eisenhower's views on the prospects for an early capture of Rome. Two days later Lord Louis Mountbatten, a good friend, stopped off en route to New Delhi to assume command of the Burma-Thailand theater. Mountbatten sought Eisenhower's advice on running an Allied command, then at dinner brought Eisenhower up to date on the situation in London.

Doubts persisted in London about OVERLORD, and the wisdom of an ironclad commitment to it at the expense of ongoing operations in Italy. In view of recent German reverses, who could say that by May 1944 OVERLORD would be necessary? On the other hand, who could be sure that the

Germans would not recover on all fronts, or that satisfactory Russian military cooperation with the Allies could be worked out, either of which would make OVERLORD impractical? Invasion planning was in the doldrums until a solution could be found to unforeseen shortages of landing craft that would soon hamper operations in all theaters. In British minds, the landing-craft situation raised additional questions about the ANVIL landings in the south of France, a contingency agreed upon at Quebec before the Americans and British could evaluate the possibilities in Italy and the Balkans, and the outcome of the summer battles in Russia.

On the fourth the chairman of the War Production Board, Donald Nelson, stopped off on his way to Moscow for talks about Lend-Lease scheduling. Nelson explained the thinking behind the sudden spate of optimistic war forecasts in the Allied press and semipublic suggestions that OVERLORD might prove unnecessary, after all. In London he had been briefed on detailed plans for POINTBLANK, the combined American-British strategic-bombing offensive against Germany set to be in full swing by late November. The Air Staffs, pleased by the results of recent raids on German cities and industrial targets, planned to follow up with concentrated attacks on ball-bearing and airframe plants for several weeks, which would open the door to the potentially decisive attacks on "morale targets" and critical industries. There was talk the war would be over by Christmas, and Nelson did not doubt it.

U.S. Secretary of the Navy Colonel Frank Knox, a visitor on October 6, discounted the Air Staff plans. He told Eisenhower that the American Joint Chiefs were convinced that the cross-Channel invasion of France would prove necessary. Knox intimated that Army Chief of Staff General George C. Marshall would probably be leaving Washington shortly to assume command of the invasion forces in England, despite newspaper gossip to the contrary.

Harrison Salisbury, London manager of United Press, stopped over on his way to Moscow. General Brehon Somervell, a candidate to succeed Marshall as Army Chief of Staff, also visited on his way to Moscow. In addition, Eisenhower received Niles Trammel, president of NBC, and General Leonard "Gee" Gerow, an old Army friend, now in command of the 29th Division in England and awaiting Corps command in the cross-Channel invasion. On the fifteenth Secretary of State Cordell Hull passed through on his way to Moscow, accompanied by W. Averell Harriman, the newly designated U.S. ambassador to the USSR. Harriman confided that Marshall's appointment was set, which he felt would end the suspense and make his job of dealing with the Russians easier.

Later that day Eisenhower kept an appointment with Secretary of the Treasury Henry Morgenthau, a meeting of special significance. Eleven months earlier, Morgenthau had been the leading critic in the Cabinet of the so-called Darlan Deal, the accord struck between AFHQ and Vichy

Defense Minister Admiral Jean-François Darlan during the Allied landings at Casablanca, Oran and Algiers, code-named TORCH. In exchange for Darlan's aid in persuading Vichy officials to call off French armed resistance against the Allied invasion force, Eisenhower had agreed to appoint Darlan civil administrator of the French colonies in North Africa and leave in place a host of incumbent pro-Vichy colonial officials.

The Darlan Deal had been Eisenhower's precarious baptism in wartime diplomatic politics. With news of it, the American and British press harshly denounced the bargain, accusing AFHQ and Eisenhower of "trucking with fascism." In the prolonged uproar, Roosevelt and Churchill had been moved to consider disavowing the accord, but deferred, reluctantly, to Eisenhower's entreaties that the cooperation of the Vichy officials was indispensable to the success of TORCH and protection of Allied supply lines stretching 900 miles from Casablanca to central Tunisia. Over Morgenthau's objections, Roosevelt had belatedly endorsed the accord, calling it a "temporary expedient justified solely by the stress of battle." But the Vichy controversy had remained intense all winter, ending only with the Axis capitulation at Tunis in May.

Now, however, the Darlan episode was a fading memory. Morgenthau, who had urged Eisenhower's relief from command over the affair, arrived bearing a private note from the President that obliquely confirmed what Eisenhower had surely anticipated: a meeting with Roosevelt, Churchill and Stalin was imminent, and Secretary of State Cordell Hull was traveling to Moscow to arrange the details. Soon the three powers would reach final decisions on the grand strategy for 1944, which Eisenhower assumed meant the long-planned cross-Channel invasion of northwest France. "Dear Ike," Roosevelt wrote:

> Henry Morgenthau, Jr. will be in the Mediterranean area soon and I hope you will be able to give him all the information in regard to currency exchange in economic matters. Also give him the lowdown on the attitude of the French.
> Don't tell anybody it is possible that I may see you in a little over a month— possibly in North Africa.
> My best wishes to you,
>
> Franklin Roosevelt

The October lull at AFHQ was both unexpected and unwelcome. The parade of visitors underscored the 600 miles separating Algiers and the battlefront to the northeast. Logistics had not kept pace with the advance. And so while the St. Georges remained the nominal nerve center of the Allied war effort, General Alexander's 15th Army Group Headquarters in Naples gradually assumed real direction of the battle.

In Algiers, the battle seemed to grow more remote with each day. Talk in the city centered on the struggle between General Henri Giraud and De Gaulle for control of the Algiers-based French Committee of National Liberation, capped by De Gaulle's bid that month to consolidate the civil and military affairs of the committee under "a single strong executive." A solitary barrage balloon on the Bay of Algiers was a remnant of times when the ancient harbor and city lay within range of German airfields in Tunisia and Sardinia. Other remnants were the heavily armed sentries at the St. Georges Hotel, and the anti-aircraft nests surrounding the Villa dar el Ouad, Eisenhower's private cottage in the outskirts set on a hill overlooking the alabaster city.

In the privacy of the villa, Eisenhower chafed at his confinement. He restlessly deplored the "military tendency to become entrenched in a single location" and directed his staff to begin laying plans to transfer AFHQ offices to Naples. Naval Commander Harry C. Butcher, his aide-de-camp, listened sympathetically and faithfully chronicled these complaints in the detailed dairy he had been keeping for months, complaints that were familiar, and understandable.

Butcher had been a close and trusted friend for eighteen years. Raised and educated in Iowa, he had gone to Washington in the twenties, originally as a journalist for an agricultural publication. Charming, shrewd and a raconteur, Butcher rose quickly in Washington, showing a knack for making influential friends, among them New Deal Press Secretary Stephen Early, FDR confidant and fellow Iowan Harry Hopkins, and Milton Eisenhower, a high-level official in the Department of Agriculture, who in 1928 introduced him to his older brother Major Dwight Eisenhower, then a student at the Army War College.

Butcher had first known Eisenhower as an extroverted staff officer, a low-stakes poker player, a hail-fellow-well-met at Prohibition parties, known for his lusty, atonal rendition of "Abdullah Bulbul Amir" to the thirty-eighth verse. Later, in the mid-thirties, Butcher had known Eisenhower as an ambitious, hard-driving assistant on the personal staff of Army Chief of Staff Douglas MacArthur. In early 1942 Butcher, by now a vice president at CBS, had again met Eisenhower, this time when he was a brigadier general on Marshall's staff spending eighteen hours a day on the Far East crisis and on negotiations with the British on the American military build-up in England. In June 1942, when he was appointed to command the European Theater of Operations, Eisenhower had asked Admiral Ernest King to depart from strict protocol and permit Butcher, now a commander in the U.S. Navy, to serve as his aide in London. King consented, and so Eisenhower and Butcher embarked for England together.

In the fifteen months since, Butcher had kept the diary, served as staff troubleshooter and handled the press, and had taken upon himself the job of looking after Eisenhower's well-being. And now, in October 1943,

Butcher fretted that Eisenhower, smoking four packs of cigarettes a day, sleeping intermittently, plagued with a chronic cold and worn down by two years of continuous pressure, was near exhaustion.

The past four months had been the most demanding of all. Since the Axis surrender at Tunis on May 31, Eisenhower had commanded the assault on the offshore Italian island of Pantelleria, the massive eight-division landings on Sicily and the ensuing thirty-day campaign to clear the island. In early September, he had conducted the clandestine Italian armistice talks, commanded the British Eighth Army landings at Taranto and Calabria, followed by the U.S. Fifth Army landings at Salerno, which proved to be a near disaster.

Salerno cast a long shadow over Allied deliberations and would do so for months. The German stand at Salerno, some worried, was just a foretaste of what the Allies could expect if they tempted fate by landing in northwest France. Eisenhower, on the other hand, attributed the near catastrophe to more technical factors—namely, his inability to command adequate resources from higher authority. This stemmed from two basic problems: first, American-British differences over objectives in Italy heightened by the fluid situation after Mussolini's overthrow, a situation that could not be helped; second, the growing reluctance to subordinate the air wing in support of land operations, which was due, in Eisenhower's opinion, to indecision about objectives, overconfidence about the effectiveness of strategic air operations and to reluctance in both Allied capitals to delegate essential authority to a theater commander.

Would Salerno would prove to be unique? Allied indecision had been understandable. The final decision to invade the Italian mainland, reached at the mid-August Quebec meetings, had coincided with Italian surrender overtures, which held out prospects ranging from full Italian help in occupying Italy as far north as Florence to the breakdown of talks and all-out Italian resistance backed by German reinforcements moving south through the Brenner Pass. Churchill had seized on the negotiations to press for ambitious landings and a dash on Rome. Marshall and the American Joint Chiefs, concerned about the German build-up, had opposed the risk of an expanded military commitment in the Mediterranean that might jeopardize the mid-October deadline for withdrawing aircraft, divisions and landing craft earmarked for POINTBLANK and OVERLORD. Finally, the two sides had compromised and ordered Eisenhower to mount landings in Italy but without amending the October deadline or adopting a clear set of objectives beyond forcing an Italian capitulation. Meanwhile, six heavy-bomber groups needed in Italy had left for England for POINTBLANK.

Anticipating trouble, Eisenhower had waged a long and unsuccessful fight to delay the transfer, clashing with the U.S. Eighth Air Force commander, General Ira Eaker, and the ETO commander, General Jacob Devers, and with Marshall himself. When final appeals failed, Eisenhower, anticipating determined German resistance and last-minute Italian problems, had been forced to scale down ambitious plans for landings near Rome and to settle on the more cautious choice of Salerno, 120 miles to the south, the largest port within range of tactical Allied air cover based in Sicily, and within reach of the British Eighth Army's secondary landings planned at Calabria and Taranto.

For this, Eisenhower would be criticized for overcaution, but by D-day (September 8), even Salerno had become a risky objective. After the landings at Taranto, the hastily mobilized German Tenth Army had moved south of Rome into the vicinity of Salerno. As the landings proceeded, the Italians bowed to Eisenhower's threats to publish the facts of the negotiations and surrendered, but the government took flight, ending any hope of Italian assistance. Finally, the Luftwaffe had intercepted the invasion convoys, so the U.S. Fifth Army went ashore minus the advantages of surprise or preliminary bombardment by supporting battleships, cruisers and bombers. Within hours of the landings, British X Corps at Salerno and the U.S. VI Corps at Paestum faced three German divisions, and within forty-eight hours, German Field Marshal Albert Kesselring had contained the northern beachhead and formed a five-division counterattack, launched on the twelfth.

Few would forget the twelfth of September. That day the American 36th Division at Paestum barely prevented the Germans from crossing the Calore River and splitting the beachhead. In the emergency, Eisenhower had ordered the 82nd Airborne, originally set to seize the airfields in Rome, to reinforce the beachhead. Other units, collecting in Sicily and North Africa for transfer to England, were embarked on spare LSTs and sent to the beaches. General Alexander had flown off to the Italian naval base at Taranto to urge British General Bernard Montgomery to accelerate the overland advance of his Eighth Army. Admiral Andrew Cunningham dispatched eighteen Royal Navy battleships, cruisers and destroyers into Salerno Bay to direct withering shore bombardment against the German counterattack while the Air commander in chief, RAF Air Chief Marshal Arthur Tedder, orchestrated all available aircraft in the Mediterranean theater.

Air and naval intervention had eventually stopped the elements of six panzer divisions, proof that the Allies could respond to crisis, even a crisis resulting from high-level indecision. But the margin had been narrow, and in the critical moments of Kesselring's counterattack on September 12, Eisenhower had found himself negotiating with the Combined Chiefs of Staff in Washington for return of the air groups, a position he resolved he would never find himself in again.

Butcher had meticulously recorded the four anxious days Eisenhower spent pacing the offices in Tunis and Algiers, monitoring the reports and rumors from the beachhead: a garbled message that General Mark Wayne

Clark had withdrawn Fifth Army headquarters from the beach and had re-embarked his command ship; a false report that Clark had decided to evacuate VI Corps; German communiqués, usually reliable, describing the U.S. 36th Division at Paestum "in headlong flight." Finally, by the seventeenth the British Eighth Army and U.S.-British Fifth Army had joined up, and the Allies moved up both coasts toward the Trigno and Volturno rivers.

And so the crisis passed, but it seemed destined that troubles would plague the campaign in Italy. The German Tenth Army, after a vigorous stand at Salerno, had conducted a series of effective delaying actions and purchased time for the construction of strong defenses in rugged terrain behind the Garigliano and Sangro rivers blocking the approaches to Rome. The Fifth Army had entered Naples on October 1, but at the cost of 12,000 casualties in a three-week campaign, and by mid-month the advance had stalled. After the initial wave of relief, gloom descended over Allied staffs in London, Algiers and Washington. Instead of a quick advance to Rome, the Allies faced an extended battle in terrain heavily favoring the defense, a perceived setback compounded by less dramatic German successes in the eastern Mediterranean, which nullified the Italian surrender as a factor in grand strategy and undermined Allied unity on the eve of talks in Moscow.

The latter reverses were felt keenly in London. In the confusion of early September, Churchill had dispatched British troops of General Sir Henry Wilson's Mideast command to take over the Italian garrisons on the Dodecanese islands of Cos, Samos and Leros, preparatory to an attack on Rhodes. Churchill had hoped to clear the eastern Mediterranean at little cost, and to induce Turkey to enter the war on the Allied side, thereby bolstering the British case for a Mediterranean-based "third front" at the forthcoming conferences. Then, on October 3, German troops staging from Greece stormed Cos. With word of the assault, Churchill and the British Chiefs of Staff (BCOS) resolved to salvage Cos, Leros and Samos by drawing on air support and eventually ground reinforcements from Italy to bolster General Wilson's understrength Mideast command for a counterassault on Rhodes. In the Salerno controversies, however, Marshall had served notice that the Americans would oppose any commitments that jeopardized the mid-October timetable for transferring troops from Italy back to England. Marshall viewed Rhodes as potentially just such a commitment, particularly if the Germans matched the Allied build-up in the area.

Within hours of the German assault on Cos, Churchill appealed to Eisenhower informally to spare bombers of the U.S. Twelfth Air Force to support the British garrisons, a move that involved jurisdictional problems, though the procedure was not unusual. By October 1943, Churchill had grown accustomed to by-passing the Anglo-American Combined Chiefs of Staff to deal directly with Eisenhower, regarding him in his capacity of Mediterranean commander in chief as somewhat of a "constitutional monarch."

While 75 percent of the troops assigned to AFHQ were British, 80 percent of the casualties sustained in North Africa and Sicily had been Empire troops. Aware of this and of his junior position relative to his nominally subordinate British deputies, Eisenhower had tirelessly endeavored to accommodate the British and Churchill. Thus he provided air units of the U.S. Twelfth Air Force "on a very temporary basis," only to withdraw them at Marshall's suggestion forty-eight hours later. On the ninth Eisenhower formally declined to endorse the British proposals for landings on Rhodes, much to Churchill's disappointment.

Years later Eisenhower would defend himself, pointing out that his approach had been strictly military. Since it was unlikely that the Combined Chiefs of Staff would replace resources borrowed from Italy for Rhodes, Eisenhower had to consider whether AFHQ had adequate air, naval and ground resources to maintain their garrisons in the Dodecanese Islands without jeopardizing objectives in Italy. The answer was no.

All week the situation in Italy deteriorated, raising doubts that even the modest objectives set for the Italian campaign were attainable. As recently as October 4, Eisenhower had confidently predicted to Marshall that Rome would be in Allied hands by the end of the month. Then, on the ninth, the U.S. Fifth Army identified three new German divisions south of Rome, a "drastic change," as Eisenhower put it, which dashed lingering hopes that the German Tenth Army, after mounting brief resistance, would continue to withdraw northward. The German Tenth Army now matched the Fifth and Eighth armies in ground strength on the Gaeta–Termoli line, backed by an equivalent German force patrolling northern Italy. Only Allied air and naval supremacy, estimated to be the equivalent of ten divisions, provided the tactical edge at the front.

At a conference in Tunis that day, called at Churchill's behest to discuss the Dodecanese situation, Eisenhower, Clark and Alexander and their Middle East counterparts evaluated all aspects of the Mediterranean situation. Alexander could not even rule out the possibility of a German counteroffensive in Italy and spoke of an "all-out" offensive to break the Gaeta–Termoli line to improve the Allied position involving aggressive tactics such as amphibious end-run landings. Sparing even one division with armored elements for Rhodes would "preclude" such tactics, and the naval commitment in holding the threatened islands would be "prohibitive." All agreed that preparations for Rhodes would tie up the bulk of Eisenhower's available air forces for weeks. In short, a campaign in the eastern Mediterranean would be an unacceptable drain on Allied resources needed in Italy, barring a change of heart in the Combined Chiefs of Staff on the timing of transfers to England, which seemed unlikely in view of Marshall's attitude.

Afterward Eisenhower sent the Combined Chiefs of Staff, in Washington, a detailed report of the meeting. In it he reviewed the problems in Italy and summarized the unanimous conclusion: that available Mediterranean re-

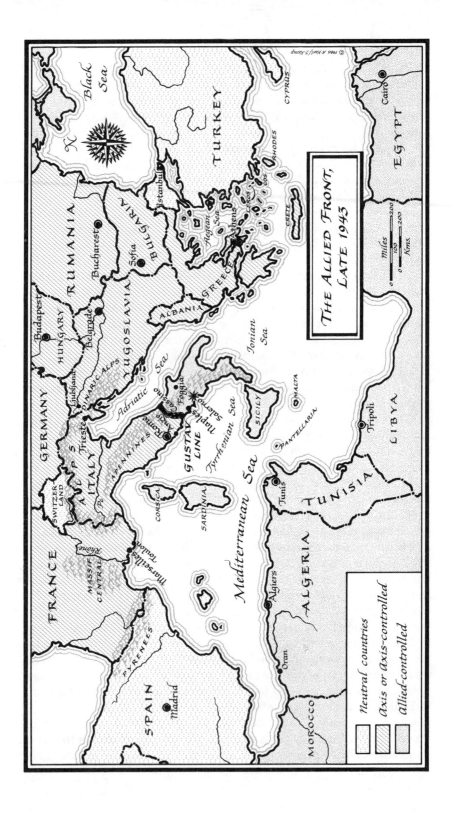

THE ALLIED FRONT, LATE 1943

Neutral countries

Axis or Axis-controlled

Allied-controlled

© 1986 A. Karl / J. Kemp

sources were not adequate for Italy and for holding the Dodecanese; that this reduced matters to a choice between "Rhodes and Rome"; that "to us it is clear that we must concentrate on the Italian campaign."

The unhappy sequel came the following day. British Foreign Minister Anthony Eden arrived in Algiers bearing Churchill's urgent appeal for Eisenhower to consider half measures such as maintaining a "foothold" on Cos and Leros. But Eisenhower did not come back from Tunis right away, having decided at the last minute to accompany Alexander to Naples, then to continue on to the Eighth Army front for a firsthand look at the Sangro River battle. In frustration, Eden "gave up" and returned to London.

Churchill would give up less easily. By the time Eisenhower returned to Algiers, Cos had fallen, signaling the high-water mark of eastern Mediterranean operations. But as long as Leros held on, Churchill would refuse to accept the situation as settled and would appeal several more times for Eisenhower's help in persuading Marshall to change his mind. When, inevitably, 5,000 crack paratroopers surrendered at Leros four weeks later, Churchill criticized Eisenhower's withdrawal of aircraft on the fifth and his refusal to lend his support afterward. Eight years later in his memoir, Churchill would still reproach Eisenhower for casting away "glittering prizes" on the eve of talks with the Russians.

And so, by mid-month, as the visitors came and went, Anglo-American debate had resumed on grand strategy. With word of Eisenhower's telegram on the ninth, Churchill had instructed the British Chiefs to begin drafting a battery of Mediterranean initiatives for the Allied-Soviet meetings ahead. Eisenhower's staff in Algiers had gone to work on plans for winter operations in Italy. Did the prospective gains in the eastern Mediterranean and Italy in the next several months justify a deeper commitment of Allied resources there and the risk of delaying preparations for OVERLORD?

In Italy, Montgomery's Eighth Army was in possession of the airfields at Foggia, from which the Mediterranean-based Fifteenth Air Force could wage POINTBLANK missions against southern Germany and Austria. Mussolini had been overthrown, deepening Berlin's diplomatic and political isolation. Ten frontline German divisions backed by ten divisions north of Rome were engaged at the Garigliano and Sangro rivers. The threat of counteroffensive receded, but by mid-month further progress in Italy inescapably required slowing up the transfer of troops to England, as Alexander had warned as early as the ninth of October. At a minimum, Churchill was determined to take Rome, seventy miles distant. Marshall questioned the purpose of Rome, and Roosevelt was undecided.

Anticipating the President's arrival in North Africa and a major debate in the CCS, Eisenhower canceled all appointments between October 21 and 25, and left Algiers for a closer look at the Fifth Army sector on the Garigliano River. There, he observed the snarl and chaos brought by the

early onset of winter rains. Sandy plains had turned into impassable marshland, creeks were overflowing, and all bridges and causeways across these
barriers had been destroyed. Eisenhower toured Naples and its harbor,
which after three long weeks of repairs had been salvaged as a functioning
port. The retreating Germans had abducted hundreds of hostages, destroyed the telephone exchange and telegraph office, demolished bridges
and roads, and had blown five holes in the aqueduct serving the city, forcing
city officials to ration water. For good measure the Germans destroyed the
city library and the Royal Society manuscripts, and wrecked a sanatorium.
Two complexes, identified as possible sites for a future AFHQ, could not
be inspected because of delayed-action explosives, a foretaste of the winter
campaign in Italy.

Eisenhower proceeded to Tunis for another round of meetings with Alexander and the 15th Army Group staff. By now the group discounted the
danger of a German counteroffensive because of the dismal conditions that
hampered the Allied advance. Alexander posed a new problem: that of
German retreat northward behind the Gustav Line, thus gaining a shorter
and more defensible position covering Rome, a maneuver that would enable
the Germans to hold in Italy while releasing troops to other fronts. In his
opinion, constant pressure in the next six months would be necessary to
prevent these German transfers.

That day Alexander sketched plans for seaborne amphibious flanking
attacks on the Eighth and Fifth Army fronts, plans that would involve
sixty-eight OVERLORD LSTs, the 82nd Airborne, and other units set for
transfer to England. Alexander told Eisenhower that he would inform the
British Chiefs that he deemed these steps "essential." Eisenhower and
Alexander finally settled on a proposal to keep the OVERLORD LSTs in Italy
until December 15, an unavoidable compromise.*

Weary and in low spirits, Eisenhower returned to Algiers, one week shy
of the first anniversary of the Allied North African landings, to wait. With
Allied-Soviet talks imminent, control over the theater would soon drift
upward into the austere chambers of the Combined Chiefs of Staff in the
Federal Reserve Building in Washington. That week Eisenhower endorsed
Alexander's proposal and fired off an aggressive appraisal of operations in
Italy, carefully evaluated in terms of the requirements for OVERLORD.
Privately, however, Eisenhower was far from optimistic about prospects in
Italy.

Returning from Naples and a search for new headquarters, Butcher
brimmed with frontline anticipation of the liberation of Rome, but he found
Eisenhower fatalistic. Over dinner Eisenhower confided that the Allies, in
his opinion, were stalemated in Italy, adding that the present war of attri-

---

*The CCS approved this extension on November 6. See Churchill, *Closing the Ring* (Boston:
Houghton Mifflin, 1951), p. 213.

tion was an "inevitable phase in any successful campaign." He reminisced about the Allied halt at Bizerte in December 1942, imposed on the Allies by the surprise German reinforcement of Tunisia, and by the weather, a prelude to a long uncertain winter, then victory in May. Eisenhower confided to Butcher that he would not consider risking the Fifth and Eighth armies in open battle in the Po River Valley that winter even if they were reinforced. Realistically, the Allies would be fortunate to have Rome by Christmas. More realistically, by Christmas he expected to be entrenched on a strong winter line south of Rome and holding.

MOSCOW

By the opening of the Foreign Ministers Conference in Moscow, events confirmed that the Red Army held the initiative in all sectors on the eastern front. Twelve weeks had passed since the stunning repulse of Germany's third and final bid for victory in Russia in the tank battle at Kursk. On the rebound, a confident and replenished Red Army, mustering a colossal force of over 330 divisions, sustained a summer offensive, having remained in close pursuit of the Germans through the Ukraine, pressing inexorably toward its ancient capital city of Kiev.

As the foreign ministers arrived, the Red Army launched covering attacks from bridgeheads over the Dnieper River and for a breathtaking interval in late October threatened to isolate 500,000 German troops in retreat between the Sea of Azov and the Dnieper bend. By a series of desperate improvisations, the German Army Group A formed a front west of Kiev, guarding the gateway to Rumania and Bulgaria. On November 6, as the Red Army entered the ruins of Kiev, Stalin assumed the title of marshal and, in a rare radio address heard by the delegates and the Soviet people, declared that "victory is near." On behalf of the Red Army in over two years of war, Stalin claimed the destruction of 14,000 enemy aircraft, 25,000 tanks and 4 million German casualties, including 1.8 million killed.

The three-power Foreign Ministers Conference carried on its business in the euphoric Russian capital. Nightly, fireworks lit up the Moscow skyline heralding the recapture of towns and villages in the Ukraine. Throughout, the Soviets staged a blunt display of a newfound confidence, contrasting sharply with their anxious agitation for a second front only months before. Greeting Cordell Hull's arrival in Moscow, *Pravda* broke eighteen months of silence and confirmed that the USSR would claim all territory acquired under the Nazi-Soviet Pact of 1939, including the Baltic States, western Poland and Rumania. "The frontiers of the Soviet Union," wrote *Pravda,* "can be the subject of discussion no more than, let us say, the frontiers of the United States and 'the status of California.' "

For sixteen days Cordell Hull and British Foreign Secretary Anthony

Eden met with Molotov in sessions at the Spirdonovka Palace. The delegates managed a display of unity, quickly shelving a number of questions that had been plaguing the alliance in 1943. Since Moscow's recall of ambassadors from London and Washington in July, the Western Allies had carefully monitored Soviet propaganda statements distinguishing sharply between the Nazi leadership and the German people, moves reminiscent of the Nazi-Soviet pact that rekindled concern about Soviet willingness to negotiate peace terms with "acceptable elements" in Germany. Reviving this question, several weeks before the conference Moscow had announced sponsorship of a Free Germany Committee, composed of exiled German socialists and Army officers captured at Stalingrad, pledged to building a new Germany, "free, independent, united . . . a just and better place." Hull now worked for and obtained Molotov's endorsement of Roosevelt's Casablanca unconditional-surrender formula, laying to rest months of rumors.

In the busy plenary sessions Hull also gained Russian endorsement of the proposed United Nations Organization and the principle of "sovereign equality" for all UN member states. The three-power delegates agreed on the first partition of post-1938 Germany by recognizing an independent Austria and according her "liberated" status at the eventual peace conference. The USSR consented to take a seat both on the Italian armistice commission and on the Eden-sponsored European Advisory Commission formed to draw up occupation zones and peace terms for Germany and the German satellites. In a startling behind-the-scenes development, Stalin spoke to Hull about eventual Russian military help against Japan.

The fate of Eastern Europe, a sensitive matter, was sidestepped. Harriman, years later, wrote critically that Hull dismissed the importance of East European territorial and political issues as "piddling little things" and a "Pandora's box of infinite trouble." Both he and Eden questioned Hull's circumspection about Poland. Earlier in the year Moscow had broken relations with the London-based Polish government-in-exile after the London Poles entertained Nazi claims charging the Red Army with responsibility for the murder of 10,000 Polish officers found in mass graves in the Katyn Forest, near Smolensk. They had vainly urged Hull that the time to arrange reconciliation between Moscow and the London Poles was in October 1943, when the Soviet Union had need of the West, and *not* at the eventual peace conference, when the Red Army would have occupied Eastern Europe. But Hull refused to raise the Polish matter or to discuss Balkan issues, and so as the Moscow sessions ended, Harriman was convinced that a storm over the future of Poland, Czechoslovakia, Bulgaria, Hungary and Rumania "had merely been postponed." Too much, he thought, had been seemingly conceded on two false premises: that the Soviet Union had the ability to win the war without effective Allied help; and that there was the slightest chance, Soviet wartime propaganda notwithstanding, that the Russians would stop short of "pulverizing" the German state.

To the world at large, however, the Moscow conference was a success. The aging American Secretary of State returned to a hero's welcome in Washington. In an address before a Joint Session of Congress, Hull proclaimed a victory for the Atlantic Charter* and the principle of collective security embodied in the United Nations. He optimistically declared to a hopeful Congress that the United Nations meant that at the end of the war, "no longer will there be need for spheres of influence, for alliances, for the balance of power or any of the 'special arrangements' " characteristic of Europe's tragic past. But redemption of Europe's past depended on ending the war first—the conference business on which Hull did not report.

Behind the scenes Hull, Eden and Molotov had negotiated arrangements for a summit parley set for Teheran in late November. Simultaneously, American and British military delegates sounded out their Russian counterparts on military matters and probed for an accurate reading of Soviet military strength and intent. So far the Red Army had proven resilient in the battles in the Ukraine, belying the numbing estimates of Russian losses sustained since the Nazi invasion, estimates that had been filed by the American and British military representatives left behind at the conclusion of the conference to open permanent missions. Russian military and civilian dead exceeded 20 million. Casualties of all kinds exceeded 30 million. The cities, towns and villages of the Ukraine, the Crimea, White Russia and the Caucasus were in ruins. At least 40 percent of Russian industry was destroyed. The military missions also noted that despite its Ukrainian disasters, the German army (consisting of four Army Groups with 250 divisions, including 24 panzer types), held the Dnieper and a deep arc of fortresses north of the Pripet Marshes, bulging southward from Leningrad to Vitebsk.

What did Russian losses of this magnitude mean? No one knew, though the answer in military terms would have a decisive bearing on OVERLORD, whose success was improbable without an active eastern front. Plainly, these numbers meant that a formal Russian-German "settlement" was impractical. This left other possibilities, however. Some believed that the USSR, nearing terminal exhaustion, would ultimately prove unable to sustain operations beyond the prewar Soviet borders, thereby leaving the Western Allies to deal with Hitler on their own. Alternatively, in view of the ferocious Russian drive toward Kiev, it seemed possible to a handful of Allied observers that the Soviets, pressing on in an exalted state, might attempt to play a lone hand and spurn cooperation with OVERLORD, a contingency long discounted in Allied deliberations.

Yet diplomats encountered disquieting signs that the Soviets might be contemplating abandonment of the two-year quest for the second front. Ominously, Stalin and Molotov, flushed with the news from Kiev, had reacted indifferently to Eden's hints of yet another postponement of OVER-

---

*The joint statement of war aims issued by Churchill and Roosevelt in August 1941.

LORD into the summer of 1944. Observers carefully noted that Stalin in his November 6 talk publicly acknowledged U.S. Lend-Lease shipments for the first time and strongly praised the Allied war in Italy, as a sort of second front.

Nonetheless, the second front dominated the military agenda. General John R. Deane, the U.S. military representative, and General Sir Hastings Ismay of the British Chiefs, in discussions with members of STAVKA, the Soviet high command, perceived little change in Soviet policy. In keeping with the Soviet line since June 1941, STAVKA representatives had single-mindedly insisted on OVERLORD by May 1, 1944. Ismay, Deane and the Soviet staff stipulated that the planned invasion of France, by posing a direct threat to the Saar and the Ruhr, would compel the Germans to commit the maximum number of defenders and thus provide the most direct relief for the eastern front. In turn, Deane and Ismay had reminded STAVKA that OVERLORD still involved serious military risks for the Western Allies, and they had meticulously outlined the conditions set for the success of OVER-LORD by COSSAC, the OVERLORD planning group in London: that an invasion of northwest France could succeed provided the Allies had air superiority; that there were no more than twelve mobile German divisions in France or three mobile divisions in the vicinity of the beaches on D-Day; that it "must not be possible for the Germans to transfer fifteen first-quality divisions during the first two months of operations." Fulfillment of the latter two conditions would depend, in part, upon the timing and scale of simultaneous Red Army operations in the spring of 1944. Typically, STAVKA representatives had offered no information about Russian plans.

"Yesterday's conference considered the *only* point of the Soviet agenda," Harriman wired Roosevelt, "namely the war on the second front—both officers [Deane and Ismay] did an extremely competent job in outlining and explaining our plans and showed willingness to answer freely any and all questions. Deane was precise in defining the conditions which must be precedent to their fulfillment . . . he appeared to satisfy and win the confidence of the Soviet delegates."

Within the week, Churchill aboard the H.M.S. *Renown* and Roosevelt aboard the U.S.S. *Iowa* were steaming toward Cairo and a brief preliminary conference before making their way to the scheduled summit with Stalin in Teheran. The British and American political and military chiefs, traveling separately, knew that at Teheran the future course of the war would be determined, resolving for good the two-year controversy over the proposed landings in France upon which all else rested. But it was now a question not just of how the war would be fought, as all sides well knew, but how it would be won—and the shape the world would take afterward.

Churchill and the British Chiefs urgently looked forward to Cairo as a last chance to spell out the military and political consequences of an inflexible "lawyer's bargain" to be struck with Stalin on the date and size of the proposed invasion of France. Undaunted by setbacks in Italy, Cos and Leros, Churchill intended to press ambitious designs for the Mediterranean: landing craft for operations in the Aegean; a program of military aid and other blandishments for Turkey to join the Allied side; aid to the partisans in Yugoslavia; the capture of Rome and stepped-up offensives in Italy; and reconsideration of plans for secondary landings in southern France (ANVIL), attached at Marshall's insistence at Quebec in August as a supporting operation for OVERLORD. Churchill did not rule out ANVIL in all circumstances, but he deplored the inhibiting effect that shipping shortages would have on Mediterranean operations that winter, which he was convinced would yield big gains at little cost, though admittedly at the risk of a slight delay in OVERLORD.

Many suspected otherwise. According to the numerous legends that have grown up around the events of November 1943, Churchill, convinced of ultimate victory, adopted an outright Balkan strategy, based on Italy, aimed at taking up positions in eastern Europe to block a Russian invasion of central Europe—charges Churchill would vehemently deny in the years ahead. Did the British support OVERLORD? Churchill would reply that only "simpletons" questioned it. Yet Churchill was determined to have a winter offensive in Italy at the expense of delaying OVERLORD if necessary, and in order to arrange a winter offensive he was apparently satisfied to build suspense about British consent to hosting the invasion.

Evidently, Churchill's support for Italy rested on several factors. First, British prestige was heavily invested in Italy. Second, British postwar interests in Eastern Europe were a factor. Third, the safety of OVERLORD. Churchill intended to insist at the outset that all sides be clear about the preconditions set for the success of the cross-Channel operation, as well as the steps to ensure the safety of Allied forces committed to OVERLORD in all its phases. Churchill intended to stress all of this, confident that doing so would prove helpful in hammering out Allied-Soviet military cooperation as well as setting the desired tone for discussions about the postwar future of Germany, France, Poland, the German satellites, Greece, Yugoslavia and Italy. Unlike the Americans, Churchill was sure the Russians wanted OVERLORD, and that the Allies could freely bargain with the Russians over Allied fulfillment of the second-front pledge, which, from the British standpoint, had always been carefully qualified.

For two years Churchill and the British Chiefs had been forthright about the military risks in crossing the English Channel. As Churchill was fond of pointing out, these very risks had deterred a German invasion in 1940 and thus accounted for Britain's existence. By November 1943 the military risks as seen in London were still substantial despite the German setbacks in Russia. These setbacks, which, in bringing the outlines of victory into focus, also underscored Germany's hopeless prospects on the eastern front and the idea that only by inflicting a massive defeat on the Allies could the Germans hope for a stalemate. Significantly, the German ground strength in the west had been built up since July. Meanwhile, in the climate of war optimism, the original Allied plans for a 48-division Allied build-up in England had been scaled back to 37 divisions, a force vulnerable to containment by the estimated 52 German divisions already in France and Belgium.

Both sides agreed that the eastern-front activity would be critical. It was apparent that the Germans, overextended along a 1,500-mile eastern front, were capable of holding a straightened and shortened rear line, thus freeing reserves that would provide a decisive margin in France. Little could be done to prevent this in the next six months—the point was to try to keep the Germans from carrying out this maneuver at the time of the landings as the Allies placed troops ashore, then at critical points afterward in the ensuing battle of France.

But even though the Americans and British agreed about the importance of Russian military cooperation, differences remained on other points, such as how specific Russian assurances had to be and the proper approach toward obtaining these assurances, both linked to more serious differences about the importance of the invasion and the objectives in talks with the Russians. In short, realistic about the military hazards of OVERLORD, the British were also realistic about what OVERLORD stood to accomplish. OVERLORD was no longer necessary to ensure Russian survival, nor was it clear OVERLORD was essential to defeat Germany. OVERLORD would hasten victory, but it would also ease the Russian task of consolidating their victories in the east—and come at great risk to the Allies. Hence, Churchill opposed unconditional pledges about OVERLORD such as a fixed date, or pledges to overlook opportunities in Italy, or to slight British interests, which were as important as American and Russian interests. Churchill intended to parley with Stalin, not curry favor, to assert British views, to negotiate for specific Russian pledges and, above all, to retain flexibility.

With the Americans resisting him on many of these points, Churchill on October 23 had cabled Roosevelt with a request for a preliminary U.S.-British conference to consider the "new facts" that had arisen since their talks at Quebec. Two weeks later, Churchill's views had taken the form of an aide-mémoire placed before the Combined Chiefs of Staff on Armistice Day, November 11, just as the Roosevelt party boarded the *Iowa* in Hampton Roads, Virginia. "The point of issue," wrote the British Chiefs, "is how far what might be termed the sanctity of OVERLORD is to be preserved in its entirety, irrespective of developments in the Mediterranean theater." The paper cited encouraging new developments since Quebec—the Italian surrender, the unforeseen Russian successes, Germany's wavering diplomatic position in Finland and the Balkans, Turkey's preliminary moves toward entering the war. "In these changed conditions," the British Chiefs wrote, "we feel that the consideration of adjustments of, if not actual departures from, the decisions taken at TRIDENT and QUADRANT is not only fully justified, but positively essential." These new circumstances required flexibility—no commitments at Teheran to arbitrary dates or numbers of divisions to be committed in France. Since Germany was stretched —possibly to the point of military and political collapse—it was essential to attack "remorselessly and continuously" in "any and every area," including Italy and the Mediterranean.

If his purpose was to generate suspense, Churchill succeeded. Robert Sherwood, in his account of Roosevelt's stormy transatlantic voyage aboard the *Iowa,* noted that Marshall, Brehon Somervell, Thomas Handy and the other Army generals departed Hampton Roads "trained to anticipate and prepare for all kinds of trouble." The November 11 aide-mémoire touched emotional currents that had been building for months, particularly the suggestion that Germany was on the verge of military and political collapse. Few believed it, and, anyway, barely two weeks had elapsed since the Moscow conference and the tenuous Allied-Soviet accord on unconditional surrender, which in spirit foreclosed talk of anything except a fight to the finish leading to total German defeat and occupation.

In November 1943 British candor about the hazards of OVERLORD was no longer welcome. Suspicion of British motives, particularly at the U.S. Army level, was profound. Few believed that Churchill sought to bolster OVERLORD in any way. Indeed, that he sought to cancel it seemed straightforward enough. The British, in Marshall's opinion, unless firmly committed to a certain time and date, would always find ways to put off preparations for OVERLORD.

Army views had crystallized at the Casablanca conference ten months earlier. There, Colonel Stanley Embick of Marshall's OPD Staff had circulated a paper that reflected the consensus in Army and War Department circles. In it, Embick charged in effect that since April 1942 America had been led down the "primrose path" by Britain's "agreements in principle" to OVERLORD; that under cover of these agreements the British, satisfied with stalemate on the eastern front, pursued a traditional balance-of-power strategy aimed solely at preserving the Empire and British interests in a postwar world. British designs in the Balkans and the Mediterranean, he charged, were not war measures against Germany, but aimed at checking the Soviet advance into these regions.

Several months later Secretary of War Henry Stimson had articulated the companion view—that the British lacked the vigor to mount the decisive offensive. Shortly before Quebec he had written Roosevelt a lengthy letter warning the President against any further delay in adopting OVERLORD and urging the appointment of General George Marshall to command the operation. On a trip to London in July, Stimson had concluded that the Americans could not rationally hope to cross the Channel and come to grips with the Germans under a British commander. He had warned Roosevelt that "the shadows of Passchendaele and Dunkirk" still hung too heavily over British imagination to permit this, and accounted for their "terribly dangerous" theories that Germany could be beaten by a series of attritions in northern Italy, in the outer Mediterranean, in Greece, in the Balkans, in Rumania and other satellite countries, thus delegating the military burden to Russia.

A passionate advocate of OVERLORD, Stimson was aware of the narrow margin in Allied resources and the stakes of failure. But Stimson had visions that without OVERLORD the United States and Britain would be mired in peripheral theaters and locked out of the decisive battles, having defaulted on their best chance to assume a major role in the fighting against Germany. OVERLORD involved risks and sacrificing certain postwar territorial advantages, but without OVERLORD he foresaw the erosion of Allied standing in Europe, the loss of Allied self-respect, the collapse of postwar cooperation and ultimately Roosevelt's policy amid endless recriminations over the Russian victories.

Deadlines approached. For the invasion to be a big factor in the defeat of Germany, it would have to be launched soon; 1944, the year of decisive battles, would also be an election year. With the Germans in retreat, American sentiment would run high in favor of operations in the Pacific. Isolationists might re-emerge and play on understandable fears by questioning any policy at this stage of the war that did not pursue ostensible advantages against the Russians. "We are facing a difficult year at home with timid and hostile hearts ready to seize and exploit any wavering on the part of our war leadership," he had warned Roosevelt. "A firm resolute leadership, on the other hand, will go far to silence such voices. The American people showed this in the terrible year of 1864, when the firm, unfaltering tactics of the Virginia campaign were endorsed by the people of the United States in spite of the hideous losses of the Wilderness, Spotsylvania and Cold Harbor."

Stimson's point was well taken, but presumably well understood by the British themselves. Thus, one must assume that his purpose was to broach a related problem, that of the impact of British views on the Americans: how long would the Americans who would be mobilizing the bulk of men and resources be willing to heed British doubts and misgivings?

Specifically, an unspoken problem raised by both the Embick memorandum and Stimson's letter was the President's personal resolve on OVERLORD. Roosevelt's long-standing susceptibility to British views had led to serious clashes with Marshall and Stimson over how to handle the all-consuming problems of mobilizing Allied resources and Russian military and political cooperation. Stimson's strictures had not always been welcome or considered practical; indeed, after months in eclipse, Stimson was not listed on the roster of passengers aboard the *Iowa*. Arguably Roosevelt's gradualism with Congress and his susceptibility to British views on North Africa and Italy had brought the Allies to this point—a summit including all three major powers convened to weigh OVERLORD as a practical design and a basis for future cooperation, provided Moscow did not turn around and suggest alternatives or disclaim OVERLORD, a growing concern.

On the voyage, this concern intensified. A cable reached the *Iowa* from General Deane in Moscow reporting fresh signs that "the Russians want to end the war quickly and feel they can do it." Deane cited Stalin's recent speech, the Eden-Molotov exchanges, and being "bombarded" with inquiries by Soviet military staff about inaction on the Italian front. Deane warned Marshall and Roosevelt to be on guard for an abrupt Russian shift on the question of the second front.

The Deane cable, unlike the British aide-mémoire, caused a minor flurry, evidently because the idea of Russian opposition to OVERLORD was still relatively new. The Army staff, according to Sherwood, had left Hampton Roads determined to get their way against the British, not the Russians. Consistently overridden on matters of grand strategy in two years, the Army planners attributed past decisions in favor of the Mediterranean to superior British staff work and had prepared their case to meet British arguments—not Russian. A staff of one hundred and fifty officers sailed aboard the *Iowa* armed with dozens of intelligence reports and position papers, including a 38-page document spelling out the fundamental U.S.-British differences in strategy and philosophy toward the war.

"This is the one contingency for which we have no plan," Marshall quipped upon reading the Deane cable. But unlike FDR's chief of staff, Admiral W. D. Leahy, and Harry Hopkins, who both took the cable seriously, Marshall attached little importance to it, perhaps doubting that the Russians had failed to foresee the extent of their successes in the Ukraine or that Soviet policy was so capricious as to change on the basis of local successes in the Ukraine. But the Deane cable did bear out Marshall's feeling that after twenty-four months of high-level military conferences, American and British staffs had exhausted the subject of grand strategy.

Accordingly, the four-day Anglo-American discussions at Cairo were fruitless. Determined to avoid "ganging up on Stalin," Roosevelt had invited Molotov to sit in on talks at which the British had hoped to hammer out a common negotiating stance for the conference. When Molotov was unavailable, Roosevelt, over British objections, invited Chiang Kai-shek to Cairo for extended talks about the Chinese theater. Chiang's presence inhibited discussion of the November 11 aide-mémoire or the latest wrinkles in Russian thinking. The Americans met British proposals for extended amphibious operations in the Mediterranean with American-Chinese plans for a major amphibious attack into Burma to open overland supply routes from the Bay of Bengal to Chungking, China's landlocked wartime capital. Eisenhower flew in to brief the CCS on Italian operations and conditions in Yugoslavia. But nothing could be decided and Marshall turned aside efforts of General Sir Alan Brooke, chief of the Imperial General Staff, to discuss the ambiguities in recent Soviet statements, predicting that "Stalin would probably simplify the problem."

TEHERAN

Sunday, November 28, 1943. At four o'clock the delegations gathered in the main conference room of the Empire-style Russian legation in Teheran, a large yellow brick building surrounded by Sikhs, Red Army guards and U.S. Army MPs. From the spacious (70-by-40-foot) conference room, the delegates could see the Elburz Mountains in the distance and Mount Demavend. The oak conference table was round to avoid problems of seating protocol.

Franklin Roosevelt at sixty-one was the youngest leader present. He had not wanted to travel the entire distance to Teheran and had told Stalin in October that his limit would be Basra, Iraq, even though he would be glad to travel 6,000 miles, "ten times the distance," for meetings with the Soviet General Secretary. Communication links between Teheran and Washington were unreliable, and communications were important in view of his constitutional duty to sign or veto bills within ten days of passage by Congress and the fact that Congress remained in session.

But Stalin, in reply, had observed that while communications between Washington and Teheran were unreliable, communications between Moscow and Teheran were good and as such were essential to supervise developments on the eastern front, which offered the USSR "a once in 50 years opportunity" to thrash the German army in Russia. When Stalin offered to send Molotov to Basra in his place, Roosevelt deferred to Harriman's advice not to regard the Russian position as entirely insincere, especially in view of "the supreme importance of a meeting now."

Churchill at sixty-nine was the oldest of the three. His urgent desire was to avoid hard-and-fast commitments on the timing and scale of OVERLORD. For this he needed the backing of Roosevelt and the sanction of Stalin. But he was depressed about the probable outcome of Teheran, "beleaguered, not by his enemies, but by those same rescuers who threatened to push him into the background along with the power and prestige of the entire British Empire."

The conference at Teheran was Stalin's first trip outside the Soviet Union since 1912, when he had met secretly with Lenin in the Polish city of Cracow. Wearing the light-beige tunic of a marshal with large gold epaulettes, Stalin cut an unlikely figure; small, frail and taciturn, Stalin led a delegation of four—Molotov; an old revolutionary crony, Kliment E. Voroshilov; his trusted interpreter, Pavlov; and an unidentified secretary.

As the meeting came to order, Roosevelt, as chairman of the conference, noted the "auspicious" circumstance that the three sides had come together.

"We are sitting around this table for the first time as a family with the one object of winning the war," he said. He told Stalin of the relationship worked out between the British and the Americans since the fall of France. It was to "publish nothing but to speak our minds very freely."

"In such a family circle," he added, "we hope that we will be very successful in achieving constructive accord in order that we maintain close touch throughout the war and after the war."

Churchill spoke next. "We represent here a concentration of great worldly power," he said. "In our hands we have perhaps the responsibility for the shortening of this war. In our hands we have, too, the future of mankind. I pray that we may be worthy of this God-given opportunity."

Stalin in his role as host took "pleasure in welcoming those present. . . . I think that history will show that this opportunity has been of tremendous import. . . . now let's get down to business."

With a pointer and a large map of the Pacific, Roosevelt offered a survey of the war in Asia, a struggle in which the United States was bearing the main burden. The effort against Japan was absorbing the majority of American capital ships and a million men—a war of attrition against Japanese naval combatants and merchant shipping. He informed Stalin of the plans he and Churchill had discussed in Cairo to drive the Japanese from Burma and to open the supply lines to Chungking. Roosevelt then briefly addressed the problem of immediate concern to all three: OVERLORD. A million troops would be in Britain by the end of 1943 and 1.25 million by March of the following year. After seizing a beachhead, the Allies intended to "proceed inland and liberate France." He noted that planning for this complex operation had encountered many problems, which were slowly being resolved. OVERLORD was *possible before August 1.*

"The Channel is such a disagreeable body of water," he added. "No matter how unpleasant, however, we still want to get across it."

"We were very glad it was an unpleasant body of water at one time," Churchill added.

Having hinted that he would favor a postponement until August, Roosevelt continued in a vein that surprised his advisers. The President told Stalin that it was difficult to set a definite date for the attack because of landing-craft bottlenecks and the weather. In the event of a postponement, he asked, how could the Allies in the Mediterranean be of assistance to the Red Army? Roosevelt presented Stalin with several choices: stepped-up attacks in Italy, an invasion in the northeast Adriatic to aid Tito, or operations in the Aegean aimed at inducing the Turks to declare war and join the Allies.

The President's improvisation, in which he briefly associated the American position with Britain's, caused a startled Harry Hopkins to scribble a note to Admiral King asking the Chief of Naval Operations if he had any idea who had promoted "that Adriatic business" to the President. King turned and whispered, "As far as I know, it is his own idea."

Stalin spoke next. He welcomed the news about the Pacific theater. As he had told Hull in October, the Soviet armies in Manchuria were defensive —Soviet forces needed to be increased threefold to undertake an offensive. But when the war ended in Europe, "then by our common front we shall win."

Stalin then rendered a lengthy discourse on the eastern front. He told of the elaborate preparations for the summer offensives, but admitted that the Soviets had been surprised by the extent of their successes. The German lines, considerably weakened by the winter campaign, had buckled unexpectedly under the pressure of Russian attacks launched along a broad front. Stalin cautioned that an estimated 22 German motorized divisions were currently counterattacking near Kiev. He further cautioned that despite the Russian victories, the Axis maintained 260 divisions in Russia, many more than in 1942—6 fresh German divisions had just arrived from France and Italy. "How can you best help the Soviet Union?" he asked rhetorically.

As for the western front, Stalin said the Soviet Union considered Italian operations valuable as a way to open shipping lanes in the Mediterranean, but he added it was "not considered that operations in Italy are of great value to further the war against the Axis—they are of no further great importance as regards the defeat of Germany." Also, in Stalin's opinion, Turkey and the Balkans were "distant" issues for the Western Allies. Stalin suspected that Hitler had reinforced Italy in the early stages because "he knew that nothing can be decided there," and merely angled to stall a decisive offensive elsewhere. This left "northwestern or southern France." Stalin confirmed that Soviet military authorities believed it would be better to use northern France for invasion purposes, "but it must be expected that the Germans will fight like devils to prevent such an attack."

Churchill assured Stalin that OVERLORD was settled U.S.-British policy and described the amphibious and other forces scheduled to arrive in the British Isles by May 1944 for an operation of unprecedented magnitude. There was, in other words, no question about OVERLORD. The question was, What could be done in the meanwhile? Were there any operations in the Mediterranean that the Soviets felt would justify any delay in OVERLORD, however slight?

"The Soviet Union has never regarded that the Mediterranean is of secondary importance," Stalin replied. "It is of the first importance, but not from the point of view of invading Germany."

Churchill pursued his theme. As the Allies pressed toward the Pisa–Rimini line, north of Rome, opportunities would open up for a third front in southern France or alternatively in Yugoslavia. Indeed, Italy was itself a "third front," one that should be exploited. For instance, operations in the eastern Mediterranean would enable the British fleet to sail into the Black Sea and support the Russian flank anchored there. In this event,

Turkey might enter the war and thus cause a political "turnover" in Bulgaria, which would force a German evacuation of Greece and jeopardize the enemy's position elsewhere, such as in Hungary, which was already putting out genuine peace feelers. The Prime Minister sought Soviet views on these points, as "these were questions on which the Soviets had a special point of view and special knowledge." Churchill cautioned that Allied plans in the eastern Mediterranean would mean a delay of one to two months in launching OVERLORD. Accordingly, the British and American governments had deliberately kept their minds open on these issues until they could consult the Soviet government.

At this point, Roosevelt reminded Churchill of the "further project of moving up to the Northern Adriatic and then northeast to the Danube." Churchill agreed, adding that once the Allies had "destroyed the German Armies south of the Apennines in the narrow part of Italy," the Allied Armies would be able to advance to points where they could either strike into southern France or, as the President had just suggested, attack northeast from the head of the Adriatic.

Stalin then addressed a series of questions to Churchill:

Q.: Am I right in thinking that the invasion of France is to be undertaken by 35 divisions?
A.: Yes. Particularly strong divisions.
Q.: Is it intended that this operation should be carried out by the forces now in Italy?
A.: No. Seven divisions have already been or are in the process of being withdrawn from Italy and North Africa to take part in OVERLORD. . . . After they have been withdrawn, about 22 divisions will be left in the Mediterranean for Italy or other objectives . . . for an operation against southern France or . . . moving from the head of the Adriatic towards the Danube . . . in conformity with OVERLORD. Meanwhile, it should not be difficult to spare two or three divisions to take the islands in the Aegean. . . .

Stalin asked Churchill about the operation in the south of France. Churchill replied that it had not been planned in detail, but "the idea was that it might be done in conformity or simultaneously with OVERLORD."

Stalin also asked how many Anglo-American troops would have to be allotted to the eastern Mediterranean to support Turkey in the event Turkey entered the war.

Churchill estimated two to three divisions, several flak regiments and twenty air squadrons, whereupon for several minutes Stalin and Churchill talked about the entry of Turkey into the war. Churchill conceded that Turkish participation might require that an Allied garrison be stationed on Turkish soil, and possibly a two-month postponement of OVERLORD. Stalin conceded the value of Turkish entry into the war but pronounced himself skeptical about the Turks' entering the war except by the "scruff of the neck." The Turks had played "fast and loose" with the Allies and the Axis.

"Neutrals regard all belligerents as fools," he said. "We must prove to them that if they do not enter the war, they do not reap the fruits of victory."

Stalin admitted that he had little interest in Turkey, and he turned the subject back to OVERLORD and France. He remarked that he did not think it "worthwhile to scatter the British and American forces," sending some to Turkey, others to southern France, yet others to northern France and others to the Atlantic. OVERLORD should be the "basis of operations in 1944 and others considered diversionary." As for ANVIL, Stalin suggested that once Rome had been captured, perhaps the Mediterranean forces could attack southern France from Corsica, in which case the two invasions could establish contact. Indeed, perhaps an invasion into southern France should *precede* OVERLORD.

Churchill emphasized that the failure to take Rome by January would be a crushing political setback in Parliament—among other things, he could justly be accused in Parliament of failing to render adequate aid to Britain's Soviet ally that winter. Churchill doubted that the airfields on Corsica could be developed in time to support landings in southern France before OVER-LORD.

Stalin, however, believed that OVERLORD on balance held out the greatest possibilities "especially if supported by southern France," which would be possible, he suggested, if Allied strength in Italy were reduced to ten divisions, leaving Rome to be taken at a later date.

As the first plenary session closed, the three leaders touched briefly again on Turkey, then agreed to arrange a military conference between Voroshilov and the Anglo-American military advisers the following morning, Monday, November 29.

Historians have written that the opening plenary session of the twenty-eighth vindicated George Marshall, who, ironically, was not present, though the session opened an hour late; the story, often told, was that he had been sightseeing and had not been informed of the time the meetings would begin. Many of those who were present assumed that Stalin had brought a small entourage in order to avoid being overheard by his military advisers. Likewise, Roosevelt may have been reluctant to have Marshall witness his brief effort to support Churchill's quest for an interim Mediterranean strategy.

The mystery of Russian intent aroused by the Deane cable and recent Soviet statements dissolved. The Soviets, as they had for two years, still favored a second front. Moreover, Stalin had shown restraint. He had politely suggested OVERLORD and termed it helpful—presumably he intended to offer military cooperation to assist the operation, though he had indicated nothing about Russian plans. To the extent that Stalin had intended to do so all along, the first plenary session vindicated Churchill.

Crucial points had to be clarified—for example, specifics about Russian support. The importance of the May 1 date for OVERLORD in Russian thinking was unclear. The true basis of Stalin's interest in southern France was also unclear: whether the Soviets conceived landings in southern France as militarily inseparable from OVERLORD or favored this merely as a way to divert the Italian theater forces away from the Balkans, and in either case, whether Stalin would link all Russian cooperation to ANVIL. In discussions that night at the British legation, General Alan Brooke vainly insisted that Stalin had liked the idea of ANVIL landings in southern France merely because they would open the Balkans to occupation by the Red Army. Brooke reminded Marshall of Eisenhower's latest appraisal of southern France, which he had termed a "necessarily isolated and small scale operation" that compared unfavorably as a diversionary plan to the "Balkan belt" concept of engaging sixty German divisions from Zagreb to the Riviera. Likewise, Brooke adamantly opposed an ironclad commitment to OVERLORD on May 1. A late spring thaw in Russia might frustrate the best intentions—only by waiting for early summer could all sides be reasonably certain that conditions would permit coordinated operations on both fronts. Brooke urged straight talk about the preconditions affixed to OVERLORD: the defeat of the Luftwaffe; no more than twelve German mobile divisions in France or three divisions in the vicinity of the beachhead on D-Day; and preventing the transfer of fifteen German divisions to France—conditions that rested upon an all-out Russian effort coinciding with OVERLORD.

The following morning, for five and a half hours, Brooke, Leahy, General Marshall and British Air Chief Marshal Charles Portal sought from Voroshilov, the lone Russian, clarification of the vital points raised the night before. Brooke undertook the burden of the argument. He reminded Voroshilov of the six months that would elapse between Teheran and the earliest moments at which OVERLORD could be launched. He explained the constraints on Allied plans such as the shortage of LSTs and other landing craft essential for amphibious landings. LSTs were needed in Italy and the Pacific, with OVERLORD probably consuming the remainder. Southern France could not be guaranteed without diverting landing craft now available for flanking operations in Italy. With Marshall's backing, Brooke observed that an isolated attack into southern France preceding OVERLORD would court defeat. He spoke about the hazards of OVERLORD itself, again backed by Marshall, who noted that the Red Army had crossed many rivers but as yet had not attempted a body of water like the Channel. "Withdrawal behind a river is a failure," Marshall told Voroshilov, "but failure from the sea is a catastrophe."

Brooke and Marshall talked in vain because Voroshilov had no brief to reveal Soviet plans. But he had questions: landing craft, this constraint on Allied plans—did the U.S. and Britain have a plan to alleviate this problem? Would Turkey's entry into the war diminish the importance of OVERLORD in Allied eyes? Voroshilov revealed that Stalin was indifferent to other operations except as they bore on OVERLORD. For instance, the previous day, Stalin had suggested an attack into southern France. "Marshal Stalin does not insist on this," he said, "but he does insist on the execution of OVERLORD on the date already planned."

The first plenary session had been cordial. But in limited dealings with the Russians since 1941, American and British diplomats had noted sharp swings in mood from session to session, a phenomenon that deepened the air of mystery about the workings of the Soviet government. Some believed the Russians practiced unpredictability as a deliberate tactic. Others surmised that Stalin was obligated to clear policy with an inner clique of the Politburo or was anxious to impress his colleagues in the presence of foreigners. But Stalin was in Teheran without advisers, and so few were prepared for his abruptness on the twenty-ninth. Suddenly Stalin's openness to suggestions was gone, and his new mood caught Roosevelt and Churchill off-balance.

The second plenary session opened on a solemn note, marred by an accident. In a hall outside the conference room, Churchill unveiled a fifty-inch bejeweled Sword of Stalingrad, commissioned by King George VI to commemorate the great Russian victory, and presented it to Stalin. The sword, forged at the Wilkinson Sword Foundry by eighty-three-year-old Thomas Beasley, was a token of British esteem for the measureless Russian sacrifice in lives and property in the common cause. In silence, Stalin drew the sword, kissed the blade and handed it to Voroshilov, who fumbled and dropped it to the floor. Voroshilov hastily retrieved the sword, placed it in its scabbard and passed it to the Red Army guard of honor, who turned and marched away in silence.

The three full U.S., British and Russian delegations were present for the climactic plenary session. There was no agenda. General Alan Brooke and General Marshall opened with a brief summary of the military committee meetings that morning. No conclusions had been reached. A second meeting had been set for the morning of the thirtieth—no decisions about Balkan operations or southern France or Italy could yet be reported. Marshall recited the difficulties concerning the availability of LSTs and other landing craft that had plagued the planning for OVERLORD throughout. Alan Brooke offered a more detailed rundown on the discussion, concluding with a reminder of the conditions attached by COSSAC to the OVERLORD plan: defeat of the Luftwaffe; no more than twelve German mobile divisions in France and no more than three divisions in the vicinity of the beaches or reinforcement by fifteen divisions in the first two months. Alan Brooke elaborated on the concern, "shared by the Americans," that the Germans in Italy might suddenly withdraw northward to the Pisa–Rimini line in Italy, which would free divisions for other fronts, the concern at the heart of the British proposals. He briefly recapitulated the points raised about

Italy, southern France, Yugoslavia, Turkey, Rhodes and Greece. Voroshilov confirmed Brooke's version of the committee conference, and the decision to raise these matters "further at the next meeting . . ."

"Who will command OVERLORD?" Stalin interrupted.

Churchill and Roosevelt replied in unison that it had not been decided.

"Then nothing will come of these operations," Stalin snapped. "Who carries the moral and technical responsibility for this operation?"

Roosevelt identified the British General Frederick E. Morgan, administrator of COSSAC, the vast OVERLORD planning apparatus employing over 3,000 American and British officers and technical experts.

STALIN: Who has the executive responsibility for OVERLORD preparations?
ROOSEVELT: We have decided the names of all the commanders except that of Supreme Commander.
STALIN: General Morgan might say that all things are ready—however, when the Supreme Commander reports, he, the Supreme Commander, might not think that everything necessarily has been accomplished by the Chief of Staff. There must be one person in charge.

After a pause, Churchill told Stalin about his talks with Roosevelt at Quebec, where the two sides had agreed that the commander should be American. Though England provided the base for this operation, OVERLORD was the supreme operation of the war, and England, acknowledging the larger American contribution, had warmly consented to place her armies under an American commander. Churchill predicted the appointment would be made "within a fortnight."

Ruffled by Stalin's abruptness, Churchill then spoke for ten minutes on the larger questions before the group. The conference was "unique in the eyes of 1.4 billion people," he said. There was an urgent need to settle outstanding military and political questions—first, how the Allied Mediterranean force could assist in laying the foundation for the final offensive against Germany. He was not suggesting cancellation of OVERLORD, or even a postponement, but the possibility of one for the sake of easy gains in the eastern Mediterranean in the next six months that would bring Turkey into the war, further overextend Germany and hasten victory. In his opinion, there were three or more methods of assisting OVERLORD without undue delay. For instance, retaining a two-division amphibious lift in the Mediterranean would make both an offensive on Rhodes and flanking operations in Italy possible, involving no more than a six- to eight-week delay. Or the Allies could extend help to Tito's partisan forces, which were holding down 30 German and 12 Bulgarian divisions in Yugoslavia and Greece, a powerful force that might otherwise provide the Germans with a sizable reserve for commitment in France. Also, if the Turks entered the war, the Bulgarian units would be tied down—Churchill would be returning to Cairo with the President and would be seeing President Ismet Inönü of

Turkey. He needed to know the answer to an important question: If Turkey declared war on Germany, and Bulgaria then declared war on Turkey, would the Soviets declare war on Bulgaria? If not, Churchill foresaw obstacles to Turkish entry into the war on the side of the Allies. . . .

> STALIN: . . . As soon as Turkey comes into the war we can consider that the matter is closed. The USSR will take care of Bulgaria. If Bulgaria declares war on Turkey, the USSR will declare war on Bulgaria. Even under these circumstances Turkey will not enter the war.

Stalin pressed. He did not care any longer about projects involving two or three Allied divisions in Turkey, and he saw "no disagreement on this point."

"Turkey, Rome, Yugoslavia, all of these, are relatively unimportant," he said. "We, the USSR, find OVERLORD the most important and decisive. It is true that the USSR needs help which is why the representatives of the Soviet Union are here at this conference—the Soviets expect help from those who are willing to fulfill operation OVERLORD." The three questions before the group, he continued, remained the date of OVERLORD. The Russians would agree to May 1, no later. Landings in southern France—whether two or three months earlier or simultaneously with OVERLORD "all the same." Lastly, the appointment of a commander—on this, the Soviets would wait a week. The choice of a commander, of course, was a matter between the British and American governments, but the Soviets wanted to "know his name." The Soviets believed that until a commander was appointed, no success from OVERLORD, particularly in the matter of organization, could be expected. "The USSR does not enter into the matter of this selection but the Soviets definitely want to know who he will be."

As he ticked off his questions, one, two, three, Stalin forced the issue. The undercurrents of hostility and suspicion threatened the unity of the conference. When Roosevelt reminded Stalin of the thirty Axis divisions tied up in the Balkans, Stalin interrupted. According to Soviet intelligence estimates, there were eight German divisions in Yugoslavia, five in Greece and three in Bulgaria, for a total of sixteen. "There are twenty in France," Stalin said. "I will not agree to OVERLORD later than May 1."

Churchill protested that "many great possibilities in the Mediterranean should not be ruthlessly cast aside." Stalin replied that Mediterranean issues were "diversions." Churchill protested that for the British to be idle for six months before OVERLORD would lay Britain open to the reproach from the Soviets of allowing the Red Army to bear all the burden of the land fighting, whereupon Stalin denied he wanted the British "to think that the Soviets wish them to do nothing."

Churchill vehemently criticized Stalin's bland indifference to the hazards confronting OVERLORD. He reminded Stalin of the conditions for success: defeat of the German Luftwaffe; no more than twelve German mobile divisions in France on D-Day; three at the beaches; preventing the transfer of fifteen first-quality German divisions to France in the first sixty days.

> STALIN: And if there are thirteen mobile divisions in France on D-Day, will this rule out OVERLORD?

Stalin drove the point home. He announced that he and his two aides, Molotov and Voroshilov, had studied President Roosevelt's proposal in the plenary session for an ad hoc committee to take up the question of Balkan partisans and had concluded that "there is no need for a committee." The conference faced three issues: the dates of OVERLORD and landings in the south of France, and the identity of the commander. Stalin was in a hurry and was needed in Moscow to supervise the front and to stand watch over the developing crisis near Kiev.

For several minutes the group wrangled about the ad hoc committee while all sides gathered their thoughts. Finally Stalin peered across the table at Churchill. "Are the British thinking seriously of OVERLORD only in order to satisfy the USSR?"

Churchill defiantly replied, *"Provided* the conditions previously stated for OVERLORD are established when the time comes, it will be our stern duty to hurl across the Channel against the Germans every sinew of our strength."

The second plenary session at Teheran demonstrated beyond doubt that Stalin would discuss nothing seriously until he had an Anglo-American commitment on OVERLORD, including a commitment to abandon all Mediterranean projects east of Italy. "No more can be done here," Churchill exclaimed to his physician, Lord Moran, who chronicled the mood of gloom and futility that descended upon the British delegation. Portal and Brooke spoke of leaving Teheran before dawn. The Americans were somber, but the next morning, as the heads of government met privately in twos at the Russian legation, Marshall, Brooke, King, Portal and Leahy convened a rump session of the Combined Chiefs of Staff. On behalf of Roosevelt and Churchill, the CCS issued directives to the newly formed British 21st Army Group and the U.S. 12th Army Group in Britain scheduled for activation in OVERLORD. The great cross-Channel invasion of Europe, conceived in the weeks after the fall of France, and planned for over three years, was on.

Separate meetings between the principals went on the next morning in which Roosevelt, Churchill and Stalin discussed the OVERLORD question off the record. The purpose of the plenary session set for the afternoon of the thirtieth was to repeat, for the conference record, what Stalin, Roosevelt and Churchill finally affirmed to one another in the private sessions and to bury the antagonisms that erupted on the afternoon of the twenty-ninth.

General Alan Brooke again opened the session. He carefully briefed Stalin on the conclusions reached by the Combined Chiefs only hours before. It was decided, he said, that the "Anglo-American forces would launch OVERLORD during the month of May, in conjunction with a supporting operation against the south of France, on the largest scale that would be permitted by the landing craft available at that time."

Churchill said, "It is of course understood that we shall keep in close touch with Marshal Stalin and the Soviet military authorities in order that operations may be coordinated."

"I understand the importance of the decision reached by the Anglo-American staffs," Stalin replied. There would be "difficulties in the beginning and possibly dangers"—most of all, at the beginning of the attack, the Germans would attempt to transfer divisions in from the eastern front "to meet it and to prevent its success. . . . To deny the Germans freedom of action," he said, "the Soviets will undertake to organize a large-scale offensive against the Germans in May in order to contain the maximum number of German divisions on the eastern front and remove difficulties for OVER-LORD."

Roosevelt added that he and Churchill would decide upon the command for OVERLORD in Cairo. The three leaders then briefly discussed the agenda for the December 1 session, and approved the text of a communiqué to be issued at the conclusion of the conference. The plenary session adjourned.

In the less formal atmosphere of the dinners and luncheons at Teheran, Stalin, Roosevelt and Churchill talked about the immense political ramifications of the military bargain being worked out. On the night of the twenty-ninth at dinner, the group discussed the Tito-Mihajlović clash in Yugoslavia, the Rumanian and Hungarian peace overtures, terms for Finland, and the Polish boundaries. At later banquets they discussed the UN, British politics, the sensitive question of American domestic opinion on the East European problem, similar British concerns about Poland, Russian concerns about secure postwar borders, French politics, the now doubtful status of the French colonies and the diminished postwar role for France envisioned by the three, as indicated by the exclusion of the French from the conference. The three sides agreed on the basics, but a troubled future was implicit.

To Churchill's chagrin, specifics were hard to come by. Stalin repeatedly sought to couple the treatment of France with that of Poland, thereby inviting the Allies to assume a free hand in France, which was to be liberated by Allied forces, and asserting in turn his own freedom of action in Poland, which was to be liberated by the Red Army. Stalin left open the possibility of Polish elections and eventual inclusion of the London Poles in some way. Since the object of Soviet policy in Poland appeared to be the containment of Germany, Stalin wanted a "strong" Poland as a buffer against future German expansion, a Poland ruled by a friendly government that would protect land lines of communication between the USSR and the Soviet occupation zone in Germany. Also, a defensible frontier meant Soviet annexations of Polish territory offset by Polish annexations of Germany along the so-called Curzon Line, which also had the troublesome effect of creating a Czech-Russian border, thus conferring buffer status upon Czechoslovakia, too. The Soviet position on Eastern Europe emerged: Stalin would insist on "friendly" neighbors. As for Germany, Stalin was pessimistic about the prospect of reforming the German people and confirmed that, notwithstanding propaganda broadcasts, the Soviets intended to break Germany up into a number of small states.

No one disputed that Germany should be divided up, which was the crucial point of the conference. How to do it produced debate. On the night of the thirtieth, Churchill spoke of severing warlike Prussia from the rest of Germany, which was to be linked with Hungary and Austria in a Balkan federation. Roosevelt suggested a more elaborate seven-way partition. Stalin preferred Roosevelt's plan.

Throughout, Churchill pressed his idea that a more moderate solution could be found or would have to be found. A policy with the single-minded objective of crushing the Germans would harm Europe as a whole, and become itself a source of further difficulties. Yet Churchill did not dispute that unless the Big Powers could be assured of national survival, no real basis existed for independent policies pursued by France, Germany, Italy, Yugoslavia, Bulgaria, Poland, Rumania, Czechoslovakia, Austria, Belgium and Turkey. Churchill and Roosevelt hoped that the Russians would be satisfied with Polish territorial concessions and suggested that political independence for Poland would be in the best interest of Russia, in terms of both Russian security and relations with the West. Stalin did not see any contradiction. He explained that Soviet policy was for a strong, independent and friendly Poland, mindful that Poland had been a corridor for German invasion of Russia twice in twenty years, with the latest one not over.

Repeatedly the discussion returned to Germany and Russian fears of a German recovery, which Stalin expected "within fifteen to twenty years." Stalin pressed his view that merely defeating Germany in this war would not be enough: only radical long-range political, military and economic controls could prevent a German revival. How could this be done?

"Nothing is final," Churchill remarked at one point. "The world rolls on. We have now learnt something. Our duty is to make the world safe for at least fifty years by German disarmament, by preventing rearmament, by supervision of German factories, by forbidding all aviation and by territorial changes of a far-reaching character." In his opinion, the question came back to whether Great Britain, the United States and the USSR could "keep a close friendship and supervise Germany in their mutual interest."

> STALIN: There was control after the last war but it failed.
> CHURCHILL: We were inexperienced then. The last war was not to the same extent a national war, and Russia was not a party at the Peace Conference. It will be different this time . . .

Eisenhower observed the Cairo and Teheran conferences from the sidelines. On November 17 he had flown to Malta to greet Churchill on board the H.M.S. *Renown,* bound for the conference. There he learned that the British would be reopening issues of grand strategy at Teheran. His chief of staff, General William Bedell Smith, lingered for talks with Brooke and returned to Algiers with details and a prediction from his staff that the forthcoming conference would be the "hottest one yet." On the twentieth Eisenhower had flown to Oran and had been at pierside to greet the U.S.S. *Iowa.* He had accompanied the President to Tunis, dined alone with Roosevelt that night at the presidential villa, and spent the following day guiding Roosevelt over the Tunisian battlefields.

During this picnic outing, Harry Hopkins remained behind for a talk with Harry Butcher. Hopkins and Butcher were friends who in their limited contacts in the war had achieved a relationship based on frankness. It had been Hopkins who had taken Butcher aside at the Casablanca conference, at a moment when Eisenhower's position at AFHQ was in doubt because of the Darlan incident, to present Butcher with the facts of life. Hopkins had then advised Butcher that Eisenhower should "forget the political hullabaloo" and concentrate on Tunis, noting that "if General Eisenhower seizes Tunisia by May he will go down as one of the great generals in history." When Butcher asked, "And if he doesn't?" Hopkins had smiled.

Now, on November 22, Hopkins was bearing pleasant news. Eisenhower was in the President's favor and would be returning to Washington as chief of staff under the current plan in which Marshall would command OVER-LORD. However, Hopkins warned Butcher that the British might "wash out" on OVERLORD at Cairo and Teheran. Everything was in the balance.

Eisenhower spent the twenty-third in Algiers at work on the brief he would deliver at the CCS meetings in Cairo. After a short meeting with an assistant to Navy Secretary Knox, an Illinois attorney named Adlai Stevenson, Eisenhower left the office on an inspection tour. Thus, he was out of touch when word reached Algiers of a Stateside radio broadcast by the columnist Drew Pearson in Washington revealing that General George S. Patton had violated military law by slapping American enlisted men in field hospitals at the height of the Sicily battles in August. According to Pearson, Patton on two separate occasions in August had upbraided and slapped GIs recovering from "nervous exhaustion" in full view of hospital staffs. Pearson's report and the ensuing disclosures that week exposed a long-simmering crisis at AFHQ.

Eisenhower had known about the incident for weeks. When first informed of the slapping episode, he had dispatched his "eyes and ears," General Everett Hughes, to investigate the circumstances, which, if true, constituted a court-martial offense against Patton. Armed with the Hughes report and affidavits filed by medical personnel who had witnessed the incidents, Eisenhower had fired off a personal and informal reprimand to Patton, and had required him to apologize personally to the two soldiers and to avoid repetition. Then, reluctant to lose Patton, Eisenhower had asked Demaree Bess of the *Saturday Evening Post,* Charles Daly of CBS and correspondent Quentin Reynolds into his tent at Amilcar, Tunis, to invite their cooperation in suppressing the story. He disclosed the full facts and offered his own view of Patton's motives and his opinion of Patton's importance as an Army commander, leaving the matter to their discretion.

Patton had been a problem for Eisenhower in both North Africa and Sicily. Temperamental and vain, he had not gotten along with his British colleagues and held himself above his fellow Americans. By his aggressive tactics, however, Patton had revived II Corps in the demoralizing aftermath of the German attack at the Kasserine Pass, and gone on to develop the Seventh Army and lead it to a dazzling string of victories in Sicily.

At the St. Georges Hotel, Butcher had chronicled Eisenhower's thinking in the Patton matter. Privately, Eisenhower had deplored Patton's methods as "severe and wrong," but early on he had intimated to Butcher he would do anything not to relieve him. Eisenhower suspected that Patton's tirade had been a deliberate step to shake up the Seventh Army—and if it had not been deliberate, Eisenhower could cite many instances in history of commanders in the field of battle literally "going crazy" at the sight of the dead and wounded. In either case, "one-third of every army is composed of born leaders and one-third skulkers," he said. Patton knew that occasionally leaders and fighters had to coerce, even shame the others to fight. Eisenhower told Butcher he would keep the matter confidential.

In the three months since, the story had gradually become common knowledge in the theater, along with other stories of Patton's alleged cruelty and insensitivity. Quentin Reynolds had dropped by Eisenhower's office one afternoon to tell him that 50,000 troops in the Seventh Army "would gladly shoot Patton." Finally, after Sicily, Eisenhower had placed Patton on probation and dispatched him to Corsica in command of a shell Seventh Army headquarters as part of a deception intended to draw German intelligence to the possibility of quick Allied attacks on southern France. But Eisenhower continued to recommend Patton for command of an Army group in OVERLORD.

Pearson's disclosures on November 23 were an embarrassment for AFHQ, especially in the eyes of correspondents who had kept quiet only to be unmasked as partners in a conspiracy of silence. In Eisenhower's absence his chief of staff handled the inquiries and compounded AFHQ's problems. Bedell Smith told reporters the literal truth: that Patton had received no official reprimand from Eisenhower. Smith neglected to mention Eisenhower's blistering letter to Patton and orders to apologize personally to the individuals and staffs involved.

Although they were to meet within twenty-four hours, Eisenhower and Marshall corresponded with each other for the record. Responding to Senate calls for an investigation, Marshall wired Eisenhower from Cairo on the twenty-third to seek clarification of the facts. Eisenhower dictated a private letter for Marshall's use in coordinating explanations at the War Department. He described the stellar performance of the Seventh Army and Patton's "absolute refusal to accept any excuses for delay or procrastination" in the rapid Seventh Army advance through Sicily. Investigation revealed that Patton had momentarily lost his temper in encountering "two unwounded, repeat unwounded patients" in tent hospitals, whereupon he had ordered Patton to apologize, but he had left him in command with the "net result . . . that the Seventh Army had high morale throughout the Sicilian campaign . . . "

> To sum up: it is true that General Patton was guilty of reprehensible conduct with respect to two enlisted men. They were suffering from a nervous disorder and in one case the man had a temperature. After exhaustive investigation, including a personal visit to Sicily, I decided that the corrective action as described above was adequate and suitable in the circumstances. I still believe that this decision is sound. As a final word, it has been reported many times to me that in every recent public appearance of Patton before any crowds composed of his own soldiers, he is greeted by thunderous applause . . .

On the twenty-fourth Eisenhower flew to Cairo for the Combined Chiefs of Staff meetings at the Mena House Hotel. He briefed the American and British Chiefs on the prospects of reaching the Po River that winter, and on the relative merits of Italy-based offensives into southern Germany and the Balkans. Eisenhower estimated that operations to the Po River would involve at a minimum a sixty- to ninety-day delay in transfers of landing craft to England for OVERLORD. That night he attended Thanksgiving dinner at the Mena House with Marshall, King and the American staff. His tired appearance prompted Marshall to suggest that he take a vacation for several days. "If your subordinates cannot do [the work] for you," Marshall told him, "you haven't organized them properly."

Accompanied by a small group of personal staff members, Eisenhower left Cairo the next morning for a tour of the Nile and the Holy Land. The group visited Luxor, built on the ancient city of Thebes. They visited the Valley of the Kings and, on the day of Roosevelt's departure for Teheran, flew to Jerusalem for several days at the King David Hotel and a tour of Bethlehem and Gethsemane. On the trip back to Algiers, Eisenhower stopped over in Cairo, where he met briefly on December 1 with Elliott Roosevelt, the President's son, who had been at Teheran for the first three days and returned with the advance party.

By now Eisenhower and Elliott Roosevelt were well acquainted. Roosevelt, who commanded a photo reconnaissance flight wing in Europe, had been a frequent guest at AFHQ, and was soon to be engaged to Ruth Briggs, Smith's personal secretary. Now Elliott Roosevelt gave Eisenhower an insider's view of the conferences to date. From the American point of view, talks had gone all right—Churchill had been "turned aside," and Stalin was in the driver's seat. There would be no extended U.S.-British operations in the eastern Mediterranean without Soviet approval. The cross-Channel invasion was set, though command arrangements had not been worked out. Late that afternoon, Eisenhower returned to Algiers.

It was an anxious wait. On December 1, AFHQ grappled with security problems. Reuters in Stockholm and Lisbon flashed reports that Churchill, Roosevelt and Stalin had met at Teheran, reports that were picked up within several hours by OWI in Washington, Reuters in London, Radio Ankara and Radio Berlin. Eisenhower and Smith decided not to impose censorship lest the theater press corps interpret the action as confirmation that the conference had taken place. That night Eisenhower cabled Marshall, now back in Cairo, to recommend that the presidential party cancel plans to rejoin the *Iowa* at Oran and consider flying back via the central African route.

The next six days in Algiers passed slowly. Eisenhower left the St. Georges Hotel each day at noon. On several occasions after lunch at the villa, he rode horseback. On the third day he spent the afternoon with Smith hunting partridge and discussing the future.

Eisenhower expected that soon he would be returning to Washington to replace Marshall as Chief of Staff. At long last, he was resigned to the change. He had been prepared to request, if asked, that he remain either in the Mediterranean or serve under Marshall as an army group commander in OVERLORD. But he had long since known that the British would insist on a British commander in chief in the Mediterranean, that General Omar Bradley was slated for army group command and that the President would probably recall him to Washington whatever his wishes. Several weeks before, Smith back in Washington on AFHQ business had raised the matter of Eisenhower's future with Marshall and the President and, on Eisenhower's behalf, had politely discouraged the notion of Chief of Staff only to return with word that "unfortunately, the President seems set on you." This had been confirmed by the President himself in their private talks on

November 20. But nothing was official, and, in Cairo, Eisenhower had detected procrastination.

Eisenhower dared to hope that he would be tapped to lead OVERLORD. In the six days between his return to Algiers and the arrival of the homeward-bound presidential party, as was his custom in times of tension, he fired off a spate of personal letters to friends and family. Each night he wrote his wife, Mamie. On the third he wrote Milton, who after eight years at the Department of Agriculture and the Office of War Information had recently assumed the presidency of Kansas State University. In a long letter Dwight praised Milton's inaugural address and discoursed at length on his faith in education as an answer to the ills afflicting the world. Eisenhower wrote his son, John, then completing his final year at West Point, to console him about his poor marks in discipline and military hygiene. "I have a hunch that if you are to look up my own West Point standing in the two subjects," he wrote, "you would find that my grades were lower than yours . . . I repeat that I was never a star student myself, so possibly my ideas of educational training are not too valuable." He wrote a chatty letter to his parents-in-law, "Pupah" and "Min" Doud, thanking them for the "care packages" and clippings from the Denver *Post* about their golden wedding anniversary. He replied to a letter from a cousin living in Junction City, Kansas, who had written with news about his brother Earl and his long-lost maternal uncle, Luther Stover, now living in Kansas.

Butcher's diary contains details of a dinner Eisenhower hosted for the personal staff at the villa on the night of December 4. Smith; a young Army aide, Major Ernest "Tex" Lee; Eisenhower's secretary-chauffeur, Kay Summersby; and Butcher gathered for what all sensed was a farewell.

The staff had been together for a year, through the Darlan affair, the successful TORCH landings, Sicily and Salerno. Now it would be breaking up. Eisenhower recounted the gist of his private talk with Roosevelt in Tunis three weeks earlier. The President leaned definitely toward Marshall for OVERLORD—in the President's opinion, Marshall, the Chief of Staff who had organized the American Army, deserved the historic credit that would befall the man who led the Allied force into battle, mindful that the soldiers best remembered in history were the field commanders. For instance, the man on the street could name General Grant, but few could name Halleck, Lincoln's Civil War Army Chief of Staff.

Eisenhower told the group he agreed with the President. He felt grateful for the chances that had come his way: in two short years he had risen from lieutenant colonel to full general, an ascendancy he had never expected. He had had ample time in the limelight, and his experiences in North Africa and Italy would be invaluable in Washington. And he was grateful to have been able to command troops, a soldier's highest aspiration.

As he talked on, Eisenhower reminisced about George C. Marshall. His favorite story concerned his service in Marshall's Operations Division in the spring of 1942, a hectic time divided between negotiations with the British on European operations and the siege at Bataan and Corregidor. Eisenhower recalled being summoned by the Chief of Staff one afternoon in late March for a talk about promotions. Marshall warned him that he would be spending the war at a desk in Washington and that as a staff officer he would probably not be in line for promotion.

Eisenhower recalled boldly replying that he (Eisenhower) did "not give a damn about his [Marshall's] promotion plans," that he (Eisenhower) would do his duty, and if that locked him to a desk, then "so be it," whereupon he had stood up and strode to the door, where he had caught himself. As he looked back "feeling rather foolish," he detected a flicker of a smile on Marshall's face as the Chief of Staff returned to the papers on his desk. The very next Monday, notice of promotion to Lieutenant General was on his desk. Eisenhower was convinced the outburst, though impulsive, had set him on his course.

Butcher, in his gentle Iowa accent, nudged Eisenhower. He had said many times that Ike would be "the best or worst Chief of Staff in history." Butcher predicted that his "notorious abomination of politics would be an appealing trait with the House and Senate in Washington"—but he lacked Marshall's patience and diplomacy, which had been instrumental in winning congressional support for the President's program.

Eisenhower excused all present from any obligation to return with him to Washington. "I will be carried up to Arlington in six months anyway," he said with a shrug. The group enjoyed a good laugh.

That night, in full expectation from hour to hour that his appointment as Chief of Staff would come, Eisenhower wrote his wife, his fourth letter in as many days:

> I miss you terribly. What is going to happen as the result of all rumored changes in command, etc. I don't know. But no matter what does happen—I do hope I can have a visit with you before too long. I know I am a changed person —no one could be through what I've seen and not be different from what he was at the beginning. But in at least one way I'm certain of my reactions—I love you! I wish I could see you an hour to tell you how much!

At the Mena House Hotel in Cairo, Churchill, Roosevelt and their staffs met to resolve the lingering military issues. Right away it became clear that in view of commitments to OVERLORD, a supporting invasion of southern France, and vigorous prosecution of the Italian war that winter, landing craft were not available for both Churchill's planned offensive into the eastern Mediterranean and an amphibious assault in the Bay of Bengal. Reluctantly, Churchill and Roosevelt decided to set aside both.

Meanwhile Churchill and Eden received President Ismet Inönü of Turkey to warn him that unless the Turks declared war at once, Ankara would have no seat at the peace conference and would thereafter receive "treatment accorded neutrals." Inönü was skeptical of Russian assurances at Teheran and concerned that Russian intervention would come too late to protect Turkish cities against Luftwaffe reprisals staged from Rhodes. With control of the Dardanelles looming as a major postwar Russian preoccupation, Inönü also had misgivings about accepting Soviet aid or in any way being beholden to Moscow. The British had been chased from the Dodecanese and could therefore provide no guarantees. The Turkish government backed out.

Roosevelt and Churchill turned to the matter of command for OVERLORD, which they had promised Stalin would be settled within the fortnight. According to several postwar accounts, the British Chiefs favored Marshall because of his immense prestige in Britain, and the belief that Marshall could ensure that unlimited American resources would be committed to the formidable undertaking. Yet the appointment was not really a question to be worked out between the Americans and the British, but one to be worked out by Roosevelt in consultation with Churchill. As agreed at Quebec, designation of the command was ultimately the President's responsibility.

By now it was obvious to the British that Roosevelt's mind was not made up. Reportedly, in early November Roosevelt had been ready to appoint Marshall but had procrastinated. Marshall's prospective departure for London had been under fire since September in the Hearst press and among isolationist critics in Congress opposed to his replacements—to General Somervell, owing to his role as an early organizer of WPA projects, and to Eisenhower on grounds of suspected pro–New Deal views and the possibility that he was being groomed as Roosevelt's running mate in 1944. Such criticism had prompted Roosevelt's sudden warning to the press in mid-September "not to go out on a limb" in predicting who would go to London, the first real sign that Roosevelt was reconsidering.

Harry Hopkins knew that the President had grown dependent on Marshall's presence in Washington and his ability to handle Congress. Likewise, Admiral King, chief of naval operations, and JCS Chairman Admiral Leahy questioned whether Marshall could be spared from the Combined Chiefs of Staff, where he had led the struggle against deep Allied involvement in the Mediterranean to the detriment of OVERLORD. By implication, all three questioned Eisenhower's effectiveness in carrying on Marshall's work and Marshall's usefulness as a theater commander. Similarly, General John "Blackjack" Pershing, who had known both Marshall and Eisenhower as staff officers, advised Roosevelt in a letter that sending Marshall to Europe would be a "fundamental and very grave error in our military policy" in breaking up working relationships at both levels.

There was no doubt that the Chief of Staff expected and desired command of the army he had organized, and the chance to implement the OVERLORD plan, which bore his stamp. There are stories that Marshall had packed his large Pentagon desk, once belonging to Union Cavalry Commander Philip Sheridan, for shipment to London. In October, Marshall had summoned General F. E. Morgan to Washington for several planning discussions and had begun filling out the roster of American commanders for OVERLORD. George Marshall, who epitomized the best in American military leadership, deserved command of OVERLORD, the greatest military operation in the history of the United States Army, and the most coveted command of the war.

Behind the scenes in Cairo and Teheran, Roosevelt worked on proposals to reward Marshall and at the same time retain both him and Eisenhower in roles in which they had demonstrated effectiveness. Before Teheran, Hopkins had circulated an idea whereby Marshall would assume overall command of both OVERLORD and the Mediterranean front, with Eisenhower and Alan Brooke serving under him as army group commanders. According to this scheme, Marshall and the CCS would deal one to one on the Middle East, Italy, southern France, the Balkans and northern France, a procedure Hopkins felt would ensure maximum coordination of the two theaters and adequate resources for France. A second proposal was essentially the same: to award Marshall command of OVERLORD while retaining him as a member of the Combined Chiefs of Staff.

Whether Roosevelt expected the British to go along with such a sweeping delegation of power to Marshall is unclear. The precedent offered for the first proposal was the authority granted Field Marshal Ferdinand Foch over the western front and Italy in 1918. In casual discussions before Teheran, however, the British had shown little enthusiasm for the proposal. Citing the "multifarious aspects of the war," including its economic and political aspects, the British had noted that the proposed delegation of power to any single individual would be "quite vast" and rejected the Foch precedent as "superficial." Churchill remarked that there was no single officer, "without getting into personalities," qualified to act as broker between the United States and Britain over such diverse interests. Churchill further warned that such an appointment would be read as notice of imminent victory and sap the determination of the Allied populations.

After Teheran, Roosevelt pressed the second idea—command of OVERLORD for Marshall, who would retain his seat on the Combined Chiefs of Staff. On December 4 the Combined Chiefs formally considered the President's proposal. Again the British balked, noting that should the commander of OVERLORD vote in the Combined Chiefs, CCS oversight of the critical European theater would in effect be nullified, upsetting the formal mechanism through which the United States and Britain had pooled resources and coordinated policy for two years. Plainly, the British would not allow fusion of OVERLORD command with the CCS. This recast the question solely to whether Marshall should be spared from Washington to command OVERLORD.

Thereafter Marshall's personal prestige may have been a handicap, perhaps the decisive one. First, the British had not yet nominated Eisenhower's successor. Having served notice that they would favor prosecuting Italy vigorously, the British might feel compelled to offset Marshall's presence in London with Brooke in Italy. Such a move might accentuate the rivalry between the two fronts, and obstruct the natural flow of resources from Italy to OVERLORD. Second, for two years at numerous conferences, Marshall had borne the brunt of the strategic arguments with the British. In prevailing over British objections, Marshall had expended goodwill. Could he serve effectively as a subordinate to Brooke on the CCS? Did Marshall the advocate have the political skills to handle the highly political task of satisfying the British and making an Allied force mesh? The British might be less reluctant to compromise with Eisenhower.

There was much else to be said for Eisenhower. For a year he had carried out missions in the Mediterranean close to British hearts. He had achieved popularity among the British and a reputation for fair-mindedness. Many questioned Eisenhower's abilities as a strategist and considered him overcautious. But the British had worked well with him and the record was one of unbroken victories in the field with an Allied force. North Africa and Italy had been an important proving ground for the policy of integrating forces in a single-command organization, and as BBC correspondent Chester Wilmot put it, Eisenhower's command had proven that for the first time in history an Allied command was possible, "inspired by a spirit of unity and common purpose which would override international prejudices and inter-service rivalries."

Eisenhower had proven in the Darlan affair and recently in the handling of Patton that he would not shrink from accepting responsibility and relieving higher authority of direct involvement in controversial matters, a factor bound to grow in importance as the war progressed. Finally, the President had to consider the consequences of failure, which would be greatly magnified if OVERLORD was commanded by Marshall. In view of the admitted risks, there were advantages to holding Marshall in reserve in the event the U.S. Army was required to retrieve a disaster. Significantly, both of the proposals rejected by the British at Cairo had called for intermediate commanders—buffers between Marshall and a potential failure of the cross-Channel assault.

On the night of the fourth Roosevelt, facing the clear alternative of appointing Marshall to London or retaining him in Washington, deputized Hopkins to take the Chief of Staff aside and sound out his views. Would he, Marshall, prefer command of OVERLORD or remaining in Washington as Chief of Staff? "I shall accept any decision the President would make," Marshall replied.

On December 5, Roosevelt and Churchill left the Mena House Hotel in a jeep for a ride near the pyramids and a private talk. The President told Churchill that he had not made up his mind about Marshall and Eisenhower. According to his account of the talk, Churchill recalled being surprised, but resisted the temptation to remind Roosevelt that at Quebec the British, in ceding command, had assumed that Marshall was the choice. Churchill scrupulously avoided expressing any preference, but he assured Roosevelt that the British would be satisfied with Eisenhower.

That afternoon Roosevelt and Marshall met. The President asked his Chief of Staff to make a decision. Marshall told his biographer, Forrest Pogue, that the President added, "I don't think I could sleep at night with you out of the country." General Marshall remained silent, asking for nothing and offering nothing in return.

On the night of the sixth the British Chiefs formally rejected the proposal to accord the commander of OVERLORD a seat on the CCS. With the conference about to end, Roosevelt moved to consummate the Teheran understandings. Apparently, Roosevelt could not bring himself to inform Marshall of his final decision outright. That night, twenty-four hours short of the second anniversary of Pearl Harbor, Roosevelt summoned Marshall to his hotel suite to assist him in drafting a message.

As the story goes, Marshall drew up a chair, took out a pencil and paper and began jotting down the President's dictations. "From the President to Marshal Stalin," Roosevelt began. "The appointment of General Eisenhower to command of OVERLORD operation has been decided upon. Roosevelt." The President inspected the piece of paper and, in his own handwriting, inserted "immediate."

Without a trace of emotion, Marshall gathered the note and walked to Message Central at the Army Signal Corps Headquarters in the Mena House Hotel. Inadvertently, after filing the message with the duty signalman, Marshall left the document behind. Thirty minutes later the Chief of Staff returned, retrieved the paper and placed it in a military pouch to be dispatched to Algiers for Eisenhower's safekeeping. At the top of the page Marshall had written:

Cairo . . . December 7, 1943

Dear Eisenhower:

I thought you would like to have this as a memento. It was written very hurriedly by me as the final meeting broke up yesterday, the President signing it immediately.

G. C. M.

December 7. Eisenhower and Butcher took breakfast together in the Villa dar el Ouad. The Cairo meetings were over, and the two men awaited a flight to Carthage to greet the presidential party, which would return as planned to Oran. Bedell Smith phoned from the St. Georges Hotel with the text of a confusing message from Marshall asking Eisenhower to submit his personal requests promptly to him in Washington.

Eisenhower, with this vaguest hint of the great responsibilities before him, flew from Algiers to Al Aouina in Tunis. He stood on the tarmac below the ramp and greeted each guest in the presidential party as he disembarked from the *Sacred Cow*—Harry Hopkins, Admiral King and Roosevelt's son-in-law, John Boettinger. Finally the President, in his wheelchair, was hoisted backward down the ramp.

Eisenhower and Roosevelt shook hands and climbed into the presidential limousine for the short ride to the "White House" for a visit. Seated in the rear of the limousine, Roosevelt turned to Eisenhower. "Well, Ike, you are going to command OVERLORD."

Eisenhower was poised. "Mr. President," he replied, "I realize that such an appointment involved difficult decisions. I hope you will not be disappointed."

On that day, December 7, the communiqué of the Teheran conference was released to the world simultaneously in Washington, London and Moscow, confirming that the great meeting had taken place. Only three reporters had been present at Teheran: Edward Nglay of the Chicago *Sun*, Lloyd Stratton of the Associated Press and John Willis of Reuters. With the lifting of censorship, they filed dispatches based on a glimpse of the three leaders at a picture session on the steps of the Russian legation. In the pictures Roosevelt, somber and wrapped in a black cape, held a cigarette. Stalin, in his marshal's tunic, cradled a pipe. Churchill, in a blue airman's uniform, smoked a cigar.

In the communiqué, there was no mention of the United Nations. Many were quick to point out that the vague, almost subdued tone of the document contrasted with the visionary themes of similar proclamations issued in World War I. But the Teheran communiqué brightened the Christmas season in Allied capitals, for it meant that America, the USSR and Britain had met and coordinated plans, overcoming two years of dangerous military and political isolation, and consolidated the anti-fascist coalition, thereby foreclosing Germany's one chance of gaining a military stalemate. The postwar ramifications were unclear but hopeful.

"Out of this meeting there came a strange document," *Newsweek* ventured to comment later that week, "printed in full in the box on this page. The document is strange for this reason; it touches not one concrete question that is troubling the statesmen of the world, and yet, if it can be believed, it solves them all. . . . "

We, the President of the United States of America, the Prime Minister of Great Britain and the Premier of the Soviet Union have met in these four days past in this capital of our ally, Tehran, and have shaped and confirmed our common policy.

We express our determination that our nations shall work together in the war and in the peace that will follow.

As to the war, our military staffs have joined in our round table discussions and we have concerted our plans for the destruction of the German forces. We have reached complete agreement as to the scope and timing of operations which will be undertaken from the east, west and south. The common understanding which we have reached here guarantees that victory will be ours.

And as to peace, we are sure that our concord will make it an enduring peace. We recognize fully the supreme responsibility resting upon us and all the nations to make a peace which will command good will from the overwhelming masses of the people of the world and banish the scourge and terror of war for many generations.

With our diplomatic advisors we have surveyed the problems of the future. We shall seek the cooperation and active participation of all nations, large and small, whose people in heart and mind are dedicated, as are our own peoples, to the elimination of tyranny and slavery, oppression and intolerance. We will welcome them as they may choose to come into the world family of democratic nations.

No power on earth can prevent our destroying the German armies by land, their U-boats by sea and their war planes from the air. Our attacks will be relentless and increasing.

Emerging from these friendly conferences we look with confidence to the day when all the peoples of the world may live free lives untouched by tyranny and according to their varying desires and their own consequences. We come here with hope and determination. We leave here friends in fact, in spirit and in purpose. Signed at Tehran, December 1, 1943.

Roosevelt Churchill Stalin.

JOURNEY HOME

The next several weeks in Algiers were busy as Eisenhower tried to firm up his departure for London. With twenty-six weeks to assume direction of the most complex military operation of the war, Eisenhower was anxious to consult with the COSSAC planning staff and to supervise the deliberations of his OVERLORD deputies. Revisions to the COSSAC plan were inevitable, and Eisenhower knew that no proposed revisions would receive a hearing in the Combined Chiefs of Staff until they had been brought before him and his deputies seated in conference in London and formally endorsed by them.

But it was not to be. There was transition business to wrap up. Formal announcement of the appointment was on hold while both sides maneuvered for the next round of the OVERLORD debate. After receiving word of his appointment, Eisenhower had flown on with the presidential party to Malta and Sicily to consult with Roosevelt. Then, back at the St. Georges, Eisenhower greeted Brooke and the Prime Minister, who passed through on his way to Marrakech for a year-end rest. General Brooke lingered to talk about the conferences, British billets for OVERLORD and Alexander's latest proposals to break the stalemate in Italy by amphibious assault along the coast that would involve yet another extension of the deadline for the LSTs earmarked for England. This would have a ripple effect on all plans because of the landing-craft problem, delaying preparations for both ANVIL and OVERLORD. Brooke's visit was notice that the Combined Chiefs in Cairo had miles to go in working out differences over exactly what had been decided.

ANVIL was a case in point. In the American view, notwithstanding Stalin's "open-mindedness" in the discussion stages, a large-scale ANVIL had become fixed Anglo-American-Soviet policy when it was offered by Roosevelt and Churchill on November 30 and was met by Stalin's reciprocal pledge of a supporting Russian offensive. In American eyes, ANVIL amounted to a pledge to subordinate the Mediterranean front to France, *the* assurance that the Allies would commit all necessary resources to France. In the British view, Teheran had produced two clear-cut decisions: first, an Anglo-American commitment to open a front in France; second, British consent to curtail military operations in the eastern Mediterranean basin aimed at bringing Turkey into the war in exchange for American consent to drop plans in the Bay of Bengal, which together ensured adequate resources for the assault against France with a reserve to press the campaign in Italy. Churchill had been clear about Rome. Landings in southern France, while agreed upon, were a commitment of lesser stature, an expedient to ensure that Mediterranean operations would support OVERLORD when the time came.

The Teheran military conclusions overlooked Rome, for which Churchill had a simple explanation, later set forth in his memoirs. At Teheran everyone had been under the impression that the fall of Rome was imminent—none had contemplated, much less foreseen, the disappointing results of Alexander's November offensives. Churchill recalled not only his solemn pledge to Stalin that the Allied forces "would not stand idle" for six months, but his warning that the failure to take Rome would, among other things, expose Churchill to parliamentary reproaches that British forces were failing to render aid to the Red Army. Stalin had not denied that Rome had to precede ANVIL, since, logically, failure to take Rome could only be attributed to a German stand south of Rome in sufficient strength to accomplish the diversionary purpose of ANVIL.

But Churchill would explain that even the early capture of Rome would not have resolved the matter. In the British view, since OVERLORD and ANVIL were conceived as mutually supporting, ANVIL was binding insofar as its military assumptions were valid: that it would prove practical to launch the two operations simultaneously, and that in May 1944 ANVIL would turn out to be the best option among the many available to prevent German concentrations against OVERLORD. To say that ANVIL was a firm commitment valid in any and all circumstances would be to say that ANVIL was a political commitment, not a military undertaking. Churchill rejected any such idea, or related idea, that ANVIL amounted to a sort of open-ended pledge to reinforce France from Italy. Literally speaking, long-range objectives for Italy and France had *not* been settled because they could not be.

Once again, Eisenhower found himself on the spot. Though he was headed for a rival theater, Eisenhower remained commander in chief in Italy. Meanwhile, Churchill hoped to commit Eisenhower before he left for London and stepped up Italian operations, operations in line with his appraisals filed as Mediterranean commander in chief in early November before Cairo. Then Eisenhower had strongly affirmed the strategic importance of the Po River and the sixty-division Balkan "belt" idea, and had reaffirmed their importance at the first Cairo conference. In London, Eisenhower would be reminded of this and reminded of the fact that he had once called ANVIL, with its landings 500 miles from the English Channel in an area confined by the rugged Massif Central, a "necessarily isolated and small scale operation."

Eisenhower faced other unresolved problems, such as command of the strategic air forces in the OVERLORD period. Personnel choices lagged. Evidently, to sidestep the debate over Rhodes, Marshall had flown directly from Cairo to the Far East. From MacArthur's headquarters in Brisbane, Marshall sent Eisenhower a long list of suggestions for filling army and corps command slots by juggling the Italian and OVERLORD command billets among Generals Clark, Truscott, Patton, Devers and Eaker. After weeks of negotiations, Eisenhower would prevail on most of Marshall's requests. He would fail, however, to achieve prompt clarification of the "puzzling" CCS decisions on air command arrangements, a problem linked procedurally to ANVIL by an elaborate command setup for POINTBLANK, which the Americans seemed to have accepted in order to secure autonomy for the air forces, and by the British to ensure a review of ANVIL.

U.S. Army Air Corps Commander General Henry "Hap" Arnold called on Eisenhower, as did General Carl "Tooey" Spaatz, commander of the U.S. Eighth and Fifteenth air forces. The topic of discussion was the as yet undefined role of the strategic air forces in OVERLORD. As expected, the CCS in ordering POINTBLANK had officially subordinated air policy to the needs of the invasion. But in so doing, the Combined Chiefs had omitted dates and procedures wherein the strategic air forces earmarked for POINTBLANK would pass to Eisenhower's command. In the latest strategic air force directive, the first target priority set was the defeat of the German air force, a "preliminary" to OVERLORD. Other priorities served the wider objective of POINTBLANK first spelled out at Casablanca calling for the "progressive destruction and dislocation of the German military, industrial and economic system, and the *undermining of the morale of the German people to a point where their capacity for armed resistance is fatally undermined.*" The clause embodied the idea, pushed by Arnold and RAF Air

Chief Marshal Charles Portal ever since, that the air arm, if unleashed, stood a chance of achieving an outright military decision over Germany, thus rendering a land invasion unnecessary.

Conflict seemed inevitable. Until now, strategic air policy had more or less been compatible with the limited claim on the strategic air forces by ground operations in North Africa and Italy. OVERLORD would be different, and Eisenhower intended to call for support on a scale eclipsing all other operations to date. Targeting policy would be at stake, as well as a crucial point of command, particularly command of the London-based U.S. Eighth Air Force. Eisenhower's ability to function in London as more than an American Army task group commander and messenger between the British, the Americans and rival services based there would hinge on many factors, but particularly on his success in securing command over all American forces in England, including the air forces. Experienced in coalition politics, Eisenhower knew that command of the assigned British forces would be subject to BCOS review at all levels. He would have to negotiate for British compliance with his directives, and to do so effectively, he needed unequivocal ascendancy over all American forces in Britain, land, air, sea.

On close inspection, Spaatz and Arnold had devised a formidable barrier in the complex Cairo command formula. Under it, British Bomber Command and Spaatz, in dual command of the London-based U.S. Eighth Air Force and the Foggia-based U.S. Fifteenth Air Force, had been placed under British Air Chief Marshal Charles Portal, who, as CCS "agent" for POINTBLANK, coordinated all targeting priorities, with no specific timetable for the eventual transfer of the strategic air forces to Eisenhower's command at SHAEF. Significantly, even the Americans who had argued long and hard for committing all resources to the invasion had hedged. According to a separate American JCS directive issued after the Cairo conference, Spaatz was to pass command of the American forces to Eisenhower at a "date to be named later" *by the CCS,* a provision that reinforced the idea that the Americans could abide by the British sense of when a transfer would be appropriate. When would this be? It stood to reason the British could approve the transfer when and if they were satisfied with all aspects of OVERLORD policy, including ANVIL, on which both sides were far apart.

In short, the directive was more than an expression of the customary air staffs' desire for autonomy. The arrangement was backed by a coalition of formidable men, including Churchill, Portal, Spaatz, Arnold, Harris, Jim Doolittle, Brooke and, by implication, Marshall and Roosevelt. Plainly, POINTBLANK was to be given full rein that winter. The directive was also a sign that neither side had resolved basic misgivings about staking all on a land invasion of France or about the idea of delegating real authority to an Allied supreme commander. All of this pointed to the conclusion that Eisenhower's selection on December 6 was a compromise, as much the fruit of indecision at the highest levels as of resolution. In retrospect, frequent suggestions that Marshall's appointment might have averted the command problems facing Eisenhower in December 1943 were naïve.

Meanwhile Eisenhower attended to old business in Algiers. On the thirteenth, Assistant Secretary of War John J. McCloy arrived from Washington on an eleventh-hour mission to curb De Gaulle's abrupt purge and arrest of a number of leading pro-Giraud colonial officials, a preliminary to his final consolidation of complete power over the Algiers-based French Committee of National Liberation (FCNL). McCloy conveyed the President's demand that Peyrouton, Boisson, Noguès and other officials who had defected with Darlan in November 1942 not be brought to public trial.

By now Eisenhower was eager to shed his role as a mediator between London, Washington and the rival FCNL factions led by Giraud and De Gaulle. In the weary months spent at work on French problems, Eisenhower had, assisted by Harold Macmillan of the British Foreign Office and Robert Murphy of the State Department, managed the gradual shift toward De Gaulle, mainly with British backing. In the course of it, he had gained a grudging admiration for the intransigent De Gaulle and his quest to restore French authority and power. The American favorite, General Henri Giraud, had gradually lost out. Giraud had concentrated exclusively on military matters to the detriment of politics, absenting himself from Algiers at critical moments in the power struggle that summer, including the entire month of July, which he had spent in Washington negotiating arms deliveries for the French forces in Italy and Algeria. In his absence De Gaulle had subordinated Giraud's military command to the FCNL structure, commenced the purge of pro-Darlan officials, and ramrodded provisions through the FCNL, reducing Giraud's political power to a simple veto.

American apprehensions remained. Roosevelt proceeded cautiously on recognition owing to misgivings about De Gaulle's ambitions, his anti-Americanism, and evident concern that formal recognition of a provisional French government might accelerate Soviet moves in Poland, a concern soon to be heightened by Harriman's warnings that Moscow was on the verge of forming a new Polish committee to implement the Curzon Line. From the American point of view, any action by Eisenhower advancing recognition of De Gaulle would be suspect, and yet the French situation was an important bridge to the British, who increasingly identified De Gaulle and a strong France as essential to their own future. There was a bright spot —De Gaulle's fate was linked to ANVIL. Southern France was to be the point of entry for French forces in the Mediterranean in order to avoid political and military complications inherent in utilizing large French forces in the invasion battle. This meant that British opposition to ANVIL might not be so unbending, after all. Down the road, Eisenhower could perhaps see a progression: step-by-step inclusion of the Gaullists in OVERLORD, followed by British support for ANVIL ushering in new mutual confidence and a solution to the air problem.

By mid-month, Alexander's 15th Army Group Headquarters finished work on bold proposals for a two-division Fifth Army "end run" to break the stalemate in Italy. The plan, operation SHINGLE, included amphibious landings at Anzio, thirty miles south of Rome and sixty miles behind German lines, with the objective of turning the German Nineteenth Army flank anchored on the Tyrrhenian Sea. About to depart the theater, Eisenhower was reluctant to take a position on a matter that could look very different to him in his new capacity. But the recently extended deadlines on withdrawal of the OVERLORD LSTs approached:* 104 LSTs were available in Italy; 88 were needed for transporting two divisions to Anzio in the first wave, the minimal force which General Clark had estimated in November could operate independently of the main body of the Fifth Army for about seven days; and 68 LSTs were scheduled to depart Naples for Britain, leaving a deficiency of 52 for Anzio, assuming no extension of the OVERLORD deadline.

The Anzio plan, operation SHINGLE, had first been drawn up in early November. The 15th Army Group regarded the towns of Anzio and Nettuno as ideal targets for an amphibious attack. Situated together on an undefended coastal plain near Rome, Anzio and Nettuno were nestled close to the Alban Hills, the last barriers athwart the southern approaches to Rome. In the original idea, landings at Anzio would come in the climactic stages of an offensive launched as the Fifth Army entered the town of Frosinone, twenty miles south of Anzio. According to the Fifth Army plan, VI Corps, when assured of quick linkup with the Fifth Army, would fall out of line, board at Naples, and after surprise landings at Anzio, advance boldly inland to seize the Alban Hills and threaten German road connections to Rome, forcing the German Tenth Army to retreat and abandon Italy south of the mountainous Pisa–Rimini line. The plan, as originally conceived, offered the best chance of reaching Rome quickly. Beyond Rome, Alexander might reach the Po River Valley by spring, where his forces would be poised to threaten southern France, or Yugoslavia and southern Germany through the Ljubljana Gap, in which event supporting operations for OVERLORD might be reappraised.

But times had changed. Historian Martin Blumenson shows how by December, SHINGLE entailed major risks. Alexander's late November offensive had stalled, raising the possibility that the Germans could successfully reinforce the area and isolate the landing force at Anzio before the Fifth and Eighth armies could break through the German Tenth Army and link up. In that case, Allied forces in Italy would be divided between two major

*At Cairo, the CCS had postponed the December 15 deadline one month.

battles south of Rome, with a beachhead forced to draw on transports for supply over the beaches, disrupting the redeployments back to England and preparations for ANVIL indefinitely.

With a review set for Christmas in Tunis, Eisenhower flew back to Naples for another week-long tour of the Sangro–Cassino front and conferences with Clark, Montgomery and Alexander. There he observed firsthand the conditions that rendered the original SHINGLE plans obsolete. Clark's Fifth Army was stalled on the Garigliano River, sixty miles from Anzio, with no prospects of reaching Frosinone. The Eighth Army campaign was epitomized by the December "river fighting." On December 10 the British Eighth Army crossed the Moro. Eighteen days would pass before the same army breached the Ortana River line, a scant two miles beyond the Moro. The Riccio River was next, and then the Pescara.

By Christmas the Italian theater G-2 section had concluded that the Germans were too strong to permit SHINGLE in its present form. The German Tenth Army, well entrenched behind the Garigliano River, could spare an estimated three divisions to defend Anzio, and two others, the 29th and 90th panzer divisions, had moved into reserve south of Rome, into positions to respond quickly. The two forces were deemed capable of roping off the Anzio beachhead until fresh units drawn from the newly formed German Fourteenth Army in northern Italy arrived. At best, SHINGLE might force a breakthrough on the Garigliano, but SHINGLE and a Fifth Army offensive would probably not be mutually supporting for weeks, much less days.

By Christmas Eve, with ANVIL implicitly at stake, the Americans and British divided sharply in the CCS. On the twenty-third, Eisenhower and Bedell Smith visited the Caserta Palace, in Naples, the newly proposed AFHQ site. According to Butcher, they were tense and depressed. Eisenhower invited Smith to his quarters for a private dinner, whereupon the chief of staff abruptly refused. Tempers flared. "No chief of staff ever refuses the invitation of his commanding general to dinner," Eisenhower scolded Smith. Smith offered to quit. Eisenhower replied, "Fine," telling Smith for the first time that the British and Marshall had opposed his transfer to London anyway. It was a momentary skirmish, resolved by a handshake on Christmas morning as they flew off to Tunis and meetings with Churchill, Alexander, Fleet Admiral Sir Andrew Cunningham, Air Chief Marshal Tedder and General Maitland Wilson, the newly designated supreme commander, appointed by Churchill as Eisenhower's successor at AFHQ.

Ostensibly Churchill had arranged the meeting to unite Eisenhower and Wilson so as to ensure a smooth transition in Italy, but the wide-ranging discussions seemed timed to commit Eisenhower on SHINGLE before he left for London and began submitting claims for OVERLORD. Exhibiting the defiantly gloomy mood that he had assumed since Teheran, Churchill spoke of his determination to resume a full-scale offensive in Italy. He politely demanded SHINGLE by January 15, having weighed the hazards confronting SHINGLE and accepted them. The Prime Minister was not deterred by the prospect of an isolated Anzio cauldron, nor was he concerned that preparations for ANVIL might be disrupted, since the feasibility of ANVIL depended on securing Rome first. An "end run" strategy provided the only chance of breaking the winter stalemate, and so Churchill insisted on it.

Martin Blumenson notes that Eisenhower was "reluctant even to participate in the discussions." After several hours of talks he gave ground and agreed to endorse another extension for the LSTs that were due to leave Italy imminently. Afterward Churchill cabled Roosevelt with a detailed account of the meeting in which "Eisenhower and all of his high officers" had finally agreed that it would be "irrational" not to retain fifty-six LSTs for the "three weeks" necessary to mount SHINGLE, LSTs destined otherwise to sit in English ports all winter.

Four days elapsed. In his reply Roosevelt cautioned Churchill that Stalin would have to be consulted if there was any "delay or hazard" to ANVIL, whereupon, confident of success, he approved SHINGLE. On the same day, however, Marshall summoned Eisenhower back to Washington for a rest and talks, dashing Eisenhower's hopes for a quick getaway to London.

On December 30, as Butcher made arrangements for the return trip, Eisenhower forlornly wrapped up his affairs in Algiers. He met with De Gaulle to discuss the arrests of former Vichy officials and plans for equipping French units to participate in ANVIL—meetings of which there are several versions. Butcher called it a "love fest." In his diary Stimson described Eisenhower's version rendered in Washington several days later. According to Stimson, Eisenhower claimed that he had finally gained De Gaulle for the Allied cause: De Gaulle had pledged no public trials for Flandin, Peyrouten and Boisson, and no executions. In his own version, De Gaulle claimed Eisenhower for the cause of Free France. He recalled that as they shook hands, Eisenhower manfully confessed American errors from the beginning of the U.S. relationship with De Gaulle dating back to 1940, especially American errors in the Darlan affair, intimated to De Gaulle that he (Eisenhower) had been falsely warned against him (De Gaulle). Eisenhower now "recognized that this judgment was mistaken," that he needed De Gaulle's help and had "come to ask for it." "At last!" De Gaulle quoted himself. "You are a real man, as you know to say 'I was wrong.'"

On New Year's Eve, 1943, without announcement or the formality of a farewell at AFHQ, Eisenhower concluded fourteen months of service in Algiers. He, Butcher and Sergeant Mickey McKeogh, his orderly, left Algiers aboard a B-17 Fortress for Marrakech and a third conference with Churchill in the luxurious Taylor Villa at the base of the Atlas Mountains. Montgomery flew in to report on the COSSAC planning sessions in London, which he attended as the newly designated 21st Army Group commander. The group discussed Bomber Command's role in OVERLORD and SHINGLE, and expanding the assault phase (NEPTUNE) as recommended by the working group in London.

Montgomery had closely inspected the COSSAC plan, and his reaction had been "that of any trained soldier": the primarily British COSSAC staff, working within stringent, unrealistic landing craft and troop limitations set at Quebec, had succeeded in defining the variables governing tactical success or failure of the landings. Otherwise, the plan bore the stamp, as Chester Wilmot later wrote, of the "atmosphere of doubt which prevailed in Britain about the whole OVERLORD project."

As of December 30 the NEPTUNE plan, covering the assault phase of OVERLORD, envisioned smaller-scale landings at Normandy than the landings at Salerno and Sicily. Problems had to be faced at once: strengthening the NEPTUNE assault from three to five divisions, and extending the narrow 25-mile invasion front centered on Bayeux, Normandy. Montgomery's view was that a decision to expand the assault had to be made at once and reallocations settled for troops, support ships and landing craft so that planners could get to work quickly. An obvious source for these reallocations would be Italy—Montgomery urged prompt cancellation of ANVIL.

At 4:15 A.M. on January 1, 1944, Eisenhower departed Marrakech and Africa. Airborne over the Atlantic, he vaguely complained to Butcher that the arrangements at AFHQ, as he relinquished command, seemed "highly unsatisfactory." He was particularly disturbed to learn that his successor, General Maitland Wilson, had decided to continue to base AFHQ in Algiers. But he admitted he felt personal relief. He trusted he would be dealing less with French politics and with Churchill's constant meddling in military affairs, since, he explained, the Prime Minister at Tunis had "practically taken tactical control of the Mediterranean."

The War Department imposed complete censorship on the trip. A three-week absence from London on the heels of Roosevelt's Christmas announcement would, if known, have confirmed prematurely what to COSSAC planners in London and the Combined Chiefs of Staff in Washington was a foregone conclusion: the May 1 target date discussed at Teheran was unrealistic. The Western Allies would observe the strict letter of the "May" pledge at Teheran, but this now meant the end of May. In the wake of Teheran, the Americans apparently had come around to General Brooke's approach toward ensuring a concurrent eastern-front offensive. To protect the thirty-seven-division force, the Allies would rely on the June weather in Russia in addition to Russian pledges, and now debated only the method and timing of presenting the fact of the postponement to Moscow.

And so Eisenhower was homeward bound over the Atlantic as the year 1944 opened, a year destined to bring forth a new world. Indicating the global sweep of the war, the Allied press that day carried battle communiqués reporting on military developments from Kiev to Brisbane.

American-Japanese air battles raged off the Arakan coast. In Italy, as the British Eighth Army fought toward Pescara, the Fifth Army resumed the attack toward the Garigliano. Near Kiev the Red Army, having checked the German counteroffensive, launched fresh attacks toward the prewar Polish frontier at Lvov. U.S. Eighth Air Force bombers struck industrial targets in the Ruhr and the low countries. Progress was evident on all fronts, but all looked westward to the English Channel, and the invasion of France. In Berlin, Hitler, in his New Year's proclamation, braced the German people for invasion on both fronts. In it he reviewed the five-year history of the war in Europe, provoked by England's "300-year-old practice of British-made European wars." Hitler taunted the British at length for the alliance with the "devil of Bolshevism," which, he predicted, would betray England, no matter what the outcome. Hitler pledged a fight to the finish in a struggle overriding all humanitarian considerations, one leaving "no victors and vanquished but only survivors and annihilated."

Years later Mamie recalled her husband's restless visit. It was his first trip to the United States since leaving Washington eighteen months earlier to assume command of the American forces in England. As Eisenhower had warned her in December, he was a changed man. Physically, he was older. His chain-smoking had aggravated bouts of colds and bronchitis. What was left of his blond hair was turning gray; he had thickened around the waist and in the face, and his voice was deeper.

In private Eisenhower seemed somber and hard to approach. Two days after arriving home, the couple traveled through a snowstorm to West Point for a brief reunion with their twenty-year-old son, John. The tight-knit Eisenhower family spent six hours aboard a train docked at East Shore Station below the West Point plain. John brought several friends along for a dinner party. Afterward father and son talked about West Point, John's forthcoming graduation in June and his ideas about a service branch. For the first time his father's official concerns could not be discussed, and John noticed that Eisenhower's "no nonsense life of the past 18 months had sharpened his manner somewhat," though he could not measure the change precisely—the last time father and son had seen each other was for a few hours shortly after Eisenhower's surprise appointment to command the European theater in June 1942, an appointment that had lifted him out of thirty-one years of staff work. John noted that his father seemed preoccupied and impatient to get on with the conferences in Washington.

From West Point, Eisenhower flew on to Manhattan, Kansas, for a brief clandestine reunion with his eighty-two-year-old mother, Ida, Milton, and his eldest brother, Edgar, an attorney in Tacoma, Washington. He returned to Washington for ten days of meetings, private luncheons and dinners, at which he sounded out official Washington for support, and surveyed the scene in the American capital.

Eisenhower and Butcher soon found that they had many adjustments to make also. Butcher noted in his diary that for both men, returning to Washington was a jarring experience. Only the Wardman Park Hotel, which they had both known as a hub for New Deal politicians, seemed familiar. Mamie had set up house in an annex of the Wardman and furnished it with her husband's favorite keepsakes: the silver tea service Eisenhower had painstakingly saved for, buying a piece a year since their fourth anniversary, in 1920; two blue Chinese rugs purchased while they were in the Philippines; the family piano; and his favorite overstuffed chair in the living room. She displayed their bound set of Harvard classics, purchased in the early 1930s, in a bookcase next to several framed French prints acquired when they had lived in Paris on the Rue d'Auteil twelve years earlier. But the city beneath the third-story window, like the returning soldiers, had been transformed.

The Eisenhowers had first known Washington during Eisenhower's stint as a student at the Army War College in the Coolidge era, then later in the depths of the Depression years, a time when the city moved at the slower pace of its predominantly Southern, Tidewater character. During the years 1926–35, Eisenhower had made his reputation as a staff officer under Generals George Van Horn Moseley and MacArthur, years described by Mamie in letters written to her mother in Denver. In them, she had noted Ike's long hours of work but seemed otherwise content with a comfortable and secure life—she had described Ike riding the nickel trolley from the Wyoming Apartments on Connecticut and 22nd to the War Department at the State, War and Navy Building next to the White House; the fishing and boating Saturdays on the Potomac; Sunday School for John before brunch and afternoon polo at Fort Myers with the George Pattons; for Ike and George, an occasional overnight goose-hunting trip to Aberdeen, Maryland; and the evenings at the Wyoming Apartments listening to boxing from the Uline Arena; Ike's steady advancement. The Eisenhowers had been building for retirement out West, she confided, when in January 1933 MacArthur, as chief of staff, asked Eisenhower to serve as his assistant. This meant an extended stay in Washington, "a shock to us," as Mamie complained cheerfully, adding "but when the Chief of Staff puts it up to you, there is nothing else to do—besides we are comfortable here and could be loads worse off." Mamie assured her mother that the news "was a marvelous compliment to Ike," and that if "anything should pop up in China," Ike would be on the ground floor "to hop right off," noting "it would kill him if another war broke out and he didn't get in it—surely in this army we can never tell or make plans."

Eleven years later Washington was a wartime capital, tense, expectant, humming to the pace set by the proliferating war agencies that regulated an industrial and wartime complex producing annually 100,000 aircraft and over 20,000 tanks, and industrial output levels which were double prewar production and which far outstripped the combined production of Japan and Germany. Prefabricated housing accommodated the crush of wartime employees. Temporary buildings stood on the Mall, and near the Ellipse. Small wartime factories sprouted through the city, particularly northward in the Maryland suburbs. The War Department, located in the temporary buildings on Constitution Avenue when Eisenhower first had reported for work at OPD in January 1942, had moved across the Potomac into the Pentagon complex, a five-story building with five concentric rings, housing a labyrinth of offices built over a 200-yard concourse for buses and taxis.

Few in Washington had begun to focus on the forthcoming invasion, however. In his diary, Butcher grumbled about "dirges of sacrifice" on the home front, and the sharp contrast he found at private cocktail parties between the "universal hatred of Japan" and the ambivalence about the European war, which many of his friends considered to be over. Indeed, newspapers and weekly magazines freely speculated about an imminent German collapse. Prominent reports indicated that the German satellites were sounding out the Allies on surrender terms in awareness "that Germany has irrevocably lost the war." Newspaper headlines heralded the punishing Eighth Air Force "third front" bombing sweeps over the Ruhr, Silesia and Berlin. Analysts compared German military straits in the Ukraine and Poland with the western front in November 1918, when the German General Staff, fearful of invasion and internal revolt, abruptly pushed the Berlin Socialists forward to arrange an armistice.

James Byrnes, Henry Stimson and other top government officials campaigned against complacency fed by predictions of early victory. Even General "Hap" Arnold, in an article for the Washington *Post* at midmonth, cautioned that the Eighth Air Force aerial offensives were no substitute for a ground invasion of Europe, that they could only make the invasion "as economical as possible." However, many of Arnold's subordinates were less constrained. In early January the Washington *Post* correspondent Edward F. Folliard disclosed a confidential report by General James Doolittle on the Pantelleria raids in June 1943 leading to the surrender of the 12,000-man Italian garrison which had "proven conclusively that no agency can stand up under the prolonged, uncontested bombardment of purposely selected objectives." Doolittle's confidential report was more congenial than Administration propaganda on behalf of a National Service Law, and provided hope that "the invasion of Europe might not be the awesome thing it has come to be."

Criticism of the Roosevelt Administration, building since Cordell Hull's voyage to Moscow in October, was growing. James Byrnes, director of the Office of War Mobilization, and his controversial deputy, General Lucius Clay, battled congressional pressure to begin reconversion of aircraft and shipping plants for civilian use. Organized labor, headed by Philip Murray of the CIO and the United Mine Workers' president, John L. Lewis, threatened nationwide rail and coal strikes against wage freezes. A coalition of labor and business leaders opposed plans unveiled in the President's State of the Union message for a National Service Law and other measures for "total mobilization" for the offensives planned in 1944. And 1944 was an election year, an unknown factor in assessing war policy. Gradually, for the first time since December, politicians and editorialists ventured doubts about U.S. policy toward the Russians, doubts reinforced by Moscow's campaign to force the Allied hand on the Polish boundary problem raised at Moscow and Teheran.

As lead columns of the Red Army rolled toward Rumania and crossed the pre-1941 Polish border at Dubno, Moscow announced the details of a territorial "compromise" on the western frontier, a "modified Curzon Line." To compensate Poland for the western Ukraine and Belorussia, annexed by Russia in 1939, Moscow now weighed a grant of Prussian territory on the Baltic for Poland, including Pomerania, "according to the degree of friendliness shown by the Polish government." Barnett Nover of the Washington *Post,* in a long article, analyzed Moscow's "ominous" excursion into the territorial question, hitherto shelved lest "premature discussion split the ranks of the U.N." He detected signs in the Moscow "compromise" that the Soviets were tinkering with the "fatal mistake" of equating "subservient" neighbors with "friendly" neighbors. Aroused by an unconfirmed report by the "diplomat correspondent" of the London *Observer* that the United States and Britain had in fact endorsed the Curzon Line at Teheran, the powerful Republican Senators Robert Taft and Arthur Vandenberg set a congressional probe into the Polish question and the "secret understandings" at Teheran.

Roosevelt's vulnerabilities were apparent. Even before Pearl Harbor and before Hitler "honored" his pact with Japan and declared war on the United States, the President had succeeded in educating the American public about the need to combat Germany, to participate in European affairs and to sponsor a future-oriented United Nations. But he had done so by minimizing the risks of a cross-Channel invasion and by minimizing likely Soviet postwar gains, expedients forced on him by domestic opponents unwilling either to back U.S. intervention on terms short of a clear-cut victory without compromise of American principles or to support full mobilization which might have enabled Roosevelt to accomplish this. Indeed, mobilization plans had been curtailed steadily from peak Army estimates in June 1942 calling for a 300-division Army to the current Army ceilings frozen at 90 divisions, with powerful pressure to divert many of these units to the Pacific.

Russia was the question mark. For weeks the *Newsweek* columnist Ernest Lindley had been warning about the gulf between casual popular expectations of a decisive American victory in Europe and the military means available to secure it, a potentially rich future harvest for political revisionism. Lindley proceeded to write off American-British differences, which had once been so troublesome. Differences remained in areas such as policy toward India, agricultural subsidies, civilian air transport, "nothing that would arouse American opinion." But a total victory for the United Nations left another great power to be considered—Russia. Hopes for establishing international peacekeeping would depend on the position of the Soviet Union—its absence from international organizations would leave peacekeeping bodies "incomplete." However, terms for Russian participation had yet to be discussed, which, according to Lindley, accounted for the visits of British diplomats to Washington in recent months. Until the British had hammered out a satisfactory U.S. commitment to a European position, Whitehall would be forever on the lookout to discuss spheres of influence with the Soviet Union as a hedge against being abandoned to face this new colossus alone. Seemingly, Lindley did not consider the Russians a threat as such, unless transformed into one by default or carelessness, but appearances would count heavily, appearances of Russian restraint and cooperation.

And so by January 1944 Roosevelt's war policy was buffeted: by reawakening isolationists ready to bid for control of the Republican party at the July convention; by disgruntled labor leaders tired of wage controls imposed on a work force that produced at 250 percent of 1941 levels; by expectations of quick victory despite irreversible reductions set on Army mobilization levels that in December 1942 had been dictated by these very expectations; by shortages in landing craft, particularly the LST, due to imperfect estimates, production bottlenecks, and to allocations controlled by the Navy, as well as Chief of Naval Operations Admiral Ernest King's "private war" on Japan and plans for the Nimitz-MacArthur "island hopping" offensive in the Gilberts and New Britain that winter. Prodigious U.S. industrial output obscured the military hazards of the invasion itself. Because of capital-ship production for the Pacific, there would be no substantial reserve of LSTs and other specialized landing craft to provide for adjustments in OVERLORD plans, and by late summer of 1944, the Allies would face a shortage of reserve divisions on every front.

Eisenhower made his rounds in Washington incognito. Mamie recalled that by six o'clock each morning her husband was cooking his own eggs and bacon, and pacing about the tight kitchen annex of their Wardman Park apartment. McKeogh would arrive at seven. Forty-five minutes later Colonel Frank McCarthy of the War Department came to the back door to escort her husband on his daily rounds. Eisenhower would leave the hotel through the service elevator, wearing a plain army cap and a trench coat to conceal his insignia. He rode to appointments in a staff car with curtains drawn over the windows.

Throughout, Bedell Smith in London kept in close touch with the early OVERLORD planning sessions in the British capital. Returning from his visit to Marrakech, Montgomery presented two proposals. First, he decided to endorse a significant strengthening of the OVERLORD assault, from three to five assault divisions, with two in floating reserve, and wider use of airborne elements. Second, Montgomery would recommend that ANVIL be canceled to be sure of adequate resources for the expanded assault in light of SHINGLE. Smith warned of a British paper, circulated by Air Chief Marshal Portal and the British Air Ministry for eventual submission to the Combined Chiefs of Staff, that sought to dictate in detail the targeting procedures and staff organization of the British Second and U.S. Ninth tactical air forces, forces assigned to OVERLORD. The Portal plan presupposed strict guidelines and restrictions accompanying later contributions to SHAEF by British Bomber Command and the U.S. Eighth and Fifteenth air forces.

Eisenhower and Marshall met several times in Marshall's Pentagon offices. Claiming he had gained Churchill's agreement "in principle" at Marrakech about eventual control of Bomber Command, Eisenhower was indignant about the British effort to dictate air procedures in advance. Marshall was sympathetic and admitted that he had intended, if named supreme commander, to insist on unfettered command of the strategic air forces to the extent of "denouncing in the public press any arrangement short of unification." But Marshall had not been named supreme commander, so the question remained whether the Chief of Staff would now insist on Eisenhower's behalf.

Eisenhower tactfully probed for Marshall's support. The answer would unfold in the coming few weeks and would be a qualified "yes." The American Chiefs of Staff would provide everything necessary to sustain OVERLORD as the supreme operation of 1944. But Eisenhower's personal authority over the air forces appeared to depend on a number of factors. Marshall's purpose in recalling Eisenhower to Washington was to emphasize that the American Joint Chiefs naturally expected him, as the senior American in Europe, to bid for maximum resources, specifically to take the lead in pushing ANVIL to fruition. Marshall briefed Eisenhower fully on Teheran and ANVIL. He emphasized several points: first, the U.S. Army wanted the port of Marseilles as a port of disembarkation for the divisions training in the U.S. earmarked for France. Second, in his opinion, ANVIL would prove to be an essential diversionary front in France, especially if launched simultaneously with OVERLORD. Third, without ANVIL, the French divisions in Italy and those forming in Algeria would not find transportation to France. Fourth, another advantage of Marseilles was its proximity to the Italian front, which would permit reinforcement of France from Italy as necessary. Lastly, the Soviets had been assured the operation would take place. Marshall encouraged Eisenhower not to feel constrained in his requests for either operation, since in his opinion OVERLORD and ANVIL were inseparable. In short, the Chief of Staff intended to retain a strong voice over the pace of concessions to the British. Would Marshall await the outcome of SHINGLE before committing himself on air command? "Ike still has the air problem to lick," Butcher concluded at mid-month.

Obviously, a problem Eisenhower faced would be to develop personal independence of Marshall. A factor in the coming debates would be his reluctance to assert himself against the tall, austere Chief of Staff, a man who exerted a considerable hold over all who worked with him, reinforced by his aloof manner and towering authority in Washington. Marshall was an enigma. No matter how long or intimate his working relationship was with anyone, Marshall kept his distance. He addressed subordinates by surnames, except for Patton, whom he called by his first name, and at times even by his nickname, Georgie. Omar Bradley later described Marshall's practice of keeping his staff on edge by demanding much and meeting failure with chilling silence, a trait well known to Eisenhower in his six months at OPD with Marshall after Pearl Harbor.

Marshall's strength was his reputation, however. Like his contemporaries, Eisenhower had developed at a distance what he called "unlimited admiration" for Marshall, fostered first by General Fox Conner, young Eisenhower's commanding officer and mentor in Panama during the early twenties. Conner had served with Marshall in Pershing's AEF; and in long conversations in Panama, Conner had often spoken to Eisenhower of the inevitable world conflict ahead, in which the United States would "have to fight beside allies." Leaders would have to combine strategic sense with a knack for overcoming nationalistic considerations. Conner always came back to the name of George C. Marshall as just the man who might be equal to such a task.

Marshall's reputation reached commanding heights in 1940–41, when he was credited with the near single-handed achievement of prewar mobilization and adequately preparing the Army for the outbreak of the war. Foresight and organizational ability were characteristics of the man who at the close of World War I began a file of evaluations of officers he considered potential commanders should war begin again. Among the names in George Marshall's file was that of Dwight David Eisenhower, a man whom he had met only twice before Eisenhower's arrival in December 1941 to head up his war plans group.

Another problem Eisenhower faced would be his dealings with the President. Here the challenge was not in establishing personal independence, but in discerning the President's wishes in a highly charged diplomatic and political atmosphere. According to his calendar of appointments, Eisenhower met three times with Roosevelt at the White House for talks about De Gaulle and U.S.-French relations still mending from the U.S. role in the Darlan deal. In the third meeting the highly sensitive problem of German occupation policy came up.

Like many of his military contemporaries, Eisenhower harbored mixed feelings about the President, the consummate politician. In the early days of the New Deal he had admired Roosevelt's firm leadership, as evident in letters Eisenhower sent to "Pupah" Doud. Later he had been disillusioned by Roosevelt's Court-packing plan and his purge of Southern Democrats in 1938. Nevertheless, he respected Roosevelt's wartime leadership, a respect mingled with feelings of personal gratitude and wariness.

Shortly after Pearl Harbor, Eisenhower had joined OPD as an expert on the Philippines and found himself in charge of the President's sensitive correspondence with MacArthur, the purpose of which was to defuse MacArthur's defiant stance on the Philippines and Asia, a job not without ironies or impact on future American politics. Eisenhower worked effectively, and attributed his rapid rise thereafter to Roosevelt, but work in the service of the President had never been easy. During the Darlan affair he had endured the President's slow endorsement of his actions, the OWI statements harshly critical of the Darlan deal uncensored by Washington, and the "savage press attacks" a month later over the appointment of Peyrouton as mayor of Algiers. During the stalemate in central Tunisia in the winter of 1943 the President had held up Eisenhower's promotion to four stars, so that for several months he was outranked by his entire array of British AFHQ deputies. In a letter to his son, John, on the Darlan matter, Eisenhower had written:

> I am a Lieutenant Colonel of the regular Army, and I think a pretty good one. . . . temporary promotion has not, I trust, unbalanced my judgment. . . . at any moment, it is possible that a necessity might arise for my relief and consequent demotion. If so, you are not to worry about it . . . *modern war is a very complicated business* and governments are forced to treat individuals as pawns—if it becomes expedient to reduce me, I would be the first to recommend it.

In the chaos of wartime Washington that January, the executive mansion remained an island of tranquillity. The White House was in need of repairs and paint, notably at the base of the ground-floor windows. The residence seemed strangely empty with the President's large family away, and without Harry Hopkins, who after Teheran had gone to the Mayo Clinic to recover from a serious illness.

Of his third and final visit with the President on January 12, Eisenhower later wrote a careful account. He entered the Roosevelts' second-floor bedroom and found the President, dressed in a gray bathrobe, propped up in a plain mahogany four-poster. On a bedside table there was a large stack of memoranda and reports. Officially the President was confined to bed with influenza, but Eisenhower could detect the advanced symptoms of sclerosis, described at Teheran by Churchill's physician, Lord Moran. The President's physical condition had declined sharply in the four weeks since the trip to Malta and Sicily.

Eisenhower stood at the foot of the bed and awaited his invitation to sit down. First he had a personal request for an autographed picture from his chauffeur-secretary, Kay Summersby, who had driven the President on their tour of the battlefields at Carthage. Roosevelt cheerfully inscribed the photo.

Strangely, the subject of OVERLORD, on which the outcome of the war depended, did not come up. Instead Eisenhower listened attentively while the President discussed the controversy heating up between Stimson, McCloy, Hull and Morgenthau over the political and economic future of Germany. Roosevelt intimated that he leaned toward "hard" peace terms, or partition of the German nation and a heavy schedule of reparations levied on German industry for the costs of war. He briefly surveyed the subjects to be taken up by the European Advisory Committee, formed at the Moscow Conference in October and set to convene in London that month to hammer out plans for a three-power occupation of Germany.

Roosevelt was dissatisfied with the prospective U.S. zone in Bavaria and the Rhineland. He reminisced about his days as a student in the Rhineland, where he had acquired a knowledge of Germany firsthand. He described Bavaria, which he had once toured on a bicycle, as a land of Baroque castles, of nothing but "scenery and tourists." The United States should insist on access to the Baltic seaport of Hamburg and avoid the problem of running supply lines through France, and Roosevelt expected British opposition.

Eisenhower offered a suggestion. Perhaps a clash over Hamburg and Bavaria could be averted if the United States and Britain decided to administer the zones jointly—a dual policy in the western zones might avoid confusion. "Ike, the matter of occupational zones has been decided," the President replied merrily. Eisenhower ventured to say that perhaps the Allies should establish an administrative capital at the geographic junction of the American, British and Russian zones to promote a common occupational policy. Roosevelt reminded Eisenhower, "Such matters are of concern to politicians, not generals." Whereupon, Eisenhower recalled years later, "I subsided."

As the two men were joined by the First Lady, Eisenhower rose for the introduction. "Ike," Roosevelt asked, "do you like the title Supreme Commander?"

"I like the title, Mr. President," he replied. "It has the ring of importance —something like Sultan."

Roosevelt laughed, bid Eisenhower "*Adiós,*" and wished him good luck.

Twenty-four hours later, with little resolved by the sojourn home, Eisenhower and Butcher left Washington. Thanks to strong seasonal tailwinds, the transatlantic flight took only thirty hours, including refueling stops at Bermuda and Terceira, the Azores. Two weeks earlier, on the flight from Marrakech to Washington, as the same aircraft passed through the three-mile limit of San Miguel, in the Azores, a Portuguese anti-aircraft battery had briefly opened fire, forcing the plane to divert. This time Eisenhower slept through most of the uneventful flight while Butcher sat in the forward compartment with the pilot.

At midnight on the fourteenth, Eisenhower and Butcher landed at Prestwick Field in Scotland, greeted by Colonel James Gault of the Scots Guard. Gault, a veteran of Eisenhower's pre-TORCH London staff in 1942, was a treasured friend. A balding investment banker, Gault had decided to leave his business once again to serve as Eisenhower's British military aide and Butcher's British counterpart.

Gault had several pleasant surprises. First, he had made direct arrangements with Services of Supply Commander General J.C.H. Lee to have the comfortable sleeper "Bayonet," Eisenhower's private rail car in 1942, at nearby Ayr station for the train trip to London. Second, he had located a suitable apartment in London. Third, Air Chief Marshall Tedder had agreed to relinquish Telegraph Cottage, Eisenhower's onetime country residence, when the planned shift of Supreme headquarters from downtown London to the Kingston suburbs was complete.

Eisenhower's aversion to big cities was well known. In the six months that he had spent in London in 1942, he had gained notoriety and popularity among his troops by conspicuously spurning lavish quarters and avoiding London society. A widely told story was of his first visit to the stately Claridges Hotel in June 1942, when taken aback by the furnishings trimmed with black, gold and pink, Eisenhower had called the place a "funeral parlor," vowed to aides that he would "not fight this war over teacups," and moved to a small unpretentious flat. This time, after searching for several weeks, Gault had located a modest townhouse in Mayfair close enough to Whitehall and the temporary SHAEF offices at Grosvenor Square for overnight stays in London during conferences with Churchill or the British Chiefs.

The all-day train ride through Thornhill, Carlisle, Preston and Birmingham came to an end at eleven-thirty on the night of January 15, 1944, when "Bayonet" pulled to a stop several hundred yards short of Primrose Hill station. In the dense fog the party could barely make out the silhouettes of Eisenhower's personal staff waiting at the sidings. Afterward the motor caravan inched along at five miles an hour, with MPs marching on foot with flashlights to prevent an accident. Orange beacons marking the main thoroughfare glowed strangely along the crescents and curves of Regents Park and Oxford Circus on the way to Hayes Lodge on Chesterfield Street near Berkeley Square.

After midnight the group reached the three-story townhouse located in a fashionable but declining residential area yielding to a proliferation of movie theaters, penny arcades, stores and office buildings. Gault had furnished the dwelling tastefully and modestly with antique Pembroke and gate-leg tables, and a twelve-seat dining table for conferences. Mrs. Mc-Carquodole, the landlady, would accept only a pound sterling a month and had refused a three-month term, asking that the lease read "until the cessation of the war with Germany."

By the sixteenth, Eisenhower was at work at his temporary Grosvenor Square offices. Problems had mounted up large and small—the lack of a headquarters organization, the empty command slots, tactics for the assault, and the still undetermined schedules for ships and landing craft. Within twenty-four hours of his arrival he again communicated with Marshall about a battery of requests to fill out the roster of American generals in command of the three American armies, twelve corps and sixty divisions eventually scheduled to fight on the western front.

At his new offices Eisenhower received General Omar Bradley, a West Point classmate who would command the U.S. First Army in the OVER-LORD assault, with headquarters at Bristol. He also received General J.C.H. Lee, to whom he delegated authority for supply and administration of the U.S. forces in Britain. In the next several days he made courtesy calls on Prime Minister Churchill at 10 Downing Street, King George VI and Queen Elizabeth at Buckingham Palace, and on General Alan Brooke at the chambers of the Imperial General Staff overlooking the Horse Guards.

As General Conner had foreseen twenty years before, a task rivaling grand strategy in importance would be to surmount inter-Allied differences. Like Marshall, Brooke would prove to be a formidable challenge for Eisenhower. The two men were opposites; Eisenhower open and friendly; Brooke reserved, clever, critical and with a habit of staccato speech, which Eisenhower and many other Americans found disconcerting. Famous for a temper he fought to keep in check, Eisenhower met his match in the acerbic Brooke. They disagreed often, "sharply and vehemently" in Eisenhower's words, though Eisenhower often conceded that Brooke was a "brilliant soldier."

Brooke had long been a critic of American concepts for the cross-Channel invasion. In wartime conferences he was the leading proponent of the British-backed peripheral strategies that were deeply rooted in Britain's island position and its centuries of mercantilism, reinforced by the Great War, in which Brooke as a highly decorated gunner had seen firsthand the devastation wreaked on inexperienced British troops by the formidable Germans. The lessons of the Great War had been confirmed by his experiences in the battle of France in June 1940, along with his distrust of American views as untested militarily. In the early debates, Brooke had vigorously opposed a premature strike at Germany through France, as it smacked of the strategies of 1915. He had pushed the British strategy of economic, political and military attrition looking to indirect thrusts against exposed portions of the Nazi empire, Dakar, Libya, Iraq, Greece and Italy, before an eventual return to France. Brooke had modified his position in 1943 and had briefly aspired to command OVERLORD himself. He would remain poised between the two views, though in January he resumed his role as skeptic and spokesman for BCOS views on Italy.

At 47 Grosvenor Square, Eisenhower continued to receive his principal advisers. One of these was Admiral Bertram Ramsay, naval allied commander in chief renowned for his role in the miraculous escape of the British expeditionary force from Dunkirk and later for his command of the Allied Naval Task Force at Sicily. There was also Air Chief Marshal Sir Trafford Leigh-Mallory, in charge of fighter command during the Battle of Britain and now Allied air commander in chief—air consisting currently of the assigned forces, the U.S. Ninth Air Force and British Second Tactical Air Force.

General Bernard Law Montgomery, commander of the 21st Army Group, failed to pay personal respects to the Supreme Commander—a sign of troubles to come. On the morning after Eisenhower's arrival in the British Isles, Montgomery had been away to address the U.S. 29th Division in Scotland. According to prominent accounts of the speech published in London, Montgomery had declared that it was a great personal honor for him to "take command of the British Army and American Army of which General Eisenhower is to be Supreme Commander," a categorical and somewhat misleading statement that caused a stir at 47 Grosvenor.

Montgomery as 21st Army Group commander would command American and British forces in the NEPTUNE assault. But at Quebec the CCS had omitted a "ground commander in chief" in the charts drawn for the OVERLORD command organization, a departure from the procedures in North Africa and Italy, apparently designed to make way for Marshall's direct command over the ground forces in the later stages of the campaign until the American ground force build-up in France warranted a U.S. 12th Army Group and thus a U.S. ground commander serving as a co-equal to Montgomery.

Organization charts still omitted the job of ground commander in chief. But Eisenhower's appointment reopened the issue, and Montgomery's open-ended remarks hinted at challenges ahead. So did London press reactions to the news of Eisenhower's presence in England. All week, friendly editorials in the *Daily Mail,* the *Times* of London and the *Express* welcomed Eisenhower, a popular American figure, back to the British Isles as the first foreigner in English history to have direct command over British forces in war. Then a series of articles in Beaverbrook's *Express* revealed that Eighth Air Force and Bomber Command operations based in the United Kingdom, contrary to popular belief, had not come under the command of the Supreme Commander. Britain's eight daily newspapers highlighted Montgomery's speech and ran feature-length profiles on the British deputies at SHAEF, all veterans of the campaigns in Egypt, Libya and France, and notably "battle proven," in contrast to the relatively inexperienced Americans. Indeed, the British press in January 1944 trained an unusually intense spotlight on potential troubles, particularly since it was widely known that 1944 would be the invasion year. A mood gripped London, Anthony Brown later wrote, "that was both fearful and carefree as it was said to have been at the Guards Ball before Waterloo."

Meanwhile, on the seventeenth, Eisenhower by proclamation established Supreme Headquarters Allied Expeditionary Force (SHAEF). He met with General Morgan to review the COSSAC plan as the planning agency passed out of existence. The Public Information Division that day "confirmed" the Supreme Commander's presence in London, hours before Eisenhower received a throng of reporters accredited to SHAEF for photographs and a press conference. Tactfully Eisenhower refused to contradict Montgomery or to clarify command arrangements following the landings except to caution that correspondents would be unwise to "go out on a limb" in predicting future command arrangements.

Afterward he greeted several hundred officers in the auditorium at 47 Grosvenor Square. In his first talk to the large staff, Eisenhower's theme was a summons to "erase nationality." Butcher's account reads:

> He recalled that at AFHQ British officers had worked under Americans of less rank and vice versa and had done so chiefly for the good of the cause. He said his door was open to any staff members and that he preferred to do business informally rather than formally. However, he expected staff members to remain integrated with their chiefs of sections and Chief of Staff, but asked their indulgence if he failed to know as much about a given phase of operations, particularly on the technical side, as the experts, and if he advances an idea which had already been considered and accepted or rejected, not to be hesitant about giving him the facts. No commander, he intimated, can know everything and that is the reason for having a staff. He recognized several faces from the previous operations and especially welcomed them to the new AEF. He complimented all on the splendid work which had already been done.

2

The "Bill" for OVERLORD

THE COSSAC plan, completed on January 17, 1944, represented over three years of planning and information-gathering for an operation conceived from the start as the supreme Allied military effort of the war. For as Franklin Roosevelt had reminded the American people as early as September 1942, victory over Germany could come only by winning decisive battles in the heartland of Europe. By this the President had meant to say in advance that the forthcoming North African and Italian campaigns could only be preliminaries, and that the time would come for a decision to mount the invasion of France. Reaching that decision had been a battle of its own, an internal one and much bound up with Allied self-confidence. It was a battle still going on in January 1944 as Eisenhower arrived in London, and was destined to last the rest of the war.

One has to review the story of how OVERLORD developed to understand the challenge Eisenhower and his colleagues faced, and the forms that challenge would assume. The concept of OVERLORD had evolved over a period of three years, undergoing many changes. It was to be one of the last great attacks of the war, predominantly American, but it would also be the fruition of British ideas sketched out within weeks of the fall of France in June 1940.

Indeed, one might say that Dunkirk and the ensuing fall of France marked the true beginning of the OVERLORD saga. In military terms, Dunkirk dispelled illusions that the task of dislodging the Germans from their European conquests would be simple. In practical terms, the German occupation of all western Europe gave rise to the need for an Anglo-American invasion somewhere if Europe was to be liberated. And in political terms, the British-French defeat, in June 1940, in exposing the weakness of the European democracies and the consequences of American noninvolvement made it incumbent on the survivors—the British and the Americans—to regroup and to mobilize not only an adequate but a maximum military effort in order to redeem the prestige of Democracy. After Dunkirk, American intervention in Europe became a matter of time so long as Roosevelt remained in office. And Dunkirk had coincided with the rise to power of Sir Winston Churchill, a man who was defiantly committed to a fight to the finish with Hitler in order to save "our own British life, and the long continuity of our institutions and our empire," and who, even after the German attack on Russia, considered it not "worth a place on the cabinet agenda" that "Britain join the spectators . . . who might watch with detached interest, or even relish, a mutually destructive struggle between the Nazi and Communist Empires. . . . "

The earliest British plans, undertaken by Lord Louis Mountbatten's Combined Operations, had necessarily been small-scale. In the summer of 1940 Britain "stood alone," braced for a German invasion, and Churchill had probably not exaggerated when he warned a secret session of Parliament in late June that British survival probably hinged on the outcome of American elections that November, for in Churchill's view everything depended upon Roosevelt's support. Indeed, years later, COSSAC officials would look back on Mountbatten's Combined Operations planning work as an "academic exercise." It had been apparent early on that a military campaign to break the German hold on Europe was not practical without massive U.S. military intervention, an active eastern front to fill the void in ground strength left by the French capitulation. Roosevelt's re-election settled the issue of U.S. support, hence British survival, at least for a while; but active U.S. military intervention on an adequate scale for invasion remained to be seen, and Russia was isolated by the terms of the Nazi-Soviet pact.

The U.S. intervention had evolved in steps. Step one had come shortly after the 1940 election when Chief of Naval Operations Admiral Harold Stark framed the "Europe First" concept—that should war break out between the United States and the Axis powers, the American war effort could concentrate on the defeat of Germany, the stronger of the two Axis powers. By January 1941, secret American-British military conferences (code-named ABC) had begun in Washington to plot joint military strategy. The result was "ABC-1," a resolution embodying the Europe First strategy. But this amounted to little more than a decision to pool American and British military resources *"in the event"* of U.S. intervention. In January 1941 Roosevelt pushed a program of military assistance called Lend-Lease through Congress, a measure short of outright U.S. military intervention and presented to Congress as a substitute for it.

U.S. mobilization had been under way for eighteen months. From a force consisting of little over three divisions and 17,000 airmen in 1939, the United

States mustered the equivalent of thirty-four ground divisions by late spring 1941. But the United States was neutral, American forces were distant from the scene of battle, separated from the vital front by the Atlantic Ocean, patrolled by U-boats, and Roosevelt was faced with a virulent isolationist campaign led by the America First Committee. Tensions between the United States and Japan ran high, meaning that war would probably break out in the Far East first and be likely to win the unified support of Congress, in contrast with the cause of aiding Britain, which commanded strong support within the American leadership, but divided the electorate over Britain's "hopeless" prospects.

In this uncertain context, British planners had taken the lead in formulating Allied grand strategy. British doctrine consisted of throwing an air and naval "ring" around Europe, nourishing political resistance groups on the Continent, limiting military operations aimed at lopping off exposed portions of the German empire and then ultimately returning to the Continent after a significant breakdown of Nazi military and political controls. British military strategy thereafter never deviated from "peripheralism," an approach rooted in Britain's history as a balancer, in limited British aims in the conflict which amounted to restoring the pre-Depression political and military status quo in Europe, in the uncertainty in 1940–41 about Russian and U.S. military intervention, and in reluctance to devise strategies going beyond what the British were capable of without direct U.S. and Soviet military intervention. The Mountbatten group went to work on mounting a series of raids on French installations, and in the course of two years succeeded in devising many of the tactics and strategies that would determine the success of the OVERLORD invasion. But the impetus for the more ambitious idea of a frontal assault on German-held Europe, finally adopted, would be American, and reflect a more American approach, one rooted in America's disposition to intervene in European affairs decisively in the name of far-reaching goals or to abstain from Europe altogether.

But would the Americans intervene? The Americans, with a productive economy and unlimited resources, were capable of conceiving operations on a far larger scale than the British. Yet intervention in Europe was a divisive issue in American politics, and so the commitment of American resources would never match American boldness in strategic thinking. This constraining factor, along with Roosevelt's determination to reconcile U.S., British and Russian war aims, would account for American willingness to compromise. The result would be a smaller-scale invasion, launched later than the Americans had hoped, but far more ambitious than the earlier British plans had envisioned. Working out the compromise had proven to be a difficult process, however. All in all, whether American and British resources and objectives could be effectively harnessed, and Allied moves coordinated with the Russians, still remained to be seen as Eisenhower took up command in London in January 1944.

THE EARLY DEBATES

It had been evident early on that working out Anglo-American differences would take time. Though secrecy protected the ABC staff talks in early 1941, British proposals for intermediate military steps in North Africa and the Middle East revealed skepticism on both sides. Within the highest levels of the U.S. military establishment, there was a heritage of anti-British sentiment. The Navy recalled British diplomacy in the twenties aimed at limiting rival fleets while the Army nurtured memories of problems in 1918, and of postwar British intrusions into the Americas afterward. Both were critical of Britain's role as a "balancer," and the effortless German victory in 1940 did not diminish the idea held by many Americans that Great Britain would concentrate on the protection of British "postwar interests, commercial and military." The Joint Army-Navy planning committee in January 1941 had gone so far as to warn against "entrusting our national future to British direction," advice that bolstered Navy advocates of a Pacific First strategy and Army planners who formulated the controversial Victory Program, which envisioned a war in which the United States would practically go it alone in Europe by mobilizing a massive force of 210 divisions backed by huge fleets of ships and aircraft. Neither service reflected Roosevelt's middle position—a Europe First policy in close alliance with the British and eventually the Russians, in line with realistic but ambitious American mobilization levels. Early on, Roosevelt had exhibited his susceptibility to British views, a source of consternation to the military, and a source of congressional concern that American intervention in Europe would be "self-defeating," first in propping up a decaying British empire, and eventually by promoting the expansion of Russia in Europe.

Step two in the saga of U.S. intervention had been the German attack on Russia, launched on June 22, 1941, which in Stimson's words had been "an almost providential occurrence." The German-Russian war opened the door to preliminary British military moves in Egypt, Greece and North Africa, and set the stage for eventual U.S. military participation. For a while, however, serious domestic controversy arose over a policy of aiding Communist Russia against the Germans. Under the impact of Hitler's early successes against Russia, the Roosevelt Administration managed to include the Russians in Lend-Lease, but U.S. military intervention was another matter, particularly since the scale of the eastern-front battles made it obvious that the Americans could not effectively oppose the Germans militarily without Russian cooperation. Inevitably, powerful support arose for the idea of doing nothing, for the reason that Russian communism was a greater threat than German fascism, and/or that it would be advantageous for the Allies to allow the two totalitarian giants to wear each other down. One might say that the German attack on Russia confronted Congress with the issue it would have had to resolve sooner or later: whether Nazi domination of Europe was such a threat to American security and the American way of life as to justify attempts to defeat Germany by allying not only with the British but with the Soviets. In the critical test of Roosevelt's policy, legislation to extend the military draft for one year and keep American mobilization on track passed the House of Representatives on August 12, 1941, by one vote.

In the wake of this narrow verdict, the outlines of U.S. participation had come into focus. Debate over intervention underscored the precariousness of Roosevelt's Europe First policy. The draft-extension controversy left no doubt that U.S. military force levels would fall well below Operation Victory* estimates of the 200-plus U.S. divisions needed to fight the Germans without Allies. Close dealings with Allies would be necessary, and yet it was the prospect of becoming an ally of the Soviet Union that had nearly provoked Congress to dismantle the American military build-up. Accordingly, Roosevelt knew, if he had not always known, that he would have to handle the Russian issue carefully, and sidestep political and territorial issues affecting postwar relations with the USSR where possible, at least until the distant day when American forces were heavily engaged against the Germans and the need for U.S.-Soviet cooperation became self-evident. Until then, Soviet moderation would be crucial in the cause of mobilizing U.S. intervention in Europe—signs indicating that the Soviet Union would respond to U.S. suggestions for postwar world order. This fact accounted in part for Roosevelt's determination from the beginning to deal with the Russians on a friendly basis, and lent urgency in Washington to opening a military front against the Germans. The sooner the Americans approached the Russians about a military alliance backed up by firm plans for intervention, the easier it would be to achieve real mutual confidence. Mutual confidence would make political dealings with Moscow less necessary, would quiet congressional criticism, afford greater odds of military success and lay the foundations of postwar cooperation.

In military terms, these facts translated into an American strategy that placed a premium on quick, decisive victory, direct aid for the eastern front and avoiding the diversion of precious American resources to remote theaters or to battlefields on the periphery of Europe. The stakes were high. Indeed, the importance of dealing with the Soviet Union on American terms may have accounted for the fact that American military estimates persistently underestimated Russian staying power and, correspondingly, empha-

---

*Operation Victory was a War Department study in late 1941 on the military and industrial requirements for a war in Europe.

sized both the urgency of Allied steps to relieve the situation on the eastern front and the importance of such aid to the Russians. In any event, the Russian "problem" injected a certain rigidity and lack of realism into American military planning, which meant problems with the British. But without the Russian problem, U.S. military intervention in Europe was impractical, and without U.S. military intervention as an eventual goal, it was questionable whether Roosevelt could sustain Lend-Lease and other aid for Britain. Early on, the British would learn to live with American "rigidity" on strategic issues, but not without qualms.

The Russian problem came up at the meetings between Churchill and Roosevelt at Argenta Bay, Newfoundland, in August 1941. There the two leaders met for talks about Asia, "ring" operations in Europe, and the problem of working out a basis for Allied-Russian cooperation. Many question marks surrounded the idea of an Allied-Soviet alliance. With the Red Army in retreat in all sectors, American-British assessments of Soviet intentions and strength differed sharply. The Americans were braced for disaster on the eastern front. The British were anxious about the Russian setbacks and eager to start assistance flowing to the Russians, but confident that the Russians would recover and eventually defeat the Germans. Therefore, Stalin's need for Allied aid was unclear, as were the terms he would be able to set for close cooperation. Significant American-British differences, also rooted in differing national outlooks, toward the Russian question cropped up over what the Allies could offer. With the Russians in retreat, the British perceived that circumstances were auspicious to begin work on a settlement of postwar territorial and political issues, and, moreover, thought that diplomatic concessions might be a sufficient basis for Allied-Soviet relations. But the Americans favored military aid and, in any case, favored a hands-off position on diplomatic questions. Differences emerged as the Americans and British worked on the technical problems of aiding Russia, interim military operations and contingency planning in the event that war broke out in the Far East.

Although the military talks were inconclusive, Roosevelt and Churchill proceeded to approve the Atlantic Charter, a statement of war aims in which the two sides affirmed the "four freedoms," as well as a commitment to free trade, international economic cooperation, and collective security against aggression and territorial aggrandizement. Publication of the charter on the eve of the draft-extension vote was designed to alert Congress to the inevitability of U.S. intervention and the Soviets to the existence of like-minded U.S. and British policies, which the Russians were invited to endorse, thereby marking the beginning of negotiations for a common policy to defeat Hitler.

Relations with the Russians were difficult from the start, however. Even as the Red Army fell back 600 miles on all fronts in late 1941, Stalin indicated to American and British emissaries that postwar Russia would accept nothing less than full recognition of Russian territorial gains under the Nazi-Soviet pact, including the Baltic States, Poland and Bessarabia, and harsh terms for Germany, including the loss of East Prussia, and the Sudetenland and a heavy schedule of reparations—at a minimum. Meanwhile the Russians campaigned vigorously for a second front, and gave notice in effect that Soviet restraint on diplomatic questions would depend in great measure on the timeliness and effectiveness of Allied military aid. In the months before Pearl Harbor, Roosevelt, confined to a policy of Lend-Lease, remained aloof on all diplomatic discussions. The British were unhappy about forgoing productive talks and dismayed by the rigidities imposed by U.S. public opinion. But they did not press, since American support for Britain was at stake. British deference to Roosevelt's political approach in the fall of 1941 set the precedent for a British-inspired military strategy and American-inspired diplomacy toward the Russians, which were characteristic of Allied policy until January 1944.

Meanwhile, concern about German progress toward Moscow triggered the earliest War Department planning for operations in Europe. The problem was to devise a military strategy that combined aid to Russia with an efficient use of American resources. War now appeared inevitable in the Far East, and so War Department planning recognized that Pacific commitments would exert a major claim on American military resources. Indeed, bipartisan support for American involvement in Europe could probably not be sustained without a vigorous effort in the Far East. All these factors led to consideration of an invasion of the Continent via England.

In *Crusade in Europe,* Eisenhower described the planning under way when he joined the War Department shortly after Pearl Harbor. He recalled that planning focused on northwestern France by a process of elimination, and described the rejected Allied options: Allied forces moving directly to the Russian front via Murmansk or Iran; offensives through the Mediterranean, southern France or the Iberian Peninsula. All of these were deemed inadequate on political or military grounds. It may have been a paper drawn up by Lieutenant Colonel Edwin E. Schwein in the fall of 1941 that first identified northwestern France as an American objective. At the height of the Russian military crisis, Schwein explored methods of opening a diversionary front and came to the conclusion that an invasion of France would prove to be "the only possible method of approach to an ultimate victory of the democracies," and that the area in France that would divert sizable German forces was "the area of northern France between Dunkirk and Le Touquet." Thereafter, the War Department pushed a strategy of concentration, and opposed peripheral operations advocated by the British for the sake of avoiding piecemeal commitments that would disperse Allied military strength available for 1942 and 1943 operations.

This represented War Department thinking at the high-level U.S.-British conferences (ARCADIA) held in Washington shortly after Pearl Harbor to reaffirm ABC-1. The meeting went forward amid the backdrop of Japanese victories in Hong Kong, Burma, Thailand, Singapore and Java and equally significant news that the Russians had opened a massive offensive in the Moscow area, inflicting a major defeat on the German Army Group Center. These events imperiled the Europe First assumptions of ABC-1, and produced far-ranging conversations on how to proceed.

On behalf of the War Department, General Marshall resisted "dispersion" of Allied resources to the Mediterranean, a theater which offered only indirect benefits and which could not be secured without substantial commitments of troops and shipping. Roosevelt, however, was receptive to the British-sponsored operation GYMNAST, a plan to relieve the threat to the Middle East and expel the Axis from Africa in a giant pincer movement staged from Egypt and North Africa.

In a fateful judgment, the President decided that the same factors weighing against diplomacy with Russia would mandate opening a front against German troops in 1942 at the latest. The immediate problem was to prevent Pacific First pressures from overwhelming ABC-1 by default. Likewise, it became apparent that the President believed a war psychology against Germany would have to be built up, even at the expense of steps to concentrate resources for a land offensive in Europe. British views were a factor. Roosevelt could not overlook the fact that the British were partners and that Britain would provide the base for an Allied invasion of the Continent. Nor could he overlook the strategic importance of the Mediterranean theater or its importance in terms of sustaining British morale, as operations there held out hope of a future in which the British would not be barred from areas of traditional interest. In short, Mediterranean operations were attainable and strategically important, and they provided a way of opening a front in Europe quickly. But the Mediterranean theater could only be of secondary importance in military terms—like the Pacific. Accordingly, the two sides tacitly agreed to balance resources between the Mediterranean and Pacific thereafter. But, for the moment, covering the Pacific and firming up Australia as a Pacific base took priority, a task that would take several months. Apparently ruling out a land offensive in western Europe before 1943, the conference tentatively adopted GYMNAST.

ARCADIA was significant in many ways. Despite strong feelings in Washington against Europe First, Roosevelt and Churchill, whose differences were "of emphasis and priority rather than of principle," reaffirmed ABC-1. They formed the Combined Chiefs of Staff (CCS), a "committee in action" to consist of the American and British Chiefs of Staff with a permanent seat in Washington charged with making allocations of manpower and supplies, and coordinating global military policy over five theaters of war. The Americans assumed primary responsibility for the Pacific theater and the American hemisphere. The British assumed charge of the Mediterranean and South Asia. The CCS reserved the question of supervision over the vital European theater, because of its importance and the need for a coordinated policy there. But the Far East emergency had to be handled first. Even GYMNAST was on hold, and months would pass before the Americans and British could begin to work out a semblance of a military policy in Europe.

The ensuing debates of 1942 were the most significant of the war, debates in which Eisenhower participated first as a planner and later as a theater commander. Eisenhower's attendance at ARCADIA as a planner had marked the beginning of his quick rise in the inner councils of the Alliance. Weeks before, he had been summoned to Washington to serve as an assistant to General Leonard T. Gerow, whom he eventually replaced as chief of Marshall's War Plans staff, a selection based on Eisenhower's expertise on the Far East and his experience as a former staff assistant to MacArthur in Manila. Immediately, Eisenhower had found himself embroiled in the Far East crisis, in charge of monitoring the flow of supplies and troops to Australia with special responsibility for the sensitive task of handling presidential correspondence with MacArthur, who was determined to overturn Europe First and force the Roosevelt Administration to wage an all-out defense of the Philippines. In personal terms, the assignment was full of ironies. Having faithfully served MacArthur as a staff officer for six years, Eisenhower now found himself enlisted by MacArthur's arch rival, Roosevelt, and would eventually be castigated by his former chief as one of the "faceless staff officers" who frustrated the defense of the Philippines.

Accounts of Eisenhower's months in Washington attest to the extraordinary pressures on him and his staff as the War Department struggled to contain the Far East crisis and to resume long-range planning. That winter Eisenhower commuted between the Munitions Building and his brother Milton's home fifteen miles away in Falls Church. The day began before the first light when he made coffee and cooked himself breakfast while he read the morning newspapers. Usually he returned from the office around ten o'clock, when each night his sister-in-law, Helen Eaker Eisenhower, served dinner and his six-year-old niece Ruthie greeted him at the door with the evening paper and slippers.

Aksel Nielsen, the Doud family financial consultant and a lifelong friend, was an occasional guest at Milton's that winter. Years later he recalled that the warmth of Helen Eaker's hospitality, and Milton's comradeship, cemented the bond between the two brothers permanently. The two Eisenhower brothers collaborated closely, on Dwight's memoranda at War Plans, and on the dozens of papers connected with Milton's painful six-month stint as a coordinator of the Japanese Relocation Authority, the agency responsible for quarantining the Japanese-American population into camps amid the anti-Japanese furor after Pearl Harbor. Unlike their earlier collaboration in 1930s, there was nothing leisurely about these nocturnal sessions, which lasted for two intense hours or so, before a highball and bed.

In his account of the winter of 1942 in *Crusade in Europe,* Eisenhower recalled the high stakes riding on even the most routine decisions, such as his own in late January to arrange the transport of the entire 15,000-man New Caledonia Garrison from Charleston, South Carolina, to Brisbane by way of Brazil aboard H.M.S. *Queen Mary.* The vessel was to make the voyage without armed escort, an acceptable risk since the refitted *Queen Mary* was swift enough to outrun German U-boats. Eisenhower was mindful, however, that in making the ship available, Churchill had warned Marshall that in the event of mishap, there were lifeboats and rafts for only 8,000 men.

Thereafter Eisenhower suppressed all thought of the *Queen Mary* until War Plans received the intercept of a cable from the Italian embassy in Brazil to Rome reporting that the ship had docked in Rio de Janeiro and was believed to be proceeding into the South Atlantic. Dreading that this information had been passed to the German U-boat command, Eisenhower was tempted to alert Marshall. Deciding that nothing could be done, he kept the news to himself.

For two weeks Eisenhower slept fitfully, and it was only when word reached Washington that the *Queen Mary* had arrived safely in Australia that Eisenhower told Marshall about the cable and his two-week vigil. "Eisenhower," the Chief of Staff replied, "I received that intercept at the same time you did. I was merely hoping that you might not see it and so I said nothing to you until I knew the outcome."

Then, on February 16, Eisenhower formally replaced Gerow and assumed charge of the overall planning effort. An invasion of Europe had not been forgotten—indeed, the idea was widely shared among Eisenhower's colleagues at War Plans, including General Thomas Handy, General Joseph McNarney and Colonel Albert Wedemeyer. Eisenhower's War Department diaries of the time reveal the intense in-house discussion of a European invasion even at the height of the Asian emergency, and competition over authorship of the idea that all sensed would be of historic magnitude. But everything depended on stepping up lagging troop mobilization, the production of ships, airplanes and landing craft, and overcoming the political and diplomatic hurdles to a build-up in England.

It was in these circumstances that the OVERLORD concept assumed shape. By February 1942 a "guiding concept" was becoming essential if the Allies were ever going to halt the rush of resources to the Far East. Simultaneously, worries about a Russian collapse were imperceptibly shifting to concern about the consequences of Russian survival and recovery without prompt and effective Allied intervention. The situation in Russia was unclear, but, in any case, time was of the essence.

Historian Mark Stoler has shown how detailed planning for an Allied invasion of Europe was prompted by the spate of separate-peace rumors coinciding with the close of the Russian winter counteroffensive in mid-February 1942, which left the German army intact and deep within Russia. On February 23 in an order of the day, Stalin omitted mention of the Allies altogether and blamed the war on Hitler, not the German people, which was widely interpreted as a signal that the Russians were willing to negotiate. Simultaneously, Ambassador Maxim Litvinov in Washington warned Under Secretary of State Sumner Welles that without the opening of a second front the Soviet Union would have to quit the war. These events had a galvanizing effect, though how literally threats of a separate peace were actually taken is unknown.

By now, War Department assessments had become slightly inconsistent. On the one hand, they emphasized the dire Russian straits and the need for prompt Allied military help. On the other, they acknowledged the overriding importance of the Red Army to American plans for European operations and the consequences of a separate peace, which reflected backhanded respect for the first military force to check Germany. The Red Army had borne up well over the winter, and Russian-German negotiations were plausible. But Russian survival without negotiations was also plausible, and it was hard to conceive that the millions of Russian casualties to date would not pose an insuperable barrier to negotiations. In short, the War Department would not dismiss the possibility of German-Russian negotiations, nor could it overlook another possibility—namely, that the Russians felt isolated, and that only through timely action could the Allies hope to influence Soviet political and military policy long-range. Significantly, as second-front agitation resumed, 1941 talk of "aid" turned to talk of military operations to "aid" the Russians in such a fashion as to ensure Russian survival and to guarantee that the Russians understand the importance of the aid rendered. But was direct military aid possible? Certainly not, at least not any time soon.

By late February, Allied military planning was in disarray. The Americans were mobilizing, but the bulk of resources were still flowing to Australia and Southeast Asia to stem the Japanese offensive. Meanwhile, the British reinforced North Africa in response to a German drive to clear the British out of Egypt and the Middle East. In short, the Allies lacked resources for opening a major front in 1942 and faced the problem that even existing resources would be drawn into remote theaters, facts obvious to the Germans, and presumably to the Russians as well. In this context, Russian pressure seemed to have a long-range objective: not direct aid as such right away, but steps in 1942 that would make direct help in 1943 feasible, something within the realm of possibility provided the Allies avoided extended commitments to remote theaters and commenced timely preparations, without which it was possible that an invasion would be put off not one year but two—until 1944.

This raised GYMNAST and the Far East, the issues faced at ARCADIA. At

ARCADIA, the Allies had decided to shore up Allied positions in Asia and the Middle East. But this entailed potentially deep commitments that would drain off resources without advancing preparations for an invasion, for invasion planning would require that the Allies in effect confine military operations to holding actions in Australia and to defending fall-back points in the Middle East.

Other advantages of a strictly defensive strategy in 1942 were apparent. A methodical build-up in England would not only make a 1943 invasion possible, but have the additional effect of forcing the Germans to garrison France by late summer or fall of 1942 and to this extent relieve the situation in Russia indirectly. Alternatively, with the Allies committed in remote theaters that the Axis could defend economically, the Germans could plan eastern-front operations in confidence that there would be no threat to France before mid to late 1943 at the earliest, meaning that they would know they had a clear shot at Russia in 1942, and probably a third one in 1943.

Paradoxically, then, practically any Allied military action in 1942 stood to increase the burden on Russia, not lessen it. The Russians faced a crisis in 1942, in any case, but again Allied action in 1942 was probably not the real aim of Russian pressure. The issue was an Allied invasion in 1943, and what separate-peace hints and second-front agitation seemed to suggest in unison was that Allied actions in 1942, inconsistent with plans for an invasion in 1943, would, in jeopardizing Russian survival, convince the Russians that they had no choice but to seek their own military and political solutions —for what would be the point of relying on allies willing to take great risks with Russian survival or who were indifferent to costly stalemate?

All of this reinforced feelings in the War Department that GYMNAST would be a great mistake. To invade North Africa would be to commit forces in a remote theater that the Germans could tie up with a minimal commitment of forces on their part. The operation would risk a Russian collapse or a separate peace, or noncooperation, any of which would rule out an invasion of Europe. Significantly, as he assumed formal charge of Marshall's OPD staff, Eisenhower took up the cause of U.S. aid for Russia, couched in the standard terms of assisting Russia through the difficult summer months ahead, but qualified by the proviso that U.S. aid be extended in such a way that Moscow would "recognize its importance." Thus, Eisenhower bridged the two possibilities: first, that of a Russian collapse in the summer; second, that the Russians would survive the summer against the full force of the German army. The point, in his opinion, was to concentrate on attainable steps that would enhance the prospects of Russian survival, and set the stage for invasion. But soon Eisenhower, in his diary, was lamenting the chaos in military planning, and the sense of complacency about the importance of Allied military steps about to be taken.

Decisions were approaching that would govern procurement, shipping, training and mobilization schedules for the rest of the year, and the essential task was to commence the build-up in England, and yet everywhere he looked there were problems. The Navy Department opposed interfering with operations to halt the Japanese advance. The President had indicated that a 1942 preliminary operation against Germany of some kind would be necessary to ward off Pacific First pressures. Would the President consider alternatives to GYMNAST? Other possibilities might satisfy the President's requirements and be consistent with a build-up in England that year, such as small-scale cross-Channel raids, or perhaps large-scale air operations in western Europe. Cross-Channel raids would court defeat. Anything larger than a small-scale landing party putting ashore for several hours was likely to be overwhelmed by the Germans at practically every point along the west European coast. Would the President accept failure? To date, failure in the Far East had galvanized demands for revenge against Japan, and, it stood to reason, setbacks might do the same in Europe. But as events would show, Roosevelt judged that whereas Pearl Harbor had energized the country against Japan, failure in Europe would demoralize the war effort against Germany, and so all operations undertaken against Germany would have to succeed. But for the moment the President's views were unclear.

Indeed, Roosevelt would never spell out his views systematically or over-rule the War Department categorically. In the winter of 1942 Roosevelt may have been anxious to use the War Department initiative as a counterpoint to Navy pressures or simply reluctant to make any decision at all. Roosevelt faced many unknowns: how far the Japanese would press; congressional politics in the spring session; whether GYMNAST, an operation that entailed diplomatic risks, was feasible; the exact situation in Russia.

Congressional manuevers were on everyone's mind that month. In his diary, Eisenhower narrated bits and pieces of the ongoing controversies over reorganization of the War Department in the wake of leaks of Operation VICTORY estimates to the isolationist press and congressional pressure to clear the air of insinuations that the War Department conspired to expose the Navy to defeat at Pearl Harbor for the sake of maneuvering America into war in Europe. As February came to a close, debate on 1942 operations started up in earnest, pitting General Marshall against Admiral King with the White House in the middle, seemingly content to allow re-argument of the ARCADIA decisions.

Meanwhile, Eisenhower took charge of drafting the "guiding concept" for the War Department. In an undated memo late that month, he sketched a two-step approach; first, identification of those "vital tasks that must be performed by the United Nations in order to avoid defeat"; second, to pick the point at which the United States should attempt operations with "maximum promise of defeating the Axis." Essential tasks to avoid defeat included, in order, securing the North American citadel, keeping England in the war, assisting Russia "to stay in the war as an active participant," and lastly, action to prevent the junction of Japanese and German forces in the

Middle East, a contingency that caused the British great concern. In Eisenhower's opinion, the security both of North America and England was assured by forces in place, which reduced the real issue before the Allies to finding ways to "conduct such operations as will directly and indirectly assist in taking the pressure off of the Russian armies." In sum, the vital task in Eisenhower's view was commencing a build-up in England looking to cross-Channel invasion presumably in 1943 or late 1942, if necessary, which in either case would force the Germans to garrison France that summer.

Eisenhower's "vital tasks" memo in effect revived the Schwein memo of September 1941, but without specifics, a measure of how far Pearl Harbor had pushed planning away from Europe. Disorganization was rife. There were estimates that the United States would be capable of mustering 600,000 troops backed by 6,500 aircraft in England by fall. But the estimates varied from week to week, and were subject to many limitations, such as the construction of special landing craft that interfered with Navy capital-ship construction programs. Competition between the War Department and the Navy Department was intense. Eisenhower's diary jottings describe the jostling for resources, and heated clashes with Admiral Ernest J. King, the Pacific First advocate whose role in Anglo-American debates ahead was to be a persistent reminder of the stringent limitations imposed upon European operations. Nonetheless, the War Department fought on, in hopes of clarifying Roosevelt's 1942 edict, convinced, as Stimson put it, that "the only way to get the initiative in this war is to take it."

On February 28 Eisenhower submitted a second document to Marshall, entitled "Strategic Conceptions and Their Applications to the Southwest Pacific," the origin of the controversial SLEDGEHAMMER proposal to land Allied troops in northwest France that fall. In it Eisenhower updated the case for assuming the defensive in the Far East and forgoing an invasion of North Africa. Noting that Japan had successfully penetrated the Dutch East Indies and was in possession of all the oil and rubber stores she sought, Eisenhower suggested that the Japanese offensive had run its course. He proposed a delaying action in the Dutch East Indies, token assistance to the beleaguered Bataan garrison, and maintenance of sea communications with Australia. Proceeding, he drafted a list of what were "necessary" and "desirable" goals for U.S. planners in the months ahead, a list that omitted Far East and North African objectives entirely from the "necessary" category. The necessary task, he repeated, was the "retention of Russia in the war as an active enemy against Germany" by extending Lend-Lease, and "the early initiation of operations that will draw from the Russian front sizeable proportions of the German Army . . . conceived and so presented to the Russians that they will recognize the importance of the support rendered. Air, *possibly ground attack from England, is indicated.*"

Eisenhower's timely memorandum made its way through the various planning echelons of the American military establishment. On March 7, the JCS called for assistance to the Soviet Union, which was "actively and aggressively opposing Germany," while observing "strict economy in other theaters." Soon the Combined Chiefs, having weighed the impact of the Japanese offensive, and the lack of merchant shipping urgently needed for Lend-Lease and for Red Sea service to Egypt, termed GYMNAST "obsolete." Meanwhile, Marshall, Arnold and Stimson met with Roosevelt in the Oval Office to urge that the build-up in England begin at once to "put an end to dispersions."

By now the President had backed away from North Africa for reasons that are not entirely clear. Apparently Roosevelt was anxious to forestall British pressure to pursue talks with the Russians on a treaty recognizing postwar Soviet absorption of the Baltic States. Simultaneously, emissaries of the Provisional Polish Government in London warned that if the Allies did not land in Europe quickly, the Soviet Union's western neighbors would have no choice but to look to Russia and not to the Allies. Apparently, Marshall's views were a factor, along with congressional pressures in the wake of MacArthur's defeat in the Philippines. In any event, on the ninth Roosevelt sent a cable to Churchill in which he laid GYMNAST to rest and proposed that the combined Chiefs of Staff immediately assert jurisdiction over northwest Europe, a procedural step that would set up a framework for discussions about a build-up in England.

A week later, the issue was joined between the United States and Great Britain amid a clamor of second-front agitation by Soviet officials, including diplomat Andrei Gromyko on tour in the United States to address second-front rallies in Madison Square Garden, New York, and in Washington. On the sixteenth the Joint Chiefs of Staff formally endorsed the build-up in England, code-named BOLERO, adding that the Allies should "at once decide on a clear course of action, and execute this decision with the utmost vigor." Sir John Dill, permanent representative to the CCS, tabled a British counterproposal hastily drafted in response to Roosevelt's message of March 9, which included proposals for landings in the summer of 1943 near Le Havre but "under conditions of severe deterioration of German military power."

This passive British concept apparently looked to the revival of GYMNAST. Anglo-American differences were wide. On March 24 Marshall directed Eisenhower (who had just been promoted to lieutenant general) to draft a paper that would attempt to reconcile the British and American approaches. Eisenhower found little in common between the two proposals and responded a day later in a memorandum entitled "Critical Points in the Development of Coordinated Viewpoint as to Major Tasks of the War," in which he listed several reasons for undertaking an American build-up in the British Isles at once: the relatively short sea line of communication enabling the United States to deploy forces abroad quickly; the need to defend

England anyway; the possibility that a build-up in England would force Germany to garrison the French coast; the advantages of an early invasion there, such as the superiority of land communications in northwest Europe essential for sustained operations; the prospect of gaining local air superiority from forward air bases in southern England; the ability to employ "a major portion of British combat power"; and the timing in light of Germany's current preoccupation in Russia. Eisenhower cautioned that such a plan would depend on "complete agreement" within the Combined Chiefs of Staff and "husbanding of combat power." But Eisenhower saw no worthwhile alternative to BOLERO in Europe and predicted that failure by the British to agree would force abandonment of Europe First and the adoption of a strategy of all-out war against Japan.

Whether Eisenhower was the first to come up with this troublesome "either-or" is unknown. Marshall and King would brandish the threat of a Pacific First strategy in talks with the British intended to discourage British hopes for U.S. support on British operations in the Mediterranean. The threat seemed plausible; the Pacific war commanded wide support in Congress, all-out mobilization in Europe was still a completely untested idea, and it seemed doubtful that Congress would support a diversion of U.S. resources to areas of British interest exclusively. The threat also embodied the notion that peripheral operations, by delaying invasion and risking Russian support, would probably rule out eventual Russian cooperation, which was indispensable for an early invasion of western Europe, the truly worthwhile Allied objective.

But an "either-or" approach did not sit well with the President, who would eventually disavow Marshall's use of it. In his opinion, the approach antagonized the British unnecessarily and foreclosed discussion of attainable and perhaps useful steps in 1942. Also, an either-or approach implied something that was not true—that Roosevelt was willing to abandon Europe First in any circumstances or to pretend that he would.

In time it would become apparent that Europe First was more than a military strategy, that it was the very foundation of Roosevelt's war policy, and as such became an even more urgent priority in the President's mind the more domestic pressures threatened to overtake it. Roosevelt's war aims were always the subject of debate, but the crucial point would emerge in 1942: that Roosevelt's Europe First priority was fixed, not subject to change because of military or diplomatic factors and events, and linked not to any single military strategy in Europe but to the best European strategy available.

Military factors were far from irrelevant. The relative strength and proximity of Germany plus the importance of Russian cooperation and the need to aid Russia were important. But one senses, in retrospect, that even a Russian collapse or a Russian policy of noncooperation with the Allies would not have altered Roosevelt's emphasis on Europe. That priority was a function of the special significance of Europe in American politics, and the ominous significance of Europe's Depression-era lapse into fascism and the rise of Germany which had persuaded American liberals, including Roosevelt, that fascism in some form might come to be seen as the "wave of the future" for Depression-era America. In this sense, German expansion, only a figurative threat to American physical security, posed by its example a threat to the social and political fabric of America which had to be met first by the containment and then by the isolation of the Nazi regime, and eventually by war backed up by the largest-scale intervention possible in alliance with the British and the Russians. All this, despite British imperialism, which inspired little real support in America, and despite Soviet Communism, which, though expansionist, held no substantial attraction for the Western world as such. The fact that implementing the Europe First priority would be hard did not mean that Pacific First was an acceptable alternative. To the contrary, the very fact that Europe First was difficult made it all the more essential, since the goals of defeating Germany and prevailing over German apologists in America in whatever guise were one and the same. Seemingly, the point dawned slowly on the War Department, which approached the problem of Europe First only in military terms, an oversimplification. By and large, it was Roosevelt, Stimson and Marshall who debated the means of carrying out Europe First, a debate that General Eisenhower observed from the sidelines where he was in charge of drafting the supporting memoranda and position papers to accompany Roosevelt's unfolding policy.

One feature of Roosevelt's policy appeared to have eluded Marshall. Because Europe First was a political problem, the main practical hurdle Roosevelt faced was not keeping the Russians in the war but maintaining congressional support for Europe First through the off-year 1942 elections. Evidently Roosevelt was concerned that without an operation of some kind in progress against the Germans, the election might become a referendum on Europe First. The military and diplomatic arguments against 1942 operations were impressive, but would become academic if Roosevelt could not first solve the domestic political conflict. Elections were none of Marshall's business, but soon his rigid advocacy of a purely military solution would pose difficulties for Roosevelt in his effort to promote GYMNAST as a worthy operation for American forces. But all of this was to come. Meanwhile the President kept his own counsel, allowing Marshall for the moment to come forward with ideas.

Debate raged on. An early hint of the President's final position came on March 25. On that day Stimson and Marshall carried Eisenhower's memorandum to the White House for Roosevelt's approval. Roosevelt approved but was inclined simply to submit the document to the Combined Chiefs of Staff, a move that Hopkins feared would result in the proposal being "pulled to pieces and emasculated." When Roosevelt agreed to withhold the proposal temporarily, Marshall returned to the War Department and ordered Eisenhower to draft a more detailed study that might be presented in London to the British.

At once, the entire War Plans machinery was set to the task of turning out a specific plan based on estimates of the British forces available, Channel tides and weather, selection between various alternative ports, the readiness of the U.S. Army, shipping and special landing craft restrictions. By April 1 Eisenhower had produced a historic document, later known as the "Marshall memorandum," which outlined two military operations around which the build-up (BOLERO) would be organized. The main proposal was ROUNDUP, an invasion of France in early 1943 with 48 divisions: 18 British and 30 American. SLEDGEHAMMER was a contingency plan for small-scale landings in late 1942 for the dual purpose of securing a small bridgehead in France for future operations and drawing off German strength in Russia in the event of an eastern-front emergency that summer.

Whether the War Department considered SLEDGEHAMMER a serious proposal or not has been a subject of debate ever since. The high-risk contingency plan plainly underscored the propaganda role of BOLERO by forcing all to confront the urgency of aid to Russia and emphasizing the importance of "concentration" to accomplish this. Otherwise, the SLEDGE-HAMMER proposal appeared mainly designed to fulfill the President's 1942 deadline, perhaps tendered in hopes that "adoption" might be followed by postponement, or very small scale operations in France that summer.

SLEDGEHAMMER dramatized one point: that in strictly military terms even a failed small-scale cross-Channel attack in 1942 linked to a build-up in England would be better than successful Allied operations elsewhere that would simply disperse American military assets and assure the Germans of no early invasion of France. ROUNDUP was plainly the preferred solution, a deliberate build-up in England looking to 1943. A warning was implicit: that 1943 was not only the earliest possible date for an all-out invasion but the best and possibly the only practical date. By 1944, the real alternative to 1943, either the USSR would be out of the war, ruling out invasion altogether, or victorious or winning and thus indisposed to cooperate with Allied landings, which, in any event, would be hazardous, since even heavy German attrition in Russia would not necessarily guarantee Allied superiority in France. But the SLEDGEHAMMER idea ran counter both to British views and to Roosevelt's concept of what American politics would allow.

Soon it became evident that Roosevelt would accept no defeats in Europe, regardless of Russian demands for a second front. In mid-April, Roosevelt might have called a halt to the debate—once again, that he did not do so remains a mystery. Apparently he questioned whether the British understood the urgency of making preparations for an invasion from the American point of view. Roosevelt evidently agreed with the moral lurking in the proposal: that Europe First could become less meaningful, if not meaningless, unless the Allies resolved to fight on a big scale when and where it counted. ROUNDUP gave Roosevelt a means to offset Pacific First pressures. And backing it enabled Roosevelt to avoid saying no to Moscow and, above all, kept his government harnessed to the goal of opening a front against Germany somewhere in 1942.

In any event, Roosevelt readily endorsed BOLERO and Marshall's mission to London, perhaps rationalizing that land operations in Europe in 1942 might prove feasible. In any case, the British would have to contribute most of the forces and provide the base for SLEDGEHAMMER. British consent was doubtful, and a British refusal would enable Roosevelt to avoid taking sides between Marshall and King. Hopkins accompanied Marshall, apparently to make sure that London, in hearing out Marshall, understood Roosevelt's view in full.

Predictably, at the first April conference the British, who found themselves uncomfortably cast as referees over an in-house American argument, were evasive and reluctant to say no. Marshall and Hopkins found Brooke and Churchill eager for BOLERO and in favor of SLEDGEHAMMER "in principle" but skeptical about a number of points: whether it would work; whether it would aid Russia; whether the situation in Russia was really all so desperate.

After the London trip Marshall and Stimson embarked on an all-out fight for SLEDGEHAMMER, a fight destined to leave a legacy of misunderstanding and frustration that would still be evident in early 1944. In the next five months the British remained committed "in principle" to SLEDGEHAMMER but opposed in fact. They found themselves maneuvered into emphasizing the obvious hazards of the operation, a fact that would thereafter stigmatize the British as overcautious and deviously anti-Russian. The spectacle of American disunity shook British confidence, by impressing them with the precariousness of Europe First and Roosevelt's hold over U.S. policy. Simultaneously, the British had to contend with Roosevelt's ongoing refusal to back diplomatic discussions with the Russians, especially as it became obvious that effective military operations were not possible in 1942 or 1943. On the other hand, the British could not question the President's assessment of American domestic politics, an assessment which, though it ruled out talks with Moscow, reopened the door to GYMNAST. In hindsight, one might say that Roosevelt's handling of Pacific First pressures and organizing support for a European invasion rivaled his accomplishment in building pro-Allied sentiment after 1939. But the costs of permitting an extended debate would be high. The British would emerge from the debate offended and wary, the Russians cynical. Roosevelt's equivocations would, in time, erode his own authority somewhat, since he would cede the image of boldness and vision to the military, which formulated and pushed the invasion plan to fruition. Indeed, Churchill would later rank the civilian-military confrontation in the SLEDGEHAMMER debate as equal in significance to the wartime Anglo-American debate itself. The SLEDGEHAMMER debate would undermine both Roosevelt and Churchill, who finally had to impose North Africa on their military advisers and thus take responsibility for postponing the invasion until 1944, which would occur in improved military circumstances for the Allies but with grudging and provisional Russian military and diplomatic cooperation if any—seemingly the worst of all worlds except for one without Europe First and without an invasion at all.

This disheartening scenario unfolded rapidly in late June and early July 1942. As the SLEDGEHAMMER debate peaked, the German offensive had resumed in Russia. Initial German successes inspired new fears of a Russian collapse and led to a brief outpouring of pro-Russian sympathy in the West. The 1941 battles had left the USSR without the Ukrainian granaries, the Donets industrial basin, and all of White Russia west of Vyazma. Now two German army groups overran Rostov in a drive for the Caucasus. For a time the entire Russian line wavered under the blow of a German southern flanking thrust aimed at severing communications between Moscow and the Black Sea, Iran and the Caspian Sea. As the offensive began, Molotov toured Allied capitals to plead for an immediate second front to alleviate the desperate Russian plight. Whether the Allies actually feared a Russian collapse, and again whether the Russians actually expected a second front to materialize, has been debated ever since. The Molotov mission did, however, succeed in exposing Allied doubts and drawing the Allies into pledges that would prove embarrassing when the settling of postwar accounts began in late 1943.

Churchill resisted all pledges to Molotov. His bland assurances to Molotov that the Allies would "fight on" in the event of a Soviet collapse implied British confidence deep down that the Soviets would survive the summer fighting, and indeed would recover and win the war. Thus the British promised nothing. Roosevelt, however, was reluctant to say no. At his meeting with Molotov, Roosevelt overruled Marshall and promised Molotov a second front in 1942. Molotov took this to mean a version of SLEDGE-HAMMER, which Roosevelt did not dispute in so many words. Roosevelt was vague about objectives. He resisted language that would have categorically committed the United States to landings in northwest France, but he was specific about 1942. Molotov heard what he wanted to hear; but what he actually heard must, in retrospect, have been little more than what was becoming apparent to Roosevelt's staff and the British: that the President was determined to mount a military operation somewhere before the elections wherever the Allies could be guaranteed success. By now GYMNAST had re-entered the picture, so Roosevelt probably had GYMNAST in mind in his talks with Molotov. If so, Roosevelt was being disingenuous with Molotov and he knowingly accepted the risk of the serious problems with the Russians that later materialized. Presumably Roosevelt was devious for good reason. To begin with, his 1942 deadline was still not fully understood or accepted by the War Department. Second, even British military authorities were beginning to question the purpose of GYMNAST. Evidently anticipating intense arguments ahead, Roosevelt may have pledged a second front in order to bind his government to the 1942 deadline. By not specifying GYMNAST, Roosevelt also avoided the complications of allowing the Russians to reject the idea in advance, which would have left the Allies with the choice of mounting GYMNAST in defiance of explicit Russian objections, or doing nothing. In short, Roosevelt's choice was between hypothetical cooperation with the Russians in 1943 and domestic support for operations in Europe of any description. In the circumstances, he had no choice at all.

The Molotov-Roosevelt communiqué announcing that the two sides had reached "full understanding" on a second front spurred a visit to Washington by Churchill for talks. Churchill found Roosevelt accommodating, but beleaguered by his military staff. After hard discussion, final decisions were put off until July, but an invasion of North Africa seemed indicated. Intense debate continued, pitting Churchill against Marshall, which again Roosevelt might have forestalled but did not. Several weeks of debate ensued, climaxing with Marshall's return to London in July to confront the British over SLEDGEHAMMER a second time. By July, however, the real suspense was whether Marshall would agree to back down and defend GYMNAST against Pacific First pressures. Defusing the issue took months, and Marshall would never relent graciously, a stance that probably advanced the cause of OVERLORD but weakened Marshall's chance to command the operation.

Meanwhile, just as Churchill arrived in Washington, Eisenhower left Washington for London as Roosevelt's surprise choice to assume command of BOLERO. During the next several weeks Eisenhower privately and publicly made the arguments for SLEDGEHAMMER on behalf of the War Department. Butcher's account relates the endless meetings and dinners with Portal, Admiral Pound, Brooke, Ismay, and later with Churchill, at which Eisenhower and Clark haggled over the meaning of Alan Brooke's condition that "deterioration of German morale" should precede a 1942 assault.

Butcher's diary portrays Eisenhower at his Grosvenor Square office hard at work coordinating the campaign of public pressure behind a SLEDGE-HAMMER-type assault in 1942. ETO staff planners worked around the clock to assemble information, tables, factual data to assist American negotiators in the weeks ahead. In time, Eisenhower sensed the futility of debate, but not before he had emerged from his obscure role as a planner and staff officer to become a commander and public figure.

The transition occurred in the July 20 issue of *Life* magazine, which featured the U.S. build-up of American troops in England, an editorial call to arms for a second front to save Russia, and a prominent profile of Eisenhower. In the editorial, *Life* joined the crescendo of press commentary

©1986 A.Karl/J.Kemp

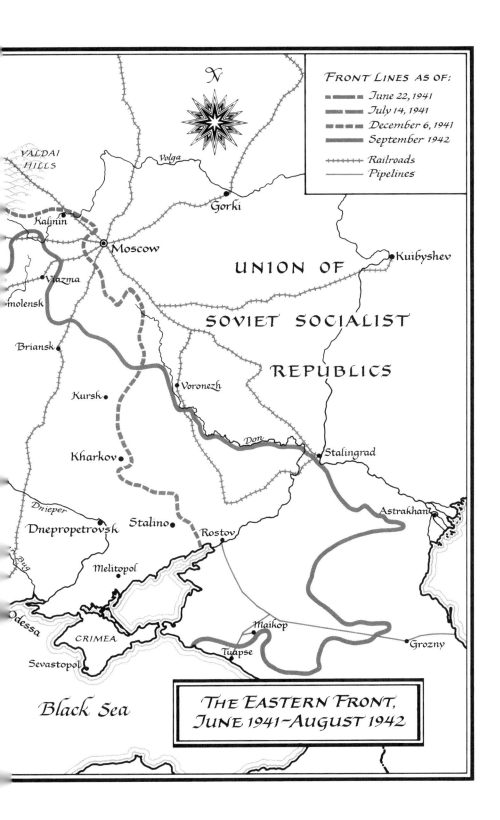

FRONT LINES AS OF:

- June 22, 1941
- July 14, 1941
- December 6, 1941
- September 1942
- ++++++ Railroads
- ——— Pipelines

N

VALDAI
HILLS

Volga

Gorki

Kalinin

Moscow

Kuibyshev

Vlazma

Smolensk

UNION OF

SOVIET SOCIALIST

REPUBLICS

Briansk

Kursk

Voronezh

Don

Kharkov

Stalingrad

Dnieper

Dnepropetrovsk

Stalino

Rostov

Astrakhan

Bug

Melitopol

Odessa

CRIMEA

Maikop

Grozny

Tuapse

Sevastopol

Black Sea

THE EASTERN FRONT,
JUNE 1941–AUGUST 1942

demanding that the governments of the United States and Great Britain launch a second front for the sake of preventing a German victory in Russia. The thrust of it was to castigate those two Allied governments for temporizing in the face of catastrophe. *Life* criticized official complacency about Russian losses and reminded its readership that a "Golden Hour of preparation" was "daily being bought with the lives of fresh thousands of Russians." *Life* belittled official statements in London and Washington that drew attention to the far-flung obligations of the British and American armies in the Mediterranean, the Middle East and the Pacific, acknowledging that technically the war was worldwide, but with a "decisive battlefield"—not Egypt, where the British Eighth Army faced three panzer divisions of Rommel's Afrika Korps, but Russia, where the Red Army handled the "367 remaining estimated German divisions," an exaggeration probably attributable to ETO estimates provided by Eisenhower's headquarters, which cooperated closely with the article.

Life's call to arms was a kind of public introduction of Dwight Eisenhower. Readers opened the magazine to a large photograph of an unidentified general at his desk, leaning back in his chair, dressed in plain khaki and gesturing animatedly with a cigarette. In the description of Russia's agony below and the inadequacy of Allied military efforts, the text identified the "man above" as "the American who is probably going to fix this."

Life complained that like the Allied war effort to date, General Eisenhower's credentials were vague. He was a "big, bland Kansan," a tank expert who had never seen combat, appointed to direct the American build-up in England because of a reputation for staff work and his performance in the Louisiana military maneuvers shortly before Pearl Harbor where he had shown himself to be the "coolest and most capable officer in the field." *Life* called Eisenhower "the closest thing the United States has to a Pershing in this war"—faint praise. Stronger praise was the assertion that Eisenhower "knows what he is doing," building a force that would "probably lose" its first encounter with Germany, but would inflict some "unpleasant surprises."

The articles had no byline. They contained dozens of photographs taken in Ireland of American tank maneuvers and of GIs in basic training, indications that *Life* had received the full cooperation of ETO. *Life*'s comments about the Russian situation faithfully paraphrased the War Department position summarized in the memos drafted by Eisenhower for U.S. Army Chief of Staff George C. Marshall's use in London that week. The *Life* magazine profile would be a source of charges that Eisenhower was too pro-Russian, though the impact on readers may have been the opposite: the article was powerful ammunition both for the interventionist War Department concerned about the consequences of Allied inaction *and* a Pacific-minded Navy Department, impressed by the futility of North Africa and fatalistic about the chances that American intervention would ever come off in Europe on a scale matching the eastern front, much less what the U.S. Navy was in a position to accomplish in the Far East. But by the time the article appeared the President's wishes were evident, and Eisenhower had all but abandoned SLEDGEHAMMER, with regret.

The London conference was over before it began insofar as 1942 operations went, but the spectacle was unforgettable. Marshall, King and Hopkins arrived on July 20 under specific presidential instructions to reach a decision on operations somewhere in 1942 and to adopt GYMNAST if SLEDGEHAMMER proved impractical. Immediately the party divided up, with Hopkins proceeding to the Prime Minister's estate at Chequers for a weekend with Churchill, and Marshall going to Claridges for conferences with Eisenhower and his ETO staff.

In *The Hinge of Fate,* Churchill published the text of Roosevelt's negotiating instructions, which he implied that Hopkins had shown him that weekend. The FDR historian James McGregor Burns called Roosevelt's instructions "ambivalent." Churchill termed them "masterly," for the text was a cloaked but unmistakable assurance from Roosevelt to Churchill that he had no intention of allowing the U.S. Army to stampede the Combined Chiefs and himself into a cross-Channel adventure in 1942. First, Roosevelt called SLEDGEHAMMER a matter "of such grave importance that every reason calls for accomplishment of it," then steadily, point by point, stripped Marshall of all negotiating power vis-à-vis the BCOS, beginning with Marshall's pretense that SLEDGEHAMMER was the only alternative to adoption of a Pacific First strategy. The President imposed a 1942 deadline to consider a feasible operation against the Germans to be evaluated in light of "the world situation as it exists at that time," then gave Marshall one week to reach agreement.

Marshall struggled manfully nevertheless and drove a hard bargain for his consent, with Admiral King's help. King throughout predicted that the United States would refuse to curtail efforts in the Far East for the sake of "ring" objectives in Europe and at one point even threatened to deny U.S. naval protection for convoys to North Africa. The British made light of King's "idle threats" which reflected his pro-Pacific attitude and which they were confident did not represent Roosevelt's views, but they never felt confident enough to ignore them. Indeed, among the terms forced on the British by the Americans was an agreement to amend ABC-1, wherein both sides endorsed the dispatch of U.S. landing craft and capital ships for an American offensive on Guadalcanal.

Thereafter, it was all downhill for SLEDGEHAMMER. Turning to the merits of the proposal, Clark and Eisenhower, charged with presenting the feasibility of a twelve-division attack on Cherbourg late that summer and maintaining a permanent hold in France, could not vouch for the success of the operation in good conscience. SLEDGEHAMMER would be launched with odds Eisenhower estimated at 1 to 2 against successful landings and 1 to 5 against maintaining a beachhead. Eisenhower loyally argued that the stakes justified the risks, urging, "we would be guilty of one of the grossest military blunders of all history if Germany should be permitted to eliminate an Allied Army of 8,000,000 men, when some stroke of ours might have saved the situation." But by late July the argument meant less than it had before the onset of the German summer offensive. Initial German territorial gains were impressive, but the Germans by then had turned away from the main Russian forces and veered southward toward Stalingrad and the Caucasus. In short, the British could rely on American studies to show that SLEDGE-HAMMER would fail and have no effect whatsoever on the Russian front. British estimates of 60 days to organize SLEDGEHAMMER suddenly became 120 days; when pressed, Brooke noted that the British were expected to provide the bulk of the forces for SLEDGEHAMMER, forces that the BCOS chose not to commit to a bloody cross-Channel fiasco or a "success" that would leave Allied forces penned up in the Cotentin Peninsula, cordoned off in a "bomb and shell trap" under constant Luftwaffe and artillery pounding all winter.

In this spirit, the conference adopted GYMNAST (now TORCH): large-scale landings in Morocco and Algeria, "behind" a British Eighth Army offensive set for October. At Marshall's insistence, TORCH would be contingent on a review of SLEDGEHAMMER set six weeks hence in light of the eastern-front situation. But few expected a material change in Russia that would justify SLEDGEHAMMER, and the conference led to "forward action" on Sardinia, Sicily and the Italian mainland as well as other methods of exploiting TORCH—precisely the deep commitment to Mediterranean operations Marshall was determined to avoid. In CCS-94, the document embodying the decisions of the conference, Marshall exacted British stipulations obliging the Combined Chiefs to shed any pretense that North Africa could be considered a suitable base for future operations in Europe. TORCH was to be a "defensive" operation aimed at shoring up positions around the periphery of Europe, a very limited operation resting on doubtful premises, which would be tested in the next several weeks.

Marshall reserved an opening to reconsider TORCH anytime before September 15 if severe Russian setbacks in the next few weeks compelled desperate action to ease German pressure on the eastern front. Marshall probably had another contingency in mind: that events would demonstrate conclusively that the Russians had survived round two of the German-Russian war and compel a last-minute reassessment of the "defensive" strategy chosen by the Allies. But the main factor weighing in favor of TORCH was U.S. domestic politics, and this factor was not likely to change. Perhaps Marshall's seemingly futile effort to reserve this opening had a deeper purpose, that of highlighting the doubtful value of TORCH in anticipation of future debates. Next time, should the British urge exploiting TORCH in the Mediterranean, Marshall, in opposing it, would be armed with stipulations the British had accepted characterizing TORCH as secondary and defensive. When the time came, CCS would have to either go along with U.S. proposals or, consistent with its own appraisal, default.

The London conference boded ill for U.S.-British relations. For the Americans, the conference had been deeply frustrating. The American attitude was that the British were to blame for blocking proposals that might have laid the groundwork for invasion in 1943, that the British had gotten BOLERO for nothing, and now, secure in the knowledge that American military and economic backing was assured, would exploit their new-found security to further purely British interest in the Mediterranean. Likewise, the London conference left an aftertaste of British cynicism in response to Marshall's display of misdirected anger: after all, SLEDGEHAMMER was not really feasible, in that the Americans had insufficient troops to commit to the operation, yet American politics required that it appear feasible. Marshall's intransigence had been disheartening; a bad omen for future give-and-take. Perhaps the most discouraging revelation of all had been Allied military weakness, from which all else stemmed. In fact, the Allies could do nothing to help the Russians in 1942, apparently much to British as well as American regret. The steps required, in Roosevelt's judgment, to preserve Europe First probably ruled out invasion in 1943 as well, which left the question of an invasion at any time in doubt. Indeed, in Eisenhower's snap opinion, it was a given that an invasion had been ruled out for 1943 and probably for good. In any event, in Eisenhower's words, the Allied role had become "a waiting one rather than a positive one."

Debate bubbled on. Marshall departed London in a huff, having refused command of TORCH and having delegated responsibility for TORCH and SLEDGEHAMMER planning to Eisenhower. With SLEDGEHAMMER kept in planning status for the next six weeks, the War Department waged a rearguard fight against TORCH, resulting in Stimson's isolation from major decisions and an enervating "transatlantic essay contest" over TORCH objectives, which hampered Eisenhower's ability to identify resources and firm up prospective landing sites in North Africa.

Churchill grimly flew on to Moscow to inform Stalin of TORCH. For weeks the Soviet press had publicly criticized the Allied military as "wholly unconvincing" and vowed that the Soviet government "would not acquiesce in the postponement of a second front in Europe until 1943." Churchill endured Stalin's taunts about Allied reluctance to fight Germans, but he arrived in Moscow empty-handed. Soviet-Allied relations, never good, were headed toward lows reminiscent of Nazi-Soviet pact days.

The TORCH-SLEDGEHAMMER debate ended shortly afterward. Coinciding with Churchill's return to London on August 18, Combined Operations under Lord Louis Mountbatten hurled the Canadian 2nd Division against the French coastal port at Dieppe. Except for consultations between

Mountbatten and Eisenhower in July, the "Dieppe raid" was a purely Commonwealth action, independent of ETO. Officially the British government would call the Dieppe raid a "reconnaissance in force," a probe to test German reaction time and defensive techniques, and to rehearse for the eventual invasion against northwest France. Another stated purpose was to draw the German Luftwaffe away from Russia.

In 1975, however, Anthony Cave Brown, in *Bodyguard of Lies* drew upon newly opened British Special Intelligence files to build a persuasive case that the Dieppe raid had, in fact, been a planned failure, a sacrificial expenditure of 3,000 lives to embarrass opponents of North Africa, testimony to the power of Marshall's advocacy. Brown's case is strong. Dieppe was first approved as Operation RUTTER on May 13, then canceled on July 8, the day Churchill wired Roosevelt with what he thought would be accepted as the final British rejection of SLEDGEHAMMER. On July 15 Dill cabled from Washington warning Churchill that Marshall had not given up the fight and would reopen the issue once he arrived in London. The Prime Minister then revived Dieppe, now code-named JUBILEE. The second round of deliberations on the raid was kept within a narrow circle of planners and certain members of the War Cabinet. No minutes were kept of the meetings. The objective set for the raid was hazardous: a frontal assault on a coastal city held by the German 110th Field Infantry Division, with confirmed knowledge that the 10th Panzer Division nearby at Amiens was capable of reinforcement within a matter of hours. According to Brown, British deception measures drew attention to the Dieppe area instead of away from it, as would routinely be expected. Commando raids were launched in the vicinity of Dieppe ninety-six hours before the scheduled attack, ensuring that the defending 110th Division would be at maximum alert when the attack came.

In the late evening and early morning of August 18–19, 1942, the Canadian 2nd Division, consisting of six battalions, attacked seven points along the beach, including the Dieppe Casino. The assault force encountered a fully prepared enemy. The Canadian 2nd was quickly pinned down under hostile fire at the breakwater, and most units never reached the beaches. Hundreds died aboard landing craft, and of 6,150 men who landed, 3,500 were killed or captured in the six-hour engagement.

The raid would influence techniques and tactics chosen for the OVERLORD plan presented to Eisenhower on January 17, 1944. The raid also impressed planners with the efficiency of German defenses, the dangers of frontal assault on a port city "and the consequent need for concentrating the greatest possible weight on the initial assault." But evidently the main point of Dieppe was not to test techniques for 1944 but to demonstrate the futility of further argument over SLEDGEHAMMER in August 1942.

If so, JUBILEE had the intended effect on Eisenhower. His wartime files contain scant references to the Dieppe raid, but one such reference was a reply to Marshall in which Eisenhower assured the Chief of Staff that ETO would tone down publicity about the fifty American Rangers involved in the assault, and avoid giving the impression that Dieppe was the opening campaign of an earnest effort to land and stay in France.

Thereafter, Eisenhower shifted focus to TORCH. Forty-eight hours after the surviving remnants of the decimated Canadian force limped back to Southhampton, Eisenhower found himself replying to a letter from his old mentor, General Fox Conner, on the 1942 situation. In it Eisenhower assured Conner that he agreed with him "as to the immediate task to be performed by the Allies [relieving pressure on the Russians]":

> I have preached that doctrine earnestly for the last six months—to everyone who would listen to me. I have never had any trouble getting academic concurrences; but there are plenty of difficulties to be encountered when you bring up the question of actual operations. Actually, the whole thing seems to me to be absurdly simple. I believe in direct methods, possibly because I am too simple-minded to be an intriguer or to attempt to be clever. However, I am no longer in the places where these great questions have to be settled. My only job is to carry out my directives as well as I can. I sincerely trust that I will be able to do my duty in accordance with your own high standards.

AFTERMATH

In his memoirs Winston Churchill minimized the SLEDGEHAMMER decision. He called the plan a victim of "strategic natural selection," implying that SLEDGEHAMMER had withered away in the manner of bad ideas. "I did not have to argue against SLEDGEHAMMER myself," he wrote, "it fell of its own weakness." But elsewhere in his six volumes on the war, he defended no other decision so vigorously as his rejection of SLEDGEHAMMER and his insistence on TORCH. At the time, Churchill and the British may have sensed danger in being "right" about 1942, for eventually there would in fact be an invasion and the Americans would then prove to have been "right." The British, who knew they could not match American resources and would thus have to rely more and more on persuasion and prestige, would thereafter bear the onus in American and Russian minds of having forced TORCH and postponed the invasion by twenty-three months.

Accordingly, Churchill, rankled at what he felt were partisan conclusions drawn by the American Chiefs, attempted to blame Guadalcanal for the failure to mount a 1943 ROUNDUP. During an overnight visit at Chequers, in mid-September, Eisenhower was drawn into a heated discussion about TORCH-ROUNDUP. Churchill would not hear of the idea that TORCH had ruled out ROUNDUP and told Eisenhower that in Harriman's presence he had assured Stalin that TORCH would aid systematic preparations for 1943. Churchill returned to the subject over and over that night, asking Eisenhower why in the world 13 divisions in North Africa should have any effect whatsoever on Operation ROUNDUP, which envisaged 50 divisions or more. In his report to Marshall, Eisenhower recalled that he "went over with him all the additional costs in the opening of a new theater, and establishing a second line of communications, and building up a new front and base facilities and in the long turnaround for ships."

Thereafter, cross-Channel planning waned. Churchill pressed on, berating the British Chiefs in November for the "frightful gap" between what military staffs had considered within the realm of possibility in July 1942 and how little was actually being planned. But little would be done, and Churchill's travail illustrated the truism that it was one thing to foresee frustration, another to experience it. Twelve months of uncertainty lay ahead.

In October 1942, Montgomery's Eighth Army had launched the El Alamein offensive and on November 8, two days after the off-year U.S. elections, Allied forces successfully landed at Casablanca, Oran and Algiers under Eisenhower's command. German reinforcements blocked advances in Tunisia, thus extending the North African campaign by six months. The high command would be absorbed in the Darlan affair all winter. In the field, American generals and troops would weather their first test, but troop inexperience and poor coordination among the Americans, British and French took their toll in time and lives.

Meanwhile, on November 19 the Russians launched a two-prong counteroffensive over the Volga that encircled the German Sixth Army at Stalingrad and imperiled the 600-mile retreat of German forces in the Caucasus. In the next six weeks, amid the news of Stalingrad, the Allies took stock. In December, Churchill aired the problem of 1943 with Roosevelt, and challenged American decisions to scale back BOLERO and reinforce the Pacific. Separately, the newly formed U.S. Joint Strategic Survey Committee in Washington had drawn up a paper recommending the build-up of a balanced U.S.-British force in Britain in preparation for a decisive cross-Channel assault before the end of 1943. The JCS approved the paper, then presented it to the British, who countered with proposals for expanded Mediterranean operations in 1943, and pushing the invasion off to 1944.

The turning point on the eastern front at Stalingrad dramatized the intractability of Roosevelt's problems. Full-scale participation in operations against Germany were essential to fulfill American war aims as Roosevelt conceived them. And yet every step toward an invasion raised new problems. By January 1943 the magnitude of the Russian victory at Stalingrad signaled that Germany had been contained, which reduced both the Allied incentive to mobilize and the Soviet incentive to cooperate, and inhibited Roosevelt's ability to approach the Russians about cooperation. U.S. Army ground combat strength in numbers approached its peak that month. Second-front emotions cooled, and anti-Russian sentiment reappeared in the U.S. press for the first time since 1941.

In the wake of Stalingrad, the Germans announced total mobilization. Even if insufficient to recapture the strategic initiative on all fronts, German force levels would rise, and might prove sufficient for a defensive strategy in Russia with a margin left over for ground superiority in the west for some time to come. Allied planners could anticipate a situation wherein German losses in Russia would be offset by new recruits, a more efficient military policy in Russia, and Allied cutbacks. Thus one could foresee a cycle of greater Allied military reliance on the Russians just as domestic pressures mounted against concessions to the Soviets, abetted in turn by dwindling Soviet inhibitions about asserting their postwar aspirations and plans. In January 1943 Stalin declined Roosevelt's invitation for a meeting on American soil to discuss Lend-Lease, U.S. bases in Russia, the Far East war, and other U.S.-Soviet concerns; then, two months later, he broke relations with the London Poles over the Katyn Forest allegations.

On the other hand, these were problems Roosevelt and Churchill had probably foreseen and would have faced even without TORCH in 1942. Indeed, TORCH yielded important gains in North Africa and temporarily silenced debate over Europe First, buttressed in retrospect by Roosevelt's highly controversial unconditional-surrender declaration at Casablanca. The declaration served several purposes; first, that of improving relations with the Russians at the outset of a trying year of waiting; second, that of binding Congress to large-scale operations in Europe eventually, thereby heading off congressional pressure for cutbacks in war production. Churchill's hand in drafting the controversial declaration, often credited with extending the war, is unknown, but he approved.

At Casablanca, the Anglo-American debate centered on ROUNDUP versus extended operations in the Mediterranean, with the issue implicitly 1944. The British again "won," and the JCS consented to Sicily next. But the two sides also decided to establish the combined command and planning organization in London known as COSSAC "to plan for small-scale raids, a return to the continent in 1943 under conditions of German collapse, a limited operation in 1943 to secure a bridgehead on the continent for later exploitation, and last an invasion in force in 1944." Another rearguard struggle waged by Marshall on behalf of a 1943 "ROUNDHAMMER" was not set aside until a series of June conferences in Algiers hosted by Eisenhower, at which plans for the invasion of Sicily were approved, looking toward the invasion of Italy in September.

At Casablanca the CCS faced rigidities in invasion planning that it had not realistically faced before. Troop limitations would place a premium on Allied air and naval strength. Thus, the CCS devised POINTBLANK, the Allied combined bomber offensive with the strategic task of winning the battle of the Atlantic, gaining air superiority and securing "the progressive

destruction and dislocation of the German military, industrial, and economic system, and the undermining of the morale of the German people
to a point where their capacity for armed resistance is fatally weakened."
Significantly, both sides resisted unified air command for reasons of politics
and technical differences between the British night-bombing techniques and
U.S. daylight precision bombing. The British argued that daylight bombing
was too costly and pressed the Eighth Air Force to join the RAF in night
bombing designed to destroy "whole critical industrial and military areas."
General Arnold balked, and the POINTBLANK directive bridged both approaches, setting priority for submarine-construction yards, the aircraft
industry, transportation targets, oil and "other enemy war industry."

Eight weeks later COSSAC commenced in a climate of skepticism. As
the story went, shortly after Casablanca, as he handed COSSAC Chief
General Frederick Morgan a BCOS outline draft of the cross-Channel
plans, Brooke had remarked, "Well—there it is. It won't work. But you
must bloody well make it work." Morgan, affable and zealous, quickly
became the central figure in the planning effort.

By late spring, COSSAC objectives were amended to delete operations in
late 1943. Morgan was to carry out "an elaborate camouflage and deception
scheme," keeping alive the expectation of a large-scale cross-Channel operation in 1943 but to plan for "a full scale assault against the continent in 1944
as early as possible." COSSAC assumed charge of elaborate deception
operations staged in support of Mediterranean operations, and to test techniques for the main event, in which the Allies would seek to ensure the
strategic dispersion of German troops by a campaign of political warfare,
subversion, economic warfare and deception "in order to undermine the
German will and ability to fight, and pin down forces wherever they might
be found." Diversionary operations, under the code name COCKADE, consisted of feints that summer in the direction of the Brest peninsula (WAD-
HAM), simulated preparations for attack against Norway (TINDALL), and
threats toward the Pas-de-Calais (STARKEY), aimed to test German responses and to prevent German withdrawals from France to Italy and
Russia.

Both the Americans and British came to place much store on deception.
The British LCS—the coordinating and planning agency for all deception
and intelligence activities—drew up plans for feints and deception on a
global scale, the result of several signal successes in 1943. Operation ZEPPE-
LIN, a cover plan for Sicily, included strategies to plant false information
about attacks in two areas: (1) in Greece, in preparation for a thrust via the
Balkans; (2) in Sardinia, as jumping-off point for invading southern France.
ZEPPELIN played on German skepticism that the Allies would ever risk a
frontal attack and Hitler's belief that Churchill would eventually be "obsessed by the desire to prove in 1943 the validity of his grand strategy in 1915,
of a decisive assault against enemy-occupied Europe from the Southeast."

PLANNING OVERLORD

At the June conferences in Washington the CCS, in ordering an invasion of Sicily, formally set priority for ROUNDUP (soon to be OVERLORD). Over Brooke's objections, the CCS set a target date of May 1, 1944, a date chosen to precede the probable date of a 1944 Russian summer offensive by several weeks and set early enough to exploit four months of summer campaign weather.

Meanwhile, differences re-emerged as COSSAC attempted to arrive at firm estimates of Allied resources for the forthcoming invasion. The Americans urged that plans be drawn on the basis of *maximum* forces available, but the British opposed this and instructed Morgan to plan on the basis of *available* forces. Tentative strength for OVERLORD set at Washington called for 29 American and British divisions reinforced by 7 divisions to be withdrawn from the Mediterranean in mid-October 1943. The "American reserve," consisting of divisions forming in America and available for direct shipment to France would be in the range of 40 divisions, depending on how the invasion progressed. Hence, Morgan described the prodigious planning effort that summer as a process of drawing up a "map which starts at one end with San Francisco and ends at the other end in Berlin." COSSAC charted plans for the movement of every plane, landing vessel and soldier, and devised the tactical studies and cloaking operation deemed essential to the success of OVERLORD.

That summer, as COSSAC steadily expanded, Morgan contended with interservice rivalries, subtle British opposition and American skepticism about the predominantly British organization. Marshal Arthur Harris of RAF Bomber Command refused to cooperate with the organization. Morgan dealt with a skeptical British War Cabinet and a Prime Minister who grumbled about commitments so far in advance of something not certain to happen. An American planning agency under ETO Commander General Frank Andrews and his successor Lieutenant General Jacob Devers also held aloof. Within the integrated British-American agency, Morgan gradually surmounted American suspicion that British planners, committed to Mediterranean strategy, would worry too much about the "butcher's bill" in France, admittedly a deep "preoccupation of the British government and their Chiefs of Staff." Morgan recruited American members of the COSSAC staff from G-5 (plans sections) at ETOUSA (European Theater of Operations, U.S. Army). Finally the ETO commander, Lieutenant General Devers, assumed a role in the planning until General Omar Bradley's appointment in October to command the newly formed U.S. First Army with its headquarters in Bristol.

Next to troops, landing craft availability was the critical factor in assault planning. Production of specialized craft for opposed landings was new in warfare and had begun in earnest only as recently as the spring of 1942, to be cut back shortly after the TORCH decision. Since foreseeable production levels would force tightly balanced allocations to Italy, the Pacific and England, and raised the question of increasing production of landing craft, the British requested increases in American production, since the British, already at maximum production, could not provide an extra margin. Admiral King held out against increases that would delay capital-ship and ocean-escort programs needed for the build-up and for his "private war" in the Pacific. The British called King's refusal "short-sighted," and in May 1943, presented a proposal calling for the lift needed for a ten-division landing force. Finding that the required 8,500 landing craft was an impossible goal given U.S. production schedules, British estimates kindled American suspicion that the British would never support the assault, a logical inference in view of "British arguments at the Washington conference for further operations in the Mediterranean and of their openly expressed doubts as to the feasibility of a cross-channel invasion unless German strength in the west could be drastically reduced." King and Marshall agreed to accept landing-craft production rates as a "limiting factor" in all planning. By mid-summer, COSSAC planners had identified landing craft sufficient for a five-division assault phase: three divisions in the assault and two in the floating reserve with a second follow-up of two divisions achieved by turnaround of the first craft plus miscellaneous other craft. According to historian Gordon Harrison, "these planning figures were accepted without significant debate and it was agreed that General Morgan would be ordered to confine his plan to the detailed allotment of 4,504 landing ships and craft which planners' figures said would be available."

Morgan's estimates were based on the "feeling" of what an assault would require, since no detailed tactical plan had yet been prepared. Estimates did not take into account loss or damage to craft in the assault, turnaround time and the need for close-support craft. But the estimates pegged OVERLORD as a smaller-scale landing than Sicily or Salerno.

Adoption of ANVIL at Quebec in August was an additional burden on landing-craft resources. Tentative inspection of the landing-craft problem made it apparent that ANVIL would call on ships tentatively allocated to the Pacific and the Mediterranean, especially if the OVERLORD assault was expanded. The British, determined to police past understandings that resources for the Pacific and Mediterranean be balanced, pressed a jurisdictional point—that while technically ANVIL would be mounted by AFHQ with Mediterranean resources, ANVIL and OVERLORD would form a whole. Allocations for ANVIL from the Mediterranean would have to be balanced out against the Pacific ledger.

By the fall of 1943 Churchill and the BCOS, partly to firm up the demarcation between France and the Mediterranean, began to assert the strategic possibilities of the Mediterranean theater with various proposals for a "Balkan belt" and landings in the Adriatic and in the Dodecanese, a strategy that was abandoned at Cairo in exchange for the cancellation of the American-sponsored Andamans operation. In the SHINGLE debate, Churchill reasserted the jurisdictional line between France and Italy, since, among other things, ANVIL had assumed a life of its own and threatened to submerge the campaign in Italy altogether. Conceived originally as a diversionary one-division "feint," ANVIL evolved into a plan for full-scale American-French landings designed to deploy ten otherwise "idle" American and French divisions in the Mediterranean. Since the British were not to participate in ANVIL, the ANVIL issue centered not so much on whether the British would approve, but on how far the Americans would go in cutting back U.S. support for Italy.

Inevitably, debate over ANVIL quickened after Teheran as the British felt the pressure of American economic and military predominance in OVERLORD and tallied up the results of the conference. Churchill was determined to slow down American withdrawals from the Mediterranean. Even at the height of the ANVIL controversy, however, it would never be clear to Eisenhower that the British actually opposed ANVIL or considered the Balkan strategy a practical design. First of all, British views were not uniform, and a debate was evident between Churchill and his advisers about the wisdom of opposing ANVIL to the end and thereby forgoing control of OVERLORD, thus confining British say to control of the Mediterranean theater. Brooke and the BCOS reckoned with the practical limits on developing the Italian campaign without U.S. support, the dangers of OVERLORD to which the British would contribute fifteen Empire divisions, and the certainty of U.S. support for France, an advantage for British troops who would be sent there. Influence over OVERLORD meant say over the vital theater and over postwar issues. But in Churchill's opinion, nourishing a third front based on Italy was essential as a contingency should OVERLORD prove impractical, and as an asset in his dealings with the Soviets, as well as in protecting British interests in the area. By January 1944, the uncertainty of Churchill's views was discernible, however, and more than once Eisenhower would find himself in the middle of an in-house British argument.

The landing-craft shortage was real, however, and one can speculate whether the ANVIL controversy would ever have reached the point it did had the Allies possessed ample stocks. After Quebec, as he undertook a re-examination of the OVERLORD plan with the idea of increasing the size of the OVERLORD assault, Morgan learned that the minimal number of landing and support craft originally guaranteed was not available. Morgan reported the shortages to the BCOS—which raised the issue of production schedules again and spurred a vain search for new sources of landing craft in hopes that painful choices might be avoided. Eventually, the U.S. War Production Board agreed to a 35 percent increase in landing-craft production, which merely meant that existing production schedules would be fulfilled. Thereafter, curing the shortage of LSTs without curtailing operations in other theaters would involve a delay in OVERLORD until the summer of 1944, which was apparently the reason for Roosevelt's brief effort to back OVERLORD "before August" at Teheran. Indeed, just as the CCS issued the directive for OVERLORD, Roosevelt personally ordered Nelson and Byrnes to cancel plans for new LST construction.

Thereafter, shortages and hard choices were unavoidable. OVERLORD in May 1944 meant that landing-craft availability would be a matter of stretching existing resources, through reallocations from the Mediterranean or the Pacific, comb-out of training facilities in the United States, and expedients such as increasing loading and serviceability rates. By the time of Eisenhower's arrival in London in January 1944, revised plans called for an expanded assault at Normandy by five divisions with two in reserve to be sure of a wider front on D-Day and the quick capture of Cherbourg. And with SHINGLE set for mid-month, landing craft did not appear to be available for both ANVIL and a widened OVERLORD assault.

By fall 1943, COSSAC was a going concern. Along with responsibility for military planning, Morgan had assumed executive authority over French civil affairs, planning for the German occupation, psychological warfare, and operational control for RANKIN, a contingency plan to occupy Berlin in the event of a sudden German military or political collapse. COSSAC directed reconnaissance missions in northwest Europe, and coordinated elements of the French resistance.

By now the British had set up Army, Navy and Air commands for the invasion. The Second British Army, First Canadian Army and British 21st Army Group had functioning headquarters, and became Morgan's principal source of advice on Army problems. In September the CCS had appointed RAF Air Marshall Trafford Leigh-Mallory to command the AEAF.* A month later the CCS named Admiral Bertram Ramsay commander in chief of the naval forces.

Gradually, most aspects of the OVERLORD plan became fixed. Normandy, one of the earliest features of the plan, had been ratified at the all-British RATTLE conference, held at the Hollywood Hotel in Largs, Scotland, on June 28, 1943, called to explore the problems confronting the cross-Channel project. Since then, the integrated COSSAC staff had painstakingly compiled studies of logistics, ship schedules, terrain, hydrographic details, intelligence, command, tactical deception, and studies of special factors such as tides, moon and weather suitable for tactical naval and air support for the landings in Normandy.

As in their choice of northwest France, planners had selected Normandy by the process of elimination. Mountbatten's Combined Operations had

*Allied Expeditionary Air Forces.

defined the prerequisites for any landing site; firm beaches were necessary for landing armored elements in the first wave with adequate roads and exits leading away from the beaches; landing sites had to be within range of British and American fighters based in southern England, and within overnight sailing distance from Bristol, Plymouth and Portsmouth. The combined assault forces would eventually include over 4,000 ships of all descriptions to transport the invasion forces across the Channel under cover of darkness. The site would have to be suitable for naval fire and air bombardment capable of destroying or neutralizing beach defenses, and for a quick Allied rate of build-up, in an area where Allied forces could be sure of exceeding local enemy strength long enough to seize a major port.

This last consideration ruled out the beaches in the Pas-de-Calais at Boulogne, Dunkirk and Calais, the textbook choice initially favored by Combined Operations planners in 1942. Visible from Dover on a clear day with field glasses, the Pas-de-Calais region afforded a quick turnaround for the naval convoys, direct support by long-range artillery batteries stationed along the Dover coast, and proximity to Rouen and Le Havre, a close cluster of port towns, and the approaches to the lowlands and the northwestern German frontier. The lack of flat, hard ground inland suitable for airfields and steep escarpments rising behind the best beaches were drawbacks, but the fatal drawback was the importance of the area to the Germans.

Since 1942 the bulk of German units in France had been deployed there and the region had been developed as the main link in the beltlike German Channel defenses from Le Havre to Bremen. By January 1944, eighteen divisions of the German Fifteenth Army garrisoned the Pas-de-Calais. Assault landings on this position might have succeeded. But in posing an immediate threat to the hinge of German defenses in France, landings would have eliminated the factor of German indecision about committing reserves against the bridgehead. The hope was that if the German high command believed it could hesitate for several days without exposing crucial objectives, it might do so, handing the Allies an edge in the race to build up forces in the landing zone. Normandy was close to the Fifteenth Army concentrations at Calais, but this counted for less than it appeared to on a map. The proximity of the two areas meant that the Germans could not rule out the possibility of simultaneous landings at both, a possibility to be exploited in deception plans. Likewise the AEAF staff was at work on plans for an air campaign on the French rail system to magnify the impact of air interdiction on D-Day which would aim primarily at impeding Fifteenth Army movement. Many air experts, however, now questioned the effectiveness of bombing transport systems, and Eisenhower knew that a big debate on air policy was inevitable.

In its deliberations, COSSAC had eliminated Holland and Belgium as too distant from England. Le Havre, at the mouth of the Seine, lay close enough

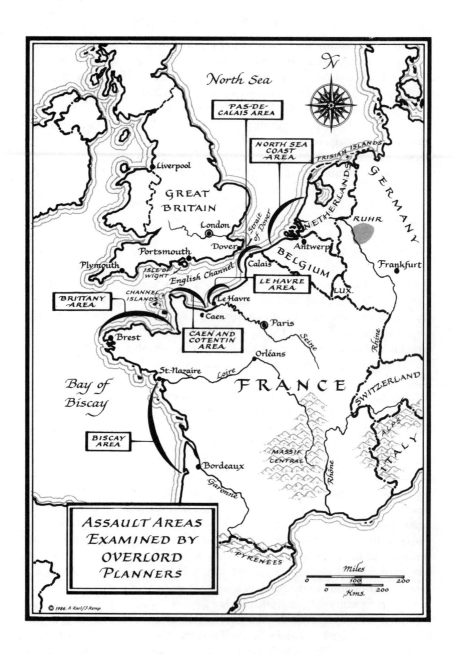

North Sea

PAS-DE-CALAIS AREA

NORTH SEA COAST AREA

FRISIAN ISLANDS

Liverpool

GREAT BRITAIN

GERMANY

NETHERLANDS

RUHR

London

Strait of Dover

Dover

Antwerp

Portsmouth

BELGIUM

Frankfurt

Plymouth

ISLE OF WIGHT

Calais

English Channel

LE HAVRE AREA

LUX.

CHANNEL ISLANDS

BRITTANY AREA

Le Havre

Caen

Paris

Seine

Rhine

SWITZERLAND

Brest

CAEN AND COTENTIN AREA

Orléans

FRANCE

St. Nazaire

Loire

Bay of Biscay

ALPS

ITALY

BISCAY AREA

Bordeaux

MASSIF CENTRAL

Rhône

Garonne

ASSAULT AREAS EXAMINED BY OVERLORD PLANNERS

PYRÉNÉES

Miles

0   100   200

0   100   200

Kms.

© 1986 A·Karl/J·Kemp

to southern England, but the beaches in that region are fragmented by the Seine estuary. COSSAC considered the Bay of Biscay, close to the ports of Brest, St.-Nazaire and Lorient, a region exposed to Atlantic storms, and the distances involved meant a long turnaround time for ships.

This left the beaches of Normandy, at the neck of the Cotentin Peninsula. Normandy, defended by the understrength German Seventh Army, encompassed the port towns of Colleville and Vierville. Sheltered from the Atlantic by the Cotentin Peninsula, the beaches were considered wide and hard enough. Between three and five assault divisions could be landed with two following up, including armored elements to spearhead an early breakout. Planners noted that in the Caen–Falaise plain south of Caen, rolling unwooded terrain was suitable for rapid construction of airfields and armored operations. A good lateral road and rail network ran from Cherbourg along the invasion front capable of sustaining a break-out offensive either way: south toward the Breton ports or east toward Paris.

But Normandy presented problems. A Normandy beachhead would be vulnerable to isolation in the hedgerow country. Ports were a problem. Cherbourg, the best port in the area, had barely enough capacity for the American build-up on the western flank. The COSSAC plan estimated thirty days for the capture of Cherbourg by the Western task force (American) because of the systems of river barriers at the neck of the Cotentin Peninsula, time enough to enable the German garrison to demolish the facility, which could mean at least another three weeks to salvage the port.

These facts had inspired one of the most remarkable elements of the NEPTUNE plan. While seizing and rehabilitating Cherbourg, the 21st Army Group would have to improvise delivery of the 600 tons per day needed to maintain each Allied division on the line. Air drops and beaching LSTs offered a partial answer; the rest of the answer was the Allies' decision to construct components of two artificial ports the size of Dover, one for the American sector, one for the British. On D-Day, the Royal Navy would haul the components across the Channel and assemble them in seven days under enemy fire behind the British beaches at Arromanches and the American beaches at St.-Laurent. The artificial ports (MULBERRY), proposed first by Mountbatten's Combined Operations staff, would consist of a number of components—large 200-foot caissons (PHOENIX) sunk to serve as an outer breakwater. Seventy-four merchant ships would steam in company with the invasion force, to be sunk in the shallow waters (GOOSEBERRY) to provide 8,000 yards of inner breakwater. Prefabricated docks, a maze of floating quays, steel runways and piers (WHALE) would be anchored to the beach.

There were doubts that MULBERRY would work. The job of hauling 50,000 tons of steelwork, one million tons of concrete, 6 miles of bridges and 120 miles of steel cable was immense. The ports would be vulnerable to enemy fire and Channel storms. Yet COSSAC had seen no alternative, and had actually listed MULBERRY among the preconditions for OVER-LORD, albeit one withheld from the Russians at Moscow and Teheran. Evidently the British and the Americans did not agree completely about the importance of MULBERRY. Also, the Allies had decided not to disclose Normandy to the Russians, and MULBERRY would reveal Normandy by indicating that the Allies intended to mount landings not dependent on capturing a major port.

Nothing would be spared to protect the secret of Normandy. At RATTLE, the group had approved FORTITUDE, a series of deception plans, a more intricate scheme than the deceptions at North Africa, Sicily or Salerno, indeed a "strategic" plan in scale. In the best case, FORTITUDE would keep German divisions tied down from Norway to Marseilles. At a minimum, FORTITUDE was supposed to induce the Germans to hold back the Fifteenth Army reserve at Calais by bluffing secondary landings there using elaborate stratagems. In FORTITUDE north, the fictitious British Fourth Army with headquarters in Edinburgh would prepare for an "invasion" of Normandy. Then, after D-Day it would "move" south to join Patton's fictitious First U.S. Army Group (FUSAG) assembling for landings at Calais. Unlike the British Fourth Army, FUSAG consisted of real forces scheduled to follow up through Normandy: the First Canadian Army, three U.S. divisions, and a follow-up force of four armored and four infantry divisions of Patton's U.S. Third Army set to be activated by D plus 30.

Eisenhower, Montgomery, Patton and Bradley all doubted the effectiveness of deception operations and were reluctant to place much store by them. The 21st Army Group questioned COSSAC estimates which held that FORTITUDE south would "pin down" the neighboring Fifteenth Army for a month. The feeling was that German reserves at Calais would move according to the availability of German reinforcements from other fronts to replace Calais, or when assured that the Allied build-up in Normandy had reached the point where secondary landings could be ruled out, at which point the best deception plans in the world could not stop an all-out effort to defeat the bridgehead. Also, FORTITUDE required Russian cooperation, which remained a question mark. At Teheran, declaring "truth deserves a bodyguard of lies," Churchill had presented JAEL, the plan for global deceptions and diversionary operations for OVERLORD. The military conclusions of the conference had called for an Allied-Soviet deception strategy in 1944 featuring two elements: (1) to suggest that the Allies and Russians intended joint operations in Scandinavia and the Balkans, and (2) to put over the idea that the Americans and British would not launch a cross-Channel attack until after the Russians had launched a summer offensive in July. But the Soviets were skeptical about deception plans in general. To enlist Russian cooperation, John Henry Bevan, head of the LCS, flew to Moscow with his U.S. assistant Lieutenant Colonel William H. Baumer on January 29, 1944, to present Plan JAEL. The Russians stalled on talks for ten days. Then, after Bevan, Baumer and Deane explained the idea of the plan, the Soviets appeared to accept. An Allied-Soviet agreement to coordinate global deception would be initialed on March 6, 1944, but according to Burrows, the Russians "hated and distrusted the whole thing."

It was difficult to look beyond D plus 30, and few did so. Planning proceeded on two assumptions: that the Allies would have the initiative in the assault phase; that the Germans were capable of matching or exceeding Allied ground strength in all phases after the landings. The most economical line of defense was the coast, but within the preconditions set by COSSAC the Allies could probably get ashore quickly and move inland to gain space for the build-up. Planners assumed that overall enemy strength in the west by May would rise to between 50 and 60 divisions, including 12 mobile divisions. On D-Day over half the German divisions would be "static" divisions, immobile units capable of limited offensive action. The pre-positioning of German armor would be a key element in success or failure in the battle of the beachhead.

Thereafter, the pace of German reinforcements would be the critical factor. After successful Allied landings, the Germans would evaluate the eastern and western fronts and consider an all-out response in the west depending on the mix of threats and opportunities confronting them. Containment of the Allied bridgehead would buy time for an all-out German effort to destroy the invasion. Would the Germans attempt to do it? Allied air superiority could hamper such an effort, and extended German lines of communication would also weigh against it. Yet the Germans might be tempted to take risks on the smaller western fronts. And the more threatening the Allied concentrations, the more likely German attention would be drawn westward to France, a factor in the "indirect" choice of Normandy and tentative plans to orient the invasion force southward toward Brittany, away from the German frontier instead of northeast along the Channel coast.

All of this illustrated what by early 1944 was a truism: that short of the blow leading to a German capitulation, success for the Allies would always be a mixed blessing. There were optimists who doubted that any German leader, even Hitler, would have the power to implement a policy that risked reverses in the east, but no one could assume it, and Allied forces would, in any case, encounter greater and greater resistance as they advanced on Germany, and would face danger in the event of a Russian pause. Likewise, the paradox of success would conceivably apply to the eastern-front offensive as well, for a major Russian success, in dramatizing hopeless German prospects there, might tempt the German leadership to take greater risks to eliminate the smaller western front in the desperate hope of reversing fortunes. By the time such possibilities might arise, the Allies were to be well established north of the Loire and along the Seine. But no one could predict the timing and scale of Russian actions precisely, and, realistically, the chances for the kind of close coordination between the two fronts that would ensure that the German armies on both fronts would be engaged at the right times and kept off-balance had ended in 1942.

Finally, COSSAC grappled with the problems of command. British and U.S. troops would land on separate beaches in keeping with their separate logistical and administrative systems. Morgan had proposed unified ground command under a Britisher until the American build-up justified a separate army group command, whereupon the Supreme Commander would assume command of the American and British army groups. Montgomery's 21st Army Group had been designated to coordinate the assault, but Eisenhower's appointment reopened the issue of an overall ground commander in chief. Precedents in North Africa, Sicily and Italy favored a British commander in chief, but the British Army in the Mediterranean was the preponderant force. In OVERLORD the American forces could predominate and 1944 would be an election year, a point against an integrated ground command under the British. On the other hand, overlapping command procedures provided some assurance that the Allied high command would not break up under crisis pressures as it had in June 1940.

The crucial command problem left open by COSSAC concerned the air forces, a matter to be resolved by the CCS. By January 17 the Combined Chiefs of Staff had still not worked out the text of Eisenhower's directive, and Eisenhower's air problems had become part of a wider debate over Eisenhower's powers in general. The British sought to limit Eisenhower's powers to precise terms, and to broaden the jurisdiction of the naval, air and ground commanders under him, all Britishers. The British favored limiting Eisenhower's assigned tasks to the attainment of a lodgement area in France in anticipation of future negotiations over Italy versus France. The American Joint Chiefs favored bolder, more permanent objectives. Debate would last another month, and the crucial issue of air command would still not be settled.

The air issue involved complex military and political factors and would be fought out at several levels: the size of the assigned forces, the relationship of SHAEF and the strategic air forces, not to mention French politics, and the role of the Supreme Command itself. These issues were interrelated, and novel. No commander had laid claim to the strategic air forces before. Only Marshall could have done so without prolonged debate. Resistance would be strong, since strategic targeting possibilities in late 1943 were greater because of improvements in air technique. But OVERLORD was more hazardous and complex than any operation attempted to date, and ground superiority would never be assured. Air, sea and ground coordination was essential. Exceptions would be made for certain British units not performing tasks directly related to OVERLORD, but beyond this, exceptions might lead to more exceptions and breakdown of air-sea-ground coordination altogether. Moreover, direct command over all American forces would be the key to Eisenhower's ability to act. In practical terms, Eisenhower would be coordinating American and British forces, and this inevitably meant negotiations with the British and Montgomery. Eisenhower intended to approach those negotiations as the man who spoke for all the American forces in England. To a lesser degree, Eisenhower would be negotiating with his American subordinates as well, and visible exceptions made for any major forces, especially American, operating in England would undermine disciplined American acceptance of Eisenhower's authority. This was unspoken, but a fact nonetheless.

The stakes were not so obvious at first glance, nor was the significance of Eisenhower's formal control over the Eighth Air Force. In the past Eisenhower's command had functioned well with informal arrangements and decisions by consensus. For instance, in AFHQ days, Eisenhower and General Spaatz had readily cooperated on air problems. Targeting policy in OVERLORD, as before, would be a day-to-day procedure worked out between committees of technical experts with priorities settled by consensus. Salerno had proven the adaptability of AFHQ in a crisis. But OVERLORD would be a prolonged test of the alliance, magnified by unprecedented hazards and persisting doubt, in view of German reversals, that OVERLORD was sound military and political strategy, or even necessary.

As of late 1943, the question of whether OVERLORD was really necessary or desirable was growing, not diminishing. As each day went by, many wondered whether the Germans could postpone defeat much longer. That they lacked the power to stop a determined Russian offensive would become apparent in time, as well as the fact that they were helplessly overextended elsewhere but powerless to yield ground. German ability to stave off air attack and merciless pounding of German industry and cities had deteriorated irreversibly. Allied and Russian campaigns in progress seemed adequate to defeat Germany sooner or later, and though a successful OVERLORD stood to defeat the Germans sooner rather than later, this was by no means certain. Nor was it certain that the Germans could not exploit the peculiar hazards of cross-Channel landings and local Allied weakness in France to defeat OVERLORD. And for the sake of undertaking the most hazardous operation anyone could conceive of in 1944, the Allies were confining operations to Italy and France, which stood to fall into Allied hands anyway, at the cost of gains in the Balkans and eastern Mediterranean and with no guarantees that doing so would in fact improve matters with the Russians.

In command terms, doubts of this kind presented Eisenhower with a formidable challenge. His task was to fuse American and British forces and competing service branches within each force into a cohesive unit. In theory, this would be easiest to accomplish when a sense of common danger was high and, correspondingly, most difficult as the common danger receded. But it was apparent that the actual situation Eisenhower would confront was something in between, for the Allied operations about to be undertaken would be hazardous, despite the imminent German defeat-in-the-making. This meant that hopes would persist to the end that the obstacles might suddenly dissolve, hopes mixed with resentment of the seemingly unnecessary dangers courted at such a late hour of the war.

Soldiers at all levels sensed the paradox; as a German defeat seemed more inevitable every day, the Allies could not be sure that their chosen course guaranteed that they would win on their own front. Would OVERLORD fail? The invasion might succeed but this would leave the battle of France, and little choice except to press on with a hazardous and expensive advance on the Ruhr.

In short, had the need for OVERLORD been self-evident as a means to defeat Germany, the hazards it presented might have been a unifying factor and Eisenhower's authority might have been unquestioned with or without clear lines of authority over both forces. The necessity of OVERLORD was not self-evident, however. The obvious dangers faced would be met with resolution, but mixed with a sense that courting dangers at this stage of the war was pointless or that the hazards would prove to be illusory, which would breed grievances and balkiness. In the circumstances, Eisenhower's task was to extend his personal authority over all air, ground and sea forces in England and to consolidate it, unlike the days at AFHQ, where he functioned best by coordinating rival authorities. His power to act and to negotiate was at stake, and the crucial test of it would be control of the American Eighth Air Force, at least in the early stages of OVERLORD.

By January 1944, troubles were evident. Eisenhower's Air Command, including RAF General Trafford Leigh-Mallory, an experienced fighter commander, was inexperienced in strategic air and not deemed suited by Arnold, Portal and Spaatz to be in formal charge of selecting targets for strategic bombers. At Christmas the BCOS had submitted a draft directive dictating the organization of the AEAF, giving notice that even Eisenhower's latitude over tactical air forces was a given. January 1944 was the heyday of talk that the U.S. strategic air forces in England and Italy, if allowed to conduct operations against German aircraft production and oil refineries for twenty or thirty clear operational days, might finish the war. Eisenhower had not forgotten that just before the first Cairo conference, Spaatz had intimated to Butcher that he considered OVERLORD "neither necessary nor desirable." Arnold, Harris and Portal shared the feeling, and the "puzzling" air-command formula hammered out at Cairo reflected it.

Evidently, the purpose of the Cairo arrangement was to keep the strategic air forces from being diverted from POINTBLANK in the next several months. How soon Portal and the CCS would decide that the "preliminary" tasks for OVERLORD had been fulfilled was unclear. Achieving air superiority, the "preliminary" to OVERLORD, would take time, and it would be an effective preliminary for an all-out campaign on German industry too.

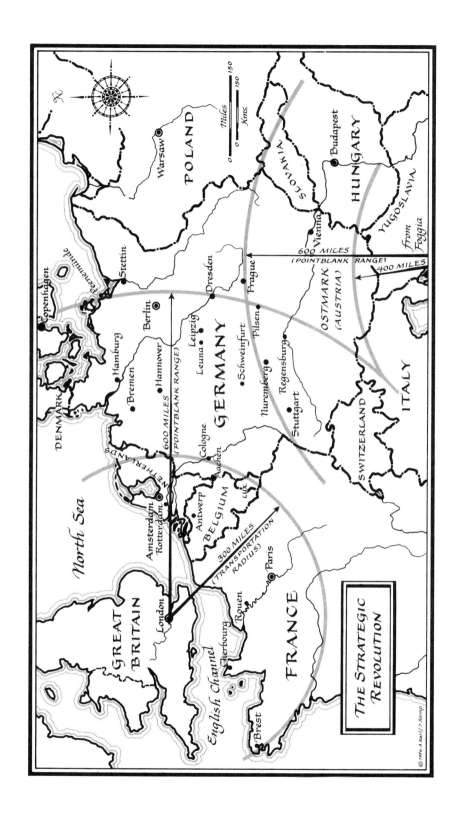

THE STRATEGIC REVOLUTION

© 1986 A.Karl/J.Kemp

GREAT BRITAIN

North Sea

English Channel

London

Amsterdam
Rotterdam

NETHERLANDS

Antwerp

BELGIUM

Lux.

Aachen

Cologne

600 MILES
(POINTBLANK RANGE)

300 MILES
(TRANSPORTATION RADIUS)

Cherbourg

Brest

Rouen

Paris

FRANCE

SWITZERLAND

DENMARK

Copenhagen

Peenemünde

Stettin

Hamburg

Bremen

Hannover

Berlin

Leipzig

Leuna

Dresden

Schweinfurt

Pilsen

GERMANY

Nuremberg

Regensburg

Stuttgart

Prague

ITALY

OSTMARK
(AUSTRIA)

Vienna

SLOVAKIA

HUNGARY

Budapest

YUGOSLAVIA

600 MILES
(POINTBLANK RANGE)

400 MILES

from Foggia

POLAND

Warsaw

Miles

Kms.

0   150

0   150

Issues of national prestige were at stake. The British in January claimed that Bomber Command would never be subordinated to SHAEF, likening it to the "Home Fleet." Assuming the British balked, Arnold and Spaatz were bound to raise the issue of even-handed treatment for the American Air Forces and other questions as well, such as the fairness of asking the Americans to assume sole responsibility for bombing French transport targets, and what sense it made to divert American bombers from tasks the CCS deemed vital for the British.

The battleground would be targeting policy. In January 1944 the AEAF staff placed the finishing touches on the transportation plan. It was the brainchild of Dr. Solly Zuckerman, a professor of anatomy, described as a "small, mysterious man with an old unpressed tweed suit." As a consultant to AFHQ, Zuckerman had done detailed studies of the bombing at Pantelleria, Sicily, Salerno and the raids on the marshaling yards at Rome. In January 1944, working at AEAF headquarters in Stanmore, Zuckerman applied the lessons of the Mediterranean to "conditions prevailing in northwest Europe." His conclusions formed the basis of a plan calling for an all-out eight-week campaign to create a "railway desert" from Bonn, Düsseldorf and the Ruhr, thence north and west through Antwerp, Amiens, Paris and Normandy.

According to his estimates, continuous bombardment of maintenance sheds, repair yards, and depots—no fewer than 72 targets, 33 in Belgium and France, and another 39 in western Germany—would reduce the French rail system to 33 percent efficiency. Then on D-Day, air interdiction would take up the slack and isolate the battlefield, slowing up the strategic movement of German armor and infantry toward Normandy. For instance, in January, the 9th and 11th panzer divisions were at Bordeaux and Marseilles, the 2nd SS Panzer Division idled near the Spanish border, and elements of three panzer divisions were being refitted near Paris, Brussels and north of Antwerp. These units were distant enough so that the breakdown of rail transport in France might impede the arrival for perhaps as long as three weeks, buying precious time to enlarge the bridgehead. Such a plan, if it worked, would render crucial assistance to OVERLORD. Would it work?

Even the SHAEF staff was skeptical and raised the questions heard endlessly in the weeks ahead. Would the Luftwaffe rise to defend transport targets? Would a bombing campaign on the French, Belgian and German rail net succeed in eliminating "slack" in the rail system? Even assuming that such a plan could achieve a 40 or 50 percent reduction in efficiency, could the Germans make do with the rest? What would stop the Germans from redistributing reserves when the object of the air plan became obvious? Could the goal of slowing replacements be better served by careful selection and interdiction of specific units and targets around D-Day? And what about the French? The plan contemplated a ruthless assault on French transport installations that would destroy property and lives, and take a toll in French goodwill and cooperation in the years ahead.

On the other hand, POINTBLANK, too, had its skeptics. Beginning in late spring 1943, the air forces had waged war on sixty enemy industries, including "morale" targets, submarine construction yards and bases, airframe plants, aircraft assembly plants, ball-bearing plants, oil refineries, synthetic-rubber plants, tire plants and military-transport-vehicle plants. Results of the U.S. daylight offensives had been disappointing, at heavy cost in the deep-penetration raids. Gradually the Germans had dispersed aircraft-industry plants beyond fighter escort range, and less than 10 percent of the estimated 22,667 tons of bombs dropped by the Eighth Air Force from July 1 to November 15, 1943, on the German aircraft industry had struck targets. As recently as October 1943, U.S. Eighth Air Force daylight raids had been suspended following attacks on the Schweinfurt ball-bearing plant in which 60 of the 291 bombers had been lost to enemy ground fire and fighters.

To date, German morale had withstood the shock of massive city-destruction raids on Hamburg, the Ruhr and Berlin. Reports by visitors returning to neutral capitals documented the capacity of the Germans to maintain essential services and business as usual despite the massive raids —morale in some ways improved, and the bombings reinforced the premonition of total destruction in store for Germany as the only alternative to victory far more convincingly than the "unconditional surrender" slogan which German propaganda exploited to justify all-out mobilization.

Actually, Allied raids had been carried out in haphazard fashion; preoccupation with North Africa, Italy and the battle of the Atlantic shipping lanes had permitted only sporadic efforts on cities and industry to date. Some criticized the emphasis on "area bombing" over centers of armaments production. Certain raids—such as the May 7, 1943, attacks on the Ruhr dams and the July raids on Hamburg—might have succeeded in inflicting permanent damage had they been followed up. Experts blamed respites in the "start and stop" policy for the miraculous reorganization and dispersal of German war production, which reached wartime records by November. And though early results in the Battle of Berlin, ordered in late November, fell short of claims that the campaign would end the war, the Eighth Air Force and Bomber Command could show that the deep-penetration raids took a heavy toll on German operations on all fronts and diverted the Luftwaffe away from both fronts to home defense. The air forces were just reaching peak mobilization techniques of American daylight and precision bombing, and nighttime British terror bombing on German cities had gradually been refined through the development of homing devices like radar pathfinders and Oboe, and for advanced fighters brought into service to sustain distant all-weather operations day and night. New bases were on line in Italy, and negotiations proceeded with the Soviets for bases in Russia to permit two-way bombing runs over the Balkans. By January the advanced P-47 and P-51 long-range escorts arrived in numbers, capable of accompanying the American Liberators and Fortresses 800 miles into Germany. Finally, the Cairo command arrangements, in uniting the Eighth and First air forces under Spaatz, Harris and Portal meant central targeting from remote bases.

Years later Spaatz wrote on the significance of Cairo and listed the ancient principles of war embodied in the POINTBLANK directive: widely dispersed air bases afforded *"maneuver and surprise"*; bombers drawn from these bases were capable of *"concentration"* on targets chosen as "most vital to the enemy's war potential"; the manned bomber epitomized the military principle of *"economy by force,"* in the unique ability of bombers to strike "decisive objectives" without "being compelled to disperse its force on numerous objectives of secondary importance." Lastly, at Cairo, the Combined Chiefs devised command arrangements that achieved *unity of command.* But the unity forged at Cairo meant fragmentation of SHAEF, and separation of air, naval and sea components of the Allied military effort.

Who would win? The claim of air operations on the imagination of the Allied high command was strong, even discounting the Air Force claims as typical service-branch exaggerations. Visionary ideas were often not susceptible to proof, and failure might become the rationale for greater effort, not less. Not only had forecasts of total destruction of the German economy proven false, but German fighters were reappearing in alarming numbers by the end of 1943, which would prolong POINTBLANK's "preliminary" mission in OVERLORD. Important nonmilitary interests were at stake, and Eisenhower faced formidable institutional obstacles owing to the unique standing of the air forces. For two years Arnold, Portal, Harris, Spaatz and Doolittle had operated under broad directives that accorded the air forces virtual independence and great prestige, magnified by the status of the air wing as the one service branch waging war directly on the German homeland and the covert hope that the invasion might thus be averted.

In Washington, Marshall had hedged. General Arnold, who had been touring Air Force installations near his home in Sonoma, California, had been unable to confer personally with Eisenhower about the eventual transfer of the U.S. Eighth and Fifteenth air forces to SHAEF. Eisenhower and Arnold had talked by phone and Eisenhower had indicated his "strong views" that the American and British strategic air forces come under his command. He had told Arnold of his talks with Churchill in Marrakech about Bomber Command in which the Prime Minister *"had not rejected the desirability of the measure,"* and indeed had predicted that, in time, "control of *all* operational aircraft should go to Eisenhower." But Arnold had cautioned Eisenhower that Churchill would be contending with strong Air Ministry objections. Arnold's evasiveness was a sign that Eisenhower's best hope would be compromise as the invasion deadline drew nearer.

A key figure in a compromise would be Eisenhower's deputy, RAF Air Chief Marshal Arthur Tedder, a man who had shown a knack for handling inter-Allied and inter-service problems at AFHQ. Tedder, who had served

Eisenhower as air commander in chief in Africa, Sicily and Italy, was a friend. He has been described as a man of boyish good looks and a quiet, taciturn manner, pronounced since the loss of his eldest son during the Battle of Britain. Tedder enjoyed wide professional respect: a Luftwaffe appraisal at the time rated him Eisenhower's superior in energy and intellect.

Tedder's career fit the pattern of most of the Air Barons. He had been one of the handful of British officers to transfer from the Army to the Royal Air Force when it was formed as a separate branch under Lord Trenchard in 1916. He commanded an air squadron in France and between the wars attended the Imperial Defense College; later he became director of the RAF Staff college. He had quickly risen to prominence in the North African campaign, where he had perfected a "chessman's talent" for coordinating ground action and air support. But, like Leigh-Mallory, his knowledge of strategic bombing was theoretical, not practical. And like his air colleagues at the Air Ministry, Tedder at first questioned the Zuckerman findings about the effectiveness of attacks on transport, and for the moment appeared reluctant to do battle with the BCOS, braced for the "peaceful invasion" of Britain by 1.5 million American troops by early March.

On January 17 Morgan bequeathed Eisenhower unfinished business. Along with the air problem, Eisenhower had to worry about CCS approval for increasing the strength and size of the assault. In early January, estimates of enemy strength in the invasion area had been upgraded. The Germans were placing anti-landing obstacles below the high-water mark, and new coastal batteries were under construction as part of a "thickening" of the invasion crust. Eisenhower would also have to confront the problem of ANVIL, the landings at Marseilles. At Christmas, Churchill had served notice that the British would insist that Rome take priority over ANVIL. Marshall discounted the importance of Rome. SHINGLE would claim allocation of landing craft, and the risks of Anzio raised doubts about the ability to disentangle ANVIL-designated landing craft in time for OVERLORD and ANVIL, which the Americans suspected was Churchill's real purpose. Recriminations in the event of continued stalemate south of Rome would erode the spirit of compromise and Eisenhower's quest for command of the strategic air forces.

But time marched on. As the planning phase was wrapped up, 50 percent of expected U.S. ground troops were already in Britain, and arrival of the rest on schedule was set. U.S. corps and army headquarters were established. U.S. naval organization for the assault was also set. The specialized programs for training troops for the amphibious assault were well under way. By January the components for the MULBERRY harbors were under construction in slips, yards, remote harbors and inlets throughout England.

Preliminary phases of OVERLORD had begun, including air and sea actions. Propaganda and sabotage operations were integrated into a "combined offensive aimed at softening the German resistance." COSSAC began low-level leaks to press and radio about mundane items, such as promotions and engagements, to confirm the presence of fictitious units and falsify the intentions of real units. In the closing weeks of 1943, Patton, in charge of the shell Seventh Army, had shuttled from Corsica to encourage rumors of a Seventh Army invasion of northern Italy, then to Malta, then to Cairo for discussions with the British about an invasion of Greece, then to Palermo at Christmas to plan Adriatic operations. In early January 1944, Patton quietly disappeared, to reappear in England at the end of the month and in secrecy assume command of FUSAG and the imaginary landings at Calais. In Edinburgh, Colonel R. M. "Roy" McLean already commanded the phantom Fourth Army preparing for the "invasion" of Norway. Wireless traffic simulated the presence of units and military installations—calls for tank parts, petrol dumps, pipelines and hospitals. Commando raids were carried out against Norwegian coastal towns and industrial targets, along with intensified aerial reconnaissance of the area. British intelligence agents "confirmed" Fourth Army plans through double agents lionized in the histories of the secret war published thirty years later with code names like Garbo, Brutus, Treasure, Tricycle and Van Loop, in intelligence jargon the "first violins" of the FORTITUDE orchestra.

Would OVERLORD succeed? Beyond a point, the Allies could be at the mercy of unknowns. In December 1943, Allied reconnaissance had first spotted construction of launching sites for the V-I rocket at Cherbourg and Calais. Intelligence knew about the range and direction capabilities of the V-I rocket, but lacked information about the destructive power of the warhead. German propaganda hinted at other secret weapons in readiness. Eisenhower was among a handful of men with knowledge of the laboratory race to harness the energy of the atom, hinted at occasionally in scientific magazines and journals.

Would FORTITUDE contribute? How would the Germans rearrange their dispositions between now and May? Would MULBERRY work? Components had been tested by the Royal Engineers and technicians of the British War Office. But artificial harbors had been tried before, and by January 17 there were labor problems and delays in construction of the project sufficient to raise doubts. Problems with MULBERRY were a factor in Montgomery's call for expanding the NEPTUNE assault with two assault divisions by airborne troops. The speedy capture of Cherbourg was essential. Would POINT-BLANK ensure local air superiority as promised? Without local superiority, tactical surprise would be lost and the enemy would be able to muster distant reserves for counterattacks before the Allies gained a secure foothold. Otherwise, Allied sea and air superiority would provide a margin in overcoming initial resistance. An estimated 1,200 warships would command the sea, including 23 cruisers, and 7 battleships. Ten thousand heavy and medium bombers, protected by screens of fighters, would saturate German defenses during the assault. In the east, would the Russians attack on time and in sufficient strength?

Finally, Eisenhower's supreme decision to attack would depend on the weather, the unknown and unknowable factor in the planning for D-Day that could make or break years of effort. The Allies could calculate the right combinations of tides and hours of moonlight suitable for airdrops and landings, but not the weather. However, the Allies possessed a major advantage in this regard. Dominant westerly patterns could be tracked in Canada and Newfoundland, which gave the Allies earlier and more reliable long-range forecasts than was available to the Germans—potentially a big asset in achieving surprise if bad weather patterns obscured favorable trends. To exploit the advantage, by January the Allies were engaged in "the weather war"—a low-key campaign to neutralize German weather stations in Norway and the Channel Islands.

There were ample grounds for confidence. Except for the behemoths identified in France—the 130th Panzer Lehr and the 9th and 10th SS Panzer —German formations were not as strong as they had been in 1940. The Wehrmacht lacked mobility on all fronts, and had long since passed its peak. Three years of war had reduced the efficiency of the Luftwaffe on all fronts. The Germans in Normandy would be relying on extended communications. But the German army remained a well-equipped force, particularly in tanks, manned by an officer corps and enlisted ranks marked by superior skill and courage. The field divisions, panzer and panzer grenadiers, packed more offensive power than American, Russian and British counterparts and were capable of turning Normandy into a "bomb and shell trap" if well placed. Only so much could be done to prevent this, and whether or not the Germans deduced Normandy beforehand could only be surmised by the presence or absence of three mobile divisions in the vicinity of Normandy on D-Day. German strategic priorities would be deduced by the number of mobile divisions in France, and success would also depend on air superiority and the morale of Eisenhower's armies. It had become a familiar refrain: air superiority, no more than three mobile divisions at Normandy on D-Day, or twelve in France or reinforcement by another fifteen. What if these preconditions were not met? And if they were? "These conditions having been fulfilled," wrote the COSSAC historian, "it was thought that OVERLORD would have a reasonable chance of success."

SUBMISSION OF THE BILL

In the week after Eisenhower's arrival in London the OVERLORD commanders met with the COSSAC staff to carry out the transition and to define OVERLORD needs to be presented to the Combined Chiefs in the form of a "bill" for the invasion. In Eisenhower's first five days in London, he and Morgan met daily to hammer out the final recommendations submitted by the COSSAC staff in time for the meeting set between Eisenhower and his deputies at Norfolk House on January 21.

Historic Norfolk House was to have been the hub of pre-invasion planning and operations. A three-story Georgian-style mansion, built on the site where King George III had been born, it derived its name from the long line of dukes of Norfolk who had served as earl marshals of England since the Battle of Hastings, in 1066. Located near Piccadilly, within five minutes of the government offices at Whitehall, Norfolk House bordered St. James's Park, an exclusive area closed to all Londoners except tenants of St. James's Square, enabling principal commanders and deputies to come and go in secrecy.

Because Norfolk House was close to Whitehall, routine SHAEF deliberations there could be susceptible to oversight by the British Chiefs. Hence, plans were afoot to relocate SHAEF to the suburbs near Eighth Air Force headquarters in Kingston, reserving Norfolk House for the most formal gatherings, such as the one that convened at ten-thirty on the twenty-first to draw up the final air, ground and naval "bill" for OVERLORD.

General Eisenhower chaired the meeting. Air Chief Marshal Arthur Tedder, deputy supreme commander, was present. Montgomery attended, accompanied by his peacemaking chief of staff, Major General Francis "Freddie" de Guingand. Others present included Morgan, Bradley, Ramsay, Leigh-Mallory, Bedell Smith and Rear Admiral Kirk. General Carl Spaatz, commander of the U.S. Eighth and Fifteenth air forces, was a notable absentee—his Eighth Air Force was crucial to a unified command, which also depended on SHINGLE, set to start within forty-eight hours in a climate of pessimism.

The U.S. Fifth Army offensive across the Garigliano toward the Rapido River and the Liri Valley was now ten days old, but sixty miles still separated the Fifth Army from the landing front at Anzio. The day before, British X Corps on the north had crossed the Garigliano, drawing southward the 29th and 90th panzer grenadier divisions held in reserve near Rome. This raised eleventh-hour concern about a hot reception for General John Lucas' VI Corps, built up from a 20,000-man force in the original plan to three infantry divisions, armored divisions, various parachute, tank commands and Ranger units totaling 110,000 troops in a drastically revised plan insisted upon by Churchill as "essential for a decision in Italy." Decisive success and Rome would fulfill Churchill's preconditions set for ANVIL, and dramatize the possibilities of exploitation northward toward the Po. But few expected it and the probable casualty was ANVIL, and mutual confidence. Eisenhower's principal deputies had long since concluded that ANVIL would mean unacceptable shortages of landing craft for an expanded assault in any case, without reallocation from the Pacific; Marshall and the American Chiefs disagreed.

At the Norfolk House meeting, General Montgomery was the first to speak. On behalf of the 21st Army Group, he presented the Army conclusions. Montgomery briefed the group on recent preparations in the German Seventh Army sector, which emphasized the need to obtain "quick success" on D-Day. In Montgomery's opinion, assault by three divisions backed by two follow-up divisions on D-Day as currently called for "was not sufficient to achieve this object." The virtues of "concentration" on a three-division front would, in his opinion, be offset by the probability that a narrow front would simply ease the German tasks of identifying the Allied objectives and acting quickly to contain the invasion force. Landings by five divisions with two follow-up divisions and airborne attacks would enable the landing force to "emerge quickly and strike hard and deep." A wider front would disperse beach defenses, relieve congestion in the bridgehead, stretch local reserves and place strong forces on the western flank on D-Day capable of moving quickly beyond the neck of the Cotentin. Montgomery favored airborne drops on the American right flank—he reminded the group of British efforts in June 1940 to exploit the "natural moat" formed by the Vire-Douve rivers along the landward approaches to Cherbourg. Montgomery emphasized the importance of Cherbourg. The 21st Army Group did not wish to be dependent on the MULBERRY harbors. A strong western flank would position forces for a quick push to Cherbourg and south toward the Brest peninsula and additional ports.

In summary, Montgomery assured the group he had approached all questions from a standpoint of seeking the "minimum resources necessary to make a proper success of the operation." But the 21st Army Group questioned whether sufficient naval resources were on hand to make best use of the assigned forces—and "as at present planned, OVERLORD was not a sound operation of war." A five-division assault was essential, but naval resources for it were missing and not in sight unless ANVIL was abandoned. Accordingly, Montgomery recommended cancellation of ANVIL.

Eisenhower agreed with Montgomery's view on the importance of Cherbourg and on widening the assault, but he cautioned the group that ANVIL could only be canceled "as a last resort." Alluding to his talks with Marshall in Washington, Eisenhower spoke to the group of ANVIL's advantages. The Russians expected the operation to take place; without ANVIL, seven French divisions now training in North Africa would not have a port of entry into France. For these reasons, in his formal recommendation due by early February, he could not recommend that ANVIL be canceled or reduced to a threat unless he was convinced that OVERLORD "could not otherwise be successfully mounted." Eisenhower's casual dismissal of the idea that a simultaneous ANVIL and OVERLORD would be mutually supporting passed without comment.

Admiral Bertram Ramsay discussed the naval ramifications of Montgomery's five-division proposal. First, a wider assault would mean more shipping and congestion in the ports of southern England, a drawback particularly if the German V-1 rocket sites under construction near Cherbourg, Calais and Antwerp became operational. Second, whereas a three-division assault force based along the Channel could move within twenty-four hours' notice, a five-division force would stage from points as distant as Bristol on the Irish Sea and could move only with sixty hours' notice. This, inherently, meant a certain built-in gamble on the weather conditions. Third, widening the front would bring the assault forces and the cumbersome LSTs within range of German 155-inch shore batteries at Pointe du Hoc and Le Havre during off-loading phases, requiring increases in bombardment escort ships and minesweepers. Fourth, additional assault shipping and craft would be required: 120 LCTs, 43 LSTs and 60 LCIs. To Ramsay, it was obvious that the 21st Army Group would be many LSTs short if ANVIL went forward: even without ANVIL, there would be deficiencies until early June, and in June, ANVIL and OVERLORD could not be mounted simultaneously without additional lift from "Pacific waters." His "short conclusion" was that a five-division assault was not possible in early May. A compromise four-division assault was possible in early May by spreading out allotted naval forces. Ramsay reminded the group that since the landings required moonlight, the alternative to an early May date was early June.

Leigh-Mallory briefed the group on the Zuckerman plan. The "critical factor" in NEPTUNE was the rate of German reinforcement, he said. Destruction of the rail systems feeding the Normandy area would delay reinforcements. Leigh-Mallory described the details of the SHAEF plan: an eight-week program concentrating first on servicing stations and signaling systems from Paris on an arc northeast through Orléans, Tours, Saumur, Nantes and Rennes, then concentration on the marshaling yards at Lisieux–Falaise–Caen–St.-Lô–Carentan. Six to eight weeks were needed to reduce rail traffic to 30 percent efficiency within a hundred-mile radius, thereby hampering the flow of German reinforcements from other fronts at the critical stages of OVERLORD. He therefore hoped the Allied Air Force would be "brought to strength by April 1st."

Preliminary bombing would seek to "segregate" the landing zone from enemy air. All airfields within 110 miles would be attacked—beginning with the workshops, and other necessary buildings, then the airfields and runways. Leigh-Mallory noted that if ANVIL was canceled, he stood to gain an extra eight air squadrons from the Mediterranean airborne units in the assault. Parenthetically, ANVIL would be a factor in the airdrop plans: Leigh-Mallory noted that cancellation of ANVIL would give a margin of safety by providing extra transport for the two-division drop in the Cotentin area, and the British 6th Airborne in the Caen area.

The judgment was unanimous. All of Eisenhower's advisers urged a postponement, strengthening the assault and cancellation of ANVIL. But the long-range benefits could not be ignored: enhancing Soviet-Allied cooperation, opening a new front in France, employing idle troops, and securing a conduit for emergency reinforcements from the Mediterranean in the event of crisis in the battle of France after the assault.

After lunch the group reassembled at three o'clock. Most of the meeting was off the record, and so it is not known what conclusions were reached on ANVIL, which was the subject of discussion. There were two solutions, both difficult. The first, favored by the BCOS, was to maintain ANVIL on a one-division basis as a "threat," as originally planned. The second was postponement, a solution that offered something for both sides: a postponement would keep the project alive, as the Americans would surely demand, and afford time for the seizure of Rome while bolstering the case for modification or cancellation, assuming the British wanted cancellation, which Eisenhower did not.

At the close of the afternoon session, the group edited the cable drafted by Smith for transmission to the Combined Chiefs of Staff in the form of a "bill" setting forth OVERLORD's requirements. The group agreed that the "bill" should include a "positive statement that OVERLORD must have in the initial assault five divisions landed simultaneously since: (1) the present plan of attack was too much of a column, (2) additional width of the front would be necessary, (3) that it is absolutely necessary to secure post facilities, (4) that it is necessary to seize the tactical advantage . . . at the earliest possible time, (5) that it is desirable to get behind the barrier on the Cotentin Peninsula by a large and strong force." Eisenhower approved, and suggested that the draft telegram read so that the CCS would "see OVERLORD as it is seen in London," and include a strong statement to the effect that "the success of the OVERLORD operation is the crisis of the European war for both the U.S. government and the British government, and that it must not fail but must be a complete success."

Forty-eight hours later, the "bill" went out in two parts. In a cable to the Combined Chiefs of Staff, dated January 23, Eisenhower proposed a five-division assault to place Allied forces east of Caen and west of the marshy Vire estuary on D-Day. According to revised figures, this meant an additional 72 LCILs, 47 LSTs, 144 LCTs, 5 cruisers, 24 destroyers, a number of additional miscellaneous amphibious craft and 8 fighter squadrons, all to be assembled in Britain at D minus 28 "at the latest." In the key passage, Eisenhower broached ANVIL. "Ideal would be a five-division OVERLORD and a three-division ANVIL," he wrote, but if both proved impossible, he would accept a five-division OVERLORD and a one-division ANVIL, "being maintained as a threat until enemy employment justifies its active employment," a contingency that he urged "only as a last resort, and after all other means and alternatives have failed." Eisenhower passed along Montgomery's views in favor of meeting the May 1 target date as "ideal" for exploiting summer campaign weather, then endorsed postponement rather than risk failure "with reduced forces on the earlier date," a formality.

Part II was air. Two days before, Arnold had apologized in a note for his absence from Washington, but thanked Eisenhower for his news about Churchill. The Army Air Corps commander again cautioned that the Prime Minister's "strong support" might be necessary to surmount the opposition within the British Chiefs to U.S. supervision over Bomber Command. Since Eisenhower would be obligated to petition the Combined Chiefs for command or use of the air forces, Arnold asked to be informed in advance, and to be given the details of the SHAEF air plan so that he could study it and, he hoped, be of help and "support" it.

On the twenty-third Eisenhower briefly thanked Arnold for his expressions of support. Since arriving in London, he continued, he had broached the problem of air command with his planners, who had tentatively concluded that Eighth Air Force daylight precision bombers would probably prove more "directly useful" to OVERLORD than the British night area bombers. However, he would bid for both and anticipated no trouble. "I am perfectly willing to avoid terms and language that may startle anyone," Eisenhower wrote, "but there can be no evasion of the certainly that when the time comes, the OVERLORD commander must have the full power to determine the missions and priorities for attacks by all forces." In the event of trouble, he assured Arnold, his convictions would be "clearly spelled out before the CCS" and communicated periodically to Arnold.

Meanwhile, the VI Corps landings at Anzio went forward. To the end, G-2 reports warned that the Germans would consider landings by a corps "an emergency to be met by any and all the available resources and strength available to the German High Command in Italy." Accounts attest to the misgivings of the commander, General John P. Lucas. At the stormy conference on January 9, at 15th Army Group Headquarters in Caserta, Lucas had protested his assignment, which he sardonically compared with Gallipoli "with the same amateur on the coach's bench." Alexander had blandly brushed aside Lucas' doubts, confident that the Fifteenth Air Force would be able to take care of German reinforcements, and that VI Corps could "sustain itself independently" for as long as it took to link up. The German Tenth Army reserve formations south of Rome "lacked balance and organization in their dispositions," he said. Alexander conceded that the isolation of 110,000 troops was a risk, but an "unavoidable one."

And so it went on the night of the twenty-second. Fifty thousand troops of the British 1st and U.S. 3rd plus two follow-up divisions sailed from Naples. The convoy evaded detection and reached the objective uneventfully. The landing forces encountered only sporadic opposition in the move ashore. For a day nothing stood between VI Corps and the Alban Hills, the supply route for the German Tenth Army and the gateway to Rome, an illusory opportunity that inspired high hopes in the first press reports. But field reports reaching Washington and London told a different tale, one of decisive German actions and hesitant VI Corps actions that quickly turned the tide.

The German Tenth Army quickly passed to the defensive. Three divisions left the Garigliano–Pescara and fell back north to the Anzio bridgehead while Fourteenth Army reserves poured south from the Po. Mindful of Salerno, and separated from the main force by sixty miles, Lucas decided against ordering movement inland and instead secured the beachhead against counterattack. This cautious decision inspired rumors in British quarters that American General Mark Clark, in defiance of Alexander, had arbitrarily reversed VI Corps–Fifth Army roles and confined Lucas to an orderly build-up in the hope that VI Corps, by drawing off the Tenth Army, might open the road to Rome for Clark's Fifth Army. In any event, instead of moving aggressively inland to cut Tenth Army supply lines, VI Corps entrenched in the narrow perimeter at Anzio.

Within forty-eight hours of the landings, two German divisions blocked the key road intersections inland at Campoleone and Cisterna. By the night of the twenty-fourth, the bridgehead was only seven miles deep and twenty miles wide. Lucas' first effort to move inland thirty-six hours later was met at Cisterna by elements of eight German divisions, including the 715th Field Division, drawn from southern France. It was the beginning of a long siege.

RESPONSE

Portions of the "bill" met no opposition. On the thirty-first the CCS authorized widening the Normandy assault, while omitting to specify the sources of the additional landing craft. Churchill and Roosevelt had corresponded off and on about postponement, and had agreed two weeks before that a late-May date would still be "May," in keeping with the Teheran understandings. Even if the landings were delayed until early June, preliminaries would be under way and the Soviets would probably not quibble over seventy-two hours. But Eisenhower's early victories in the CCS left the hard issues standing: ANVIL and control of the strategic air forces.

Illusions that the air problems would solve themselves were quickly dispelled. CCS approval of a wider assault coincided with a new POINTBLANK directive in which the CCS advised Portal that preparations for direct support of OVERLORD "should be maintained without detriment to the Combined Bomber offensive," then directed Leigh-Mallory's AEAF to provide support for POINTBLANK.

Meanwhile the British and American Eighth Air Force staffs at offices in nearby High Wycombe and Bushy Park wrapped up preparations for the next phase in "the Battle of Berlin," code-named BIG WEEK. This would be a series of deep-penetration raids against the German capital and targets

ranging as far east as Stettin deploying in mass the P-47 and P-51 interceptors. The air staffs brimmed with anticipation about the first chance to
engage the Luftwaffe in extended combat with concerted attacks by the
Eighth and Fifteenth air forces and Bomber Command. The mathematics
of attrition would consolidate uncontested supremacy in the skies over
Germany, whereupon the Fortresses, Liberators and Lancasters would be
free to roam at will deploying, as Spaatz later put it, "the first war instrument of history capable of stopping the heart mechanism of a great industrialized enemy."

Attempts by Leigh-Mallory and Tedder to work out an informal system
of consultations with Portal and Spaatz for setting bombing priorities
quickly broke down. In meetings with Harris, Spaatz and Portal at Leigh-
Mallory's Stanmore offices called to set up a permanent targeting committee, the conferees found little common ground. There were personality
clashes. Spaatz later told Portal that he simply would "not take orders"
from Leigh-Mallory. Both sides agreed that German air force targets should
command "first priority" but disagreed on what these targets were. Leigh-
Mallory argued that the Luftwaffe could rise to defend against systematic
attacks on transport. Bomber Command representatives countered with a
plan for several "independent" targeting committees and presented data to
prove the inappropriateness of British night techniques for rail targets.
Tedder challenged the authenticity of the data. Harris lectured Tedder that
to divert the bombers would be to "commit the irremediable error of
diverting our best weapon from the military function for which it has been
equipped and trained to that which it cannot effectively carry out." Portal
warned Tedder that CCS approval of the commitment was probably necessary. Eisenhower urged Tedder to keep the informal committee discussions
alive, hinting that to satisfy Spaatz he might accept a substitute for Leigh-
Mallory as the putative supervisor of the transportation plan—namely,
Tedder. Eisenhower's contemplated step—to by-pass his air commander in
chief for the sake of compromise was risky, and heightened the tense mood
within Eisenhower's fledgling command.

Butcher noted the pervasive blanket of security shrouding 20 Grosvenor
Square as Eisenhower went about his schedule of appointments, including
a wave of security restrictions levied by Eisenhower on staff dealings with
the press in the wake of the press stories on the as-yet-unsettled command
arrangements for air and ground. Eisenhower's routine Tuesday luncheons
at 10 Downing Street resumed upon the Prime Minister's return from his
month in Marrakech. The Prime Minister's mood that January was defiant
and his presence in London underlined the command problems. Eisenhower
resumed his quest to relocate SHAEF well outside the city center near the
Eighth Air Force compound at "Widewing."

Troubles cropped up on several fronts. Butcher chronicles Smith's complaints over dinner at Hayes Lodge about the ongoing press build-up for

Montgomery, now being hailed as Britain's greatest soldier since Wellington. The publicity touched a sensitive chord from AFHQ days, when Eisenhower and his staff had often found themselves by-passed and overshadowed by Alexander and the 15th Army Group Staff. Smith told Eisenhower
that "being realistic," the British press would again try to damn Eisenhower
with faint praise for his skills as a coordinator, and "insinuate that the
British have cleverly accepted an American as Supreme Commander but
have infiltrated British commanders for land, sea and air." He predicted
that SHAEF could soon be on the "defensive" across the board.

No one disputed him. Eisenhower, Butcher and Smith were accustomed
to these periodic press campaigns, semiofficial expressions of British views.
The practice of training the spotlight on the inner workings of the Allied
Command to build up British personalities and positions in important
command debates was common. But experience with the British press made
the reports no less unwelcome. Eisenhower's hands were tied. He could not
contradict the British press, nor could he silence British colleagues. As a
coalition commander, he was obliged to accept even faint praise and build
on it.

Restraint was a burden for Eisenhower and his American subordinates,
who occasionally found it frustrating and incomprehensible. The intense,
hard-driving Smith lapsed early. Smith called on Brooke at his chambers
late in January to present a number of SHAEF requests for British staff
officers being held at AFHQ. The list included General K. W. Strong,
Eisenhower's G-2 after Kasserine Pass, and Lieutenant General Humphrey
Gale, Eisenhower's former chief of administration at AFHQ, favorites of
Brooke, Alexander and Wilson. Brooke lectured Smith tartly about "raiding AFHQ" and his own duty as Chief of the Imperial General Staff to look
after the needs of OVERLORD *and* Italy objectively and impartially. "I am
responsible," Brooke said, "and there will be no string pulling." Smith
stalked out. Eisenhower made the apologies, then called Smith on the
carpet. "Maybe the war is getting on my nerves, or my ulcers, or both,"
Smith explained.

The episode bothered Eisenhower too. Several days later he buried his
dismay in a memo. Eisenhower was upset that his accomplishments were
portrayed as political and diplomatic rather than military, and he particularly disliked the label "cautious." He sketched a list of his bold decisions:
TORCH; launching Salerno on a shoestring; his decision to salvage II Corps
for the closing attack on Tunis; his command decision in favor of Salerno
over eleventh-hour British pleas for Taranto, which had worked. "To all the
C-in-C must go the great share of the operational credit," he noted. "But
it wearies me to be thought of as timid, when I've had to do things that were
so risky as to be almost crazy. Oh hum . . ."

On the cold foggy afternoon of January 26 General George S. Patton
arrived in secrecy to assume his role in the QUICKSILVER deception while

awaiting activation of the U.S. Third Army after D-Day. Butcher was on hand to greet Patton's C-47 at the airfield and escorted Patton back to Eisenhower's billet at Hayes Lodge for a talk with Eisenhower about Patton's responsibilities, now that he was provisionally restored to favor.

In the wake of the soldier-slapping disclosures, Eisenhower had been moved to warn his old friend about the impact of the episode on the U.S. Senate, on liberal opinion in the United States *and* on the British, as he had done after less publicized instances of trouble. For instance, the British professed not to understand Patton's impetuous, even deliberately outrageous, manner. Eisenhower had counseled Patton to avoid the appearance that he acted "on impulse and not upon study and reflection," and had offered tips like counting to ten when tempted to speak and cultivating a "certain sphinx-like quality upon occasion."

In the weeks after the soldier-slapping incident, Patton had atoned lavishly. Several days after the Pearson broadcast he wrote Eisenhower contritely; then, perhaps with a premonition of Eisenhower's appointment, sent along a copy of Osborne's *The Norman Conquest,* a history of the long-ago Norman invasion of the Sicilian coast. In his cover note Patton praised the Norman conquest of Sicily with an understrength force and approvingly noted the invaders' abilities as "meticulous planners."

Patton, now described by Butcher as a "master of flattery," arrived in London humbly grateful and eager to go to work. On his circuitous route to London by way of Washington, he had called on Mamie at the Wardman Park, had knelt and offered thanks to her for her husband's forgiveness and patience. The mood carried over into dinner at Hayes Lodge.

Patton was not happy to be on the sidelines during the landings, but he was grateful to learn he would eventually command the U.S. Third Army. Patton pledged he would be a team player and lingered after dinner to trade stories about Army friends and Civil War history, a favorite pastime from Washington days. "Ike, as you are now the most powerful man in the world," Patton said, "it is foolish to contest your views." Eisenhower tossed off the compliment with a shrug.

"General Patton has just been in my office," Butcher wrote two days later, "and, while visiting reemphasized that Ike is on the threshold of becoming the greatest general of all time—including Napoleon."

The Anzio battle raged on. With VI Corps and the Fifth Army still separated by fifty-five miles, Alexander and Clark flew to the bridgehead to inspect the situation. A German counteroffensive was in the offing, and so Alexander ordered a switch to defensive tactics beginning February 1, a decision that converted Anzio into a pocket under fierce artillery fire with Allied casualties at a rate of 2,000 per day.

Predictably, a mood of recrimination descended over the military staffs in Washington and London. Insinuating that the British were satisfied with stalemate and the demise of ANVIL, the American Joint Chiefs peppered the 15th Army Group with requests for an explanation of Alexander's failure to use elements of the 82nd Airborne, which had been detained at AFHQ for the specific purpose of participating in SHINGLE. The JCS also questioned the waste of crack British airborne units on the Eighth Army line as infantry, and other misuses of special forces. Churchill rebuked Alexander for his failure to assert his authority over the American-led VI Corps and asked why he failed to order aggressive moves into the Alban Hills in the first thirty-six hours of the landings.

The question of ANVIL arose again. Landing-craft schedules, drawn on the basis of a three-week battle at Anzio, were in disarray, though British surveys of the landing-craft problem revealed that Eisenhower would lack adequate lift for the revised five-division assault plan regardless of the situation at Anzio. In British eyes, this raised the hitherto unspoken problem of the overall shortages due to landing-craft commitments for MacArthur's New Gloucester campaign, attributable in British minds to election-year concerns. The solution seemed straightforward: an American decision to provide reinforcements from the Pacific, or American agreements to cancel ANVIL forthwith so that Eisenhower's planners could get to work confident of timely transfers of excess landing craft currently in the Mediterranean.

Finally, on February 4 the BCOS formally pushed for the prompt fulfillment of OVERLORD requirements spelled out in Eisenhower's January 23 "bill," complete with a proposed directive for Wilson instructing him to consider that ANVIL "as planned is cancelled" in light of Eisenhower's increased needs. The BCOS urged Washington to consider a "new factor of the highest importance"—that the Germans had not withdrawn north of Rome as expected when the three powers had adopted ANVIL, but instead had decided to fight south of Rome "to the utmost of their capacity," giving Wilson a chance to "pin down their [German] forces and to commit them still further."

The BCOS suggested a three-step plan: first, recasting ANVIL as a one-division "threat" sufficient to contain three German divisions on the Riviera; second, fulfillment of Eisenhower's needs from current surpluses in Italy; third, prosecution of Italy "with utmost vigor." For good measure, the BCOS criticized the whole ANVIL concept as a diversion from Italy, a campaign likely to engage German forces in an operation "not strategically interwoven with OVERLORD" owing to vast distances between northwest France and the Riviera. Notably, the BCOS stopped short of proposing outright cancellation.

In Washington, a highly technical debate ensued over British figures showing an absolute shortage of landing craft for an expanded assault. The JCS rejected the estimates as inflated, and all conclusions based on them pessimistic. First, postponing OVERLORD until late May meant an extra month of landing-craft production. Second, the JCS opposed leaping to premature conclusions about Anzio. Third, if shortages were found to exist, King was ready to spare U.S. vessels from the Pacific provided there were assurances that these ships were earmarked for ANVIL and not Yugoslavia. The Americans professed to be open-minded, but Marshall informed Eisenhower of his personal view that a campaign in the Balkans would be an inferior substitution for ANVIL. For the British, flexibility in the Mediterranean was the key point. The British disliked the idea that they had to guarantee in advance how Wilson would develop American reinforcements: the British could point to the fact that both sides had agreed to expand the OVERLORD assault, and both sides had approved SHINGLE, which, incidentally, had confirmed the British hunch that stepped-up operations in Italy would themselves accomplish the diversionary purposes of ANVIL.

But times had changed. American open-mindedness about Italy had vanished. In American eyes, stalemate at Anzio confirmed the worst premonitions about the "indirect" advantages of operations up the boot in Italy. ANVIL, on the other hand, would be a conduit for direct reinforcement of France, it would aid dealings with the Russians and, conceivably, become a fallback in the event the Germans suddenly massed strength on the Channel, jeopardizing OVERLORD. And since vigorous American opposition, followed by reluctant support for British ideas in the Mediterranean, was a well-established pattern, the JCS wanted the British to make no mistake about American determination this time.

What were Eisenhower's views? Apparently Washington was concerned by the possibility that Eisenhower had succumbed to British pressure. From a distance, a Brooke-Eisenhower deal did not seem far-fetched. Eisenhower and Brooke both had called for reviving the idea of conducting ANVIL as a one-division "feint," and Marshall was struck by the irony of a British motion to reinforce Eisenhower "forthwith," after months of campaigning for relief from rigid timetables on transferring LSTs from Italy. The sudden turnaround seemed more than curious, and King and Marshall resolved to match it by becoming "Mediterraneanites," retaining all requested LSTs in Italy—at least until the technical questions were cleared up and Wilson had firm orders to mount ANVIL.

Immediately, OPD landing-craft experts were in transatlantic telephone contact with SHAEF with reports on U.S. landing-craft production schedules for April and May, which by King's estimates were sufficient for a two-division ANVIL and an expanded OVERLORD, at least by LST standards set for Marine operations in the Pacific. For several days SHAEF and the War Department explored ways of retaining both operations. One suggestion was to exchange armored landing craft earmarked for ANVIL for unarmored craft in OVERLORD. Planners explored basic assumptions—for instance, the feasibility of an 85 percent serviceability rate instead of the 70 percent rate fixed by the British. Planners worked on the idea of cutting down the number of tanks and trucks in the assault waves so that the landing craft would accommodate more troops. But calculations in London left the expanded OVERLORD and two-division ANVIL short, even given an extra month of production. According to Ramsay, extra production would not alleviate the critical shortage of LSTs. Time was also a factor as Montgomery's representatives insisted new craft would have to be in Britain six weeks before D-Day for proper training, which meant that late-spring production from America would not be available on time.

On the sixth, Eisenhower's fatalistic tone about ANVIL in a message to Marshall brought matters to a head over Eisenhower's role. In it, Eisenhower emphasized time: the need to identify landing craft for a widened assault in time to make plans and preparations. Eisenhower noted that Anzio raised doubts in his mind that forces would "be disentangled in time to put on a strong ANVIL," though he assured Marshall that he took some comfort that bitter fighting south of Rome would "in some degree compensate for the absence of ANVIL."

In a stern reply, Marshall conceded two points. First, he assured Eisenhower that he considered him the best judge of OVERLORD's requirements. Second, Marshall privately conceded that in the event Lucas and Clark failed to link up by April 1, ANVIL would "be practically abandoned." But he was concerned about the conflicting estimates of landing-craft shortages, and reluctant to decide now that Wilson would not be north of Rome by April 1. Wrong estimates would leave American and French troops idle— unnecessarily. The Chief of Staff posed a question: Did Eisenhower personally consider the requested allocations "absolutely imperative"? Marshall urged Eisenhower to weigh all factors carefully—he assured Eisenhower that he would use his influence "to agree with your desires," and that his real interest was only to be sure that " 'localitis' is not developing and that the pressures on you have not warped your judgement."

"Localitis" in Marshall's army was a reproach. Also, Marshall's offer to conform to Eisenhower's wishes right away was a probe: was Eisenhower open-minded about his own estimates or was he committed to them? And there was a loophole: Marshall's pledge to use his personal influence did not commit Admiral King or the President. Privately, Eisenhower sensed another element in Marshall's attitude—reluctance to delegate. In a memo to himself, Eisenhower indulged in a rare outburst aimed at Marshall and what Eisenhower perceived as his reluctance to help. In it, he reviewed his frustrations in recent weeks; the drift in completing the command billets in December; the inconvenience of Marshall's ten-day trip to Australia after Cairo, Marshall's campaign on behalf of Generals Eaker and Devers, Eisenhower's opponents in the Salerno air quarrels, and the inconvenience of his summons back to Washington so that he could be instructed on ANVIL, which had kept him away from weeks of crucial preliminary sessions in London.

As of the seventh, Eisenhower awaited a formal directive; control of the strategic air forces was doubtful, and shortages linked to ANVIL, he now feared, would be trumped up into a full-blown crisis over a setback in Italy, which both sides had foreseen in December. SHINGLE was stalemated, and "we can't close our eyes to that, no matter how much we shout about 'principles and agreements,' " he wrote. "With Italy requiring an allotment, it looks like ANVIL is doomed. I hate this—in spite of my recognition of the fact that Italian fighting would be some compensation for a strong ANVIL."

On the eighth Eisenhower composed a reply to Marshall in which he carefully set out the common ground. First, he agreed that the crucial point was to deploy all troops in the Mediterranean usefully, a point he assured Marshall he had stressed with the British along with the advantages of ANVIL. Eisenhower also agreed with Marshall that without Rome by April 1, the Allies would find themselves committed south of Rome "with everything." He was concerned about the time element.

"To disabuse your mind about my own personal approach to this problem," he continued, "it was not until I had formed my own conclusions on these matters [ANVIL] and had submitted a long telegram to Washington that I learned that the British Chiefs of Staff more or less went along with my own views, except that I believe some of them have never attached the same importance to ANVIL as I have." Eisenhower admitted to "inescapable" compromises in the past for the sake of "unity of purpose and effort," but denied that anyone had urged his views on him, or that he was "particularly affected by localitis." What he had meant to convey on January 23 was that OVERLORD "represents for the U.S. and the U.K. a real crisis in the European war. . . . Real success should do much to hasten the end of this conflict, but a reverse will have opposite repercussions from which we would recover with the utmost difficulty." In closing, Eisenhower recited his needs: landing craft for a five-division assault heavily reinforced with armor, two months of intensive air attacks on French rail targets, control of the Air Force, an airborne division in the first wave, sixty days in which OVERLORD absorbed "everything the U.N. can possibly pour into it," and a timely commitment to those requests.

The next day Eisenhower followed up with an apology to Marshall for his defensiveness abut "localitis." He enclosed a list of names for still unfilled corps command billets—endorsed by Bradley. Eisenhower intimated to Marshall his "struggle" to relocate SHAEF outside London, and commiserated over the reports from Anzio, disclosing in passing that the SHAEF air plan was about to become "doctrine" at a Supreme Commander's conference set for the following day, at which he also expected to "fix our recommended dates for the passage of command of Strategical Air Forces to this Headquarters."

On the tenth Eisenhower and Marshall spoke by transatlantic phone.

They arranged a visit by OPD experts to hammer out the facts about the alleged shortages in OVERLORD. Then, on the eleventh, the American Chiefs abruptly designated Eisenhower as the American JCS "agent" in future discussions with the BCOS on ANVIL. On its face, this was a substantial delegation of power, which took Churchill and Brooke agreeably by surprise and became the basis of legends that the JCS considered Eisenhower "the only person whom the Americans were prepared to accept as arbiter, between the claims of OVERLORD and ANVIL." On the other hand, the move promoted Eisenhower out of his natural role as an advocate for SHAEF into one of spokesman for the views of Marshall, King, Arnold and the President, applying the brakes on compromise.

On the twelfth, at a meeting with Leigh-Mallory, Eisenhower officially "approved" the SHAEF air plan. Two days later the Combined Chiefs approved Eisenhower's directive, a historic document that set forth his tasks to the degree that both sides could agree on them. The omissions revealed the unresolved business at mid-month.

At British insistence, this directive required Eisenhower to train forces and make plans to exploit RANKIN, a contingency plan to exploit a sudden German military withdrawal from France or a sudden collapse of Nazi controls. The CCS denied Eisenhower authority to communicate directly with STAVKA, the military missions in Moscow. The American Chiefs inserted a clause stipulating that SHAEF would command ANVIL, and directed Eisenhower to "submit timely recommendations compatible with this regard."

The two sides compromised on the definition of Eisenhower's task. Five weeks before, a British draft was prepared instructing Eisenhower to gain a lodgement area in France "from which further offensive action *can* be aimed at the heart of Germany." The Americans had rejected it. The British then rejected as beyond Allied means the open-ended American counter-proposal directing Eisenhower to gain a lodgement area suitable for operations "striking at the heart of Germany." The final version, never to be altered, directed Eisenhower to be designated Supreme Commander, Allied Expeditionary Force, to "enter the continent of Europe, and in conjunction with the other United Nations, undertake operations aimed at the heart of Germany and destruction of her armed forces." The CCS did not define "heart," or "other United Nations," leaving room for interpretation, and for the inclusion of the Soviets as a factor in Allied military planning.

Eisenhower received no command authority over the strategic air forces; indeed he was reminded of the concurrent military activities of the Allied sea and air forces operating under the POINTBLANK directive and he was invited to "recommend any variation in these activities which may seem to you desirable." The command annexes were silent on Bomber Command and the Eighth Air Force. Eisenhower received no air annex.

3

Widewing

AND so by mid-February, as the Combined Chiefs of Staff formally designated Eisenhower Supreme Commander, fundamental questions remained: when and whether the CCS would take the next step and delegate the authority necessary to Eisenhower to carry out OVERLORD and to sustain the operation. Gradually it had become plain that answers would not be forthcoming until, from the point of view of the CCS at least, decisions were necessary or possible.

It was apparent that fundamental doubts persisted about OVERLORD. Indeed, an aspect of the ANVIL debate was to become clearer that week: that the Americans and British debated ANVIL in part with an eye toward the problem of what to do should German moves in the next several weeks rule out OVERLORD as impractical. Evidence of this included Marshall's designation of Eisenhower as JCS "agent" for ANVIL, and the CCS decision —at Marshall's behest—to designate Eisenhower commander of the ANVIL forces, an action evidently designed to emphasize that the JCS considered an invasion of southern France the only acceptable alternative to an invasion of northwest France, should OVERLORD prove to be impractical. Likewise, BCOS' refusal to be pinned down on ANVIL implied that the British would reserve the right to insist on expanded Italian operations as an alternative should OVERLORD be ruled out. Historians can only conjecture about this aspect of the ANVIL controversy. But it was an aspect, and the question as Eisenhower saw it, was how long the two sides would continue to entertain doubts about OVERLORD. There would never be perfect certainty about OVERLORD. Since the Germans had the ability to reinforce France, an irrevocable commitment to OVERLORD was not possible until the troops were ashore in France. Even so, the question remained: How long would the CCS heed caution and decline to delegate to Eisenhower the necessary authority to carry out OVERLORD? To wait too long would leave

Eisenhower insufficient time to establish clear lines of authority at SHAEF and convey doubts to Eisenhower's subordinates both about CCS determination to see OVERLORD through and about Eisenhower himself, which would confirm a depressing premonition in mid-February that the Allies were capable of resolute action only in situations like Salerno and Anzio, reverses in a secondary theater.

And so Eisenhower was impatient. He had already privately resolved that a postponement of ANVIL was inevitable and had said as much to Marshall. Soon Smith would broach the idea of ANVIL as an alternative to OVERLORD in discussions at Norfolk House. Eisenhower in turn would forbid discussion of it and never again would the suggestion appear in the record of his Supreme Commander conferences. But Eisenhower could not tell the CCS what to decide, and to confront the CCS with its own doubts would raise suspicion that Eisenhower had doubts of his own.

Predictably, the ANVIL debate hardened. In American eyes, ANVIL remained a symbol of Allied determination to concentrate all available resources in France, and talk of alternatives, logical or not, seemed to them tantamount to going back on basic commitments. On the other hand, for the British, ANVIL was evolving into a test of how far the British, and all those the British represented, were to be bound beyond the letter of agreements entered into with the Americans and Russians. At Teheran the British had painstakingly reserved the right to reassess ANVIL in light of the availability of landing craft in May, a significant caveat, and to say that ANVIL was fixed in ice would be to say that British reservations at Teheran were not to be taken seriously, a proposition Churchill rejected.

Thus, Eisenhower's task was to defuse the wider aspects of ANVIL and to narrow the ground on air issues by April 1, the informal deadline set for him by Leigh-Mallory's request for the transport plan by that date. First, British assurances were now needed to the effect that France had unquestioned priority. On the part of the Americans, assurances were necessary to the British that the Americans did not consider ANVIL a fixed agreement; that the Americans would review it in good faith and in no way considered ANVIL a commitment to withdraw all U.S. support from Italy or to relinquish Allied say on political questions which the British labored to keep open by retaining flexibility on ANVIL. Finally, Eisenhower had to eliminate insinuations of bad faith that had cropped up on the landing-craft problem, the subject of meetings for two weeks in the wake of Eisenhower's designation as JCS "agent" on ANVIL.

Meanwhile, General John E. Hull and Rear Admiral Charles M. Cooke arrived in London. They were OPD staff experts on the landing-craft problem, formally sent to assist Eisenhower in ANVIL negotiations in a "purely advisory" capacity. At ten o'clock on the morning of the fourteenth, in the drafty third-floor conference room at Norfolk House, Eisenhower, Smith, Ramsay, Leigh-Mallory, Cooke, Hull and fifteen staff members went to work on landing-craft schedules for OVERLORD and ANVIL, mainly to agree on a set of facts. It was an unspoken fact that Hull and Cooke had flown in from Washington to evaluate the integrity of SHAEF landing-craft estimates, and so Eisenhower hoped that the discussions might at least narrow arguments to the extent of eliminating American insinuations of bad faith levied at SHAEF and the British in early February.

As the meeting came to order, Eisenhower stressed the "great importance" of OVERLORD. He invited all present "to study our demands for landing craft to support this operation . . . carefully." He explained that the misunderstandings between Washington and London were "technical calculations," mainly naval, which he was confident would be cleared up if "points of difference are approached in a considerate attitude." Ideally, he said, *all* LSTs now in the Mediterranean would stay there and OVERLORD's needs might be met from "other sources."

Cooke read and circulated a paper that set out the points of disagreement and options for overcoming deficiencies. There ensued a long discussion typical of the formal conferences at Norfolk House—conferences outwardly arcane and technical in the written record, which obscured the inherent drama of discussions so critical to the fate of the alliance and the course of the war.

What deficiencies if any had to be made good for a five-division OVERLORD assault and a two-division ANVIL as planned? Which planning assumptions should the group adopt for calculating serviceability and estimated losses of landing craft? Could the Allies safely double-load personnel transports on vehicle carriers for the landings? Would the danger of German artillery and air bombardment be greatest then, or did the element of surprise enable the Allies to run risks? Would additional tactical bomber wings and destroyers mitigate risks by silencing the massive German coastal batteries between Le Havre and Cherbourg? Could estimated deficiencies due to "attrition" be alleviated by expedients? Had calculations overestimated discharge times for the LCIs and LSTs? Could juggling serviceability and availability ratios—paper judgments—transform the situation?

As it turned out, Admiral Ramsay's landing-craft estimates bordered on the overcautions based on past experience. The issue was the margin in loading below "theoretical maximum" to be accepted in the landing phase in view of the threat of German shore-battery fire on D-Day. Ramsay defended his estimates—unlike past operations, he said, German air and artillery fire would reach maximum on D-Day with battery fire intensifying between H plus 3 and H plus 6 and reaching "maximum intensity at noon." He had decided that overloaded vessels on D-Day ran too great a risk of heavy casualties at sea. Every man lost at sea would "jeopardize the operation," Ramsay said. Troops double-bunked aboard crowded vessels for three or four days would arrive at the beaches "not . . . physically fit."

Ramsay spoke of the uniqueness of OVERLORD as the supreme operation of 1944, which no one disputed. But it was not clear that the sailing distances involved or German shore defenses constituted an unprecedented hazard. Thus, as Eisenhower put it, a consensus arose in favor of "increased loading," taking a look at expedients and examining the shortages more closely.

But shortages did exist. An exhaustive discussion focused on the shortages of the versatile LSTs, the decisive point. Short of double-loading and double-bunking, the most generous computations fell thirty-two short for a five-division OVERLORD by late May. There was very little "give" in ANVIL as planned, and all knew that VI Corps at Anzio was fending off counterattack by elements of ten German divisions and no one could predict how long Anzio would drain off Mediterranean shipping.

Eisenhower repeatedly assured Hull and Cooke that he was anxious to "do everything in our power to avoid landing craft from that theater just because we could use *a little more* for OVERLORD"—that is, he would oppose small increases for OVERLORD achieved at the expense of drastic reductions in ANVIL, unless, of course, "it was absolutely essential for ensuring the success of OVERLORD."

Cooke indicated that ten of the 32 LSTs *might* be provided from U.S. training programs, and felt that LST capacity could be increased by juggling serviceability rates. Ramsay replied he was "reluctant to rely on probabilities" and judging by past experience refused to deal with certainties in the planning stage. He was not sure that serviceability figures were not already "over-optimistic"—British maintenance facilities were overtaxed, given the probability of additional losses when the LSTs in Northern Ireland set sail for southern England on the eve of the assault. Eisenhower agreed, adding "in no uncertain terms" that he would have no hesitation, in the end, about requesting the Combined Chiefs in his capacity as JCS "agent" and Supreme Commander to compensate for deficiencies by withdrawals from ANVIL. In sum, OVERLORD was 32 LSTs short, but 10 *might* be available from U.S. sources, leaving a "deficiency" of 22 LSTs. ANVIL would claim 77 LSTs, from which 22 might be spared, which he felt he could support on grounds that OVERLORD was the all-out operation. Eisenhower doubted that General Henry Wilson would consider ANVIL feasible without the 22 LSTs—but it might be worth a try. Eisenhower wished Hull and Cooke success in their meetings with the 21st Army Group on the problem, and assured them he was available "day or night to discuss these matters." The meeting recessed.

The talks on the fourteenth represented progress. First, there was no longer any dispute that shortages existed for a five-division assault. Second, there was no dispute that OVERLORD preparations took absolute precedence over ANVIL. For instance, no one had urged double-bunking for the assault in the "all-out" operation. SHAEF won round one by establishing that shortages existed that had to be fulfilled from the Mediterranean or *"other sources."* Round two, however, was another matter—that of bringing both sides to act on these estimates in a timely way that would lead to an overall settlement.

Anzio overshadowed the meetings. For days, Alexander and the 15th Army Group weighed desperate measures to break the siege at Cassino and link up with the bridgehead. Trenchfoot, frostbite, cold winds and mud at Cassino and Anzio had rendered Allied armored superiority useless. With the Fifth Army bogged down at Cassino, five U.S. and British divisions were isolated and threatened with defeat in detail. That week, to break the Cassino stalemate, Alexander ordered the bombardment of the ancient Abbey of St. Benedict, which had been converted into a German strongpoint on the promontory overlooking the town and dividing Fifth Army positions. On February 15, 254 Fifteenth Air Force heavy bombers pounded the monastery, destroying it (except for the tomb and cell of St. Benedict), to no avail.

The sixteenth was a day of crisis. In Cassino the crack German 1st Paratroops Division moved back into the abbey, occupied the ruins as a fortress and fought Fifth Army attacks to a standstill. In Anzio, elements of four panzer divisions massed at Campoleone on the northern edge of the perimeter and overran the British 56th Division as it relieved the British 1st, spreading confusion through both units. A second attack to the south drove a deep wedge into the positions held by the U.S. 45th Infantry Division, bringing the German 88 guns nearby within range of the beach.

The reverberations were felt that night in London. An orderly at Hayes Lodge roused Eisenhower from sleep with a copy of a night telegram from Alexander to Brooke describing the desperate conditions at VI Corps Headquarters, dispatched without consulting Clark. In it, Alexander complained that negativism and depression had set in, and proposed drastic steps—the sacking of Lucas and the appointment of a British Corps command, since "no single American in the theater" was in his opinion capable of restoring VI Corps morale and moving inland.

Eisenhower and Brooke talked by phone. Eisenhower informed him that he might spare Patton for a month but cautioned that American command policy was the business of Clark and Devers. Eisenhower warned Brooke that Alexander contemplated a step that would precipitate "a grave crisis" between the Americans and British.

The situation at Anzio stabilized. In the next several days, VI Corps trained its artillery on the heavily congested German roads. A desperate stand by the U.S. 3rd Division at the Carreceto Creek checked the German onslaught, but repeated attacks to break the Cassino line failed and stalemate deepened. In the CCS, the Anzio crisis rekindled intransigence on ANVIL. In British eyes, American refusals to take account of the battle raging south of Rome were arbitrary, as the intensity of the fighting vindicated the

February 4 BCOS proposal in which the British had formally suggested that the diversionary purposes of ANVIL could best be served in Italy. In American eyes, stalemate again emphasized the futility of pouring additional resources into an indecisive battle for Rome, which, in Marshall's words, "weighed lightly in the balance" against other military problems facing the Allies.

In the chambers of the Combined Chiefs in the Federal Reserve Building on 14th Street in Washington, Admiral Ernest King, in his dual role of Chief of Naval Operations and Commander in Chief of the Fleet, emerged momentarily as the primary American spokesman. Confronted with a similar impasse in the past, the American Chiefs had turned to King to strengthen the U.S. position by threatening revisions in the basic Europe First strategy by "going Pacific." All week King insisted he would not lightly sacrifice reinforcements for Nimitz and MacArthur, that he consented only for the sake of ANVIL. He insisted on British assurances that rearrangement of the landing-craft schedules in the United States, Britain and Naples left enough for a two-division lift in Naples for ANVIL, and that ANVIL preparations proceed.

King's Pacific First threat recalled the intensity of earlier battles in 1942 and tripped up Eisenhower's moves to work out ANVIL on a basis acceptable to the British—postponement, with full reconsideration of ANVIL in light of the circumstances prevailing in late spring. In Eisenhower's mind the ingenuity of both camps in evading the main issues—the OVERLORD build-up and his command authority—was cause for despair, and at moments, his patience lapsed.

In the next several days, Smith barely restrained Eisenhower from taking up Marshall's gauntlet and declaring that a decision on ANVIL had now become "absolutely imperative." But a decision was not imperative yet, and an effort to push for one would, in Smith's view, simply convince Washington that "we changed our minds too quickly." In short, Eisenhower, as JCS "agent," was committed to do his best on behalf of ANVIL, and unless he moved Churchill beyond his "pledge" to Stalin on Rome, relations with Marshall would unravel. Grounds existed for compromise: an unequivocal American endorsement of Rome, in exchange for British support for ANVIL in principle that would weigh heavily in future discussions of Italy versus ANVIL. But who would take the first step?

Meanwhile, Hull and Cooke made the rounds at SHAEF to hammer out the landing-craft question. The February 14 session had narrowed the ground. Hull and Cooke conveyed Washington's basic terms: until some operation in the nature of ANVIL was on the books, no compromise was possible. "No compromise" meant no U.S. allocations from the Pacific to cover shortages, leaving it up to Eisenhower and Wilson to parcel out existing stocks. Compromise meant ANVIL.

In the next ninety-six hours the group worked out the terms of a "trade" wherein 20 British LSTs and 21 British LCIs would be drawn from Italy by April 1 in exchange for 6 American AKA troop carriers. This would leave Wilson short, but the idea was that LST deficiencies in Italy would eventually be made up by U.S. units sailing direct to Italy from America that would be drawn from current stocks, new production and Pacific allocations.

There were obvious advantages: first, certainty that Eisenhower could count on withdrawals from ANVIL to arrive on time in England, whereas no one could count on the arrival of American units on time. Second, the AKA, a large lumbering ship, was less seaworthy in rough waters and technically more suitable for the Tyrrhenian Sea and Anzio. The trade would satisfy ANVIL deficiencies only "in part," effective on April 1, when, presumably, the CCS would weigh the returns from Italy and Russia. In terms of sailing distances, the trade was senseless; evidently its main purpose was to substitute American vessels for British in the Mediterranean and thereby inhibit Wilson's planning by limiting the number of British vessels at his disposal for operations such as landings in Istria. The American distrust implicit in the scheme was unfortunate, and the compromise meant delaying the arrival in England of LSTs. Eisenhower was wary, but the alternative was impasse, and so he approved. Eisenhower set a meeting for the eighteenth to formalize the deal to be presented to the BCOS on the nineteenth, then presumably forwarded to Washington as a recommendation which he would submit in his capacity as JCS "agent."

On the eighteenth Eisenhower, Ramsay, Leigh-Mallory, Cooke, Hull and a larger group including Montgomery reassembled at Norfolk House to approve the Hull-Smith conclusions. Eisenhower opened the meeting by noting that the technical questions of landing craft had been discussed back and forth at the staff level and that the time had "come for a command decision" on the problem of landing-craft availability for a five-division OVERLORD.

Smith presented the paper worked out with Hull and Cooke. He noted that the problem was "whether or not we could provide an adequate lift for OVERLORD with flexibility . . . allowing sufficient ships and craft to remain in the Mediterranean [for a] two-division assault for ANVIL." Smith described the exchange: 6 large AKA transports currently in England for 20 LSTs and 21 LCIs in Italy by April 1. The exchange reflected "technical problems of loading and tactical questions of flexibility," he said, and the urgency of proceeding.

Eisenhower's British deputies fell into line. On behalf of the 21st Army Group, Montgomery accepted the "compromise . . . fully cognizant of the urgent necessity for reaching a final decision."

Ramsay also endorsed it, cautioning that it added "to the complexity of an already complex naval situation."

Leigh-Mallory approved on behalf of the AEAF provided the transfer did not retard the timely arrival of fighters to get fighter fields in operation.

In the discussion that followed, Eisenhower's impatience about putting off the transfer was obvious. He pressed Smith to explain why a decision could not be made right away. Smith confessed his reluctance to make any firm commitments before April 1, and for the first time raised the unspoken. Smith noted the problem of German preparations in the Fifteenth and Seventh Army sectors, and the possibility of fresh German mobile reinforcements. The German build-up had already reached the "critical point," he said, and OVERLORD might become "impractical," forcing the Allies to shift the center of gravity to Italy and to enter France through the southern coast.

Eisenhower angrily replied that he wanted a decision "now," and again polled the group. De Guingand, Montgomery's chief of staff, said that the Army must "know at this time precisely what craft they can plan on." Ramsay agreed. Cooke and Hull seemed to agree with de Guingand and Eisenhower, but Cooke suggested that the decision might be made "now," with a provision that the ships remain in Naples until April 1 for "refitting." Eisenhower replied that "changed conditions," such as a situation requiring the Allies to invade southern France in lieu of northwest France, were a matter for reconsideration of the Combined Chiefs, not SHAEF.

Smith pressed on. He reminded Eisenhower of another reason for delay —the inability, as yet, to identify the source for the ten LST deficiency which nobody had solved yet. To transfer ships for a five-division assault still represented a "gamble" of sorts. Eisenhower agreed that the ten missing LSTs had to be identified somewhere—he suggested attaching a statement in the memorandum drawing attention to the problem—but he disagreed that the exchange was a "gamble" and would forbid talking about OVERLORD in those terms.

In a message to Marshall on the morning of the nineteenth, Eisenhower observed that the recent crisis in Italy had all but ruled out ANVIL as planned, but his message was private and personal—an attempt to explore his personal latitude and to condition Marshall for postponement. Nor did Eisenhower look forward to presenting the compromise to Brooke.

Eisenhower proceeded to Whitehall that morning with the nine-point memorandum. In the meetings with Brooke and Cunningham, he stressed what the memorandum offered the British. First, deficiencies in OVERLORD would be made good from ANVIL reserves, just as the BCOS had foreseen. This all but guaranteed postponement. Second, he would look to Washington for at least seven of the estimated ten to fifteen LSTs needed from "other sources." He personally assured Brooke he considered a "successful conclusion" to Italy an "essential prelude" to OVERLORD.

Eisenhower was also "convinced" ANVIL would be of great assistance to OVERLORD and warned Brooke he intended to recommend a directive for

Wilson charging him with making "a maximum effort" to mount the operation. Eisenhower did not think a two-division ANVIL had become impossible yet. He explained that the ships withdrawn from Naples by April 1 should be British in the "interest of balancing the national lift for both OVERLORD and ANVIL." Eisenhower added that in the event ANVIL proved impractical, he would have no hesitation about calling in all landing-craft surpluses in the Mediterranean (American and British) over and above one division, in keeping with the objective of ANVIL as a supporting operation for OVERLORD.

Brooke assured Eisenhower the BCOS would make a "maximum effort" to mount ANVIL. However, Brooke noted "indications" that ANVIL preparations were already interfering with Wilson's conduct of the campaign in Italy. A number of American units had been withdrawn for "amphibious" training. Airfield construction in Corsica absorbed resources. Brooke further observed that to earmark ten divisions for ANVIL now would leave Alexander with a "narrow margin" in his quest for Rome. Brooke recalled his warnings in Cairo that Italy, ANVIL and OVERLORD would all be "skimped" in the end—precisely his concern now. Then Admiral Andrew Cunningham raised the sensitive problem of exchanging British and American LSTs. He was "doubtful" that British ships would be refitted and sailed for England by April 1—he had always calculated that new American LSTs would sail directly for England instead of the Mediterranean.

Discussion ensued—Smith and Cooke explained that the American vessels were being configured with special davits suitable for Mediterranean conditions. Cunningham was still skeptical that British LSTs could refit in time. At one point Brooke assured Eisenhower that he supported a "diversionary operation" in southern France after OVERLORD to deploy French troops, and suggested that Wilson be directed to conduct a "study of possible operations" in southern France. Eisenhower asked Cunningham to clarify whether the problem of withdrawing British LSTs by April 1 would hold good if ANVIL was canceled. Cunningham said that "every effort" would be made to return the ships and to see that they were manned by experienced crews "as far as possible." Eventually the group accepted the nine-point memorandum, subject to several provisos affixed by Brooke and Cunningham which negated it.

As the meeting ended, the question of who would "give," the Americans or the British, remained unanswered. After Eisenhower left, the BCOS remained in session and drew up a list of conclusions and forwarded them to the CCS in Washington, conclusions that muddied the situation. The BCOS agreed to study the LST-AKA exchange, but opposed steps that would "skimp" both theaters. In the event ANVIL was canceled, the BCOS pledged "all possible steps" to transfer Mediterranean ships back to England for OVERLORD. The BCOS called it "unthinkable" to strip Wilson of ten divisions for the sake of ANVIL and urged a directive specifying that

Italy would have "priority" over all Mediterranean operations, and a prompt decision on ANVIL—the BCOS termed the chances of mounting ANVIL "negligible."

Abruptly, on the twentieth, Eisenhower received a terse three-paragraph note from Montgomery in which he appeared to back away from his endorsement of the exchange only two days before. Montgomery cited a report by the War Office Operations Directorate on conditions in Italy—troops were fatigued, in need of regrouping and "generally . . . not too well situated for getting on to Rome and beyond." In the circumstances, Montgomery suspected that withdrawing troops for ANVIL would be impractical, and he could not see the point "in cutting ourselves down" for the sake of an operation unlikely to happen.

The next day Montgomery followed up with a note describing a talk he had just had with the Prime Minister at Chequers on OVERLORD preparations. Churchill had encouraged Montgomery to move strongly for an immediate strengthening of OVERLORD, noting that in view of the German stand at Anzio, Italy had become a "major war" and that the Riviera landings "would come at the expense of it." According to Montgomery, Churchill felt that the "major war" under way in Italy had accomplished the work of ANVIL. Speaking for himself, Montgomery urged Eisenhower to "make a definite decision to cancel ANVIL" at once, which would enable the Mediterranean command to devote full attention to fighting Germans in Italy, whereupon he predicted that the British landing craft would be released "at once." In sum, Montgomery hoped Eisenhower would agree to "throw the whole weight of our opinion into the scales against ANVIL" for the sake of "two really good campaigns—one in Italy and one in OVERLORD."

In his careful reply, Eisenhower conceded that "events of the past week have influenced my general conclusions very strongly along the lines you suggest." He cautioned Montgomery against simple answers, however; postponement was likely, but he predicted that the Allies would land in southern France "sooner or later" because of the well-known advantages of such a move. Second, no naval reinforcements except those approved on the eighteenth were necessary, so he opposed a "tremendous rush" in deciding for or against ANVIL.

Meanwhile, Marshall's response to Eisenhower's February 19 cable was negative. Furthermore, Marshall had shared Eisenhower's message with Admiral Leahy, who shared it with Roosevelt, who instructed Leahy to draw Marshall's attention to the fact that "we are committed to a third power and I do not feel we have any right to abandon this commitment without taking up the matter with the third power." Roosevelt broached this problem in a cable to Churchill in which he recalled that the Allies had given Stalin "a promise that OVERLORD would be launched by May and supported by the strongest practicable landing in the south of France at about the same time and that he [Stalin] agreed to plan for simultaneous Russian attacks on the Eastern Front."

On the twenty-second, armed with the latest JCS message asking for a "clear cut statement of basis for your agreement or disagreement" with the BCOS paper, Eisenhower returned to the conference with Brooke, at which he hoped to secure what he decided was the minimum: British support for a directive to Wilson that postponed ANVIL but kept token ANVIL preparations alive. Brooke consented to wording that would direct Wilson to weigh ANVIL among other alternatives after Rome, and direct him to *plan* the operation provided that "planning" ANVIL did not interfere with Wilson's operations. Even this was yielded reluctantly, coupled with suggestions that Eisenhower be "candid" in his dealings with the American Chiefs.

Eisenhower tried to put the most optimistic light on the American point of view. He explained the real JCS concern—merely that canceling preparations for ANVIL would strip the Allies of flexibility in the event of dramatic changes, such as a sudden German withdrawal north of Rome to the Pisa–Rimini line, freeing forces for France. Eisenhower assured Brooke that he personally felt ANVIL was the best of several choices for a diversionary operation—not the only one—*after* Rome, and *after* the withdrawal of the twenty LSTs and LCIs, whichever came first. As JCS "agent," he would accept a directive for Wilson ordering that the operation be planned, provided planning did not interfere with Rome.

Brooke noted that planning was *already* interfering with operations to link up the Fifth Army and Anzio. Brooke reminded Eisenhower that ANVIL was *not* the two-division landing as the Americans commonly referred to it, but a two-division landing with eight follow-up divisions, a ten-division commitment that would reduce Wilson's forces in Italy by 33 percent. Wilson's reluctance to commit reserves and relieve exhausted divisions in the battle stemmed in part from his awareness that soon he might have to part with a third of his force.

For the first and last time, the subject of Teheran appeared in the minutes of Eisenhower's meetings that winter. Eisenhower assured Brooke that it was his understanding that the American position had not been set inflexibly on ANVIL at any fixed level of forces. He predicted the JCS would accept any diversionary operation "worthy of the name of the largest scale possible after meeting requirements for the Italian campaign." Eisenhower added that he intended to do nothing to inhibit Wilson's use of American reinforcements in the Rome battle, and otherwise hinted he favored alternatives to ANVIL. But he could not support canceling ANVIL—yet.

Brooke detected common ground. If Eisenhower indeed felt that ANVIL was *not* necessarily a ten-division operation, and *not* necessarily against the south of France, maybe Wilson could be instructed "to continue planning operations to contain the maximum number of enemy forces in the Mediterranean" with the resources available after meeting his needs in Italy, and

Brooke *hoped* ANVIL as conceived would be possible as the best of several alternatives.

Eisenhower relented. Brooke's terms were not unreasonable, and Eisenhower may have hoped that Roosevelt would accept if Marshall and King would not. If so, as of February 22 Eisenhower was still underestimating American support for ANVIL and Roosevelt's new aloofness on military questions. Or perhaps Eisenhower was anxious to prove his open-mindedness in British eyes, in hopes that even if the Americans rejected his amendments, the British would be disposed to trust Eisenhower's future recommendations on the as yet unexplored approach of postponing ANVIL. If so, Eisenhower was gambling on the possibility that the British, after OVERLORD, would come to see ANVIL in the way the Americans saw it. Eisenhower may have read British views perceptively, but he was laying himself open to British charges that he had misled the British. In any case, by the twenty-second, with Montgomery re-entering the fray as a spokesman for Churchill, Eisenhower was on notice that ANVIL would soon be dividing his command internally if something did not give quickly.

A quick, intense debate in the CCS followed over the Eisenhower-Brooke memorandum. The American JCS quickly found fault with the accord. The JCS acknowledged that postponement of ANVIL was likely in view of the stalemate at Anzio, but indicated that they would insist on a firm target date even while reinforcing Eisenhower with an additional six LSTs and twenty LCIs currently in Italy. The British opposed hampering Alexander's efforts to link up VI Corps and Clark's Fifth Army.

Under the shadow of an extended impasse, Eisenhower was tempted once again to call a halt to the whole argument by formally recommending postponement, a move that would probably decide it, albeit at a great price in Marshall's confidence. At a long and arduous meeting on February 26 at Norfolk House, Eisenhower intimated that he contemplated the even more drastic step of sending a message to the CCS calling ANVIL "impossible." He was not swayed by reports that President Roosevelt had endorsed the American-British LST switch, which in Smith's words meant that additional landing craft were a "near certainty." Near certainty was not good enough—Eisenhower was skeptical and weighed sending the message anyway to be sure of the LSTs within the next three weeks. Smith strenuously urged Eisenhower to do nothing, and Eisenhower held back.

CCS approval of the Eisenhower-Brooke memo followed, but it was to become effective upon a review of Wilson's directive set for the twentieth. This meant that debate had merely been put off. Indeed, as Marshall intimated in a cable to Eisenhower, the United States and Britain agreed on one point only—that the "state of uncertainty should be terminated." But in late February 1944, uncertainty permeated every aspect of American-British relations concerning war policy with no end in sight. Certain problems could be negotiated, many could not. For instance, it was a fact that an irrevocable decision on ANVIL could not be made until at or near the time of OVERLORD, and even then it would be, as Smith had put it, a "gamble." Months of discussion left matters where they had been left at Cairo—the Americans insisted on ANVIL, the British insisted on Rome, with neither operation possible by June.

Indecision dramatized the anomalous situation confronting the Allies— that after three years of preparations, a supreme Allied effort against Germany still could not be mapped out on the basis of Allied resources; that the military campaign ahead would depend on the ebb and flow of remote battles in Russia, meaning that the Allies awaited the outcome of events in the next several weeks involving the Germans and Russians over which they had no control. And magnifying the frustration was a growing awareness that Germany's military defeat was all but assured. Talk that 1944 would be 1918 all over again seemed to be justified, though the contrasts between the Allied situation in 1944 and 1918 were as pertinent as the comparisons; unlike the situation in 1918, the Allies lacked a firm Continental base or control over the largest force in the field facing Germany. Allied strategy, in the circumstances, was predicated on faith that the German-Russian war would develop in ways that fulfilled the preconditions set for Allied success in an operation that appeared to court risks that seemed excessive in terms of defeating Germany.

As things stood, in late February, German Army Groups B and G mustered fifty-two divisions between Marseilles and Dunkirk, a force exceeding in ground strength the Anglo-American Army mobilized in England for the invasion, with no guarantee that the Germans would not substantially reinforce France in the next three months, or later as the invasion battle proceeded. Would this happen? German and Russian decisions would soon tell the story.

The mystery now absorbing the Allied leaders in mid-February was the continuing refusal of the Germans to yield untenable positions in Russia in the face of a determined broad-front Russian winter offensive. Four German army groups clung to exposed salients north of the Pripet Marshes and west of Rumania, apparently to shore up the morale of the German satellites. How long would these "political" objectives take precedence over Germany's chance to defeat or deter OVERLORD? It was felt that a timely withdrawal back to the Riga–Odessa line from salients deep in Baltic Russia and along the Black Sea would actually improve German defensive positions in the east and yield a strategic reserve of as many as sixty divisions for use on both fronts. Presumably, German decisions to economize in the east would be unmistakable and would be evident soon enough to afford time for adjusting Allied plans, exactly as Smith had had in mind on the eighteenth. But timing was critical, and this raised a second mystery—the ongoing Russian winter offensive. In short, the sooner the Russian attacks tapered off, the sooner the Germans would reassess the two fronts and reach irrevocable decisions about France, determining the success of the landings. Also, because Russian preparations were known to be methodical, the sooner the current offensive stopped, the sooner preparations for the Russian summer offensive would start and the more confident the Allies and Russians would be that the Germans would not have freedom of action in the critical stages of the invasion battle.

The eastern war was not a "lightning war." Like the summer and fall attacks of 1943, the January Russian offensive had been methodically planned as a series of assaults up and down the front—applying, then easing pressure until gaps opened for exploitation, a panoramic feat reminiscent of Foch's massive offensives on the Marne in 1918. Artillery and aircraft had been brought up behind the lines to permit deep exploitation through points where the German army buckled, and offensives were rarely pushed to the limit. The Russian summer offensive would probably unfold the same way. As Deane warned the CCS on February 27, reassembling would take time, and if everything was to be set by mid-June, the Russians would have to pause soon in order to avoid outrunning their communications.

The January offensive in the Leningrad sector had pushed the German Eighteenth Army back behind Lake Ilmen. Then, as the Germans stabilized the north, the Russians carried out violent attacks along the entire front. In the center, a four-prong offensive launched in late December west of Kiev and southward against the German salient on the Dnieper bend rolled on. By mid-February, two Russian fronts* had encircled two corps of the German Eighth Army and cut the lateral railroads running from Lvov to Odessa, all capped by annihilation of the Korsun pocket on February 17, a "little Stalingrad," in which 100,000 Germans were killed or taken prisoner.

The offensive proceeded. Farther south, Malinovsky's First Ukrainian Front drove the German Sixth Army from the Dnieper bend and unhinged the German Seventeenth Army defenses covering Sevastopol. In Poland, the weather remained cold and clear, and dispatches indicated a larger-scale broad-front offensive under way toward Lvov. In the critical sector at Vinnitsa near the Lvov–Odessa railway, the German First Panzer Army, repulsed at Korsun, was suddenly encircled from the north by Zhukov and the south by Konev's Second Ukrainian Front, which opened a gap for deep exploitation. For several days the First Panzer Army, supplied by air, fought westward across the rivers Dniester and Prut. And with the First Panzer Army consumed in the confusion of the Russian breakthrough, there were reports of a general collapse south of Lvov, tales of abandoned armored vehicles, Rumanian and Hungarian divisions surrendering without firing a shot, and of disorganization and apathy spreading through German

*A Russian "front" was roughly the equivalent of an Allied "army group."

ranks. How far would the Russians exploit their success?

But even as the Russians advanced, the Allies gained considerable diplomatic leverage when it became apparent that the Balkan States would attempt to surrender through the Allies in hopes of avoiding a Russian invasion. As the Red Army crossed the Dniester and Prut, overtures from the Hungarian regent, Admiral Horthy, and Miklós Kállay, president of the Hungarian Council, reached London, via the Vatican and contacts in Cairo, seeking clarification of unconditional surrender. Overtures also reached London from King Michael and Marshal Ion Antonescu of Rumania through Ankara and the Vatican. These overtures specified two things: first, the German satellites were eager to surrender to the Allies; second, an Allied military presence would probably be necessary, either in the form of Allied airborne landings in Rumania and Hungary or preferably a major land offensive through northern Italy into southern Germany and the Balkans.

With the Allies south of Rome, placing forces in Rumania and Hungary was impractical. But this might not be so forever, and to maintain contacts with the Balkan governments had obvious advantages in dealings with Moscow on Poland, Greece, Yugoslavia and Turkey. Predictably, the Americans and British divided over the question of "informing" Moscow of the overtures. Churchill, who was preparing a grand scheme for apportioning occupation duties between the British and Russians in the Balkans, prevailed, and Eden informed Molotov of the overtures.

Meanwhile, Allied-Soviet military coordination languished with little prospect of improvement. For weeks General John Deane and General Brocas Burrows had consulted STAVKA to discern Russian plans, without success. Following published accusations in *Pravda* that Allied agents in Cairo and Madrid had contacted German agents about a separate peace, negotiations foundered on FRANTIC, the "shuttle" bombing program staged to and from bases in Russia by the Fifteenth Air Force, designed to permit two-way bombing raids over industrial targets in southern and eastern Germany, which, incidentally, would enable the Fifteenth Air Force to reconnoiter the Russian front. STAVKA representatives met all military inquiries by Deane and Burrows with questions about exact Allied plans for launching OVERLORD: dates, beaches, divisions, and so on, about which neither man could provide information. In turn, General Antonov arranged for Deane and Burrows to receive written summaries of STAVKA military communiqués one hour before release to the world press.

Foreseeing situations like this as early as Christmas 1943, Eisenhower had volunteered to assume personal responsibility for communicating directly with STAVKA on all questions affecting OVERLORD so that any problems of coordination might be solved soldier-to-soldier. In early February, Eisenhower volunteered again, only to receive his directive which specifically forbade SHAEF-STAVKA contacts. Eisenhower would try again, but with

Allied-Soviet military coordination in limbo, and the Russian offensive moving ahead full steam, long-range planning entered a kind of twilight zone.

Butcher chronicled the tensions of February. The days passed slowly, days of endless appointments on staff and administrative matters at Grosvenor Square, followed by conferences lasting into late afternoon capped by working dinners and an occasional evening out. Butcher noted the talk around the office about Anzio, which dampened spirits already chilled by February skies perpetually darkened by rain, banks of clouds and fog. Routine worries included the daily reports of transatlantic convoys bearing troops and supplies, concern about "secret weapons," ANVIL, the French and air problems.

Predictably, as BIG WEEK approached, attempts to hammer out working arrangements between SHAEF and the air staffs faltered. Eisenhower maintained his optimism, since, as he had learned long before, not to acknowledge a crisis often avoided one. So far, in eighteen months, the Combined Chiefs had invariably met Eisenhower's essential needs, and Eisenhower seemed outwardly confident that the CCS would do so eventually in this case too. Occasionally Butcher noted snippets of trouble, such as word that Arnold and Spaatz were still "skeptical" about "dissipating" a strategic weapon in a tactical role. Butcher noted that British Air Ministry talk did not "jibe" with Churchill's pledge in Marrakech, though, he added, things would "probably work out alright" and Eisenhower seemed confident that he and Spaatz would "see eye to eye in an emergency." Eisenhower did not elaborate on the reasons he was so confident about "emergency" cooperation, and he was mindful that Spaatz, like many of his Air colleagues, still considered POINTBLANK "not merely as a prerequisite to OVERLORD, but as a perfectly feasible alternative to it. . . ."

By mid-February, POINTBLANK was in full swing. Results were good. Deep down, Eisenhower and most of the high command may have suspected that the grandiose Air Force claims were not far from the truth, particularly in the European theater. As a trained infantry officer, Eisenhower instinctively recoiled from the idea of heavy reliance on air power, and he was skeptical that the air forces had mastered the problem of concentrating on relevant targets. But he could not dispute the value of POINTBLANK, and air superiority was essential to OVERLORD.

As debate picked up, Eisenhower bided his time sensing that the passage of time was on his side, to a point. The flaw in the Air argument had always been time. The concept of strategic bombardment as a war-winning strategy could not be pursued indefinitely, for the invasion of Europe was scheduled for May in conjunction with the Russian ally. Soon the problem of how the air forces could best assist in gaining a lodgement in France would have to be faced, and the psychology of the argument would begin to shift. Eventually, the Air staffs would have to reckon with the SHAEF argument that if the transportation plan kept as much as a single mobile division away from Normandy, even for as little as twenty-four hours during the "dread interval" at the beaches, the preliminary air effort would render useful aid to OVERLORD. SHAEF, however, had to reckon with the counterargument that this was carrying OVERLORD logic to the extreme, as well as with skepticism that transport targets could be attacked effectively and opposition to the idea of committing the full weight of the strategic air forces to particular tactical objectives. Conceivably, to do so for weeks before the landings would not affect the positioning of a single division. Debate would go on along these lines. Eventually the approaching deadline might change the tone of the debate, making a compromise of some kind seem inevitable. Should this new tone emerge by April 1 or before, Eisenhower would know that the time had come to assert himself on the issue.

As time wore on, Eisenhower concluded that he would have to rely on Tedder and accept a compromise arrangement falling short of outright command over Bomber Command and Spaatz. The British would insist on autonomy for Bomber Command in any arrangement. Spaatz, backed by Arnold, would insist that an exception be made for the Italy-based U.S. Fifteenth Air Force and probably hold out for a specific deadline on transferring the Eighth Air Force back.

Meanwhile, SHAEF and the Air staffs drew apart. "I am afraid that having started as a confirmed optimist, I am steadily losing my optimism as to how this is all going to work out," Tedder warned Portal on February 22. "I am more and more being forced to the unfortunate conclusion that the two strategic forces are determined not to play." Tedder warned Portal that "a split on the question of the control of air forces might well, since the issues are very clear, precipitate a quite irremediable cleavage."

On the twenty-second, Spaatz was in Foggia to coordinate the movements of the Fifteenth Air Force in BIG WEEK. The attacks had begun two days earlier, aided by a break in the weather. An Arctic high-pressure system prevailed over the skies of Europe for the next week, dissipating the low clouds, turbulence, haze and dust that ordinarily shrouded Silesia, Berlin and the industrial towns of the Ruhr Valley. On Sunday, approximately 1,000 American bombers, escorted by P-51 Thunderbolt fighters, struck an aircraft-component plant at Brunswick and an ME-109 plant at Leipzig, followed that night by the RAF Lancasters. Coordinated Eighth and Fifteenth Air Force attacks came on Tuesday, and for the next forty-eight hours American B-17s and B-24s by day and the British Lancasters and Halifaxes by night carried out continuous missions over Berlin, Stuttgart, Saarbrücken, Cologne, Dortmund, Essen, Kassel, and ranging as far east as the Polish border just east of Stettin. On Thursday, in daylight, 226

Air Force bombers struck Schweinfurt, followed that night by 734 Lancasters and Halifaxes. On Friday, 2,000 planes struck Regensburg, Augsburg, Furth and Stuttgart, climaxing a week of raids on every known airframe plant in Germany.

Press reports focused on Berlin. Once again, heavy Allied raids on Berlin had hit the Reich Chancellery, the Tiergarten Zoo and most of the government buildings. Chaos reigned in the city and was magnified by shortages of essential supplies, disrupted communications and the crush of thousands of homeless. Raids shattered windows in two million dwellings, and momentarily paralyzed essential hospital and first-aid services, which provoked German threats to suspend the Geneva Convention and shoot all Allied airmen captured on sight.

The assault on Berlin prompted Hitler's recall of bombers from other fronts to stage the "little blitz," a series of retaliatory strikes on London later that week. For the first time in eighteen months, the depleted Luftwaffe bomber force managed to penetrate the British fighter and flak defenses, driving the citizens of London back to bomb shelters. German bombers struck St. James's Square, Kingston Way, and scattered random destruction throughout the city, shattering windows at the Admiralty, 10 Downing Street and Norfolk House.

The accent was on nonchalance. Butcher, part of an Air Force poker ring, described a game held in Spaatz's Park House apartment shortly after Spaatz's return from Foggia. Grim and serious-minded at work, Spaatz was a generous and popular host, in keeping with his celebrity as the dual commander of the Eighth and Fifteenth U.S. strategic air forces. When German night attacks disrupted the game, Spaatz excused himself, grabbed a notepad and stepped out on the balcony to record his observations, the stuff of legends in a war-weary capital.

In the first several days, the military results of BIG WEEK could not be tabulated accurately because of cloud cover in certain areas and problems with night photography. In the battles raging that week, air losses were light, and claims of downed German interceptors were high—attributed to the use of P-47 and P-51 long-range interceptors. On the morning of the twenty-eighth, Zuckerman warned Tedder that his personal contacts in both the Air Ministry and the Eighth Air Force had told him that "interest in the Transportation Plan was waning." The Air staffs, encouraged by the performance of the new interceptors and anxious to follow with an assault on oil refineries, sensed again that with twenty to thirty clear days of operational weather, the Eighth Air Force and Bomber Command might paralyze the German war economy and force a German collapse on all fronts. Zuckerman conceded the optimism was "to some extent justified and might prove to be in fact true," but he urged "from our point of view, however, the vital factor is time."

That night, Eisenhower and Smith attended a dinner given by Churchill at 10 Downing Street for the British Chiefs of Staff. The Eisenhower-Brooke accord was forty-eight hours old, and represented progress insofar as Eisenhower had succeeded in persuading the Americans to accord the Italian campaign "overriding priority" in the Mediterranean, at least until linkup of the Fifth Army and VI Corps.

Churchill had a legendary habit of keeping his guests up late regaling them with stories and speeches, and on the night of the twenty-eighth he was in peak form. The friendly but emotional discussions that began at dinner lasted past one o'clock and ranged over the disappointing news from the Anzio front, the Russian-Finnish peace negotiations, Rumanian peace feelers, De Gaulle, air policy and ANVIL. American-British differences permeated the discussions, differences that had begun to take a toll on the unity of the British Conservative-Labour coalition.

Then, as the conversation turned to air policy, Eisenhower reminded Churchill of their talks at Marrakech, which had left him with the impression that he would receive control of Bomber Command. Churchill retorted that the Cairo directive had envisioned no such thing. What Churchill had meant was that he anticipated that Eisenhower would command the American strategic air forces and that British Bomber Command would work "in conjunction" with SHAEF, not under SHAEF. Churchill had never foreseen that Eisenhower would "command the whole air effort." Churchill reminded Eisenhower that Britain was playing host for the invasion and that her sensibilities were of some moment. He likened British Bomber Command, Fighter Command and Coastal Command to the Home Fleet as symbols of British prestige and independence.

As Eisenhower and Churchill argued the point back and forth, British misgivings about bombing French targets emerged. Churchill also revealed that Harris and Spaatz balked at the idea of taking orders from Leigh-Mallory, who was considered an outsider in the strategic bombing fraternity at the Air Ministry, abrasive personally and inexperienced except in fighter techniques. Harris and Spaatz *had* indicated an interest in working with Tedder, who still operated without portfolio, though plainly any arrangement with Tedder would be more in the nature of "supervision," not "command."

Eisenhower was "flabbergasted" to learn of personal difficulties between Leigh-Mallory and the British Air Ministry, since the Air Ministry had insisted on his appointment. And since the Combined Chiefs had long intended to vest SHAEF with control "at an appropriate date," he could not see the objection to working through SHAEF and an Air commander in chief designated by the British. "Why did we give you Tedder?" Churchill said. "Why?" Eisenhower replied, adding he had been led to expect command of the strategic air forces, and if the CCS equivocated on all-out support of OVERLORD, he might "have to pack and go home."

Around two in the morning, Churchill produced the text of a three-point compromise: first, that Eisenhower submit the SHAEF plan and specific air needs to the CCS; second, that Eisenhower agree to place Air Marshal Tedder over the forces temporarily or permanently assigned to SHAEF; third, that Tedder "supervise" Spaatz, Harris and Leigh-Mallory co-equally, effective when Eisenhower and Air Chief Marshal Portal hammered out an agreement on targeting priorities.

Eisenhower demurred. The procedure seemed cumbersome, and Churchill was asking Eisenhower to concede a lot at the outset. First, the suggestion that Eisenhower formally submit SHAEF needs to the CCS was redundant, and therefore a veiled invitation that he omit Bomber Command in his request on grounds that British night-bombing techniques were too imprecise for transport targets. The Americans would strenuously object. Second, Eisenhower was not sure the Americans would accept Tedder's assumption of a formal role. Third, timing was a problem: Churchill was asking Eisenhower to renounce his maximum position on command *before* Eisenhower and Portal discussed targeting priorities.

Churchill's sudden interest in the situation was encouraging, however. The compromise had advantages. Churchill was convincing when he said the British would not yield control of Bomber Command, and this would all but rule out direct command of the Eighth Air Force. The term "supervision" offered a way around this, however, and it established SHAEF primacy. British confidence in Tedder was encouraging, and the idea of direct negotiations with Portal was more promising than continuing the existing liaison committee arrangements. Eisenhower was not sure that Portal supported the transport plan, but he had reason to question whether Portal would support Eighth Air Force proposals for following up BIG WEEK.

Eisenhower returned to Hayes Lodge that night uneasy and depressed. Would Arnold and Marshall go along? Eisenhower was apparently concerned that Churchill's procedure would break down and accomplish little more than convince the Americans that Eisenhower was too reliant on the British and unable to withstand Churchill's pressure. Afterward Eisenhower told Butcher about his threat to "go home" and British hypersensitivity on Bomber Command. But time was ebbing away, and shortly afterward Eisenhower conferred with Tedder and urged him to open talks with Portal at once, and to prepare an outline of the SHAEF plan for CCS approval, telling him it was essential to act before the Prime Minister was "in this thing with both feet."

In the next several days, as Tedder took charge of the negotiations, Eisenhower faced in-house problems. Five months earlier, Leigh-Mallory had assumed the portfolio of Allied Air commander in chief in the expectation of supervising the overall air effort. Despite misgivings, Leigh-Mallory's AEAF staff had pushed the transport plan. Predictably, Leigh-Mallory did not warm to the idea of stepping aside, though easing matters was the fact that Leigh-Mallory was a British appointment and had the British to blame for his tacit demotion.

Leigh-Mallory persisted, and clumsily submitted a long list of SHAEF targets to the BCOS on his own, all of which were disapproved politely except for a raid set by Portal on Trappes in the western suburbs of Paris to test "the feasibility of attack on rail centers." Butcher noted Eisenhower's chagrin. "Just when I think I have the air problem licked," Eisenhower complained, "someone else's feelings are hurt and I have another problem to settle."

For a week, Tedder and Portal met daily to hammer out the wording of a directive to supersede the January directive. Anxious to narrow the issues, Eisenhower decided to excuse Bomber Command tacitly by instructing Tedder to accept BCOS reservations attached to any targeting directive. "Reservations would exist in practice upon the power of my command," he told Tedder, "whether called Supreme or not." In doing so, Eisenhower gambled fatefully on Portal's tact and willingness to meet Tedder halfway.

By the first week of March the "little blitz" on London came to an end. Its petulance and ineffectiveness magnified the dimensions of the Allied victory in the minds of analysts at Uxbridge, Stanmore and Whitehall who tallied the results of the BIG WEEK raids from reconnaissance photographs and after battle reports. It would later be estimated that for a week 90 percent of Germany's tire production had temporarily come to a halt. An estimated 70 percent of the then operating airframe plants were permanently destroyed. Raids on synthetic-oil plants were effective. The Luftwaffe had been up in force to defend the airframe, oil and steel plants, and had sustained heavy losses—estimated at 1,200 aircraft, a blow particularly in the loss of trained pilots. Subsequently the Eighth Air Force learned that the Luftwaffe had slashed pilot training that month from 260 to 110 hours in order to expedite replacements, which was bound to degrade Luftwaffe performance over time.

"The German fighter force will never be as strong again in the foreseeable future as it was two weeks ago," Spaatz wrote on March 5 in the preamble to a document spelling out the details of an Eighth Air Force plan to attack German synthetic-oil refineries. Even at peak strength the Luftwaffe had not effectively resisted daylight precision bombing of Germany from end to end. In Spaatz's opinion, what in January had been conjecture was "now a certainty"—that Germany was "powerless to prevent the destruction of any system of targets . . . selected . . . as our real aim."

Spaatz's memo of March 5 opened the month-long debate over targeting. In it, Spaatz proposed a new set of POINTBLANK priorities for a campaign aimed at the critical petroleum and synthetic-oil industry which would call on 50 percent of the strategic bombers based in England. In the memorandum (classified for thirty years), Spaatz as a courtesy requested Eisenhower's "concurrence" in a program that "must favor a RANKIN," or a German political and military collapse. Two factors in his opinion could vitiate this opportunity—sudden adverse weather, and redundant targeting that would usher in the law of diminishing returns.

For the "oil plan," Spaatz offered sweeping claims: 23 synthetic-oil plants and 31 oil refineries processed 90 percent of German oil stocks, all identified and confirmed by air intelligence. With fifteen good visual days for the Eighth Air Force, and ten days for the Fifteenth Air Force, he estimated that overall German oil production could be cut by 50 percent, leaving the military operating under drastic economies, 33 percent short of minimum needs. Spaatz envisioned German armored formations frozen in place on all fronts, which in his opinion would be "an important factor in the decision of the German High Command to continue resistance after D-Day." Additionally, attacks on the synthetic-oil plants and refineries would draw in German air defenses and permit a strong secondary effort on ball-bearing plants, rubber factories and airframe plants that would be capable of slashing the output in each category by 65 to 80 percent.

Predictably, SHAEF technical experts were skeptical of the "oil plan," and the BIG WEEK findings. The strategic air forces commanders by now had developed an irrepressible habit of overpromising. There were detectable weaknesses in the fine print; several of the primary targets listed were synthetic plants in the Ruhr, by-passed earlier by the Eighth Air Force because of smoke, haze, heavy ground-based anti-aircraft fire and other problems not solved by the P-47 and P-51. The deep targets south and southeast of Berlin were deemed highly hazardous. On the ninth, Tedder and Portal agreed on a draft directive assigning Tedder as Eisenhower's "agent" to "supervise" Spaatz, Harris and Leigh-Mallory. Eisenhower's authority would be "subject to intervention by the CCS if necessary to impose additional tasks on him" and the entire procedure would be reviewed after OVERLORD. Finally, Tedder and Portal stipulated that the time was rapidly approaching when objectives in Germany "must give way to the needs of OVERLORD."

But the procedure would not become effective until Eisenhower, as CCS agent for OVERLORD, and Portal as CCS agent for POINTBLANK, agreed on target priorities. On this point, Portal and Tedder failed to make progress. Portal was personally skeptical that the transport plan would be effective, though he indicated no real enthusiasm for Spaatz's alternative, and the thrust of his doubts was the hitherto unspoken problem of French casualties in the bombing of French civilian targets.

In any event, Portal and Tedder eliminated a number of collateral points that might have been raised to disrupt the negotiations. Command procedures, though cumbersome, were resolved consistent with Eisenhower's determination to bring the U.S. Eighth Air Force under the SHAEF umbrella, albeit under his "supervision." Issues, such as the location of Anglo-

American Air staff conference sites, and who would attend and in what capacity, were tossed aside. The stipulation about the impending priority of OVERLORD was a first and significant step toward orienting the air discussions away from hushed talk at High Wycombe about the "strategic revolution" heralded by BIG WEEK, and toward the problems of the inevitable invasion.

On March 10, Eisenhower decided to bring the air dispute to a boil. At the Supreme Commander's conference in Norfolk House that morning, he chaired a discussion on a wide-ranging agenda, including a proposed ban on diplomatic communications in the British Isles; French civil affairs and SHAEF authority to deal with De Gaulle's FCNL; ANVIL; and the Tedder-Portal accord, which Eisenhower endorsed. To force the issue, Eisenhower directed Tedder "that the time . . . has come for . . . operations of the 9th Air Force to be directed toward the preparations for . . . OVERLORD."

Afterward Leigh-Mallory issued orders to General Lewis Brereton of the Ninth Air Force, with copies forwarded to Spaatz, declaring that it was "the wish of the Supreme Commander" that the Ninth Air Force, hitherto engaged in escorting POINTBLANK missions, revert to the exclusive control of the commander, Allied Expeditionary Air Force. Specifically, AEAF P-38, P-47 and P-51 fighters would no longer be escorting bombers of the Eighth Air Force over Germany, but would be escorting Ninth Air Force bombing operations on French rail targets. Leigh-Mallory assigned General Brereton seventy-eight transport targets in northwest France, Belgium and west Germany. As a "second priority," the Ninth Air Force was to support POINTBLANK "indirectly" by striking targets with "maximum diversionary effect" in France and Belgium. Leigh-Mallory's action served two purposes: first, it provoked a dispute between Spaatz and the Ninth Air Force to be brought before Tedder, Eisenhower and Portal for adjudication, thereby activating the Churchill procedure; second, Leigh-Mallory might gain several days of uninterrupted time to conduct a number of additional trial runs in Belgium and France to rebut adverse JIC findings on the Trappes raid.

Spaatz promptly challenged Leigh-Mallory's actions. In a letter to Eisenhower, Spaatz conceded that the "diversionary targets" assigned Ninth Air Force medium bombers might engage German fighters, but noted that Leigh-Mallory had failed to coordinate the timing of these missions with Eighth Air Force Headquarters. Spaatz complained that Leigh-Mallory lacked authority to reassign Ninth Air Force P-47s and P-51s in light of the CCS directive in January that defined the primary mission of the Ninth Air Force as the "support [of] our heavy bomber operations." By the twentieth, Eisenhower had suspended the Ninth Air Force attacks and "ruled" in favor of Spaatz. Portal set a review of the matter at the Air Ministry at the end of the month.

SETTLING IN

Six weeks had passed since Eisenhower's arrival in London, and the invasion vigil had now begun. In late February the gathering American forces continued to arrive in England at the rate of 150,000 per month to join their British, Canadian, French and Polish comrades in the interminable wait for the decision to go that would come with the right combination of predicted weather, tide and moon.

Meanwhile, SHAEF moved from London to the Eighth Air Force cantonment in Bushy Park, in the London suburb of Kingston, code-named Widewing. There the Eighth Air Force Technical Air Staff had drawn plans for the now routine 1,000-bomber daylight raids over Germany. Eisenhower had hoped that proximity of the two staffs would promote informal coordination, but he was mainly eager to set up camp in an area free from the distractions of London and BCOS supervision. When Smith told him about the grumbling among the staff over the move to a suburb, Eisenhower vowed that he would go to Widewing "alone" if necessary, and again complained around the office about the "military tendency to become entrenched in one's location." The move, held up for four weeks, proceeded in stages and became official on Sunday, March 5, the day Spaatz submitted the oil plan. The shift to Widewing, complete by April 1, marked the inauguration of a new era at SHAEF.

The monster complex, home base for 1,600 U.S. and 1,229 British officers, consisted of a cluster of Nissen huts, a PX building and tents under dingy camouflage in a large park barricaded from the suburban village adjoining it by a ten-foot stone wall. SHAEF set up offices in the "C" Building. The "G" staffs for administration, operations, intelligence and supply set themselves up along a long dim corridor. The cement floors were bare, and the offices damp and unheated, obliging the staff to wear long socks and long underwear. The mild discomfort and austerity at Widewing set the desired tone for the workday. While he liked a warm, friendly atmosphere away from the office, Eisenhower insisted on strict, smooth-running procedures at headquarters.

The circumstances were ideal for organizing a staff capable of concentrating on the problems of invasion. The order of the day was routine, predictability, collegiality, loyalty to the principle of Allied unity and loyalty to SHAEF, which, in time, would become an entity capable of weathering the twists and turns of mood and emotion in the Allied camp and make its weight felt in Allied councils. In March 1944, SHAEF powers remained a subject of sharp debate and delegations of authority would come gradually and sparingly. At Widewing Eisenhower bided his time; as a staff member would later put it, he was a "watchman waiting to see where any trouble military or political arose."

Shortly after the move, Brigadier General Kenneth Strong arrived from

AFHQ to rejoin SHAEF as Eisenhower's G-2, a position he had first assumed in Algiers in the wake of the Kasserine Pass setback in February 1943. In his memoir, *Intelligence at the Top,* Strong described Widewing and the procedures Eisenhower adopted to mold American and British officers and men into a single effective unit.

The stress was on calm efficiency. A sharp military bearing and scrupulous care for personal appearance was mandatory, including ties, shined shoes, military tucks, and pressed clothes in all offices. As Strong recalled, several British colleagues found adjusting to the "Continental" practices at SHAEF difficult at first, but most eventually found them "simple to understand and effective." An unaccustomed feature of the staff system was delegation. Through Smith, Eisenhower allowed the staff to make decisions and trusted subordinates to make the right ones. The mixed senior staff assumed responsibility for the hiring and firing of American and British officers alike. In this respect, the heads of the "G" staff divisions at SHAEF enjoyed much wider individual responsibility than was customary in the British system.

The tone of staff operations was "Continental," but the goal was collegiality. Eisenhower instituted a system of American coffee breaks in the morning and British tea in the afternoon. Some felt that the weight of Eisenhower's sanctions fell heaviest on the Americans, over whom he had direct administrative power. Indeed, Patton and Bradley would question Eisenhower's "even-handedness" in all aspects of SHAEF, claiming he bent too far backward to appease the British. But in Strong's opinion, Eisenhower's procedures bolstered morale and "unity of command"—as he put it, Eisenhower was determined that unity be the reality of his command, not just "a pious aspiration thinly disguising national jealousies, ambitions and recriminations of high-ranking officers."

Eisenhower's problem in maintaining American-British unity in the military staffs and commands has often been minimized or overlooked altogether. But the task in 1944 had grown more complicated after two years of war, not less. In England the frightfulness of standing alone in the 1940–42 period was a fading memory, and so the "peaceful invasion" of the arriving American troops seemed less welcome than before. And with British safety assured, the American presence was more a reminder of the compromises the British had been pushed into in order to survive, and of the steady loss of British influence in Allied councils, revealed emphatically in late 1943 at Teheran. Indeed, U.S. ground forces in France would eventually predominate in the invasion force. The American Eighth and Fifteenth Air Force dominated the combined bombing offensive. The Americans asserted the dominant claims of OVERLORD, and attempted, in British eyes, to extend the "tyranny" of OVERLORD by subordinating the British-dominated Italian theater, facts known to few but sensed by the population at large.

In retrospect, Churchill's policy toward the Americans, which has been subject to many interpretations, seems inseparable from the crisis in British morale occasioned by British awareness of their dependence on foreign help, a problem Churchill recognized early on. The consequences of this realization had been impressed on Eisenhower in North Africa. There, Eisenhower had learned that he could discount British proposals on occasion, but that he would ignore the deeper sources of British dissatisfaction at his peril.

Accordingly, Eisenhower directed the Americans to adopt the manners of guests—a policy that bred some resentment in American ranks and a certain amount of patronizing criticism of Eisenhower by the British, criticism that Strong rejected as "ill-informed." American battle morale was a factor in the policy. As Eisenhower saw it, an extra ounce of courtesy never hurt, and in practical terms, courtesy, in minimizing incidents, would tend to shield the American command and the GIs from unnecessary British criticisms, which would reinforce the GIs' dissatisfaction.

Eisenhower's attention to the problem was well known. He approved procedures for all American commands that emphasized discretion and courtesy. Every soldier received a booklet instructing him on British customs and habits. He ordered division commanders to encourage troops to tour the war-torn areas in the vicinity of American bases, and to be sure that GIs kept a neat appearance in public. Commanders were to discourage their troops from frequenting local bars, and act sternly against houliganism and brawls. ETO encouraged servicemen to use the USO and Red Cross facilities, and to invest surplus pay in war bonds to avoid antagonisms bred by higher GI pay.

Many stories attested to Eisenhower's tireless attention to good relations between the American and British peoples. One story, often told, involved an American Army officer accused of provoking a pub fight over a woman by calling a British soldier "a British S.O.B." When the officer defended himself, Eisenhower is alleged to have replied, "Calling him an S.O.B. was OK, but you called him a British S.O.B," and to have ordered the officer sent home by slow boat and demoted. Years later, Butcher doubted the story and others like it, but the tale circulated widely with Eisenhower's approval.

Eisenhower occasionally answered letters on the problem and took time out to enlist both "home fronts" in the cause of better relations. In February a British woman had written to complain about an unnamed American officer who insisted on being billeted in a home where he could have a private bath. Eisenhower thanked her, and assured her that the "colonel to whom you refer would have a most uncomfortable ten minutes if he should ever express, in my hearing, his disinclination to accept proffered hospitality unless a private bath were involved."

In another case a British citizen wrote to describe an incident aboard a bus in Hertfordshire: an American officer had gotten on a bus smoking a cigar and an Englishman had told him that smoking was not allowed on the bus. The writer quoted the American officer as replying, "Don't be so typically English; you ought to be in an institution." Eisenhower again thanked his correspondent, and assured him he was "completely right in assuming that the matter of maintaining a firm Anglo-American partnership for the purpose of winning this war lies close to my heart." Eisenhower asked him to make an effort to identify such offenders in the future. Letters poured in from the American home front also, offering suggestions and seeking advice. In thanking a sixth-grade class in Roanoke, Virginia, for his copy of "The Last Will and Testament of Adolf Hitler," Eisenhower, as requested, described what a sixth grader could do on behalf of loved ones serving in England: first, to pledge allegiance to the flag each Monday; second, to say "a short prayer" for the safety and welfare of the fighting men of the U.N. throughout the world; third, to work after school to purchase war savings stamps; fourth, to urge their parents to buy war bonds; fifth, to write friends in England and assure them "that everyone at home is working and sacrificing all the time to help win this war in the shortest possible time"; sixth, to learn about government programs for saving scrap metal; and finally, to study U.S. history from the beginning in order to "appreciate the rights and privileges our country has given us and so that he would always be ready to meet his own obligations to our country whether in war or peace. . . ."

Coalition politics was a full-time job. At the day-to-day command level, coalition politics meant that decisions were collegial, arrived at after extended consultations with both sides, often at the cost of satisfying clear-cut results, to the dismay of both camps. But the diffusion of authority in the Allied high command was a reality, and Eisenhower suspected that categorical assertions of his authority would only expose how tenuous it was. For better or worse, policy-making would involve surmounting American and British vetoes at every step, in addition to the usual problems inherent in running a large military organization.

Accordingly, Eisenhower indulged his more flamboyant American and British subordinates—namely, Patton and Montgomery. Montgomery was particularly troublesome. "The introverted product of his mother's perfectionist discipline in the Victorian household of his father, the Bishop of Tasmania," as historian Russell Weigley has described him, General Bernard Law Montgomery was a man who rarely admitted error. By temperament, he was a disruptive element in an Allied command. Like his mentor, Brooke, Montgomery made little attempt to conceal his sense of superiority over the inexperienced Americans, including Eisenhower, who had missed service in France in 1918 and had become acquainted with strategy, tactics and command belatedly in the campaigns of 1942-43 by virtue of promotions earned by staff work, not trial in battle.

Only Patton seemed immune to this sort of carping, despite his anti-British outbursts and his well-known distaste for Montgomery. Patton was popular in London, partly because of his cultivation of aristocratic manners, which scandalized his fellow Americans, but mainly because of his record of heroism in World War I, which seemed to set him apart from the ordinary run of American officers. By contrast, British assessments of Eisenhower were more reserved. He seemed youthful, a learner and "eager to cast aside conventions and get on with the job," as Strong put it. But his inexperience mattered. As his son, John, later put it, by now Eisenhower's inexperience "was less significant than it seemed," and a professional soldier would readily have agreed that "little connection exists between the command of an infantry regiment on the battlefield and planning for a massive amphibious operation." However, appraisals were not always so reasoned, and "Eisenhower would have given a great deal for the prestige of having been shot at."

Complicating matters with Montgomery, Eisenhower's request for General Alexander was generally known. This accentuated Montgomery's stature and implied that he was selected partly to keep the Americans uncomfortable. Montgomery's "indiscretions" came naturally, but many seemed to be deliberate acts of official discourtesy as well. Eisenhower deplored the troubles provoked by Montgomery's fractiousness, but Montgomery's charter at SHAEF, backed by Brooke and Churchill, was no less secure than Eisenhower's charter backed by Marshall and Roosevelt, a fact known to both men. In their own fashion, however, Eisenhower and Montgomery got along. At the working level, Eisenhower and Montgomery, under rival pressures from home governments, were cast as powerful antagonists and almost obliged to act as such. At the same time, both were aware of their interdependence, a fact perceived by Smith and Montgomery's "peace making" chief of staff General Francis "Freddie" de Guingand, who time after time intervened to retrieve seemingly impossible situations between the two men.

Coalition politics also involved intricate dealings with the CCS, Marshall and Churchill. According to Strong, it was in his relation with his superiors that Eisenhower demonstrated his real mastery. Strong would contrast Eisenhower with Von Moltke of the German high command in World War I whose narrow professionalism had rendered him unfit to deal with the Kaiser and the German War Cabinet. Eisenhower was a veteran of War Department politics, and this equipped him to stand his ground or concede to superiors as the situation required. Eisenhower's authority would always be nebulous. Technically, he was accountable to the Combined Chiefs of Staff in Washington. But as a draftsman of the CCS proposals at ARCADIA, Eisenhower knew as well as anyone else that relations between the CCS, field commands and both governments were undefined.

The CCS drew up recommendations for Churchill and Roosevelt, who acted "jointly" through it. As a practical matter, Churchill and Roosevelt had recognized that formal accord on many details would be impossible and undesirable—therefore, the two men resolved to delegate many of the details of strategy making to the CCS, who in turn delegated powers to Eisenhower. Significantly, there was no provision for failure to agree about military and diplomatic questions, and so the CCS procedure was strongly biased against second thoughts. Indeed, short of a breakdown of the whole process, formal delegations of power by the CCS would be practically irreversible, a factor in the ongoing debates over ANVIL and Eisenhower's powers over the strategic air forces. Eisenhower was asking both sides to make all but irreversible commitments, mindful that grants of authority would necessarily leave wide room for interpretation, and the job of interpreting policy necessarily involved day-by-day consultation with Marshall and Churchill, though occasionally he would act on his own without consultation, as he had done in the Darlan case. Indeed, when to act on his own and when to consult higher authority had often been Eisenhower's most crucial decision, and would be again.

Complicating matters, the Anglo-American alliance was about to admit a third partner. By March 1944, Eisenhower knew he had not left French problems behind him in Algiers as he had hoped. Invasion planning involved hammering out a policy for liberated France, and achieving a working relationship with De Gaulle's French Committee of National Liberation (FCNL) in a sea of conflicting pressures. Roosevelt remained suspicious of De Gaulle, who was determined to carry out a policy of self-determination for postwar France; he was wary of trouble with De Gaulle while the U.S. Army fought on French soil, and wary of provoking premature Russian moves in Poland by measures perceived as "imposing" De Gaulle on the French people. Meanwhile the British had become doubly eager to recognize De Gaulle, not only as the guarantor of a strong non-Communist postwar France to offset the growing power of the Russians and Americans, but as a partner and close ally in inter-Allied dealings with the Americans.

American-French relations deteriorated, especially after Teheran. There, high-level negotiations had taken place over military operations to liberate France, but were conducted without French representation. The spectacle seemed to offer convincing proof for De Gaulle that the Allies would not be willing to put up with an effective French authority, at least for the duration of the war. Likewise, the conference was proof that the Allies intended to settle the crucial postwar issues, including issues of vital interest to France, before the peace conference, not afterward.

In the circumstances, American insistence on democratic elections before fully recognizing French authority seemed to be more than unawareness of French problems; indeed, it signified distrust at best, and at worst an intention to thwart a French recovery. By January, De Gaulle struggled against a superpower "condominium," an unintended but all-powerful system of American-Russian direction over postwar spheres in Europe implied by Stalin's designs on Poland and his casual equation of France and Poland at the conference. De Gaulle was said to be braced for a repetition of the Darlan affair—Allied military rule over France through discredited institutions intended to deny the French any opportunity to restore French society or political life.

Churchill sharply disagreed with De Gaulle's assessment of American motives, but he was concerned that Britain not be blamed for the American non-policy. Churchill felt that Russian policy in Poland was a foregone conclusion, and he was convinced that to abstain in France risked a Communist takeover there or permanent alienation of the non-Communists. For the moment, the Prime Minister deferred to Roosevelt's sense of timing, but eventual British recognition of the FCNL was, in his mind, inevitable.

As for the timing of Allied recognition, the Soviets would not be bystanders. With influence over a large and subservient Communist party in France, Moscow was capable of easing or disrupting De Gaulle's rise to power and the SHAEF occupation. The future of France as such was a matter of indifference to Stalin, and his support for De Gaulle had nothing to do with approval of the Free French. Indeed, at Teheran, Stalin had scorned De Gaulle's pretensions of French greatness and his bid to gain a place for France in Allied councils, several times remarking that he regarded Marshal Pétain as representing the true soul of France. The basis for Stalin's proffered exchange was obvious: Soviet support for De Gaulle, along with a quiet Communist underground, in exchange for reciprocal cooperation in silencing the pro-London Poles when the time came to reconstitute Poland by "democratic elements" living in Moscow. And even if the issue was academic, De Gaulle flaunted his Soviet backing to bolster his prestige and bargaining power with Washington. Churchill, meanwhile, trained the spotlight on the Polish problem, staking out a position that evolved into a general condemnation of settlements that excluded exile authority in the name of democracy.

Eisenhower was thrust into the middle of all this. "Recognition" was beyond his power, so he was limited in dealings with the FCNL, though he considered it the only vehicle through which to deal with French problems. Eisenhower wanted to accommodate Churchill and the British, but as always, he approached the problem in military terms. The military realities were, as Eisenhower saw it, (1) an Allied occupation of France, however efficient, would be a waste of Allied manpower; (2) French fighting divisions should be used for this purpose and in the battle of France; (3) the Allies needed the cooperation of the French Resistance, which only De Gaulle could arrange. Eisenhower had qualms about dealing with an assertive French authority, but reports from France forecast imminent civil war between the collaboration and Resistance forces. French civilian authority would be essential to police the area, to assist SHAEF in maintaining the security of land-based communications, and to provide civilian labor so that the Allied armies would not have to become garrison troops. Finally, De Gaulle's claim to represent France was impressive and would probably bear up. He dominated "the external resistance," with uncontested control of Lebanon, Syria, Algeria, Morocco, Chad and Dakar. De Gaulle commanded the French divisions in North Africa slated for ANVIL, and the FCNL had exclusive contact with the "army of the shadows," the French underground, estimated to number 150,000 men under arms. This fact alone made him indispensable in organizing the short-term reconstruction of France, which De Gaulle intended to do by taking every opportunity to assert French participation in the liberation of France.

Eisenhower steadily incorporated the FCNL into SHAEF affairs. By Christmas he had won De Gaulle's trust and his agreement to subordinate seven French divisions to AFHQ without a seat on the CCS in exchange for a "major role" in the forthcoming liberation of France. In Washington he had tactfully pressed the dual problems of FCNL representation at SHAEF and civil affairs planning for France after the liberation, which required that some kind of agreement be made between the Allies and De Gaulle. Eisenhower also gained the impression that the President, despite his aversion to De Gaulle, was biding his time and would endorse gradual steps that would be justified on military grounds just as he had in the Darlan affair. Eisenhower, back in London, began to pressure the CCS for clarification of his authority to deal with the FCNL.

Progress was slow. On January 14 Hull notified Eden that official U.S. policy was for SHAEF to exercise complete military control of France and that Washington would refuse to negotiate with De Gaulle over civil affairs or extend recognition to the FCNL. On January 19 Eisenhower cabled the Combined Chiefs of Staff disclosing that it was essential that plans be crystallized concerning civil affairs in France, and urging that De Gaulle be allowed to designate a representative with whom Eisenhower could enter into immediate negotiations. Roosevelt's response via McCloy was to authorize Eisenhower to deal "informally" with representatives of the FCNL on matters affecting the Resistance, a grant that Eisenhower construed liberally. On January 22 he met with General François d'Astier de la Vigerie, military representative of the FCNL. Eisenhower agreed to rearm Resistance groups with SHAEF assets and place senior French officers on his staff as advisers. Eisenhower told D'Astier he expected to have a French division of 7,500 to 10,000 men take part in the liberation of France and urged intensification of effort for tactical and political collaboration.

Then the trouble started. Following up, D'Astier sent Eisenhower a letter on February 7 sketching broad lines of possible action by French Resistance, including sabotage and small attacks in battle zones and sabotage in German zones of communications. D'Astier asked Eisenhower to select zones for Resistance activities and specify where he envisioned attacks and what arms could be expected from SHAEF. This raised a difficult point; Eisenhower could not disclose the objective of OVERLORD to D'Astier or to any representatives of the FCNL. Mutual confidence on this point would become the supreme test of French-Allied relations.

Pessimists worried that the French army under the FCNL might actually turn into a hostile force during the battle of France, a reason for equipping the ANVIL divisions and General Leclerc's 1st French Division with U.S. arms. It was not far-fetched to imagine that De Gaulle, bitterly anti-American over Roosevelt's lack of support in 1940, actually opposed Allied liberation of his country.

But the feeling was that even assuming that De Gaulle was reliable, the FCNL was not. A number of leading figures of the FCNL had lived in the unoccupied territory of southern France before TORCH. Several had been recruited from the Vichy colonial administrations. The attitudes and purposes of many FCNL members were complex and unpredictable. German intelligence had easily penetrated the group, and since it was impossible to know who among the French could be trusted, no one would be trusted, including De Gaulle. In March the unprecedented ban on all diplomatic communications emanating from the British Isles was aimed at the French as well as the Russians.

Meanwhile, French participation could be kept to a minimum. The British and Americans would coordinate most of the details of French participation in OVERLORD. SHAEF organized men, transport and aid for Resistance groups funded by the British. Resistance activities would include sabotage and terrorism confined to areas believed to be battle zones. Prior to D-Day, the task of the Resistance was to supply information on German troop movement and to conduct sabotage of railways. As the saying went, the value of Resistance work was to be considered a "bonus" and not to be taken into account in operational planning.

Since D-Day could not be disclosed, military talks eventually broke down. As for French military participation, the French insisted on the right to by-pass SHAEF and to intercede with the U. S. and British governments —in lieu of CCS representation. The Allies refused to admit the French to the CCS, or to accord any special rights. Negotiations proceeded under a directive, sent March 15, giving Eisenhower permission to consult with the FCNL but specifying that this involved no recognition of the FCNL and that in return the committee must guarantee the re-establishment of all French liberties. Under the directive, France, unlike Norway, Belgium and Holland, was to be governed as a military zone, which was logical, since France was going to be a battlefield. But the issue had passed beyond logic. Compounding the ambiguities, Roosevelt revealed this to a mid-March press conference, remarking that France would be "Eisenhower's business" and that he would deal with the FCNL groups "depending upon conditions."

In April, declaring that no French authority would be valid unless acting in the name of the FCNL, De Gaulle would move decisively to establish his undisputed upper hand over postwar France. In early April, he would dismiss Giraud from all posts, assume personal command of the army and convene a provisional Consultative Assembly in Algiers to begin work on economic plans and the post-Vichy legal code, on the theory that Vichy, as the first government in French history to cede sovereignty to a foreign power, was illegal, and its official laws and decrees were criminal and of no effect.

On April 9, Secretary of State Cordell Hull would issue a statement, which Eisenhower interpreted as a softening of the American position, on establishing civil authority in France. Eisenhower requested CCS approval to initiate conversations with General Pierre Joseph Koenig, D'Astier's replacement as the FCNL representative. While waiting for approval, talks would resume on an "informal" basis, for a while, carefully skirting the political issue. But almost immediately the FCNL would order Koenig to discontinue the talks in retaliation for the diplomatic ban.

Gradually, diplomatic concerns began to fade. At four o'clock each morning, the night duty officers briefed the oncoming intelligence staff watch on overnight military developments; the movement of German air, naval and army units in the previous twenty-four hours; news from Italy and the eastern front. At seven-fifteen the staff would gather these reports and cables from Washington, London and Army Group Headquarters and brief the morning staff meeting chaired by Smith, which included General Leigh-Mallory, General Harold "Pinky" Bull, G-3 Operations, Air Marshal James Robb, General Humfrey Gale, and General Kenneth Strong as SHAEF G-2. Routinely, each officer reported on the activities in his respective "G" departments, and the staff decided what to present to Eisenhower.

Eisenhower would arrive around nine and the staff would join him, Tedder and occasionally Spaatz in conference. Eisenhower was all business —"keen and analytical," as a colleague once put it. He exhibited "phenomenal quick mindedness" and a capacity to "shift gears with lightning speed from one subject to another, ready to digest and deal with a whole stream of complex issues."

The military briefings came first. Years later General Strong recalled Eisenhower's practice of requiring oral briefings instead of written reports, a technique to avoid being overwhelmed with detail—for fear that something of importance might slip by in a stack of papers. Moreover, Eisenhower could judge the demeanor of the reporting officer for signs of doubt often not conveyed in a written report, and of overreliance on special sources of intelligence, a problem ushered in by the revolution of information technology since 1939.

One such special source was ULTRA, the code name for the supersecret intelligence gleaned from the deciphering of the German Enigma machine by British intelligence agencies. ULTRA was one of the most closely held secrets of the war, which was finally revealed in the spring of 1974 with the lifting of the thirty-year ban on disclosure. Historian and former ULTRA analyst F. W. Winterbotham's *The Ultra Secret,* published that year, would describe how the British broke the German diplomatic and military codes and speculate on ULTRA's impact on the course of the war.

Four years before, British intelligence had penetrated the puzzle of the German Enigma machine used for transmission of encrypted diplomatic and military message traffic. The technical feat had involved the construction of a "universal machine" that could "imitate or interpret the performance of each of the thousands of Enigmas that would come to exist in the Wehrmacht . . . to extrapolate the constant keying procedure that every major German command ordered every day and every night, year in and year out; and capable of making an almost infinite number of mathematical calculations at speeds far beyond human ability."

The early work had been accomplished in August of 1939 by a team of British mathematicians and cryptanalysts working in a secluded Victorian mansion called Bletchley Park. By 1942 the Bletchley group had cracked the German code in its entirety. Decrypting machines, the so-called Bronze Goddesses, decoded top-level German communications on military plans, and the very highest level traffic from OKW (Oberkommando der Wehrmacht)* to commanders, political dispatches to governors, field commanders' reports to OKW and Luftwaffe signals. A team of intelligence analysts decided on the priority of the ULTRA data, and on who should be allowed to see the messages.

All ULTRA messages were destroyed on delivery, so there are no records of Eisenhower's day-to-day use of ULTRA intercepts. Winterbotham pointed out that Allied commanders reacted in different ways to ULTRA. Montgomery "resented" it, while Patton saw ULTRA as a "new tool" for aiding the swift advance of his armies. "Those with rigid ideas on orthodox methods of fighting an enemy seemed to think it was not quite right to know what the enemy was going to do," he wrote. "Those, on the other hand, with more flexible minds were ready to take every advantage the information offered them." According to Winterbotham, Eisenhower, Spaatz, Alexander and Patton were commanders with the flexibility to take advantage of this new intelligence source.

There were inherent limitations on the use of ULTRA. Corroborating evidence was necessary, because at no point could anyone be sure the Germans were not on to the penetration of the Enigma system. All intelligence sources were somewhat susceptible to the inherent problem that intelligence evaluation would be corrupted and the results misleading be-

*The German high command.

cause of a tendency in intelligence staffs to confine their inquiries to questions the high command wanted answered, and to reach conclusions that would confirm those already reached at the command level. But in late winter of 1944, ULTRA provided important details of day-to-day exchanges between OKW and Paris which shed light on German priorities and strength along the Atlantic Wall all carefully checked with underground sources and reconnaissance. ULTRA tracked German knowledge of Allied intentions and preparations, and intercepts revealed that Allied plans were the subject of an intense debate at all levels of the German high command, as portentous as the debate in London.

The debate pitted two of the most renowned personalities of the Wehrmacht—Field Marshal Gerd von Rundstedt, OB West, and the upstart General Erwin Rommel of desert-warfare fame. Both were well known to the Allies. Rundstedt, the austere Black Knight of the Prussian Junker class, remained Germany's ranking field marshal not yet identified with a major defeat, and a crucial link in the strained relationship between the regular army and the Nazi party. Von Rundstedt had planned the lightning campaign against Poland in 1939, and commanded an army group during the thirty-day rout of Marshal Beck's Polish forces. In September 1940, Von Rundstedt had commanded Army Group A in France South, which later conquered Kiev, Kharkov and Rostov before he retired after a clash with Hitler, whom he reportedly held in disdain.

Recalled three months after Pearl Harbor when German army intelligence warned of a lightning American-British thrust across the Channel, Von Rundstedt had taken charge of devising a solution to the problem of defending an extended 3,000-mile coastline with an average force of fifty divisions, usually newly forming or understrength and refitting after service in Russia. In this role, Von Rundstedt had grown defeatist and tired, but he had stayed on, a symbol of long-ago German triumphs in France, and of Wehrmacht support for Hitler.

As the practitioner of "blitzkrieg," Von Rundstedt was a proponent of strategies of fluid defense. His doctrines for over two years stressed containment of the Allied beachhead, then destruction by counteroffensive. A seeming exception to this doctrine was Von Rundstedt's orthodox emphasis on the defense of Calais, a fact that implied a lack of confidence in his ability to call on strong reserves. Another explanation, further suggested in several recent histories, may have been poor German army intelligence, which caused the Germans to exaggerate Allied strength in Britain, hence Allied abilities to launch both a frontal assault at Calais and diversionary landings.

But in either case, the Germans would not risk exposing Calais, a vital position that served variously as a communications link between Germany and forward positions elsewhere in France, a collecting ground for reserves, and a rear line in the event of an Allied success west of the Seine. Unless assured of wholesale reinforcement from Russia, Von Rundstedt knew that the bulk of his reserves would be tied up there. In a sense, therefore, Calais was the key to German intentions: to the degree that Calais figured in German planning, the Allies could form an estimate of how confident Von Rundstedt was about being reinforced.

Without the prospect of major reinforcements, Von Rundstedt's doctrines seemed obsolescent. He would lack troops and air strength to make a success of ideas applicable perhaps in 1940–1941, but less so now, especially with Germany's loss of air superiority. And, by March, it was not only questionable that Von Rundstedt would have adequate reserves, but that he would have control over the reserves he had. All this, despite Hitler's new priority for the west outlined in a November 1943 directive and signaled in his New Year's Day proclamation. Rommel, committed to a more aggressive policy of defending France at the beaches, was ascendant, which meant that coastal defense would be dangerously upgraded but also that German command arrangements would leave no one effectively in charge of the invasion front, a hopeful development.

In this context, the combination of Von Rundstedt's notions of fluid defense and Rommel's effort to upgrade the coastal defenses suggested that the Germans would attempt to improvise a holding action pending eventual reinforcement. When would reinforcements be available? No one knew, but Von Rundstedt's skill and experience in past campaigns commanded respect, and a short-term strategy of containment appeared to be within his means. The timing and strength of reserves sent to France would tell the story, and to a lesser degree the ability of the high command to respond efficiently to the invasion.

In December, Rommel had made a highly publicized tour of the Atlantic Wall, the first step toward supplanting Von Rundstedt and implementing a more economical defense strategy of repelling invasion at the coast. Like Von Rundstedt, Rommel was a well-known and respected adversary. Like Von Rundstedt, he was said to favor negotiations with the West, after the Germans proved their mastery over the Allies by repelling the invasion.

Accordingly, Rommel was determined to implement changes and to infuse the command with energy and determination. Moreover, as one of the few officers of the German high command with considerable experience in Africa and Italy, he had high respect for Allied fighting ability. He warned his colleagues that the invasion would be a battle of an altogether different character from that on the Russian front. Salerno, in his opinion, demonstrated that in view of Allied naval and air superiority, the Wehrmacht lacked the ability to organize a successful counteroffensive against a bridgehead once it was established. Hence, Rommel emphasized the urgency of defeating the invasion at the beaches in the first twenty-four hours, which he believed would be "decisive."

Rommel's influence altered the Allied problem. First, German preparations would greatly increase the hazards on D-Day. The defense of Calais would be somewhat downgraded by the Germans, and other possible landing areas would be taken into account. Rommel set about to "thicken" the coastline crust, to narrow the divisional frontages, and to position reserves closer to the beaches. But so far OB West was being forced to make do with the reserves on hand, a hopeful sign.

At the time of Rommel's Christmas tour, divisional frontages in some sectors averaged 100 miles or more. Now units were bunched up. Fixed fortifications would greatly enhance the value of garrison troops, so Rommel directed the construction of a 5- to 6-kilometer defense belt from Denmark to Brittany to be complete by June. Rommel deemed landings possible in several places and at short intervals, with the "main" landings possible anywhere between the Somme and the Seine and at the Pas-de-Calais. Eventually Rommel would choose Normandy, as would Hitler, but the lack of reserves, compelling a forward defense, also ruled out any strategy that exposed the Calais sector.

By March, Rommel had assumed command of Army Group B. Feverish preparations were observable in all sectors. Crash programs were started to construct a series of resistance nests behind extensive mine fields, underwater obstacles and fortifications at the beaches. Rommel's ambitious plans would fall short, however, leaving wide distances between fortified points. The hour was late. Arguments raged away within the high command and among the overlapping echelons of command—army, navy and Organisation Todt, the German construction force. Shortages of labor and cement held up construction of the Atlantic Wall in the Fifteenth and Seventh Army sectors, all complicated by the divided command arrangements.

By late April, Rommel commanded the Army Group B, the Seventh and Fifteenth armies, with the right to by-pass Von Rundstedt and appeal directly to OKW. The Seventh and Fifteenth armies in turn controlled three panzer divisions, but OKW formed a special headquarters to control a three-division panzer reserve kept in the Paris area. Von Rundstedt, charged with responsibility for the defense of France and the Low Countries, could be without command over naval units or the Nazi-dominated Luftwaffe. The Luftwaffe controlled coastal anti-aircraft units and parachute troops; the navy controlled ships and shore installations and coastal artillery. The SS retained administrative and disciplinary powers over SS units, and the military governor in Paris retained control of the occupational garrisons, although he was nominally subordinate to OB West.

Would the Germans reinforce France? SHAEF had reports that few outside the Nazi inner circle were willing to run risks on the eastern front to defend France against invasion. Allied intelligence circulated reports that the non-Nazi German military leadership, while unwilling to write off the war yet, might oppose an all-out effort to defeat the Allies at the expense of Russia. Some military leaders hoped the Allies would reach Berlin before the Russians if worse came to worst, and rumor had it that Von Rundstedt favored this approach. Eisenhower was unwilling to place any credence in these reports.

Meanwhile, the more pressing problem was German strategy in France, the subject of a somewhat reassuring "appreciation" issued by the Combined Intelligence Staff on March 17. In it the CIS assessed the likely German response to the invasion, including an evaluation of the all-important question of German reserves for the battle of France. First, according to the CIS, the Germans were likely to attempt to hold their most economical line of defense—the coastline. Second, the widely scattered reserves already in France would probably not come into play in the early stages of the invasion battle. The CIS deemed it unlikely that the Germans would evacuate the area at the mouth of the river Scheldt, the port city of Brest or the Channel Islands, since the troops retrieved by evacuation would not offer returns commensurate with denying the Allies these points. This also held true for Italy, Holland, Belgium, northern Italy and Norway, where evacuation would be time-consuming and do nothing but expose essential objectives without materially increasing German strength. The issue therefore came down to the Russian front and German willingness to cut their losses there and fall back on the Riga line. So far this had not happened, and the report noted that in the event of a "serious crisis" in the east, the Germans might be "compelled" to take risks in the west until the eastern front was "stabilized." This was by no means a unanimous view, however. At about the same time, Montgomery's chief intelligence officer issued a report remarking on the German refusal to withdraw to the "narrow 'throat'" between the Baltic and Black seas. "For the moment it would seem. . . that the enemy is courting further and deepening disaster in the east to retain a good chance in the west," he wrote, "a strange gamble militarily, made intelligent politically by the prospect of a compromise peace if the Western decision bore fruit: in short, more and more Stalingrads in the hope of one Dunkirk. . . . "

Meanwhile, Deane and Burrows filed disquieting reports on the scale of violence on the eastern front. Deane reminded Washington about the Russian practice of methodical preparations and noted that Russian attacks, instead of winding down in preparation for mid-June, had increased in intensity, and the most recent conscription call-ups in Russia were being trained for July. Soviet attacks raged all month. Marshal Georgi Zhukov, defender of Stalingrad and architect of the Ukrainian offensives in 1943, left Moscow for Kiev to assume direction of four Russian army groups south of the Pripet Marshes. Zhukov's Army Group advanced on the Carpathian passes and the Hungarian plain. In the center, Konev crossed the Dniester into Rumania on the northern flank of Malinovsky's drive to capture Odessa and isolate the German forces in the southern Ukraine.

As the Red Army crossed the Dniester on a broad front and touched the

Carpathian mountains, the Rumanians and Hungarians showed signs of "super jitters," as Butcher put it. In Budapest, the Horthy regime abruptly arrested seventy Hungarian officers and issued writs for fugitives under Nazi protection accused of murdering 2,500 people in Ujvidek, Yugoslavia, in January 1942. This gesture—a dying act and relegated to the middle pages of Western newspapers—was quickly submerged in German countermeasures to "protect Hungarian independence."

The German high command acted decisively at mid-month to stem the political-military crisis in the east. The 1st and 2nd SS Panzer Corps left France. The Germans combed out infantry formations in Denmark and Norway to join the battle in Galicia and shore up positions in the wavering Balkans. On March 19, Panzer Lehr occupied Budapest and, uprooting the Kállay government, obtained Horthy's pledges of cooperation. Gradually, the 1st Panzer Corps broke its encirclement in Galicia, and by early April, Zhukov would be checked at the Yablonitza Pass, stopped by an early thaw, fatigue and a desperate German stand.

German countermeasures in Hungary provided a grim foretaste of what to expect in the months ahead. By March, many in London and Washington had come around to the idea that modification of "unconditional surrender" or such tactics as publishing lists of war criminals who would be shot on sight might divide and demoralize the German leadership and lead to an armistice. Whether and how political ferment in Germany should be encouraged was a growing and divisive issue. Again, Eisenhower was a skeptic. Intelligence historian Ladislas Farago in *Burn After Reading* would charge after the war that Eisenhower, when informed of MI-6, SOE and OSS contacts with an anti-Nazi conspiracy in the highest reaches of the Wehrmacht, indicated no interest whatsoever, despite rising sentiment in both capitals for a reassessment and what Brown would call a "moment of extraordinary opportunity"—a chance to negotiate a "mutually acceptable" surrender that would avoid the loss of lives and treasure of OVERLORD.

Did a "mutually acceptable" basis for a negotiated peace exist? Eisenhower's skepticism about the whole subject apparently rested on several grounds: first, the danger and futility of pinning hopes on a conspiracy he suspected was exaggerated; second, and more important, what he perceived to be the fundamental policy questions at issue. OSS kept Eisenhower thoroughly briefed on the so-called Schwarze Kapelle, which consisted of a ring in the German Abwehr, the counterintelligence service of OKW, a pocket of conspirators in the Home Army and in the Army Group commands on the eastern front documented through contacts in Berne, Stockholm and Lisbon. No one in touch with these contacts could doubt that anti-Hitler sentiment existed in the Army, but the "conspiracy" was remarkable not by its size but by how small and isolated it was. Moreover, Wehrmacht opposition had not formed until the Germans met reverses on the eastern front, and presumably reflected not misgivings with Nazi methods but disillusionment about impending catastrophe and hopes of evading retribution for the Nazi occupation policy in Russia in 1941–43. But the real problem concerned the aims of the conspiracy itself, for the object of a coup and armistice negotiations was not surrender and making amends, but finding a way out of fighting a two-front war in order to avert invasion by the Soviets. As things stood, a new government backed by a wounded but unbeaten German army mustering 260 field divisions in possession of most of central Europe was no more likely to accept responsibility for reparations to Russia or to accept partition than the current regime. Indeed, the overtures reported to Eisenhower and other Allied leaders were explicit that the Germans considered that they and the Allies had a common enemy in Russia; and what the Germans sought was tacit Allied aid against Russia and a change in Allied policy, not in German policy. Hence even Churchill, an advocate of a short war and a conciliatory peace which kept Germany more or less intact, appeared to part company with critics of unconditional surrender. Churchill favored a moderate peace and rehabilitation of Germany, but on Allied terms, and he wanted the process to begin with a German initiative, a German change of heart leading to a purge of the Nazis and unconditional surrender to the Allies and Russians, thereby initiating a process of atoning for the crimes and the misery inflicted by the Germans on Europe.

Was there a middle position? Some thought that a simple "clarification" of unconditional surrender reassuring the Germans of their future would undermine German combat morale and hasten military surrender. But as long as the German aim was to avert invasion, it was hard to imagine terms that would reassure the Germans without renouncing Allied aims or bringing on a break with the Russians; it was hard to see how any "clarification" could avoid confusing the political issues and undermining Allied combat morale more than German morale, and hard to see how Churchill's scenario, which involved a genuine act of submission by the Germans, would work in practice. Again, the absence of a broad-based resistance to Hitler was telling. For over a dozen years the Nazi party had systematically eliminated or silenced the clergy, the labor unions, the universities and liberal political opponents. SHAEF specialists, now at work on plans for a military government, had so far been unable to identify any domestic source of civil authority in an occupied Germany not heavily implicated in Nazi policies. It stood to reason that the Germans knew this best of all and would see little to be gained by vague provisional offers. A fight to the finish seemed much more likely—or, as Eisenhower put it, "If you were given two choices —one to mount a scaffold and the other to charge twenty bayonets, you may as well charge bayonets."

In the event, the German occupation of Hungary that March stripped the Horthy regime of its last vestiges of independence and rendered the Hungarians powerless to resist any measures forced on them by the Germans to bind them to a desperate fight to the finish. Soon, word seeped out to the world press that Horthy's ban on Jewish deportations had ended, that the concentration of Jews into central locations had begun, and that the shipments of an estimated one million Hungarian Jews to Auschwitz would soon begin at the rate of twelve thousand per day. The War Cabinet looked on, amazed (in Churchill's words) by "no doubt the 'greatest and most horrible crime ever committed in the whole history of the world . . . done by scientific machinery by nominally civilized men in the name of a great state and one of the leading races of Europe." Barter transactions were futile, however. In May, Eden would disclose the crisis in Commons. This spurred an approach by Himmler, allegedly "to enhance his credentials as a negotiator" in which he offered to free all one million Jews in exchange for ten thousand Allied vehicles. Nazi contacts confirmed Himmler's fantastic proposal through Waadah, the clandestine Jewish rescue agency. The War Cabinet grimly wrote off the "offer" as a cynical joke and/or ploy to arouse Soviet suspicions of separate peace talks, since the negotiations were to begin with contacts "between high Nazi officials and upper-level American and British officers to discuss a separate peace between Germany and the Western Allies." Waadah representatives flown to Istanbul for talks would be taken into custody by British agents, thus ending negotiations, whereupon "the extermination of the Hungarian Jews was allowed to proceed."

By March, Eisenhower spent increasingly more time on the road. He had plans to visit each of the thirty-seven divisions now in England scheduled to take part in the invasion. His role as a commander of troops has often been overlooked in the accounts of high-level wartime politics.

The experience was still new. At the outset of the war he had no actual experience in commanding a divisional or corps unit. After command of a large tank training center at Camp Colt, Gettysburg, in 1918, he had gone on to twenty years in staff assignments and command schools. Conscious of his inexperience, Eisenhower adopted a prosaic attitude toward command, describing his role occasionally as managerial, a link in a vast organizational chain performing a specialized task. But he was proud of the Alliance and his unique role as a commander of American and British troops. For years he had aspired to command military forces and he found it a humbling, almost obsessive experience. Eisenhower would insist on being seen personally by the troops who would bear the risks of injury and death in the invasion, and he assumed special responsibility for looking after the morale of his combined force.

In one of his earliest memos of the war, Eisenhower in July 1942 had dictated an extended account of an overnight visit at Chequers for a conference with Churchill on TORCH. In it he described the private quarters built overlooking a central living room under a towering ceiling, and a staircase adorned with paintings, sculptures and books. Eisenhower's description was eloquent testimony to his veneration of England and British traditions. As a Midwesterner born in the farm country of central Kansas and raised in the strictures of the German Pennsylvania Mennonite sect, Eisenhower admired the refinement of the structure. As a military man, he noted that the ancient estate, reserved for the use of the Prime Minister, had once been owned by a sister of Cromwell.

Eisenhower was given the second-floor Cromwell suite. Too excited to sleep, he spent the night reading a book on Cromwell, who inspired many of Eisenhower's references to the problems of morale and command. "Belief in an underlying cause," he later wrote in *Crusade in Europe* "is fully as important to success in war as any local spirit or discipline induced or produced by whatever kind of command or leadership action." He recalled that Cromwell's "Ironsides" had marched into battle singing hymns with an iron discipline fortified by an "inner conviction that never deserted them in any kind of dramatic crisis," the essence of the first great citizen army in history.

England in March 1944 remained an inspiring place despite the dreary postwar prospects her people faced. Production on a wartime basis since the late 1930s had choked off the private economy and forced the British to liquidate foreign holdings. Through central planning, the British had expanded munitions sixfold in three years, reducing British life to a regimen of hard work. Dry statistics told the story: of 23.5 million men and women available in the work force, 5.2 million served in the armed forces, 7.8 million served in the civilian war effort, barely 10.4 million sustained the economy. Imports were down 50 percent and expenditures on nonmilitary items off 45 percent from prewar levels. The British leadership resisted the slide and deplored the "grey uniformity of a world civilization" that awaited them. But none questioned the war effort.

On the road at least once a week, Eisenhower took time to observe and get to know the divisional commands, and to become familiar with the weapons and techniques of the invasion. On an early trip Eisenhower, Brooke and Gault visited Saxmundham, Suffolk, the headquarters of the British 79th Armored Division. The 79th was Brooke's special project as chief of the Imperial General Staff, formed to develop advanced armored techniques for the OVERLORD invasion and placed under the command of General P.C.S. Hobart, the British pioneer in armored technique.

Hobart's innovative use of British armor in OVERLORD was to be almost as revolutionary as the first appearance of British tanks at Cambrai in 1917. Hobart was a tall, bespectacled soldier whose turbulent career paralleled the experience of pioneers in the development of tank warfare elsewhere. Like Patton, De Gaulle and the German tank expert Heinz Guderian, Hobart as the commander of the First British Tank Brigade in the thirties had been a leading theoretician of the role of armor operating independently of infantry, and had clashed with conservatives in the War Office. He had spent the early days of the war in North Africa in command of the British 7th Armored Division. Then, after clashes with Wavell and Wilson, he had gone into early retirement. After the fall of France, Churchill had recalled Hobart and granted him a broad charter to develop armored techniques in the belief that the troops "should be carried into battle behind armor and be given mechanical means for accomplishing their tasks."

Eisenhower observed the fruits of Hobart's efforts: a duplex drive tank (DD), an amphibious tank capable of steaming through the water at 4.3 knots, and equipped with flamethrowers and minesweeping equipment. The DD was designed for the British sector around Ouistreham and Arromanches, stretches of flat sandy beach where the lead elements could expect early counterattacks by German armor. On his return to London, Eisenhower contacted Bradley and encouraged him to requisition similar equipment for the American assault regiments.

As time went on, Eisenhower attempted to cement a personal bond with his troops. At each stop he carefully inspected the division and base organization, the conditions of the campsites, the mess halls, the quartermaster organization and the barracks, and addressed the troops in an informal, political-stump style. When speaking to British troops, he talked of the close character of the Anglo-American alliance with emphasis on the special ties of culture and history. With American troops, Eisenhower was less formal. Inspecting columns of troops, he would stop and talk with every fifth or sixth soldier, drilling each on his job, occasionally pausing to ask soldiers about their background—where they lived, what their interests were, and if they happened to be Westerners, about cattle ranching and fishing. Newsmen and photographers were kept at a distance, so only a scant record of these encounters survived.

On the road, Eisenhower also renewed friendships with old Army friends and colleagues. Gault wrote an account of another early visit—to Gerow's 29th Infantry Division Headquarters in Norton Manor, now headquarters for V Corps, consisting of both the 29th and 1st infantry divisions. Gerow was his oldest and best friend in the theater, and V Corps headquarters would provide a haven in moments of anxiety more than once.

On the trip through the south English countryside, Gault observed the remarkable conversion of the sleepy area into a bustling cantonment of supply dumps, tent cities and vehicle pens stretching inland twenty-five miles from the coast. Everywhere, they passed theaters and dance halls, bars, pubs and clothing stores, evidence of the "peaceful invasion" affecting millions of British citizens who lived near prohibited military areas, airfields and ammunition dumps on the Salisbury Plain.

Eisenhower and Gerow were opposites. Gerow, trim and meticulous, was a chronic worrier. Eisenhower, hale and robust, had a gregarious and confident manner. But the two men shared similar thinking and tastes, and had similar prewar professional reputations as staff officers. Twenty-eight years before, in the summer of 1916, Eisenhower and Gerow had first served together in the 19th Regiment based at San Antonio. In 1926, they had been classmates at the Leavenworth Command and General Staff School. They had formed a two-man study group in Eisenhower's tiny attic. Eisenhower had graduated first in his class by less than one-thousandth of a grade point ahead of Gerow, a performance that marked both for command responsibility. During the 1930s in Washington, the Eisenhowers and Gerows had been neighbors in the Wyoming Apartment Building on Connecticut Avenue overlooking the statue of General George McClellan.

Their gradual wartime falling out was typical of Eisenhower's slow alienation from his old Army colleagues. Seemingly, it was chance that had propelled Eisenhower into the spotlight and consigned Gerow, having accumulated a reputation as an "unlucky" general, to the purgatory of risky battlefield assignments at sensitive points. Eisenhower narrowly avoided this fate. In the summer of 1940, Gerow, then at Marshall's War Plans Division, had invited Eisenhower, recently back from MacArthur's staff in Manila, to join him in Washington. After much thought, Eisenhower had decided to refuse and accept command of a field regiment at Fort Lewis, Washington, an unremarkable decision that caused a drastic reversal in the fortunes of the two men. It had been Gerow's misfortune to be in command of OPD on December 7, 1941, when the Japanese surprise attack fell on Pearl Harbor. Four days later, Eisenhower, serving as Third Army chief of staff at Fort Sam Houston, received orders to become Gerow's assistant in charge of East Asia, and eventual replacement.

Inevitably, Gerow's reputation had been tarnished by Pearl Harbor. Following the breakdown of Washington-Tokyo negotiations in late November 1941, War Plans had been responsible for sending out the stages of alert to all Pacific commands, including Pearl Harbor. The Roberts Commission, appointed to investigate the circumstances of the Japanese assault, turned up improper acknowledgment by Pearl Harbor military authorities and found Gerow had failed "to follow through," implicating him in the chain of oversights that enabled the Japanese to move four aircraft-carrier task forces undetected from Honshu to Oahu. Mystery surrounded the whole Pearl Harbor question, and Gerow's role in it. There were hints that Gerow had shouldered the blame to cover up a high-level conspiracy to withhold warnings from Pearl Harbor in order to magnify the disaster and propel America into war. Eisenhower suspected as much. In a letter shortly after his promotion to four-star general, Eisenhower conceded to Gerow that he could "never get over the feeling, one I have held ever since I was a second Lieutenant, that in every respect you have deserved recognition far above myself. . . . You must know, as I do, that certain fortuitous circumstances, more than any indication of peculiar merit, were responsible for my advancement."

Gerow had spent weeks testifying before the Roberts Commission in early 1942. Thereafter he became one of the handful of general officers who "irrevocably" lost Marshall's favor, though he had received the 29th Division in February 1942 after relinquishing a reorganized War Plans Division to his successor, Dwight Eisenhower. As the 1944 election year heated up, Gerow could look forward to periodic recall back to Washington to appear before congressional committees.

Now V Corps trained for assault landings across the beaches between Vierville-sur-Mer and Port-en-Bessin, the most dangerous of the five OVERLORD beaches. Code-named OMAHA, the beaches featured 110-foot cliffs, and steeply sloping bluffs blocking exits in many sectors—easily fortified by artillery strongpoints and pillboxes. Aerial reconnaissance in early March slowed a rapid thickening of the Atlantic Wall fortifications in all sectors. The German preparations were a cause of general worry, particularly for V Corps, since OMAHA, a relatively isolated beach, received top German priority.

Gault also described a field trip to Sandhurst Academy, near Camberley, Surrey, where Eisenhower addressed the graduating class of British officer candidates on the morning of March 11, 1944. After breakfast Eisenhower and Gault left Kingston on a chilly, sunny, springlike morning. The outing was a welcome relief from command problems and worries. Eisenhower looked forward to seeing Sandhurst, an institution founded about the time of West Point to train regular officers for the British Army. In the war emergency, Sandhurst had abandoned the full-course curriculum, and postponed all plans for expansion in order to rush through officer candidates for frontline duty similar to the accelerated program at West Point.

That morning Eisenhower delivered a rare public address, recorded in full by an Army Signal Corps technician who also took films of the event. After observing the passing out in review, Eisenhower, standing behind a modest podium erected on the old Capital building, extemporaneously delivered a commencement address on the responsibilities faced by the graduating class.

Eisenhower began with a recital of the unbroken record of good relations between America and England since 1812. He sketched the history of the military alliances of 1917 and 1941. The success story of American-British relations was due, in his opinion, to a common enemy, but to common values, too. Never before had the forces of evil been pitted more distinctly against those of decency and respect for humankind. The Allies fought on the side of decency, democracy and liberty.

Eisenhower predicted eventual victory. He described the formidable forces arrayed against the Germans. While the Russians hammered back the Germans in the Ukraine and inflicted upon them still further losses, the great Allied air arm pounded Germany by night and by day from the west. But the war still had to be won, and won as quickly as possible with the minimum losses in lives and property . . . and

> any person, whether at the plough or with a gun at the front, who fails to do his full duty every day and every hour, must forever bear on his conscience that he has contributed some incalculable amount to the agony and sacrifice that our two countries must endure.
>
> It behooves us, then, to think what these duties are . . . particularly our own. Our governments arrange that the resources of these great Allies are used in such a way as to inflict the greatest punishment upon the enemy and accomplish his defeat. It is for the High Command by air, sea and land to see that these resources are placed into action properly led, organized and maintained, to win these victories. The High Command can do no more than to put you in action in the best possible way, under the best possible conditions, and to make sure that you are well supplied, well cared for, and everything is done for you in the way of getting you ammunition, food, clothing and everything that you need. But upon your shoulders rests the real responsibility.
>
> You young men have this war to win. It is small unit leadership that is going to win the ground battle and that battle must be won before that enemy of ours is finally crushed. It is up to you men to give your units—whether it is a tank crew, platoon, or becomes a company—leadership, every hour of the day, every day of the week. You must know every single one of your men. It is not enough that you are the best soldier in that unit, that you are the strongest, the toughest, the most durable, and the best equipped technically. You must be their leader, their father, their mentor even if you are half their age. You must understand their problems. You must keep them out of trouble. If they get in trouble, you must be the one to go to their rescue. That cultivation of human understanding between you and your men is the one art that you must yet master and you must master it quickly. Then you will be doing your duty and you will be worthy of the traditions of this great school and of your great country.
>
> To each one of you I wish Godspeed and Good Luck. If I could have my wish as I stand here today, feeling honored as I do in the tribute paid me, I would say this: If I could only meet you all somewhere east of the Rhine and renew the acquaintanceship of this pleasant morning.
> Good Luck. . . .

DECISIONS

Back in London, at the Supreme Commander's conference on March 13, Eisenhower, for the first and last time, acknowledged his command problems in the presence of his deputies. He told Ramsay, Leigh-Mallory, Tedder, Montgomery and the staff about the "hold up" in the expected transfer of the strategic air forces to SHAEF. Objections had suddenly developed in Washington over the word "supervision" to characterize Tedder's authority. General Arnold was insisting the British agree to the word "command." Eisenhower trusted the whole problem would prove to be a misunderstanding, but reminded the group it was important "that these air forces . . . be placed under his control. . . . "

The news could not have come as a surprise, though Eisenhower's mention of it in a full conference with his deputies and advisers probably did. Montgomery, Ramsay, Leigh-Mallory, Tedder and Smith knew about Eisenhower's reluctance to talk about inter-Allied and command problems. But the problems were obvious. A formal explanation had become necessary in view of the uncertainty surrounding air policy, and the shipping shortages which had a "marked effect" on Army planning. Also, Montgomery, Ramsay, Leigh-Mallory and Tedder, Eisenhower's British subordinates, had spoken in favor of the transport plan, and Eisenhower needed help.

The March 20 review set for ANVIL approached. The review of the transport plan called by Portal at the Air Ministry was set for March 25. The invasion deadline also approached, and basic issues remained: whether Allied resources would be mobilized and deployed efficiently; whether the CCS would allow Eisenhower to consolidate his authority, or permit his authority to become a hotly debated subject at every turn in the invasion battle; in other words, whether the Allies would make the irreversible commitments necessary to sustain the invasion, or would try to proceed with caution to the end, allowing current "misunderstandings" to persist and stand in the way of yielding direction over air, naval and ground forces to a single Allied authority.

In the next several days, misunderstandings persisted over the terms "command" and "supervision." Arnold opposed any loose arrangements and refused to believe that Eisenhower had accepted them, a point clarified by the BCOS, which disclosed that Eisenhower had drafted the Tedder-Portal protocol in his own hand. Responding to Marshall's query, Eisenhower professed bewilderment about the controversy and explained that the British Air marshals had "so well and clearly understood" that operational authority over assigned forces would "reside in me" that questioning the phrase "supervision" had "never occurred to me." Arnold backed down, with the two sides settling on the word "direction," effective upon approval of the transport plan, which would involve Portal's approval, then CCS approval, then War Cabinet approval target by target.

By now, the air issue was mired in French politics. The War Cabinet questioned the effect of the transport plan on French-Allied relations in view of U.S. determination to keep De Gaulle at arm's length. To Eden it seemed illogical and self-defeating to direct a ruthless bombing campaign against French cities and villages while locking out French authority during the pre-invasion period when, presumably, it would be asked to explain the policy to the French people. Surely such a policy would emphasize the expendability of French lives and undermine relations with the FCNL, which was "already looking to Russia more than we would like." The British would insist on a procedure in which the War Cabinet would review each proposed target and apply a rigorous standard of civilian casualties. Whether the British would find themselves able to participate was also conjectural, since "precision bombing" was an Eighth Air Force specialty.

On it went. Logically, as time passed, Eisenhower's position would be strengthened. Under the pressure of the invasion deadline, the Americans would be compelled to face up to the postponement of ANVIL and concede priority for Wilson's assault on Rome, and the British would reciprocate with statesmanship on Bomber Command that would, in turn, isolate Eighth Air Force objections to the plan and end the suspense. But the pressures seemed illogical, and fundamental uncertainty seemed to persist on both sides, as was apparent in the hard-and-fast positions taken on ANVIL, and reluctance to confront the air question.

At mid-month, the BCOS again complained that preparations already under way, including construction of airfields on Corsica, hampered Wilson's preparations for an offensive to link up with Anzio. On the eve of the ANVIL review, Alexander filed a pessimistic estimate announcing that an attempt to break the Sangro-Cassino line and linkup of VI Corps and the Fifth Army could not even be mounted until mid-May, which pushed ANVIL off until late July at the earliest. This rekindled American JCS doubts about the worth of taking Rome, which aroused BCOS objections about "rigid" positions on operations that would pin down troops in the Mediterranean three months hence.

In support of Rome, the British cited the ongoing battle and intelligence intercepts indicating German determination to stand south of the capital. To earmark forces for ANVIL would "hamper" Wilson, and offer no assurance that ANVIL could engage German troops on a comparable scale, resulting in "nullification" of the Italian theater. The Americans replied that the Germans were capable of a sudden withdrawal northward—that as few as nine divisions of the German Tenth Army could contain the Allies north of Rome, releasing fifteen divisions to other fronts. Marshall's staff produced the scholarship: 48 million tons of equipment would have to pass through the European ports to support the OVERLORD divisions in France; the logistical experts estimated that the Allies would need Antwerp, the Brittany ports, Le Havre and Marseilles. The Americans envisioned a "pincers" in France to converge at the Loire. General Frank N. Roberts, in a memorandum, argued variously that ANVIL's advantages included avoiding "political difficulties" with the French, utilizing spare American and French divisions, avoiding a "costly, unremunerative" advance in Italy, as well as avoiding "the thorny politics of the Balkans" and the "use of occupational forces in Austria, Hungary and South Germany"—points that both emphasized the American-French character of ANVIL and broached the problem of Russian views.

Marshall reminded Eisenhower of the Russian factor in a cable on the seventeenth about the impasse. Observing wistfully that "the basis for a final decision" was "no better than a month ago," he raised two specific concerns: first, the "possibility if not the probability" that the Germans in "taking desperate measures which they certainly will do to crush OVERLORD" would withdraw to the Riga line; second, in light of MAGIC intercepts indicating that the Germans still anticipated landings either in the northern Adriatic or southern France, he expressed concern that stopping preparations would trigger a rearrangement of forces "to your great disadvantage." Marshall left it to Eisenhower to decide which was more important.

Once again, Eisenhower offered to communicate directly with STAVKA about all military problems, including the factors in favor of a postponement of ANVIL. Washington refused. Churchill opposed separate military channels of communication on such a vital issue. For several days Churchill and the BCOS stood by for an emergency trip to Washington to hammer out the problem. As an alternative, Eisenhower hoped to dispatch Smith back to Washington to impress on Marshall that ANVIL as planned was not practical and that indecision was having a "marked effect" on planning. Roosevelt declined to host the meeting, however, and the Smith idea evaporated under the pressure of urgent business.

Finally, on the twentieth, Eisenhower, in an unspectacular decision, decided to recommend postponement of ANVIL formally and revive the transfer of LSTs to England. In a background message to Marshall, Eisenhower explained that given his current lift, there were LSTs for the first three phases of D-Day, and none for the next three days. The only foreseeable source of reinforcements he knew about was the Mediterranean—and stalemate at Anzio tied up practically all the remaining lift, rendering ANVIL "as conceived" not possible. On the twenty-first, Eisenhower and Wilson filed simultaneous formal recommendations. Eisenhower issued a call for twenty-six LSTs in Italy, up six from February, noting that he had hitherto been "willing to live with shortages identified on the assumption of a strong ANVIL which no longer obtained." Wilson appealed for a ruling on the availability of shipping and troops for the linkup offensive set for May 15, then recommended cancellation of ANVIL and later reconsideration of it after Rome, along with other options, including pursuit into central Italy and landings at the head of the Adriatic to strike at German communications in Italy and the Balkans.

The CCS could not dispute the unanimous judgment of both theater commanders, and so the recommendations settled the question of postponement. But Wilson's cable revived suspicions that the British were angling to tie up forces until after OVERLORD when a belated Italian offensive would absorb all Mediterranean resources, thwart ANVIL and salvage resources for a Balkan strategy. Marshall criticized Wilson's delay and told Dill flatly that he considered ANVIL the "test of the alliance"—that is, the JCS would insist that ANVIL preparations be kept alive in some form and probably require the operation to go forward.

On the twenty-second, Eisenhower returned to Whitehall for a conference in hopes of persuading Brooke to meet Marshall partway. Brooke was unyielding. The CIGS complained about hampering Wilson, and noted once again the fact that ANVIL involved not two assault divisions but two assault divisions plus eight follow-on divisions for a total of ten, or one third of Wilson's force. Cunningham raised Eisenhower's request for twenty-six LSTs. As for sending British ships back to London instead of U.S. ships direct from the States, Cunningham noted that serviceability was still low because of SHINGLE—"nothing" would be available until late April. However, if ANVIL was cancelled, Eisenhower could rely on twenty LSTs and could keep the six AKAs. Cunningham felt that the simplest solution, of course, was to keep the British LSTs where they were and to dispatch U.S. vessels destined for Italy straight to the U.K. However, he was reluctant to rehash this, "since the Americans have rejected it so many times in the past."

Eisenhower conveyed Marshall's concerns about a rapid German retreat in Italy, and his concern that Wilson and Alexander contemplated a "diminution" of the offensive effort in Italy. Brooke was confident the Germans could not withdraw north of Rome between then and May 15; intelligence confirmed it. Brooke urged Eisenhower to consider the effects of a decision "nullifying" Wilson's capacity to support OVERLORD with an offensive on Rome. Eisenhower left.

Things continued downhill in the next forty-eight hours. Confronted with a unanimous judgment by the field command, the JCS, as expected, approved a postponement and endorsed Eisenhower's request for the twenty-six LSTs in Italy. This left the problem of LSTs for Italy and Wilson's directive. Once again, King offered to compensate for shortages by diverting additional landing craft from the Pacific *provided* the British accepted a July 10 target date for ANVIL. The American JCS declined Cunningham's offer to transfer the six AKAs back to England for OVERLORD. Dill reported back to Brooke that the atmosphere in Washington was "excellent," but that the Americans made it clear that extra landing craft were offered with great reluctance, which meant "material delay in the Pacific." The JCS remained convinced the Germans would not hesitate to abandon Italy, if necessary, leaving nine divisions in Italy and transferring fifteen elsewhere. Finally, Dill noted that Washington was reluctant to approach the French or the Russians about postponement.

In a memorandum for the record on the twenty-second, Eisenhower finally confessed his discouragement to himself. First, ANVIL was now "out of the question"—at least as originally planned. Eisenhower recited his steps to salvage ANVIL in accordance with Marshall's wishes and otherwise assured himself of his objectivity, but it had been "striving for the impossible." Meanwhile, he faced acute shortages of gunfire support and the twenty-six LSTs in Italy. Second, Eisenhower described the latest twists and turns on the French problem: the formidable task of civil administration, which could be achieved only through De Gaulle, in his opinion, but this too was unresolved. Finally, Eisenhower briefly narrated the story of the air dispute—first, the British suspicions early on that he would try "to seize all air and apply it very locally." He recited his assurances that he would exempt Coastal Command, his willingness to substitute Tedder for Leigh-Mallory, disrupted by Arnold over a matter "I considered settled a week ago, after many weeks of argument. . . . "

" . . . I have recommended to General Marshall that a word be adopted that leaves no doubt in anybody's mind of my authority and responsibility," he closed. "The actual air preparatory plan is to be the subject of a formal meeting on Saturday, March 25, between Portal, Spaatz, Harris, Leigh-Mallory, Tedder and myself. . . . If a satisfactory answer is not recorded I am going to take drastic action and inform the Combined Chiefs of Staff that unless the matter is settled at once I will request relief from this command."

In the next seventy-two hours, Spaatz and Tedder cross-filed closing briefs. Spaatz filed a revision of his oil plan, updated to incorporate the negative conclusions of the London-based JIC, which, he was confident, had discredited the transport plan. The study, based on data gained in the test raids on Trappes, Le Mans and Amiens, made a number of points: first, that the repair capacity of the French rail network was unlimited; second, that military traffic in Belgium and France consumed only 20 percent of capacity, leaving an ample "cushion" to transport military traffic on D-Day; third, that a far shorter period than eight weeks would be adequate to achieve the 100-mile-radius "railway desert" envisioned in the Zuckerman plan, and that a more ambitious program would be a futile diversion of resources from morale and industrial targets. Interdiction of rail communication as a "tactical" objective was "not considered."

Spaatz proposed five priorities: oil, fighter and ball-bearing industries, rubber production, and lastly, bomber production. He described the advantages of oil targets—90 percent of Axis output was concentrated in 31 refineries; that 14 refineries produced 80 percent—limited raids could reach most of the refineries, and so petroleum was a "target system" the Germans would have to defend in force. Finally, he noted that "no action by the Combined Chiefs of Staff is necessary" to implement the plan, a bonus that avoided the problem of establishing new headquarters and new procedures, which Portal had campaigned against for over six months.

Tedder responded in a memo on behalf of SHAEF. Tedder carefully reviewed the main points: first, he denied that he proposed to alter the basic POINTBLANK priority—that of achieving the defeat of the German air force —since "Air superiority during the assault and subsequent operations" was fundamental. But the time had come to entrust SHAEF with the task of directing the air forces in this fundamental task. Second, Tedder dwelled on the speculative aspects of the oil plan. He disputed that the bombing of oil refineries "in the short time available" could affect German capacity to respond to OVERLORD; that is, an overall deterioration of the German war effort did not address the basic problem, that of opening a land front, the sole concern of all services "during the assault and subsequent landing operations." Third, the SHAEF plan offered maximum support of land operations by aiming at maximum disruption of enemy rail traffic in the invasion area. As distinguished from the indirect benefits of an overall deterioration of the German position that might or might not affect the local outcome, the SHAEF plan held out the prospect of direct aid to the landings —*if* begun at once. Systematic attacks were necessary on repair centers and marshaling yards if the tactical plans were to succeed.

And thus the issue was joined. The meeting came to order at three on the afternoon of March 25. Around the table in his office at the Air Ministry sat Portal, Eisenhower, Harris, Spaatz, Tedder, Leigh-Mallory, observers from the War Office, technical representatives from the Air Ministry, and representatives from the Ministry of Economic Warfare. Portal acted as chairman, and recognized each man in turn around the table.

The first item on the agenda was the transport plan. In his clipped tones, Tedder summarized his points: that SHAEF did not question top priority for GAF (German air force) targets; that the question technically dealt with second priority—use of air resources not deployed against GAF targets. In urging adoption of the transport plan by April 1, Tedder did not say how long operations would last. Presumably this would be the subject of future negotiations.

Tedder disputed the JIC estimates of the rail "cushion" and the condition of the French railroads—his reports indicated that French railways were inefficient and highly vulnerable if bombed systematically. This would canalize traffic, strain existing repair facilities and strip the system of flexibility. Then, on D-Day and afterward, German reserves would be forced to travel by road and would be materially delayed in reaching the front— *provided* extensive bombardment began well beforehand. In summary, Tedder cautioned that he did not wish to claim too much for the plan. It would not prevent *all* traffic from getting through. The object was to weaken the system and enhance the effects of the all-out tactical plan on or about the time of the invasion. But any reduction in German traffic would aid the invasion and justify the priority.

Tedder had presented an extreme case. It was difficult to measure the effect on Normandy of a wide-ranging campaign against rail targets. Likewise, it was hard to measure the value of any reduction in German traffic which Tedder insisted justified diverting the strategic air forces from their primary mission of attacking the German war industry and fighting capability as a whole. By same token, the assembled group could not precisely measure the effects of an oil campaign, and dared not dismiss the value of direct aid in the landings, however small, nor could they ignore the Supreme Commander's wishes.

Portal commented. The air chief of staff told the group he was persuaded the transportation plan would have a "serious effect" on the efficiency of the French rail system. But would redeployment of reserves in the closing weeks nullify it? Did the German Seventh Army in Normandy have adequate stocks of equipment on hand for the critical first week of the battle? And what would deter the German military authorities from simply canceling civilian traffic in northwest France and using all railway equipment for military purposes? General McMullen of War Office Intelligence disputed Tedder's point about the vulnerability of the French rail system. He agreed it was vulnerable, particularly because of the dependence of Normandy on coal shipped from Lens and Lille. However, McMullen noted recent reports of as many as 45,000 Organisation Todt workers pressed into service on the railways. He guessed that makeshift servicing units could keep the system moving in an emergency. At best, Allied bombing would achieve a 20–30 percent reduction in rail traffic, leaving a sufficient "cushion" for some military traffic. He noted that "some" reduction might not be enough to leave the Germans short of essential needs. Would delay of a day or two matter? McMullen recalled that attacks against the supply lines in Africa and Italy had not cut the flow of essential stores to the central Tunisian front, and he questioned Zuckerman's findings about Italy. Attacks on rail targets had delayed troop formations for two or three days, but they invariably "got through."

Tedder distinguished Normandy from North Africa. In Normandy the Germans would not be able to cut off civilian traffic, which doubly burdened the system. Sir Arthur Noble of the JIC agreed that the Germans would have to feed the local population, since "starvation of the region would embarrass their military effort." But the recent grain harvest had already been distributed in northwest France. And he estimated the French *economic* contribution to the German war effort was about 10 percent, consisting mostly of coal and raw materials. *This* economic traffic could be suspended easily for five weeks.

At this point Eisenhower spoke up. He suggested the group approach the question slightly differently—that is, in terms of his directive and the question of how the air arm could best support OVERLORD. The first five to six weeks would be critical for OVERLORD, he said, "getting and staying ashore." OVERLORD was the all-out operation, and the greatest role for the air that he could imagine would be to hamper enemy movement in the critical phases. Short-range tactical bombers and fighters *might* take over after the landings, but this left the question of the role of the strategic bombers in the meanwhile. In his opinion, a campaign commencing April 1 would reduce overall efficiency, "canalize" the traffic, impose strains on the system, which might break down when the tactical bombers came into

play, and "delaying the arrival of one division would be worthwhile."
Eisenhower noted that there were twelve panzer formations in France now,
and Allied success was "conditioned on no more than twelve," and three
near the beaches. He agreed with Air Marshal Tedder that delaying a single
armored division on D-Day would be worthwhile, and questioned whether
the oil plan would accomplish this. In fact, Eisenhower saw no alternative
to the transport plan.

General Kennedy of the Ministry of Economic Warfare agreed with
General Eisenhower's statement of the problem, but questioned the usefulness of a drawn-out campaign aimed at reducing the efficiency of the whole
system, a far too ambitious goal and a "waste" if unsuccessful. Kennedy
doubted that the Zuckerman plan in Italy had had any material effect on
enemy movement. Perhaps a *less* ambitious plan over a smaller area might
be more directly useful. Kennedy conceded that delaying even one division
in the critical period would make rail targets "attractive." As an aside,
Kennedy noted that the present plan was the work of civilian railway
experts, accustomed to looking at enemy transportation problems through
the lens of problems in England and in the last war, in which the problems
were "quite different."

Eisenhower granted that exact calculations were hard to make. The point
was that one plan attempted to reduce the efficiency of German transportation, the other did not. According to everything he had read, there were two
ways the air forces could contribute to OVERLORD: first, the defeat of the
German air force, and second, by "hindering transportation." Parenthetically, Eisenhower regretted Kennedy's complaint that the War Office had
not yet been consulted by SHAEF on the transportation plan. Continuing, he
reminded Kennedy that estimates varied on the effectiveness of any such
effort. But his feeling was that whether the estimates were completely accurate or not, "some reduction in traffic, however small, justifies adoption."

Kennedy and McMullen conceded there would be *some* reduction, but
doubted it was possible to estimate how much. McMullen felt the Germans
could improvise and would "not be seriously embarrassed" by transportation attacks, whereas disruption of oil refineries would have a direct impact
on the German war effort.

Discussion in this vein developed several points: Eisenhower's views about
the value of even minimum results; that estimates about the effect of rail
attacks was speculation at best; that depending on the estimates accepted,
the two programs need not be mutually exclusive. Throughout, Spaatz
demurred. His views on the rail plan were best summed up in his memorandum, and ably presented by Kennedy and McMullen. As discussion turned
to the alternative, Spaatz rendered a brief defense of the oil plan.

In short, Spaatz doubted that a strategic-bombing offensive on the rail
lines would affect the landings or hinder the arrival of reserves from other

fronts or undermine Germany's military effort as a whole. On the other hand, a campaign on refineries and synthetic-oil plants would force the Germans to economize on all fronts and paralyze resistance on all fronts eventually. Spaatz doubted that German fighters would attempt to defend transportation targets, and so adoption of the SHAEF plan could afford the Luftwaffe a badly needed respite. Admittedly, the oil plan was of little direct help to the invasion itself, but he doubted the transport plan would help either.

Spaatz took questions. If POINTBLANK achieved the promised reduction in German oil stocks, when did he favor a decisive effect? Six months. Were the strategic results of rail attacks comparable? No. Spaatz did "not expect the Transportation Plan to have a decisive effect within any measurable length of time." General Lawrence of the Ministry of Economic Warfare raised a "critical exception" for Whitehall to consider. He noted that three months of oil strikes might result in a 25 percent cut in petroleum, but no one could forecast how the German high command would apportion the cut among the fronts. Lawrence noted that General Spaatz was talking about generalized results—reports from Normandy indicated that the Germans maintained large stocks in the west, "so that the effect need not be immediate." Lawrence estimated that *some* effects of the oil plan would be "noticeable within four to five months on the western front," but even this was uncertain.

Portal interjected for the record that "conclusively" the oil plan would be of no help whatsoever in OVERLORD during the first critical weeks, and the tide turned.

Gradually, deep skepticism emerged about Eighth Air Force projections. Few had disputed them in November and December, but this was the moment of decision. Schemes to gain a knockout blow from the air that had been relevant minutes before suddenly seemed beside the point, and Air estimates accepted for months suddenly seemed unreliable. This reduced the pre-OVERLORD question to narrower ground: not whether strategic air attacks punished Germany, but whether they would aid OVERLORD. This depended on two factors: petroleum stocks and rail capacity. If in fact petroleum stocks in Normandy were adequate, rail lines would be the only target system rendering direct aid to OVERLORD.

In the ensuing discussion, guided by the austere, humorless Portal, the lack of unity between the Air staffs was striking. Hitherto silent, Harris spoke up. He professed his desire that the British Bomber Command "be of help." But Bomber Command worked at night against area targets. Precision nighttime bombing required exact conditions for the Oboe Pathfinder and certain moon periods, so the task was "quite beyond the capacity of my command." Harris noted that German cities were transportation centers, so city attacks would contribute, conceding, however, that impact on transport would be entirely "fortuitous."

When Portal demurred, Eisenhower rapidly assured Harris that the real issue concerned the role of the Eighth and Fifteenth air forces and that the "Transportation Plan meant very little change for Bomber Command"— a concession. Eisenhower then proceeded to offer Spaatz a concession: a time limit. Eisenhower emphasized the five to six critical weeks, his willingness to reassess the air situation as it developed, and to relinquish air command "as the first critical situation in OVERLORD is passed."

Spaatz protested that a program diverting up to 50 percent of his force had to produce *some* attrition of the Luftwaffe, or he would fail in his primary mission to "win the war of attrition against the German Air Force." German fighters would rise en masse to oppose attacks on synthetic plants, and deep-penetration raids would not preclude attacks on the rail system. On the other hand, the transportation plan would afford Germany ten precious weeks to recover from the effects of the February and March disasters.

At this point, Portal reminded Spaatz that no one disputed first priority for German air force targets—the group was discussing several priority missions. Moreover, Portal agreed that "the Germans would certainly not resist isolated attacks against rail centers, though things would be different if they perceived an all-out attack on the rail system." It was clear, in Portal's opinion, how the air forces could render direct aid to OVERLORD. The technical aspects would have to be worked out between Tedder and Spaatz, mindful that the program would have to produce the mandatory attrition of German fighters. However, Portal was "convinced that attacks on German Air Force targets would in themselves achieve this," which narrowed the question of rail targets versus oil targets.

Portal had a question for Eisenhower. Would destruction of the French railroads retard the Allied pursuit?

"We should not consider it," Eisenhower replied. "The Germans shall certainly destroy the railroads as they retreat."

As the discussion continued in this vein, the participants sensed that this, the March 25 meeting, was a major step. One of the biggest hurdles to adoption of the SHAEF plan had been a united front between the Air staffs against the transport plan. What accounted for it? Eisenhower was not sure, but he closely observed Portal's objective manner, which foreclosed further debate on the merits of the two plans and narrowed the issue to that extent. In gratitude and admiration, looking back on Portal's performance twenty years later, Eisenhower would rank him with Churchill, Marshall, Dulles and Major General Fox Conner as one of the five greatest men he had ever known.

In closing, Portal cautioned Eisenhower about a number of unresolved problems. He informed Eisenhower of the recent RAF estimates of as many as 160,000 or more French civilian casualties in an all-out campaign on rail centers with or without forewarning. The matter of French casualties was a delicate one and would have to be raised with the War Cabinet. Eisenhower assured Portal that he appreciated the importance of this consideration and would raise it himself with the British government.

Then Portal, like a judge on the bench, rendered a summary of the discussion. Over the objections of most of the 21st Army Group staff, Harris, Spaatz, and many of his colleagues at the Air Ministry, Portal on behalf of the CCS directed Spaatz and Tedder to evaluate the technical aspects of rail bombing in conjunction with the German air force targets and to report the results to Eisenhower. He asked Tedder to prepare a draft directive, to be approved by General Eisenhower and himself, urging Tedder to consult the military transportation experts. The meeting ended.

Was this the long-awaited break? Twenty-four hours after the Air Ministry talks, Eisenhower returned to conference with Brooke in hopes of firming up a compromise on a directive for Wilson. Eisenhower urgently hoped the British would accept King's "offer," or at least agree to keep ANVIL in planning status, which the JCS would insist on. This was not too much to ask in view of the postponement approved on the twenty-fourth, which guaranteed a review of ANVIL "near or at the time of OVERLORD," as the British had insisted ever since Cairo.

Imminent landing-craft shortages in Italy had recast the issue slightly. If the British continued to insist on "flexibility," U.S. LSTs for Italy appeared to be out. This meant an extended postponement and further "strengthening" of the British case. But this could only serve to exacerbate the issue by pointing up Washington's anxiety about arousing the Russians and cornering the Americans into assuming full responsibility, for the operation was a potentially explosive step in light of election-year politics and divided opinion in Roosevelt's Cabinet over the Russian problem. Otherwise, Eisenhower would see to it that ANVIL was adjusted to British satisfaction.

It was a forlorn meeting, typical of many ahead. As expected, Brooke liked Admiral King's "offer" but rejected the preconditions, which amounted to the "pointing of a pistol." The Chief of the Imperial General Staff told Eisenhower once again that he would not commit to a scheme of operations four or five months in advance. Eisenhower urged Brooke to consider the political pressures on the American Joint Chiefs and the Cabinet, which accounted for King's demand that he know in advance that the reallocation would wind up in France. Eisenhower reminded Brooke of recent talk of a MacArthur presidential candidacy and recent moves in the House to bring a resolution to the floor calling for an "immediate all out Pacific offensive and allocation of sufficient U.S. resources in support thereof." Eisenhower saw nothing devious about the proposal; the American Joint Chiefs were out on a limb, and landing craft could not be spared for anything except protection of U.S. forces in France. Furthermore, Eisenhower was sure the JCS was concerned about launching "the strongest and most ambitious amphibious operation that the military situation would then permit" so as to introduce an additional threat against the European mainland and so as to accomplish the greatest possible support for OVER-LORD; this did not mean a fixed idea of any particular place or time.

Brooke seemed unmoved. He was offended by King's "blackmail" and weary of Washington's inability to work out Pacific problems. Brooke reminded Eisenhower that the whole problem of landing craft stemmed from U.S. inability to carry out "Europe First" completely, the basic policy agreed upon long ago at ARCADIA. He reminded Eisenhower that Wilson still did not know what troops he could commit to Alexander's May 15 offensive to link up the Fifth Army and VI Corps. This might nullify the Mediterranean: it proved to his satisfaction the folly of conducting war by "lawyer's agreements."

Eisenhower groped for compromise. At one point he intimated to Brooke that he agreed completely with Wilson's assessment of the importance of Rome and Wilson's optimism about pinning down German forces afterward. Cunningham asked Eisenhower if he would be willing to endorse Rome. Eisenhower was not sure he could do this, but he was "willing to go along with the sense that the decision as to actual place [for ANVIL] would be made closer to the time."

Finally Eisenhower, Brooke and Cunningham hammered out a compromise directive according to "overriding priority" for Rome and omitting ANVIL by name. First, Wilson would be directed "to contain maximum number of enemy forces." Second, Wilson would receive additional lift by July 10, with operations to be determined at a later date. Brooke agreed not to oppose the construction of Corsican airfields, a concession to American feelings.

In his message to Marshall afterward, Eisenhower beseeched the Chief of Staff to accept Brooke's off-the-record assurances. Eisenhower revealed that Brooke had insisted that overriding priority in Italy would be joining up the VI Corps and the Fifth Army, but he had agreed that "*no* repeat *no* particular geographical location, including Rome" had military significance compared with AFHQ's primary duty of carrying on operations "of maximum support to OVERLORD." Second, Brooke had predicted that by early July a two-division amphibious operation in the Mediterranean would prove necessary to support OVERLORD. Third, Brooke had agreed that the best objective would probably be southern France if the Germans suddenly withdrew to the Pisa–Rimini line, but that if the German Tenth Army fought on in the vicinity of Rome, the CCS might select "the exact place later." Eisenhower noted that the BCOS had been polite and "grateful" for Marshall's views, adding that he now suspected the whole three-month affair was just a matter of emphasis. Eisenhower had carefully weighed Brooke's demeanor, and told Marshall he suspected that what kept the BCOS from agreeing to ANVIL on the spot had been a desire to "prevent a complete freezing of ideas as to where and in what ultimate strength."

A settlement was imminent. The JCS promptly rejected the compromise directive, however, and for a while it appeared that the progress achieved on the twenty-fifth would unravel. For the next week, Spaatz fought on against paying "too great a price . . . for the certainty of very little." Then, on the thirty-first Eisenhower decided to assure Spaatz that the Fifteenth Air Force would be exempted from the program, an important concession. He also assured Spaatz he would give first priority to the overall mission of destruction of German military *and* economic system, gave Spaatz permission to launch a series of heavy attacks on the German oil industry in early April and back the oil plan as the top priority in June.

Portal meanwhile continued to issue directives to the Eighth Air Force and Bomber Command. He cautioned Tedder that the transportation plan could not be official policy until the British War Cabinet approved the plan after consideration of the wider political issues. War Cabinet objectives centered on the RAF technical study showing that even early warning, issued by dropping leaflets over French population centers, would not avoid killing 40,000 Frenchmen. Simultaneously Lord Cherwell, paymaster general, conducted a technical study that confirmed the RAF findings: fifty thousand tons of bombs dropped on the lowlands and northern France would leave 40,000 dead and 160,000 civilians wounded. These estimates, revised substantially downward two weeks later, formed the basis of the Joint Intelligence Committee's findings that the bombing must be extremely "accurate" both to be effective and to avoid civilian casualties. Translated, the Cherwell and JIC reports meant that only Eighth Air Force precision bombers operating by day could accomplish the job, a task still not approved officially by the CCS.

Churchill intervened on April 3. In a letter to Eisenhower, he announced that the War Cabinet had taken "a rather grave and on the whole adverse view" of the program in light of the RAF study. That day, Eisenhower and Churchill again met to discuss Wilson's directive, now ensnared in debate over the level of ANVIL preparations that King would accept before approving the transfer of landing craft and British insistence that the directive include a positive statement about Rome after linkup at Anzio, four weeks off.

In the next several days, Eisenhower for once became privately critical of the British. He could understand their anger about King's "offer," which implied that the Americans suspected the British had ulterior motives in refusing to consent to a firm target date for ANVIL. At the same time, Eisenhower sensed that the JCS had now gone as far as it would and should go—the next step was the cancellation of ANVIL, which Washington was unlikely to accept and, in Eisenhower's view, was probably premature. Moreover, by April, post-invasion planning at SHAEF was beginning to focus on the long-range advantages of a secondary front based on Marseilles in the battle of France and the advance to the German frontier. The advantages were formidable, and Eisenhower could not discount the possibility that the British would eventually support ANVIL—as a practical matter, the British could not ignore their investment in France.

Debate wore on into mid-April, then suddenly stopped. Churchill pushed the Eisenhower-Brooke compromise to the end, at one point exchanging messages with Marshall on the ANVIL problem as the President stood aloof, reported to be vacationing in South Carolina to recover from influenza. Then on the fourteenth, Eisenhower, having referred the problem of War Cabinet objections over French casualty estimates to the CCS, received a directive assigning him control of the strategic air forces until the invasion was "securely ashore." Simultaneously, the CCS split the difference on ANVIL. In Wilson's final directive, issued on the nineteenth, Rome received "top priority in current Mediterranean operations," with a review of ANVIL set for June 15. The CCS ratified Wilson's plans for a mid-May offensive while at the same time directing him to maintain an "effective threat" against the Riviera sufficient to contain the German Army Group C. However, the Americans refused to re-allocate any Pacific shipping, which pushed both ANVIL and Istria into the remote future. This decision infuriated Brooke, who privately vowed history would never "forgive them [the Americans] for bargaining equipment versus strategy and for trying to blackmail us into agreeing with them by holding the pistol of withholding landing craft at our heads." More of this would be heard later—but for now the debate subsided, and the leadership began to close ranks, a move begun in retrospect by Churchill on February 28, accelerated by Portal's performance at the Air Ministry on March 25 and, apparently, assisted throughout by Eisenhower's restraint.

In this way, the pre-invasion command crisis passed, though the command settlement amounted to little more than a truce reached under the pressure of events and the approaching invasion deadlines. What did it mean? Looking back on it, Eisenhower would derive many lessons from the debates of February–March 1944: the main lesson, as he later put it, was that the clearest and most reliable judgments are invariably reached "in the calm." In late 1943 the Americans, British and Russians at Teheran, not under pressure of operational deadlines, had devised a plan for the quickest resolution of the war in the interests of all. The plan possessed a relentless military and diplomatic logic which all had seen in November, only to find themselves temporarily divided over adopting the necessary and inevitable measures necessary to carry it out.

As for Eisenhower's contribution toward arranging this truce, the record is not clear. One might say that Eisenhower's approach had been a characteristic one: one that focused on the problem of reconciling the British first, all the while deferring as many divisive long-range problems as possible for the sake of concentrating on the immediate issue. This approach inevitably meant disillusionment and future troubles, but in retrospect it was probably Eisenhower's only course. And so, as the command crisis passed, Eisenhower could not have failed to recognize that the command truce was temporary, and that the hard part was ahead.

4

Invasion

THE days passed slowly. The wait for D-Day was agony. Mamie Eisenhower, back at the Wardman after spending several weeks in Texas, endured her fifth invasion vigil of the war. In the times before, she had detected a pattern in her husband's letters. Usually his letters were busy and chatty descriptions of office routine, mutual friends and social highlights. She had learned that when he became sentimental, or observant, he was telegraphing the imminence of a major attack.

Eisenhower's letters home in January and February seemed usual enough. He had described being "decked out in my best" for his call on King George at Buckingham Palace. He had complained about a number of articles lost in the move from Algiers, including a St. Christopher's medal sent to him by a schoolgirl in Canton, Ohio. In another he described Hayes Lodge, and discussed their 1943 tax returns. On Valentine's Day he observed the twenty-eighth anniversary of his call on her at 1216 McCullough Street in San Antonio to present his class ring.

His notes were testimony to his growing fondness for the British. He introduced a number of important people he had gotten to know and expected Mamie to get to know after the war. He described a dinner at Claridges in late February hosted by his good friend Admiral Andrew Cunningham, once a colleague at AFHQ and now First Lord of the Admiralty. The surprise party had involved a dozen British military and diplomatic colleagues, and Cunningham had capped it with a glowing tribute to Eisenhower, which left him speechless. Eisenhower described the George III silver salver presented to him, inscribed by all present, including Harold Macmillan, a friend and future Prime Minister of England. Eisenhower had the salver insured, placed it in a London bank vault, and sent Mamie the photostated copies of the documents.

In March his notes became irregular and short. He apologized for his lapses in writing home and asked her to be patient. He reminded her of the letters he received from mothers asking about their sons "missing in action," begging his help, but always asking that he do nothing that would add to his burdens or in any way interfere with them. "The more people suffer, the more truly considerate they become," he wrote. "How I wish this cruel business of war could be completed quickly," he wrote several days later, "a man must develop a veneer of callousness that lets him consider such things dispassionately, but he can never escape a recognition of the fact that back home the news brings anguish and suffering to families all over the country. Mothers, fathers, brothers and sisters, wives and friends must have a difficult time preserving any comforting philosophy and retaining any belief in the eternal rightness of things."

In early March, reminiscing about their engagement party at the Garden of Allah near the theater on Alamo Plaza in San Antonio twenty-eight years earlier, he wrote:

> . . . The days are getting much longer. In this northerly climate there is a great difference between the length of summer and winter days, so the daily change is quite noticeable. It never really gets warm, though—even in July.
>
> My days are always full. Even when I think I have a couple of hours to myself, something always happens to upset my plans. But it's right that we should be busy —as long as we can retain some time to think. And thinking must be done some time during a day when a man is fresh. After 7:00 P.M. I never seem to have an original thought—although one night at 2:00 A.M. I came out with an idea that the P.M. [Churchill] seized upon as tops. The fact was, I was only trying to think of something that would settle the matter and allows us to go home. . . .

Then came early-spring weather and reports of a gradual stabilization on the eastern front, which dashed lingering hopes on both sides of the Atlantic that the Germans would be defeated before summer. Press reports noted the stepped-up bombing attacks on German communications centers, the evacuation of civilians from coastal areas and sudden restrictions on diplomats and press in the British Isles. Neutral capitals—Madrid, Stockholm, Lisbon and Ankara—became rumor mills about invasion dates and places. Many calculations were being made, noted the *Nation,* "their accuracy can be checked when the first Allied soldier wades ashore on the first continental beachhead. But no one doubts that the attack will come soon, or that the last phase of the war is about to begin."

Gradually, friends and relatives corresponding with Eisenhower awoke to the building anticipation of the invasion in America. For a year Eisenhower and his eldest brother, Edgar, had been exchanging letters, and quarreling as usual. Quick with advice from an older to a younger brother, Edgar had complained regularly that winter about the tidal wave of publicity engulfing Ike and the four brothers on the details of their lives from birth in Texas and Abilene to their upbringing in rural Kansas, sentimentalized in books and articles in tones borrowed from Mark Twain.

Edgar, a top-flight Tacoma tax attorney, was a self-made millionaire and did not warm to the notion of being known as somebody's "brother." He politely accused Dwight of encouraging the publicity, informing him that he was tired of movie producers, magazine journalists, and newspaper men inundating him with requests for anecdotes about their boyhood.

Suddenly in April, Edgar, sobered by the appalling responsibility confronting his brother, began to cooperate with journalists. He wrote Dwight to ask him if he could take a minute to draw up a list of the several incidents he remembered best about their boyhood. Edgar volunteered to fill in the rest. Sensing friendliness, Dwight replied that he simply had no time, but good-naturedly reminded Edgar, "You could run faster, hit better, field better, tote the football better and do everything except beat me at shot gun shooting . . . so it looks to me that if you have to tell any stories about our boyhood, you will have to tell them that I was just the tail to your kite."

In reply, Edgar did not tease his brother about the curtailment of his civil liberties, the rationing and the inconvenience. ". . . all the signs point toward an early invasion of the continent," he wrote, "and I hold my breath until I read about the number of casualties we have suffered. I know the venture will be costly, but I am confident that every conceivable protection to our boys will be made by you before the march commences. I sincerely hope that the attack will be successful and that war will come to a sudden end, and the cost in lives will not be too great."

By April the move to Widewing was complete. Gault still maintained Hayes Lodge for nights in London, but Eisenhower's full-time residence was Telegraph Cottage. There he lived privately, even reclusively, protected by his close-knit staff, surrounded by the memories of autumn 1942, which he had spent there.

Telegraph Cottage, at the intersection of Kingston Road and Coombe Lane, stood along a row of houses at the end of a driveway guarded by a white pole gate manned by one armed sentry, a veteran of World War I. The small five-room Tudor-style house was set on a ten-acre plot, with a modest truck garden in the back, surrounded by forests. The existence of the cottage was almost completely unknown to anyone outside of Eisenhower's immediate personal entourage. As the story goes, Ambassador Harriman visiting the cottage in October 1942 for a planning session had been asked not to disclose its whereabouts to his daughter, Kathleen.

The main section included a tiny living room heated by a fireplace and furnished with two chairs, a mahogany sofa and a bridge table. A glassed-in porch in the back looked out on a garden and trees separating the cottage and a golf course. Telegraph Cottage was a sanctuary, and serious books were banned along with all traces of work. Only the Sunday London newspapers and Eisenhower's bedtime Westerns were allowed. Eisenhower, who considered himself lazy by nature, occasionally talked about his plans for after the war. Somewhere out west, he hoped to find a rustic place like Telegraph Cottage where he would fish, tend cattle and horses. Or maybe he would move back to Telegraph Cottage.

According to Butcher, the cottage inspired Eisenhower's first sketch as an artist. The idea of painting was probably suggested to him by Tedder, though later versions of Eisenhower's interest in art would carefully post-date his earliest efforts to 1947 to avoid suggestions that he had emulated the British. Eisenhower remarked to Butcher that spring that the features of Telegraph Cottage seemed expressive of England as a whole. It was a remote, dilapidated, drafty English cottage, with a floor plan no different from thousands of other "Nash" homes built in the area. It was weary but comfortable, and there, he said, "I feel free."

Inevitably, Eisenhower's off-hours at Telegraph Cottage would lead to speculation about his relationship with Kay Summersby. Rumors of an affair circulated in London and Army circles in Washington, which blossomed after publication of Summersby's suggestive book in 1948 based on a sketchy diary she had started in June. Summersby would expand her tale in 1976 and allege a love affair, though without giving details. Butcher would deny aspects of her story, but few disputed her version of the routine at Telegraph Cottage. However far it went, the two were attached. Eisenhower was under tremendous pressures and in need of company. Beyond this, the truth was known only by them, and both are gone.

Years later Mickey McKeogh was offended by Summersby's books and perturbed by her effort to portray herself as an "exclusive concern." "Mickey" McKeogh had been with Eisenhower since Third Army days in the summer of 1941 at Fort Sam Houston, Texas. The son of a New York City policeman, he had been a bellhop at the Plaza Hotel before volunteering for the Army in 1940. Utterly devoted, he faithfully tended to Eisenhower's needs twenty-four hours a day. Eisenhower, in turn, treated him decently and fairly, "like a father." As far as Mickey was concerned, everyone was a member of a "family," sharing equally in Eisenhower's successes and disappointments and contributing more or less equally to Eisenhower's well-being. McKeogh denied that Telegraph Cottage was a "home for two." In McKeogh's view, Summersby was a valued member of the staff, but not his "type." He remembered a number of scrapes with her, and a few good times as well. She was "nice, unmilitary, and very emotional." In McKeogh's opinion, Eisenhower needed unmilitary types like her to relieve the austere and disciplined routine he otherwise led. At times, however, her nonmilitary qualities intruded on Mickey's keen sense of his place within the headquarters setup; Kay had a habit of crossing jurisdictional lines to order Mickey and some of the other personal orderlies around. Once, Mickey recalled appealing to Eisenhower for relief. "Bear with her," he had replied, "she's not a very well person."

The staff had mourned with Summersby in late 1943 when her fiancé was killed by a land mine in North Africa shortly before she was to be married. But living with tragedy was inescapable in wartime, and Kay gradually regained her spirits. Eisenhower's admonition suggested that there might be something special about Kay, however. Either she was special to Eisenhower, or her personal tragedy affected him in a special way, a concern that lifted him out of his own preoccupations. In time, McKeogh became satisfied that it was his duty to accept Kay in accordance with the General's wishes, and he conceded years later that while Summersby exaggerated the tale of romance, there could be no exaggeration of her importance on the staff.

Butcher presided over a personal staff picked for its discretion and loyalty and forged during the Darlan storm, Eisenhower's most vulnerable moment. There is evidence that members of Eisenhower's TORCH staff broke ranks over the Eisenhower-Darlan accord or fell away during the winter stalemate in Tunisia. Smith, Butcher, McKeogh and "Skib" Summersby had stood firm. Butcher's most vivid stories deal with Eisenhower's anxious months in the winter of 1942–43. He would recall that the African campaign was frustrating and tense, a prolonged test of Eisenhower's restraint, which he abandoned privately only once, on the night following the Axis surrender at Tunis. For several hours, over bourbon and branch water, Eisenhower and Butcher sat up to compose an oracular telegram to MacArthur acknowledging MacArthur's perfunctory congratulations over a victory that netted 300,000 German and Italian prisoners. Butcher later explained that for Eisenhower, Tunisia was a supreme moment. He had been a worker in the vineyards on MacArthur's staff, denigrated as an "aide," though he often wrote MacArthur's speeches. Having now achieved a victory on his own, he was afraid MacArthur would not notice. At about three o'clock, Butcher recalled, the two applied the finishing flourishes on the stately document and staggered off to bed. The following morning before his first appointment, Eisenhower, the diplomat as always, ran the document through the shredder at the St. Georges.

At Telegraph Cottage, Eisenhower's staff was on hand at breakfast. The group reassembled at supper. Routine bridge guests included T. J. Davis, a staff colleague who had been with Eisenhower in Manila and Washington. Summersby was the official hostess. Omar Bradley was an occasional guest. Ruth Briggs, Smith's personal secretary, often filled in as the fourth. Butcher kept score in games played for modest stakes at threepence per hundred points. McKeogh hovered about, emptying ashtrays and keeping the peanut dish full. McKeogh also made sure Eisenhower's bedside table was stacked with chocolate, Chesterfield cigarettes and pulp Westerns.

Eisenhower's taste for Western novels was known and talked about in wartime London, a taste he made no effort to conceal. He enjoyed the lore of the Old West, which he had learned growing up in Abilene, once notori-

ous as the terminus of the Chisholm Trail and the domain of Wild Bill
Hickok. Actually, the Hickok era had ended twenty years before Eisenhower's boyhood in the 1890s. Abilene by then had settled down as one of
many conventional Main Street towns dotting the Kansas City–Denver rail
line at the turn of the century, set apart from the others by its town lore,
cheerfully embellished by the older folk as the years went on. Eisenhower's
boyhood was uneventful, a time of hard work and monotony relieved by
baseball, football and, by Eisenhower's account, daydreaming about escape
into the wider world that he had learned about in books and at school.

Who was he? Biographies and articles on Eisenhower appearing that
spring delved into the circumstances of his youth. Little was known about
it. Several years before Eisenhower's birth, the Eisenhowers had left a
secure and prosperous life as farmers in the Lykens Valley of central Pennsylvania to resettle in central Kansas, where they met reverses leading to
a drastic break with the past. The Eisenhower ancestors had been Menno-
nites in the German Palatinate; they had settled in Switzerland to escape
religious persecution in the sixteenth century. From Switzerland, the Eisenhowers emigrated to America in 1732 and settled in the German-speaking
"Pennsylvania Dutch" regions near Lancaster. First the Civil War, then
industrialization encroached on the Mennonite community. That and personal tragedy prompted Eisenhower's grandfather to join the Mennonite
migration to the rich farmlands of central Kansas.

But as the biographers discovered, the encroachments had been irreversible. Eisenhower's father, David, described as an inquisitive, rebellious spirit,
grew up restless with Mennonite strictures and the prospect of a lifetime of
farming. First, David Eisenhower broke with long-settled custom to seek
higher education, attending Lane University near Lawrence, Kansas, for a
year where he met and married Ida Stover. Then, in a fateful step, David
sold his land to raise capital for a store in the town of Hope, Kansas. In
the depression of 1888 the store went bankrupt, and Eisenhower lost his
entire investment. Deep in debt, he left Kansas temporarily to work as a
manual laborer on the TKM railroad in Denison, Texas, where Dwight
Eisenhower was born, the third of six sons, on October 14, 1890.

The interlude of failure was considered so disgraceful by his parents that
Eisenhower grew up in almost complete ignorance of it. On his cadet
registry of West Point, Eisenhower would erroneously list "Tyler," Texas,
as his birthplace, and not until 1943, thanks to the enterprising efforts of a
local reporter for the *Denison Texas Herald,* did he learn of his actual
birthplace, a small unshaded frame house on stilts near the TKM terminal.

Thereafter, the Eisenhower family gradually recovered. After two years
in Texas the Eisenhowers returned to Abilene, where David Eisenhower
accepted a job as a foreman in the local creamery at low wages and saved
every penny he could. The Eisenhowers accumulated enough savings to buy
a small house south of the tracks on three acres, where they raised vegeta-

bles and kept a horse and several cows. Life was comfortable but austere.

Daily life for the children was described as being full of chores and schoolwork. Social life revolved around the newly impoverished Mennonite community in the area. In 1944, townspeople could still recall the Eisenhower boys as grade-schoolers selling surplus vegetables in town to purchase necessities. In high school, Dwight took a job at the Belle Springs Creamery, where his father worked six days a week. He pulled ice, washed cans in the butter rooms and ran a compressor, which ground ice into powder. Company records show that occasionally he drew goods in lieu of pay, including shoes to work on the wet cement floors of the butter rooms. Young Eisenhower developed physical strength, a capacity for hard work, and a determination steeled by a strict and domineering father, who "lived in the shadows of an early failure." By contrast, Ida was described as a serene, deeply religious person who imparted tolerance and optimism to her sons. Both parents had education, and valued it. As the story went, Dwight wanted to go to West Point for the free education and the adventure, braving the disapproval of his Mennonite parents. But his parents permitted it. Eisenhower wasted no time at West Point in impressing his instructors and fellow students as a young man marked for advancement.

After dinner at Telegraph Cottage, Eisenhower occasionally took "constitutionals" down Coombe Lane with Summersby or Butcher. Summersby would later describe Eisenhower as a lonely kind of person, accustomed to hard work and little fun. Eisenhower experienced his share of disappointments—his missed service in World War I, the death of his first son, "Icky," aged four, in 1922 at Fort Meade, where the Eisenhowers had become acquainted with the George Pattons and General Fox Conner. Eisenhower spent sixteen years as a major in the peacetime Army, slowly climbing through the Army school system and staff assignments. As a staff officer, he became a self-described "draft horse," unspectacular but indispensable, in the service of the War Department, MacArthur and then Marshall.

And so all had turned out well, and by April 1944, Eisenhower looked back on Abilene fondly. He credited many of his successes to the character-developing experience of "being needed" as a youth and contributing real work toward the survival of the family. Occasionally he talked about his family, particularly the "characters," such as Dwight's uncle, a man by the name of Abraham Lincoln Eisenhower.

Like his brother David, "Abe" left farming for a varied career as a veterinarian and preacher of the Gospel, and like David, he had lost heavily in the depression of 1888. There the similarity ended. After his store failed, David's spirit of enterprise had vanished. For Abe, a failed veterinary practice had merely been a preliminary. At about the time the state began to enforce rules about licensing and professional training, as Eisenhower put it, Abe met an itinerant evangelist preaching on a street corner in Abilene and experienced "full salvation." It was told that in the space of a few days

Abe rented his two-story house on Fourth Street to David with an option to buy, converted a Conestoga wagon into a mobile home equipped with chairs, tables, four cots and a gas stove, dubbed his contraption the "House of Pilgrimage," and with his new wife sailed off into the Oklahoma Territory embarked on a career of preaching the Gospel.

From Oklahoma, Abe had journeyed to California, then to Iowa and Ohio, then back to Kansas and Oklahoma, spreading the Gospel and defying his misfortunes. A well-known yarn about Abe was how he had broken up a July Fourth celebration in nearby Herington, Kansas, with a stem-winding sermon on Job, hellfire and brimstone. Uncle Abe's fame spread. In Oklahoma, Abe and his wife opened an orphanage for abandoned children, alcoholics and unwed mothers, which was still open in the spring of 1944, testimony to their perseverance.

Several times, entertaining guests at Telegraph Cottage, Eisenhower repeated yarns about Abe, a reminder of his humble origins, which his British hosts found interesting and endearing. But he remarked once to Summersby that he regarded Abe as more than a colorful vagabond of the American West. "I always thought there was a lesson in Abe's sermons," he told her, "but I'm damned if I've ever been able to figure out what it is. I know the old man was mighty proud of himself, the way he could raise an audience out of dust, so to speak."

The wait continued. Butcher kept busy with the diary and provided constant companionship to relieve Eisenhower's tremendous inner tension. He noted Eisenhower's complaints about an incessant ringing in his ears, a symptom of hypertension. What Butcher knew, and what the doctors were withholding from the General, was an alarming rise in his blood pressure, which the doctors were attempting to treat surreptitiously by supplementing medication prescribed for Eisenhower's chronic cold. Butcher arranged with the superintendent of nearby Richmond Park for Eisenhower to ride on horseback through the park trails on days when visitors were not allowed. He acquired badminton equipment, which he kept in the garage, and coaxed Eisenhower occasionally into playing several holes of golf at the Castle Coombe course on the other side of the woods. But Eisenhower's intermittent efforts to relax never took him away from official worries very long.

As time went on, a detectable aimlessness crept into Butcher's account, reminiscent of October 1943 at the St. Georges. He chronicled gossip about the flow of visitors passing through London to and from Cairo, Algiers, Moscow and Washington. As before, talk centered on the home front in America and the eastern front—only this time there were no conferences in the offing. Lloyd Stratton of the AP passed through on his way back from Moscow with a report that the Russians seemed "thoroughly united and fanatically prosecuting the war both on the home front and battle fronts."

But Stratton expected the Russians to let up after regaining all prewar Russian territory, whereupon the war would become a "high-level military affair."

April was political primary season in America. The withdrawal of Wendell Willkie, who had opposed Roosevelt in 1940, threw the Republican race open, enlivened by the disclosure of correspondence between MacArthur and Congressman Arthur Miller of Nebraska in which MacArthur apocalyptically denounced New Deal policies as threatening the American way of life and criticized Roosevelt's undue concern over the European war, which he, MacArthur, considered practically won.

From afar, Eisenhower privately sympathized with MacArthur, who, in his opinion, had been "used." But his former chief's criticism of war policy touched a sensitive chord in London. Skeptics of American intentions, strengthened by the latest round on ANVIL, noted the episode and other signs that American "rigidity" on strategic and political issues would continue with or without a Roosevelt victory in the fall. By now the BCOS had abandoned an "attrition" strategy against the Germans for a new and more aggressive pursuit strategy, with emphasis on a range of bold stratagems designed to force a quick decision over Germany. The meaning of this shift in thinking is debatable, but it was expressive of the one point on which all Londoners agreed: that hopes of minimizing the political, moral and economic damage in Europe would depend on a "short war," ending by the fall of 1944 at the latest.

From the Channel Islands to Istanbul, Europe cowered under German occupation, poised between the Russian invasion and anarchy. Reports, based on the eyewitness accounts of visitors returning from Paris and Berlin to the neutral capitals Madrid, Stockholm, Lisbon, Berne and Ankara, described the terror of the bombings, the agony of Hungary and the agony of France with the elevation of Darnard and Henriot in the Laval government, one small step short of direct German rule over France through a Nazi *Gauleiter.* Sentiment in London rose for action to bring the Germans to their senses in the hope of halting their suicidal course.

Behind the scenes, Churchill urgently pushed for talks with the Russians on the unfinished business of Poland, Hungary, Rumania, Bulgaria and Greece, and served notice of new initiatives in a controversial speech in Parliament aimed at nipping an incipient Conservative party revolt. In it the Prime Minister criticized rigid responses to complex issues to be faced in the coming months and declared that, in his opinion, as the war progressed it had "become less ideological." Churchill aroused criticism in London and Washington with kindly words spoken about Turkey and Spain, capped by a tribute to the "military and material contributions" of the Free French, who, he declared, had assumed fourth place in the ranks of the Alliance.

Butcher noted the questions cropping up about the President's health.

General Albert Wedemeyer paid a call at Widewing on his way to New Delhi, where he was to become deputy Allied CINC under Mountbatten. He had recently been to Hyde Park; the President, who had seemed ill and preoccupied, appeared worried about D-Day, about congressional criticism of his foreign policy, wage and price controls, and "secret diplomacy." Wedemeyer told Eisenhower that the Office of War Information was adjusting broadcast policy to prepare the American people for high casualties.

In mid-April, newly appointed Under Secretary of State Edward Stettinius visited London for talks with Eden, Churchill and the Foreign Office. Officially, Stettinius was responding to complaints about the lack of interaction between second-echelon American and British diplomats due to the almost bimonthly meetings that had taken place between Roosevelt and Churchill before Teheran. Stettinius was also in London to be introduced as Hull's probable successor and to become familiar with the array of problems soon to confront the Allies: France, and dealings with De Gaulle; the United Nations; discussions with the Russians on Poland and the Balkans; postwar Russian territorial claims; and arrangements for the international monetary conferences set for the summer.

Stettinius had news of the political situation and a behind-the-scenes report on the President. At one point Stettinius told Butcher that Roosevelt was slipping, a man grown indecisive, and unable to concentrate under the pressures of his job. Stettinius disclosed that there were Cabinet members who felt the President "would go down with tremendous prestige if he were to announce at the Democratic National Convention his decision not to be a candidate again and at the same dramatic moment recommend General Marshall for the nomination." Stettinius felt the President could assume a role in the United Nations, where he would retain his "dominant position on postwar matters."

During his visit Stettinius also described the intense debate over unconditional surrender. Personally, he was critical of the President's "rigid" stance on unconditional surrender and told Eisenhower that many in Congress and the Cabinet suspected that the policy had outlived its usefulness as a "vote of self-confidence." In his opinion, the policy accomplished nothing except to bind the German people more tightly together with the Nazis, harden resistance on all fronts and undermine the possibilities of a revolt within Germany, perhaps originating in the antagonism between the Wehrmacht and the SS.

There are conflicting versions of a meeting between Eisenhower, Smith and Stettinius on a formal approach to the JCS for a "clarification" of the policy. Farago's version depicts Smith as the prime mover and Eisenhower as "noncommittal" and reluctant to participate. In a cable to the Joint Chiefs in Washington, Stettinius related that Eisenhower and Smith favored a "clarification" of the policy, such as a statement of principle indicating the Allies' intent to restore religious freedom, trade unions and conditions of "law, order, and property rights" in Germany as a military measure calculated to create a climate of acceptance in the army and in the population toward capitulation.

By April, the consensus at SHAEF favored this step. The argument ran that such a statement might do some good and would not alter the existing situation, since, after all, the Allies were fighting for all of these things. But would the Russians approve? Moscow had long been "open-minded" on unconditional surrender, and Stalin had approved the policy at the Moscow foreign ministers conference at Hull's request. But even though the Soviets remained ostensibly open-minded, now did not seem to be the time for the Allies to initiate a revision of it. Indeed, as General Deane of the military mission in Moscow would later write, many Russians still suspected that talk of OVERLORD was an elaborate deception plan. Even to raise the question of terms for Germany was a sensitive matter, made more so by the Balkan overtures about which Churchill was keeping Moscow closely informed in his quest to apportion British-Soviet responsibilities for occupation policy in the Balkans.

By April, another factor had to be considered. The Soviets were talking about plans for reconstructing Russia with the help of German prisoners of war and repatriated Russian nationals who had fought or worked on the side of Germany. Talk about giving the Germans an "out" would raise doubts in Russia that the Allies intended to cooperate with Russian plans by repatriating Russian nationals or by refusing the surrender of eastern-front units who, when the time came, might try to evade deportation to Russia by surrendering on the western front, where the Geneva conventions were in full force. The morale factor had to be considered also—whether Allied troops would interpret a change as Allied generosity or an admission of Allied weakness.

Afterward Roosevelt rejected the Stettinius proposal and instructed Hull to inform "all involved" that the subject was not even to be considered without his approval, since he was unwilling to assure the Germans about their future or that the Allies would oppose Moscow's demand for German forced labor at the end of the war to "restore the devastated areas in Europe." Nonetheless, the JCS and SHAEF grappled over a text of principles that would be acceptable to the Russians and effective in conveying to pro-peace elements in Germany a reassuring picture of postwar German society.

Smith and Phillips at SHAEF later came up with a half step: approaching Moscow about an amnesty proclamation for "nationals serving under compulsion" in the German army in France to be issued by the United Nations for all "non-volunteers" who surrendered at the first opportunity. SHAEF proposed to target the Russian nationals serving in German static divisions south of Cherbourg.

Roosevelt was mildly attracted. In May, he opened the matter for comment by Eisenhower and the military staffs, hoping either to find a firm military rationale for proceeding or to silence the JCS. In particular, Roosevelt had doubts "as to the ability of the Allied High Command to back up any promise that might be made merely on behalf of the United States and Great Britain." Eisenhower urged Smith to pursue the question of a three-power statement of principles that acknowledged Soviet demands for German labor. "The difficulty," Eisenhower explained, "arises in writing something that may be acceptable to the Russians . . . and at the same time not be so harshly interpreted by the German nation as to allow German propaganda to denounce the statement as an intention to enslave the whole Axis. If we cannot surmount this obstacle, then we had better drop the whole matter and let it ride as it is. . . ."

The unconditional surrender controversy was inseparable from the climate of doubt that persisted at all levels. BBC correspondent Chester Wilmot, who would accompany the British 6th Airborne on D-Day, later described the "listless air of uncertainty" in the camps springing up in southern England.

Had the British Army recovered wholly from the defeats of 1940-41? Brooke and Churchill had long been unsure, and had therefore been reluctant as recently as Teheran to submit sixteen divisions to the hazards of a cross-Channel assault. Field commanders were skeptical of the ability of infantry and light armor to penetrate mine fields and fortifications of steel and concrete manned by well-trained troops in the best of circumstances. Would the Allies achieve surprise? The odds seemed stacked against it, for it appeared that the invasion date could be deduced by tidal and weather conditions. The topography of the French Channel coast allowed for an assault of great size in only a few places, and it was hard to believe that the assemblage of such a large assault force could be kept hidden or that security would not be breached by someone. The arrival in England of a fresh American division each week could not be concealed, nor could the ongoing concentration of 70,000 vehicles, 7,000 guns and 4,000 ships along the south coast of England from Bristol to Ipswich. The enemy might be kept confused during the preparatory stage, but by H-Hour the Germans would surely know that Normandy was *the* assault. Wilmot wrote of a "deep, unspoken dread" about the coming assault on the Atlantic Wall. "The [British] people had hardened themselves to endure what must be endured," he wrote. "There would be no shrinking from sacrifice, since their resolution was far stronger than their fear, but they could not altogether dispel from their hearts the memories of Passchendaele, Dunkirk and Dieppe."

Would the raw American units weather the supreme challenge of an all-out German defense of France? Inexperienced and uncertain leadership had exacted a stern penalty in central Tunisia, at Salerno and in the battle raging at Anzio. Barely twelve months had elapsed since the Kasserine disaster. Casual discipline, indifferent morale and intermittent patrolling had contributed directly to the tactical surprise achieved by the Germans in central Tunisia. In the wake of Kasserine, Eisenhower had sacked II Corps Commander Lloyd Fredendall, but still rebuked himself for his weakness in failing to send Fredendall back to the United States reduced in rank.

The ongoing stalemate at Anzio was part of the Kasserine legacy. Weeks earlier, Wes Gallagher, the AP correspondent at AFHQ, had passed through with word about the play-it-safe attitude in the field commands. "Eisenhower is missed," he said. "A commander to say 'Go ahead, the responsibility is mine.' " Several weeks later, following his relief due to "extreme exhaustion," Major General John P. Lucas visited 47 Grosvenor to brief the staff about what, according to Harry Butcher, "might be called 'The End Run That Was Blocked.' "

Lucas described the Anzio operation in detail: VI Corps practice landings at Salerno beforehand had revealed the inexperience of the assault divisions; VI Corps had been fortunate at first when German counterattacks against the 3rd Division sector had been within range of naval gunfire, and later when the counteroffensive at Campoleone happened to hit reinforced positions. Lucas noted that the German high command could always be expected to make mistakes, and yet the German troops seemed strangely "filled with optimism" about eventual victory. Of Lucas, Butcher wrote, "He seemed to be a soldier carrying out orders with which he was not in sympathy." Unlike the landing at Anzio, experienced units would lead the OVERLORD assault. Eisenhower chose the battle-hardened U.S. 1st and 4th divisions and Montgomery chose the British 50th and 7th Armored as lead divisions. But the 29th Division, also set to land at OMAHA, was fresh, and the final FABIUS rehearsals that month would rekindle doubts about the training and fitness of inexperienced American units.

Several security scares occurred. A famous one had domestic political overtones. In March, employees at the Army Mail Sorting Office in Chicago broke open by accident a set of documents mailed from England by Sergeant "Thomas P. Kane" of SHAEF Ordinance G-4 to his sister that contained the target date, the Normandy landing site and build-up data. At first General Thomas J. Betts of SHAEF G-2 and General Clayton Bissell, War Department G-2, suspected that "Kane," a soldier of German extraction, had attempted to leak OVERLORD to the isolationist anti-Roosevelt Chicago *Tribune,* which had allegedly assigned a reporter in England to break the story. (Of course, "scoops" of military plans had occurred before.

Shortly before Pearl Harbor, the *Tribune* had leaked details of the classified "Operation Victory" estimates.* Later the *Tribune* disclosed in print that the Americans had broken the Japanese naval code.) After an exhaustive investigation, "Kane" was cleared of espionage, confined to quarters and placed under surveillance until after D-Day.

Another case involved General Henry Jervis Miller, quartermaster general of the Ninth Air Force and a 1915 classmate of Eisenhower and Bradley at West Point. At Claridges Hotel in April, General Edwin L. Sibert, counterintelligence officer of ETO, overheard Miller repeat over drinks at Claridges a complaint that supplies were "not getting through" from the States and could not until after the invasion in mid-June. Sibert reported the case to Bradley, who informed Eisenhower. After his arrest, Miller, from "the hospital," appealed to Eisenhower on the basis of friendship to be sent back to America at his current rank to await "such action as the fates have in store for me." In his reply, Eisenhower told Miller he regretted "sitting as a judge" in a case involving a friend, but that he was persuaded by testimony compiled by Sibert of two corroborating witnesses that he was guilty of a serious breach of security. Eisenhower denied the appeal, and ordered Miller reduced to colonel and sent back to the United States.

A bizarre mishap occurred in May when a gust of wind blew twelve copies of the "OVERLORD order" out the window of the British War Office into a crowd of pedestrians. Staff and clerks raced into the street, finding eleven of the twelve copies, "Two agonizing hours passed," recalled John Eisenhower in *Allies.* "Finally a stranger walked up to the British sentry on the opposite side of the street and handed him the missing copy. The man's identity was never known."

Perhaps the strangest security scare of all would surface in early May. The London *Daily Telegraph,* read by millions, published one of the more popular and challenging puzzles offered by Britain's eight national daily newspapers. On May 2 a British staff member at SHAEF noticed Seventeen across: "One of the U.S."—answer: "Utah." Two weeks later, a clue in the *Daily Telegraph* puzzle read: "Red Indian on the Missouri"—answer: "Omaha." ETO counterintelligence chief General Sibert alerted Scotland Yard and British MI-5 counterintelligence about the puzzle. The author, a schoolmaster living in the London suburb of Leatherhead by the name of Leonard Sidney Dawe was placed under surveillance.

Meanwhile, overseas cabling privileges were denied all but a few trusted newsmen. Every phone call made by a soldier or official, every letter in sensitive areas of Britain, every telegram was liable to monitoring. Travel in and out of and visits to England and Scotland were forbidden to all but a few. SHAEF instituted a special procedure for all documents revealing the place or time of the invasion. They were labeled BIGOT—the highest

*See Chapter 2.

security classification—a term that reversed the letters of "To Gib" stamped on papers of the officers who had gone to Gibraltar for TORCH.

Eisenhower appealed to the Combined Chiefs, Roosevelt and Churchill to limit any statements pertaining to D-Day to expressions of "good wishes and encouragement to the Allied troops," avoiding mention of the NEPTUNE area, and above all saying nothing that would imply that Normandy was to be the supreme effort. SHAEF, still monitoring the debate within the German high command, was aware of the success of FORTITUDE so far in confirming the Pas-de-Calais as a primary or secondary Allied target. Under the terms of the diplomatic ban, all communications between ambassadors and representatives accredited in London, except for the American government, passed through British cipher, an unprecedented suspension of the tradition of confidential communications between diplomats and their home country. The British government imposed these restrictions reluctantly. Debate over the length of the ban lasted for several weeks. On March 10 the British War Cabinet had banned unauthorized travel and imposed modest restrictions on communications. Since it affected the French, Churchill urged that the ban be short. Eisenhower insisted on a lengthy ban lasting several weeks after OVERLORD. When Churchill balked, Eisenhower requested Brooke to present the matter to the British War Cabinet, saying he felt "bound to say frankly that I regard this source of leakage as the gravest risk to the security of our operations and to the lives of our sailors, soldiers and airmen." Finally, on April 15, Churchill and the War Cabinet endorsed a ban extending into the post-invasion period.

Perhaps the most sensitive security question of all was informing Moscow of the details of OVERLORD. Mutual suspicions had re-emerged since Teheran. FRANTIC negotiations lagged. After Bevan's mission on BODYGUARD, STAVKA began "bombarding" the liaison officers with inquiries about times, troop strengths, objectives, and so on. Lieutenant General Brocas Burrows again asked the CCS for permission to send his naval and air attachés to London for a briefing and a marked map, warning that "the Soviets will never forgive us if OVERLORD is postponed." "He [Burrows] has been assured that we intend to stick by our agreement at Teheran," Butcher wrote irritably, "and advised to keep his shirt on." It had not been forgotten that Soviet Ambassador Ivan Maisky in October 1942 had disclosed TORCH to British reporters several weeks before the North African landings. Many wondered deep down whether the Russians might be content with stalemate or disaster in France after a major battle that kept the Germans busy for a couple of months.

Finally, on April 7, the CCS gave Burrows and Deane permission to inform Marshal Antonov of STAVKA that the date was May 31 "with two or three days' margin on either side to allow for weather and tide." Deane and Burrows received no information about the size of the assault or about the landing area, only the date. Deane and Burrows conveyed this information to Antonov, who thanked them and promised a reply within two days.

Instead, two weeks passed. On April 23, Antonov sent Burrows and Deane a terse three-paragraph note: the Red Army General Staff was satisfied with the date selected; the Red Army would attack simultaneously. In the third paragraph, STAVKA requested Burrows and Deane to so inform the CCS. On this tenuous basis, the eastern and western fronts became, "irrevocably, one war."

With notification of STAVKA on April 7, the preparation phase of OVER-LORD came to a close. That day at Group Headquarters in Kensington, Montgomery presented the 21st Army Group plan to a small assemblage, including Eisenhower and Churchill, a dress rehearsal for a more formal review set for mid-May. Working with teams of "syndicates" of ground, air and naval experts, Montgomery's staff had coordinated the tactical assault plans submitted by Bradley and Dempsey in late February.

In the final tactical plan, five assault landings would occur on the Cotentin Peninsula, running from east to west: SWORD Beach at Ouistreham near Caen, assigned to the 3rd British Infantry Division supported by the British 6th Airborne; six miles west, JUNO Beach at Courseulles, assigned to the 3rd Canadian division; fifteen miles farther west, the 50th British Division would assault GOLD Beach at Arromanches. British Empire forces would stage from the easternmost ports near Portsmouth to maintain a Canadian-British line of supply running from England to the Continent. Fifteen miles west of GOLD Beach, V Corps, consisting of the 1st and 29th U.S. Infantry divisions, would assault OMAHA west of Bayeux. West of Carentan, the 4th U.S. Infantry Division would assault UTAH Beach in tandem with 101st Airborne drops farther inland to secure the causeways over the inundations behind the beaches, and the 82nd farther east at Ste.-Mère-Eglise to gain bridgeheads over the Douve and Vire rivers.

In the landing phase, the objective would be a quick linkup of the American, British and Canadian forces, then swift expansion overland to exploit tactical surprise. On the left, or eastern, flank, the British would seize the town of Caen on D-Day and cross the Orne River assisted by the British 6th Airborne Division dropped on the east bank of the river to seize the bridges. British and Canadian forces would seize Bayeux and the surrounding road nets and high ground, holding the center of the five-beach lodgements to protect against a German counterattack along the Allied "seam." Then the British forces would move sufficiently far inland to seize the Caen plateau, terrain suitable for forward air bases and tank warfare, essential positioning for the battle of breakout. On the western flank, the American forces at OMAHA would move inland quickly to provide flank protection for the UTAH landings and seize the Cherbourg–Paris road running through the small town of Carentan, a vital road artery that would link all five beachheads. In the west, VII Corps at UTAH, supported by the 82nd and

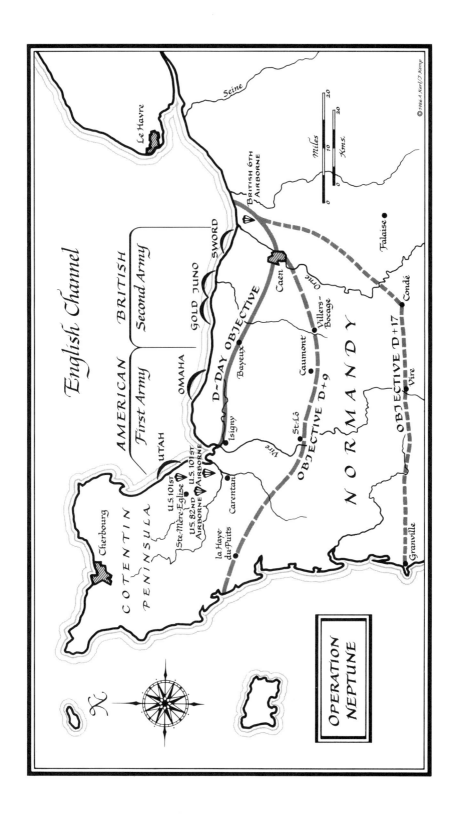

101st U.S. airborne divisions, would attack westward to cut off the Cherbourg Peninsula. Tactical surprise and rapid movement would be vital to success to prevent the Germans from containing the bridgehead long enough to form a powerful reserve for counterattack.

With the 21st Army Group ashore, the Allies would have a foothold, which could be exploited eastward, south or southwest, and Montgomery would confront the problem of breakout. Each sector presented a different problem. In the British sector at Caen, armor could move overland through the Caen plain toward the Seine and Paris. At first glance, the area offered the best potential for expansion and exploitation. Battle conditions in the Caen–Falaise flat terrain would be highly favorable to the Allies where air superiority and mobility could be at a premium. By contrast, the American sector was difficult terrain, suitable only for infantry. South of OMAHA and UTAH beaches, the Normandy countryside turned into the bocage of hedgerow farmland and earthen dikes put up by Norman farmers centuries before to mark property boundaries, maintained since to protect orchard land against gale winds from the Atlantic. The small square plots, an acre or less in places, formed natural defenses against armor, and could be held economically by infantry and anti-tank defenses.

The terrain features had obvious implications. The German Seventh and Fifteenth armies would fear breakout most through the Caen sector and would probably mass forces backed by the Fifteenth Army in the Pas-de-Calais. The Germans would probably economize on the western flank in attempting to exploit the natural defenses of the bocage. Thus, an attempt to break out in the east would be a frontal assault whereas breakout in the west would be more indirect, and possibly less arduous.

Montgomery would later claim categorically that long before the invasion he had planned a "feint" at Caen and breakout in the American sector. Foreseeing that the British armored forces, poised at Falaise, would draw the German mobile forces into battle, he claimed that he had planned all along to exploit German weakness on the western flank by a power drive by the Americans, supported by the ruthless employment of air forces.

Montgomery's plan would be the subject of the most heated controversy of the Normandy battle, a controversy fully developed during the actual fighting itself. Critics would accuse him of covering up a failure to break out at Caen, a plausible charge for several reasons. First, actual breakout plans were tentative, and according to Russell Weigley, Montgomery "was always careful to search what the written record would show he promised in advance." Sketchy COSSAC plans, written in 1943 before the addition of UTAH Beach, had forecast breakout at Caen, which was good tank terrain and the shortest road to Paris. But the COSSAC idea, based on the assumption of a three-division invasion front, was probably obsolete by April—a fact overlooked by Montgomery's detractors. Much would be made of the fact that British assault formations were to be heavily equipped with armor to be employed offensively in seizing Caen quickly by D plus 1, and of Montgomery's forecast on April 7 that his troops would be "knocking about" deep inside the Caen plateau on D-Day. There is evidence that Montgomery in the late stages of the campaign considered a British breakout, but that he did so only after repeated American attempts to break out in the western sector had failed, and after the bulk of the German Fifteenth Army had entered the Normandy battle depleting the German reserve east of the Seine. Whether Montgomery had a change of heart or not is debatable, but in either case the idea of a British breakout would be an improvisation considered after the landings, and not as part of a master plan, all bearing out Montgomery's postwar contentions.

Otherwise, the evidence supports Montgomery's version of his intentions —as far as he went. At the Supreme Commander's conferences and on April 7 Montgomery spoke of breakout and expansion into Brittany in a wheeling movement pivoting on the British flank. Phase lines drawn up by 21st Army Group planners envisioned a gradual expansion of the British flank beyond Caen toward Argentan–Falaise while planning assigned top priority to the capture of Cherbourg and the Brittany ports as ports of entry for the U.S. divisions training in America. No comparable projections existed for Boulogne, Calais, Dunkirk or Dieppe. Every British unit scheduled to participate in the battle of France was already identified in the OVERLORD plan and scheduled to enter France via Normandy.

But all this left the question of how Allied strategy in Normandy would be implemented. Specifically, what would be the necessary scale of the "feint" at Caen necessary to "contain" German forces in that sector and support the American breakout effort? Eisenhower, who helped to generate the controversy over Montgomery's alleged failure to break out at Caen apparently did so not because he quarreled with Montgomery's concept of a containing action there, but because he questioned Montgomery's willingness to carry through the containing action at Caen with sufficient vigor. In short, Eisenhower did not anticipate an Allied breakout through the British sector, but it "certainly . . . was General Eisenhower's impression that Montgomery intended a major offensive effort on the Allies' eastern flank, not merely an absorption of German reserves."

All of this raised an unspoken aspect of OVERLORD strategy: who would bear the greater burden of casualties? This factor weighed particularly on the British, saddled with mounting war debts, a depleted industrial base, and weakened by 500,000 Empire casualties since 1939. Montgomery was leading into battle Britain's last reserve of troops, sixteen divisions intermixed with Polish and Canadian units, an indication that Britain had reached the end of the mobilization line. By contrast, fresh armored replacements would begin arriving from the United States in July and infantry replacements in August. Montgomery, with the acquiescence of SHAEF and Marshall, was prepared to accept greater casualties in the American sector, a factor in his "master plan" calling for breakout through the bocage and in British acquiescence, so far, in command arrangements wherein the Americans would form an independent army group command under Eisenhower after the breakout. In turn the British, "held" to a vigorous diversion at Caen, forced eventually to agree to ANVIL and impressed by the danger of venturing off toward the German frontier without a unified land command, would reopen the command issue, with fateful consequences.

Meanwhile, advance planning went forward for the subsequent battle of France. Logistical and mobilization plans had to be brought in line with post-landing objectives. Thus, by the end of April, SHAEF began filing "appreciations" of post-breakout plans with the CCS looking toward a wheeling movement southward into the Brittany ports, then eastward along the Loire to the line of the Seine. By D plus 90, the British army group on the north would be facing the lowlands, with the Americans on the right flank facing Verdun and Frankfurt.

Thereafter, the Allies would wait and see. Dempsey's Second Army and Crerar's First Canadian would advance along the coastal plain of northern France and through the Low Countries toward the Belgian port of Antwerp. The American First and Third armies would attack through Paris and central France, drawing abreast of the upper Rhine with the mission of protecting the southern flank of the British and Canadian forces. ANVIL forces would link up on the right flank of the center group to form a "broad front" advance to the German frontier. But "adoption" of this broad-front strategy was tentative—no detailed plans existed beyond D plus 90. Smith would later describe the conferences at Widewing in April at which Eisenhower and his staff sketched out a broad-front strategy. Eisenhower would recall these meetings also and, like Montgomery, categorically insist that everything *after* Normandy went precisely as planned. But, like breakout strategy, grand strategy was not firm because it could not be. According to estimates submitted to the CCS, sixty-eight Allied divisions would be stationed along the Seine by late fall 1944, supplied by the Breton ports, poised for an offensive to the German frontier by early spring of 1945.

The significant feature of Eisenhower's tentative post-Seine strategy was his concept of a two-prong offensive. Both prongs—one British, one American—were to be kept strong and capable of arriving at the Rhine in sufficient strength to cross. Montgomery's front was to have "priority," which amounted to British supervision of an American army in lieu of unified ground command. Otherwise, by managing the flow of supplies, Eisenhower would be able to adjust and reverse the roles depending on British progress along the waterways and canals in Belgium and Holland, and on American progress toward Strasbourg and Frankfurt.

Likewise, the "broad front" was a flexible but cautious concept, aimed at clearing all of France and forgoing the advantages of concentration in attack. Post-Normandy plans were aggressively phrased but vague and had to reckon with the possibility of a German counteroffensive and the need to shore up flanks east of the Seine, another factor in favor of ANVIL. But the British would eventually turn the tables on the broad-front strategy and sharply criticize it as overcautious and demand that Eisenhower concentrate his forces in a single thrust to force a decision through a sector of his choice. But, like the broad front, the "pencil thrust" was apparently tailored to suit defensive needs as well, at least as the British conceived them. A prominent feature of Montgomery's single thrust was a single overall ground commander, a device, by implication, to maintain a say over the American army in order to avoid a repetition of the breakdown in French-British conditions attending the German offensive in June 1940. In this sense, the enervating debate that would arise over Berlin in August 1944 was a debate over pursuit strategy and defensive strategy fought out on a narrow but significant point: whether the greater source of danger to Allied security in the winter of 1944 was an exposed southern flank or whether it was divided command arrangements. Eisenhower would attempt to compromise on command by offering Montgomery informal authority over the American forces adjoining the British. Rejecting compromise, Montgomery would attempt to force adoption of his command proposals by launching his ill-fated offensive into Holland in September 1944.

In short, Eisenhower intended to proceed methodically, not boldly. SHAEF strategy would serve the dual purpose of pursuit and survival. The British would later charge, in effect, that Eisenhower, well in advance, discounted early victory, and by extension lost the opportunity to seize critical objectives deep in central Europe, particularly "prestige" objectives like Berlin, Vienna and Prague. The allegation had a basis; had the Allies hoped to reach these objectives, their plans might have looked to early capture of the North Sea ports instead of Brittany and anticipated the possibility of sending ANVIL forces to northwest France in order to concentrate Allied resources north of the Loire for a thrust toward the Ruhr.

Had Berlin, Vienna and Prague been ruled out? No one could predict the actual state of things by late 1944. But Eisenhower's "broad front" strategy did presume that the battle of France, like OVERLORD, would be hard fought and closely linked to events in the east, that strong defensive positions would be essential at each stage in the event of Russian reverses or a prolonged Russian slowdown, and finally, that the eventual invasion of Germany would necessarily be coordinated with the Russians.

This final point raised basic questions. When would coordination with the Russians cease to be necessary? And what then? Eisenhower would insist that his approach to this problem was "military," in keeping with his directive calling for operations in conjunction with the other United Nations "aimed at the heart of Germany and the destruction of her armed forces." Eisenhower interpreted this clause in the wide context of his consultations with Churchill, Marshall and Roosevelt and the ongoing European Advisory Committee talks on the delineation of occupation zones and communications with the Russians. Eisenhower would construe his directive as an order to wage war on Germany in coordination with the Russians until the Allies and Russians achieved the earliest possible destruction of the German army—which meant until a formal German capitulation, occupation by the Allies and Russians of their respective zones, and the actual surrender of all German military forces. Military strategy would be tailored to these ends while being mindful that the Germans would probably try to avoid surrender to the Russians and fight on, if encouraged by Allied actions and statements suggesting that they had something to gain by doing so. Therefore, coordination with the Russians would probably always be necessary if for no other reason than to demoralize German resistance. Moreover, postwar cooperation was an objective implied by the EAC zones. Eisenhower would "coordinate" with Moscow at least until Roosevelt and Churchill decided to amend his directive.

But Eisenhower would be faulted for failing to seek clarification of his directive in the interval after Roosevelt's death when decisive action might have won Berlin and Prague. Did Eisenhower faithfully interpret Allied policy?

The Combined Chiefs of Staff had framed an ambiguous statement of policy. The CCS, in rejecting narrower British versions of Eisenhower's proposed directive, had assigned Eisenhower a mission extending chronologically from invasion to the destruction of the German armed forces. But the CCS did not define what "destruction" of the German armed forces meant. Operations were to be aimed at the "heart" of Germany. But what was the "heart" of Germany? Even the generals did not agree on the meaning of a term that was, ostensibly "military" but was laden with political significance.

Smith, drawing together many of the interpretations of the word, later wrote of "two hearts" of Germany: the first was the industrial "heart," including the Ruhr basin and the Saar coal-mining region on the west bank of the Rhine, which were declining in importance as Germany rapidly dispersed strategic industries to Austria and Silesia to shield war production from the POINTBLANK onslaught; the second "heart" was the political and administrative hub of Berlin, also a prestige objective located deep inside the prospective Russian zone of occupation.

At the outset, SHAEF "chose" the narrower interpretation, though the two objectives were not mutually exclusive. Eisenhower would later claim that the SHAEF choice of the Ruhr was made on "military" grounds in the belief that the German army would fight for the industrial centers of the Saar and Ruhr in order to prolong resistance. Thus, by attacking the Ruhr, the Allies would also be observing Clausewitz's dictum that one should always engage the mass of enemy forces, a dictum that shaped post-breakout strategy.

Elaborating, Smith later recalled occasional staff discussions that spring about a campaign plan against the Ruhr that envisioned assaults from the north across the lower Rhine and the south through the Frankfurt corridor in a classic double envelopment maneuver inspired by Count Alfred von Schlieffen's analysis of Hannibal's victory at Cannae. A double envelopment, in theory, was the ultimate objective of any campaign—annihilation of enemy forces by encirclement. But in practice, few considered double envelopment a practical or relevant objective. It had been achieved twice since 1900: by the Germans against the Russians over vast empty spaces at Tannenberg in August 1914, and again by the Germans at Kiev in September 1941. Therefore, critics would later argue that encirclement of the Ruhr industrial complex was poor strategy when selected, then needless when implemented in the conditions of German military disintegration facing Eisenhower in April 1945. By persisting in an encirclement strategy, Eisenhower dispersed Allied strategic power available for a Berlin thrust. That Eisenhower "chose" the Ruhr ahead of time, then adhered to this choice long after German resistance had evaporated on his front suggests that Eisenhower's decision to eschew Berlin had been political and set far in advance. On the other hand, Eisenhower's "choice" of the Ruhr in advance justified the two-prong strategy that would implement it; thus it could be argued that Eisenhower had chosen the surest method of protecting the flanks of his forces, and this would suggest that Eisenhower's decision to encircle the Ruhr but forgo Berlin was last-minute, based on his on-the-spot judgment of the situation.

In April 1944, all of this was in the distant future. Improvisation was inherent in any plan, according to another eminent German military theoretician, Count Helmuth von Moltke, who once observed that a plan was valid only until the enemy made his first move. By mid-April, the Allies were anxiously looking for clues of the enemy's first move. A German "recovery" was under way in France. Units returning from Hungary resumed the watch on the Channel. In April, ULTRA monitored the dispute between Von Rundstedt, Hitler and Rommel over the deployment of the panzer reserves north of the Loire—whether, as Von Rundstedt urged, the mobile forces should be held in reserve near Paris and Le Havre, or, as Rommel urged, closer to the invasion front.

An intense guessing game was on about the Allied objective. Von Rundstedt wavered. He anticipated an understrength landing to gain a large port, possibly Le Havre and Cherbourg, with Brest and Boulogne secondary, followed by a "main thrust" on Pas-de-Calais. Shipping distances and the V-1 batteries installed at Antwerp would be a decisive factor in Allied strategy, in his opinion. Rommel, who had originally anticipated the Somme, suspected Normandy. Indeed, Normandy gained ground in German estimates throughout April, particularly after the withdrawals of landing craft from Naples had proceeded apace, ruling out southern France and the Bay of Biscay. In time, Rommel persuaded Hitler, who, on May 6 issued instructions to OB West in Paris to attach "particular importance" to Normandy and the defense of Normandy, and to report plans for meeting landings there. German defenses at Normandy were to be sharply upgraded, and the panzer reserve moved forward. But the Fifteenth Army stayed at Calais.

In his diary Butcher made veiled references to these intercepts. He described a lunch with Smith at Widewing shortly after the intercept of Hitler's instructions on Normandy. Smith seemed tired and depressed. He vowed to Butcher that he would never be a chief of staff again, and that he looked forward to retiring quickly from the Army as soon as the war was over. He confessed that he had premonitions of disaster.

Butcher did too. Radio Berlin was broadcasting "any day." From the details obviously available to the Germans about ship concentrations in southern England and Wales, it seemed implausible that the invasion plan had not been pieced together. The range of Ninth Air Force fighters was a clear geographical limitation, the sailing distance in darkness for the Western convoys at Bristol and Cardiff another.

Smith told Butcher he did not think that getting ashore would be the real problem: ULTRA wireless intercepts revealed that in fact the German high command remained divided between Normandy and Pas-de-Calais as the likely invasion point. After the landings, Smith expected the Germans to release the Fifteenth Army promptly. He predicted that the counteroffensive would be organized with the same speed and skill Kesselring had exhibited at Anzio and Salerno. The chances of weathering the German counterattacks? The whole issue might come down to the cloud cover dictating the effectiveness of air interdiction against enemy reinforcements. The odds—"Fifty-fifty."

His desk calendar shows that Eisenhower was now taking off at least two days a week. To his staff he seemed fatalistic, saying, "Someone has to make the decision and I suppose I'm it." As the wait wore on, Eisenhower in private became nervous, impatient. He was chain-smoking and drinking fifteen cups of coffee a day. At meals he would sit and tap his hand restlessly on the dinner table. Afterward he and Butcher would toss a football, play badminton or shoot target practice at tin cans strung by one of the houseboys. Eisenhower complained of a sore left eye, diagnosed as the result of overwork and healed by applications of hot packs. The ringing in his left ear would not go away and he lost weight. He was not sleeping at night. Several times McKeogh looked in and found Eisenhower sitting up in bed with the lights out, staring out the window.

The rehearsals proceeded. On the night of April 25, accompanied by Bradley, Tedder and Butcher, Eisenhower boarded "Bayonet" for an overnight train ride to the town of Slapton Sands on Lyme Bay in Sussex to observe Exercise TIGER, the dress rehearsal for the American Assault Force O. En route, while visiting the sprawling vehicle depot at Salisbury, Eisenhower talked to Smith by phone and learned of remarks by Patton before the Knutsford Women's Auxiliary "Welcome Home Club" near Headquarters at Peover Hall in Kent. According to sketchy British newspaper reports, Patton bragged about the 170,000 Italians and Germans dispatched to the "infernal regions" by his Seventh Army in Sicily. After teasing the group about the morals of the GI, Patton called for a quick victory in Europe so that the Seventh Army could "get a chance to go on and kill Japanese." He applauded the women of the auxiliary for maintaining the American-British friendship club in view of "the evident destiny of the British and Americans to rule the world."

At Widewing, General "T.J." Davis, SHAEF PR director, spent a busy morning on the twenty-sixth trying to contain press inquiries and insert "and the Russians" into the transcript of Patton's remarks. British reaction was tolerant, but in Washington, New Deal liberals and isolationists alike joined newspapers in denouncing the indiscretion and demanding Patton's dismissal. In Eisenhower's absence, Smith took charge. For months the War Department had warned SHAEF of a backlash in Washington against the wartime publicity for American generals and militarism fed by MacArthur's dalliance with the Republican party. Patton's transgressions were serious. He had been warned to keep a low profile, and to say nothing. Smith handled the wave of inquiries from Washington, and re-enacting the Sicilian affair, dispatched Everett Hughes to collect Patton's version of the events.

Aboard "Bayonet" that night, Eisenhower, Gerow, Bradley, Tedder and Butcher avoided the divisive subject of Patton. Exercise TIGER had been "disappointing." Because of the weather, H-Hour had been postponed. Beach engineer coordination had broken down; movement by the LCVPs and tank craft had been confused. Several of the experimental Duplex Drive amphibious tanks sank in the Channel chop, and air cover, timed precisely in the plan to precede the landings, was late and erratic.

For months Gerow, a worrier, had suppressed his misgivings about OMAHA. However, two days earlier a group of Ninth Air Force fighter bombers had strafed and bombed construction gangs laying mines and obstructions. A detonation had triggered a string of fourteen "sympathetic" underwater explosions, confirming that mine fields were now being laid below the high-water mark. Gerow talked on pessimistically about OMAHA Beach; the 155-inch-gun emplacements on both flanks would oblige the Navy to discharge landing craft eleven miles at sea, while the 110-foot escarpments blocked access inland. Tedder suggested that the group consider accepting the risk of an occasional "short," and permit bombing within two hundred yards of the beach. Gerow objected. The timing of the naval gunfire support, bombing and off-loading schedules was too inexact—

the cruisers and battleships operated within an acceptable three- to four-minute margin of error; close bombing sorties would narrow the margin to two minutes.

Eisenhower thought that the extensive mining in the OMAHA sector was a good sign. In his opinion, this showed that the Germans did not trust the capacity of their armored divisions to counterattack.

"You should be optimistic and cheerful," Eisenhower told Gerow. "Behind you will be the greatest fire power ever assembled," he said.

"I am not pessimistic," Gerow replied, "just realistic."

Late that night the second and third waves of Exercise TIGER met disaster. Nine German E-boats staging from Cherbourg attacked a convoy of LSTs discharging units of VII Corps in a practice night landing. The LSTs, without escort, were unable to conduct evasive maneuvers. The E-boats sank two LSTs and damaged a third. In the ink-black night, 97 sailors and 441 soldiers died.

The E-boat attack at Lyme Bay reduced the entire OVERLORD LST reserve to zero. Because the topographical features of Slapton Sands resembled those of both OMAHA and UTAH, there was worry that the German navy had gathered important clues to Allied intent. Rumors were rife that several of the E-boats had cut engines and hauled prisoners out of the water. For forty-eight hours two BIGOT officers were unaccounted for,* so SHAEF imposed censorship on the incident to avoid alerting the Germans to its importance. General T. J. Betts, deputy chief of SHAEF Intelligence, led a team of investigators at Slapton Sands to interview survivors and tour hospitals to locate the missing. Divers in Lyme Bay finally retrieved the bodies of the missing BIGOT officers, thus ending the security scare.

Meanwhile, Eisenhower returned to London and the Patton matter, resolved not to come to Patton's instant defense as he had in the Sicilian affair. Heedless of repeated warnings about indiscretions, Patton had acted in a manner seemingly calculated to humiliate Eisenhower, Bradley and the American command and to provoke a test of his indispensability in England. This time, Eisenhower would be guided by the War Department.

In the next seventy-two hours Eisenhower sent three cables to Marshall indicating that he intended "stern disciplinary action" and would not object if the War Department determined that "retention of General Patton would diminish the confidence of the public and the government" in SHAEF. Eisenhower decided to accept General Courtney Hodges, a Bradley protégé, as Patton's replacement at the Third Army. Hughes, under orders to hear Patton's side of the story, filed a report. Patton claimed that he had included the Russians and told Hughes that he suspected a "frame-up." The Welcome Home Club had assured him he spoke "off the record." Strangely, the

*A "BIGOT officer" was an officer who had access to NEPTUNE secrets.

news had slipped out despite censorship and the presence of a representative of the British Ministry of Information.

"I leave the matter entirely to your decision," Marshall told Eisenhower on the thirtieth. "You carry the burden of responsibility as to the success of OVERLORD. . . . between us, we can bear the burden of the present unfortunate reaction. . . ." On May 1, Eisenhower, after dictating a blistering reprimand for the record, summoned Patton to his offices at Widewing. Eisenhower chastised Patton so severely that the noise could be heard by the sentries down the hall. Patton wept, offered to resign and left shaken. That night he confided to his diary: "I feel like death." After deliberating for forty-eight hours, Eisenhower dispatched a reprieve. Informing Patton that the War Department had delegated complete responsibility in the matter, Eisenhower admonished Patton that he would assume responsibility for retaining him one last time "solely because of my faith in you as a battle leader and from no other motives."

As the Patton affair reverberated in the world news, the Russian winter/spring offensive ended. In southern Poland, the Russians mopped up pockets of resistance. Elements of the German Fourth Army, isolated in the Crimea, fell back into Sevastopol for a desperate siege. A brief ceremony in Washington, D.C., symbolically inaugurated the next phase of the war. In the ornate ballroom of the Mayflower Hotel on Connecticut Avenue, Ambassador Andrei Gromyko presented the Order of Suvorov to Secretary of State Cordell Hull, who accepted on behalf of General Dwight Eisenhower. Gromyko offered the decoration in grateful appreciation for the long-awaited second front. The award, according to *Time* magazine, was one of the three highest Soviet military decorations, named for the legendary Aleksandr Suvorov, hero of the Russo-Turkish war of 1773–74 at the battle of the Rimnic River, conqueror of Warsaw, and leader of the Russian army checked by Napoleon at the Alps.

With the decoration, Eisenhower received a pension of twenty rubles a month ($3.85) and a red passbook entitling him to free passage on the subways and buses of Moscow. For the first time since July 1943, STAVKA communiqués announced no Red Army attacks in progress.

MAY

The May 1 issue of *Time* magazine featured a cover story on General Omar Bradley, commander of the American forces mustering in England for the assault on *Festung Europa*. The article was a flattering profile of the tall, lanky, soft-spoken "GI General," born in Clark, Missouri.

Like his classmate Eisenhower, Bradley was among the officers who missed World War I and had considered leaving the Army. He had spent thirteen years of his career as an instructor at West Point, mostly at the

Infantry School at Fort Benning, and at Leavenworth. At Fort Benning, Bradley had first caught the eye of Colonel George Marshall, who entered his name in the book he kept of promising officers (which included Eisenhower). Like Eisenhower's, Bradley's career had consisted of a succession of minor posts in no way predictive of his current responsibilities over the American ground forces in England.

Time recited Bradley's victories as a corps commander in North Africa and Sicily, which led to his appointment to command of the U.S. First Army in England. *Time* praised his qualities of steadiness and sound practical judgment now credited with offsetting Patton's erratic actions in Sicily. The opening sentence of the article, beneath an aerial photograph taken above Dover of "the far shore" at Calais, read: "When?"

Elsewhere, *Time* disclosed President Roosevelt's return to Washington after four weeks at Bernard Baruch's 23,000-acre plantation, Hobcaw Barony, north of Charleston, South Carolina. White House physicians, prompted by press stories drawing attention to the President's slack appearance and bearing, pronounced the President to be in excellent shape after a needed rest.

The press noted SHAEF's announcement of Patton's presence in England. *Time* contrasted his conduct and Bradley's habits of discretion, and reputation for compassion. *Time* noted recent revelations by anonymous veterans of the Seventh Army illustrating Patton's contempt for helpless civilians in Italy. The articles on Patton gave vent to lingering complaints that Patton, having weathered the Knutsford affair, was "tolerated as an eccentric genius solely because he was considered indispensable."

Newsweek described a recent incident at the SHAEF offices in London. Twenty-three-year-old Private First Class Walter Thorpe came to the door of 20 Grosvenor Square and announced to the sentries, "I'd like to see the General [Eisenhower] if he is not busy. Tell him I'm from Abilene, Kansas." Ten minutes later the large brass-paneled oak doors swung open. Thorpe, once employed as a druggist at Roy Eisenhower's pharmacy in Junction City, Kansas, was escorted into the General's office for a twenty-minute talk. Thorpe told reporters afterward that he had asked for a token so that his buddies would believe him. Eisenhower wrote a brief note in longhand:

> Dear Thorpe,
>   I am delighted that, as a fellow citizen of Abilene, Kansas, you called on me at my office to see me today.
>   [signed] Dwight Eisenhower

Sentries stood watch outside the War Room at Widewing. On a wall were displays of the most closely held secret of the Alliance—a large map of the Cotentin Peninsula and of the five beaches marked as targets of the assault:

the VII Corps objective UTAH Beach, west of Carentan on the north bank of the Vire, the 82nd and 101st Airborne drop zones; OMAHA Beach between Vierville and Colleville; GOLD Beach east of the picturesque seaside village of Arromanches; JUNO Beach at the road junction at Courseulles; SWORD Beach, between Caen and Ouistreham, drop zones for the 6th British Airborne Division in the flats northeast of Caen, a university and cathedral town often called the Athens of Normandy. The map also displayed the hydrographical details of the beaches, the depressions and shallow depths of water, the location of barriers, mine fields, large German gun emplacements, pillboxes and coastal artillery. Early one morning Butcher stood alone gazing at this map just after he had requested of Rear Admiral Alan R. Kirk, commander of Task Force O, that he be allowed to join the assault force. As he examined the map, Butcher suddenly became conscious that Tedder, smoking a pipe, watched him.

"How far out before we can begin wading?" Butcher asked.

"The shallow depths make good mine fields," Tedder replied.

The War Room map by early May displayed the reshuffling of German units north of the Loire and the ongoing German "recovery." The 77th Field Infantry Division moved up into the Cotentin. The 5th Parachute Division arrived in Rennes. The 9th and 10th SS remained in Poland, but the 1st SS, the Adolf Hitler Division, had returned to the west and refitted in Belgium. The 2nd SS returned to Bordeaux. The 21st Panzer Division, a veteran of the Afrika Korps, moved up from Rennes to Caen. The mighty 130th Panzer Lehr, composed of four panzer grenadier battalions and two tank battalions, returned from Budapest. Instead of detraining at the ordinary bivouac at Verdun, Panzer Lehr continued on to Chartres, a day's march from the beach. The 116th Panzer Division remained anchored at nearby Mantes-Gassicourt, due east of the 12th SS Panzer held in close reserve at Bernay, Gacé, Dreux and Evreux.

In Normandy, German Seventh Army defenses bunched up. A regiment of the crack 346th Infantry reinforced the 711th Coastal Division at Bayeux, while the remainder of the 346th garrisoned St.-Lô. The 30th Mobile Brigade moved into Coutances on the western coast of the Cotentin. Infantry formation, on the Brittany Peninsula, inched northward toward Cherbourg. Evidently the Germans had ruled out all landing sites except Normandy and the Pas-de-Calais. Instead of facing six divisions on D-Day, the Allies would face eight, with four more within forty-eight hours of the beach.

On the second, Ambassador Harriman stopped over on his way back to Moscow after an extensive round of talks in Washington to report on the "runaround" he was getting on the Polish situation. Harriman briefed Eisenhower. In Harriman's opinion, Stalin meant what he said when he denied that Moscow desired to "hand-pick" a Polish government—but this rested on what Harriman believed was a naïve assumption that the Poles would greet the Russians as liberators. Harriman had been obliged to warn the President that as things stood, the Polish solution would be a "completely Soviet one." As he later recalled, Harriman found Eisenhower "grown in stature" since their last meeting, brimming with constructive ideas about improving liaison between SHAEF and STAVKA. Harriman had good news: STAVKA planned an "all-out attack" to coincide with OVERLORD, but he had no specifics.

The Allied high command, in conferences and gatherings, now resolved to banish fears and countenance optimism. Omar Bradley told me thirty-two years later that after May 1 no one spoke a word of failure. "The invasion had to succeed, and so there was no thought given otherwise." In a meeting with the Dominion prime ministers, Churchill claimed that given his way, "the layout of the war would have been different and he would have rolled up Europe from the southeast to join hands with the Russians." The Prime Minister had hoped to avoid the massacres of the Great War but was overruled. He now "hardened towards this enterprise."

In *Crusade,* Eisenhower described the ritual exchanges at his weekly luncheons at 10 Downing Street. Churchill would tease Eisenhower about his optimism: "General, it is good for commanders to be optimistic, else they would never win a battle. I must say to you that if by the time the snow flies you have established your 30-odd divisions now in Britain safely on the Normandy coast and have the port of Cherbourg firmly in your grasp, I will be the first to proclaim that this was a gigantic and wonderfully conducted military campaign.

"And," he would add, "if you have seized Le Havre and control the Contentin Peninsula and the mouth of the Seine, I will proclaim that this is one of the finest operations in modern war.

"And if by Christmas you have liberated our beloved Paris, so that she may regain her life of Freedom and take her accustomed place as the center of Western European culture and beauty, I will proclaim that this operation is the most grandly conceived and best conducted known to the history of war."

"Prime Minister," Eisenhower would reply, "we expect to be on the borders of Germany by Christmas, pounding away at her defenses. When that occurs, if Hitler has the slightest judgment of wisdom left, he will surrender unconditionally to avoid the complete destruction of Germany."

By May, the transportation plan was in full swing. The Eighth and Ninth air forces struck transport targets on a wide arc through western Germany, the Low Countries and France. The early returns were encouraging. Skeptics had not taken into account weaknesses in the French transport system stemming from prewar neglect of maintenance and repair facilities and then from German requisitions. The Germans had taken measures to protect the railroads—instituting a strict system to restrict rail shipment to only crucial military supplies—but the system was "in decay" and repairs were not keeping pace with the damage inflicted by Allied bombers. Vichy claims of civilian casualties ran far below the 80,000–160,000 casualties feared.

To all the world, the intensified air campaign signaled invasion. Radio Berlin taunted the Allies about the large concentrations of troops and ships in southern England, and promised that German bombers would soon pay a call. British Bomber Command joined in and conducted continuous sorties over France and western Germany. To the Britishers living in East Anglia below the flight path, the low drone of the overhead Lancasters, Halifaxes, Fortresses and Liberators around the clock meant an invasion soon. Surely, Allied air forces could not sustain the intensity of the air attacks for long. It was said later that the Angel of Mons reappeared to women in Caddington in the night sky, just as she had before the battles in Flanders in 1914. Local authorities explained that flares and searchlights were being tested, but Caddington was sure it had been revisited. Having endured four years of hardship and disruptions with a fatalistic determination to see the hateful war through, the British public now briefly re-experienced the enthusiasms of 1914, thirty years before.

The world press speculated about the time and place. Some predicted that the Allies would land on May 10, the fourth anniversary of the German attack on Belgium and Holland. *Arriba* in Madrid published a prediction based on the tides for Monday, May 15, or Tuesday, May 16. The Nazi press claimed that the attack could come anytime between May 6 and June 7. American newspapers debated the possible landing sites: St.-Nazaire, Cherbourg, Le Havre, Dieppe, Boulogne, Dunkirk and Calais.

Gradually, word reached most of Eisenhower's grade school and high school friends living in remote central Kansas. They were proud that one of their number was leading the most important Allied attack of the war. The Curry sisters sent letters. Ruby Norman Lucier, an old high school flame, wrote. Reporters combed Abilene for stories. Magazines that month profiled the six Eisenhower brothers, and their mother, Ida Eisenhower, now widowed and living with a nurse-companion in the Eisenhower home on southeast 4th Street. Stories noted that Ida Eisenhower, AP "Mother of the Year" in 1943, had been born in the Shenandoah Valley and raised in the River Brethren Faith as a pacifist. When reporters asked her if she was proud of her son, her stock reply was, "Which one?" Had he been a good boy? Dwight, her third son, had been "difficult, but a good boy." Had Ida and her husband, David, opposed Dwight's decision to go to West Point? " 'It is your choice,' " she had told him.

"I must say that mother is getting to be quite a wit if she is suggesting that I should be the one to testify as to whether I was born during the day or during the night," Eisenhower chuckled in a note to his aunt Hannah Amanda Musser on May 4. "The only thing she ever told me about the occurrence was that I was born during a fierce thunderstorm and it was to that coincidence she always blamed my liking for lightning and thunder-storms as a child. I still don't see, though, why the doctor from Chicago should ask her such a question by telegram."

When his personal replies to the Curry sisters and several businessmen in Abilene were published by newspapers, Eisenhower summoned the Judge Advocate General to look into legal recourse against the invasion of privacy. Butcher was amused by Eisenhower's naïveté. But then, after all, Ike had been cloaked in censorship during his trip to America, his only one since arriving in London twenty-four months earlier. Eisenhower had never faced the civilian press, and had no way of evaluating the press build-up.

Captain Everett "Swede" Hazlett, a boyhood friend, set the standard of friendship. Swede, a professor of English at the University of North Carolina in Durham, had been a schoolmate in Abilene. The wellborn son of an Abilene doctor, Swede had reached out and befriended the six Eisenhower brothers, who hailed from the poor South Side of the Union Pacific tracks.

Hazlett emerged as an important figure in books and articles that spring. According to legend, shortly after graduating from high school, he and Ike decided to apply to Annapolis. Together, they studied for the entrance exams while Ike supervised the night shift at the Belle Springs Creamery. Then Dwight discovered that he had become ineligible for Annapolis because of age, so the two went their separate ways in June 1911—Swede to Annapolis to become a midshipman, and Ike to West Point as a twenty-year-old cadet. But the friendship endured. The two corresponded off and on, having seen each other three times since: at an Army-Navy game in 1913, in Panama in 1922, and in Washington briefly in 1935. Eisenhower and Hazlett had resumed corresponding during the war.

In the spring of 1944 Ike and Swede had been exchanging gossip about old friends, barbs about the Army-Navy rivalry, and occasional observations about the global war. In one letter Eisenhower discoursed on education, which, in keeping with the progressive spirit of the day, he saw as the solution to the world's ills. Impressed, Hazlett had shown the letter to several professors at UNC, who, in turn, had distributed it to the Board of Visitors, who passed it to the local congressman, who had written back seeking permission to place the letter in the *Congressional Record*. Swede knew to suppress it.

Somewhat later than Mamie and Edgar, Hazlett sensed the imminence of the invasion. In May, politicians and ministers throughout America announced plans for days of prayer. American newspapers carried Eighth Air Force and Bomber Command communiqués. Bomb lines formed a diagonal across the northwest quadrant of France, a clear preliminary. "God bless you, Ike," Swede wrote, "and God give you success in the giant operation ahead of you. I have never been much on prayer—but of late I have found myself slipping a bit. Perhaps it is age—and perhaps it is the magnitude of the job ahead of you, and all of us. Anyway, I'm squeezing, and pulling and praying."

In southern England 2,876,000 officers and men organized into thirty-nine divisions plus air, medical, transport, and communications units waited "tense as a coiled spring" set to move to concentration areas, then marshaling areas and finally the assault areas. Someone remarked facetiously that only the barrage balloons floating over the coastal port and depots kept the island from sinking under the weight of the preparations.

Eisenhower and his staff worked around the clock tending to last-minute details. On May 8, Eisenhower met with Stark, Spaatz and Bradley to formalize D-Day and resolve Army–Navy–Air Force requirements for H-Hour. The ground forces would have preferred night landings to curtail enemy observation, but the Navy needed darkness to transmit the Channel, then daylight for ship-to-shore bombardment. A moon phase was necessary for airdrops and preliminary bombardment.

As Bradley later recalled, because of the mines and obstacles below the half-tide mark along the entire invasion coast, tides were a critical factor. Mine fields blocked the inland passes behind the beaches, and in several sectors the German Seventh Army had erected six- to twenty-foot seawalls. Landings at low tide would force the assault waves to disembark and thread through mines and obstacles under machine-gun fire. At high tide the assault waves would ride in over them. But tides were swift along the Normandy coast, and early waves of landing craft riding in at or near high tide would have little time to discharge their cargo. Accordingly, H-Hour would fall on a rising tide. Bradley reported on the experiments conducted to determine the time that engineers would require to clear lines through the obstacles. The tides rose at the rate of one foot per fifteen minutes and the math was "simple": engineers could blow a path through the obstacles in water two feet deep, or at thirty minutes after low tide.

A rising tide at daybreak, coinciding with the right moon phases for the planned airdrops, would occur on June 5, 6 and 7. "Y-Day," code-named HALCYON, was June 1, the day on which the invasion force was scheduled to be in readiness. D-Day was therefore HALYCON plus four, five and six. The ideal—HALYCON five, June 6—offered the most minutes of daylight after low tide. Eisenhower asked the group to consult their staffs and report back by May 15, whereupon he could notify the CCS and army groups of step one of the attack order.

Eisenhower's final order to proceed would depend partly on the wind, clouds and sea conditions. The postponement from May until June had increased the probability of good weather in line with Army, Navy and Air Force minimal conditions: airborne drops required winds no higher than Force 3 (8–10 miles per hour) or a cloud layer thicker than 6 to 10; the bombers needed a cloud base above 3,000 feet; the landing force required seas with waves no choppier than three or four feet, low fog and cloud density.

The staff at SHAEF joked nervously about the "agreed weather report." This referred to the daily weather analysis prepared by civilian meteorologist Group Captain Dr. John Stagg, on loan to the Royal Air Force, along with his American-British group of experts drawn from the Admiralty, AEAF Headquarters Stanmore, the Eighth Air Force and the Air Ministry meteorologist at Dunstable. The Stagg Group enjoyed a major advantage over German weather services, which were confined to data fed from Ireland and Norway. To predict the predominantly westerly weather patterns, the Allies worked with information gleaned from a string of weather stations in Northern Ireland, the Faerö Islands, Iceland, Greenland, Labrador, Gibraltar and the eastern United States, information checked against dossiers of probabilities compiled from years of weather records. Normally, weather over the Channel could be reliably predicted about forty-eight hours in advance, meaning a built-in twelve-hour gamble according to Ramsay's requirements for the coordinated movement of the over 4,000 naval craft.

Heavy responsibility rested on the austere Stagg. He had rehearsed his prediction daily since reporting to COSSAC in November. Then, in recent weeks, at the Supreme Commander's conferences on Mondays, Stagg routinely presented an experimental five-day forecast based on a Thursday D-Day to enable all to gain confidence in the accuracy of the forecasting. All hoped for the best: an accurate forecast of good weather. Second best was an accurate forecast of bad weather, which would probably force postponement until mid-June, the next correct combination of tide and moon. Next was an inaccurate forecast of bad weather, which might lead to an unnecessary postponement to mid-month. Still worse, a mixed forecast. All dreaded a wrong forecast of good weather.

Adverse weather would curtail close support of gunships and the air force. High surf would turn the precision landing schedule into a snarl, meaning unnecessary losses of men and equipment, and delays in moving inland. At worst, bad weather spelled disaster—sluggish off-loading, disorganization in the Channel and effective enemy countermeasures under cloud cover.

May 1944 was a near-perfect month—day after day of blue skies, gentle two- to three-knot winds and a smooth Channel surface. With a premonition, Butcher complained to his diary that the perfect weather felt sultry, "like Iowa before a storm."

Meanwhile, Churchill launched a last-minute effort to restrain the transport plan, now 50 percent complete. Photographs confirmed the pinpoint accuracy of the daylight attacks, and the chaos inflicted on the French rail system. Movement by railroad measured by the January–February Railway Index fixed on a scale at 100 now ran at 38. The JIC recommended continuation without restriction unless there were overriding political considerations. Nonetheless, Churchill decided to impose a limit of 150 casualties per raid unless Washington assumed full responsibility for the "carnage."

Churchill and the War Cabinet also debated the importance of the V-1 missile sites, soon to be operational between Cherbourg and Antwerp. The Allies lacked essential information about the V-1. The missile was believed to be a 440-mile-per-hour ramjet frame with a 4,000-pound warhead. The RAF and the Eighth Air Force had flown 30,000 sorties against "ski sites" since November 1943, and had managed to knock out 65 of an estimated 96 launchers under construction. Estimates varied widely about the effectiveness of the V-1. Morgan had studied the V-1 threat to coastal harbors and the problem of dispersing the invasion fleet to Scotland, and had concluded that in view of the warhead size, V-1 attacks on the shipyards in Portsmouth and Southampton would cause about the same damage as aerial bombardment, and that the weapon was one of the "smaller hazards of war to which OVERLORD is liable." Churchill, however, despaired about the impact on a war-weary British public of any prolonged bombardment by remote-controlled missiles, and decided the threat to British morale overrode military factors. In a letter dated the twenty-eighth, Churchill informed Eisenhower that the War Cabinet had taken an "adverse view" of the list of proposed targets and would simultaneously insist on upgrading CROSSBOW, the air campaign on German V-1 sites situated along the Channel coast.

In his reply Eisenhower rejected formally any formula restraining operations based on estimated casualties. Civilian casualties were "inherent in any plan for the full use of Air power to prepare for our assault," he wrote. Vichy claims of civilian casualties so far were much lower than JIC estimates, evidence of the accuracy of the Eighth Air Force pinpoint bombing. Eisenhower regretted the "considerable misunderstanding" concerning the transportation plan, and understood "the gravity of the issues raised."

The issue was France and De Gaulle's presence in London on D-Day. On May 8, Eisenhower and Churchill met privately at 10 Downing Street. Apparently they agreed to coordinate steps; first, Churchill would protest the bombing, but American approval of the transport plan would be Eisenhower's cue to reopen the question of agreement on civil affairs with the FCNL to offset the impact of the bombings. Both were aware of the parallels with Darlan when Roosevelt had reluctantly yielded to "military necessity" urged on him by Eisenhower with Churchill's support. Eisenhower and Churchill expected Roosevelt to do so again, if pushed.

The luncheon was memorable. Apparently, Eisenhower and Churchill discussed the latest intercepts from Normandy, which impressed both with the finality of the operation. Later that day Churchill told Brooke that he had remarked to Eisenhower as he left, "I am in this with you to the end. If it fails, we go down together."

On the ninth, Churchill cabled Roosevelt to place before him War Cabinet "anxiety" about French casualties. His colleagues questioned "whether almost as good military results could not be produced by other methods." Eisenhower had forewarned Marshall, and had assured him of his undeviating support for the plan on grounds of military necessity. Accordingly, on the eleventh, Roosevelt called the casualties "regrettable," but he was "not prepared to impose from this distance any restriction on military action by the responsible military commanders that in their opinion might militate against the success of OVERLORD." That day Eisenhower reopened the problem of a civil affairs agreement with De Gaulle.

In a message to the Combined Chiefs, Eisenhower spoke of the "awkwardness" of De Gaulle's decision to break off all negotiations on currency matters, civil activity and resistance policy. He warned of "acute embarrassment to the Allied forces" without French cooperation on forming security battalions to safeguard communications, currency questions, organization of civilian police and civilian labor. He offered two solutions: first, to invite De Gaulle to London for the invasion period; second, to allow General Koenig to communicate with Algiers by French cipher, an exception to the diplomatic ban that would signal the special trust and confidence felt toward the French committee. Eisenhower urged that the situation be handled as a matter of "utmost urgency and that it be considered as far as possible on its military aspects."

On the thirteenth, Roosevelt clarified Eisenhower's guidance in dealings with the FCNL. He assigned Eisenhower the "additional tasks" of being certain the FCNL did not seek to impose political choices on the French, and he was to keep in mind that the policy of "free determination" was to be preserved "in substance and in spirit." The President did not want Eisenhower involved with the committee "on a political level," and again directed that occupation policy be strictly military. Roosevelt then conceded the main point by choosing not to contest the "overriding necessity" of De Gaulle's presence in London.

Churchill issued the invitation. In no mood to obscure his triumph, De Gaulle would impose conditions, first refusing Churchill's formal offer on May 23. Three days later, De Gaulle in Algiers would proclaim the FCNL as the provisional government of France, and himself as president, meaning there could no longer be any evasion of De Gaulle's claims in dealing with the FCNL. A day later, Roosevelt would surrender tacitly, and through the FCNL naval representative in Washington invite De Gaulle to Washington for talks, in effect conferring status on him as the provisional head of state.

At mid-month, Eisenhower embarked on a whirlwind trip to bases and depots to inspect troops, and to meet with division and corps commanders for a last time in accordance with his own directive calling on all commands to meet regularly with troops, to be seen, and to dispel nameless fears based on German propaganda claims about the strength of the Luftwaffe and of the Atlantic Wall. Eisenhower toured the Burtonwood depot with Spaatz, then flew to Northern Ireland to review the 10th and 11th infantry divisions at Newcastle, the U.S. XV Corps and the British 8th Infantry Division. At Bangor he inspected the U.S.S. *Texas, Quincy, Tuscaloosa, Arkansas* and *Nevada,* contributions by Admiral Ernest King as part of the final resolution of the ANVIL controversy. Soon the entire command joined in a hectic round of visits and inspection trips similar to the closing days of the political campaigns in Eisenhower's future. Their mission was to inspire confidence in assault forces, emphasizing "the stark and elemental facts as to the character of our Nazi enemy, the need for crushing him if we are to survive, and, finally, to drive home the fact that we have defeated them before and can do it again. It is only necessary to steel ourselves to the task. . . ."

On May 15 the final review of the OVERLORD plan took place at the 21st Army Group headquarters located in the Georgian red-brick St. Paul's School in Kensington, which Montgomery had attended as a child. In the offices of the High Master, which the young Montgomery had been forbidden to enter, he had set up his command post. In an auditorium across the hall, Montgomery played host to the large assemblage of commanders and aides.

Formal invitations had been sent out. King George VI was the honored guest, and the gathering included Churchill, Eisenhower, Tedder, Brooke, Field Marshal Smuts, Leigh-Mallory, Ramsay, Patton, General Miles Dempsey, commander of the British Second Army, and over 150 commanders of air, sea and land units participating in D-Day. No representative of the FCNL or from any of the governments-in-exile headquartered in London attended, so the review was a strictly Anglo-American event. The purpose of the meeting was morale—to infuse the leadership with the spirit of victory about a perilous military operation which, daily, passed from their effective control. The FABIUS rehearsals were complete. The eight assault divisions had gathered in the ten-mile concentration areas.

In retrospect, May 15 was the high tide of Anglo-American unity. Both sides would assert vindication in the plans presented that day: the Americans, who had pressed for OVERLORD since March 1942, and the British, who had attached the preconditions for success. The final OVERLORD plan was of mixed character: an assault against objectives within 300 miles of the Ruhr and the Saar which, if successful, would open the most direct routes to the defeat of Germany, but which would be shaped by British doctrines of indirect assault with emphasis on airborne and seaborne elements.

The assemblage sat on rows of narrow benches in a balcony overlooking a plaster relief map of Normandy and the Cotentin Peninsula. The map, the width of a city block, exhibited the terrain features of the towns and farms, including the flat plains southeast of Caen, the hedgerow fields honeycombing the bocage behind the "American" beaches, and the marshy Vire estuary. Markers fixed the location of German units. The II SS Panzer Corps was back from Budapest. Six divisions of the Seventh Army held Normandy —two coastal divisions, one opposite each sector, the 91st Field Infantry Division at St.-Lô, a second field division at Coutances and the crack 21st Panzer at Caen. The three-division panzer reserve stood near Paris under direct OKW command, a sign of persistent indecision within the German high command.

One by one, the principal commanders of OVERLORD spoke. Spaatz read a paper describing the unexpected success of the transport-bombing plan. Never a supporter of it, Spaatz was still critical of the diversion from oil targets in Germany. His delivery was halting and, in the opinion of witnesses, confused. Air Chief Marshal Harris briefed the group on the RAF Bomber Command raids on V-1 sites in France, Belgium and Holland. Leigh-Mallory outlined the complex air plan aimed at neutralizing the beach defenses and acting as a screen for the invasion force. Ramsay explained the procedures of coordinating the movements of the nearly 4,000 naval craft berthed throughout England and Scotland. The armada would rendezvous at a point south of the Isle of Wight, called "Piccadilly Circus," before proceeding along precise courses to the American and British landing zones. "It seemed to most of us that the proper meshing of so many gears would need nothing less than divine guidance," recalled Admiral Deyo, commander of Bombardment Group for Force U. "A failure at one point could throw the momentum out of balance and result in chaos. All in that room were aware of the gravity of the elements to be dealt with."

Bradley described the American tactics at the beach. The invasion craft would be led by minesweepers, proceeding in darkness to clear channels, followed by the LCVPs with engineers and sappers, then the Ranger battalions to scale the cliffs in the American sector to take out the coastal batteries. Then the infantry. Then the vehicles.

Then Montgomery took center stage. With a pointer he traced the maneuvers of the 21st Army Group on the Normandy mock-up. Rarely photographed at ground level, he wore his customary padded shoes to cover his shortness. A distinct blend of spinster and hawk, Montgomery relished the grand occasion, as the notes of his remarks show.

Montgomery, the professional, could not suppress his delight that his intelligence reports had confirmed that the 21st Army Group faced Rommel, whom he characterized as "an energetic and determined commander" but "too impulsive" to fight the "set piece" battle. Under Rommel's supervision, the Germans had thickened the coastal crust, increased the number of infantry divisions not committed to beach defense to seal off the coast, and had redistributed the panzer reserve. Rommel's ascendancy meant "OVERLORD is to be defeated at the beaches."

Sixty enemy divisions were in France, ten panzer type and twelve field infantry, mobile type. Montgomery expected the enemy to concentrate first against the British to prevent a breakout into the Caen plateau, while relying more on the natural defenses provided by the farms and hedgerows in the Cotentin. Moreover, concentration at Caen would economically preserve the link between the German Seventh Army in Normandy and the German Fifteenth Army in the Pas-de-Calais.

Montgomery predicted that the race would begin by noon, D-Day, when the Allies could look forward to the arrival of the 21st SS Division at Lisieux. By dusk the 17th SS Panzer Grenadier would arrive from Rennes. By the first night the assault force of eight Allied divisions would be facing seven battle-worthy German divisions, and so it was essential to gain space rapidly before the enemy could bring up sufficient reserves. Armored columns must penetrate quickly, to "peg out claims well inland," upsetting enemy plans and gaining ground for the follow-up divisions. "Meanwhile the air must hold the ring, and make very difficult the movement of enemy reserves by train or road toward the lodgement area."

By D plus 2, Panzer Lehr would arrive from Tours, and the 116th Panzer Division from Nantes. By then, Montgomery believed, the Germans, having evaluated the size of the committed force, would regard OVERLORD as the "overriding menace" requiring the concentration in Normandy of all available formations. The Allies could then expect thirteen divisions to begin moving toward the NEPTUNE area, including the Fifteenth Army panzer reserve at Amiens, Toulouse, Bordeaux and at Sedan in Belgium, and eight or more infantry divisions from western Brittany and the Pas-de-Calais. By the fifth day, with fifteen Allied divisions ashore, the Germans "will have achieved the ingredients of a counterattack"—twenty-four divisions, sufficient infantry to guard the flanks, and nine panzer divisions "available for the blow" launched on a line Caen–Bayeux–Carentan. The critical points would be Bayeux, the seam of the American and British fronts, and Carentan, between UTAH and OMAHA. Until both objectives were secure, the landings would be "awkwardly placed." Alternatively, the invasion would be secure when the Allies controlled the main enemy lateral road, Grandville–Vire–Argentan–Falaise–Caen.

"The problem?" Montgomery asked in closing.

"The enemy is in position, with reserves available.

"There are obstacles and mine fields on the beaches; we cannot gain contact with the obstacles and reach them.

"There are many unknown hazards.

"After a sea voyage, and a landing on a strange coast, there is always some loss of cohesion.

"The solution!

"We have the initiative.

"We can rely on the violence of our assault, our great weight of supporting fire, from the sea and air.

"The simplicity of our plan.

"Our robust mentality and morale. We shall have to send the soldiers into this party 'seeing red.' We must get them completely on their toes; having absolute faith in the plan; and imbued with infectious optimism and offensive eagerness. Nothing must stop them! If we send them into battle in this way—then we shall succeed."

As Montgomery took his seat, Churchill rose. The Prime Minister conceded to the group that for years he had had his doubts. He recalled his visions of the Channel running red with the blood of British soldiers, extinguished like the generation of British officers at Ypres and Passchendaele. But he was "hardening toward this enterprise." Tapping his cupped left hand, Churchill said the time had come to banish doubt, to have confidence in the fruits of three years of planning, and to rally behind OVERLORD. Then others, one by one, contributed words of determination.

Slightly ahead of schedule, King George rose to depart. He asked the Almighty's blessing on OVERLORD, then passed down the front row, shaking hands with the distinguished guests and pausing to speak with Eisenhower, who had delivered a brief introduction. Eisenhower's deep Kansas voice broke the silence. "Your Majesty," he said, "there will be eleven thousand planes overhead on D-Day, and OVERLORD is backed by the greatest armada in history. It will not fail."

Decisions were now upon Eisenhower. On the seventeenth he informed the CCS of "Halcyon plus 4," confirmed by Ramsay as the day offering the precise combination of moon, tides and weather. U.S., British and Canadian assault forces prepared to move up into the concentration areas from Felixstowe to Cardiff. The assault ships moored in Shoreham, Portsmouth, Weymouth and Torquay took on trucks, hospital equipment, bulldozers, food, clothing, field kitchens, rolling stock, assault craft and armor. A ten-mile zone marked off by barbed-wire fencing surrounded assembly areas, patrolled by two thousand special counterintelligence officers. Officers and soldiers inside the zone were not scheduled to learn of the ultimate destination in France until the end of May, when each command would be issued aerial photographs and special models simulating the terrain features and the German defenses at the Normandy beaches. Equipment, including gas masks, would be issued to the troops in the event the Germans, known to possess large stockpiles of poison gas, decided in desperation to breach the international conventions banning gas warfare.

Eisenhower decided to open a forward headquarters in Portsmouth in order to be close to the troops in the first week. Supreme Commander conferences could take place at Southwick House, a country mansion on a hill overlooking the bustling port, which served as operational center for Allied naval headquarters. Commander Quinton Brown, the headquarters commandant, wanted Eisenhower to choose between overnight accommodations aboard a rail car or a tent encampment in the area. Because a rail car might be a burden on the local commands, Eisenhower asked for a trailer camp. Brown organized the camp situated in a wooded area a few hundred yards from a school building two and one half miles from Southwick House and seven miles north of Portsmouth. It consisted of a ring of tents to house the personal staff, and trailers with large maps and Teletype machines next to a tent set up for Stagg and the Anglo-American weather staff.

Brown located a comfortable caravan (trailer) equipped with a living room, a galley and a study, which Eisenhower decorated with pictures of Mamie and his son, John, who still knew nothing of the arrangements his father had made with Marshall for him to travel to England by ship for a visit after his graduation ceremony. Signal Corps installed a large switchboard and three phones: a red phone, the direct link to Washington; a green phone, connecting the trailer with 10 Downing Street; and a black phone, connecting the trailer and Southwick House.

In his last full week at Widewing, Eisenhower wrapped up. Day by day he reviewed the air reports, weighing the timing of moves to isolate the Normandy area and stepped-up resources to increase the efficiency of the attacks. Intercepts and underground sources reported desperate calls from German transportation authorities for an additional hundred trains per day and a rush on needed repairs. On May 23, Vichy Radio conceded that the French rail system was "in complete chaos." Marshaling yards and repair shops were rubble. But traffic was getting through, prompting a Ninth Air Force test bombing run against a 200-meter span bridge in the western outskirts of Paris. The mission was a success—for several days Spaatz, Brereton, Leigh-Mallory, Tedder and Cunningham of the British Second Tactical Air Force debated an AEAF plan to reduce the thirty-six rail and road-bridge targets over the Seine northeast of Paris. Spaatz objected that a "bridge busting" campaign would "slaughter thousands" and could not be carried out with precision. Eisenhower decided to hold off.

In the next several days Eisenhower held meetings with representatives of the Belgian, Dutch and Norwegian governments-in-exile to sign agreements providing for civilian authority in the liberated territories effective when the Allied troops arrived. To the end, SHAEF reached no agreement with De Gaulle's FCNL, since this would have involved formal recognition.

On the night of the twenty-second, Elliott Roosevelt was a dinner guest at Telegraph Cottage. Butcher described the evening of bridge and Roosevelt's stories about his recent experiences in Moscow in the FRANTIC negotiations.

Roosevelt brought up the travail of the military missions in the attempt to get information about the unknown war in the east. But the eastern front was a war of unbelievable brutality and suffering. Members of the Russian high command were complaining to him that the Red Army "suffered more casualties before breakfast every morning than the Allies suffered in a month." Forty percent, maybe more, of the country was destroyed, and 16 million, maybe 20 million, left dead by the receding Nazi armies. Roosevelt attributed the losses to the policy, early in the war, of salvaging the army by fighting on with armed partisan bands of old men, women and children. But he had heard stories about a ruthless German campaign of mass murder, documented in the Soviet trials of captured German SS officers accused of atrocities at Krasnodar, Kiev and Kharkov.

Eisenhower asked Roosevelt if he had received special treatment in Moscow. "Being a son means nothing," Elliott replied. For instance, Stalin's son had been captured by the Germans. Stalin had refused to offer to exchange German prisoners for him, and had allowed the twenty-year-old private to die in a Nazi prison camp.

"Stalin is a stickler for keeping his word," Roosevelt added. "The test for Britain and the United States is keeping their word on the second front."

"I'm not certain precisely what commitments have been made," Eisenhower replied, "but I assure you there will be no welshing on the second front."

Eisenhower took the twenty-third off. In a letter home he described taking a horseback ride alone through Richmond Park. He described the flowers, birds, the hordes of rabbits, pheasants and partridge tumbling through fields of flowers resembling the bluebonnets of Texas.

Eisenhower instructed Mamie about the graduation gifts he was sending back for John. He was entrusting John with several documents, his Russian decoration, a silver ladle, an original set of Parker pens, and left it to Mamie to choose between a four-star insignia or a set of "Ike" pins suitable for mounting—and engraved with the inscription "To his son, John"—to avoid embarrassment. "You are to keep the extra set," he closed. "I hope this is clear."

On the twenty-fourth, Eisenhower kept routine appointments. On the twenty-fifth, he and Gault visited Middleton's VIII Corps, destined to spearhead the American drive to isolate the Cherbourg Peninsula, then returned to Bushy Park for conferences on the twenty-sixth with Eaker and Spaatz on the Ninth Air Force proposals. Eisenhower ordered the "bridge busting" campaign on the Seine River bridges to proceed.

At noon that day, Eisenhower left for Buckingham Palace and a private luncheon with the King and Queen to pay respects, another memorable day. Few grasped Eisenhower's reverence for the English royal family, which had honored him with friendship and hospitality.

The King, afflicted by ill health since youth, was notoriously quiet and shy and was hampered by a speech impediment. According to a story told by staff members, the King and Eisenhower in Tunisia had once ridden together in a jeep for several hours in complete silence. On the twenty-sixth, however, King George was gregarious. Over lunch, served buffet style in an upstairs apartment, the three reminisced. The Queen told Eisenhower for the first time about something that had happened on his tour of Windsor Castle two years before. As it turned out, the guide, Colonel Sterling, had forgotten that the King and Queen were on the grounds. The couple were sipping tea in a garden when they suddenly heard Sterling, Eisenhower and Clark approaching. The royal couple had not wanted to intrude, so they had knelt on hands and knees behind the hedge until the Americans had walked by. Now the three shared a good laugh.

Back at Widewing, Eisenhower told Butcher about the luncheon. During the dessert course he did not notice that his napkin had fallen to the floor. Yet he felt no self-consciousness or embarrassment when the King mentioned it to him. "It could have been like visiting a friend in Abilene," he told Butcher.

That night, having directed subcommanders to be informed of D-Day, June 5, Eisenhower departed Telegraph Cottage by train for a short visit with Gerow at V Corps Headquarters. The ten-mile concentration zones were now sealed off. Mail to and from the marshaling zones was impounded. Contact with relatives and friends was limited to dire emergencies.

Several days earlier, V Corps Headquarters had been transferred from Norton Manor to Somerset, Cornwall. The shift took place on a chilly morning warmed by the sun at midday, described years later by a young War Department historian, Forrest Pogue, assigned to go ashore with a company of the 175th Infantry in Assault Force O on D-Day. Pogue recalled how, earlier in the day, he and a number of officers had been summoned to the briefing tent to be given copies of the assault plan and to examine the photos and maps of OMAHA. Pogue noted how the pillboxes, strongpoints, mine field, anti-tank emplacements, shore guns and terrain resembled the layout of the training grounds used that month. At least the far shore no longer seemed to be such a "dark unknown," he thought, though it looked "unpromising."

Pogue described the peaceful hills of southern England along the way to Somerset, and the awesome sight as he crested a hill and saw the roads below jammed with equipment, vehicles carrying assault tanks, trucks, waxes for waterproofing, personnel carriers and troops on foot, all streaming south. In the woodlands he counted many partially concealed airfields and remembered best passing a quaint country house with a sign on the front door, "Tea for sale." As the lorries passed through the narrow streets of the little villages, townspeople lined the way cheering and waving goodbye and good luck.

From a promontory near Southwick House, Admiral Ramsay daily watched these caravans, some of which stretched a hundred miles from the bivouac zones. Ramsay, determined to maintain calm, had arranged a cricket game for his staff on the lawn at Southwick House on Y-Day, June

GERMAN STRENGTH
IN FRANCE ON D-DAY

North Sea

GREAT BRITAIN

London

Bristol Channel

Bristol

Portsmouth

Cherbourg

Caen

Brest

St-Nazaire

Bay of Biscay

Bordeaux

English Channel

Calais

Antwerp

Brussels

NETHERLANDS

BELGIUM

GERMANY

Rhine

Moselle

Meuse

Paris

Seine

ARMY GROUP B

Loire

ARMY GROUP G

FRANCE

MASSIF CENTRAL

Rhône

SWITZERLAND

ALPS

ITALY

Marseilles

Mediterranean Sea

PYRENEES

SPAIN

GERMAN:
Infantry divisions
Panzer divisions

ALLIED:
Infantry divisions
Corps

Miles
0   100   200
0   100   200
Kms.

© A·Karl/J·Kemp 1986.

1, the day he was to assume control of all naval operations in the Channel. "It is a tragic situation that this is the scene of a stage set for terrible human sacrifice," he remarked to an aide as he watched one convoy. "But if out of it comes peace and happiness, who would have it otherwise?"

COUNTDOWN

May 27. A clue in the *Daily Telegraph* puzzle read: "Bet some big wig like this has stolen some of it many times." The answer: "Overlord."

This installment of the Dawe puzzle coincided with a critical development in Normandy: 21st Army Group intelligence and SHAEF G-2 confirmed that the German 352 Field Infantry Division had moved from the vicinity of St.-Lô into the OMAHA sector. Eisenhower spent the day with Gerow at Norton Manor. One can assume that Eisenhower and Gerow discussed the situation, and that Gerow agreed with Eisenhower's evident decision to withhold the information from the commanders of the 1st and 29th divisions.

For days Eisenhower had brooded over the fate of the American airborne drops, which had never been a settled feature of the plan. At the first Supreme Commander's conference in January, Leigh-Mallory had voiced his misgivings. In the best of circumstances, landings in the swamps and hedgerows of the Cotentin would be disorganized and perhaps ineffective in retarding German movement into the UTAH sector. Secondly, flying low at an altitude of 1,000 feet, the 915 transport aircraft for two divisions would be forming a conveyor belt in nearly ideal moon conditions for anti-aircraft batteries beneath. Since then, the U.S. drop zones had been shifted and expanded. With the addition of UTAH Beach, the 101st had been assigned to land behind UTAH on the east coast of the Cherbourg Peninsula in support of the 82nd drops farther west to get a jump on isolating Cherbourg.

That day, with word of German reinforcements near UTAH, Bradley and Brigadier General James Gavin, commander of the 82nd Airborne, had decided to drop the 82nd Division closer to the 101st so that the two divisions could operate in mutual support. The 101st now would capture the causeways and destroy bridges and locks on the Douve River on the southern flank of UTAH Beach. The 82nd would jump on both sides of the Merderet River to capture Ste.-Mère-Eglise, thus cutting the main road and the Carentan–Cherbourg railroad, and capture bridges across the Merderet and the area beyond it to clear the beaches.

May 28. McClure's division at SHAEF revived the stillborn proposal for a limited amnesty for the Russian, Polish, Belgian, Norwegian and Dutch national elements pressed into service in the German army and labor force who surrendered "at first opportunity." McClure and playwright Robert

Sherwood, who temporarily headed up OWI operations in London, met to draft a "fireside chat" to be read by Eisenhower shortly after the landings calling on the German army to lay down arms. The proposal was sent to the White House and adopted reluctantly by Roosevelt, then rejected by Churchill, who complained that such a declaration would seem as if "we were begging before we have won the battle."

May 29. SHAEF wired Washington and all commands in England setting "Exercise Hornpipe Plus 6" and "Halycon 4," signals that the invasion was in readiness. Given acceptable weather, D-Day was set for June 5. Marshall cabled with news that the Combined Chiefs had set a meeting in London for the weekend of June 12 to review ANVIL, tentatively set for July 10. The CCS also intended "to be on hand in case major decisions by the CCS are necessary," arising from one of two circumstances: an early setback with time remaining to re-embark the assault force; a serious German counter-attack in the first seven or eight days with ground preponderance.

By now Eisenhower had authorized Tedder to focus Ninth Air Force strikes on airfields and roads in the Normandy area. Concentrated bombing in one sector or another would scarcely be noticed and, if noticed, probably discounted. Enemy concentrations were already at the limit—the 709th Infantry Division occupied Cherbourg; the 91st and 352nd field infantry divisions had moved up to the base of the Cotentin, along with the 716th, a parachute regiment, and the 243rd Division in reserve. The 21st Panzer Division remained south and east of Caen. Outside of the zone, five field-quality infantry divisions marked time on the Brittany Peninsula south of St.-Malo, opposite eighteen divisions, the heaviest concentration north of the Seine near Amiens, Boulogne, Calais and Dunkirk.

At Widewing, Tedder chaired a stormy commanders-in-chief conference attended by Leigh-Mallory, Smith, Morgan, Gale, Bull, Strong and De Guingand. Two problems had to be dealt with at once. First, the bomb line. The 352nd in position behind OMAHA threatened Force O in the center of the invasion front. Instead of meeting four understrength garrison batta-lions as expected, the 1st and 29th divisions would be landing opposite two first-rate field regiments without warning. Tactical support measures had to be upgraded.

The bombers were confined to a period between ten minutes before first light to forty minutes after sunup; H-Hour began at dawn plus forty-five minutes and could not be postponed. In view of these restrictions, close air support would not neutralize all enemy shore batteries. Should the Ninth Air Force extend time over target by accepting the risk of a 500-yard bomb line? Because of the extreme hazard of "shorts," the group decided finally that the matter would have to be taken to the Supreme Commander.

The second question dealt with the airborne drops. For Leigh-Mallory, the movement of the 352nd Field Division in the OMAHA sector settled matters. He warned the group of disaster as waves of transports ran the gauntlet of searchlights and heavy flack.

Seconded by De Guingand on behalf of the 21st Army Group, Tedder ruled that UTAH was essential, and that the airborne landings "were an acceptable risk." Leigh-Mallory afterward phoned Eisenhower to inform him that, after study, he had concluded that the reinforced German positions behind UTAH Beach were "too great a hazard to overcome." Casualties would be "abnormally severe," he said, amounting to the "futile slaughter" of two airborne divisions. By his estimate, 50 percent of the paratroopers would be dead before the landings, and 70 percent of the gliders destroyed. His recommendation: Cancel the American airborne drop.

Eisenhower reached Bradley at his headquarters in Bristol. Bradley stated that he could not order the landings at UTAH without the airborne drop. Without it, UTAH would be virtually isolated against the reinforced German defenses, increasing the likelihood of a local disaster, which he doubted could be confined to UTAH Beach, since repulse on any front would permeate the force. Eisenhower talked with General Ridgway, who was scheduled to parachute in with the 82nd. Ridgway seconded Bradley and probably turned the tide against radical last-minute revisions of the UTAH plan.

For Eisenhower, it was a difficult moment. Apparently, Leigh-Mallory was reluctant to assume responsibility for American casualties. More important, he appeared to question fundamentals of the plan. As yet, Leigh-Mallory had spoken to Eisenhower only by phone, so the depth of his convictions were not clear. Eisenhower decided to let him exercise his right to go on record; late that night he phoned Leigh-Mallory and told him that he was ordering the airborne attacks. He reminded him of his right to object to this decision in writing.

May 30. A clue in the *Daily Telegraph* crossword puzzle read: "This bush is the center of nursery or revolutions." The answer: "mulberry."

After a night of sporadic sleep, Eisenhower went into conference with Tedder, General Handy, Admiral Cooke and Colonel McCarthy of Marshall's Advance Staff, after which he dispatched a message to the Combined Chiefs of Staff urging the JCS to deploy the resources of joint security control to clamp down on security breaches. Similar action had been ordered at SHAEF and by the British security organization.

Leigh-Mallory's written protest arrived at midday, hand-delivered. In it he apologized for increasing Eisenhower's problems "at the present difficult time," and said he would be "failing in my duty to you if I did not let you know that I am very unhappy about the U.S. airborne operations as now planned for the night of D-1 D-Day."

Leigh-Mallory recited the hazards: the sorties over the Cotentin Peninsula; the lack of armored protection on the underbelly of the C-47 aircraft; the "probability of scatter landings," the lack of cohesion sure to follow that would undermine an orderly assault at UTAH. Leigh-Mallory did not confine his criticism to the airborne assault. He called UTAH Beach logically "unsound," adding that if airborne landings were a condition for VII Corps success, the whole western flank was too hazardous. His conclusion fell short of any clear-cut recommendations; however, he predicted trouble and results far short of what Eisenhower expected, noting that if success of the UTAH assault depended on the drops, the landings would be "seriously prejudiced."

Leigh-Mallory's careful wording suggested that his real purpose was to disavow responsibility for American airborne casualties. Butcher flew into a rage and hurled Leigh-Mallory's "Casper Milk-toast" protest into the diary, doubtlessly reflecting Eisenhower's reaction. Still, Eisenhower spent the entire afternoon at Telegraph Cottage reconsidering the matter, in what he later described as his most agonizing moment.

Could the plan be changed? Eisenhower recapitulated the arguments pro and con for the airdrops, the decision to expand the assault to which they were linked, along with the goal of quickly seizing Cherbourg, all of which were deemed crucial to OVERLORD. Eisenhower had canceled 82nd Airborne drops during Salerno and might have done so again. He had to consider that the destruction of two airborne divisions in the course of the airdrops would be a great burden, but he could not ignore Bradley's views that any changes now would depress Eisenhower's subordinates and open the door to more changes and panic on the eve of the assault. The drops would have to proceed. Eisenhower phoned Leigh-Mallory, acknowledged his letter and ordered the airborne drop.

June 1. The *Daily Telegraph* crossword puzzle that morning read, 15 down: "Brittania and he hold the same thing." Answer: "Neptune." That day MI-5 (British counterespionage) finally took Dawe and his co-author, Melville Jones, into custody. After questioning, they were released and MI-5 ruled that the whole matter was one of the most fantastic coincidences in history. But the *Daily Telegraph* puzzle had not been a complete coincidence. Forty years later Ronald French, a pupil at Dawe's school, would emerge with a story he had sworn never to tell. French described how Dawe would routinely assemble the pupils in his study and assign them to fill in blank crossword puzzles and write clues. At the time, French and fellow pupils spent afternoons at nearby American and Canadian camps where soldiers freely used the code words, not always knowing what they meant. French wrote several of these words in Dawe's blank forms. Years later he remembered MULBERRY in particular because of the nursery rhyme. After his release, Dawe searched out French. When the boy admitted what he had done, Dawe told him to burn anything he had written down about the soldiers and swear on a Bible that he would never tell the story.

Would the weather hold up? Thursday, June 1, dawned "dull and gray." The meteorologists at Portsmouth traced a rapidly changing weather pattern developing over the Atlantic. A high-pressure ridge over Iceland was forcing depressions southward, and a high-pressure system over the Azores was weakening. "Fairly optimistic," Stagg noted in his diary that morning, "but obviously a very marginal and difficult situation."

That evening Stagg informed General Bull, G-3, of the shaky consensus. Weather prospects for the middle of the following week were "not good." Deep depressions were forming between Newfoundland and Ireland, making predictions "hazardous." Stagg told Bull that Widewing and the Admiralty were sharply divided over short-term forecasts.

Stagg suggested that the Supreme Commander be informed of the disagreement. "For heaven's sake, Stagg," Bull exclaimed, "get it sorted out by tomorrow morning before you come to the Supreme Commander's conference. General Eisenhower is a very worried man." But clearing weather over south England made Stagg's pessimistic report appear overcautious. "Weather forecasts while still indefinite are generally favorable," Eisenhower cabled Marshall that night. "I will keep you informed on this point. Everyone is in good heart and barring unsuitable meteorological conditions we will do the trick as scheduled."

That night Admiral Ramsay telephoned from Portsmouth with the news that Prime Minister Churchill now insisted upon accompanying the invading force across the Channel on D-Day. The matter had come up several times that spring, and in each case Eisenhower had discouraged the Prime Minister's romantic notion. Were Churchill's ship to be hit by a torpedo or a bomber, at least five neighboring ships would have to come to the rescue —five ships that otherwise would necessarily proceed and concentrate on gunfire support duties and protection of the convoys of troops. According to Ramsay, the Prime Minister seemed "set on the idea." As Prime Minister and Administrative Chief of the British Navy, Churchill had the power to induct himself into the Navy for the twenty-four hours or so of the invasion.

Eisenhower was sympathetic. He told Ramsay he understood Churchill's natural desire to share the dangers of the invasion force. But Churchill's presence would be an intolerable personal burden and disruption. Eisenhower asked Ramsay to tell Churchill his request had been "disapproved."

Forty-eight hours later Churchill petulantly decided not to accompany the force ashore. Meanwhile, King George had informed the Prime Minister that if Churchill went, the King would feel obligated to go also. In his memoirs, Churchill made it plain that he deferred to the Crown, not to Eisenhower.

. . .

June 2. The seventy-two-hour countdown began. Stagg and the weather staff were still sharply divided over the forecast. The U.S. services at Widewing predicted clear weather. The monitoring stations reporting through the Admiralty and Air Ministry indicated that the entire North Atlantic area was covered by weather depressions, a pattern "sluggish and slow to show its hand," Stagg wrote, "favorable from a wind point of view though very uncertain about cloud." He could not rule out the possibility of gale-force winds or of 900-foot cloud ceilings, practically ruling out air-ground support and airborne operations.

At nine o'clock that night, Eisenhower chaired a Supreme Commander's conference at Southwick House, Portsmouth. The scene would be re-enacted many times in the next several days. Eisenhower, Montgomery, Tedder, Leigh-Mallory, Ramsay and Smith sat on sofas and easy chairs informally arranged in a ring in the first-floor library of Southwick House next to the War Room.

At nine-thirty Stagg entered to brief the group. He called the weather "untrustworthy" and a potential menace, though the forecast was by no means unanimously accepted by the staff. The picture was "finely balanced," he said, but tipped "on the favorable side."

Eisenhower: "Well, what do *you* think?"

Stagg: "If I were to answer that, sir, that would make me a guesser, not a meteorologist."

The meeting recessed early. Confronting a twenty-four-hour deadline on a decision to postpone landings set for the fifth, Eisenhower ordered weather briefings two times a day. "The weather in this country is practically unpredictable," Eisenhower complained in a memorandum for the record.

> For some days our experts have been meeting almost hourly and I have been holding Commanders-in-Chief meetings once or twice a day to consider the reports and tentative predictions.
> While at this moment, the morning of June 3rd, it appears that the weather will not be so bad as to preclude landings and will possibly even permit reasonably effective gunfire support from the Navy, the picture from the air viewpoint is not so good.
> Probably no one that does not have to bear the specific and direct responsibility of making the final decision as to what to do can understand the intensity of these burdens. The Supreme Commander, much more than any of his subordinates, has been kept informed of the political issues involved, particularly the anticipated effect of delay upon the Russians. He likewise is in close touch with all the advice from his military subordinates and must face the issue even when the technical advice as to weather is not unanimous from several experts.

June 3. Clear skies prevailed all day, but forecasts were still bad. The weather staff remained bitterly divided over the short-term forecast and a new possibility—that a benign weather system sandwiched between the depression might arrive and last the three days required for the landings and initial build-up. But no one was sure of it, and so the debate went on all day. And by evening Stagg found himself faced with what he later described as a "ridiculous" situation: at the Supreme Commander's conference that night, he was expected to present an "agreed" forecast for the five-day period covering D-Day, and yet no two of his experts could agree on a forecast for the next twenty-four hours!

As the Supreme Commander's conference reconvened at nine o'clock in the evening, bombardment ships berthed at Clyde, Scapa Flow and Belfast were under way. Ships carrying the American western task forces idled in the Irish Sea.

As Stagg recalled, the tension was "palpable" in the room. Eisenhower, "serious and unsmiling," listened while Stagg presented a picture "disturbed and complex," potentially "full of menace." According to the Dunstable forecasts, weather would permit close-shore naval bombardment, but low cloud cover would make air support operations "improbable." Stagg was disturbed about the longer-range forecast of high winds and low visibility.

Several asked Stagg about forecasts for a prediction for Tuesday and Wednesday. Stagg talked about the "benign high" detected between the low-pressure areas forming over Iceland. However, he could not "differentiate one day from another" in the invasion period. The services were unanimous about bad weather on the fifth.

Eisenhower reminded Stagg that he had been optimistic the night before. "Is there just a chance that you might be a bit more optimistic tomorrow?"

Stagg replied the balance had "gone too far to the other side for it to swing back again overnight tonight."

With predicted level 4–5 winds and a 1,000-foot ceiling, Leigh-Mallory proposed a postponement. Eisenhower polled the group. All agreed. To cover a possible last-minute improvement, Eisenhower directed the remaining American assault forces in port to embark, and set a review at 4:30 A.M., eight hours hence.

By now, exceptional weather patterns over the Atlantic had reduced the reliability of any estimate from the standard twenty-four to forty-eight hours to six to twelve hours. An L-5 condition had moved into the Channel area. "In all the charts for the forty or fifty years I had examined," Stagg wrote, "I could not recall one which at this time of the year resembled this chart in the number and intensity of the depressions it portrayed at one time." The weather patterns were typical of winter weather in the North Atlantic, and yet the night outside his tent was starlit, clear and cool.

At the 4:30 meeting, Eisenhower asked Stagg if he foresaw a change. "No change, sir," he replied.

Ramsay asked Stagg when the cloud cover was due to appear.

Stagg: "By 8 or 9 A.M., four or five hours from now."

Stagg withdrew from the room.

Montgomery was anxious to launch the attack on the fifth, despite the poor forecast. Leigh-Mallory reminded Eisenhower about air support. Bradley had refused to land the 4th Division at UTAH without 101st and 82nd Airborne drops—decent flying conditions were essential for the airborne assault. Ramsay reminded the group that a decision had to be made within thirty minutes in order to halt the sortie of the main force and to order a turnaround of the other ships and landing craft already under way.

Montgomery backed away, and Eisenhower ordered the postponement without dissent. Smith immediately wired the CCS and all commands the code words indicating the postponement and phoned 10 Downing Street. Simultaneously, orders went out to the entire fleet, steaming toward "Piccadilly Circus," ordering units to return. Several elements of the task force steamed on oblivious of the order. As late as nine the next morning, a formation of 138 ships carrying the U.S. 4th Infantry Division steamed twenty-five miles south of the Isle of Wight, not having acknowledged the signal to stop. British Coastal Command dispatched a Walrus biplane to find the convoy and to signal it to reverse course and return to port. When the convoy ignored radio warnings, the Walrus crew dropped a canister on the main deck of the lead ship. The task force reversed course, narrowly averting compromise of the operation.

June 4. By ten, clouds appeared over southern England and the wind rose. Gale warnings in the Channel were issued at eleven. Meanwhile Churchill, Smuts, Ismay and Bevin arrived at Eisenhower's tent camp with De Gaulle, who had just flown in from Algiers aboard Churchill's private airplane. De Gaulle was now to be informed of D-Day and of his opportunity to cooperate by broadcasting a D-Day message to the French people urging obedience to SHAEF instructions.

The De Gaulle matter had become complicated. On the night of the first, the British War Cabinet had ventilated last-minute misgivings about the French Resistance and De Gaulle. There were memories of Giraud in 1942 when American and British ideas of what the French people wanted had proven false. Would permitting De Gaulle to broadcast as president of the Provisional Government of France be ineffectual? Churchill overruled all objections, assuring the Cabinet that De Gaulle was a good gamble and would cooperate. But as Churchill and Eisenhower were soon to learn, one did not invite Charles de Gaulle to deliver a prepared text.

De Gaulle had arrived in London in an intransigent mood, suspicious of a Darlan case in the making and determined to assert his authority over France. Earlier in the day, a "bristling" De Gaulle had conferred with Churchill and Eden over lunch. Churchill had attempted to put him in a cooperative frame of mind, reminding him that for quite some time France might consist of a "few people under fire." Churchill urged him to accept Roosevelt's invitation to visit Washington. De Gaulle had been "quite willing to do this" and had told Roosevelt so, but he was anxious first to know "who was to administer liberated France." De Gaulle would not submit his qualifications to Roosevelt, for he had nothing to ask of Washington "or, for that matter, Britain." Churchill had reminded De Gaulle that in the event of a split between the FCNL and Washington, Britain would always choose Washington. He had been honored to promote the cause of the FCNL as the de facto authority in France, but if De Gaulle sought "the title deeds to France, the answer was 'no.' "

The mood carried over into the visit at Portsmouth.

Eisenhower handed De Gaulle copies of the talk De Gaulle was to deliver over BBC, and his own talk to be broadcast immediately after the landings. De Gaulle objected to Eisenhower's message, which failed to mention his name or the Provisional Government of France, of which he was president. De Gaulle noted that the SHAEF message implied that the Vichy orders should be obeyed until more permanent arrangements could be made. Also, it overstressed obedience to SHAEF instructions, as though SHAEF intended military occupation of a liberated country. The message De Gaulle was to read resembled remarks drafted for King Haakon of Norway and Queen Juliana of Holland, and acknowledged SHAEF military authority.

Eisenhower led the French leader on a "Cook's tour" of the War Room and briefed De Gaulle on Normandy and the follow-on landings at Calais. Thus, as late as the fourth, SHAEF was still unwilling to take De Gaulle into its complete confidence, and carefully preserved the FORTITUDE deception.

Afterward Eisenhower, De Gaulle and Churchill walked outside in the rain up a cinder pathway leading to the signal tent, according to Butcher, in order to give De Gaulle "the elbow room . . . to wave his arms."

> Ike did some too, and in due course they returned, went into the War Room, and we heard Anglo-French dictation to one of Churchill's secretaries. De Gaulle was to broadcast when called upon, but had wanted Ike to take out of his speech any reference to his, Ike's, control of law and order amongst his, De Gaulle's, Frenchmen. That's where it was left on Sunday evening.

Eisenhower could not change the text of his D-Day message. Recordings were set to be broadcast, and over a million copies were printed, ready to be dropped from aircraft across France on D-Day. Eisenhower was unwilling to share his temporary authority in the battle zone. De Gaulle refused to endorse Eisenhower's text or to deliver his own.

On it went. Twenty-four hours later, Smith met with Koenig in a last-minute attempt to iron out differences. Koenig was empowered to discuss changes in Eisenhower's statement, nothing more, and he insisted on the deletion of a section referring to the "free choice of governmental representatives" following the liberation of France. Smith insisted that no substitutions or rearrangements were possible. Koenig replied that he understood, but in turn De Gaulle "in these circumstances" was unable "to make a statement following that of General Eisenhower."

Smith threatened to proceed with the original program "minus any statement from General De Gaulle," a bluff. Koenig saw through it, and the upshot was that De Gaulle would tape a BBC broadcast of his choice beamed on the night of the sixth in which he called for obedience to the "orders given by the French government and by the French leaders it has appointed."

"The storm gathered in fury," Wilmot wrote of the fourth, "and it seemed that all the months of preparation would be nullified by the one factor which could not be harnessed by the plan."

Nerves were strained, particularly aboard the American ships, on which the troops had been entombed for as long as seventy-two hours. With word of the postponement, Bradley and Kirk discussed what their response would be if they were polled for a recommendation about postponement beyond the sixth. The seventh could be marginal—beyond the seventh, the choice was whether to postpone OVERLORD until mid-month, or attempt it in daylight on the eighth or ninth. At first Bradley favored mid-month instead of daylight landings on the eighth and ninth, which would rely exclusively on naval and air firepower. On the other hand, a postponement for two weeks for the sake of favorable tide and moon conditions meant a shorter summer campaign and risked German reinforcements in the interval. The U.S. First Army was expected to seize Cherbourg and lead a breakout through the bocage country of Normandy, a task bound to be complicated by delay. Finally, Bradley feared leaks and the impact of a long wait on the morale of his troops. Bradley consulted Gerow and Collins, who agreed that waiting fourteen more days would unbearably prolong the tension among his troops and that "an overdose of daylight had become . . . preferable to the ordeal of a long delay."

Much the same ran through Eisenhower's mind. After a quick supper he returned to Southwick House, rubbing in his pocket the seven lucky coins he had carried first in the caves of Gibraltar, where he spent the night of the invasion of North Africa. Luck in the weather would be crucial because he, too, had concluded that delay would have disastrous consequences. The assault troops, fully briefed and ready, would have to disembark and return to Plymouth, Dartmouth, Torquay and Devon. A two-week or four-week postponement, as he later wrote, would give the German Seventh Army time to complete construction of the defenses in the Normandy area, and Eisenhower could not overlook the vaunted V-1 "secret weapons."

Above all, Eisenhower weighed the effects of a letdown. In four earlier landings Eisenhower had never ordered a two-week postponement, and so he could not measure the effect precisely. However, the Leigh-Mallory episode was an example of what he could expect at the command level. Also, Eisenhower had to consider the Russians. For two weeks Moscow would probably be convinced that the Allies were not and had never been serious about landings in France, and might even attribute the eventual landings to Soviet diplomatic harassment of London and Washington. This was significant because post-invasion cooperation had not been worked out. For these reasons, it was hard to see how OVERLORD, conceived as a decisive step to seize the initiative, could be stopped.

Deliberations resumed. At nine-thirty Group Captain Stagg returned to the bare library at Southwick House to report a development. He described how the syndicate of weathermen had discerned a cold front west of Ireland around 1 P.M. that was due in the area by dawn of the sixth. The benign high between the cold front and a following depression was a weather phenomenon typical of winter—not June. But there it was, all the services agreed, and the "break" in the storm might hold up for as long as thirty-six hours. Seas would be moderate and the cloud cover might lift, although heavy aerial and naval bombardment might still be impossible. With the lessening of winds beginning midnight Monday, the landing craft would have an "inconvenient time of it," but conditions would not be chaotic. Clouds would move in Tuesday night, and he cautioned that the weather would remain "unsettled" that week.

Air Chief Marshal Leigh-Mallory asked Stagg if he had consulted AEAF meteorologists. Stagg had, and they agreed on "almost perfect visual bombing weather from Monday evening to early forenoon Tuesday."

In Leigh-Mallory's opinion, conditions for the airborne troops to commence at midnight the night of June 5 would only be "moderately good," and the same held for the heavy bombers the following morning. Thus it passed to Tedder to sound a more optimistic note.

Tedder asked Stagg how personally confident he was of the forecast he had just presented. Stagg was "quite confident" that a fair interval would follow tonight's front.

As Stagg left the room, Tedder remarked that he thought heavy and medium bombers could use the gaps in the weather, but he considered the decision to go "chancy." Eisenhower's two advisers on the crucial air element had hedged.

Admiral Ramsay pointed out that conditions were satisfactory for naval bombardment. He reminded the group that a postponement beyond the sixth probably meant two weeks. Ships would have to return to port to refuel and could not turn around by the seventh. In several hours he would have to issue a "provisional warning" to Admiral Kirk if the invasion was to proceed on the sixth. If they are recalled, "there can be no question of continuing on Wednesday."

"I would say go," Montgomery said. Smith agreed. Conditions *might* be good, he said. If so, the weather news could prove to be a real break; the Germans would be lulled by less accurate forecasts. "It's a helluva gamble," Smith added, "but it's the best possible gamble."

The room was silent for two minutes.

"The question is," Eisenhower mused, "how long you can allow this thing to just kind of hang out there on a limb?"

Silence.

"I'm quite positive that the order must be given."

A small crowd had collected outside the room. Stagg talked to an Admiralty colleague who waited with a set of signals for each contingency, go or stop.

"He alone is the one to say," wrote Kay Summersby in her journal several minutes later, "we will go."

A final review was set for four-fifteen the following morning. Shortly before, Eisenhower rose from a fitful sleep. As he later recalled, the tent camp shook and shuddered in a gale, so he woke up thinking that at least the decision to postpone from the fifth to the sixth had been the correct one. On HALYCON plus four, the armada would have crossed ninety miles of turbulent seas. In the off-loading, landing craft would have capsized, causing confusion and loss of life. Storms would have grounded the paratroopers. Air support would have been nonexistent. The storm outside his window enhanced Eisenhower's confidence in Stagg, and in his own judgment and good fortune. Eisenhower was a man who had faith in his hunches, a trait he looked for in other commanders.

As the story goes, for the final time, the respective air, ground and naval commanders in chief arrived bundled in windbreakers and overcoats and umbrellas to fend off the horizontal sheets of rain. All present wore battle dress except for Montgomery, who wore his trademark light-brown corduroys, a pullover sweater and black beret. In the interval of seven hours, the principals of OVERLORD had individually become reconciled to the inevitability of the decision.

Stagg had more good news, welcome fortification. His prediction for a break in the storm still "held good." The little changes reported were "in the direction of optimism." Cloud cover: three-tenths, height, 2,000 feet; winds between force 3 and 4. In the course of the meeting, the pressure of the rain against the windowpane seemed to lessen. Eisenhower promised Stagg a "big celebration if the forecast comes off."

Leigh-Mallory conceded that the marginal air conditions might work against the Germans. Reconnaissance aircraft would be grounded and the Luftwaffe response to the landing force sluggish. Smith raised a question:

Could the Navy gunners spot in this visibility? Ramsay said "Yes."

The ships had been launched, and this time there would be no order to turn back. After a final pause, as though to assure himself that he had taken the step in all due deliberation, Eisenhower closed, "Okay, we'll go."

And so, with three words, Eisenhower irreversibly set the forces of OVER-LORD in motion. Many have narrated this decision—few have evaluated it. Years later Admiral Friedrich Ruge, Rommel's naval adviser that night, would reflect on it. He would note that Eisenhower, on the strength of a weather forecast, decided to launch the invasion on the sixth instead of postponing it until the nineteenth without having to clear that decision with higher authority. By the morning of the fifth, the Allied high command operated with "clear responsibilities at every level," in contrast to the faction-ridden German high command. Friction existed, as might be expected, but the organization functioned well, owing in part to Eisenhower's personal qualities as well as to the efficiency of the military organization itself. Ruge concluded that Eisenhower's decision that night was "one of the truly great decisions in military history."

Allied good fortune would hold. Accounts of the German high command describe the mood of skepticism that the Allies would invade before the Russian summer offensive, expected at the end of June. The Germans would also be victims of faulty intelligence. As German records later revealed, the Luftwaffe, in charge of predicting weather patterns, had not operated far enough westward of Ireland to detect the clear break in the weather charted by Stagg's group. Early on the morning of the fifth the German naval command concluded that the inclement weather ruled out imminent threat of invasion. Conditions were so poor that the Germans canceled air reconnaissance missions over the southwestern ports in England and routine E-boat operations, which might have detected the mine-sweeping flotillas trolling into position to clear channels to the beaches.

Rommel awoke on the morning of June 5 to the sound of wind and rain at his quarters in Château de La Roche Guyon outside Paris. Meteorological prediction held that the weather would force at least a two-week delay. Rommel left on an auto trip on which he planned to visit Obersalzburg to speak personally to Hitler about manpower and equipment shortages in Normandy, planning to request two more panzer divisions, an anti-aircraft corps, and a Nebelwerfer (rocket-launching) brigade to reinforce Normandy.

Earlier in the day, OB West had reported to all commands that "as yet there is no immediate prospect of the invasion." For most of the day and evening, a majority of the Seventh Army divisional and corps commanders were away from command posts attending a battle-problem session in Rennes to determine solutions for theoretical enemy landings beginning with parachute drops, followed by landings at Normandy.

Meanwhile at Portsmouth, group commanders returned to the seclusion of their quarters. The rains continued all night. Early that morning Eisenhower motored to nearby Portsmouth to bid farewell to the embarking British 3rd and 50th divisions, and returned to the trailer camp for lunch.

According to Butcher, the two of them played crackerbox checkers. Butcher told yarns about Senator Bilbo, the well-known Mississippi demagogue who had once beaten his good friend Senator Pat Harrison in a primary. Harrison had been advised that the trouble with his campaign was that he was "too damn honorable and should use Bilbo's tactics." Eisenhower laughed heartily, and so, as Butcher wrote, "We talked, during lunch, of senators and skunks and civet cats."

That afternoon Eisenhower went to a makeshift press room at the tent caravan, to brief the four correspondents accredited to SHAEF: Robert Barr of BBC; Stanley Burch of Reuters; Ned Roberts of UP; Red Mueller of NBC. Eisenhower "nonchalantly" revealed that OVERLORD had been irrevocably launched. The reporters received the news in an off-hand way, "a study in suppressed emotion which would interest any psychologist," according to Butcher.

Late that afternoon Eisenhower entertained the thought that all would not go well. He tore off a small sheet of paper from a desk pad and scribbled a note that he intended to release in the event he or the CCS ordered abandonment of the beachhead:

> Our landings in the Cherbourg–Le Havre area have failed to gain a satisfactory foothold and I have withdrawn the troops. My decision to attack at this time and place was based upon the best information available. The troops, the air and the navy did all that bravery and devotion to duty could do. If any blame or fault attaches to the attempt, it is mine alone.

Before Sicily, Pantelleria, North Africa and Italy, Eisenhower had drafted a similar statement. He had made it a practice to keep a copy in his wallet for ready reference, though in the crush of events he had usually forgotten about it.

Late in the day Eisenhower decided to visit the 101st Airborne Division at Newbury—one of two units Leigh-Mallory had predicted would suffer 80 percent casualties. Eisenhower rode in the lead car with Jimmy Gault, followed by Smith, Butcher, Lieutenant Leo Moore, a reporter, with Butcher, Mueller and Roberts in a second car. The ninety-minute trip was tortuously slow in the flow of trucks and troop carriers, weaving past checkpoints through the choked avenues of Portsmouth. At dusk the wind abated and the clouds lifted.

The party arrived unannounced to avoid disrupting the embarkation aboard the C-47s. The stars on the running board of the automobile had been covered, but the troops of the 101st quickly recognized Eisenhower and the word passed. Many have described how Eisenhower wandered through the formless groups of soldiers, stepping over packs and guns. The faces of the men had been blackened with charcoal and cocoa to protect against glare and to serve as camouflage. He stopped at intervals to talk to the thick clusters of soldiers gathering round him. He asked their names and homes.

"Texas, sir!" one replied. "Don't worry, sir, the 101st is on the job and everything will be taken care of in fine shape."

Laughter and applause. Another soldier invited Eisenhower down to his ranch after the war.

"Where are you from, soldier?"

"Missouri, sir!"

"And you, soldier?"

"Kansas, sir."

"And you, soldier?"

"Texas, sir." Cheers, and the roll call of the states went on, "like a roll of battle honors," one observer wrote, as it unfolded, affirming an "awareness that the General and the men were associated in a great enterprise."

Eisenhower walked General Maxwell Taylor to the ramp of a C-47 airplane to shake hands, then returned to his car parked at some distance from the field and drove to the nearby 101st Airborne Headquarters. He and his staff stood on the roof of the building to watch the swarms of C-47s pass overhead in the clearing night, bound for France. Eisenhower returned to Portsmouth.

"Here then, we reach what the Western powers may justly regard as the supreme climax of the war," Churchill later wrote about the night spent in the War Room Annex in the bunker below St. James's Square, sipping brandy with his secretary, Jack Colville. "Though the road would be long and hard, could we doubt that victory would be gained?"

"It is very hard to believe that in a few hours the invasion starts," Brooke wrote, seated alone at his chambers at the Horse Guards. "I am very uneasy about the whole operation. At best it will fall so far short of the expectations of the bulk of the people, namely all those who know nothing about its difficulties. At worst, it may well be the most ghastly disaster of the whole war. I wish to God it were safely over."

Roosevelt extended his weekend with friends at Camp Shangri-La in the Catoctin Mountains. Marshall extended his weekend in Leesville, Virginia, leaving word with his staff not to send messages to Eisenhower, since there was nothing further the War Department could do.

In Portsmouth, Eisenhower, Butcher, Summersby, Tedder, Smith, Gale and Whitely sat around a small table drinking coffee. Nobody could think of anything to say, so they sat in silence. Finally Butcher said, "The hell with it," rose and went to bed. Slowly, one by one, the party dispersed. Eisenhower returned to his trailer to pass the five or six hours before news of the airborne drop.

The Allies were on the move everywhere that night. Alexander's offensive, launched on May 14, rolled on. After two weeks of violent attacks, VI Corps and the Fifth Army had at last linked at Cisterna. Then Clark turned in pursuit of the German Tenth Army northward to the Caesar line, joined by the Eighth Army, which advanced through the Liri Valley. On the fourth, lead elements of the U.S. 88th Division had entered Rome's Piazza Venezia.

The sudden German retreat north of Rome appeared to bear out Marshall's contention that the Germans would quickly fall back to the Pisa–Rimini line to release troops for other fronts. Debate over Italy would resume—whether to pursue to the Po River valley, or to consolidate and launch ANVIL, a debate that would depend on the outcome in Normandy.

That night Eisenhower dictated brief congratulatory telegrams to his friends at AFHQ on the imminent fall of Rome, a splendid moment. He cabled Clark, Cunningham, Wilson, Alexander and Eaker, congratulating all for the "brilliant success" they had achieved and assured each of his "continuing confidence in you and your ability." He asked to be remembered to his friends on the AFHQ staff, promising they would "soon meet" in the heart of the enemy homeland." Part of the impulse to congratulate AFHQ must have stemmed from his awareness that within twenty-four to seventy-two hours he would either be receiving congratulatory messages in return or, along with the CCS, be engaged in the most frantic deliberations of the war to retrieve an ill-timed invasion that had wrecked Allied hopes for defeating Germany in 1944, 1945 or even 1946.

Eisenhower perused reports. He read a report based on a State Department cablegram relaying reports filed by the American legation in Stockholm describing conditions in Europe that night. According to "reliable Swedish sources," morale within Germany was being steadily undermined. The report described rumors of leadership upheavals within the army, criticism of Nazi officials, and the latest rumors of clashes between Hitler and the older generals of the Wehrmacht who were eager to sue for an armistice in hopes that the Allies would reach Berlin before the Russians.

Hamburg has left only about one hundred homes with more than one floor, Stockholm informants stated. Complete destruction of 80% of Düsseldorf is reported. In Leipzig 80% of the factories are stated to be out of production, and 50% of the population is reported to have been evacuated. Rapid deterioration of the food situation is reported. There is demoralization of railway traffic. . . .
   An early end of the war, through a successful invasion, is hoped for by the German population, it is reported. . . .

By the night of the fifth, U.S. and British medium bombers had succeeded in cutting 18 of the 24 bridges across the Seine, isolating temporarily the Seventh and Fifteenth German armies in northwest France. According to intelligence reports, Allied bombers now claimed 5,400 locomotives and placed an additional 1,700 locomotives and 25,000 wagons damaged and out of action. In the region Nord, traffic ran at 13 percent of January levels, and 30 percent throughout France.

The transport plan aroused protest. In the past week, Pope Pius XII had endorsed an appeal issued by a number of French priests protesting the "indiscriminate" bombing of France. Vichy propaganda warned the population that air-raid damage was nothing compared with what the "liberators" had in store should France be turned into a battlefield. But several French refugees reached London and related that Parisians were reacting to the bombing with sorrow, not indignation. The report noted: "The recent increase in the air offensive is definitely linked in the people's minds with the idea of the second front and this is a big factor in maintaining morale."

In the months ahead, SHAEF military summaries would be published daily describing unit location, enemy identification, casualties, and weather. The first of these summaries eloquently testified to the vast movement under way: 48 British Mosquito fighter-bombers had attacked Domfront, St.-Pierre and Thury-Harcourt that day; 1,136 heavy bombers had been ordered to attack coastal batteries in the landing sectors. Otherwise, all was in suspense. The report continued:

ORDER OF BATTLE

1. *ENEMY (In contact).*
None.
2. *ALLIED.*
BRITISH.

Formation	Location
Second British Army	Afloat
XXX Corps	Afloat
50 infantry divisions	Afloat
7 armored divisions	Afloat
51 infantry divisions	Afloat
I Corps	Afloat
3 infantry divisions	Afloat
3 Canadian infantry divisions	Afloat

UNITED STATES

First Army	Afloat
V Corps	Afloat
1st Infantry Division	Afloat
29th Infantry Division	Afloat
2nd Infantry Division	Afloat
VII Corps	Afloat

| 4th Infantry Division | Afloat |
| 90th Infantry Division | Afloat |

Under cover of darkness, four thousand American, British and Canadian ships of all types—six battleships and eighty destroyers, freighters, ocean liners, tugs hauling components for the MULBERRY harbors, minesweepers, hospital ships—bending and buckling "slowly, ponderously" in the gray chop converged at "Piccadilly Circus." There, the armada pivoted southward in five lanes, which would branch into ten channels near the Normandy coast. That night each of the 175,000 members of the Allied Expeditionary Force received a small slip of paper suitable for being folded into a wallet. On it was printed Eisenhower's Order of the Day for June 6, 1944.

In early February, General Raymond Barker had first called attention to the need for a proclamation on D-Day. He had proposed that the Supreme Commander tell the soldiers about their enemy, what was expected of each, and that he affirm his belief in a victorious outcome of the battle. The several drafts, and Eisenhower's handwritten corrections, survive. Eisenhower's deletions and militantly phrased substitutions hardened the graceful, complex message aimed at the world to convey the spirit of the great crusade launched on Hitler's Europe. Eisenhower deleted a recital of past victories, for clearly, OVERLORD was a beginning. In defining the purpose of the invasion, he struck out "overthrow" and inserted "the elimination of Nazi tyranny."

"I think General Eisenhower's changes have made a decided improvement," Barker minuted Smith. "I like especially the last phrase in paragraph two: it expresses just the thought I wanted to get in but couldn't quite achieve."

In three years the grand design had taken shape. In the months since January, the tentative phrases and qualifications had fallen out. And now Eisenhower spoke to the armada and the world with certainty about the severe German response awaiting the invasion force and of his faith in final victory:

> Soldiers, sailors and airmen of the Allied Expeditionary Forces!
> You are about to embark upon the great crusade, toward which we have striven these many months. The eyes of the world are upon you, the hopes and prayers of liberty-loving people everywhere march with you. In company with our brave Allies and brothers in arms on other fronts you will bring about the destruction of the German war machine, the elimination of Nazi tyranny over the oppressed peoples of Europe, and security for ourselves in a free world.
> Your task will not be an easy one. Your enemy is well trained, well equipped and battle hardened. He will fight savagely.
> But this is the year 1944! Much has happened since the Nazi triumphs of 1940–1941. The United Nations have inflicted upon the Germans great defeats, in open battle, man to man. Our air offensive has seriously reduced their strength in the air and their capacity to wage war on the ground. Our home fronts have

given us an overwhelming superiority in weapons and munitions of war, and placed at our disposal great reserves of trained fighting men. The tide has turned! The free men of the world are marching together to victory!

I have full confidence in your courage, devotion to duty, skill in battle. We will accept nothing less than full victory!

Good luck! And let us all beseech the blessings of Almighty God upon this great and noble undertaking.

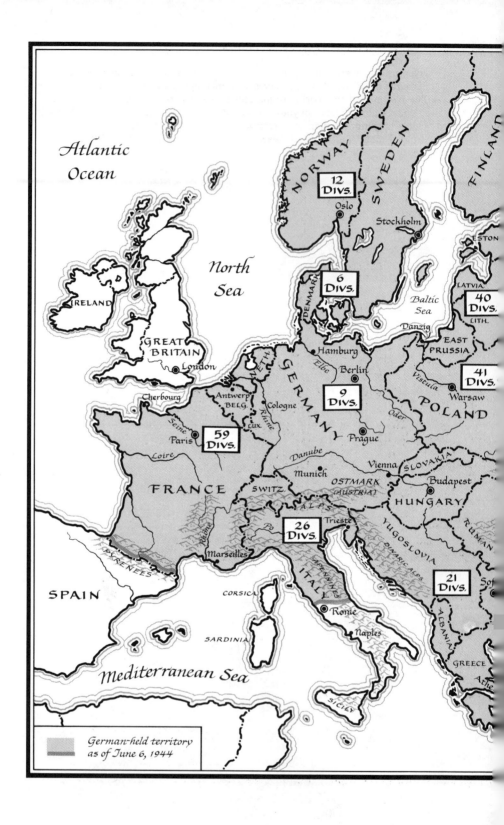

Atlantic
Ocean

North
Sea

IRELAND

GREAT
BRITAIN
• London

Cherbourg

NORWAY

Oslo

SWEDEN

Stockholm

FINLAND

ESTON.

LATVIA

LITH.

Baltic
Sea

Danzig

12 DIVS.

6 DIVS.

40 DIVS.

DENMARK

Hamburg

Elbe

Berlin

GERMANY

Prague

Oder

Vistula

Warsaw

EAST
PRUSSIA

POLAND

41 DIVS.

9 DIVS.

Antwerp
BELG.

Cologne

Rhine

LUX.

Seine

Paris

Loire

59 DIVS.

FRANCE

SWITZ.

Danube

Munich

Vienna

SLOVAKIA

Budapest

HUNGARY

RUMAN.

OSTMARK
(AUSTRIA)

ALPS

Po

Trieste

26 DIVS.

Rhône

Marseilles

YUGOSLAVIA

DINARIC ALPS

21 DIVS.

Sof

PYRENEES

SPAIN

CORSICA

ITALY

APENNINES

Rome

Naples

ALBANIA

GREECE

Athe

SARDINIA

SICILY

Mediterranean Sea

German-held territory
as of June 6, 1944

DISTRIBUTION OF GERMAN DIVISIONS, JUNE 6, 1944

6 DIVS.

35 DIVS.

Kms.
0   400

Miles
0   400

Leningrad

Volga

Moscow

Vitebsk

UNION OF SOVIET SOCIALIST REPUBLICS

Kursk

UKRAINE

Don

Kharkov

Stalingrad

Kiev

Dnieper

Rostov

Dniester

Caspian Sea

Odessa

CRIMEA

Sevastopol

Bucharest

Black Sea

ULGARIA

Istanbul

IRAN

Ankara

TURKEY

IRAQ

SYRIA

CRETE

CYPRUS

© A.Karl/J.Kemp 1986

Normandy

D-DAY

AT thirty minutes past midnight, as Eisenhower's trailer returned to Portsmouth, the first wave of C-47 transports carrying elements of 82nd and 101st airborne divisions reached the landing zones south and west of the sleepy villages of Ste.-Mère-Eglise, Pont l'Abbé and Carentan. An hour later, in the operations bunker of the German 84th Corps at St.-Lô, General Erich Marcks was celebrating his birthday with members of his staff when he was called away by reports of "unusual air activity" from Caen to Cherbourg. General Richter, commander of the 716th Infantry Division, phoned with news that British paratroopers had landed east of Caen. Richter spoke with authority. Several soldiers of the British 6th Airborne had landed on the lawn of 716th Infantry Division Headquarters and had been captured. Other reports told of drops in the Coutances–Valognes–St.-Lô triangle. Airdrops, sixty-three miles apart.

Signs had accumulated for the watchful throughout the previous evening. After the nine o'clock news broadcast announcing the fall of Rome, the BBC transmitted its nightly string of code messages to the French Resistance. "I am looking for four-leaf clovers. . . . The tomatoes should be picked. . . . The dice are on the table. . . . It is hot in Suez. . . . The children are bored on Sundays." Then, the second line of the Verlaine couplet: "Pierce my heart with a dull languor." Since June 1 the French Resistance and Gestapo counterintelligence had been waiting for this missing piece of the couplet, since it keyed carefully laid plans for demolitions in support of the invasion. The German Fifteenth Army staff, informed of the transmission, placed troops in the highest degree of readiness and signaled all commands that the invasion was about to start.

At his headquarters in Château St.-Germain, Von Rundstedt, called away from dinner, discounted the news of the broadcast. The Verlaine couplet had been broadcast in early May and had proven to be a false alarm.

Weather reports still predicted inclement weather for the sixth, and the latest intelligence reports confirmed that Allied preparations were not complete. By the night of June 5, Von Rundstedt had become convinced that the Allies would wait for the opening of the Russian summer offensive. "Does anyone think the enemy is stupid enough to announce his arrival over the radio?" he exclaimed to a guest. Von Rundstedt, "slightly tipsy," retired to his room.

The aging field marshal's skepticism set the pattern for the fateful German lack of response in the next three hours as time was lost for organizing countermeasures that might have repulsed the invasion at the beaches. Ruge, Rommel's naval adviser, would write: "A kind of coma appears to have descended on all those who might have changed the course of events by realizing some hours earlier what was happening." At 1 A.M., forty miles west of Paris at Army Group B Headquarters, in the Château de La Roche Guyon, Chief of Staff Hans Speidel received a call from Colonel Antoine Staubwasser of Army Group B Intelligence, who told him about the BBC messages. Speidel instructed Staubwasser to check with OB West about placing the Seventh Army on alert. Staubwasser would later recall that he spoke with an unidentified staff officer at St.-Germain-en-Laye shortly afterward who told him not to alert the Seventh Army or LXXXIV Corps.

Heavy Allied bombing attacks pounded naval stations from Cherbourg to Dunkirk. Several stations still active erroneously reported intercepts of major enemy naval forces headed for Cap d'Antifer, near Dieppe. At 1:50, Naval Group West, headquartered in the Bois de Boulogne in Paris, flashed an invasion warning. OKW (the German high command) discounted the report.

Eventually the sequence of alerts would become a matter of dispute. General Bodo Zimmerman, OB West operations officer, later claimed that Army Group B was on full alert from midnight on. Phone logs eventually recovered would indicate that as of dawn on June 6, OB West had alerted the First, Nineteenth and Fifteenth armies. Legends arose about Speidel's inaction in the face of warnings, particularly his oversight in not placing the Seventh Army on alert, but it is doubtful that Speidel's failure to follow up on the warnings was critical to the outcome of the D-Day battle. From 1 A.M. on, two battalions of the 21st Panzer, 716th Infantry and a battalion of the 91st Field Landing Division had been engaged in combat for an hour. Shortly after 2 A.M., the Seventh Army chief of staff, General Max Pemsel, on his own initiative, placed the Seventh Army on local alert, then notified its commander, General Friedrich Dollman, who quickly returned from Rennes. German hopes on D-Day would hinge on prompt deployment of reserves to the area from other sectors.

As it turned out, the weather played a crucial role in gaining precious hours for the invasion force. Rommel and others, who had carefully studied the Allied techniques at Salerno and Anzio, believed there would be no

landings without favorable forecasts for five days. The "benign high" between the low pressure fronts detected by Group Captain Stagg eluded
German meteorologists to the end. Admiral Helmuth Krancke, German
naval commander in OB West, had been so certain that no attack would
occur if the wind exceeded twenty-four knots, and the waves five to eight
feet, that he had canceled aerial coastal reconnaissance patrols.

At 2 A.M. Krancke, visiting the U-boat base in Bordeaux, was informed
of the BBC Resistance alerts, the airborne drops and of intense bombardment of radar sites between Cherbourg and Le Havre. Having long anticipated landings in the Pas-de-Calais, Krancke ordered a flotilla of torpedo boats to patrol near the mouth of the Seine to investigate the radar
reports. No patrols left Cherbourg. Meanwhile, the gale and low clouds
masked the transit of the mightiest armada in history—59 convoys
stretched out for over a hundred miles converging on the invasion coast.
Behind the gale, clearing and windy weather was due at daybreak.

Finally, around 2 A.M. the German command reluctantly responded to
the portents of the unfolding invasion, which, so far, did not conform to
preconceived German notions of what the Allies would do. By then Von
Rundstedt, in a bathrobe, had arrived in the War Room at St.-Germain to
monitor the developing situation and to weigh the critical question of
deploying the armored divisions in the Army Group B sector. Von Rundstedt knew well that any decision would take time to implement, because
he still lacked clear authority to deploy the panzers. Army Group B retained tactical control of the 21st, 2nd and 116th panzers, subject to OKW
approval. OKW retained direct control of the I SS Panzer Corps, consisting
of the 1st and 12th SS Panzer Lehr. Von Rundstedt might have initiated the
movement of panzers on his own and cleared this step with OKW later, but
he did not, evidently because he was still doubtful that full-scale landings
would occur there.

For an hour or so, Von Rundstedt wrestled with the immediate problem
of deciding whether the reports were accurate, and, if landings were in
progress, where and on what scale. Von Rundstedt hesitated. Landings in
the Calais–Boulogne–Dunkirk sector had long been an article of faith, but
the confirmed reports on his desk that night were of enemy activity in the
Seventh Army sector. Moreover, Von Rundstedt had long hypothesized,
indeed conceded, that the Allies would achieve tactical surprise somewhere
along his 3,000-mile front. The coastal fortifications, in his view, served the
purpose of slowing up the invasion force to afford time to organize a
deliberate counterattack, a view that in the closing arguments with Rommel
had largely prevailed. Indeed, Rommel's frantic last-minute entreaties for
the 12th SS Hitler Jugend and other units in Normandy had been refused.
The invasion was to be repelled methodically: first, the Germans would
define the flanks of the assault; second, the Germans would contain the

assault as infantry and armored reserves moved up; then, and only then, would the Germans launch a massive counterthrust.

But a question undoubtedly occupied Von Rundstedt's mind that night: Did Army Group B have the power to contain, then destroy, the invasion in such a methodical fashion? Minute by minute, as additional information reached the German nerve center at St.-Germain, the pattern of Allied airdrops began to weigh against the more comforting assessments. At 2:51 Von Rundstedt, now suspecting a major attack, ordered his staff to notify OKW in Berlin and Obersalzberg of the airdrops, but he took no other action right away.

The stage was set for the critical deliberations at St.-Germain, Berlin and Obersalzberg over countermeasures that would determine the course of the battle in the "fearful interval" ahead when the Allied landing forces would be struggling ashore against German defenses in the effort to consolidate a foothold in France. Most historians agree that a chance remained for the Germans to defeat the landings at the beaches, but this required a resolute commitment of the OKW reserve and 15th Army panzers within the next several hours. By daybreak Allied bombers would seriously hamper the movement of German armor by day, and only a few hours of darkness and early-morning mist were left to protect the movements of the nearby 12th SS Panzer Division and the more distant Panzer Lehr at Chartres, the spearheads of a counterattack in the event of a major landing.

Finally, at four-thirty, Von Rundstedt, satisfied that landings were in progress and "were to be expected at dawn," split the difference. First, he ordered the 12th SS Panzer Division and Panzer Lehr to commence movement toward Caen, an order that left the 116th and 2nd panzers in place. Second, he decided to observe protocol and inform OKW, perhaps anticipating that OKW would overrule his limited action and thereby absolve him of responsibility for holding back the I SS Panzer Corps. In his cable to OKW, Von Rundstedt assessed the reports cautiously, noting that "*if* this is actually a large-scale enemy operation," prompt movement of the 1st Panzer would enable the reserve to "enter the battle on the coast during the day." Von Rundstedt settled back to await OKW's decision.

An hour passed before Colonel General Alfred Jodl, OKW chief of operations, was informed of Von Rundstedt's cable. OKW read the same weather reports and knew of the BBC action messages and that similar alerts had proven false before. OKW also knew that Allied airdrops of men and supplies for the Resistance were commonplace. Predictably, Jodl was unconvinced that the activity was not part of a massive deception to conceal Allied landings in the Pas-de-Calais area, an idea supported by the pattern of enemy bombing and naval activity reported that night.

At six-thirty, "not yet fully convinced that here and now the real invasion had begun," Jodl called St.-Germain and ordered Von Rundstedt to halt the movement of the 12th SS Panzer at Lisieux, and to cancel orders for

Panzer Lehr altogether. Von Rundstedt acquiesced, and so, as dawn broke over the continent of Europe on June 6, a combination of the weather, two years of German preparation for landings elsewhere, and German reluctance to commit precious reserves in France conspired in favor of Allied success on D-Day. As Wilmot noted, at Caen on the sixth, the British would encounter 146 tanks and 51 assault guns of the 21st Panzer. Had Panzer Lehr and the 12th SS moved out for Normandy at 5 A.M., the British might have faced another 500 tanks and 100 assault guns, along with 40,000 panzer grenadier infantry before sundown on the sixth and a full-scale counterattack late in the afternoon or the evening of the same day.

But again, this turn of events, while fortuitous, was just a start. Gaining a foothold on D-Day had always been considered a lesser problem for the Allies than expansion of the lodgement area. German indecision opened the door to the Calvados in the early hours of the sixth, but time remained to slam it shut depending on many factors, but above all on Hitler's willingness to spare reserves from Calais and other theaters. Meanwhile, the invasion forces had much to fear from orderly German countermeasures, and from Von Rundstedt, a formidable and dangerous adversary.

Just before dawn in London, De Gaulle, Smith and the CCS finally ratified the outlines of an accord ensuring that De Gaulle would broadcast to the French people on D-Day. Eisenhower could not change the text of his own statement, and so De Gaulle would not disclose the text of his own. However, General J.F.M. Whiteley and General Pierre Joseph Koenig, commander of the French forces in England, proceeded to execute an agreement whereby Koenig placed the FFI (Force of the French Resistance) under SHAEF command.

Whether the French Resistance would obey any military authority at all was questionable, but the accord represented progress. Most important, it set the precedent for SHAEF control of regular French army units under De Gaulle's command, a crucial step. In the accord, both sides sidestepped the problem of a French seat on the CCS.

De Gaulle, anxious to prevent Communist elements in the Resistance from seizing power, accepted SHAEF's policy of "no general uprisings" on D-Day, a policy that also guaranteed that the Resistance would not be sacrificed in aid of deception plans. All in all, the compromise was a long stride toward recognition, both by restoring cooperation between SHAEF and the Algiers committee, and in carving out a role for France in the Alliance.

Dawn in England was eerie. Brooke in his diary remarked on the irony that life went on as usual on the streets beneath his window. According to Commander Thompson, the Prime Minister "was much on edge." Mrs. Churchill had joined her husband in the war bunker shortly after midnight, and they sat and talked quietly.

Knowing of Eisenhower's private torment about the fate of the 101st and 82nd Airborne, Butcher had asked Lieutenant Colonel Hugh Barkley of the AEAF to call with the first available reports of the returning transports. Each half hour that night, Butcher awoke drowsily. Had he heard from Barkley? No. At six-forty, H-Hour at UTAH and OMAHA, he lay awake staring at the drab tent ceiling over his cot. The telephone rang. AEAC Air Marshal Leigh-Mallory was on the line asking to speak with Eisenhower. Butcher told him Eisenhower was asleep and could not be disturbed. Butcher then hitched up a scrambler to get Leigh-Mallory's report on the 101st, 82nd and 6th airborne divisions.

Butcher took down the news on a scratch pad; of the 850 American C-47s airlifting the 82nd and 101st, 21 were lost. Four gliders were unaccounted for. Of the 400 transports ferrying the British 6th Airborne, 8 were lost. There had been little flak and no fighter opposition. Enemy air was active near Le Havre, a sign that the deception had worked.

Elated, Butcher dressed and scurried down the cinder path to Eisenhower's trailer, where he found Eisenhower propped up in bed reading a Western with a full ashtray at his bedside. As they discussed Leigh-Mallory's report Eisenhower was interrupted by a call from Admiral Ramsay. According to Ramsay, the winds had not abated, but sun breaking over the Normandy coast had given the British destroyers, battleships and cruisers fair visibility for naval gunfire support. The fleet was proceeding according to plan, but in choppy seas under skies fair to cloudy.

So far, naval groups had not encountered the magnetic or pressure mines deployed near Le Havre, and the beach obstacles seemed less serious than had been feared. Ramsay reported only a number of isolated instances of contact with the enemy during the night. At 5:15 the eastern flank of bombardment force D had been attacked by several E-boats from Le Havre, which then turned back. A Norwegian destroyer was lost; in all, there was an "air of unreality" as the immense invasion force arrived at the French coast. As yet there was no evidence of increased German radio, telephone traffic, or even reports of German air reconnaissance.

An hour before, the first of over 10,500 sorties flown by the RAF and the American Eighth and Ninth air forces struck batteries and strongpoints along the Normandy coast. The air attacks had given way to the battleships, cruisers and destroyers, which pounded coastal positions until the first assault waves arrived within 3,000 yards of the shoreline. As planned, the Navy yielded to hundreds of fighters and fighter-bombers, which swept in to cover the assault waves in the final minutes. By 7 A.M. the assault began and D-Day became "a soldier's battle."

"At 0800 there are still no reports," the First Army diarist complained in the journal he kept aboard the *Achenar,* an LST eleven miles offshore:

There is blue in the sky above, and the sun is out, but there is a strong breeze blowing, and our procession of LCIs, marching in two columns behind us, dip and toss in the white caps. Also in the procession is a lumbering LSD, landing ship dock, which can accommodate a half-dozen smaller craft in its innards and repair them. Ahead of us are two destroyers proceeding carefully through the mine-swept channels past flag buoys; overhead are Thunderbolts and a mission of 36 B-26s returning from a job done in France.

The continuous drone since 4 A.M. of bombers returning from France alerted the residents in south England to the attack. The word spread. With word that Radio Berlin had announced that four parachute divisions had landed between "Le Havre and Cherbourg," Eisenhower and his staff in Portsmouth debated whether or not to issue a communiqué. Butcher phoned Smith at Widewing, who insisted that the communiqué await 21st Army Group confirmation that lead elements were moving inland. Over coffee around a makeshift table in a neighboring tent, Eisenhower sat with Bull, Strong and Butcher. They talked excitedly about the air and naval reports. Strong believed that the Berlin report was a sign that NEPTUNE had achieved "tactical surprise." Where was the Luftwaffe? The E-boats hurled against bombardment squadron D seemed to be reacting to an expected assault on Calais—perhaps the deception plan would prove to be a gigantic success, after all.* The group drew optimistic conclusions from the lack of reports from the landing area, deciding that the silence meant that the commanders at the scene were busy expediting the movement ashore. Only a crisis would be referred to higher command, or so they hoped.

Eisenhower drafted a quick message to Marshall in Washington, who was scheduled to arrive at Prestwick, Scotland, in forty-eight hours:

> I have as yet no information concerning the actual landings nor of our progress through beach obstacles. Communiqué will not be issued until we have word that leading ground troops are actually ashore.
>
> All preliminary reports are satisfactory. Airborne formations apparently landed in good order with losses out of approximately 1250 airplanes participating about 30. Preliminary bombings by air went off as scheduled. Navy reports sweeping some mines, but so far as is known, channels are clear and operations proceeding as planned. . . .

Afterward Eisenhower left for 21st Army Group forward at nearby Broomfield House to confer with Montgomery, who made it clear he wished to be free of visitors. Montgomery told Eisenhower that "my place is ashore," and that he intended to cross the Channel that night to set up an advance command post. The British and Canadian forces had been off-loading for an hour. Montgomery had no hard information, except that the airborne drops had been satisfactory. The preliminary bombardment had

*See Chapter 2.

gone off on schedule. Channels were clear of mine fields and "proceeding as planned." On this basis, Montgomery was satisfied that the leading elements were probably ashore.

"At 0930, exactly as promised," wrote the First Army diarist, "we hear the first communiqué over the radio, very vague, as was to be expected, stating only that landings are being made on the north coast of France." He continued:

> At 0945, General Eisenhower broadcasts his message; telling the people of France to act only if they have received definite order to act, and assuring the people of other occupied countries that their day will come. He was followed by King Haakon of Norway and other United Nations leaders. . . . we slow down to six knots as we approach a huge convoy ahead. "Now is sub time, if ever," says the Chief Engineer. It is a beautiful warm day, but getting rougher every minute.

During the ten decisive hours of NEPTUNE, beginning at H-Hour 0640 on June 6 until twilight, Eisenhower and SHAEF headquarters would receive the barest of information, but this was the result in part of technical factors. Bradley, who spent the anxious hours aboard the U.S.S. *Augusta,* later recalled the technical problems of remaining in contact with Portsmouth. After the issuance of the communiqué, so many messages jammed SHAEF switchboards from citizens, politicians and friends, that the SHAEF communicators simply fell twelve hours behind in transcribing the radio traffic. A decoding machine broke down at 21st Army Group forward.

According to Summersby, Eisenhower spent most of the day in his trailer drinking endless cups of coffee, "waiting for the reports to come in." Few did, and so Eisenhower gained only sketchy details for most of the day about the British beaches, UTAH and the crisis at OMAHA, where for several hours the fate of the invasion hung in the balance.

The British landings went smoothly, though gains fell well short of Montgomery's confident prediction of a 30-mile advance to Falaise on D-Day. The beaches along the 25-mile sector were flat and firm, minus the steep escarpments and inundations behind the American beaches. But owing to unusual tidal conditions, the British task forces had to land one hour after sunrise, and Dempsey, anticipating alert opposition by the 21st Panzer and 12th SS divisions at Evreux, resolved to concentrate on establishing strong defensive screens.

Most of the fighting in the British sector occurred at Caen. Before sunlight, the British 6th Airborne successfully established a bridgehead east of the Orne and managed to divert two battalions of the 21st Panzer. The British 3rd Division met light resistance at the beach, then pushed inland at midday along the Caen Canal to join with the British 6th Airborne. Vehicle congestion at the beaches plagued the later waves. Commander General J. T. Crocker, informed that the 21st Panzer had occupied the city, ordered cautious tactics. Late that afternoon the British 3rd met the first shock of an armored counterattack and drew up to secure its positions short of the northeast suburbs.

At JUNO, the Canadian 3rd Division encountered rough seas and well-entrenched German defenses. Small units by-passed machine-gun nests, anti-tank defenses and mine fields, then fanned out behind the coastal strip westward to link with the British 50th near the town of Courseulles, and east toward the British 3rd. Follow-on units cleared the pockets by noon, and the Canadians pressed toward the Caen–Bayeux road, within three miles of the D-Day objective set at Carpiquet airfield. At GOLD, the British 50th weathered strong resistance at the beach. Stopped short of the towns of Bessin and Bayeux, the 50th, followed by the 7th Armored, secured Arromanches and blocking positions in the northern suburbs of Bayeux, to cover the precarious American V Corps bridgehead to the west.

The decisive battles that day unfolded on the American flank. At UTAH, Barton's 4th Division off-loaded uneventfully. The island of St.-Marcouf, four miles from the landing zone, was not garrisoned as feared, and so the force achieved surprise. Owing to a navigational error, the first waves off-loaded at beaches 2,000 yards south of the planned objective against thinly manned outposts that were demoralized by the shock of the naval bombardment and isolated from the mainland by inlets. The first waves stormed through obstacles across 500 yards of open beaches between the waterline and the first entrenchments, but encountered only sporadic fire. The amphibious DD tanks, launched from close in, by-passed the entrenched fortifications, crossed the causeways and quickly reduced strongpoints behind the lagoons with the aid of elements of the 101st Airborne. Fifteen waves were ashore by 9:45, and Admiral Moon cabled Portsmouth with the news that Force U had "arrived transport area without incident," 21,000 troops and 1,700 vehicles pressed past several large German pockets of resistance, to within a mile of the town of Ste.-Mère-Eglise, held by elements of the 82nd Airborne.

Indeed, the airborne drops were a factor in success at UTAH despite heavy casualties and initial confusion in the night drops. Many of the heavily loaded paratroopers drifted down into the inundations and swamps and drowned. Many others were killed by heavy ground fire. Scattered over a wide sector, and short of artillery and ammunition, the two airborne divisions spent most of the night regrouping, cut off from one another by miles of hedgerow in the Normandy bocage. Troops organized into makeshift platoons and squads, then roamed the Cotentin Peninsula toward their objectives. Isolated groups of men cut telephone wires, shot dispatch riders and kidnapped messengers, paralyzing German small unit commands. The 82nd managed to take Ste.-Mère-Eglise and to establish a pocket along the Merderet. Several companies of the 101st succeeded in securing the southern end of the four causeways linking UTAH Beach with the mainland. The price might seem high, but the two divisions would have an impact on the battle, narrowly vindicating Eisenhower's judgment.

The supreme test of the D-Day landings came at OMAHA Beach, where the troubles had begun well before H-Hour. Uncertain that naval and air bombardment could reduce the heavy coastal artillery batteries in the area, Bradley had ordered the disembarkation of the 1st and 4th divisions into assault craft eleven miles offshore in choppy seas. As H-Hour approached, the assault forces of the 1st and 29th divisions, showered by sea spray and buffeted by rough seas, were chilled and exhausted. In three- to six-foot seas that swamped the assault boats ferrying the anti-tank guns and jeeps, one battalion of DD tanks did not attempt to launch. Of the twenty-nine DDs launched in the other battalion, twenty-two sank in the four-foot seas with crews aboard, and five others were destroyed by beach fire.

Meanwhile, low cloud cover had prevented effective naval bombardment. Air operations were also ineffective because of the poor visibility and skillful concealment of enemy positions. Planes had to fly under the clouds, as low as 2,000 feet and up to 7,000 feet, with another solid layer above that; low-flying pilots could not see shore until a few minutes before crossing it and braved dangerous congestion in the area. Once bombs had been dropped, there was no time for the pilots to see if targets had been hit, and soon the whole shoreline was obscured by smoke. General Helmuth Kraiss, commander of the German 352nd, responded vigorously to the forewarnings of landings in his sector. By daybreak the 352nd manned the escarpments and trenches blocking the cart-path exits inland to Colleville, St.-Laurent and Vierville. Facing elements of eight regiments instead of four, and denied effective air and seaborne support, for a time V Corps was outmatched.

According to the many accounts of the battle, for seven hours the battle at OMAHA was touch and go. The progress of the 116th Regimental combat team, which landed between Vierville and St.-Laurent, was typical. Severe shore-battery fire showered the assault during the last half mile before touchdown. A direct hit sank one landing craft in the leading company, a second foundered. The rest went aground on a sandbar several yards from the seawall. The 116th waded under heavy fire in five feet of water past the dead and dying. One by one, the survivors darted over the open beach to the seawall, the only defense against the fire; many of those who could not make a decision to cross the open space of beach met death at the water's edge.

In the first half hour, hundreds died in the sea or on the beach. The rest clung behind the tanks on the beach or dug in. The noise at OMAHA that morning was said to be so terrible that most could not think or function beyond heeding their instinct to run or hide. For a while it seemed that everything had gone wrong: the air bombardment had missed its targets, the naval shelling had had little effect; most of the DD tanks were lost at sea or destroyed on the beach; the infantry were scattered and badly weakened; the vital demolition crews had been decimated and were unable to clear the beach; the presence of the German 352nd Division had been unexpected.

The American commanders still offshore had little idea of what was going on, but by 10 A.M. they could see the congestion at the beaches and Gerow's reports were "mostly confirmation of trouble." Meanwhile, Omar Bradley, aboard his command ship, the U.S.S. *Augusta,* dispatched Major Chester Hansen to take a look. Ninety minutes later Hansen returned with a firsthand report of what appeared to be a disaster in the making. The second, third and fourth assault waves were stacked up behind the first. OMAHA Beach was a scene of disorganization, with most of the troops pinned behind obstacles under enemy fire, surrounded by flaming vehicles, dead and wounded. Hansen could report no progress in scaling the bluffs between the strongpoints where just about then a handful of men under makeshift leadership, braving enemy fire and mine fields, had started up the relatively undefended slopes. Indeed, the many accounts of OMAHA would tell of the countless instances of courage under fire, which gradually turned the tide sometime after 11 A.M., shortly after Hansen had turned back for the *Augusta.* Small groups of six to ten men, motivated by the example of a handful who under pillbox fire impetuously stormed past enemy positions, began to inch forward in single file through mine fields toward the bluffs with heavy weapons, tanks, jeeps or other equipment. Meanwhile General Clarence Huebner, commander of the 1st Division, ordered the destroyer gunships back into the line to direct fire against the enemy gun emplacements. As the morning haze began to lift, the naval bombardment honed in accurately on German targets to provide relief.

The progress was not evident right away, however. At noon, with his latest reports terming the struggle "still critical," Bradley weighed writing off OMAHA as lost and diverting the follow-up 29th Division east to GOLD Beach and evidently, broached the idea to the British 21st Army Group. Brooke, in his diary, grimly chronicled the reports of failure by the eastern U.S. Corps "practically along its whole front" and the request "to land on our Western beaches." It was at noon that Bradley conferred with Gerow and Huebner aboard the *Ancon.* With the second tide, a force of 25,000 men and 4,400 additional vehicles was due to arrive at the transport area of OMAHA Beach.

Should the follow-up waves land at OMAHA? It was apparent that the fate of the western flank was in the balance. Bradley knew that if he wrote off OMAHA he could not consider sending more divisions to UTAH Beach, since the American forces there would be twenty miles away from the British zone, cut off except by sea. To reinforce UTAH would mean that widely separated American and British fronts would be operating virtually independently, vulnerable to "defeat in detail." As for casualties, rerouting the follow-up units at OMAHA involved writing off elements of the 29th and 1st at OMAHA, the 4th at UTAH, the two airborne divisions. The Americans would be forfeiting Cherbourg and a chance to move quickly toward Brittany, and Americans going ashore on the British beaches would jeopardize the British objectives by compounding confusion in the British zone.

Accordingly, Bradley decided to order the second wave to land at OMAHA, a decision that resembled Eisenhower's decision six days before to order the 82nd and 101st Airborne drops. Bradley's reasoning was similar: every local action had a crucial bearing on success along the whole invasion front; annihilation of the center beach meant writing off the western flank, which in turn would overload the British sector and greatly simplify the German task of containing and defeating the invasion. The invasion had to succeed, and so the parts would have to fit the whole.

Shortly after a grim noon situation report, Bradley was fortified by a radio message reporting that Navy gunships had silenced a number of enemy positions. Gerow reported penetrations through the bluffs at five points, and spearheads at the Vierville–Colleville road. Fortunately, no German counterattacks materialized, owing to a momentous miscalculation by Kraiss, who, confident that the situation at OMAHA was under control, had dispatched a regiment back to the scene of the reported airdrops at Carentan, and a second to the high ground near Arromanches. Indeed, for several hours Kraiss and his staff apparently believed that the American landings had been repulsed, and issued a report to this effect at 1:35.

Word of the crisis at OMAHA reached Eisenhower at 1:30 P.M. through the Navy, which had observers on the scene. "I could see from his questions he wished he were running the 21st Army Group," Butcher noted, "so he could do something about it himself, but from where he sits, he just can't step in." Eisenhower authorized a risky measure in support of Bradley's decision. Despite the persistence of haze and cloud into the early afternoon, Eisenhower authorized AEAF tactical bombers to carry out instrument bombing in the sector, risking "shorts" falling on the advanced American positions.

Gradually, due to the sheer weight of air and naval gunfire support, German attrition, local superiority in numbers and the bravery of the 1st Division, the Americans developed preponderance at OMAHA. The First Army diarist chronicled the evolving success:

By 1300 we can sight land—a thin purple haze some 25 miles away. At 1400 we pass the *Augusta,* and an hour later reach the transport area, some twelve miles offshore. At 2000 we take aboard the first wounded—an officer from the 1st Division, and later on, several enlisted men. The waves are so high it took an hour to land one from an LCI in a stretcher's buoy. Early reports from land are none too encouraging. And, when before 2100 the *Achenar* moves within four miles off Omaha beach, the angry flashes of fire from the cliffs above are clearly visible without the use of glasses. The American battleships, the *Texas, Nevada,* and *Arkansas;* the French cruiser, *Enterprise,* and numerous destroyers of all nations are laying in a murderous fire, both on top of the cliffs and in the enemy's rear, and the town of Port-en-Bessin which marks the boundary between the First Army and Second British Army is ablaze in several spots. One of the first reports of V Corps ends: "God bless the American Navy."

On June 6, Allied air superiority was such that the Luftwaffe was barely able to mount one hundred sorties along the entire coast. Obliged to rely on ground reconnaissance, the German command in Normandy was cut off from vital information for much of the day. Seventh Army Headquarters did not learn of the landings at UTAH Beach until 4 P.M., and not until nightfall did the 352nd revise its claim to have repulsed the invasion at St.-Laurent, which accounted in part for the failure to reinforce the 352nd and exploit the first and last German opportunity to divide the invasion front. German countermeasures were most effective in the eastern sector between Bayeux and Caen which the German high command regarded as an immediate threat to German Seventh Army communications.

At midafternoon, ten hours after Jodl's "Hold fast" edict, reliable evidence available to the Germans defined the flanks of the assault. The German high command still procrastinated, aided by Allied deceptions calculated to cause the Germans to hesitate before committing the panzer reserves and units of the Fifteenth Army. Allied intelligence leaked the news of Marshall's forthcoming visit to London so as to imply that the American Chief of Staff wished to be in the city to confer with Patton. Action alerts went out to the Resistance in Belgium and northern France, and intelligence teams parachuted into Le Havre, Calais and Dunkirk while the Allies conspicuously assembled dummy landing craft and ships at British ports in the Thames estuary.

The effect of these measures is unknown, but the specter of landings at Calais probably reinforced the German inclination to procrastinate. By 11 A.M., the German Fifteenth Army and nine panzer divisions from Marseilles to Antwerp stood by, fueled and ready, for orders to embark for Normandy. Jodl's edict stood despite frantic appeals by Marcks and Rommel for prompt reinforcement. Finally, at 2 P.M., after hosting a luncheon for the new Hungarian premier, General Dóme Sztojay, at Klessheim Castle near Obersalzberg, Hitler ratified Jodl's decisions, then took up the problem of landings in Normandy.

By midafternoon, Von Rundstedt maintained that the landings were diversionary, and that a main effort was imminent in the Pas-de-Calais area. This enabled Hitler to put off considering the basic issues involved in releasing the Fifteenth Army infantry and armored reserves and to focus on the more immediate problem of ensuring that Allied penetrations did not jeopardize critical German positions in northeast France. Normandy was considered dangerous, however, particularly the British bridgehead threatening Caen which was the vital road and communications link between the German Seventh and Fifteenth armies. Accordingly, Hitler ordered Caen to be held at all costs and met Von Rundstedt's request to place 12th SS Panzer and Panzer Lehr under the Seventh Army, coupled with instructions to "have the enemy in the bridgehead annihilated by the evening of 6 June," a characteristically unrealistic and ambiguous order.

In retrospect, Hitler's actions on the sixth suggest that he doubted the Germans would defeat the invasion and therefore decided early on merely to contain the bridgehead with the idea of handling the situation later. First, Hitler was still holding back armor, and the armor he ordered into action late that afternoon would arrive too late to repel the landings on the sixth as Rommel wished. Second, by committing armor to the line in the role of infantry, Hitler complicated Von Rundstedt's task of systematically collecting armor for counterattack later. Above all, the order concentrated German armor on the British flank, which, from the German point of view, was the key defensive sector in the area. There the bulk of German armor would remain during the whole Normandy campaign, much to the frustration of Rommel and Von Rundstedt, neither of whom had considered a strategy of containment feasible. But the deeper question, as both Rommel and Von Rundstedt knew, involved Hitler's willingness or ability to part with reserves elsewhere, which might have enabled the Germans to deploy counterattacks without inhibition.

In any event, the impact of Hitler's order to hold Caen was felt quickly at GOLD Beach. Rommel, in touch with his headquarters by phone and sensing his one chance to defeat the landings, ordered the 21st Panzer, partially engaged east of the Orne, to counterattack "regardless of reinforcements" and hold a wedge between the British and Canadians for a counterattack on the seventh "which must reach the beaches without fail." Late in the afternoon, fifty tanks and a battalion of infantry of the 21st Panzer left the northern suburbs of Caen and marched through a gap at Périers to relieve a German strongpoint at Douvres blocking the junction between the Third Canadian and the Third British. By dusk, German spearheads reached the coast at Luc-sur-Mer and relieved a two-mile pocket of German defenders, cut off from communications all day, and established a corridor that threatened the British flank in the Orne Valley. British glider-borne troops and light tanks of the British 6th Air Landing Brigade dropped into the area before night fell to reinforce the British 6th Airborne. "All that night, Crocker's divisions stood to, expecting a large-scale attack," wrote Wilmot, "while darkness gave the German army cover which the Luftwaffe could not provide."

By evening, the Atlantic Wall had been tenuously breached on a fifty-mile front. Eisenhower, Tedder, Leigh-Mallory and Ramsay gathered in the library, where forty-eight hours earlier Eisenhower had launched OVER-LORD. Reports were gathered up and discussed. All the bridgeheads were short of their objectives, though objectives had been framed ambitiously to avoid a repetition of Anzio.

The next ninety-six hours would be Germany's big chance. In the center of the invasion front, V Corps, after a full day of combat, held a sliver of coast 1,000 yards deep at points. Confusion in the first waves hampered all succeeding waves, and had prevented a sustained advance inland toward the objectives at Fort Port-en-Bessin and Caumont. V Corps beaches remained within easy range of German artillery, and the piles of wreckage hampered resupply. Major gaps existed on both sides of OMAHA. Ten miles separated V Corps and the 50th British to the east at Bayeux and seven miles separated V Corps and Force U to the west, while most elements of the 82nd and 101st Airborne were still out of contact and dispersed over a hundred-square-mile sector. Several days would pass before these divisions could reorganize and fight as coherent units.

On the eastern flank, the problem was space. The British 3rd Division prepared to meet renewed counterattack by the 21st Panzer Division, reinforced by the 12th SS Hitler Jugend. The Second Army bridgehead was only three miles deep at the slenderest points, eight miles deep at the thickest but short of Caen and the Carpiquet airfields. Leigh-Mallory and Tedder, who were anxious to gain space for the construction of airfields, would often recall Montgomery's bold prediction that the open terrain southwest of the Caen sector would be in Allied hands by the night of the sixth. In view of the evident German decision to stand at Caen, the British Second Army had little prospect of soon reaching Caen or the open terrain beyond.

On the bright side, every assault division was ashore, with all signs positive for the seventh. The German reaction had been oddly haphazard. Less than 400 enemy aircraft sorties had been reported in the invasion area, well below expectations, and German countermeasures had been indecisive, especially at OMAHA. In his most anxious moments, Eisenhower had worried that the kind of resistance encountered at OMAHA would occur along the entire invasion front. Casualties ranged between 10,000 and 15,000, a fraction of the 75,000 casualties feared, and under cover of darkness, engineers were at work sweeping away the beach obstacles and wreckage in all sectors to expedite the off-loading of troops and supply.

The group cautiously pronounced NEPTUNE a success. In Tedder's opinion the Allies had, in fact, achieved "tactical surprise," judging by the virtual absence of the Luftwaffe over the beach, the confused response of the German navy and the level of resistance at the shoreline in every sector except OMAHA. But the Allies needed space, which meant linking up the beachheads quickly. To expedite steps to join up OMAHA and neighboring sectors, Eisenhower made plans to cross the Channel by ship for visits with Montgomery and Bradley the following morning.

. . .

Throughout the sixth, people in London, Washington and New York had followed the news by radio and newspapers. At noon Churchill, accompanied by his wife and Montgomery's brother, addressed an expectant Parliament. In his speech, Churchill built suspense by dwelling at length on Clark's great triumph in capturing Rome, then turned to the invasion, which had been anticipated for so long.

I have also to announce to the House that during the early hours of this morning the first of a series of landings in force upon the European continent has taken place. In this case, the liberating assault fell upon the coast of France. An immense armada of upwards of 4,000 ships, together with several thousand smaller craft, crossed the Channel. Massed airborne landings have been successfully effected behind the enemy lines, and landings on the beaches are proceeding at various points at this present time. The fire of the shore batteries has largely been quelled. The obstacles that were constructed in the sea have not proved so difficult as was apprehended. The Anglo-American allies are sustained by about 11,000 first-line aircraft, which can be drawn upon as may be needed for the purpose of the battle. . . . So far the commanders who are engaged report that everything is going according to plan. And what a plan! This vast operation is undoubtedly the most complicated and difficult that has ever taken place. It involves tides, winds, waves, visibility, both from the air and the sea standpoint, and the combined employment of land, air and sea forces in the highest degree of intimacy and in contact with conditions which could not and cannot be fully foreseen.

The three-line communiqué SHAEF issued at 3:30 Eastern Daylight Time reached Washington and New York eight hours after Roosevelt's fireside chat announcing the fall of Rome. As the first bulletins came over the radio, workers leaving the night shift drifted into churches to pray. Others learned of the news at breakfast. Daily newspapers published extras featuring the latest bulletins and reports. The Los Angeles *Times* published a large map depicting Allied landing areas east and west of the Somme. The Philadelphia *Inquirer* stopped presses in order to print a full page of bulletins and sketchy accounts of the action. A massive gathering at Madison Square Garden in New York City convened to pray for the invasion, an impromptu counterpart to the high religious ceremonies held that morning in London at St. Paul's and at Westminster Abbey. There were wild rumors about the official estimates of casualties ranging from several thousand to several hundred thousand—nobody knew. Richard C. Hottelet of UP filed an eyewitness dispatch after a twenty-mile flight along the coast in a Ninth Air Force Marauder reporting that the invasion had been unopposed, though later dispatches hinted at heavy fighting in the American sectors.

"Well, I think this is a very happy conference today," Roosevelt said at a morning press briefing for over two hundred correspondents at the White House. "Looking at the rows of you coming in, you have the same expression as the anonymous and silent people this side of the desk who just came in before you—all smiles." Roosevelt added, "The war is by no means over yet." Eisenhower was "up to schedule," he said, "but you don't just walk to Berlin: the sooner this country realizes that, the better."

By evening Roosevelt knew of the near disaster at OMAHA, and of the uneven progress in the British sector. To preserve the fiction of the FORTI-TUDE deception plan, SHAEF had asked the White House to refrain from proclamations or speeches indicating that Normandy was the primary ob-jective. Accordingly, Roosevelt in a second fireside chat within twenty-four hours spoke of the success attained "thus far" and revealed to his nation-wide audience that he had turned aside the urgings of many to "call the nation into a single day of special prayer," implying that a larger and more dangerous effort lay ahead. Yet, as he closed, Roosevelt conveyed finality.

Almighty God: Our sons, pride of our nation, this day have set upon a mighty endeavor, a struggle to preserve our Republic, our religion and our civilization, and to set free a suffering humanity.

Lead them straight and true; give strength to their arms, stoutness to their hearts, and steadfastness in their faith.

They will need Thy blessings. Their road will be long and hard. For the enemy is strong. He may hurl back our forces. Success may not come with rushing speed, but we shall return again and again; and we know that by Thy grace, and by the righteousness of our cause, our sons will triumph.

They will be sorely tried, by night and by day, without rest—until the victory is won. The darkness will be rent by noise and flame. Men's souls will be shaken with the violence of wars.

For these men are lately drawn from the ways of peace. They fight not for the lust of conquest. They fight to end conquest. They fight to liberate. They fight to let justice arise, and tolerance and good will among all Thy people. They yearn but for the end of battle, for their return to the haven of home.

BUILD-UP

June 7. Follow-up divisions on the night of the sixth battled congestion particularly in the OMAHA sector, as the 1st and 29th fought inland against stiff opposition by the German 352nd. For a time, U-boat sightings in the western approaches disrupted off-loadings in both American sectors. But by morning the forces packed into the five bridgeheads became formidable armies knitted together by a reliable seaborne line of communications. And 1,160 RAF heavy bombers were out in the night pounding airfields, roads and German troop concentrations, followed at first light by 1,100 Eighth Air Force heavy bombers, which struck rail bridges and roads from the Loire to the Orne.

All waited for signs of a decisive German move. Prompt enemy action on the morning of the seventh backed by reinforcements drawn from all sectors of France might simultaneously have denied the Allies critical roadways and essential space while maintaining strong forward positions for a counteroffensive to destroy the invasion. For, as Eisenhower would put it, once the Allies held Cherbourg, Brittany and breathing space south of Caen, "we will be there to stay."

In the next seventy-two hours, answers to many questions would be indicated in the movement of German reserves, particularly the infantry of the Fifteenth Army at Calais. Such a movement would signal preparation for a major German counteroffensive in France backed by strategic withdrawals from Italy and the East. The Fifteenth Army dominated the waking thoughts of Eisenhower and his colleagues, who were determined to seize the interval to gain ground in all sectors and link up.

On the sixth and seventh Eisenhower found very little time to write. Eighteen months before, in the caves of Gibraltar, he had passed anxious hours dictating running appraisals to Marshall. This time he even overlooked a letter home, barely managing to dispatch a congratulatory telegram to his son, John, whose graduation ceremonies at West Point were on the sixth. To Mamie he had sent "much love . . . as time has not permitted letter writing recently and probably will not for a while but I know you understand." Except for the brief report sent at 8 A.M. on the sixth, Marshall and the CCS heard nothing. In the next few days Eisenhower's appointments log would be atypically blank.

Instinctively, the responsible commanders of OVERLORD tried to withdraw into cocoons of staff, as they, including the Supreme Commander, wished no diversion from their obsession with the problems in Normandy. Throughout the sixth the atmosphere at Southwick House had briefly resembled an election-night headquarters. Eisenhower had emerged to talk to reporters, who noted he looked a bit "rough around the edges" with fatigue but happy. Earlier in the day, Morgan had interrupted Eisenhower as he studied the large gray-green nautical plot in the adjoining War Room to offer congratulations. "Well, Freddie, you started it," Eisenhower said as they shook hands.

Soon the spell wore off. Leigh-Mallory, who had attempted to contact Eisenhower shortly after dawn with the first reports of the returning Ninth Air Force transports, sent a three-paragraph letter congratulating Eisenhower on the courage of his decision, saying "it is sometimes difficult in this life to admit that one is wrong." Eisenhower accepted the letter, but never replied. Leigh-Mallory had been only partly wrong, as the reports reaching Eisenhower late that night indicated.

Indeed, Leigh-Mallory's apology was almost as unwelcome as his official protest, for it said nothing about the heavy casualties actually incurred or the contributions of the 82nd and 101st, which no one could gauge yet. The Leigh-Mallory episode guaranteed close scrutiny of Eisenhower's decision to risk two airborne divisions on a dangerous mission in the one sector where the Allies had known ahead of time that resistance at the beaches would probably be slight. Had Eisenhower risked lives unnecessarily?

By the morning of the seventh, Eisenhower also carried the burden of the near rout of V Corps at OMAHA due, in part, to his decision to withhold word of the presence of the German 352nd. Unlike Leigh-Mallory, Gerow had communicated his qualms orally to Eisenhower, and had otherwise kept silent. Eisenhower was not outwardly moved by loyalty to his friends, or by vindictiveness, but in his way, he was both loyal and unforgiving, especially at times like June 6–7. Eisenhower rarely dwelled on the faults of men who fell out of favor, but such men usually disappeared quickly. Leigh-Mallory's usefulness was impaired. He would linger for three months, subordinate to Tedder, who had in any case assumed direction of the air-war effort, then depart France for the India-Burma theater, after a reorganization of the air forces in September resulting in the abolition of the AEAF. Likewise, Eisenhower quietly resolved to reward Gerow with command of an army—if all turned out.

Meanwhile, Montgomery boarded H.M.S. *Faulknor* and directed his chief of staff, De Guingand, to investigate arrangements for transferring 21st Army Group to a forward headquarters in the British sector pending Eisenhower's permission to go ashore. That would come when Eisenhower was confident there would be no repetition of Salerno when Clark had attempted to re-embark. Corps and divisional commanders, obligated to "go down with the ship" had gone ashore the night before.

June 7 was a day of tactical adjustments. Allied objectives were threefold: first, to expedite the build-up; second, to gain space at Caen; the third, and overriding, problem was to link up the beachheads in a solid, mutually supporting line. But poor weather hampered air and naval operations. The seas were choppy and gray, under a 2,000-foot cloud ceiling. Ammunition ran low, and traffic snarls had developed in all sectors, which delayed the arrival of supplies and troops.

Montgomery and Bradley met aboard the *Augusta* to discuss the German pockets at Carentan and St.-Aubin, and to work out the urgent measures necessary to link up and expand the bridgehead before the Germans could organize strength in the center. The 352nd Field Infantry Division, reinforced by the 6th Parachute Regiment, had taken strong defensive positions in Carentan on the lateral road connecting OMAHA and UTAH. Bradley and Montgomery identified Carentan as the key to the American sector—a small fishing village south of the river Douve, flanked to the west and south by heavily inundated marshland. With elements of the 101st Airborne and 29th Division bogged down near the town, Bradley agreed to orient VII Corps west to support Gerow, which amounted to suspending attacks across the Cotentin and forgoing a quick effort to relieve the isolated 82nd Airborne bridgehead on the Merderet. In turn, Montgomery was concerned about V Corps losses, and the wide gap between the British XXX Corps and

Gerow. Bradley agreed to reinforce Gerow's left wing to link up with the British 50th at Bayeux.

Two hours later Eisenhower pulled up aboard H.M.S. *Apollo* for a talk with Bradley and Kirk aboard the U.S.S. *Augusta* about OMAHA and the American sector. As Bradley later recalled, Eisenhower first teased him about the lack of reports on OMAHA on the sixth. With mock innocence, Bradley told Eisenhower about the twelve-hour backlog at Portsmouth which had still not acknowledged all radio traffic from the *Augusta*. Eisenhower ratified Bradley's decision to put UTAH on hold for the sake of achieving a quick linkup between Collins and Gerow.

Near Arromanches, Eisenhower met with Montgomery aboard the H.M.S. *Faulknor* to discuss the worrisome problem of Caen in light of the evident German decision to mass forces there. Eisenhower was mindful that the length of the Orne River would be the surest barrier against the German Fifteenth Army—the bridgehead would not be safe as long as the Germans held a bridgehead on the western bank of the Orne. Meanwhile the British were blocked by the 21st Panzer and a regiment of the 12th SS Panzer which had arrived at night. German strongpoints held out at Douvres and Luc-sur-Mer, and German artillery still commanded the Périers Ridge in the narrow but dangerous German wedge between JUNO and SWORD.

Montgomery reported troubles with Leigh-Mallory and the Eighth Air Force, which he had assumed was available to strike "choke points" in the region so as to disrupt the arrival of German armor. Spaatz was refusing to accept the 21st Army Group target lists, claiming that bombing "choke points" would entail severe civilian casualties and extensive destruction of buildings. Eisenhower scheduled a conference with Spaatz and Leigh-Mallory at Southwick House that night.

A mishap held up Eisenhower's arrival back in Portsmouth. After re-embarking, Eisenhower asked Captain F. A. Grindle, commander of the *Apollo,* to pass close to shore for a look at the British beaches. Navigating shoal water, the *Apollo* struck a sandbar. With a violent shudder the ship jerked free, but the propellers and drive shafts were bent. The party transferred by barge to H.M.S. *Undaunted,* and finally got back to Portsmouth at ten that evening.

En route, worried that Grindle would suffer for a blunder for which he himself felt responsible, Eisenhower asked Admiral Ramsay to intercede. Ramsay, who had been on the bridge, was critical of Grindle's effort to force the sandbar instead of cutting engines and raising the stern. An inquiry was inevitable, but Ramsay would write a "kind" report and predicted Grindle would get off with a reprimand. "Good naval officers have a reprimand or two on their records," he assured Eisenhower.

Two days later Butcher and Gault would call on Grindle at Portsmouth, where the *Apollo* sat in drydock. Butcher consoled Grindle with the news that the *Faulknor* with Montgomery aboard had run aground behind the

British beaches shortly after the rendezvous on the seventh. Butcher reported back to Eisenhower, who "volunteered to send a brief note to his old friend Sir Andrew Cunningham on Grindle's behalf."

By the evening of the seventh, intelligence reports indicated the enemy was on the move. Twenty-four hours after the landings, the German high command had virtually written off Biscay and southern France as the focal points for major action, and shifted all eyes toward the Channel coast. Positions south of the Loire and on the Mediterranean coast were stripped of all but garrison troops to concentrate the full weight of the field divisions in northwest France. The 2nd SS Das Reich had left Toulouse. The 2nd Parachute Corps and 17th SS Panzer Grenadier Division left Poitiers. Panzer Lehr moved up from Chartres. The Adolf Hitler 1st SS left Antwerp. Intelligence closely watched the 711th and 134th infantry divisions, drawn from the Calais area, which crossed the Seine to join the 21st Panzer at Caen.

It was for this very moment that Eisenhower had demanded and obtained unfettered control of the air forces. There was no time to haggle over civilian casualties or property damage or better strategic uses of the air forces. Everything was subordinate now to the exigencies of OVERLORD. On the night of the seventh Eisenhower directed Spaatz to target road junctions, major highways, along with rail centers, airfields, bridges and depots, and to make Normandy a "zone of isolation." By the morning of the eighth, the U.S. Eighth Air Force bombed villages and towns on the roads leading to Normandy to slow down the arrival of enemy reinforcements. It was to be, as Anthony Cave Brown later wrote, "one of the most brutal uses of aerial power in history."

All commands went to work. RAF Bomber Command pounded rail lines running through Paris from western Germany. The U.S. Eighth Air Force by day leveled the bridges, rail and road junctions near Normandy, joined by the AEAF, which on the eighth alone flew 3,573 sorties over railway centers, coastal batteries, bridges and radar installations in Caen, Villers-Bocage—the gateway town to the bocage—and the road junctions at St.-Lô.

The merciless pounding cut a swath of destruction through Normandy and left in its wake eerie anomalies—a lone cathedral here, a barn there, anomalies highlighting rather than relieving the pattern of chaos and devastation; it slowed down but did not stop the 12th SS Panzer, the 351st, the 711th and Panzer Lehr, which arrived in strength at Tilly on the eighth to block the 1st Division–XXX Corps advance toward Caumont.

June 8. "Reports from the beaches are satisfactory," wrote Kay Summersby in her journal that morning, another day of sullen overcast weather. "The buildup is good but E. says it's not fast enough."

Anxiety began to permeate the command. That morning Eisenhower dictated a memo for Bedell Smith giving instructions for answering letters and cables. Smith was to use restraint until there was the linkup along the five beachheads and "obvious" progress toward Cherbourg and Caen. Messages were to be kept short, cordial and noncommittal in revealing information, Eisenhower wrote. "Pomposity, overoptimism, overpessimism" were to be carefully avoided.

Later that morning, yielding to the request of SHAEF PRO (Public Relations Office), Eisenhower consented to greet the press "off the record." On the way to the PRO tent at Southwick, Eisenhower confided to Butcher that he "hardly knew what to say to them." Butcher had a suggestion: to say nothing that would spur false optimism on the home front as the pronouncements after Anzio had done.

At his press conference Eisenhower weaved between candor and evasion, sensed by all the assembled reporters. Responding to questions about the near disaster in the American sector, Eisenhower told of the "accidental" presence of the 352nd at OMAHA. Over and over again, he talked about the importance of the weather in the next several days, strangely as though to suggest the temporary powerlessness of the Allied high command while it awaited a decisive German move. Low cloud, winds and the fluid front lines interfered with air strikes against enemy concentrations moving toward the beaches. Risking disclosure of FORTITUDE, Eisenhower took the reporters into his confidence and revealed that the enemy "evidently still seemed to expect landings elsewhere," which was "desirable for us since it will probably keep divisions fixed awaiting these threats." He called the landings "hazardous" and closed the conference, in which, Butcher wrote, he was "animated only when he talked about the possibility of good weather." "You fellows pray for it, too," Eisenhower said as he left.

Shortly afterward Butcher told Smith about the digest of clippings he had seen summarizing the American press reports and editorials. While these were factual, Butcher sensed that the press was "leading us into overoptimism at home," adding that he thought it would be wise to "let the enemy be overoptimistic—it's better to go into the game as an underdog." Smith agreed, and summoned the correspondents into the PRO hut for an impromptu conference to render Eisenhower's warnings more explicit.

Butcher describes how Smith briefed the reassembled group about the problems faced in Normandy, particularly the supply problem. Smith sketched the facts: the unloading was twelve to twenty-four hours behind schedule. There were supply deficiencies at OMAHA—instead of D-Day target calling for off-loading 2,400 tons over the beach, only 100 tons had actually been off-loaded. Smith informed the group about the serious gaps between the sectors, especially the gaps east and west of OMAHA Beach. Radio contact had still not been established with elements of the 82nd, which were thought to be holding a bridgehead across the Merderet against heavy counterattack. "Caen was to have been taken on D-Day," Smith told them, "and at this moment we are still fighting for it, in fact being pushed back by counterattack." He conceded that the German build-up had been slower than expected, and "so perhaps the bad break of the weather has not been fatal."

Meanwhile, V Corps pushed south toward Caumont, but advances elsewhere were slow. The 82nd Airborne west of the Merderet River established tenuous contact with VII Corps while maintaining control of Ste.-Mère-Eglise and a bridgehead across the Merderet. Gebhardt's 29th Division took the seaside village of Isigny and marched toward Carentan as elements of the 101st Airborne attacked eastward from the Carentan Canal.

Similarly, SHAEF summaries spoke of "strong resistance along the whole front." German strongpoints continued to hold out behind British lines, while the British 6th Airborne tenaciously held the Orne bridgehead against violent and continuous attacks. By nightfall the battle for Caen appeared to be stalemated, and Lieutenant General Miles Dempsey spoke of his "worry about a premature advance which might unbalance the entire invasion force."

By the ninth, with the British blocked at Caen and the extreme eastern front stalemated, attention focused on the center and the towns of Tilly, Villers-Bocage and Caumont along the American-British boundary. Rommel and Dempsey simultaneously planned offensives there. Caumont was the "seam" of the Allied front, and from the German point of view, the place where Allied coordination might crack under pressure of German counterattacks. The U.S. 1st Division, after linking with the British XXX Corps, had pushed south and exposed a seven-mile flank, which had to be closed. Simultaneously, Dempsey had concluded that Caumont was the sector fluid enough for rapid expansion, which might enable XXX Corps to envelope Caen from the west. Adding urgency to this, SHAEF reported "considerable night activity" in Caumont–Tilly–Villers-Bocage, occupied by the lead regiments of Panzer Lehr and the late arrivals of the 12th SS Panzer. Dempsey ordered spoiling attacks at Tilly to engage armor and exploit the lack of field-grade infantry there and to close up ranks for Gerow's left.

A tug-of-war ensued. Dempsey wanted strong American support for his right flank, but Bradley suspected Dempsey of overcaution, and resisted. Moreover, Bradley was much concerned that Gerow and Collins had still not linked up. Sparing American forces to shore up Caumont–Tilly would mean delay in taking Carentan and linkup along the American front. Early on the ninth Montgomery and Bradley met at Port-en-Bessin to work the problem out.

Montgomery presented Dempsey's proposed offensive at Caumont and suggested that Bradley reinforce the V Corps sector. Bradley recognized the danger in the German preparations at Tilly–Caumont but again resisted the idea of weakening his effort to take Carentan. Montgomery then sketched his view of how the campaign would go, and precipitated the beginnings of the controversy over strategy in the Normandy campaign that would last for weeks.

By now Montgomery had concluded that the German armored build-up at Caen was a hopeful sign, but leaned to the idea that Caen should be formally abandoned as an immediate objective of the Normandy campaign. In his view, the Second Army could maintain limited attacks there and engage the panzers, thereby preventing the kind of build-up attempted at Tilly. Montgomery went on to predict to Bradley that he expected the real break to develop in the American sector. Indeed, he noted several times that the development of the battle emphasized the importance of Cherbourg as a port used to gain room for the American build-up, a truism and in Bradley's opinion a veiled way of saying that Montgomery was critical of American progress. Actually, Montgomery's optimism about Dempsey's sector seemed well founded and his general approach seemed justified, but Bradley found it troublesome. From his point of view, Montgomery seemed too ready to excuse Dempsey's caution at Caen, too complacent about British progress, and all too eager to commit him to long-range plans, which seemed very premature.

Master of the set-piece battle, Montgomery on the ninth demonstrated that he was determined to link early Allied maneuvers to a broader concept. Moreover, his views stated on the ninth concerning Caen and the likely development of the campaign were not new or startling. They seemed no more than logical in view of the early commitment of German armor at Caen, which suggested that the Germans, without a quick victory in Normandy, would try to contain the bridgehead and concentrate their energies on Caen. This would open the door at Cherbourg to rapid expansion of the American bridgehead southward toward Brittany, which, again, had been foreseen. But again, on the ninth, with all commands scrambling to consolidate the slender foothold in France, Montgomery's attempt to commit Bradley to a particular scheme of operation seemed premature, and it implied that he either thought that the Americans were not trying hard enough or was suggesting that the British should not be expected to push hard on the eastern flank.

In retrospect, there is little doubt that Montgomery was making a basic statement of military policy. Indeed, he would soon spell out his views in a letter to Brooke, apparently to equip Brooke and the BCOS for handling problems in talks with Marshall and King that week. Likewise, the Montgomery-Bradley exchange alarmed Eisenhower somewhat when he heard of it, and accounted for his early attempts to oversee the battle carefully. Like Bradley, Eisenhower felt that Montgomery seemed unduly cautious, though Eisenhower could not quarrel with facts nor question a plan that in principle had been accepted by all commands in April. Nor did Eisenhower "misunderstand Monty's strategy," as Brooke and others would allege when Eisenhower began to pressure 21st Army Group for action to strengthen the "containing actions" at Caen. It was simply that the issues —casualties, and the unresolved question of overall ground command after the landings were secured—were difficult to discuss seventy-two hours after the assault.

Throughout the ninth a violent battle raged along the slopes and orchards north of Tilly as XXX Corps attempted to extend a "right hook" to envelop the Norman capital from the west. The Canadian 3rd Division was repulsed and driven back by elements of the 12th SS and Panzer Lehr. That night Churchill directed the BCOS to draft plans for a secondary landing in Brittany for consideration by the CCS as an alternative to ANVIL and a contingency in case Normandy became a cauldron.

In London and Berlin, June 9 was a day of strategic reappraisals. Eisenhower spent the day in conference. Early that morning he motored to an undisclosed location in the western suburbs of London to brief Marshall and King on the situation in the bridgehead. He spent the early afternoon at Widewing reviewing a list of court-martial sentences with General Betts. Churchill and his entourage arrived at Bushy Park in the afternoon for a briefing, and to talk about Churchill's latest communications with Stalin on the timing and scale of the Russian summer offensive.

Forty-eight hours before, Stalin had responded perfunctorily to Churchill's cable informing him of the invasion. Deane and Burrows in Moscow had pressed Antonov for details of Soviet plans, but the Russians maintained an air of mystery. Churchill had since exchanged two messages with Stalin, who seemed impressed by the magnitude of the invasion, and on the ninth had intimated that an offensive would start in the Leningrad area and "speed along the long line until the whole front is ablaze." But Stalin had said nothing concrete, so the scope and objectives of the offensive remained to be seen. Eisenhower told Smith to draft a congratulatory telegram to be sent to Vasilevsky when "we are assured that the Leningrad attack is a big one."

Simultaneously, fateful deliberations were under way in the German high command. For two days Rommel, sensing the outcome, had desperately attempted to organize a full-strength counterattack at Caumont–Tilly to regain Bayeux, convinced that this was the last chance to isolate major pockets of the landing force and defeat the invasion. Likewise Von Rundstedt, impressed by the sheer weight of the invasion, had begun to doubt that Normandy was a diversion or that the Seventh Army, backed by armor, could successfully contain the bridgehead. Gradually he had come around to Rommel's idea that Fifteenth Army infantry was now essential for flank protection and to extricate the 12th SS and 21st Panzer from combat around Caen.

But OKW remained adamant on the question of the Fifteenth Army infantry. Ruge later described Rommel's agony as all requests for infantry replacements fell on deaf ears at OKW and the German chance to defeat the landings slipped away. On the night of the sixth, Rommel had asked for several Fifteenth Army regimental combat teams "to be followed by all the infantry divisions [holding] the second line in Calais." OKW refused. Rommel requested the 2nd Parachute Corps in Brittany—request denied. Rommel requested the 9th Panzer Division at Marseilles under Army Group G—request denied. Rommel insisted that the main objective of the landings would be to seal off the Cotentin and to seize Cherbourg as a major port, and found himself arguing with OKW, which was apparently persuaded by FORTITUDE that landings at Boulogne were imminent.

On the seventh, OKW had instructed Rommel to "contain the American bridgehead," and focus on the hinge at Caen with armor released to the Seventh Army sector for that specific purpose. OKW stubbornness was bolstered by the pattern of Allied bombing and reports of action messages sent to the French and Belgian underground in preparation for landings at Calais. That day OKW did release the 17th SS Panzer Grenadier Division in Brittany to "rope off" the Americans in the Cotentin, but the mass of panzers was directed to stay in the Caen sector and defend the vital road arteries, permitting lateral communications between the Seventh and Fifteenth armies.

Finally, on the seventh, Von Rundstedt intervened. Having evaluated the amount of supply coming over the beaches, and the units identified in the build-up, including the 82nd Airborne, the U.S. 1st and the British 7th Armored, he decided that Normandy was an all-out effort. Meanwhile the Germans had recovered a briefcase full of VII Corps plans chained to the corpse of an American officer near Carentan. The same day, near OMAHA, the Germans found a briefcase containing the entire scheme of maneuver and the U.S. order of battle. It seemed odd that the documents, stamped "Destroy Before Embarkation," were taken ashore, and the Germans suspected a trap. But Von Rundstedt accepted the discovery as authentic, informed Hitler of it on the eighth and obtained OKW permission to commence the movement of eight panzer divisions to Normandy.

By the eighth Hitler and OKW confronted Von Rundstedt's appeal for the Fifteenth Army infantry reserve—five field-grade divisions—which posed the wider question of the reserves to be made available for the sake of a decision in France. Hitler procrastinated, declaring at first that he was unwilling to expose Calais and Dunkirk because V-1 sites located there, and scheduled to become operational by the end of the week, might compel a quick second Allied landing to neutralize the threat. But this evaded the thrust of Von Rundstedt's appeal.

Again, so long as the Allies had large uncommitted forces in England, divisions released from the Fifteenth Army at Calais for use in Normandy would have to be replaced, presumably with troops from other fronts. The question was whether to oblige Von Rundstedt to make do in Normandy with the Seventh Army, which would keep the Fifteenth Army on station to protect the Calais region against secondary landings and to act as a theater reserve. Von Rundstedt doubted that the Seventh Army would hold Normandy, so Hitler had to weigh the risk of a setback there against the dangers elsewhere. Specifically, Hitler had to reckon with a Red Army threat to Lvov and Brest-Litovsk, a hinge connecting an eighty-division salient extending deep into central Russia and the Baltic States. In short, now that the Allies were showing their hand, should the Germans accept risks in the west for the sake of holding round four in Russia, or should risks in Russia be accepted in order to gain a decision in France? Hitler faced the question on June 9 and finally resolved it in favor of the former on grounds that were not clear.

Perhaps there was nothing to decide. Hitler and OKW had long foreseen Allied landings and had carefully worked out troop priorities accordingly. In light of subsequent events, the survival of the Nazi regime would depend on Hitler's total commitment to stemming the Russian summer offensive. Yet the decision to accept risks in the west clearly went against the grain of Hitler's pronouncements since November, and Hitler made his choice reluctantly.

Twenty-four hours earlier, OKW had released the Fifteenth Army infantry reserve to Normandy, a decision that might have spelled doom for the Allies. At his noon conference on the ninth, Hitler endorsed orders transferring the 9th and 10th SS Panzer divisions from Poland to France. But Hitler exhibited doubt and set a conference for midnight to review both decisions. Then, at midnight between the ninth and the tenth, Hitler, backed by Jodl, ordered OB West to pass to the defensive, to strengthen the Fifteenth Army at Calais in anticipation of Allied landings there and to halt the movement of the panzer and infantry divisions from Pas-de-Calais to Normandy.

News of Hitler's decision reached Von Rundstedt and Rommel during the night and brought both field marshals to the brink of tendering their resignations. According to F. W. Winterbotham in *The Ultra Secret,* ULTRA intercepted the messages flashing back and forth between OKW and St.-Germain. As Brown says, Hitler's order suspending "Case Three" elicited bitter protests from Rommel and Von Rundstedt and quiet exultation in London, where all suspected this meant the beachhead was safe. According to Brown, Marshall, the American Chiefs and the BCOS were in conference at the war bunker beneath St. James's Park on the morning of the tenth when informed of the intercepts. For two days, situation maps had displayed the movement of German troops and vehicles toward Normandy, along with the transfer of fighter and fighter-bomber bases. The atmosphere, according to Anthony Wingate, a witness, was one "heavy with tension and pipe and cigarette smoke combined with a faint aroma of good whiskey."

Then Joan Bright (a secretary who kept the most secret intelligence file) knocked on the door and said there was a message. . . . Brooke and Marshall went to have a look. They were all smiles . . . there it was. Hitler had cancelled Case Three. We'd won, and what an astonishing moment that was. We knew then that we'd won . . . there might be heavy battles, but we'd won. . . .

But had the Allies "won"? Hitler's decision was far-reaching and, arguably, it set the course of the summer campaigns and perhaps of the war itself. In short, as optimists had predicted, Hitler had found himself constrained from sacrificing ground in Russia to mount an all-out effort against the landings in France. But the tactical success of the landing phase did not mean that the Allies would easily overcome German efforts to contain the bridgehead, or that the Germans would not turn their full attention to France sooner or later.

Indeed, Albert Speer in his account of Hitler's thinking at the time would shed additional light on Hitler's decisions on the night of the ninth. Speer would suggest that both Hitler and OKW underestimated the staying power of the Allied forces in France and were willing to accept risks in Normandy based on misplaced confidence that even after losing France, the Germans could restore the situation in the west at will. Speer's reliability as a source is suspect, and his account sounds like rationalization on Hitler's part. But he would go on to explain that Hitler's view had little to do with logic and facts, such as the balance of divisions, ships and planes in the west, but instead rested on memories of Munich and the German victory over France in 1940, events that confirmed Hitler in his contempt for democracy as a system that, in his view, enfeebled the fighting spirit of a nation.

In the next forty-eight hours Rommel, General Geyr von Schweppenburg and Von Rundstedt improvised without the infantry of the Fifteenth Army. Army Group B set about vigorously to organize a last-ditch counteroffensive at Caen with the forces available, and to strengthen the German wedge at Carentan. Though reinforced by the 17th SS and the 2nd Panzer, Rommel by the tenth confronted an impossible problem of his own making in extricating the panzers committed against the British at Tilly and north of Caen. Eisenhower, Montgomery and Bradley played the Allied trump of strategic air in tactical support of the ground forces.

Along the "seam" near Caumont, Huebner's 1st Division was across the Aure River but exposed well forward of Bucknall's XXX Corps. With preparations behind schedule for the drive on Cherbourg, Bradley ordered all necessary measures to link up V Corps and VII Corps at Carentan as quickly as possible. "If it becomes necessary to save time," he told Collins, "put 500 or even 1,000 tons of air on Carentan and take the city apart. Then rush it and you'll get in." Soon, the 29th Division at Isigny occupied the flatlands east of the Carentan Canal while glider infantry reinforced the 101st Paratroopers advancing on the town from the southwest. On the morning of June 10, Bradley had moved to a CP set up at Pointe du Hoc. That afternoon, having received a false report that OMAHA and UTAH had been joined, Bradley set off in a jeep to find Collins, only to be forced back by sniper fire. The 17th SS joined the siege at Carentan to relieve the encircled German paratroopers, and Carentan held out in a desperate fight until dawn on June 12.

Eisenhower, on the tenth, had met briefly with De Guingand. When Eisenhower complained that Montgomery had not sent his daily radio message about the way the battle was going, De Guingand conveyed Montgomery's complaints about air-ground coordination and Montgomery's worries about the pressure of German panzers on the British front which hampered Dempsey's attempt to close up on Gerow's left flank at Caumont. Eisenhower ordered the AEAF into the battle at Caumont to break up preparations for a German attack, and German accounts confirm that Allied bombers wore down the German efforts to assemble for a counter-attack.

German accounts have described the impact of AEAF interdiction on German preparations and the orderly movement of armor. Arriving forces had to detrain at night a hundred miles from the front and take shelter in orchards and farmhouses by day. Even movement at night limped along at four miles per hour with constant detours, consuming precious gasoline. General Fritz Bayerlein, Rommel's chief of staff in Africa and commander of Panzer Lehr, would describe the road from Chartres to Normandy as a "fighter-bomber race course." Panzer Lehr straggled into Tilly minus forty petrol wagons, ninety trucks, five tanks and with hundreds of casualties, all before entering battle. The 2nd SS Das Reich and other divisions from Biscay and Brittany experienced harassment by French guerrilla bands, which blew up bridges and rail lines, mined roads and sniped at vehicles, slowing the transit to a crawl.

The constant bombardment also had a demoralizing effect on the troops and officers of the Seventh Army. The relentless air attacks emphasized the absence of the Luftwaffe, held back that week to defend synthetic-fuel plants against the oil blitz launched by Spaatz in late May and stepped up beginning June 8. Allied domination of the skies was also a reminder of how tenuous German Seventh Army communications were and seemed to spell doom, but the German troops fought courageously. Abandoned to his own devices by the high command, Rommel attempted to scrape up three panzer divisions while holding Carentan, Isigny, Caen, Tilly and Caumont. Then on the ninth Rommel passed to the defensive "from the Orne to the Vire" to wait for the II Parachute Corps, Panzer Lehr, the 12th SS Panzer and 21st Panzer for an attack coordinated by Von Schweppenburg's Panzer Group West Headquarters.

Meanwhile, Bucknall's XXX Corps launched spoiling attacks at Tilly and Caumont while the AEAF pounded strongpoints and road nets, throwing scheduled movement into confusion. General Erich Marcks was killed when his truck was caught on an open road by fighter-bombers. British intelligence tracing wireless signals located Von Schweppenburg's field tent in an apple orchard near the Norman town of La Caine. Before nightfall on the tenth, the low clouds broke and several dozen AEAF fighter-bombers swept the area, destroying the encampment, killing or wounding the entire staff and severely wounding Von Schweppenburg. Command of the 1st SS Panzer Corps passed to SS General Sepp Dietrich, who hesitated. On the eleventh, amplifying instructions came from OKW Berlin, finally canceling any contemplated counteroffensive toward Bayeux by Army Group B, and directing Rommel to hold Caen "at all costs." By the twelfth the Germans entrenched along the fifty-mile front as the 101st re-entered Carentan and VII Corps spearheads entered Montebourg, then opened the drive across the Merderet River to isolate the Cotentin. By the fourteenth OKW had written off Cherbourg, and ordered the garrison to defend the port "to the last tin of rations and the last round of ammunition," then to convert it "into a heap of ruins."

Ruge, who later recounted these events step by step, described the gloom that descended over the Army Group Staff. The lines were yielding slowly but steadily under Allied air, ground and naval pressure—counterattacks mounted in the Caen sector had yielded "limited gains" and at far too great a cost. The stillborn effort to attack the seam at Caumont was depressing, attributable to OKW's frivolous neglect of Normandy and a dangerous underestimation of the Allies. Few of Ruge's colleagues believed the bridgehead could be contained for long or that Germany had the capacity to wage a two-front war, despite Germany's historic advantage of interior lines.

And so while Eisenhower paced Widewing and Portsmouth in solitude, and while Montgomery formulated a "right hook" to envelop Caen from the west, Rommel and his staff brooded over the impending Allied success in consolidating the bridgehead. In Ruge's words, these facts and the heavy reverses in the east made it clear to a group of patriotic Germans that time was running out if they wanted to "avert a complete catastrophe for their people." Narrow hopes had been pinned on Von Schweppenburg's ability to gather reserves for a quick counterattack to relieve strongpoints along the coast that were still holding out, hopes shelved by the mischance at his headquarters and then snuffed out by subsequent OKW orders halting all counterattacks and passing to the defensive in Normandy. According to Ruge, it was on the eleventh that Phase One of OVERLORD became history. "The Third Front had become a fact," he wrote, "and the fate of the Third Reich was sealed."

· · ·

As the battle of the bridgehead reached its climax, fleets of oceangoing tugs towed the immense steel caissons, floating roadways, pontoons and cause-ways for the MULBERRYs at Arromanches and St.-Laurent. Assembly had been under way since the eighth, and by the end of the first week, the two artificial harbors provided a port of disembarkation for 74,000 troops, 10,000 vehicles and 17,000 tons of weapons, food, fuel and armored vehicles bringing needed relief in the build-up.

The GOOSEBERRY breakwaters held up under a stiff northwest wind, permitting thousands of small craft to beach and to ferry light stores of food, clothing and ammunition at Courseulles, Ouistreham and Port-en-Bessin. Montgomery's May 15 estimate at St. Paul's that by D plus 4 sixteen Allied divisions would be facing twenty full-strength German field divisions now seemed, in retrospect, pessimistic. The situation actually confronting the Allies at the end of the first ninety-six hours appeared bright indeed. Sixteen Allied divisions ashore faced only ten German divisions, with reinforce-ments from Brittany, the Paris area, Biscay and Marseilles moving at a rate of thirty miles a day under the cover of darkness.

On the tenth Montgomery had informed Churchill that the American and British sectors were ready to receive visitors, saying, in so many words, that the Allies were in Normandy to stay. The grim facts, apparent to Ruge, Rommel and Von Rundstedt by the night of the tenth, were sensed simul-taneously in the Allied camp. The SHAEF weekly intelligence summary on land operations for the week noted that "the outstanding feature to date of the operations on the continent is the unexpected ease with which the much vaunted 'Atlantic wall' defenses were broken through, and this despite the very adverse weather conditions."

As recognition of this fact rippled through London and Washington, reactions were sober. Churchill vaguely wrote of having been "surprised" at the ease of the landings, and by German reluctance to counterattack in the early hours with the speed and élan for which the German army had become renowned in 1939. OKW, instead of concentrating against the obvi-ous threat, had scattered forces up and down the coast of France. "How strange," he mused, "that the Germans, now on the defensive, made the same mistake as the French in 1940 and dispersed their most powerful weapon of counterattack," referring to the five panzer divisions north of the Loire which, if dispatched to Normandy before June 8, might have driven the invaders into the sea.

In the years ahead, many would attribute this "miracle" to FORTITUDE, though in retrospect the German high command would have been rash to commit the forces at Calais to the defense of Normandy in the early hours of the attack unless confident of reinforcements. Until the other twenty-three OVERLORD divisions in southern England off-loaded in Normandy, the Allies in fact possessed the landing craft and troops to mount secondary landings at Calais or elsewhere—indeed, Churchill's idea of secondary landings in Brittany had come up in the CCS talks that week.

The real "miracle" had been Hitler's decision on the night of June 9–10 to contain the Allies in Normandy, which stemmed from his inability to order withdrawals from Russia. Hitler was "looking east," and rearranging his armies in France in hopes of clinging to essential positions, and he was presumably willing to sacrifice the German Seventh Army if necessary. But again, how long would this good fortune last? Complacency was the danger facing the Allies in the next several weeks. Indeed, on the tenth, shortly after ULTRA intercepts confirmed that the bridgehead was safe, Eisenhower had independently directed SHAEF G-3 to go to work on contingency plans for landings in Brittany in the event of "stabilization" in Normandy.

But optimism was running high. As early as the sixth, Brooke and the BCOS at the weekly COS meeting approved a brief but very significant statement by the Joint Intelligence Committee (JIC), a brief but important assessment that speculated on the prospects for the second front and its impact on Germany. In it the JIC portrayed Germany as fatally overextended and therefore incapable of collecting reserves to wage an effective campaign in France. Reviewing the German plight theater by theater, the JIC doubted that German evacuation of territory would prove practical anywhere, even in the east, except possibly in Norway and "southern Greece as far as the Mount Olympus line." Withdrawals everywhere else exposed vital objectives, and would result either in the loss of critical resources or in political upheavals in the German satellites, in Scandinavia and in Germany herself.

For instance, only by maintaining garrisons in Norway and Finland could the Germans be sure of access to Swedish ore. The extended belt of German fortresses deep in central Russia covered Finland, hence Norway and Sweden, and so they would not be evacuated. Similarly, withdrawal north of the Po River would bring the industries of southern Germany and Austria within range of continuous Allied aerial bombardment. Then, too, the Germans had to stand fast in Rumania to retain access to the oil fields at Ploesti, and so on. In this way, the JIC discounted the chances of major German reinforcements in France, and unless the Germans could deny the Allies air bases in France, neither a prolonged defense of France nor even a prolonged defense of the Siegfried Line, for that matter, would be possible. Dispatched to SHAEF, 10 Downing Street, the military mission in Moscow and to the White House, the JIC appraisal concluded that while it could not estimate precisely when German resistance would collapse, "viewing the picture as a whole . . . Germany's defeat should occur before 1945."

The JIC assessment was not entirely welcome at SHAEF. As he filed it away in his diary, Butcher labeled the report "interesting." Perhaps it was that the tone of the report seemed overoptimistic and premature in view of the fact that the American and British armies still struggled to consolidate a foothold in France. The conclusions rested on several debatable assumptions. First, it was debatable that the Germans would not risk access to raw materials for the sake of radical moves to improve the desperate German situation outlined in the report. Second, the report overlooked the possibility that Germany would be able to form a reserve from as yet untapped sources of manpower in Germany. Third, it assumed that the defense of the eastern front would always take precedence over moves to defeat the Allies. Finally, the JIC neglected a basic fact that in Eisenhower's mind was the key to long-range German intentions: that in June 1944, Germany was not protecting an overextended empire but struggling to avert "obliteration." The optimism of the report was not atypical, given the post-invasion euphoria, but optimism is rarely the basis of an objective intelligence report. Indeed, one might say that the JIC report seemed reminiscent of British appraisals months before on the eve of the Teheran and Cairo conferences, and if so, it was a hint of a British campaign in the offing to revive all the old questions about ANVIL and France, a sign of troubles to come.

Were the Germans at the brink of collapse? The reappearance of the idea of a German "collapse" before the end of the year was significant in several ways, and it coincided with fresh rumors of an anti-Nazi revolt led by "conservative elements in the Wehrmacht" and the Home Army preliminary to armistice negotiations. Such reports appeared to presuppose that the Allies would encourage a coup and could take it into account in military planning. Did the British and Americans take seriously the reports reaching London of an imminent anti-Nazi coup? Would the British, who appeared to set much store by them, base military policy on them?

Brown shows how shortly after the invasion the British MI-6 and American OSS were in contact with German emissaries in Stockholm and Madrid about prospects of a coup planned by the Beck conspirators and Wehrmacht generals, including Rommel and Hans Speidel, his chief of staff. Once again, Eisenhower, among others, still doubted, or chose to doubt, that OSS in Geneva was in contact with a genuine resistance group. Did the British disagree? Apparently so, yet Major General Sir Kenneth Strong, SHAEF G-2, would later write that he did not think an organized conspiracy existed, an opinion shared by Anthony Wingate of MI-6. "We received frequent reports about the German opposition," Wingate would tell Brown years later. "But the political authorities decided that no reliance could be placed on these. It had been decided long since that the war could only be ended by military means. Therefore, we did ask ourselves about the use that we could make of these contacts in order to assist our strategic deception operations. We decided that such overtures were examples of defeatism and of course where you have disaffected elements they are more liable to accept information which was to the disadvantage of Hitler. . . ."

Wingate's recollection implies that Churchill and the British took little account of a German conspiracy and perhaps they did, except as a diplomatic tool in Churchill's dealings with Washington and Moscow on military cooperation and postwar questions such as France, Italy, Norway, Yugoslavia, Poland, Greece, and occupation policy for Germany. But the idea of a German coup had more than symbolic and diplomatic importance as subsequent British efforts to maintain contact with the Beck group would show. The importance of a "conspiracy" in Germany would soon blossom into an issue between Eisenhower and the British.

Butcher's chronicle also refers to political problems cropping up in the week after the landing. An immediate problem involved the French. During the CCS meetings, the British served notice that they hoped the period of Allied military government over liberated France would be short. Eden broached the problem with Marshall that weekend at Chequers—specifically the problems of U.S.-issued currency in Normandy and De Gaulle's recent treatment by SHAEF. Marshall "worked Eden over" about French obstructionists who made trouble while American boys fought for the liberation of France and warned Eden of a "wave of indignation . . . that could sweep the whole damn British Foreign Office" if the British broke ranks on the French issue.

Eden was impressed by the intensity of Marshall's determination to approach De Gaulle as a military question, yet he and others in London could not help noticing the questions suddenly cropping up in the American press that week about the consequences of a long war and a military approach which took little account of postwar politics. Even amid the rejoicing over the early military communiqués heralding the success in Normandy, American editorials suggested that the era in which the Americans could brush off British urgency about confronting postwar political problems was drawing to a close. For instance, *Life* editorialized that week about the momentous transition in American life heralded by D-Day. The magazine noted that "With the establishment of a firm lodgement on the continent, we are now the most powerful nation on earth," and proceeded to raise questions about a policy devised before anyone in Washington had fully appreciated this fact, a policy that could end only in the total destruction of the German nation and economy. *Life* reminded its readership that history's lessons demonstrated that "power employed for its own sake is a fatal intoxicant that undermines the victor with moral defeat," and in this vein recalled Saint Augustine's commentaries which had traced the beginning of Rome's moral decay and its fall thereafter to the extermination of Carthage in 143 B.C., an act of brutality that reduced subsequent Roman conquests to "feats of empty militarism." Pax Romana, *Life* noted, had been a peace "by virtue of force of arms." By Carthage, *Life* meant Germany. By Rome, *Life* meant the United States, which would possess the power of Imperial Rome by the end of the war and necessarily confront choices that would determine whether

America would sponsor a peace governed by force, or a settlement based on consent.

In broaching the problem of postwar recovery, *Life*, by implication, questioned Russian influence over Allied strategy and the frontal strategies the magazine had once demanded in introducing Eisenhower to its readership twenty-four months earlier. The *Saturday Evening Post* had been frankly critical of the relentless bombardment of German industry in the Ruhr and the Saar, industries that might prove essential in the reconstruction of Europe after the war, and noted that destruction of the fruits of a free-enterprise industrial system was a self-defeating policy for a nation itself committed to the principles of free enterprise. Neither magazine offered advice about how to end the war, but the period of fighting "a profoundly political war without mentioning the war's political bases," as Charles Bolte of the *Nation* put it, was ending.

Meanwhile the Allies were awaiting news from Russia about the promised summer offensive set to coincide with OVERLORD. Major General John Deane, in London for the CCS meeting, told of walking the streets of Moscow on the sixth and having been surprised by the pro forma announcements and the business-as-usual reactions by ordinary Muscovites. More to the point, Stalin's congratulatory telegram on the sixth had neglected to clarify Red Army plans for the concurrent offensive. He had expressed "the joy to us all" in the Kremlin over the invasion news, extended "hope of further successes," and indicated vaguely that the "summer offensive of the Soviet forces organized in accordance with the agreement at the Teheran conference" would develop "by stages" on "one of the important sectors of the front" leading to a "general offensive" by July about which he would "not fail to inform . . . in due course." Evidently, hard news about Russian intentions awaited confirmation of favorable developments in Normandy.

Churchill, a day later, had replied to Stalin with a detailed description of the invasion battle which included an account of the crisis at OMAHA, the weather conditions that hindered the build-up, the battle at Caen, plans for secondary landings in the Brest Peninsula, and the MULBERRY secret. "But, all this waits on the hazards of war," Churchill added, "which, Marshall Stalin, you know so well." In his reply on the ninth Stalin praised "the valiant British and American armies" and extended warm wishes "for further successes," then closed with news that "tomorrow June 10, the first stage will open in our summer offensive on the Leningrad front."

It was this message that Churchill had relayed to Eisenhower at their meeting at Widewing on the ninth. According to Butcher, Stalin's message initially electrified SHAEF, since a Russian offensive from the Black Sea to the Baltic, if sustained, would probably bar German reinforcement of Normandy all summer.

Finally, on the twelfth, with word of a thirty-mile Red Army penetration between Lake Ladoga and Finland on the Mannerheim Line, Eisenhower told Smith to dispatch the congratulatory message to Vasilevsky which he had placed "on hold." In it Eisenhower praised "the magnificent performance of the great Red Army" which had been a "constant source of inspiration," wished Vasilevsky "great success" and pledged that SHAEF "daily" would bring more troops "into the fighting line" in the joint effort to bring the "final destruction of Nazi tyranny."

The scope of the Red Army attack remained to be seen, however. Eisenhower's message crossed a third wire from Stalin to Churchill, in which Stalin intimated that a stepped-up tempo of operations was imminent, inspired by OVERLORD, for which he extended unrestrained congratulations. "As is evident," Stalin declared, "the landing conceived on a grandiose scale has succeeded completely. . . ."

> My colleagues and I cannot but admit that the history of warfare knows no other like undertaking from the point of view of its scale, its vast conception, and its masterly execution. As is well known, Napoleon in his time failed ignominiously in his plan to force the Channel. The hysterical Hitler, who boasted for two years that he would effect a forcing of the Channel, was unable to make up his mind even to hint at attempting to carry out his threat. Only our allies have succeeded in realizing with honor the grandiose plan of the forcing of the Channel. History will record this deed as an achievement of the highest order. . . .

In these unsettled circumstances, the Combined Chiefs of Staff turned to post-OVERLORD matters, including ANVIL. In sessions on June 11, 13 and 14, Brooke, Marshall, King and Portal found that they had difficulty looking beyond the exigencies of OVERLORD, and quickly affirmed that Mediterranean operations would hinge on success in Normandy. The group framed a directive for Wilson in which the CCS confined the Fifteenth Army Group pursuit beyond Rome to the Pisa–Rimini line.

The Americans made an apparent concession. Marshall suddenly entertained two alternatives to landings in Marseilles, where, he conceded, "the strength of the coast defenses and the unprofitable line of advance up the Rhone Valley" might enable the Germans to delay economically the progress of the invasion in force. The alternatives were CALIPH, landings at Bordeaux, and landings on the Dalmatian coast. Apparently CALIPH was a British-sponsored compromise solution to the ANVIL problem. Sufficiently detached geographically from Italy, CALIPH stood to protect the dignity of AFHQ as an independent theater of operations, and to provide more direct support for the invasion force than landings in Marseilles. Secondly, CALIPH was not ANVIL—a crucial procedural point in British eyes.

The records provide little insight into Marshall's sudden openness to a landing at the head of the Adriatic. The talks were conducted in a blaze of

Anglo-American cordiality, so Marshall may have wished to be open-minded. Marshall may also have been reluctant to rule everything out pending word of the Russian summer offensive, or he may have been sensitive to election-year criticism of ANVIL. CALIPH may have appealed to the Americans because of Churchill's support, the off chance of stalemate in Normandy and the never-ending problem of ensuring that American forces did not become bogged down in secondary efforts at the risk of OVERLORD.

Marshall's lapse was reminiscent of his support for Brooke in the military-committee discussion with Voroshilov at Teheran. His implicit distrust of Moscow was a ray of sunlight for Brooke, who scented vindication. "It was interesting to listen to Marshall explaining *now* why the Germans fought in central Italy," Brooke noted in his diary, adding, "he [Marshall] seemed to forget that I had given him all these arguments several months ago." The CCS had placed southern France in its "proper perspective," or so Brooke thought. For the moment, the CCS directive for AFHQ instructed Wilson to plan on any of the three alternatives, to be selected dependent upon "(a) the progress of operation OVERLORD with the forces now assigned to it, (b) the direction and degree of success of the forthcoming Russian offensive, (c) the German reactions to (a) and (b) above."

Finally, on June 12, Eisenhower escorted Marshall, King and Arnold on a tour of the American zone. The usual low-lying morning fog and chill of southern England lifted by seven o'clock, an hour after the dawn rendez-vous of high-level VIPs at Cosham station for the train trip to Portsmouth. Colonel Jimmy Gault accompanied Marshall, King, Arnold and Eisenhower aboard the U.S.S. *Thompson* and kept an account of the voyage to the far shore where "everyone experienced a thrilling and satisfying feeling of putting their feet for the first time on France."

The Channel was placid and blue, and there were few signs of war until the barrage balloons came into view above the ships anchored near the shoreline. The day was perfect for Marshall's return to the land where he had made his legendary reputation as Pershing's operations officer in 1918 at the Meuse–Argonne and St.-Mihiel. For Eisenhower, the inspection of the "tiny realm" in Normandy was of equal significance. He enjoyed playing host to a man whose concept he had carried to fruition, and to be able to do so was the mark of his new stature within Allied councils, for his role was changing from that of a coordinator brokering rival conceptions of strategy to that of a commander over the largest single military force in the field.

As always, Eisenhower's influence was difficult to measure, but it had grown perceptibly in the past several weeks. Soon, personal changes in Eisenhower would also be evident. "D-Day cemented his personal confidence," Kevin McCann, a speech writer and friend, would recall three decades later. Eisenhower, a son of the Kansas plains, cautious and given to self-doubt in Africa and Italy, had demonstrated in Normandy that he could make and back up a momentous decision "with the best of them." In Africa he had been satisfied at times to be outranked by his nominal British subordinates, to serve as coordinator between rival services within his theater, in part because he had not always been confident of his own judgment. This had now changed.

At eleven-fifteen the *Thompson* docked at MULBERRY "A" amid the hustle and bustle of vehicles off-loading which formed a vast conveyor belt from the sea to OMAHA Beach and up its bluffs, now swept clean of most obstacles and debris. At the First Army Headquarters near Pointe du Hoc, the VIP group joined Gerow and Bradley, who briefed the gathering during a luncheon of K rations.

There were problems. MULBERRY "A" and OMAHA were still under enemy artillery fire. The two-division VIII Corps attacks to cut the base of the Cotentin Peninsula and cover Collins' attack on Cherbourg, set for the nineteenth, had encountered rough going. The newly trained 90th Division had failed to expand the 82nd Airborne bridgehead over the Merderet, apparently due to overcaution by its commander, who was soon to be relieved. Bradley would reorganize the attack by dropping the 90th back to protect the flank of the veteran 90th Division off-loading at UTAH. The bridgehead lacked depth everywhere, but the German Seventh Army seemed to lack coherence and to be coping "at all costs with the immediate situation."

In his briefing, Bradley spoke of his satisfaction over how the battle had developed in his sectors. He had expected a flood of German infantry to arrive on the heels of the German armor. Instead, only two divisions had arrived from Brittany, which he attributed in part to the bombing of the Loire and Seine bridges and enemy knowledge that the Allies were capable of further landings. In any event, the infantry divisions, which might have been most useful to the enemy in the hedgerows of the Cotentin, had not shown up, and soon the build-up would reach a stage where there would be no point along the Normandy front from which Von Rundstedt could safely withdraw troops. Pilfering troops from the British front near Caen to reinforce the American sector would risk a tank breakthrough on the British flank. And as he would later write, the enemy could not risk St.-Lô or an American breakthrough that would pin down German forces in the Cotentin and "finish forever his hope for arresting and thereafter destroying our beachhead."

That day a seesaw battle raged at nearby Carentan. After lunch, news arrived that the 101st Airborne Division had taken Carentan, followed by word of major counterattacks spearheaded by the 17th SS Panzer Grenadier. Foreseeing the German move, Bradley had reinforced the 101st with two regiments. The VIP party traveled on to the village of Isigny, destroyed in the V Corps attack westward, then returned to OMAHA later in the afternoon. Gault noted the high morale of the commanders and that the units hummed efficiently as they moved supplies and troops ashore in a "workmanlike atmosphere of getting the job done," all in "excellent spirits and full of quiet confidence." The skies on the ten-mile bridgehead were clear of enemy planes, visible proof that the aerial campaigns of early 1944 had gained the Allies complete superiority and evidence that "the cat's hold" on the beachheads had become "a panther claw."

As the VIP party rolled along in a phalanx of jeeps, the troops cheered Eisenhower. "There's Ike," several shouted, "the old man himself!" As they saluted and waved, Eisenhower expansively waved back.

Aboard the U.S.S. *Thompson* during the return transit, Marshall talked to Eisenhower about his postwar future as Army Chief of Staff. "Why do you think we have been pushing you?" Marshall asked him. "When the war is over, I expect that you have ten years of hard work ahead of you."

"General," Eisenhower replied, "I hope then to have a long rest."

A day later, Second Lieutenant John Eisenhower arrived at Prestwick, Scotland, after an ocean crossing aboard the H.M.S. *Queen Mary* with the U.S. 7th Armored Division. Knowing that the invasion period would place Eisenhower under the most relentless pressure of his life, Marshall had thoughtfully arranged the visit. In his three-week furlough between gradua-tion and his duty station with the 71st Infantry Division at Fort Benning, John Eisenhower would become reacquainted with his father and his en-tirely new and complicated life. As Eisenhower senior later wrote: ". . . contact with such world figures as Stalin, Churchill, De Gaulle, Adenauer, Khrushchev, Dulles, Patton and Marshall—to name a few—has given me a certain loneliness and difficulty in making small talk."

John's startling initiation had come a week before at the West Point commencement ceremonies on June 6. Instead of spending the day with fellow cadets and family, he and Mamie were confronted by photographers and reporters clamoring for pictures and comment about events in France. A black limousine had whisked the two away from the celebrations early, closing off the easy camaraderie between John and his classmates, including those whose own fathers served as general officers in Italy and France.

John had long been ambivalent about his decision to follow his father through West Point. Since childhood he had nurtured ambitions to write, perhaps to become a novelist or a journalist. As a teenager in the Philippines he had acquired a taste for the remote outposts of American civilization and a desire to explore. He returned from the Philippines at seventeen with a suitcase full of imaginary dispatches "filed" as a correspondent for the New York *Herald Tribune*. After completing high school at Fort Lewis, he had responded to eighteen years of "persuasion" and become a cadet at West Point, but he had not abandoned his ambition completely. Still bristling over the sudden intrusion of reporters at his graduation, John sensed that June 6 had put off his writing ambitions even further.

At Prestwick, John entered a strange new world. Colonel "Tex" Lee, a member of Eisenhower's personal staff, was on hand to greet him and escort him to London. England in June 1944 was a "romantic and heroic place," and John later described the excitement of the train ride from Prestwick and his first view of London. Aboard "Bayonet," Lee brimmed with reports of the battle in Normandy. On their arrival John witnessed a city enveloped in the high drama of invasion. All the while, the British went about their business in a matter-of-fact way, braving an uncertain future with a courage that impressed the Americans who visited the city.

At Widewing on the fourteenth, the two Eisenhowers enjoyed a reunion in the General's drafty, cement-floored office. They were occasionally interrupted by the crush of briefing officers and reports from the front, which gave John a chance to observe his father in this new setting. He observed Eisenhower's crisp efficiency in moving along dozens of projects, and was dazzled by the scope of his responsibility. That day Eisenhower was at work on the problem of the late supply convoys at OMAHA and divisional allotments on the First Army flank. He chaired a planning conference, consulted with the British Foreign Minister on De Gaulle's abrupt visit to Bayeux on the thirteenth, and attended a briefing on the performance of German and Allied divisions along the front.

In the next several days the Eisenhowers spent the late afternoon and evenings with guests at Telegraph Cottage. There were reunions with "Uncle Everett" Hughes and Patton over dinners that John's father cooked in a tall chef's hat on the new patio behind the glassed-in porch, followed by serious after-dinner bridge games attended by hosts of orderlies. John noted that a slight "military barrier" had grown up between father and son. During a twilight stroll through the woods behind the five-acre Telegraph Cottage compound, John, walking to his father's left, posed a question. "If we should meet an officer who ranks above me but below you, how do we handle this? Do I salute first, and when he returns my salute, do you return his?" John knew he raised an unresolved point of Army protocol which his father sidestepped with a smile. "John, there isn't an officer in this theater who doesn't rank above you and below me."

Little by little, the post-invasion euphoria was wearing off. The day before John's arrival in Britain, a new era of warfare opened as the first German V-1's struck targets in Brighton, Kent and London, bringing the ancient city once again within the zone of fire. In the first attacks on the twelfth, ten rounds were fired, of which four reached England causing minor damage. Though MI-6 cautioned that June 12 had simply been a misfire and worse was to come, many suspected that the V-1 had been a bluff, after all.

Talk that the V-1 was an elaborate hoax ended on Thursday, June 15. That day, thirteen V-1's fell on London, followed three days later by a major attack in which rockets exploded at five-minute intervals, striking the Guards' Chapel at Wellington Barracks, several blocks from 10 Downing Street, Buckingham Place and Parliament, killing 80 officers and family members and wounding 120. Fearing panic in London, Churchill cut short a stay at Chequers to assume charge of the V-1 countermeasures, beginning with the evacuation of Parliament to Church House for the duration of the war.

Later attacks that month would demonstrate that the V-1, though of limited effect militarily, was an effective terror weapon. Underlying concern about the V-1 were worries that the rate of fire might dramatically increase, or that the now proven V-1 was only the first in a series of new weapons about to make an appearance. The ramjet V-1 was closely linked with the development of liquid-fuel rockets and associated in a general way in the minds of military planners with other new weapons, such as the V-T proximity fuze being developed in America, new kinds of gas and superweapons like the atom bomb also being developed in America with the aid of scientists who had escaped Hitler's Europe. The War Cabinet met daily to discuss V-1 countermeasures and British retaliation. On the eighteenth, the matter came before Tedder, who "directed" the Eighth Air Force and Bomber Command under POINTBLANK. That day the BCOS, exercising rights reserved in the Portal-Tedder accord, formally requested Eisenhower to revise his air directive and place CROSSBOW—the anti–V-1 campaign— at the top of the targeting priority list.

Eisenhower and Tedder were reluctant to divert bombers for CROSSBOW. The V-1 projectiles fired that week flew under 8,000 feet at a speed of only 250 miles per hour, well within the capacity of RAF interceptors, and the early V-1 attacks struck mostly residential areas and posed little hazard to the air and naval complexes on the southern coast. Harris skeptically noted that an effort to bomb all the launching sites on the Channel coast would involve 10,000 sorties, the loss of 100 airplanes, and 650 trained personnel. But as the attacks intensified, worries about British civilian morale could not be overlooked, and at Churchill's request Eisenhower ruled that V-1 sites would have "first priority over everything except the urgent requirements of the battle." This meant that transport targets surrounding Normandy would retain first priority while CROSSBOW moved up to second priority, ahead of strategic attacks on German ball-bearing plants, airframe plants and synthetic-oil refineries.

For a while in late June, over 20 percent of the strategic sorties would be directed against V-1 sites in the Pas-de-Calais. The War Cabinet rejected proposals for gas attacks, severe reprisals on Berlin or a public ultimatum threatening to "write off" a German village for each V-1 attack on the ground that the Allies, in effect, would be "negotiating" with the enemy, and committing themselves to an extended diversion of strategic bombers from POINTBLANK targets in Germany. The V-1 remote control missile was a sinister phenomenon, another step toward broadening the battlefield to include noncombatants so widely noted by military historians and journalists since 1914. But soon it was clear that "as both a terror weapon and a means of defeating the Allied build-up, the flying bomb was not decisive."

The weapon had nuisance value—indeed, several times that week, air raid sirens and the distinct buzz of an approaching missile sent dinner guests at Telegraph Cottage scurrying to a small, moundlike cement bunker built at Churchill's insistence behind the rear porch. In his diary, Butcher chronicled the first time the group was awakened by a V-1 alert. Eisenhower declined to take shelter, vowing he was not going to succumb to concern about his personal safety and wind up spending every night of his life shuttling back and forth between his room and a shelter below ground. But the terrific impact of a hit two hundred yards away convinced him otherwise, and the entire household retired to the bunker.

Meanwhile, letdown began to creep into the accounts of the battle. In Normandy, progress was steady but slow. Within seventy-two hours of Eisenhower's tour of OMAHA, the American and British armies had been linked up, along the sixty-mile front, but they remained short of the post–D-Day "phase lines" drawn up in April to estimate progress inland.

At SHAEF, concern centered on the British sector. Twenty-first Army Group plans had envisioned tank columns pushing well south of Caen by D plus 14 to gain airfields and force a campaign on terrain where the Allies would reap the full benefit of air and mobile superiority. At Villers-Bocage, the 12th SS repulsed the British 7th Armored, blocking Dempsey's "right hook." German armor also blocked the Canadians at the Carpiquet airfields; and Caen, a D-Day objective, seemed beyond reach. Prospects for the deep bridgehead beyond Alençon and Argentan by D plus 25 were, as Tedder put it at a conference at Stanmore on the fourteenth, "remote." The air barons were critical of the slow pace in building up tactical airfields, and irritated by persistent 21st Army Group requests for tactical air support. At Stanmore, Air Marshal Arthur Coningham, commander of the Second British Tactical Air Force, ventured to say that the withdrawal of the British Seventh Armored behind Tilly was a "severe setback," and that in fact the Army plan had "failed" because of undue caution. Indeed, by the fourteenth, lead elements of the 2nd Panzer from Amiens were identified, bringing to four the number of confirmed panzer divisions on the Second Army front. In the battle for Villers-Bocage, U.S. V Corps artillery intervention had prevented a rout, but the British had been forced to retreat and Dempsey warned that Caen could be taken "by a set piece assault and we do not have the men or ammunition for that at this time."

It was said that like many of his RAF colleagues, Coningham, a gruff, physically imposing man, nursed grudges against Montgomery, with whom he had served during the Eighth Army campaigns in Egypt and Libya. Montgomery's high-handed treatment of the air staffs in North Africa had grated, as had the enormous press build-up of Montgomery, beginning at the battle of El Alamein. But the problem was the tone of Dempsey's orders and appraisals, combined with Second Army requests for heavy air intervention in the siege of Caen which seemed to confirm Coningham's frank criticism of Army leadership. That day the Stanmore group discussed 21st Army Group proposals for an "aerial offensive" southwest of Caen to build up frontline morale. An unidentified participant gasped, "Cassino!"

On the fifteenth, with wind of Montgomery's new strategy for an aggressive defense near Caen, Eisenhower scheduled a trip to the British sector. The recent shift of emphasis in 21st Army Group thinking implied that the British halt at Caen had become permanent, and that, furthermore, Montgomery intended to use only a fraction of the British troops ashore offensively.

At 9:05 both Eisenhowers left Portsmouth aboard a C-47, escorted by thirteen P-47 Thunderbolts. They landed at an airstrip near Bayeux and motored to Montgomery's headquarters, a cluster of tents and trucks in the garden of a château on the outskirts. Aides informed Eisenhower that Montgomery was at Grandcamp in conference with General Bradley and would not be back until four o'clock in the afternoon. Adamant about not disrupting the routine of his subordinate commanders, Eisenhower accepted Montgomery's absence graciously. In the eyes of others present, however, Montgomery's absence appeared to be a deliberate discourtesy, a poor omen for future command relations in Normandy.

The entourage continued on to General Dempsey's Second Army headquarters for a firsthand report on the Second Army setback at Tilly. Dempsey complained about obstruction by air officials at SHAEF, who were reluctant to deploy aircraft in direct support of ground troops. According to John's journal, Tedder "quickly called the airmen into a conference to straighten out the matter and especially to avoid any misunderstandings which might hamper the functioning of their set-up later on." Dempsey briefed Eisenhower on plans for a second assault on Villers-Bocage, set for the eighteenth.

The Supreme Commander's party idled away the afternoon. They lingered for lunch at Dempsey's headquarters, then toured Bayeux, which, unlike the majority of Norman villages or towns, had escaped serious damage. The homes were picturesque and many of the windows were adorned with flowers. The open spaces in the suburbs were green and relatively untouched by the artillery and ground fire. John noted that Normandy, cultivated by the Germans as a breadbasket, had been spared the privations of the German occupation.

John found the attitude of the French people "sobering," however. Instead of "bursting with enthusiasm," they "seemed not only indifferent, but sullen." British jeeps and lorries, rumbling through Bayeux on the way to the front five miles distant, passed unacknowledged by townspeople. There was little evidence of an outpouring of pro-Allied sentiment following De Gaulle's visit the day before for speeches and a parade. The wariness of the townspeople in Bayeux surprised John, who had been raised on the lore of the AEF arrival in France twenty-seven years earlier when the First Division paraded down the Rue de Rivoli and the Champs-Elysées in Paris on July 4, 1917, singing "Marching Through Georgia" to shouts of *"Vive l'Amérique!"* The same division had narrowly averted destruction at St.-Laurent six days before.

The prosperity in Bayeux impressed John Eisenhower, as did the absence of evidence of the battle he could hear five miles away. As a six-year-old in 1928, on Sunday outings with his father, he had toured the trenches along the Meuse and Aisne, littered with helmets and bayonets a decade after the Great War. As a boy, he had imagined the great charges across no-man's-land, and he had difficulty picturing current tactics which dispersed men and equipment over such wide distances.

British impressions of liberated France in June of 1944 were similarly subdued. On a tour with Churchill in the British sector on the twelfth, Brooke had noted the devastation of Valognes, Montebourg and the villages in the Orne Valley, and the sad countenances of the Normans, who believed "we were bringing war and desolation to their country." No one could be sure the Allied invasion had succeeded. If it had, De Gaulle's arrival would mean liberation from the Germans, but it would also mean heavy fighting first and the onset of civil struggle in France as the Vichy structure of petty officials and police inevitably collapsed.

As the jeep bumped along, John raised all of this with his father. "Despite everything a soldier is led to believe," Eisenhower observed, "populations usually want to have as little to do with a war going on around them as possible." In his experience, wherever military formations passed, the population kept their eyes downward. "Of course," he mused, "one cannot expect the people to wave flags for several weeks after the arrival of our troops."

At four o'clock the two Eisenhowers returned to the 21st Army Group encampment. Dressed in his turtleneck sweater and tanker's beret, Montgomery greeted them cordially and led them on a tour of his command post, a wood-paneled trailer captured during the Libyan campaign that had once belonged to Rommel. Montgomery lived in the solitude of a rustic camp, isolated from his main 21st Group Command center. He had with him only a small personal staff: an American liaison officer, two British aides, a Canadian PA (personal assistant), and a British MA (military assistant). A signal detachment and a security guard equipped with black American jeeps rounded out the entourage. Dusty and fatigued, John retired to a nearby tent for refreshments as the two generals stepped up a short ladder into the cabooselike trailer and drew the panel door shut.

The Eisenhower-Montgomery conference on June 15 was significant, their first since Hitler's decisions on the night of June 9–10. German dispositions confirmed an intention to hold at Caen, guarding communications with Paris and Belgium while slowly yielding ground in the American sector. This gave the Allies a period of grace, which they had to exploit decisively as fresh reports indicated that the 1st SS from Antwerp and the II SS Panzer Corps, which had detrained in Lorraine, were on the march to Normandy.

That day, Eisenhower approved Montgomery's policy of "taking the firm defensive" at Caen: by this, Eisenhower understood Montgomery to mean continuous attacks to engage German mobile forces so as to frustrate their attempts to disengage armor and substitute infantry in order to gather armored reserve for counterattack. After the U.S. VII Corps cleared Cherbourg, both men looked to expansion of the American lodgement southward into Brittany, which would gain "breathing space" while stretching an already overextended German line to the breaking point. Again, Montgomery spoke of the long-range possibilities. Before the landings, no one had known whether the enemy would defend Normandy with significant forces or withdraw. The German decision to contain the bridgehead, which meant slow progress now, also meant that Normandy would probably evolve into the decisive battle in France. The German Fifteenth Army would enter the fray step by step, though presumably the Allies would maintain preponderance. And as Bradley pushed out, it was conceivable that victory would come with dramatic suddenness and possibly result in rolling up the Germans in France.

Eisenhower agreed that the long-range possibilities were impressive, since without reinforcements the Germans could hardly hope to contain the bridgehead, and failure to do so would probably lead to a German collapse in France. However, the short-term problem remained: that of coordinated American-British action to pin down German armor in the British sector so as to ease Bradley's passage to Brittany. In Eisenhower's opinion, the bridgehead was not deep enough on the British flank. To his way of thinking, all the lessons of Salerno and Anzio had shown that "there could be no halt until the deepest and widest bridgehead was won." Eisenhower readily conceded to Montgomery the difference between a plan and "hoped-for results," but the British Second Army had not gained enough ground. In turn, Montgomery seemed to step back from his commitment at St. Paul's that the Second Army would "crack about and force the battle our way." He spoke of "balance" and "maneuver," and of stratagems to draw in enemy forces along the Orne, then to induce "excessive resistance at one point to stretch and break [the Germans'] lines at another" in a battle he felt would eventually result in a decisive victory over Von Rundstedt's overextended forces.

The meeting was exploratory. Eisenhower, like Bradley, agreed with the essentials of Montgomery's basic policy, but the potential for misunderstanding was there. Indeed, Montgomery and Brooke would gain the impression that though Eisenhower "made himself responsible for his Lieutenant's strategy . . . he never seems wholly to have understood it." That plan was, according to Montgomery, "to pull the Germans on to Second Army so that First Army can extend and expand," as spelled out in the phase lines followed up by the quick seizure of Cherbourg and the Brittany ports, to be followed up by defeating the Germans between the Seine and the Loire. Eisenhower agreed, but differed with Montgomery on one aspect of strategy: tactics on the British flank. Whereas Montgomery appeared to favor "pulling" the German forces on the British Second Army, Eisenhower favored a more aggressive approach of *pushing* out with the British Second Army in order to engage and pin down German forces at Caen. Time was an important factor in Eisenhower's thinking also.

The Eisenhowers flew back to Portsmouth. In his diary, Butcher described the V-1 bombardment and the somewhat disappointing news of fighting in Russia. "The Russians are advancing in the Karelian Isthmus but have not started offensives in other sectors," he wrote. "In the meantime, intelligence reports that Germans are moving an infantry division from as far away as Jutland to France. Perhaps the Russians are waiting for the German movement Franceward to gain momentum before they begin their wallops."

In the next forty-eight hours, progress was steady in the American sector. Shortly after the 9th Division kicked off, General Eddy informed Bradley that the German Seventh Army was gradually conceding the Cotentin Peninsula north of Coutances. Two German divisions had fallen back to reinforce Cherbourg, while two others formed a defensive line across the neck of the peninsula to block expansion toward Avranches and Brittany. On the seventeenth General Collins telephoned to confirm that the 90th and 82nd had formed an eighteen-mile screen across the peninsula, sealing Cherbourg off from further German reinforcement.

Collins, a veteran of Guadalcanal, quickly formed VII Corps into three columns to advance north. Barton's 4th Division attacked along the northern coast. The 79th was in the center. On the left, Eddy's 9th jogged a full 90 degrees north in twenty-two hours. At 3 A.M. on the eighteenth, VII Corps attacked. Eddy's quick swing provided the impetus for a fast advance up the peninsula, and disrupted German efforts to organize the static troops in the hills east of the harbor.

In his first Normandy directive issued on the nineteenth, Montgomery ordered attacks to take Cherbourg and the resumption of Dempsey's right

N

Cherbourg

Montebourg

Merderet

Ste-Mère-
Eglise

6

Barneville

Douve

La Haye-
du-Puits

Carentan

Isig

79   8   90   4
                    83

243   353   91   2 SS
                    17 SS PG

Périers

1   3 2

9   4

30

5 PARA

LEHR

St-

3

Taute

Coutances

ALLIED FRONT
AS OF:

━━━━━ Morning, June 10, 1944
━━━━━ Midnight, June 30, 1944
- - - - - Midnight, July 24, 1944

SITUATION AS OF
MIDNIGHT,
JULY 24, 1944:

──o── Army boundary
──•── Corps boundary

116   Infantry division
6   Allied armored division
2   German armored division

GERMAN

SEVENTH

ARMY

Granville

Avranches

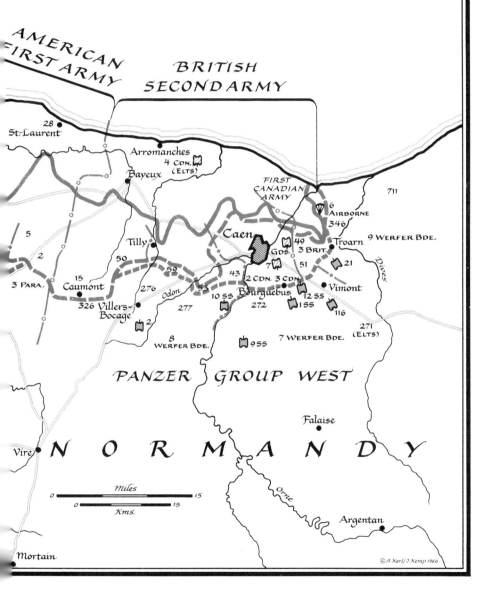

English Channel

THE BATTLE OF NORMANDY

AMERICAN FIRST ARMY

BRITISH SECOND ARMY

St-Laurent 28

Arromanches

4 CDN. (ELTS)

Bayeux

FIRST CANADIAN ARMY

711

6 AIRBORNE

346

9 WERFER BDE.

5

2

Tilly

Caen

49

Gds. 3 BRIT

Troarn

50

52

43

7

51

21

Dives

3 PARA.

15

Caumont

276

Odon

53

2 CDN. 3 CDN.

Vimont

326 Villers-Bocage

277

10 SS

Bourguebus

272

12 SS

1 SS

116

2

271 (ELTS)

8 WERFER BDE.

955

7 WERFER BDE.

PANZER GROUP WEST

Falaise

N O R M A N D Y

Vire

Miles

0   15

Kms.

0   15

Orne

Argentan

Mortain

© A. Karl/J. Kemp 1986

hook on Caen, which, though optimistic in tone, emphasized the avoidance of danger and exposure. In his summary of the battle to date, Montgomery applauded the linkup of all five beaches on a continuous front, and noted that Dempsey and Bradley had retained the initiative. Twenty-five British and American divisions were ashore and being kept at full strength via reinforcement, and "we are at a strong point administratively." Montgomery's conclusions were troublesome; he portrayed the setback at Tilly as part of a master plan and minimized the stalemate at Caen. "At present," he wrote, "our armies are facing in different directions. Once we can capture Caen and Cherbourg and all face in the same direction, the enemy problem becomes enormous."

> The actual threat in Normandy then becomes a big anxiety and it will probably take precedence over other potential threats, e.g., the Pas de Calais. It is then that we have a mighty chance—to make the German Army *come to our threat,* and to defeat it between the Seine and the Loire.

Late on the eighteenth, as Dempsey prepared to launch VIII Corps attack over the Odon, a northwest wind, at a 4- to 5-level force, swept down upon the Channel from Norway to usher in overcast and a cloud base at 2,000 feet. By the evening, the wind at Portsmouth began to freshen. That night the rains began, and Montgomery, still awaiting the arrival of the entire British VIII Corps, called off attacks in the Caen sector.

By the next morning, the 4- to 5-level breeze had turned into gale-force winds 6 to 7. SHAEF weather service at Stanmore, unable to pick up weather patterns over Norway and Scandinavia, had not detected the front. Bradley recalled his surprise on awakening "to an ominous wind, a leaden sky, and a cold scaley rain that tore at the tent flaps." By nine, Montgomery had confirmed the postponement on the British front, and Eisenhower had canceled plans to fly to France for a visit.

Meanwhile Admiral Ramsay had dispatched hundreds of tons of supplies for the St.-Laurent and Arromanches MULBERRYs to make good on the shortages accumulated since the sixth, specifically to alleviate a critical ammunition deficiency in the American zone. As the weather worsened, unloading stopped and the small craft towing cargo from south England tried to take refuge near shore. Craft in the vicinity of the beaches hid behind the GOOSEBERRY breakwaters. The winds rose, and by nightfall MULBERRY "A" began to disintegrate. The outer breakwaters dragged against the current, the caissons shifted, and ships in port dragged anchor.

Ramsay phoned Eisenhower at Telegraph Cottage to report inclement weather and severe damage to the MULBERRY "A" moorings. In his weather memo the next morning, Group Captain Stagg described the catastrophe that would have overtaken NEPTUNE had the landings been put off to mid-month, sudden gale winds and heavy seas making landings impossible. Eisenhower scribbled: "Thanks, and thank the Gods of war we went when we did!—D.E."

TROUBLES

Between the nineteenth and twenty-third, a series of gales swept the Calvados coast, wreaked havoc in the bridgehead, forced suspension of all off-loading and postponement of Dempsey's enveloping offensive toward Caen for a week. For a while the heavy seas and winds seemed to imperil the Allied hold on Normandy itself, a gloomy backdrop for the closing arguments on ANVIL, which Churchill meanwhile brought to a climax within ninety-six hours after the CCS recessed in harmony on the fourteenth.

In retrospect, CCS unity on the fourteenth had been superficial. In the brief afterglow of the landings, it had been easy to forget that Marshall's open-mindedness and the entire accord were contingent on fast-breaking events, and that hard choices had to be faced soon. From Marshall's point of view, progress in Normandy (article [a] of Wilson's directive) was still uneven as the Chief of Staff arrived in Naples for conferences with Wilson and Alexander on ANVIL. The Russian summer offensive (article [b]) had not begun, a fact trumpeted by Radio Berlin, which broadcast the text of a lecture delivered by Field Marshal Keitel before the National Socialist Indoctrination of Officers in Sonthofen predicting "that the Russians would not attack until the Western Allies had obtained greater success." Limited-scale attacks near Leningrad gave few clues to the scope of Russian intentions.

Behind the scenes in London, the BCOS and the War Cabinet debated the next British move, mindful that in a matter of weeks the combination of ANVIL, the American political conventions and an all but certain German disaster in Poland would submerge British positions on Poland, Rumania, Bulgaria, Hungary, Turkey, Yugoslavia, Greece and even Italy. Brooke's diaries allude to this debate, which encompassed basic points of war policy; specifically, the meaning of Germany's loss of dominance in Europe. Britain had fought six wars in a century to prevent a single power from dominating Europe. As Brooke put it, should British policy begin to look toward building up Germany against the Russian threat years hence? Concern about Russian power raised all the old questions about American rigidity on timely negotiations with Moscow and new ones that apparently divided the BCOS and the War Cabinet. For instance, the British military leadership was beginning to doubt the profitability of standing on the sidelines in OVERLORD and France, where things might be decided quickly for the sake of building up Alexander's summer offensive in Italy. Brooke cordially questioned the purpose of pursuing operations in Italy much further, and by implication questioned both Churchill's judgment and his ability to deliver results any longer in his special relationship with Washington.

In turn, Churchill opposed undermining Alexander's progress north of Rome, for it opened new strategic possibilities. Also, Churchill by now had gone to work to enlist Roosevelt's support for initiatives to combat Russian "intrigues" in Italy and the Balkans, as well as his support for a British-Russian arrangement formalizing occupation duties in that area in which Churchill hoped to salvage Greece as a British responsibility. He hoped to wrap things up before the Russian summer offensive in Rumania, but above all before any final agreement on ANVIL. As the CCS meetings of mid-June had broken up, Churchill's Balkan initiative was still pending. Meanwhile, the State Department remained reluctant to endorse anything "savoring of spheres of influence," while the Russians, though open-minded, were reluctant to agree to arrangements the Americans could not endorse. This stand-off, by freezing Allied-Soviet diplomacy in the Balkans, seemingly implied Allied sanction for Soviet efforts to provide "coherent direction" in the politics of the region. Nor was Churchill appeased by Roosevelt's vague countersuggestions for three-power consultative committees to handle occupation problems in the Balkans or his tentative consent to a three-month "trial effort" carefully framed to meet American objections and avoid connotations of spheres of influence. As for ANVIL, in Churchill's view the critical point now was timing, doing nothing irrevocable that would hinder his effort to hammer out a bargain with Stalin; he was determined, in his words, to "bring order out of chaos" and not to acquiesce in the "communization of the Balkans and perhaps of Italy." And apart from that, Alexander's sudden hundred-mile advance north of Rome that week raised a new problem—that of halting a successful 15th Army Group offensive in progress. British—especially Churchill's—prestige was at stake.

Suddenly the tentative ANVIL accord collapsed. At a meeting in Naples on the sixteenth, Wilson confronted Marshall with sharply upgraded landing-craft estimates for a three-division ANVIL and a questionable estimate that unless troop withdrawals from the 15th Army Group began by June 28, a mere twelve days away, ANVIL would have to be postponed from early August until mid-September. With Alexander in pursuit of the German Tenth Army south of Lake Trasimeno, Wilson opposed any interruption of his progress, and had decided to recommend cancellation of ANVIL and "exploitation through the Ljubljana gap into the plains of Hungary," which he felt would be "a less direct but more effective" method of assisting OVERLORD.

Wilson's estimate of the time needed to collect forces for an operation planned since August 1943 seemed fantastic. For SHINGLE, two assault divisions had been organized from forces engaged in a siege on the Sangro within three weeks of CCS approval. The practical effect of delay until mid-September would be to cancel landings at Bordeaux as well, which were to be coordinated with the later phases of OVERLORD, and delay in Marshall's book just meant more delay. Marshall repudiated the AFHQ assessment, then warned Wilson that he had long regarded Marseilles as the essential port of entry for 40 to 50 divisions training in America. Marshall returned to Washington for the final showdown on ANVIL.

Was a compromise possible? Evidently, Churchill doubted it, but he was not finished arguing the matter. To Wilson's formal proposal, submitted on the nineteenth for cancellation of ANVIL and a campaign for pursuit through the Po River and the Ljubljana gap, Churchill affixed the goal of seizing Vienna. In so doing, Churchill chose the most flamboyant method possible for pressing the British case, for nothing faintly as ambitious had been set for OVERLORD.

There is no doubt that Churchill personally framed the Vienna objective. His bid "to renew the war of position and maneuver," long proposed by the British Chiefs, now brought him into conflict with Brooke, the architect of the Mediterranean strategy, and even with Wilson, who as Mediterranean commander in chief would be required to defend the Vienna plan on military grounds. Wilson questioned whether 21 to 30 Allied divisions could be profitably deployed into the southern Alps. Both Brooke and Wilson opposed ANVIL, but they also opposed Vienna as impractical and bound to "stir up all of Marshall's old suspicions about British policy in the Balkans," as Brooke put it in his diary. As Brooke told Churchill on the twenty-second, in an attack on the Ljubljana Gap, Alexander "should have three enemies instead of one": the topography, the weather and the Germans. The scheme, in Brooke's opinion, seemed predicated on German disintegration, a very poor basis on which to draw up military plans and commitments. So far Brooke, Dill and Wilson had gained concessions by constantly defending Italian operations in terms of aiding OVERLORD by pinning down German reserves that would otherwise be shifted to France. Within these strictures, Brooke proposed to protect Alexander.

For Eisenhower, whose recommendation was due shortly, the building crisis on ANVIL came as a surprise and disappointment. Eisenhower had been highly encouraged by the CCS meetings at which Marshall had taken the initiative in trying to hammer out a compromise, a significant change from March, when the American Chiefs had talked in terms of ironclad commitments. Apparently, Eisenhower was attracted by the idea of CA-LIPH. The operation satisfied Eisenhower's requirements for reinforcements; it meant opening a front close to the scene of major battles that summer; it would avoid difficulties with the British over Marseilles, which in British eyes was too remote from Normandy and too close to Italy.

Eisenhower had everything to gain by compromise. He was no more

eager to see Alexander's offensives halted in midstream than to relinquish
the ten divisions he expected to get in ANVIL. Among other things, Churchill had long hinted that an active theater in Italy would tend to turn British
attention away from France and mean fewer problems with Montgomery.
With this in mind, Eisenhower indicated to Wilson on the sixteenth that he
would actually prefer Bordeaux to Marseilles, but that if Bordeaux proved
impractical because of the constricted beaches, "the comparative merits of
the ANVIL assault are better known to you [Wilson] than to me."

But chances of compromise collapsed on the nineteenth. As the storm
broke over the Channel, General Wilson had responded to Eisenhower in
a long document devoted to raising a "fundamental issue of military policy." Wilson began by informing Eisenhower of his talks with Marshall,
who had "brought out for the first time a point which seems to me to be
of paramount importance, not clear to me from previous telegrams, namely
that there are between 40 and 50 divisions in the United States which cannot
be introduced into France as rapidly as desired or maintained there through
the ports of northwest France or by stages through the United Kingdom,
mandating, 'another major port' in France." Wilson had concluded that
Bordeaux was too small and probably "too hazardous" as well, despite the
presence of only one German division in the area. Therefore the choices
narrowed to two—Marseilles and Trieste. Wilson went on to say that the
strategic problem of sacrificing Alexander's pursuit in order to secure port
facilities for the extensive American build-up in France

> seems to me to face the Combined Chiefs of Staff with a decision as to whether
> our strategy in the coming months is to be aimed at the defeat of Germany this
> year, or, while making every endeavor to defeat him this year, at assuring his
> defeat in the first half of 1945.
>
> I assume from your telegram that the danger of your bridgehead being forced
> back into the sea is now past; and therefore that the strategy best calculated to
> assist the success of OVERLORD is to produce such an effect on enemy resist-
> ance thereto that your advance through France is *fast* and *continuous*. To strike
> a blow which may cause the enemy to divert or withdraw divisions from France
> and at the same time face him with the *prospect of defeat this year* appears to me
> to be the best way of doing this.

Wilson elaborated at length on the military factors involved in this strategic question. ANVIL would be "impracticable" until August 15 "without
prejudicing the operations in progress"; ANVIL would impose a six-week
pause and a halt south of the Pisa–Rimini line, and break up a first-class
fighting machine "in which cooperation between ground and air has
reached an exceptional and increasing degree of efficiency after months of
hard work"; pursuit in Italy held out "really decisive results" should the
present success in Italy be exploited "through the Pisa–Rimini line across
the Po and then to advance towards southern Hungary through the Ljubl-

jana Gap." Wilson enclosed an extended forecast: a mid-July attack on Florence, a bridgehead across the Po by August, and by the end of the month a strike toward Venice followed by a march on Trieste and Ljubljana in conjunction with amphibious assaults and paratroop operations to mount the Alps.

Wilson's communication dispelled any lingering thought that the enervating ANVIL dispute would end quietly. In practical terms, Wilson's removing Bordeaux as a compromise choice apparently narrowed Eisenhower's remaining choices to three: to endorse ANVIL in August or later, which meant relinquishing ten divisions until fall; to endorse operations in the Adriatic, which meant relinquishing ten divisions altogether; to endorse ANVIL at the expense of halting Alexander in his tracks and all the trouble which that entailed. But in narrowing the issue, Wilson confronted Eisenhower with this unavoidable fact: *any* compromise would embarrass AFHQ operations. And in raising "fundamental issues" of military policy and the prospect of putting off victory until 1945, Wilson hinted that the British would not be evasive about the wider implications of ANVIL, which included passive acceptance of a Russian invasion of the Balkans and a drawn-out winter campaign that would result in the destruction of central Europe and Russian domination of the area.

Eisenhower could not have failed to recognize that Wilson's message was one of the most significant of the war, a political and military document comparable to the long-ago "Marshall memorandum," which he himself had drafted. Significantly, as in the Marshall memorandum, the most striking feature of Wilson's challenge was its unreality. First, Wilson assumed that the American Joint Chiefs would suddenly consider Vienna or completely reassess the method of committing 40 to 50 American divisions in Europe with the Normandy battle at its height. Second, he insisted that a Vienna strategy was a practical alternative, which even the BCOS knew was not so. Third, he assumed that the Allies had the power to devise a timetable for ending the war, a suggestion that could stem only from special knowledge of Russian intentions or of a German "collapse." This unreality suggested that Wilson's document, like the Marshall memorandum, was not so much a "military" proposal to exploit an illusory Allied freedom of action but an attempt to influence policy months, perhaps years, hence.

There the similarities ceased. First, whereas Marshall in 1942 had confronted the British with the possible consequences of failing to face the possibility of a German victory over Russia, Wilson, with Churchill's backing, confronted the Americans, and Eisenhower in particular, with the consequences of not facing a Russian victory over Germany. This opened the whole range of issues and responsibility for their postwar consequences in terms that no one had faced before in so many words. Second, whereas debate over the Marshall memorandum had occurred before the commit-

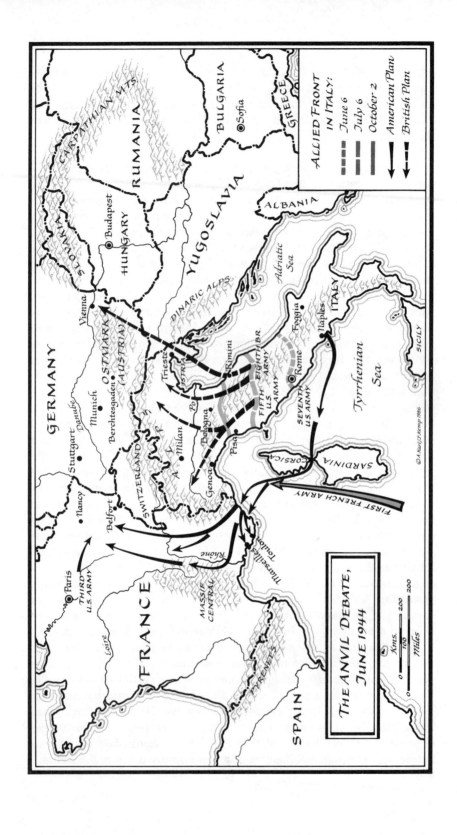

THE ANVIL DEBATE,
JUNE 1944

ALLIED FRONT
IN ITALY:
June 6
July 6
October 2
American Plan
British Plan

©A.Karl/J.Kemp 1986

ment of major forces in the field, Wilson's wire raised fundamental questions of military policy at a time when significant forces were actively committed to battle. Third, whereas in 1942 the British had been in a position to resolve an internal American quarrel over the second front by assuming blame for turning Marshall down, the reverse was not true. Perhaps a compromise of sorts was possible, but the Americans could not accept responsibility for the loss of eastern Europe, and because of their growing preponderance in Europe, they would not have to accept it.

But in practical terms it was evident that the Americans, specifically Eisenhower, would have to assume the sole onus of ANVIL, which had been agreed upon at Teheran and which in Marshall's mind was the key to Allied-Soviet cooperation. Churchill intended to make this decision as painful as possible, and for Eisenhower, choosing ANVIL would indeed be painful. For months Eisenhower had promoted compromise on ANVIL and had gone out of his way to prove his impartiality and the open-mindedness of the American Joint Chiefs to alternatives to the point of hinting that he and the American Chiefs would support "any diversionary operation" worthy of the name when the time came, *including* one in the Adriatic. Of course, no one in the months following Teheran had foreseen that a diversionary operation in the Mediterranean might halt Alexander's 15th Army Group offensive in progress, nor had Eisenhower anticipated the slow initial progress in Normandy, which made forgoing the reinforcements ANVIL would deliver through Marseilles unthinkable. At least Wilson had stopped short of calling ANVIL impossible, and one virtue of the wire—perhaps a passing one—was that confining debate to Italy versus France in the next several months would distract attention from potential differences between Eisenhower and Montgomery.

In retrospect, one might say that Eisenhower was encountering his first real brush with American politics as well. For, as yet, the American government had not begun to prepare the American public for the political consequences of the European war. Indeed, as the election year wore on, Europe First still rested in part on exaggerated promises of likely American gains in Europe, the ease of the Allied war effort, and minimizing the prospect of Russian gains. That the Americans should reject Vienna on June 19 was obvious to Eisenhower, who was commanding an Army battling the Germans in Normandy. He needed reinforcements, and assurances of close Russian cooperation in the coming weeks and months. Perhaps this was obvious as well to the Congress and the American public, which for the first time confronted the prospect of heavy casualties in France. But the Congress and the American public had not been consulted step by step on the details of war policy, and might therefore be receptive to suggestions down the road that "concessions" to the Russians had not been inevitable or necessary in June 1944.

Years later I talked with General Lucius Clay, who in the summer of 1944 had left the Office of War Mobilization to join SHAEF as deputy in Normandy for administration and civil government. We discussed the bearing of such wartime debates as ANVIL on Eisenhower's eventual entry into politics. Clay, as Eisenhower's most intimate counselor between 1945 and 1952, would be one of the few figures to bridge Eisenhower's military and political careers. He readily acknowledged the implications for Eisenhower's political future of likely postwar charges that high officials had treasonably accepted Soviet influence over Allied military strategy, charges that originated in Eisenhower's arguments with the British beginning in late June 1944. I asked Clay if Eisenhower perceived these political implications at the time, and whether he was in fact aware that he was being marked as a future political figure. Clay replied, "Of course."

At Portsmouth on June 20, Eisenhower still looked for ways of reviving CALIPH, which, whatever its military merits, would allow the British to reopen the question of Alexander's eventual objective by maintaining an agreeable separation between the two theaters. His formal recommendation was on hold, pending consultation with Marshall and a meeting set with Churchill on the twenty-third. Twice on the twentieth Eisenhower communicated with Marshall about developments in Normandy and the Wilson memorandum.

First, inclement weather on the twentieth had again forced most shipping from southern England to turn back. Heavy waves pounded the Calvados coast and seriously damaged MULBERRY "A." Over five hundred vessels were beached in both sectors. Eisenhower warned Marshall that "new conditions" caused by the "large percentage of loss" of traffic and small craft in the Channel underscored the importance of the "quick capture of Cherbourg," which required all-out naval and air support. He observed that the storm, by bringing operations to a standstill at Caen and permitting the Germans to regroup, was bound to have an impact on the planning for Italian operations. He assured Marshall that "wandering off overland via Trieste to Ljubljana repeat Ljubljana is to indulge in conjecture to an unwarrantable degree *at the present time*," and promised that "detailed reports and new estimates will go forward to the Combined Chiefs of Staff as quickly as possible." Eisenhower concluded:

> AFHQ apparently fails to appreciate that achievement of a successful bridgehead in France does not repeat not of itself imply success in operation OVERLORD as a whole. In spite of any local successes achieved in northern France, operation OVERLORD will be in urgent need of any assistance possible from elsewhere for some time to come.

An exchange of messages between SHAEF and Washington ensued, and Eisenhower quickly learned that neither Marshall nor Churchill would permit him to straddle the issue. Marshall cabled Eisenhower to remind him that AFHQ had "gained an advantage" by being first to approach the CCS and that Eisenhower's views were essential to offset the impact of the British. Marshall supported Eisenhower's informal views and he encouraged Eisenhower to follow up in the CCS, assuring him that he and his colleagues in the Joint Chiefs were in complete accord and believed that "there should be no delay in getting a firm decision."

In four lengthy conferences on the twenty-first and twenty-second Eisenhower explored all angles: landing-craft availability; AFHQ estimates; the toll of storm damage on the Normandy build-up. By the night of the twenty-second Eisenhower, having weighed the military and political factors, had made up his mind to act. He met with Lieutenant General Sir James Gammel, Wilson's chief of staff, who was in London to assist the BCOS in its deliberations. Eisenhower told Gammel he "wanted ANVIL . . . [and] that he was against an attack into Hungary via Trieste."

Early on the twenty-third, Eisenhower returned to London for a private meeting with Churchill at 10 Downing Street. John accompanied him and would later describe his introduction to the Prime Minister in the gloom of a midmorning downpour. "This is the worst weather I have ever seen in my life," Churchill grumbled as he ushered the two Eisenhowers into 10 Downing Street for a tour. "They have no right to give us weather like this!"

Eisenhower and Churchill retired to the War Room for a conference. The mood was reminiscent of Tunis at Christmas, but with the roles reversed. Lacking a specific plan like SHINGLE on which to peg the British claim in Italy, Churchill opposed ANVIL, the existing military plan . Churchill made his point—that nothing must interfere with Alexander's pursuit of Kesselring, that all would be lost if the CCS ordered Wilson to start withdrawals by the twenty-eighth. Churchill cited Wilson's estimates that pursuit up the Italian peninsula, by threatening southern Germany, would prevent the transfer of at least five divisions to France, but that preparations for ANVIL would compel an Allied pause lasting six to twelve weeks, permitting Kesselring to regroup and fortify the Gothic Line. Even Wilson's immediate objective, the Pisa–Rimini line, would then be in doubt, which would be unacceptable.

Eisenhower agreed with Churchill that Alexander's success would have a favorable impact in France. But he questioned Wilson's estimates of the time it would take him to organize ANVIL, an operation planned for almost a year. He felt that Alexander's offensive might succeed despite preparation for ANVIL. Eisenhower was willing to talk about a compromise landing site, but progress was slow in Normandy, and so Eisenhower was in no position to turn down timely reinforcements from any source. Eisenhower accepted August 15 as a compromise date. But Churchill was not satisfied, and in parting, he asked Eisenhower to consult Smith before submitting his views to the CCS.

John would recall that heated discussion did not diminish the personal affection between Eisenhower and Churchill, noting, "their friendship was all the more remarkable, because the ultimate war objectives of the British and Americans were in many ways divergent." The two Eisenhowers took their leave and "sloshed out through the rain to the waiting car."

Back at Portsmouth, on the night of the twenty-third, Eisenhower directed Smith to draft a formal statement of his views endorsing ANVIL. In the cable dispatched that night, Eisenhower weighed the technical factors for and against ANVIL. He discussed the availability of landing craft in southern England to satisfy Wilson's request for fifty additional LSTs for a vastly upgraded three-division ANVIL assault despite reported German withdrawals from the Marseilles area. Eisenhower raised the problem Alexander would have in destroying German forces south of the Pisa–Rimini line. He cited the advantages of deploying French divisions in North Africa through Marseilles and the importance of Marseilles on his southern flank after the OVERLORD armies had seized France north of the Loire and prepared to cross the Seine. ANVIL would also tap the resources of the French underground in southern France. Eisenhower cited the impact of the gale winds on off-loading at the OVERLORD beaches, which was bound to cause an unforeseen delay in gaining Brittany. The overriding factor, however, was the character of OVERLORD. Eisenhower summarized Wilson's cable and his discussions with emissaries from Wilson's AFHQ headquarters; then he indicated "the factors which emerge from our conversations":

A. OVERLORD is the decisive campaign of 1944. A stalemate in the OVERLORD area would be recognized by the world as a defeat, and the result on Russia might be far reaching. It is imperative we concentrate our forces in direct support of the decisive area of northern France.

B. ANVIL, with an invasion in the Bay of Biscay precluded, then provides the most direct route to northern France where the battles for the Ruhr will be fought. Moreover, ANVIL initially will contain an appreciable number of German divisions, will give us a port through which reinforcements from the U.S. can be deployed, and will open a route for an advance to the north where these reinforcements can fight on the main battlefield of France.

... Our forces in Italy do not directly threaten an area vital to the enemy who, therefore, has the initiative in deciding whether or not to withdraw out of Italy.

... France is the decisive theater. This decision was taken long ago by the Combined Chiefs of Staff. In my view, the resources of Great Britain and the United States will not permit us to maintain two major theaters in the European war, each with decisive missions.

One day later the American Chiefs endorsed Eisenhower's views and called General Wilson's proposals for northern Italy and the Balkans "unacceptable." The British balked, so in the next several days American-

British arguments resumed, along the same lines as those that had divided the Allies in the March debate over ANVIL.

The British questioned the need for ANVIL in view of the complete success of the Normandy landings and Alexander's advance. American arguments ran the same as before: that Marseilles would be a necessary port of embarkation for the U.S. divisions in America; that Marseilles would be a useful conduit for Free French troops; that ANVIL would divert German resources from northwest France; that it was essential to concentrate on the decisive campaign and avoid overextension by venturing into the Balkans; that the Russians expected the operation to happen.

For four days the weather had been too inclement for flying and the seas too rough to permit Eisenhower to board and disembark from a destroyer. Each morning between the twentieth and the twenty-third Eisenhower rose, received the weather reports and canceled planned visits to American and British sectors to assess the damage of the storm.

Protected by the Calabran reef, the Arromanches MULBERRY had fared well in the four days of storms, but the American MULBERRY, exposed to the northerly winds, waves and swift currents, had been destroyed. OMAHA Beach was littered with wrecked landing craft, random sections of the MULBERRY and tons of other debris, and wreckage. By the twenty-first, unloadings had ceased completely, and by the twenty-third were five days behind schedule, with the ammunition and vehicle situation "bad." Eisenhower warned Marshall that "our situation is *not repeat not* as good as we had reason to expect it would be," and renewed a plea that Admiral King maintain the three battleships, two cruisers and twenty-six destroyers on station which the Navy now proposed to return to the Pacific.

Despite the Channel storm, VII Corps had advanced slowly up the coastline of the Cotentin Peninsula to the outskirts of Cherbourg. The garrison commander, General Karl Wilhelm von Schlieben, issued an order to his officers and troops warning that "withdrawal from present positions is punishable by death," and empowering leaders "to shoot at sight anyone leaving his post because of cowardice." Three U.S. divisions raced against the clock to prevent the Germans from carrying out the wholesale demolition of the port facility, though five days would pass before Collins' VII Corps could break through the German outer perimeter, and the battle raged house by house, street by street. Ninth Air Force saturation bombing failed to dislodge firmly entrenched Germans, whereupon Bradley called on Admiral Kirk to dispatch gunships to level the Fort du Roule bastion, a crucial strongpoint guarding the Cherbourg harbor entrance. On the twenty-fourth the gale weather broke, and Eisenhower departed for Normandy for his long-postponed inspection of the American sector and for consultation with Bradley. By 8 A.M. the two Eisenhowers and a large party had boarded a destroyer for a quick trip to the French coast. South of Portsmouth the entourage moved with a long line of LSTs steaming in formation for Normandy, readying to beach and discharge 10,000 tons of weapons and supplies within twenty-four hours of the abatement of the storm.

The group spent the day at Bradley's First Army Headquarters, located in an apple orchard on a hill overlooking the small town of Isigny. At lunch John enjoyed a reunion with "Gee" Gerow, who was present to brief Eisenhower on the V Corps sector at Caumont. General Henry Crerar, commander of the First Canadian Army, joined the group for a long and sober discussion about future plans. Eisenhower and Bradley discussed for the first time the problem of an American breakout, which both anticipated would eventually occur in the St.-Lô area just to the west of Caumont.

But breakout strategy was still academic until Bradley could solve the immediate problem—Cherbourg—and regain lost momentum. As Bradley recalled, Eisenhower was "moody," and particularly anxious that Bradley push VIII Corps toward Coutances before Collins was finished at Cherbourg in order to capitalize on Dempsey's Odon River offensive, a "right hook" aimed at Caen set to resume on the twenty-sixth. So far the Allies were prevailing in the battle of the build-up and the German containing rope was "under strain." Significantly, the Germans had not been able to take advantage of the storm to organize a reserve for a counteroffensive or to reinforce Bradley's front, but Eisenhower urged Bradley to take advantage of the opportunity "which may not obtain too long."

Otherwise, the day was upbeat. After lunch the entourage took a jeep ride through Isigny to inspect the U.S. 83rd Infantry Division, which had off-loaded at OMAHA that morning. Deriving a lesson in human nature, John noted a contrast between French attitudes in the American zone that day and the attitudes he had observed nine days earlier at Bayeux. Isigny, seized on the eighth of June, had been subjected to the most withering naval gunfire since the British fleet blocked Kesselring's counterattack at Salerno. Yet, unlike their unscathed neighbors in Bayeux, the Norman fishermen of Isigny seemed friendly and robust as they gathered along the road and waved cheerfully at the Eisenhowers' caravan of jeeps winding its way to the 83rd Infantry Division bivouac. In Bayeux the villagers had been cautious because they were afraid of what *might* happen, whereas the people in Isigny had nothing to lose. John mentioned the contrast to Bradley, who was seated next to him. Bradley smiled, and recalled that when the 17th SS had counterattacked at Carentan on the thirteenth, many of the villagers had hauled in the French tricolor they had hoisted twenty-four hours earlier to hail the American arrival. "John," he said, "the people are now convinced that the Allies are here to stay."

Eisenhower and Bradley took time out to inspect the troops of the newly arriving 83rd Division. In his memoirs, Bradley described the typical encounter as Eisenhower moved briskly down the line of assembled troops.

"Soldier, how many experts do you think you have in your rifle squad?"
"Three, sir, I think."
"You think? Soldier, you had better know, dammit. Know exactly what you've got."
(To another.)
"And how many experts do you have?"
"Four. I am one of them, sir."
"Good, that's fine. Where are you from?"
"Kentucky, sir."
"Got a good squad?"
"Best in the company, sir."
"Does the rest of the company think so?"
"Well. . . . , sir."
"Stupid bunch of people are they?" (Laughter.)

The Eisenhowers left for Portsmouth invigorated by the visit. Airborne, they gazed on the storm wreckage at OMAHA, a spectacle to behold. Three hundred hulls of all descriptions littered the American beaches and were only slowly being plowed away by teams of engineers. "There was no sight in the war that so impressed with the industrial might of America as the wreckage on the landing beaches," Eisenhower later wrote. "To any other nation the disaster would have been almost decisive; but so great was American productive capacity that the great storm occasioned little more than a ripple in the development of our buildup."

By the night of the twenty-fourth, reports reached London and Washington of massive Russian attacks on the heavily fortified German garrisons east of Minsk in central Russia. The Soviets reported gains of eighty miles and the near encirclement of Vitebsk along with other fortresses at Orsha, Mogilev and Bobruisk, signs that the Soviets had opened a supreme drive to clear White Russia before advancing into the Balkans. Soon, the Russians would issue an uncontradicted claim that 25,000 German prisoners had been captured in the first ninety-six hours of the attack, among them, for the first time since Stalingrad, German general officers.

Meanwhile the ANVIL debate intensified, with positions hardening in both camps. Back from Normandy, Eisenhower explored contingency plans for landings in Biscay and Brittany, now anxious about the possibility of stalemate in Normandy. He met with Generals Frederick Browning and Lewis Brereton about the possibility of deploying an Allied airborne army in England in an effort to break out of the lodgement area. He attended conferences at Widewing with Spaatz, and took a long inspection trip to Guildford and Exeter, spending the night of the twenty-fifth with Patton, who, like Eisenhower, was restless with the slow progress on the front. Returning to London, Eisenhower attended several conferences with Churchill at 10 Downing Street as the ANVIL debate closed in a storm of acrimony.

British hopes rose after Field Marshal Jan Smuts returned from a tour of AFHQ and reported that Alexander and Wilson, still in pursuit south of Lake Trasimeno, anticipated "no difficulty in the breakthrough to the Po," which, if coordinated with the Russians, might "constitute as serious a threat to the enemy as Eisenhower's advance from the west." For a while Churchill may have entertained visions that Alexander's progress might convert the Americans and stave off the inevitable, for on the twenty-seventh, responding to the American Chiefs, the BCOS raised a host of fresh objections to ANVIL.

In view of the "decisive" nature of northwest France, the BCOS seriously doubted the "wisdom of General Eisenhower releasing landing craft for ANVIL," since General Wilson's latest estimate was that fifty-five additional LSTs were necessary for a suddenly expanded three-division planned assault against the depleted German garrison on the Riviera. The BCOS questioned the "adequacy of air resources in the Mediterranean" to cover the pursuit of Italy and ANVIL simultaneously. Officially the BCOS accepted Wilson's estimate that in order to meet a mid-August deadline, withdrawals would have to begin within ninety-six hours and concluding that "the withdrawal now of forces from Italy to achieve this target date is unacceptable to the British Chiefs of Staff." As an alternative, the BCOS suggested that the overburdened Fifteenth Air Force drop supplies to the Maquis in southern France and that Wilson maintain a "feint" on Marseilles.

"The British proposal to abandon ANVIL and commit everything to Italy is unacceptable," came the fierce JCS reply twenty-four hours later. The American Chiefs disposed of the British case point by point. According to U.S. information, the German force being hounded out of Italy was "whipped"—a mere shell—so the twenty-one divisions Alexander would retain after ANVIL were sufficient to handle the four battle-worthy German divisions left in Kesselring's Tenth Army. The American Chiefs asserted that only "ill-advised determination of Hitler to fight south of Rome" had justified delay in ANVIL in the first place, and predicted that German policy was bound to change "if and when" German generals ousted the Nazis. And should Kesselring's remaining forces do the logical thing and retire behind the Alps, the JCS predicted the Allies would derive a "negligible result from our large Mediterranean forces." The American Chiefs went on to call the BCOS estimates of AFHQ air resources an unacceptable view of "warmaking on the Allied side which is a most serious reflection on the fighting ability of our ground forces." Finally, the JCS noted that General Eisenhower, "the man responsible for the success of OVERLORD," had been consulted and was prepared to spare all necessary landing craft from southern England to make the operation possible, concluding with some of the strongest words in the history of the Anglo-American coalition:

> It is deplorable that the British and U.S. disagree when time is pressing. The British statements concerning Italy are not sound or in keeping with the early end of the war. The U.S. desires to put as many U.S. divisions in France as soon as possible. Progress by Alexander in Italy does not contribute to this. General Wilson wants a decision by 27 June. There is no reason for discussions except to delay a decision which must be made.

Churchill fired off a message to Roosevelt that day in which he complained about the "arbitrary" tone of American proposals. He pleaded that despite everyone's willingness to "help Eisenhower," the principle of concentration of force at the decisive point should not ruin "all our great affairs in the Mediterranean, and we take it hard that this should be demanded of us." Likewise, the BCOS called for "patient discussion to avoid a false step" and urged the Americans to weigh Wilson's point concerning the choice between victory in 1944 or 1945. "The foundation of our strategy should be the continued use of maximum forces wherever the enemy can be induced to fight," the BCOS warned.

> History will not forgive commitment of substantial forces to an operation which will not mature for three critical months and pay small dividends for three more. British Chiefs see no prospect that they can advise his Majesty's government contrary to the stand they have adopted to date.

By the end of June the Alliance had seemingly reached a complete impasse, unable to agree even on basic facts. The American Chiefs were alleging that the German Tenth Army had been reduced to four combat divisions. The British Chiefs claimed that OKW had reinforced the Tenth Army with four OKW divisions, and predicted that OKW would dispatch six more. The British argued that an attack through the Ljubljana gap would divert as many as five divisions from France. Eisenhower countered that an Allied campaign into the Alps would enable the Germans to release troops from Italy to reinforce France.

In a testy cable on the twenty-eighth, Churchill raised several heretofore unspoken issues with Roosevelt, issues that accounted for the hard choices facing the Allies—shortages of American combat reinforcements due to mobilization decisions, and the heavy service and rear-echelon component in the 550,000 troops scheduled to arrive in August. Churchill dismissed alternatives to Italy, specifically "the bleak and sterile Toulon-Marseilles operation," which could not "even with great success, directly influence the battle of 1944," he wrote, which raised "a grave question whether we should ruin all hope of a large victory in Italy and condemn ourselves to a passive role in that theater."

The Prime Minister was done. At a War Cabinet meeting on the twenty-ninth, Churchill, in peak form, announced to his colleagues that he was ready to press on and do battle with the Americans on Alexander's behalf. There were no takers. First, reports from Russia, requiring careful study, indicated that a gigantic attack had developed north of the Pripet Marshes and that the German line in Russia was broken on four fronts. Meanwhile, the news from Normandy was uneven—beaches in certain sectors were still under German artillery fire, Cherbourg was still in enemy hands, and Dempsey's Odon offensive was stalled. Brooke suggested a new approach —saying to the Americans, "All right, if you insist on being damned fools, sooner than fall out with you, which would be fatal, we shall be damned fools with you and we shall see that we perform the role of damned fools damned well."

Afterwards, Churchill phoned Eisenhower and Smith. To each, he sadly acknowledged "the definite purpose of the U.S. Chiefs of Staff to mount an ANVIL." Churchill said the British Chiefs of Staff would probably make one more effort to convince Marshall of the Trieste move, but that they would not permit an impasse to arise, and would, consequently, agree to ANVIL.

Eisenhower informed Marshall of this news, whereupon Roosevelt cabled Churchill to thank him for his latest message conveying the detailed views of Alexander and Smuts on the merits of a campaign on Vienna. "For several natural and very human reasons," Roosevelt wrote, "Smuts and Alexander overlooked two factors involved in Vienna." First, how Vienna "infringed" on grand strategy; secondly, "for purely political reasons over here, I could never survive even a slight setback in OVERLORD if it were known that fairly large forces had been diverted to the Balkans." Finally, Roosevelt was "mindful of the agreement with Stalin on the attack on southern France and his views favoring this assault and viewing all other operations as unimportant."

> At Teheran we agreed upon a definite plan of attack. Now that we are fully involved in our major blow, history will never forgive us if we lose precious time and lives in indecision and debate. My dear friend, I beg you to let us go ahead with our plan. If we can't agree to direct Wilson by 1 July to do the job as quickly as he can, we must send a message to Stalin at once.

Having elicited a rare admission of Stalin's influence in Roosevelt's thinking, the Prime Minister won a moral victory of sorts. On July 2 the CCS issued a directive to Wilson instructing him to launch ANVIL by August 15, though few doubted that Churchill would return to the subject. AFHQ would lose troops, but events were becoming fluid in Russia and time remained for Churchill to explore minimum terms: alternate landing sites outside the Mediterranean that would avoid the connotation that the Allies were afraid to revise plans without consulting Stalin or that Churchill was powerless to talk Roosevelt out of directing all of Alexander's forces into France. On the second, with landings set in six weeks, the Prime Minister petulantly stipulated that ANVIL be rechristened DRAGOON—"done," he later wrote, "in case the enemy had learnt the meaning of the original codeword."

STALEMATE?

As the Channel storm abated, the true picture on the eastern front was anyone's guess, though many sensed that the course of the war was being altered hourly. As Brooke put it, the Germans now were "bound to pay the penalty for their faulty strategy," a strategy that had perplexed the Allies for months but that exposed massive German forces in Russia to defeat and at the same time curtailed Hitler's ability to form reserves in the west, seemingly the worst of both worlds.

In short, the faulty German strategy to which Brooke referred consisted of Hitler's risky and stubborn refusal to abandon the two deep German salients in central Russia and east of the Carpathians, a refusal that accounted for his decision on June 9 to contain the Normandy invasion and not to reinforce France at the expense of Russia. Orthodox strategy for months had called for a German withdrawal to the Riga line and other steps to form a strategic reserve that might have enabled the Germans to wage a prolonged defense of the homeland. But it had become increasingly evident that the Germans saw little point in waging a prolonged set-piece defense of their own borders. And so little about German military strategy made sense from an orthodox point of view, a fact only slowly and grudgingly conceded by many in the Allied high command.

In retrospect one might say that the far-flung German deployments in Russia dramatized the "either or" situation facing Hitler and the Germans. Having gambled all on an attempt to conquer Europe, they had left little room between triumph and total disaster and saw little alternative except to undertake risks on all fronts in the desperate hope of regaining an upper hand by holding, against all odds, seemingly untenable positions from which victorious offensives might eventually be staged. Perhaps there were many Germans who questioned whether this logic applied equally to the West. But all Germans had to contend with the Allied policy of unconditional surrender. No one could question that Germany was in a "do or die" situation in Russia, or that what it would now take to restore the Russian front was likely to undermine the situation in the west long enough to convert the western theater to a "do or die" situation also.

And so the alternative to prevailing on all fronts was total defeat. In June 1944 this was plainly so in Russia, where the Germans had to maintain territory and the illusion of strength for the sake of German morale, and to prevent the defection of Rumania, Bulgaria, Hungary and Finland. In conventional military terms, this meant overextension of precious resources kept in Russia at the risk of a threatening Allied build-up in France, which, as Hitler evidently reasoned, would be confronted in due course when all shades of German opinion grasped the futility of thinking in terms of compromise with the Allies and recognized the "either or" situation confronting Germany.

Very few high-ranking Germans were comfortable with this logic. Inside accounts of the German high command show that Hitler's military advisers were aware that the German hold on both salients in Russia was tenuous. In December 1943, 30 depleted divisions on the eastern front had been erased from OKH ledgers, and during the February–March crisis, Germany had sustained another 800,000 casualties in the Ukraine. With the remaining 170 divisions stretched out over a winding 1,500-mile front and with vulnerable lines of communication running through a countryside infested by well-organized paramilitary partisans, wrong guesses meant the quick loss of 5 divisions, and a strategic miscalculation imperiled 70 to 100 divisions.

Even Hitler's most loyal military advisers shrank from these facts. Colonel General Jodl, OKW Chief of Staff, had been overheard in the course of a long, tedious briefing during the March crisis saying sarcastically that at least none of the Russian successes to date had had a "directly fatal effect." Jodl, joined by Field Marshals Walther Model, Kurt Zeitzler and Fritz Erich von Manstein, before being sacked in the OKH shake-out in March, had suggested straightening and shortening the front in order to form reserves. But Hitler's policy was to hold everywhere, and those around the Führer comforted themselves that such "Stand fast" orders had worked in the past, and that the Russians had been gravely wounded also. "They [the Russians] are bound to wear themselves out," Hitler had remarked in March. "After all, there is no reason to think they are like the mythical giant who grew stronger every time he was struck down! We have lived through many situations which all had thought were beyond repair, and it later turned out the Russians could be brought under control."

Were German hopes so completely unfounded? "Stand fast" tactics had restored the German line west of Moscow in the winter crisis of 1941 and at Rostov in January 1943, where the sacrifice of the German Sixth Army had successfully covered the orderly withdrawal of two army groups and restored the front when the slightest step backward might have degenerated into chaotic, panicky retreat. Indeed, despite the standard expressions of contempt for Hitler's "intuition," Allied generals, including Eisenhower, also greatly feared his influence on the battle. As Wilmot put it, free of a restraining orthodoxy, the Führer often derived more imaginative battle solutions than his generals, who were bound by custom and inhibited, in many cases, by deep misgivings about the all-or-nothing course to which they had been committed. But to stand fast in Russia in June 1944 meant surmounting the seemingly inexhaustible resources of the Soviet Union, their 5 to 1 superiority in men, tanks and airplanes at any selected point and Soviet willingness to absorb casualties also at a 5 to 1 rate.

By early June the German high command was debating the point where the Russians would mount their prime attack. After clearing the Ukraine, the bulk of the Red Army had wheeled northward toward the sensitive Lvov–Brest–Kovel sector southeast of Warsaw. Like Calais, Lvov was a communications center; it linked the segments of the German front north of the Carpathians. A successful Russian drive in Galicia would unhinge two German army groups strung out north of the Pripet Marshes with their backs to the Baltic. Accordingly, 37 divisions, including 11 panzer types between Lvov and Kovel were bunched in a 200-mile line from the base of the Carpathians through Lvov in eastern Galicia to the Vistula at Brest-Litovsk, the staging point for BARBAROSSA in 1941. By contrast, one panzer and 33 infantry divisions of the Army Group Center held the 500-mile Minsk salient from Kovel to Vitebsk in a belt of isolated strongpoints at strategic road and rail junctions, covered on the southern flank by the impassable Pripet Marshes.

Army Group Center, lacking "defense in depth," was highly vulnerable. Field Marshal Ernst Busch, who commanded Army Group Center, had successfully contained winter attacks at Vitebsk but had come to doubt the ability of his army group to withstand the shock of a summer offensive. Unlike Rommel in Normandy, Busch urged withdrawal—from Vitebsk to Napoleon's line on the Berezina, only to be refused, evidently because withdrawal from Vitebsk meant withdrawal from the Leningrad sector, the defection of Finland and losing control of the Baltic.

By mid-June, the German high command was faced with a riddle somewhat similar to what it had faced in France before D-Day. Amid "disturbing and . . . unmistakable" signals, the Germans girded to meet the blow at Brest and Lvov much as Von Rundstedt had organized his defenses at Calais in anticipation of an Allied landing there. But as Russian attacks began in the Leningrad area, signs appeared that the Russians were preparing a frontal attack on Vitebsk, distant from the bulk of German reserves.

Suddenly in mid-June the elite Russian Fifth Guards Army appeared at Smolensk. German intelligence estimated the presence of 4,500 Russian aircraft opposite the Army Group Center sector hundreds of miles east of the "decisive hinge" at Brest. Overruling Busch, Hitler minimized the threat and massed reserves in the Kovel–Brest–eastern Galicia sector. But, as Hermann Gackenholz, historian of Army Group Center, later noted in a critical commentary, Hitler had correctly deemed the Galician sector as the danger point, but he "incorrectly gauged the manner in which STAVKA, the Russian high command, intended to force a decision." This miscalculation in military terms left thirty-three German divisions immobile and exposed in such a way as to risk a disaster exceeding Stalingrad and the defeat inflicted by Germany on France in 1940, to which the imminent Russian victory would be compared.

Just as OVERLORD was gaining a foothold in France, the fateful countdown began in the east. On the fourteenth of June, as the CCS in London wrapped up its deliberations and Marshall left for Italy and discussions with Wilson, a meeting described by Gackenholz took place at OKH Headquarters in Minsk involving all the German army group staff and army group chiefs of staff in Russia. According to Gackenholz, only Army Group Center, consisting of 400,000 men organized into the Third Panzer Army and Fourth and Ninth infantry armies could "submit clear proofs" of an imminent offensive on their fronts. And, he wrote, "sober and unprejudiced appraisal of the situation made it impossible for Army Group Headquarters to suppose that, in view of the extended linear front it was manning, it could possibly cope, without adequate reserves, with the expected large-scale attack." But Hitler again denied Busch's requests to commence immediate German withdrawals behind the Dnieper and Berezina rivers though he agreed to place a panzer division in reserve behind Bobruisk, a threatened stronghold on Busch's southern flank.

Thereafter, in Gackenholz's words, Hitler's solution in the east was to wait and to "belittle the lack of resolve" of his eastern-front commanders. Having denied Busch permission to organize a "mobile defense" of the sector, Hitler designated Vitebsk, Orsha and Mogilev as "strongpoints," and demonstrated again his ability to brush aside Wehrmacht qualms and his willingness to expend a limitless number of lives for desperate ends. Finally, it was Keitel's speech at Sonthofen predicting no Russian attacks until the Allies achieved gains in Normandy that signaled doom for Army Group Center. Gackenholz recorded that a "spirit of resignation" overcame the Army Group Command as the staff in Minsk was left to "wait and see how things would develop."

It was in these circumstances that Hitler had entertained fresh pleas by Rommel and Von Rundstedt for the release of the Fifteenth Army infantry at Calais for action in Normandy. Hitler refused, deeming the Caen sector easily defensible so long as the Caen–Pas-de-Calais highway remained open to permit the flexible and rapid movement of reserves to threatened sectors. Hitler spent most of June at Rastenburg, in East Prussia, gazing at situation maps portending the annihilation of forces in Russia several times the size of the German Seventh Army in Normandy, an obsession shared by the German Army high command to the detriment of a well-coordinated strategy in the battle of the Normandy bridgehead.

Finally, on June 17, Rommel persuaded Hitler to visit France for a conference at Soissons, in the bunker constructed in 1940 for the Führer's use as a command post for the invasion of England. According to Speidel's account, Hitler seemed nervous and distracted, monopolizing the conversation as he rambled on about the V-1 and other miracle weapons. Plainly, he intended no reinforcements for France until he knew the outcome of round four in Russia, and found it painful to be questioned about this decision.

Rommel urged Hitler to reconsider. He described Normandy as a "killing ground," as bad as anything on the eastern front. Despite the lack of Allied progress on the map, the situation was growing more desperate by the hour because of the lack of reinforcements and complete Allied air superiority. Rommel recalled the failure of the June 11 counterattack, and predicted that by waiting at some point along the sixty-mile line stretching from Cherbourg to the Orne, the combination of American and British manpower, sea bombardment and strategic air power would produce a rupture. And a major crack in the German defenses would bring the full weight of overwhelming American and British firepower and mobility into play.

Hitler and Rommel rehashed the issue of Caen. Was the city a pivot for American operations in the Cotentin or a base for British attacks toward the Pas-de-Calais? Hitler claimed that he still expected landings in the Pas-de-Calais, an evasion which in practical terms meant that he could not afford a deeper involvement in Normandy or release units held in reserve at Calais which had to be replaced. The Fifteenth Army was to stand and await the "main landing" at Calais—that is, to be kept intact in order to hold the Seine River after the inevitable sacrifice of the Seventh Army and supporting armored units.

Rommel persisted. Convinced that containment would fail, he recommended drastic measures: either a counteroffensive at Bayeux or a prompt retreat to successive river lines: the Seine and the Somme, then the West Wall. Hitler and Rommel discussed the possibilities of a counteroffensive at the slenderest point of the American zone. Hitler liked the idea, but again refused Rommel latitude over his reserves in France, and refused him permission to withdraw from Normandy, predicting that the V-1 blitz would soon break British morale. According to Speidel, Rommel then confronted Hitler: "Do you believe this war can be won?"

Hitler shouted back, "Look after your invasion front, and don't bother about continuation of the war."

A day later, OKW learned that the U.S. 9th Division had isolated the 91st and 77th divisions at Cherbourg. Hitler denied Von Schlieben permission to withdraw into the fortifications of the Cherbourg citadel, and arbitrarily marked off a line east of the city to be held to the last man. Von Schlieben wired back appealing for permission to surrender "in view of the great superiority of the enemy aircraft, tanks, and artillery and now finally the naval bombardment." Hitler refused Von Schlieben's plea, ordered Cherbourg held to the "last round of ammunition," then directed Rommel to "strike into the rear of the first American Army advancing on Cherbourg and relieve Cherbourg."

Futile exchanges of this kind confronted Von Rundstedt and Rommel with the unpleasant fact that OKW considered Army Group B expendable and led to the incident responsible for Von Rundstedt's abrupt retirement. In late June, upon receipt of fresh OKW orders to counterattack at Bayeux, Von Rundstedt phoned Keitel to tell him that a counteroffensive, in the circumstances, was impossible. "What shall we do?" Keitel replied, whereupon Von Rundstedt snapped, "Make peace, you fools, what else can you do?"

Within three days of this conversation, Von Rundstedt stepped down, on grounds of ill health, and was replaced by Field Marshal Hans Günther von Kluge, a veteran of the eastern front and one-time commander of the Army Group Center in Russia. The shift was intended to infuse the command in France with fanaticism, and was accompanied by stern measures, including a court-martial inquiry into the surrender of Cherbourg on June 26 in defiance of Berlin's orders. SS General Paul Hausser was appointed commander of the Seventh Army to replace General Friedrich Dollman, a suicide. Hausser, the first SS officer ever to command a Wehrmacht army, quickly set about to sprinkle SS NCOs through the ranks in Normandy who were empowered to shoot anyone who abandoned his post and to recommend reprisals against next of kin in Germany. Allied frontline units quickly felt the impact of this maneuver, which was duly reported in the SHAEF intelligence summary, kindling talk of "stabilization" in Normandy.

On the night of June 21, as Montgomery issued his directive ordering the capture of Cherbourg and Caen, an estimated 240,000 Russian partisans in the Minsk area set off 10,500 demolition charges and destroyed rail links west of the city—a portent of the impending attack. As the American and British commanders sorted out the toll of the great storm, OKH inventoried the forces assembled opposite Army Group Center in central Russia. Coordinated by Marshal Zhukov as commander in chief, and Chief of Staff Marshal Alexander Vasilevsky, 166 Red Army divisions gathered. On the northern flank of the army group, in the open land surrounding the isolated German strong point of Vitebsk, the First Baltic Front (18 infantry divisions and 9 armored divisions)* faced the 3 divisions of German VI Corps. The mission of this force was to sever the 2 army groups and to encircle the Third Panzer Army at Vitebsk, thus serving as the northern prong of concentric offensives aimed at the annihilation of the army group and the recapture of Minsk, and the recovery of Russia's prewar frontier. In the center at Orsha, a key supply base, 7 divisions of the Fourth German Army faced the Second White Russian Front, consisting of 16 infantry divisions,

*Once again, a Russian "front" is roughly equivalent to an Allied army group.

2 armored divisions, and the southern wing of the Third White Russian Front, including 25 infantry and 11 armored divisions. At Bobruisk in the south, the Russians assembled the First White Russian Front, consisting of 23 infantry divisions, 7 armored divisions, 27 infantry and 6 tank formations drawn up on the flank of the German Ninth Army. Spearheading this force was the elite Fifth Armored Guards Army, poised to exploit the thin strip of tank terrain between Bobruisk and the northern edge of the Pripet Marshes.

The weight of the Russian concentration was directed at the weakened flanks, and so, even before the opening round was fired, the army group's position was, according to Gackenholz, "critical." On the evening of June 22, waves of fighter-bombers pounded Vitebsk as the First Baltic Front attacked the northern shoulder of the Third Panzer Army. The following day, assaults opened all along the 250-mile front backed by 400 pieces of artillery per mile. Units drawn from the Kovel–Brest sector had turned up on the flanks of the army group, and by midday of the twenty-third, Russian armor was pouring past the "strong points," and Vitebsk was quickly "pinched off" between converging thrusts by the two northern Russian fronts. The attack swiftly spread southward in a frontal assault against the Fourth Army, followed the next day by attacks on the Ninth Army, which covered the German rear line along the Dnieper and Berezina.

By the twenty-fourth, the Russians severed the Minsk–Moscow highway, isolating Vitebsk. On the same day, the Russians isolated portions of the Third Panzer Army and threatened the rear of the German Fourth Army, which withstood a frontal assault again. According to Gackenholz, as late as the twenty-fourth, time remained to save the bulk of the Third Panzer Army and a coherent defense might still have been possible if the Third Panzer Army attacked southward and the Fourth Army fell back behind the Berezina. But all of this depended on Hitler's willingness to authorize withdrawal from Vitebsk and give his officers wide latitude to cope with the situation. That night, Hitler instead issued a personal order to General Georg-Hans Reinhardt, commander in chief of the Third Panzer Army, that Vitebsk was "to be held at all costs," whereupon army commanders, ignoring OKH instructions, followed their individual conscience and began initiating "veiled" withdrawals.

By the morning of the twenty-fifth, only a general withdrawal from White Russia offered hope of salvaging the Ninth Army, by-passed at points and threatened at Bobruisk; the Fourth Army, threatened from the rear; and the Third Panzer Army isolated since midday on the twenty-fourth. Under this pressure, Hitler authorized withdrawal in the Fourth Army sector, but again ordered the Third Panzer Army to hold Vitebsk, an order reaffirmed that night as the last remaining road link between Vitebsk and Minsk was cut off by forward spearheads of the Third White Russian Front. In the

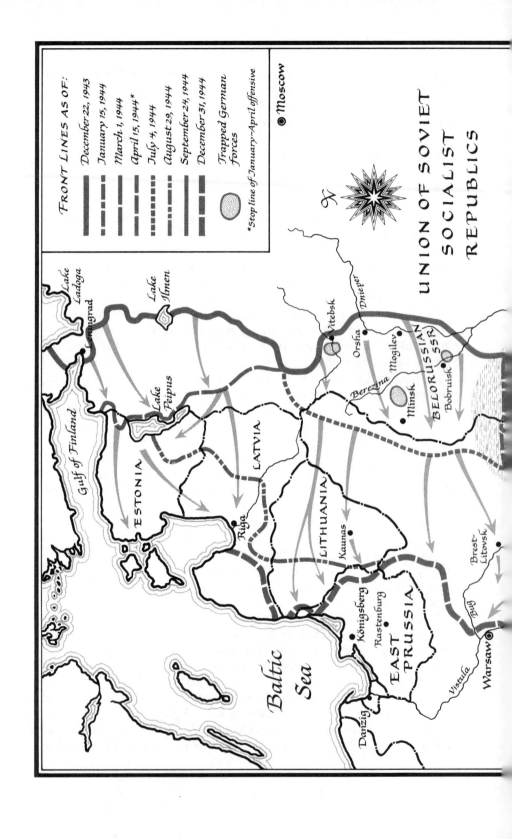

FRONT LINES AS OF:

December 22, 1943
January 15, 1944
March 1, 1944
April 15, 1944*
July 4, 1944
August 29, 1944
September 24, 1944
December 31, 1944

Trapped German forces

*Stop line of January–April offensive

Moscow

UNION OF SOVIET SOCIALIST REPUBLICS

Lake Ladoga
Leningrad
Lake Ilmen
Lake Peipus
Gulf of Finland
Baltic Sea
ESTONIA
LATVIA
Riga
LITHUANIA
Kaunas
Königsberg
Rastenburg
EAST PRUSSIA
Danzig
Warsaw
Vistula
Bug
Brest Litovsk
Vitebsk
Orsha
Mogilev
Minsk
Bobruisk
Berezina
Dnieper
BELORUSSIAN SSR

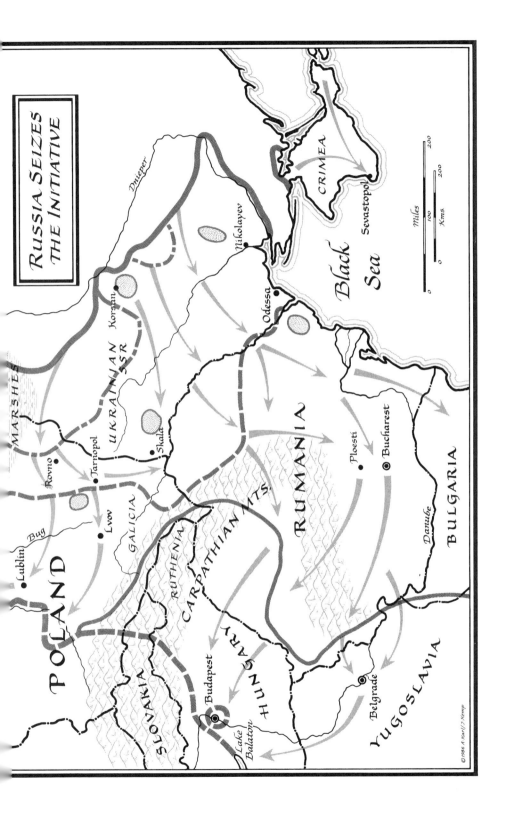

RUSSIA SEIZES
THE INITIATIVE

POLAND

MARSHES

Lublin

Bug

Rovno

Lvov

Tarnopol

GALICIA

RUTHENIA

SLOVAKIA

Budapest

Lake
Balaton

HUNGARY

CARPATHIAN MTS.

Skala

Korsun

UKRAINIAN
S.S.R.

Dnieper

Nikolayev

Odessa

CRIMEA

Sevastopol

Black

Sea

RUMANIA

Ploesti

Bucharest

Danube

BULGARIA

Belgrade

YUGOSLAVIA

Miles

100   200

0   200

Kms

0

© 1986 A.Karl/J.Kemp

maelstrom Hitler, reacting hysterically to the defeatism of his OKH staff, directed the neighboring Army Group North to support the Third Panzer and ordered the 206th Infantry Division, a force of 10,000 men, to hold Vitebsk "until it is relieved."

Here Gackenholz pauses in his commentary to reflect on Hitler's remarks. He notes that the Führer, in ordering the relief of Vitebsk, was either exhibiting a "lack of insight" or being "cynical." Or perhaps Hitler was reluctant to admit to those present that a "force stronger than his will was shaping the conduct of the war." In any event, Hitler's miscalculations had allowed the Red Army to break into open terrain behind German lines in White Russia, where it threatened Minsk and the army group communications, as well as "new and far-reaching objectives" in the direction of Warsaw and the German frontier. In Gackenholtz's opinion, Germany perished that night.

In correspondence between Churchill, Roosevelt, Eisenhower, Marshall, Brooke and Smuts, there is scant reference to the Russian destruction of the German Army Group Center in a matter of five days while the British and Americans remained pinned in a sixty-mile strip of northwest France. Information was sketchy, or perhaps the omission is an instance of what Butcher had called "suppressed emotion that would interest a psychiatrist." Nor would any of the memoirs link the building emotions in London and Washington in early July 1944 to the ensuing destruction of three German armies, the erasure of twenty-five German divisions and 300,000 men in the first of two big Russian attacks that summer. Churchill would recite these events in a pro forma way in *Triumph and Tragedy* at the end of a chapter on the Balkan controversies. Eisenhower would barely refer to the Soviet victory in *Crusade in Europe,* written in 1948, by which time he may have had second thoughts about his wartime gestures of respect for the Red Army and goodwill toward the Soviet Union.

For the next four weeks the Allied press would watch on with admiration, and a touch of unease. How far would the Russians go? It seemed safe to predict that the Russian armies would pause and consolidate after encircling 100,000 soldiers of the army group at Minsk on July 4. But a second wave of Russian mobile armies pierced an improvised rear line southwest of Minsk, and "their [the Germans'] reduced forces were inadequate to cover the space, which became wider as the Russian bulge grew deeper." On July 14 Konev's long-awaited offensive against the Lvov sector would open at last, to be followed by resumption of the drive in Rumania which had stopped at the Carpathians in April.

What did it mean? Among other things, the Russian invasion of Poland was on, so a Russian solution in Poland was imminent. Accordingly, Churchill, anxious to clarify the status of his Balkan initiative, pressed for meetings with Roosevelt in Washington to be followed by a three-power meeting with Stalin in Scotland. Stalin begged off, saying he was too busy coordinating the front and would be unable to leave Moscow, though he heaped praise on the Allies for the fall of Cherbourg, noting:

> Allied forces have liberated Cherbourg, thus crowning their efforts in Normandy with another great victory. . . . We wish you new successes.
> Concerning our offensives, it can be said that we shall not give the Germans a breathing space, but shall continue to widen the front of our offensive operations by increasing the strength of our onslaught against the German Armies. You will of course agree with me that this is indispensable for our common cause.
> As regarding the Hitlerite flying bombs, this expedient, it is clear, can have no serious importance either for operations in Normandy, or the population of London, whose bravery is known to all.

Shortly, Eisenhower would receive a note from Harriman in Moscow telling about the "intense" interest the Red Army Staff had in the film SHAEF had sent the military liaison office in Moscow of the OVERLORD invasion. Two marshals and two hundred or more generals and staff officers witnessed the film. In postscript, Harriman intimated that he had seen Stalin that day, who was describing OVERLORD as an "unheard-of achievement."

Harriman may have been the unwitting conduit of an implied affront, for if OVERLORD had been an "unheard-of achievement," what words could describe the still greater victory on the eastern front? John, preparing to return to the States, recalled in the closing days at Telegraph Cottage his father's impatience and growing frustration as newspapers daily trumpeted the unfolding successes of the Russian army, a reaction that John described as a case of "professional envy." Indeed, as June closed, it was hard to escape comparison—Gault called them "warranted and irresistible," as did Butcher. But the problem confronting Eisenhower was to sort out the military implications and take action.

How would the German defeat unfolding in central Russia alter the situation in Normandy? Eisenhower had to weigh every possibility in the harshest light for the Allies. First of all, essential information was lacking, but it was clear that an attack launched from deep in Russia would fall short of decisive objectives. Second, what mattered was not how badly the Germans were defeated in a single battle, but how long the Russians and Germans would remain engaged and on what scale. Plainly, the collapse of the German Army Group Center would force economies and, by eliminating the big salient in central Russia, tend to accomplish the radical shortening and straightening of the German lines, and dramatize the futility of the German situation in Russia somewhat earlier than expected. Months before, in weighing the hypothetical case of a major German reverse in the summer battles, 21st Army Group intelligence had speculated that such a defeat would dispose the Germans to run greater risks in Russia for the sake of one Dunkirk on the smaller front in France.

On the other hand, there was a growing feeling at SHAEF and in London that it was becoming "illogical" for the Germans to fight. The SHAEF report referring to the sprinkling of SS NCOs throughout the Seventh Army had gone on to say that these stiffening measures, though effective, "cannot . . . insure his unit against the effects of Allied guns and bombs, they cannot put right a transportation system that is on its last legs, they cannot conjure up relief from non-existent formations." To many, it was axiomatic that whether the Germans would persist beyond all logic in bringing ruination to their country, while inflicting tragic losses on the Russians and Americans and British, depended on whether Hitler remained in power. Lively speculation began in the press on when and whether the Wehrmacht could rise up, depose Hitler and call off the war to avert catastrophe.

But again, the optimistic scenarios assumed that wide segments of German society had something to gain by an anti-Nazi uprising, or that the Germans would soon conclude they had exhausted every avenue short of unconditional surrender. And the fact remained, as Colonel General Jodl would observe to his Allied interrogators after the war, that after Minsk a German counteroffensive to destroy thirty Russian divisions on the eastern front now meant nothing, whereas defeating thirty Allied divisions might knock Britain and the United States out of the war. In this vein, Montgomery in his second directive issued on June 30, speculated on future possibilities:

It is not clear whether Hitler proposes to concentrate great strength in northwest Europe so as to annihilate the Allied forces in Normandy. He may decide that this is a good proposition; in order to achieve success he may be quite prepared to give ground gradually in the Russian front, and to accept reverses in that theater. His policy in this respect will emerge in due course. For the present it is quite clear he has reinforced the Normandy front strongly, and that a full-blooded counterattack seems imminent.

And so as June closed, debate bubbled on over the likely consequences of the events in Russia. Would events on the Russian front propel rational men to rise up in Germany? As Smuts put it, the Germans, having lost the invasion battle, and with her armies put to rout in Russia, and "knowing what to expect from a Russian invasion, will decide for concentrating on the Russian front. This will help ease our task in the west."

Brooke agreed. As he wrote in his diary at the close of a War Cabinet discussion on postwar plans in Germany, the Russians were "not entirely European." It stood to reason that because of Germany's natural affinity with the West, the Wehrmacht would force a policy of blocking the Russians in Poland. Churchill was not so sure, but in the wake of ANVIL he adopted the argument and used it in dealings with the Americans, hoping to shake them out of their complacency toward the Russians and the urgent need for talks with Stalin to hammer out occupation arrangements in the Balkans. "An intense impression must be made upon the Americans that we have been ill-treated and are furious," he minuted Ismay on July 6. "If we take everything lying down there will be no end to what will be put upon us."

Inevitably, differences between Eisenhower and the British cropped up over updates from OSS Berne on anti-Nazi ferment and plans for an attempt in mid-July on Hitler's life, which was to be followed by an anti-Nazi coup by elements of the Wehrmacht and the Home Army. Once again, Eisenhower did not want even to discuss the subject, as he had indicated "disgust at dealing with German generals." According to Farago, Eisenhower refused even to make a "serious effort . . . to procure specific information about the fantastic ferment in the very core of the German High Command" which included high-ranking officials in Paris. Farago would explain that Eisenhower and Smith, after the invasion, concluded that no conceivable German government existed, even one headed by a German counterpart to the Italian Badoglio, who had handed Eisenhower Italy's surrender on "a silver platter," with which Eisenhower would deal on any basis other than "unconditional surrender." In this way, as Farago put it, Eisenhower and SHAEF undercut the very active conspiracy in the Home Army by spurning interest, and not supporting measures that might have equipped the conspirators to approach their colleagues in the Wehrmacht, and Abwehr, and in the influential circles of business and politics who were now disposed to surrender short of abject capitulation and occupation by the Russians. Eisenhower was opposed to negotiations "even if it meant winning the war without further bloodshed," and was concentrating "on the strictly military aspects of the war he was expected to win by strictly military means."

Indeed, Gault described a lunchtime visit by Lord Halifax, British ambassador to the United States, at advance SHAEF headquarters in Portsmouth which Eisenhower apparently construed as an effort to sound out his views on the OSS reports from Berne. After a long friendly talk about trout fishing and Halifax's experiences while viceroy of India, Eisenhower, Halifax and Gault, joined by Smith, discussed Allied policy in the event of a German army putsch. Halifax thought this was likely, but Eisenhower discounted the possibility. When Halifax raised the postwar fate of the German leadership, Eisenhower "mentioned the Spanish explanation" of being "shot while attempting to escape, adding that the expeditious disposal of Hitler and his cohorts would remove a source of embarrassment for the Allied governments, and save the time and effort required for a tedious trial."

When Halifax suggested that Hitler and the General Staff posed two different questions, Eisenhower and Smith disagreed, though all three agreed that the problem of the General Staff would "be left to nature" if the Russians overran Germany. But "Ike repeated his views that the German General Staff regards this war and the preceding one as merely campaigns in their dogged determination to first dominate Europe and eventually the world," Gault wrote. "He [Eisenhower] would exterminate all the general staff. Or maybe they would be concentrated on some appropriate St. Helena." Smith explained to Halifax that imprisonment would accomplish very little, since it would probably lead to eventual release of the prisoners "because in six or eight years, our own publics again would grow soft-hearted and conciliatory." Halifax asked Eisenhower how many officers he meant by the German General Staff. Eisenhower answered, "About 3,500," adding he would include "all leaders of the Nazi party from mayors on up and all members of the Gestapo."

For good measure, Eisenhower speculated that justice might be done if the zones of occupation in Germany were temporarily assigned to the nations overrun by Hitler: he would give Russia the largest portion, and split the remaining portions among the Czechs, Yugoslavs, Poles, Danes, Norwegians, Greeks and the French.

The Normandy battle raged on. In drizzly, muddy weather the Allies confronted stiffening German resistance in both sectors while hampered by shortages of ammunition in the wake of the storm. By the end of June a major salvage effort was under way to make the port of Cherbourg functional.

But progress was slow and Eisenhower was beginning to detect caution on the part of both Bradley and Montgomery. Bradley, who had hoped to launch a major attack toward Coutances and Brittany simultaneously with the siege of Cherbourg, had sharply curtailed plans. First, in the Cherbourg battles, infantry-tank and air-ground coordination had been poor. Unable in any case to launch a major effort until VII Corps could join the line at the Taute River, Bradley scheduled an intensive four-day training program on hedgerow fighting and the "urgent need for the development of an aggressive spirit in the infantry soldier," and set Middleton's VIII Corps attack toward Coutances for July 3.

Similar news came from the British sector, where bad weather delayed the arrival of VIII Corps and the preparations for Dempsey's long-awaited Second Army "blitz attack" toward Villers-Bocage to envelop Caen from the western approaches. On the twenty-sixth, VIII Corps, led by the 15th Scottish Division, opened a drive between Caen and Tilly to seize a bridgehead over the Odon River and the ridge behind the river. Simultaneously, Canadian I Corps resumed the drive on the Carpiquet airfields, suspended since the sixth, and British I Corps launched a diversionary attack southward from the "airborne bridgehead" east of the Orne River to cut the Caen–Falaise road. But thick ground mist and heavy rains curtailed air support. Dempsey slogged through hedgerows, then rammed up against the 12th SS Hitler Jugend, which, according to Wilmot, "fought with a tenacity and a ferocity seldom equaled and never excelled during the whole campaign." The Scottish 15th breached the Caen–Tilly road and opened a corridor for the 11th Armored attack across the Odon, but counterattacks by elements of the 21st and 2nd panzer divisions developed the following morning. The British 11th Armored gained a tenuous bridgehead over the Odon River and Dempsey poured reinforcements into the bridgehead (covering an area 4,000 yards by 2,000 yards), which provoked a "violent and immediate German reaction." By the twenty-ninth, daylight photo reconnaissance identified elements of eight panzer divisions concentrated against the Second Army Odon River bridgehead, including six SS units. Dempsey decided to consolidate, and in clearing skies, RAF fighter-bombers, Navy gunships, and pinpoint artillery blunted a counterattack by the 10th SS and a regiment of the 1st SS at the village of Cheux. The Odon bridgehead held.

With Bradley's offensive down the west coast of the Cotentin set to start on July 3, no one was talking stalemate yet. As Eisenhower put it in a talk with Smith and Bull at Widewing, the necessary "additional ports" in Brittany *should* be taken by "land assault," meaning that he expected the U.S. First Army to strike as planned through the German defenses to occupy Brittany. Indeed, when measured in terms of the troop build-up and the trend in fighting, the Allies were gradually winning, and sooner or later they would achieve the necessary preponderance at a select point and achieve breakout. But the Allied advantage was a temporary one. Soon— by mid-July in Smith's opinion—the Allies would reach the "acme" of their relative strength, and by mid-July the Germans were likely to be reassessing the decisions of June 9–10 which had left the door in France ajar.

A looming problem was supply—too much of it. By late June the sixty-mile bridgehead was still only five miles deep at points. If the bridgehead could not be expanded soon, the small lodgement area would be choked with men and machines. Soon there would not be room for the fresh American divisions in England and America, which would then either have to stand idle or be sent elsewhere. Eisenhower was mindful that ANVIL would inevitably be reconsidered at the last minute, and that Italian operations would grow in attractiveness if Alexander kept up the pace and the Normandy stalemate continued. Eisenhower was also aware of another possibility: if too much time elapsed without progress on the ground, as Bradley put it, "airmen who still believed Germany could be defeated by air power alone could emerge in commanding roles leaving the Allies mired in fruitless stalemate."

By now Coningham and Brereton were at work on a plan for employing airborne troops in a "strategic" envelopment of a select point along the German line. SHAEF and the BCOS considered an airborne operation in tandem with secondary landings at Quiberon Bay near St.-Malo. But the use of the British 6th Airborne, U.S. 101st, and the 82nd Airborne, which now comprised the First Allied Airborne Army, would be an emergency measure, and so Eisenhower leaned against it.

But as the days wore on, expansion of the Normandy bridgehead had turned into a slow and costly campaign. German armor blocked the good tank terrain. Elite paratroopers and field infantry were entrenched in the hedgerows. SHAEF anxiously monitored the movement of the II SS Panzer Corps as a possible key to German intentions, mindful that a sudden shift of armor into the American sector opposite St.-Lô might presage stepped-up transfers from Calais, which, in turn, would signal large-scale transfers from other theaters. So far, in addition to the panzers, six German infantry divisions had arrived from the Netherlands, Italy, the southern coast of France, and the Bay of Biscay. None had departed for Poland. A G-2 summary noted that the 9th and 10th SS panzer divisions had entered the battle at Tilly in piecemeal fashion and that Rommel had "frittered away strength trying to plug the gaps created by continuous Allied pressures." But time was slipping away.

The mood of unease at SHAEF deepened with the arrival of Montgomery's updated directive on June 30, his first since the opening of the Russian offensive, and the halts at Coutances and west of Caen. The document capped a difficult week and was a prelude to trying times in Normandy. In it, Montgomery elaborated on the "broad policy" he had sketched for Eisenhower in their discussions on June 15, but in new circumstances. At that time, Montgomery had spoken in terms of pulling in the Germans on the left along with "rapid expansion of the lodgement area." Since then, the enemy had successfully reinforced on Montgomery's left, but the lodgement area had not expanded.

The staffs at SHAEF, at the First Army and at Montgomery's headquarters now confronted a problem Eisenhower had hoped might not come up —that of a fully coordinated Anglo-American offensive to pierce an established defensive line launched from D-plus-5 lines five weeks after the landings. Bradley was ready to launch a frontal offensive in four stages beginning on the third, but few expected a decisive success.

A "breakout offensive" presented problems not addressed in any plan to date—political problems. OVERLORD planners had anticipated a deeper bridgehead on D-Day, and rapid movement inland in the first week, enabling the American and British armies to act in a loosely coordinated fashion after the landings. Instead, Eisenhower was faced with having to mount a large-scale set-piece land offensive involving intimate coordination of the two armies.

Serious political problems were implied in a coordinated offensive by two armies, one British, one American, which might be summarized as follows: only one army could be assigned the primary mission and thus be accorded

Eisenhower relaxing at the
St. Georges in the fall of 1943.
U.S. Army

OVERLORD

Eisenhower at the Italian front in mid-October 1943 to evaluate the situation with (left to right) Major General Lucian Truscott, Lieutenant General Mark W. Clark, and Major General John P. Lucas, who would eventually command VI Corps at Anzio. *U.S. Army*

Eisenhower and Patton in North Africa shortly before the fall of Tunis. "Sometimes obsequious and sometimes arrogant," John Eisenhower wrote of Patton, "several times he would have been replaced except for his passion for pursuit of a defeated enemy, in which role Patton was irreplaceable." *U.S. Army*

November 20, 1943. Dinner with President Roosevelt in Tunis shortly before the first Cairo conference. Generals Carl Spaatz and Walter Bedell Smith are to Roosevelt's left and his son Elliott is opposite. *U.S. Army*

Roosevelt and Churchill with the Combined Chiefs of Staff, January 1943. Seated, left to right: General Henry Arnold, Admiral Ernest King, Churchill, Roosevelt, Field Marshal Alan Brooke, Admiral Dudley Pound, General George Marshall. Standing, left to right: Brigadier Vivian Dykes, General Hastings Ismay, Admiral Louis Mountbatten, Major General John R. Deane, Sir John Greer Dill, Air Chief Marshal Charles Portal, Henry Hopkins. *U.S. Army*

The Big Three at Teheran. *U.S. Army*

Teheran, November 29, 1943. Churchill presenting the sword of Stalingrad to Marshal Joseph Stalin. *UPI/Bettman News Photo*

Two days after his appointment to command OVERLORD, Eisenhower confers with Roosevelt aboard *The Sacred Cow* en route to Sicily.
U.S. Army

Mamie and West Point cadet John Eisenhower, Christmas, 1943. *Eisenhower Family Collection*

Christmas meeting at Tunis at which Eisenhower reluctantly endorsed SHINGLE. Also present were General Maitland "Jumbo" Wilson (on Churchill's left), Air Chief Marshal Arthur Tedder (second row, second from left), General Harold Alexander (second row, center) and General Walter Bedell Smith (second row, far right).
British War Office

London, January 1944. The SHAEF high command. Left to right:
General Omar Bradley, Admiral Bertram Ramsay, Air Chief Marshal
Arthur Tedder, Eisenhower, General Bernard Montgomery, Air Chief
Marshal Trafford Leigh-Mallory, Major General Walter B. Smith.
U.S. Army

The air dispute: General Henry "Hap" Arnold confers with Air
Chief Marshal Charles Portal. *U.S. Army*

Air Chief Marshal Arthur
Tedder and General Carl Spaatz
in early 1944. *UPI/Bettman
News Photo*

On the road. Eisenhower handling a Browning machine gun
on an inspection trip outside
London, February 5, 1944.
U.S. Army

"The peaceful invasion."
American GIs in southern
England, late winter, 1944.
*Frank Scherschel, Life Magazine,
©Time, Inc.*

Telegraph Cottage, picture
taken circa 1922. *Eisenhower
Family Collection*

Major General Walter Bedell
Smith, chief of staff, SHAEF.
Though he lacked a college
education, Smith enjoyed a
reputation for brilliance and
effectiveness as a staff officer.
But Smith's brusque and often
tactless manner led to early
clashes with Field Marshal
Alan Brooke and the British.
Source unknown

Eisenhower, photographed with his staff before the Darlan crisis. Butcher at front left; McKeogh, rear, second from left; Kay Summersby on McKeogh's left and next to Colonel, later General, T. J. Davis. *Margaret Bourke-White, Life Magazine, © Time, Inc.*

Eisenhower as a plebe at West Point, 1912. *Eisenhower Family Collection*

ORIGINS

The Eisenhowers outside the family home in Abilene circa 1907. Left to right: Milton, David, Dwight, Ida and Earl. (Missing: Arthur, Edgar and Roy, who had already left home.) *Eisenhower Family Collection*

Newlyweds Dwight and Mamie Eisenhower, 1916, San Antonio, Texas. *Eisenhower Family Collection.*

Eisenhower's first son, David Dwight, who died in January 1922 of scarlet fever at the age of four. In his retirement years, Eisenhower would call Icky's death "the greatest disappointment and disaster in my life, the one I have never been able to forget completely." *Eisenhower Family Collection*

To my Pal Johnnie Eisenhower

Fox Conner

29 Jan. 1924

Eisenhower's mentor General
Fox Conner in January 1924.
Photo is inscribed to his "pal
Johnnie," Eisenhower's second
son, born several months after
Icky's death. *Courtesy of John
Eisenhower*

John's third birthday, August
3, 1925. *Eisenhower Family
Collection*

Eisenhower family reunion at Abilene, Kansas, in June 1926, several weeks after Eisenhower graduated first in his Leavenworth class. Back row: Arthur, Edgar, Dwight, Roy, Earl, Milton. Front row: David and Ida.
Eisenhower Family Collection

Year abroad. Reims, France, 1928. Mamie and close friend Mrs. George Horkan, photographed in front of the cathedral within blocks of the schoolhouse where seventeen years later Eisenhower would receive the German surrender.
Eisenhower Family Collection

Photo of Tyne Cot Cemetery, near Ypres, taken in 1928 by Eisenhower while on a tour of battlefields with the American Battlefield Movements Commission. *Eisenhower Family Collection*

The Eisenhowers and Mrs. William Gruber somewhere in southern Germany in early 1929 on Eisenhower's only tour of Germany before the war. *Eisenhower Family Collection*

Back in Washington in the early thirties, Eisenhower, a self-described "draft horse" in the service of MacArthur, stands outside his office in the State War and Navy Building (now the Executive Office Building). *Eisenhower Family Collection*

With MacArthur at Fort McKinley, the Philippines, early 1937. *Eisenhower Family Collection*

(Right) Father and son at tennis courts in Baguio, Philippines, February 1937. *Courtesy of John Eisenhower*

Eisenhower on the stand at his farewell review, Manila, December 1939. *Eisenhower Family Collection*

Lieutenant Colonel Eisenhower, chief of staff, IX Corps, poses at his desk, Fort Lewis, Washington, early 1941. *Eisenhower Family Collection*

A mother's pride. Ida Eisenhower at home in Abilene sometime in 1943. *Eisenhower Family Collection*

Field Marshal Erwin Rommel supervising the laying of obstacles along the French coast. His experiences in North Africa and Italy had convinced Rommel that an Allied invasion could not be defeated unless defeated at the beaches, and his advocacy of a forward defense led to conflict with OKW and OB West Von Rundstedt. *Courtesy of Eisenhower Library*

Field Marshal Karl Rudolf Gerd von Rundstedt. As OB West since 1942, Von Rundstedt had grown tired and defeatist and yet he continued to advocate the relatively ambitious approach of defeating Allied landings by means of a well-prepared armored counteroffensive in the mold of his 1940 victories over the French and British. *U.S. Army*

INVASION

Mid-May 1944. In the weeks before D-Day, Eisenhower and General Bernard Montgomery, shown together here, embarked on a series of eleventh-hour trips to meet with troops and "make absolutely clear to our men the stark and elemental facts as to the character of our Nazi enemy, the absolute need for crushing him, if we are to survive, and, finally, to drive home the fact that we have defeated him before and can do it again." *U.S. Army*

June 5, 1944, at dusk.
Eisenhower pays an eleventh-
hour call on the troops of the
U.S. 101st Airborne. Butcher
(in naval uniform) and Colonel
James Gault (on Butcher's left)
watch on. *U.S. Army*

June 4, 1944. Eisenhower,
Churchill and De Gaulle confer at Portsmouth. In the heat
of discussion, Eisenhower and
De Gaulle went outside,
where, according to Butcher,
"there was enough elbow
room for De Gaulle to wave
his arms and talk." *U.S. Army*

the prestige of the victory; the other army would have to undertake the support mission, which by its nature would involve heavy casualties and none of the compensating gains. Eisenhower, Montgomery and Bradley recalled well the serious problems caused by relegation of the American Army to hard and thankless support roles in Tunisia and Sicily.

But the problem could probably not be avoided—something Montgomery appeared to anticipate on the thirtieth. On the one hand, he was the first to suggest in writing the possibility that the Germans might choose to "annihilate" the bridgehead even if this meant further sacrifices in Poland. Then, having raised the danger, he proceeded to nullify steps to avoid it by offering a plan with vague objectives that implied criticism of Bradley, a sign that Montgomery anticipated difficult negotiations over roles and missions in the breakout offensive. Montgomery carefully phrased his directive to shield his command from criticism by, among other things, justifying his decision to consolidate the Odon bridgehead.

Montgomery recalled at length that his broad policy had "always been to draw the main enemy force in the battle on our eastern flank, and to fight them there so that our affairs on the western flank could proceed the easier." Bearing out the success of this policy was the build-up opposite the Second Army at Caen of "a formidable array of German Panzer divisions—eight positively identified and possibly more to come." Battlefield strategy would therefore remain unchanged and be guided by two principles. First, Montgomery proposed to retain the initiative by "offensive action" and disclosed First Army plans to launch all four corps in an offensive southward toward Avranches, starting Monday, July 3, the preliminary to entering Brittany and a "wide sweep" north of the Loire. Second, the army group was to "have no setbacks," particularly on the eastern flank, where an enemy success "might have direct repercussions on the quick development of our plan for the western flank." Thereupon Montgomery rearranged British 7th Armored Division boundaries to form a reserve in anticipation of a "full-blooded enemy counterattack," then delegated to the British Second Army three limited tasks: "(a) to hold the main enemy forces in the area between Caen and Villers Bocage; (b) to resist setbacks; and (c) to develop operations for the capture of Caen as opportunity offers—and the sooner the better." In his list of specific tasks, Montgomery had assigned the offensive role to the First Army in such unequivocal terms that, except for a British corps attack on Caen proper set for the eighth, the British Second Army virtually passed to the defensive.

The political problems of arranging a coordinated offensive were implicit in a talk at Grandcamp between Montgomery and Bradley on the morning of the thirtieth called by Montgomery to discuss Bradley's offensive set for July 3. Within hours of having promulgated a justification for Dempsey's caution at Caen, Montgomery caught Bradley off-balance by unveiling a SHAEF–21st Army Group contingency plan entitled LUCKY STRIKE, described as "a general operation to exploit [German] army weakness by drawing east with our major forces." Certain features of LUCKY STRIKE were consistent with Montgomery's directive such as his emphasis on the importance of Bradley's offensive through the bocage. Otherwise, LUCKY STRIKE appeared to contemplate a complete change in the plan Montgomery's directive had spelled out. First, it downgraded the importance of Brittany and instead looked to a British offensive to break out southeast of Caen toward Falaise after the Americans had "cleared the greater part of the bocage." Then the American Army would shift its weight from Coutances on the coast toward Caumont in the center in order to assume a supporting role in a British breakout offensive, due east, led by Dempsey, Crerar, and elements of the U.S. First Army to encircle the remaining Germans west of the Orne, then to pursue to the Seine and into Calais to seize the V-I sites. LUCKY STRIKE did, however, envision an offensive role for the rest of the American forces upon several conditions: first, that no appreciable German resistance remained in Brittany or between the Allied line and a line Laval–Le Mans–Chartres; second, that no enemy armor remained south of the Loire at the time of breakout. In this case, and only then, Montgomery would write off objectives in Brittany and wheel American arms to "block" the Paris–Orléans gap in support of the British Second, Canadian First and U.S. First Army advance without pause along the Channel. Also, Montgomery told Bradley that LUCKY STRIKE, among other things, would require that present command arrangements remain in effect "indefinitely."

Once again, LUCKY STRIKE purported to address a situation that Montgomery had brought up in the course of explaining his strategy several weeks earlier—that in an extended battle in Normandy, German forces east of the Seine might be pulled in west of the river, which would raise the ante in Normandy and make an Allied breakout harder, but would hand the Allies a chance to defeat the Germans decisively west of the river Seine. LUCKY STRIKE was a plan for exploiting this eventuality, an adjustment in breakout plans looking to a massive coordinated battle west of the Seine that shifted the main emphasis to the British sector. But this shift would occur *later,* only *after* German forces had moved opposite Bradley, not before, and it was to be followed up by a British-led, American-supported offensive to exploit Bradley's gains in the bocage presumably while the British trained troops and formed reserves.

Was LUCKY STRIKE a serious plan? Bradley could not deny that as German forces drifted in from Calais, LUCKY STRIKE conditions seemed to be taking shape, either by design—as Montgomery would later assert—or by default. For it was hard to imagine that Montgomery had deliberately raised the ante in Normandy, and hard for Bradley to imagine that Montgomery, waging such a cautious battle at Caen, was really so eager to mount the vigorous breakout assault by British forces implied in the scheme even should Bradley's upcoming offensive draw in German reserves from the Caen sector. In no circumstances could the Germans afford to give up Caen, which meant that any strategy looking to a British "breakout" would necessarily involve a frontal British assault through Caen, and, if followed up, a frontal assault on the strongest backup German positions. Finally, the notion implicit in LUCKY STRIKE that Montgomery would retain command over significant American forces after a breakout, especially one achieved by American forces, was unrealistic and something Bradley was resolved to "resist . . . to my utmost, even to the point of resignation."

But Bradley could not discount LUCKY STRIKE altogether. By the thirtieth, there was growing British skepticism that the Americans would advance boldly through the Normandy bocage and rising sentiment in London to do something about the V-1 sites at Calais. The conversation was unpleasant, and the mood "oppressive," reminiscent of Africa days when Bradley, as II Corps commander, had been relegated to support missions and had found himself obliged to sit and wait for British instructions. Nor could Bradley discount Montgomery's proposal to continue the current command setup. Bradley later told his aide Major Hansen that he was sure Montgomery would now bid to retain overall ground command when Patton assumed command of the U.S. Third Army. Bradley for his part expected to command the newly formed U.S. Twelfth Army Group directly under Eisenhower, who would then relieve Montgomery of overall direction of the land battle. Bradley, a veteran of the Mediterranean war, had long anticipated and prepared for an eleventh-hour British effort to derail these plans, though he was sure that Marshall would oppose such a British attempt. But Eisenhower had still not set the date for activation of the Third Army or expressed himself officially on the command setup.

But it remained to be seen precisely how Montgomery's bid for retaining command would take shape—indeed whether Montgomery intended to bid at all, and whether LUCKY STRIKE was a military plan, a talking point, or, again, speculation on Montgomery's part about how he would maneuver American forces after a breakout. Perhaps the real significance of LUCKY STRIKE was not the plan as such but the idea that perpetuating the current command arrangement and a British offensive—*any* offensive—were linked; that Montgomery, anticipating Eisenhower's pressures in the next few weeks for a supporting British offensive in an American breakout attack, was setting his price, a high one.

This latter interpretation of the Bradley-Montgomery meeting, when he heard of it, seemed plausible to Eisenhower for several reasons. Like Bradley, Eisenhower had no reason to doubt that Montgomery's June 30 directive represented Montgomery's true thinking; it called expansion of the American sector mandatory, to be followed up by seizure of the Brittany ports. The British had adequate port and MULBERRY capacity for their build-up; the Americans did not and American troops were essential "to sustain an eastward push." Second, Eisenhower discounted the V-1's as a military problem or as an objective, and suspected that Montgomery did also. Finally, whether it was practical or not, Montgomery could not accept the British casualties inevitable in LUCKY STRIKE. By late June, Eisenhower had reports that the British were combing out the RAF, Navy and supply corps for 90,000 infantry replacements to prevent the breakup of five or more divisions.

What would Eisenhower offer Montgomery in the way of command concessions? Not much. Based on past experience in the Mediterranean, Bradley assumed that the British would find ways to run every theater of war; however, he overestimated Eisenhower's ability to accommodate the British if not his willingness to do so. But Normandy was not Tunisia or Sicily. In France the Americans were becoming the dominant force. Since 1944 was an election year in the United States, this weighed heavily against perpetuating British command over American forces. Also, Eisenhower had already demonstrated in the air-command dispute in March that he would tenaciously seek to expand his own command authority, and his direct authority over American troops would be at stake.

In the next several days, Eisenhower went into action. Evidently, to sidestep the command problem as a bone of contention, he decided to hold up activation of the Third Army. In view of the British replacement crisis, Eisenhower sent word to Montgomery that U.S. divisions of Gerow's V Corps at Caumont were available to support Dempsey's Odon River offensive. Then Eisenhower made arrangements for an extended trip to Normandy to confer with Montgomery and Bradley, but before leaving, he conferred with Tedder several times.

For some time Tedder, as Eisenhower's deputy commander, had been acting as an adviser without portfolio whose specific task was to serve as Eisenhower's agent at the daily Stanmore air meetings. Tedder, in February, had rendered indispensable assistance, and he was going to be asked to do so again on a very difficult assignment—helping to arrange a large supporting British attack for an American breakout that did not involve significant command concessions on Eisenhower's part. This would involve bringing British pressure to bear on Montgomery for offensive action at Caen or, at a minimum, neutralizing British opposition to it.

It was becoming more and more obvious that the British did not present a wholly united front. Churchill's arguments with the BCOS over Italy versus France were apparent, and the British were not immune to the same interservice rivalries that afflicted the Americans. For instance, British air marshals, including Tedder, Coningham, Bottomley and Portal, had taken the lead in criticizing 21st Army Group failures, especially Dempsey's inability to gain space southeast of Caen suitable for forward air bases. They knew that the OVERLORD plan had called for eighty-one fighter-bomber and heavy-bomber squadrons based on the Continent and twenty-seven operational airfields by June 30, or D plus 24. Thirty-eight squadrons were ashore, dispersed at five narrow airstrips, two of which remained under German artillery fire. The British air marshals were also irked by 21st Army Group's requests for heavy air support for limited objective attacks, and more or less agreed with Spaatz that direct air support of the ground battle was a "waste" of a strategic asset. In short, the British air marshals were becoming impatient with Montgomery's progress, particularly in the Caen sector.

Tedder's views were conventionally British and typical of an airman. He did not question JIC findings that a German military collapse was likely by December. Like many, he had expected the Germans to retire to the Seine in order to gather reserves for the eastern front. Tedder shared the anxiety of the War Cabinet about the V-1 bombardment of the British southern coast, and favored ideas bandied about in recent days to reinforce the Second Army for a drive to clear the Channel coast of the V-1 sites. He had been under the impression that Montgomery had promised bold tactics in the British sector to acquire elbow room in the Caen arena, which would position him to press along the Channel coast to neutralize the V-1 sites, and suspected Montgomery had reneged. Finally, like Brooke, Tedder may have harbored doubts that the Americans would ever mount a successful push through the bocage. In short, though Tedder's views were not especially relevant to the developing issues between Bradley and Montgomery, and his approach was different from Eisenhower's in almost every respect, Tedder and Eisenhower nevertheless agreed on two basic points—one, the bridgehead was in trouble; two, it was essential to keep Montgomery rolling on the eastern flank.

At an exploratory meeting in Portsmouth on June 30, Eisenhower solicited Tedder's views about Montgomery's directive. Tedder was critical of it. Montgomery, in going on record with his "broad policy," was evidently sensitive to charges that the 21st Army Group had met a reverse, yet he was reluctant to take aggressive steps at Caen. Eisenhower asked Tedder if he would be willing to put his views on record. Tedder was willing. Eisenhower encouraged Tedder to feel at complete liberty to communicate directly with Montgomery by message or in person on air problems or "anything you might wish to discuss."

Tedder emerged from the meeting as Eisenhower's closest adviser in dealing with Montgomery on air-ground problems, with a mandate to mobilize appropriate public and private pressure on Montgomery for sustaining the attack at Caen. Eisenhower's policy was, as he later expressed it, for simultaneous, mutually supporting offensives by the Americans and British moving "shoulder to shoulder, with honors and sacrifices equally shared." Grave misunderstandings were in the wind, and Montgomery would write later, "I do not think that great and good man [Eisenhower], now one of my greatest friends, had any idea of the trouble he was starting. . . ."

"For the moment, Montgomery is expecting a heavy counterattack, but is confident he can defeat it," Summersby noted in her office journal on the thirtieth. "Meanwhile, he [Eisenhower] is just waiting."

A day later, with hopes that Bradley's attacking forces would reach Avranches, Eisenhower embarked for Normandy and a four-day visit, most of which he spent in the American sector inspecting troops, hospitals, and field conditions. "The first impression," wrote Gault, "was of rain and mud as it had been raining hard for the last few days." The dreary impression was a lasting one, based on an extended look at the grim conditions of Normandy, which the VII Corps commander, General "Joe" Collins, the hero of Guadalcanal, likened to the jungles of the southwest Pacific.

By now the Normandy battle had evolved into a slow struggle for control of key road junctions, fought through narrow bottlenecks flanked by marshes and against an enemy taking maximum advantage of hedgerows, which formed deep trenches and thick walls blocking off air and artillery observation. To date, the superior mobility of the American Sherman tank was being nullified on a battlefield carved up into 150-yard plots. Slower, more heavily armed German Mark V and Mark VI Panther-Tiger tanks appearing in large numbers gained a decisive advantage in head-on engagements. And again, unseasonable weather was a handicap, limiting air support and producing mud which, as Butcher put it, was "reminiscent to Ike of Tunisia in the wintertime."

When and where would the break come? Eisenhower spent the evenings of his visit at First Army Headquarters with Bradley, Collins and Gerow mapping out plans. American feelings ran high about Montgomery. To these men, Montgomery's caution at Caen had one explanation—saving British lives. "This consideration," Collins told me years later, "was always uppermost in Montgomery's mind." Coaxing the British into a major attack at Caen would be difficult, and it was apparent to the Americans that one was needed.

Since mid-June, as Bradley recounted in his memoir, the U.S. First Army had been searching for "a hole," the first opening in the German defenses through which the Americans could pour accumulated infantry and armored units to break through and roll up the German lines. In the hedgerow country stretching from Bayeux to Cherbourg, territorial gains were not enough; an orderly German retreat would simply oblige the First Army to fight the same battle for another set of hedgerows. To avoid this, the Americans would have to abandon broad-front tactics and attack so suddenly and fiercely at one point that the Germans would not be able to organize defenses to the rear. Armor would have to by-pass strongpoints and drive deeply along the north–south roads, and sever lateral communications between the breakout sector and the German reserves east of Caumont.

The most promising objective was St.-Lô, identified by Bradley as the hinge of the Cotentin campaign on June 24. Located on a rise overlooking the Vire Valley, "not only did its tall, bombed church mark the center of a road junction vital to Rommel," he wrote, "but the town itself straddled a crosscut road that ran from Bayeux on the Calvados coast to Coutances on the west shore, thus severing the Normandy shoulder from the main body of France." By taking St.-Lô and then dashing with armor to Coutances, the Americans would cut the rear of most of the Seventh Army, shorten the First Army line, and assume positions for a deep advance into Brittany. But the Germans had also realized the importance of St.-Lô and were massing reserves there.

By early July the 17th SS Division and the 2nd SS Panzer Das Reich held the westward approaches to St.-Lô, forcing Bradley to lead with an attack toward Coutances and the western road junction at La Haye-du-Puits on the Atlantic coast, a far less promising approach. Secondary attacks by Corlett's XIX Corps and Collins' VII Corps would push out from the Carentan marshes and converge at St.-Lô, which would improve the First Army position. In short, Bradley expected a slow, costly overland battle of attrition, through "perfect defensive terrain."

On July 2, Eisenhower and Bradley continued on to Montgomery's headquarters for a talk about Bradley's imminent four-corps attack toward Avranches. At this meeting, Montgomery again raised LUCKY STRIKE, noting the developing opportunity to defeat the Germans west of the Seine. "Political considerations are obvious," Major Hansen wrote afterward.

July 3. Phase one of the U.S. First Army battle for position opened in fog and rain. "This was the day in which the attack was to start," wrote Gault forlornly, "and if one had tried to select a more depressing morning, it would have been, I think, impossible."

Visibility and ceiling were zero at daybreak, so air sorties were canceled. With partial clearing at noon, Eisenhower mounted a hundred-foot German flak tower to observe Middleton's VIII Corps in action through binoculars. From there, he could look out over the green woods and hedgerows in the direction of the coast and see St.-Lô.

That afternoon Eisenhower, Gault and Bradley toured Cherbourg. The defending German 71st Division had not sunk many hulls in the Channel, so the damage at first glance did not seem as extensive as the demolition of Naples. But the electrical and heating plants at the port were useless, the loading cranes had been dismantled and broken up, and the Germans had mined the Channel from end to end. The rehabilitation of Naples had taken three days. Cherbourg would take six weeks.

The group visited the Fort du Roule, the scene of a last-ditch German siege. They inspected a V-1 bunker, a large, well-camouflaged structure fortified in concrete. "Isn't it facing New York?" someone gasped. "Knowing the devilish German scientific mind," wrote Gault, "you speculated on whether they were going so far as to split the atom."

The rains continued. By nightfall, VIII Corps had gained 4,000 yards in two sectors, reaching the La Haye-du-Puits–St.-Saveur-le-Vicomte road. But the troubled 90th Division, after an advance of 3,000 yards, fought off counterattacks and stopped as the disappointing day drew to a close.

July 4 was the same. "No surprise to us," wrote the First Army diarist, "cloudy with intermittent rain. We have quite given up hope of ever seeing the sun for more than a few minutes at a time—so fickle has been the weather, so quick a change from a cloudless sky to hard-driving rain." At noon, in accordance with Bradley's wishes, every non-concealed First Army artillery position was to fire one round at the German line to commemorate Independence Day. Eisenhower and Bradley left the lunchroom at twelve sharp to listen to the roar of 1,000 artillery pieces from Caumont to Cherbourg.

By afternoon the battle reports were poor. The half-strength 82nd Airborne was resisting counterattack, and the 90th Division had again been checked. Collins' VII Corps attacks jumped off but made slow progress. Late in the afternoon, touring an Air Force fighter field, Eisenhower on a whim asked the Ninth Air Force commander, thirty-seven-year-old General "Pete" Quesada, to take him up in the rear seat of a Mustang P-51. Bradley was extremely unhappy with the idea and asked Eisenhower not to do it. "All right, Brad," Eisenhower snapped, "I'm not going to fly to Berlin."

For forty-five minutes, with Quesada at the controls, the Mustang flew west over the American-German line, then south, then dipped northeast toward Paris, and into German-occupied France. From the co-pilot seat, Eisenhower raptly gazed down on the panorama. Typically, troop concentrations were widely dispersed because of modern artillery and air technique. The wide spacing of units in World War II accounted for the "loneliness" of the battlefield spoken of so often by veterans of that war— something that placed such a high premium on small-unit leadership. "Except for occasional flashes of enemy artillery," Eisenhower told Gault afterward, "it was a peaceful scene."

THE OFFENSIVE

Bradley's slow progress opened a month of discontent—a "difficult time," as Eisenhower later put it. Gradually, concern spread to all quarters that the cross-Channel invasion, as had been feared, would bring the return of the trench warfare of 1916–17. By July, newspapers still could not report significant progress on the fifty-mile front, only five miles deep near the Carentan marshes.

Spirits sank in London, where to meet the V-1 threat, civil defense officials undertook to evacuate over one million women, children, elderly and ill from downtown London to the countryside. The migration strained transport systems and held up shipments to the Continent. On June 27 Home Secretary Herbert Morrison had reported to the War Cabinet that over 200,000 houses had been damaged or destroyed by the V-1 and that broken windows and shattered sewage systems threatened serious epidemics unless fixed by winter.

The distinctive buzz emitted by the pilotless aircraft shortly before dropping on random targets at any time of day or night had injected a new element in the war of nerves. In his diary Butcher wrote that "most of the people I know are semi-dazed from loss of sleep and have the jitters, which they show when a door bangs or the sound of motors from motorcycles or aircraft are heard." Widewing and Telegraph Cottage attracted more than a fair share of alerts. On one night alone, Butcher counted twenty-five V-1 explosions between 7 P.M. and 1 A.M. Routinely, Eisenhower, Summersby, Butcher, Gault, McKeogh and Hunt retired to the stark white-walled shelter to spend the night in sleeping bags or on cots.

After experimentation, RAF Coastal Command devised methods to interdict the missile over the water, which was necessary because even a downed rocket would explode upon impact with the earth. The Ministry of Home Defence coordinated the massive shift of anti-aircraft batteries along a fifteen-mile strip of coast between London and the sea for use in cloudy weather when radar and fighters were less effective.

Fighters and anti-aircraft together would down 46 percent of all V-1's fired. Of the 10,500 V-1's launched at England, an estimated 25 percent flew off course because of malfunction. Roughly 20 percent penetrated British defenses and hit targets, claiming 10,000 lives and 1.1 million homes, including parts of the Royal Lodge, Windsor Castle and the Hampton Court Palace.

These figures, while grave, did not justify prolonged diversion of strategic bombers. SHAEF stood by its conclusion that the V-1 was neither an effective "city destruction" weapon, nor very useful militarily. Within five days of giving "first priority" to V-1 sites, Eisenhower sent a memorandum to Smith reminding his chief of staff that the Allies had sixty to ninety days to make maximum use of the air; he enclosed a list of operations he wanted carried out to exploit "the one important factor in which we enjoy tremendous superiority." Eisenhower forwarded to Tedder a memo from Spaatz complaining that CROSSBOW was a "diversion" from the main task of wearing down the Luftwaffe and bombing German industry. "Instructions for continuing to make CROSSBOW targets our first priority must stand," he wrote. "But I think it would be well to issue an overall policy that, when we have favorable conditions over Germany and when the entire strategic air forces cannot be used against CROSSBOW, we should attack—(a) Aircraft industry, (b) Oil, (c) ball bearing, (d) Vehicular production."

· · ·

CROSSBOW peaked on the nights of July 4–5 and 7–8 in two intensive raids on launching sites and storage depots at Calais. On the fifth, 227 Lancasters dropped six-ton "earthquake" bombs, but the sites escaped damage. V-1 attacks resumed, and CROSSBOW was quietly downgraded, with Churchill's tacit consent.

At a press conference Eisenhower put the best light on this decision. He expressed sympathy for the plight of the British population. He conceded that the flying bombs, if equipped with infrared-type guidance systems, might have great military possibilities someday. For now, though, he said he did "not like them and everyone with whom I talk shares this feeling." The flying bomb was "a nuisance" and the military had resolved to "get on with its work and pay no attention to it."

Meanwhile, the War Cabinet resolved to push the British flying bomb program. "What will be their application in our hands?" Air Chief Marshal Bottomley asked Tedder that week. "In their present form they are a toy," Tedder replied, "but their development will profoundly affect both war and peace."

As Bradley's slow assault toward La Haye-du-Puits proceeded, Hanson Baldwin, military correspondent of the *New York Times,* reported that the contrast between the speed of the Russian and Anglo-American advances had become "a sort of grim jest in Normandy," where "it is said that we shall soon have to adjust our artillery fire to avoid laying down a barrage on the Russians advancing from the east." By July 4 the Third Panzer Army, and the Ninth and Fourth infantry armies, a force the equivalent of the German Army Group B in northern France, were paper formations written off by OKH as having "no further combat value whatsoever," submerged as they were in a flood of 116 Russian infantry divisions, 6 cavalry divisions, 16 mechanized infantry brigades, 42 armored brigades, backed by 4,500 tactical bombers in the skies overhead. On one day alone, 57,000 German army prisoners were paraded through the streets of Moscow, marching, Churchill wrote, "who knows whither."

That week Hitler, in a funeral oration for General Hans Dietl, killed in the retreat, declared, "May his example inspire many officers and generals. May they learn to banish any idea that a struggle in which the fanaticism of a nation is engaged might end otherwise than in victory." Hitler's remarks, aimed evidently at defeatism in the ranks, was taken as confirmation of a Nazi-Wehrmacht rift. Berlin announced Von Rundstedt's relief, an unprecedented action. SHAEF intelligence further noted Goebbels' exaggerated claims about the effectiveness of the V-1, a sign "that Germany is in a state of crisis."

[Goebbels] seems to be deliberately taking a short-term advantage at the cost of a later severe disillusionment of the German people when peace does not come and air raids on Germany do not cease. Analysis of Goebbels' technique in the past makes it seem astonishing that he should thus deliberately court disaster. Secondly, Goebbels is also courting disaster by founding his invasion propaganda for Germans on the thesis that losses will drive the Allies to make peace at no distant date. These two aberrations cannot be explained even by supposing that Goebbels is casting caution aside in view of this belief in defeat, for as long as he continues to function he must act as if he believed that Germany would survive, and therefore must retain his old principle of caution.

The War Cabinet took a hopeful view of such reports. Informed by the OSS that an attempt on Hitler's life would occur on the fifteenth or twentieth of July, Deputy Prime Minister Clement Attlee rose in Parliament on July 6 to say:

> So far as His Majesty's Government are concerned, it has repeatedly been made clear in public statements that we shall fight on until Germany has been forced to capitulate and until Nazism is extirpated. It is for the German people to draw the logical conclusion. If any section of them wants to see a return to a regime based on respect for international law and for the rights of the individual, they must understand that no one will believe them until they have taken active steps to rid themselves of their present regime. The longer they continue to support and to tolerate their present rulers, the heavier grows their own direct responsibility for the destruction that is being wrought throughout the world, and not least in their own country.

Attlee spoke just as the FORTITUDE deception expired as a factor in the Normandy campaign. July 6–9 presented the last moon-and-tide combinations in July suitable for landings at Calais. Patton, whose presence was necessary in Normandy to ready his headquarters for activation, landed at OMAHA Beach on the sixth and was greeted by hundreds of GIs, whom he addressed from the rear of a jeep in colorful language that quickly made the rounds in Normandy. To sustain the flimsy pretense of FORTITUDE, Marshall decided to provide the chief of the U.S. Army Information, General Lesley McNair, as Patton's "replacement" at FUSAG. Meanwhile, Patton's presence in France had to be explained, so Eisenhower directed Smith to "leak" that Patton had been replaced by the most capable and experienced senior American commander, General Lesley McNair.

But FORTITUDE, in the circumstances, was a matter of leaving no stone unturned, for the idea of a secondary Allied landing at Calais was becoming less and less plausible. Twenty-nine of the thirty-seven OVERLORD divisions were ashore in Normandy. After replacing Von Rundstedt, Von Kluge, a veteran of the eastern front, had successfully set about to bolster the center and western flanks in anticipation of Fifteenth Army reinforcements. Forty-eight hours after Attlee's speech, Hitler issued orders for LUTTICH, a seven-panzer-division night offensive at Caen. ULTRA intercepted the cables between OKW and Army Group B about preparations for the offensive, as well as the cable releasing the 116th Panzer at Amiens and five infantry divisions of the Fifteenth Army for duty in Normandy, which apparently marked the end of the "main landing" at Calais as a factor in OKW thinking.

Finally, on the seventh, as Major General Charles H. Corlett's XIX Corps launched attacks toward St.-Lô, Eisenhower wrote Montgomery and for the first time in writing acknowledged the possibility of a stalemate. In response to Montgomery's revised directive of the seventh, Eisenhower recalled their long-ago struggle on behalf of the transport plan when both of them had "demanded from the air . . . that they delay the arrival of enemy forces in the NEPTUNE area." Eisenhower noted that the air forces had succeeded "magnificently."

"Very soon we will be approaching the limit in the capacity of the ports now in our possession to receive and maintain American troops," Eisenhower wrote. "Thereafter it is possible for the enemy to increase his *relative* strength; actually he seems to be doing so already."

Eisenhower was "familiar with [Montgomery's] plan of generally holding firmly with your left attracting thereto all of the enemy armor while your right pushes down the Peninsula and threatens the rear and flank of the forces facing the British Second Army." Eisenhower supported the plan wholeheartedly but questioned whether it had been given a fair test. The advance on Coutances was "slow" and "laborious," because of the nature of the country and the impossibility of employing air and artillery with maximum effectiveness, and also the "arrival on that front of reinforcements."

In view of this, Eisenhower had concluded that the time had come to use "all possible energy in a determined effort to prevent a stalemate or facing the necessity of fighting a major defensive battle with the slight depth we now have in the bridgehead." He reminded Montgomery that a major full-dress attack on the left flank had not been attempted, and that the Allies needed depth and "elbow room"—at least enough territory to protect the SWORD Beach from German artillery fire and to secure suitable airfields.

"I am myself quite happy about the situation," Montgomery replied. He assured Eisenhower that he had been working "throughout on a very definite plan," consistent with his determination to keep the initiative and "to have no setbacks."

Three things were now "vital."

1. We must get the Brittany peninsula.
2. We do not want to get hemmed in to a relatively small area.
3. Third, we want to engage the enemy in battle to write off his troops and generally to kill Germans. Exactly where we do this does not matter so long as (a) and (b) are complied with.

Montgomery reminded Eisenhower that Dempsey had drawn eight panzer divisions onto VIII Corps at the Odon River. He, too, was disappointed with the First Army advance, which had "been slower than I thought would be the case." Montgomery knew the country was "terribly close, the weather has been atrocious, and certain enemy reserves have been brought in against it." In closing, Montgomery informed Eisenhower that Dempsey's attack on the western half of the city was under way that hour, and that Dempsey was at work on plans to exploit bridgeheads over the Orne Canal, which he expected to be in British hands by nightfall.

"Of one thing you can be quite sure," he closed, "there will be no stalemate."

> If the enemy decides to concentrate very great and overwhelming strength against us, that will take a considerable time; and during that time we will relentlessly get on with our business; we are very strong now and need not delay any longer for buildup purposes.
>
> I shall always ensure that I am well balanced; at present I have no fears of any offensive move the enemy might make; I am concentrating on making the battle swing our way.
>
> Yrs ever
> (sgd) MONTY

That day, the British I Corps entered the western suburbs of Caen behind a force of 467 Lancasters and Halifaxes, which dropped 2,560 tons of explosives on German positions. To avoid "shorts," the RAF bombers observed a 6,000-yard bomb line, so the screen of fortified villages in the northern suburbs escaped preliminary bombardment. I Corps fought through house to house, then stalled in the city proper, picking its way through deep craters. Rubble choked the roads. Bulldozers could not clear the debris in time to prevent the German 21st Panzer from withdrawing safely behind the Orne. That night the 21st, reinforced by the 1st SS, fortified positions on the eastern bank, and the following morning attempted to cross the canal. Montgomery canceled a British VIII Corps attack set for the next day.

Churchill received congratulatory cables from Stalin and Roosevelt on the fall of Caen. The Allied press hailed the Caen "breakthrough" as the first major victory since Cherbourg. On the ninth a proposal reached Eisenhower's desk from the SHAEF psychological warfare division proposing that Stalin, General Wilson and General Eisenhower issue simultaneous orders of the day proclaiming the hopelessness of the German cause in the east, west and south and that Germany was finished as a military power, "and that the German High Command knows it."

But behind the scenes, there was little rejoicing. At Chequers on the ninth Churchill spent the morning scolding Eisenhower about ANVIL and the press stories originating from SHAEF critical of Montgomery. Gloom descended over the Army staffs: with 1,000 tanks, and backed by the mightiest air attack since Cassino, I Corps had failed to capture a single bridgehead over the Orne; Montgomery's eastern flank was securely based on the west bank—nothing more. In the field, the SHAEF G-2 weekly summary noted the tales of fanatical German resistance drifting back through the ranks, resistance that withstood the best-laid aerial bombardment yet. "While his troops are exhausted and his local reserves gone," noted G-2, "the enemy's tenacity remains."

On the tenth Montgomery issued a new directive, in which he recapitulated his "broad policy" and defiantly ruled out any change in plan, conceding that in view of enemy reinforcement at St.-Lô, "operations of the Second Army must therefore be so staged that they will have a *direct influence* on the operations of the First Army, as well as holding enemy forces on the eastern flank." In addition to Brittany, he wanted "depth and space" in both flanks, the airfields near Caen, and unceasing attacks "by *both* First and Second Armies." Hints of a concession appeared in the appendix outlining the barest outline of a fresh proposal.

> The [Second] Army will retain the ability to be able to operate with a strong armoured force east of the ORNE in the general area between CAEN and FALAISE.
>
> For this purpose a Corps of three armoured divisions will be held in reserve, ready to be employed when ordered by me.
>
> The opportunity for the employment of this Corps may be sudden and fleeting; therefore a study of the problems involved will be begun at once.

On the tenth, Montgomery and Bradley met again and agreed on the rough outlines of the first genuine Anglo-American attack of the war, an attack compelled by the growing threat of stalemate. For a brief moment, stalemate in Normandy was an equalizer. According to Bradley, the two men affirmed that the situation was not as desperate as some believed, and noted that the Germans had not succeeded in substituting infantry for panzer divisions at Caen, and that the remaining defenses extending to the west coast were stretched. The tenacity of the German defense could not substitute for real strength forever, though Bradley confessed discouragement about the slow advance toward La Haye-du-Puits and St.-Lô. But the main offensive by VIII Corps down the Coutances road had ended, which meant a western breakout would have to originate from start points west of St.-Lô, which he did not expect Corlett's XIX Corps to reach for ten days.

Montgomery presented the outlines of GOODWOOD, the plan hinted at in the directive of July 10—a six-division attack sprung from the "airborne bridgehead" east of the Orne to seize the Bourguébus ridge southeast of

Caen and threaten Falaise, to begin after a "feint" from the Odon bridge-head on the sixteenth. Unlike LUCKY STRIKE, GOODWOOD was to be a support offensive timed to precede an American attack from St.-Lô by forty-eight hours so as to fix German attention on Caen. Forty-eight hours later, Bradley would approve operation COBRA, the companion breakout attack at St.-Lô.

COBRA, as the code name connoted, was to be sudden, lethal and unconventional. By July 12, Bradley had set aside many of his earlier expectations. The search for the textbook "first opening" had met with no success, and "broad front" tactics were proving to be unsuitable for the hedgerow country. Accordingly, Bradley and his First Army staff devised a simple and original solution capitalizing on the one resource the enemy lacked: air power.

With COBRA, Bradley abandoned the search for an opening or soft spot in the German line as such. Instead he would create one by concentrating overwhelming air power on a small sector, or "carpet." Instead of attacking simultaneously with several corps on a wide front with supporting and main attacks, COBRA would strike with one corps through the narrow sector opened by the strategic air force. There was little artistry about COBRA, no intricate maneuvers except for the problem of assembling the seven-division strike force secretly at night. Yet the COBRA idea in its particulars had eluded everyone so far.

Bradley later wrote that the COBRA concept came to him in a flash of clarity as he observed the bombing of Fort du Roule in late June. Air support had gotten a bad name at Cherbourg because of "shorts" falling over the American 4th Division that inflicted casualties, damaged morale and undermined confidence between the infantry generals and airmen. Still, Bradley had been fascinated by the spectacle of 250 bombers sweeping over Cherbourg, and had closely observed the results. A siege that might have lasted two weeks had lasted two days. If 250 airplanes could support a ground attack, why not 300 or even 1,000?

Accordingly, First Army planners were on the search not for a "first opening" but for a lateral road, "one that could double as a boundary for the assault units, and as a demarcation line for the aircraft flying in over the battle to distinguish the friendly from the enemy side." The precise point would be near several intersecting highways along which armored columns could dash through enemy lines and fan out through the Normandy bocage.

Two roads running north–south intersected the St.-Lô–Périers road held by advance elements of Panzer Lehr, which was moving into the area from Caen. On the twelfth Bradley marked off the "carpet," a point 6,000 yards by 2,000 yards two miles west of St. Lô, where 1,500 light and heavy bombers of the Eighth Air Force would lay 4,300 tons of explosives, and open the way for infantry to assume defensive positions at the shoulders, followed by a motorized infantry division to dash forward to defend road nets, followed by two armored divisions bound for Coutances. First Corlett's XIX Corps would have to capture St.-Lô, which, if it remained in enemy hands, could be the springboard for a counterattack. Montgomery had already initiated a request for all-out bomber support for GOODWOOD, and on the thirteenth Eisenhower went to work to line up the Eighth Air Force and Bomber Command for similar use in the Orne Valley.

"Ike spoke to Beedle [Smith] about using Bomber Command for area bombing of enemy concentrations in the battle line," Butcher wrote that night. "If an area half a mile in diameter could be saturated in the RAF manner at night, the infantry in a quick attack could then practically walk through. He [Eisenhower] said this technique should be pressed and developed."

So for the first time since June 6, Montgomery, Eisenhower and Bradley had tenuously coordinated post-landing attack plans. Montgomery was thinking in terms of a diversionary attack that would risk substantial Empire casualties to create an opportunity for the U.S. First Army, an indication of the stakes riding on the attack. Eisenhower's uncharacteristic management of the land offensive would also be indicative. Known for his affability, his abilities as a negotiator and his talent for reconciling differences among strong personalities, Eisenhower in the days ahead was about to set aside customary practices that had served him well before. Perhaps the most obvious change in the several days would be his unwillingness to rely on Montgomery's word that Dempsey would mount large-scale diversionary attacks in aid of COBRA as indicated.

The reasons were political, which is to say that while Bradley and Montgomery had come to an agreement about what the military situation required, this was no guarantee that military factors would prevail and that the combined offensive would come off. What the military situation required was coordinated action: an all-out American attack assisted by a sustained and potentially expensive attack on the eastern flank first to arrest the German build-up opposite Bradley and second to block German efforts to mobilize forces to oppose Bradley's breakout once achieved. But the politics of the situation raised doubts in Eisenhower's mind that precise coordination would come easily if at all.

Indeed, political factors weighed in favor of caution and delay on all sides. In Bradley's case, delay once Dempsey's attacks started would give the Germans a chance to reinforce Caen and enhance the odds of a clear breakthrough at St.-Lô at minimum cost. In Montgomery's case, caution and then delay would tend to assure that Bradley would move out as promised and, secondly, give the British a chance to assess Bradley's progress, hence the need for a sustained and costly diversionary attack or the possibility—albeit remote—that Bradley's attack, in drawing off German strength, might open the door for a British breakout at Caen. A standoff of this kind could not be ruled out, particularly since the British, over whom Eisenhower exercised only formalistic authority, had drawn the thankless assignment and were expected to strike first.

Was Eisenhower overreacting? The Montgomery-Bradley accord rested on certain contingencies. At least ten days would pass before Bradley's forces would be ready for an American offensive, ten days in which anything could happen. In his directive of the tenth, Montgomery had preserved an escape hatch by terming the situation in the Orne Valley a "fleeting opportunity," and had closely centralized all GOODWOOD planning under himself. Eisenhower also had to consider that in view of the military situation the Bradley-Montgomery meeting had been belated and not in the spirit of meeting a crisis head-on. The possibility of a military stalemate had been real since the British 7th Armored setback at Tilly on June 12. Yet four weeks passed before anyone acknowledged trouble in the bridgehead, in stark contrast to the alert coordination at Salerno and elsewhere in the Mediterranean where military crisis invariably had a unifying effect. In short, the Normandy invasion was shaping up as a very different kind of campaign, one in which military crisis was divisive at all levels.

Since ANVIL and the July 4 trip to Normandy, all signs had pointed to trouble with Montgomery and the British. Montgomery had raised and then soft-pedaled LUCKY STRIKE, and declined Eisenhower's offer to place an American armored division under Dempsey. Word was about that the British War Office had informed the Second Army that replacements would cease in several weeks. Meanwhile, Brooke had weighed in emphatically behind Montgomery's "right hook," and Churchill, distracted by hopes for a quick conference with Roosevelt, kept suitcases packed to fly to Washington at a moment's notice.

On the ninth, at Chequers, the Prime Minister had hinted to Eisenhower that he was considering another try to abort ANVIL-DRAGOON in light of Alexander's steady advance past Lake Trasimeno. He scolded Eisenhower for his turnaround on ANVIL, then discussed the fresh reports from Berne predicting an imminent army takeover in Germany. Eisenhower, citing business, had declined to stay for lunch and left early for Portsmouth for an afternoon of appointments. Then on the tenth Halifax had come, and Eisenhower received him warily as an emissary from the Prime Minister to sound out the Supreme Commander on negotiations with the German high command. The Halifax visit bore out Eisenhower's suspicion that Montgomery, already under instructions to "conserve" British troops, was under pressure to curtail British operations pending an imminent "collapse" in Germany.

And by now, Tedder had moved to the forefront. Back from Normandy, Eisenhower had asked Tedder, now on record against Montgomery's "dilatory" methods, "to keep in the closest possible touch" with the 21st Army Group, not only to see that Montgomery's requests were satisfied but also "to see that they had asked for every practicable kind of air support." He also had asked Tedder to remain in touch with Portal and the Air Ministry, to hear out complaints about the conduct of the battle and to keep Eisenhower informed. After Eisenhower's Normandy visit, Tedder, according to Butcher, began to "pressure" Eisenhower to form the U.S. 12th Army Group and to assume personal overall command of the land battle—in effect, to demote Montgomery.

Indeed Tedder, on the seventh, had "pushed" Eisenhower to send the message to Montgomery complaining about the drift of German panzers toward Caumont and the arrival of infantry reinforcements at St.-Lô. According to Butcher, Tedder urged a much stiffer message than the one Eisenhower actually sent, and had "objected" to the conciliatory language as too indirect, a "reflection" of Eisenhower's impatience, not a forthright statement of it.

Tedder's "pressures" grew. Back from Chequers on the ninth, with word of the repulse of the British I Corps at the Orne Canal, Eisenhower met with Tedder and solicited his opinion about the scale of the British attack involving one instead of the two corps Montgomery had talked about on the eighth. "Company exercises," Tedder replied, contemptuously noting that Montgomery still had not mounted a single attack involving more than two or three divisions. Tedder warned Eisenhower that Montgomery would never commit his entire mobile force in a coordinated action unless he was ordered to do so. But ordered by whom? That night Tedder, with Eisenhower's consent, phoned Air Chief Marshal Portal, just back from the Continent, to solicit his opinion about Montgomery's "victory" at Caen. Portal agreed that he was deeply concerned about the "stagnation" setting in at the bridgehead, attributable, he thought, to Montgomery, "who could neither be removed nor moved to action."

Montgomery's July 10 directive, couched in defiant tones, was the turning point. Thereafter Tedder coordinated the "whispering campaign at SHAEF," and became a prime mover in the "air-ground dispute," an intense two-week internal war of words pitting the air marshals—Portal, Coningham, Harris, Tedder and Bottomley—against Montgomery and the 21st Army Group staff. The dispute was "mediated" throughout by Eisenhower, but it seems to have been Eisenhower himself who had actually inspired the quarrel through Tedder and encouraged the low-level publicity, which shook London for days.

By July 11, background stories appeared in the British press revealing that the air commanders, long dissatisfied with Montgomery's inability to seize the airfield terrain near Falaise, disputed the claims of victory at Caen. There was veiled criticism of Montgomery's overreliance on air support, and the lack of aggressive thinking at the 21st Army Group. Soon the "air-ground" dispute widened into more general criticism of Montgomery, including low-level accusations that Montgomery had deliberately misled the Air Ministry and SHAEF by exaggerating his intentions at Caen to get air support.

SHAEF joined in. Deputy Chief of Staff General Frederick Morgan, author of the old COSSAC plan, mingled with newsmen and criticized Montgomery for "incurable defensive-mindedness." Reporters were informed confidentially of the original plans calling for an advance to Lisieux and Alençon *before* the American seizure of Avranches. Chief of Staff "Beedle" Smith revealed to staff associates that Montgomery had originally intended a "drive across the Orne from Caen toward the south and southeast exploiting in the direction of Paris," and for one reason or another, "had fundamentally changed his plan on June 30th." Hints of Eisenhower's personal dissatisfaction with Montgomery, and trouble between Montgomery and the air staffs, appeared in the American and British press.

Since the "air-ground" dispute fixed attention on the British Second Army siege at Caen, some, including Bradley in 1951, would suggest that the controversy was nothing more than a ruse to draw German attention away from St.-Lô. A "quick exoneration" of Montgomery from the press criticism in mid-July, Bradley explained, would have exposed the true strategy which formed the basis of Allied plans. But Bradley formed his impression of the mid-month controversy from afar in Normandy.

But the British side of the story, as it has emerged since 1951, revealed the intense emotion aroused in the British high command, which perceived the SHAEF "ruse" as pressure aimed, in Wilmot's words, at "undermining [Montgomery's] plan of command." Montgomery, the target, bitterly wrote in 1958 of his difficult days after July 9 and the sharp deterioration in British-SHAEF coordination brought on by the public campaign to cast doubt on his conduct of the battle. Montgomery castigated Coningham and Tedder for nursing old grudges from Eighth Army days by demanding action at Caen, and castigated the "displaced strategists" at SHAEF, meaning Morgan, whose COSSAC plan for a breakout toward Paris had been discarded in January 1944. "He [Morgan] considered Eisenhower was a God," Montgomery wrote. "He placed me at the other end of the celestial order. So here were the seeds of discord."

"Eisenhower and I were poles apart when it came to the conduct of war," Montgomery continued. "His [Eisenhower's] creed appeared to me to be that there must be aggressive action on the part of everyone at all times. Everybody must attack at all times. My military doctrine was based on unbalancing the enemy while keeping well-balanced myself. . . . I gained the impression that the senior officers at Supreme Headquarters did not understand the doctrine of balance in the conduct of operations. I had learnt it in the battle fighting since 1940, and I knew from experience how it helped to save men's lives."

Montgomery thus pointed up the less publicized but no less important issue—casualties. By July 10 the Allies were fighting a major war of attrition in Normandy, with casualties for both sectors pushing past 100,000. Mont-gomery and his British subordinates could point to the dire pre–D-Day estimates as proof that the policy of "balance" was saving lives, but few were listening, particularly not the Americans. SHAEF policy was to re-lease "Allied" casualty figures, but as casualties approached 100,000 killed and wounded, most knew the Americans were absorbing more than the British, despite the fact that for the moment the American and British forces were roughly equal in size and that Dempsey faced the bulk of panzers.

As casualties mounted, so did American pressure for a formal accounting and action to rectify the 2 to 1 disparity between American and British losses with more aggressive British operations at Caen. One week before the Democratic National Convention, Secretary of War Henry Stimson visited London and met three times with Eisenhower to talk about De Gaulle, ANVIL and reaction at home over the casualty lists, which for the first time brought home to Americans the cost of the European war. In three private meetings with Eisenhower, Stimson warned that Montgomery's leadership of American ground forces was aggravating the problem and urged that Eisenhower proceed with the formation of Bradley's 12th Army Group and assume direct control of the land battle.

Eisenhower expected the British to bid for greater control at SHAEF sooner or later and was reluctant to foreclose their claim, which he sensed would be essential for future coordination. Stimson's "pressure" in mid-July, which injected American election-year rigidities into the equation, was unwelcome, but as a practical matter, American public opinion in an elec-tion year would not long tolerate a British general in command of an Allied force who was reluctant to commit British troops to battle.

The British were very wary of Stimson's visit. The Secretary of War had visited London once before—in the summer of 1943—on his mission to evaluate British firmness on the second front, and on his return to Washing-ton, he had urged Roosevelt to claim command of OVERLORD for the Americans and Marshall. As Marshall's most ardent backer in the Cabinet, Stimson was in London not to look for ways of minimizing American casualties per se, but to look for ways to make heavy casualties acceptable to the American public. His arrival in mid-July was a warning to the British that the "casualty ratio" might emerge as an issue in British dealings with the Americans.

Churchill, who did not want OVERLORD command issues foreclosed, girded for trouble. Shortly before Stimson's arrival, he solicited a memo from Smith spelling out the facts about post-OVERLORD American mobili-zation plans, which Churchill was anxious to have in order, first, to rebut the validity of Marshall's claims about the feasibility and importance of a Mediterranean front in France and, second, to reinforce awareness at SHAEF of the facts about Britain's wartime mobilization effort, which in his opinion compared favorably with the American effort. After all, whereas Britain was at full mobilization with female conscripts and a universal service law, the Americans were not fully mobilized and Congress had voted down a universal service law. The British Home Office was moving heaven and earth to scrape up 90,000 infantry replacements to avoid disbanding five divisions and their service and support components. American manpower had only begun to be tapped. Churchill wanted it understood by Smith and Eisenhower that even though Britain had assumed the role of spelling out the hazards of operations such as OVERLORD, he wanted no mistaking of the fact that the British sacrifice in relative terms exceeded the American war effort so far.

In his memo, Smith confirmed that American mobilization levels, frozen at eighty-eight divisions since August 1943, meant that the flow of divisions would slow to four in the D-plus-90 to D-plus-120 period, and to zero afterwards. "A far larger Army than we now have or possess will be needed to advance through Germany and France, unless there is a total collapse on the Russian or German front," Churchill observed.

A week later, Churchill dug in. "I am sure demands will be made in America for the publication of the American casualties, which are presently greatly in excess of our own," he wrote Ismay. He hoped Eisenhower's "broad-minded plan" to publish "Allied casualties" would survive, but he doubted it. "I am particularly anxious that the Canadian casualties, though stated separately, should be included in the British publication of casualties; otherwise they will be assumed to be part of the American casualties. The point is of Imperial consequence."

And so the elemental question of casualties hovered over the final preparations for GOODWOOD-COBRA. Montgomery had tacitly accepted the secondary role in the coming offensive and so he would go first to "draw the German army onto the British flank at Caen." Meanwhile, twelve divisions of the U.S. First Army slowly advanced on a broad front through the swamps of the lower Vire and Taute, converging on St.-Lô at the rate of 1,000 yards and 1,000 casualties a day. VIII Corps, attacking from La Haye-du-Puits southward, gained five miles in seven days over terrain that nullified American tank and air superiority. Fatigue was widespread, ammunition was short, and Bradley had issued a call for 25,000 additional infantry reinforcements to fill out depleted formations.

On July 12, Montgomery, after conferring with Bomber Command to arrange for a massive aerial bombardment along the corridor selected for GOODWOOD, informed Eisenhower of the details. The Odon feint would begin on the fifteenth, and work up to the attacks east of the Orne that would follow on the seventeenth, which he understood could come roughly twenty-four hours before a heavy American attack west of St.-Lô. According to Tedder, the message contained welcome "evidence of a change of mind," or did it? First, Montgomery assured Eisenhower that on Monday the seventeenth his eastern flank "would burst into flames" with "far-reaching results," but since he would require the full weight of air power on the seventeenth, good weather was "essential" and "we will wait for it if Monday is bad." Second, Montgomery asked Eisenhower to bar visitors, as "this next business will require all of our attention," which suggested that having nothing further to discuss, he did not want to see Eisenhower. Third, he asked SHAEF to "keep information of the intended operation very secret."

The message was curious, particularly the puzzling request for secrecy, which laid to rest Bradley's cheerful assumption that Montgomery was planning a "feint" at Caen. The request to conceal the preparations for GOODWOOD meant either that he had suddenly given up on Bradley and revived plans for a British breakout at Caen—which Eisenhower tended to discount—or that he was hedging about mounting an effective diversionary attack, which Eisenhower understood to mean a major attack preceding COBRA designed to fix German attention on Caen. Bearing out the latter possibility was Montgomery's mention of the weather and a possible postponement. Eisenhower foresaw troubles to the end.

On the thirteenth, Eisenhower canceled his appointments at Portsmouth and quickly returned to Widewing for a meeting with Tedder. The two men discussed Montgomery's message and drafted a reply. In it, Eisenhower told Montgomery that he was "so pepped up concerning the promise of this plan that either Tedder or myself or both will be glad to visit you if we can help in any way." All the air support Montgomery wanted on the seventeenth was available. An American armored division was also available.

That day Montgomery postponed GOODWOOD twenty-four hours because of Corlett's inability to advance and develop the left pincer for COBRA at St.-Lô. He sent Eisenhower terse notification of the change, along with a message to Tedder repeating that he wished to receive no visitors.

Eisenhower, sensing hesitancy, replied that he understood "the proposed timing of the impending operations," and approved the postponement. He added:

> With respect to the plan, I am confident that it will reap a harvest from all the sowing you have been doing during the past weeks. . . . I am not discounting the difficulties or the initial losses, but in this case I am viewing the prospects with the most tremendous optimism and enthusiasm. I would not be surprised to see you gaining a victory that will make some of the "old classics" look like skirmishes between patrols. . . .
>
>   As ever,
>   Ike

According to Butcher, in the next forty-eight hours, mounting press speculation about the possibility of Second Army operations east of Caen coincided with tiresome "negotiations with the British" over the whole range of censorship policies. A major point of contention was SHAEF's sudden decision to adopt the U.S. War Department practice of publicizing American units "in order to bring personalities in the news that brings the war effort closer to the people," as Eisenhower put it. The British felt the publicity would assist the enemy in identifying Allied units.

At dinner on the fifteenth Eisenhower intimated to Butcher that he had tried to institute a uniform policy throughout his Allied command for two years and had yielded to the British view "not particularly because he believed in it," but for the sake of administrative unity. "But now," Butcher wrote, "he feels the time has come when he must fall in with the U.S. demands at least so far as U.S. troops are concerned."

Press speculation about a breakout to Paris bubbled on, eliciting a sharp protest from Montgomery through Smith on the sixteenth as the Canadian II Corps opened its attacks from the Odon bridgehead. Eisenhower replied with a lengthy defense of U.S. War Department policy on censorship, policy toward VIP visits to war sectors, and releases about individual battalions, regiments, divisions and commanding officers which the Americans hoped to publicize for the benefit of hometown consumption. In closing,

> Beedle tells me your headquarters has requested our cooperation in suppressing early news of your forthcoming attack, particularly as to its size. Naturally you have my complete and full support in this purpose especially since newspapers, recently, in the absence of spectacular news, have been doing a lot of speculating that has been uncomfortably close to the truth. However, the general situation in that flank is rather obvious to both sides and any attempt to stop speculation would have been futile. . . .
>
> As ever,
> Ike

The strains of mid-July were telling heavily on Eisenhower. Butcher chronicled the return of all the pre-invasion symptoms—the sleeplessness, the ringing in the ears, signs of fatigue in the company of his private staff. GOODWOOD, a set-piece six-division assault in the tradition of El Alamein, an attack that Britain could no longer afford, was destined to be launched amid a blaze of publicity on Monday, July 17. Eisenhower regretted the pressure he had felt compelled to apply on Montgomery, a man he deeply admired. Montgomery, pushed into a diversionary attack billed as the breakout, would be diminished, then further diminished when Bradley stepped up to army group command to serve as his equal. Tedder, who had undertaken the role of Eisenhower's liaison with Brooke and Montgomery, was risking friendships, as was Morgan.

After a three-week lapse, Eisenhower resumed writing home. He told Mamie about John's visit and about the many people who had complimented him since about his son. Weeks before, he had cautioned Mamie against following John to Fort Benning during his training period. "Undoubtedly he has some feeling (at least subconsciously) that he has always been carefully watched over. He is wondering how he will do 'on his own.' So he must be . . . on his own before he comes up against really critical problems. I know how you feel about him . . . but I think brief visits are more advisable than any long stay."

The letter apparently elicited a tart response from Mamie. Eisenhower wrote again several days later to apologize for upsetting her with advice about John. He went on to describe his dreary and "humdrum existence," disrupted by V-1 alerts. He was saddened by the death of one of his office staff and of several British friends in a recent V-1 attack. Occasionally Eisenhower indulged in a few thoughts about life after the war. He wanted a normal existence again; or, he caught himself, "maybe there is no such thing—but I keep thinking there is and want to go back to it." He remarked how much had happened in such a short time: "The time races by and you wonder where it has gone. While I often feel that I cannot remember the time when I was not carrying this burden, I feel, on the other hand, that it was only yesterday that we were at Fort Myer together, and you stood by the flagpole to wave goodbye."

"How glad I'll be when this is over," he added in a brief note on the sixteenth. "In the meantime, one simply doesn't dare think about the sacrifices and losses."

By the night of the seventeenth the Allies had reason to anticipate success in Normandy, for they were prevailing in a campaign of attrition. Estimates agreed that German losses were about equal to Allied losses—115,000 killed and wounded in the six-week campaign to date. On the Allied side, 903,061 American troops and 663,295 British troops in 34 divisions had landed through the beach ports along with 330,000 vehicles. Of the 28 German divisions, three had been destroyed and six reduced to less than 50 percent effectiveness. Replacements from German training depots had arrived slowly, fatigued from running a gauntlet of air bombardment and harassment, day and night. The German army group in Normandy by mid-July was stretched, plugging holes and holding on like a losing poker player forced to double each hand, as Eisenhower later put it. Lacking protection in the air and outgunned, the Germans were timing their capacity to hold on, and could not risk a retreat over the plains of northern France.

But since the end of the July 7–9 moon-tide phase and thus the prospect of landings in Calais, Rommel had been rearranging the front to dig in for the long siege and the arrival of reinforcements. Panzer Lehr had broken off the engagement at the Odon bridgehead and moved in behind St.-Lô. The II SS Panzer Corps drifted westward toward Caumont; the 2nd Panzer and the 116th Panzer, ariving from Amiens, moved into reserve south of

Caen. After Caen on the ninth, the Germans weighed the possibility that the Americans would attempt a breakout and were reinforcing the sector.

The assault commenced in stages as Canadian attacks from the Odon bridgehead on the fifteenth drew the 9th SS Panzer Division, a battle group of the 1st SS and the 2nd Panzer. For a precious seventy-two hours the Odon attack froze enemy movement west of the river Orne.

Dempsey was next. Intended originally as a mass assault east of the Orne to rush Falaise, GOODWOOD was aimed at the Bourguébus ridge, the heights commanding the eastern Caen suburbs. Montgomery reminded the VIII Corps commander, General Richard O'Connor, on the fifteenth that the eastern flank was "a bastion on which the whole future of the campaign in northwest Europe depends. It must be a firm bastion; and if it were to become unstable, the operations on the western flank would cease." For the moment, however, it was essential to halt the westward drift of German panzers. Two infantry corps would clear the flanks while VIII Corps spearheaded the attacks along a narrow 1,500-yard corridor between rows of fortified villages, then advanced up the slope through several screens of prepared defenses.

On the night of the seventeenth, VIII Corps crossed special bridges hoisted over the river, entered the "airborne" bridgehead seized by the British 65th Airborne on D-Day, then turned south. Surprise was lost. Luftwaffe reconnaissance dropped flares and illuminated the night crossings. As the story goes, General Sepp Dietrich, a veteran of the eastern front, had learned to press an ear to the ground at night to detect the low rumble of tank treads passing over limestone. The German defenses in the Orne Valley were alert and ready, reinforced that night by elements of two panzer divisions.

On July 18 at first daylight, 1,599 medium and light bombers of the RAF pounded the forward infantry defenses in the net of fortified villages between the western suburbs of Caen and Troarn, opening a day of turbulent emotion in Normandy, Portsmouth and London. For two hours the earth shuddered with the impact of 7,000 tons of explosives. At 7:45 the Canadian II Corps on the right rushed past the dazed German defenses into the eastern suburbs of Caen while British I Corps infantry marched toward Troarn. In the center the 11th Armored led the charge on a 1,500-yard front through the corridor toward the slopes of the Bourguébus ridge. Within three hours the 11th had reportedly gained six miles and reached the slopes. The mood of exultation at 21st Army Group Headquarters spurred Montgomery to make a rash announcement that "troops of the 2nd Army attacked and broke through into the area east of the Orne and southeast of Caen" and confirming that the Second Army was "now operating in the open country to the south and southeast of Caen."

"E. [Eisenhower] just wants Montgomery to keep pressing forward," wrote Summersby at her desk as a luncheon conference broke up in Portsmouth.

The elation did not last long. Heavy resistance had developed at Vimont, and Dempsey, who observed the attack through binoculars, knew by II A.M. that the assault had not penetrated the prepared defenses. Six German defense screens stretched out at least twice the expected depth of four or five miles. The British 11th Armored reached the high-water mark at noon, piercing the German line on the north slope of the ridge. Then disorganization at road centers, slow movement over the cratered roads, and counterattacks on the flanks imposed a halt. A panzer battalion of the 1st SS reinforced the ridge by noon, followed by battle groups of the II SS Panzer Corps dispatched east from the Odon bridgehead.

"I am willing to lose 200–300 tanks to take the ridge of Bourguébus," Dempsey had said beforehand, "but I cannot risk the infantry." As a last resort Dempsey ordered the follow-up 7th Armored to drive relentlessly in behind the 11th, but the attack failed to get under way until dusk. By nightfall the Canadians continued through the eastern suburbs of Caen, but the battle for the corridor had degenerated into a battle over strongpoints. The 11th Armored stalled at the ridge, with a loss of 126 tanks, over one half of its armor.

At 9 P.M. Tedder phoned with sketchy news of German reinforcements at Troarn and Caen. Gloom descended on Portsmouth, where most of those present, including Eisenhower, assumed that Montgomery after meeting slight resistance had drawn up. Eisenhower was personally angry with Montgomery, who had pledged an offensive, not an attack. Telling Tedder he was tired of Montgomery always wanting to "draw up his administrative tail," Eisenhower scheduled a trip to the bridgehead the following day.

After midnight Butcher spent four hours decoding a personal message from Montgomery, who elaborated on Tedder's report. In it Montgomery "rejoiced on his gains," informed Eisenhower of his decision to consolidate the seven-mile penetration east of the Orne and passed along, without explanation, the surprising news that Bradley had postponed COBRA twenty-four hours, from the twentieth to the twenty-first. In view of Bradley's postponement, Butcher suspected that Eisenhower might wish to delay his visit to the front. Despite the early hour, at 4 A.M. Butcher scurried with the text of the message. He found Eisenhower in a deep sleep. "It won't affect the trip," he grumbled upon hearing the news, then fell back to sleep.

July 19. The trip to France was off. Eisenhower's B-25 at Thorney Island was grounded by a "fog which touched the ground," according to his pilot, Major Larry Hansen. For twenty-four hours, consultations with Montgomery hung fire, and essential information was lacking.

Eisenhower spent the morning pacing his office. He was not surprised by the limited gains. His concern was getting to the bottom of the implied connection between Montgomery's halt and Bradley's postponement. Did Montgomery suspect Bradley of lying back? The minimal forty-eight-hour separation between the two attacks was a form of assurance to Montgomery that the secondary assault at Caen would not be exposed to undue losses. Meanwhile, GOODWOOD was stationary amid reports of major counterattacks along the flanks of the GOODWOOD corridor. Montgomery at an early morning briefing startled the press by pronouncing his "satisfaction" with the results of an offensive he now called a "battle of position."

The news of the halt came as a shock at SHAEF, where it was widely believed that Montgomery had gone through the motions and now proposed to sit. At Widewing and Portsmouth the corridors rang with indignation. Rumors circulated that Dempsey had actually broken through the last German screen north of the ridge and deliberately stopped. Tedder, pacing excitedly, offered to lay before the BCOs his views in writing in support of "anything Eisenhower wished to do about Montgomery for not going places with his big armored push." Leigh-Mallory and Coningham, who had arranged to support the attack with the most elaborate aerial bombardment in history, smoldered. Gault noted talk about sacking Montgomery and speculation about potential replacements, an "impractical" suggestion, he noted, because strict British censorship practices had "limited the field of available replacements to a handful."

Eisenhower's forebodings grew after a talk with Churchill, who called to demand that SHAEF lift a ban on visitors to the front and permit him to visit Montgomery, warning that he would otherwise make a "War Cabinet issue" of it. Soon Eisenhower received a cable from Montgomery asking for an urgent conference the following day "alone."

Churchill, eager to get the facts, dispatched Brooke to Normandy late that afternoon after the fog had lifted to consult with Montgomery. According to his diary account of the meeting, Brooke warned Montgomery about the strained reaction to his press conference and of the "tendency of the Prime Minister to listen to suggestions Montgomery played for safety and was not prepared to take risks." Montgomery replied to Brooke that he was "delighted with his success east of Caen." In the course of his explanation, Montgomery complained that Stimson's tour of the American sector had prevented Bradley from "getting out battle orders on time"—hence the American postponement from the twentieth to the twenty-first. The implication was that Bradley had unjustifiably delayed COBRA.

Pleased and enlightened, Brooke asked Montgomery to clear up a slight misunderstanding. The Prime Minister's anger was due in part to a false impression that Eisenhower had merely been conveying Montgomery's wishes in asking the Prime Minister to stay in London. Montgomery complied. Brooke hand-carried Montgomery's handwritten note back to Churchill. Later that night, Churchill called Brooke to say he was "delighted with Montgomery's letter and felt rather ashamed of himself for all he had said."

Confined to Portsmouth awaiting a dinner appointment with General Alexander Surles, director of Pentagon Public Relations, Eisenhower spent the afternoon in bed reading. Butcher described him as "blue as indigo" over the lack of progress at Caen, resting fitfully, reading Westerns, trying to pass the day quickly, waiting to get ashore.

July 20. One of the most fateful days of the war dawned clear in Normandy. It was sultry in Chicago, Illinois, where the Democratic Convention gathered to nominate Roosevelt for a fourth term and Senator Harry S. Truman as his running mate to replace the ousted Henry A. Wallace. It was also a sultry day in Berlin, where the ring of German Home Army conspirators prepared to seize communications throughout Germany and Europe. Word of Hitler's assassination was expected by one-fifteen that afternoon.

By now the Home Army conspiracy had been warned by military sources in Paris that the front was about to burst in Normandy. Limited time remained to act before the Germans had nothing to offer the West in return for an armistice, and all sides pressed on irresistibly to implement unconditional surrender. A government of Social Democrats was set to assume power under General Ludwig Beck, who had resigned in 1938 as Chief of Staff in protest over the German occupation of the Sudetenland. A majority favored continuing the war in the east while offering the Allies free passage to Berlin. The issue was clear and urgent: Would Germany respond to Attlee's summons and begin to make amends to a devastated Europe and earn her way back into the family of civilized nations?

Low cloud and fog grounded all flights at midmorning. "Even if I have to swim, I have to get across the Channel," Eisenhower told Butcher at nine-thirty as he summoned the SHAEF command aircraft. By eleven, Eisenhower was airborne, and within the hour he was locked in private conference with Montgomery, grilling him for an explanation of his halt at Troarn and making his displeasure known in no uncertain terms. Eisenhower wanted the attack resumed at Caen and was determined to erase promptly any misunderstanding about Bradley's intentions toward COBRA.

Eisenhower found Montgomery "very pleased" with the results of GOOD-WOOD. The Second Army had gained a precarious foothold east of the Orne, had diverted the 116th Panzer, uncommitted two days before, and the 2nd Panzer and the II SS Panzer Corps which had been drifting toward Caumont. He was "full of confidence" about COBRA, and convinced a "single annihilating stroke" at St.-Lô would roll up the German Seventh Army. Emphasizing "balance," Montgomery reminded Eisenhower of the truism "If everyone attacks, nobody can exploit," which implied that Montgomery may have been angling for LUCKY STRIKE after all. Shortly after Eisenhower's departure and before the arrival of the Prime Minister, Montgomery ordered Dempsey to withdraw the British armor into reserve. GOODWOOD was over, with British losses in thirty-six hours totaling 500 tanks and 4,000 men.

Eisenhower proceeded to Grandcamp for discussions with Bradley, Collins, Gerow, Spaatz and Brereton, who had spent the afternoon poring over final plans for COBRA. Though Corlett was just then clearing the town of St.-Lô after an exhausting twelve-day advance, Eisenhower ordered COBRA to proceed on the twenty-first, whereupon Air "Ops" were issued to all commands at three-thirty. Eisenhower, tense and expectant, returned to Portsmouth in time for dinner. "Monty says it is up to Bradley to go ahead," Summersby wrote in her journal.

Weather predictions for the twenty-first were bad and the extended forecast uncertain, so Leigh-Mallory indicated a second twenty-four-hour postponement of COBRA, which became official at 11 P.M. Even Butcher sensed trouble that night. Montgomery had delivered the secondary attack at Caen, and now, locked in meetings with the Prime Minister, he was not likely to resume until COBRA was under way. Eisenhower retired early to the trailer, while Butcher recapitulated the events of the day: Montgomery's stunning halt at Caen, Bradley's troublesome postponement at St.-Lô, Eisenhower's dash for the Continent that morning, the ongoing "air ground dispute" and the second postponement of COBRA. "How he [Eisenhower] will handle this situation remains the principal suspended interest to the diary at the moment," he closed.

Throughout the night, sketchy news reached London about the uprisings in Berlin, Breslau, Vienna, Prague, Munich, Paris and Athens set off by late-afternoon reports that the Führer had been killed by a bomb concealed in a briefcase in a conference room at his East Prussian headquarters. The conspirators, for a time, controlled large sections of the government quarters in Berlin. Then, at six, Nazi radio confirmed the attempt on Hitler's life, adding that he had escaped death and suffered only "slight bruises" and superficial wounds from the effects of the explosion. The Home Army had formed a provisional government under General Ludwig Beck, but confronted with conflicting reports, hesitated to act.

At 12:30 A.M. Hitler in Berlin emerged to address Europe and the German people by radio. "If I speak to you today," Hitler said, "it is first in order that you should hear my voice and should know that I am unhurt and well and secondly that you should know of a crime unparalleled in German history." The Führer recited the bare details of the attempt on his life, which had killed or severely wounded several of his closest associates. His own survival was, he said, "confirmation of the task given to me by Providence to continue in the pursuit of the aim of my life, as I have done hitherto." Hitler exonerated the German people and the Wehrmacht, which he called on to stamp out traitors with "obedience typical of the German army." He warned listeners not to heed orders issued by "a very small clique of criminal elements, which will now be exterminated quite mercilessly."

Hitler's exoneration of the Wehrmacht rang hollow, and it was thought to be significant that in the ensuing announcements made that night, representatives of the armed forces were omitted from the roll call of loyalty pledges offered by Grossadmiral Karl Dönitz of the Navy and Hermann Göring of the Luftwaffe. But roundups of suspected anti-Nazi dissidents went on through the night in Budapest, Vienna, Berlin, Paris and Prague.

There is no record that Eisenhower was informed of the assassination attempt that night. Churchill was aboard H.M.S. *Enterprise* returning from his conference with Montgomery when he learned the news. Although he maintained a buoyant demeanor in the next few days, Churchill suspected at once that any chance of an army takeover was ended, and with it, hopes of averting the protracted war that would leave Europe a "charnel house," bankrupt Britain, and demoralize the Continent for a century.

In *Triumph and Tragedy*, Churchill would describe the scene in the wardroom at midnight where a group of officers gathered around a piano to sing songs, including the chorus of "Rule Britannia." The Prime Minister asked the assemblage if anyone knew all the stanzas and discovered that no one did. He then stood and recited the words, and in his account of that night reprinted them in his book "for the benefit and the instruction of the reader," a testament to Britain's growing isolation so plainly linked to Germany's suicidal course.

> The nations not so blessed as thee
> Must in their turn to tyrants fall,
> Whilst thou shalt flourish great and free
> The dread and envy of them all.
>
> The muses still with freedom found
> Shall to thy happy coast repair
> Blest Isle with matchless beauty crowned
> And manly hearts to guard the fair.

COBRA

July 21. COBRA was poised to strike. On the western flank, Middleton's VII Corps had reached the Taute River, the staging point for an attack southward along the Cotentin road. In the center, "Lightning Joe" Collins' VII Corps, consisting of three infantry, one motorized infantry and two armored divisions, had closed the Périers–St.-Lô road; XIX Corps assembled at the outskirts of St.-Lô, and to the extreme east, V Corps under Gerow had taken Tourniers. On the same day, General Brereton assumed command of the Allied airborne forces, a combined American-British corps consisting of the airborne units used for D-Day and other airborne troops arriving in Europe, giving the Allies the ability to envelop the thin German defenses in Normandy if COBRA did not gain a quick breakout.

In the past week, several GIs had invented and shown to Bradley a simple device that would greatly ease the task of armor. With German tetrahedra attached to the bows, the U.S. T-30 Shermans could slice through the mounds of hedgerow without pause. In *Crusade in Europe,* Eisenhower later described the "simple invention that restored the effectiveness of the tank and gave a tremendous boost to morale throughout the army." By the morning of the twenty-first, 30 percent of Collins' tanks had been equipped with the device.

But to gain a decision at St.-Lô, Bradley knew he had to seize the roads, and that tanks had to stream down these roads quickly. This depended on precision timing of the planned aerial bombardment and cratering in front of the assault force to avoid "shorts," the absence of a deep German reserve behind the forward infantry defense, and above all, good weather.

According to the First Army diary, with the rain falling "in cats and dogs," Bradley at his morning conference told his division commanders he had no plans that day "other than to try to keep dry." Few even seemed aware of the attempted assassination of Hitler. Rumors of a gas attack swept through V Corps that morning and were traced to a German artillery shot near an ammunition dump which had touched off dynamite, emitting head-ache-causing fumes. The First Army diarist noted local counterattacks along the St.-Lô–Périers road and a rare appearance of the Luftwaffe after lunch. Panzer Lehr reinforced the line west of St.-Lô near VI Corps start points for COBRA. "The enemy undoubtedly smells something coming," noted the diarist.

At Portsmouth, reactions to events in Berlin were subdued. Radio Berlin reported fifty summary executions, including those of Beck and Count Klaus von Stauffenberg, the would-be assassin. Himmler assumed command of the Home Army, and Goebbels, as the new Reich Plenipotentiary for Total War, convened a military tribunal to investigate allegations of Wehrmacht complicity. Butcher wrote that he was "excited about it," though no one else was. Eisenhower, who barely paid attention to the news, reminded Butcher that eleven SS divisions were now on the line in Normandy. General Strong, who in 1938 had been the British military attaché in Berlin, observed that the brutal measures announced that morning would probably be popular. "Germans like a strong man," he said. "Severe action to obtain discipline even by widespread purge makes the German feel that he is being led by strong men."

Strong and Eisenhower were suspicious of the whole affair. It was conceivable that Hitler had trumped up the incident to gain a pretext to shake up the General Staff. Only a day earlier, there had been neutral press reports of mutiny in several divisions of Army Group North pinned against the Baltic. According to sources in Stockholm, Himmler's appointment had been set a day before the "bomb." Eisenhower believed that Hitler would exploit the aborted coup to demand even more drastic sacrifices of the German people. "German resistance, in other words, would stiffen, not collapse?" Butcher asked.

"Correct," Strong replied.

By now difficulties were cropping up in all quarters. Several days before at an air conference, Portal warned Tedder that the air marshals were impatient with progress in the bridgehead—most of them were weary of tying up strategic bombers in direct support of the ground forces, a role for which heavy bombers were ill designed. Portal reminded Tedder that the transport plan was a temporary measure to protect the invasion force while it went ashore. Technically the bridgehead was "safe" in light of Montgomery's recent assertion that Rommel, without substantial reinforcement, lacked the power to defeat the bridgehead. Portal wanted to resume POINT-BLANK, as did Spaatz, who felt that SHAEF was wasting a precious asset, and predicted that the American and British people would soon begin to question "tying up tremendous air power to plow up fields—in front of an army reluctant to move."

Admiral King, with Roosevelt's election-year assent, had transferred most of the battleships, destroyers and cruisers from the English Channel, stripping SHAEF of an important support weapon that was still needed to pin down several German divisions in the Orne Valley. There were rumblings that soon the lodgement area literally would be too small for the mass of idle American divisions in training in the United States and awaiting shipment to Europe. General Gale had warned that without a second deep-water port to complement Cherbourg, the OVERLORD build-up would "collapse." Port Director Lord Leathers warned SHAEF that unless Cherbourg could be opened soon and receive the growing accumulation of ships standing offshore at UTAH and GOLD, he would propose stockpiling American equipment in the British Isles. Eisenhower had swiftly rejected Leather's assessment and convened a conference to expedite special measures to open Cherbourg.

By nightfall there were signs that the offensive was unraveling. In the wake of his meeting with Churchill, Montgomery issued a new directive. The Second Army had gained a "good firm bridgehead beyond the Orne," he wrote, which meant that the army group had gained the "ability to penetrate strongly in that sector when desired." Now it was "vital that the western flank should swing southward and eastward. . . . the whole weight of the Army Group will therefore be directed to this task." In the brief appendix listing Army tasks, Montgomery ordered VIII Corps back across the Orne to rest and refit for attacks on or about August 3 in the Caumont sector.

German armor was disengaging east of Caen and drifting westward, and with word that COBRA was off another twenty-four hours because of forecasts of heavy rain, Eisenhower knew he was going to have to demand resumption of the attacks east of Caen. Tedder arrived that night, and the two men calmly went to work on a reply to Montgomery. In it, Eisenhower summarized their talk on the twentieth; first, he acknowledged the "serious political questions" involved in resuming attacks at Caen, including British casualties and "the seriousness of the reinforcement problem for Dempsey." But "for the moment at least," Eisenhower urged Montgomery to consider that political problems paralleled the military factors.

Eisenhower reminded Montgomery of his letter written long ago (on July 8) in which he declared that "we are now so well situated that we can attack the Germans hard and continuously in the relentless pursuit of our objectives." Eisenhower still agreed with this, and the main objective in Brittany was best achieved by relentless and "simultaneous" attacks in all sectors now that Allied strength was at its zenith. "Time is vital."

In his reply Montgomery denied "any intention of stopping offensive operations on the eastern flank." For that reason he had regrouped, firmed up the sector facing due east with the Canadian Army, and reorganized the Second Army to "devote its main attention to offensive action toward Falaise," which would unfold in stages beginning with an attack by the British I Corps at Troarn on July 25. Meanwhile, he was forming a reserve. His note ended with:

> "See para. 14 of M-512 which provides for a force to exploit any success gained. Does above assure you that we see eye to eye on the main military problem. If *not repeat not* do please let me know.
>
> We are apparently in complete agreement in conviction that vigorous and persistent offensive should be sustained by both First and Second Armies. General offensive action is further indicated at this moment because of evidence that enemy must utilize SS troops to ensure effectiveness of other units.
>
> Yours ever,
> Monty

July 22. At an off-the-record press conference in Portsmouth, Eisenhower expressed his disappointment that the campaign was not progressing rapidly and deplored speculation about an imminent armistice and "talk of postwar plans." To the assembled reporters, he downplayed the possibility of a German collapse, predicting that "the defeat of Germany would be military." Asked about his year-end prediction before leaving Algiers that the European war would end in 1944, Eisenhower explained that he had "intended it more as a challenge than as a prediction." By July 22, the blame for failure to achieve victory in 1944 loomed as a major point of contention between the Americans and British, and so Eisenhower specifically instructed reporters not to print the question or the answer, lest "the qualifications be overlooked."

July 23. A difficult day. Summersby's journal reads: "Meeting—the War Room. Attack again postponed. . . . Letter from Tedder greatly concerned regarding lack of progress on land-front." Time was running out at St.-Lô. The 116th Panzer had pulled back into reserve south of Caen. The 2nd Panzer inched toward Caumont, and the II SS Panzer Corps left the Bourguébus ridge and crossed the Orne.

Tedder pressed an eleventh-hour campaign to hold Montgomery to a resumption of the offensive in the British sector. In a talk with Brooke that day, Tedder charged that Montgomery had thrown away a "historic opportunity" to exploit the disorganization of German defenses in the wake of the failed coup. He warned Brooke that SHAEF was losing faith in Montgomery, and that he had personally urged Eisenhower to "act at once" to form the two American armies and to assert direct command over the land battle. Tedder forwarded to Eisenhower his BCOS letter in which he enunciated the grievances of the air marshals against the cautious Army leadership. He did so, he wrote, because he realized the difficulties of Allied command and hoped that "the expression of my views as your immediate British subordinate may be of some assistance to you to support you in any action you may consider the situation demands."

Tedder's appeals apparently made little impression on Whitehall, however. The War Cabinet was still concentrating on the implications of the failed German putsch, for even the most confirmed optimists conceded now that the Nazis were entrenched. The assassination attempt on Hitler coincided with a notable hardening by Moscow on a variety of issues, including the Turks, Poland and the hoped-for British-Russian arrangements on the Balkans that Stalin had called off earlier in the week, citing American "doubts regarding this question." With Marshal Konev close to Warsaw, the Russians were about to take a far-reaching step on Poland. Members of the Polish Lublin National Liberation Committee forming in Moscow would soon announce that Poland would scrap the constitution of 1935 and revert to the constitution of 1921. The critical difference between the two was a provision in the 1935 constitution, now defunct, providing that a Polish government in wartime could perpetuate itself "even if in exile." The measure came shortly after Roosevelt's acceptance address to the Democratic National Convention and his departure for meetings with MacArthur in Honolulu, sparing the President political embarrassment over this rebuff to the exiled Polish government in London.

July 24. COBRA, set to go at midday, was again postponed because of fog and rain. Bradley waited until the last possible moment before making the decision, worried that the teeming concentrations of troops opposite Panzer Lehr would compromise American plans. Moreover, Bradley knew that his forces could not tolerate delay much longer, and sensed the difficulties with the British.

At Grandcamp, preparations had hummed along for the attack all morning. Joined by Brereton, Ridgway and six war correspondents, Bradley motored to his forward headquarters at noon, preparing to issue the orders at any time before 3 P.M. But with fog still clinging to the ground, foursomes of P-47 dive bombers, far off course, strafed and bombed along the Périers road, striking forward positions of the American 30th Infantry Division. A squadron of B-17s flying north–south instead of east–west dropped clusters of bombs "short" over the American lines. Orange flares thrown up to warn the bombers away were lost in the dust and smoke. For thirty minutes the U.S. division was pinned in foxholes under American bombardment. By one o'clock, word arrived that Leigh-Mallory and Bradley had called off the attack.

By one-forty Bradley and his staff had rushed to 30th Division Headquarters to restore shaken morale. The death toll was seventeen dead, eighty wounded. The mistaken bomb run had not only knocked out a regiment of the 30th Division, but had betrayed the narrow sector marked off for the attack, handing the Germans an opportunity to place a defensive screen south of the Périers road.

Bradley was also shocked by the north–south course flown by the bombers over the lines instead of the parallel course agreed upon with Leigh-Mallory on the nineteenth at a Stanmore conference. On the phone with Leigh-Mallory, Bradley learned that the bombing pattern over the "carpet" had not been inadvertent. In fact, Eisenhower had approved it when he was told that planners had discovered the air sorties would take ninety minutes longer if flown on a parallel course and expose the bomber group to unacceptably heavy flak. No one at AEAF had informed VII Corps or First Army, and so late that afternoon Bradley flew on to London for a stormy conference with Leigh-Mallory, who held that unless the pattern was perpendicular, AEAF would simply refuse to fly. Grimly, Bradley returned to France.

That same afternoon, Eisenhower learned that Montgomery had set aside plans to launch a supporting British I Corps attack on Troarn. Butcher described the luncheon aboard the H.M.S. *Victory,* at which the main topic of conversation was GOODWOOD and the British manpower situation. According to Butcher, their "friends at Naval Headquarters" spoke of the grim facts of Britain's ebbing manpower, describing the drastic steps to comb out supply units, the RAF and the Navy to find the 90,000 needed replacements. British formations, when depleted, were being cannibalized and written off. The word was that the British high command was "so conscious of Britain's ebbing manpower that they hesitate to permit an attack where a division might be lost."

Afterward, Eisenhower received De Guingand at SHAEF forward for a talk about Montgomery's postponement and the situation on both flanks. Eisenhower warned De Guingand that time was running out. Without a supporting British attack and continuous action on the Caen front, there was a risk that the Germans would be able to concentrate reserves on the eastern flank of VII Corps, which was supposed to advance heedless of risk toward Coutances. At length, Eisenhower conceded that British casualties and reserves were a legitimate concern. Nonetheless, Montgomery had to understand his own problems—that he and Bradley were under pressure from the War Department to conserve American lives too. But the crucial point was that action was needed now—COBRA was set to go for the twenty-fifth, weather permitting. Worn down by four months of unbroken strain, Eisenhower and Smith slipped away for some fishing at the country estate of Ivan Cobbold in Suffolk.

Would the British attack? Evidently, Eisenhower's meeting with De Guingand had an effect. That night a lengthy letter arrived from Montgomery outlining in detail his plans for resuming the offensive in the British sector. In it, Montgomery described the "quite frightful" weather that had practically shut down air operations and turned the area southeast of Caen into a sea of mud. Montgomery proceeded to restate his intentions spelled out on the twenty-first in language that had become all too familiar. He wrote of the "definite and continuous" threat being maintained at Caen in anticipation of the "really big victory" on the western flank. Montgomery then outlined an intricate four-tier offensive bracketing the Orne and featuring heavy attacks in the Caumont sector in order to block German efforts to assemble forces against Bradley and to form new lines in the St.-Lô area, all set to climax with a four-armored-division attack "to create complete chaos in the Falaise area, destroying everything seen and generally to put wind up the enemy" on August 4, eleven days hence.

Once again, the concession appeared in the closing paragraph, cloaked by Montgomery's terse recapitulation of Bradley's latest postponement and a personal request that Bradley, in view of poor forecasts, set a 6 P.M. H-Hour if necessary to get COBRA rolling on the twenty-fifth. He reiterated his concern about the weather and the major problems he foresaw in lining up his forces for the push to Falaise. *Despite* all of this, however, the multitiered "left-right-left-right" would commence with Canadian attacks east of the Orne beginning at 3:30 A.M. on the twenty-fifth, several hours away.

Meanwhile, Eisenhower had asked Butcher to make arrangements for a trip to Normandy by 10 A.M. the following morning, and had taken the usual step of dispatching a letter to Bradley through Montgomery, his superior, knowing it would be read by both and understood by both to mean that COBRA was definitely set for the twenty-fifth:

Dear Brad,

My high hopes and best wishes ride with you in your attack today, which is the largest ground assault yet staged in this war by American troops exclusively. Speaking as the responsible American rather than the Allied commander, I assure you that the eyes of our whole country will be following your progress and I take full responsibility for answer to them for the necessary price of victory. But a breakthrough at this juncture will minimize the total cost. General Montgomery's plan calls for a vigorous and continuing offensive by the other armies in the line, thus allowing you to pursue every advantage of an ardor verging on recklessness and with all your troops without fear of a major counteroffensive from the forces the enemy now has on this front. All these attacks are mutually supporting and if Second Army should secure a breakthrough simultaneously with yours, the results will be incalculable. Good luck to every one of you.

At I A.M. Butcher answered the secure phone. The Prime Minister wished to speak to Eisenhower but did not want to disturb his sleep. Butcher walked down the cinder pathway and paused at Eisenhower's door. Hearing nothing, he concluded that Eisenhower was reading and opened it slowly. The room was dark, but before Butcher could tiptoe out, Eisenhower sat upright, grabbed the phone and took the call. "Prime Minister, what do your people think about the situation over there?" Eisenhower asked. Butcher left.

Churchill and Eisenhower talked for thirty minutes. According to Butcher, Churchill had a lot to talk about—first about the combined attack set for the morrow and Montgomery's agreement to bolster Canadian II Corps with several British divisions and, second, about the Prime Minister's "exuberance" over the reports of "disarray in Germany." Churchill had news that Hitler had instituted the Nazi salute in all Wehrmacht formations, a practice bound to kindle resentment between the army and the party.

Churchill's enthusiasm over the signs of "German disarray," may not have been very convincing to Eisenhower, but his larger point was clear: he seemed to be reproaching Eisenhower for remarks in recent days that indicated insensitivity to the fact that patriotic Germans had acted. "For the first time he [Ike] seemed enthusiastic" about the signs of "German collapse," Butcher wrote afterward. "I think he caught some of the PM's exuberance." De Guingand called from Montgomery's headquarters to confirm that British units would "bolster the attack" by Canadian II Corps.

July 25. It was a gray dawn along the fifty-mile front in Normandy. Reports of the Russian drive on Warsaw continued to stream in, and as the Germans yielded ground in Poland, shocking secrets came to light. American correspondents at Minsk filed stories telling of irrefutable evidence of mass slaughter and atrocities, which would spur an outraged New York *Herald Tribune* to editorialize that the government "responsible for such mass atrocities should be exterminated." That day, Hitler would promulgate his Total War decree empowering Himmler and Goebbels to comb every reserve of German manpower in transport, business, agriculture and government service to form Volksturm, or People's Divisions, for the defense of the Reich, a draconian measure soon followed by the Kinship Hostage decree on August 1, formally making families liable for the performance of kin on the battlefront.

But would these measures work in time?

In Normandy, the German troops fought bravely, but pessimism had set in among the command. Many, including Rommel and Von Kluge—rumored to have been killed or wounded by Allied bombers on the seventeenth—had come under suspicion of complicity in the plot against Hitler. Little by little, from the German point of view, the situation had deteriorated to the point of hopelessness. Reinforcements were on the way, but would not arrive in time to stave off the disaster that the German command in Normandy sensed was about to engulf the Seventh Army. On the St.-Lô front, despite the reinforcement in recent days, SS General Paul Hausser held only three battalions in reserve. He lacked real power in the form of the superior tanks, superior artillery and aerial superiority that had provided the Allies with a decisive edge in every engagement so far.

By the night of July 24, the German high command surmised that yet another dose of Allied air power was being readied for breakout attempts that week—a new, if not revolutionary, development against which the Germans were finding themselves powerless. This was ironic, since it had been the Germans who had perfected tactical bombers as an artillery and reconnaissance weapon in Poland, France and Russia. But German close air-ground support doctrines seemed quaint compared with the Allied bombardment of the invasion coast on D-Day, at Cherbourg on the twenty-sixth, at Caen on July ninth, and at Troarn on the eighteenth, bombardments that marked the arrival of air power as a weapon of decisive power on a field of battle. Indeed, within days of his arrival in France, Von Kluge had concluded that Allied air power could in itself come close to breaking the German front. "It is immaterial whether such a bomb carpet strikes good troops or bad, they are more or less annihilated," Von Kluge warned Hitler. "If this occurs frequently, then the power of endurance of the forces is put to the highest test, indeed it becomes dormant and dies."

The U.S. First Army diarist chronicled an interrogation of a young, highly intelligent German private, "a likely member of a G-3 staff." The interrogator posed a hypothetical question: If he were an American general, how would he break the German line? "In a few terse sentences," according to the diarist, the German private outlined a massive air strike to destroy the German line at a select point, enabling the Allies to walk through, "obviously without knowledge that 'his plan' had been worked on for many days previous."

Forewarned by the abortive attack at noon on the twenty-fourth, Hausser of the Seventh Army had concluded that instead of attacking on a broad front the Americans would switch and attempt an assault on a narrow front several miles west of St.-Lô. In the early-morning light, a battle group of the 2nd SS rushed in on the western flank of Panzer Lehr to wait. In the American camp, word circulated excitedly through the division and corps headquarters in Normandy that the attack was "on." Battalion staffs assembled for a final review, received mimeographs of the "op plan" and dispersed to make ready.

It was none too soon because for days, correspondents had been pestering Bradley and his staff about the slow advance on St.-Lô. Some had tried to get him to admit the Americans were stalemated but he had denied it. Were the Allies engaged in a "sit down" policy waiting for the Russians' attack to exhaust itself in Poland? Bradley had assured the correspondents that the Americans were "guileless" and suggested they "withhold [their] verdict."

Several days before, Bradley had decided to brief the press on COBRA. He had described it as a "quick power drive" to be conducted at tank speed and planned to the hour so that failure of the assault divisions to reach the first-day objectives would seriously jeopardize the entire plan. Two thousand bombers of the U.S. Eighth and Ninth Air Force would punch the hole, Bradley said. The 9th and 30th U.S. infantry divisions had drawn the assignment to rush in and guard the shoulders, backed by the 4th Infantry. Then "the Big Red One," 1st U.S. (Motorized) Infantry Division, would barrel through, followed by the 2nd and 3rd armored divisions, "breaking without mercy," ignoring their flanks, by-passing all strongpoints, and rolling into the enemy's rear in order to cut off the forces facing VIII Corps and to block the arrival of enemy reinforcements from the eastern sector. Meanwhile, VIII Corps, protected overhead by Ninth Air Force fighters and bombers, would launch an armored blitz and "sweep south . . . past Avranches," where it would turn the corner into Brittany. "Tanks will be lost," he had said, "but we have overwhelming strength and the attack must be pushed."

Was an Allied breakout imminent? Years later, Bradley would describe three Russian observers invited to witness COBRA, a "curious" delegation consisting of a youthful admiral and two Red Army generals whom he described as keen and conspicuously correct. Along the way, Bradley witnessed a telling scene, evidence of the savage hatreds on the eastern front. Near the front the group stopped at a German POW cage, whereupon one of the generals, "his face set in a chilly stare," hailed a German officer of the 17th Luftwaffe Division captured the day before west of St.-Lô. The Russian broke into fluent German: "And, *Herr Hauptmann,* what do you think will happen to Germany after we win the war?"

The paratrooper, "tall and hard-muscled," faltered, then stiffened. Germany, he assumed, would "probably be broken up into little pieces."

"Not Germany," the Soviet officer said, speaking slowly, "not Germany, *Herr Hauptmann*—but Germans!"

The war resumed. Butcher had turned in late after a poker game with a couple of AP and BBC reporters. They had listened to the awesome sound of the Eighth Air Force moving into action in Normandy. "Scads of aircraft overhead," he wrote that morning, like the sound of orchestras tuning up in the pit, first the "sweet basso profundo in various numbers of voices from solo to quartet, to sextette and finally to the great massed a capella choir. 'Twas sweet music. . . .

"This morning the chorus continues as a gay refrain to echo death to enemy. Cripes, I'm getting high-falutin' . . . must have been the good night's sleep."

Witnesses say that at precisely 0936, 350 P-47 fighter-bombers of the Eighth Air Force arrived over the 2,500-by-6,000-yard "carpet" to bomb and strafe Panzer Lehr strongpoints. At 0958, the low drone of 1,500 B-17s and B-24s, each carrying forty 100-pound fragmentation bombs, became audible. To the naked eye, the approaching waves were dots, then clots of bombers lined up twelve by three. At 1000 GIs and generals alike stopped in awe to watch first the slow, lumbering gait of the bombers running the ack-ack, forming a conveyor belt flying rectangular patterns over the carpet. Parachutes appeared under one plane, parachutes snapped in the tail of another, and a third burst into flames. Then the crackle-pop of explosions, the deep rumble of the trembling earth which obliterated individual sounds, followed by a billowing wall of smoke and dust that swallowed the land.

The markers began drifting northward with the breeze toward the American 30th Division on the western flank, 1,500 yards behind the road. At 1015, as the second wave approached, Bradley and Eisenhower, who had just arrived, received reports that several units of the 9th and 30th infantry divisions were receiving direct hits. Nothing could be done, and on it went for almost an hour. At 1058, the last wave of bombers, 396 B-25s, arrived to comb the sector before 1,000 artillery pieces opened fire.

Through binoculars, Eisenhower witnessed the stupendous inferno and its aftermath. Four unscathed German tanks near the St.-Lô–Périers road hoisted white flags. Surviving German soldiers stumbled around in the dust, flames and confusion, deaf and demented by the noise and the flash. By noon the small sector crisscrossed by hedgerows earlier that morning resembled a "moon landscape." German communications had ceased, and most of the infantry, artillery and tank position had been buried or flattened, except for those in small corridors spared by pre-design for the American armored advance.

But there was no American advance. The bombardment had shocked and dazed the forward American divisions, destroying two battalions of the 30th

Division Headquarters amid reports that General Lesley McNair, who had insisted on witnessing the bombardment from a forward position, was missing. Bradley found General Leland Hobbs, commander of the 30th Division, shaken and angry. "Shorts" for the second day in a row had killed over a hundred Americans with many uncounted. To Hodges, Hobbs complained, "We're good soldiers, Courtney, I know, but there's absolutely no excuse, no excuse at all. I wish I could show some of those boys, decorated with everything a man can be decorated with, some of our clearing stations." By midafternoon a Chicago *Tribune* reporter informed Hodges of the reports that a general "up the road" had been killed. Medical corpsmen on the scene had identified McNair by the three stars on one shoulder. The body of Lieutenant General Lesley McNair had been hurled eighty feet from a slit trench.

Late-afternoon reports were bad. The infantry had trouble organizing an advance and navigating the bomb craters. Miraculously, scattered German strongpoints in the pocket returned fire backed by artillery entrenched two miles behind. By dusk, with reports that the 2nd SS and 17th SS had intervened on the western flank, Eisenhower left Bradley's command post discouraged. With McNair's death confirmed, and at least a hundred U.S. troops of the 9th and 30th divisions killed and six hundred wounded by friendly fire, Eisenhower told Bradley as he departed that he had "lost all faith in bombers acting in support of the ground force. That's a job for the artillery. I gave them a green light this time. But I promise you it's the last."

After dinner, Bradley reached Eisenhower by phone with a fresh report of the attack, which had gotten under way at six.

The 9th, a 2,300-yard gain.

The 4th, a 1,200-yard gain.

The 30th, a 1,300-yard gain.

Smith remarked, "The slow beginning might be the harbinger of a good end."

July 26. The day of suspense. By morning, sketchy reports indicated that the German line west of St.-Lô had been pierced. The remnants of Panzer Lehr had withdrawn southeastward, and counterattacks led by the 2nd SS at the base of the carpet were easily brought under control. The dimensions of the American success were still unknown when Eisenhower met forlornly with Churchill for lunch at 10 Downing Street. Churchill had initiated the meeting, but Eisenhower used it to resume his campaign for an all-out supporting offensive east of the Orne with late word in that the Canadian II Corps had been repulsed at the Bourguébus Ridge and had stopped to consolidate.

Over lunch, Eisenhower frankly complained about the difficulties caused by Montgomery's conduct of the land battle, which had caused complaints over a disproportionate share of American casualties. Afterward Churchill reached Alan Brooke and told him that Eisenhower was "tired of Montgomery's always stopping to draw up his administrative tail, and wanted Monty to get on his bicycle and start moving."

But by late afternoon the reports indicated improvement. Troops of the 9th, 4th and 30th infantry divisions had opened a gap between the towns of St.-Gilles and Marigny. Sensing an opportunity, the VII Corps commander, General Lawton Collins, reached a command decision to unleash the 2nd and 3rd Armored, although VII Corps held neither town. Collins, dashing from unit to unit, swung a column of tanks seven miles down the Marigny–Coutances road past demolitions, roadblocks and strongpoints backed by low-flying Thunderbolts called in against enemy strongpoints. By three, according to Bradley, a bare twenty-four hours after the jump-off, "we sensed that the initial crisis had passed, and that the time had come for bold exploitation of a breakthrough."

"My news this evening on Bradley's attack is very sketchy and I have none at all on what's going on in the Second Army front," Eisenhower wrote Montgomery that night. "However, I know the troops are fighting for all they are worth and I am certain the enemy will somewhere crack under the pressure," adding that Churchill at lunch had "repeated over and over again that he knew you understood the necessity for 'keeping the front aflame,' while major attacks were in progress."

July 27. In a hectic and confusing morning the dimensions of the opportunity became plain at both Bradley's and Montgomery's headquarters. The German Seventh Army reeling under a two-prong American assault could not organize a front. Bradley hurriedly left his morning staff conference to urge "Collins to throw everything in and keep pushing, for Boche was apparently on the run." The 17th and 2nd SS divisions west of St.-Lô abandoned the attempt to cut the VII Corps attack at the base and floundered about. Middleton was reporting a "slow but definite withdrawal eastward in front of VII Corps." With six divisions in the jaws of a converging attack toward Coutances, Bradley summoned Gerow, Corlett and Collins to implement phase II of the attack—coordinated assaults by Corlett and Gerow toward Vire to disrupt any attempted retreat by the German panzers and infantry west of St.-Lô. Phase III was imminent—a four-division dash for Granville, then Avranches, gateway to the Brittany Peninsula coordinated by General Patton, who paced impatiently at Middleton's headquarters waiting, worried "that the war would be over before he got in it." Infantry riding tanks, half-tracks and motorized artillery poured through the Marigny–St.-Gilles gap all day, blitzing through the hedgerows toward Coutances, completing the isolation of the German LXXXIV Corps by dark.

Churchill hosted a dinner at 10 Downing Street that night to unite Eisenhower and Brooke for the first time in weeks. Bulletins arrived throughout the evening. VII Corps had entered Coutances, while VIII Corps on the move through Périers and Lessay was cutting to pieces the remnants of six

German divisions desperately trying to filter back through American lines to the German main body forming on the Vire River.

For most of the evening, the usual "reserve" between Eisenhower and Brooke was apparent. Brooke, whose clever, testy manner was alien to Eisenhower, Marshall and the other Americans who crossed swords with him, lectured the Supreme Commander about the rough handling of Montgomery and demanded amends. "It is equally clear that Ike has the very vaguest conception of war!" he wrote Montgomery the following day.

> I drew his attention to what your basic strategy had been, i.e., to hold with your left and draw Germans onto the left flank whilst you pushed with your right. I explained how in my mind this conception was being carried out, that the bulk of the armor had been kept against the British. He could not refute these arguments and asked whether I did not consider that we were in a position to launch major offensives on each front simultaneously.

Brooke continued:

> I told him that in view of the fact that the German density in Normandy was two and a half times that on the Russian front whilst our superiority and strength was only in the nature of some twenty-five percent as compared to three hundred percent Russian superiority on the eastern front, I did not consider that we were in a position to launch an all-out offensive along the whole front.

But Eisenhower had disagreed with Brooke's comparison with the eastern front, and Churchill, for once, had been inclined to agree with Eisenhower's arguments.

> Now as a result of all this talking and the actual situation on your front [Brooke concluded], I feel personally quite certain Dempsey must attack at the earliest possible moment on a large scale. We must not allow German forces to move from his front to Bradley's front, or we shall give more cause than ever for criticism.

Montgomery had already acted. Late in the afternoon of the twenty-seventh, the 2nd and 116th panzer divisions had disengaged at Caen and conducted a forced march to Vire, the key road junction east of St.-Lô, where the Germans would establish an improvised line to cover the Seventh Army withdrawal and to threaten the flank of the American breakthrough. The departure of the two panzer divisions alerted Montgomery to the opportunity presented by the First Army penetration. At a late-afternoon battle conference he had directed Dempsey to reassemble O'Connor's VIII Corps as quickly as possible and "to step on the gas for Vire" to disorganize German efforts to regroup. By nightfall the Normandy front was ablaze, from the eastern bank of the Orne to Coutances.

Eisenhower spent the next three days in Portsmouth waiting impatiently for news. The dinner conference with Brooke at 10 Downing Street had been difficult, a sign of the feelings aroused in recent weeks. His old friend T. J. Davis stopped to tell about a dinner party he had attended on the night of the twenty-seventh where his British hostess had become so incensed with the constant BBC news reports on the American breakout that she had gotten up and switched off the radio. "This shows that while Ike has reasonably good teamwork in the military," Butcher wrote, "his example has not affected deep-seated national instincts and probably never will."

Waiting for news, Eisenhower brooded about the implications of the aerial display he had witnessed at St.-Lô on the twenty-fifth, which inspired forebodings as well as admiration. In a letter to his wife, written after a visit to the villages near St.-Lô that had been ground up in the bombardment, Eisenhower called the German a "beast" for having provoked him to order it. Eisenhower, depressed, sensed that by his use of the bombers the "moral ascendancy" the Allies had intended to establish over the Germans in Normandy had somehow eluded them. But the air technique displayed by COBRA was a qualitative advance, something the Allies could not ignore in the coming battles of France and Germany.

Accordingly, Eisenhower deputized Tedder to bring the air commanders together "to elucidate lessons learned from the attacks by Montgomery and Bradley on the 25th." The Allies "possessed a power of breakthrough," he said, "and we must learn how to use it."

Tedder in the next three days canvassed Spaatz, Harris, Eaker of the Fifteenth Air Force and Portal, all of whom had been astonished by the terrific demonstration put on by the U.S. Eighth Air Force. Eaker still maintained that bomber support of ground operations applied only to amphibious landings and to "special situations." Spaatz added that too frequent a use of heavy bombers would "act as a drug and eventually provide an antidote." But everyone was hedging.

Meanwhile American troops swarmed over the main roads between Coutances and Vire, advancing at will while Montgomery hastily organized the two-corps British drive toward Vire to break up German attempts to form a line. Bradley, on the twenty-eighth, tossed caution to the winds and decided against any consolidation phase at Coutances. Patton, "supervising" VIII Corps, received the green light to push through a gap at Coutances and to drive armored columns to Avranches and into Brittany.

And by Saturday, July 29, as British spearheads reached the suburbs of Vire, Patton's 4th Armored, having covered twenty-five miles in thirty-six hours, entered Avranches and established a bridgehead over the bridge at Pontaubault. The twin blow triggered Von Kluge's desperate warning to OKW that the Seventh Army flank "had collapsed" and that the front had been "ripped open." ULTRA intercepted the message, and Churchill, when told of it, gave a "quiet grunt of satisfaction."

Eisenhower received the news at Portsmouth after a quiet dinner with

Admiral and Lady Ramsay. On Sunday, the thirtieth, according to Summersby, "E. slept late this morning, the first time." At noon Eisenhower, Tedder and Gault met for a quiet lunch to talk over plans and decided that the time had come for Gault to visit Normandy and to find a suitable location for a forward headquarters in France.

6

Pursuit

Wᴇᴇᴋᴇɴᴅ situation reports continued to be good. By Monday they indicated a victory in Normandy of dimensions unforeseen a week before when rain and fog had forced repeated delays in Cᴏʙʀᴀ, delays unanticipated even as late as the twenty-ninth, when Bradley, assuming the German Seventh Army would establish a north–south line based on Vire, cautiously ordered Collins to consolidate at Coutances. Leaders in London, Portsmouth and Washington awoke from weeks of military stalemate that day, and debate resumed in a new and fluid situation.

"August—the month when wars usually start," Brooke mused in his diary on the first. "I wonder whether this one may look like finishing it instead?" Thereafter, Brooke complained about the laborious weekly Chiefs of Staff meeting at Whitehall on Monday, August 1, at which the group tediously disposed of an agenda drawn up in the weeks of stalemate and setback: committee reports on the buzz-bomb threat, the resettlement of women and children into the London suburbs, and the weekly JIC report, prepared before St.-Lô, assessing the depressing implications of the abortive German putsch.

As the hours wore on, Brooke's mind wandered to the news from France. With Coutances and Avranches in Allied hands, he expected Bradley to push south to the Brest peninsula and to clear it quickly, whereupon the Germans would be flanked and have little choice except to withdraw behind the Seine. Yet in view of Allied mobility and air preponderance, it was hard for Brooke to see how the Germans could organize a defense of the Seine or, for that matter, it was hard to see how the Germans could hold the Somme or Marne or any other line in France. Now seemed to be the moment for bold action—if ever. And yet Brooke elsewhere noted that Deane and Burrows, who had just returned from Moscow, had discouraging reports on efforts to set up a military "staff center" in Moscow, and that news reports confirmed a Red Army slowdown east of Warsaw.

On the night of the first, Churchill, seizing on the weekend news, resumed war on ANVIL-DRAGOON. He summoned Eisenhower to 10 Downing Street to present an array of British proposals improvised that weekend to exploit the promising situation on all fronts: proposals to airlift supplies to the pro-London Polish patriots battling Nazi panzers in the streets of Warsaw, to reinforce guerrilla operations in Yugoslavia, and to airlift two British divisions into Athens to preempt a pro-Communist EAM takeover in the wake of a German pullout; and finally, a last and best offer for a compromise on ANVIL-DRAGOON, a proposal to shift Wilson's ten-division landings from Marseilles to Quiberon Bay, Brittany, which was the prime subject of Churchill's talks with Eisenhower that night.

Churchill's eleventh-hour compromise proposal could not have come as a surprise. As recently as July 9, Churchill had hinted he could reopen the issue. In the next two weeks the Prime Minister was planning to fly to Naples for talks with Tito and the Greeks, talks that would be undermined by launching DRAGOON as planned. Finally, on the night of August 1, the Allied high command faced "new facts" in the military situation that once again provided a basis for reopening a host of dormant military issues.

But did the Allies actually face "new facts"? Eisenhower's conversation with Churchill that night was reminiscent of earlier discussions—the Tunisia conferences in December, the late-June conferences at 10 Downing Street during the storm, and their talks in July. Like the others, it was destined to be a source of misunderstanding, and so Eisenhower came prepared.

Eisenhower was open-minded and conciliatory—just how conciliatory is unknown. Facing the formidable task of restoring mutual confidence with Montgomery, Eisenhower had every incentive to find common ground, though the evidence is mixed on behalf of Churchill's claim that Eisenhower actually initiated the Brittany compromise and came to him bearing a draft message for Marshall formally proposing it. Eisenhower had much to gain in a compromise on ANVIL-DRAGOON, and a direct reinforcement of the American flank with landings in Brittany had obvious advantages if Bradley met a sudden and unexpected reverse in exploiting the breakthrough at St.-Lô. On the other hand, stalemate seemed unlikely. D-day for ANVIL-DRAGOON was only fifteen days away, and in a new and fluid situation, the natural course was to rely on set plans.

In any event, what is certain is that Churchill that night endeavored to place before Eisenhower the implications of ANVIL-DRAGOON. First, the long Normandy siege had taken a toll on mutual confidence. Second, ANVIL-DRAGOON, now imminent, would halt Alexander's offensive south of Florence in circumstances causing many to wonder whether a diversionary operation to support OVERLORD was necessary. Third, Eisenhower was about to activate Patton's Third Army, meaning that if things went according to plan, Montgomery would soon be relegated to an army group command. In short, the Americans were getting their way on Italy as well as on France, and this imbalance was certain to undermine British prestige if not Churchill's leadership, and certain to redound to Eisenhower's disadvantage in time.

Who suggested Brittany is unclear, but Churchill liked the idea and he urged Eisenhower to give it every consideration. Brittany would concentrate forces quickly on Bradley's right flank and aid in the current offensive. Landings in Brittany would also permit Wilson and Alexander to plan Alex's next step with assurance that the 15th Army Group in Italy would not be called upon constantly to support operations in nearby southern France. As always, one of Churchill's growing misgivings about Marseilles was that it falsely implied to others—Tito, the Greeks, the Russians—that the Allies had settled on southern France as *Alexander's* objective after the 15th Army Group reached the Po.

Eisenhower was receptive, but again, the pros and cons were finely balanced and his answer was necessarily an hour-to-hour thing. Was a shift from Marseilles to Brittany practical ten days before a three-division landing? Was Churchill angling for outright cancellation? Most important, what should Eisenhower assume about the ongoing Allied breakout? Would Bradley's momentum carry the Allies past the Seine? Logistical schedules were based on plans for an extended Allied pause and build-up west of the Seine lasting three weeks or more, then a major battle to cross the Seine.

In this latter case, a landing in Brittany could strengthen Bradley at just the right time and place, giving him needed reinforcements and fresh ports. But Eisenhower was at this moment considering a major change in plan, SHAEF's version of LUCKY STRIKE wherein Patton's Third Army would assume a spearhead role and dash through the open German flank to roll up the Germans and pursue them across the Seine. In this case, Third Army reinforcements arriving from Brittany would be superfluous, whereas landings in southern France would open a new front on the Allied right flank, ready to march north and link up east of the Seine. This maneuver would probably force the Germans to evacuate all garrisons south of the Loire and permit the Allies to push eastward practically without inhibition. And in considering such a bold scheme, Eisenhower had also to consider that German resistance in the weeks and months ahead would depend on the flow of German reserves to the west, which would be affected by the pace of Russian operations in Poland and Rumania.

Late into the night, Churchill insisted that in *either* case DRAGOON was futile and that he could not understand American support for it. Even the reduced German First Army at Marseilles was capable of containing DRAGOON in the rugged Rhône Valley, and this would be a waste of ten divisions Eisenhower might otherwise deploy on Bradley's right flank to exploit the situation in Normandy. Churchill emphasized how "strange" it would appear if the Allies walked away from a "glittering opportunity to reinforce Bradley." But would reinforcement of Bradley be necessary?

By the next morning, August 2, evidence mounted of a decisive victory in the making, which meant the end of the Normandy battles along with any chance that Eisenhower and Churchill might suddenly compromise the ANVIL-DRAGOON dilemma. Along the coast, Collins' VII Corps and Middleton's VIII Corps had by-passed pockets of resistance north of Coutances, and pushed seven divisions through Avranches supported by continuous close air support, which overwhelmed enemy defenses and disrupted night movement. As he officially assumed command of the Third Army, Patton had found a German flank "dangling loosely and in distress," and his forces were poised to march into Brittany as planned, or to exploit the developing opportunity to dash southeast into open terrain where the full weight of Allied armor and air superiority could be brought to bear.

By the second, Patton had pushed through the Avranches-Pontaubault bottleneck. General Wade Haislip's newly formed XV Corps had attacked southeast from Avranches toward the towns of Mayenne and Laval, posing a threat to the rear of the German Seventh Army. Brittany remained Patton's primary objective, but should Dempsey and Hodges seize Vire, and Bradley make good his seizure of Avranches, Patton could operate safely toward Paris–Orléans, while Montgomery, in conjunction with Hodges, would stage east of Caen and, in Eisenhower's words, concentrate on the "task of completing the destruction of the German Army, at least that portion west of the Orne, and exploiting beyond that as far as we possibly could."

And so the situation weighed against accommodating Churchill, and this may have accounted for Eisenhower's request for Marshall's help that day in handling a difficult command problem. Though he had now formally assumed command of the 12th Army Group, Bradley remained officially subordinate to Montgomery pending Eisenhower's assumption of overall ground command, and Eisenhower wanted to keep things that way for a while. In a message to Marshall on the thirtieth, Eisenhower had predicted that a lengthy transition period would be necessary—thirty days or more —before SHAEF could transfer communications and staff to a suitable location in France. Two days later, for the record, Eisenhower confided to Marshall that he had personally approved Montgomery's "policy of taking up a firm defensive and containing action at Caen" while Bradley took Cherbourg and wheeled southward. He, Montgomery, and Bradley had been of a "single mind" about destroying "substantial portions of the enemy in our immediate front so as to have later freedom of action."

But were real concessions to Montgomery possible? According to Butcher, Eisenhower arrived back in Portsmouth that night slightly depressed about the last-minute complications he was sure Churchill would raise about DRAGOON. Over dinner, Eisenhower intimated vague details of his talk with Churchill, which had lasted for three hours. The Prime Minister had been cordial, but as Butcher noted afterward, Eisenhower was "increasingly concerned about . . . the feeling that the questioning and apparent dissension might cause a rift in the unity of the Allies at a time when success is almost within our grasp." Eisenhower was exasperated that the British in particular did not seem satisfied with victory; they were concerned about "how it is to be achieved." Meanwhile, Butcher faithfully chronicled Eisenhower's complaints as the general paced restlessly over the cinder pathways at the tent camp waiting for news from France. "Ike is impatient," Butcher wrote, "repeat impatient, I mean impatient."

On the second, intercepts of enemy traffic confirmed that Middleton's VIII Corps was "to hell and gone" in Brittany. The 6th Armored Division at Granville and the 4th Armored Division marched toward Brest through incoherent enemy groups fighting independently. In Normandy, after regrouping at Coutances and Avranches, Collins' VII Corps passed through the town of Mortain and opened a ten-mile corridor for Corlett's XIX Corps and Haislip's XV Corps. Meanwhile, the 79th Division advanced toward the town of Fougères, the first step of what was to develop into a plunge into the open French countryside southwest of the German Seventh Army. Small German pockets barred the way to Le Mans and the German supply dumps at Alençon.

Meanwhile, Eisenhower awaited clues of German intentions. Would they form new lines, attempt to retreat or counterattack? In his opinion Von Kluge's logical choice was to hold the Caen shoulder, then pivot southeast with the badly mauled Seventh Army, and deploy armor to cover a phased retreat behind the Orne and the Seine. A second and less feasible choice would be to attempt to stretch out on a north–south line based on Vire in hopes of containing Patton's Third Army west of the Orne River, a maneuver that depended on Von Kluge's ability to reinforce the town of Vire by panzers withdrawn from the British sector, which risked a collapse at Caen. The third and most radical choice, implied by the flow of Fifteenth Army reinforcements into Caen and German resistance at Vire, was a counterattack at Avranches or south against Patton's isolated spearheads in a bid to reverse fortunes dramatically with one bold stroke.

On the second, Von Kluge and Hitler grappled all day with the choice between withdrawal and a bold strategy of counterattack. ULTRA intercepted Hitler's order to gather up all of the panzer divisions in Normandy, "regardless of their present commitment," for a counteroffensive toward Mortain and the sea to sever Patton's columns from the American main body. Hitler specified that Von Kluge's preparations were to be deliberate; he was not to attack until the 9th SS, 10th SS and 12th SS had extricated themselves and joined up near Vire and a Luftwaffe reserve had arrived in France, as "the decision in the whole battle of France depends on the success of this attack."

According to Winterbotham, some discounted the so-called order as a bluff. Tedder phoned Winterbotham at Bletchley to ask "in view of the extreme importance of Hitler's signal" if he could be sure it was authentic. Winterbotham later phoned back with word that the message was written "in Hitler's own distinct style and language," and that "there was no reason to doubt it on any score." Significantly, General Bradley would later claim that ULTRA provided his field headquarters "nothing about German plans until the eve of LUTTICH three days later," which suggests either that Eisenhower withheld the exchanges from both men so as not to inhibit the Laval–Mayenne thrust or that Bradley simply forgot or discounted them, owing to doubts that the beleaguered German command in Normandy was prepared to carry out Hitler's order. To Bradley, a counteroffensive seemed to be the least likely course the Germans would take, a deliberate sacrifice of troops and equipment. That night, ULTRA intercepted Von Kluge's protest that "to the best of my knowledge and conscience, the execution of this order means the collapse of the whole Normandy front." Von Kluge urgently requested OKW to "re-examine the matter and bring it to the Führer's attention." He insisted that armor was the backbone of the German defense at Caen and that further withdrawals of armor from Caen meant the collapse of the whole front.

Was a German retreat imminent? An argument between Von Kluge and Hitler ensued. "My money was on Hitler," Winterbotham later wrote, "and his obsession to show his doubting armies that he still remained a genius and to rekindle the Hitler myth." German postwar accounts would attribute Hitler's obstinance to his isolation in distant East Prussia, where he made decisions by looking at maps "without taking into consideration the difficulties involved in the field of executing the decision," including necessary means, time and space, the "elements of strategy fundamental for success."

On the other hand, OKW historian P. E. Schramm, in a postwar essay, would portray the planned Mortain counterattack as a logical extension of the Normandy battle. By his June decision to starve Normandy, Hitler had long since accepted the risk of collapse in France, so that the attack on Mortain, should it fail, would leave the Germans no worse off than Hitler had originally anticipated. After the Allies had accumulated sufficient matériel to hold, Schramm explained, some hoped a breakout might be delayed by several months, and when it came, that the army group might "resist through delaying actions" and "contain the enemy by counterattacks at least and not lose the initiative completely" while the means to seize the strategic initiative would be developed. Moreover, an intermediate line between the Vire River and the Seine could only be temporary cover for the

Somme, and the Somme temporary cover for the Albert Canal and the West Wall, and so Hitler had in fact nothing to lose. Also, as Jodl would later recall, many in the German high command felt that the U.S. Army had "not proven its superior skills in the field," and that an American Army, less experienced and less dangerous than the British Army, might buckle under pressure. Jodl would add in hindsight that "the picture changed completely with the breakthrough where we experienced an operation that was first-class, courageous, with long-range operational aims carried out more like our German methods than those of the English or French."

On the third, as Eisenhower proceeded to France for discussions with Bradley and Montgomery, ULTRA intercepted Hitler's reply politely rejecting Von Kluge's arguments and indicating that "the attack to split the American forces must be carried out" to cut the twenty-mile Avranches corridor with "at least four" panzer divisions. Confirming ULTRA, German efforts to defend staging areas for an armored attack were detectable near the town of Domfront near Vire amid signs of covert German preparations for a pullout.

In the next ninety-six hours the German decision had a predictably dampening effect on Eisenhower and Bradley, but they responded boldly. Over the weekend, Bradley had outlined plans for a "war-winning drive," an American version of LUCKY STRIKE which after seizure of the Brittany peninsula looked to a "long" envelopment by Patton's Third Army through the Paris–Orléans gap, thence northward along the Seine toward Calais to link up with Dempsey and envelop the Germans west of the Seine. By the third, confronted with evidence of a German counteroffensive, Bradley had grown somewhat cautious. He was insistent about the capturing of the Breton ports and concerned about the safety of Avranches, but he opposed the idea of consolidating his forces or of drawing back Patton's forces southeast of Avranches, which were poised to push east and operate against the German flank. Bradley felt that holding the threatened sector at Avranches with air power and a single division, the U.S. 30th, was an acceptable risk, since five American infantry divisions and two armored combat commands were operating just north of Avranches. Eisenhower agreed, and reminded Bradley that in the event that local German counterattacks succeeded in temporarily isolating American forces south of Avranches, supply by airlift could provide 2,000 tons of supplies daily.

In deciding against consolidation at Avranches, Eisenhower and Bradley initiated the long-awaited war of movement in France. Haislip's XV Corps would move southeast toward Rennes–Laval, protected on its left by the newly formed XX Corps, which was to attack southward toward the Loire. That afternoon Bradley ordered Patton to send minimum forces into Brittany and to drive his main units eastward toward Laval, Le Mans and Chartres while the U.S. First, British Second and Canadian armies maintained relentless pressure in Normandy to prevent the Germans from disen-

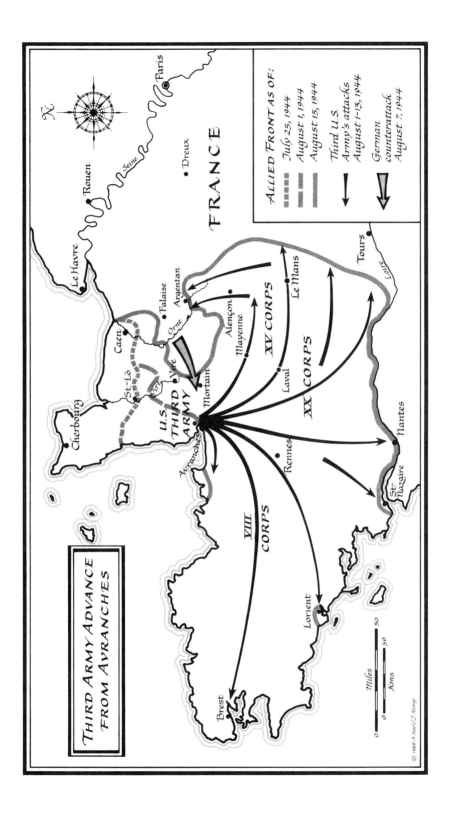

THIRD ARMY ADVANCE FROM AVRANCHES

ALLIED FRONT AS OF:
- July 25, 1944
- August 1, 1944
- August 15, 1944

Third U.S. Army's attacks August 1-13, 1944

German counterattack August 7, 1944

FRANCE

Paris
Dreux
Rouen
Le Havre
Seine
Falaise
Argentan
Caen
Orne
Alençon
Mayenne
Le Mans
XV CORPS
Vire
St-Lô
Mortain
Laval
XX CORPS
Tours
Loire
U.S. THIRD ARMY
Avranches
Rennes
Nantes
St. Nazaire
Cherbourg
VIII CORPS
Lorient
Brest

Miles
Kms.

© 1986 A. Karl / J. Kemp

gaging armor at Caen. Almost overlooked in the excitement was Eisenhower's decision to delegate the capture of Brittany to a single corps, Middleton's VIII Corps, which irrevocably sealed the issue of ANVIL-DRAGOON and set the stage for endless British-American difficulties ahead.

August 3 was a day of decision. Over the weekend, Montgomery, also thinking ambitiously, had revived the 21st Army Group's version of LUCKY STRIKE, a rival "war-winning" plan for a 21st Army Group drive eastward over the Seine *assisted* by American armor, which was to advance along the north bank of the Loire to block the Paris–Orléans gap. But whether LUCKY STRIKE was practical or desirable was slightly beside the point. The point was that Montgomery, like Eisenhower, grasped the changes ushered in by the American breakout that permitted—indeed obligated—the Allies to modify original plans and to act boldly. Like Eisenhower, Montgomery was thinking in terms of a decisive battle west of the Seine, which he believed should be fought now even at the expense of the early capture of Brittany, which would either fall into Bradley's lap without a fight or become irrelevant in a battle of pursuit that would open up ports along the Channel coast. Meanwhile, the problem was (a) to protect Bradley's columns operating south of Avranches and (b) to prevent the Germans from forming a defensible north–south line. Accordingly, Montgomery ordered Dempsey to step up the Second Army attacks in the Caumont sector and, at the same time, set TOTALIZE, a resumption of the Canadian attack over the Bourguébus ridge and down the Caen–Falaise road, to begin the night of August 7–8.

Though fundamental differences were implicit in the rival "war-winning" plans drawn up by Bradley and Montgomery on the weekend, both army groups were on the march and the tactical decisions reached on the third were complementary. Thus, for an interval of two weeks or so, Eisenhower's command would be marching in lockstep. Bradley would retain weakened forces at Mortain while building up forces south of Avranches behind Von Kluge's left flank and launching an offensive. Montgomery, while building up forces for a major attack east of the Orne, would maintain the pressure at Caumont on the right flank of the German armored concentration threatening Avranches.

The American offensive was well under way before Eisenhower's return to Portsmouth that night. Patton's tank columns rumbled through the open French countryside toward Le Mans. By the next morning, as Summersby noted at the conclusion of a War Room conference at Portsmouth, the intercepts and dispatches were all good and "looking very much like the newspapers."

Eisenhower would have preferred to bide his time on ANVIL-DRAGOON, at least until the German counterattack materialized and he could be sure the Allies were on the verge of a drive to cross the Seine. But the August 15 deadline approached, and Churchill, who knew that time was on the side of ANVIL-DRAGOON, could not wait any longer.

Brooke's diary sheds light on the ongoing argument between himself, Churchill and others over the wisdom of challenging DRAGOON at the last minute. Brooke was supportive, particularly when he heard that Eisenhower had been the one to suggest the Brittany idea. On the whole, however, Brooke was in favor of cutting losses in Italy and refocusing all British efforts in France, having concluded that since the bulk of Allied resources would be committed in France eventually, to remain aloof would be to relinquish a real say over a campaign that Brooke now felt might prove to be decisive in the next few weeks.

In turn, Churchill waged a valiant struggle. The Prime Minister doubted that the British could neglect Alexander's Italian campaign without a loss of self-confidence and prestige, doubted that the Allies could afford to liquidate their position in Italy, doubted that Normandy would prove to be "decisive," and perhaps Churchill was also wary of competing for control in France. After all, high-level competition between theaters was one thing: competition between forces *within* a theater was another, and carried with it the potential for a breakdown in coordination on vital points. Determined to be optimistic in his dealing with the Americans, Churchill would oppose the tactic of dwelling on American "errors" entailed in such a contest and was sure that Eisenhower agreed with him. However, to avoid all these issues, Italy had to be kept up as a rival theater, and so Churchill was depending on Eisenhower to accept some kind of compromise on DRAGOON.

On the fourth the British went in both directions. First, the BCOS offered a motion calling on the CCS to instruct Eisenhower to bolster the 21st Army Group for an all-out sweep along the Channel coast, a far-reaching move that opened CCS debate over strategy in France for the first time since January. The motion was notice that the BCOS would continue to support Montgomery in overall ground command and notice as well that the BCOS had carefully reserved its position on the new phase of operations ahead that had been vaguely touched upon in Eisenhower's directive. Also on the fourth, over Brooke's objections, the BCOS instructed General Wilson in Naples to make ready for a last-minute decision to land the DRAGOON force at Quiberon Bay. In a cable to Roosevelt, Churchill proposed that DRAGOON be directed into the "main and decisive battle," then cabled Eisenhower to inform him that he had personally contacted the President, "backing up your suggestion." The American Joint Chiefs protested Wilson's instructions and cabled Eisenhower asking for his view, whereupon Churchill arranged an eleventh-hour luncheon meeting with Eisenhower in Portsmouth the next day, with advisers present.

The Portsmouth luncheon, lasting six hours, was one of Eisenhower's most difficult experiences in a difficult year. Gathered around a conference table at the tent camp, Churchill, Admiral William Tennant and Admiral Sir Andrew Cunningham faced Eisenhower, Tedder, Smith and Ramsay. Cunningham's presence was significant. A stout supporter at AFHQ, Cunningham had hosted the Claridges reunion in February, and more recently had been Eisenhower's regular dinner guest at Portsmouth. Cunningham personified Anglo-American cooperation, and his presence, along with Brooke's absence, was evidence that Eisenhower was facing emissaries from a pro-American camp whose ability to deliver was now in question.

By all accounts, Eisenhower was on the defensive throughout. At the moment of decision, Eisenhower found himself uncomfortably urging plans he had questioned himself in the earlier debates. Eisenhower had repeatedly affirmed the value of Italy, and just as often had been ambivalent about the strategic possibilities of ANVIL, and its usefulness as a supporting operation for OVERLORD. Moreover, OVERLORD *had* succeeded, or so Churchill insisted until dark, arguing that what "ANVIL was meant for is already gained."

The seven-month ANVIL-DRAGOON controversy, after many twists and turns, had been reduced to a very narrow and seemingly minor question— the landing site. Churchill was not proposing a postponement, and disclaimed any thought of keeping in Italy the ten United States and French divisions slated to participate in DRAGOON. But Marseilles was remote from the front in Normandy. To direct troops there would weaken an Italian offensive in progress, and thus seemed to presuppose a concept of how Alexander's nearby forces would proceed after reaching the Po River.

On it went. Churchill maintained that troops landing in Brittany could be in action within two weeks on Patton's right flank, whereas a landing in Marseilles, 500 miles from the main battle, might be contained in the Rhône Valley until late autumn. Marseilles violated the military principle of "concentration," and landings there precluded chances of "finishing up Hitler this year."

In response, "Ike said no, continued saying no all afternoon, and ended saying no in every form of the English language at his command," as Butcher later put it. In the ninety-six hours since their last meeting, Brittany had become a secondary objective. Landings there would be absorbed in a rearguard struggle over minor ports and would be distant from the main front east of the Seine. Eisenhower cited the latest intelligence reports indicating that the Riviera coast was now virtually undefended. He doubted that the German garrisons in southern France had the power to contain Devers' 6th Army Group, the force intended for DRAGOON.

In short, as Eisenhower saw it, the German First Army at Marseilles was a potential menace only if by-passed. So despite his earlier ambivalence, now at the moment of decision he argued that a new front in southern France would clear all France of potential flanking threats to extended operations. A major Mediterranean port could efficiently supply operations in the Saar and the Vosges, and Marseilles would accelerate the arrival of fresh divisions from America that might otherwise stand idle or be sent to the Pacific. And unless Eisenhower could recommend Brittany on "military" grounds, he would not recommend it at all. For good measure, Eisenhower denied that DRAGOON foreclosed "finishing up Hitler this year."

The unspokens were many: the Russians and the meaning of Konev's abrupt pause on the Vistula ten miles east of Warsaw, which coincided with the Polish uprisings in Warsaw. Did this mean that the Russians were deliberately leaving to the Germans the task of suppressing the Polish opposition? Other unspokens were the growing sense of British powerlessness, Churchill's eroding authority, the American election year, and declining mutual confidence as military success magnified the opportunities and risks on the western front.

Debate lasted for hours. To Eisenhower's chagrin, Smith broke ranks and joined Churchill and Cunningham. Tennant, Tedder and Ramsay vigorously supported Eisenhower. Even twenty-three years later, in an interview with Alistair Cooke, Eisenhower would recall the painstaking details as though it had been yesterday:

Cooke: You know, somewhere Churchill defines democracy as "The occasional necessity of deferring to the opinions of others." I think this is a definition that must have had great meaning for him when you came to the conflict about going up through the south of France. . . . Churchill was suddenly overcome with this great desire to go up through Austria—to send Alexander through Austria. Would you tell us about that, General?

Eisenhower: Yes, in my headquarters, Churchill had with him my great friend, Admiral Sir Andrew Cunningham, who believed as his Prime Minister did. . . . The real thing was, were we going to win the war just as fast as we could with one great big powerful blow, with the aid of a secondary attack from the south? Or were we going to delay the completion of the war for other purposes? I strongly believed that the Allied armies, moving up from the D-Day beaches, should be supported by an army to come up from the Mediterranean. And that such a southern port should be open to us for later troop arrivals from the States. This military action was approved by *all the allies at the highest levels.* The troops for ANVIL-DRAGOON—the code name for the attack from the south of France —were to be withdrawn from Italy. Of course, that meant slowing our northern advance in that country. . . .

Brooke chronicled the tremendous sense of disappointment in the BCOS when news came that Eisenhower not only had never sent a telegram to Marshall on Brittany but "strongly opposed . . . any change in the South of France plan." There were mumblings of "double cross" and bad faith. A similar mood reigned in Portsmouth. After cabling Marshall with a detailed summary of his talks and assuring him of his "unwavering" support of ANVIL-DRAGOON, Eisenhower darkly predicted to Butcher that

Churchill would "return to the subject in two or three days and simply regard the issue as unsettled."

Butcher also noted signs of dissension betwen Churchill and the British Chiefs. Late on the fifth, word reached Portsmouth of Wilson's rejection of the BCOS-proposed shift to Quiberon Bay as "unwise," citing the problem of off-loading and reloading hundreds of ships. Wilson now endorsed AN-VIL-DRAGOON outright because of the more rapid convoy turnaround time between Naples and Marseilles, and "thus," Butcher put it sharply, "the Prime Minister was rebuffed by his British Allied Commander."

In Normandy, enemy actions and ULTRA still pointed to a German attack at Avranches. German resistance was fierce at Vire, Mount Pinçon and Domfront, and near Mortain, where the U.S. 30th Division encountered reconnaissance elements of the 2nd Panzer Division, spearhead of the northern shoulder. By the morning of the sixth, with Patton's columns ranging deep into the French countryside and Gerow in the outskirts of Vire, ULTRA eavesdropped on the latest German exchanges over what to do. Depressed by Allied air superiority, the American capture of Mortain and the deteriorating situation at Vire, Von Kluge pleaded for permission to concentrate mobile units on the southern flank to blunt Patton's drive and cover a German withdrawal behind "the Seine or further."

As the German H-Hour approached, evidence abounded that Von Kluge, on his own authority, was extricating troops under cover of complying with orders. As Montgomery noted in a directive issued that night: "From the general trend of enemy movement it appears he is falling back, unwillingly, to some new line." Enemy movements would "make no difference to us," Montgomery declared, and he urged his armies to "be prepared to attack the enemy quickly, whenever and wherever he may stand to fight; he must not be given time to 'settle in' on any positions. . . . We must follow him up with speed wherever he withdraws, and allow him no respite." Confidence bordering on euphoria also gripped First Army Headquarters as German disarray in Normandy became apparent. The First Army diarist recorded rumors of a "now or never attempt" at Avranches, and in describing Gerow's seizure of Vire, and Patton's seizure of Vannes, St.-Malo and Laval, noted the "strong possibility" of a Third Army sweep past Le Mans toward Alençon which "may yet succeed in drawing tight the string around his neck."

That day, euphoria, kept under wraps since St.-Lô, burst into public print. First Army G-2 Colonel B. A. "Monk" Dickson, told a press gathering that he doubted the German forces in Normandy could hold out "more than four to eight weeks as a fighting machine," and predicted that "the current situation may change with dramatic suddenness into a race to reach a chaotic Germany." Similarly, in the British camp, on the eve of TOTAL-IZE, a two-corps assault against the "door" at Mount Pinçon, commanders at all levels incautiously predicted an imminent German collapse on all fronts. Most prominently, Montgomery's chief of staff, General "Freddie" de Guingand, revealed to newsmen that the British were "decimating the Panzers on the British front," and that German reserves were stretched and "successfully interdicted at the Seine by Allied air."

Quickly intensifying beyond all reason, British high-level optimism that week assumed the air of an official campaign. Even Butcher, a confirmed optimist, began to wonder, and he carefully noted Eisenhower's misgivings about loose talk of victory, reminiscent of the euphoria surrounding July 20. By H-Hour for LUTTICH, Butcher was calling "this kind of talk . . . most unfortunate," noting that "if the war doesn't end in three weeks—and it probably will not—the public will have been led up a blind alley. . . . I told Ike about this super-optimism and he lamented it, but said there was little he could do."

Shortly after midnight, August 7, the German assault commenced. The XLVII Panzer Corps at Domfront, under cover of darkness, launched an attack without artillery preparation toward Mortain. The vanguard 2nd Panzer Division gained seven miles through the tired, understrength and evidently unsuspecting 30th Division at Mortain. By dawn, protected by low fog, German armored reinforcements poured into the area. The Germans seized Mortain and overran the 30th Division command post, opening a dangerous gap which, if exploited, might have reached the coast.

For twenty-four hours Hodges, Bradley and Collins were worried about the safety of VII Corps and a German breakthrough, which would have made the position of twelve U.S. divisions south of the Avranches bottleneck "logistically untenable." The near disintegration of the 30th Division was sobering, as was the shock of encountering a determined enemy after so many weeks, something Bradley attributed to enemy "habits of discipline and obedience." But on August 7 the German attack was snared in the crosswinds of doubt within the high command and plagued by bad fortune. The 120th Regiment of the 30th Division heroically clung to "Hill 317," a 1,030-foot promontory by-passed in the night attack. From the heights, the 120th directed withering artillery fire on the German flanks. The Germans failed to exploit a dangerous gap in the American line near the town of St.-Hilaire before the U.S. 35th Division and 4th Division could move up. The fog lifted early that day, and by noon, in dry, cloudless weather, ten squadrons of British Typhoons and American Thunderbolts swept the roads and pummeled heavily congested intersections.

By midday the attack had reached dangerous proportions, but the magnitude of the opportunity it provided the Allies was apparent. With Patton's forces in the clear and the German lines about to buckle at Caen and Vire, the Germans had committed four panzer divisions and supporting infantry in a deep salient. With the forecasts promising continued fair weather,

Bradley decided that the German counteroffensive, already slowing up, could be contained by remnants of the 30th Division and by air power, a defense that he apparently kept weak in the hope of luring the Germans deeper into the trap.

Bradley was amazed. To Hansen, he remarked that LUTTICH was "the greatest tactical blunder I've ever heard of," and muttered that the enemy "had better straighten out on our front or he'll be terribly embarrassed one of these days." But Bradley moved cautiously. The day before, he and Patton had met to discuss the possibility of either a "long" or a "short" envelopment by Patton's Third Army. Instead, he proceeded to divide up the Third Army east of Le Mans, deciding to send Haislip's XV Corps north to operate against the German flank at Alençon and Argentan, with XX Corps venturing east toward the Paris–Orléans gap, a compromise which left every option open but which has been criticized by military historians as failing to capitalize fully on the German blunder.

The criticism would hold that the Allies should have proceeded boldly to encircle the Germans either at the Seine or in Normandy, moves that, if successful, might have completely erased two German armies. The former required a prompt decision to push Patton's full strength toward the Seine; the latter would have involved an attack toward Argentan–Falaise by both of Patton's corps and postponing the push for the Seine. But in either case, encirclement was a big "if," and the principals—Eisenhower, Bradley and Montgomery—would finally decide against it in favor of a "mix": an effort to compress the German flanks, coupled with a bold advance by Patton in hopes of racing the Germans to the Seine, along with a series of small encirclements later on to mop up remnants of the German army left behind in the retreat. Montgomery and Bradley questioned the point both of "strategic envelopment" or of the chances of pulling it off, as did Eisenhower. To a degree, one might say that Eisenhower, Montgomery and Bradley exhibited undue respect for a mortally wounded enemy at a moment of rare opportunity. On the other hand, other strategies available on August 7 stood to inflict large if not comparable numbers of casualties on the Germans while minimizing Allied losses. And with a significant victory within reach of the Allied group on both flanks, no one saw the point of courting tactical risks barring an opportunity to win a "decisive" victory, which none of the principals foresaw—yet. Accordingly, Bradley and Montgomery devised a strategy of least risk—not blocking but compressing the inevitable German retreat through a corridor bounded by the towns of Argentan and Falaise that the Allies could comb over with air and artillery.

Controversy would persist, though Bradley's Mortain decision was routine in World War II. In Russia and Italy the Germans had repeatedly demonstrated little fear of strategic envelopment and had repeatedly shown their ability to break an encirclement line. Bradley and Montgomery, backed by Eisenhower, doubted that an Allied line formed behind the

German rear could withstand a determined retreat by as many as nineteen German divisions. As he put it several times that week, Bradley preferred a "solid shoulder" at Argentan to a "broken neck." From this, Montgomery and Bradley, with Eisenhower's full backing, did not deviate, though in the latter stage of the battle, with the German retreat well along, the American and British armies would perform the ritual of encircling the remnants of LUTTICH at Falaise–Trun–Chambois.

On August 7, Patton flamboyantly protested the decision. Euphoric over the rapid Third Army advance and anxious to "seize the unforgiving minute," Patton agitated for pushing both of his corps due east toward the Orléans–Paris gap. The apostle of bold maneuver and attack, Patton urged that the air-armor advantage worked only with "incessant and apparently ruthless driving on the part of the ground commander," views later echoed by many German commentators who claimed that an Allied dash to seize the Seine crossings that week might have sealed all exits for the German Fifth and Seventh armies.

In *Crusade,* Eisenhower intimated that he welcomed competing temperaments, such as those of Bradley and Patton. He credited this combination with often producing better than expected results. Eisenhower recalled the lineup of American field commanders on August 7: in Patton, he wrote, the Allies had a "great leader for exploiting a mobile situation"; on Patton's left, Eisenhower had placed the "sturdy Hodges to continue the pressure on the Germans." In both armies were "battle-tested corps and division commanders who could be depended upon in any situation to act promptly and effectively without waiting for detailed instructions from above." In Bradley the Allies had a leader who encouraged a spirit of aggressiveness in his field commanders but who conducted the battle with balance and prudence. In commenting on criticism of Mortain, Eisenhower pointedly noted that "Patton was an operational commander—not an overall commander."

But a tremendous Allied victory was unfolding. In a message to Marshall on the night of the seventh, Eisenhower confidently indicated that the enemy counterattack at Mortain had already been defeated. And with the Canadians attacking toward Falaise and XIX Corps entering Vire, Bradley had gained "practically an open flank." Eisenhower disclosed to Marshall his plans to swing elements of the Third Army toward the Paris–Orléans gap, while the bulk of it swung north toward Argentan–Falaise to destroy the German Seventh Army east of the Dives River. Meanwhile, Bradley would secure Brittany with VIII Corps. Exceeding even the rosiest expectations of April and May, Eisenhower predicted to Marshall that the Allies would soon be in a position to seize Seine crossings, and then to pursue to the Somme, while clearing the Seine ports and beyond.

However, gains were not keeping pace with expectations. Moreover, it was a truism by now that an Allied victory was incomplete without major political and military controversy over what to do next, and the Mortain battle would soon prove to be no exception. On the seventh, Eisenhower would find himself courting involvement in yet a second controversy only hours after the closing debate on DRAGOON. Eisenhower, already concerned that military policy might be overwhelmed by political maneuvering and recriminations, spent much of the day in conference with Treasury Secretary Henry Morgenthau, who was in France to discuss occupation and mobilization policy, and to sound out Eisenhower's views on a major issue before the Cabinet: the Morgenthau plan for postwar German administration.

This meeting was destined to be a source of recurring rumors about Eisenhower's hand in the so-called Morgenthau plan, a blueprint for a hard-peace occupation policy in postwar Germany. Eisenhower's role in formulating it would first surface on the eve of the 1948 primary season, and then resurface in the 1952 campaign and in the fall of 1953 on the eve of the Army-McCarthy hearings when Communist spy allegations were again leveled against Morgenthau's aide, Harry Dexter White, who was present that day.

Amid rising "soft peace" sentiment in Washington, Morgenthau arrived in Normandy under somewhat of a cloud. Many factors accounted for a new trend in U.S. policy: the elections; the events of July 20 and German defeats on all fronts; growing unease over the Russian advance in Poland and recent signs of a Soviet lone-hand approach on the Polish question; and, perhaps most important, recent Allied successes. The focus was a national press debate that had started up over unconditional surrender—what the phrase meant, and what it implied about the future of Germany and Europe; specifically, whether the aim of destroying fascism, which no one quarreled with, was inseparable from a policy of destroying the German state. By August many were arguing that unconditional surrender was prolonging the war, and speculated that the Germans, if assured about their future, would seize the chance to give up rather than bring on the invasion of the Fatherland. But if the policy was abandoned, would Allied-Russian cooperation unravel? Would modification of the policy have the intended effect on the Germans of producing a real change of heart?

These were questions that the Allied high command had confronted in May, when Eisenhower had discouraged "soft peace" statements that might erode the unity of his command or undermine combat morale. The appeal of such a policy in Moscow had also been a factor, which was still a consideration on August 7. Konev's halt at the Vistula had become an extended pause marking the end of a 400-mile Red Army advance from the Dnieper. Meanwhile, secondary Russian offensives had opened in Rumania and Hungary, which meant that action on the crucial Polish front was not likely to resume anytime soon. Eisenhower anticipated hard fighting ahead.

According to Morgenthau's account, Eisenhower took the lead and persuaded him and his aide, Harry Dexter White, to return to Washington to draw up a "Carthaginian" occupation policy, which Morgenthau claimed he did and promptly sold to Roosevelt. Morgenthau quoted Eisenhower as minimizing the Soviet problem, predicting that the USSR would press modest postwar claims, having "all she can digest, and . . . problems of her own which will keep her busy until long after we are dead."

Was Eisenhower the inspiration behind the Morgenthau plan? Eisenhower would never deny it in so many words, though his version of his August 7 meeting with Morgenthau would differ somewhat. When Morgenthau's recollection of this meeting first surfaced in late 1947, Eisenhower directed his Pentagon staff aides to search the files for documented evidence to support or refuge Morgenthau's version. When the search turned up very little, Eisenhower's aide Colonel Craig Cannon dictated a memo that summarized Eisenhower's recollection of the meeting. In it, Cannon quoted Eisenhower as having recalled that he had told Morgenthau that the German people should be made to feel a sense of responsibility for the war, and that German welfare should take a backseat to the welfare of Germany's victims. But he had denied making suggestions to flood the Ruhr mines, to create German industrial plants for shipment to Russia or to "pastoralize" Germany. The Morgenthau controversy would haunt Eisenhower's early career in politics, however, again illustrating the continuity in postwar politics of the old prewar debates about the wisdom of defeating Germany in alliance with Russia.

Hours after the Eisenhower-Morgenthau meeting, the Canadian II Corps, deploying novel techniques of nighttime bomber support, rumbled through the Bourguébus ridge and extended spearheads three miles down the Caen–Falaise road. ULTRA overheard Von Kluge's pleas for permission to break off the attacks of Mortain, and Hitler's unequivocal orders to gather up all the armor remaining in Normandy and to resume the offensive at Mortain by August 11. As the German tug-of-war continued, the 9th, 10th, and 12th SS divisions were on the move from Mount Pinçon toward the salient, reinforced by the 9th Panzer Division drawn from Bordeaux and reorganized under a special panzer group headquarters charged by Hitler with carrying out the attack. Allied commanders on the scene noticed, however, that Von Kluge was committing the panzers at the shoulders of the Mortain salient, a preliminary to retreat.

On the eighth, Eisenhower and Bradley met along a roadside near the town of St.-Sauveur-Lendelin to consider adjustments in the "short envelopment plan." Bradley conveyed Patton's "coolness" to the idea of a limited attack in Argentan. Again, Bradley felt that Patton was ignoring the threat of German armor, and that Patton's desire to drive on to Falaise to link with the Canadians and complete the encirclement ignored the ability of the Germans to break out of such a trap. Bradley's plan was for Walker's XX Corps to continue westward while Haislip's XV Corps swung toward Argentan with Collins' VII Corps moving up in support. According to Smith, Eisenhower approved the maneuver "with a nod" and again assured Bradley that in the event the Germans attacked and penetrated to the coast, supply by airlift could provide Patton's lead columns 2,000 tons per day. In a phone conversation with Montgomery that afternoon, Eisenhower approved Montgomery's decision to set the American-Canadian boundary at Argentan, a line fifteen miles distant from Falaise and Crerar's spearheads, and which provided Von Kluge the corridor for his escape—yet another tactical decision destined to be criticized as overcautious and unimaginative. But Bradley, Montgomery and Eisenhower were mindful of Allied losses in Normandy, of German desperation and superior numbers, of German willingness to trade whole armies for space and time, facts borne out in recent weeks by events in Normandy and Russia.

In the next seventy-two hours, Eisenhower waited while Churchill provoked a final conference on DRAGOON. On the sixth, he had dispatched a lengthy appeal to Hopkins in Washington asking him to raise DRAGOON with Roosevelt, who by now had left Washington for a highly publicized postconvention conference with MacArthur at Pearl Harbor. Hopkins' reply had been "far from comforting," however. The presidential confidant had predicted that the President's reply would "be in the negative," that Roosevelt personally backed Eisenhower in the "sure conquest of France," and that "to change the strategy now would be a great mistake." With "no more to be done about it," Churchill petulantly summoned Eisenhower to 10 Downing Street for a private talk the night of the ninth to assess the wreckage of his nine-month crusade to salvage the Italian campaign.

The mood was dark. For several hours the developing victory at Mortain seemed far away, almost incidental alongside the reports from Warsaw, the peace rumors in Rumania, Bulgaria and Finland, foundering British diplomacy in Yugoslavia and Greece, and Roosevelt's untimely departure for Hawaii, which sealed the fate of DRAGOON. Denied a conference with Roosevelt, Churchill was about to depart for Naples for talks with Tito. He wanted Eisenhower to know how gravely DRAGOON undermined his situation. He wanted Eisenhower's personal assurances that as eventual commander of the DRAGOON force he would not call on Alexander further unless it was absolutely necessary.

To get these assurances, Churchill deployed every device at his command. He accused the Americans of an arbitrary, even domineering attitude toward the British, and of wielding "actual and potential strength as a bludgeon in conference." He predicted hard times ahead, wept, and dramatically warned that DRAGOON might compel him "to lay down the mantle of my high office."

Eisenhower was embarrassed, but his hands were tied by policies made jointly by the President and the Prime Minister. Stoically, Eisenhower cited the critical passages of his directive issued in February. The Combined Chiefs of Staff had charged him with proceeding into "the heart of Germany and destroying Hitler's armed forces." Eisenhower had evaluated DRAGOON in these terms and had concluded that it was "essential to concentrate our forces to push through France into Germany." He conceded that wars were "waged for political purposes," but he lacked political authority and therefore authority to make what would have amounted to a political recommendation to the CCS to shift DRAGOON to Brittany. Eisenhower favored DRAGOON, and would continue to do so unless Churchill went to Roosevelt "to get his agreement to change my orders," since despite the unfolding victory in Normandy, the long-range success of OVERLORD was in no way assured.

As he later put it in a note, Eisenhower regretted the Prime Minister's sense of being bludgeoned, and he denied "any desire on the part of any responsible person in the American war machine to disregard British views or cold-bloodedly to leave Britain holding an empty bag on any of our joint undertakings." Eisenhower asked Churchill to understand the American position. British views had prevailed in 1942 and in 1943, and in this light, he personally did not consider the American views "intemperate" because of "long and persistent support of ANVIL." Finally Eisenhower reminded Churchill that he depended on his support. For sentimental and practical reasons, Eisenhower hoped that everyone would "adhere tenaciously to the concepts of control brought forth by the President and yourself two and one half years ago."

Two days after Churchill's departure, Ismay was a dinner guest in Portsmouth. According to Butcher, the evening was cordial. In the company of guests and staff, Ismay and Eisenhower bantered about the Prime Minister's eccentricities in conferences: Churchill's pacing about as he talked, his obliviousness to chairs, lamps or crystal, and his routine use of tears and humor to make a point.

After dinner, Ismay took Eisenhower aside to ask him what he thought about a plan to send Alexander British reinforcements for an offensive north of Florence. Eisenhower's reaction was "negative," since he saw no way around a policy of concentrating all available forces in France in the next several weeks. Eisenhower agreed that Alexander's *present* force level would be necessary to sustain an attack into the Po River Valley, which he supported in light of recent press speculation about Nazi plans to convert the mountains of Austria, northern Italy and southern Germany into an SS citadel for carrying on a guerrilla struggle for decades, the so-called National Redoubt. On this tentative basis, Eisenhower and Ismay resolved the subject. Ismay left Portsmouth with the "strong impression" that while Eisenhower opposed reinforcement of Alexander, he would try not to lay claim to British units for France, and would not oppose British replacements for Alexander.

As he departed London for his talks with Tito in Naples, Churchill would grandly "adopt" ANVIL-DRAGOON. Liberated from the protocol surrounding D-Day, the Prime Minister on August 15 would don a flak suit and ride a British destroyer into battle with the first wave, a gesture that conveyed good sportsmanship. But in thus accepting an operation challenged by the British in every waking moment since Teheran, the Prime Minister conveyed that he was a soldier and was therefore loyally conforming to decisions irrespective of the wisdom or unwisdom of the operation as he saw it, which was to say that he believed that history would question DRAGOON, and that he expected the Americans to accept the consequences.

But had compromise on ANVIL ever been possible? In retrospect, it seems curious that Churchill had persisted with an idea, in the name of British prestige, that would only fail. By so doing, Churchill had gained time for Alexander but not enough time to bolster the British position in his talks with Tito that week. Likewise, Churchill had gained debating points on issues bound to grow in importance, but debating points could not substitute for results, and in gaining them, Churchill mainly succeeded in dramatizing the crisis in Anglo-American relations and his inability to resolve it.

In any event, the closing ANVIL debate would prove to be both a symptom and a cause of future troubles, particularly for Eisenhower, who in the wake of Normandy faced a formidable task of restoring his command. The debate was a symptom of the hardening of views on all sides amid rising frustration over the prospect of an all but certain victory over Germany along with prolonged battles in the meantime, while the Nazis restored control in the wake of the abortive July 20 plot. More than ever, Eisenhower would be depending on Churchill's restraining influence as the focus of British attention shifted from Italy to France. For a while, however, Churchill would be either disinclined or unable to exert a restraining influence, as British skeptics of American willingness to compromise were apparently vindicated. It seems more than coincidental that a mere forty-eight hours after Churchill's departure for Naples, Montgomery would launch his fateful bid to retain overall ground command in the name of winning the war by late 1944 with a strategy based on France instead of Italy.

Trying times were ahead, which was not surprising. In the best of worlds, the Germans, seeing the error of their ways, would have found means of overthrowing the Nazis and making formal amends to forestall invasion and a prolonged war for control of central Europe, but this possibility, if it had ever existed, perished on July 20. One slender hope remained as Von Kluge's retreat from Normandy began on the night of the eleventh, the hope that the German high command might opt for an informal "collapse" by piecemeal surrender in the field and passive resistance to Nazi decrees. POW interrogations that week confirmed reconnaissance reports that the German command had neglected rear lines on the Seine, Somme and Marne, and that the vaunted West Wall on the German frontier from

Holland to Switzerland was in disrepair. Reports from neutral capitals still indicated that the German high command, under no illusions that Allied terms would be easy, circumspectly hoped that the Allied invasion of Germany would come quickly and that the Allies would reach Berlin first.

Indeed, there are several accounts of tenuous German efforts to contact Allied emissaries that week as the Normandy campaign crashed to its climax. There is an undocumented account that on August 15 Von Kluge drove away from his forward headquarters for twelve hours in an attempt to rendezvous with emissaries from Patton's Third Army. Von Kluge's plan, according to this account, was to discuss unconditional surrender of his whole front, provided the Allies agreed to move through it quickly into Germany. Allegedly, however, Von Kluge's motor caravan was sidetracked by an American fighter-bomber attack, and in order to avoid suspicion, the German commander was forced to return to his headquarters before making contact. Brown reveals documentation that came to light in 1974 of an overture on August 11, 1944, passed through the German embassy in Lisbon. OSS Berne reported to the President and the Joint Chiefs a German businessman in Lisbon who passed word that the "German General Headquarters" was ready to surrender unconditionally to the Allies to meet all industrial and territorial demands, provided the Allies "act at once to occupy the Reich and keep out the Soviet." OSS Chief Allen Dulles in Berne recommended special attention to the overture "in view of the channels employed and the apparent sincerity of the source." Apparently no record of action taken exists.

Despite a Normandy victory, formidable obstacles to a surrender of any kind remained: first, Allied doubts that genuine forces of resistance to Hitler existed in Germany, and if they did exist, whether the Allies shared common ground with them and could risk entertaining their overtures; second, German skepticism that the Allies would exploit piecemeal surrender in a satisfactory manner and assure them that the Russians could be kept out of Germany. But Allied assurances—clear enough to guarantee passive occupation of Germany—meant an Anglo-American rupture with the Russians, something the Allies in the end could not accept. Or perhaps the whole idea was highly improbable—that fifty Allied divisions, on their own, would venture 300 miles from the Normandy base to the German frontier, would then venture another 300 miles from the German frontier to the Elbe River through hostile territory and then accept the "surrender" of a 300-division German army that had not been beaten by Allied arms.

The devastation of much of Europe in the winter of 1944 was now foreseeable, and responsibility for it was part of the ongoing debate as Churchill left for Naples. In the privacy of his staff at Portsmouth that week, Eisenhower grimly predicted a German recovery in the west even as the Canadians and Americans compressed the Falaise–Argentan pocket. As Eisenhower put it to Butcher, the Allies faced at least "one more battle" at the

Rhine, if not west of the Rhine. Ambitious plans for exploiting victory in Normandy were in the wind, but Eisenhower was hardly convinced that the Allies could operate beyond the Seine because, beyond the Seine, logistical constraints would be a big factor.

Indeed, staff studies hastily drawn up for pursuit beyond the Seine noted the problems: 20,000 tons a day were being off-loaded through the constricted beach ports at Cherbourg, but delivery of supplies east of the Seine would require time to rehabilitate railheads, roads and bridges. Comm-Z had drawn up plans for a round-the-clock truck convoy system in the American sector, but this was only makeshift, in Eisenhower's words, before an "enforced slowup of our advance which must eventually occur while we improve maintenance facilities for a further offensive that would be sustained for a considerable period." Eisenhower sensed that the Normandy battle would prove to be less than decisive, a theme he stressed in messages to Marshall and in letters home to Mamie at mid-month. "Always be optimistic and courageous," he wrote Mamie, "but not expectant. . . . every victory, even a partial one is sweet—but the end of the war only comes with the complete destruction of the Hun forces."

PURSUIT

In the field, rumors of a German surrender persisted as Dempsey and Hodges, having absorbed a smaller Mortain counterattack on the eleventh, pushed eastward against the salient with Crerar and Patton closing the flanks. At a press conference on the twelfth, called to announce that the 35th Division had taken St.-Hilaire and relieved the 120th at Hill 317, the new First Army commander, General Courtney Hodges, was bombarded with questions. When would the Allies be in Paris? Would the German army be destroyed west of the Seine? Was the German Seventh Army purposely committing suicide? What were the chances of a "break" in German morale? Hodges "refused to be trapped," wrote the First Army diarist, answering "frankly all questions which concerned his Army front but refused to be drawn into the strategical picture, on which the correspondents always seek the 'answers.' "

By the twelfth the Americans and British attacked in all sectors. The Canadians pressed for Falaise as the Third Army entered Argentan. In the area bounded by Falaise, Argentan and Mortain, eight divisions of the German Seventh Army and Fifth Panzer Army, compressed into a corridor twenty miles by ten miles, struggled to escape.

In the next several days, as the weather continued hot and dry, Allied bombers flew continuous sorties over the Falaise–Argentan cauldron. A haze of dust formed over the latticelike roads but provided scant protection for the Germans by day. The aerial pounding finally prevented any movement of traffic, forcing the Germans to dismount their vehicles and flee on foot. Air observers returned with reports of panic and slaughter: German columns abandoned thousands of trucks, half-tracks, self-propelled guns and tanks on the roads between Falaise and Chambois. The haul of captured and destroyed equipment was tremendous: 220 tanks, 160 assault guns, 130 anti-aircraft guns, 130 half-tracks and 2,000 horse-drawn trucks, leaving thousands stranded in a footrace for the Seine against the motorized American infantry. In seven days, 10,000 Germans would die in the Falaise pocket, and the "encirclement," completed at Chambois–Trun on the nineteenth, would bag another 50,000 prisoners. But estimates were that more than half the men in the Falaise cauldron escaped to safety that week, and in weighing the significance of the victory, no one could overlook that German lines had held east of Caen. The absence of formal surrenders in the field signified a lesser victory than Stalingrad or Tunisia.

Bradley's decision to funnel a German escape in lieu of cutting it did not sit easily. As early as the eleventh, the Allied boundary formally drawn through Argentan by Montgomery had seemed overly cautious. That day Haislip's XV Corps approached Argentan with four divisions, including Leclerc's 2nd French Armored, where, according to Montgomery's instructions, they were to draw up and wait for the Canadians. Near Argentan, Haislip met the expected resistance by the 352nd Division, remnants of Panzer Lehr, the 9th Panzer and the 116th Panzer. But as Collins' VII Corps closed the Mayenne gap farther back to link up, Haislip's way to Falaise and linkup with the Canadians seemed open.

A struggle ensued between Eisenhower and the American field commands. Spurred by Haislip, Patton agitated for permission to proceed to Falaise while there was still time to get into position to cut the German retreat. The Argentan boundary appeared to be cautious in the extreme, even suspect in Third Army ranks as a SHAEF-British plot to reserve the glory of liberating Falaise, a 21st Army Group D-Day objective, for Crerar and Montgomery. Patton, flirting with defiance of the boundary, placed the U.S. 4th Armored on standby for a plunge north of Argentan against the flank of the German corridor.

At a meeting in Condé on the thirteenth, Eisenhower, Montgomery and Bradley reviewed the problem and decided against altering the boundary. They would not attempt to halt the torrent of Germans stampeding eastward. Bradley later recalled that to close the gap, Haislip's inexperienced XV Corps would have to venture twenty miles beyond Argentan, all the while threatened on its western flank by German armor. Bradley doubted that one American corps could withstand the flood of retreating Germans.

On the fourteenth Patton, determined to take Falaise, recklessly dispatched columns of the U.S. 4th Armored Division eight miles north of Argentan, only to call them back when Eisenhower and Bradley again refused to permit XV Corps to venture beyond Argentan. Eisenhower stood at Bradley's side and monitored his conversation with Patton that afternoon. Patton demanded permission to continue. Bradley refused, and explained the Allied boundary problem somewhat disingenuously, telling Patton that even if the American forces succeeded in reaching Falaise, Bradley was "reluctant to chance a head-on meeting between two converging armies," which was a "dangerous and uncontrollable maneuver . . . unless . . . each is halted by prearranged plan." When Patton vowed to transit the gap and "drive the British into the sea and give them another Dunkirk," Bradley reminded Patton that the enemy was pulling out and ordered Patton to "button up and get ready for him."

As he ordered Patton to stop, Bradley decided to detach two of Haislip's divisions at Argentan to angle wide of the German escape, an abrupt return to the "long envelopment" discarded on the third that divided Haislip's southern pincer and effectively ended any chance of closing the gap. This decision commenced the Allied-German race for the Seine, where Bradley proposed to cut the German retreat in a series of piecemeal actions.

The race was on. By the fifteenth, as VII Corps reinforced Haislip at Argentan, XV Corps divided up, with two divisions breaking contact with the enemy to make for the town of Dreux on the Seine to harass the German flight over the river. Meanwhile, V Corps, "pinched out" at Vire, regrouped, then moved up on Haislip's right in order to close the pocket eight miles east of Argentan at Chambois later that week. South of Argentan, Patton directed Cook's XII Corps toward Orléans and Walker's XX Corps toward Chartres in a dash to preempt German efforts to form a line covering Paris. This set the stage for spectacular ground gains in the next week and the liberation of Paris.

Restraint at Argentan took a toll, particularly on the spirit of command unity that Eisenhower was seeking to restore. Bradley's adroit handling of Mortain in refusing to panic and retract his right wing on August 3 would be obscured by criticism of his failure to follow through and to capitalize on Hitler's strategic blunders. Montgomery's error in overestimating for days on end the Canadian pace toward Argentan was also criticized. Montgomery and Bradley, backed by Eisenhower, had not deviated from their cautious design adopted on the third for exploiting Normandy west of the Seine, but admitting this to their respective staff and commands became difficult in the heady days of breakout and pursuit.

In the sudden excitement generated by Patton's dash from Avranches, even Bradley, reflecting the emotions of his staff, would succumb to second thoughts about Argentan. Beneath his placid exterior, Bradley was sensitive to slights, real or imagined, aimed at the American command by the British. At Condé, Montgomery had again broached long-range plans. Although he endorsed Bradley's caution at Argentan, Montgomery had vehemently opposed his follow-up plan to commit the Third Army toward the Paris-

Orléans gap and had pressed his latest version of LUCKY STRIKE calling for concentration of massive strength north of the Loire and a British attack over the Seine into Calais, thence through the lowlands and into Belgium, with Patton's armor moving due east in support of Dempsey.

With the Canadian First Army stalled north of Falaise, Dempsey stalled at Mount Pinçon, and Patton in the open, Montgomery's revival of LUCKY STRIKE again struck Bradley as a calculated insult aimed at American generalship, and as stubborn reluctance on Montgomery's part to realize that the American breakout at St.-Lô had ended any chance that Montgomery would remain in command of the ground forces. Once again, however, more was involved. Montgomery's talk about a big thrust through Paris pivoting northeast with "emphasis on the left," north of the Ardennes, was not an academic proposition, for once again Montgomery was "looking ahead." He told Bradley that he envisioned capturing Calais, Ostend, Dunkirk and even Antwerp, 250 miles distant, with its twenty-eight miles of docks and a rail system linking all of Belgium and Holland. Montgomery was sanguine—indeed, he predicted that a solid mass of forty divisions could cross the Rhine and invade Germany. Montgomery's manner was intransigent, and his timing, three days after Eisenhower's closing talk with Churchill on DRAGOON, suggested that Montgomery's ideas were not just ordinary proposals.

Confirmation that Montgomery would vigorously oppose Eisenhower's assumption of overall ground command came seventy-two hours later, on the seventeenth, when a very different Montgomery met a second time with Bradley at 21st Army Group Headquarters to coordinate Haislip's maneuver and Dempsey's drive for the Seine. Montgomery no longer displayed the air of meticulous caution that he had shown three days before at Condé. Since then, the ongoing German collapse in France had recast the problem as one of organizing a pursuit offensive through France and strategy afterward, which raised a host of points discussed before but left unresolved. Crerar's Canadian columns had resumed their advance through Falaise toward Argentan and Chambois–Trun. Dempsey regrouped for a drive to the Seine while Haislip's XV Corps forces reached the Seine at Dreux. Patton's spectacular gains toward Orléans and Chartres continued through fragments of the German First Army, which beat a hasty retreat from Biscay. Two days before, on August 15, the DRAGOON landings under Devers had put to shore near Marseilles against scant opposition, and readied a ten-division blow northward up the Rhône Valley.

Accordingly, at Condé on the seventeenth, Montgomery went straight to the point. He reminded Bradley that the Allies now faced the problem of pursuit, which would require quick decisions and "above all, a plan." Montgomery proceeded to sketch plans calling for a British-led American-supported pursuit offensive toward Belgium.

Montgomery spoke in visionary terms. He opposed Patton's deep drive south of Paris to link with Devers' 6th Army Group, calling it a dispersion of armored strength away from the main battlefront, where he was sure the Allies had an unprecedented opportunity, in the wake of a decisive victory west of the Seine, to push through France and beyond before the Germans could organize a front. But this was provided that the 12th and 21st army groups stayed together "as a solid mass of some 40 divisions . . . so strong that it need fear nothing."

Specifically, Montgomery proposed that the British clear the Pas-de-Calais and Flanders, and advance toward Antwerp with an American army group protecting Dempsey's southern flank. The whole movement would pivot northward from Paris, no less than a "Von Schlieffen Plan in reverse," with Patton's Third Army *"positioned"* at Orléans–Troyes–Châlons–Reims–Laon and a right flank "thrown back along the Loire." In all circumstances, Montgomery insisted "we must not reach out with our right to join [DRAGOON] and thus unbalance our strategy," which, he argued, must look to securing bridgeheads over the Rhine by October, quickly seizing the Ruhr, and springing twenty divisions for a bolt over the north German plain toward Berlin.

Many of the features of the plan Montgomery sketched were familiar, many were not. Once again, as at Tunisia, Sicily, Salerno, and in Normandy, Bradley noted that Montgomery claimed the primary mission for the British Second Army, with the Americans relegated to secondary tasks. Bradley again suspected that the true inspiration of the plan was Montgomery's "ego," bruised in the "air-ground dispute," and that his main purpose was to rehabilitate his reputation by retaining control of the First Army and using it to secure British successes.

On the other hand, by injecting Berlin, Montgomery ventured into the realm of grand strategy. Indeed, Bradley's report to Eisenhower on the Fougères talks left no doubt that Montgomery had sketched the outlines of a major initiative with the objective Berlin and ending the war. Soon it would be apparent that problems between Eisenhower and Montgomery were about to pass the point of minor adjustments and evolve into a battle over fundamental military policy, which would raise doubts that the Allies in the coming weeks would possess the first prerequisite of military strategy —unity of command.

Meanwhile, in an effort to dampen rumors of German surrender, and to extend an olive branch to Montgomery, Eisenhower flew to London on the fifteenth to address a rare press conference at his Grosvenor Square offices. The big news that day was his consent, at Marshall's suggestion, to lift censorship on Patton's command of the Third Army, which thereby confirmed the existence of two American armies operating in France and meant that Bradley's promotion as Montgomery's "co-equal" could not be put off for long. Significantly, Eisenhower refused to elaborate on the com-

mand implications. He spoke "feelingly and earnestly" about the cooperation of land, sea and air forces in the Normandy battle with special emphasis
on the heroic British effort at Caen. Eisenhower also warned the packed
conference against heeding peace rumors, and deplored predictions that the
war would be over in a matter of weeks, observing that "Hitler and his gang
have nothing to lose by enforcing prosecution of the war." Eisenhower
warned against overestimating the significance of dramatic territorial gains
in the next several weeks.

Because the transcript of the conference was heavily edited by censors,
the impact of Eisenhower's warning was blunted, and the gesture Eisenhower aimed at Montgomery and the British was too be undermined by bad
fortune. Shortly after the press conference, in a talk with his old friend Wes
Gallagher of the Associated Press, Butcher suddenly relaxed his guard.

Butcher knew that SHAEF-press relations had not recovered from the
second Patton incident, and he was defensive about a spate of Hearst-press
articles critical of Eisenhower as a "figurehead." Reflecting Eisenhower's
private frustrations, Butcher disclosed to Gallagher what Eisenhower had
left unsaid at the press conference: that Bradley, in command of an army
group since the Avranches breakout, had been exercising complete control
over the American forces and had effectively functioned as Montgomery's
"co-equal" under Eisenhower.

Gallagher's dispatch triggered an inter-Allied press controversy. First the
British newspapers erupted with a round of editorials deploring Montgomery's "demotion," followed by a series of American editorials deploring the
implied British criticism of Eisenhower and Bradley. Eisenhower tried to
salvage the situation. On the seventeenth, in response to press inquiries
about Bradley's status, Smith, directed by Eisenhower, denied that Bradley
was as yet in any way "co-equal" with Montgomery and refused to say when
Bradley ever would be "co-equal." Reaction in Washington was prompt.
Unenthusiastic about Eisenhower's public emphasis of Montgomery's overall role in coordinating the Normandy battle and breakout, Marshall informed Eisenhower of the Hearst articles, and of widespread comment in
the American press about Eisenhower's use of British subordinates as land,
sea and air commanders. Marshall assured Eisenhower that "the astonishing success of the campaign up to the present moment" had evoked "emphatic expressions of confidence in you and Bradley." Accordingly, he
urged Eisenhower to accelerate plans to set up forward-command facilities
in France in order to assure ground command promptly. In the same
message, Marshall put off Eisenhower's routine request to promote Bradley,
at least until the "transition period" ended and Bradley assumed responsibilities commensurate with his new rank.

The Gallagher leak meant a crisis in Eisenhower's intimate official family.
Eisenhower was polite and sympathetic toward Butcher, who undoubtedly

had tried to protect Eisenhower's interests as he thought best. But Butcher's position as a confidant, friend and member of the SHAEF household had become untenable, at least for a while.

As Bradley and Montgomery met on the seventeenth, Eisenhower asked Butcher to replace the ailing T. J. Davis as head of SHAEF PRD in London. In their parting meeting, Eisenhower was pleasant but firm. He assured Butcher that his assignment was "temporary," and gave him a standing invitation to return to his headquarters as a guest. Butcher was packed and gone by dusk, and the role of confidant quickly passed to Jimmy Gault, who was to neglect the office diary and close history's eyes to the hour-by-hour record of the critical months ahead.

On notice of a command crisis, Eisenhower spent the next several days at work on a myriad of diplomatic and political problems. Montgomery's talk of Berlin was just one of the many British proposals flooding Eisenhower's desk that week, including proposals to airlift paratroopers into Athens, proposals to airlift commandos and supplies into Warsaw, where German panzer forces intervened to suppress Polish uprisings, and fresh proposals for landings at Trieste and Istria to flank the Gothic Line north of Florence, all ideas pegged to the prospect of an imminent economic-military collapse in Germany.

Visitors arrived from stateside with news of controversies in Washington. Assistant Secretary of War Anna Rosenberg visited to discuss demobilization policy. Navy Secretary James Forrestal passed through London and took time out to talk over occupation policy with Eisenhower. Morgenthau was by now circulating the "Morgenthau plan," the scheme for the political dismemberment and the "pastoralization" of Germany. In a wide-ranging talk, Forrestal informed Eisenhower of the controversy over Morgenthau's views in the Cabinet, and the growing consensus in Washington that the Soviets could not be trusted and were resolved "to destroy representative government." Forrestal's trip was perhaps a sign of pre-election jitters, and concern about the impact on the voters of embarrassing Russian actions in Poland.

Meanwhile, with the liberation of Paris at hand, Allied policy toward De Gaulle had to be clarified. As things stood, Roosevelt still opposed formal recognition of the FCNL (French Committee of National Liberation) and wanted De Gaulle's role downplayed. This became the subject of a tense conference among Eisenhower, De Gaulle, and Eden at the new SHAEF forward compound in Tourniers on the twentieth.

Since Eisenhower's stormy confrontation with De Gaulle long ago, on June 4, the French problem, while debated back and forth between Washington and London, had been relegated to military government specialists at SHAEF. Now the ongoing German collapse west of the Seine pushed

France to the forefront, raising the practical question of how to govern France and how far to go in assisting the Gaullists.

By the twentieth the city of Paris was in turmoil. With news of Patton's dash, workers five days before had called a general strike. The pro-Communist FFI had moved in open defiance of German authority to seize buildings throughout the city, presumably in hopes of vying with De Gaulle over control of Paris. That day, with Haislip's XV Corps expanding the Nantes bridgehead and Patton extending a flank to Fontainebleau southeast of Paris, the FFI had entered negotiations with the German occupational authority for a cease-fire. The beleaguered German command recognized the FFI as combatants in exchange for a seventy-two-hour cease-fire to evacuate German troops and the Paris garrison.

From De Gaulle's point of view, timely moves were essential to preempt a Communist takeover of Paris, and according to his biographer, Brian Crozier, De Gaulle also suspected a Darlan deal in the making, which would amount to a regime of direct Allied military rule through local Vichy authority. Aware of his importance in recruiting French divisions, and confident of British support, De Gaulle was pressing stiff terms for his cooperation with the Allies: virtual autonomy for French forces under SHAEF, American aid, the prompt occupation of Paris and restoration of French sovereignty in the military zones.

One month earlier, Roosevelt had all but recognized the Gaullists by receiving De Gaulle in Washington, but this was not enough, and the JCS still balked at Eisenhower's appeals for a formal revision of his pre-D-Day directive to include permission to conclude a civil affairs agreement with De Gaulle. At Tourniers on the twentieth, Eisenhower tried to temper De Gaulle's demands and gain latitude. He discouraged flamboyant actions by De Gaulle and warned that without a pledge of quick elections, there could be no formal U. S. recognition. As for Paris, Eisenhower indicated that in military terms it might be better to postpone entering the city indefinitely. Eisenhower cited military planning estimates that supplying the city would divert an estimated 4,000 tons of food and oil supplies daily.

Eisenhower was bluffing, and the bluff would be short-lived. The FFI armistice with General Dietrich von Choltitz, the commander of the German garrison, was set to expire on the twenty-third, a deadline of sorts on De Gaulle's ability to take Paris without widespread civil disorders. By the twenty-first, underground emissaries warned SHAEF and De Gaulle that Choltitz had orders to "destroy all bridges over the Seine and to devastate the city," and that he had directed that Paris be wired for systematic demolition. Through Swedish emissaries, Choltitz had indicated that he personally opposed the orders and preferred to surrender the city to regular Allied forces, presumably to avoid capture and summary execution by the FFI.

Meanwhile, Leclerc's French 2nd Armored Division had landed ten days before and had moved into the battle at Chambois as part of Gerow's V Corps. On the twenty-first Leclerc broke contact with the Germans and withdrew to regroup near Le Mans to prepare for the march to Paris. According to the First Army diary, Leclerc, under Gerow's orders to "stay put," angrily paced Army headquarters demanding permission to proceed to the French capital. Gerow kept Leclerc on hold, but Eisenhower's balancing act dissolved the next day when Marshal Alphonse Juin threatened in writing to order Leclerc to Paris with or without SHAEF approval, which would have been a bad precedent in French-SHAEF relations. As a veteran of MacArthur's staff, Eisenhower was familiar with the general's dictum that a military commander must never issue an order that will not be obeyed.

Later on the night of the twenty-second, twenty-four hours before the armistice was to lapse, Eisenhower met with Juin, Bradley and Koenig at Tourniers. Paris was in chaos. Power stations were out, and food was in short supply. Juin beseeched Eisenhower to negotiate with Choltitz and spare the City of Light. The treasures of Paris would be demolished, and French unity destroyed in civil war, eventualities that could be avoided only by a resolute French administration.

Mindful of the Darlan affair, Eisenhower decided that he was empowered to act. Mindful also that the Darlan case had been a military expedient to stop Allied-French fighting, Eisenhower needed a military rationale acceptable in Washington that went beyond assuring the safety of Allied communications. He finally decided that the German garrison in Paris constituted a "menace to the Allied flank," and directed Bradley to eliminate it, using the French 2nd Armored if possible. In a message to the CCS that afternoon, Eisenhower explained that while he preferred to by-pass the city, the Germans would soon be evacuating Paris, "like it or not." That night Leclerc's 2nd Armored moved out for Versailles and the western suburbs of Paris to await expiration of the Choltitz-FFI armistice with orders to "reinforce" the FFI, which, by decree, was not incorporated into the French army under SHAEF. Hodges assigned the U.S. 4th Infantry Division to accompany Leclerc, and Eisenhower placed both units under V Corps, thereby bestowing the title of American liberator of Paris on General Leonard T. Gerow.

Meanwhile, on the nineteenth and twentieth, Eisenhower had convened meetings at his new Normandy headquarters to hammer out plans for crossing the Seine, a step involving intricate logistical problems and the formalization of longer-range plans for joining up with the DRAGOON forces now ashore without incident at Marseilles and pursuing the defeated remnants of four German army groups to the German frontier.

The big question that night was how far Montgomery would carry the plan he had sketched for Bradley on the seventeenth. With it, Montgomery had served notice that he would oppose a thrust by Patton to link up with Devers' 6th Army Group forces and plans to form a solid southern flank, which, in Eisenhower's view, was essential and the reason he had ultimately backed DRAGOON. In the tumult of mid-August, Eisenhower intended to adhere to the "broad front" concept sketched months before, the concept Montgomery now challenged. Would Montgomery accept compromise?

Ominously, Montgomery was absent, and represented by his peacemaking chief of staff, General "Freddie" de Guingand, who would virtually live at Tourniers for the next forty-eight hours. De Guingand later wrote that he was consciously attempting to bridge a potentially serious gulf between Eisenhower and Montgomery over strategy, now complicated by the Gallagher leak and the nationalistic considerations involved in Montgomery's imminent "demotion."

The hour was late. The Tourniers conference was a belated attempt to work out differences in a new phase of the war ushered in by the breakout. With tentative contact established between the Polish armored division and the U.S. 90th Infantry Division at Mount Ormel near Chambois, and with most of the Seine west of Paris in Allied hands, "for all practical purposes the OVERLORD campaign to secure a lodgement area in western France between the Seine and Loire ended . . . ten days ahead of schedule." But the Allied high command confronted basic problems of ground strategy that were not close to being worked out, and a vigorous debate was imminent. The debate would begin with an effort to assess what the Germans were doing and the magnitude of the opportunity Eisenhower and his advisers faced on the twentieth: Were the Germans merely retreating from France or was Germany on the edge of defeat?

Eisenhower's decision to cross the Seine was accepted without dissent. However, the group reached a shaky compromise on operations east of the Seine. There would be two thrusts: first, a "main effort" toward Amiens–Mons–Liège led by Montgomery's 21st Army Group with the U.S. First Army in support; a secondary thrust by Patton's Third Army through Verdun–Metz. Bradley's pivotal 12th Army Group, mustering on the Seine and capable of turning northeast or southeast, would divide, with the U.S. First Army proceeding toward Belgium and Patton toward Metz and the Saar to link up with DRAGOON at Dijon, a pattern that conformed with Eisenhower's long-standing, broad-front intentions outlined at staff conferences in London before the invasion but one that Montgomery had rejected on the seventeenth by demanding that the Allies orient all forces toward Mons–Liège–Antwerp.

Were the Germans nearing defeat? The strategic issue involved a basic choice between concentration of Allied striking power for the sake of quick pursuit toward a single objective or a general advance to consolidate victory in France. The strategic question was also inseparable from the command

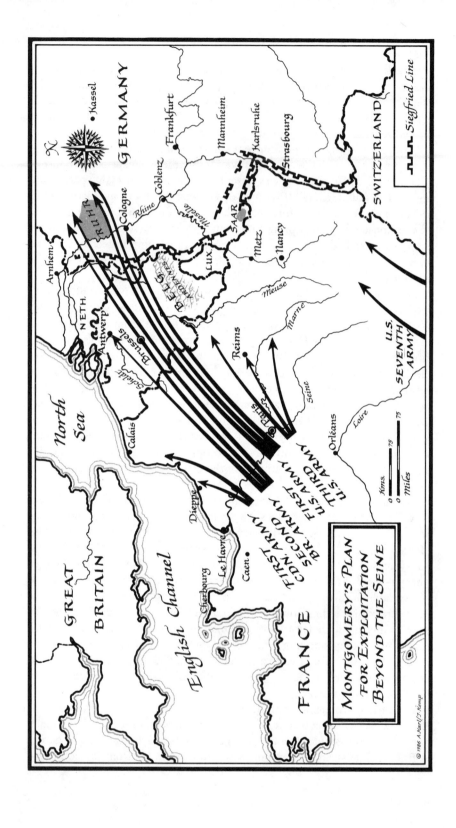

GREAT BRITAIN

North Sea

English Channel

FRANCE

Cherbourg
Le Havre
Caen
Dieppe
Calais

NETH.
Antwerp
Brussels
Schelde

Arnhem

BELGIUM
ARDENNES

LUX.

Paris
Reims
Orléans

GERMANY

Kassel
Cologne
Coblenz
Frankfurt
Mannheim
Karlsruhe
Strasbourg
Metz
Nancy

RUHR
Rhine
Moselle
SAAR
Meuse
Marne
Seine
Loire

SWITZERLAND

U.S. SEVENTH ARMY

CDN. FIRST ARMY
BR. SECOND ARMY
U.S. FIRST ARMY
U.S. THIRD ARMY

Siegfried Line

Kms. 0   75
Miles 0   75

MONTGOMERY'S PLAN FOR EXPLOITATION BEYOND THE SEINE

© 1986 A.Karl/J.Kemp

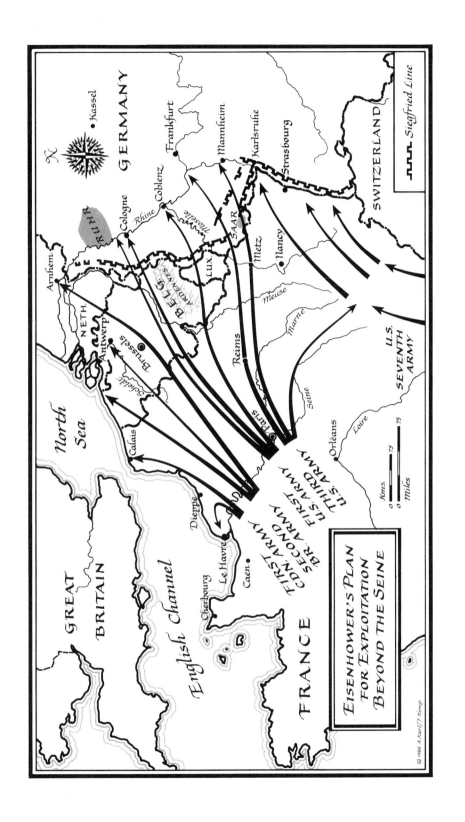

EISENHOWER'S PLAN
FOR EXPLOITATION
BEYOND THE SEINE

problem: whether the two army groups—the British and American—would concentrate on a single objective under the tight control of a single overall Ground C-in-C, as Montgomery demanded, or whether the Americans and British would now proceed to clear France of Germans preliminary to what Eisenhower foresaw as a methodical battle for control of the Rhine and "linking up the whole front to prevent the costliness of establishing long defensive flanks."

As usual, Eisenhower groped for compromise. For one thing, integrated command procedures of some kind were essential simply to avoid confusion among American-British-French forces. Hence, Eisenhower had placed the Leclerc division under Bradley and now indicated that an American corps would operate with Montgomery's 21st Army Group at all times, which would avoid complete segregation of either army group. Eisenhower was also mindful of an issue that he suspected concerned Montgomery: that as the Allies approached the German frontier and the Germans formed a front, setbacks would tempt national forces to operate independently and leave each force isolated, fending for itself, which was the history of the Anglo-French coalition in 1940. Thus, Eisenhower assigned two divisions of Corlett's XIX Corps to support Dempsey's imminent offensive over the Seine. He decided that Montgomery was to have first call on Brereton's newly formed Allied Airborne Army to spearhead pursuit operations into Calais against the drastically reduced German Fifteenth Army. Montgomery would have supply "priority." Eisenhower privately told De Guingand that while his own personal command over the ground forces was unavoidable, he anticipated delay in implementing it and was amenable to the idea that Montgomery would retain "liaison" and coordination powers over the American First Army. However, British command of the U.S. First Army was not possible.

On the twenty-first, as De Guingand carried the accord back to 21st Army Group Headquarters, Eisenhower cabled Montgomery to elaborate. He assured Montgomery that First Army attacks toward the Seine were going well and that soon Hodges would be able to swing forces north in support of Dempsey's Seine crossings due to start in a week. He asked Montgomery to examine 21st Army Group needs—air support, the First Allied Airborne Army, American ground units. As for command, "the existing system is undisturbed until a date which will be communicated to you as far in advance as possible." Eisenhower was "aiming at September 1st." Twenty-four hours later De Guingand returned to Tourniers with Montgomery's ten-point letter rejecting the plan in every particular but leaving the door open by requesting a face-to-face meeting to hammer out the problems "without Chiefs-of-Staff present."

Eisenhower's conference with Montgomery at Condé-sur-Noireau on August 23 was perhaps the most significant meeting of the summer campaign.

Forty years later it seems doubtful that Eisenhower expected to resolve the command problem then and there, or that Montgomery would have yielded quickly on major points of command and strategy which he had only fully developed on August 17. Therefore, the meeting was mostly exploratory, to enable Eisenhower to evaluate the source of Montgomery's objections, and to explore a compromise. It failed.

Montgomery was in a brusque mood. He imperiously dismissed Smith from the conference room to talk alone with Eisenhower. For almost an hour, he spoke from the typed document sent through De Guingand, having arranged the meeting not to exchange views but to bolster his demands for a "firm and sound plan" grounding Patton east of Paris and concentrating all available strength in his own 21st Army Group, which he considered essential for exploiting success in Normandy and ending the war. An intransigent Montgomery foresaw that Eisenhower's broad-front policy meant that the American and British front lines would "very soon be stretched." Montgomery perceived a fleeting opportunity to win the war. But supply was a looming constraint on all operations west of the Seine, and to defeat Germany, the high command had to choose one thrust line and concentrate fuel and ammunition behind it.

Montgomery insisted that the Normandy campaign had been a great victory, but that it "must be followed up." All of his military training told him that with "the whole line advancing and everyone fighting all the time, the advance would inevitably peter out," the Allies would fail to achieve a decision, the Germans would recover "and then we would be faced with a long winter campaign with all that entailed for the British people." Montgomery declared that the 21st Army Group was not strong enough to accomplish the tasks outlined at Tourniers on the twentieth. Eisenhower agreed, and suggested that American support would be available for Dempsey's Seine crossings and subsequent operations to clear Calais. Montgomery declared that coordinated operational control was essential. Again Eisenhower agreed. But by this Montgomery meant "*unified* control" under a single ground commander in chief, a factor so important that if American election-year public opinion posed a problem, Montgomery was prepared to serve under Bradley. The point, in Montgomery's opinion, was that the Normandy arrangements were battle-proven and made even more sense for the weeks ahead, when tight coordination would be necessary. Eisenhower would have enough on his hands sitting on a "lofty perch" and coordinating all the political and logistical problems at SHAEF.

Eisenhower disagreed. He pointed out to Montgomery that future battles would be fought on a far larger scale. Each of the army group commanders would function as a land commander, and only the Supreme Command could hope to consolidate the actions of these fronts and the political-logistical problems Montgomery spoke of.

Montgomery pressed on. Specifically, he urged that Patton, on the move through the Paris–Orléans gap, wheel north from Troyes and leave the Saar objectives to the 6th Army Group moving unopposed up the Rhône River Valley. Montgomery over and over again urged that a forty-division mass, with "nothing to fear," would be capable of jumping the Seine, seizing the Channel ports and V-bomb sites, crossing the Belgian frontier, then attacking the Ruhr and advancing beyond the Ruhr to Berlin. Eisenhower disagreed, and recited the offer he had sent through De Guingand.

Eisenhower was unwilling to give Montgomery an American army of at least twelve divisions and effective control of Patton, which would sacrifice position and reduce Bradley's army group to the Third Army. First, Eisenhower felt that this would be unsound strategy. Second, he warned Montgomery that "public opinion in the States would object." He knew that Dempsey needed flank support for the Seine crossings, and so, as he indicated, Corlett's XIX Corps stood by to help, along with Brereton's Allied Airborne Army. Dempsey would have "preference" in supply, and no matter what the command arrangements, Eisenhower would see to it that Montgomery retained "operational coordination" over the northern flank of the Allied advance. Montgomery's overall plan had merit; indeed Eisenhower liked it so much that he would consider giving it priority, though he cautioned that election-year politics ruled out formal overall British ground command, particularly in light of the heavy casualties he anticipated. Patton was "carrying the ball," rolling up gains and winning great acclaim in America. Eisenhower would not stop him. Montgomery pronounced himself flabbergasted that American public opinion would require unsound military strategy, and again insisted on First Army support beyond the Seine to the Brussels–Liège–Charleroi line and beyond to Berlin. "He [Eisenhower] listened quietly," Montgomery wrote, and the meeting ended.

And thus began the great debate of 1944 over rival plans for exploiting victory beyond the Seine, a debate that has never been resolved. Much has been written weighing whether or not Montgomery's proposal to stop Patton and consolidate the mass of offensive power for a bolt toward the Ruhr on a single front might have succeeded. Often overlooked is the fact that Eisenhower never considered the single-thrust idea—only ways to derail it. The assumptions behind Montgomery's idea were false, in Eisenhower's opinion, and even if Montgomery's assumptions were valid, the command arrangements he proposed had become politically impractical in Normandy. But the thrust of Eisenhower's position was military; in short, in Eisenhower's opinion, the Germans were disorganized but far from defeated and could never be defeated by the allies alone. And because the Germans were not defeated, they were able to form a front and frustrate any effort to sustain an offensive beyond the Rhine. Moreover, Montgomery's proposal to "concentrate" Allied forces in a single offensive would actually simplify the German task of organizing a front by eliminating German uncertainty over deciding where to defend. Thus, Montgomery's talk of defeating the German army and driving to Berlin with forty Allied divisions was "fantastic"—Eisenhower would not even consider it. The idea was heedless of supply considerations, the lack of functioning ports, and the urgent need in Eisenhower's opinion to push out the right flank to establish contact with DRAGOON and establish a coherent line with secure flanks behind which the Allies could regroup.

Eisenhower left the meeting with a premonition of trouble. A discouraging revelation was Montgomery's intransigence, which augured poorly for close military coordination in the next several weeks. Indeed, the military facts seemed obvious, and so Montgomery's talk of Berlin suggested that he was interested not in accommodating differences but in making demands. This suggested a parallel between Montgomery's performance and Wilson's abrupt propaganda in favor of Vienna several weeks before, which suggested in turn that Montgomery was acting not in his capacity as an army group commander, but at the behest of the BCOS, which, for diplomatic and political reasons as well as military ones, was likely to force the issue at length and raise others as well that would eventually spur competing American counterproposals and erode Eisenhower's authority.

Much was to come, but on the night of the twenty-third, Eisenhower knew that he was caught between two "musts." Over and over, Montgomery had insisted that the British "must" was different from the American "must," a "difference in urgency, as well as a difference in doctrine." British morale, the British economy, and postwar Europe, which vitally interested the British, required victory in 1944—"no later." But like the British "must," the American "must" was also urgent, a plan for military victory that went forward under arrangements commensurate with the American contributions in men and supplies. Potentially the problem, like ANVIL, was insoluble, and by the night of the twenty-third, Eisenhower lacked word of Soviet willingness to set up a military staff center, which meant that he was not sure that the Allies would have the luxury of time to work all this out. Indeed, Butcher's parting entry that week casually noted SHAEF's request that the CCS ask STAVKA to grant SHAEF "access to research centers and experimental stations overrun by the Russians in Germany, the better to prosecute the war against the Japs . . . ," a veiled reference to SHAEF's sudden uncertainty about the Russian timetable for resuming operations over the Vistula.

On August 24 Eisenhower phoned Bradley with orders to cross the Seine and push his left wing northward in support of Montgomery. He sent messages to Montgomery and Marshall in hopes of finding common ground and averting an airing of the command issue.

In his cable to Montgomery, Eisenhower summed up their talks with the accent on the positive. He was "enthusiastic" about the prospect of taking Antwerp and threatening the Ruhr. Eisenhower confirmed that Montgomery would have authority to coordinate Bradley's left wing, and disclosed that Bradley was on his way to Condé with instructions to "bend every effort towards speeding up the deployment of his forces in that direction."

To Marshall, Eisenhower sent a summary of plans for crossing the Seine. He predicted easy crossings in all sectors, but cautioned that there were not "sufficient strength and supply possibilities to do everything we should like to do simultaneously." Marshall could expect a major British drive northeast to "complete the destruction of the principal concentration of enemy force now in this region," which would entail U.S. First Army support operations and British command of several U.S. units. Eisenhower regretted the unavoidable delay in Bradley's assuming overall ground command, but assured Marshall that as a practical matter Bradley had long been operating "with a considerable degree of independence," and the change would be "really more obvious than real." Eisenhower added a personal sidelight. Churchill had cabled from Naples with a glowing account of U.S.-British cooperation in the DRAGOON landings "and a generous prediction that developments in Normandy . . . might eclipse the Russian victories to date . . . When I think of all the fighting and mental anguish I went through in order to preserve that operation," he closed, "I don't know whether to sit down and laugh or to cry."

On August 24, east of Falaise at Chambois, a final German attempt to break through the Polish and American forces failed, ending the battle of the Falaise pocket. At the Seine town of Elbeuf, XIX Corps converged with Canadian II Corps, netting the equivalent of five more German divisions, and south of Elbeuf, XV Corps seized a second Seine bridgehead at Nantes. German rear guards held crosspoints near Elbeuf for two days and bad weather intervened to cover the German flight over the Seine in small boats and rafts, but Field Marshal Walther Model's brief, desperate effort to organize a river line collapsed. Meanwhile, Patton's columns by-passed resistance with stunning speed; XII Corps entered Fontainebleau, igniting rebellion in Paris, and XX Corps, after a three-day battle in Chartres, drove spearheads a hundred miles southeast of Paris toward Troyes, a stunning drive that heralded the liberation of Paris and the collapse of German resistance in France.

Was the war over? The events of the next seventy-two hours would be reenacted elsewhere in France often in the next three weeks. Leclerc's columns slowly advanced through immense throngs of men, women and children choking the boulevards of the western Parisian suburbs. German stragglers emerged from hideouts to surrender and escape the summary vengeance of the FFI. Though nominally in control of the central city, the German army was nowhere in evidence, a scene that prompted Leclerc to remark that everything seemed like 1940 in reverse, "complete disorder on the enemy side, their columns completely surprised." By midnight on the twenty-fourth, French spearheads had moved into Paris under cover of darkness and French forces occupied the Hôtel de Ville. The main body of the French 2nd Armored reached the city at dawn on the twenty-fifth.

Rapturous demonstrations broke out in the city punctuated by a chorus of church bells that proclaimed deliverance from France's long night, and by sniper fire between Resistance units and collaborators. Paris emerged "from the shadows" that week, but the outbursts of relief and joy in the next several days would not conceal the scars of German occupation. Collaborators were dragged into the streets and paraded about to endure the taunts of compatriots. Crowds circled and jeered while Parisians shaved the heads of women accused of consorting with the enemy.

In the confusion, the tug-of-war between De Gaulle and SHAEF continued. On the twenty-fifth, as De Gaulle took residence in the Hôtel de Ville and prepared for his formal entry the following day, two authorities vied over who was in charge of Paris: Gerow, acting as Paris Allied military commander, and General Leclerc, appointed by De Gaulle French governor of the city. Leclerc accepted Choltitz's surrender in the name of the FCNL and proceeded to parade the French 2nd Armored in a show of force. Gerow, ensconced in a separate headquarters in Montparnasse countermanded the order and told Leclerc to "proceed with cleaning up the city" of Germans.

Dual control by Gerow and Leclerc could not last long. While they clashed over measures to maintain order, SHAEF and Gaullist emissaries hammered out the terms of a civil affairs agreement between the FCNL and SHAEF, ready by afternoon and initialed by Eisenhower without consulting Washington in order to "provide a secure rear area" for the Allied armies. Under it, SHAEF would deal with De Gaulle as the de facto leader of a provisional French government reserving power over a "forward zone," temporarily consisting of the entire country but eventually to encompass only the battlefronts. Late that night, arrangements were made for Eisenhower to pay a ceremonial call on De Gaulle's offices at the Ministry of War.

The following morning Eisenhower left Tourniers for Paris. At another time, his journey might have been a triumphant occasion. But no crowds would greet the Supreme Commander in Paris such as the ones that had greeted General Pershing twenty-five years before. The wounds of the French defeat in 1940 were too fresh and deep, and anxiety about the future of France was too intense.

But the occasion was memorable. Thirty-three months before, Eisenhower had risked his career in the Darlan affair, and now he had been accorded the great honor of extending de facto recognition to the Free French, something he could not have imagined sixteen years before, when he lived at Pont-Mirabeau working on the manuscript for General Pershing's *Guide to the American Battlefields in Europe.* Eisenhower had fond memories of his sunny apartment on the right bank of the Seine, known to old Army friends as "Chez Eisenhower," a hostel in 1928–29 for a constant stream of friends passing through Europe. He had fond memories of the trips on Sundays with six-year-old John to inspect the nearby battlefields of the Great War. On these tours, Eisenhower had become intimately acquainted with the battle terrain of eastern France, which Mamie, looking back, would attribute to the hand of fate. The Eisenhowers that year had explored Belgium, the Rhineland and the ancestral Palatinate region of Germany, where the next battles would be fought. Above all, in his year in Paris, Eisenhower had observed the demoralization of postwar France, accentuated by Aristide Briand's vain effort to bind the Allies of the Great War to a system of collective defense against a possibly resurgent Germany, an effort that foundered on American and British isolationism and the malaise of the Great Depression. Eisenhower approached the problem of postwar France with a measure of understanding, perhaps sympathy.

On August 26 the Supreme Commander's caravan moved with the flow of troops toward Paris by way of the battlefields at Falaise, Trun and Chambois. Accompanied by staff and Merrill Mueller of NBC, a veteran of the trip to Newbury on the night of the invasion, Eisenhower took time out to witness the wreckage and slaughter at Falaise. From a bitterly contested ridge near Chambois, he observed the panorama of tanks, caissons, half-tracks and horse-drawn artillery pieces littering the narrow road running through Chambois. In the tremendous air and artillery pummeling, ten thousand Germans had died, along with thousands of horses and mules. Yet the burial details shuffling through the debris were reminders of the thousands who had escaped, and of Radio Berlin's frantic proclamations that week calling the Falaise battle a noble achievement of German arms in buying time for the "German miracle" being organized. Radio reports also confirmed that Field Marshal Model, who had earned a reputation as an expert in restoring shattered fronts in Russia, had replaced Von Kluge, who, according to Swedish sources, had been under suspicion for complicity in the July 20 conspiracy and had committed suicide. Eighteen new divisions were forming in Germany, and a hundred fortress infantry batallions had become replacement batallions with new mobilization measures in the wind, including the formation of a reserve army of twenty-five divisions. German tank production was at record levels, and in the bombing respite afforded German industry during the Normandy campaign, aircraft deliveries reached wartime heights.

On the way to Chartres, Eisenhower called at 21st Army Group Tactical Headquarters in Gacé to invite Montgomery to join him in Paris. Montgomery was absent, and according to his staff, would be too busy to accompany Eisenhower on the twenty-seventh. Perhaps Montgomery wanted to avoid a meeting with Eisenhower and Bradley together where he would face pressure to compose his differences with American strategy, or perhaps

Montgomery was on British Foreign Office instructions to stay away so that Eisenhower's call on De Gaulle would be an undiluted American gesture of recognition. In any event, Eisenhower proceeded to Chartres for an overnight stay with Bradley.

In Chartres, Eisenhower visited the exquisite Gothic cathedral, which had miraculously been spared in the three days of fighting around the city. The next morning, Sunday, August 27, Eisenhower and Bradley motored into Paris under heavy guard, avoiding Versailles and other scenes of sporadic rearguard fighting between FFI guerrillas and collaborators. Friendly crowds of onlookers greeted the Eisenhower caravan at an impromptu stop at Notre Dame, delaying Eisenhower's arrival at De Gaulle's offices.

At their meeting on August 27, Eisenhower found De Gaulle to be typically austere, already clothed in the authority he had assumed upon entering the city forty-eight hours before. De Gaulle presented Eisenhower with a list of urgent needs—food, supplies, uniforms to issue to the Free French forces, and help against "unruly elements," including the Communist wing of the FFI that still roamed throughout the city. With plans to disarm or draft Communists into the French army and form new divisions, his government needed additional military equipment. De Gaulle asked for the temporary loan of two American divisions to parade through the city in another show of force to suppress revolt.

Eisenhower readily consented, and, in explaining the maneuver to Washington, would note that Paris was a "good road network" betwen the American position and German defenses east of the city. Two American divisions, the U.S. 28th and 4th Infantry, marched down the Champs-Elysées the following afternoon to become the first units in American history to participate in a ceremonial parade and enter battle on the same day.

De Gaulle consented to review the parade but otherwise acknowledged American help as little as possible. He joined Bradley and Leclerc in the reviewing stand and led the procession down the Champs-Elysées, then excused himself early from the ceremonies at the Tomb of the Unknown Soldier, setting a pattern of two decades of dealings with the Americans and Eisenhower.

In the years ahead, De Gaulle would take no note of the occasion, much to Eisenhower's disappointment. In 1959, on the eve of discussions with Soviet Premier Nikita Khrushchev in the second postwar crisis over Berlin, a still sentimental U.S. President Dwight Eisenhower would propose that his visit to Paris for consultations with French President Charles De Gaulle begin on August 27, the fifteenth anniversary of their conference at the prefecture. De Gaulle, newly restored to power in France and embarked on his course of leading France out of NATO, suggested a later date, and so the anniversary faded into obscurity.

. . .

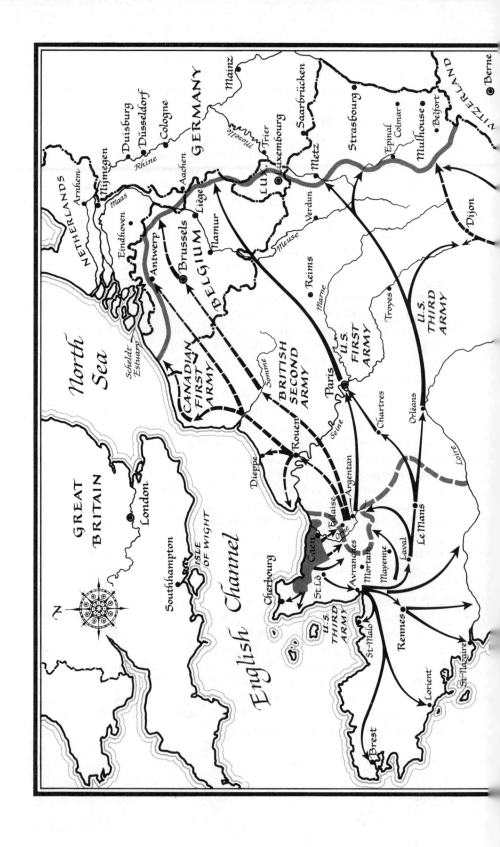

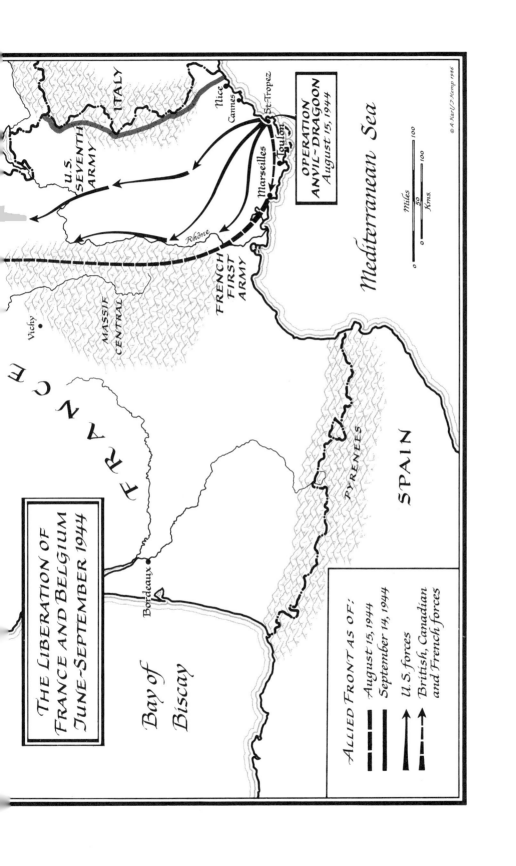

THE LIBERATION OF
FRANCE AND BELGIUM
JUNE–SEPTEMBER 1944

OPERATION
ANVIL–DRAGOON
August 15, 1944

U.S. SEVENTH ARMY

ITALY

Nice
Cannes
St-Tropez
Toulon
Marseilles

Rhône

FRENCH FIRST ARMY

Mediterranean Sea

Vichy

MASSIF CENTRAL

FRANCE

Bordeaux

Bay of Biscay

PYRENEES

SPAIN

© A. Karl / J. Kemp 1986

Miles
0   50   100
Kms.
0   100

ALLIED FRONT AS OF:
August 15, 1944
September 14, 1944
U.S. forces
British, Canadian
and French forces

The Allied pursuit across France was continuing. By the night of the twenty-fifth, Eisenhower's armies had formed up along the Seine. The First Canadian held Elbeuf south of Rouen, poised to sweep the Channel ports. On the right near Vernon, a rejuvenated British XXX Corps, built up to seven divisions under the aggressive leadership of General Brian Horrocks, moved into four Seine bridgeheads. Generals Corlett, Collins and Gerow of the U.S. First Army bracketed Paris. East of Paris, Patton's XX and XII Corps stretched out 140 miles from Fontainebleau to Troyes, ready to cross the Seine and Marne to link with Devers' forces in rapid pursuit of the German Nineteenth Army up the Rhône Valley.

On the twenty-sixth, from south to north, the Allied broad-front offensive commenced in earnest. Both of Patton's corps struck eastward from the Seine bridgeheads. In the center, XII Corps reached Château Thierry and crossed the Marne on the twenty-seventh, and a day later crossed the Aisne at Soissons and dashed unopposed for Sedan and the Meuse, flanked on the north by Gerow's V Corps. Corlett's XIX Corps assembled at Nantes, then marched for the Somme east of Amiens on the right of Montgomery's massive set-piece attack, which commenced the twenty-ninth.

All watched in amazement as Horrocks' XXX Corps attacked beyond the Seine from four bridgeheads, then crossed the Somme on the run, pushing through the bedraggled remnants of twenty German divisions of the Seventh and Fifteenth armies. Horrocks, determined to exhibit British prowess in pursuit, by-passed pockets of German resistance and rolled on, covering 200 miles to the Belgian frontier in six days. Capturing the mood of excitement, the U.S. First Army diarist chronicled the almost constant breakdown in communications between First Army Headquarters and lead elements, and the frantic press inquiries for news. The self-effacing general Courtney Hodges declined all requests for interviews, telling his aide-de-camp, "Winning the war is the thing right now."

And on it went. In a two-week interval, new disasters had engulfed Germany everywhere. Except on the Vistula, the German army was on the retreat on every front. In Rumania a two-prong Red Army drive swept through Ploesti and encircled two German armies, a disaster on the scale of Mortain. The USSR declared war on Bulgaria, whereupon the Bulgarians surrendered, followed by the Finns. The Rumanians surrendered, declared war against Germany, then suddenly joined the Red Army in an offensive to cut off the German garrisons in Greece and southern Yugoslavia.

Day by day the Allied high command remained locked in debate over the meaning of the apparent German collapse. As the advance proceeded, Montgomery stepped up his criticism of the lack of plans to capitalize on German disarray, warning Eisenhower that strategy would soon become "unstitched." In turn, with his formal assumption of command over the ground forces set for September 1, Eisenhower continued to hold out for fluid command arrangements in hopes of maintaining harmony with Montgomery and defusing BCOS anger over the switch. But Eisenhower's ability to extend concessions was limited, and he divided 12th Army Group supplies equally between Hodges and Patton, holding to his view that the Allies were exploiting a passing chance to press forward in all sectors so as to consolidate a defensible line behind which his armies could refit. Events seemed to bear out Montgomery more and more, but Eisenhower was determined to hold to this approach as long as Germans in the field continued to follow orders and withdraw toward the German frontier rather than surrender. Again, as to whether the Germans would succeed in organizing a front, Eisenhower believed they would do so because they had no choice—perhaps his single most controversial judgment of the war, one questioned by the Americans as well as the British.

In Bradley's words, all sides were in search of "a meaningful clue" to enemy intent. Dempsey's rapid progress into Calais and over the Somme was evidence that the Germans either were engaged in an informal surrender or were powerless, as were Hodges' easy crossings of the Seine. In support of his more cautious view, Eisenhower had only sketchy evidence of German preparations on the frontier, but he monitored less-noticed actions that week at Brest, Dunkirk and Calais, where isolated German garrisons were fighting to the last round of ammunition. And, by the twenty-eighth, intelligence reported a threatening concentration of panzer units drawn from Bordeaux, Marseilles and Italy collecting near Dijon on Patton's extended right flank.

Determined optimism seized the Allied command at all levels, however. Patton insisted to Bradley that with "two corps up and one corps back" advancing on a line Metz–Nancy–Epinal, "we can be in Germany in ten days." But while Patton's columns ranged wide of German units, Patton's G-2 on August 28 cautioned that despite the crippling of German communications and disorganization, "the enemy nevertheless has been able to maintain a sufficiently cohesive front to exercise an overall control of his tactical situation. His withdrawal, though continuing, has not been a rout or mass collapse." But most ignored such assessments, and soon Eisenhower found himself battling with emotional appraisals of the situation stemming from the elation over the breakout in Normandy, the official optimism of Whitehall and the British sense of "urgency," which Churchill might have restrained but did not. Within the next few days the formidable optimism in the BCOS was matched by similar feelings even among some of Eisenhower's closest advisers.

Eisenhower's chief of staff, General Walter Bedell Smith, wavered. Major General Whiteley and SHAEF G-2 General Kenneth Strong, realists after the failed conspiracy, became guarded optimists. Strong's daily intelligence report inventoried the shattering German losses in the two and a half months culminating in the Falaise disaster: 300,000 dead and captured, 200,000 isolated in the Atlantic ports and the Channel Islands, and 2,200 tanks lost. By SHAEF estimates, this reduced enemy forces north of the Ardennes forest to the "equivalent" of two weak panzer and nine disorganized infantry divisions, all in full retreat. South of the Ardennes, two panzer grenadier and four poor infantry divisions were joined by the equivalent of a division extricated from Bordeaux and two from Marseilles. Tedder, who did not succumb to the optimism, shuttled back and forth between London and Tourniers, and later wrote that amid all the victory talk that week he sensed the Alliance was headed for a "grave split." Differences over strategy and assessments of the Germans were symptoms of an erosion of common purpose and trust, of the ability to approach problems logically caused by an accumulation of disagreements but aggravated by the determined victory campaign orchestrated by Whitehall.

In the climate of euphoria, middle ground between Montgomery and Eisenhower vanished, though the form their disagreement would assume was unclear for several days. On the twenty-ninth, notified of imminent meetings between Churchill and Roosevelt in Quebec, Eisenhower made one more attempt at conciliation. In a preliminary directive to all commands, he acknowledged signs of enemy "internal dissension" and collapse, and called on all to "seize this opportunity by acting swiftly and relentlessly." Eisenhower prominently recited the terms of Montgomery's "priority," including command of an American corps, and twice mentioned Montgomery's power to coordinate his own forces and Bradley's, noting that the left wing of the First Army had advanced east of Amiens–Lille "with the principal offensive mission of assisting [Montgomery] in the destruction of enemy forces south of the Somme."

But this was as far as his concession to Montgomery went. Eisenhower confirmed that Bradley would divide his forces north and south of the Ardennes Forest, and advance to the West Wall on a line from Aachen to Trier, while Patton's Third Army crossed the Meuse beyond Nancy, linked with DRAGOON and strengthened its southern flank against the reported concentration of German forces on the upper Moselle. Finally, Eisenhower ordered Montgomery to take Antwerp, perhaps the key feature of the directive.

In retrospect, Eisenhower's order, unremarkable at first glance, constituted a challenge. At Condé, among the benefits Montgomery had held out for his single thrust into Germany was the prompt seizure of Antwerp. In ordinary circumstances, opening the vast Belgian port and clearing the winding 75-mile Scheldt approaches would be a lengthy and expensive operation, but Montgomery had indicated that this might now be done both quickly and inexpensively. Mindful, however, that existing SHAEF contingency plans for Rhine crossings had set as a precondition that Antwerp be in Allied hands and functioning by September 15, Montgomery had demanded that the U.S. First Army aid him in taking the port city, which would enable Dempsey's Second Army to push on northeast of Antwerp toward the Rhine.

Eisenhower assigned Montgomery the objective, but he did not assign the American troops to assist in taking the objective. Thus, Eisenhower conveyed several things. First, it was a reminder that as of the twenty-ninth, Montgomery was the only responsible Allied commander who anticipated that the Allies were in a position to threaten the Ruhr soon, so it was up to him to make this possible. Eisenhower could not arbitrarily exclude an extension of the battle into the Ruhr, but he was skeptical and therefore under no obligation to assist a Ruhr operation in its early stages. Second, that Eisenhower was not sure that Montgomery had worked out an apparent contradiction in his thinking. The validity of Montgomery's overall plan appeared to rest on the prospect of a sudden, one-time opportunity to exploit a disorganized and demoralized enemy. It was inconsistent to say on the one hand that Germany was too disorganized to form a front, and on the other to acknowledge that a major diversion of forces would be necessary to secure an objective like Antwerp. Eisenhower assumed that the Allies faced a determined enemy and did not expect such an enemy to surrender important objectives like Antwerp easily. The German high command could afford to cut losses at the Seine and arguably the Somme, but was unlikely to hand over a major port by September 15 capable of sustaining fifty divisions within fifty miles of the German border without a prolonged siege, and again, until he was convinced that German resistance had degenerated to the point that Montgomery suggested, Eisenhower saw no point in reorganizing the whole front. In short, Eisenhower was giving Montgomery an opportunity to accomplish several things simultaneously: first, to satisfy a precondition for a Ruhr–Berlin offensive; second, to surmount Eisenhower's skepticism about Montgomery's plan as a whole.

The British reaction was negative, and the turmoil set off by Eisenhower's attempt at conciliation and his Antwerp order in the August 29 message would spawn numerous caricatures of him as an "arbiter," a man balancing the interests of rival subordinates and unwilling to "make the decisive choice," as historian Arthur Bryant put it, which alone could "turn the option of difficulties that is war into victory." His Antwerp order would be the basis for charges that Eisenhower was a staff officer with "little knowledge of the realities of the battlefield," "obsessed" with logistics, and so on.

The BCOS opposed Patton's operations toward Metz–Epinal, but particularly opposed Montgomery taking Antwerp in the manner ordered. The imperative task in British minds was not to test the assumptions of Montgomery's plan, but to *act* on them. Evidently, the BCOS questioned the relevance of Antwerp in current operations as well as the idea that Antwerp was a precondition for the Ruhr, an idea that had originated with SHAEF, not the BCOS. The BCOS felt that concentrating supplies in one sector would do the trick, and that even a demoralized enemy might succeed in blocking the Scheldt approaches and destroying the docks, making the port unusable for some time. Thus German resistance at Antwerp could stall Montgomery's momentum by forcing him to divert forces to its capture.

In any event, Brooke's account of a BCOS meeting on the thirtieth summarized the British consensus: that Eisenhower's August 29 message made a review of basic military strategy and command procedure at Quebec "inevitable"; that Eisenhower's decision to assume command and his plan to split the American force and link up with DRAGOON would "add three to six months to the war."

The next day Brooke flew to Condé for talks with Montgomery, which he described in his diary. Significantly, Montgomery was not wholly dissatisfied with Eisenhower's August 29 directive; indeed, he was pleased that Eisenhower had ordered the U.S. First Army to advance north of the Ardennes and to support Dempsey's drive through Belgium. Brooke found Montgomery not unsympathetic to the "political pressures" on Eisenhower to build up Bradley's army group and to maintain the American armies on a separate axis of advance.

Meanwhile Eisenhower was in London for talks with Churchill. On the thirtieth the Prime Minister was in a somber mood, depressed by his visit to Italy. Perhaps aware that Eisenhower was uncomfortable with Montgomery's sudden independence, Churchill mentioned to him Wilson's complaints about General Clark's habit of by-passing AFHQ and reporting directly to Washington. The Prime Minister also informed Eisenhower that he had decided to make Montgomery a field marshal, the first such promotion handed out in the field, but necessary lest the public interpret Montgomery's diminished responsibilities, forty-eight hours hence, as a demotion. Churchill ran over the list of pending British proposals: paratroop drops in Athens to preempt an EAM takeover, aid for the Warsaw uprisings, reinforcements for Alexander and landings in Istria, talks with King Peter of Yugoslavia, and discussions in Moscow on shuttle-bombing bases, which would require a permanent military staff.

The next day Eisenhower emerged at a press conference, his last for three months. Before a massive gathering at Grosvenor Square, he deplored talk of Montgomery's "demotion" and castigated newspaper criticism of Dempsey's alleged caution at Caen, where "every foot the Germans lost at Caen was like losing 10 miles anywhere else." Eisenhower briefly commented on the imminent command shift, revealing that the new arrangement had been understood and "accepted from the beginning." Eisenhower appealed to the assembled correspondents for their cooperation in quelling overoptimism on the home fronts. He reminded the press that Germany could quickly draw on garrisons in Norway and Denmark, and on units extricated from Finland. He spoke of "one more battle" ahead, the campaign to break the

Siegfried Line defenses, whose duration would depend "on the condition of the German troops arriving there."

As he left the conference Eisenhower encountered Butcher, who had been in charge of the arrangements. He suggested that the two of them drive to Telegraph Cottage for lunch and a visit, about which Butcher dictated an account.

Away from the flow of information at SHAEF for several weeks, Butcher was eager to be brought up to date. As they motored through Kensington, Butcher told Eisenhower of the talk at the British Ministry of Information about press pool arrangements for the drive to Berlin. Eisenhower told him "not to count on it." Eisenhower ruminated on the problem of "curing overoptimism" in the Allied press and reminded Butcher that optimists were overlooking important facts: overextended supply lines as the Allies moved over the Seine and beyond the D-plus-90 phase lines where they had expected to spend the winter. Port capacity was low. The improvised truck convoys and airlift on line could probably not deliver enough petroleum to cross the Rhine, let alone reach it. Eisenhower mentioned the ongoing battles at Brest, St.-Nazaire, Lorient, and the reports in recent days of German armor collecting near Dijon opposite Patton's spearheads. "Invitably we will be checked," he told Butcher.

After a pleasant lunch in the tiny sitting room of the cottage, Eisenhower flew back to France and seclusion in a new forward headquarters located near Granville, a small Breton village overlooking the abbey of Mont-St.-Michel on the Atlantic coast. It was there, far from the front lines, that Eisenhower would implement the August 20 decisions, one of his most controversial actions of the war. When in later years he referred to the virtue of adhering to decisions reached "in the calm," he spoke of March 1944, but also of the period now beginning, an interval when the situation on the front changed hourly like a kaleidoscope as the Allied advance rolled over SHAEF's winter phase lines, over the Somme, the Marne and over the Meuse, through clusters of German troops, past the British battlefields and stations of World War I: Amiens, Passchendaele, the Argonne, Ypres, Verdun, shutting out the ghosts of summers past.

As he settled in at Granville on the night of August 31, Eisenhower was troubled. High-level meetings at Quebec were imminent, and so he cabled Marshall to endorse Churchill's urgent concern, voiced at their meeting the day before, about reports of German preparations in the so-called Alpine redoubt and to urge support for Alexander's effort to preempt German preparations by an attack north from the Po. Eisenhower told Marshall he hoped good would come of the talks in Quebec, because he noted "little instances that seemed to indicate that the Allies do not work together so effectively in prosperity as they can in adversity. Any backward step in the progress we have made along this line would be a pity."

. . .

September 1. Veterans of the German high command would later agree that bold Allied moves that week might have penetrated the German frontier defenses and ended the war. To his postwar interrogators, Jodl described the difficulties facing the German high command. Under Hitler's ongoing edict to counterattack in Normandy, the military had been severely restricted in preparing for the defense of the Seine, the Somme and the German frontier. "The action of the supreme command upon events in the west was extremely limited," Jodl recalled. "It scarcely had any reserves available and only with reserves can strong influence be exercised. . . . for days there was just a general directive, to fight as stubbornly or hold or gain as much ground as possible in order to seal the gaps in the fronts and to gain the necessary time for the West Wall to receive armaments for its defense." Jodl also suggested that determined movement on the Paris–Reims–Luxembourg axis toward Frankfurt, where a single reconnaissance battalion of the Sixth Panzer Army patrolled the Saar frontier, would have penetrated the toughest sectors of the West Wall. But while indicating that concentrated Allied attack *might* have succeeded anywhere, Jodl stopped short of saying that the Allies could have won the war in September 1944.

By now, Field Marshal Walther Model, mastermind of German recoveries at the Dniester in March 1944, Lvov in April 1944, and Warsaw in July, had replaced Von Kluge. He now faced, by consensus, a task rivaling his earlier challenges because of his lack of ready reserves and the woeful neglect of the West Wall, the so-called Siegfried Line, the defenses from Krefeld to Karlsruhe, which were of limited value in organizing a defensive front in any case. The West Wall, constructed in 1937, had been designed not for static defense but as a springboard for German offensives. The Germans had long considered fixed fortifications detrimental to the fighting spirit and thus a "doubtful asset," and had designed existing forts to enhance the defensive potential of the hilly, heavily forested western approaches. Accordingly, depths varied considerably—from forty forts per 1,000 square yards in the Saar and Rhineland to a string of isolated bunkers covering the Maas River north of Aachen. And by September 1944, even existing emplacements needed upgrading. Mine fields were gone, barbed wire and other obstacles had been stripped for the Atlantic Wall, and the remaining pillboxes, anti-tank ditches and fortifications were overgrown by shrubbery and grass.

Necessary preparations started late. Again, according to Jodl, a major problem had been to persuade Hitler to authorize defensive preparations. For most of July and August, OKW had been unable to persuade Hitler to leave his East Prussia headquarters, where he had supervised the German retreat in Poland and Rumania. Even after Mortain, Hitler stayed in Rastenburg and evaded responsibility by blaming setbacks on sabotage of his orders and Kluge's rumored treachery. Finally, on the thirty-first, armed with Model's estimate that the Dijon–Somme line was lost without immediate reinforcement by six nonexistent panzer and twenty-five infantry divisions, Jodl prevailed on Hitler to concentrate on the problem of the West Wall. As Jodl later recalled, at a situation conference in Rastenburg he coined a slogan: "The best is to have such a position [rear line] and not need it. It is also good if you have no rear position and don't need it. But if you need a rear position and don't have it, that is a catastrophe!"

The Rastenburg meeting on August 31 might be called the true beginning of the "German miracle." Assets were canvassed: 600,000 soldiers returning from France, 18 new divisions forming since late July, 100 fortress infantry battalions, and 10 panzer brigades from the eastern front. Ready forces extricated from southern France included several panzer–panzer grenadier types, including the crack 106th Panzer Brigade and the Luftwaffe, and accelerated preparations for the West Wall. Then, on September 1, Hitler decided to relegate Model to command of Army Group B, covering the critical sector north of the Ardennes, and to recall Von Rundstedt as OB West, charged with holding Belgium north of the Scheldt and the West Wall from Aachen to Metz to the Vosges.

Von Rundstedt's recall has been described as a political step, a measure to recommit the wavering officer corps and stem the popular disillusionment that had set in after the failure of the V-weapon campaign. Von Rundstedt also signaled Hitler's determination to resume the offensive in the west eventually. Author of great victories in Poland, France and Russia and spared defeat in Normandy by his timely "retirement," Von Rundstedt technically remained Germany's one unbeaten field marshal. Now he would return to the scene of his 1940 triumphs against the French when Germany fought unaided by allies except for the pact of convenience with the Soviets. For the moment, however, Von Rundstedt's task was to organize a front. The situation seemed difficult, even desperate, but he could bank on the assistance of one factor lacking in Normandy: that German logistical problems were simple and that Allied logistical problems, by comparison, were more complex. The German high command was confident that Eisenhower's columns would soon outrun supply lines and the Allies would be forced either to concentrate on one objective or to pass to the defensive.

Meanwhile the U.S. Army diarist noted on the first that both Corlett's XIX Corps and Collins' VII Corps continued to drive to the north unimpeded. By midnight they were "not many miles from the Belgium border." Resistance everywhere was light, and German soldiers were "bewildered and lost by the sweep of American armor and methodically being mopped up." The diarist noted Bradley's efforts to cope with mounting supply shortages. Patton's dash was consuming 400,000 gallons of petroleum daily, while Third Army receipts, at first running at 200,000 gallons daily, had sagged to 25,000 gallons because of priority for Hodges and difficulties in transporting gasoline to the front.

Supply was the main subject of Eisenhower's conferences at Granville as he assumed command of the ground armies on the western front, a problem that might be summarized as follows. First, the Allies had ample stocks of ammunition and petroleum on the Continent. Despite the crowded bridgehead, during the Normandy battle the American build-up had fulfilled plans for eighteen U.S. divisions with 25,000 supporting soldiers, each requiring 500 tons of ammunition, food and oil. But in quartermaster terms, since August 8 the Allies had advanced 260 logistical planning days in three weeks. Comm-Z deliveries from Cherbourg to Chartres had peaked on the twenty-ninth of August at 7,000 tons per day, thereafter to decline. In line with Montgomery's priority, Eisenhower on August 29 had adjusted the available American tonnage in favor of Hodges' First Army operating on Montgomery's left, but this would soon ground Patton. Eisenhower now reassessed this priority in light of German opposition developing in Patton's sector on the Langres Plateau. But the Quebec summit was imminent, in which Eisenhower's authority and instructions would be reviewed, and so support for Patton had to be weighed against the risk of appearing to backtrack on Montgomery's "priority," which would enable Montgomery to blame his lack of progress on Eisenhower, not the Germans.

Eisenhower anticipated a slowdown soon. On the first he approved plans to shift SHAEF main headquarters from Widewing to Versailles. With General Raymond Barker, he reviewed drafts of antifraternization regulations for Allied soldiers in Germany, and received Spaatz for dinner to talk over Portal's motion to reclaim command of the strategic air forces and resume POINTBLANK. Spaatz found Eisenhower lukewarm about opposing Portal. Apparently Eisenhower was unwilling to outbid the Air Ministry for control of the heavy bombers and content to rely on informal understandings with Spaatz.

September 2. Accompanied by Hoyt Vandenberg, Eisenhower flew from Granville to Chartres for talks with Patton and Bradley about supply allocations in Bradley's favor. The American generals were in a rebellious mood over the gasoline shortages, Montgomery's "extravagant supply requirements," and his single-thrust plan, which all seemed so reminiscent of Tunisia and Sicily, obliging U.S. forces to "sit out the war on a defensive front." Bradley and Patton, who were dubious of trusting Montgomery with any offensive task at all, were ready to match Montgomery's war-winning talk point by point. At Chartres, Patton clamored for permission to drive on to Frankfurt. Bradley urged no letup while the Germans were on the run, "even for a minute," as the Germans "would have nothing left to fight with" if pushed now. On the defensive, Eisenhower at first was "pontifical" and, quoting Clausewitz, lectured his two lieutenants on the probable course of the battle of Germany ahead that would consist of a vast maneuver to envelop the Ruhr from the north and south to destroy German capacity to wage war. When Patton and Bradley saw that Eisenhower's concept left room for sustaining the current American offensive, tempers calmed and the group got down to business.

As he later recalled, Bradley explained that his real worry was that Montgomery's "priority" might lead to "overriding priority" and a deal allowing for British command of the First Army. Significantly, Bradley did not really dispute Eisenhower's choice of emphasis on this "offensive to the north," and he stood willing to spare troops to support the British offensive —within limits. Bradley warned Eisenhower that American public opinion "would not tolerate Montgomery in command of the U.S. 1st Army." Moving on, the three discussed the worrisome reports of German armor gathering in the Epinal area evidently for the dual purpose of masking the German withdrawal south of the Loire and threatening Patton's right flank. Linkup with DRAGOON would ease the situation, but this would not occur for at least two weeks. Meanwhile, Bradley urged that Corlett's XIX Corps and Collins' VII Corps, along with Hodges' northernmost units, orient eastward away from the British toward the Aachen gap north of the Ardennes Forest, which would enable Gerow's V Corps to advance into the Ardennes Forest and to extend support for Third Army crossings over the Moselle and pursuit as far as Mannheim–Frankfurt–Coblenz.

Eisenhower was in a bind. He favored reinforcing Patton, especially in view of Patton's immediate problem, which was to disrupt German preparations at Nancy–Epinal, but he would have grave difficulties with the British should he in effect cancel Montgomery's priority at the very moment he endorsed it. Thus, Eisenhower could not resolve the supply issue categorically to Bradley's satisfaction, which would have involved slowing up Hodges' northernmost units on Montgomery's flank. He agreed, however, to ground a corps—Corlett's XIX—and to consider transferring one of Corlett's divisions to reinforce the Moselle front, but this had to be done carefully. Patton, officially, was to conduct an "active defense," with the understanding that if engaged, he would be resupplied, a contingency which Eisenhower did not mention in his forthcoming directive and which was not implemented until after Brooke's departure for Quebec on the fifth. Afterward Bradley, left in suspense, phoned Hodges with orders that XIX Corps and VII Corps north of the Ardennes were to "curl up" to await further developments, placing First Army support for Montgomery on "hold." The First Army diarist that day noted "so many changes in the First Army direction that indeed there seems at times as if those 'on top' do not have an altogether clear and consistent conception of the direction from which they want to cross the German frontier."

On the flight back to Granville, Eisenhower had a brush with death, an episode destined to assume importance in the legends surrounding the days ahead. With Eisenhower's command C-47 grounded at Chartres with a broken muffler, Captain Dick Underwood had commandeered a small two-seater L-5 liaison plane for the return flight. As the plane approached Granville the weather along the winding Breton coast turned windy and sullen. Since the L-5 was low on gasoline, Underwood doubted that he could locate the airstrip through the cloud cover, and decided to set the plane down on a beach as close to the Granville villa as possible.

Underwood successfully landed the airplane. But the beaches near Mont-St.-Michel had been mined by the Germans, and neither Eisenhower nor Underwood could remember whether demolition teams had cleared the area. While the two men carefully inched over the soft sand toward the road, Eisenhower slipped and fell, painfully wrenching his right knee. With Underwood's help he hobbled to the road, where the two hailed a jeep and rode back to the cottage.

That night, back in his villa at Mont-St.-Michel, Eisenhower was bedridden in severe pain. The Army physician summoned to examine the knee prescribed a rubber brace and extended bed rest, orders that Eisenhower would fitfully observe, fueling Montgomery's disingenuous charge that Eisenhower that week was "completely out of touch with the battle" and therefore unable to evaluate the developing opportunity in Belgium. According to Summersby, who was with him throughout this week, by the following morning a convalescing Eisenhower was already back at work in bed phrasing the crucial passages of a formal directive to be issued forty-eight hours hence.

"E. stays in bed all day on account of his leg," Summersby wrote the next day. "E. is adamant that he will not allow SHAEF to put in A. [American] directive boundaries. . . . He says that it must be an Allied problem, and that we've got to continue on that basis."

September 3. News from the Continent confirmed Brooke in his determination to challenge Eisenhower's "broad front" plan. Early that day Horrocks' XXX Corps crossed the Belgian border spearheaded by the Guards Armored Division, which made for Brussels, and the 11th Armored making for Antwerp. German resistance "was scattered and incoherent, and its collapse . . . accelerated by the Belgian underground," wrote Wilmot. A conviction formed that day at all levels of the British command that the war was over, and the British initiative, under way for two weeks but hitherto lacking specific contours, began to assume shape.

The JIC, which had first predicted a 1944 victory in June, was completing a report, to be published coinciding with the British departure for Quebec, in which it itemized German straits and flatly predicted that resistance "under the control of the German High Command is unlikely to continue beyond December 1, 1944, and may end even sooner." This assumption guided planning that day at 21st Army Group Headquarters for a British offensive northward into Holland to flank the West Wall, seize a Rhine bridgehead, and with First Army support to seize the Ruhr and proceed to Berlin.

Apparently Montgomery gave little hint of a specific plan-in-the-making at his meeting that morning with Bradley, called to "coordinate" the movements of VII Corps and XIX Corps. However, Montgomery's plan was a significant one, for it would elevate his differences with Eisenhower from the level of pure abstraction.

On the third, the newly appointed British field marshal was pleasant, "cooperative," and seemingly unruffled by Bradley's report of his talk with Eisenhower the day before, including the news that Corlett's XIX Corps would pause after reaching the Belgian town of Tournai instead of advancing in support of Dempsey. Tournai was one of many Airborne target areas overrun that week by Brereton's newly formed Allied Airborne Army.

According to Bradley, Montgomery spoke to him in passing of an operation through Holland to seize the highway bridge at Arnhem, but seemed impressed with Bradley's views about the difficulty of the Dutch countryside, laced with canals and dikes, and reports that German units returning from France were converting Holland into a vast encampment. Thus Bradley would later learn of operation MARKET-GARDEN only indirectly, through a British liaison officer attached to 12th Army Group Headquarters —in retrospect, a deliberate affront on Montgomery's part aimed at impressing Bradley with his subordinate status as far as the British were concerned.

Outline plans drawn up for MARKET-GARDEN that week represented Montgomery's largest and most imaginative venture of the war, a plan conceived with eventual victory in Europe as "certain as anything in war can be." Much has been written about MARKET-GARDEN, and it is important to review its essential features. First, the plan was to flank the West Wall by dropping three divisions of Brereton's Allied Airborne Army in Holland to seize the bridges and canals over the Maas at Grave and Eindhoven, the Waal at Nijmegen, and the Ijssel at Arnhem. The drop would be timed to coincide with Dempsey's arrival at the Dutch frontier. Second, with the Airborne troops holding the bridges and canals, three British corps, spearheaded by Horrocks' XXX Corps armor joined by the British XII Corps on the left flank and the British VIII Corps on the right, would rush from starting points on the Meuse–Escaut canal through the Airborne bridgeheads along a single highway, relieving the Airborne divisions to clear a pathway for an offensive over the Rhine into the north German plain. A significant feature of the plan was that the British would by-pass Antwerp, and delegate its capture to American forces. Even more significant was the scale of MARKET-GARDEN. Montgomery proposed to commit fourteen British Empire divisions and 150,000 men, a force rivaling Bradley's combined strength in the First and Third armies. MARKET-GARDEN was no small-scale operation, but rather, in Bradley's words, "an attempt by Monty to almost unilaterally launch a full-blooded thrust to Berlin."

Indeed, MARKET-GARDEN was to be the preliminary in Montgomery's proposed forty-division thrust over the lower Rhine into the north German plain. The design was daring, even "brilliant," as Bradley put it. But on close inspection, Bradley was skeptical and, in recalling his reaction years later, chose his words carefully; MARKET-GARDEN was to be an "attempt" to advance through Holland preliminary to a drive into northern Germany which Montgomery hoped to accomplish "almost unilaterally." When he heard about it, Bradley doubted that the "attempt" was very practical, and he suspected that the point in initiating the maneuver was not to win the war but "to force Eisenhower's hand on the U.S. First Army."

Bradley's logic seemed impeccable. The key feature of MARKET-GAR-DEN was that it involved a major reorientation of Dempsey's advance, which in time would force Eisenhower to reorient the rest of the Allied forces as well. First, as of September 3, the British VIII Corps was grounded at the Seine owing to maintenance problems, which would diminish Montgomery's ability to mount the operation without U.S. aid. Meanwhile Dempsey's other corps marched northeast toward Belgium on the left flank of the U.S. First Army, closely supported on *its* left by Corlett's XIX Corps, which marched on the left of Collins' VII Corps on the left of Gerow's V Corps, which stretched out to cover Patton's left flank. Now, instead of continuing the northeasterly advance into Belgium, Dempsey would swing due north into Holland in a maneuver that would open a wide gap between the British and American forces. Assuming strong German resistance, the maneuver would practically force XIX Corps north to cover Dempsey's right flank, which would draw Collins northward to cover XIX Corps, which in turn would draw Gerow northward from the Ardennes, and so on down the line, eventually forcing Patton to break off his advance over the Moselle in order to operate north of the Ardennes.

Bradley assumed there would be heavy German resistance to Rhine crossings, and so he also assumed that the result of Montgomery's maneuver would be not to reinforce success but to prevent failure. On close inspection, the risks of MARKET-GARDEN, even in the best of circumstances, were formidable. Three airborne divisions were to drop into widely separated zones along a sixty-mile corridor in densely defended Holland. The entire scheme required a quick breakthrough by the ground units and split-second coordination over dozens of canals and rivers along a single road running through Holland. Even a disorganized enemy might disrupt the intricate timetables, and disruption at any point would unravel the whole. Therefore, in the likely event of a setback, the U.S. First Army and eventually the Third Army would be drawn north to assist in operations initiated by the British in an ill-conceived battle, with the effect of completely rearranging the front and halting Patton in his tracks, accomplishing de facto what Montgomery had been proposing for weeks. Bradley therefore resolved to oppose MARKET-GARDEN. On military grounds, the plan seemed pointless. On political grounds, he was determined to resist the idea of awarding Montgomery control over American troops in the aftermath of a British-instigated military crisis that served no good purpose. To an extent, Bradley would succeed. Although the plan would go forward and produce results similar to what Bradley foresaw, the result would not strengthen Montgomery's position.

Indeed, as events would show, there was more to MARKET-GARDEN than a simple plot by Montgomery to force Eisenhower's hand by initiating an ill-advised military maneuver, a fact that Bradley would concede toward the end of his life. At the time Bradley, under pressure of events, did not pause to look beyond the short-term military implications. For instance, it struck him as out of character that the cautious Montgomery would support such a bold plan, but Bradley did not question that Montgomery was the author of the plan. Likewise, Bradley, soon satisfied that Eisenhower opposed the plan as deeply as he himself did, was surprised when Eisenhower not only approved it but ordered Montgomery point-blank to carry it out even after it became apparent that Montgomery was looking for a way to back down on it. Years later Bradley would confess that the whole episode was a mystery to him, though he was convinced for the rest of his life that the operation had been a mistake, at least in military terms.

In retrospect, there are mysterious aspects of MARKET-GARDEN, but the whole affair seems less mysterious in the context of other Anglo-American debates. Bradley was not a veteran of the ANVIL-DRAGOON controversy, and so he had no way of seeing the similarity between Montgomery's audacious plan to take Berlin and Wilson's audacious plan for Vienna, nor perhaps the parallels between MARKET-GARDEN and Marshall's long-ago SLEDGEHAMMER proposal in the summer of 1942 to mobilize a second front in France to assist Russia. Bradley was right in saying that MARKET-GARDEN was a very far-ranging plan. Like Vienna and SLEDGEHAMMER, it was also provocative, visionary and impractical for all the reasons Bradley cited, and thus, like the others, presumably devised more with the idea of raising basic issues of war policy than as a plan for current action. Eisenhower, a veteran of the SLEDGEHAMMER and Vienna controversies, could not have failed to note the similarities between these and MARKET-GARDEN. Nor could he have overlooked the dissimilarities which made MARKET-GARDEN a disruptive excursion into grand strategy and which probably accounted for his eventual and surprising approval of MARKET-GARDEN—not as a way of appeasing Montgomery but to oblige Montgomery either to back down and admit that MARKET-GARDEN had been unrealistic all along, or to carry it out and endure a personal as well as a tactical setback. In either case Eisenhower would thus be able to silence tendentious talk of victory in September.

The similarities between MARKET-GARDEN and the earlier debates over the proposed invasion of France in 1942 and the thrust toward Vienna are clear. Like them, MARKET-GARDEN was visionary and impractical. It coincided with a period of deep strain in inter-Allied relations. In view of recent debates over Vienna, MARKET-GARDEN appears to have been the upshot of an internal British quarrel over strategy objectives, much as SLEDGEHAMMER stemmed from an intra-American quarrel. Like SLEDGE-HAMMER, it was a sign of frustration over Allied weaknesses at yet another critical turning point of the war, this time with victory "as certain as anything in war could be" but with no end in sight in the actual fighting. Finally, like its predecessors, MARKET-GARDEN was a promising political tool in the inevitable debates ahead—assuming, of course, that Eisenhower disapproved it so that its basic premises, which Eisenhower dismissed as "fantastic," were not put to the test.

As for the dissimilarities, Eisenhower could not help reflecting that the earlier debates had involved decisions apportioning forces *between* theaters argued out at the highest levels of the alliance. By contrast, MARKET-GARDEN would involve a debate between Allies within a theater of war where huge forces operated near the German frontier in circumstances that required *maximum* coordination of all fronts, not endless haggling over objectives. Likewise, SLEDGEHAMMER had centered on ways of committing Allied forces more effectively *in concert with* the Russians at the onset of a long war against Germany, whereas MARKET-GARDEN was a visionary proposal based on the assumption that the Germans were finished, that Allied-Soviet cooperation was no longer necessary, and that the Allies were momentarily free to decide among themselves who would take Berlin, and so on.

In this way, MARKET-GARDEN was more than premature. It was disruptive of sound strategy, and of the disciplined acceptance of Eisenhower's directives by the British and potentially even by the American forces in the field should the British succeed in kindling debate over such long-range objectives as Berlin or attempt to assign blame for failing to reach Berlin in September 1944. One can assume, however, as Eisenhower did, that the real object of MARKET-GARDEN was not to disrupt the alliance but to encourage close American-British cooperation. But for the British such cooperation meant British command over significant American forces in a highly fluid situation on the German frontier. Berlin was not what the British had in mind; what they wanted was a dominant voice within the Allied command. But MARKET-GARDEN, the method chosen by Montgomery to achieve this result, was unfortunate, for it implied unwillingness on the part of the British to accept Eisenhower's word that American and British operations would be closely coordinated, or, as Bradley put it, it reflected a determination to "force" Eisenhower's hand on the First Army.

Accordingly, MARKET-GARDEN raised a host of unpleasant choices for Eisenhower. First, Eisenhower could reject MARKET-GARDEN categorically on military grounds, as Bradley urged, which would assure the Allies of Antwerp but saddle his command with the full onus of scuttling what the British insisted was a feasible design to end the war in September 1944, spurring endless recriminations and competition for the leading role in the next go-around. Second, Eisenhower could approve MARKET-GARDEN, revising his "broad front" decision by wholehearted adoption of Montgomery's strategic plan, which would probably startle the British as well as the Americans and distort military policy in the process. Third, Eisenhower could negotiate with Montgomery on the basis of MARKET-GARDEN and Berlin in hopes of defusing the issue, but this would involve making concessions beyond those he had already made, and set the bad example of rewarding intransigence by negotiating under duress, which could not pass unnoticed by the Americans.

Lastly, Eisenhower might approve MARKET-GARDEN but without modifying his broad-front policy. This would disrupt Eisenhower's plans, though not decisively, and silence debate in the process by forcing Montgomery to either back down or carry through. If Montgomery carried through and failed, Eisenhower might be open to charges that he had not supported MARKET-GARDEN adequately. But in theory, if MARKET-GARDEN was feasible, it stood to reason that the Allies could advance anywhere in whatever strength; that is, if Montgomery was right that 40 Allied divisions "need fear nothing" in a march on Berlin supplied from bases 700 miles away through enemy territory when enemy forces still numbered 260 divisions on all fronts, then it was hard to see why, say, the 15 divisions of Montgomery's 21st Army Group could not do the same thing by themselves. In either case, MARKET-GARDEN presupposed that superior German forces would simply dissolve. Weighing all the military factors, including deferring the capture of Antwerp, Eisenhower felt that the Allies could afford to test this proposition—if Montgomery insisted.

Again, it is not certain when Eisenhower got wind of the plan, but as the British advanced into Belgium on September 3, he apparently sensed that something was brewing and was anxious to dispel any illusions that his broad-front intentions sketched out on the twenty-ninth were subject to change. What Eisenhower presumably hoped was that he could dissuade Montgomery in advance from proposing a scheme which Eisenhower would have to approve but which would end, were it carried out, in disaster. On the third Eisenhower dispatched Ramsay to Condé for a meeting with Montgomery to remind him of three things as his forces approached Antwerp: first, the "opening" of Antwerp by September 15 was a precondition for an invasion of Germany and Berlin; second, the "opening" of Antwerp meant seizing the docks and clearing the seventy-mile estuary; third, "opening" Antwerp was the responsibility of forces *already* assigned to the 21st Army Group and Eisenhower could go no further on command arrangements that on September 1 had become final.

Meanwhile Dempsey's columns advanced through Belgium at thirty miles per hour. In the towns, throngs choked the streets, cheering and dancing in unrestrained joy. Dempsey pushed on, and by late afternoon the Guards Armored Division passed through Brussels to another tumultuous reception through streets deserted only an hour before as the Germans evacuated.

The Guards Armored Division passed through Brussels that night and pushed spearheads toward Louvain while the 11th Armored rolled for Antwerp.

South of Brussels, the American VII Corps scored a significant and unheralded victory. ULTRA had confirmed that large detachments of the retreating German Fifth and Seventh armies were headed toward the Belgian town of Mons and might be encircled if Collins' VII Corps suddenly angled north toward Corlett's XIX Corps. Collins struck north, and in a quick twenty-four-hour engagement he and Corlett trapped the remnants of twenty disorganized divisions, 25,000 men, and opened a sixty-mile gap in German defenses.

On it went. That night General Strong's SHAEF intelligence report contemptuously downgraded German strength, and revamped the divisional order of battle to substitute "equivalent" formations for "nominal" units. Since Mortain, intelligence claimed the equivalent of five panzer divisions destroyed and six others badly mauled, the "equivalent" of twenty infantry divisions eliminated elsewhere, twelve divisions severely depleted, and four divisions written off in the isolated fortresses of Brest, Lorient, Le Havre, St.-Nazaire, and the Channel Islands. Intelligence noted scattered forces assembling along the Rhine, makeshift armored brigades, fortress infantry battalions, auxiliary battalions and Luftwaffe troops scraped up from the eastern front, and rear-echelon installations including the 100,000 men of Army Group G, dismissed by SHAEF as the "equivalent" of a single division at Dijon. This optimistic view carried over into the fourth, the day called by historian Martin Blumenson the "critical date of the European campaign."

September 4. In Granville, Eisenhower met Devers to discuss Patton's Third Army and the mechanics of linkup between Devers and the transfer of the 6th Army Group to SHAEF. That day Eisenhower published his intentions in his first formal directive as land commander.

In it he appeased the victory fever in his preamble but otherwise adhered to plan and set the course of debate for months. He spoke of the apparent German collapse but affirmed that his policy remained the "destruction of the enemy forces which meant hunting down and destroying the German

Army where it stood rather than exploiting the freedom of action to seize fixed objectives." Eisenhower predicted that the German army would attempt to concentrate its reserves in defense of the Ruhr and the Saar and would "regard the approach to the Ruhr as the most important." Accordingly, he formally assigned Montgomery "priority," but in doing so ruled out a single thrust and set two preconditions to an invasion of Germany: first, the opening of Antwerp; second, that the enemy be engaged in battle and driven from the west bank of the Rhine so that the Allies could stage operations into Germany with the benefit of firm defensive flanks behind the Rhine.

Thus, on the fourth, the Supreme Commander made his views official that had been outlined on August 29. Whether his intentions would be proven or disproven by events was a question Eisenhower himself seemed to raise, and doubts rose while the high command waited for a definite break in the military situation as the Allies neared the German frontier.

Reports from the battle all day indicated that the Germans appeared stunned, unable to organize a stand anywhere except at river crossings and road junctions. There were reports that German troops, demoralized by poor communications and severe shortages of weapons, panicked and were abandoning equipment and looting supply installations.

At First Army Headquarters, where Bradley awaited confirmation of Eisenhower's plan to reinforce Patton, a state of suspended animation was palpable in the First Army diarist's account of the day. The diarist enviously chronicled Dempsey's triumphal reception in Brussels, along with the less dramatic reports from the American sector; Corlett's XIX Corps idled at Mons, waiting for word whether to support Dempsey in Belgium or to detach forces to Patton in Lorraine to preempt German preparations at Epinal and Dijon. Bradley and Hodges conferred with SHAEF about detaching Corlett's 79th Division and sending it to Lorraine but "no hard or fast decision was forthcoming." The diarist noted that Bradley spent most of the day waiting at his new headquarters in Laval. That afternoon he posed for the Marchioness of Queensbury, commissioned by *Life* magazine to paint portraits of the British and American high command. The marchioness stayed for a cocktail and dinner, then began a sketch of Ninth Air Force Commander General "Pete" Quesada. "The general consensus," noted the diarist, "is that she has done a fairly competent job, although the General [Bradley] feels he has been made a little too sad."

In Granville, Eisenhower was dining quietly with Spaatz when the news arrived that the British 11th Armored Division had entered and captured Antwerp. A second jolt came soon after in the form of Montgomery's dramatic night letter proposing that he and Eisenhower meet the next day so that Montgomery could "put before you certain aspects of future operations and to give you my views." Montgomery enclosed a ten-point outline of his plan without specifics, and informed Eisenhower curtly that the conflict had now "reached a stage where one really powerful and full-blooded thrust towards Berlin is likely to get there and thus end the German war." A choice between his thrust and Patton's thrust was "vital," and if the Allies persisted with a compromise solution and split maintenance and resources "so that neither thrust is full-blooded, we will prolong the war." Montgomery considered the problem "simple and clearcut," a "matter of such vital importance" that he felt sure Eisenhower agreed that a decision in favor of a single thrust under Dempsey was "required at once."

September 5. Early the next morning Eisenhower summoned Admiral Ramsay to Granville to gather the facts about Antwerp. The facts were startling. Late on the fourth the British 11th Armored Division, upon reaching the outskirts of Antwerp, had discovered Germans "nowhere in evidence." General G. P. Roberts, commander of the 11th, pressed his columns through the city, and captured the 1,000-acre harbor intact, including the quays, locks, drydocks and rolling stock. For some unexplained reason, however, Roberts had failed to proceed across the Albert Canal or west to South Beveland and down the Walcheren causeways to secure the Scheldt approaches, without which the harbor was useless.

Roberts' failure to follow through would seem even more mysterious in the next twenty-four hours as reports indicated that the German Fifteenth Army had withdrawn in panic through Breskens and Walcheren. But a closer inspection of the situation would reveal that the Germans were drawing back to form a garrison along the Scheldt approaches and reinforcing the northern suburbs and the Albert Canal. The implication was that Montgomery, sensing a major battle for the approaches, had stopped Roberts to avoid being drawn into battle there, for his intention was to delegate the task of opening the port to the Canadians and Americans. Thus, to an extent, the "fall" of Antwerp was less than met the eye despite the excitement surrounding the event, excitement comparable to that surrounding the first reports of the attempt on Hitler's life.

The facts had to be sorted out, and on notice that Montgomery was prepared to take the fateful step of proposing a concrete plan to exploit the fall of Antwerp, Eisenhower decided to decline Montgomery's request for a meeting on the fifth. Instead, he sent a message to Montgomery to ask him to clarify the situation at Antwerp, adding that he endorsed Montgomery's idea of a powerful thrust for Berlin, though he cautioned that he did "not, repeat not, agree that it should be initiated at this moment to the exclusion of all other maneuvers." Eisenhower referred Montgomery to his directive of the fourth, in which he listed the preconditions for such a move, and settled back to wait.

Was the war over? Eisenhower could not deny that Antwerp was a significant victory—indeed, he had personally set Antwerp as the test of

German intentions, and the event brought him face-to-face with the question: Did he dare alter the scheme of advance he had laid out on the twenty-ninth of August? Did he dare not to?

As of September 5, Antwerp was technically not open, but Montgomery's seizure of the port intact momentarily shook Eisenhower's confidence in his judgment of German intentions. Indeed, as he had in other moments of self-doubt, Eisenhower that afternoon dictated a memorandum for the record to clarify his thinking.

First, he summarized the German situation. The German defeat *"seemed"* complete, he noted. The Allied armies were "advancing at will subject only to the requirement for maintenance," though maintenance was stretched to the limit, as had been foreseen for weeks.

He then proceeded to recite the story of his recent encounters with Montgomery, and to review in his own mind the case for his "broad front" strategy; that "from the beginning with the substantial destruction of enemy forces in France," he had favored advancing rapidly on the Rhine through the Aachen gap in the north and the Metz gap in the south to take advantage of *all* available lines of communication for the purpose of stretching enemy defenses, and bringing the southern forces onto the Rhine between Switzerland and Coblenz to establish secure flanks. Was this approach still valid? Again, Eisenhower had little to go on except mixed reports and his hunches. Three questions confronted him, which he touched on in passing.

First, were the Germans defeated on all fronts? The Allied advance was dramatic, but the Russians were checked at the Vistula, and Alexander's offensives were winding down. The answer was no.

Second, were the Germans defeated on the western front and in fact surrendering? Again, the Germans were withdrawing, but as yet no major field surrenders had been reported, and major sieges raged at Brest, Dunkirk, Calais, Le Havre and Ostend. The Germans were collecting armor on the Langres Plateau to threaten Patton's right flank and block Devers' progress up the Rhine. The answer, therefore, was "Probably not."

Third, could the Germans form a western front capable of prolonged resistance? To date, the Germans had been powerless to resist the Allied advance through France. Evidence was confusing, but any answer had to take into account four factors: first, that Allied striking power would soon diminish; second, that the Germans, if determined to resist, would have better communications and far more incentive than ever before to use them efficiently; third, the consequences of overcaution and prolonging the war; fourth, the consequences of overoptimism and forming military plans accordingly. Eisenhower's answer was "Probably not."

In short, Eisenhower was abiding by his judgment resolved in the "calm" of late August. Until someone came up with news indicating a definite "break" in German resistance along the German frontier, Eisenhower would assume that the Germans intended to defend it and were able to do so. But the news of Antwerp had altered the situation in one sense: Eisenhower could no longer be sure of his ability to reinforce Patton's sector without endless difficulties with the British, but a sector was threatened on the fifth by fresh German arrivals at Dijon and Epinal. In the memo for his files, Eisenhower grumbled about Montgomery's "usual caution" in having refused to operate in Belgium without First Army support for his southern flank, which had forced Patton to ground his main body near Paris for several days, and then to venture east with spearheads. But it was plain to him that he now deemed it important "while supporting the advance eastward through Belgium to get Patton moving once again so that we may be fully prepared to carry out the original conception for the final stage of the campaign."

Eisenhower spent the rest of the day rushing various projects to completion. At noon he ordered Corlett's XIX Corps to release the U.S. 79th Division for Patton's Third Army. Fatefully, Eisenhower authorized new supply allocations, dividing Bradley's 7,000 tons evenly between the U.S. First and Third armies, a move that appeared to suspend Montgomery's "priority" in all but name twenty-four hours after he had solemnized it in his first directive.

"The decision on the 79th division is final and it moves to Third Army starting tomorrow," noted the First Army diarist.

> In the XIX Corps sector there is no other change except that the 113th Cavalry has pushed its reconnaissance well forward. . . . In the VII Corps sector the 1st division is still cleaning up the pocket of Germans west and south of Mons, and the total of dead and prisoners was established today to be 20,000. Hospital arrangements have been made to transfer an Evacuation Hospital into the area in order that medical treatment may be given many German wounded. . . . The 39th Infantry which has crossed the Meuse, one of the places the General [Hodges] expected the Germans to stand if indeed they could stand anywhere, reported tonight encountering small armor, tank, motor and flame-thrower fire . . .

By the night of the fifth, Eisenhower and Montgomery, the two men who might have joined hands to keep operations balanced, were on a collision course spelling months of troubles at SHAEF. Time remained. Montgomery, in his telegram to Eisenhower on the night of the fourth, had taken a long step by formally proposing Berlin, but he had Eisenhower's directive and had still not taken the step of formally proposing MARKET-GARDEN, the plan he had in mind to back it up. Eisenhower had also taken a long step in dividing the tonnages between Hodges and Patton equally, for it handed Montgomery an alibi for British setbacks in case events changed his mind in the next several days. There matters stood, and Eisenhower would spend the next three days with his personal staff recuperating at Granville from his knee injury.

What would Montgomery do now? The British pressures on Eisenhower are well documented but British pressures on Montgomery are not, and it is unclear whether Montgomery's rash mention of Berlin on the night of the fourth was his idea, perhaps prompted by Brooke, or whether, as may have been the case, it was uttered on Brooke's direct orders, perhaps to see how Eisenhower would react to this challenge, a challenge too audacious to approve, but too flamboyant to be ignored. Ominously, Churchill, a man who might have restrained Montgomery, departed for Quebec on the morning of the fifth.

Meanwhile, British preparations for the Quebec summit had concluded in an angry mood, heightened by the frustration of victory in France which brought the end in sight with no assurance that it would occur quickly. On the third and fourth, the War Cabinet had mulled over Moscow's sudden declaration of war on Bulgaria, upending Allied-Bulgarian armistice talks in Cairo, and the Russians' flat refusal to permit British airlifts to aid the pro-London Polish Home Army in Warsaw, even while Konev's armies continued to idle a mere ten miles away on the Vistula. The War Cabinet was troubled by Tito's insolence, by Alexander's halt south of the Po and by the American "hands off" attitude toward all these questions, including Roosevelt's expressions of "official distress" over the Warsaw situation but his failure to follow up with diplomatic support.

On the transatlantic voyage aboard H.M.S. *Queen Mary,* Churchill voiced concern about exaggerating the German crisis, but did not press his case. In his diary, Brooke described the discussions over the JIC report, over plans for withdrawing Empire troops from Europe, and other issues which "though justified by events . . . must await the next few days." Churchill was still depressed, distracted, petulant with his staff, uncertain of himself and his ability to deal with Roosevelt and Marshall, and accusing Brooke at one point of preparing to "frame up . . . with the American chiefs against him." Girding for a showdown with the Americans, Churchill directed his aides to produce statistics and tables demonstrating that British Empire troops still outnumbered American troops in Europe, a "strong basis on which we approach this conference." Churchill was still determined to stop any further taxing of Alexander's campaign in Italy, and to suggest Vienna, along with landings on the Istrian Peninsula to join up with Tito's Partisans.

Churchill and Brooke aired the issue at a Chiefs of Staff meeting on the eighth, shortly before arriving in Quebec, a meeting at which Churchill cautioned Brooke against approaching the Americans on the basis of a 1944 German collapse. The JIC report, in his opinion, erred on the side of optimism. It overlooked shortages of transport and petrol and other factors bound to slow up the advance, and "the pace could not last." Churchill pointed to strong German resistance reported at Dieppe, Boulogne, Brest and St.-Nazaire, and fresh reports of battles along the the Albert Canal and Patton's front at Metz. He personally doubted that the 21st Army Group could advance in force beyond Belgium until it "dealt with the Germans to the north of Antwerp," and predicted that the Germans would organize the Siegfried Line. He urged that the "fortifying and consolidating effect of a stand on the frontier . . . not be underrated." But Churchill did not insist, and the chance passed that the CCS would endorse Eisenhower's September 4 directive or otherwise foreclose MARKET-GARDEN.

For Winston Churchill, the British arrival in Halifax on September 10 was outwardly a personal triumph: the first two-way Anglo-American conference in a year, and proof at first glance that the Americans could now do business with the British, even in an election year. Many more "triumphs" followed, a breathtaking string of concessions, casually dispensed by Roosevelt and the American Joint Chiefs in four days of meetings that marked the dismal conclusion of Churchill's year-long quest for a genuine third front.

Throughout, Brooke puzzled in his diary over the "wonderful spirit of cooperation" greeting every British proposal and the discussions proceeding "much easier than expected." Tentatively Brooke attributed this to natural feelings of cordiality in the afterglow of victory in Normandy. Leahy, Arnold, Marshall and King seemed mellow and relaxed, anxious to please and to accommodate. When Churchill proposed that nothing be withdrawn from Alexander until Kesselring's defeat, the Americans agreeably "surrendered" and suggested that landing craft would be available for an invasion of Istria. In the military conclusions, the American Chiefs formally endorsed Alexander's offensive north of Florence, and agreed to review Italy in light of the outcome and "the views of General Eisenhower." The American JCS appreciated Churchill's candor about taking Vienna so as to block the Russian advance into central Europe, and, indeed, urged him to plan it.

The British had arrived "sticky about their possessions in the Pacific" and braced to battle unnamed "troublemakers" in the American JCS who reportedly opposed their participation in the Pacific conflict. Churchill found his offer of the British fleet for use in the Pacific "no sooner offered than accepted," though General Arnold was hesitant about calling on RAF help in the strategic bombing offensive against Japan. The CCS issued a directive restoring Portal as CCS "agent" for POINTBLANK and endorsed THUNDER-CLAP, a series of saturation raids on German synthetic-fuel plants, airframe factories and Berlin, aimed at paralyzing Nazi political administration and knocking out the German economy. The CCS endorsed Eisenhower's report on plans for extending his two-prong offensive to "press on with all speed to destroy the German armed forces and occupy the heart of Germany," and on American initiative "invited Eisenhower's attention to the advantages of the northern line of approach into Germany, as opposed to the southern, and . . . to the necessity for the opening up of . . . Antwerp and Rotterdam."

Through Eden, Eisenhower had recommended a plan to extend the life of SHAEF into the occupation period in the hope that the armistice would not witness a return to business as usual. Both sides were hesitant about Eisenhower's "fresh and original" idea, but the discussion prompted by it led to quick agreement on zones of occupation. The British claimed north-west Germany encompassing the North Sea ports. The Americans deferred and accepted Bavaria, Württemberg and Baden, with Russia getting the rest. To the end, Roosevelt was wary of running American military lines of supply through a Gaullist France, evidently anticipating problems with France and perhaps reciprocal Soviet demands for lines of supply through Poland. Roosevelt asked for an enclave in the North Sea port of Bremen, and when the British approved, Roosevelt indicated that he would permit a French zone of occupation, a sign that American recognition of De Gaulle was not far off.

The Americans were hesitant about British plans to airlift commandos to Athens, but approved. Roosevelt exhibited interest in Churchill's talks with Tito, and seemed grateful to Churchill for his willingness to pioneer a relationship with the Yugoslav Communists. The JCS approved airlifting supplies and weapons for the beleaguered Polish patriots in Warsaw, with or without Russian approval, just as the news reached the conference of Stalin's sudden decision to advance into the eastern suburbs six weeks after having arrived at the Vistula and halting there, which had enabled the Germans to arrest or slaughter two-hundred thousand Poles. The group exchanged views on the atom bomb and settled on "full collaboration in the military and commercial application of atomic energy after the defeat of Japan," pending congressional approval. And so, as Churchill reported to Attlee, the conference closed "in a blaze of friendship," even with Vienna "fully accepted here."

What accounted for the American change of heart? No one knew, but the British could not help noticing that a high-level American reappraisal of the Russians was under way. Harriman and Deane in Moscow warned that in light of the rapid pace of Russian moves to recognize the Soviet-backed Lublin committee as the provisional government of Poland, the policy of Soviet-American friendship was getting nowhere.

Apparently the President's health was also a factor. Roosevelt's optimism about dealings with the Russians seemed undiminished, but he was not up to his usual self and the new consensus on the Soviets seemed to be forming around him. The Roosevelt Administration had faced the sudden appearance of anti-Communism in the presidential election campaign, which seemed to bother the American staff but not the President. In any event, the American change of heart was welcome, if belated. With the Rumanians, Finns and Bulgarians at Russia's mercy, northern Yugoslavia overrun, and

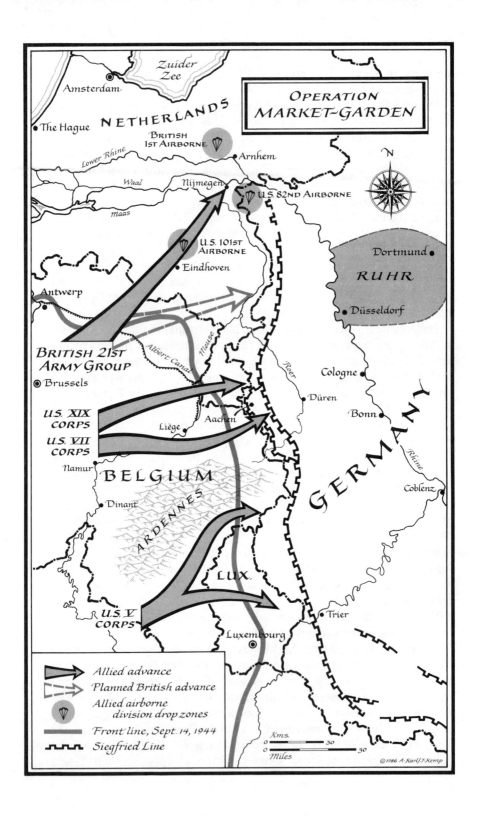

OPERATION MARKET–GARDEN

Zuider Zee

Amsterdam

The Hague

NETHERLANDS

Lower Rhine

BRITISH 1ST AIRBORNE

Arnhem

Waal

Nijmegen

U.S. 82ND AIRBORNE

Maas

U.S. 101ST AIRBORNE

Eindhoven

Antwerp

RUHR

Dortmund

Düsseldorf

BRITISH 21ST ARMY GROUP

Brussels

Albert Canal

Meuse

Roer

Cologne

U.S. XIX CORPS

Liège

Aachen

Düren

U.S. VII CORPS

Bonn

Namur

BELGIUM

Rhine

Coblenz

Dinant

ARDENNES

GERMANY

LUX.

U.S. V CORPS

Trier

Luxembourg

Allied advance

Planned British advance

Allied airborne division drop zones

Front line, Sept. 14, 1944

Siegfried Line

Kms.

0   30

Miles

0   30

©1986 A. Karl/J. Kemp

the Polish opposition stamped out in Warsaw, it was very late in the day to expect much from a fluid quid pro quo approach to the Russians. The timing of the American shift suggested concern about putting the best light on past misunderstandings rather than a real change of heart, since the Americans knew that the British could not act on their proposals. Brooke carefully noted to himself that Alexander would be lucky to launch Istria landings by February 1, and that the Americans knew it. The Americans applauded British foresight and approved Churchill's proposals in spirit, yet, according to Brooke, "the tragedy is that the Americans, whilst admiring him [Churchill] as a man, have little opinion of him as a strategist."

Churchill's discomfiture may have accounted for the bizarre sidelight for which the conference is remembered—Anglo-American approval of the so-called Morgenthau Plan. The "plan" presented at Quebec was still little more than a declaration of intent in line with the principles of a hard peace. Roosevelt favored it. Churchill would recall in 1953 that when he was told of the Morgenthau Plan he "violently" opposed it, but accounts of the conference show Churchill firmly in Roosevelt's corner, in favor of "making Germans stand in soup lines" and pastoralizing the country.

To his stunned entourage at Quebec, Churchill blandly explained that Morgenthau had convinced him that Britain deserved a chance after the war to protect her export markets and to rehabilitate her economy at German expense. More likely, Churchill had evaluated the American lineup. The President, strong in spirit, was haggard and ill, and Morgenthau did not seem to speak for anybody. Thus Churchill could assume that the Morgenthau Plan would never be adopted whole, and so he could lend moral support for this relic of Casablanca days, reciprocate for American approval of Vienna and let the Americans sort it out.

The American response made it very unlikely that Churchill would weigh in on the side of restraint in Holland. The military staffs on both sides were impatient to get on with ending the war quickly, and Churchill was not about to discourage them. In the appendix to *Triumph and Tragedy,* Churchill reproduced a memorandum to Ismay on September 14 dictated four days after Montgomery's formal presentation of MARKET-GARDEN to Eisenhower on the tenth and Eisenhower's approval of it on that day. In the memorandum, after weighing the pros and cons of submitting a plan for demobilization of the British Army beginning in December based on the JIC report, Churchill instructed Ismay to inform the Chiefs of Staff committee in London that while he was "very doubtful" the German war would end by the end of 1944, he approved the "practical steps you propose to take, subject to Cabinet and Defense Committee agreement. You may therefore submit your paper to the Cabinet as you wish."

Years later Eisenhower and Bradley both conceded that MARKET-GARDEN was a brilliant if impractical plan and acknowledged the potential advantages had MARKET-GARDEN succeeded in seizing a wide corridor through Holland and gaining a bridgehead at Arnhem. Whether the plan succeeded or not, a British advance into Holland would have had redeeming aspects, for it would have enveloped Antwerp from the north, reduced German positions west of the Maas, utilized the Airborne, idle since Normandy, and cut off the German forces collecting in western Holland and Rotterdam. Even Bradley conceded that two northern thrusts, one by Horrocks and a second by Corlett and Collins in support, might have reached as far as Amsterdam and gained a bridgehead over the Rhine. But this would have drawn V Corps northward to cover the Ardennes, thereby forcing Patton north and away from panzer concentrations at Epinal and quick linkup with the Seventh Army.

But as an operation of war, MARKET-GARDEN somewhat resembled GOODWOOD—a bid for a decisive breakout through one of the most vital and densely defended areas on the German frontier. Dempsey would take on the largest German troop concentrations intelligence could locate on the western front, a force lacking heavy equipment and exhausted but battle-worthy if determined to resist. Like GOODWOOD, MARKET-GARDEN, by engaging German reserves, stood to ease Bradley's job in certain sectors, but Bradley was sure that Montgomery did not intend a repetition of GOOD-WOOD, in which the British served a supporting role.

Bradley's opposition hardened between September 5 and the tenth as the German "miracle" began in earnest. That week Allied columns approached the German frontier and encountered stiffening resistance from the upper Moselle to the Escaut canal. New battle groups, hastily assembled, arrived to close gaps and counterattack in many sectors, particularly in the south on the Langres Plateau and the Moselle. How this was achieved would emerge in the German accounts, which emphasize the fall of Antwerp as the event that finally electrified the Germans.

Initially, on the second, after recalling Von Rundstedt, Hitler approved a general directive abandoning the Somme and authorizing the German army to give up terrain "inch by inch but to avoid encirclement," but to make a stand at Dijon to cover the withdrawals of the First and Nineteenth armies from the Mediterranean and the Biscay coast. Then came the fall of Antwerp, which, according to Schramm, was the event that dispelled German lethargy. "For the first time," Schramm wrote, "the enemy succeeded in capturing a port in good condition . . . a success the German Command had always tried to prevent . . . although the mouth of the Schelde was still blocked by the German forces." Coordinated action began at once. Model assumed charge of operations north of the Moselle, then sent the Fifteenth Army to block the Scheldt and six battalions of the newly formed 1st Parachute Army to man the Albert Canal and seal off the sixty-mile breach between Antwerp and Maastricht. Meanwhile Hitler ordered Von Rundstedt to assemble the forces on the upper Moselle, and "regardless of local losses to advance deep into the American east flank, [to attack] in a northwesterly direction from the Epinal area." Hitler granted Von Rundstedt "carte blanche" to act, whereupon "the old man [Von Rundstedt] set about his task with the coolness and efficiency of a man who knew what he was about," organizing a line running along the Maas in the north, the Siegfried Line in the center, the Moselle River and Vosges mountains in the south, and from behind these positions mobilizing the remnants of his old forces and new recruits into an army.

Some questioned the realism of Hitler's order to counterattack in the Lorraine. But as Schramm explained, among Hitler's "irrevocable principles" was that withdrawal affected the power of resistance and caused other withdrawals, a principle "which provoked much criticism but in several cases actually had the effect that fronts looked upon as lost were held, and counterattacks, considered as impossible, were successful." For weeks the high command had held back on assembling panzer brigades, believing a success was obtainable if armor was "not wasted for support of the front, but committed at a point where they would meet weak resistance." Evidently, Model's frantic late-August estimates of the infantry and armor needed to man the Somme–Dijon line had been an effort to claim this reserve. In Lorraine, Hitler proposed to probe the American flank for weakness while consolidating a forward base of operations on the American flank. According to Schramm, this was another link in the chain of events leading to the coming winter counteroffensive in the west.

And so, by the night of September 4, the Germans had begun to rally. They took advantage of lengthening Allied supply lines while their skillful evacuation from the Seine was galvanized at all levels by the harsh logic of the German predicament that September, for there was no way out short of total victory or defeat. Years later General Gerhardt von Schwerin, commander of the 116th Panzer, would tell postwar interrogators his own story, one typical of the German army that week.

After dusk on the fourth, at a meeting at LXXXVII Corps Headquarters at Vise, south of the Dutch-Belgian border, amid the news from Antwerp, Schwerin received instructions to commit the 116th Panzer to the relief of the Liège fortress.

In contact with the German opposition before the July 20 attempt on Hitler's life, Schwerin opposed continuation of the war. At his divisional headquarters later that night, he assembled his officers. Calmly and "without fear of betrayal," he explained that he had concluded that the high command persisted in a policy of "madness and suicide," which could only mean the destruction of Germany. He told the group he would retain command of the division only if in so doing he might help end the war on a tolerable basis, and only if the officers present wanted him to remain. By "a tolerable basis" Schwerin meant ensuring the survival of a unified German state.

All urged Schwerin to stay. To begin with, it was plain that no future could be salvaged for Germany unless the German army checked the current Allied advance. Late that night a reconnaissance detachment and tank battalion of the 116th moved out for Liège, followed by the entire division at dawn on the fifth. The 116th Panzer entered the fray at Liège, withdrew, then swung north to Aachen to take part in the bitter siege with VII Corps for Aachen and control of the Stolberg gap. The 116th would fight on that autumn, and would eventually spearhead the Fifth Panzer Army in the German counteroffensive through the Ardennes Forest in December 1944.

This was the tale of midweek: German disarray, then sudden recovery— in the south, sudden concentrations of German armor at Lunéville; in the north, prompt reinforcement of Walcheren Island and the Albert Canal, which spurred Montgomery's angry complaints to Eisenhower through emissaries of the inability of Corlett's XIX Corps to advance "in support of British operations." A pattern of "stiffening resistance" became evident within twenty-four hours of the fall of Antwerp as the Allied pursuit across France neared Germany and merged, as Blumenson put it, "imperceptibly into a war of position."

For a while, however, nothing could dispel the irresistible "champagne atmosphere." Butcher, now with SHAEF Public Relations in Paris, complained privately that censorship had relaxed practically to the point of breakdown. Preparing for a PRD briefing on the seventh, Butcher urged General Edward C. Betts to brace reporters for a hard battle at the West Wall. Betts agreed, but at the briefing succumbed to the mood of the gathering. Asked whether the First Army dash would break through the Siegfried Line, Betts replied, "Why, of course we'll go right through it." Both wire services quoted General Bedell Smith in Paris as saying that "militarily, the war is won."

On the seventh, in overcast weather, Horrocks' XXX Corps, after the forty-eight-hour pause at Antwerp, resumed the Belgian offensive toward Holland. The spearhead 11th Armored gained a bridgehead over the Albert Canal at Beringen, then encountered lead elements of the newly formed German 1st Parachute Army. For two days, XXX Corps struggled to maintain the Albert Canal foothold against a fresh influx of German infantry. North of the canal, Horrocks pushed the last eighteen miles house to house through Navy and parachute units scraped up and sent to man the Meuse Escaut Canal and the start point for MARKET-GARDEN.

All commands hummed with complaints about supply shortages, but the evidence is that Bradley and Montgomery coped. Eighty percent of the lavish divisional tonnages set by field manuals arrived by truck and plane. The First Army diary, an important chronicle of the war, brimmed with optimism. The diarist noted the many predictions of victory in a week or ten days with good weather. There were also self-deceptions: BBC reports of rumors that Hitler was dead, reports of efforts by Von Rundstedt to capitulate, false reports of Dempsey's capture of Roermond, The Hague, Maastricht and Utrecht, some of which originated with Allied black propaganda radio channels. On the seventh, VII Corps, after regrouping at Liège, launched "the all-out drive to the Rhine." Collins, "itching for more territory to conquer," turned north, crossed the Meuse at Liège and Namur as he headed for the West Wall at Aachen with Gerow on his right, retracing Von Rundstedt's 1940 assault backward through the Ardennes Forest.

Then doubts began to creep into the First Army diary, talk of "handicaps" faced by troops having advanced ceaselessly since St.-Lô and now battling shortages of gasoline and ammunition with each mile toward the German frontier. Bradley, who estimated that his army group had sufficient gasoline and ammunition to operate for ten days, became cautious as Gerow and Collins drew up to the German frontier. G-2 was saying that the Siegfried Line was thinly manned, but Bradley wondered, "Could we believe that?"

In the south, Bradley had banked on sheer momentum to carry Patton's Third Army over the Moselle. A direct line to Mainz via Metz was Patton's set objective, and as historian Russell Weigley wrote, "Remote objectives had always served the Third Army well." Attacks on September 6 quickly foundered in the maze of forts and strongpoints surrounding the Metz citadel held by a rejuvenated German Nineteenth Army. General Walton Walker's XX Corps enveloped the fortress north and south from bridgeheads over the Moselle. But the guns of Fort Driant rained down fire and prevented the building of bridges while elements of the 3rd and 15th Panzer Grenadier, the 17th SS Panzer Grenadier and 106th Panzer Brigade moved up to contest the Moselle bridgeheads.

The battles of Metz and Nancy raged on between the fifth and tenth. With a strengthened XV Corps and French troops, Patton attempted to seize and enlarge footholds east of the Moselle. But ammunition was low, and intelligence reported the ongoing arrival of enemy units in the forest of Parroy fifteen miles east of Lorraine. That week, the Fifth Panzer Army reappeared, and six divisions and four brigades were reported to be building up in the Lunéville area. By the eleventh, the Third Army was involved in a "hard fight south of Nancy" to force the Moselle, and prepared to meet counterattacks.

All of this meant that hourly the MARKET-GARDEN idea was becoming more and more untenable. Montgomery's proposal to go off on a 40-degree tangent into Belgium would divert troops and supplies from the battles at Aachen and Antwerp. It would expose a large British force to defeat or stalemate. The time was approaching when ideally Eisenhower and Montgomery would have taken the situation in hand, but just as the need for common action became apparent, the odds of achieving it receded, a sign of the intractability of inter-Allied differences aroused by the frustrations of Normandy, the tantalizing prospect that the war was ending but the awareness, deep down, that the war was not ending.

Meanwhile, Eisenhower waited. All week, he and Montgomery avoided each other, perhaps sensing that a premature encounter could only commit them to a plan destined to end in failure and in recriminations likely to impair military plans and their own ability to function. For Montgomery, the failure of MARKET-GARDEN would further diminish him and probably even undermine his standing at Whitehall as well as his position as the Britisher with whom the Americans had to do business in northern Europe. For Eisenhower, such a failure would raise questions in Washington about his "grip" on the situation. Thus, both had incentives to pool their resources and come together on a sensible plan to secure positions on the German frontier for the inevitable pause ahead, but the difficulties were, in retrospect, insurmountable.

By now, Montgomery apparently reasoned that to discard MARKET-GARDEN would be to admit that the offensive rationale for gathering forty divisions under his command did not exist. Without insisting on MARKET-GARDEN, he probably feared that he would get no additional American troops and that he might even lose the American corps he had. Moreover, Churchill's departure for Quebec removed the one man from the scene who might have intervened to restrain Brooke's emissaries and members of the "stay behind" War Cabinet who pressured Montgomery that week to take Holland and keep the Berlin issue alive. In short, Montgomery probably felt that he had no recourse but to press on in the hope that Eisenhower would turn the plan down, and if not, that he would somehow make the best of a bad situation.

Significantly, Montgomery did not follow up on his Berlin message of September 4 in the five-day period that he would later insist was the critical moment of decision on the western front. Perhaps Montgomery hoped that the pattern of stiffening German resistance would convince Eisenhower that he had no alternative but to reject MARKET-GARDEN. On the other hand, Eisenhower was keeping his distance from Montgomery perhaps in the hope that the pattern of stiffening German resistance would convince Montgomery that he had no choice but to drop Berlin and scale down his objectives to focus on the Ruhr and Antwerp. For if Eisenhower refused MARKET-GARDEN and its promise of Berlin, history might never forgive him.

And so Eisenhower and Montgomery were at an impasse, and MARKET-GARDEN, an operation that probably neither man wanted, was very likely to go forward at the risk of annihilating the airborne units and postponing necessary projects elsewhere. Perhaps the two men were fatalistic, mindful of parallels between the current impasse and earlier situations when the Americans and the British had grappled with divisive questions, in particular 1942, when a divided American government turned to the British to take responsibility for deciding against opening a second front in France, which had led to the disastrous token landings at Dieppe, ordered by Churchill to discredit SLEDGEHAMMER after the fact.

Did these parallels occur to Eisenhower and Montgomery? No one knows, but it is one of history's ironies that Eisenhower and Montgomery had both been on the scene in London when Marshall persisted to the outer limits for SLEDGEHAMMER only to plunge the Allies into the crisis leading to Dieppe and the sacrifice of the Canadian 1st Division. In the summer of 1942 Eisenhower had been Marshall's key assistant in the SLEDGEHAMMER debates and in this capacity had become acquainted with Lieutenant General B. L. Montgomery, who at the time was Mountbatten's chief planner in charge of Dieppe. In these roles, Eisenhower and Montgomery had first met and begun their strange personal relationship. In these roles, too, they had learned about the complexities of inter-Allied politics and the timeless facts of military leadership in time of war in which the elements of strategy —concentration of force, unity of command, maneuver, surprise, security, simplicity and well-defined objectives—do not always present themselves in neat packages, and thus generals are obliged to choose their moves on the basis of some elements at the expense of others. One might say that in September 1944 "unity of command" was in conflict with all the other strategic elements, but unity of command came first.

This truism had been on Eisenhower's mind for weeks. Indeed, three weeks before, at his press conference announcing activation of Patton's Third Army, he had done his best to dampen the rift caused by the "air-ground" dispute in mid-July. That day Eisenhower appealed for unity and cooperation between the three service branches of the various forces under SHAEF. He went on to "castigate" those who were underestimating the hard tasks ahead as representative of the kind of thinking that would prolong the war. At several moments Eisenhower reflected philosophically on operations to date, and spoke frankly about the hard choices he and his colleagues had faced recently. "One of the duties of a general is to determine the best investment of human lives," he remarked at one point. "If he thinks the expenditure of 10,000 lives in the current battle will save 20,000 later, it is up to him to do it."

Meanwhile, Eisenhower and Montgomery waited. Eisenhower was bedridden at Granville. Montgomery was secluded in Amiens absorbed with matters on the front and unable to leave his post. Montgomery would later allege that Eisenhower was out of touch with him, and that poor communications at Granville left the front directionless at a moment when a clear choice between Dempsey and Patton might have brought victory in the west. Eisenhower's communications during his sojourn at Granville were poor, but Montgomery's claim seems disingenuous. He would cite as proof the fact that Eisenhower's September 5 reply, pouring cold water on Berlin, reached 21st Army Group Headquarters late and in two parts, on the seventh and ninth. Yet other messages reached Granville by courier and telephone all week, and there is no record of any attempt by Montgomery to remedy the communications breakdown when his headquarters allegedly received "part two" of Eisenhower's September 5 message two days before his headquarters received "part one." Despite his knee injury, Eisenhower held daily conferences, attended luncheons and received visitors. At the end of the week he journeyed to Rennes on the eighth, then to Chartres and Paris on the ninth.

The ninth was a long day for Eisenhower. On his way to Brussels, he visited Middleton's VIII Corps Headquarters in Rennes. There, Eisenhower supervised formation of a new Ninth Army Headquarters under General William Simpson, a force slated for insertion on Hodges' northern flank as a buffer between the U.S. First Army and the 21st Army Group. In Rennes, Eisenhower conferred with Generals Middleton and Bradley about the siege at nearby Brest. Isolated 350 miles west of the Siegfried Line without hope of relief, a 40,000-man SS garrison, led by General Hermann Ramcke, had fought VIII Corps to a standstill in a "patient, grinding, probing action lurching from strong point to strong point"; VIII Corps had advanced from hills and ridges to the city wall, where three divisions, reinforced by heavy artillery and the newly formed XXIX Tactical Air Command, had failed to break the German resistance. Some felt the garrison should be roped off and contained. Brest was a considerable diversion of First Army effort, an instance were Bradley and Eisenhower seemed unduly bound by the remnants of pre-OVERLORD planning.

The port had assumed new importance, however. Bradley was determined that the SS not win, and that Middleton "take Brest in order to maintain the illusion of the fact that the U.S. Army cannot be beaten." Eisenhower agreed, but he was also interested in the battle as a demonstration of German morale and determination to fight on. Eisenhower approved Middleton's plan to carry out the siege to its conclusion, regardless of opportunities beckoning eastward. Ten days would pass before Ramcke gave up, and with the German surrender, plans for rehabilitating the port would be scrapped.

On the ninth, before flying to Laval to spend the night with Bradley, Eisenhower, citing Brest, warned the CCS in Quebec that resistance, thought to be nearing collapse earlier that week, was "stiffening somewhat as we approach the German frontier." Eisenhower voiced concern that German Fifteenth Army garrisons along the Scheldt would "delay the utilization of Antwerp as a port and thus will vitally influence the full development of our strategy."

Bradley later recalled that he made Eisenhower spend the evening "rehearing all my objections to MARKET-GARDEN." Bradley recalled Dempsey's apparent blunder in failing to clear the Scheldt on the fourth. Bradley warned that since the 12th Army Group could not spare forces to open the

Scheldt, MARKET-GARDEN meant putting off Antwerp indefinitely. Bradley further reminded Eisenhower of recent ULTRA intercepts confirming that elements of twenty German divisions were regrouping in Holland, including the II SS Panzer Corps in the Arnhem area. MARKET-GARDEN would *increase* rather than *decrease* Allied flank exposure on the Rhine by "opening a gap" between the 12th and 21st army groups.

Earlier in the day, Montgomery had wired Eisenhower to protest his latest directive. He had again charged that XIX Corps was "unable to advance properly for lack of petroleum," and had cited Dempsey's additional need for 500 three-ton trucks plus 1,000 tons per day by airlift. Of the promised airlift of 1,000 tons a day, Dempsey had received 750 tons total. But "I submit that a reallocation of our present resources in every description would be adequate to get one thrust to Berlin," he had written. But it was "difficult to explain things in a message like this." Eisenhower and Montgomery set a meeting for the tenth in Brussels.

September 10. Opposed to MARKET-GARDEN by now, General Miles Dempsey visited Montgomery shortly before his meeting with Eisenhower to urge him to drop MARKET-GARDEN and to go with an alternative plan (COMET), which called for a 21st Army Group offensive supported by airborne elements stretching northeast toward Venlo–Wesel instead of due north. Dempsey was concerned about the wide gap MARKET-GARDEN would open between the Second Army and XIX Corps. He sketched the dangers of going off on such a tangent with firm assurances the Americans would fill the gap, and confronted Montgomery with the "disappointingly slow" progress of XXX Corps and the fact that the German First Parachute Army was fighting effectively. Horrocks had gained a second foothold over the Albert Canal, but XXX Corps spearheads were just now reaching the Meuse–Escaut start line with little prospect of being joined there by the rest of the 2nd Army Group. The British VIII Corps was immobile at the Seine, and British XII Corps was heavily engaged at Le Havre, which left only Horrocks' two armored divisions for the armored push through Holland, a risk particularly in light of Dutch underground reports indicating heavy rail activity in the Arnhem area, and panzers refitting at Eindhoven and Nijmegen. Montgomery gave Dempsey the impression that the problem was out of his hands. Montgomery spoke of War Office interest in capturing The Hague and destroying the German V-2 sites in Holland. Montgomery reminded Dempsey that unless the 21st Army Group used the 1st Allied Airborne Army promptly, Eisenhower would assign it to Bradley.

The tenth was an autumnlike day, sunny and cool. Eisenhower was still convalescing, and so the meeting occurred aboard his command C-47 at the Brussels airport in the presence of Tedder, Gale and De Guingand with Montgomery's approval, either because Montgomery was speaking for the record or perhaps in the vain hope that Eisenhower's advisers would influence him against the operation.

The tense discussion opened with an effort to agree upon essential facts. Eisenhower asked Montgomery to concede that Antwerp was not "open." Montgomery asked Eisenhower to admit either that he had never intended "priority" for the 21st Army Group or that SHAEF orders were "not being followed" by Bradley. Montgomery cited Corlett's XIX Corps, suddenly grounded for lack of oil and stripped of a division he learned was to be sent south to reinforce Patton. The Supreme Commander denied that he had ever meant "priority" to mean "absolute priority," and reminded Montgomery that XIX Corps had crossed the Dutch frontier with ample petroleum to reach the Rhine. Finally, Eisenhower and Montgomery stipulated that Antwerp was not "open," and that German resistance was "stiffening all along the front." The meeting got down to business.

Montgomery proceeded to lecture Eisenhower, Tedder and Gale in schoolmaster fashion about a strategic picture that had become "jerky and disjointed." With maintenance split evenly between Patton and Hodges and the Allies attacking everywhere, he predicted the Allies would succeed nowhere.

As Montgomery ran down the list of their recent exchanges in rude, insulting terms, Eisenhower cut him off: "What you are saying is this; if I give you all the supply you want, you would go straight to Berlin, right? Berlin is three hundred miles from your front—you would require division after division to protect your flank. The beachhead can't supply a thrust into Germany."

Montgomery countered that the 21st Army Group could "supply them, all right" if it was given what it needed.

Eisenhower reminded Montgomery that every contingency plan on Berlin required that Antwerp be operational by September 15. Montgomery insisted that the seizure of Berlin, the administrative and political heart of Germany, would bring a quick end to German resistance and that an advance to Berlin via the Ruhr was immediately possible. Then, calling it "the last chance to end the war in 1944," Montgomery outlined MARKET-GARDEN.

He described in detail the daring plan to march three British corps over an airborne carpet in Holland. One may suppose that Eisenhower, like Bradley, was impressed by the imaginativeness and scope of Montgomery's plan. But the underlying assumptions did not make sense, and it became evident to Tedder, who had flown in from London to act as witness, that Montgomery was not wholehearted in his presentation. Indeed, by all accounts of the meeting, including his own, Montgomery did not put the case to Eisenhower as forcefully as he could have.

Montgomery conceded to Eisenhower that he faced "stiffening resistance" everywhere. He spoke of probable delays in organizing Dempsey's forces of a week or more. Montgomery could not predict when VIII Corps and XII Corps would be ready. As yet, with two armored and four infantry divisions, Dempsey was expected to punch through an intricate and densely defended system of causeways and bridges across the Rhine, then spearhead an Allied offensive onto the Ruhr. Even with American support he could not do it, and this seemed obvious to everyone.

Responding to these signals, Eisenhower gave Montgomery an opportunity to back off from Berlin. He reminded Montgomery that even if MARKET-GARDEN succeeded, Dempsey would have to stop and "turn instantly" to clearing the Scheldt. Antwerp was essential, and taking the Bevelands and Walcheren Island would be long and costly. Eisenhower was prepared to offer Montgomery "any assistance" to clear the Scheldt estuary if Montgomery would make it his first priority.

Montgomery persisted in calling Berlin the "prize" of the war, and predicted he could get there with adequate support, whereupon Eisenhower approved MARKET-GARDEN. As he would recall privately twenty-two years later, "I not only approved MARKET-GARDEN, I insisted upon it."

The meeting broke up. Montgomery returned to Amiens to plan the operation and Eisenhower returned to Granville. That night Bradley phoned Eisenhower to learn the outcome of the talks. As he later recalled, he detected right away in Eisenhower's evasiveness that he had approved MARKET-GARDEN, and hotly disagreed with Eisenhower's characterization of the plan as "an incident and extension of our eastward rush to the line we needed for temporary security."

Years later Bradley and other critics of this decision would claim that "a real military commander" in Eisenhower's place would simply have ordered Montgomery to take Antwerp, an action that might have spared the crack British 1st Airborne and avoided thousands of casualties in the eventual assault on Walcheren Island to open Antwerp, an operation rivaling the Sicily invasion in scope. But a "real military commander" in Eisenhower's shoes would not have lasted two months in his job, as events would show. Evidently, in Eisenhower's judgment, delaying the opening of Antwerp would pose problems that would be minor compared with allowing any further discussion of Berlin. The debate had to end, and so, barring a change of heart on Montgomery's part, MARKET-GARDEN was on, which did not mean Montgomery's ideas had prevailed.

Butcher wrote the following day that "Ike is thinking in terms of advancing on a wide front to take advantage of all existing lines of communication." Butcher, a visitor, described Eisenhower's version of Montgomery's bold idea of a march through Holland followed by an attempt "to threaten Berlin itself." He noted that Eisenhower seemed enthusiastic, but that he seemed just as concerned about the battles at Metz and Aachen. Though "excited" about a Rhine bridgehead, Eisenhower told Butcher that Berlin was "*not,* at the moment, to have priority over other operations."

Eisenhower spent the vigil in Granville. There was little of the turmoil of mid-July. He remained in bed for several days, still recuperating, and tended to routine items. A headquarters transfer to Versailles was under way. Promotion lists were due, and demobilization planning had started. Evacuation of German prisoners, the French rail program, air bases in France, and the details of the Sixth Army transfer from Alexander to SHAEF were all pressing. Word of a new CCS directive resuming POINT-BLANK under Portal, news that four months earlier might have shaken the foundations of his command, came and went.

On the eleventh Bradley came for lunch to discuss "the entire field of next month's operations." The two men also talked about MARKET-GARDEN. Bradley lobbied for lifting the supply constraints hampering Patton in the Moselle battle. Alarmed by the costs of Montgomery's fantastic design to "flank" the West Wall, Bradley felt duty-bound to repeat the consequences of MARKET-GARDEN: it would fail. It might force XIX Corps away from the battle for the "West Wall bridgehead" battle at Aachen. Eisenhower "silenced" Bradley's objections.

Eisenhower confirmed that Corlett's XIX Corps would operate on Hodges' flank, and that supplies would be evenly divided between Hodges and Patton until the fourteenth. Patton had forty-eight hours to "become so heavily involved I might reconsider," but otherwise a September 14 deadline on Patton's operations was mandatory. On the fifteenth all requested maintenance and airlift would be available for Dempsey's Second Army, and as Bradley recalled, Eisenhower "wanted MARKET-GARDEN on time"—September 17, 1944.

General Everett Hughes, an old friend, was a visitor that week. In his diary he described the gathering of friends, Summersby and Colonel Tex Lee, who joined him in tackling Eisenhower "about the growing public relations problem—the need to play up the American side of the battle in France." Eisenhower explained to Hughes that American leadership had to be "low key" if things were to work after the war in Europe. Hughes reminded his old friend that he (Eisenhower) would not be spending the rest of his life in Europe. Eisenhower demurred.

On the twelfth came Montgomery's first warning of a postponement. In a message, he warned Eisenhower that his decision that the northern thrust toward the Ruhr was not to have priority over other operations was bound to have "certain repercussions." Having investigated the lagging maintenance situation, 21st Army Group planners had concluded that "large scale operations by Second Army and the Airborne Army toward the Meuse and Rhine cannot now take place before 23 September at the earliest and possibly 26 September," and a delay inevitably meant "heavier resistance and slower progress." Since a prompt MARKET-GARDEN was "basically a matter of rail and road and air transport," Montgomery assured Eisenhower that he was doing what he could "to get on with the business." But "*no great results*" could be expected "until we have built up stocks of ammunition and other requirements."

"E. is sending Bedell to see Monty to find out just what we have to do," wrote Summersby that morning. Smith and Gale flew to Brussels that afternoon to tell Montgomery that Eisenhower had decided to strip three U.S. divisions of maintenance in Normandy and to assign the extra transport to supplement the British supply routes. In a follow-up message the next day, Eisenhower approved all arrangements "emergency in character and . . . temporary" to meet the September 17 deadline. He disclosed that Comm-Z agreed to provide 500 tons by air and another 500 tons by truck, and informed Montgomery that he had directed Bradley to establish an advance command post in Belgium and to set up direct communications between the 21st Army Group and First Army. Afterward, Eisenhower issued to all commands an "amplification" of his earlier directive, a carefully drafted document that placed the Eisenhower-Montgomery controversy on record so that no one could mistake what was being tested in Holland.

In it, Eisenhower looked back in time. He recalled the situation on August 20 and the factors governing his broad-front decision that day at Tourniers. An alternative he had considered was to concentrate "all resources behind a single *knife-like and narrow thrust,*" in the hope that "whatever force we can maintain" could advance and bring "the capitulation of that country [Germany]." Instead, he had chosen to order Allied forces to seize suitable positions where they would regroup and build maintenance facilities capable of sustaining "the great bulk of our forces on the drive into Germany." Citing recent talks with Bradley, Montgomery and Ramsay, Eisenhower had concluded that the early capture of deep-water ports and improved maintenance facilities were prerequisites to "a final all-out assault on Germany proper." Bad weather, due shortly, could paralyze operations east of the Rhine, and without improved communications a "speedy and prolonged advance by forces adequate in strength, depending on bulk oil, transport and ammunition is not a feasible operation." Eisenhower indicated that Dempsey's imminent high-priority attack through Holland would seek to gain a Rhine bridgehead. The Second Army would have first claim on "all forms of logistic support" until October 1. Montgomery's mission thereafter would be to secure Antwerp and the other Channel ports from which "lines of communication radiating therefrom can give adequate maintenance to the Northern Group of Armies deep into the heart of Germany." Eisenhower said nothing about Montgomery's "priority," and thus left Montgomery to wonder whether a reverse in Holland would in fact terminate it.

On the fourteenth Montgomery sent Eisenhower word of more problems. In a directive issued to the 21st Army Group earlier that day, Montgomery retreated from his bolder proclamations of recent weeks. For the first time he acknowledged the importance of Antwerp and assigned the task of clearing the Beveland approaches to the Canadian First Army. Silent on Berlin, Montgomery set the Ruhr as the objective of the 21st Army Group attacks, and while he called the Ruhr a "step on the northern route of advance into Germany," strangely said nothing about MARKET-GARDEN.

Along with a copy of this directive forwarded to Granville, Montgomery enclosed a conciliatory message to the Supreme Commander. In it, he praised SHAEF's hard work and cooperation in solving the Second Army supply problem, adding that he would be needing an extra 500 tons daily delivered by special lorry until October 7, an extension of six days. Montgomery again assured Eisenhower that MARKET-GARDEN was on for the seventeenth, barring rain.

Sensing an opening, Eisenhower sent Montgomery a long personal and confidential wire in which he speculated about operations after seizure of the Ruhr, the Saar and Frankfurt. Since his policy was to pursue the German army and defeat it, Eisenhower tried to anticipate where the Germans would try to organize a front after losing the Ruhr and the Saar.

Looking down the road, Eisenhower did not rule out Berlin as a possibility. "Clearly, Berlin is the main prize," he conceded, "the prize in defense of which the enemy is *likely* to concentrate the bulk of his forces." Accordingly, after quickly seizing the Ruhr and the Saar, Eisenhower assured Montgomery that he would consider a rapid thrust for Berlin as one of several alternatives that might be pursued, though strategy at that point would have to be coordinated with the Russians. Other choices, as he saw them, would include a drive toward Lübeck and Kiel to cut off German forces in Denmark-Norway. Another would be to advance to Brunswick–Leipzig–Dresden in central Germany, which were important industrial areas. Another would be a southward drive on a Nuremberg–Regensburg line toward Munich, a city of "transcending political importance." If the Russians failed to reach Berlin, Eisenhower suggested an offensive toward Berlin via the Ruhr by Montgomery's forces or Berlin via Frankfurt by Bradley's forces. Though it was "not possible at this stage to indicate the timing of these thrusts or their strengths," Eisenhower encouraged Montgomery to think it over.

Meanwhile, Eisenhower sent Marshall an account of recent operations and future plans for use at Quebec. He recited his decisions since August 1 and the debate accompanying each step. Eisenhower told Marshall of Montgomery's sudden "obsession" about rushing his army group to Berlin, which study had exposed "as a fantastic idea." He assured Marshall he had rejected the idea, adding that he had agreed to provide Montgomery strength to seize a Rhine bridgehead in airborne operations set for the seventeenth "unless weather prevents." Eisenhower assured Marshall that he had nonetheless chosen the profitable alternative of pushing forces to the Rhine on all fronts before an extended pause to refit and reinforce.

Looking into the future, and anticipating that Russian pressure would not be sustained on the current scale, Eisenhower predicted a major battle for control of the Rhine. He hoped to gain the West Wall, then pierce the Rhine barrier at the Ruhr and take the Saar, and finally undertake an "unremitting advance against the heart of the enemy country." Phase one would be hard going, however, and "the big crash to start that move may prove to be a rather rough affair."

MARKET-GARDEN was a very unpopular decision in American circles to the end. Told to assume the defensive from Nancy to Luxembourg on the fourteenth, Patton fumed in his diary: "Monty does what he pleases and Ike says 'yes, sir.' Monty wants all supplies sent to him and the First U.S. Army and for me to hold. Brad thinks I can and should push on. Brad told Ike that if Monty takes control of the XIX and VII Corps of the First Army, as he wants to, he, Bradley, will ask to be relieved . . . Ike feels that we think he is selling us out but he had to as Monty will not take orders. So we have to . . ."

The battle along the German frontier under way at Aachen and Prüm was sobering. Although all commands possessed ample stocks of gasoline and ammunition to reach the Rhine, there was weariness in Allied ranks, a marked revival of German resistance, and mounting signs that after the 325-mile advance from St.-Lô, the Allies were losing momentum.

In the week before MARKET-GARDEN at Prüm and Aachen, German units written off weeks before reappeared. Fresh German units opposed VII Corps crossings of the Meuse at Liège. Collins attempted to pierce the West Wall through the Stolberg–Düren corridor south of Aachen, but reconnaissance units were stopped on the twelfth. In midweek, Collins ruptured the West Wall in two places, and coordinated attacks by XIX Corps and VII Corps widened the "West Wall bridgehead" in the forests south of Aachen, then met the 116th Panzer Division and Fifteenth Army infantry sent to seal off the penetration "or die in the attempt," as *Newsweek* put it.

In the Ardennes Forest, Gerow gained contact with the Third Army at Luxembourg and crossed the German frontier at Stalzemberg on the night of the eleventh. A two-division attack on the fourteenth penetrated the West Wall in two places, then met elements of the 1st SS Panzer Corps and 2nd Panzer Division. By the eighteenth the Germans were mounting large-scale counterattacks, and Gerow, lacking the strength to consolidate his hold on the West Wall, called off the V Corps offensive and withdrew.

Farther south, heavy rains and mud slowed Patton's operations, which enabled the Germans, feverishly at work on restoring the West Wall, to regroup. Metz did not yield and by midweek a crisis had developed in the

Nancy sector. American XII Corps attacks from Moselle bridgeheads at Nancy preempted a Fifth Panzer Army attack, forcing the Germans to commit units piecemeal; XII Corps entered Nancy on the fifteenth, and Haislip's XV Corps seized a Moselle bridgehead below Epinal. But as Haislip reached out to link with the French II Corps, he encountered German armor and stopped. Within seventy-two hours German counterattacks in the Nancy–Epinal sector had developed into the largest tank battles since Caen. As Schramm would later put it, a German thumb at Epinal–Nancy pressed against the extended American wrist. The question was whether the American fist would give way to the pressure of the thumb or whether the thumb would be forced to withdraw for fear of being cut off. Air intervened, and by the twentieth Patton held Lunéville and Nancy, and, having forced the Fifth Panzer Army to fall back, scored a defensive victory by preventing the Germans from turning his southern flank on the Marne. And so it went in the countdown toward H-Hour, amid forecasts of clear skies and cool autumn weather in Holland.

In his postwar account, Bedell Smith recalled that "not long before the drop," on Friday morning the fifteenth, General Strong visited his office to discuss a disturbing hunch. Four German panzer divisions had been out of contact since Mortain—specifically, Strong had in mind the 9th and 10th SS, two divisions extricated from the Falaise pocket. He had no proof, but the 2nd SS Panzer Corps had to be "somewhere." By the process of elimination and his "sixth sense" as an intelligence officer, Strong connected his hunch to Dutch underground reports about retraining activity and the build-up of heavy AA flak in the vicinity of the highway bridge at Arnhem.

Smith immediately arranged a meeting with Eisenhower, who, according to Smith, weighed Strong's deduction "with the greatest care." Eisenhower had questions. Did Strong have proof? Strong was not aware of any photographic evidence of panzers in the Arnhem area. Eisenhower decided to take no action, but he instructed Strong and Smith to visit Montgomery in Brussels forthwith to present their report.

In Brussels, Montgomery also considered Strong's warnings carefully, but, committed by his own pronouncements, he had hardened on MARKET-GARDEN. Montgomery doubted that the 9th and 10th SS were battle-worthy and claimed he was more concerned about the Dutch terrain and "adequate maintenance."

That night Eisenhower penned a friendly letter to Montgomery. He said he had read Montgomery's latest 21st Army Group directive and praised it as "in exact accordance with all the understandings that we now have." He predicted that Dempsey would win a major victory, and promised Montgomery all the troops and supplies that could be "efficiently employed in the battle." He apologized for the snags in delivering the extra 500 tons a day to Dempsey, but he had been assured that the problem had been worked out with Comm-Z and that supplies would begin arriving by dawn the seventeenth. Eisenhower intimated that about the twentieth he would be moving his forward headquarters from Granville to Versailles, where he expected to be hosting a "major conference." He would know "the exact location later" and "pass it on." He closed: "Best of luck—Ike."

MARKET-GARDEN

In the next forty-eight hours Eisenhower caught up on his correspondence home. To his brother Earl, now an engineer in Charleroi, Pennsylvania, Eisenhower good-naturedly apologized for the publicity engulfing his brothers in recent months. He agreed with Earl's complaint in a recent letter that home-front press coverage was too optimistic. Eisenhower assumed casualty lists were being published, however, and "that alone should be able to keep people in their sober senses with respect to the job we have to do."

Eisenhower affectionately thanked the Douds for a recent letter describing their golden wedding anniversary celebration in Denver, signing his letter, as he had for twenty-eight years, "Your devoted son." To P. A. Hodgson, his football teammate and West Point roommate, Eisenhower ascribed his recent injury to his "good knee." "Darned annoying," he wrote, that "after practicing for more than 30 years to protect one leg, to reverse the process completely."

Hodgson knew all about Eisenhower's old football injury. In 1915 Hodgson had profiled his friend Dwight in the West Point yearbook, *The Howitzer.* He described how "Ike," once acclaimed by sportswriter Walter Camp as a potential all-American, had endured his bitter disappointment: Dwight "merely consents to exist until graduation sets him free. At one time he [Ike] threatened to get interested in life and won his 'A' by being the most promising back in Eastern football—but the Tufts game broke his knee and the promise."

In a letter to his mother that week, Eisenhower described the war in France as a "hard, tough struggle," redeemed by the hope that "this time the job is done well enough that your grandchildren, in their time, will at least be spared going through a second war experience." He asked Ida to give everyone in Abilene his warm regards, and looked forward to the great day when he could go back to Abilene and renew the friendships he had prized so much as a boy.

Ida Elizabeth Stover had been born in the Shenandoah Valley west of the Blue Ridge Mountains in 1862, two years before Philip Sheridan's infamous scorched-earth attack, which succeeded in destroying the valley's usefulness as a Confederate granary and making it a base for invasion of the North. Her parents, though pacifists, had offered sanctuary in their home to Confederate soldiers fleeing Sheridan's cavalry. Too young to remember the fighting, she had been raised on stories of the Civil War, and grown up in the misery left by Sheridan's campaign. These stories she had passed along to her sons.

Finally, to Mamie, Eisenhower apologized for the long lapse in correspondence. He explained that he had been very busy, despite the impressions given by the press, which left him wondering "how the people at home can be so complacent about finishing off the job we have here." He described his recent trips to Paris and Brussels, told Mamie about his plans to move to Versailles and his hope that he could avoid staying in Paris for very long, reminding her that he preferred "camps to cities." At least Paris and Brussels had escaped serious damage, he wrote, "Amiens the same . . . but some of the larger towns have been pulverized. . . . I always feel sad when I face the necessity of destroying the homes of my friends! The German is a beast."

At Granville, Eisenhower assumed responsibility for an operation which he opposed as futile, yet which he had insisted upon. "We were inordinately proud of our airborne units," he later wrote of Sunday, September 17, 1944. "But the interest in that battle had its roots in something deeper than pride. We felt it would prove whether or not the Germans could succeed in establishing renewed and effective resistance—on the battle's outcome we would form an estimate of the severity of the fighting still ahead of us."

By noon, in a low haze, RAF and Eighth Air Force bombers and fighters ranged the length of Holland pounding enemy dumps and barracks; 5,500 planes and gliders followed, ferrying 34,000 British and American troops representing, in Wilmot's words, the "last, slender chance of ending the German war in 1944." But even advocates of MARKET-GARDEN knew that the chance, if it ever existed, had long since passed.

Early reports from Holland were better than expected. All 20,000 troops in the first wave reached the drop zones safely. Enemy flak and fighters harassing the return flights claimed only thirty transports and bombers. On schedule at 2:25, Horrocks' XXX Corps launched attacks down the single road connecting Escaut, Eindhoven, Nijmegen and Arnhem. Up the road General Maxwell Taylor's 101st assembled and seized bridges over the Son and Uden, while farther up, the 82nd Airborne successfully captured the Maas bridge at Grave.

As the story goes, troubles and mishaps plagued the British 1st Airborne at Arnhem from the beginning. Owing to dense flak defenses, General Robert Urquhart had selected drop zones eight miles northwest of the Arnhem bridge. With reinforcements and artillery set to arrive in stages, the drop zones had to be held, compelling Urquhart to divide up his force. The Armored jeeps were lost in transit, so the assault battalions had had to proceed to the Arnhem bridge by foot, which took four hours.

By late afternoon the 9th SS Hohenstauffen Division attacked Urquhart's airhead on the north bank of the river and encircled the assault battalion on the north end of the highway bridge. But the situation deteriorated rapidly and attempts to storm the far side of the bridge failed. Urquhart's reconnaissance patrols entered the city and found it heavily defended by tanks and self-propelled guns. By happenstance, Field Marshal Model had been in Arnhem on the seventeenth, and had quickly assumed personal direction of countermeasures on the scene. At a conference in Rastenburg that night, Hitler decided to reinforce the Fifteenth Army in Holland, and by the next morning a panzer brigade, three infantry divisions and dozens of units scraped up from depots, the Home Army and the Luftwaffe flowed into Holland from Cleve and Emmerich.

On the eighteenth, misfortune continued to plague MARKET-GARDEN. A low-pressure weather front moved in over England. Dense fog delayed for five hours the departure of reinforcements and glider-borne artillery. Supply drops at Arnhem were wide of the drop zones, and the forces protecting the airhead remained out of contact with the bridge. Held to a six-mile gain on the first day, Horrock's XXX Corps armor broke through to Eindhoven while the 101st Airborne entered the town from the north. But traffic congestion and bottlenecks along the corridor slowed movement, and progress by XII Corps and VIII Corps on the flanks was depressingly slow. At Nijmegen, due to reports of enemy armor and the presence of the II Parachute Corps in the Reichswald Forest, Ridgway postponed the assault on the 600-meter span bridge to await Horrocks' arrival. By nightfall the first of a series of German counterattacks from the Reichswald Forest was under way, and MARKET-GARDEN was in trouble along the entire length of the corridor.

By the night of the eighteenth Montgomery knew he faced a setback in Holland. Despite the successful Allied airborne landings and apparent surprise, German countermeasures held XXX Corps to six miles in the first day and denied Dempsey two of the three bridges. As of the eighteenth, the Germans held the Maas bridge at Nijmegen, and had strongly reinforced positions along the corridor north of Nijmegen. The advantage of conducting airborne operations in close proximity to British air bases had been nullified by weather. More important, the very first hours of combat had rendered Montgomery's basic assumption false: that the Germans in September 1944 were either ready to surrender or too disorganized to form a strong front. Dempsey had met a determined enemy.

Historians agree that the main object of all operations from the night of the eighteenth on was to relieve the British 1st Airborne, consolidate the Maas bridgehead by capturing Nijmegen while minimizing losses, including Montgomery's inevitable loss of prestige in the eyes of the British and the Americans. As late as the nineteenth in messages to Eisenhower, Montgomery defiantly pressed his plan for taking Berlin and resisted suggestions that he concentrate on Antwerp. He hotly complained about supply shortages and transport, as well as the lack of flank support for

Corlett's XIX Corps, which idled on the Albert Canal at Maastricht next to VII Corps idling at Aachen. But Montgomery's fury was spent, and despite personality differences and recent controversies, Eisenhower's problem now was to find a way to allow Montgomery to close ranks before the setback opened the floodgates to political pressures from both sides. Montgomery's supply complaints were not without foundation and touched off explosions in Granville. Eisenhower summoned General J.C.H. Lee, commander of Comm-Z on the nineteenth for a stern talk. Deliveries had dropped to 17,000 tons per day instead of a promised 30,000 tons, arousing suspicion of widespread pilfering and black-market skimming. Eisenhower also opposed the bloated echelons of supply personnel moving into Paris, and, according to Summersby, put Smith to work afterward on a "policy of having a commandant for the Paris area . . . It will have to be someone who is tough."

News in the next forty-eight hours continued to be bad. On the nineteenth, Horrocks' XXX Corps linked with the 82nd Airborne at Grave and proceeded on to Nijmegen in hopes of quickly securing a Maas bridgehead. On the afternoon of the twentieth, XXX Corps armor lunched into Nijmegen and "crunched through the debris-littered streets in fierce assaults." A battalion of the 82nd Airborne in light canvas assault boats under smoke and artillery cover flanked 500 German defenders on the span bridge and stormed the Maas bridge. By 6:45, twenty-four hours behind schedule, U.S. troops hoisted an American flag on the north end of the bridge, which spurred the British Guards Armored through the last wall of defenders holding on the south bank. But five miles north of Nijmegen, XXX Corps, bogged down in the rain, encountered an anti-tank screen along the single-lane road and stopped.

By the second, with the two British follow-up corps stalled south of Eindhoven and struggling with elements of ten German divisions for control of the road, Dempsey was reluctant to push the Nijmegen breakthrough. The pause lasted another twenty-four hours, and by the twenty-second Dempsey and Montgomery had abandoned plans to "exploit" beyond the Zuider Zee, and had turned their full attention to measures to consolidate the salient. That day the Dutch underground reported that the 9th Panzer Division had cleared the northern end of the Arnhem bridge and pocketed the main body of British troops in a tight perimeter of 1,000 yards by 2,000 yards west of the city. Overcast skies prevented resupply. Only 53 of the 110 planes airlifting the Polish brigade were able to discharge troops. Casualties were heavy, and according to Urquhart, relief was "vital" within twenty-four hours.

The grim news from Holland, marking the end of the summer battles, caused little commotion. Most had known deep down that the war would go on into the fall and winter. That afternoon, at his new main headquarters in the annex of the Trianon Palace Hotel at Versailles, Eisenhower convened the jury. Twenty-three generals, admirals and air marshals were present, including Tedder, Leigh-Mallory, Spaatz, Smith, Ramsay and Bradley, the largest such gathering since the pre-Normandy review at St. Paul's in May. A conspicuous absentee was Montgomery, represented by his peacemaking chief of staff, General de Guingand.

A defiant Montgomery later explained that he knew he was not popular at SHAEF or with the American generals because of his views and "thought it best to keep away while the matter was being further argued." In the eyes of some, Montgomery, facing a major setback in Holland, simply could not endure a gathering called to hash over the consequences. Butcher noted that the SHAEF office pool was taking bets on whether Montgomery would attend in person or "plead concentration on the battle" and send De Guingand, with long odds quoted in favor of the latter. But Eisenhower did not seem surprised or offended by Montgomery's absence, an act of self-preservation which was the important thing now.

It was De Guingand who coined the formula enabling the group to set aside differences and do business. As of the twenty-second, the British Second Army held seven of the eight bridges in Holland, and so MARKET-GARDEN was a "ninety percent success." The failure to punch through to Arnhem on time was attributable to bad luck, weather and supply, but even if supplied, Dempsey could have gained the bridgehead at Arnhem but "not more." And so the issue now was future operations in the face of stiffening resistance on the German frontier. De Guingand presented Montgomery's plan for exploiting Dempsey's gains in Holland, wherein the Twenty-second Army would throw a "left hook" southward on Venlo and Roermond aimed at Düsseldorf, supported by a converging "right hook" by the First Army. Bradley submitted a rival plan emphasizing four points:

1. The port of Antwerp is essential.
2. In considering any move into Germany we are faced with the fact that such a move must be made in great depth.
3. The enemy must be kept engaged on a very wide front in order to keep him from concentrating in front of the main effort.
4. In supporting the primary 21st Army Group thrust, the American armies should either concentrate on Cologne or Frankfurt.

Bradley proceeded to recommend a wide envelopment of the Ruhr via offensives north of Düsseldorf and secondary offensives north of the Saar. Bradley endorsed priority for the northern thrust, but urged "an advance . . . made by all armies, each supporting the main thrust, the main thrust also getting priority as to concentrated effort and priority in supply." All murmured approval. A British initiative to seize Berlin was no longer on the table, and so by consensus the aim of current operations was the capture of the Ruhr via offensives staged north and south of the Ruhr.

Discussion centered on the role of the American First Army, the key to the month-long command dispute. Should Hodges be emphasizing operations on his left toward Cologne in close support of the British or on his right toward Frankfurt in support of Patton? With Dempsey's fourteen divisions heavily engaged in a forty-mile salient on both flanks by elements of twenty German divisions, including four panzer types, and unable to spare troops to assist the Canadians at Antwerp or to eliminate threats east of the Maas, all favored Cologne.

The September 22 discussion set the framework for debate that fall and winter. The group stipulated the limits on the eventual Ruhr thrust to be carried out under the direction of the 21st Army Group. The road and rail network north of the Ardennes would sustain thirty-five divisions over the Rhine, and with eighty divisions due by late winter a secondary thrust would be desirable and possible to draw German defenders away from the Ruhr. "To gain the capability of concentration," Eisenhower would insist on preliminary operations to clear the west bank of the Rhine in its entirety. Looking down the road, should the Germans retain a hold on staging areas west of the river, fully half of the eighty Allied divisions due in Europe by May 1945 would be engaged in defensive tasks.

At the close, the group turned to measures to aid Dempsey. Eisenhower ordered Patton's Third Army to cease aggressive operations, and placed the entire sector south of the Ardennes Forest on the defensive. The U.S. First Army was to nudge northwest and detach a corps to "assume responsibility for the southern sector of the [British] 2nd Army." Eisenhower ordered the American VIII Corps, fresh from the siege at Brest, to move into the thinly held Ardennes Forest to protect Hodges' right flank. In summary, Eisenhower emphasized the main points "to be accepted by all": first, an additional deep-water port, either Antwerp or Rotterdam, was necessary to sustain a power drive into Germany; second, all agreed that "the envelopment of the Ruhr from the north by the 21st Army Group supported by the 1st Army is the main effort of the present phase of operations," wording that satisfied De Guingand, who sent a message to Montgomery informing him of the "excellent" conference.

Afterward, in a conciliatory message to Montgomery, Eisenhower elaborated. He reminded Montgomery that Patton "contained" a heavy concentration of armor at Lunéville, that Hodges was heavily engaged at Aachen, and as the First Army shifted northward, a gap would appear south of Aachen in the Ardennes Forest, where the Germans might inflict a "nasty little Kasserine if the enemy chooses at any time to concentrate a bit of strength." This accounted for the key omission of the conference: U.S. forces could not be spared to aid Montgomery's effort to open Antwerp. In closing, Eisenhower urged Montgomery to consider the present offensive in Holland "bold when compared to our general maintenance situation." Eisenhower hoped the two of them would be in close touch in the coming weeks, since he found "without exception, when all of us can get together and look the various features of our problems squarely in the face, the answers usually become obvious." He urged Montgomery not to hesitate "for a second to let me know at any time that anything seems to you to go wrong, particularly where I, my staff, or any forces not directly under your control can be of help. . . . of course we need Antwerp."

In the next four days, fierce battles raged along the airborne corridor. At two points near Eindhoven, II Parachute Corps retook portions of "Hell's Highway," then fell back. Panzer reinforcements poured into Holland through the Arnhem area. Finally, on the night of the twenty-fourth, Dempsey decided against a final effort to reach the Neder Rijn and sent word to Urquhart ordering the remnants of the British 1st Airborne to evacuate the town of Arnhem and fall back to safety behind XXX Corps lines. Twenty-four hours later, in the rain and under cover of darkness, the survivors slipped through the woods in groups of ten and shuttled over the Rhine in fifteen rubber rafts, leaving behind 7,500 dead, wounded and missing.

The end came on the gray, rainy afternoon of September 26 as King George flew into the Dutch salient to decorate the 2,163 survivors of the British 1st Airborne. General Urquhart read a letter from Montgomery praising their gallantry in action in the heroic tradition of the British Army. But all was not lost. "As regards Arnhem," Churchill wrote Smuts several days later, "I think you have the position a little out of focus. The battle was a decided victory, but the leading division, asking, quite rightly, for more, was given a chop. I have not been affected by any feeling of disappointment over this and am glad our commanders are capable of running this kind of risk."

By the close of September the British Second Army had seized seven of eight bridges along the sixty-mile corridor, and had "split" the German Fifteenth Army. Put another way, Dempsey's Second Army was in a deep salient constricted on all sides by canals and rivers. Dempsey had not succeeded in flanking the West Wall as hoped, and the British did not threaten the Ruhr. That Montgomery had failed in his strategic purpose was slowly and grudgingly being accepted.

On the twenty-fourth, SHAEF intelligence, after weeks of optimism, had first conceded in the fine print that the balance of accounts between nominal and true German strength had suddenly become "more and more complicated," owing to new elements "confusing the issue":

1. Hitler's refusal to disband gutted divisions.
2. The low combat morale and readiness of "make-believe divisions" formed that week in Holland.
3. The sudden flow of troops not yet incorporated into existing units.

Resistance in Holland that week bought time for German reinforcements flowing in from Norway, Denmark, Italy and Poland and from recruiting stations in Germany. Soon the 48 "nominal" divisions, equaling 25 "equivalent" divisions, would number 48 full-strength infantry divisions, backed by 13 armored divisions organized into six armies, facing 56 Allied divisions dispersed along a 400-mile front from Holland to Switzerland, as Bryant put it, "like Gamelin in 1940." The analogy with 1940 would lurk in all planning thereafter.

Inevitably, the disillusionment would trigger repeated examinations into the facts and illusions surrounding the Normandy battle and the pursuit through France. American sources, particularly Bradley, would criticize Eisenhower for having appeased Montgomery too long in Normandy, and later. Bradley did not question the Allied halt on the German frontier, citing supply shortages. But he criticized MARKET-GARDEN as "a massive assault in the wrong direction at what was probably the most crucial moment on the German front." Dempsey had by-passed the Scheldt when the approaches to Antwerp might have been cleared easily, and forced the Allies to sacrifice gains at Aachen and Nancy.

British and German criticisms focused on Eisenhower's earlier decisions of August 20 and September 4. Wilmot would claim that unequivocal decision by Eisenhower as late as September 4 to stop Patton's advance and to exploit Montgomery's seizure of Brussels and Antwerp might have "torn the weak German front to pieces and ended the war in the winter of 1944." Wilmot in 1951 would charge that the Americans exaggerated logistical problems as a constraint on Allied operations in general, noting that 50 percent of American divisional supply requirements should have been adequate to sustain pursuit of a battered enemy. Citing German sources, Wilmot also claimed that a twenty-division Allied thrust through Holland launched on time should have been powerful enough to cross the Rhine and seize the Ruhr. Instead, Dempsey's three corps had been unable to operate simultaneously, and Corlett's XIX Corps, Montgomery's flank support, had sat the battle out on the Albert Canal. All of this was attributable, according to Wilmot, to Eisenhower's determination to move on a broad front, his inability to restrain Patton and especially his anxiety to bring about an early linkup with the ANVIL forces. An unspoken in the criticism is the assumption that the German high command at one point had been prepared to open the western front, and that Eisenhower, unwilling to plan operations on this basis, had passed up a glittering opportunity to win the war. But criticism in this vein is incomplete, since it focuses on Eisenhower's earlier decisions, thereby neglecting the question of why Montgomery proposed MARKET-GARDEN on September 10 *after* the fleeting opportunity had passed and why Eisenhower approved it then. The unavoidable conclusion is that while a "glittering opportunity" may have existed for a week or so in late August, such an opportunity was not the basis for the British decision to propose MARKET-GARDEN, and therefore almost beside the point in the complex politics surrounding the whole affair. And so what was the point of the controversy? In retrospect, it would appear that long-range aims were a major issue, but that perhaps the major issue had been command—how the Allies would organize themselves to weather the dangerous period ahead. Debate would persist for years.

Eisenhower's version, which sidestepped many of the issues, appeared in 1948. Bradley's version appeared in 1951, as did Wilmot's biting criticism of Eisenhower's broad-front decision in his *Struggle for Europe.* In 1953 Churchill washed his hands of the controversy. In *Triumph and Tragedy* he observed noncommittally that "strategists may long debate these issues." But by then the Prime Minister was being circumspect, for in 1953 the Americans and British were reaping the whirlwind of Senator Joseph R. McCarthy's use of wartime British arguments against Roosevelt, Marshall and, by implication, Eisenhower, arguments that amounted to accusations that the American high command, having won the war in the west, had unaccountably turned over the fruits of victory in Europe to the Russians. Publication of Churchill's last volume came shortly before the Army-McCarthy showdown over congressional access to U.S. Army files and presumably eventual access to Army documents, including then President Dwight D. Eisenhower's wartime papers and correspondence.

After McCarthy's censure, Churchill's retirement and the Suez crisis of 1956, which was an episode with marked similarities to MARKET-GARDEN insofar as the British were once more counting on American support to achieve a political goal, British circumspection again ended. In early 1958 Montgomery would publish his memoirs, proclaiming himself to be "an unapologetic advocate of MARKET-GARDEN," and associate himself with Wilmot's assessment that the failure to win in September 1944 was due primarily to Eisenhower's broad-front stategies. Brooke would follow two years later with an account suggesting the deeper current in British thought, that victory had been disallowed by American election-year politics. Both magnified the stereotype of Eisenhower as a man who, in Brooke's words, "inclined one way then the other . . . an arbiter balancing the requirements of competing Allies and subordinates rather than a commander."

In late September 1944 the feeling was one of futility. From July onward there had been growing evidence that the Germans would fight to the bitter end. Slowly the inexorability of a ruinous war, in which solutions defied the most imaginative and valiant minds, was becoming apparent to all.

It was a time reminiscent of St. Georges in Algiers a year before. Eisenhower moved into winter quarters at the gloomy château in St.-Germain on the outskirts of Versailles that had been occupied by Von Rundstedt on the night of the invasion. Eisenhower quickly became restive over the "military tendency to become entrenched in one location," and put his staff to work to locate a forward headquarters closer to the front. He also directed a second crackdown to root out complacency in all rear echelons, particularly in the Services of Supply (SOS). On the twenty-eighth, aware that Comm-Z had defied his earlier instructions not to set up a headquarters in Paris, Eisenhower summoned Lee for a second conference in the Trianon. Eisenhower told Lee that he would not tolerate large echelons of constabulary soldiers basking in comfort in Paris. He told Lee to find ways of "getting Comm-Z out of Paris ASAP," and to bar unauthorized personnel from the city "no matter what their rank." Eisenhower wanted an inspector general to comb SOS for able-bodied replacements, and wanted "someone who was tough," according to Summersby.

Eisenhower was shaken and disappointed about the setback at Arnhem. Among other things, a fall campaign meant that his son, John, would join a unit in Europe, something he had not had to face before.

Indeed, for several weeks he and Mamie had been corresponding about John's eventual transfer to Europe. Among other things, Eisenhower had learned that John had suddenly decided to apply for the paratroopers at Fort Benning, and he had tried to discourage him, reminding him about his chronic inner-ear problem. On September 27 Eisenhower notified Mamie that John in his latest letter had finally shown the good sense to drop the idea. In the same note, Eisenhower told Mamie that he frankly hoped John would be assigned to Europe, where "I could at least keep track of him, which would be something," though he hotly denied knowing anything about John's possible transfer to the 71st Division under Brigadier General Willard Wyman, a friend from Fort Lewis days.

Several days later Eisenhower cabled Colonel Charles Gailey, his chief of staff from OPD days, to request that someone at the Pentagon approach John and ask him if he would object to being assigned to a theater commanded by his father. Eisenhower explained to Gailey that this would enable him to keep track of John without his knowledge, "which would mean a lot to me, to say nothing of his mother."

In his directive on the twenty-fifth, Bradley ordered Patton to assume a "holding mission" on the Moselle and to improve Third Army positions for the assault on the Metz fortress. Four days later Haislip's XV Corps transferred to the Seventh Army, which reduced the Third Army from three to two corps. That day Eisenhower informed the CCS that the central and southern groups of armies (DRAGOON) had linked up, forming a continuous Allied front from the North Sea to Switzerland. Despite heavy losses, the enemy had "succeeded in establishing a relatively stable and cohesive front located approximately on the German frontier," and was "taking every possible measure to mitigate his difficult position and there are no signs of collapse in morale or in the will to defend Germany." A day later, SHAEF intelligence circulated a report conceding that despite the hopelessness of the enemy position, the Germans had "fared better than might have been expected," and that in Holland after the initial shock, the Germans had rebounded "with credit" and "may well cherish hopes of a more considerable success."

In heavy fighting that week, at Aachen, Eindhoven and Metz, the shape of the western front changed little. Supposedly, at the point of capitulation in early September, the Germans had successfully fortified the West Wall running from the lower Rhine through the Vosges, the Eifel, the Roer and the Maas, pierced by the First Army at Aachen, where the Germans massed reserves.

Enemy intentions were unclear. Would the Germans maintain the pressure at Nijmegen by drawing on armor currently backing up Aachen? The concentration of armor at Metz and west of the Vosges showed a "steady intention of forming two large armored groups to be used as mobile reserves, one for each army group, while the line is stabilized with infantry alone." The SHAEF report recited the many unsuccessful German attempts to accomplish this since June 6 and discounted success now, but the threat bore watching.

Fall Campaign

I N the wake of MARKET-GARDEN, Eisenhower remained at Versailles for an extended review of the military situation. For the first time since May, he attended daily full-dress staff conferences to deal with the crisis in Holland, to inventory Allied problems elsewhere and to map out strategy for the next few months.

By October the Allied situation was "uneven." With the Second Army in Holland extended along the Nijmegen corridor and attacked on both flanks, Dempsey spoke of a "dismal picture" mirrored in all sectors by shortages of ammunition and petrol. Farther south, Bradley's armies were stalled at the Meuse and the Moselle, well short of the intermediate objectives Eisenhower had spelled out in his September 4 directive. Devers' 6th Army Group had arrived at Dijon in strength, west of the Vosges.

After an operational pause lasting several weeks, the Allies faced a choice of resuming the offensive or staying put for an extended period to rest, refit and await the build-up of American and French forces. The decision involved political and military factors. Opening Antwerp was a high priority. Elsewhere, battle conditions were favorable for attacks to exploit a passing opportunity to drive the reinforcing Germans back from potential staging areas for counterattack. Because of thin German defenses in the Vosges, Devers' forces had a chance to reach the Rhine and establish a strong defensible southern flank. But choosing the sectors to emphasize raised sharp differences of opinion. For instance, Montgomery would oppose any operations south of the Ardennes at the expense of his effort to clear Antwerp and reduce German salients along the Maas in Holland. Montgomery needed First Army support to accomplish these goals simultaneously, but First Army support for Montgomery would weaken Hodges' campaign in the Aachen sector, which would weaken Gerow, which would weaken Patton's efforts to take Metz, and so on down the line.

A new issue overshadowed Eisenhower's early-October conferences: Allied manpower, a problem foreseen and discussed quietly since July. Eisenhower had to consider that assuming the offensive would involve heavy casualties at the very moment he and his commanders faced a slowdown in the flow of trained replacements and new divisions, a halt that would persist for months.

The manpower issue was a sensitive one in Washington and hard to raise. One possible solution would be to call on Alexander's army group for reinforcements, a measure the CCS had considered at Quebec and reserved for future consideration in light of Alexander's progress. But this solution, however tempting, raised political problems. Eisenhower could not recommend it without seeming to go back on understandings with Churchill, who remained set on a Vienna offensive. These and other factors had to be weighed, so no final decision was possible until there was a full canvass of Allied leadership and field commanders.

As the month opened, the Allied high command was on the move. Marshall was due in Versailles for a visit in early October. Churchill and Brooke prepared to journey to Moscow for talks with the Russians on military cooperation and a host of diplomatic problems. As the Red Army rolled on through Rumania and Bulgaria, Churchill hoped to formalize Stalin's backing for a British solution in strife-torn Greece caught between Communist EAM forces and monarchists; he declared that Greek political arrangements could not wait for the American election or the more remote possibility of a Big Three meeting. Nor could arrangements in Poland, and Churchill was determined to confront Stalin personally with Moscow's "gross inhumanity" in refusing to allow an Allied airlift to assist Polish patriots battling Germans in the streets of Warsaw while Soviet troops continued to idle on the Vistula. The Americans were standoffish, "determined," as Brooke put it, to do "nothing that might injure the prospects of an American-Russian working understanding which was his [Roosevelt's] recipe for the future governance of mankind."

Indeed, in October 1944, important Anglo-American political differences persisted. The consensus at Quebec on German occupation policy, atomic-secrets sharing, the Far East, Poland, France and the Balkans seem tentative in retrospect. On the other hand, the conference had been notable insofar as the American and British military staffs had found themselves drawing together on most aspects of military policy, a fact that emerged in Eisenhower's separate talks with Brooke and Marshall at Versailles.

Brooke visited on the fifth. Surprisingly, Brooke was critical of Montgomery's offensive in Holland, and of Montgomery's ongoing refusal to concentrate on Antwerp. This was welcome, but it was also a sign that Montgomery's stock had sunk in London and a hint that Brooke harbored doubts about Montgomery's future usefulness as the senior British officer in northwest Europe. In his diary Brooke described his cordial visit with

Eisenhower at his St.-Germain château and the situation conference held in an ornate office in the Trianon annex. Eisenhower who "ran the conference very well" briefed the group on his three-step strategy: first, opening Antwerp; second, an offensive to clear the Rhine north and south of the Ruhr; third, an eventual advance over the Rhine toward Berlin via the Ruhr or Frankfurt while Devers' 6th Army Group threatened Munich "as a cover plan." On Holland, a conciliatory Eisenhower "nobly took all blame on himself, as he had approved of Montgomery's suggestion to operate on Arnhem." Brooke, in turn, agreed that Monty's Holland strategy was faulty, and that instead of carrying out his advance on Arnhem, "he [Montgomery] ought to have made certain of Antwerp in the first place."

On the sixth, as Brooke left, Marshall arrived accompanied by War Mobilization Director James Byrnes for discussions about Italy and the replacement problem made urgent by the prospect of a fall and winter campaign on the German frontier. In thirty-six hours of conferences, Eisenhower, Marshall and Byrnes deliberated on all aspects of the manpower problem, which was to exert such sway over American thinking in the next few months. On the eve of the elections, the Administration was contending with an increasingly powerful anti–National Service lobby made up of big labor, the National Association of Manufacturers and the National Chamber of Commerce. As usual, the Administration confronted powerful pressure to divert American forces to the Far East, so reinforcements above and beyond current schedules posed political problems, and Marshall would oppose anything that needlessly inflamed the manpower issue—specifically, anything that could call into question the overall ninety-division mobilization ceiling set in June.

And so manpower was a source of potential conflict between Eisenhower and Marshall, which might be summarized as follows: Marshall had global responsibilities but was narrowly accountable to President Roosevelt, whose main concern was maintaining domestic support for the war, support that was waning and likely to diminish further should casualties increase. Winning the war in Europe took precedence over all, but Marshall and the War Department wanted no part of the usual demand by a theater commander for ten divisions more than he needed, especially since a call for divisions would involve Congress and would inevitably bring on a review of manpower policies and war policy in general. On the other hand, Eisenhower's territorial responsibility was narrower but his accountability much broader. His job was to reconcile differences between Roosevelt and the British to maintain balance in Allied councils, and to make room for De Gaulle's France, too. As German reinforcements mounted up, should a need for troops develop, Eisenhower could not be sure that he would not have to turn to the British and French for new divisions, and he was not sure that he could do this without turning to the Americans or guarantee that half-measures, such as accelerated replacements and new regiments not attached to divisions, would be enough. Nor could Eisenhower guarantee Marshall that he would turn to the Italian theater for fresh divisions first before approaching Washington. Finally, with the balancing of diplomatic accounts already under way, and postwar influence to be measured in part by troops deployed and casualties incurred, the British were contemplating fresh call-ups and encouraging the French to follow suit. Eisenhower welcomed it, and he was in no position to rule out making concessions to obtain fresh French and British units for his theater.

A related problem was strategy. Marshall, as yet, had not taken a firm position on Eisenhower's strategy. Presumably, as long as Eisenhower's strategic plans and Marshall's ninety-division mobilization ceiling were in harmony, Eisenhower could assume he had Marshall's backing. On the other hand, should the two come in conflict for any reason, Eisenhower could assume that Marshall would be inclined to question Eisenhower's plans and even the command setup. Confirmation of this was Marshall's attitude of determined optimism that he conveyed to Eisenhower and Bradley throughout his stay in Versailles and on his later tour of Nancy, Metz, Ninth Army Headquarters in Arlon, Eindhoven and XIX Headquarters at Maastricht. Indeed, Marshall intimated to Eisenhower that the JCS was considering an "end the war" directive, which would include authorizing a series of one-time extraordinary steps to "play things to a conclusion": return of the strategic bombers to SHAEF; authorized use of the VT fuze* and other advanced weapons systems; and accelerated dispatch of existing units and replacements to France. Meanwhile, Marshall and Byrnes closely examined the ETO setup. Of the more than 2.7 million Americans in Europe, 437,000 were Air Force personnel and 740,000 were attached to Comm-Z. Slightly more than 50 percent of the remaining 1.233 million were combat soldiers. Hence, SHAEF calls for U.S. divisions would inexorably begin with close scrutiny of SHAEF waste and duplication, of ETO leadership, Allied battle leadership, and so on.

Eisenhower solemnly pledged every expedient to combat waste and duplication, and before Marshall's departure ordered yet another thorough comb-out of Comm-Z to find able-bodied soldiers for the front. Eisenhower decided to offer soldiers under court-martial an opportunity to earn pardons with frontline service, and weighed a proposal to offer blacks serving in segregated service battalions an opportunity to volunteer for the front. Generals Lee and Smith were opposed to such a radical departure in ETO procedures and Eisenhower acquiesced.

The early-October conferences produced consensus on one point. Montgomery's 21st Army Group offensive in Holland, fought over difficult terrain and threatened on both flanks by a well-entrenched enemy, was the kind of luxury the Allies could no longer afford. As things stood, Montgom-

---

*The VT fuze was an artillery homing device used in the closing days of the war.

ery was unable to give full backing for the Canadian drive to clear the approaches to Antwerp. Antwerp would simplify the problem of resupply and reinforcement of ETO. American support was not available, however. Hodges' First Army battled to enlarge the First Army "West Wall bridge-head" at Aachen, which, in threatening Cologne, drew German armor from Patton's sector, which in turn eased pressure on Devers' brand-new 6th Army Group, which readied a drive to the upper Rhine. That week, a touch-and-go battle raged in the mud and rain around Aachen. Corlett's XIX Corps pushed toward Jülich to encircle Aachen from the north while Collins, southeast of Aachen, waged a fierce yard-by-yard battle for the ridges and hills of the Stolberg corridor.

Would Montgomery now relent and direct 21st Army Group energies toward the capture of Antwerp? Throughout Marshall's stay, Montgomery stubbornly held out for the support of American XIX Corps and signaled his reluctance to consolidate in Holland. In his post–MARKET-GARDEN directive, despite assigning the "vital" objective of Antwerp first priority, Montgomery had nonetheless allowed Dempsey to maintain his attacks southwest along the Maas toward Krefeld–Venlo, while the rest of the British Second Army held Nijmegen. The First Canadian Army, engaged at Breskens and South Beveland, received the lowest logistical priority in the 21st Army Group. By October, Holland and Antwerp had assumed symbolic as well as military importance, and Montgomery was reluctant to draw back or in any way concede the futility of his actions there.

During Marshall's tour, Eisenhower and Montgomery fenced vigorously. On the sixth, triggering a round of hot exchanges, Hodges informed Demp-sey that Corlett's XIX Corps, owing to shortages of ammunition and petro-leum, could not assist the British Second Army attack on Krefeld. Mont-gomery promptly advised Eisenhower that the September 22 plan was in jeopardy, and summoned Bradley and Hodges to Brussels for a conference on Holland. That night Montgomery informed Eisenhower that British Second Army operations against the Ruhr were impossible without Ant-werp, as well as a secure bridgehead north of Nijmegen and the west bank of the Maas, and since he lacked the troops to accomplish these intermedi-ate steps simultaneously, he would need fresh U.S. divisions to open Ant-werp. Eisenhower dispatched Tedder to Brussels to get the facts about 21st Army Group logistical support for Crerar's Canadian First Army.

On the eighth Eisenhower sent a message to Bradley, with a copy to Montgomery, in which he observed that 21st Army Group commitments were "too heavy" owing to unforeseen enemy reinforcement in Holland. First, Eisenhower authorized Bradley to use XIX Corps in Hodges' attack at Düren–Aachen. Second, Eisenhower shifted the newly formed Ninth Army Headquarters from Arlon to Maastricht, a step which meant that the Ninth Army would *eventually* be positioned to pass back and forth between Bradley and Montgomery as events dictated.

Montgomery and Bradley sharply disputed Eisenhower's meaning. Bradley interpreted Eisenhower's message as revoking 21st Army Group priority. Montgomery hotly denied any such reading of Eisenhower's message. Ramsay and Tedder returned to Versailles with word that Montgomery had effectively grounded the First Canadian Army and put off scheduled operations for Antwerp until November 1. Eisenhower informed Montgomery of Tedder's report, adding that while he did not presume to know best "where the emphasis lies within your army group," the Allies were "squarely up against the situation . . . anticipated for months," and without Antwerp by mid-November, operations would come to a standstill. Of Montgomery's assigned tasks, Eisenhower rated Antwerp "of the first importance" and urged that the Canadian operations proceed with full 21st Army Group support.

In his reply, Montgomery demanded XIX Corps. Protesting Tedder's "wild statements" concerning his operations "about which he can know nothing, repeat nothing," he claimed the Canadian attacks at Breskens and South Beveland were well supplied and making progress, which he would follow up until Antwerp was open for shipping. By the same token, Montgomery recalled that at the SHAEF conference on the twenty-second it had been "laid down [in the minutes] that the *main* effort of the present phase of operation is the attack against the Ruhr." As he had indicated two days before, the 21st Army Group could not simultaneously (a) sustain the Ruhr offensive, (b) defend the Nijmegen salient, and (c) open Antwerp without getting "stretched."

"I was careful to state in my telegram that I hoped the report was not, repeat not, correct," Eisenhower replied to Montgomery on the tenth. "I am glad that my concern was not, repeat not, justified and regret taking your time for something you already had in hand." Eisenhower offered Tedder to help examine Dempsey's air needs, and indicated that he would do his utmost in "providing you temporarily with extra strength."

Negotiations over XIX Corps resumed. On the twelfth, after Marshall's visit, Montgomery summoned Smith to Brussels and presented him with a memorandum recklessly reviving his August 23 proposal: that Eisenhower be relieved of the day-to-day burden of ground command and be free to sit on his "lofty perch" and coordinate the political, diplomatic, air, sea and ground efforts in the European theater. Evidently Montgomery, for all of Eisenhower's attempts to accommodate him, was coming to the end of his rope, spurred no doubt by Brooke's growing criticism of MARKET-GARDEN and of the state of affairs in Holland generally.

By now General Marshall was aroused. Returning to Versailles after visits to Verdun, Luxembourg, Aachen and Eindhoven, Marshall was more convinced than ever that the German salients in the Vosges and Antwerp had to be eliminated in order to gather reserves and cover gaps between Hodges and Patton. He had listened to Montgomery's litany of complaints and had returned to Versailles impressed by Montgomery's "overwhelming egotism." Marshall extended his return visit by thirty-six hours to lend his support as Eisenhower drafted his reply to Montgomery's wire—the one in which he urged that Eisenhower sit on a lofty perch. It was Marshall's first intervention on a theater matter.

With Marshall at his side, Eisenhower formally rejected Montgomery's August 23 command proposals and related military operations. "The questions you raise are serious ones," he wrote. "However, they do not constitute the real issue at hand. That issue is Antwerp." Eisenhower intimated that both Brooke and Marshall favored a "flat order" to give precedence to the Canadians at Antwerp.

Eisenhower went on to say that he was now willing to provide XIX Corps to aid Crerar at Antwerp, but that this was his limit. As for the command issue, Eisenhower found himself in "emphatic agreement" with Montgomery's concept of a single command being in charge of the ground battle on each battlefront; that is, he favored Montgomery's command over the battle front in Holland, Bradley's command over the battlefront in the Ardennes, and Devers' command over the battlefront south of the Ardennes. "Normandy is history," he continued. No single commander could keep a "battle grip" over a 400-mile front from Switzerland to Holland, but if Montgomery disagreed, then it was his duty to refer the question "to higher authority for any action they may choose to take, however drastic." On a point of nationalism raised in Montgomery's letter, Eisenhower recited instances of his past willingness to place American forces in the 21st Army Group: he had, after all, supported MARKET-GARDEN, given Montgomery liaison powers over Bradley, and he lent XIX Corps now. Despite "inescapable national differences," Eisenhower expected all commands to "meet their military problems sanely, sensibly and logically, and, while not shutting our eyes to the fact that we are two different nations, produce solutions that permit effective cooperation . . . and effective results. Good will and mutual confidence are, of course, mandatory."

Eisenhower's habitual pleasantries were notably brief. "These are my plans, and the reasons therefore stated in the frankest possible way," he closed. "Like all other plans in war, they are subject to modification if unforeseen conditions occur, but I am certain that under them all of us can operate effectively and with full cooperation. . . . Ike."

A day later Montgomery canceled Dempsey's attack on Krefeld and decided to reinforce II Corps to support the Canadian First Army at Breskens and the Bevelands. Finally, on the sixteenth, Montgomery passed to the defensive in Holland, giving Antwerp "unequivocal priority." In informing Eisenhower of this action, Montgomery pledged "one hundred percent" support for Eisenhower's plans and his views on command. Having given his own views and received his answer, Montgomery vowed Eisenhower would "hear no more on the subject from me."

. . .

In the next few days, Eisenhower retraced Marshall's steps from 6th Army Group Headquarters at Vittel to Brussels to inspect the front and confer with Bradley, Simpson, Hodges, Patton and Montgomery. Eisenhower's odyssey began auspiciously on October 14, his fifty-fourth birthday. *Time* magazine profiled the Supreme Commander, reporting that since Normandy "Eisenhower has not visibly aged . . . but he gives a subtle impression of having grown bigger as a man and as a commander. For lack of exercise, he is slightly thicker around the middle and there are often tired lines under his snapping blue eyes. But he is very fit. . . . Even in times of crisis, he is relaxed, genial and confident on the surface—whatever goes on underneath."

October 14 happened to be the day of King George's tour of the U.S. sector. The British monarch joined Eisenhower and the American senior command for luncheon at First Army's tented headquarters near Verviers. Despite the mud surrounding the austere dining hall, spirits were high at the luncheon. While Patton boasted of his exploits in Mexico and Africa, Eisenhower teasingly kept him to versions that were at least somewhat near the truth—to the delight of the group.

When the luncheon concluded, Eisenhower motored with Bradley to his forward headquarters in Luxembourg. As they drove through the city Bradley noted the numerous banners proclaiming the duchy's national slogan: "We wish to remain what we are." The day ended at the Alfa Hotel with a big, gaily decorated birthday cake baked especially for Eisenhower by a chef in Paris.

The situation elsewhere was not so cheerful. Devers was grounded in rain and mud. Walker's XX Corps hammered away at the historic city of Metz, inaugurating the slowest phase of Third Army operations in the war. For a time XX Corps infantry held portions of the Fort Driant stronghold, but after a four-day battle withdrew under German shelling. In private Patton's normal buoyancy faded. In his diary Patton confided that his forces fought three enemies—the Germans, the weather and time. Of the three, Patton rated the weather the worst. As autumn rains drenched the western front, sick rates from trench foot and pneumonia exceeded battle casualties, with no improvement in sight. A long pause was inevitable, but in halting, Patton intended to "rectify the line, thereby maintaining the offensive spirit in the troops so that when we attack, we will not be pacifists."

Bad news continued. On October 17, with the bulk of the defenders safely extricated, electricity out and food gone, the 2,000-man German garrison surrendered the ruins of Aachen. With bomber support curtailed by low clouds, Collins' attempt to push on to Düren and the Roer River failed. Crerar's slow struggle through the inundations at Breskens and the Bevelands fared little better. Montgomery set a November 1 target date for an air-naval-amphibious assault on the outermost garrison at Walcheren Island after a novel attempt by the RAF to "sink" the island by destroying the twenty-foot seawalls.

When would the Germans quit? In eight weeks they had lost territory amounting to three times the size of the Reich proper and had sustained over two million casualties. But the German army, having survived, regrouped behind the system of forts, rivers and mountains. The Organisation Todt hurriedly filled gaps in the West Wall with anti-tank ditches, trenches, weapons installations and mine fields, preparations reminiscent of the Atlantic Wall fortifications. SHAEF intelligence reported that the Germans were drawing reinforcements from Norway and the eastern front to man the West Wall, and conceded "the western front is more stable now than it has ever been and a great deal of hard fighting will be necessary before the hard crust of enemy reistance is overcome." Intelligence reports noted that for the first time in twenty-four months, the Germans were forming a strategic reserve. Aerial reconnaissance detected unusual activity at Düsseldorf, Bonn and Cologne, strangely "lit up" at night, a fact which for several days "baffled" First Army G-2. There were rumors of rebellion and of SS-army armed clashes for control of the Rhineland cities, rumors discounted finally with identification of the Fifth Panzer Army and the vanguard of the newly forming Sixth SS Panzer Army near Cologne.

All commands braced for the impact of drastic new German mobilization measures announced that month. By decree of SS-Chief Heinrich Himmler, the Germans combed industry and drafted the entire able-bodied male population between sixteen and sixty into a newly designated Home Army. On the eighteenth, in a speech commemorating the anniversary of the Battle of Leipzig, Himmler warned the world that the invasion of Germany meant "rivers of blood" and sacrifices "equivalent to national suicide," a theme echoed by Hitler in a proclamation issued that same day calling for "the second great total effort" of Germany.

Hitler's proclamation was significant. After twenty-four months of unremitting reverses, he attempted to bring Germany full circle back to simpler and better times. In particular, he recalled the triumphs of 1939 and 1940, when the Germans, "trusting in our own power," had defeated France and Britain with the belated help of Italy and a passive front in Poland, which implied that vaguely Germany proposed to turn back the clock to Nazi-Soviet-Pact days. Obviously, overt Nazi-Soviet collaboration was out of the question, but with the Russian pause at the Vistula entering its tenth week, with the full Allied hand displayed along the Rhine and the Po, and with Germany's long-range projects bleak if not hopeless, the Germans jeopardized very little by candor.

In Brussels on the eighteenth, Eisenhower, Bradley and Montgomery weighed the situation. The strategic decision confronting the Allies that month was closely balanced. On the one hand, Eisenhower's commanders were reluctant to push an autumn offensive to the limit. Tactical constraints included Allied ammunition shortages, German reinforcements and poor weather conditions, which would curtail air support, swamp side roads, and flood rivers and streams in Holland and the Rhineland. As noted, manpower was a constraining factor. All commanders were under orders to slash service components to the bone for extra troops—including Spaatz, who mobilized 10,000 air force personnel to fill out infantry formations. But the slow arrival of scheduled Allied reinforcements made any strategy risking large casualties hazardous, at least until the Allies could plan in confidence on resumed Soviet activity in Poland. Until then, the temptation was strong to retrench, yield to the strategic air forces on the western front and ride out the threat of counteroffensive.

Weighing against a pause, however, were three arguments. Again, the Allies had been stopped not only short of staging areas for an invasion of Germany but short of defensible positions in many sectors. Dempsey's Second Army would not be secure on either flank until the Germans were driven from bridgeheads over the Maas. North of the Ardennes, Bradley could not sustain an offensive until the First Army cleared the Hürtgen Forest and reached the Roer River line. The thinly held Ardennes sector was vulnerable, Patton's Moselle bridgeheads were insecure, and Devers was short of the Vosges Mountains. Second, offsetting the manpower problem somewhat was the fact that many German units arriving that month had been hastily mobilized and lacked adequate training. While the casualty ratio was ordinarily three to one in favor of the defensive, Bradley, Simpson, Hodges, Patton and Montgomery all agreed that remaining on the attack would inflict double the usual casualties on the Germans, all the while exploiting relative German weakness to draw closer to the West Wall and the Rhine.

Finally, Eisenhower had to weigh the factor of morale. Passing to the defensive was likely to erode combat morale and efficiency. Moreover, experience to date in Africa, Italy and Normandy suggested that an Allied coalition could not long remain on the defensive. Any intimation by Eisenhower now that he considered the German build-up too costly to attack would be the signal to start planning for a German counterattack, and this would breed American unease about the reliability of the British in the north and the French in the south. It would also stimulate British unease about the Americans and the French, and French unease about the Americans and the British. Shaping up was the second great battle of the second front, one fought in less favorable circumstances than the first, to be waged without the benefit of pre-invasion unity along a battle line associated in recent history with a British-French disaster. To step back now would be to accept Hitler's invitation to turn back the clock to 1939–40, and so the Allies would attack.

Thereafter Eisenhower and his advisers turned to planning the offensive. Hard choices were inevitable. The primary objective would be to draw in and commit German armored reserves upon the opening of the port of Antwerp. Because of supply problems and the German Fifteenth Army threat on Dempsey's northern flank, Antwerp remained an urgent priority. Capture of the port would cut shipping turnaround distances by two thirds and provide docking facilities to supply the entire front north of the Ardennes. But as Simond's reinforced Canadian II Corps slowly reduced the Breskens pocket and opened the attack on the Bevelands, it was clear that securing the Scheldt approaches, an operation requiring coordinated air, land and amphibious assault, would engage Dempsey's entire reserve, leaving a weakened force to concentrate on clearing the British left flank on the Maas. Montgomery's seventeen divisions faced an estimated twenty German divisions, including four panzer types, which precluded extensive operations elsewhere until mid-November. Montgomery had now absorbed all available British Empire troops, the Polish divisions and the Canadian Army, and so Eisenhower considered reinforcing the 21st Army Group. Antwerp was bound to fall in time, however, and so Eisenhower decided to concentrate American forces in the Aachen sector, where German armor would be engaged and pinned down.

By mid-October, XIX Corps and VII Corps had breached the West Wall and enveloped the urban maze of Aachen, drawing in elements of the Fifth Panzer backed by the Sixth Panzer Army. In widening the "West Wall bridgehead," the Allies threatened Cologne, and by pressing attacks there stood to prevent German concentration against the more vulnerable Ardennes and Moselle sectors. Before the Aachen bridgehead could be developed as a springboard, however, bitter fighting lay ahead through the densely wooded Hürtgen, where the enemy enjoyed the advantage of good defensive terrain. On the southern edge of the forest the German Seventh Army held five dams at the headwaters of the Roer with the ability to isolate American bridgeheads west of the river by opening the sluices and flooding the Roer Valley.

An autumn offensive meant accepting the "calculated risk" of thinly manning the Ardennes sector and others farther south. Patton's prospects were poor. Until the Third Army controlled Metz, the Germans would block the valley of the Moselle. Patton's right flank faced the strongest sections of the West Wall. As the tour ended, Eisenhower decided to transfer Haislip's XV Corps to the Seventh Army to reinforce Devers' more promising two-prong attack through Saverne and Belfort to the Rhine against the understrength First and Nineteenth armies in the Vosges. Moreover, in pushing the 6th Army Group *now,* Eisenhower hoped to avoid difficulties with the British later, who were prone to question any commitment in the area. Operations in every sector shaped up as a matter of adequate artillery, ammunition and replacements, and close coordination between Allied staffs.

. . .

By the third week of October the American press acknowledged that the Germans had formed a front west of the Rhine, and the Allied victory talk drained away. At Versailles Eisenhower found himself entrenched at headquarters, as he had vowed he would not be.

Years later one of Bedell Smith's deputy chiefs of staff at Versailles, Air Marshal James Robb, would describe the setting. Eisenhower's office was a long narrow room divided halfway along by a partition, not up to ceiling height. On the near side as visitors entered, Captain Kay Summersby sat at her desk. Robb noted that in England before TORCH, then later in North Africa, Summersby had been the general's driver but that she had now been promoted to secretary, a "very responsible post for an English girl to hold." On the opposite side of the room the Supreme Commander worked with his back to a blazing log fire. Eisenhower's desk was close to the fireplace, adorned with pictures of Mamie and the President. Behind his chair was a stand holding three flags: the American, the Union Jack and a flag with the SHAEF crest on a white silk background. "Along the partition is a sideboard, bare except for one or two family photographs and a carafe of water," Robb wrote. "On the desk itself is a large box of cigars open, with a clearly printed notice 'Help yourself' stuck on it. I never saw anyone do so, and although the General does not smoke cigars, I noticed that the numbers left in the box went down steadily each day. The visiting firemen no doubt take the notice at its face value."

In letters home Eisenhower wrote Mamie about the more routine concerns stacked high on his desk after his trip to the front. He sketched his new surroundings at St.-Germain and Versailles, the latest stop on a wartime odyssey that was taking him through the fabled places of Europe. On the eighteenth he described his trip to the front. He admitted that the weather had been chilly, "but I'm comfortable enough, because I can keep dry and wear enough clothes," adding, "anyone in this war, that has the slightest temptation to bemoan his lot or feel sorry for himself should visit the front line soldier!"

On the nineteenth, Eisenhower arrived at the office early in order to squeeze in a letter home before sound technicians arrived to record a broadcast for the victory war bond drive and the British Empire celebration of the Battle of El Alamein. In his note Eisenhower apologized to Mamie for his infrequency in writing in a roundabout way by telling her of his growing problem of keeping up with his personal and official mail. He described hundreds of letters he was receiving from mothers, hospital patients, children, old folks, and the trouble he had finding competent help in answering all of them.

On the twenty-third Eisenhower assured Mamie he had not had a "high time" on his birthday, as reported in the press. He briefly thanked her for the belated birthday candy, toothbrushes and socks, then told her of a telegram that had just arrived announcing the death in action of the son of

Seventh Army Commander General Alexander M. Patch. "God, how wearying and wearing it gets."

As the 1944 elections approached, questions arose in the American press about strategy east of Paris, and the impact of untimely speculation about the Morgenthau Plan and hard-peace schemes, now called "most unfortunate in terms of hastening the end of the European phase of the war." War weariness set in on both sides of the Atlantic.

Behind the scenes, deteriorating Allied-Soviet relations and the elusive problem of military cooperation moved to the top of the Allied agenda as the British delegation returned from Moscow. In Moscow Brooke had chronicled the endless discussions on Yugoslavia, Greece, Rumania, Bulgaria, the Far East and Poland, despairing that all the postwar talk was "neglecting the problem of finishing the war." Military cooperation, the vital point in Brooke's opinion, was apparently among the topics Stalin proposed to reserve for a three-power conference on wider issues to be held that winter somewhere in Russia.

In October the Red Army entered Belgrade and pressed on toward Budapest. But these advances were of secondary importance. Only operations on the Polish front ranked in importance with the western front. In the military discussions, General Alexei Antonov, otherwise forthright, was evasive and noncommittal about the Russian timetable in Poland. The Russians prepared to clear pockets at Riga, and Latvia on the Baltic flank, and expel the Germans from Russian soil in time for the anniversary of the Bolshevik revolution on November 7. But weather uncertainties made forecasting an all-out offensive in Poland impossible. As for Japan, STAVKA was "prepared to discuss plans now."

Undaunted, Churchill offered de facto recognition of pro-Soviet occupational regimes in Rumania and Bulgaria, claimed Greece as a British responsibility, and reserved the Allied position on Hungary and Yugoslavia, technically non-neighboring states and of lesser interest to Stalin. On Poland, Churchill urged Stalin to accept the Curzon Line in lieu of imposing a political settlement there that would imperil Allied-Soviet relations. But Stanislaw Mikolajczyk, the leader of the London Poles, on hand in Moscow for the talks, was not in a position to accept territorial or political compromises on behalf of the London Poles, and so Churchill made little headway. During the conferences, the Germans finally snuffed out Polish Home Army resistance in Warsaw, which further weakened the Allied hand in Poland as well as the British position in Churchill's talks with Stalin about the "sad tangle" in eastern Europe. Mid-course, Roosevelt cabled Stalin a reminder that Churchill spoke on behalf of Great Britain only, and that he himself looked forward to three-way meetings in late November.

Thereafter, Stalin was willing to discuss minor accommodations between London and the Lublin Poles, and seemed in no hurry to recognize the

Lublin Committee as the provisional government of Poland. But since the Russians had sponsored the Lublin Committee, Churchill did not doubt that Soviet recognition of Lublin as a provisional government was a matter of time. The Polish discussions fortified earlier British impressions of Soviet postwar views; the big factor underlying Stalin's position on Poland, as before, was the problem of the occupation of Germany. Churchill and Stalin discussed German partition and the "merits and drawbacks" of the Morgenthau Plan. Nothing was resolved, but Stalin anticipated a lengthy period of military occupation in Germany which could be sustained only through Poland, meaning that firm arrangements there with a friendly Polish government would be necessary to protect Soviet communications and rear lines. Toward the close of the meetings Stalin indicated that the Russian offensive toward Budapest "needed Allied help," and personally endorsed Alexander's latest plan for a ten-division assault on the Adriatic coast. With the 15th Army Group bogged down on the Gothic Line between Bologna and Rimini until February, Stalin's gesture seemed hollow.

At one session, Churchill ventured a deal. He scribbled down a list of Balkan territories and apportioned British and Russian "interest and sentiments" by percentages: Rumania 90–10 Russia; Bulgaria 75–25 Russia; Greece 90–10 Britain; Hungary and Yugoslavia 50–50. Stalin marked the paper with a check. Churchill urged that since some might protest such a "callous" resolution of the Balkan problem, the paper should be burned. Stalin replied, "You keep it."

"Stalin will get what he wants—the Americans have seen to that," Churchill told his physician and confidant Lord Moran afterward. But he was of two minds about the Russians. "Of course," he told Moran, "it is all very one-sided. They [the Russians] get what they want by guile or flattery or force. But they've done a lot to get it. Seven or eight million soldiers killed, perhaps more. If they hadn't we might have pulled through, but we could not have had a foot in Europe. Besides, I want nothing except Stalin's friendship. . . . When this fellow goes you don't know what will happen. There will be a lot of trouble."

Moran noted that seemingly Russia would have things all her way in Europe after the war. "Oh, I don't think so," Churchill replied.

The Moscow conference brought the diplomatic and military problem of De Gaulle to the fore. In the near future the Soviets would resolve the political situation in Poland, which meant that further delay in France could only erode De Gaulle's hold on the Allied position. By October, instability stalked France. The trials of Vichy collaborators had opened and De Gaulle was contending with intense left-wing political activity, including acts of violence. Severe shortages of coal, gasoline and other raw materials hampered industrial recovery, causing widespread disillusion aimed at Allied military and civilian authority.

While Churchill was meeting with Stalin, Eisenhower's negotiators were hard at work on the terms of full U.S. backing consistent with Roosevelt's insistence that the French people be given unqualified freedom of choice at the end of the war. Eisenhower particularly urged De Gaulle's help in mobilizing the FFI and conscripts into regular units to help alleviate the Allied reinforcement problem, which he knew would be a big mark in De Gaulle's favor in Washington.

De Gaulle was troublesome to the end, however, and attached his usual conditions: a French seat on the EAC (European Advisory Commission), Lend-Lease, a French occupation zone, and assurances that France would gain the Saar and Westphalia. Eisenhower once again found himself in the middle between the French and Marshall and Roosevelt, who were evaluating Eisenhower's ability to handle De Gaulle without compromising American political and military interests.

On the seventeenth, on a British motion, the CCS solicited Eisenhower's views on conditions in France and on the military pros and cons of expanding the zone of the interior under De Gaulle's administration. On the twentieth Eisenhower conferred with Ambassador Jefferson Caffery, recently designated representative to the de facto French authority, who sent a recommendation back to Washington that day on the problem of recognition. In it, Caffery reported that, in Eisenhower's opinion, the "forces of disorder" threatened Allied rear lines of communication. Second, Eisenhower had observed that the Allies would avert much criticism that winter if French authorities were made responsible for distributing food and fuel supplies and for preventing strikes in essential industries. For instance, Allied coal deliveries would be 33 percent of what German deliveries had been. Third, both believed that it was not in the interest of Great Britain or the United States that "a single power dominate the European continent." On the twenty-third the State Department endorsed these views and Eisenhower and Caffery signed a new, more detailed civil affairs agreement with De Gaulle which expanded the zone of the interior and recognized the FCNL as the provisional government of France.

Signs of doubt in Washington mounted. Shortly after Marshall's return from France, the JCS stunned the British representatives in the CCS with a comprehensive proposal asking "whether or not we should conduct the war in France during the next two and one half months on the basis of playing everything to a conclusion." The Americans followed up with the "end the war directive" Marshall had spoken of that would include authority to use the supersecret VT, or proximity, fuze, accelerated shipment of twelve American regiments not incorporated into divisions, new ammunition priorities, and, finally, revision of the month-old Quebec POINTBLANK decision providing for the return of the strategic bombers to Eisenhower's control for attacks to isolate the Ruhr and to provide direct support of Bradley's Aachen offensive.

The motion came as a slight surprise to Eisenhower and Bradley, who had both been confident that Marshall, having witnessed conditions at Metz, Aachen, and in Holland, understood that a victory within two and a half months was impossible. Presidential politics seemed involved when news arrived a day later of a Roosevelt campaign speech in Philadelphia, in which while promising harsh terms for Germany, he all but backed away from the Morgenthau Plan.

On the eve of the elections, Roosevelt and Marshall seemed anxious to present Congress with the prospect of success. On his visit to Versailles, Marshall had made it plain that new U.S. divisions for ETO were out of the question, and so it appeared that Marshall was determined to discourage SHAEF mobilization requests, whether prompted by battlefield losses or by coalition politics. The "end of the war" directive was formal notice in effect to Eisenhower that he had a heavy burden of proof to justify requests for additional divisions and reinforcements.

British rejection was quick. In the CCS, Dill cautioned that without control of Antwerp, restocked ammunition, fresh U.S. divisions and other preparations, a premature end-the-war offensive would extend hostilities "well into 1945," as if whatever the Americans wanted, the British wanted the opposite. In the brief POINTBLANK debate, a similar turnaround was evident. On behalf of Spaatz's oil plan, Tedder, the architect of the transport plan in Normandy, opposed Marshall's proposal for concentrating the air effort on the Ruhr and the battle areas, cautioning against literal applications of the lessons of France and Belgium to frontline conditions in Germany. Eisenhower informed Marshall that air operations in direct tactical support on the battle line would be curtailed by weather and that he considered "hammering constantly at the enemy's oil" a better alternative. The motion died.

The POINTBLANK argument was more symbolic than real and did not last long. The oil offensive under way since June would continue, as would "area" attacks and attacks and close support of land operations, all of which could be waged simultaneously because of the location of the Allied front lines. Portal strongly urged that concentration on targets "behind" the front would be more likely to shorten the war than waging all-out support strikes for the land battle, but the two objectives were not inconsistent. For instance, Operation QUEEN, an all-out aerial blitz planned in support of Bradley's Roer offensive would occur within range of targets that were key communications links between the Ruhr and the rest of Germany. Accordingly, as 1,000 bomber raids commenced on Duisburg, Bonn, Kassel, Mainz, Mannheim and Stuttgart, the Eighth and Ninth air forces flew record numbers of air-ground sorties in support of the First and Ninth armies' push in the Aachen sector.

But with operations at a standstill in all sectors, and a long hard battle for Antwerp likely, Eisenhower wanted no illusions about the fall offensive.

On October 23, Eisenhower attempted to bring the CCS debate to a quick close. In a message to Marshall, Eisenhower conceded the possibility that fresh infantry replacements might "produce the desired break and . . . wind up the war more quickly." He wanted infantry replacements, but he was hesitant to accept Marshall's offer of the regiments because he was looking to a time when circumstances permitted shipment and utilization of *"complete* divisions available." In the same message, Eisenhower declined unlimited Eighth Air Force air-ground support, and in a message to Arnold later that day declined Arnold's offer to transfer the Twelfth Air Force from Italy to France, assuring him that "in this field at least [air] things are going very positively at present."

Meanwhile, Eisenhower corresponded with General Wilson on the subject of prospects in Italy. Wilson had written to describe conditions in Italy and to tell Eisenhower that frankly he doubted Italy could contribute materially to Allied progress in the next several months. At the time, Churchill was still attempting to reinforce Italy with three divisions, but now even Churchill's staff planners opposed the idea and leaned to the idea that "Italy must now adapt to the steadily increasing needs of OVERLORD." Indeed, there was talk in London of withdrawing the U.S. Fifth Army and several British divisions from Wilson to form a strategic reserve in Holland. In any event, Wilson told Eisenhower he suspected that a Russian offensive in the Balkans would have a bigger bearing on Kesselring's actions than Alexander's operations. In passing, Wilson noted that the Russian offensive toward Belgrade and Budapest was making "good progress" against "soft stuff," and he wondered about Poland and "how they will tackle solid resistance when deprived of the assistance of the resistance."

"I share your curiosity about the Russian purpose," Eisenhower noted in his reply. "When he [the Russians] launches a full-out attack in his center it could be most encouraging to see a real advance along the Warsaw route. I hope he gets something big started very soon."

About then, Eisenhower received Butcher for a visit. Having just concluded a tour of PRD facilities, Butcher gave Eisenhower a firsthand impression of the American field staffs. He noted that amid the grand surroundings at the Trianon in Versailles and the melancholy trappings of the villa at St.-Germain, Eisenhower seemed tense, still on the mend from his knee injury and shaken by his recent tour of the front. Butcher told Eisenhower about a witticism, attributed to Patton, and circulating in the American command, calling Eisenhower "the best general the British have." Butcher had seen Patton recently, who denied the "best British general business." Indeed, Patton had told him that he personally was convinced that Eisenhower had chosen the "correct strategy" in September. But Patton did not deny that his staff or certain other American commanders felt that Montgomery's failure at Arnhem had tied up airborne troops that might have gotten Metz and Antwerp, and the Americans to the Rhine.

Butcher also told Eisenhower of his talk with Congresswoman Edith Rogers during her recent tour of hospitals in the Paris area. Rogers had mentioned press rumors at home to the effect that Churchill had talked Eisenhower into Holland to delay a major victory until the eve of the elections.

Eisenhower was unconcerned about Patton. Strong partisanship, at least at the Army level, was a healthy sign. He assured Butcher the Holland rumors were false. Intimating details of his recent exchanges with Washington, Eisenhower also told Butcher that operations were entering a "static" phase at least until the build-up was complete. Not widely known was the fact that despite German casualties since June, the Germans now outnumbered Allied combat troops, with the margin growing. Eisenhower recalled Tunisia in December 1942, when a similar offensive had outrun supply lines short of "decisive" objectives and forced a pause to absorb the German response. If the Tunisia parallel held, a round of diplomatic conferences similar to Casablanca would occur under the cloud of a major German counterattack.

Butcher, now a communications specialist, mentioned the elaborate press facilities at Spa, Belgium. "That is a sector where the Germans might easily counterattack," Eisenhower cautioned. "You might find your transmitters in German hands." He told Butcher that he had decided to hold the Ardennes lightly, and that the Germans could "swing a push through that sector if they chose."

Eisenhower told Butcher a cheerful story. Quietly in late September, he had sent 3,000 reinforcements to Italy and received a thank-you from their mutual friend Field Marshal Alexander. "War is such a dirty business and costs everyone so much, that occasionally I find relief in the incidental bright spots in the dreary picture," Eisenhower said.

Meanwhile, Eisenhower was at work on the late-October offensive with Ramsay, Spaatz, Kirk, Tedder and Smith. All agreed now that constant pressure in all sectors would wear down German strength, whereas by waiting, the balance would gradually tip against the offensive. All but Montgomery favored operations in every sector. Bradley "greatly desired to attack in the 3rd Army [Patton's] sector," pointing out that German defenses south of the Ardennes were less developed and that the Rhine was an attainable objective there. British opposition was intense, and so Eisenhower assigned priority for the First and Ninth armies' effort on Krefeld–Cologne–Bonn on the British right flank, through the Hürtgen Forest, confining Patton to attacks on Metz "when logistics permitted."

On the twenty-eighth, rejecting Montgomery's latest plea for a "left hook" against the Ruhr, Eisenhower promulgated his long-awaited "three phase" directive. Phase one was to be the battle west of the Rhine, closing the river and "taking advantage of any opportunity to seize bridgeheads."

Montgomery, after opening Antwerp, would swing from Nijmegen south-east to support Hodges' left wing as the First Army advanced from Aachen to Cologne. Secondary attacks south of the Ardennes were to draw strength from Aachen, clear the Rhine south of Cologne, push the Germans out of Alsace, occupy the Saar, and gain Rhine bridgeheads for a thrust through Frankfurt.

In phase two, Allied operations would aim at "the capture of bridgeheads over the Rhine and the deployment of our forces on the east bank" with the main effort on the Ruhr with a subsidiary American effort. Montgomery would decide the "extent of operations necessary to clear western Holland . . . based on military factors and not upon political considerations," while Bradley deployed forces over the Rhine in strength. Eisenhower called phase three "the advance from the Rhine," without elaboration.

Eisenhower thus shed all but the pretense of priority for Montgomery. In the first phases, Bradley and Montgomery were to operate "in conjunction," but Montgomery's coordinating powers were gone, and Eisenhower returned the 1st Airborne Army to Bradley. For the phase-two "main effort" north of the Ardennes, Eisenhower set no specific objectives, and by indicating his dissatisfaction with Holland, implied that Montgomery would remain in a supporting role. On phase-three objectives, he left a complete blank, which sidestepped the problems of Army troop objectives, Berlin and other divisive questions.

Eisenhower's October 28 directive aroused Whitehall. Brooke privately complained that the planned offensive lacked any prospect of getting farther than the Rhine, and that Eisenhower had adopted a strategy of attrition. Brooke's diary contains evidence that discussions had begun concerning a British command shift: Wilson to Washington to replace the ailing Field Marshal Dill, Field Marshal Alexander to step up and replace Wilson with Clark stepping up to replace Alexander, with perhaps Alexander, a known favorite of the Supreme Commander's, going to Paris as Eisenhower's land commander or deputy. Such a step would position a British Command officer between Eisenhower and the Army troops, but eliminate the factor of Montgomery's personality and possibly satisfy American objections about formal designation of a Ground C-in-C. There was talk of trench warfare, heavy casualties, hints of a potential repetition of 1940 brought on by Eisenhower's refusal to halt Patton and concentrate the 12th Army Group north of the Rhine. But there were no formal protests. Apparently Brooke saw no point in further discussion until events had their say and the CCS could evaluate the success of Eisenhower's offensive.

As the wait resumed. Eisenhower caught up on routine matters. He reviewed disciplinary cases, promotion lists, consulted Robert Murphy on the French occupation, and approved antifraternization regulations effective in the Aachen zone. By late October, Eisenhower again played host to a parade of visitors from Washington and London who arrived with news of Quebec, the Morgenthau controversy, the Dumbarton Oaks Conference,* word of Roosevelt's failing health, and the elections.

Gerow returned from Washington, where he had appeared before the Roberts Commission still investigating Pearl Harbor, with a pessimistic appraisal of the replacement situation. Basil O'Connor, president of the Red Cross, and Anne McCormick, columnist for the *New York Times,* came for an interview. General Joseph McNarney visited to discuss replacements, as did General Lucius Clay, who passed through Versailles on his way back to Washington to resume service under Mobilization Director James Byrnes after several months as administrator of the Normandy base.

Clay was an old friend, an associate from Manila days. Trim at forty-seven years with jet-black hair, Clay had emerged with a reputation as one of the Army's top administrators during his service as Somervell's director of material, a skill attributable in part to his knowledge about politics. His father, Alexander H. Clay, had been a senator from Georgia for fourteen years. His wartime assignment with Somervell had acquainted him with Congress, and his Washington savvy destined that he would be Eisenhower's political counselor in two national political campaigns.

In Army circles, among the liveliest topics of speculation was postwar occupation policy, which remained the subject of an intense Cabinet-level quarrel pitting Stimson and Marshall versus Morgenthau over what policy should be and who should carry it out. In short, the War Department opposed a long period of military rule in the occupational period, arguing that the Army was not equipped to perform the essentially civilian function of postwar reconstruction. No matter what the outcome, however, technical factors pointed to a long period of military rule. First, there was the problem of establishing order. Second, the President, acting as Commander in Chief, could do what he had to do in the early stages of the occupation without involving Congress and civilian agencies. Certain problems were more suitable for military administration, such as denazification and nonfraternization, which would entail a thorough canvass and rooting out of the German leadership. Inevitably, whichever course Washington took would have to consider the Soviet demand for a harsh policy of reparations, including the handover of Russian nationals and German veterans of the eastern-front units designated for slave labor to rebuild the shattered Russian economy. Again, civilian and political agencies were not equipped to perform these essentially military functions. All signs pointed to the likelihood that Eisenhower would serve as military governor for several months, maybe longer, and that the job of military governor would embroil Eisenhower in political controversy sooner or later.

---

*Dumbarton Oaks was the international conference in Washington called to work out postwar currency problems.

In October the journalist Drew Pearson had broken the details of the Stimson-Morgenthau clash over the treatment of Germany. A wide spectrum of conservative and liberal opinion variously criticized the Morgenthau Plan on grounds that the policy would induce the Germans to resist to the bitter end, and that as a matter of fundamental decency and good sense, America should not participate in a policy of wanton destruction of German industry and livelihood. The financier Bernard Baruch, citing the tragic effects of the Versailles Treaty, announced that he would oppose draconian reparations, and joined a growing number of politicians questioning the moral implications of a Carthaginian peace and terrorizing the German people.

Behind the scenes, Morgenthau had steadily lost ground in his clash with Stimson and Marshall. Proposals for internationalization of the Ruhr and converting Germany into a "pastoral state" still had emotional appeal, but it was doubtful that a hard peace would remain popular for long. The President wavered, and Churchill's baffling views in favor of the Morgenthau Plan were not taken seriously. McCloy and Stimson were ascendant, in favor of a transitional period of military government for Germany, rehabilitation of German industry to ensure the flow of reparations and, above all, closer Pentagon–State Department liaison to infuse "greater realism in postwar thinking," a theme echoed by Forrestal and Harriman, who by now was urging a complete reassessment of Russian policy. Back in Washington for the elections and consultations after Churchill's visit to Moscow, Harriman had warned the Cabinet that the Russians were "under the impression we have given them the green light to settle things in their neighborhood as they wished," that the Soviet definition of friendliness was "hand-picked governments to ensure domination on grounds of security," and that Moscow's attitude was hardening into arrogance and a go-it-alone position in the belief that "she [Russia] has won the war for us." In this climate, there were second thoughts about accommodating each and every Russian demand in Germany, even in the early phases of an occupation.

But the Allies—specifically the Americans—could move only so fast even with sensible adjustments to occupation planning, such as it was. The German problem was complex. It involved such questions as the balance of power in Europe, the postwar European economy, and striking an appropriate balance between a punitive policy and reconciliation. Above all, the problem of what to do in Germany was a European concern, primarily a matter of what the British, the French, but particularly the Russians would tolerate in the rebuilding of Germany. Reconstructing the German economy had to be weighed against European concerns about a German revival, and good sense held that reconciliation toward Germany was a matter to be decided by Germany's victims, not the victors. Moreover, in October 1944 a "hard peace" policy was still the thread linking the Allies and the Soviets. Even sensible discussion of alternatives carried with it the danger of eroding political and still critical military cooperation, and even inter-Allied cooperation might be jeopardized by an American initiative calling for a more practical approach.

Indeed, at least as things were seen in Europe, a realistic American policy on Germany seemed to be beside the point. Few, including Churchill, doubted that American policy would be realistic eventually or that the Americans were committed in Europe, where they were needed, especially with Republicans as well as Democrats now advocating involvement in Europe. The question therefore was not whether but how: how much latitude the Americans, whose help was indispensable, would leave to those closest to the scene. In retrospect, Churchill's surprising approval of the Morgenthau Plan at Quebec was meaningful as a polite but unmistakable reminder that the British would resist changes in American policy toward Germany that they did not initiate, for no one could accuse Churchill of not being sensible on Germany.

In any event, all was in limbo. By October 1944 SHAEF was already involved in such matters as reconstruction planning and denazification in conquered zones. A CCS directive issued September 17, 1944, reflected high-level indecision. Paragraph 3 read: "Pending the receipt of directives containing long-range policies, your objectives must be of short term and military character, in order not to prejudice whatever ultimate policies may be later determined upon."

Appendix C of the directive had tentatively sketched out economic policy. Eisenhower was directed only to "assume such control of existing German industrial, agricultural, utility, communication and transportation facilities" as necessary to end war production, to assure the maintenance of a central supply to prevent starvation, to quell sabotage and to create stable conditions to permit the rapid redeployment of troops to Japan. Even the question of returning art looted by the Nazis was deferred. Anticipating Russian demands for reparations, the CCS had directed Eisenhower to "make a survey to determine the extent to which local productive capacity and local supplies are or can be made available for export for relief and rehabilitation in the devastated areas of Europe." The Americans and British debated whether to wield reparations and economic aid as a tool in negotiations with the Russians, but no one as yet doubted that Moscow in the end would demand and receive a heavy bounty from all zones.

The European Advisory Commission's recommendations for occupational zones were soon to be adopted, but the EAC proposal for a policy of "coordinated administration" under a central control commission consisting of the Russian, British and American commanders located in Berlin was less certain. SHAEF, meanwhile, assumed all judicial, executive and legislative powers in the occupied sector of Germany, which was to be treated "as a defeated enemy nation." According to the directive:

The clear fact of German military defeat in the inevitable consequences of aggression must be appreciated by all levels of the German population. The German people must be made to understand that all necessary steps will be taken to guarantee against a third attempt by them to conquer the world.

The CCS, in an updated directive issued in October specified the provisions: the occupation authority would arrest all General Staff Corps officers when found. A new economic directive required Eisenhower not to take "steps towards the economic rehabilitation of Germany," a somewhat academic order, since the anticipated conditions in Germany included anything but a rapid, early recovery.

Hinting at Eisenhower's eventual appointment as military governor, Assistant Secretary of War John J. McCloy wrote the Supreme Commander on October 25:

In the course of the public discussions of the subject all appreciation of the hard work and thinking which had already been done in connection with the administration of Germany was lost. Many people came forward with "plans" who were utterly innocent of any realization of the extent and complexity of the problem. One "Plan" which was rather rapidly produced was the so-called "Morgenthau Plan." There were certain aspects of this to which the Secretary of War objected in his capacity as a member of the Cabinet Committee appointed to give general guidance on the subject. Inevitably, the press and others oversimplified the issue as to "hard" and "soft" schools and immediately there is speculation as to who would be the High Commissioner and whether he would be of one school or another. Mr. Morgenthau had his candidates and others had theirs.

Once again, the debate on the Morgenthau Plan would be among the earliest U.S. political controversies to involve Eisenhower. General Lucius Clay, as Eisenhower's deputy and then successor in Germany, would also be deeply involved in the question of German rehabilitation, and perhaps because of the sensitivity of this issue would become Eisenhower's indispensable political counselor in the late forties and in the early years of the Eisenhower Administration. And as the 1944 elections approached, Eisenhower sensed the eventual pressures that would build on him to remain at the center of events after the war and to become active in politics.

By late October Governor Thomas E. Dewey, the Republican candidate, had broadened his attacks on New Deal "defeatism" to encompass pro-Communism. Throughout 1944 the Republicans had claimed the anti-Communism issue and had carefully built up a long-range foreign policy position on it, notice that the long-postponed referendum on American intervention in Europe, still on hold pending a German collapse, would soon occur in some form. Dewey attacked the "indispensable man" theme, neglect of MacArthur, the CIO-Communist influence on Roosevelt, and the effectiveness of war policy and diplomacy conducted in secret. Polls indicated a close contest, evidence that despite the outward consensus achieved after Pearl Harbor, the war had changed attitudes less than one might have expected. The odds favored the President and his reassuring themes of sustaining New Deal reforms and of avoiding the errors of World War I by ensuring a secure-peace settlement before the armistice. But enthusiasm for the President was muted, and the response to Dewey, as Sherwood wrote, was a sign that "it [the war] was to be the first in American history in which the general disillusionment preceded the firing of the last shot."

Eisenhower's letters home were studded with comments about the presidential campaign. He was grateful not to be involved. He had been surprised by MacArthur's foolishness in having permitted his name to be used by the Republicans before Dewey's nomination. Though the MacArthur boomlet had faded, removing "Europe first" as a campaign issue, several books that fall documented MacArthur's case for Asia, which identified MacArthur as a man to watch, and, by implication, Eisenhower as the counterpoint.

For the first time Eisenhower, Republican-born, a non-voter by Army tradition, favored Roosevelt. His name had briefly surfaced in political circles in late 1943 as a potential running mate for Roosevelt in the event MacArthur won the Republican nomination. Eisenhower's views and background seemed conventional enough, though he qualified as "a political unknown." To politicians, journalists and friends passing through Paris who sounded him out about his views, he revealed a rural-Kansas, conservative, anti–New Deal bias, but one not deeply held. His experiences in the peacetime Army and in Washington in the thirties reflected another dimension; privately, Eisenhower had supported the New Deal until 1938, and had praised Roosevelt as "a great war leader."

Eisenhower's stature was growing. Visitors brought news of the good impression his low-key manner made on the American public. Butcher described a visit in July by General Alexander Surles, chief of Army Public Relations, who discussed with Eisenhower the negative reaction to MacArthur's meddling. Surles congratulated him for the modest and dignified balance he struck in his own publicity. "Don't let anyone change you," Surles remarked, intimating that Eisenhower and Marshall stood "one-two" in popular esteem.

After MARKET-GARDEN, Surles had written to say that despite the setback, Eisenhower's stature was "higher than ever." Eisenhower's prominence would be measured tangibly by the curiosity of the press and the myriad requests for appearances and endorsements by civic groups, foundations, politicians and journalists, all of which Eisenhower kept at arm's length.

Years later Butcher could recall only one fleeting political discussion with Eisenhower during the war. Once in Algiers, when the subject came up, Butcher mentioned to Eisenhower that his short nickname was "ideal for headlines," and had reminded him that victorious foreign wars produced a "desire for generals in the White House." Eisenhower agreed, but he admonished Butcher never to raise the subject again or to discuss it with anyone, perhaps mindful that potential political power might be an asset in drawing attention to the needs of his theater, and that, as MacArthur was proving every day, any overt attempt to wield political influence was self-defeating.

Butcher's public relations sense was good, but the historical parallels he suggested were imprecise. In the nineteenth century, soldier-aristocrats had gone on to the presidency after winning heroic reputations for part-time service in border wars. And, of course, there was Grant. World War I, a different kind of war, had produced no more than a brief boomlet for Pershing, something Eisenhower remembered well because of the year he spent on Pershing's staff in Washington. Grant had been the only career military officer to become President, a man thrust forward by the special circumstances of political and social breakdown occasioned by the Civil War. In any case, Eisenhower opposed the idea of military men in politics even in extraordinary times, and if a General-President was inevitable, Eisenhower did not want to be the man responsible for setting a precedent, a feeling reinforced by wartime associates Hopkins and Harriman and later by Senator Robert Taft, who devoted his postwar senatorial career to alerting the republic to the corrupting effect of war on a democracy and the dangers of militarism.

But as Butcher had indicated, speculation was inevitable, and it con-tinued to crop up in his diary as well as in Patton's diary, in which Patton measured his old friend Eisenhower from afar as a potential politician. Patton's views were based on what he saw in Eisenhower's contacts with soldiers and small groups. But no portrait of Eisenhower as a politician or as a man with political views emerged in these accounts.

What *were* Eisenhower's political views? No figure except Marshall and the President was as firmly identified with "Europe first," and yet beyond this there was a mystery about Eisenhower that would persist even as political groups became active on his behalf after the war and journalists delved into his past for clues.

But the clues would not reveal a consistent picture of Eisenhower. His politics have been described as "standard American," yet his politics took shape in a foreign war. Edward R. Murrow had called Eisenhower the "personification of the American middle class," and yet Eisenhower was a career soldier and his boyhood had been spent in purposeful poverty. The many contrasting interpretations of Eisenhower were a symptom of Eisen-hower's pragmatic bent and absence of systematic views on politics except on Europe, and even here there was irony. It was ironic, for example, that Eisenhower, who for eight years had served MacArthur as a staff assistant, four of which were spent in Manila, found himself running the European theater and cast as MacArthur's counterpart. There were other ironies as well: that Eisenhower, a youth from isolationist rural Kansas, would rise to prominence as an "internationalist" in the services of a reform President who sponsored the beginnings of a welfare state, which was anathema to rural America. It was also ironic that Eisenhower, the son of German-speaking parents, would emerge as a historic leader of a holy war against Germany. Eisenhower's preferences remained typical of a small-town Kansan who prized thrift, individualism, hard work and achievement, but his positive outlook was tempered somewhat by the memory of the hardships that had overtaken the Eisenhower family, and an eccentric distrust of lawyers inherited from his mother, Ida.

Only after his death would the veil lift on Eisenhower's days in the peacetime Army. Mamie's regular correspondence with her mother, "Min" Doud, survive, as do a handful of Eisenhower's letters to his father-in-law and a few diaries that Eisenhower had kept in the thirties. In them, a sketchy picture emerges of Eisenhower as a man who moved with the times and adapted readily to the conventional, if unsystematic, views of the Depression-era Army. Eisenhower shared a widespread skepticism toward all politicians, combined with a discreet interest in politics, an isolationist preference in foreign policy, admiration for national planning and the firm recovery measures implemented by the first Roosevelt Administration. Indeed, shortly after the 1933 inaugural, Eisenhower had declared his full approval of the President's "100 days" in his diary jottings, pronouncing himself ready to follow where the President would lead. Major Eisenhower had applauded the isolationist tack of the early Roosevelt Administration during the Depression-era international trade wars, noting once that "the best way to get out of trouble is to deal within ourselves—adjust our own production to our own consumption—and cease worrying about foreign markets except those necessary to pay for essential imports . . . shut others out and proceed scientifically to adjust economic activity within our own country so as to enhance the general standard of living to the greatest extent possible."

In his day, Eisenhower became a defender of Roosevelt's centralizing measures, which he felt would inspire confidence and insulate national recovery from special-interest groups and "the pernicious influence of jealousy." As the Depression wore on, Major Eisenhower found himself skeptical of both business and labor, and toyed with the idea of "temporary socialization of the country" administered through a "supreme centralized authority" as the "coldly efficient way to recovery." But Eisenhower was also skeptical of a national welfare system, an attitude that reflected MacArthur's view as well and became more persistent as the New Deal launched welfare and pro-labor reform measures. Eisenhower shared the doubts of his contemporaries about the chances of democracy in the United States or anywhere else, which he felt depended on bringing a measurable prosperity to the great majority of people living within the system. Eisenhower compared the political implications of the American Depression with the "terrible systems in vogue" in Italy, Turkey, Germany and Poland. Like many of his Army contemporaries, he found himself mildly admiring Mussolini's successes in reviving Italy, as distinguished from the frantic posturing of Hitler's Germany.

For Eisenhower, as for many other Americans, Hitler's Germany had been the special case that finally dispelled the Depression-era inwardness in the American attitude. Many were reluctant at first to take Nazi bombast seriously, and Hitler seemed to be a comical figure. And yet early on, Germany in the grip of the Nazis appeared to be launched on a course of no return, a realization that dawned with the German reoccupation of the Rhineland, the promulgation of the Nuremberg Laws, the frantic pressure on Austria leading to the *Anschluss,* the constant pressure on Poland, France and Czechoslovakia which seemed partly explainable in terms of recent history but strangely modern and sinister as well, especially as German success led to success, and the peoples of Europe began looking for a way out of war.

Debates over the significance of the emerging German nightmare had occurred in places as far away as Manila. By 1938, as he found himself gradually falling out with MacArthur, Eisenhower had been restless for a change. It is perhaps significant that Eisenhower was in Washington on official business in September 1938 during the crisis days of Munich, which exposed the demoralization of France and England. Munich came as a deep shock for many, including Eisenhower. On returning to Manila, upon learning that he was finished as a member of MacArthur's staff, Eisenhower had resumed his diary and speculated on the meaning of events in Europe. He had revived old acquaintances in Washington in hopes of getting a transfer to field duty, and he corresponded with "Gee" Gerow, Mark Wayne Clark, Haislip and Patton. Much of this correspondence has survived and records the ruminations of these officers on the strategies and techniques to be deployed in the coming war, a war that had become inevitable when Germany scorned the Munich accords and absorbed the whole of Czechoslovakia in the spring of 1939.

Then, as Hitler grabbed more and more territory while the great powers looked on, Eisenhower began to grasp the dimensions of the disaster about to engulf Europe and became convinced that Americans could not avoid the war to purge Europe of the Nazi terror. According to his son, John, Eisenhower had sensed early on that his proficiency as an officer would give him a prominent role in the second American Expeditionary Force. Perhaps Eisenhower had sensed as well that the nightmare in Europe would absorb him and his generation for the rest of their lives. Having missed service in the Great War, the prospect of war in Europe vindicated long years of service and Fox Conner's advice years before in Panama that the Great War had only ended in an armed truce. But it was apparent that the second AEF, unlike the first, would be marching off not to France and glory but to lend American weight to salvaging a continent bent on self-destruction. Then, on September 3, 1939, in the wake of Hitler's attack on Poland, England and France declared war and the struggle began.

"This evening we have been listening to broadcasts of Chamberlain's speech stating that Great Britain was at war with Germany," Eisenhower wrote that night. "After months and months of feverish effort to appease and placate the madman that is governing Germany the British and French seem to be driven into a corner out of which they can work their way only by fighting. It's a sad day for Europe and for the whole civilized world— though for a long time it has seemed ridiculous to refer to the world as civilized."

> If the war, which now seems to be upon us, is as long drawn out and disastrous, as bloody and as costly as the so-called World War, then I believe that the remnants of nations emerging from it will be scarcely recognizable as the ones that entered it. Communism and anarchy are apt to spread rapidly, while crime and disorder, loss of personal liberties, and abject poverty will curse the areas that witness any amount of fighting. It doesn't seem possible that people that proudly refer to themselves as intelligent could let the situation come about. Hundreds of millions will suffer privations and starvation, millions will be killed and wounded, because one man so wills it. He is a power-drunk egocentric, but even so he would still not do this if he were sane. He is one of the criminally insane, but unfortunately he is the absolute ruler of 89,000,000 people. And by his personal magnetism, which he must have, he has converted a large proportion of those millions to his insane schemes and to blind acceptance of his leadership. Unless he is successful in overcoming the whole world by brute force the final result will be that Germany will have to be dismembered and destroyed.

By late October 1944 the weather was relentlessly pro-German. Eisenhower told Butcher that he "hoped and prayed there would be a short spell of good weather to bring relief from mud, rain and snow, so tanks and infantry could take the offensive and be aided by our great superiority of air power," but it was not to be. Rains swept Holland. Six inches of fresh snow covered the Ardennes.

From Antwerp to the Swiss frontier, the fighting was slow. The infantry measured gains in yards. No one was especially surprised, but no one except Devers had expected to reach the Rhine. The bitter German defense spurred Eisenhower, in private, to vow in frustration that he would "make the German wish that he had gone completely back to the Rhine at the end of his harried retreat across France," a vow that became more defiant as the weeks wore on.

In the north, the battle of Antwerp raged. Breskens fell on October 26. For six days the 2nd Canadian Division, joined by the British 52nd, fought through the fixed fortifications of South Beveland, preliminary to the large-

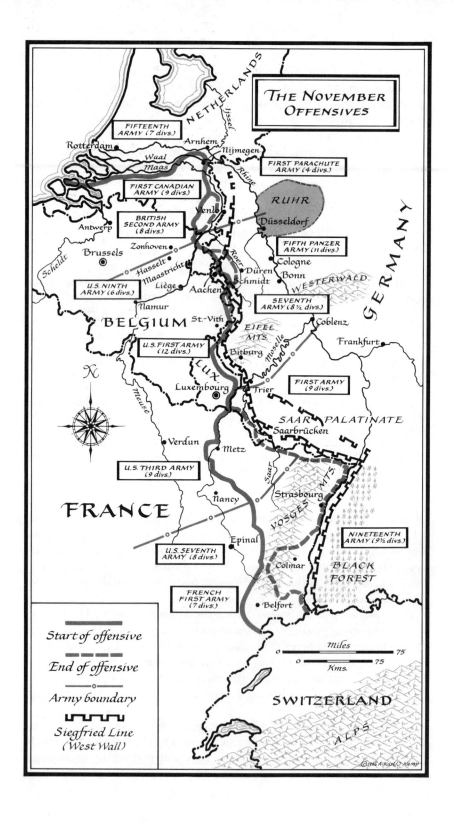

THE NOVEMBER
OFFENSIVES

NETHERLANDS

Rotterdam

FIFTEENTH
ARMY (7 divs.)

Arnhem

Nijmegen

Waal
Maas

Rhine

FIRST PARACHUTE
ARMY (4 divs.)

FIRST CANADIAN
ARMY (9 divs.)

Venlo

RUHR

Düsseldorf

BRITISH
SECOND ARMY
(8 divs.)

Zonhoven

Antwerp

FIFTH PANZER
ARMY (11 divs.)

Cologne

Roer

Brussels

Hasselt

Maastricht

Düren

Schmidt

Bonn

WESTERWALD

GERMANY

Scheldt

U.S. NINTH
ARMY (6 divs.)

Liège

Aachen

SEVENTH
ARMY (8½ divs.)

Namur

St-Vith

Coblenz

BELGIUM

EIFEL
MTS.

Frankfurt

U.S. FIRST ARMY
(12 divs.)

Bitburg

Moselle

LUX.

Luxembourg

Trier

FIRST ARMY
(9 divs.)

Meuse

SAAR PALATINATE

Saarbrücken

Verdun

Metz

U.S. THIRD ARMY
(9 divs.)

Saar

VOSGES MTS.

Nancy

Strasbourg

FRANCE

NINETEENTH
ARMY (9½ divs.)

Epinal

U.S. SEVENTH
ARMY (8 divs.)

Colmar

BLACK
FOREST

FRENCH
FIRST ARMY
(7 divs.)

Belfort

Miles

0   75

0   75

Kms.

Start of offensive

End of offensive

Army boundary

Siegfried Line
(West Wall)

SWITZERLAND

ALPS

©1986 A.Karl/J.Kemp

scale amphibious assault against Walcheren Island set for November 1. A large German garrison was entrenched at Walcheren and all expected a desperate fight. Since the terrain at Walcheren was not suitable for airborne attack, the defenders enjoyed the advantage of well-laid defenses, and the high command pressed on with plans to "sink" it by destroying the surrounding sea dikes and inundating German communications, artillery positions and roads. Bomber Command took charge, and on October 27, 1,200 Lancasters pummeled the twenty-foot seawalls with earthquake bombs, inundating eighty-two square miles and isolating the Germans in the towns of Flushing, Middleburg and Domburg. The Canadian assault on the western tip of Walcheren, reinforced by the British from South Beveland, cleared Flushing, and two days later Eisenhower informed the CCS that Antwerp was open and that minesweeping had begun along the seventy-mile Scheldt estuary. Mopping up the Walcheren garrison lasted until the eighth, closing a campaign in which casualties exceeded combined Anglo-American losses in Sicily. Over 27,000 were killed and wounded.

East of Aachen, Collins' VII Corps slowly attacked toward Düren on the left flank of Gerow's V Corps, which pushed for Schmidt and the Roer dams. In the Hürtgen Forest there was a total of ten divisions on a twenty-four-mile front, the heaviest concentrations of the war. G-2 reports continued to note that along with skillful defense, the Germans were withdrawing mobile units into reserve, apparent first in the Bonn–Düsseldorf area behind Aachen.

Von Rundstedt's armies were building up from the equivalent of twenty-five understrength divisions to seventy divisions, with reports of as many as forty more forming in central Germany, making Von Runstedt capable of a prolonged stand or even counteroffensive. The once optimistic SHAEF intelligence weekly report conceded on November 5: "Goebbels can claim with some justice that the measures taken so far by no means exhausted the resources of the German nation. . . . it cannot be denied that this represents a truly colossal effort . . . undertaken in every respect as though it were the last and final spasm. The training system has been freely devoured, the sixteen year olds (next year's class) have been largely eaten into, and industry has been combed near to scalping. Beyond such a program, only the Volkssturm have been looked forward to. If the war continued for another winter, it is impossible to say that fresh waves will be created. But it is possible to wonder."

Meanwhile, the Western press tracked German political developments closely. Amid the routine reports of apathy, weariness and countless emergency decrees came word of new measures opening a new "left-wing" phase of the Nazi revolution billed by Himmler and described as a reign of "indescribable terror" against elements of the "criminal aristocracy" and business classes suspected of "capitalistic tendencies" and pro-West leanings. This had "caused a tremendous sensation in Berlin" and become "the chief topic of conversation in all quarters. After weeks of rumors came confirmation of Von Rundstedt's reappointment, followed by news from Berlin of a new Russian Liberation Committee composed of captive Russian generals. Swiss reports noted talk in the German Foreign Office about a compromise peace with Russia and a list being circulated by high governmental officials of "war criminals" to be handed over to Russians, and about the formation of a new National-Bolshevik party and "a sort of German democracy along Russian lines." The same reports indicated stepped-up persecution of centrist and socialist politicians coinciding with an easing up on Communist party activity in the Rhineland, Hamburg and Bremen.

The Allied high command was probably reluctant to make much of these curious reports. Circulating rumors in hopes of engendering Allied-Soviet distrust was standard German practice. Separate-peace soundings had been heard before and by November 1944 lacked credibility. Talk of a new "left-wing" phase of National Socialism could not be dismissed altogether, however, particularly for what it implied about German military intentions. Publicizing the "left-wing" phase of Nazism was unlikely to convince Moscow that the Nazis could be dealt with, but it did tend to suggest that the Germans and Russians had a few common interests that month. For instance, there was the matter of a Russian offensive in Poland; it was a fair assumption that the Russians were not eager to resume the war in Poland, which would be costly and divert the Germans from the west, making the Allied task easier while diverting Russians from the Balkans, where the Russians were poised to roll up big gains at low cost. It was fair to assume that the Germans, too, did not want to grapple with a Russian offensive in Poland, though from the Allied point of view, it was still hard to see what the Germans, even if assured of a reprieve in Poland, would do differently. For instance, it seemed problematic that the German army and home front, threatened by Russian invasion sooner or later, would tolerate transfers from the east to the west. On the other hand, the Allies were fighting on German soil; the Russians were not. The Germans had still not had an all-out go in the west, and it was hard to see what the Germans could lose by it.

How long could the German people fail to see "the handwriting on the military wall?" asked the SHAEF intelligence summary in its weekly report evaluating the riddle of German morale. The most skillful Nazi propaganda could not conceal the location of the front lines, or conceal the day-and-night bombardment of German cities or the lengthening casualty lists totaling 2.5 million on both fronts since April.

On the Polish front, the Russian pause on the Vistula had entered its fourth month. The Russians advanced through Lithuania, methodically pocketing twenty-six German divisions at Courland in western Latvia, and, in a secondary attack, closed East Prussia and the line of the Narew River.

In the center, the Red Army remained stationary on the Vistula, reportedly unwilling to move until Polish railways had been converted to the Russian gauge. However, the lack of Russian-gauge rail tracks did not inhibit Marshal Malinovsky's advance on Belgrade–Budapest.

Were the Russians stalling in Poland? Years later Eisenhower would speculate that Russian intelligence had somehow penetrated German military planning in the fall of 1944 and learned of German plans to wage a major offensive in the west, which accounted for Stalin's decision to stall a three-power conference. But this was speculation, and Eisenhower did not wonder about whether Russian military policy might have been influenced by such knowledge. But in retrospect, it seems more than coincidental that Soviet participation in BODYGUARD, the global deception schemes to mislead German planners, ceased on September 28, 1944.

The point, however, was academic. Whatever the Germans were up to, few in the Allied high command doubted that Moscow would be satisfied to pass the military burden to the West for a while and would exploit German weakness in the Balkans to the extent possible. As for a German counteroffensive in the west, Eisenhower and the Allied high command did not foresee the coming Ardennes counteroffensive precisely, but in one way or another the possibility had been the subject of study since mid-March 1944 and had been anticipated since the German rout in late June in Russia, for the Soviet offensive had reduced the Germans to this one choice if they were to have any hope of reversing their desperate situation. That the German situation was hopeless would not matter to those German leaders who wanted to live a few months longer or to those who might prefer death in battle to death on a scaffold.

Postwar interrogations of the Germans would reveal that the German high command was not unanimously in favor of a western offensive. OKH Chief General Heinz Guderian strongly opposed shifting eastern-front armor, with which he hoped to delay the Russian invasion. Others, while ridiculing Hitler's obsession with the history of Frederick the Great's extrication of Prussia from the Seven Years' War, would criticize him for "forgetting Frederick's patient waiting game." But in November 1944 the skeptics were in a minority. A defensive strategy, no matter how successful, could not relieve Germany of the two-front pressure or relieve German isolation by aerial embargo and naval blockade, or end the systematic destruction of German cities by aerial bombardment. Advocates of a western offensive could point to the fact that whereas the Russian threat to Silesia was long-range, Allied threats to the Ruhr and Saar were immediate, and such advocates could also point out that the Western Allies had failed in 1940 and had not borne the full brunt of the Wehrmacht since. Whatever the technical proficiency of the highly mechanized U.S. Army was in comparison with the French, the Americans, in German eyes, lacked discipline and resolution and, from afar, the Germans perceived British disenchantment. Would the Anglo-American alliance bear up under the shock of a counteroffensive? Occasionally Hitler joked that the British and Germans might join hands to expel the Americans from Europe.

As early as mid-September, as the German high command became satisfied that the crisis on the eastern front had passed, planning, confined to a very narrow circle of men, had begun for a major counteroffensive in the west. On the fourteenth of September, Hitler had first ordered Model to organize the Sixth SS Panzer Army as a reserve, with the idea of a major counteroffensive in Lorraine. When the German counterattacks against Patton's right flank failed and resulted in the loss of the Moselle, Hitler's gaze had turned northward, but his intention to launch an offensive never wavered.

As Jodl would later recall, throughout September Hitler was confined to bed with jaundice and skipped his regular headquarters staff meeting at noon and other routine appointments. Given time alone with his thoughts, Hitler cast about for a bold scheme to retrieve the August disasters and, on his own, devised the Ardennes plan. At a bedside conference in late September, Hitler sketched for Jodl the outlines of a far-ranging, multipronged plan featuring a sweep through the Ardennes to recapture Antwerp, isolate the British Second Army and force the British to withdraw, resulting in the collapse of the Anglo-American coalition. Jodl proceeded to canvass western-front commands for ideas. OKW attached a set of conditions for success: a quiet eastern front; a shift in military production priorities; operation in poor weather to hamper the Allied air force; and twenty-five new divisions by November 1 at the earliest.

In the weeks since, the preconditions had fallen into place. The Red Army in Poland turned north to attack the German Baltic salient, while Konev turned south to reinforce Malinovsky's march toward Budapest and Vienna. Twenty-five Volksgrenadier and six panzer divisions were forming. Meanwhile, at a late-September conference at the Wolfsschanze, Hitler had disclosed his conclusions about Allied plans and their implications for a winter counteroffensive. The British, in his opinion, would be occupied at Nijmegen for some time while the U.S. First Army struggled to widen the bridgehead at Aachen. Meanwhile the American Third Army would be bogged down in efforts to contain the Metz garrison while the American-French Sixth Army Group concentrated on the Belfort–Saverne gaps. This would expose a major gap in Allied lines in the Ardennes Forest. Hitler saw no prospect of change, and, according to Jodl, finally "put his finger on the map in the region of the Ardennes–Eifel and announced that through that area the great offensive would take place."

At the same meeting, Jodl presented a preliminary plan, which Hitler "accepted," that called for a main effort by three German armies through the fifty-mile sector between Monschau and Prüm supported by a secondary attack launched by the Fifteenth Army across the Meuse toward Maastricht to converge on Antwerp. Hitler assigned Von Rundstedt, a skeptic, to begin withdrawing armor forthwith along the front for training and reorganization. He would then form this armor into two armies, to be placed under direct OKW control.

In the ensuing planning phase, OKW reconsidered all the alternatives. One was to concentrate against the British salient west of the Maas close to Antwerp and thus slice along the seam of the American-British armies. A second option was a more limited attack to wipe out the First Army salient at Aachen, which would restore the West Wall and annihilate the U.S. First Army in the process. A third option was the Ardennes. Other choices included a two-prong offensive to destroy Devers' 6th Army Group, including the French First Army. In time, the second option, or "the small solution," gained the favor of the German generals, who, according to Wilmot, had earned the right to assume control of the western offensive, having restored the West Wall and protected the Germans from invasion that September. Most believed that Antwerp via the Ardennes was not a realistic choice.

Army commanders respected the military obstacles to success in the Ardennes, which seemed more formidable than before because of German overall weakness. The hilly, thickly forested region was not ideal terrain for armored operations. Tanks would be confined to a handful of roads linking the towns and cities, while the surrounding forests and defiles made traffic detours very difficult even in favorable conditions, and vulnerable to air interdiction in good weather. On the other hand, the terrain would make prompt defensive countermeasures difficult too. The wooded Eifel would camouflage the required concentration of troops, which held out the prospect of gaining surprise and quick passage over the Meuse while the Allied command hesitated as it tried to ascertain the scope of the attack and reluctantly organized countermeasures. The blow, staged far south of Holland and aimed exclusively at the American armies, would exploit the inevitable Anglo-American crisis almost as effectively as an attack in Holland, since it would arouse British doubts about intervening in the initial stages. The remoteness of the Ardennes from important objectives was itself an advantage. The German army could rely on surprise and swift, early successes, which would infuse the tired commands with confidence and sweep even the skeptics along. To be sure of this, Hitler would eventually entrust the northern flank of the attack near Liège and the U.S. First Army to the Sixth Panzer Army, designate it SS and place it under Sepp Dietrich.

In the Allied camp, premonitions of trouble brought out all the pre-OVER-LORD misgivings about the steadiness and success of the military leadership, even as the threat emphasized the interdependence of the two armies. Brooke's November diaries are a chronicle of woe as he became convinced that Eisenhower's broad-front strategy in September and November was fatally flawed. Having restrained Montgomery once out of concern for overextension and having forfeited a chance to win in September, Eisenhower was compounding matters by refusing to concentrate his forces into a solid mass that need fear nothing. November was a tense time, and Eisenhower would complain later to Marshall of Brooke's enervating "shouting" in conferences and his obsession with American command decisions, "inexperience" and mistakes.

Brooke's very specific ideas about Eisenhower's command errors were not matched by consistent suggestions of his own about alternatives. As a military strategist, Brooke probably would have questioned defensive plans that, in massing forces north of the Ardennes, would have exposed a long southern flank to the Germans. Even as a soldier, he must have known how unacceptable such a move would have been to De Gaulle, whose French forces fought in the south. Perhaps Brooke felt free to criticize because he knew criticism would not change strategy on the front and that the real issue was command: what arrangements the Americans would accept that would assure the British a voice on theater policy in the weeks ahead. Brooke's misgivings were also symptomatic of the British quandary, the growing sense of drifting along, beholden to "the colossal resources of the United States and Russia."

The British, beset by the intractable problems of near bankruptcy, war weariness, the destruction of lives and property in the bombings and the V-blitz, sorely tested Allied relations that tense month. Long-pent-up frustration with American unwillingness to back negotiations with the Russians over eastern Europe boiled over in November along with feelings that the Americans had been irresponsible critics of British diplomacy. There was gratitude for Roosevelt's help in the past, since Britain might not have survived without it. But having survived, the British assessed the costs.

By all accounts, late fall was a time of clashes. The Americans and British clashed over Italy, where the British backed the monarchists and the Americans backed the liberal Count Sforza's effort to form a Socialist government. Similar differences arose in Belgium and in Greece, where Churchill's pro-monarchy policy was repeatedly embarrassed by State Department locals who inflamed factions in Parliament and Congress against British efforts to thwart the EAM. Surveying the scene, Beaverbrook wrote candidly to Hopkins describing the "strange phase" in British public life. For the first time, Beaverbrook contended, his countrymen were experiencing uncertainty, even anxiety, about the future, due primarily to their awareness of their reliance on outside assistance, and wariness about "proceeding on their own power." Beaverbrook predicted that British elections could not be put off long and that foreign policy questions would be prominent, "for the government is now unable to deal with post-war issues. . . . the limit of the capacity to compromise has been reached."

What were British objectives? A settlement. In contrast to America's visionary but unformed aims, Churchill's postwar goals had always been definite: the restoration of something like the prewar status quo and a process of give-and-take among the major powers that would avoid the extremes of superpower collaboration and intense ideological rivalry, either of which would tend to foreclose a genuine political and moral recovery in Europe. Significantly, by the fall of 1944, several American voices were beginning to sound British-like themes in favor of restoring Europe and traditional diplomacy among the victorious powers. Perhaps the most influential of these was that of America's counselor in the Moscow embassy, George F. Kennan, who advocated Churchill's pragmatic line in the forthcoming tripartite conference. Kennan favored a frank division of Europe into spheres of influence, with the understanding that "we would keep outside of the Russian sphere, and . . . the Russians would keep out of ours." Kennan advocated drawing up a "list of the questions on which we wanted Soviet agreement, and another list of the prices we were prepared to pay." And he opposed raising issues such as Poland that were not negotiable, or accepting responsibility for what the Russians did in their sphere, admitting that the United States and Britain lacked the strength to protest effectively.

But Kennan was in a minority. The dominant view in Washington was that spheres of influence were immoral, unwise or impractical politically, and that candor about Allied weakness in eastern Europe or any consignment of territory against the will of the people was, in the words of the diplomat Charles Bohlen, "a foreign policy not possible in a democracy." By implication, there were Americans who questioned whether the British who advocated such a course were true democrats, or whether, in fact, they were not so different from the Marxist imperialists. To meet those criticisms, Churchill went to great lengths to advertise the fate of the Warsaw garrison and to enlist U.S. backing for British measures to keep Greece from falling under the EAM and "all of its malice," as Churchill put it. The British Conservative party would not permit Churchill to do less, but his actions seemed particularly aimed at influencing Roosevelt, perhaps to remind him of the inevitable give-and-take actually going on in Europe, of the differences between the Russians and British, and the urgency, in British eyes, of open covenants openly arrived at that would afford the British and Europe a measure of protection against casual policy changes by the superpowers.

In this climate, a command challenge was simply a matter of time before, during or after the mid-November Allied offensive. Moreover, in three months, Eisenhower had been tarnished in British circles. Hard decisions had somewhat eroded his reputation for impartiality. Significantly, Eisenhower's British cohorts, Morgan and Tedder, were in disfavor at Whitehall, and now, as few forgot, they had sided with Eisenhower on most major issues. With patience and forbearance, and an open-minded willingness to concede error and share credit for the fact that the Allies had passed the crucial test of OVERLORD and had exceeded even the most optimistic official forecasts in France, Eisenhower was managing the situation as best he could. He maneuvered to avoid untimely discussion of issues such as emergency command arrangements in the event of a German counteroffensive and the divisive subject of invasion objectives. The element of military uncertainty was in many ways more corrosive than full-blown crisis, and so nothing could be settled satisfactorily now. But certain problems were unavoidable, and so Eisenhower was determined to avoid the "trap" of pretending Anglo-American issues did not exist.

In *Crusade,* Eisenhower praised Brooke sincerely for his frankness throughout the war. One of Brooke's backhanded contributions was in constantly reminding Eisenhower that as an American he was considered an outsider, a welcome guest whose help was appreciated but still a guest, and a representative of a nation that stood to gain mightily in a war that, though universal in its implications, was fought mainly by Europeans against one another, tragically ruining Europe's influence in the world.

At the height of the "air-ground" quarrel in July, Milton Eisenhower had become his brother's representative in talking about a proposed M-G-M movie on Eisenhower's life with emphasis on Eisenhower's role as a modern Ben Franklin, skillfully handling the potentates of the Old World. Eisenhower had warily endorsed the project but imposed many conditions. He had warned Milton about "self-glorification" that would give the British "the right to accuse Americans of bombast and self-praise." Eisenhower explained to Milton the demands of his job. It required firmness, a "single-minded devotion to the one cause of winning the war," and "fanatical zeal" in refusing to consider anything else. Emphasizing that all of his colleagues, American and British, approached their jobs in this spirit, Eisenhower had urged that the movie company contact the Army Signal Corps and obtain pictures portraying all leaders as men "of courage, intelligence and as fully devoted as myself to the promotion of unity and effectiveness." Eisenhower had added a note of caution. Any effort to portray him as a promoter of unity in U.S.-British operations must not "lose sight of the fact that I am first and last an American—nothing else," he had written. "The fact is that no American can promote unity in a command such as mine by pretending to be British or deserting for a moment his faith in American genius and method. You must be understanding of the other fellow's viewpoint, but he must not try to win his case by false flattery or imitation."

On the eve of the offensive, Eisenhower struggled on against his retrenchment at Versailles. In her journal, Summersby chronicled Eisenhower's impatience and anxiety behind the scenes, marked by fresh crackdowns on Comm-Z amid reports of the thriving black market in supplies diverted from the front and other corruptions of war in the rear zones. An investigation of Comm-Z, pushed at Eisenhower's insistence, documented a pattern of "organized thievery," whereupon Eisenhower ordered vigorous prosecution of the offenders. Reviewing the convictions, Eisenhower ruled that enlisted men would be given a chance to purge their records by volunteering for frontline duty, and that officers be returned to the States and prison.

The 1944 elections came and went almost unnoticed in Paris. Roosevelt carried thirty-six states and 432 electoral votes, all but the Midwest; Democrats recouped seats in the House and Senate that had been lost in the 1942 Republican off-year landslide. Prominent members of the old isolationist wing went down to defeat, but isolationism had shifted focus somewhat, and the popular vote was the closest since 1916.

Afterward, Eisenhower found it necessary to defend himself to his brother Edgar, who had recently penned a long complaint about the election and the war. It was not true, he castigated Edgar, that the professional soldier liked the war in Europe. "Unquestionably any soldier would agree with almost any cynical philosophy you might care to develop respecting the progress of a civilization that allows itself to get plunged into a world war every quarter of a century," Eisenhower wrote. "The mistake that people like yourself make is in assuming that the soldier—and I mean the professional—likes it. There may be an occasional sadist or self-styled Napoleon that looks forward to such a catastrophe, but such people would be as common in civil life as in the armed forces. . . . you may see civil liberties curtailed, and developments within the government structure that are hard to bear, but the soldier sees things that, if not more terrible in their ultimate consequences, are far more terrifying and disagreeable in the immediate reactions they create."

In letters home, Eisenhower continued to share tidbits about the men he worked with and about his position, which still awed him slightly. In one letter he described gifts received from schoolchildren—a piece of white heather from a twelve-year-old boy, four-leaf clovers from an English schoolgirl, Saint Christopher medals. In another letter he consoled Mamie about her anguish over their separation and her sense of aimlessness without a specific war job to absorb her time and energies. As always, Eisenhower expressed complaints about the pace, the utter absence of relief from care, often reviewing his pledge to Mamie of a carefree life together when the war was over either in Arizona or in Colorado. Several times Eisenhower indirectly denied Washington rumors of a romantic link between himself and Summersby and scolded Mamie for listening to gossip.

Their real mutual concern was John and his imminent dispatch to Europe with the 71st Division under the watchful command of their friend General Wyman. To John, Eisenhower enclosed tips about running a platoon, encouraging him to toughen his men up with double-time marching, and always to tend to details such as warm dry clothing and precautions against trench foot. Eisenhower kept in touch with Wyman. In one letter, Eisenhower sympathized with Wyman's complaint that John, in "his anxiety to paddle his own canoe," was avoiding him to an extreme. Eisenhower assured Wyman he was confident that John would make a good soldier. John was serious, had obvious qualities of leadership and a good sense of humor and was naturally shy about profiting from relationships. Eisenhower also assured Wyman that he had no doubt that Wyman had trained a good division in the 71st. "I knew you could do that when I sent you there," he wrote, "and I have already told the War Department that I should like to see your promotion made immediately since you have already proven yourself in battle."

"Don't forget that I take a beating every day," Eisenhower wrote Mamie that day. "Entirely aside from my own problems I constantly receive letters from bereaved mothers, sisters, and wives, and from others that are begging me to send their men home, or at least outside the battle zone, to a place of comparative safety. . . .

> So far as John is concerned, we can do nothing but pray. If I interfered even slightly or indirectly he would be so resentful for the remainder of his life that neither I (nor you, if he thought you had anything to do with it) could be comfortable with him. It's all so terrible, so awful, that I constantly wonder how "civilization" can stand war at all. But, God, how I hope and pray that all will be well with him. . . . I am not fussing at you. But please try to see me in something besides a despicable light and at least let me be certain of my welcome home when this mess is finished. . . .

On the eve of Hodges' attack at Aachen, Eisenhower made another extended tour of the front to visit troops and to examine the mounting ammunition and replacement crisis. As before, Colonel Gault kept a chronicle of the trip, which included forays across the German border at Roetgen and Aachen.

From Aachen, Eisenhower motored to V Corps Headquarters for an overnight visit with Gerow, then proceeded to Ninth Army Headquarters at Maastricht, then to Brussels to meet with the Prince Regent and to deliver his first public address before the Belgian Chamber of Deputies. He went to Luxembourg for conferences with Bradley and a tour of the Ardennes Forest, the possible site of a German attack. They also discussed Patton's struggle on the Moselle.

Typical of Allied frustration was Patton's Third Army offensive at Metz, a two-prong "close penetration" of the fortress by XII Corps from Nancy and XX Corps from Thionville. Flood conditions on the Seille River delayed the attack several times. On November 8, 2,000 heavy bombers backed by 700 fighters dropped 4,000 tons of antipersonnel bombs on the Fort Driant citadel as three divisions fought their way into the city. Patton maintained his optimism, estimating that the Third Army would be at the West Wall in three days, but to his wife he complained: "It has rained every day since the first of the month and we are having a hell of a time with 'immersion' feet, about as many as from enemy fire. . . . however the enemy must be suffering more so it is a question of mutual crucifixion until he cracks."

Few quarreled with the necessity for the offensive. Bradley later deplored the cost in suffering, but noted it was west of the Rhine "that the enemy had chosen to commit his last resources, it was here that we must break his back in order to force the Rhine." Even Montgomery acquiesced in the need to reduce threatening German salients in all sectors.

Operations beginning that week were to be the source of the many comparisons thereafter drawn between the careers of General Dwight Eisenhower and General U. S. Grant. The watchword was "attrition" as the war at last began to resemble Spotsylvania and Cold Harbor, the memories Stimson had evoked to push Roosevelt toward adoption of OVERLORD at Quebec. Like the wilderness campaign of 1864, the Allied strategy of attrition had developed its "grim arithmetic." Daily the Allies inflicted 2,700 battle casualties and seized an average of 1,300 POWs, projecting to 4,000 casualties of all kinds, or the equivalent of a "new class" division every two days. At the November rate of replacement, the Germans stood to lose twenty divisions per month in combat, with an estimated capacity to refit five. Allied intelligence estimated that the Germans could mobilize an additional twelve per month in the west, meaning that the overall impact of the fall campaign would be to reduce the German manpower reserve at the rate of three divisions per month. In light of demands on all fronts, the Germans could not afford an absolute reduction of strength in the west at this rate. American losses were comparable, however, and despite Allied air and industrial might, Eisenhower's armies could not sustain these losses for very long either. And, in relative terms, without reinforcements or the reopening of Russian operation on the Vistula front, the "grim arithmetic" might actually work against the Allies—something all knew but few mentioned.

Eisenhower's first trip into Germany on a visit to the towns of Roetgen and Aachen was notable. It provided a glimpse of Germany under Allied occupation; and for Eisenhower, it was only the second time he had visited the country of his ancestors. The earlier trip through German territory had been long before, in 1929. Then Eisenhower saw the Rhineland and the ancestral Saar-Palatinate, which had slowly been recovering from the occupation and destruction of the Great War. In 1929, Eisenhower had chronicled the unexpected thrill in his discovering a land fabled in family lore as the Fatherland. In November 1944, Eisenhower returned as a conqueror in quest of clues about the people there and the task of pacification.

To the question of what sustained the Germans in November 1944, several answers were apparent. First, the evidence of coercion. American patrols encountered evidence of brutal Nazi measures: nighttime sentry platoons strung together by wire, and pillboxes manned by children, and veterans with wooden limbs fastened to cement decks. Captured documents included instructions to all commands to inform soldiers in the field that relatives of deserters were now accountable under the kinship-hostage decree. That fall, it was Nazi press policy to publish extensive personal data in the hometown newspapers of combat soldiers listed as "missing." However, the most surprising and ominous discovery was the high morale, almost exaltation, of German prisoners and the determined, almost "mystical" resistance in most sectors. The German mobilization was tapping hidden reserves—300,000 men in August, 200,000 in September and October. Many of them were from the Luftwaffe and the navy, infusing the army with higher caliber soldiers physically fit and imbued with the doctrines of Nazism more than their predecessors in Normandy, pledged to defend their homes and honor to the end.

By jarring contrast, among the civilians only misery was evident. The German population in the occupied sector around Aachen seemed eager to terminate the war. The vaunted "werewolf" partisan activity trumpeted by Nazi propaganda was nonexistent. Some, however, cautioned that Aachen was not typical, that pacifying the mixed French and German Rhineland might prove simpler than pacifying the far side of the Rhine. In any event, the first Germans encountered, objects of intense curiosity, were wearily anxious to accommodate American troops and otherwise to disassociate themselves from the Nazis, whom they seemed to fear more than the conquering Allies, who offered firm and just treatment. In a case brought to Eisenhower's attention, German civil authorities had pardoned a woman accused of harboring deserters who pleaded BBC instructions in her defense.

The tour had a hardening effect on Eisenhower. Its purpose was to gather information for the large echelons of the international press who lived and worked in Paris and relied mainly on information provided through SHAEF. Eisenhower's trip, built up in the press as Rommel's tour of the Atlantic Wall had been in December 1943, marked the beginning of a campaign to acquaint the American public with the true horrors of Europe under the Nazis.

Eisenhower's journey publicized the plight of liberated Belgium and West Holland, held hostage by the Germans. When he addressed the Belgian parliament, Eisenhower indirectly brought international attention to conditions in Belgium that had been dramatized several weeks before by the discovery of a sinister concentration camp at Breendonck on the outskirts of the city, where the Germans had kept the prewar Belgian leadership imprisoned. Within the heavy walls of Breendonck, countless inmates had died. On view were the interrogation rooms with branding irons, stoves, pulleys to suspend victims by the ankles, and blocks for smashing fingers and tearing off victims' fingernails. The subsequent publicity heightened the reports of Russian discoveries of huge extermination camps in eastern Poland, spurring Churchill's dark observation that the Allies were tiptoeing toward "an abyss" and would soon be staring into it with mixed feelings of relief at the narrow escape of some, and horror at the spectacle of those who did not escape. Every mile gained uncovered fresh evidence, in Churchill's words, of the "worst crime in the whole history of the world . . . done by scientific machinery by nominally civilized men in the name of a great state and one of the leading races of Europe."

In mid-November, perhaps as a gesture of resolve, Eisenhower placed in his desk diary a special report of an "interesting" document circulated by SHAEF G-2 on German preparations for an armistice based on the testimony of a "reliable" clandestine source, who had attended meetings in Strasbourg with Nazi party and high business officials. According to the report, dated November 20, the Nazis were privately conceding that the war was irrevocably lost and were at work on measures to salvage German military and commercial interests. At an August meeting, "principal German industrialists"—including representatives of Krupp, Röchling, Messerschmitt, Rheinmetall, Bussing and Bussing Volkswagenwerk—the German Naval Ministry and the Ministry of Armament discussed the next stage of the war. Nazi officials had briefed the group on war prospects: the war would last as long as a unified postwar Germany could be secured, no longer. The German government had endorsed prompt steps to ensure the future of German commerce by developing "contacts and alliances with foreign firms without individually . . . attracting attention." Research had begun to look into patents held jointly by American and German firms such as the Krupp patent on stainless steel held jointly with U.S. Steel, American Steel and Wire and National Tube. The conferees had endorsed a policy of easing restrictions on the export of German capital to enable firms to accumulate reserves of foreign currency. Financial concerns were obtaining titles to farmland and absorbing less prominent Nazis into inconspicuous spots in research and development offices to prevent industrial secrets from passing into the hands of the Allies and the Russians.

The report also indicated that German foreign reserves were accumulating at the Basler Handelsbank and the Schweizerische Kreditanstalt of Zurich, a meaningful detail in light of Stalin's casual suggestion to Churchill in October that the Swiss were "swine" and that the Allies could solve the West Wall problem by invading Germany through Switzerland, which was thought to be a hint of Soviet plans to invade Switzerland itself. According to Churchill, Stalin rarely spoke in such tones.

Exploiting a break in the weather, the American Ninth and First armies' offensives to clear the Roer lunged forward on November 16. The massive preliminary bombardment was ineffectual in the Aachen forests. In slow and costly fighting, Hodges' First Army advanced seven miles in two weeks. In the Hürtgen Forest near Schmidt, Gerow's V Corps, consisting of the 4th, 9th and 28th U.S. divisions, faced the bulk of German reserves and suffered the heaviest American losses of the war. Within ninety-six hours it was clear that the First Army would fall short of key objectives, leaving the Germans with bridgeheads west of the Roer River and in control of its dams.

Meanwhile, Patton's progress fell well short of the Saar Valley and breaking through the Siegfried Line. At Metz, XX Corps hacked through two panzer divisions, a panzer brigade and grenadier division and an infantry division. The Metz garrison, commanded for a time by Himmler, surrendered on November 22, ending an eight-week siege. At a cost of 29,000 battle casualties since September, Patton's Third Army pressed on and reached Saarlautern and Saarbrücken by December 1, then stopped.

In the south, the Allied offensive gained ground. Patch's Seventh Army converged on Strasbourg through Belfort and the Saverne gap, isolating 50,000 Germans in the Vosges. The understrength French First Army in snow, sleet and fog reached the Rhine at Mulhouse. But even here gains were disappointing.

General Jacob Devers, Marshall's one direct appointment, had never enjoyed Eisenhower's complete confidence. A misunderstanding quickly arose between Eisenhower and Devers over Devers' underestimation of the staying power of the understrength German Nineteenth Army in Alsace and Devers' apparent inability to control the French. Earlier in the month Eisenhower had endorsed an ambitious Seventh Army swing north to the Moselle and Devers' decision to delegate clearing the Alsatian plain to the French, all provided that "on no account" were any Germans to be left west of the Rhine and south of Strasbourg. A secure base on the upper Rhine was fundamental to any strategy of containing a German counteroffensive.

In late November Eisenhower returned to Vittel for a second meeting with Devers to insist that the French eliminate a German Nineteenth Army pocket at Colmar before the Seventh Army wheeled north toward the Saar. In Devers' opinion, the Nineteenth Army had "ceased to exist as a coherent tactical force" and subsequently permitted General Lattre de Tassigny to split French columns and compete for the honor of liberating Strasbourg. But after a token effort to clear the Colmar pocket failed, German reinforcements arrived and the pocket was destined to exert an "adverse impact on Allied operations" until it was eliminated at Eisenhower's insistence some three months later. Thus, as the offensive rolled on, it was unlikely that the Allies would achieve the aim of a secure southern flank based on the Rhine, a fact blamed in Washington on French recalcitrance and seen in London as evidence that Eisenhower lacked control of the battle.

As the November attacks raged, the specter of a setback spurred impatience bordering on panic in Washington, where the issue was casualties. The JCS remained officially optimistic and impatient to shift troops to the Pacific, but soon Eisenhower learned that the tremors surrounding the CCS "end the war" directive four weeks earlier had not been a one-time affair connected to the election.

On November 18, Eisenhower received a message from Marshall similar in tone and effect to the JCS "end the war" motion a month earlier. In it Marshall passed along a study drawn up by General Quesada's Ninth Air Force, in London, in which Quesada noted that owing to weather and German defenses, the tactical air force was proving to be of little direct use in Bradley's ongoing offensive. Quesada also noted that the Ninth Air Force had been built up into "the largest collection of fighter-bombers the world has ever seen," a tool capable of causing "the collapse of internal Germany, which will stab their armies in the back, and make our job of conquering very much less costly" if directed at isolating the German forces west of the Rhine and the Ruhr basin. Quesada noted that the Luftwaffe was incapable of coping with the strategic bombers, let alone the fighter-bombers, which could now operate with impunity over western Germany. Equipped to bomb as many as two targets, and capable of strafing at close range an additional three, 1,500 fighter-bombers could "roam the length and breadth of Germany on every day that weather permits contact flying," a technique he had seen displayed in Normandy, one which, repeated on a large scale, might crush German resistance and "make an impression on the mind of every German which he will never forget . . . live in the memories of his children and grandchildren as an illustration of the fearfulness of war."

In reply, Eisenhower tactfully indicated that the proposal had been "the subject of study by us for some time," and assured him that at Tedder's direction, fighter sweeps were being carried out incidental to ground support missions, and "the policy of wide-spread fighter sweeps indicated above will be continued."

The twentieth was a day of action at Versailles. General Lucius Clay returned for a discussion of the manpower problem. Eisenhower spelled out for Clay his urgent need for replacements. The typical American division north of the Ardennes was operating at 70 percent effective combat strength. In addition to 64,000 casualties suffered in the November battles to date, the infantry suffered from exposure, frostbite, trench foot and respiratory diseases reaching, as Bradley later recalled, "the crisis stage."

Meanwhile, word came of two developments in Washington. Marshall had slashed the ETO replacement quota from 80,000 to 67,000 men, diverting the balance to the Pacific theater. Simultaneously, in the CCS, the diplomatic accounting began with a British motion to mobilize Belgian garrison troops, a preliminary to Belgian combat formations, and to step up French mobilization, apparently deemed necessary by the British in light of congressional reluctance to grapple with the shortage of divisions in France.

Plainly, in Washington's view, talk about shortages was unwelcome. Roosevelt was conceding that there existed an "unanticipated shortage of manpower," but he suggested making up the shortfall by withdrawing troops from Italy. Marshall was adamant that American estimates be accurately drawn up, with the Air Force providing the "extra punch for victory," but this, he insisted, gave "no margin for any diversion from the main show" and, for political and diplomatic reasons, could not be altered.

The manpower question was soon bogged down in technicalities. The War Department claimed that ETO exceeded its authorized strength by an "excessive" 4 percent. General Harold Bull and SHAEF countered that accurate accounting was impossible because of troop movements. In Washington, General Thomas Handy flatly warned that the War Department, existing on a "hand-to-mouth basis," had resources "so slim that we are forced to parcel out the few remaining resources on the most frugal basis possible."

Eisenhower favored quiet diplomacy on this emotionally charged problem. He hoped to defer the issue of troops and the question of who-was-doing-more-where. His message through Clay, however, was that he could no longer promise to keep the issue under wraps or prevent it from being brought before the CCS as a formal proposal for new divisions by all three commands, at least not without progress in sounding out Moscow on Red Army intentions in Poland.

Evidently as a last resort, Eisenhower decided to approach the CCS for authority to open direct SHAEF-Soviet talks. That day he met with the Soviet ambassador in Paris, Alexander Bogolomov, ostensibly to discuss the sensitive problem of Russian nationals detained in Allied POW camps. After the meeting, however, Eisenhower sent a significant message to the CCS on German morale and proposed steps to break it, an appeal that touched off a series of obscure but important exchanges between Eisenhower, Marshall, Churchill and Roosevelt that provided a revealing glimpse of the coalition under the pressure of military setback in November 1944.

In his brief summary of operations to the CCS, Eisenhower addressed the problem of German morale, which "on this front shows no signs of cracking at present." What he described as "solid enemy resistance" was the "main factor postponing final victory which in the present circumstances can only be achieved by prolonged and bitter fighting," attributable to two factors: the habit of obedience fortified by Nazi control, and "the success of German propaganda in convincing the German people that the Allies intended the elimination of Germany as a nation." Eisenhower urged the "vital importance" of redoubling efforts to reduce the German will to resist and "using every appropriate weapon to bear to achieve this end"—including deception, propaganda "and other possible means." But, he emphasized, this was a problem SHAEF could not deal with because it lacked "relevant information and does not control all the weapons to put such a plan into effect." In sum, Eisenhower could not predict significant Allied progress at least, he implied, until someone the Russians would talk to visited Moscow to consult on the military situation.

Eisenhower's appeal on the twentieth has often been misunderstood. Some historians, notably Anthony Cave Brown, have accepted at face value Washington's interpretation of Eisenhower's references to German morale as a long-overdue proposal to modify the policy of unconditional surrender, a policy now in growing disrepute. In any event, Washington resisted Eisenhower's implication that a high-level delegation traveling to Moscow would induce Stalin to disclose his plans in Poland.

The following day Eisenhower called a full-dress press conference at the Scribe Hotel to elaborate and to nominate himself as an emissary on such a mission. Hundreds of reporters packed the conference and recorded Eisenhower's somber warnings of the German build-up.

Reminding him of his prediction of a victory in 1944, a reporter asked if he expected to "spend Christmas beyond the Rhine." Eisenhower replied, "I would like to, of course," but he promised the group that he would "never make any more [predictions]." Questioned at length on the Russian front, Eisenhower declined to state a flat opinion. He endorsed Baltic operations and Budapest–Belgrade as "fine routes," and observed that the Russians "for the moment at least" seemed to "take advantage of the situation as it exists."

Question: I have just come from the States. People are too optimistic. Can we do anything to make them less optimistic without engendering pessimism?

Eisenhower: I think that is a perfectly sound question. You don't want to promote pessimism and defeatism. Optimism—I don't know—optimism or complacency. The man thinks everything is all right and he looks around for self-interest and he forgets the job isn't quite done. I really wouldn't feel myself expert enough in this field of public psychology and public opinion to know the line that a bunch of trained newspaper people could take in doing this job. I know, myself . . . unless everybody all the way through the whole nation, including that part of the nation that is on the front and that part of it still in our homeland, unless we keep on this job everlastingly and with a mounting intensity, rather than a decreasing one, we are merely postponing the day of victory.

Asked if complacency was undermining his ability to get materials "fast enough," Eisenhower again pronounced himself "optimistic" but said he was trying to "prevent myself from being complacent. I want more things than I am getting."

Question: Has there been any indication in recent weeks of Germans transferring men from east to elsewhere westward, or even from Norway?

Eisenhower: We have known for some weeks they have been transferring troops from Norway. We have captured prisoners who have been in Norway. I have forgotten the number of divisions that have come down—what they call divisions . . . he can't spare much from the east I am sure.

Were the Volkssturm troops good? Eisenhower disliked "yes and no answers," but noted that all Germans under Nazi control were "pretty tough customers." He conceded that the Volkssturm units were "not to be compared at all with the mobile divisions."

Was there any evidence that the Germans would retreat behind the Rhine? "I have seen none," Eisenhower replied, "and I should think—and this would be merely the attitude of anyone—that had I brought that much of my force as much as he was west of the Rhine with a big river at my back where there are numerous bridges with the knowledge that the other fellow has a very powerful air force, I'd say 'This far and no farther.'"

The questioning proceeded over the whole range of topics—France, Belgium, the summer offensive—but repeatedly reporters returned to the issues of the hour: the riddle of German morale and the shock of German resistance west of the Rhine. Were the Germans on the verge of collapse? Eisenhower recalled the July 20 assassination attempt on Hitler. But since then he had seen nothing to indicate lessening of morale and he assumed that the German leadership was entrenched. "In spite of what I said about the German leaders and the Gestapo," he added, "remember this—human beings are still human. I don't give a damn if they are Nazis, they are still human and if you keep putting failure after failure on the part of his army he is going to be licked one day, and that is all there is to it."

Question: A short time ago it was generally supposed the Germans had little or no reserves inside Germany. Is the picture changed at all?

Eisenhower: We know that from everything we have been able to find out . . . they are absolutely stripping the country to make new formations, the so-called Volkssturm. Anyway, those divisions will be made up certainly of less fit, less well-trained humans than his divisions have been made up in the past. If we are correct in our estimates that he has been stretched on the Russian front, this front and the Italian front then they can't be as well equipped. In other words, the reserves he is building up may be quite effective and we must not discount them . . . but they will not be panzer grenadiers or paratroopers or SS troops.

Question: You said these troops would be most effective in prepared defenses. Is there any indication of a lot of digging east of the Rhine?

Eisenhower: You could make a quickly prepared line to defend any obstacle such as the Rhine. The Rhine is a big river, and it is practically a naval operation to cross the river.

Question: I believe [that] on November 7th, Marshal Stalin in paying tribute to the Allies in the west said that the Red Army would be in Berlin soon. That was a quotation I saw.

Eisenhower: Good for him. He will do a good job there I think.

Thus, Berlin and the whole range of military operations were apparently among the topics Eisenhower hoped to pursue in greater detail with the Russians. And if Washington and London felt unable to approach Moscow on these and other questions, Eisenhower stood ready to do so. Washington declined the offer.

On the twenty-second, Marshall countered by dispatching to Churchill and Eisenhower copies of a proposed joint declaration, approved by Roosevelt, "clarifying" unconditional surrender and directing that Eisenhower render military advice. The proclamation acknowledged the "iron discipline of the Wehrmacht and the stranglehold of the Nazi party," which distorted the truth of Allied aims in alleging that "the Allies sought the destruction of the German people and the devastation of Germany." The Allies were united in demanding military victory, but sought only "the elimination of Nazi control and the return of the German people to civilization of the rest of the world." The text noted that the German situation on the Rhine was made hopeless by "overwhelming numbers and inexhaustible resources in Poland, Czechoslovakia and Hungary" forming an "inexorable ring" of destruction. The proclamation invited the German people to cease war and "join all the people in Europe and Africa and America and in Asia in this great effort for decency and peace among human beings."

The proposal was a milestone, for twenty months after declaring unconditional surrender at Casablanca, the President appeared to be ready to explore changes in a policy now seen as prolonging the war. But like the string of disappointing triumphs at Quebec, the gesture struck Churchill as too late, as unconvincing if intended to frighten the Soviets and as unacceptable if intended to woo them. Notably, the text neglected to remind the German people that they were also "pressed" in Italy—a carrot for Stalin. Churchill furiously rejected the declaration out of hand.

On the twenty-fourth, in an emotional message, Churchill informed Roosevelt of the unanimous War Cabinet and BCOS rejection of such a statement. Churchill doubted that the Germans would be reassured by it. In his opinion, the Germans feared not the British and Americans but rather "occupation by the Russians, and a sizeable proportion of their population being transported to Russia (or as they put it, Siberia) to toil to death." He doubted that anything could be said to "eradicate this fear which is deeply rooted in them," and predicted that Stalin would probably demand several million Nazi youth, Gestapo men and SS for "prolonged work of reparation and it is difficult to say that his attitude is incorrect."

Churchill proposed to fight on. With the battle of Cologne at its peak, he wrote that he opposed any sign of weakness that would encourage desperate opposition. He endorsed Eisenhower's plan to undermine German morale "through underground methods" as, in his opinion, adequate, and opposed the "appearance of appeasement" or "confession of our errors" now. "The General Grant attitude 'to fight it out on this line if it takes all summer' appears one to which I see no alternative," he closed. "In the meantime I shall remain set in unconditional surrender which is where you put me."

Churchill dispatched a companion cable message to Eisenhower in which he explained that the War Cabinet and BCOS felt that the timing was poor for anything that might "reassure the Germans as to their future." As an aside he added:

> I have never thought your present battle would yield decisive results. But the heavy losses inflicted on the enemy by the USA 1st and 9th Armies fighting toward Venlo, also the brilliant successes which have yielded Strasbourg and the Rhine at the western frontier, and above all the great victory around Metz in the advance eastward thence, constitute a noble step toward our goal. I say this even if no further successes are gained.

On the twenty-sixth, after a message of thanks to Churchill, Eisenhower informed the President through Marshall that he opposed the joint proclamation and could recommend one only "upon some operation that would be universally recognized as a definite and material success." This he offered as his "personal view expressed without consultation with the staff."

The same day, Harriman, passing through on his way back to Moscow, arrived for a talk. He had news of his recent post-election talks with the President, who "wanted to stay out of European questions as much as possible" these days and was reluctant to concentrate on the Russian problem and the need for a "firm vigilant policy." Harriman's main point of business, however, was a prospective trip by Eisenhower to Moscow. He suggested that Eisenhower fly to Moscow for a week or so. Stalin had indicated he would see Eisenhower, but no other member of his staff. Such a gesture would have far-reaching implications, and in his wire to the CCS reporting the Harriman conversation, Eisenhower conceded, "it would be almost miraculous if ever I should find such an opportunity to leave France," though Harriman had urged that a visit "would improve coordination now and after the armistice."

The CCS refused permission, and the entire episode faded into obscurity. As a sidelight to the events of that autumn, however, the episode was significant, particularly the spectacle of Eisenhower countering Roosevelt and Marshall on a question of personal importance to Churchill, and his willingness to assume the burden of approaching Moscow.

Churchill edited out the exchanges over the declaration in the text of his massive six-volume war memoir, though he left traces of it for future inspection. Deep in the thick appendices of *Triumph and Tragedy,* Churchill reprinted a memo he sent to Eden on the twenty-sixth, among several he wrote that day on other problems, such as the forthcoming general elections, food relief for France, measures to relieve the desperate food and clothing shortages in Holland, and prize money for the Royal Navy. Churchill minuted Eden about conferring the prized Freedom of London on Eisenhower. Only four Americans in history had been so honored, the last being Wilson and Pershing in 1919.

26 November 1944
Prime Minister to Foreign Secretary:
    I consider that at the end of the winter campaign it would be appropriate for the city of London to confer its freedom upon this remarkable American General (General Eisenhower). It is obvious that no one else should be included at the time.

As the U.S. First Army offensive opened, Colonel General Alfred Jodl completed a tour of the western front after conferences with a select group of commanders on the strategies and logistics for the German counteroffensive. Jodl had presented what was still a drawing-board "concept" for a four-army assault on a fifty-mile front through the Ardennes spearheaded by the Sixth and Fifth panzer armies, to cross the Meuse, threaten Brussels and converge on Antwerp.

Consultation was necessary both for commencing preparations and ensuring compliance with Hitler's questionable decision to gamble the strategic reserve in the west. Model and the skeptical Von Rundstedt had been informed of the plan by their chiefs of staff in late October. Even within the narrow circle of the OKW planning group there was doubt. Eventually OKW refined the conditions set for success: first, no Allied breakthrough in the November offensives; second, bad weather to diminish the effect of Allied air and facilitate a massive covert build-up opposite the Ardennes; third, a quiet eastern front. Of the preconditions, the last was probably the most important. Jodl encountered deep misgivings about relying on a continued Red Army pause in Poland. And although he gained the necessary clearances insofar as all accepted the inevitability of an offensive in the west, important differences remained that may have had an important bearing on its fate.

The political leadership thought in terms of the survival of the Nazi regime. Hitler's concept of the offensive was far-ranging. The western-front commanders discounted this, and held out for a more limited military operation to restore the West Wall. There were long-range advantages in inflicting a defeat on the Allies that would bolster German prestige and buy time, provided that reserves committed to the offensive did not precipitate a crisis in Poland.

But doubts remained. Throughout November, Model, Manteuffel and Von Rundstedt complained about the "wide gulf between the wishes of the Supreme Command" and the ability of the lower echelons to put them into effect. Model argued that American divisions could offer strong resistance if First Army reserves arrived quickly from the Roer front. To the western commanders, too much depended on surprise, maneuver, and the initial shock and confusion inflicted by the infantry. They doubted that the assigned force of thirty-four divisions tentatively allotted was enough, estimating that at least ten more divisions were needed to reach the Meuse and threaten Antwerp. As Manteuffel put it, the high command was planning a "grand slam" without holding the cards. The allotted forces, in his opinion, were capable of a "small slam," including seizure of vast supply and ammunition depots at Liège. But again, the "small solution" did not address the strategic dilemma of a two-front war. Hitler, thinking in terms of 1940–41, not 1944, insisted that the practical difficulties could be overcome by the superior élan and courage of the German frontline soldier.

Gradually, all fell in line with the more far-reaching plan spelled out in Hitler's directive on November 19 in which he declared his "inalterable will" to retake Antwerp with two panzer armies attacking through the Ardennes. The plan was daring. Two armies—Dietrich's Sixth SS Panzer Army on the north and Manteuffel's Fifth Panzer Army in the center would line up opposite the lightly defended Ardennes sector with the Fifteenth and Seventh armies assuming screening positions. After the initial assault, the two armies would race through the Ardennes for the Meuse. The first army to achieve a clear breakthrough would become the spearhead, with the other assuming the role of flank protection. The Sixth SS Panzer Army, starting opposite Liège and closer to Antwerp, had the shorter distance to run, but was operating close in on the U.S. First Army. The Fifth Panzer Army would attack in a more westerly direction along Bastogne–Namur, either to protect the western flank of the Sixth SS Panzer Army or to strike across the Meuse should the U.S. First Army successfully intervene against Dietrich. The plan had every feature imaginable, including Luftwaffe support and special teams under Colonel Otto Skorzeny of English-speaking commandos dressed in American uniforms with instructions to conduct reconnaissance and disrupt communications behind Allied lines.

Everything depended on speed and surprise. In the initial stages, both armies were to fight like the German army of old, by-passing concentrations of troops and hoping that the lightning speed of the attack would both confuse the enemy and make him commit his forces piecemeal. Counterattacks would be dealt with by the supporting Seventh Army opposite Trier set to attack on Manteuffel's southern flank and the Fifteenth Army opposite Hodges' First Army near Aachen.

Even skeptics would admit that the concept and the feat of organizing the offensive was a great achievement. The German army, foundering and demoralized two months earlier, had recovered. Seventy "nominal" divisions in the west had been rebuilt and reinforced. The twenty-two divisions and four-division OKW armored reserve earmarked for the attack were at full 1944 strength. Dietrich's Sixth SS Panzer Army and Manteuffel's Fifth Panzer Army would go into battle with an eight-day supply of ammunition, 1,800 tanks and self-propelled guns, 900 combat vehicles and enough gasoline to travel 200 kilometers, with an eight-day reserve stored west of the Rhine in rail cars and supply dumps, an ample stock provided Allied bombers could be kept away.

Nazi propaganda of "last possibilities" led many to false assumptions and decisions; nonetheless, the Germans had mobilized the capacity to inflict a severe setback, aided in no small measure by Allied overconfidence. Manteuffel later disclosed that in October, in the guise of a colonel, he toured the Our River front to study tactics for the assault. He interrogated junior officers and NCOs about the American VIII Corps and learned that its men habitually remained on alert only until one hour after darkness. German night patrols routinely operated behind VIII Corps lines at night, then returned an hour before dawn, when Allied patrols resumed. Accordingly, Manteuffel recommended against elaborate artillery preparation before H-Hour and decided to attack before first light aided by the glow of artificial moonlight. "It would be silly to wake these people up," he reasoned. Let the Americans sleep, . . . only to "rise and find their foxholes . . . occupied by the Germans."

In the days ahead, the British would blame not overconfidence but Eisenhower's broad-front offensive for the imminent counteroffensive; that in foolishly persisting with stalemated attacks at Schmidt and Düren, and in authorizing Patton's stalled Metz offensive, Eisenhower exposed the First U.S. Army to near disaster. But German testimony would back Eisenhower's decision to attack in late October insofar as the American assaults on Düren–Schmidt and Metz seriously disrupted German preparations and neutralized the Fifteenth Army, which dramatized the fact that the German army, despite the autumn recovery, did not rank with its 1940 counterpart in strength or determination. Von Rundstedt, who had commanded the Ardennes offensive in 1940, would call the 1944 concept a "stroke of *near* genius" on Hitler's part, a brilliant plan but impractical.

The Germans would achieve surprise. How the Germans arranged to stage such an attack without detection would pique the interest of historians for years. Miscalculations inherent in intelligence evaluation pervaded all levels of Army intelligence, though postwar charges of an "intelligence failure" seem exaggerated. In November 1944 evaluations in the field could not be insulated from morale-boosting appraisals at the top. According to the official line, Germany was on the brink of defeat and, preoccupied with a Russian invasion, had summoned Von Rundstedt out of retirement to implement an orderly defense of the Ruhr and the western frontier. For instance, according to the November 26 SHAEF summary, Von Rundstedt's appointment was the reason for the "most logical way the enemy is now fighting his battle in the west." The report predicted local counterattacks to seal off penetrations, but nothing more. As the reasoning went, since a counteroffensive was impractical, it was therefore unlikely. Specifically, the Ardennes region was deemed an unpromising sector for the Germans, evidently because the heavily wooded massif was considered unsuitable for an Allied offensive. Allied intelligence at all levels appeared to overlook Von Rundstedt's pre-Normandy record, including his authorship of the 1940 attack through the Ardennes and the signals his appointment must have conveyed to the Russians. Reconnaissance closely followed the Sixth Panzer Army bivouacked east of the Rhine near Bonn, thought to be deployed to prevent an American breakthrough into the Cologne plain, and so on.

But the essential facts were reported and understood. Eisenhower, Bradley, Montgomery and General Strong at SHAEF did not overlook Von Rundstedt's past record, which had been well advertised by the Nazi press. Eisenhower had foreseen German concentration against the Ardennes as early as September 24, and suspected, based on his experience at the Kasserine Pass in Tunisia, that the Germans would reveal their hand at the last minute. Montgomery, Eisenhower and Bradley must have known that a First Army breakout into the Cologne plains, which would supposedly tie down the Sixth Panzer Army, was highly unlikely and that the Germans knew this too. It would appear, in retrospect, that Eisenhower's decision to man the Ardennes sector thinly did not stem from the disbelief that the Germans would attack there, but rather from a preference to accept the risk of an attack there rather than elsewhere.

In any event, by early December, Strong's daily report ventured the comment that the Sixth SS was capable of a "spoiling attack of considerable power." Von Rundstedt, Strong noted, was collecting reserves and was "sufficiently confident not to commit them piecemeal." SHAEF identified Dietrich as the commander of the Sixth Panzer, the new and honorific SS designation, and accurately placed its headquarters in Cologne. Reports closely analyzed skillful German tactics at the Roer, which emphasized "the necessity for alert OPs, listening posts, air OPs, aggressive patrolling and defense preparation for a variety of eventualities," concluding: "The German selection of the swamps west of the Meuse as a spot to employ two of his best mobile divisions alert us to the fact that the enemy cannot be trusted always to attack according to the book. He remains a clever, aggressive foe."

Premonitions, heightened by feelings of futility typified by the failure of the massive RAF bombing attacks to destroy the concrete dams at Schmidt, gradually took hold. Years later, Bradley recounted the anxious discussions about the alternatives open to the German high command with the onset of winter and poor weather. All were formally optimistic, since to admit that the Germans could mount a counteroffensive would be to admit that such an offensive might succeed. Hodges predicted the German army would try to mount a "spoiling attack" somewhere with "air, armor and infantry and secret weapons at a selected focal point at a time of his own choosing," withdraw to the Erft River west of the Roer, and then to the Rhine or perhaps "collapse." Bradley later wrote that he too continued to believe that such an attack was "only a remote possibility," a belief qualified by the alarmist views of Major General Troy Middleton, commander of VIII Corps in the Ardennes.

Middleton's four understrength divisions patrolled "the quiet front," an 88-mile stretch between the towns of Monschau and Arlon. Middleton on the scene knew that because only a few roads were suitable for tanks, air interdiction of a German attack would be relatively easy, so he optimistically spoke of a Mortain-type attack by the Germans, a spoiling action with six to ten divisions aimed at disrupting Hodges' assaults at Aachen, which, like Mortain, would be a great Allied opportunity. Bradley thought in terms of a larger-scale action. "Lacking the resources to continue our offensive and defend the Ardennes in depth," he later wrote, "my defensive plan for the Ardennes was broadly based on mobility at which we had proven ourselves unequalled rather than concentration." If they were attacked, he told Middleton, he expected him to fight a delaying action back to the Meuse while he organized an armored reserve from Patton and Hodges, which he intended to hurl against the flanks of the assault in order to win a decisive battle west of the Rhine. Bradley was sanguine, though he also recalled that at Eisenhower's prompting, he and Middleton agreed to locate no gasoline or ammunition dumps east of the Meuse. It is unclear whether Bradley or Middleton consulted Hodges about the placement of vast U.S. First Army oil dumps at Liège, a near-fatal move that undermined Eisenhower's confidence in Bradley when the blow fell.

On their early-November visit to the Ardennes, Eisenhower and Bradley had discussed the possibility of an attack there. Bradley told Eisenhower that he accepted the "calculated risk" of such an attack because Hodges and Patton could quickly release armor against the flanks, and because good flying weather would enable the Allies to retaliate effectively over the narrow, winding roadway. Bradley believed an attack could easily be contained and defeated, provided the Germans did not seize a major Allied supply dump.

Bradley's appraisal of the Ardennes was significant. Eisenhower solicited it, and Bradley, in minimizing the threat, assumed responsibility in

Eisenhower's eyes for what would prove to be an Allied miscalculation. Moreover, while it is conceivable that the German offensive took Bradley completely by surprise, it is probable that it did not, and so the question arises: Why did Bradley pass up a chance to ask for reinforcements in the area and urge Eisenhower to suspend Allied attacks in progress? The answer would seem to be that Bradley accepted the necessity of the attacks in progress, the "calculated risk" of exposing the Ardennes sector, as well as his personal responsibility not to add to Eisenhower's burdens by playing it safe and covering himself in advance against a crisis in the Ardennes.

All this was a hopeful sign. It was a sign that Bradley would not place the prestige of his army group above the need for smooth coordination in the event of a German attack in the Ardennes, because in miscalculating, Bradley also compromised his ability to resist whatever command moves, however drastic, Eisenhower might contemplate to assure U.S.-British coordination should a German attack in the Ardennes make headway. A precondition for close inter-Allied coordination had been implicit in all the debates since June—British command of large American forces. As in Normandy, it was a truism that in a future crisis, unless Montgomery commanded large American forces, he would be left to worry exclusively about protecting the all British-Canadian 21st Army Group, whatever that took.

Therefore, in an emergency, Eisenhower would probably have to meet this precondition. In a way, Bradley assured Eisenhower of his support in advance, not by pledging cooperation but by offering assessments ahead of time that would make it very hard for him to withhold it. In accepting the "calculated risk" of exposing the Ardennes Forest, Bradley accepted the fact that British cooperation might be indispensable to stem a crisis there.

And so as December came, Eisenhower was apprehensive. Privately he conceded that early results of the November offensive were a disappointment. Unusually bad flying weather hampered air support everywhere. Rains transformed the Roer, ordinarily only a minor obstacle, into a major problem, which could be overcome only by a set-piece assault reminiscent of St.-Lô. On Hodges' left, threatening German bridgeheads at Venlo and Emmerich tied Dempsey's hands. Farther south, frustration at Metz absorbed Patton, and on Devers' front the Colmar pocket remained.

Daily, Eisenhower's concern about the Russian front mounted. On the bright side, the Red Army had a well-earned reputation for methodical preparations. Preliminaries in the Ukraine in the spring of 1944 consumed two months, preparations at Vitebsk another two months. But Poland had now been inactive for four months, and there were signs of indefinite delay, called "unfortunate" by Newsweek, for "in synchronized attacks from two distant quarters, it is the cumulative moral effect that counts."

In his entry dated December 5 Butcher chronicled Eisenhower's anxiety. That night they met at the Raphael Hotel in Paris for a quiet evening of dinner and bridge in a rare evening out for Eisenhower. During the game he teased Butcher about his recent poker losses at the Eighth Air Force games, totaling $600 or so. "Oh, things are okay," Butcher chuckled. "But I could use your lucky coins."

"I've been rubbing mine pretty hard lately," Eisenhower replied.

As they talked late into the night, Butcher detected in Eisenhower a sense that his control over events was slipping away. Eisenhower seemed anxious about Hodges' inability to seize the Roer dams, Patton's postponement of a Third Army attack until mid-month, and recent British demands for new command arrangements and an equal voice at SHAEF.

Earlier that day, following formal CCS rejection of his proposed trip to Moscow, Eisenhower had filed a somber appraisal of frontline conditions. Although German divisions were arriving with only six weeks' training, contributing materially to the high German casualty rate, Allied success depended in great part on "the date and scale of the anticipated winter offensive of the Russians. I say 'anticipated,' " he had written, "because we have nothing except conjecture on which to base our ideas as to Russia's intentions."

Eisenhower had also assured Marshall that SHAEF was not growing unduly pessimistic, and that "in spite of all" the enemy was "badly stretched on this front," shifting units "up and down the line to reinforce his most threatened points," in the First and Ninth Army sectors. But efforts to take the Roer dams had failed, putting off Simpson's Ninth Army efforts to cross the Roer. Bradley had reluctantly assigned Hodges the more costly task of attacking Schmidt from the southwest, with Gerow's exhausted V Corps. Nonetheless, Eisenhower closed, "Everybody is in surprisingly good heart and condition."

With his customary optimism, Eisenhower endeavored to put the best light on rumblings within his command, which he knew would inevitably reach the CCS. Prompted by meager gains everywhere except in Alsace amounting to a "strategic reverse," Brooke and Montgomery had separately resolved to charge misconduct of the fall campaign and reopen demands for British command of Hodges' First Army. Montgomery renewed his quest for the single northern thrust to Berlin under himself as a ground commander in chief, only to find that Brooke had other plans in mind—that Bradley would step into the position as part of a broader deal with Marshall on Berlin, or that Alexander come to Paris as ground commander or as Eisenhower's "deputy." This put Montgomery under pressure to show results. Yet, Eisenhower, who had Bradley to consider, fended him off, which caused Montgomery to press his case all the harder. The turmoil would last all winter.

Within five days of Hodges' kickoff from Aachen, Montgomery had decided to test the waters. He had first raised the Command problem in a "despondent" letter to Brooke on November 6 in which he went on to describe the "unsatisfactory state of affairs in France" in dark terms. Montgomery portrayed Eisenhower as isolated and out of touch at St.-Germain, a commander issuing orders with "no relationship to the practical necessities of the battle" and lacking any grip whatever on the situation while Smith carried on the day-to-day work at Versailles. Montgomery predicted to Brooke that in "drifting along at present we are merely playing into the enemy's hands and the war will go on indefinitely." Montgomery was in a difficult position, however. Having spoken his "last word on the subject of command" in October, he was reluctant to proceed without Brooke's approval.

By now, Montgomery had reason to doubt that Brooke still considered him the man to serve as land commander. Arnhem had left scars, and he had probably also detected Brooke's declining interest in Italy, and heard talk of a new assignment for Alexander. In fact, Alexander stood out as an obvious candidate for a high position in France, given his record of service under Eisenhower as a ground commander in chief in North Africa. But if the Americans turned down Alexander, Brooke appeared to be ready to suggest Bradley, so strongly did he feel that the "set-up was bad . . . and that the war is being prolonged. . . ."

But Brooke had no set approach. First, he was reluctant to proceed, impressed as he was by the political difficulties involved and American determination to have their say. On the other hand, in his diary Brooke had noted Roosevelt's sudden admission in mid-October of unanticipated shortages of manpower and fresh troops, which had opened new vistas, since the British were in a position to provide fresh troops by consenting to transfers from Italy. Another hopeful sign had been Marshall's "wonderful telegram" in late October in which the Chief of Staff indicated that his heart was set on "finishing the war before the end of the year." All of this suggested possibilities: to appoint Alex as land commander in exchange for British reinforcements drawn from Italy; to appoint Bradley in exchange for British reinforcements but under a clear set of guidelines worked out in the CCS. Either result would assure the British of a compromise on strategy featuring strong American support for the 21st Army Group that winter and beyond. But what would induce the Americans to agree, or, for that matter, the British government?

By November, Brooke was a worried man. The British were at the bottom of a manpower barrel, and Montgomery's fifteen divisions were declining in relative importance. Meanwhile, the Allies confronted the prospect of a winter offensive, and Brooke was mindful of 1940, when Allied coordination had collapsed in the wake of a German offensive through the Ardennes

Forest. A major problem in 1940 had been disunity between the British and French commanders, similar to the disunity experienced ever since August 31, when the Americans had stripped him of direct control over all but token American forces. And, to the extent that he was "looking ahead," Brooke had to consider that Montgomery's forces alone might not be strong enough to cross the Rhine when the time came or strong enough to secure British interests in Germany, which, at a minimum, included conquest of the British zone of occupation and occupation of the North Sea ports via operations in the direction of Berlin.

How long and on what terms would the Americans continue to support Montgomery's priority? Apparently, another factor in Brooke's thinking was time—that as unfavorable as the situation was, things would never get better. British strength relative to American strength was declining, and overall Allied strength vis-à-vis the Russians had not improved since the Russian advance to the Vistula. Accordingly, Brooke and Montgomery had all but concluded that the chance that British forces would ever reach Berlin had passed, and with it, the guarantee of a major British role in the invasion of Germany. As things stood, the Russians and the Allies were equidistant from Berlin, with the Russians possessing far larger forces and a thinned-out front amid signs of a major German build-up in the west. One could not rule out a sudden improvement in the Allied position, but even if it occurred, Allied freedom of action in the coming invasion was becoming more and more circumscribed by the ongoing negotiations on occupation sectors in the EAC, which, when formally approved, would be a formidable constraint on Allied strategy.

On the other hand, Brooke did not assume that the Americans would observe the constraints implied by the EAC zones, which, in part, accounted for his growing criticism of Eisenhower's "inability to restrain Patton." On the contrary, an undercurrent in the British proposals for a northern thrust was concern about the destination of an American thrust by Bradley, which was now probably inevitable. An obvious drawback in an American thrust was that it might be ineffective. Another was that it might denude Montgomery's northern sector of support for the sake of unremunerative objectives in central and southern Germany. A less obvious concern was that Bradley would pursue the right objective, Berlin, but in the wrong way at the wrong time. From the British point of view, one factor was constant—that from the British point of view, Berlin was a useful Allied objective *provided* Montgomery's forces spearheaded the Allied offensive. Only in this way could the British be fairly certain that they would secure vital British objectives in the race for territory likely to ensue next spring. What were American thoughts? So far, the Americans had not shown their hand, but they had served notice that they would insist on a major American role in the invasion of Germany, beginning with a very large "secondary" 12th Army Group role in the Ruhr offensive that would position Bradley's forces to support Montgomery across Germany or to race him across Germany as the case may be.

Thus, Berlin loomed as a major, unspoken issue dividing the Americans and British as well as the Allies and Russians, which Brooke apparently believed was a question best worked out with Marshall—and soon. And the Berlin question presupposed that the Allies effectively dealt with the threat of a German winter offensive in the west, which was far from a given. Circumspection on this latter point lent an air of unreality to the strategy discussions that fall and provided the most dramatic illustration yet that in a coalition command only talk of an offensive is possible. But here Brooke enjoyed a slight advantage. On October 28, Eisenhower, faced with stalemate, had ordered an ambitious three-phase broad-front plan. And since Eisenhower's chances of avoiding a reverse were slight, sooner or later, confronted with the gap between plan and result, Eisenhower would be faced with having to concede faulty execution or that he was unable to devise a satisfactory plan to end the war. Presumably, Eisenhower would balk at conceding so much, but the JCS was in an impatient mood and showing signs of being receptive to criticism.

Meanwhile, Montgomery and Brooke found themselves agreeing on the need for a single-thrust strategy but differing over who should do what. More and more, Montgomery had come to see the difficulties of the ground commander idea as Eisenhower saw them. He was sympathetic to Eisenhower's problems—political and military—and concerned about the impact of a command shake-up on battle morale. Montgomery's complaints about Eisenhower were moderate, and his solutions were too limited, in Brooke's opinion. Montgomery complained about Eisenhower's strategy and his unwillingness to be more forceful with Patton, which he attributed to politics. But the criticism lacked bite and Montgomery offered little in the way of concrete suggestions beyond suggesting that he handle the problem. At one point he noted to Brooke that Eisenhower was "determined to show he is a great general in the field" and proposed to "let him do so" while all the others lent a hand to pull him through. Montgomery pressed Brooke for permission to revive the land commander idea with Eisenhower. Brooke discouraged him. "I thoroughly appreciate how unsatisfactory the situation is and how essential it is to try and rectify matters," Brooke warned Montgomery on the twentieth, "but, after having told Eisenhower 'he would hear no more from you on the subject,' you would be wrong if you reopened the matter."

Montgomery persisted, however, and on the twenty-second sounded out Brooke on a compromise he intended to present to Eisenhower: a proposal to reorganize the western front into two fronts in place of the present three-army-group structure, consisting of one front north of the Ardennes under Montgomery and one south of the Ardennes under Bradley with no land commander.

Brooke did not think much of Montgomery's compromise. In reply, he pointed out Montgomery's inconsistency in opposing Eisenhower's battle plan on the one hand, and accepting a command solution on the other that called for two fronts and left Eisenhower in full control of allocating resources between them. How could Eisenhower allocate resources without a plan? "Can you see Ike judging between the requirements of the two fronts, overriding the American clamor for their Commander being in charge of the main thrusts, etc., etc.? I can't!" Brooke conceded to Montgomery that his idea might "overcome a portion of the defects," but it omitted the essential feature: placing an intermediary—preferably a Britisher—between Eisenhower and the army groups. Therefore, Brooke was worried that Montgomery's plan would "not get at the root of the matter and the same evils will persist."

In the same letter, Brooke had gone on to inform Montgomery about rumors of "a new plot by which you are contemplating re-opening the matter with Ike by asking him whether he has any objections to your doing so! As I told you in my letter, personally, I think you are wrong in doing so. I should like a reply from you by return mail telling me exactly what you are doing and how you reconcile your new plan with everything you have said up to date." In reply, Montgomery disclosed that he had already arranged a meeting with Eisenhower on the twenty-eighth in hopes of exploring alternatives, but he assured Brooke he would do "nothing further" without his instructions.

According to Bryant, on the twenty-sixth Montgomery returned to London for talks with Brooke, in which they hammered out Montgomery's objectives in talks with Eisenhower, which were: "a) to counter the pernicious American strategy of attacking all along the line; b) to obviate splitting an Army Group with the Ardennes in the middle of it by forming two Groups (a northern and a southern) instead of the three as at present; c) to appoint a Commander for the Land forces. . . ." For the moment, by a land commander Brooke meant Bradley, who could supervise Montgomery in the north and Patton in the south. But again, whereas Brooke was determined to interpose an intermediary between Eisenhower and the army groups to coordinate the two fronts, Montgomery was willing to settle for British command of the northern front or less, with the U.S. Ninth Army under the 21st Army Group and no intermediary between Eisenhower and the American forces. This difference was crucial.

Again, it is impossible to know to what extent Brooke and Montgomery were focusing on the safety of the 21st Army Group in the current crisis or looking ahead—that is, whether they were thinking in terms of Berlin, or of withstanding the onslaught of a German winter offensive. But the basic issue in either case was the same: how to ensure that the British retained a strong voice over the Northwest European Theater of Operations and thereby the survival of British forces on the Continent in the latter case, and protection of British interests in the former.

In command terms, there were at least three ways of going about this. One way was to persuade the Americans to accept the appointment of a British deputy or land commander under Eisenhower with power to coordinate the fronts. A second way was for the British to accept Bradley or some other American in exchange for CCS understandings of American support for the British. A third way was to rely on the current setup. From the British point of view, each way had pros and cons. The first was the most direct way, but it seemed less and less practical as time wore on. By now, Montgomery saw that Eisenhower had not been exaggerating when he said that a British commander over Bradley was not possible, for domestic political and military reasons. The second way also presented difficulties from Montgomery's point of view. So far, Bradley was the candidate to step up to this position. But Montgomery did not see Bradley as the man to coordinate American and British forces or to restrain the American armies as the situation required. Montgomery felt that Bradley lacked the stature to command British forces, and he could only assume that Bradley's appointment would signal a new phase of more direct CCS supervision of the front exercised by Brooke and Marshall, which is what Brooke may have had in mind. But could the CCS broker differences likely to arise over strategy? This left the third approach of relying on Eisenhower, which was unacceptable to Brooke. The CIGS found Eisenhower's long-range plans for the invasion of Germany too passive in terms of the 21st Army Group, perhaps doubly so in view of Eisenhower's semipublic offer that weekend at his press conference to assume charge of opening direct talks with the Russians.

In sum, Montgomery was more or less satisfied with things as they were. Brooke was not. Montgomery, having fought the good fight for Berlin in September, apparently believed that Eisenhower would honor his priority and his claim on Berlin, assuming the opportunity developed. Bradley might not feel similarly bound, and what Montgomery knew better than anyone else was that a "single thrust" staged north of the Ardennes Forest could not be predominantly British. Finally, Montgomery respected Eisenhower's clear views on a land commander: that a ground commander in chief would be administratively awkward and would require months of adjustment at the wrong time. A major factor that Montgomery had cited in August in favor of a land commander now weighed against it—continuity. A time-tested procedure was in place, with clear lines of authority. In addition, since the current setup had developed in line with pre-OVERLORD understandings, Eisenhower's command, the only one of its kind in history, had acquired an aura of legitimacy. Second, another rule of coalition warfare weighed against a major command shake-up—the rule forbidding a reorganization in a crisis.

.   .   .

After Montgomery returned to Holland, Brooke pressed on, encouraged by additional signs of change in Washington on command and strategy issues. Recent JCS proposals were on his mind, evidence of healthy impatience in Washington. So was a recent article by Marshall in the December *Army-Navy Journal,* in which the Chief of Staff confessed his disappointment and surprise that victory had not come in Europe by December 7, the third anniversary of Pearl Harbor.

As the BCOS considered the situation at the end of November, Brooke found the Prime Minister hesitant, though "evidently beginning to realize that all was not well in France." Brooke argued that the Allies had sustained the first strategic reverse since the Normandy landings and that the western front was in danger of reverting to trench warfare, a state of affairs attributable to "a. American strategy, b. American organization." Brooke presented to Churchill the alternatives: Alexander going to Paris or Bradley stepping up as land commander if the Americans insisted. Churchill was open-minded but skeptical. "Ike is a good fellow who is amenable and whom I can influence," Churchill told him. "Bradley, on the other hand, might not listen to what I say." Brooke insisted that an "amenable commander is of little use, if unfit to win the war" and proposed to invite Marshall to London for talks to survey the situation. Churchill tentatively agreed but asked Brooke to "wait for a few more days before doing so."

Meanwhile, over Brooke's objection, Montgomery met with Eisenhower at his Zonhoven headquarters on the twenty-eighth. Montgomery evidently hoped to persuade Eisenhower of the need for token reform in existing procedures, if for no other reason than to stay out in front of the CCS by demonstrating their own awareness of problems in the command setup and willingness to do something about it.

The Eisenhower-Montgomery meeting at Zonhoven, only their fourth since Normandy, was marked by increased formality, indicative of the pressures on both. The two "talked in a friendly way," but Montgomery kept careful notes of the discussion. Plainly, Eisenhower and Montgomery were not discussing problems that could be resolved readily by themselves alone.

Montgomery found Eisenhower prepared to redress old grievances somewhat, but lukewarm about specific reforms. In their long talks on the night of the twenty-eighth and the morning of the twenty-ninth, the only real agreement was that the military situation was "far from good." All three army groups were short of ammunition. Rifle platoons were understrength, the U.S. reinforcement situation was bad, and British Empire casualties, numbering 75,000 since June 6, could not be replaced. Montgomery asked Eisenhower to agree that the Allies had "definitely failed since October 28th," and that they "must succeed the next time." He ritually raised the land commander idea; he suggested himself, or, alternatively, he offered to serve in a subordinate role under Bradley if Eisenhower insisted. Montgomery presented the two-front idea as an alternative in which he himself took command north of the Ardennes over Simpson, Hodges and possibly Patton while Bradley assumed command south of the Ardennes over Devers and possibly Patton. Montgomery did note that Bradley, with a thirty-division force, was not injuring the enemy substantially. Bradley was an able tactician in Montgomery's eyes, but not a strategist and too dependent on Patton. In contrast, Montgomery sought to "shape the situation," as he had in Normandy.

Discussions turned to the invasion of Germany. Eisenhower assured Montgomery of priority once the invasion was under way. He conceded the advantages of the lower Rhine and the Ruhr, but reminded Montgomery of the pitfalls of a single thrust and the benefits of two prongs, proven at Mareth and again in Normandy. Like Normandy, the 21st Army Group was up against a decisive objective with the bulk of the German defenders entrenched in the "industrial wilderness" of the Ruhr. Under cover of cloud and rain, the Germans had flooded 17 percent of the available land in Holland, converting the front into a watery maze.

Eisenhower assured Montgomery that Simpson's newly formed U.S. Ninth Army would support Dempsey, but he stopped short of offering Montgomery command of the Ninth, reserving this for future negotiation. He also refused Montgomery's suggestion that Patton's Saarland offensive set for December 3 be canceled and his divisions sent north. On a two-front command setup Eisenhower was open-minded but not enthusiastic.

In a letter to Brooke afterward, Montgomery reported everything and claimed success. Eisenhower had admitted that "a grave mistake has been made," he wrote, and was "prepared to go to about any length to succeed next time." He reported that Eisenhower had agreed "in principle" to divide the front in half, that he had favored "priority" for Montgomery's thrust, and had hinted at other concessions, though he had strongly opposed a land commander. Eisenhower had put nothing in writing, however, and so Montgomery forwarded to Eisenhower a summary of their talk. In his cover letter, Montgomery recalled how they had agreed that the October 28 plan had "definitely failed . . . that we therefore have suffered a strategic reverse. We require a new plan . . . the need to get the German war finished early is vital, in view of other factors. The new plan must not fail." Montgomery proposed a conference at Maastricht, Simpson's headquarters, on December 7, where he presumably expected to be awarded command of the U.S. Ninth Army.

"Your letter does state your conceptions and operations as presented to me the other evening," Eisenhower replied on December 1. In the body of his reply, however, Eisenhower took exception to most of Montgomery's points. First, he was uncertain about what Montgomery meant by "strategic

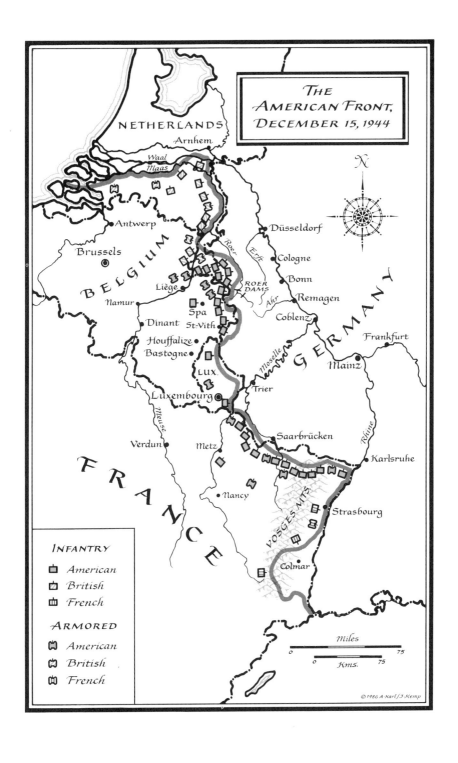

THE
AMERICAN FRONT,
DECEMBER 15, 1944

NETHERLANDS

Arnhem

Waal
Maas

Antwerp

Brussels

BELGIUM

Liège

Namur

Dinant

Spa

St-Vith

Houffalize

Bastogne

LUX.

Luxembourg

Verdun

Metz

Nancy

FRANCE

Düsseldorf

Cologne

Bonn

ROER
DAMS

Remagen

Coblenz

Frankfurt

Mainz

GERMANY

Trier

Saarbrücken

Karlsruhe

VOSGES MTS.

Strasbourg

Colmar

Roer

Erft

Ahr

Moselle

Meuse

Rhine

N

INFANTRY

□ American
▢ British
▥ French

ARMORED

▨ American
▧ British
▩ French

Miles
0   75

Kms.
0   75

©1986 A·Karl/J·Kemp

reverse," though he conceded that the November offensive would probably fail to achieve all that was hoped for it. Second, the Ruhr was an important objective, he wrote, "but never let us forget for one second that our primary objective is to defeat the German forces that are barring our way into Germany." The Ruhr was vital mainly because the German forces would fight there, and Eisenhower's undeviating policy was to pursue the Germans and defeat them where they fought. Eisenhower revealed that upon returning to Paris he had promptly put his staff to work on the two-front idea. His staff had come up with two choices: first, two fronts organized around objectives—the Ruhr and Frankfurt; second, two fronts organized on "logistical considerations." The former retained the two-prong idea, the latter envisioned a British Empire front, drawing on British supply bases, consisting of fifteen divisions in Holland and a second front, American and French, of sixty-five divisions south of Holland.

In closing, Eisenhower asked Montgomery to remember his (Eisenhower's) willingness in the past to go the extra mile. Eisenhower recalled the 500 tons per day he had given Dempsey after September 12, at the cost of grounding three U.S. divisions, which might have placed Bradley on the Rhine at Worms and pushed Patton to the Saar, clearing the west bank south of the Ardennes, and giving the Allies the "capability of concentration" now lacking. Without the measures he had actually taken in September, Eisenhower suspected that the Allies would be defending a "long narrow line of communications constantly threatened on the right flank."

Eisenhower sent a copy to Bradley, who followed up two days later with a lengthy letter to Montgomery in which he disclosed Patton's situation and plans. Patton was "containing" the Metz fortress and, Bradley indicated, even were he to pass to the defensive, the Third Army would be unable to spare a single division for Holland.

Finally Churchill yielded to Brooke and agreed to test the waters on the command problems, a decision linked to a conference with the Americans in London to hammer out a common negotiating position before talks with Stalin. On the sixth, Churchill informed Roosevelt that the time had come "to place before you the serious and disappointing war situation which faces us at the close of this year." He cited the frustrations in Italy, the "considerable delay in forcing the Rhine on the shortest road to Berlin," and the situation in the Balkans and China. "When we contrast these realities with the rosy expectations of our people," he observed, "the question very definitely arises, 'What are we going to do about it?' " Churchill urged a full-scale CCS discussion in London, "where the whole stormy scene can be calmly and patiently studied with a view to action as closely concerted as that which signalized our campaigns of 1944."

But Roosevelt was unavailable for such a meeting. In his reply, the President noted that day by day, the broad strategy adopted was developing as planned. Eisenhower's forces were "inflicting losses in excess of the German capacity to form new units," as he put it, and "chewing up the enemy's dwindling power and resources."

On December 7, the third anniversary of Pearl Harbor and the first anniversary of Eisenhower's appointment as Supreme Commander, Eisenhower joined Montgomery, Bradley, Simpson, Hodges and Tedder at Maastricht, Ninth Army Headquarters. The selection of the site proposed by Montgomery suggested the inevitable outcome of the second command debate since July—Montgomery's command of the Ninth Army. Twenty-four hours earlier, Stalin again had put off a three-way conference, deferring once more the problem of three-way military coordination and bringing the battlefield crisis closer.

There was little doubt at Maastricht that Eisenhower's British and American subordinates would pool resources to meet an emergency. Eisenhower's problem was to ensure that inter-Allied coordination came in a way that minimized the troubles involved in doing this and minimized as well the long-range impact of a military crisis, which meant conditioning the Americans for the necessary command transfer to Montgomery should the need arise.

Montgomery was tactless and difficult. Stating his views "on the problem confronting us," Montgomery raised again the single-thrust idea, an inharmonious note on the eve of the Ardennes crisis. Speaking at length, he called the Ruhr "the *only* real worthwhile objective on the western front," the north German plain opposite Dempsey the *only* sector where the Allies could force mobile war on the Germans by spring or early summer. These were factors "basic and fundamental . . . impossible to argue against." The October 28 plan "had failed to mature," and so what was required now was a "*new* plan and . . . objectives toward attainment of the master plan."

Montgomery specified three essential objectives in the weeks ahead: first, gaining intermediate objectives toward the Ruhr; second, wearing down enemy strength at a greater rate than Allied strength; third, positioning the Allies for a mobile campaign in the spring over the northern plain. Montgomery proposed that the 12th Army Group be maintained at a total strength of thirty-five divisions, operate north of Prüm–Bonn, and converge with the British 21st Army Group, operating between Wesel and Nijmegen, with the 6th Army Group "to continue operations in the Saar as far as its strength and resources will allow."

Montgomery left one major opening. He identified the Sixth Panzer Army at Bonn as the key to enemy strategy, and indicated that a "highly important factor" in winter operations could be to force the Sixth Panzer into combat, where it could be mauled and placed out of action. Montgomery implied that should the Sixth Panzer intervene against the Americans, he would moderate his demands.

Eisenhower probed Montgomery carefully on this point. He agreed to the importance of the Sixth Panzer Army and that the main objective was to "wear the Germans down and it did not matter where we did it." Was the only difference between them over how to accomplish this?

Montgomery predicted that only the Ruhr could serve the objective. The Germans were likely to defend the area in strength—fighting there would contribute "towards the attainment of the master plan."

Ironically, Montgomery's Rhine strategy might have passed for a description of Caen, when desperate German resistance had prevented a breakout, which served to undermine his military case but dramatized his intransigence. Tactfully, Eisenhower recalled Montgomery's two-prong strategy at Mareth and El Alamein. But when he suggested that he and Montgomery differed "only very slightly," Montgomery countered that "we must be clear that we differ not slightly but *widely* and on fundamental issues." Montgomery dismissed Frankfurt and insisted that if the Allies split up the resources, "neither thrust would be strong enough to obtain decisive results, the lesson of the past for which we are now paying."

The group wrangled over command but got nowhere. With a final magnanimous flourish, Montgomery offered to accept a subordinate role in a northern thrust under Bradley, but Eisenhower did not take him seriously. Montgomery's contribution to SHAEF immunity from CCS meddling— apparently unintended—was to antagonize Bradley so as to practically discredit the idea of British command over American units, by Alexander or anyone else. Montgomery received the preordained minimum: command of Simpson's Ninth Army after Gerow's four-division attack on the Roer dams set for December 13. Bradley assented and Eisenhower closed the discussion by ruling in favor of two strong thrusts, noting that existing directives governed the point, and that "if any further orders were needed, they were to be issued later."

"On the western front," SHAEF intelligence reported on December 10, "the outward surface remains comparatively unchanged, but there has been considerable stirring within the sepulchre." The report "wrote off" three German divisions, but "accepted" the presence of three fresh divisions. The Sixth SS Panzer Army remained in position behind Cologne. North of the Ardennes, formations were falling out of contact, and significant movement was under way. Farther south, intelligence had observed that the Fifth Panzer and First armies were drawing on neighboring divisions for reserves.

By the second week of December, nine panzer and five infantry divisions had slipped out of touch, and could not be located precisely because of low clouds hampering airborne reconnaissance. Conjecture about these divisions became the primary subject of the daily staff meetings at Versailles. Eisenhower and Smith repeatedly solicited Strong's views about the reserve gathering north of the Ardennes Forest. Strong guessed that the Germans were doing one of two things: either collecting a reserve to pinch off the Allied penetration at Aachen, which was his view, or, in accordance with the practice of the German General Staff, organizing a winter offensive, possibly in the Ardennes Forest.

General Strong was among the first outside of command circles to suggest the Ardennes as the German objective. Mindful that his sixth sense had proved accurate at Arnhem, Eisenhower dispatched Strong to Luxembourg to share his conclusions with Bradley. "Let them come," Bradley replied, confident that Hodges had sufficient local reserves to blunt anything the Germans might attempt in the Ardennes Forest. Bradley cited widespread evidence that German operations were severely hampered by fuel shortages, with numerous mobile vehicles being abandoned because of lack of gas.

That week, Strong circulated a top-secret intelligence digest to the army group staffs by special cipher. All copies of the report were destroyed, but Strong, in his memoir, *Intelligence at the Top,* recalled that he specifically warned that the puzzling German moves raised the strong possibility of a strike through the Ardennes Forest to relieve pressure on the Roer dams.

By the end of the week the consensus was that Von Rundstedt was in command owing to the logical way the front was being run. Bradley told a group of congressmen that Hitler obviously was out of power. "If he is ill, I wish he'd recover and take command again," he told the group. Bradley hoped that Hitler would order another desperate offensive like the one at Mortain that would enable the Allies to destroy the Germans west of the Rhine just as they had destroyed them west of the Seine.

As the curtain dropped on the fall campaign, Eisenhower at Versailles was at work on the manpower problem. He coaxed the Pentagon for administrative relief from bureaucratic-force allocations and proposed redesignating wounded soldiers in evacuation hospitals and communication troops as "non-theater personnel" in order to build up line troops without transgressing legislative guidelines. He ordered yet another "top to bottom" comb-out of Comm-Z, directing Lee to hire French civilians to spell able-bodied soldiers in menial jobs. Air force bases and other sources of idle manpower also came within the reach of the pre-Christmas shake-down in ETO.

Eisenhower maintained a flow of low-level warnings to General Thomas Handy of OPD in Washington. On the fourteenth, one week after the Maastricht meeting, Eisenhower informed Marshall that while he understood the reasoning behind War Department constraints and reluctance to accelerate the flow of trained infantry replacements to Europe, "our replacement situation is exceedingly dark." Accompanying his warnings, he renewed his request for permission to place a liaison officer in Moscow, informing Marshall of fresh identifications of eastern-front units now transferred to the west.

As usual, Soviet-Allied liaison problems were being worked out that week via talks to set "bomb lines" in the Balkans and Poland and new proposals for a shuttle base behind Soviet lines in Poland. An exchange of views about the status of the Polish Lublin provisional government remained in abeyance. Roosevelt had asked Stalin to consider a compromise solution in Poland that he hoped to present face-to-face at a working summit. Stalin, meanwhile, invited De Gaulle to Moscow and called for reciprocal three-power recognition of Lublin as the provisional Polish government to aid the Russians in suppressing Polish elements "fomenting disorder and civil war" against the Red Army.

On the fourteenth, Harriman met with Stalin and again raised the problem of Eisenhower's need to know about Russian plans for a winter offensive. Stalin agreed a "winter offensive should be launched," but was vague about the timing because unseasonably warm weather in Poland was causing ground fog that hampered artillery and air support. Stalin agreed to provide Harriman with information "after conferring with his military staff in about a week." Moving on, Stalin revived his old suggestion that the Allies mount landings in Dalmatia and that eight to ten Allied divisions "[join] up on the Russians' left" near Belgrade. In reply, Harriman recalled that Churchill "had long advocated just this Balkan strategy," but he cautioned Stalin that the winter weather in the upper Adriatic made forecasting such an operation hazardous.

By mid-December Eisenhower was a tired man. In letters home, he mused with conviction about a lazy, carefree future. In one, he told Mamie how much he was looking forward to a three-month vacation on some lonely beach "and oh, Lordy, Lordy, let it be sunny." Sharing tidbits about friends and visitors, and the endless meetings, he confessed that he was gradually becoming a "ten o'clock man." In another, he told how Christmas cards and small presents were beginning to arrive from Stateside. The packages —mostly candy and nuts—were being sent to local hospitals, though "once in a while, when the present is a lucky coin or some other trinket, I keep it myself."

That week, Eisenhower perused *Brave Men,* a book by Ernie Pyle in which he described the experience of the American GI in North Africa, Italy and Normandy.

In a note to Pyle, he said that what he liked best were the descriptions of the men on the line bearing the brunt of the battle. Noteworthy also was Pyle's description of the emotional cost of the war that he had written in late August, when it had become apparent that the Germans were defeated and that sooner or later the war would end. "I do not pretend that my own feeling is the spirit of our armies," Pyle had written. "But for me war has become a flat, black depression without highlights, a revulsion of the mind and an exhaustion of the spirit . . . to have brought little inner elation . . . only a tired sense of relief. . . ."

. . . The war in France has been especially vicious because it was one of the last stands for the enemy. We have won because of many things. . . . The victory here is the result of all the other victories . . . of Russia, and the western desert, and the bombings, and the blocking of the sea. It is the result of Tunisia and Sicily and Italy; we must never forget or belittle those campaigns. . . .

We have won this war because our men are brave, and because of many other things—because of Russia, and England, and the passage of time, and the gift of nature's materials. We did not win it because destiny created us better than all other peoples. I hope that in victory we are more grateful than we are proud. I hope we can rejoice in victory—but humbly. . . .

By mid-month Eisenhower's fatigue and his troubles with Washington were apparent. When Brooke's efforts to arrange a direct meeting with Marshall failed, Marshall, as he had done in the ANVIL dispute, deputized Eisenhower to represent American views at a round of meetings that week in London.

On the twelfth, Eisenhower flew to London for a dinner with the Prime Minister and the BCOS. Tedder and Brooke left accounts of the somber discussions over cocktails and dinner at 10 Downing Street that night. Portal, Cunningham and Brooke spoke on behalf of Montgomery's single-thrust plan across the Rhine north of Düsseldorf and urged Eisenhower to pass to the defensive south of the Ardennes.

Late into the night the BCOS pressed on. As Churchill listened silently Brooke led the arguments in the often emotional meeting, heatedly criticizing Eisenhower's "dispersion" of resources, and accusing him of "violating the principle of concentration of force." The SHAEF plan, in Brooke's opinion, simply did not reflect British urgency about ending the war. He voiced dismay when Eisenhower matter-of-factly told him that owing to the rate of reinforcement, decisive operations into Germany were not possible before May. Limited Allied strength, in Brooke's opinion, was all the more reason for concentration north of the Ardennes now. Even if reinforced, and even if the Russians resumed operations in Poland, Brooke doubted the Allies would have enough strength for two attacks deep into Germany.

In reply, Eisenhower argued that limited Allied strength, in his opinion, was all the more reason to close the Rhine along its length to gain the "capability of concentration." He had defended his actions in September and maintained that the October-November offensive had served a useful purpose. Had the Allies concentrated everything on a narrow front, they would be in trouble, as Eisenhower doubted that a line west of the Meuse and the Vosges was defensible. Eisenhower recited the terrible arithmetic of the November battles: untested German divisions had been worn down at double the ordinary rate of German casualties.

Brooke had difficulty countering Eisenhower's argument logically. The single thrust, when formulated in September, had been justified as a one-time desperate effort to exploit German military disorganization. The idea was implausible now, unless Brooke perceived sudden German demoralization and collapse, which he did not. On the night of December 12, the sensible military option was to pass to the defensive, but no one could suggest this.

Brooke persisted. A May 1945 victory was too late. Every day that passed postponed the reconstruction of the heavily mortgaged British economy, relief for Britain's war-weary population, and the end to the plight of central Europe, caught between the Russian anvil and the Allied hammer. Even to consider May 1945 would be to accept the summer of 1945, and maybe an extension of the war into 1946, which was unthinkable.

But after listening to both sides, Churchill agreed with Eisenhower that a double assault across the Rhine was only practical, a stand that so disturbed Brooke that he considered resigning the following day. Confronted later by the CIGS, Churchill blandly explained that he had taken Eisenhower's side to be a good host. That was Churchill's prerogative, of course, a reminder that the Prime Minister remained above the BCOS, and that Brooke's proposals were tools for wider purposes. The significance of Churchill's hospitality was not lost on Eisenhower, nor the passions animating Brooke.

After dinner, there were awkward silences. Eisenhower typically groped for ways of kindling the customary good spirit. Brooke, Churchill, Eisenhower, Ismay and Portal drifted into conversation about life after the war. For a while Eisenhower filibustered about his ambition: to champion the cause of Anglo-American unity after the German surrender. Despite many disagreements, the Allies fought in the shadow of a great truth, that the Allied coalition still held up after three years, an answer to skeptics who doubted that dynamic national passions could ever really be subordinated to common goals. Eisenhower, an ethnic German and native of rural Kansas, was inspired by this and pronounced himself ready to devote "the afternoon and evening of my life" to advancing this cause in peacetime.

Ismay, deeply impressed, wrote Eisenhower a day later declaring that he, too, was ready to devote his life to this cause. Churchill warmly appreciated the sentiment. Portal was silent. Brooke was sullen and seemingly bored.

Several days later the participants exchanged notes and season's greetings. Eisenhower thanked Ismay and Brooke for the "grand visit." To Brooke he added that the evening "was altogether enjoyable and I hope you did not mind my rather lengthy discussion of what I personally hope to do after the war in advancing the cause that lies so close to my heart. It is a subject on which I cannot speak sanely."

To Churchill, to whom no apologies were necessary, Eisenhower wrote:

December 16, 1944
Dear Prime Minister:

This is just a short note to send you my very best Christmas and New Year's wishes. I hope that 1945 not only brings a conclusive end to the European war, but brings you personally added success and happiness. While there is scarcely anything that could not add to your national and world stature, yet it is not too much to hope that more freedom-loving people everywhere will gain a clearer understanding of what they owe to you.

Again, my very best wishes to you and to your delightful family.

Sincerely,
Dwight D. Eisenhower

8

The Ardennes

DECEMBER 16. Before dawn the weather was warming. Low overcast and haze rising from snow cover shrouded the movement of fourteen German infantry divisions to start points backed by five panzer divisions. At five-thirty, storm battalions of three German armies "permeated" the loosely strung American fortifications "like raindrops" along the fifty-mile front between Monschau and Echternach.

In the north, between Monschau and Elsenborn, Gerow's V Corps, consisting of the 99th Division and the 2nd Armored, was making last-minute preparations to resume attacks on the Schmidt dams. On Gerow's right flank, VIII Corps defenses were stretched out dangerously. The understrength 14th Cavalry Group rested at Losheim. The U.S. 106th Division was refitting in the Schnee Eifel after battle in the Hürtgen Forest. Along the Our River, the American 28th Division and the 4th Division at Echternach farther south awaited 9,000 replacements for casualties sustained in November. The combat histories show that liaison between the units in the assault area was virtually nonexistent, and that there was no plan for the defense of the area except for Middleton's broad intent to fight a series of delaying actions, "all the way back to the Meuse" if necessary. Indeed, a kind of paralysis seems to have taken hold over the units at every echelon of command in the forty-eight hours before the attack, not unlike the paralysis that had come over the Germans in Normandy.

Then, at 5:20 A.M., announcing what would be the last major German thrust of the war, 2,000 German artillery pieces opened up along the Schnee Eifel, "walking back" toward the bridges and crossroads. Under cover of this bombardment, the infantry advanced, closely followed up by the panzers. Scattered reports of enemy probing actions in the Ardennes Forest reached First Army Headquarters at Spa by seven o'clock, followed within two hours by reports of attacks of battalion strength all along the VIII Corps front.

In Paris, Eisenhower awoke on a dull, rainy morning. As the story goes, had he been superstitious, he might have sensed the assault that was under way. At midnight the night before, he had learned that his name was included on the select five-star promotion list submitted to the Senate, along with Pershing, Leahy, Marshall, King, MacArthur, Nimitz, Arnold and Halsey. Eisenhower's last promotion had come on February 14, 1943, twenty-four hours before the German attack at the Kasserine Pass in central Tunisia, a surprise setback that had rocked the inexperienced American command and propelled Omar Bradley and George Patton to the forefront of American battle commanders.

But Eisenhower looked forward to a routine day. Bradley, grounded by fog, was due in that afternoon to discuss the results of SHAEF's latest mission to Washington on the manpower problem. So far, Eisenhower's emissaries in Washington were empty-handed. The response to all overtures was that despite recent losses, manpower in the European theater exceeded department quotas, and Eisenhower was to make do by combing out bloated Comm-Z components. In Eisenhower's opinion, however, such stopgap measures were inadequate, and by the sixteenth he contemplated drastic steps: breaking off the background talks with Washington; disbanding U.S. divisions in Europe to eliminate waste of divisional staff and support echelons; and petitioning the CCS for reinforcements, including idle divisions in the United States.

Intelligence reports that morning told of heavy rail movement in the vicinity of Bonn–Cologne. The Allies were in contact with only 54 German divisions, leaving a very high total of 20 divisions unaccounted for in the cloud and fog, including the 1st SS, 12th SS, 2nd SS, 10th SS and 9th SS divisions, which for weeks had sat like "ducks in a row" behind Cologne. German armor had just broken off contact in the Saar–Palatinate sector, leaving only two panzer and two panzer grenadier divisions facing the Third Army on the eve of Patton's Saarland offensive set for the nineteenth. The SHAEF and army group intelligence staffs unanimously felt that although it was apparent that the enemy was gathering reserves, the Germans were not yet capable of waging "major" offensive operations. General Courtney Hodges in particular had doubted anything was up, despite the pronounced movement of infantry divisions away from the Roer sector. All conceded an attack was "possible," including an attack in the Ardennes Forest, but nothing was imminent.

Before Bradley's arrival, Eisenhower was set to attend the wedding of Sergeant McKeogh to Pearlie Hargreaves, a staff secretary, at the Chapel of Louis XIV near Versailles. As he left, Eisenhower tended to a dispatch from Montgomery about operation VERITABLE, the 21st Army Group attack south and east from Nijmegen to clear the Maas set for January 12. In closing, Montgomery had asked for permission to leave 21st Army Group headquarters for several days in order to return to London for a Christmas visit with his son and talks with Brooke. Montgomery reminded Eisenhower good-naturedly of their five-pound wager fourteen months before on the date of the German surrender; Eisenhower had chosen December 1944, Montgomery spring 1945. The debt was "for payment, I think at Christmas," Montgomery wrote.

In his reply, Eisenhower told Montgomery he envied his chance to spend the holidays with his son and reminded him that the wager had nine days to run. "While it seems almost certain you will have an extra five pounds for Christmas," he wrote, "you will not get it until that day. At least you must admit we have gone a long ways toward the defeat of Germany since we made our bet on the 11th of October, 1943."

The paralysis in Belgium continued for much of the morning. Primed for the renewal of First Army attacks on Schmidt, Hodges was slow to concede that the Germans were up to anything more than "spoiling attacks." When V Corps encountered German tanks near the Elsenborn bridge, Gerow, convinced that the attack was "something big," twice asked for permission to draw up and withdraw several units north of Monschau into reserve. Hodges refused both requests.

By 11 A.M. it was apparent that the Germans had launched major attacks against the 106th Division on the boundary between Gerow and Middleton. By noon Hodges and the First Army staff at Spa had little doubt that the Germans had launched an "all-out effort" on the VIII Corps front. Hodges placed the U.S. 1st Division on six-hour alert and ordered elements of the 9th Armored to cover Malmédy and First Army installations at Spa. Hodges reached Bradley in Versailles, who agreed to prepare Simpson's 7th Armored and Patton's 10th Armored for a move to shore up the flanks of the reported penetrations.

Meanwhile, as the Germans pressed on, Gerow's V Corps sector was the scene of an early and significant American success. The mission of Dietrich's Sixth Panzer Army infantry was to overrun American forces quickly at Monschau and Bütgenbach in order to open roads for swift Armored exploitation toward the Meuse. But the warming trend had turned icy road shoulders into mud, and German traffic was snarled. The 12th SS Division, which was to exploit a breakthrough in the Bütgenbach area was committed at noon to force a breakthrough, causing a reorientation of the Sixth Panzer Army attack south toward Losheim, where the 1st SS Panzer Division had penetrated six miles beyond a line held by the U.S. 14th Cavalry Regiment and was advancing in the direction of Malmédy–Stavelot.

In the center, disaster engulfed Middleton's VIII Corps, which stretched out along the wooded hills and valleys cut by the Prüm, Our and Clerf rivers. For months, these streams of east-central Belgium had marked the line between American and German forces in the "quiet sector" of the Ardennes. By noon, waves of German assault infantry clad in green-gray had overrun the 106th and 28th divisions' outposts. Engineers had built bridges over the Our for the armored divisions, which advanced boldly. Before anyone could appreciate the significance of the reports, German infantry had encircled two regiments of the 106th, and armor had over-whelmed the 28th Division along a thirty-mile front north of the town of Vianden.

Thus, Von Rundstedt achieved tactical surprise, evening an old score. By afternoon the 106th and 28th were falling back in confusion while the neighboring 4th Division barely clung to positions at Echternach. The American reaction was one of incredulity, but by late afternoon 14 German divisions were operating in the Ardennes, a tide that would swell to an estimated 25 divisions with 600 tanks backed by 1,000 aircraft.

Meanwhile, at the Chapel of Louis XIV, the wedding guests huddled under trench coats while Butcher, resplendent in the bridge coat of a Navy captain, acted as McKeogh's best man. After the brief ceremony Eisen-hower hosted a reception for a handful of guests at the Trianon until four o'clock, when he was joined by Bradley. Eisenhower and Bradley left the reception and ducked into the War Room to discuss the manpower crisis.

An hour later Strong interrupted the meeting with word from 12th Army Group Headquarters in Luxembourg of German activity in the Ardennes. Fragmentary and contradictory reports told of German penetrations at five points on a wide front in Middleton's VIII Corps sector. Significant in Strong's opinion was the reappearance of enemy divisions long absent from the front, including the Second Panzer, and the re-formed Panzer Lehr, units last seen in the Bonn–Cologne sector. As he presented the news Strong reminded the group of his recent appraisals which had noted the threat in the Ardennes and Strong emphasized what he saw as the danger of a well-coordinated offensive aimed at Liège and the rear of the First Army, or a more far-reaching bid for the Meuse and Antwerp.

Bradley pronounced himself skeptical that the Germans would mount more than a "spoiling attack" to blunt Hodges' preparations against Schmidt and Patton's in the Saar. He and Middleton had agreed that an attack through the Ardennes could have only two objectives: (1) the quick seizure of terrain to bolster German morale, and (2) to disrupt First and Third Army preparations. All agreed that the Ardennes was poor terrain for a big attack, an area of narrow, winding defiles and roadways running northwest, against the grain of the reported penetrations. Eisenhower in-clined to Strong's view—but nothing could be done for a while, and so the group retired for an after-dinner reception at the WAC House for the

McKeoghs, champagne to celebrate Eisenhower's promotion, and several rubbers of bridge.

And so it went in the early hours of the last German offensive of the war. By dusk, with their darkest premonitions fulfilled, Eisenhower and Bradley, like their German counterparts in June, procrastinated, and unlike the Germans on the night of June 5–6, Eisenhower had little margin of territory to yield or reserves of men. After several hours of bridge, Eisenhower and Bradley returned to the War Room, where they spent the night monitoring the reports and discussing steps to be taken. Decisive action was urgent, and would come by dawn.

By midnight, an alarming picture was shaping up. Reports confirmed that Fifth and Sixth SS panzer armies were operating in the Ardennes north of the German Seventh Army, which had joined the assault attacking west and southwestward from Trier. The scale of the assault took them by surprise, but the contingency had not been completely unforeseen. Little adjustment in tactical thinking was involved, and so Eisenhower and Bradley quickly settled on a four-point plan to blunt the attack: first, shoring up the "shoulders" north and south of the reported penetration; second, blocking the westward advance by holding pivotal road hubs; third, forming a solid defensive wall along the north rim to block the Meuse; fourth, Third Army intervention against the German southern flank when possible. Ideally, these steps would prove to be effective and within the means of Bradley's 12th Army Group, and would obviate the complications of forming reserves by calling on units from other fronts, but this was far from certain.

The main problem confronting Eisenhower that night was reserves, or the lack of them. With Bradley's forces deployed for attack, Eisenhower's American reserve consisted of the 82nd and 101st airborne divisions refitting at Reims and the 11th Armored off-loading at Cherbourg. Eisenhower could not deploy the American reserve effectively or be certain of the need for reserves from other sectors until he could answer several questions. What was German strategic intent? Was the attack an all-out bid for Antwerp, or was it more local and aimed at blunting the First and Third armies' offensives, as Bradley insisted? What was the condition of VIII Corps? What was the likelihood of attacks in other sectors?

Military risks and political complications loomed wherever Eisenhower looked that night. In the north, the threat of secondary attack would preoccupy Simpson and Hodges in the Düren–Schmidt area. Horrocks' XXX Corps refitting in the Brussels area was the main unit north of the Ardennes capable of backing up rearward First Army positions, but Montgomery faced a German Fifteenth Army build-up in Holland and, plainly, for Eisenhower to call on British help would entail assurances in the form of command concessions to Montgomery if not outright command over the entire front north of the Ardennes, to be implemented under pressure of military crisis. Likewise, Patton could not reassemble the march north without stretching out the U.S. Seventh Army and probably forcing Devers' 6th Army Group back into the Vosges, which would expose the French First Army in Alsace, which De Gaulle would surely oppose. In short, the attack quickly produced a domino effect along the 400-mile front, transforming virtually independent fronts into an interlocking whole comprising American, British, and French forces each with the primary mission of self-protection.

By the morning of the seventeenth, the Allied high command was in motion. Eisenhower confirmed Bradley's decision to dispatch the 7th and 10th Armored to the shoulders of the penetration and canceled the First and Third Army attacks set to start on the nineteenth. Patton, one of the first to sense a problem in the Ardennes, was already making ready to break off contact with the German forces on the Saar River. But Patton protested relinquishing the 10th Armored to Hodges even temporarily, an early sign of widespread American reluctance to accept the news and the attending command implications, a reluctance that persisted throughout the day.

The situation quickly deteriorated. High overcast on the seventeenth prevented precise observation and hampered the use of Allied bombers against the German columns. A picture of chaos would greet Bradley back at his headquarters in Luxembourg, where his staff labored to regain touch with a fragmented command unable to cope with widespread confusion in the battle zone as command posts were overrun and German sappers cut rearward communications.

Along the northern shoulder, a seesaw battle raged at the Elsenborn ridge. The U.S. 2nd and 99th held and succeeded in tripping up the momentum of the Sixth Panzer, having forced Dietrich to commit the follow-on 12th SS to strengthen infantry attacks as early as noon on the sixteenth. But tanks of the 1st SS Division advanced twenty miles inside Belgium and approached Stavelot, eight miles from First Army Headquarters at Spa. Evacuation of the area began in confusion as clerks, cooks, mess hands, Signal Corps and Ordnance troops improvised roadblocks and strongpoints to cover an evacuation of First Army Headquarters and two vast fuel dumps containing over three million gallons of gasoline. Fortunately, at the town of St.-Vith, the arriving U.S. 7th Armored Division became the rock "on which the tide of the [Sixth Panzer] attack divided," confining elements of the spearhead 1st SS Panzer Corps to a single road in the valley of the Amblève River.

Elsewhere confusion reigned. South of St.-Vith the Fifth Panzer Army advanced unchecked toward the gap between St.-Vith and Bastogne, the two main road centers in the Ardennes. Indeed, the whole center from St.-Vith to Wiltz resembled "a no man's land as isolated American units desperately tried to delay or escape the German assault." By afternoon, with the 7th Armored in place at St.-Vith and the First Army containing Dietrich's right wing in the Malmédy–Bütgenbach area, attention began to focus on Bastogne, the crucial point in Manteuffel's sector. At Versailles, Major General J.F.M. Whiteley, Eisenhower's deputy chief of staff, was the first to alert Eisenhower to the overriding importance of Bastogne—without it, the Fifth Panzer advance would be confined to narrow roads, vulnerable to flanking attack and air interdiction. At the time, Middleton was hastily organizing a defense of the town under Bradley's orders to hold even if encircled, though Eisenhower's decision to rush reserves to reinforce Bastogne would not come until the last possible moment that night.

Meanwhile, Allied high command was in the throes of a crucial debate. The northward bias of the German attack was clear but German intentions were not, and Eisenhower confronted two interpretations, one American and one British. Throughout the day, Bradley steadfastly maintained that the Germans were engaged in a "spoiling attack" aimed at frustrating the First and Third Army offensive preparations north and south of the Ardennes, which, when contained, would hand the 12th Army Group an opportunity to inflict a major defeat on the Germans. The counterpoint was Strong's more pessimistic appraisal that the Germans were attempting a repetition of 1940. He continued to speak of the dangers of a well-coordinated offense aimed at Liège and the Meuse where the Germans had forced a breakthrough in 1940.

What were German intentions? The evidence was unclear, so it seemed possible that even the Germans did not know what they hoped to accomplish in the Ardennes. On behalf of his optimistic appraisal, Bradley could point to the fact that the German Fifteenth Army in the north opposite Aachen remained quiet while the German Seventh Army in the south at Echternach was active, and that while the Sixth SS Panzer permitted armored units to become embroiled in infantry fighting at Bütgenbach, the Fifth Panzer Army by-passed resistance and advanced rapidly toward the Bastogne–St.-Vith gap, where it would be poised to exploit northward, westward or southward to envelop Patton's Third Army. Strong's view seemed justified by the northern bias of the attack, its size and the extreme consequences should the Allies miscalculate and allow Germans to break through into the rear of the U.S. First Army. As he later recalled, Strong did not discount the American arguments, nor did he ignore the fact that Von Rundstedt's forces were weaker than in 1940. But Strong and the British had memories of German offensive prowess in the years 1940–42, whereas the Americans had encountered the Germans only in retreat. He was unwilling to say that the attack was not aimed at Liège–Brussels with the objective of destroying the entire Allied force north of the Ardennes, nor was he willing to say that the Germans could not succeed if the American First Army attempted to hold untenable positions along the northern rim for the sake of re-enacting its victory at Mortain in August.

The stakes were high. The point at issue involved no less than Bradley's control of the First and Ninth armies in that Bradley's optimistic appraisal implied that all countermeasures were within the capacity of his army group, while Strong's appraisal implied the opposite. But did the Allies dare to be optimistic? In the early stages the Allied appraisal necessarily turned on a question of fact: Did Bradley have adequate reserves to check an all-out German assault? Any doubt on this score transformed a purely military assessment into a political question: What assurances could Montgomery demand in return for parting with reserves to back up the beleaguered U.S. First Army? Presumably, Montgomery, before committing anything, would insist on overall command to make sure of his ability to transfer reserves —British and American—back and forth between the Ardennes and Holland as necessary to meet emergencies.

Gradually on the seventeenth, the scales tipped against Bradley's more optimistic appraisal. By noon twenty-four German divisions had been identified in the Ardennes, and an attack on this scale could not be justified unless the operation held out the prospect of decisive results. Likewise, Eisenhower had to reckon with Allied manpower constraints, the highly volatile situation his Allied command would face if the Germans crossed the Meuse in the First Army sector and threatened Brussels–Antwerp, and a technical factor in favor of transferring command to Montgomery—with the apparent German objectives behind the northern rim of the penetration, cautious and methodical tactics would be essential in the U.S. First Army sector, tactics which the Americans opposed and which came naturally to Montgomery. South of the German penetration the Third Army would enjoy latitude to roam and improvise, provided Patton could safely abandon the Moselle and Devers could stretch out his army group to cover Patton's right. Bradley and Patton were temperamentally better suited for counter-attack, and Eisenhower questioned whether Bradley could simultaneously devise a holding pattern in the north and aggressive tactics in the south. But the command matter was on hold pending two developments: first, a sign from Bradley that he would cooperate with the arrangement and, second, a British request that would clarify a crucial point—that the step was necessary to ensure British as well as American safety, indicating that the transfer was a temporary expedient justified by the exigencies of battle, nothing more.

Would Bradley cooperate? Bradley's initial appraisal of German intentions was a sign that the American command would not lightly abandon the idea that the 12th Army Group could handle the situation without aid and convert the German attack into a major American victory. Throughout the day, Bradley rejected all suggestions of trouble, but his grudging acceptance was a matter of time, a fact that Bradley later conceded in *A Soldier's Story,* where he recounted his long, dreary drive that afternoon from Paris back to Luxembourg City. He recalled that as the command car entered

Luxembourg he noticed a large American flag on the roof of a stone cottage. "I hope he doesn't have to take it down," Bradley remarked to Major Hansen.

"You mean we'll stay put in Luxembourg?" Hansen asked.

"You bet your life we will," Bradley replied. "I'm not going to budge this CP. It would scare everyone else to death."

The news awaiting Bradley was not good. The Sixth SS Panzer threatened Malmédy and Stavelot, the site of vast fuel dumps, which implied that the German objective was to cross the Meuse at Huy–Liège or farther west at Dinant-Namur. And yet the Fifteenth Army opposite Aachen was still quiet while the German Seventh Army at Echternach was active. The Sixth SS Panzer had permitted armored units to become embroiled in infantry fighting at Bütgenbach while the Fifth Panzer Army advanced unchecked, which again suggested that Bradley's theory that the Germans were mounting a "spoiling attack" was not so far-fetched after all. But early reports indicated that VIII Corps was not coping, and the scale of the assault was larger than Bradley had expected.

Late that afternoon, Eisenhower phoned Bradley in Luxembourg to suggest that he withdraw his forward headquarters back to Verdun. Bradley replied that he would "never move backwards with a headquarters," and that "too much prestige was at stake" even to consider it.

This exchange was significant. It fortified Eisenhower's premonition that to delay the transfer much longer might result in erratic decisions and commitments that could lead to a loss of control. Meanwhile, by entrenching himself in Luxembourg, Bradley had positioned himself away from the threatened sector in the north; 12th Army Group communications were imperiled, and since, plainly, Bradley could not direct the entire battle from his base in Luxembourg, it was fair to assume that he did not intend to.

By nightfall the command shift became imminent with Eisenhower's decision to consolidate the 82nd and 101st Airborne under Ridgway, and to direct both units to make ready for the 100-mile journey from bivouac at Reims to St.-Vith and Bastogne. With the release of the two divisions, Eisenhower was left without a ready American reserve to defend the open stretches of the Meuse between Dinant and Namur. From then on, Eisenhower's steps were aimed at accomplishing the transfer of command of the U.S. First and Ninth armies to Montgomery with as little controversy and obstruction as possible, though he continued to await a British request. Accordingly, Eisenhower ordered SHAEF to impose censorship on all First Army battle dispatches—not an unprecedented measure but an unusual one aimed evidently at discouraging speculation about a command shift and avoiding a debate in the CCS, which would hamper Eisenhower's freedom to implement it, and then to undo it when the time came. Significantly, Eisenhower gave no hint of problems in a message to General Somervell that night on the manpower problem. In it, Eisenhower acknowledged that the enemy had "launched a rather ambitious counterattack east of the Luxembourg area," but he assured Somervell that armor withdrawn from the Roer and Moselle would soon press on both flanks of the salient, and that "if this goes well, we should not only stop the thrust but should be able to profit from it." Notably, Eisenhower sent no messages to Marshall that day or the next.

In the confusion of December 17, 1944, the long-awaited German counter-offensive assumed a pattern. In the north, the Sixth Panzer Army was stalled in heavy fighting at Bütgenbach and St.-Vith, which compressed the I SS Panzer Corps into a twenty-by-five-mile salient. Hodges grappled with a "serious if not critical" situation in the Malmédy–Werbomont area, where the I SS Panzer Corps attempted to press north. Enemy columns threatened to overrun First Army Headquarters and the vast fuel dumps in the Spa area. For a time, a single company manned barricades and slowed up the Germans two miles short of Spa while transports began hauling away gasoline and Hodges prepared to evacuate First Army Headquarters farther back, to the Belgian town of St.-Trond.

In the center, the situation was fluid. German attacks on St.-Vith nearly encircled the 7th Armored while German spearheads south of St.-Vith pressed twelve miles to the Wiltz–Houffalize line. Meanwhile an all-out battle was shaping up for control of Bastogne. By the night of the seventeenth, reports placed Panzer Lehr and the 116th within five miles of the city, prompting Bradley's "Stand fast" order. Patton joined Bradley in Luxembourg to map out Third Army attacks to relieve Middleton, who had improvised a defense of the town with remnants of the 106th, 28th and 9th Armored. Patton's available forces consisted of the 4th Armored and the 26th and 80th divisions hastily formed into III Corps, and three divisions of XII Corps 100 miles away at Saarbrücken. Characteristically, Patton was unhappy about calling off his December 19 offensive. "But what the hell," he said, "we'll still be killing Krauts." Meanwhile, news of the attack filtered back to Washington and London about twenty-four hours behind the flow of reports at SHAEF. By the eighteenth, in the void left by the "news blackout," press reports based on rumors told of twenty-mile penetrations from Holland to Trier and of a serious, major winter offensive potentially "grave" and altering "the entire character of the war."

But even at the highest levels, American and British appraisals continued to differ significantly. At the Pentagon, the theme on December 18 was 1918. Marshall and Secretary Stimson, veterans of the Great War, recalled the Ludendorff offensive of March 1918, Germany's last bold effort before retreat and capitulation. Neither believed that Antwerp was in jeopardy, though they agreed that the fall of Liège and the rout of the U.S. First Army would indefinitely prolong the war. Both may also have been mindful as well of the differences between 1918 and 1944, differences that had permeated all Allied decisions since January 1944. In the summer of 1918 Allied strength in France had been growing rapidly with the infusion of the freshly deployed American Army under the Supreme Command of Field Marshal Ferdinand Foch, who directed all the armies confronting Germany. In December 1944 the American and British armies were nearing peak strength. The French were limited to eight divisions, and liaison with the massive Red Army, which provided the margin of safety, was close to nonexistent.

Hard decisions were inevitable, and as the story goes, lacking direct word from Eisenhower, Marshall decided to offer no suggestions. General George A. Lincoln of OPD and Lieutenant General Hull approached Marshall for "guidance . . . regarding how the War Department would best assist General Eisenhower in this new turn of events." According to historian Forrest Pogue, Marshall replied, "We can't help Eisenhower in any way other than not bothering him." Marshall issued an edict forbidding any messages from the Pentagon to ETO "unless approved by me."

In London the theme was June 1940. Brooke, who for months had insisted on the importance of generalship and of bold steps to seize fleeting opportunities with the precious resources at hand, now saw the tables turned by Von Rundstedt's surprise counterstroke, which threatened a repetition of June 1940, when the British had been pushed off the mainland by the collapse of the French front. He lamented the lack of reserves and American leadership, which he held to account for the crisis. Brooke, by now, was aware of Bradley's stubborn appraisal of the offensive as a "spoiling attack," of the rout of two divisions in the American center, of Eisenhower's decision to deploy the U.S. 82nd and 101st Airborne, and the absence of any set plan for restoring order in Hodges' chaotic sector. Accordingly, Brooke resolved to impose a straightforward, two-step procedure to meet the crisis. First, he was determined that the Americans abandon any illusions that they were about to mount a counteroffensive and carry out First Army withdrawals to more defensible positions. Second, he was determined to place overall responsibility on a man who could impose order and balance in a chaotic situation, namely, Montgomery. But Brooke, like Marshall, was keeping hands off.

The battle raged on. "The main point," Strong wrote in a brief circulated at Versailles on the afternoon of the eighteenth, "is whether this attack is a sign of strength or weakness." Despite rapid enemy gains, it remained to be seen whether Bradley's appraisal was far wide of the mark in classifying the attack as diversionary, or as Strong put it, "whether American appraisals of German strength are more accurate than German appraisals." Strong ventured the opinion that the German attack might be judged eventually not by the ground gained but "by the number of Allied divisions it diverts

The build-up. Troops and equipment moving ashore over the American beaches. *Source unknown (U.S. Army?)*

NORMANDY AND PARIS

Zone of isolation: a rail junction in Normandy after being pounded from the air. *U.S. Army*

Mid-June visit ashore: Eisenhower, accompanied by Second Lieutenant John Eisenhower, takes time out to chat with a GI who appears to be digging a trench. *U.S. Army*

Battle of the hedgerows. A French farmer prays over the body of a slain GI near Carentan. *U.S. Army*

Stalemate? Hedgerow battlefield in XIX Corps sector. Engineers search the road for land mines.

On July 1, Eisenhower, Bradley and Gault (on right) inspect the damage surrounding a German V-1 site near Cherbourg. "Knowing the devilish German scientific mind," wrote Gault, "you speculated on whether they were going so far as to split the atom." *U.S. Army*

Caen, the crucible. A picture of the cathedral taken shortly after Dempsey's seizure of the city on July 9. *Source unknown*

Difficult times: Eisenhower and Montgomery confer at 21st Army Group Headquarters at the height of the "air-ground" dispute. *U.S. Army*

In the aftermath of the carpet bombing of St.-Lô, Eisenhower confers with Bradley and General Elwood "Pete" Quesada. In view of the "shorts" and discouraging early results of the bombing, Eisenhower vowed to Bradley that he would forbid air support of a ground attack on that scale in the future—a vow Eisenhower would soon reconsider. *U.S. Army*

Closing the jaws. British and Canadian troops advance toward Falaise. *Source unknown*

The liberation of Paris.
Eisenhower and Bradley at the
Arc de Triomphe, August 27,
1944. *U.S. Army*

(Inset) Paris, fifteen years earlier. General John Pershing
(fifth from left) and his American Battlefield Monuments
Commission staff. Major John
Eisenhower is second from
right. *Eisenhower Family
Collection*

FALL CAMPAIGN

Battle for the Roer River. First Army troops storm German strongpoint. *U.S. Army*

(Upper left) on the road, fall, 1944. *U.S. Army*

With King George VI at Reims on Eisenhower's fifty-fourth birthday, October 14, 1944. *U.S. Army*

Inspecting troops near Aachen, fall, 1944. "I'm comfortable enough," Eisenhower wrote his wife, "because I can keep dry and wear enough clothes. Anyone, in this war, that has the slightest temptation to bemoan his lot or feel sorry for himself should visit the frontline soldier!" *Eisenhower Family Collection*

Command dispute I: Lieutenant General Omar N. Bradley, whose 12th Army Group was the bone of contention between Eisenhower and the British. Bradley's popularity with the American GIs and his willingness to assume responsibility for the "calculated risk," of thinly manning the Ardennes sector, were among the reasons Eisenhower considered Bradley his most valuable lieutenant and field commander. *Source unknown*

Command dispute II: Field Marshal Alan Brooke, conferring here with Churchill and Eisenhower at Reims in mid-November. Within the week, Brooke would launch his low-key effort to arrange meetings with Marshall for the purpose of working out a revamped system of ground command. *Source unknown (U.S. Army?)*

The calm before the storm: Eisenhower snacking with officers at a command post in Belgium, November 1944. *U.S. Army*

The German commanders. Left to right: Field Marshal Walther Model, General Josef "Sepp" Dietrich and General Hasso von Manteuffel. Of the three, only Dietrich exhibited enthusiasm for Hitler's far-ranging plans to recapture Antwerp.
National Archives: Model, Dietrich Courtesy of John Eisenhower: Manteuffel

German assault. At dawn, December 16, 1944, German infantry attacked on a seventy-five-mile front and permeated the American lines in the Ardennes Forest "like rain-drops." *U.S. Army*

Command decision: Mont-gomery, now in command of the U.S. First and Ninth armies, confers with General Matthew Ridgway about extricating American forces from the Salm River. *Source unknown (U.S. Army?)*

St.-Vith: "The rock of defense on which the tide of the [Sixth Panzer Army] assault broke and divided..." *U.S. Army*

VERITABLE. On February 8, the British drive to close the Rhine north of Düsseldorf jumps off in perhaps the worst fighting conditions of the war. *Imperial War Museum*

Closing the Bulge, January 29, 1945. Troops of the 94th Division form a human ammunition train to get shells to the front lines near Nennig, Germany. *U.S. Army, Courtesy of Eisenhower Library*

The beginning of the end. On March 15, 1945, an American observer looks down on the Ludendorff Bridge, near Remagen, from the east bank of the Rhine. *U.S. Army*

The American high command, winter–spring, 1945. Back row, left to right: Brigadier General Ralph F. Stearley, Lieutenant General Hoyt S. Vandenberg, Lieutenant General W. Bedell Smith, Major General Otto P. Weyland, Brigadier General Richard E. Nugent. Front row, left to right: Lieutenant General William M. Simpson, General George S. Patton, General Carl A. Spaatz, General Dwight D. Eisenhower, General Omar N. Bradley, General Courtney H. Hodges, Lieutenant General Leonard T. Gerow. *U.S. Army (Hodges Collection)*

THE END
IN EUROPE

March 17, 1945. Eisenhower, Patton and General Jacob Devers discuss UNDERTONE and prospects for seizing additional bridgeheads in the Mainz–Worms area. *U.S. Army*

PLUNDER: Churchill (not pictured), Brooke, Eisenhower, Montgomery and Bradley meet at Major General John B. Anderson's (second from right) XIII Corps headquarters near Rheinberg to observe British-U.S. Ninth Army Rhine crossings and to finalize plans for advance into central Germany. *U.S. Army*

Overrunning Germany. Against the westward
flow of German prisoners, American tanks
move east along the autobahn toward the Elbe
and linkup with the Russians. *U.S. Army*

Central Germany, April 1, 1945. GIs root out
isolated pockets of resistance town by town.
U.S. Army

Ohrdruf Nord. On April 12, 1945, Eisenhower, Patton and Bradley
inspect a work camp near Gotha. As Bradley puts it, "here death had
been so fouled by degradation that it both stunned and numbed us."
U.S. Army

Survivors at Buchenwald.
Photographs taken by John
Eisenhower, April 14, 1945.
Courtesy of John Eisenhower

German collapse: Troops flee-
ing the Russians at the Mulde.
Photograph taken by John
Eisenhower. *Courtesy of John
Eisenhower*

May 7, 1945. Unconditional
surrender: shortly after midnight, General Alfred Jodl
signs the instrument of surrender in the War Room at
SHAEF forward, Reims.
Admiral Hans von Friedeburg
is at Jodl's left, and behind
him is Major General K.W.D.
Strong, SHAEF G-2.
U.S. Army

Aftermath: Germany in May 1945, a scene of unrelieved desolation.
Novosti

Eisenhower, Zhukov and Montgomery meet in Berlin on June 5,
1945. *Source unknown (U.S. Army?)*

June 12, 1945. Eisenhower en
route to Guildhall to receive
the Freedom of London.
U.S. Army

Homecoming in Kansas, June
1945. *Eisenhower Family
Collection (U.S. Army)*

World traveler: on Lenin's tomb, Eisenhower, with Zhukov (at his right), Stalin and Averell Harriman, views parade through Red Square on August 12, 1945. *U.S. Army*

EPILOGUE

World citizen: General Eisenhower at the American Legion Convention, November 20, 1945. *U.S. Army*

from the vital sectors on the front," the delay, the diplomatic ferment left in its wake and the moral exhaustion and confusion attending it.

Eisenhower's timely release of the 101st and 82nd to Bastogne and St.-Vith led to the epic race for road junctions with the panzers of Manteuffel's Fifth Panzer Army. By nightfall the 101st had reinforced Middleton at Bastogne and the 82nd backed the 7th Armored Division, at St.-Vith, which had formed a strong horseshoe position along the river Salm to Vielsalm, thence east to St.-Vith, thence curling back to Werbomont.

But confusion still reigned through most of the area. On the eighteenth, the First Army diarist conceded that "the enemy line cannot be well defined," and that the corps and Army command could not "fit the pieces of the puzzle together" to form a clear picture of the battle. Some 1,348 Eighth Air Force bombers attempted pathfinder raids in hopes of disrupting enemy communications behind the Our and Clerf rivers, but it was plain that the center of the Allied line had been crushed by the main force of the enemy attack. In Bastogne, stragglers of the 28th Division arrived with "tragic tales which indicated a complete disintegration of the regimental defenses opposite the Eifel." Bastogne was cut off from First Army Headquarters, which had been nearly overrun by the 1st SS and was out of touch with the crucial battles at Stavelot, Houffalize, Bastogne and St.-Vith. Wearing American uniforms and equipped with dog tags and even paychecks, teams of German saboteurs roamed behind American lines cutting telephone wires, and attempting to misroute First Army traffic.

In the confusion, rumors were rampant. A rumor widespread in the First Army told of teams of fifty or more English-speaking assassins allegedly air-dropped in the Paris area on a mission to assassinate Eisenhower and the high command. Reluctantly Eisenhower agreed to spend the night of the eighteenth in the SHAEF compound under a large security guard of police and MPs. Heavy security was also ordered for Bradley and the other Army commanders, and the Allied high command settled in for a long winter siege.

Forty-eight hours after the attack, Eisenhower was still biding his time, awaiting a British overture to activate the command turnover and signs that Bradley would accept and support such a transfer. No signs came, even as the need for a command shift became more and more apparent.

Bradley spent most of the eighteenth in conferences with Patton at Luxembourg at work on the logistics of breaking off attacks in the Third Army sector and swinging two corps 100 miles north to relieve Bastogne and press the southern flank of the salient. To the end of his life, Bradley would insist that the transfer of his troops to Montgomery was unnecessary, claiming that Hodges' stout defense of the northern shoulder had effectively blunted the Germans within seventy-two hours after the attack. In hindsight, Bradley's claim was plausible, but by conducting all operations with Patton at his side in Luxembourg, Bradley had positioned himself to cede authority over the northern rim of the penetration and to concentrate on the relief of Bastogne. So one must assume that Bradley's defiance was a tactic to wait the British out and convince them that as far as he was concerned the transfer was reluctant, temporary, and to be accompanied by planning for eventual offensives on both flanks to defeat the German attack and to vindicate the American command.

In messages to Bradley and Devers on the night of the eighteenth, Eisenhower moved matters along. In a new directive he formally canceled Patton's Saarland offensive and declared his intentions, which were to take "immediate action to check the enemy advance," then to organize a "counteroffensive without delay with all forces north of the Moselle." Bradley's 12th Army Group assumed responsibility for the security of Namur, Liège, and Aachen and for containing the enemy east of the Meuse. Eisenhower ordered Devers to suspend all offensive operations and to assume the defense of the Third Army sector from Haguenau to Thionville. Montgomery's mission was left vague. To ensure coordination, Eisenhower convened a conference for the American commanders at 12th Army Group Headquarters in Verdun for the next morning, December 19.

Mixed news flowed into SHAEF in the early morning of the nineteenth, a crucial day of the western war: V Corps still clung to the Elsenborn ridge, and American reserves arrived in the vicinity of Liège to reinforce the northern shoulder. The determined American defense of isolated pockets and strongpoints shaped the battle and forced adjustments in the German plan, changes suggested in ULTRA intercepts and confirmed in postwar interrogations.

Postwar interrogations would confirm that on the nineteenth, with the Sixth Panzer Army heavily engaged and unlikely to seize Liège quickly, Model and Manteuffel, opponents of the "grand slam," vehemently urged Hitler to reinforce the Fifth Panzer Army sector, where Manteuffel had opened a twelve-mile breach north of Bastogne, enabling armor to pour through and sweep wide to the northwest across the Meuse at Dinant. At stake in the exchanges, several of which were overheard by ULTRA, was the deployment of two SS and three panzer–panzer grenadier-type units held east of the Rhine in the German Fifteenth Army sector. Hitler was reluctant to give up on the Sixth Panzer, but Manteuffel's Fifth Panzer Army had "won the race," and Hitler's compass was already turning south in search of strategic gains. That morning Hitler canceled a secondary Fifteenth Army offensive in Holland, and, while ordering the SS units to reinforce Dietrich, decided to gamble on Model's plan to shift the main weight of the German attack west-northwest away from the American concentrations opposite Dietrich.

This marked an abandonment of frontal tactics to produce a breakthrough and the shift to a more indirect line of approach by Manteuffel's

Fifth Panzer Army. Soon the impact of these decisions would be apparent and intensify feelings in the American camp that Eisenhower's actions that day were overcautious and needlessly hampered Bradley's ability to work out the crisis on his own. But the First Army was in disarray, Manteuffel threatened Bastogne, and German armor had broken through beyond Houffalize toward Hotton–Dinant and the undefended stretches of the Meuse.

That morning, as the battle of Bastogne opened, Eisenhower and his principal commanders converged on Bradley's main headquarters in Verdun, a meeting to become legendary in the annals of battle. For two hours Eisenhower, Bradley, Patton, Devers and Tedder deliberated in an old schoolroom stripped of furniture except for a large table and chairs facing an easel set up for Strong's maps, and a black potbellied stove, which broke the winter cold. There the alliance weathered a stern test of its ability to surmount adversity.

Once again, the outcome was perhaps indicated by the site chosen and the absentees. Hodges, reportedly suffering from exhaustion, was confined to bed at his headquarters, which had been shifted from Spa to Chaudfontaine. General Whiteley had left for London to confer with Brooke about the command setup. Montgomery, "unable to leave his command at this particular time," was represented by his chief of staff, General de Guingand, which meant that the British did not want their presence to complicate matters. The site—Verdun—was the rear headquarters that Bradley had refused to occupy.

Upon arrival at the schoolhouse, Eisenhower stepped out of his SHAEF Packard looking grave, almost ashen. As he entered the hastily improvised situation room, he appeared to brighten as he saw Bradley and Patton, old friends. In greeting them, Eisenhower urged the group to consider the situation an opportunity, not a disaster, whereupon Patton quipped, "Aw, come on, Ike, let's have the guts to let the Krauts run all the way to Paris —then we can really chew them to pieces." As the laughter subsided, Eisenhower nodded his appreciation. "George," he said, "that's fine. But the enemy must never be allowed to cross the Meuse."

This set the tone as the group got down to business. First up was General Strong, who took the floor to brief the group on the attack as seen from Versailles: On December 16 the Germans had launched an all-out attack to recover Brussels and Antwerp and to isolate the Allied forces north of the Moselle and compel a second Dunkirk. Two main thrusts had developed —one toward Liège and a second toward the Meuse at Namur. In his clipped accent, Strong sketched the parallels between the present maneuver and 1940 by way of illustrating the scope of German objectives, though he conceded that the enemy was "not nearly so strong now."

In 1940 the French and British forces had been deployed in much the same way that the Americans and British were on December 16. The French had guarded the Lorraine, the Meuse and the west bank of the Rhine opposite the Black Forest, while the British held present lines manned by the 21st Army Group along the Maas. The Germans had then struck through the Ardennes to flank the Maginot and exploit the lack of French mobile reserves, whereupon Von Rundstedt's columns swung north to encircle the British forces in Flanders. Von Rundstedt's 1940 assault with 44 divisions had grown into a 71-division offensive, which the Germans could not hope to muster now.

In the ensuing discussion, Patton argued that the German objective was actually his own Third Army. Repeatedly, Patton emphasized the "heaven-sent" opportunity to destroy the German armies, if, as he suggested, Von Rundstedt was allowed to spin through the Ardennes Forest. To this, Bradley agreed.

Patton could point to the fact that the Sixth Panzer Army was stalled at Stavelot–Monschau. And while the Fifteenth Army idled north of Aachen, the Seventh Army attacked from Trier. Devers, not Montgomery, could submit proof of offensive preparations on his front by the German Nineteenth and First armies opposite Strasbourg. On the other hand, Patton probably knew as well as anyone that the safety of the First Army came first and that Eisenhower could not heed such an appraisal—even if accurate. But his aggressive spirit pierced the overcast outside and the gloom inside, affirming that the American commanders, classmates and old friends, would handle the crisis. Indeed, in Bradley's opinion, Patton's venturesome rhetoric closed out discussion of a general withdrawal to establish winter quarters behind the Meuse and succeeded in orienting the discussion away from disaster to future contingencies by emphasizing the temporary nature of the setback. But in practical terms, Patton spoke for the Third Army only, and his attitude merely affirmed his readiness to carry out what was a preordained decision to mass forces on the southern shoulder at Arlon–Echternach for counterattack from the south. Hours before, Patton had met with his staff and approved plans to swing the newly designated III Corps north toward Bastogne, and had arrived in Verdun after leaving a set of instructions for his staff to be activated by code word.

Eisenhower, in summary, "accepted the intelligence forecast." In his opinion, the bright aspects of the situation were two: that the Germans indicated weakness in by-passing islands of resistance, and that the shoulders held firm. Eisenhower wanted counterattacks, but "not simultaneously, since simultaneous attacks are not feasible." The overriding problem was to restore the northern rim, then to increase pressure on the German salient from the south. All agreed that a key objective was Bastogne.

At this point, Eisenhower asked Patton for an estimate of when III Corps, poised eastward along the Moselle, could turn 90 degrees and march northward to the relief of the 101st at Bastogne. Confounding the conclave, Patton replied, "Forty-eight hours."

Pattons's reply "created a ripple of excitement." Did he comprehend the logistics involved in reorienting a three-division assault 90 degrees east to north? Strong understood Patton to say that three American divisions could drive through the flanks of two well-equipped German armies, something not even attempted at Mortain.

As Blumenson put it, Patton savored the "sublime moment" of his career as he had had the foresight to come prepared. Having said his piece, he excused himself and walked to an adjoining room where he phoned his headquarters in Nancy and gave the code word. When he returned, Eisenhower, surprised and delighted, cautioned that the III Corps attack was to be "methodical and sure, and not piecemeal." Patton was to attack not later than the twenty-fourth, five days away, and *not earlier* than the twenty-second.

The conversation ended with a discussion of the problem confronting Devers' 6th Army Group. To cover Patton's flank, Devers would have to "stretch out," handing an opening to the German Army Group G at Colmar opposite Strasbourg and behind strong positions along the Saar River near Karlsruhe. The First and Nineteenth armies formed a vise capable of crushing the stay-behind U.S. VI Corps and the French First Army should it become exposed on the Alsatian plain. Political considerations were involved in surrendering Alsace and Strasbourg. Nonetheless, Eisenhower wanted Devers to know that he was to withdraw promptly into the Vosges Mountains. There was no dissent.

Thus ended the historic Verdun conference. The result was a unified American and British view about the importance of cautious, methodical measures to defend Allied forces north of the Meuse and a consensus in favor of Third Army counterattacks. In a message sent to the CCS that afternoon, Eisenhower disclosed his plan to "plug holes in the north and launch consolidated attacks from the south," with Devers assuming responsibility for defending Patton's sector. But unity was fragile and a basic problem remained: that of command arrangements to carry out the strategy.

At Verdun, Bradley had mostly observed, saying little, offering nothing. This was to be the tale of the nineteenth, silence on Bradley's part and growing British concern as the First Army struggled to hold the line and the Allies felt the full impact of Hitler's decision to reinforce the ongoing Fifth Panzer Army breakthrough west of Houffalize. Montgomery, who had sent observers to the scene, was sending alarming reports to Brooke of a situation he described as "not repeat not good." With Bradley ensconced in Luxembourg and the front split in two, Montgomery predicted that a "direct order by someone" would soon be necessary to transfer command of the front. This was the situation as Montgomery, in Hasselt, received General Whiteley, Eisenhower's emissary, to discuss the command problem.

By the night of the nineteenth, a command transfer was inevitable and imminent. After Eisenhower's long, cold drive back to Versailles from Verdun, reports reached SHAEF describing an alarming deterioration in the Ardennes Forest. Manteuffel had pushed through the Bastogne–Houffalize gap toward St.-Hubert and the undefended sectors of the Meuse. Word arrived that 10,000 men of the two regiments of the 106th, out of contact since the evening of the sixteenth, had surrendered, the largest battlefield surrender of American troops in the war. The 106th and 28th had ceased to be effective units, though remnants collected at St.-Vith and Bastogne, where Middleton erected a perimeter defense, concentrated on three roads. By midday the 101st Airborne at Bastogne had been in contact with the 116th Panzer Division, 2nd Panzer Division, Panzer Lehr, the 5th Parachute Division, the Führer Escort Brigade, and a mass of Volks grenadier units opening the seesaw siege for the city.

Back in Versailles, Eisenhower learned of the near capture of the fuel dumps at Spa, which Bradley had assured him would not be located south of the Meuse. For a time a single company had stood guard while engineers hauled off two million gallons, igniting the rest, which was exactly the kind of situation Bradley had assured Eisenhower would not come up when they had discussed the Ardennes in November. Accordingly, Eisenhower sent Bradley a terse two-paragraph message reminding him of his long-ago assurances that no major dumps had been located east of the Meuse and of the "vital importance" that no Meuse bridges fall into enemy hands intact. The nudge provoked indignation in Bradley's 12th Army Group staff and defiance in Bradley, who would later cite the message as evidence that SHAEF suffered an "acute case of the shakes" and had succumbed to pessimism in directing the command turnover. Years later, confronted with Bradley's account of the emotions aroused by the telegram, Eisenhower blandly denied that the message was anything more than a "matter of routine." He recalled that Bradley had assured him a month earlier "that he had located no principal supply dumps east of the Meuse, south of Liège or north of Verdun," just as he had assured him the enemy would not reach the Meuse.

That night Whiteley returned to Versailles ready on Montgomery's behalf to place the command problem before Eisenhower. Whiteley took the precaution of conferring with Strong to enlist his support in the task. Whiteley was not sure that British pessimism was warranted, but there was a danger that Hodges and Bradley, unable to approach the British, might be left to fritter away resources in a futile effort to reassert an initiative the Americans no longer possessed.

Strong agreed. The latest dispatches indicated that the battle was in danger of getting out of hand, far more so than had been apparent that morning at Verdun. Reports traced the decisive reinforcement of Manteuffel's Fifth Panzer and its movement toward the open U.S. First Army flank at Namur, where, in Strong's opinion, major battles were likely within forty-eight hours. Whiteley and Strong weighed evidence showing that Bradley, from his forward headquarters in Luxembourg, had been out of touch with First Army Headquarters for most of the recent forty-eight hours, and unable to coordinate First Army actions along the northern shoulder. Several officers dispatched by SHAEF to prowl rear areas of the American line had returned with reports of "considerable confusion and disorganization" in the First Army sector that were unrelieved by the tales of heroism filtering back from individual American units at St.-Vith, Stavelot and Bastogne.

Between eleven and midnight, Strong, convinced "that the time had come to inform Bedell Smith about my growing doubts whether the Allies were matching up to the situation," cast his lot with Whiteley. Years later he would recall the scene as the two of them walked to Smith's bedroom and aroused the chief of staff from a deep sleep. Strong briefed Smith on the deteriorating situation, with emphasis on the evidence of breakdown in communications between 12th Army Group Headquarters and Hodges. Whiteley urged that the entire front north of the Ardennes be placed under Montgomery's command.

"Whenever there is any real trouble, the British do not appear to trust the Americans to handle it efficiently," Smith snapped. The proposal would be "completely unacceptable" to the Americans, and for good measure, since Whiteley and Strong had evidently lost confidence in SHAEF, they were "no longer acceptable as staff officers to Eisenhower." Whiteley and Strong left.

But Brooke's request via Whiteley moved the matter to decision. Smith, known for his hair-trigger temper, had reacted violently against the suggestion, but Eisenhower now had the British request that he had been waiting for. In the presence of Whiteley and Strong, Smith phoned Bradley in Luxembourg and spelled out the facts. "Dividing the front would save us a great deal of trouble, especially if your communications with Hodges or Simpson go out," he explained. Bradley replied that auxiliary circuits had been laid west of the Meuse to reopen contact between both headquarters and that the situation was "not serious enough to warrant such a fundamental change of command."

Smith asked Bradley if the arrangement would make sense were Montgomery an American.

"Bedell," Bradley replied, "in that case, it would be hard for me to object. Certainly, if Monty were an American commander, I would agree with you entirely."

This settled matters. Bradley cautioned Smith about the reluctance Americans would feel about serving under Montgomery for an extended period of time. With Eisenhower's assent, Smith assured Bradley that the U.S. Ninth and First armies would return to the 12th Army Group when the crisis abated. Meanwhile, Bradley's job would be to assume full responsibility for the Third Army offensive and make sure "Patton did not go off half-cocked."

Bradley would later rebuke himself for not standing up to Smith, but in conceding the logic of the transfer in military terms, he conceded his incapacity to act, at least without the assurance that Horrocks' XXX Corps would move up to the Meuse. Late that night Eisenhower approved the transfer effective the next morning after a conference called to draft the orders and to coordinate explanations to all parties of his extraordinary decision to transfer two American armies to British command at the height of a military crisis, one of his most important decisions since D-Day.

As the story goes, Strong rose early on the twentieth. He went about his regularly assigned duties with an ear alert for the phone call curtly informing him of his relief, a premonition fortified by the gloomy forecasts of low clouds, again canceling air intervention against the German supply columns winding through the web of roads in the Ardennes. At the 9 A.M. War Room conference, Strong learned that Smith had forgotten the confrontation the night before.

As the first item of business, Smith formally moved that the Supreme Commander assign Montgomery the U.S. First Army and Ninth Army north of the Ardennes Forest. Eisenhower approved, and in the presence of the entire staff phoned Bradley. Strong later recalled that the witnesses eavesdropped on a historic conversation, an act that in five short minutes discredited the German assumption that nationalistic fears and rivalries would inhibit prompt and effective steps to meet the German challenge. Bradley protested, but any misgivings Eisenhower may have felt were not apparent to those assembled. "Well, Brad," Eisenhower closed, "those are my orders." Afterward Eisenhower called Montgomery to confirm that he now commanded two American armies.

Eisenhower devoted the rest of the conference to the task of redrafting a carefully worded directive implementing the change and a message of explanation to the CCS. In both, Eisenhower emphasized that his eventual goal was to "launch counteroffensives without delay on each side of the enemy salient with all available forces." In areas not essential to the main purpose, Eisenhower was "prepared to yield ground in order to insure the security of essential areas and to add strength to our counteroffensive." Accordingly, Eisenhower directed Montgomery to check the enemy advance on the northern boundary of the Ardennes Forest and guard sensitive communications at Namur and Liège. Bradley received VIII Corps along with the Third Army and orders to contain the enemy east of the Meuse and to organize the relief of Bastogne.

All present that morning felt relief. At the close, General Strong, on behalf of everyone present, urged Eisenhower to respect the wishes of the security forces. He knew that Eisenhower resisted the measures as embarrassing and unbecoming. But Skorzeny's paratroopers were rumored to be in Paris with the mission of infiltrating SHAEF headquarters. Exaggerated or not, Strong insisted that no chances be taken.

As he later wrote, Eisenhower had exhibited a display of adaptability and high purpose that Strong and Whiteley conceded to each other was not likely in a British command. Defending the arrangement was now crucial. Strong urged that Eisenhower accept heavy security because, as he made clear in his memoir, "if anything had by chance happened to the Supreme Commander because insufficient precautions had been taken to protect him, the resulting chaos would have been disastrous."

"Eisenhower," he wrote, "was not expendable."

Eisenhower's timely decision removed all command barriers to containing and defeating the German counteroffensive. In a single stroke he eliminated Bradley's dual mission of containing the Germans in the north and attacking from the south. Montgomery was now able to release Horrocks' XXX Corps to man the Meuse between Namur and Dinant, which assured Hodges of British support in Belgium and the British of American support in Holland. But there was a heavy price to be paid, and the reverberations of Eisenhower's decision would be felt for months.

A significant aspect of the decision, often overlooked, was that Eisenhower had carried it out without consulting Marshall. The reasons for this are not known. Eisenhower may have been concerned that Marshall and the JCS would block it or hold it up. A second and more likely possibility was that Eisenhower believed that Marshall, while not opposed, would be reluctant to approve it in advance lest he inhibit American freedom of action later. This is not to say that Eisenhower's initiative was a harbinger of smoother relations between SHAEF and the JCS, for just the opposite was to be the case.

More and more, differences had been cropping up between Eisenhower and Marshall, and the command transfer would open a whole new list of difficulties destined to have an impact on strategy in the closing days of the war. For months, potential conflict had been implicit both in Marshall's push for a speedy conclusion of the war involving the least number of American troops and in Eisenhower's broad-front strategy. More and more, Eisenhower, who had gone to London to carry out what had basically been an American design and strategy, was contending with skepticism and impatience, which was again evident on the twentieth. Within an hour of the meeting, Churchill phoned Eisenhower to suggest the transfer and to inform him of the War Cabinet's decision to issue a fresh call for 250,000 British recruits, a gesture of resolve and support. Churchill applauded Eisenhower's decision and wished him luck. Marshall's response to the news was silence.

Was the transfer necessary? As the transfer went into effect, the first phase of the battle was ending, a phase in which, according to German plans, German forces were to have crossed the Meuse between Liège and Huy before Allied reserves intervened. The German plan had banked heavily on speed and maneuver to offset the lack of frontline divisions available and the weight of American air and ground mobility, but ninety-six hours after the attack, it was apparent that what was to have been a quick breakthrough in the Ardennes Forest along prearranged lines to be exploited by armor was evolving into a major battle for control of the Ardennes Forest itself in which the Allied build-up would match the Germans. Nevertheless, the Germans retained the initiative with twenty-plus divisions, and Eisenhower's subordinates, though unenthusiastic, accepted the command decisions and went to work.

The command transfer had been under way all morning. Montgomery's emissaries had arrived in St.-Trond before dawn for a conference with Hodges to canvass the situation in the First Army sector. Montgomery inherited a slightly improving situation. Nine American divisions were engaged in a furious battle along a thirty-mile front blocking the approaches to the Meuse between Huy and Liège, with the flash points at Monschau, Malmédy, Stavelot and Stoumont. The dangerous penetration by the I SS Corps had been blocked at Stoumont, and fuel dumps and headquarter units had been evacuated to safety. Immediately, XXX Corps, bivouacked at Hasselt–Louvain–St.-Trond began to move up behind the First Army to protect the Meuse bridges on a wide arc from Givet to Liège. Montgomery's new responsibilities also removed British objections to deploying all available American Ninth and First Army forces, a factor often overlooked. One of Montgomery's first acts was to agree to form a corps of three divisions from the Ninth Army and to place it under Hodges' nominee as "the most aggressive American Corps commander in the theater" for the defense of the western flank and employment in eventual counterattacks. The three divisions would soon number four, including the crack 2nd and 3rd armored divisions, and Hodges' nominee would be General Lawton Collins of St.-Lô–Cherbourg fame. But thoughts of counterattack notwithstanding, Montgomery was far from ready to launch a counteroffensive, as events would show.

The ensuing tug-of-war between Montgomery and his subordinate American commanders proceeded at two levels, military and political. Military issues included the question of how many units would be adequate to engage and contain the German thrust, how many units could be left in reserve, as well as the purpose of the reserve, whether the reserve was to back up a defensive line or to prepare to operate offensively. The political issue was more complex. It centered on the problem of which American or British units would be held out, which would be committed, and, by extension, the shape of the eventual counteroffensive and the pattern of future operations, which would depend in part on whether the First Army was allowed to advance into the Ardennes Forest and operate closely with Patton's Third

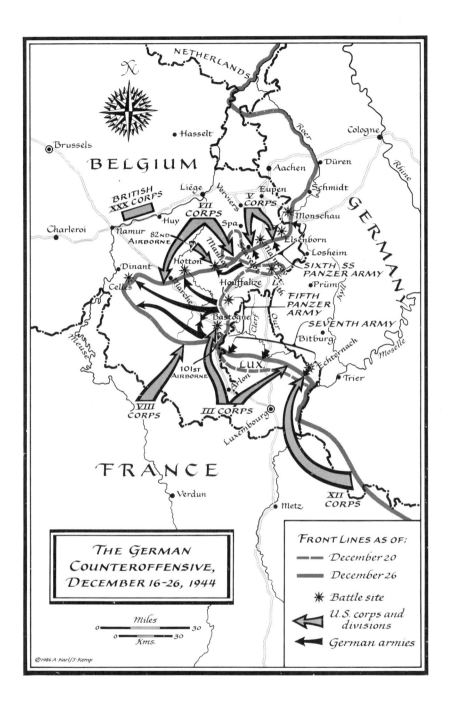

THE GERMAN
COUNTEROFFENSIVE,
DECEMBER 16–26, 1944

FRONT LINES AS OF:

- - - December 20
—— December 26

✳ Battle site

⬅ U.S. corps and
    divisions

⬅ German armies

Miles
0 ———— 30
0 ———— 30
Kms.

©1986 A·Karl/J·Kemp

Army. On the twentieth this latter consideration emerged as Montgomery, in forming VII Corps, decided to commit it in the Marche–Hotton sector, backed by XXX Corps in reserve to provide defense in depth. Hodges favored committing XXX Corps east of the Meuse at Marche and holding out VII Corps to spearhead counterattacks staged from forward positions held along the waist and base of the German salient. But American views were not unanimous, and all agreed that holding the northern shoulder between Malmédy–Monschau was the overriding objective—for the moment.

Meanwhile, at 1:30 P.M. on December 20, a supremely confident Montgomery strode into the new First Army headquarters in the Belgian town of St.-Trond like "Christ come to cleanse the temple." As he formally assumed command, Montgomery found it awkward relating to Hodges' staff from the start. An immediate question arose over whether the Americans should break off the siege at St.-Vith and extricate the 7th Armored, 9th Armored and 106th holding out there or reinforce St.-Vith as a springboard for counterattack. Hodges, "thinking offensively," was wary of evacuating St.-Vith, while Montgomery was resolved to evacuate it and straighten the line to brace for the arrival of the still uncommitted II SS Panzer Corps. In this spirit, Montgomery went to work to restore order in the northern rim, contributing, as Wilmot put it, "strong and patient handling of the chaotic situation." Refusing to hold extended positions or to permit piecemeal counterattacks, Montgomery endeavored to convert a series of local battles on the crucial northern rim into a coherent front, with Eisenhower's full backing.

An early test of Montgomery's authority arose over St.-Vith. On the twenty-first, Montgomery agreed to dispatch the 82nd Airborne to the Salm on the left of the 7th Armored, a preliminary to withdrawal. Ridgway, once at the Salm, would find himself opposed to the idea of a step backward with the 82nd division even as his forces met an assault by the full weight of II SS Panzer Corps, which appeared west of the Salm on the twenty-first. Twenty-four hours later Ridgway would sack the commanding general for authorizing preparations to abandon St.-Vith, but Montgomery would order his reinstatement and authorize retreat from St.-Vith, which began on the twenty-second, again with Eisenhower's full backing.

The stop and start over St.-Vith set the pattern of the next seventy-two hours. Montgomery set about to "tidy up" the northern rim. American field commanders, engaged in a touch-and-go battle, searched for points to counterattack, duly recorded by the First Army diarist, who chronicled the debate over Collins' role. Montgomery wanted Collins to assemble in the threatened Marche–Hotton sector, deeming local forces inadequate to stem German spearheads in the area. Collins paced First Army headquarters at St.-Trond, convinced that the high command was overestimating the threat at Hotton, a marshland where attacks would be futile and "could be broken with relatively little strength." According to the diarist, Collins was "full of his usual fighting vigor . . . confident that with the 2nd and 3rd Armored Divisions he can beat any collection that Boche would want to throw at him and that the 2nd and 3rd Armored are the two best outfits of their kind in the world, in his opinion." Long after the war, American commanders would remain sharply critical of Montgomery's overcaution, which, in their opinion, overestimated the strength of German spearheads and underestimated the resiliency and adaptability of American troops and command.

In his letter of instruction issued on the twenty-first, Montgomery compromised and ordered Collins to assemble in the Hotton sector but to be prepared to attack south, southeast, east or northeast by midnight the twenty-third. This was not enough, and years later Collins would recall that Montgomery was "certain the Germans would break through" and would have dispatched VII Corps "practically behind the Meuse" if allowed, frittering away the chance to operate against Manteuffel's armor stretched out west of Bastogne. Montgomery's refusal to deploy XXX Corps east of the Meuse was also nettlesome. As Bradley later wrote, Montgomery could easily have moved Horrocks the thirty miles or so to Marche, and his refusal to do so was a "poor and timid decision" reminiscent of the belated and cautious British moves at Vire and Falaise in August. But again, Bradley obscured an important point: that Montgomery, a Britisher, was in a position to do what no American commander committed to counteroffensive rhetoric could do—he could order American withdrawals and establish a continuous line in the north with secure flanks. Montgomery was very determined on this score and consistent. He would later recount a meeting at Louvain with Horrocks, who, like Patton, was "full of enthusiasm" and eager to allow the Germans to cross the Meuse and fight on the fields at Waterloo. Montgomery praised Horrocks' verve, but instructed him that he was "on no account . . . to allow any Germans over the river."

On it went and as the battle entered its fifth day, the First Army diarist on the twenty-first described the anxiety beneath the optimism at St.-Trond. He described the renewed fury of German attacks in the Malmédy–St.-Vith sector, the fresh reports of German paratroop drops and infiltration, the reports of heavy attacks in the V Corps sector, the reports of casualties and the overcast weather, which had curtailed air support since the seventeenth, the suspense over II SS Panzer Corps and the grim speculation about uncommitted German forces east of the Rhine. The diarist quoted First Army Chief of Staff Major General William B. Kean, who had said on Monday (the eighteenth) that Wednesday (the twentieth) would be the crucial day and that on Friday (the twenty-second) "we can tell whether we can hold or will have to further withdraw to a defense line such as the Meuse. . . ."

On the twenty-first, the battle remained fluid and uncertain. "It is impossible to tell where we stand at this point," wrote the First Army diarist.

"One minute things look good and the next minute bad." That day, the German "second wind" engulfed American defenses at four points and the battle approached a climax. At Malmédy–Bütgenbach–Monschau, twelve German divisions attacked seven American divisions in an attempt to dislodge Gerow and unhinge the northern anchor. A major battle shaped up in the Hotton area, where Collins' VII Corps assembled to blunt the Fifth Panzer Army advance. That day, the II SS Panzer Corps intervened on Ridgway's left as XVIII Corps entrenched west of St.-Vith to guard the 7th Armored Division. The fourth point was Bastogne, where the Fifth Panzer Army, having completed encirclement of the 101st and elements of the 28th divisions, probed the western approaches of the city while Manteuffel pushed his reinforced armored spearheads northwest toward Dinant.

By the twenty-second, Ridgway and Hasbrouck were falling back, and First Army Headquarters again fell farther to the rear to the town of Tongres, where it occupied a building on the grounds of the Belgian Military Academy. The German offensive had become one of the largest attacks of the war and the largest American battle in history, destined to claim 70,000 American casualties. Making matters worse, no one was sure that the Germans had committed all their available strength. Colonel B. A. "Monk" Dickson, 12th Army Group G-2, estimated that in addition to the twenty-four divisions in the salient, another thirteen were in "close reserve," backed by nine more "accepted in reserve" and possibly a dozen more from other fronts, which would amount to a build-up rivaling Von Rundstedt's in 1940. Hodges "did not entirely accept this view," Wilmot wrote, but "the knowledge that the Germans could readily commit at least six divisions against the First Army made him anxious to seal off the penetration at the earliest opportunity." Then, as the 7th Armored left St.-Vith, all eyes turned to Bastogne, the key position of the battle in the wake of the Fifth Panzer breakthrough. German control of Bastogne would open the floodgates for additional German troops threatening the Dinant–Namur sector and expose the still undefended sectors south of Dinant. One factor was in Middleton's favor: to reach Dinant before the Allies could fully organize a defense of the Meuse, it had been crucial that German armored spearheads not become embroiled in a full-pitched battle at Bastogne. Manteuffel had intended to occupy the town quickly before American reinforcements could get there. Failing this, he had ordered the vanguard XLVII Panzer Corps to rope off the town and delegate the task of rooting out the defenders to the backup waves of the assault. Manteuffel's decision, a controversial one, was a sign of German weakness, and it paved the way for the successful defense of Bastogne and a larger battle for control of the town later, long after the German momentum was spent.

Meanwhile the 12th SS Division had withdrawn from I Panzer Corps and joined II Panzer Corps in support of Manteuffel's concentrated thrust in the middle through Houffalize. OKW, pursuant to Hitler's shift on the nineteenth, ordered the Seventh Army to broaden the southern base at Echternach and Luxembourg, giving Manteuffel elbow room on his left to block the U.S. Third Army effort to relieve the now encircled 101st Airborne garrisons. Supply by air continued to be held up by poor weather, and with the western approaches thinly held, there was talk that the 101st would abandon the city and fight its way out.

Then, at 6:05 A.M. on the twenty-second, Patton's 4th Armored and 26th and 80th infantry divisions attacked north from the town of Arlon on a thirty-five-mile front over snow-covered hills and icy roads. With the ring tightening around Bastogne and German reinforcements pouring in, Montgomery was deeply concerned that Patton's attack would be bottled up and exert little influence on the Fifth Panzer Army.

All along the salient the Germans pushed for openings and attempted to end the "wild mixed fighting" to resume this advance toward Antwerp along scheduled routes. But the American lines held, and would hold again on the twenty-third, a day of clearing weather that permitted the Eighth and Ninth air forces to operate against German supply columns and depots. At Bastogne, Brigadier General Anthony McAuliffe, acting commanding general of the 101st Airborne in General Maxwell Taylor's absence, responded to a German surrender ultimatum at noon with the one word "Nuts," sounding the note of defiance in adversity which served as a rallying point for the American Army. By nightfall, XXX Corps defended the Meuse between Dinant and Liège. The 51st Scottish Division had crossed the Meuse to assume a blocking position southeast of Liège. In England, the 6th and 17th airborne divisions mustered to await Eisenhower's call. The U.S. 11th Armored, assembling in Cherbourg, readied to move up to Reims to cover the sectors of the Meuse south of Givet abandoned by the 101st and 82nd Airborne. On the right of III Corps, Patton's XII Corps marched north toward Echternach and the German Seventh Army flank, and gradually the Americans averted defeat in the Ardennes Forest.

Historians agree that by the twenty-second, six days after the German attack, the Allies had begun to prevail in the struggle for control of the Ardennes. But the fighting was touch and go, and since no one could be sure on the twenty-second that the Allies had experienced the worst, most assumed the worst and the crisis entered a new phase.

When would victory come in the seemingly endless war in Europe? The world press extended condolences to the Belgians, who had now endured a second invasion. In London the mood was grim and anxious amid the unprecedented censorship of battlefront news. In Paris the streets were empty and windows boarded up, reminiscent of June 1940. The city government ordered a curfew and posted large photographs of Colonel Skorzeny on government buildings throughout the city to aid in identifying his band of political assassins reportedly roaming the streets. In his diary, Butcher ruminated about the damage done by suppressing news of the command shift, an open secret among the correspondents at the Scribe Hotel, and chronicled the reporters' alarm and that of the French officials who predicted gloomily that the Germans would soon reach Paris.

Strong later described a similar mood at SHAEF. Marshal Alphonse Juin, on behalf of De Gaulle, visited Versailles on the twenty-second to protest Eisenhower's less noticed decision at Verdun to evacuate the Alsatian plain. As he passed an open office in the Trianon, Juin paused to gaze at the maps and documents spread over a large table. "Aren't you packing?" Juin asked the duty officer. Slowly he sauntered down the hall to Eisenhower's office.

Leaving no doubt of the supreme stakes riding on the German gamble, stories of wanton slaughter and ruthless actions circulated, including the tale of the Malmédy massacre. On the night of the seventeenth, a straggler had reached First Army Headquarters with a chilling story. While directing 7th Armored Division traffic at the Malmédy crossroads near St.-Vith, he and 150 officers and men had been taken prisoner by German tanks and infantry, marched to a nearby field and lined up. When an SS officer drew a pistol and fired two shots, he had fallen to the ground, feigning a hit when suddenly a battery of machine guns opened fire. All were killed except for a handful who hugged the snow for forty-five minutes until left behind, presumed dead.

The McKeoghs' honeymoon ended early. No sooner had the newlyweds checked into the Raphael Hotel than reports of the attack reached the city. Wherever the McKeoghs went, they were stopped on every street corner by MPs demanding identification papers. Paris swarmed with security police, soldiers and civilian police. Within a few days, the two heard rumors of attempts on Eisenhower's life, whereupon Mickey decided to return to Versailles, reminding his bride that his mother had told him, "If he [Eisenhower] doesn't come back from this war, you don't come back."

Back at the Trianon, McKeogh noted the change in Eisenhower. He seemed different—a virtual prisoner of a small army of security police who swept in over the compound, and insisted he abandon his villa at St.-Germain and move into a newly requisitioned compound adjoining the Trianon. McKeogh was fascinated to hear the Skorzeny rumors, but he quickly discounted the threat under the crush of security police and MPs which was "awesome." McKeogh later recalled feeling an "odd sympathy for any German running into those clowns."

The household staff, which had learned to sense trouble, detected the tension and kept its distance. In normal times, Eisenhower in off-hours liked to dabble with paints and to cook. The telltale signs of strain were bridge and the butts of four packs of cigarettes accumulating in the ashtray. Eisenhower's bedside ashtray that week overflowed, and McKeogh noted Eisenhower's unusual trouble sleeping.

But at SHAEF the watchword was confidence. Talk of a counterattack, which had begun virtually at the moment of the command transfer, made the rounds. Aggressive thinking was not only essential for morale, but for preventing rigidity from settling over a command laid low by months of fatigue and worry. "From the point of view of shortening the whole business . . . the fact that the Hun has stuck his neck out is the best thing that could happen," Tedder dutifully wrote his wife on the twenty-second. "It may make months of difference," he added, "but might he have waited until after Xmas?"

Among Eisenhower's first visitors that week was William E. Robinson, editor in chief of the Paris edition of the Republican-leaning New York *Herald Tribune*. Robinson had called on Eisenhower to discuss an exemption from a SHAEF directive that forbade the resumption of American business in Paris. Anxious to counter the anti-American propaganda making the rounds in France, Eisenhower granted the exemption with the proviso that the newspaper not import American civilian employees, American newsprint or American money.

The first of many meetings with Eisenhower provided Robinson with a vivid first impression. Under pressure, Eisenhower was alert, controlled and businesslike. When Robinson expressed concern about the battle raging in the Ardennes, Eisenhower seemed "unworried and unharassed." He told Robinson that he was not concerned about the outcome of the battle, and that his "thinking and planning was several weeks beyond the current situation."

William Robinson would be among Eisenhower's earliest Republican backers for the presidential nomination in 1952 and would serve as a key emissary between Eisenhower, financial contributors, the press and politicians. Like others that week, Robinson gained a lasting impression of Eisenhower's poise under pressure and his ability to look beyond the current crisis to the next one, which was testimony to Eisenhower's patience, single-mindedness and foresight.

But for Eisenhower, looking ahead was unavoidable. As the second week of fighting opened, it was still too early to be sure that the Germans would be contained, let alone to gauge the long-term effects of the counteroffensives. But with twenty-four German divisions 45 miles inside Belgium, Eisenhower had to anticipate that even in the best of outcomes, the Allies would emerge from the battle in a very different position from that on December 15, which might be summarized as follows: On the fifteenth, Allied forces had been engaged in offensives preliminary to an invasion by the 21st Army Group north of Düsseldorf, and a second one in the vicinity of Frankfurt by the Third Army and 6th Army Group. In particular, Bradley's 12th Army Group, on December 15, had been dispersed along a 230-mile front serving diverse roles; sixteen of Bradley's divisions in two armies had been operating in support of Montgomery north of the Ardennes; five divisions had manned a 75-mile defensive front in the Ardennes, while south of the Ardennes, ten divisions of Patton's Third Army had advanced beyond Metz preparing to spearhead the Frankfurt offensive. Then, on the sixteenth, the Germans attacked, and since then, all three armies of Bradley's 12th Army Group had begun to bunch up in the Ardennes while drawing other units toward the Ardennes in support.

Presumably the wholesale shift of troops to the Ardennes would be temporary, but Eisenhower could not count on it, and it was hard to imagine how a shift of this magnitude could fail to have an impact on Allied strategy if not Allied policy. First, the formidable concentration of forces that the British had strived to achieve north of the Ardennes would soon be exceeded by the concentration of American forces in the Ardennes, which would have to be undone if the Allies were to resume the now suspended next phase of Eisenhower's broad-front strategy, looking to offensives north and south of the Ardennes. Undoing the build-up in the Ardennes would be doubly complicated by a new factor; by transferring formal command of two American armies to Montgomery on the twentieth, Eisenhower had given Bradley and the American 12th Army Group command a powerful incentive to recoup by challenging existing plans, specifically by asserting an exclusively American role when the Allies resumed the offensive. Historians have not focused on this point, but it seems to be a fundamental one in understanding Eisenhower's difficult relationship with Marshall and Bradley in the complex maneuvering ahead.

In short, would the broad-front strategy weather the Ardennes? Would the Americans continue to support it? Another factor was time. The longer the battle in the Ardennes wore on, the more difficult it would be to reconstitute the December 15 front and salvage the strategies adopted in August, strategies that had been tailored to meet long-range goals as well as the short-term problem of surviving a German offensive. The longer the battle went on, the more likely it was that the Allies would emerge exhausted, out of position and behind schedule, all the while facing forthcoming, but as yet unscheduled, talks with the Russians. In the circumstances, the temptation would be strong to dispense with methodical preparations for a broad-front invasion strategy and resume instead with a single offensive from the positions the Allies then occupied. But now the Americans, not the British, would assert the predominant role in a single thrust, a thrust subject to many of the same flaws apparent in the British plans in September and more.

In short, adoption of such a single thrust would mean more than the rejection of Eisenhower's military approach, as months of debate between Eisenhower and the British had demonstrated. The single-thrust strategy advocated by the British, aimed at a fixed objective—Berlin—had always rested on either of two extreme premises: first, that the Allies were too weak to consider launching more than one invasion offensive, as Brooke had argued; second, that a German decision to fall away in the west would give the Allies sudden freedom of action, which, should they exploit it, meant opportunities to secure advantages against the Russians. No one had urged such a course in so many words, but the possibility of a German demarche in the west had long figured in the debates over unconditional surrender and western-front strategy. So far, debate had shown that a single thrust would be a departure from long-standing Allied policy, a policy based on the premise of an effective wartime alliance with the Russians that guaranteed the Allies against military isolation now and both sides later that neither would seek advantage against the other, at least until Germany had been thoroughly defeated and occupied.

Meanwhile, Butcher stopped for a visit on the twenty-third. Returning from a trip to 12th Army Group Headquarters, where he had seen chaos reminiscent of Kasserine, Butcher, like Robinson, found all in order at the Trianon. Butcher warned Eisenhower about the rumors and turmoil caused by SHAEF's blackout on military dispatches. By the twenty-third, the command shift was an open secret, and with the British press hinting of it in dispatches, Butcher suggested that SHAEF might need to get ahead of the story with an official announcement.

Eisenhower defended censorship. While he doubted the official explanation that a blackout was necessary to deny the Germans aid in locating their own frontline units, he reminded Butcher that German intelligence often relied on the BBC to trace Allied movement. Eisenhower agreed that the blackout raised suspicion that SHAEF was covering up a military disaster, but he personally saw "no need for alarm" and felt that the momentary loss of public confidence was more than offset by the potential harm in revealing the command transfer, an issue that was bound to inflame American-British-French tensions. Eisenhower assured Butcher that someday there would be a complete factual report of the "dying German thrust" as there had been after Kasserine. Meanwhile, if "all were patient, and the Lord would give us some good flying weather," all would be well. Butcher asked Eisenhower about the heavy security at the Trianon. Eisenhower was "disgusted" with the restrictions imposed by "super-cautious" security police but did not know what to do about it.

"He [Eisenhower] now knows how it must feel to be President and be guarded day and night by ever-watchful secret service men," Butcher noted. As he left, Butcher surveyed the cavernous offices at the Trianon. Through the high French windows, he watched a light snow fall, a serene sight that struck him as "appropriate for the approaching Christmas." The staff seemed calm, and going about its business as usual.

But as Christmas approached, there remained a great unknown. Were the Allies seeing the worst of it? The Russian "pause" on the Vistula had entered its fifth month. When would the Russians resume the attack? Signs were mixed, a fact duly noted in the world press. German-Russian fighting raged for control of Budapest, and Soviet communiqués noted that "several mighty Russian and Polish armies" were poised to cross the Vistula. But the Vistula had as yet not frozen over and the weather in Poland was "not cold enough." The Allied military missions in Moscow had nothing to report, and so, as Tedder later put it, "Our military, not to say political, relations with the Russians seemed most unpromising."

Eisenhower needed information about Soviet plans so that he could make plans of his own, but there were political obstacles to ascertaining Russian intentions. Apparently, a sticking point was imminent Russian recognition of the pro-Communist Lublin Committee as the Polish provisional government. Stalin had invited the Allies to join him in recognizing the Lublin Committee as the provisional government of Poland, but Roosevelt was appealing to Stalin to hold off until the three sides could meet somewhere in Russia and discuss various ideas of his own about how to handle the Polish question, a polite reminder that the Allies would consider any solution to the Polish problem premature before Red Army forces crossed the Vistula and liberated the western half of the country. Soviet silence continued.

Political barriers to approaching the Russians were growing amid talk, in Churchill's phrase, of "going to Caesar's tent." Churchill was skeptical of soliciting Soviet support, which he believed would materialize in any case, since the Russians were bound to exploit the weakened front in Poland. Second, an Allied request for Soviet plans would inevitably lead to a Soviet request for still-unformed Allied plans about which Churchill hoped to maintain an air of mystery.

But could the Allies take a Soviet winter offensive for granted? Views in Washington were less sanguine. Stimson, who took nothing for granted, spoke of reviving National Service legislation and mobilizing new troops. Having warned against excessive military dependence on Moscow, Stimson told the Cabinet he was "disturbed at Russian slowness" and worried that Moscow was "going back on us." German strength "was too close for comfort," he said, and at least ten fresh divisions might prove necessary to provide a margin of safety, no matter what the Russians did. On the other hand, Marshall flatly opposed forming new divisions and insisted that even accelerated replacements would not be sufficient if the Russians failed to act. He noted that if the Russian pause on the Vistula persisted, it would be "necessary to recast the war" with the Allied armies passing to the defensive while the "American people decided whether they wanted to raise new armies."

Meanwhile Eisenhower devised a compromise approach short of Harriman's early December proposal that Eisenhower personally travel to Moscow for talks. Plainly, Eisenhower could not leave Paris, but the Soviets might receive SHAEF emissaries. On the twenty-first, Eisenhower had cabled the CCS asking that the heads of state arrange for a SHAEF liaison party headed by Air Marshal Tedder to visit Moscow. The Russians evidently would refuse to disclose their intentions in writing, he explained, and ordinary military channels had proven insufficient so far. He had an urgent need to know whether a Russian winter offensive was imminent and would thus ease German pressure in the west, or whether the Ardennes was to be only the first of many such German attacks in the west.

Eisenhower's request posed hard questions. First, there was a problem of protocol in sending a high-ranking member of SHAEF to Moscow at the height of a military crisis. Second, and more important, Tedder could hardly go to Moscow hoping to learn Russian plans unless he was prepared to disclose Allied plans. What were Allied plans? Eisenhower's intentions, which he had not amended, called for Allied offensives to close the Rhine along its length preliminary to a main offensive north of the Ardennes and a secondary offensive south of the Ardennes with ultimate objectives— including Berlin—to be worked out in close consultation with the Russians later. But were these the intentions of the CCS?

Roosevelt, on the twenty-fourth, drafted a carefully phrased message informing Stalin that he would like to direct Eisenhower to send a staff officer "to discuss with you the situation in the west and its relationship to the Russian front in order that information essential to our efforts may be available to all of us." On Christmas Day, Stalin agreed to receive SHAEF representatives to discuss bomb lines and permanent liaison arrangements for the linkup of Soviet and Allied armies. But Stalin did not say when he would be prepared to see visitors, and Tedder's departure "as weather permitted" was held up, under British pressure, pending a favorable turn of events in the Ardennes Forest.

The wait continued, and Summersby's journal provides glimpses of tension behind the scenes at Versailles. Eisenhower's request for a high-level Allied-Soviet exchange coincided with his decision to commit the U.S. 11th Armored Division at Givet, his only reserve unit in the Third Army sector. "Strong is uneasy regarding the Russians," Summersby wrote amid reports of fresh German arrivals from the eastern front and sobering new estimates of German reserve strength. On the twenty-second, behind the twenty-four divisions identified as operating in the Ardennes, thirteen more were "accepted in reserve" and others in the Düren sector "reported in reserve but not confirmed." Day and night merged, as Eisenhower remained "pinned up" at the office under the crush of security forces.

The persistent complication was lack of troops. Surveying the reports of casualties, Smith on the afternoon of the twenty-second had mused whether the "time has come to go on record with our masters in Washington that 10 divisions are necessary if we are to win the war in Europe." Ready to request additional divisions on the sixteenth, Eisenhower had drawn back.

Having just placed two American armies under Montgomery, he was wary of proceeding with a proposal whose import would be more symbolic than practical, for Eisenhower knew that ten new American divisions were not available.

A break in the battle came on the morning of the twenty-third. A bitter cold front moved in over Belgium, nudging aside the fog and rain that had hung over the forest for a week. Pounding enemy lines and bases east of the Our, Bomber Command and 1,200 Eighth and Ninth U.S. Air Force bombers were active in the clearing skies over the battlefield. Patton's III Corps moved slowly through mine fields and demolitions, and forward columns were within twelve miles of contact with defenders of the Bastogne perimeter. Air supply of the 101st commenced, ruling out any sudden collapse of Bastogne.

But as SHAEF dug in for a long winter siege, Eisenhower girded for the struggle to maintain his authority and his control over the front. As the first week ended, the size of the salient, fifty miles deep and sixty miles wide, meant that no matter how effective the countermeasures, the Allies faced a long struggle in the Ardennes, then more hard fighting to reclaim positions abandoned elsewhere. Evidently, this accounted for an action Eisenhower took that day that was destined to become a controversial sidelight in the Ardennes saga. That morning, Eisenhower ended an eighty-year policy of automatic commutation of the death sentence for desertion by ordering the execution of Private Eddie Slovik, G Company, 109th Infantry, 28th Division. Did the circumstances justify the first execution of an American soldier for a battlefield offense since 1865?

Many would question it. Since June 6, of 40,000 desertion cases, more than 2,800 had been tried by general court-martial without executions. Slovik was a repeat offender, but critics of Eisenhower's decision would note that nothing marked Slovik's case as unusual. Notably, Slovik was not accused of assaulting an officer or comrade. According to the file Eisenhower examined that day, Slovik had appealed for another chance to "continue to be a good soldier," though he had declined a chance to earn leniency by returning to his unit. But Slovik's unremarkable background more likely than not weighed against him on a day that Eisenhower spent in conference on the manpower crisis. Slovik's unit, the 28th Division, badly mauled in the Hürtgen and again in the past week, was known as a problem division with a high rate of desertions and self-inflicted wounds. Also important was Slovik's belief that he would receive leniency. Evidently, the case was exemplary—aimed at alerting the ordinary GI to long, hard fighting ahead amid reports of units disintegrating under pressure and the mass surrender of the 106th. In a companion action, on Eisenhower's written orders, death sentences were set and carried out against three German infiltrators caught in American uniforms near Spa.

On December 23 the vagaries of the situation prompted Eisenhower's first memorandum for the record since September 5. In it, Eisenhower set forth his thinking, summarizing recent events, including the reasons for pressing the offensive in November and accepting the "possibility" of attack in the Ardennes sector. Eisenhower then recounted the steps he had taken on the sixteenth and seventeenth to contain the attack, the conferences at Verdun and the transfer of the Ninth and First armies to Montgomery. He recited the instructions he had given Bradley as he authorized weakening the Third Army front to relieve Bastogne.

> He [Bradley] must make absolutely certain of the safety of his right flank in the Trier region from which a new offensive by the German 7th Army still threatens; his attack must be by phase lines with all forces held carefully together as to avoid dispersion and waste in strength before Montgomery can join the attack from the north. . . .
>
> He has been told that above all else at this moment he must protect his right flank and make certain of the Meuse bridges. He [Bradley] definitely feels that Patton's attack, with the present object of joining up with the forces still holding Bastogne, will help in this latter mission because it will threaten the rear of all forces to the westward.
>
> Today the general instructions issued to Bradley repeat all of the above. In addition, my own staff is doing everything possible to strengthen the defense of the Meuse bridges south of Givet and to hurry up the arrival in that region of the 11th Armored Division. Instructions have been reiterated that the defenses of the Meuse are to be closely coordinated by the 12th Army Group.

Christmas Eve brought another day of good flying weather and seesaw fighting. Two thousand Allied bombers screened by eight hundred fighters pounded crowded German roads in daylight, yielding high claims in enemy tanks and transports. But III Corps, advancing through snow toward Bastogne, lost ground before German counterattacks. Things were "if anything worse than before," complained the First Army diarist. As the German Fifth Panzer rumbled on toward Dinant, anxiety arose over Montgomery's orthodox tactics at First Army Headquarters. In the Fifth Panzer sector, G-2 was predicting fresh attacks toward Verviers and Liège, and plans were drawn up to evacuate V Corps equipment in the event of withdrawal.

By the twenty-fourth, the Germans had gained room for maneuver with the withdrawal of the 7th Armored and 82nd Airborne behind the Salm River. Montgomery still lacked a continuous line, and at Tongres that day ordered Collins to hold the Hotton–Andenne line "at all costs." The Fifth Panzer Army ranged far to the west, engaging Collins' VII Corps in the Hotton sector, a series of battles in which "the German Panzers roughly handled the American divisions showing that the First Army front was still far from secure." Collins noted that German armored spearheads had outrun infantry support, however. Manteuffel's panzers were short of fuel, and his decision that day to detour Panzer Lehr and 116th Panzer back to join the siege at Bastogne was a sign that he could not count on more reserves.

Allied reserves were moving up, and weather predictions were "excellent," according to the diarist, who also alluded to the rising optimism in the field. He noted the evacuation of the 7th Armored and 106th from St.-Vith "in fairly good condition," and "fervent" plans by the surviving regiment of the 106th that the division "retain its identity rather than . . . be merged as replacements for some other division." The heroic V Corps defense of the northern shoulder was funneling the German drive "straight west, which we fear far less."

At this point, Christmas Eve, the chastened G-2 staffs were still cautious, but signs were pointing up and, significantly, American-British relations were smooth. The diarist noted Montgomery's chipper upbeat mood at his daily conferences with Hodges at St.-Trond. Two hundred British tanks arrived to compensate for American losses (to be returned "when convenient"); and the arrival of British units into the Hotton sector was a "tremendous load" off Hodges' mind. A story made the rounds about an exchange between Horrocks and Collins at their meeting to work out the defense of the Hotton–Dinant sector. Horrocks had complimented the 82nd Airborne, calling it the "best division he had ever seen in action and only regretted that his Corps, standing in reserve behind the Meuse with five divisions," was not yet able to get into the fray; that it was unfair for the Americans to take the sole brunt of this battle." The mood carried over to Christmas amid seesaw battles at Manhay, Hotton and Bastogne. "Tonight it can be said the enemy is at least temporarily halted," wrote the diarist. ". . . This does not mean, as both the General [Hodges] and General Kean realize, that he [the Germans] is going to stop attacking. . . ."

> . . . we have now had time to dig in and move our troops. General Kean impressed most forcibly on Field Marshal Montgomery this afternoon . . . in a telephone conversation that he wished to obtain at once an infantry division preferably the U.S. 102nd which could be replaced by a British division. We have the 51st Highlanders backing up our line but the General would prefer to stick in the [U.S.] 102nd to strengthen the front of the XVIII and VII Corps. . . . Field Marshal Montgomery said he would give an answer tomorrow.

Mild improvement in the battle zones was evident on Christmas Day, a day Eisenhower spent in conference in the War Room with Smith, Tedder, Bull and Whiteley with barely an hour out for a turkey dinner and opening packages from home. "You will understand from the papers we are preoccupied right now," Eisenhower wrote Mamie thanking her for the Christmas slippers and a needle threader.

Eisenhower's preoccupations were threefold: the battle at Bastogne; the reports of German armor crossing the Rhine into the German-held Colmar pocket; the incipient command crisis. Of the three, the most time-consuming was the question of command and the effort to minimize the inevitable contest between Montgomery and Bradley for control over the next phase of the battle. Eisenhower knew that restoring command solidarity would be a key factor in his ability to minimize the long-range fallout, and perhaps to avoid far-reaching command and strategy changes. Ominously, a British press campaign was already in full flower criticizing Eisenhower for events in the Ardennes. Beaverbrook's *Daily Express* went so far as to editorialize that "the knowledge that Field Marshal Montgomery was in control in Europe would be received with relief in Europe," a hint that the British were ready to disclose the highly secret command shift and push negotiations with Washington on the matter of an overall ground commander.

Unknown to Eisenhower, CCS negotiations were about to start as indicated in a paper approved by the BCOS within forty-eight hours of the German assault. In the document, the BCOS traced the roots of the December crisis to Eisenhower's failure in September to follow up adequately on the northern thrust recommended by the Quebec directive, resulting in the dispersal of his armies and the German recovery. It criticized the "lip service" Eisenhower had paid to CCS instructions in his October 28 directive, and further criticized Eisenhower's unsatisfactory brief on December 12 in which he had again endorsed a broad-front policy and advocated closing the Rhine along its length preliminary to the invasion of Germany, a policy beyond Eisenhower's means and posing "a manpower problem likely to prove insoluble."

Meanwhile, Marshall's self-imposed injunction of silence was still in effect. As of Christmas, Marshall had not commented on the command transfer. Eisenhower took this to mean that Marshall accepted the necessity of it, but that he intended to reserve his right to question or endorse the current arrangement after the fact. Marshall's silence left standing his old injunction against any significant long-range concessions to Montgomery, concessions that Eisenhower might find essential to patch up his command in the wake of the current crisis.

On Christmas Day, negotiations for the transfer of the First Army back to Bradley commenced at St.-Trond, where Montgomery and Bradley huddled for talks about the military situation. The meeting was reminiscent of the Condé talks in mid-August, but with the roles reversed. Bradley noted the improving situation and broached plans for a converging First and Third Army thrust which he felt might have decisive results if followed up. Montgomery served notice that he distrusted the idea and would not encourage it. Tactlessly, he dismissed the idea of a quick counteroffensive, saying it was "useless" to pretend that the Allies were about to turn the Ardennes battle into a great victory. The Ardennes was "a proper defeat," in his opinion, and he saw "no choice but to admit it." Montgomery spent much of the time lecturing Bradley on past mistakes. The Ardennes had been "entirely our own fault; we went much too far with our right [Patton]," trying "to develop two thrusts at the same time," neither of which had been "strong enough to gain decisive results." The Germans had seen their chance and taken it, leaving the Allies "in a proper muddle."

Afterward Bradley furiously called Smith and "let him [Montgomery] have it with both barrels," and in "no uncertain terms" demanded the prompt return of the First and Ninth armies. Bradley followed up by sending Hodges a formal letter to say he would view "with alarm" any plan carried out under British orders to surrender terrain favorable for a First Army counteroffensive.

Christmas was a day of reappraisal in all camps, as the improving Allied situation became obvious to the Germans as well. Postwar interrogations would reveal that Von Rundstedt, skeptical of the venture from the beginning, had abandoned all hope of even limited gains which had depended on rapid progress in the first forty-eight hours. Slow progress, especially in the Sixth Panzer Army sector, had exposed the flaws of a concept that matched German daring and Allied might. Moreover, American resistance had been tougher than the Germans had expected, especially at St.-Vith and Bastogne. Speed had been essential to overall success; according to the plan, reconnaissance units of the 150th SS Panzer Brigade were to have reached the Meuse bridges near Liège on D-day, to be reinforced at the Meuse by the Sixth SS Panzer Army by D plus 3. D plus 8 came and went without the hoped-for breakthrough.

Years later Von Rundstedt speculated that the Germans might have reached the Meuse had the main effort been entrusted to the Fifth Panzer Army from the beginning. Instead, Hitler had misplaced confidence in Dietrich's Sixth SS Panzer Army and entrusted it with the main role. On the very first day, Dietrich's armor had become embroiled in infantry fighting on the northern shoulder. The second waves of panzer and Volks grenadier divisions, deployed to reduce American strongpoints by-passed by the Sixth Panzer, had encountered tenacious American resistance, which had led to the improvisation of reinforcing Manteuffel on D plus 3, which came too late, particularly as it had become apparent that the Allies would not immediately withdraw behind the Meuse. Through the hole opened by Manteuffel's 2nd SS Panzer Division, OKW had poured reinforcements from the GHQ Reserve, only to be slowed by Ridgway's 82nd Airborne Division, then by VII Corps and by full-scale air intervention on the twenty-third.

But few, least of all Hitler, were ready to abandon the counteroffensive. By Christmas, there remained a chance to inflict a severe defeat on the First U.S. Army. This depended on Hitler's willingness to permit Manteuffel to wheel the Fifth Army due north and bare its flank at Dinant, and his further willingness to approve a converging German Fifteenth Army attack in the Aachen area.

But this meant scaling down expectations and settling for tactical gains. The Ardennes situation bolstered the position of General Heinz Guderian, chief of OKW, who had long opposed weakening German defenses in the east for the sake of the Ardennes offensive. At conferences in Berlin on the twenty-fifth and twenty-sixth, Guderian tried to convince Hitler that the Belgian attack had served its purpose by derailing the Allied winter offensive and creating a menace in the Ardennes Forest that would hamper Allied operations in the spring. Accordingly, Guderian strenuously urged reinforcement of the east. A reserve was needed to stem the Russian advance on Budapest, which threatened German control of petroleum and bauxite resources in the area, and Guderian warned Hitler of the urgent need for mobile reserves in Poland in view of "overwhelming" Red Army preparations along the Vistula. But having staked all on the Ardennes, Hitler spurned any talk of reinforcing Poland or accepting less than strategic victory in the Ardennes. Gambling that the Russian pause in Poland would continue until February, Hitler redirected a panzer corps from Warsaw to Budapest, then ordered a secondary offensive in Alsace to begin on New Year's Day, 1945.

By the twenty-sixth, evidence accumulated of German troubles in the Ardennes. In clear weather, thousands of Allied bombers pounded German supply lines. German prisoners had not eaten for two days, and told interrogators of recent directives ordering units to rely on captured American stores. Everywhere, German units were fighting short of ammunition and men, and vehicles were being abandoned for lack of fuel. ULTRA, which had been strongly silent before the attack, had now begun to provide intercepts that confirmed the deteriorating German positions.

According to Winterbotham, on the twenty-sixth ULTRA eavesdropped on exchanges between Von Rundstedt, Model and Manteuffel, who agreed among themselves that the capture of Antwerp was no longer feasible and groped for ways of presenting this fact to OKW. "This was a vital signal for Eisenhower who now knew at least that the attack had shot its bolt," Winterbotham later wrote. Hitler again refused his generals' advice and ordered the second counteroffensive for January 1 in Alsace. "This, too, was a vital sign both for Eisenhower and Bradley, and in it Hitler went on to say that he still believed that Antwerp could be taken," he recalled, "but both to Eisenhower and Bradley the above signs were a clear indication that the time had come for the Americans to counterattack."

In the Ardennes Forest, the Germans reorganized. The Sixth SS Panzer Army boundary was drawn east from the Our River to La Roche—in effect, passing to the defensive. Meanwhile, I SS Panzer Corps was detached and ordered south to Bastogne to join Panzer Lehr and the 116th Panzer in an all-out effort to reduce the Bastogne stronghold, and to consolidate the salient east of Houffalize. At Bastogne, the 101st narrowly contained two armored breakthroughs along the northern perimeter as patrols of Patton's 4th Armored Division gained tenuous contact from the south.

Meanwhile, columns of the 2nd SS Panzer Division had advanced to within four miles of the Meuse at Celles, where they had stopped to await fuel and reinforcements. The British 29th Armored Brigade moved in while Collins rushed Harmon's 2nd Armored Division to the scene. In the ensuing battle the Germans fell back, leaving 2,500 killed and wounded and another 1,200 captured. At midnight, 1,500 battleworthy German troops received orders to destroy any equipment to be left behind and to withdraw to the southeast to join in the battle for Bastogne. At Celles, the check of the elite 2nd SS Panzer Division marked the high-water mark of the German offensive, and the end of Manteuffel's dash for the Meuse.

In the battle for Celles, as Collins' VII Corps linked with the 29th British Armored Brigade, the Allies established a continuous front for the first time since December 16. That night the German bulge became a winding salient, extending sixty miles from its base to the constricted tip at Celles. Along the northern rim, three fully replenished American corps were entrenched, backed up by XXX Corps. In the south, two American corps mustered at Bastogne, with a third attacking the base of the German salient at Echternach.

With the immediate crisis easing, Eisenhower's imperatives were twofold: first, prompt steps to push the Germans back so as to restore the line in the Ardennes as quickly as possible; second, command unity, which meant working out an agreement on long-range steps to restore the western front in order to salvage the fragile consensus on strategy that had been worked out before the German attack. On notice of imminent CCS negotiations, Eisenhower knew that this was essential if his command was to be allowed to work its way out of the crisis and if Allied policy was to survive the shock of the offensive.

As feared, it was already apparent that restoring command unity would not be easy. Bradley had indicated that he was determined to restore his command whatever that took, while Montgomery, still in possession of the U.S. First and Ninth armies, had indicated that he was not about to make things easy for Bradley. Bradley, who had hinted the day before that he would favor bold military action to exploit the concentration of force in the Ardennes tactically and strategically, was at work on specific plans to launch counterattacks in the Ardennes involving all seven corps of the First and Third armies, which he intended to follow up with a massive far-ranging American counteroffensive. By contrast, Montgomery favored adhering to his cautious plan in the north until the Germans had actually begun their retreat, then to revert to the long-range plans adopted at Maastricht, which would involve breaking up the American concentrations in the Ardennes in order to reassemble forces for eventual resumption of the 21st Army Group offensive in Holland. The clash over command of the Ninth Army and the mission of the neighboring U.S. First Army was fundamental, and time lost in argument in the next five days would nearly destroy Eisenhower's command.

As he set meetings with his army group commanders beginning the twenty-seventh, Eisenhower characteristically found himself in sympathy with both Bradley and Montgomery. On the one hand, Eisenhower supported Bradley's fervent desire to restore his command and supported Bradley's desire to exploit the improving situation with prompt action to reduce the German salient. On the other, Eisenhower favored Montgomery's cautious handling of the delicate First Army sector and was sympathetic with what he took to be Montgomery's desire to restore the foundations of the broad-front strategy. But common ground would be hard to come by.

During a tense meeting at Versailles on the twenty-seventh, Eisenhower encouraged Bradley to think offensively, but he discouraged talk of a "hurry-up" offensive and talk of "jumping the Rhine on the run," followed by a deep thrust into Germany. But as yet, Eisenhower could not even offer Bradley guarantees about when the First Army would revert to his command, and, looking ahead, warned that in any outcome, Simpson's Ninth Army would probably remain with Montgomery, and that Montgomery could retain some form of "coordinating authority" over the First Army in line with long-standing "priority" for 21st Army Group operations.

Eisenhower and Bradley discussed the Ardennes situation at length and managed to agree on several essentials. First, they agreed that the situation had stabilized; second, they agreed that German armor, now falling back toward Bastogne, had to be engaged, then brought under air and artillery bombardment and kept from slipping away to cause fresh problems in Holland or Alsace in view of confirmed reports that German armor was crossing the Rhine at Colmar. Eisenhower approved Bradley's plans, insofar as they called for converging attacks on Houffalize to squeeze the Germans east of the Our River. As for possibilities of pursuit through the Eifel and beyond, Eisenhower was open-minded and willing to back Bradley if an American offensive developed "decisive" potential. But the 12th Army Group would have to prove itself quickly, or Eisenhower would halt it.

As Bradley left, Devers flew in to discuss the worrisome reports of the German build-up at Colmar and Karlsruhe, a reminder that the military crisis was not over. The German build-up, confirmed by ULTRA, jeopardized Eisenhower's plan to form a two-division SHAEF reserve from the 6th Army Group to cover Patton's extended line from Haguenau to Bastogne. Eisenhower again emphasized to Devers that in the event of enemy attack he was to ensure that French and American forces waged an "aggressive defense" and then withdrew into the Vosges Mountains. Eisenhower saw no point in exposing American and French forces to encirclement at Strasbourg, which would stretch the 6th Army Group even thinner and hand the

Germans a chance to recoup lost momentum. Eisenhower approved a message to the CCS on the manpower crisis, which marked the beginning of his long and complicated effort to fend off Marshall's pressure on the CCS. Hinting at future requests for American troops, Eisenhower described the current situation, its impact on planning, and his hopes of solving the problem with such expedients as equipping additional French divisions and Belgian security brigades, and using Polish troops reaching the west through Switzerland "in case of emergency." Eisenhower noted the equipment shortages plaguing the French mobilization effort. "No quicker, more economical or effective way could be found to augment our fighting power in this theater than by providing equipment for these five divisions," he noted. "If they are to be ready for full employment by early spring when we will need them, decision and action regarding their equipment must be taken promptly." By nine-thirty that night Eisenhower, Tedder, Smith and Whiteley boarded a train in the snow at Chantiers station, near Versailles, for an overnight trip to the 21st Army Group Headquarters in Hasselt, Belgium, for conferences with Montgomery.

The Hasselt meeting the next day was a typical Eisenhower-Montgomery encounter. In retrospect, Eisenhower and Montgomery were in agreement on basic aims. Both wanted to restore the front as it had stood on December 15 and salvage a strategy painstakingly worked out since July, a strategy that featured more American support for the 21st Army Group than any other plan in sight. The snags concerned method: how to proceed with eliminating the Ardennes salient; how to handle the command problem; and simply put, how to maintain mutual confidence in an Allied command. At loggerheads since Normandy and "poles apart in the conduct of war," as Montgomery put it, the odds weighed heavily against a smooth solution to the Ardennes crisis, as Eisenhower learned quickly. Tension and formality marked every move. After the intelligence briefing, Montgomery imperiously ordered Smith, Whiteley and De Guingand out of his command caravan to permit him to talk with Eisenhower alone.

Once alone, Eisenhower urged Montgomery to adjust his thinking and to support Bradley's proposals for the First and Third armies' counterattacks. Montgomery was skeptical. His harsh appraisal was that a "preventive attack would enable the Germans to take Liège and would result in heavy casualties, especially in infantry already short of replacements." As for relinquishing the First and Ninth armies, Montgomery called Bradley a tired man, and, noting that the U.S. Army had suffered "severe losses," added that it was "useless to pretend that we were going to turn this failure into a great victory." Eisenhower and Montgomery also failed to agree about the military situation. With the Germans withdrawing from Dinant and falling back toward Bastogne, they agreed that Manteuffel was not likely to mount a serious stand in the Ardennes. But British intelligence, unlike U.S. intelligence, indicated that as German pressure eased in the

Ardennes it would intensify in the Eindhoven and Aachen area—the main reason Montgomery had kept Horrocks' main body behind the Meuse. Should the First and Fifteenth German armies attack in Holland, Montgomery proposed that the British absorb the blow, then "pursue on the rebound" across the Maas reinforced by Simpson—in essence, a limited "single thrust through Holland" to threaten the Ruhr from the north.

Montgomery's worries about a German attack in Holland were groundless, for they were contradicted by firm reports of German preparations at Colmar and Strasbourg, facts known to both men. The best that could be said for Montgomery's intransigence on Holland was that Montgomery avoided the kind of hard-and-fast position that had led to past troubles. For once, Montgomery presented no grand designs comparable to MARKET-GARDEN, though he did raise the question of a British ground commander. In substance, Montgomery was now a conservative influence at SHAEF, and this enabled the two of them to reach a tenuous compromise. Montgomery agreed that if the German Fifteenth Army front stayed quiet until January 1, he would dispatch Horrocks' XXX Corps east of the Meuse and draw back VII Corps into reserve for a First Army assault on Houffalize, nothing more.

Eisenhower left Hasselt worried. Montgomery's unrestrained criticism of Bradley was a problem in that it suggested that Montgomery deep down doubted that Eisenhower would succeed in persuading Bradley to moderate his views or that Eisenhower's reasoned approach would withstand the CCS review in the offing. Montgomery's evident lack of confidence was dangerous, and suggested that he would not cooperate but would rely on his negative power to thwart changes. Montgomery, who now had no chance of becoming ground commander in chief, had the means to block others by such tactics as stalling on a First Army counterattack and by provoking the Americans generally, thus making integrated command all but impossible. To the extent that Montgomery had this obstructiveness in mind, he and Eisenhower were on a collision course. Montgomery's approach would sell the odds of genuine cooperation short if not wreck the Alliance. More important, for Montgomery to foment tensions with Bradley would reduce all issues to control of the Allied forces north of the Moselle, which would submerge the cause of reassembling the front and trying to resume as before.

Eisenhower was determined to avoid such a disaster, but command relations soon reached the crisis point. Whiteley, who had lingered at 21st Army Group Headquarters, returned on the twenty-ninth with news that Montgomery's staff had suddenly become involved with preparations to meet a German Fifteenth Army attack in the Maas salient expected on New Year's Day. Eisenhower drafted a letter, never sent, spelling out his version of the understanding that he and Montgomery had reached. The main points included (1) that German infantry divisions must not be allowed to bed down in the Ardennes and permanently threaten U.S. First and Third

Army communications; (2) that German mobile divisions must not be allowed to escape the Ardennes Forest to threaten either Holland or Strasbourg; (3) that Eisenhower approved Montgomery's idea of meeting an attack in Holland and striking the Germans "on the rebound," on condition that the Germans attacked in Holland, a contingency he dismissed in conversations with Smith as "ridiculous." In case there were no German attacks north of the Roer, the U.S. First Army was to concentrate on the Ardennes Forest and the "presence of . . . British XXX Corps, not yet employed" gave Montgomery "great flexibility," he wrote. Eisenhower placed the letter on hold, then set it aside when a message arrived from Montgomery later that day that plunged SHAEF into despair.

In it, Montgomery abruptly notified Eisenhower that Collins' VII Corps attack was off because of the "definite failure" in the Ardennes and recommended disapproval of Bradley's "hurry-up" offensive. Proceeding to "the matter of operational control of all forces engaged in the northern thrust of the Ruhr," Montgomery set two conditions for eventual success in the invasion of Germany: first, that all available forces be assigned to support the 21st Army Group advance; second, a "sound setup for command"—namely, that his power of coordination over Bradley be amended to read "operational control," phrased tightly, as "any loosely worded statement will be quite useless." Montgomery cataloged the disappointments and failures since September, then enclosed a draft directive spelling out the details of the Ruhr thrust and the new airtight command setup, warning that unless the two basic conditions were set, "we will fail again."

Summersby chronicled Eisenhower's "long and trying journey" to Hasselt, Montgomery's lack of cooperation, the growing worries about combat replacements and casualties, the still-secret command shift, the troubles with Washington, the anxious wait for Tedder's departure for Moscow, and Eisenhower's exasperation with Montgomery. "All are mad at Monty, especially Whiteley," she wrote. "E.'s one aim is to keep the staff together."

By the twenty-ninth, German infantry and panzer units were switching off along the entire length of the Ardennes, and the drift of armor from Dietrich's sector southward toward Bastogne was pronounced, a preliminary to one final battle for Bastogne before resumption of the offensive or extrication of armored forces for the eastern front. American optimism was on the rise. Collins, buoyed by the defeat of the 2nd Panzer at Celles, agitated for permission to reassemble VII Corps for counterattack. VII Corps patrols south of Manhay had advanced 1,000 yards through sparse resistance. On the thirtieth, the 12th SS left the Manhay region, ending the threat to Liège and the northern rim of the Ardennes Forest, whereupon Bradley rushed along preparations for concurrent Third Army attacks toward Houffalize to engage the twenty-seven German divisions now operating in the Ardennes. By nightfall the Third Army attack commenced just as Montgomery canceled Collins' preparations for a counterattack and ordered a postponement of the First Army offensive until January 3.

Simultaneously, Marshall broke his long silence on command matters and "violating somewhat [his] own orders to the staff here" dispatched Eisenhower a brief message. In it Marshall drew Eisenhower's attention to the talk in the British press proposing a British land commander to relieve Eisenhower of his burden in conducting the land battle. Marshall urged Eisenhower "under no circumstances make any concessions of any kind whatsoever," and assured Eisenhower that he had his complete confidence, and warned him of the terrific resentment any such action would generate at home. Marshall's vote of confidence was ambiguous, however.

At first glance, Marshall's cable was a powerful boost for Eisenhower in dealing with British pressures. At second glance, there was Marshall's injunction against "concessions" to Montgomery. In this respect, Marshall's message resembled Brooke's efforts to enjoin Montgomery's moves in late November so as to reserve all issues for the CCS, and it left the door open for a land commander by another name—Bradley, perhaps, or General Alexander designated as a deputy without portfolio.

That day, De Guingand called on Eisenhower at the Trianon to explain Montgomery's decision to postpone the First Army offensive. As he later recalled, De Guingand found Eisenhower stern and unsmiling. Flanked by Smith and Tedder at his desk, Eisenhower replied that matters had become serious. Bradley's situation was becoming "intolerable," he said. Further postponement of an offensive would cost Bradley the confidence of his troops, and would cost Eisenhower one of his ablest commanders. "Tired of the whole business," Eisenhower suggested that "it might be time for the CCS to make a decision about it."

As De Guingand recalled, Eisenhower drew two documents from his desk drawer. The first was Marshall's message ruling out dealings with Montgomery. The second was a draft cable in which Eisenhower asked the CCS in effect to choose between Montgomery's latest plan and an outline plan Eisenhower had drafted incorporating the compromise adopted at Maastricht on December 7. In this cable, Eisenhower went on to recommend that the CCS replace Montgomery with Alexander.

In short, any more delay or criticism on Montgomery's part would make a solution worked out between the two of them impossible and compel Eisenhower to take action if for no other reason than to stay abreast of the Combined Chiefs. Eisenhower reminded De Guingand that Montgomery had not been left empty-handed at Maastricht. The U.S. Ninth Army, as agreed at Maastricht, would remain with the 21st Army Group and support Dempsey's offensive north of Düsseldorf. Montgomery would retain the U.S. First Army for a transition period. Furthermore, Eisenhower had asked Bradley to locate his headquarters near Montgomery so that Montgomery could "coordinate" their northern boundary. This was the limit.

As he left, De Guingand cornered Smith and told him that he did not realize such an "extremely serious situation had developed." Smith replied that "the matter has practically reached a stage where nothing more can be done about it." De Guingand, stunned, asked for twenty-four hours to "solve the impasse," as he was certain Montgomery had no idea that things had gone so far.

De Guingand left shaken and promptly reached a phone to call Montgomery to warn that the mood at SHAEF was "bad" and to say that he had "perhaps gone a little far this time." Back in Brussels, De Guingand briefed Montgomery on the details, and would later describe Montgomery's reaction. "Montgomery appeared to be genuinely and completely taken by surprise," he recalled, and "found it difficult to grasp." When Montgomery did grasp the implications, he "looked completely nonplussed—I don't think I had ever seen him so deflated. It was as if a cloak of loneliness had descended upon him." The next morning, De Guingand took British correspondents aside in Brussels to brief them on the still-secret command shift and to warn them that it was a matter of "extreme sensitivity."

On the last day of 1944, along the northern rim of the Ardennes Forest, the front was stable. At noon, Ridgway and Collins met with Hodges for a conference lasting two and a half hours to sketch out the details of a coordinated First and Third Army attack to converge on Houffalize. In the attack, VII Corps, spearheaded by the 2nd and 3rd armored divisions, would advance toward Houffalize in company with Ridgway's XVIII Airborne Corps on the eastern flank, while the British XXX Corps reassumed defensive responsibilities in the Givet–Celles sector. Afterward, Hodges motored to Brussels for a meeting with Montgomery, where he learned of the postponement until January 3.

And so the year 1944 ended on much the same note that it had opened, one of anxiety. At the Belgian town of Tongres, Hodges and his staff at First Army Headquarters assembled in a parlor to open a case of champagne from a wine vault taken at Cherbourg. At the stroke of midnight, a burst of small-arms fire drove the group to the floor. Military police and soldiers rushed into the streets only to learn that a band of tipsy GIs had decided to celebrate with a flourish. Hodges' staff stashed the champagne, refilled the glasses with orange juice, and raised their glasses in a toast to the New Year, and "to the offensive."

In *A Soldier's Story*, Bradley described the dispiriting New Year's Eve celebration at his headquarters in Verdun. Several journalists were on hand for the subdued event. As the beverages were served for the traditional toast, *Time* correspondent Bill Walton rose to his feet and declared, "Never has the world been plagued by a year less worth remembering." Bradley nodded his assent, mentally adding, he later wrote, "and especially the last fifteen days."

By December 31, Bradley had considered resigning his command. Whatever the reasons for the command shift on December 20, and there had been good ones, there was no escaping the fact that in a moment of crisis Eisenhower had turned to Montgomery—needlessly, in Bradley's opinion. Furthermore, Bradley was convinced that Montgomery overlooked "decisive" possibilities in the Ardennes. Long-range, the American forces might recover and use the Ardennes as a springboard for a major offensive into Germany that would avenge the setback and the long train of humiliations at the hands of the British.

But was the worst over? As of the thirty-first, the western front from Mulhouse to Nijmegen remained short of replacements, threatened in all sectors, while the Allied high command remained in the dark about Russian plans. The year-end SHAEF intelligence summary reported that the Germans were hardening defenses in the Ardennes with the apparent intent of holding the sector as a base for resuming the offensive, and elements of ten German divisions had been thrown into the siege at Bastogne. Offensive preparations were evident in Devers' 6th Army Group area, where German reinforcements continued to pour into Karlsruhe and the German Nineteenth Army pocket at Colmar. On the thirty-first, Eisenhower informed the CCS of the threat to Strasbourg and of his instructions to Devers, which he suspected De Gaulle would oppose with Churchill's full support.

Would the Alliance prosper in the new year? On the thirty-first, Roosevelt, Churchill and Stalin firmed up plans for three-power talks in the Crimea to occur in early February after a preliminary Allied conference at Malta. With the approach of conferences with Stalin, debate had intensified between Washington and London over looming postwar issues. For months the two Allies had been cordially disagreeing about postwar policies toward Greece and Italy, about the Allied positions on Poland, and above all about how to approach the Russians, a topic that brought out differences which, in Robert Sherwood's words, extended "to the meaning of the Atlantic Charter itself."

Churchill returned to London from his brief Christmas sojourn in Athens, where he had hammered out arrangements for a provisional Greek government. He felt undercut by U.S. State Department leaks and an uncooperative American attitude, which in his view now amounted to unreasoning opposition to practically anything the British government proposed. In the new year, Churchill would find himself aligning more closely with the French cause, a stance that at least figuratively enlisted the British fronts in Alsace and Holland against the American center in all military discussions thereafter.

Across the Atlantic, the news of the Ardennes battle had brought 1944 to a tense close. So far, the American intervention in Europe had come at a price of 457,000 casualties, and the heaviest fighting of the war raged on as the authorities were unable to assure the public that the end was in sight.

Roosevelt, Stimson and Marshall groped for official explanations of the Ardennes counteroffensive and what it meant to the American people.

At Fort Benning, Georgia, Mamie and John Eisenhower spent New Year's Eve at the Officers Club, three weeks shy of John's departure for France with the U.S. 71st Division. John would later describe the anxious mood in the main dining room, where a radio in the corner broadcast periodic reports on the situation in Belgium. Mamie had hoped that John might not be called to duty in Europe but those hopes were now dashed.

What had gone wrong? How was it that the shattered army of a defeated nation could "rise up and scare the daylights out of us?" asked Charles Bolte of the *Nation*, who surmised that the German retreat from France had perhaps not been as disorganized as had been thought, and that military experts had underestimated the defensive value of the West Wall and the efficiency of last-ditch German mobilization measures, which tipped the "terrible arithmetic" in the west against the Allies. In the year-end summaries, the press looked beyond blame for the immediate military crisis and for the first time delved into basic issues of Allied military policy.

Newsweek recalled Eisenhower's decisions in August to advance on a broad front after the liberation of Paris which had resulted in the overextended Allied line along the Rhine. *Newsweek* columnist General J.F.C. Fuller speculated that "concentration of force," a principle "formed in every military textbook," might have converted a chain of indecisive battles in September, October and November into a single great battle. Instead, Von Rundstedt, given his chance to recover and to concentrate the German army, seized it "to gain time and cause contention, confusion, and moral exhaustion." It could be argued that Eisenhower, among those who foresaw the German recovery, had met the crisis with balanced steps and averted a potential catastrophe. But had his conduct of the summer campaign been a self-fulfilling prophecy?

Time magazine, in naming Eisenhower "Man of the Year," sounded a cautious note. Eisenhower, an accessible and popular general, had demonstrated throughout the year his steadfastness and leadership ability. A master of coalition politics, Eisenhower had bridged American and British differences, performing the feat of harnessing the military power of two sovereign nations to fight as one. Much of this was due to Eisenhower's habit of emphasizing the positive, his frankness, his knack for identifying ways around military and political obstacles, and his unquestioned objectivity and dedication. And in his unique role as commander of a combined force, Eisenhower had wielded unusual powers—not technically responsible either to Churchill or to Roosevelt, but to a combined military authority seated in Washington, which, having set the European campaign in motion, could only supervise European policy and strategy in a general way.

But the Ardennes counteroffensive seemed, in retrospect, to flow logically from Eisenhower's conduct of the summer battles. The reverberations of the setback would be felt at the Big Three meetings that winter, and well into the postwar period. Eisenhower was Man of the Year, first, because of his courageous decision to gamble on the fickle Channel weather in June, a decision that would stand high in military history, and, second, because of his diplomatic contributions. *Time* noted that classified records would eventually be necessary to shed light on Eisenhower's role as a strategist and round out the judgment.

Eisenhower spent New Year's Eve at the Trianon Palace Hotel, where he placed the finishing touches on an outline plan for post-Ardennes strategy—a slight modification of his October 28 three-phase plan—which he proposed as a basis for restoring the unity of his command. In it Eisenhower recited Montgomery's terms: command of the U.S. Ninth Army and coordinating power over Bradley's forces north of the Ardennes, but the Ardennes had imposed a condition that Eisenhower took into account. The 12th Army Group was currently concentrated in the Ardennes and could not turn its attention elsewhere until it had cleared the area and tested possibilities of closing the Rhine in its sector, though Eisenhower specified that Bradley's pursuit operations toward Bonn–Cologne would remain secondary to the main effort in Holland.

Eisenhower's outline plan presupposed several facts about his unprecedented command. First, it was impossible for the Allies to dwell on recriminations and defeat for long. Second, since the Allies were facing an extended fight west of the Rhine, resumption of the Allied offensive was mandatory. Third, the unvarnished truth, a necessary guide in drawing up military plans, was nevertheless to remain unspoken in all inter-Allied dealings. Eisenhower could not stand by while Montgomery's sudden candor about American setbacks threatened to destroy American respect for the British and himself any more than he had stood by in September when the myth of a German collapse had threatened it. Fourth, SHAEF was indispensable, as evidence mounted that the ability of the political leadership to implement military policy was approaching the vanishing point.

Along with his copy of the outline plan, Eisenhower enclosed a brief message to Bradley in which he pointed out that the mission of the imminent 12th Army Group offensive would be to clear the Ardennes only, a limited objective. Eisenhower declined to fix a firm date for the return of the First Army. He reminded Bradley that placing Simpson's Ninth Army, kept at ten-division strength, under Montgomery was settled policy.

Along with Montgomery's copy, Eisenhower sent a message in which he urged the British field marshal to read the enclosed plan "carefully." The northern thrust retained "priority," with Montgomery in command of Simpson's Ninth Army kept at ten-division strength. As agreed at Maastricht, Montgomery would have authority to set army group boundaries on his southern flank. Now it was essential to begin clearing the Germans out of the Ardennes Forest—and Eisenhower assured Montgomery "that in this matter I can go no further," closing:

> I know your loyalty as a soldier and your readiness to devote yourself to assigned tasks. For my part I would deplore the development of such an unbridgeable gulf of convictions between us that we would have to present our differences to the CCS. The confusion and debate that would follow would certainly damage the good will and devotion to a common cause that had made this Allied force unique in history. As ever, your friend,
>
> *Dwight D. Eisenhower*

COMMAND CRISIS

On January 1, 1945, Field Marshal Bernard L. Montgomery, having rendered his "frank views" on command and strategy, renounced for the second and last time his campaign to become a ground commander in chief. In a message to Eisenhower, Montgomery pledged his full support for "whatever your decision may be . . ." and expressed regret for having added to Eisenhower's burdens "in these very difficult days." But the command issue had long since transcended personality, and Montgomery's ability to resolve the controversy had steadily declined since October. Montgomery's concession, while welcome, passed virtually without notice at the Trianon.

Alsace was the prime subject of Eisenhower's day-long conference at the Trianon with Smith, Strong, Whiteley and Robb present. That morning, seven German divisions attacked southeast of the Maginot Line city of Bitche, driving the American Seventh Army back toward the main supply base at Haguenau. German armor crossed the Rhine north of Strasbourg and attacked north from Colmar. Eisenhower resolved that Devers could not afford to fight east of the Vosges no matter what De Gaulle said, and ordered VI Corps, still deployed along the northern approaches to Strasbourg, to fall back into the eastern Vosges to form a two-division SHAEF reserve.

By the second, German attacks north and south of Strasbourg gained momentum. Devers' chief of staff phoned SHAEF with news that "the German is pressing everywhere" and that Devers believed Strasbourg "was as good as lost." But VI Corps was caught in the crosscurrents of coalition politics and so the evacuation of Strasbourg was on hold pending talks with Churchill, De Gaulle and Brooke.

Eisenhower spent the second in conference with Bradley at Etain on plans for the offensive in the Ardennes Forest. In Eisenhower's absence, Marshal Juin called at Versailles to deliver a letter from De Gaulle formally protesting Eisenhower's decision to evacuate Strasbourg and threatening to withdraw the French First Army from SHAEF if Eisenhower did not reconsider. Juin insisted that the loss of Strasbourg would expose the population to reprisals, and that to lose the city *without a fight* would be a political disaster for De Gaulle's provisional government. Accordingly, the French 10th Armored Division would hold Strasbourg "at all costs," and unless the American VI Corps covered the northern approaches to the city, the French First Army would be effectively withdrawn from SHAEF. Tempers flared. Smith that night told Eisenhower that had Juin been an American, he would have "socked him on the jaw."

The French maneuver posed unattractive choices—between risking a major American force at Strasbourg to satisfy De Gaulle at the price of U.S. Third and Seventh Army security or a prudent withdrawal and a showdown with De Gaulle backed by the British. Restoring the situation in the Ardennes was first priority, and so Eisenhower informed De Gaulle that night in writing that if General Pierre Billotte did not comply with SHAEF orders, the French 10th Armored would find itself defending Strasbourg alone with support "limited to what he [Devers] can provide from the air." Eisenhower appealed to De Gaulle as one soldier to another to reconsider, but the appeal failed, and at midday on the third De Gaulle, Churchill and Brooke converged on the Trianon.

Churchill acted as witness and mediator in the stormy meeting between Eisenhower and De Gaulle in the War Room annex of the Trianon. By now the Germans had established bridgeheads north of Strasbourg, and committed armor at Colmar in a bid to reach the Saverne gap and the western Vosges to envelop 6th Army Group forces in Alsace. But the military problem could not be divorced from diplomatic and political considerations, as Eisenhower soon learned. Eisenhower's authority over French troops was largely formal, and an order to evacuate Strasbourg invited defiance, for De Gaulle had chosen Alsace as a vehicle to clarify the extent of French "sovereignty" under the new Gaullist provisional government.

Discussion lasted for hours. In the give-and-take, De Gaulle denied ever having known of the "extent of the withdrawal" contemplated in Eisenhower's orders to Devers, and demanded that the Allies hold the Marne–Rhine canal north of Strasbourg. "Nothing of what you have told me, and nothing I have written can make you think that from the military point of view I approve of your views, as they are known to me," De Gaulle said. "I should tell you frankly that the truth is just the opposite."

De Gaulle delivered a sermon. While he conceded some merit in Eisenhower's plan to shorten the lines in the south to form reserves for the north, the issue was a battle being fought in France, not Germany. "Retreat in Alsace would yield French territory to the enemy," De Gaulle said. "In the realm of strategy this would be only a maneuver, but to France, it would be a national disaster, for Alsace is sacred ground."

De Gaulle threatened to withdraw the French First Army from SHAEF unless VI Corps defended Strasbourg. Eisenhower replied that if the French First Army acted independently of SHAEF, he would lack authority to supply it, and he reminded De Gaulle that the problem was created in the first place by the inability of the French First Army to reduce the Colmar pocket as ordered in early December.

Gradually, De Gaulle prevailed. Devers' immediate safety was not in doubt. De Gaulle had concluded that he could not abandon Strasbourg and that the practical effect of a French defeat unaided by the Americans would be a political crisis practically compelling French withdrawal from SHAEF. Eisenhower could not ignore De Gaulle's judgment on this, nor could he ignore Churchill's presence, which implied British backing. And yet Strasbourg could not be held without U.S. military support, and exposing U.S. forces to risks in Alsace would not pass unnoticed by a War Department and Cabinet already prone to question whether Eisenhower was too greatly influenced by intransigent local demands and thus unable to control the situation in Europe. Heavy U.S. casualties and the likelihood of defeat for the sake of defending a French objective meant a political crisis in Washington, which was supplying the troops, tanks and aircraft for the western front.

Since the issue left little room for accommodation, Eisenhower's best hope was to bide time under a formula that preserved some flexibility. A technical point favored De Gaulle: the native soil of a military ally was under threat of recapture. In this sense, the Strasbourg question somewhat resembled the pre-OVERLORD dispute between Eisenhower and Churchill over RAF Coastal Command, which Churchill succeeded in exempting from POINTBLANK on grounds of British sovereign interests. Unlike the French, the British had been full partners in the Alliance; nevertheless, the stability of rear areas in France was essential to maintenance of the front, and Strasbourg was essential to De Gaulle's effort to ensure this.

Eisenhower, De Gaulle and Churchill finally worked out a formula wherein Devers was to be instructed to hold Strasbourg "firmly," which was well short of De Gaulle's demand that the city be held "at all costs." To Marshall, Eisenhower cited the political consequences of failure at Strasbourg, which would threaten the security of Allied rear lines of communications by undermining De Gaulle's "control of the entire French situation." In De Gaulle's presence, Eisenhower phoned Devers to give him his new instructions. "You have done the wise and proper thing," Churchill told him afterward.

Eisenhower was not so sure. So worrisome was the episode that in later years he could recount the details of the showdown from memory—De Gaulle's sermon on Alsace, fatuous, in Eisenhower's opinion, since De Gaulle had conceded the military illogic of holding Strasbourg, and unforthcoming, since he had failed to couple this demand with a pledge of more French troops or help in subduing the German pocket at Colmar farther south. In short, De Gaulle had appealed for American aid, and offered little in return.

Why did Eisenhower decide to risk two American divisions in the defense of Strasbourg? At the time, more was involved than a choice between VI Corps safety and De Gaulle's survival. By now Eisenhower apparently sensed that Marshall and Brooke were groping toward a bargain on a new command setup and a revised directive. Though Marshall and Brooke appeared to be far apart on details, they were impatient men and united in their anxiety that the current situation should not drift along. Eisenhower doubted that Roosevelt and Churchill themselves were ready to sponsor a land commander, but it was up to him to avoid the confusion that would accompany an ill-conceived CCS decision to adopt new command arrangements. For a start, Eisenhower was anxious to prove to Churchill that he had not lost his ability to balance American, French and British interests, though the balance struck that day was tentative and precarious.

All was in flux. An episode later recounted by Strong illustrated the impatience on all sides. After the meeting with De Gaulle, Eisenhower and Churchill left the War Room to find Brooke. Throughout, Brooke had been next door in Strong's office discussing the German offensive with members of the staff. He barely concealed his low regard for Eisenhower's handling of the crisis and American leadership in general, and was particularly critical of Bradley's plans to squeeze the German salient at Houffalize. Brooke predicted that the Germans, checked at Bastogne, and surely knowing now that nothing decisive could be achieved in the Ardennes, would withdraw and that Bradley's offensive, under way that morning, would prove to be redundant and unnecessary.

Strong made the case for Bradley: first, if the Germans with eight divisions in the vicinity of Bastogne succeeded in capturing the city, they might resume their offensive. Strong also believed that the Germans, if kept under continuous ground pressure, might be unable to extricate themselves so as to avert a massive defeat west of the Rhine. Strong and Brooke spread maps across the floor and vigorously thrashed out the issue with pointers. According to Strong, just as Brooke had dismissed Strong's entire concept as "hogwash," the door opened. Eisenhower and Churchill stood in the doorway and gazed over the scene of littered maps and papers. Eisenhower's face registered puzzlement, then surprise. "To me it was a rather painful occasion," Strong recalled. "Whenever Brooke and Eisenhower met," Strong later wrote, "one sensed that there was a barrier between them."

Brooke and Churchill lingered in Versailles for forty-eight hours for talks on command and strategy, discussions shadowed by preparations for the coming conferences at Malta and Yalta. Closely linked to these meetings was the Tedder mission, a trip destined to become an intense behind-the-scenes drama and a significant test of Allied intentions in January 1945.

By the third, after a stopover in London and talks with the BCOS, Tedder had flown to Naples to await clarification of the Ardennes battle before resuming his circuitous trip to Moscow via Naples, Cairo and Basra. The question Brooke and Churchill faced at Versailles was whether Tedder should be permitted to proceed to Moscow.

Tedder's mission had several purposes: first, he was to learn about Russian plans; second, his trip was to be a high-level gesture, evidently required by the Russians, which would acknowledge the importance to the Allies of a Russian attack in halting the flow of reinforcements to the western front; third, to set up permanent liaison arrangements between the two sides. A significant corollary was that Tedder's mission could not succeed unless he was prepared to disclose Allied intentions. As things still stood, Allied intentions as set forth in Eisenhower's directive of October 28 called for two thrusts over the Rhine to be preceded by a lengthy campaign to clear the Rhine along its length. Submission of this strategy and Russian "approval" would tend to tie the hands of the CCS with respect to Eisenhower's broad-front plan and the constraints implied by that plan, which included close consultation with the Russians on Berlin and a coordinated strategy for the invasion of Germany. Did Eisenhower's idea of two offensives, one to the north and one to the south of the Ardennes, an idea discussed off and on since September, remain a true statement of Allied intent?

For the moment, Tedder's absence from Versailles was satisfactory to all inasmuch as Tedder was a prime subject in confidential discussions on the command setup that night. Churchill took Eisenhower aside privately to tell him about a proposal being circulated involving Tedder's job. The idea was for Montgomery to stay where he was, and Alexander to come to Paris not as Eisenhower's "Ground Commander in Chief" but to replace Tedder at SHAEF as Deputy Supreme Commander; Tedder would then return to the Air Ministry or replace Alexander in Naples, either way a promotion for Tedder. This proposal would admittedly upgrade the British voice on ground operations, but perhaps without all the divisive implications of formally appointing a ground deputy or the administrative drawbacks of setting up new echelons of command.

The rest of the conference, devoted to strategy and manpower, ran for another twenty-four hours through dinner, breakfast and lunch. What emerged was that the British Chiefs plainly intended to initiate a review of grand strategy and command with Marshall and Arnold at Malta. Brooke intended to offer to reinforce Montgomery's 21st Army Group with several British divisions drawn from Italy, but the British, in turn, would nominate Alexander to replace Tedder at SHAEF.

It is hard to imagine that Churchill was enthusiastic about transferring Alexander or denuding Italy of second divisions. Yet Churchill seemed to support the idea, which was a measure of the toll taken by the German counteroffensive. As the three men discussed the Ardennes, Churchill "did not mince his disappointment about the battle." He informed Eisenhower that with Italy shaping up as primarily a base for the strategic bombers, many, himself included, favored Tedder there and giving Alexander a prominent position at SHAEF. Eisenhower knew of Alexander's special favor in Churchill's eyes, and since Eisenhower's esteem for Alexander was beyond question, Eisenhower readily accepted Alexander in principle. Discussion was spirited but genial. The talks concluded on the night of the fourth with the customary glass of cognac in an atmosphere of good cheer.

But much remained to be seen. Would Churchill follow up on Alexander? Would Roosevelt approve? Nor could anyone predict how long the Ardennes battle would last. As long as the main body of the Red Army idled in central Poland, the Germans could be expected to send reserves to the western front and might do so no matter what the Russians did. Past optimism had proven false, and updated JIC estimates now spoke of German resistance lingering on into 1946. Accordingly, Churchill was especially anxious to build up the French army, which he believed meant a seat on the EAC for the French and a French occupation zone—things to come. Inevitably, the manpower problem raised the question of the American divisions in Europe, a question that Churchill volunteered to raise with Washington on Eisenhower's behalf. Afterward, in a personal cable to Roosevelt, Churchill summed up his "satisfactory" talks with Eisenhower on the Ardennes and future strategy. "His Majesty's government have complete confidence in General Eisenhower and feel acutely any attacks made on him," Churchill wrote. "He [Eisenhower] and Montgomery are very closely knit, and also Bradley and Patton and it would be a disaster which broke up this combination which has in 1944 yielded us results beyond the dreams of military avarice." He continued:

> I have not found a trace of discord at the British and American headquarters; but, Mr. President, there is this brute fact: we need more fighting troops to make things move.
>
> I have a feeling this is a time for an intense new impulse both of friendship and exertion to be drawn from our bosoms and to the last scrap of our resources. Do not hesitate to tell me of anything you think we can do.

On the fourth, Tedder idled in Naples, grounded by "bad weather." That night he sent Versailles word of a very unfavorable extended forecast and a suggestion that he return to Paris should the extended weather outlook threaten further delay upon reaching Cairo. Eisenhower replied that his mission was "imperative," and ordered Tedder to proceed "as soon as the weather improves." As a precaution, Eisenhower met privately that night with UP Paris bureau chief "Red" Mueller over a drink and intimated "off the record" the historic news that direct Moscow-SHAEF liaison had been established.

Meanwhile, Churchill phoned Eisenhower with an offer. Knowing of Eisenhower's anxiety about Soviet plans in Poland, he offered to expedite matters by cabling Stalin directly for the information that would enable

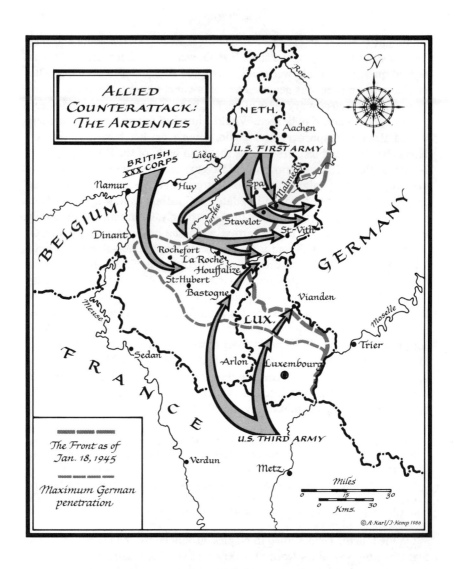

ALLIED
COUNTERATTACK:
THE ARDENNES

NETH.

Roer

Aachen

BRITISH
XXX CORPS

Namur

Liège

U.S. FIRST ARMY

Huy

Spa

Malmedy

Ourthe

Stavelot

St.-Vith

Dinant

Rochefort

La Roche

Houffalize

GERMANY

St.-Hubert

Bastogne

Vianden

Moselle

LUX.

Trier

BELGIUM

Meuse

Sedan

Arlon

Luxembourg

FRANCE

U.S. THIRD ARMY

The Front as of
Jan. 18, 1945

Maximum German
penetration

Verdun

Metz

Miles

0   15   30

0   30

Kms.

© A·Karl / J·Kemp 1986

Tedder to return to Paris. Eisenhower was appreciative, but preferred that Tedder proceed to Moscow in order to obtain the specifics that only a face-to-face meeting could provide. Shortly after the call, Eisenhower instructed Smith to inform the press pool at Versailles on the "background" of the imminent high-level visit. On the sixth, as news of the December 20 command shift broke in the world press, Smith briefed reporters at the Scribe Hotel on Tedder's trip, which he disclosed under "a severe injunction of secrecy."

Along the 400-mile western front, the battle raged on. On January 3, the long-awaited American counteroffensive had opened. Collins' VII Corps and Ridgway's XVIII Airborne Corps attacked toward Houffalize and Bastogne in subzero temperatures and four-foot snowdrifts. ULTRA revealed that Model had by now decided to end the Ardennes battle after one more attempt to take Bastogne. Patton's Third Army at Bastogne was a "knife turning in the wound," which curtailed Model's ability to consolidate his salient along La Roche–Bastogne and Stavelot–Vielsalm. Gradually Allied ground forces began to compress the German lines while air and artillery inflicted frightful losses on the Germans as, one by one, the 1st SS, 12th SS, 2nd SS, and 9th SS panzer divisions disengaged and fell back to the desperate siege at Bastogne. By the fifth, Model abandoned hope of capturing Bastogne and had turned to the problem of extricating the ten German divisions still west of Houffalize, a decision confirmed one day later by 12th Army Group intelligence, which traced the withdrawal of elite SS panzer troops away from the Bastogne area. That day, 12th Army Group G-2 General E. L. Sibert went so far as to caution the First Army to be alert "for signs of a German collapse," an observation that evoked laughter. Meanwhile eight inches of snow had blanketed Belgium, forcing a twenty-four-hour pause, and on the fifth XVIII Corps resumed toward the Salm. VII Corps made good progress along the entire front, cutting the La Roche–Vielsalm road at several points; XXX Corps joined the attack at Hotton on the left flank of the reconstituted VIII Corps, which withstood "unabated pressure" west of Bastogne. The 12th Army Group Headquarters concluded that the Germans were retreating wholesale as the reconstituted VIII Corps, including the 101st and 17th Airborne, attacked toward Houffalize.

In Alsace, the Seventh Army contained German drives south from Saarlautern and north from Colmar. The German First Army gained a small bridgehead north of Strasbourg, but no opportunity developed to employ armor as the Seventh Army withdrew safely into the Maginot Line fortifications.

Meanwhile the Germans reached the strategic decision to accept the futility of the Ardennes and to respond to the overwhelming Red Army preparations on the Vistula. Postwar interrogators would probe for the reasons for failure as the Germans saw them. Jodl and Göring would imply duplicity, citing the inability of the Fifteenth Army north of Monschau to attack on schedule, the embroilment of Dietrich's Sixth SS Panzer Army north of its intended thrust line, and other signs that field commanders had converted the offensive to their own purposes, which, after administering a shock in the west, consisted of gaining positions in anticipation of what the Germans expected to be negotiations leading to a phased surrender that salvaged German territory and a role for Germany in a postwar Europe.

There is evidence that Manteuffel and Model successfully oriented the Ardennes attack away from the grand slam to the small slam in defiance of OKW directives. It was later suggested that General Fritz Kramer, Dietrich's chief of staff, had issued operational orders aimed at Liège instead of the more westward objectives, then failed to exploit the tactical opportunities at hand when I SS Panzer Corps turned the First Army flank. Speidel, Rommel's chief of staff during the Normandy campaign, would later tell interrogators that the Wehrmacht regularly committed SS formations in battle as much as possible so as to wear down the elite formations and undermine Nazi control, a practice, he implied, that accounted for the quick check of the Sixth SS at Monschau and Elsenborn. Yet none of the principal commanders was sacked or shot, perhaps because Hitler could not admit failure, or because he now issued orders that most commanders considered impossible and therefore not worthy of obedience.

Some Germans would fault the vague and indefinite objectives. Others would fault the tardiness of the assault, ordered for mid-December instead of four weeks earlier, which might have enabled the Germans to take advantage of early-winter cloud cover. But the Allied attacks in November had severely hampered preparations, and so to this degree the Germans backhandedly credited Eisenhower's fall offensive with successfully blocking a timely counteroffensive, which might have reached the Meuse.

In any event, by January 9, it was clear to the Germans that there was little left to do except to concentrate on defending Poland and East Prussia while extricating German forces from the Balkans. Guderian, armed with new reports of the Russian build-up in Poland, resumed his plea for prompt steps to protect Silesia. With most of the German reserves in Belgium and Italy, the Russians mustered "vast forces ready to attack." On the eastern front, 133 understrength German divisions opposed approximately 450 Russian divisions. Of the 133, 30 German divisions were isolated at Memel, and another 30 strung out in the Balkans, leaving 73 to man the vast Vistula–Carpathian front, which lacked fortifications or natural barriers. Withdrawals from the west were essential to address threefold Russian superiority and to keep the Red Army out of Germany. Hitler relented, and ordered Model to give up the "area west of the Houffalize."

After Churchill's departure, Eisenhower lingered at the Trianon for a week to monitor the First Army offensive, the German attacks at Strasbourg and

Colmar, the maneuvers in London and Washington on the eve of the forthcoming conferences at Malta and Yalta, and Tedder's progress toward Moscow, which had now assumed overriding importance for Eisenhower. News of the Russian attack in Poland would be the signal that the crisis had finally passed in the west. Moreover, Tedder's arrival in Moscow would be a long step toward avoiding enervating and unnecessary debate over invasion objectives that winter, as anticipated Soviet approval of Eisenhower's intentions would weigh heavily in future Allied debates.

Summersby's account noted Tedder's slow progress. Amid reports that the Sixth Panzer Army was entraining for parts unknown at Cologne–Bonn, Churchill phoned Eisenhower on the seventh with news of a reply from Stalin. In it the Soviet leader recited the difficulties plaguing Russian preparations in Poland, including unseasonable mud and fog. Despite these difficulties, STAVKA planned "large-scale operations against the Germans along the whole central front not later than the second half of January," and said that the Allies could "rest assured that we shall do everything possible to render assistance to the glorious forces of our allies."

Had the purpose of Tedder's mission been fulfilled? Eisenhower thanked the Prime Minister, but suggested to him that more detailed information was necessary. Tedder, delayed in Cairo by an extended forecast of bad weather, again cabled for instructions and Eisenhower ordered him to "proceed."

Summersby's journal contains vignettes of the tense wait. Rumors abounded that the Germans were readying the use of poison gas in combat, and SHAEF alerted Spaatz and Doolittle to prepare for transporting gas bombs to the Continent. There were rumors too that the Germans had discovered a "ray" capable of paralyzing the engines of American B–17s and British Lancasters, and there were still other rumors of the testing and development of a "freezing bomb" observed by agents in Düsseldorf. Disheartening news reached Versailles that SHAEF emissary General Raymond Barker in Washington had told the War Department that without stepped-up infantry replacements the Allies would "lose the war," just the kind of overdramatization of the manpower problem that would shake Marshall's confidence in SHAEF. On the heels of the Barker episode, Marshall offered to provide manpower expert General Lorenzo Gasser to assist Eisenhower in his investigation of ETO duplication, coupled with the remark that the War Department would "no longer bleed ourselves much more on this side of the Atlantic to meet deficiencies on yours." Following up, Marshall offered the permanent services of Army ground forces commander General Benjamin Lear to head a new office in Paris on ETO manpower and mobilization procedures.

Meanwhile, news of the command shift had gradually leaked out to the world press. Responding to a round of editorials on both sides of the Atlantic, SHAEF, on the fifth, issued a terse one-paragraph statement noting that on December 20, when it had become apparent that the German penetration had created two fronts, Montgomery had assumed command of the northern front and Bradley command of the southern front "by instant agreement of all concerned."

The hypersensitive Bradley felt that the statement implied that Montgomery had been in command during the critical first ninety-six hours when the First Army had succeeded in holding the northern shoulder. The statement neglected to call the command arrangements "temporary," arousing suspicion in the 12th Army Group staff that Eisenhower privately wished to leave Hodges under Montgomery. This suspicion was unfounded, but the SHAEF statement, released twenty-four hours after Churchill's departure, suggested that Eisenhower had cleared the statement with Churchill and intended to proceed with the Maastricht formula, in which Simpson's Ninth Army remained with the 21st Army Group. But Eisenhower had every intention of expediting the return of the First Army to Bradley, and therefore he vigorously pushed Collins' offensive toward Houffalize—with a proviso that he could not permit the First Army to attack indefinitely in the Ardennes. Looking down the road, Montgomery's preparation in Holland would eventually begin to draw Hodges northward, and Eisenhower had pressing plans for the Third Army in the Saar, a preliminary to the secondary offensive planned south of the Ardennes aimed at Frankfurt.

Reviving the Maastricht compromise meant building up Montgomery's role as an Allied commander, which meant building up the British role in the Ardennes. On the seventh in Brussels, Montgomery summoned reporters to a press conference allegedly to clarify questions raised in public print about Eisenhower, his role and British actions along the northern shoulder of the Ardennes. Years later Bradley would concede that Montgomery probably called the press conference with the best of intentions, but months of frustration, beginning with the Normandy battle, boiled over in Montgomery's careless performance, which disrupted Eisenhower's careful formula for unity.

On the seventh, a radiant Field Marshal Bernard Montgomery engaged the world press with the tale of the Battle of the Bulge, a tale of American courage and how the "whole Allied team rallied to the call, and how teamwork saved a somewhat awkward situation." In the questioning, Montgomery claimed ample credit for "straightening out" the situation he had inherited on December 19, which he called one of "the most interesting and tricky battles I have ever handled with great issues at stake." And on he went.

Montgomery's claim—made repeatedly—that his leadership had restored a "sticky" situation in the Ardennes enraged the American leadership. Montgomery would blame the ensuing misunderstandings on the German black propaganda radio station at Arnhem, which beamed a distorted text of his remarks into American lines for the purpose of kindling command jealousies between the Americans and the British, but the mere fact that he had appeared in public to comment on the battle infuriated Bradley's disbelieving 12th Army Group staff, which also suspected SHAEF complicity in the whole affair. For instance, two days earlier Bradley had asked Eisenhower to amend the SHAEF statement to be sure his staff received credit for coordinating the first ninety-six hours of the Ardennes. Eisenhower had done nothing, which convinced Bradley aides Ralph Ingersoll and Chet Hansen that the Supreme Commander was behind Montgomery's press conference. Bradley was unwilling to go that far, but under staff pressure felt compelled to issue a clarification on the ninth, emphasizing that the command change had been "temporary," and to register a protest with Eisenhower.

Eisenhower's refusal to clarify the January 5 SHAEF statement was curious, but what Bradley did not know was that Eisenhower had warned Montgomery against deliberately provoking Bradley, on pain of recommending Alexander as Montgomery's successor. Eisenhower, infuriated by the press conference, phoned Churchill, who admitted that he had approved Montgomery's decision to meet the press. Eisenhower asked for the Prime Minister's help in quelling the "riotous sentiment of the 12th Army Group." Churchill obliged with a conciliatory speech in the House of Commons in which he noted that the Americans had engaged "30 or 40 men for every one we have engaged and they have lost 60 to 80 men for every one of us," and otherwise cautioned against claiming for the British Army "an undue share of credit for what was undoubtedly the greatest American battle of the war." But the Prime Minister declined to follow up and phone Bradley to express official regret.

The Ardennes crisis was easing, but the net effect of Eisenhower's stillborn effort to refurbish Montgomery's credentials as an Allied commander meant further trouble with Marshall, who directed a stream of inquiries about the Strasbourg affair. He informed Eisenhower on the sixth that the President had refused to receive the French ambassador, who had attempted to deliver a letter from De Gaulle appealing against Eisenhower's decision to withdraw VI Corps from Strasbourg. Eisenhower replied with a meticulous description of the VI Corps maneuver north of Strasbourg. He revealed that Devers had been told to leave reconnaissance detachments only along the Marne–Rhine canal, and at the first hint of trouble to withdraw into the Vosges Mountains.

Relations with Marshall went further downhill when on the seventh Eisenhower placed the inflammatory troop issue before the CCS. He filed a long message, weeks in the making, calling for mobilization of French divisions and urging that Washington maintain the flow of American replacements. Eisenhower went on to acknowledge that a Russian attack on Poland would force the Germans to divide reinforcements between east and west, but until such an attack was under way, the Allies had to assume that the German effort would build in intensity, ushering in "a most difficult situation, but one I feel we should face up to. In fact, it is imperative that we face this all-out German effort by an all-out effort of our own."

Eisenhower proceeded to rule out short-run expedients. He called for unallocated U.S. divisions, American divisions in Italy, increased congressional manpower ceilings, an expedited "flow of critical ammunition types and tires," plus matériel to equip the five French divisions needed in the most optimistic planning scenarios.

In a companion message to Marshall, Eisenhower recited the steps taken to fill out divisional complements within the theater. Soldiers convicted of military offenses had been given a chance to purge these records by volunteering for frontline service; Eisenhower had issued a directive through Comm-Z offering blacks, hitherto confined to maintenance and supply duty, a chance to volunteer for the front. Eisenhower had ordered a Comm-Z comb-out, the conversion of support units into infantry and the use of liberated manpower, including the French.

So far, Eisenhower had not called for mobilizing fresh American divisions, but Stimson's diaries attest to the impact at the White House of his manpower message, which portended difficulties with Congress and the British. Stimson ventured the opinion that Eisenhower, though "extraordinarily successful . . . in keeping the composite command of which he is at the head in full effect and in preserving the cordial feeling between the two armies," had lost "sight of the necessity of supporting sufficiently our national views where they were at variance with the British." For a while, Stimson favored placing the matter of new divisions before Congress and forcing Congress to "put up or shut up." He tinkered with the idea of reviving legislation for a National Service Act, a measure proposed and then quietly dropped by the White House, and a campaign for stepped-up draft quotas and laws permitting eighteen-year-olds in combat, which was also dropped. Marshall told Stimson he "flatly opposed" talk of ten new divisions "to the point where I said I would resign and asked him to tell the President this."

Thereafter the Eisenhower-Marshall correspondence, which by now "filled a good sized volume," showed signs of trouble. In his State of the Union message delivered to Congress by messenger, the President broke weeks of silence on the Ardennes. In answer to mounting criticism of the War Department and growing calls for "an authoritative interpretation of the Von Rundstedt offensive," Roosevelt characterized the Ardennes as a "setback" but focused his praise on the "indescribable and unforgettable gallantry" of American troops. As for the military leadership, Roosevelt was restrained, noting that General Eisenhower retained his "complete confidence" and "faced this period of trial with admirable calm and resolution and with speedily increasing success." Marshall forwarded a text of the message to SHAEF "by direction of the President" without comment.

In a separate message that day, Marshall acknowledged Eisenhower's two cables on manpower. His reply was technical and lengthy. In it the Chief of Staff noted that the renewal of the German offensive, and the heavy American casualties sustained, raised serious policy issues. Further noting that "we now face a situation requiring major decisions to prevent this war from dragging on for some time," Marshall asked for Eisenhower's "broad personal estimate of the resources required and the steps to be taken to bring this war in Europe to a quick conclusion."

On the eighth, the BCOS made its move. Marshall informed Eisenhower that General G. Macready of the British mission in Washington had presented a formal British motion to call on Eisenhower to submit his plans "following the suppression of the present German offensive for the conquest of Germany." The BCOS officially charged Eisenhower with violations of CCS instructions issued from Quebec, which emphasized the northern flank "toward Berlin," and for launching an offensive into the Saar instead. Macready warned Marshall that the British had bent over backwards to avoid personal criticism of Eisenhower, but in view of the Supreme Commander's "other pressing duties of supply, of political complexity, etc., command arrangements should be reconsidered."

Marshall's accompanying comments were sympathetic but noncommittal. He asked Eisenhower about the full report he had asked for earlier in the week on the European situation for use by the American Chiefs, who were now entering talks in the CCS. "Under the circumstances," Marshall wrote, "I now think that we should have those here by Thursday night so there can be some discussion by the United States Joint Chiefs before the combined meeting Friday afternoon."

On the tenth, Eisenhower sent Marshall several messages, in which he explained the whole range of operations he had directed since August and defended his actions in the Ardennes for Marshall's background use in talks on long-range plans. Eisenhower downplayed the idea that a "quick conclusion" was in the offing and indicated that he envisioned a three-phase effort to force the Rhine barrier and launch the invasion, meaning that he was reluctant to set timetables. Looking ahead, Eisenhower devoted his assessment to defending a methodical strategy of clearing German threats to the Allied flanks west of the Rhine, including Devers' flank on the upper Rhine, which would take time. At the close, Eisenhower intimated to Marshall that he had learned of moves afoot in London to replace Tedder with a ground soldier. Eisenhower doubted that this would mean "any better coordination," but he saw advantages in a deputy with ground experience who was a man of "fine personality, respected by all and willing to serve as my deputy and not repeat not under independent charter from my superiors." Alexander came to mind, but as Eisenhower understood it, Alexander was "manifestly not repeat not available." In passing, Eisenhower noted that he would lose Tedder—his principal airman—were Alexander to come to Paris. This would necessitate naming Spaatz as his Air deputy to dispel confusion about SHAEF authority over the Air Forces.

Eisenhower's message crossed Marshall's summary of a BCOS "memorandum on strategy" presented in the CCS meeting that morning. Marshall withheld the actual text, since the frank opinions stated therein were confidential expressions intended for his eyes only, but he did add that the BCOS would require that Eisenhower spell out his official views in advance of the Combined Chiefs sessions in Malta set for January 28 as a preliminary to three-power talks at Yalta. Critical of Eisenhower's past strategies, and doubtful that by spring the forces available to Eisenhower would be sufficient "for two main attacks," the BCOS proposed that all forces north of Luxembourg be organized into a main thrust under the control of "one ground commander." Marshall withheld the BCOS's biting criticism of Eisenhower's conduct of the fall campaign, and of the "improper coordination at the top" in the first ninety-six hours of the Ardennes assault. BCOS had conceded that British and American intelligence had been caught by surprise, but otherwise alleged that the German offensive had "succeeded far beyond its capacity or the advantages gained by surprise." Marshall again asked for further details about Eisenhower's plans and his reaction to the idea that the Allies lacked the strength for two offensives.

Again, that Marshall's name was inseparable from the second front and that he was the architect of the U.S. Army were not reasons to assume that Marshall and Eisenhower agreed on every particular of strategy in Europe. And Marshall's opposition to concessions to Montgomery did not mean that he opposed concessions to the British, such as appointing Alexander or adopting a strategy of concentration in the north, provided the American Army assumed an as yet unspecified but very prominent role in the closing offensives. All of this would soon become clear.

Meanwhile, on the eleventh, Marshall's response to Eisenhower's outline plan was not encouraging. Marshall praised "the soundness of your estimate and intentions," but probed further regarding Eisenhower's ideas about a deputy. He revealed that he and General Thomas Handy had debated whether to show the message to Admiral Leahy and the President "because of your last paragraph which may be taken as indicating a weakening on your part under the heavy pressure of the press and British officialdom to get some high British military official into your general management of the ground forces." Offhand, Marshall saw several pitfalls. First, the appointment would mean that "the British had won a major point in getting control of ground operations in which their divisions of necessity will play such a minor part"; second, as Marshall saw it, the appointment would complicate Eisenhower's task of "offsetting the influence of the Prime Minister." In sum, Marshall saw problems, but he neglected to demand that Eisenhower "make no concessions whatsoever," and closed with a polite suggestion that whatever the outcome of personnel discussions, Eisenhower consider augmenting his staff with an officer to function as his "eyes and ears and legs for continuous observation and discussion with top commanders along the front." Marshall recommended that he consider a Britisher as well as an American in this role.

A day later Eisenhower replied that he was "glad to get your [Marshall's] reactions," particularly about the ground deputy idea. Marshall had put his finger on a problem with Alexander that had not occurred to him—that is, that the British would win a major point. Eisenhower wanted Marshall to know that he had not meant to endorse a ground deputy as such. What he had been referring to was a deputy to function "exclusively without portfolio," responsible for "activities delegated by me" should Brooke transfer Tedder to London or Naples. Eisenhower revealed that Churchill had posed the eventuality "most secretly and personally" in the event that the CCS at Malta stripped Alexander of additional divisions, leaving him no real job in Italy. The Prime Minister had asked Eisenhower whether he would be "content" with this. "Feeling as I do toward him," Eisenhower continued, "I naturally answered in the affirmative, although I did point out that my deputy was assigned by the Combined Chiefs of Staff and that I was merely expressing a personal agreement if all these eventualities should ever come about." The eventualities seemed "rather remote," and so he had given this "no further thought." Eisenhower again cautioned Marshall that the deputy proposal would mean the loss of his principal airman, which would require him to ask the CCS for Spaatz, but this would "take some more thought on my part."

"It is almost 8 o'clock and we are still in the office," Summersby wrote in her journal that night after cataloging Eisenhower's lengthening list of meetings and trips as the Malta and Yalta conferences approached. "I really do not know how E. keeps up the pace."

An extended forecast of bad weather and engine trouble had grounded Tedder in Cairo, and warnings of snow in the Crimea had forced him to make the long journey to Moscow by train. Tedder's odyssey, which had begun in London on December 31, finally ended on the night of January 14. Tedder's mission to Moscow was unpopular in both Allied capitals, but in the end both sides permitted him to resume a dialogue suspended since Teheran, and to establish military channels that could not be opened at the political level, in retrospect an important precedent in the evolving Cold War in which contact between Moscow and the West would often be confined to nonpolitical channels.

In his memoir, *With Prejudice,* Tedder confessed to being unaware of the deputy controversy that occurred in his absence. What he did know was that by the time he arrived in Moscow, his trip had long since ceased to matter in terms of its stated purpose of finding out when the Russian attacks would begin in Poland. He recalled that as he whisked by train through the Ukrainian countryside, Soviet military communiqués disclosed details of Konev's massive assault two days before, launched from the Baranow bridgehead, opening the great Russian winter offensive. As Konev's assault veered north into the rest of the understrength forces facing Zhukov at Warsaw, 250 divisions attacked along the entire Vistula front, backed by 10,000 tactical bombers deployed "to shatter the entire German eastern front . . . [not] to gain ground, but to win the war."

It was 10:45 A.M. on the morning of January 15, 1945. After a brisk walk through the maze of anterooms and tunnels of the Kremlin, Tedder, accompanied by General Edward Betts of SHAEF and Major A. H. Birse, entered Stalin's Kremlin office, where Stalin and the Soviet Chief of Staff, Marshal Antonov, cordially received them. Having accompanied Churchill on his forlorn mission in August 1942, Tedder inspected the changes in the office where the man now called "the most powerful and mysterious world leader" lived and worked. Thirty months before, the chamber had been sparsely decorated with portraits of Marx, Lenin and Engels, and Stalin had received visitors attired in a lumpy brown coat. This time Stalin, wearing a marshal's braid, sat behind a green baize-covered desk beneath portraits of military heroes and conquerors of Russia's imperial past.

As the group went through introductions, Tedder presented Stalin a letter from Eisenhower and a box of cigars, a personal gift from the Supreme Commander.

"When do they go off?" Stalin asked.

"Not until we have left," Tedder replied to appreciative laughter as the group took seats.

According to the minutes, Stalin opened by reading from a prepared statement. The offensive under way in Poland was "large scale," methodically prepared for several months and mounted despite adverse weather conditions. Stalin recalled Roosevelt's inquiry at Christmas, and Churchill's most recent message, on January 6. "Aware of the German attack on the western front," Stalin had decided "to launch the operation regardless of the weather."

Stalin disclosed the details of the present offensive. Four fronts consisting of 250 divisions would attack in stages with the objective of reaching the Oder River just east of Berlin within eight weeks, weather permitting. Stalin "did not know whether this line would be reached or not," and alluded to an efficient ring of "stay behind" agents organized among Latvians, Poles, Rumanians and Lithuanians who were well equipped and required the Red Army to conduct a "painstaking cleanup." Stalin imagined that a similar situation existed in France and Belgium, and he expressed the hope that Eisenhower would be "especially alert to put these down." When Tedder responded noncommittally, Stalin changed the subject.

Stalin had a question for Tedder. Was there anything to the German claim that an Allied offensive over the Rhine had been set back six months? Tedder replied that the Allies "had no intention of letting up."

Tedder proceeded to describe Eisenhower's intentions—the two-prong strategy with the main crossings at Düsseldorf and a subsidiary crossing in the Frankfurt area. Tedder disclosed tentative plans for a broad-front advance into Germany, which would include a wide encirclement of the Ruhr at Kassel, reduction of the Ruhr pocket, then junction with the Russian forces in the center, perhaps near Leipzig with secondary assaults on the flanks. Tedder said nothing about Berlin, but he indicated that Eisenhower discounted the importance of "prestige" objectives, and would focus on the defeat of the German army where it stood, most likely the Ruhr. Tedder "could not be sure," but believed the invasion of Germany would probably happen between mid-March and early May. Finally, Tedder told Stalin that he had been directed to disclose firm Allied intentions on two points: there would be no major attacks over the upper Rhine into the Black Forest or any violations of Swiss neutrality.

Stalin, in reply, indicated that Red Army doctrine had always emphasized the importance of secondary attacks. The Ruhr was "obvious," he mused. "Yes, it is obvious, it is obvious to us, it is also obvious to the Germans. . . . Difficult country such as Frankfurt is not so obvious." Stalin expounded on his point at length, leading Major Birse to note his obvious pleasure with Tedder. "As he [Stalin] disliked fulsome compliments," Birse wrote, "Tedder's direct approach and avoidance of such made good impression. Also he appears to appreciate direct military contact with SHAEF and absence of politics."

As he spoke, Stalin revealed his lack of familiarity with the world outside Russia, his mastery of military detail and tactics, and his great scorn for the mortally wounded German adversary on the verge of collapse in Poland, which would conclude a war of unheard-of ferocity. Stalin was contemptuous of German leadership and the folly of the Ardennes, of Guderian's determination to maintain the "prestige garrison" of thirty now isolated divisions in Latvia pinned against the Baltic, unable to evacuate or break out, and of reports of preparations near Lake Balaton for a counteroffensive to relieve Budapest. German dispositions were "stupid," symptomatic of "stubbornness more than brains" and an unwillingness to concede that Germany was no longer a great power, but finished. Nonetheless, Stalin predicted to the group that the Germans would fight on. He agreed with Tedder's estimate that the war would not end before summer, and predicted a "break" brought on by famine, since the Red Army would soon overrun the German granaries in the east.

On the eve of Yalta, Stalin was fulsome. He commended Eisenhower's military policy as a whole, and offered advice about maintaining reserves, "readverting," as Birse put it, "to the problem of enemy agents . . . [urging] the Allies to be particularly careful in those areas which had pro-German leanings." Stalin also pledged that despite the uncertainty of weather, operations on the eastern front would be maintained in March to assist the Allied Rhine crossings.

Views of Stalin crystallized on the basis of such contacts. George Kennan, then the U.S. embassy attaché and at work on a landmark assessment of Soviet aims and Russian leadership circulated shortly afterward, assessed Stalin as a political leader and a Georgian. "Courageous but wary," wrote Kennan, "quick to anger and suspicious but patient and persistent in the execution of his purposes; capable of acting with great decision or of waiting and dissembling, as circumstances may require, outwardly modest and simple, but jealous of the prestige and dignity of the state . . . , not learned yet shrewd and pitilessly realistic, exacting in his demands for loyalty, respect and obedience; a keen and unsentimental student of men—he can be, like the true Georgian hero, a great and good friend or an implacable, dangerous enemy. It is difficult for him to be anything in between."

In line with Eisenhower's instructions, Tedder asked whether Stalin "would be receptive to a visit at a later date by General Eisenhower." Stalin seemed slightly puzzled by the request. He asked by whose authority it was tendered, and remarked that he "would not presume to invite General Eisenhower to come because he did not think it possible for General Eisenhower to detach himself from his headquarters for a visit." Stalin added that if an operational pause ensued, he would value future visits from Eisenhower's personal staff. Tedder did not elaborate, and the subject was dropped.

"We have no treaty," Stalin told Tedder as he left, "but we are comrades. It is proper and also sound, selfish policy that we would help each other in times of difficulty. It would be foolish for me to stand aside and let the Germans annihilate you; they would only turn back on me when you were dispensed with. Similarly it is to your interest to do everything possible to keep the Germans from annihilating me."

At the British embassy, Tedder filed a lengthy description of the conference. The current Red Army offensive in Poland was a massive effort and would probably lead to a significant easing of the situation in Belgium. Most encouraging had been Stalin's willingness to maintain lower-level military exchanges with SHAEF, insulated from the political currents and subcurrents in the east-west relationship. Tedder also had been impressed by Stalin's great wrath focused on Germany and no less impressed by his self-assurance, as were other foreign visitors that winter. For, as Kennan wrote, "the Kremlin chimes, never silent since those turbulent days when Lenin had them repaired and set in motion, now peal out the hours of night with a ring of self-assurance and of confidence in the future. And the sleep of those who lie within the Kremlin walls is sound and undisturbed."

In the Ardennes, cloudy weather and snow held up air support. With visibility down to 200 yards, and temperatures at zero, conditions were unfavorable for the offensive toward Houffalize, and First Army attacks advanced through well-organized enemy positions. Collins' VII Corps, built up to four divisions and spearheaded by the 2nd and 3rd divisions, attacked east of Manhay. Ridgway's XVIII crossed the Salm River on the seventh, flanked by Horrocks' XXX Corps. Gradually the situation at Bastogne eased and battle news improved, all of which corresponded to the ULTRA intercepts of the anguished exchanges between Manteuffel, Model and OKW culminating in the order to consolidate the salient and to withdraw the Sixth Panzer Army. By January 12, as Tedder arrived in Odessa, German armor had pulled back from Bastogne, and German infantry assumed fall-back positions on the Clerf–Our rivers. The First Army established firm contact with the Third Army beyond St.-Hubert, and slowly pushed toward Houffalize.

As late as the fourteenth, Eisenhower lacked word of Tedder's all-important conference in Moscow. But sketchy communiqués indicated that as many as 115 Red Army divisions were active in the Warsaw area alone and were making rapid progress. At the War Room conference, Strong presented the mounting evidence of a German withdrawal from the Ardennes. The 711th Infantry left Holland for Hungary. The German 1st Infantry left the Colmar pocket for Hungary. And, for the first time in a month, a 72-hour period had elapsed without a fresh identification on the western front. Indeed, panzer forces, withdrawn from the Ardennes and feared to be mustering east of Colmar and Aachen, were now confirmed to be heading east, with detectable rail activity and troop movements observed in the Bonn–Cologne area. The First Army lost contact with the Sixth SS Panzer Army, and, significantly, the Germans were removing all heavy equipment, which belied appraisals that the success of the German offensive had been dependent on the seizure of a major U.S. petroleum dump. German armored columns had had enough gasoline to reach objectives by operating in low gear over poor roads, and departed on their own power.

Strong also circulated a summary of a talk delivered by Hitler to his generals at Von Rundstedt's Ziegenberg castle headquarters on the night of December 12, forty-eight hours before the assault. If the report was reliable, it seemed doubtful that Hitler's authority, staked on the outcome of the offensive, would weather the withdrawal from Belgium. That night, Hitler had spoken defiantly in the presence of his generals, evidently to dispel their skepticism. Hitler had emphasized the goal of reaching the Meuse within two days, and Antwerp within three weeks. Strong observed that Allied agony must have been slight compared with the German agony of knowing, within forty-eight hours after H-Hour, that the offensive had failed.

In this context, the debate over operations after the closing of the Ardennes salient began in earnest. Once again, Eisenhower confronted rival plans of Montgomery and Bradley. Bent on vengeance and revived by the German withdrawal, Bradley wanted to use First and Third armies to push straight ahead across the Siegfried Line and then northeast to bridge the Rhine at Bonn, by-passing the Roer dams and developing a major thrust south of the Ruhr. "The clash," as Tedder later put it, "was between those who favored a continuance of the Ardennes offensive, which Bradley described as a going concern, with great possibilities, and the preparation of a heavy all-out assault in the north."

Eisenhower and Bradley met frequently that month. Each time Bradley warned Eisenhower that it would be a "grave mistake" to give up in the Ardennes on military and political grounds and insisted that pursuit through the Ardennes would have decisive results. Eisenhower was inclined to agree with Bradley. At SHAEF there was lingering anger at Montgomery, sympathy for Bradley, and disillusionment over Montgomery's extreme caution in the Ardennes, especially to his having held back XXX Corps, and a sense, as Whiteley put it, that "if you want something done quickly, don't give it to Montgomery."

But Eisenhower's views were closer in spirit to Montgomery's set-piece plans, which, to Bradley, seemed to be aimed mainly at restraining his 12th Army Group. The controversial and consistent theme of Eisenhower's post-Ardennes thinking was deliberateness. Attack strategy was to be methodical, devised in a way to eliminate every conceivable German threat west of the Rhine, and oriented toward a closely coordinated invasion and linkup with the Russians at Leipzig, and other points to be worked out. Officially, Eisenhower was unwilling to make any optimistic assumptions. He would not plan on the basis of a quick German withdrawal, and he would wait to evaluate the Russian attack before coming to conclusions. The most pessimistic assumptions pervaded SHAEF planning, highlighted by revived talk of a desperate enemy last stand in the so-called German redoubt, which Eisenhower had first weighed in August 1944 pursuant to his negotiations with Churchill over ANVIL-DRAGOON. Invasion and pursuit into Germany had to be worked out carefully with special attention to the Allied flanks and in close consultation with the Russians, doubly necessary now as the European Advisory Commission in London had placed the finishing touches on occupation zones in Germany.

In the north, Montgomery proposed a methodical two-step offensive to eliminate German forces in the Rhineland straying from the start positions of December 15 behind the Maas and the Roer. According to the Maastricht agreement, the Ninth Army would remain with the 21st Army Group, and the First Army would orient itself northward to seize the Roer dams and support Montgomery's three-phase offensive to clear the west bank north of the Ardennes. In the 21st Army Group offensive, phase one entailed a Canadian Army push south from Nijmegen in an area between the Maas and the Rhine to cut off enemy forces in the Reichswald and clear the Siegfried defenses from the east. In phase two, Simpson's Ninth Army would cross the Roer and head northeast to the Rhine while Montgomery prepared for a major Rhine crossing with the British Second Army in the north. Significantly, Montgomery's cautious scheme dovetailed with Eisenhower's overall plan to develop two widely spaced thrusts against the Ruhr and Frankfurt, and would, moreover, gradually draw the First Army away from the Ardennes, leaving the Third Army in reserve for operations south of the Ardennes.

VERITABLE-GRENADE, Montgomery's preliminary offensive to clear away German pockets west of the Maas, was weeks away, leaving ample time to proceed with Bradley's effort to drive the Germans out of the Ardennes, and, above all, time to expedite what Eisenhower sensed would be a one-time chance to resolve the problem of German pockets west of the Rhine in Alsace. In light of Marshall's impatience, the stakes were high. Plans to develop an offensive on Frankfurt would ultimately depend on a secure base south of the Moselle, and a secure base south of the Moselle depended, in turn, on a secure flank on the Rhine in Alsace, which would also tend to anchor the Frankfurt thrust and draw it south, toward Regensburg–Linz, a contingency that Eisenhower had broached with Montgomery as early as September 1944. But unless Devers and the French cleared Alsace before the CCS convened, Eisenhower could not be sure that an impatient CCS would not call off the Alsatian campaign, which would mean no secure base on the upper Rhine, no anchor for the Frankfurt thrust, and maybe no Frankfurt thrust at all, which would confine the Allies to one massive thrust in the direction of the Ruhr and Berlin.

What were CCS wishes? For the moment, the British were committed to De Gaulle's stand at Strasbourg, and this gave Eisenhower his opening to solve the problem in Alsace for good. Specifically, Eisenhower was concerned about the Colmar pocket, a source of ongoing worry in January during the battle of Strasbourg and a continuing problem at mid-month. The French, concerned mainly about Strasbourg, balked at pushing Colmar vigorously. Leclerc's American-French forces faced poorly equipped Volkssturm units in the Colmar pocket, yet could not gain ground, and Devers was reluctant to push Leclerc. Sixth Army Group emissaries directed a steady stream of requests for reinforcements, which meant trouble with Bradley, since the only practical way of reinforcing Devers would be at the expense of Bradley's drive to clear the Ardennes. But with the CCS set to meet in Malta on the twenty-eighth, Eisenhower was under a tight deadline and sensed that no matter how ardently Churchill and Roosevelt supported his invasion strategy, it was up to SHAEF to present the CCS with quick favorable results in Alsace to prove that SHAEF strategy was not a formula for inaction.

Marshall's queries triggered the most voluminous exchanges of the war, and Eisenhower supervised preparation of his formal appraisals for Marshall and the CCS for use at Yalta due by January 20. In them, Eisenhower intended to review the entire course of operations since Normandy to support his plea for "flexibility," a multiphase offensive aimed first at eliminating German resistance west of the Rhine and followed by two offensives, one toward the Ruhr, and a second toward Frankfurt, which would have the primary aim of supporting the Ruhr thrust but would simultaneously position Eisenhower's forces to pursue multiple objectives on a broad front. According to the memos on file, Eisenhower took an extraordinary interest in the task, working as editor and draftsman, constantly updating his appraisals in light of progress in the Ardennes, Alsace and the latest bulletins from Poland. Eisenhower instructed his assistant, Colonel Arthur Nevins, that the manpower problem was to be raised prominently, and to place "considerable emphasis on the location of our defensive line when we start the offensive."

In two lengthy messages, finally sent on January 15 and 20, Eisenhower spelled out the factors governing strategy and the forces necessary for a "quick decision in the west." The factors cited included the Russian offensive, the German response in Poland, the location of the defensive line when the western offensive begins, air support, and French mobilization, but the plan in every case was the same: clearing the Rhine and a two-prong invasion at the Ruhr and Frankfurt. Proceeding from the worst to best cases, Eisenhower defined the worst case as a "weak and ineffectual Russian offensive," enabling the Germans to maintain a hundred divisions in the west. Mobilization of French and additional U.S. divisions would be necessary, and, he warned, no quick decision was attainable. Middle cases assumed the Germans would reinforce the west from Italy and Norway. In the best case, with the Russian offensive a clear success, Eisenhower would contend with as few as eighty understrength German divisions tapering off gradually, though still entrenched in the "extremely formidable" natural and artificial defenses of the Siegfried Line, with the ability to operate against Allied lines of communication unless both flanks were established on the Rhine. In sum, even in the "best case," the Allies would face a situation resembling mid-September 1944 with German forces roughly equal on the ground offset by heavy Allied air preponderance. To "gain the capability of concentration," Eisenhower proposed to close the Rhine on a broad front north and south of the Moselle, a guarantee of military success predicated on the unspoken but important advantage of avoiding a premature Allied advance into Germany in order to afford time to coordinate final plans with the Russians.

In other messages that week, Eisenhower elaborated. He revived the figures agreed upon as early as the Versailles conference that had taken place after MARKET-GARDEN. In the Düsseldorf sector, rail lines and roads could sustain a maximum of 35 divisions. The forces otherwise necessary for a "quick decision" would depend on the place of the defensive line. In the "best case," and with all his own 85 divisions established on the Rhine, Eisenhower estimated that 25 divisions would be necessary to perform defensive tasks, freeing 60 for attack. With the line held in mid-January and with Alsace clear of Germans, Eisenhower estimated that 50 divisions could attack, and with the line held without Colmar, 45 could be held in reserve with 35 to attack, or forces sufficient for one thrust. Therefore, except in the best case, Eisenhower was prepared to ask for new divisions—10 additional divisions with Colmar in hand; 20 additional divisions from American and French sources with the line held at present. And should the Russian attack in Poland prove ineffective, Eisenhower would need 20 fresh divisions to close the Rhine.

The reports went on for pages, spelling out chapter and verse the bearing of eastern-front developments on western-front operations, shock treatment intended mainly to silence criticism by pointing up the real source of troubles in the west dating back three years: manpower. "The only thing to be added about plans is that they must be flexible," Eisenhower reminded Marshall. "If we jam our head up against a concentrated defense at a selected spot we must be able to go forward elsewhere. Flexibility requires reserves. . . ." Eisenhower estimated that with the forces in hand, when the good weather starts, "it may well be possible to defeat the enemy on our front, but we would be justified in expecting quick success only after we have closed the Rhine throughout its length, concentrated heavily in the north and staged a definite supporting secondary operation somewhere south of the Ruhr. Naturally this expectancy would be greater if our divisional strength were greater."

Meanwhile Eisenhower began a canvass of commanders about a directive governing operations after the linkup at Houffalize and transfer of the U.S. First Army back to Bradley. On the thirteenth he visited Bradley at Verdun to discuss a draft of a short-term directive designed to tide SHAEF over through the Malta talks. The gist of it was to spell out Eisenhower's decision to limit the "hurry up" offensive in the Ardennes to the recovery of the December 15 line, followed by resumption of First Army attacks on the Roer headwaters in support of Simpson's Roer crossing and Montgomery's VERITABLE-GRENADE attacks in three weeks. Significantly, Eisenhower's outline directive was silent on operations in Alsace, a sign that he anticipated that the CCS would not approve operations south of the Moselle.

Eisenhower found Bradley mindful of "American interests and prestige." Bradley was adamantly in favor of pushing the Houffalize assault. Throughout, he claimed that Hodges and Patton were exploiting an opportunity rivaling Mortain. Bradley looked to far-reaching operations involving seven corps and two armies. The offensive would resume with a V Corps attack southeast from Malmédy toward St.-Vith with Ridgway's XVIII Corps on the right. Meanwhile Collins' VII Corps would fall out and form a reserve for a deep First Army drive through the Eifel on the Prüm–Bonn axis supported by the full weight of the Third Army, which would attack over the Clerf River.

Bradley couched the proposal as an effort to recoup the prestige of his command, but his tone was defiant, while the scale of the offensive implied that he intended to venture into grand strategy and compete with Montgomery for control of the main thrust. But was the 12th Army Group capable of a "decisive thrust"? Historians have suggested that St.-Vith was an "opportunity of war," rivaling Mortain, but Eisenhower did not think so, and he rejected the parallel on the thirteenth. Mortain had been a battle against an enemy force with very extended lines of communications in hostile terrain favorable for armored operations. By contrast, Bradley's forces were near exhaustion and pursued a force withdrawing in good order into the densely forested terrain of the German Eifel. Naturally, Eisenhower did not doubt that Bradley's army group had the strength to build up a powerful front in the Eifel, but powerful fronts were possible in Holland and south of the Ardennes also. Eisenhower hoped Bradley would see fit to support SHAEF in organizing the fronts in Holland and south of the Ardennes, but he was not optimistic.

Meanwhile Whiteley huddled with Montgomery in Brussels to review the 21st Army Group role in the proposed directive, which formalized the points spelled out by Eisenhower on December 31. Montgomery was helpful. He acquiesced in Eisenhower's stipulations that the west bank of the Rhine be cleared in all sectors before the 21st Army Group and First Army attempted Rhine crossings. He opposed Bradley's plan to push through the Eifel and cross the Erft River as "continued for the sole reason of keeping Bradley employed offensively," but he understood and accepted the postponement of VERITABLE-GRENADE entailed in it. Montgomery accepted the temporary reduction of Simpson's strength from sixteen to twelve divisions on Whiteley's assurance that after Bradley cleared the Ardennes, the First Army would halt and form a ten-division reserve for Montgomery's offensive toward Düsseldorf. Whiteley also told Montgomery "very secretly" of Eisenhower's plans to detach five American divisions from the Ardennes for use in the battle of the Colmar pocket. Montgomery nodded.

In Versailles, Eisenhower left the office for the afternoon, having dispatched his 5,000-word cable to Marshall outlining the steps to bring the war to a "quick conclusion." At six-thirty Whiteley returned with word of Montgomery's firm approval of Eisenhower's draft directive. "These last few days have been very trying," wrote Summersby at her desk, "but the tension has lifted somewhat."

Tension remained the theme of Summersby's journal that week as she described the long wait at the Trianon—the conferences on the Ardennes and Strasbourg, the messages back and forth from Washington, and Eisenhower's long afternoons spent away from the office at the Weiller estate in fitful attempts to relax. Most troublesome were the chill in relations with

Marshall and the mystery of Roosevelt's views. From Paris, Eisenhower could keep in touch with the situation in London, but he could not predict what was happening in Washington or be sure that his views were getting through.

In his letters home, Eisenhower apologized for being "remiss" in not writing for three weeks. He trusted Mamie understood that he had been "under some stress" and that "it has been hard to sit down and to compose thoughts." Eisenhower mentioned Admiral Bertram Ramsay's recent untimely death in an airplane crash, a fine man whom she had never met. He described for Mamie his efforts to teach his new cook how to prepare pudding, meat and mush, boyhood favorites, but told her his memory had been poor and that the experiment had failed. He complained about the stifling security at the Trianon and his confinement to the adjoining Weiller estate after hours. He regretted that the snowfall that blanketed France made travel by car and air difficult and curtailed his ability to visit soldiers at the front. In one letter he reminded Mamie that only thirty-six months had elapsed since they had moved from San Antonio to Washington. "In some ways it seems like only yesterday we were making that move," he mused, "on the other hand, I cannot remember a time when I was free of these continuing problems involving staggering expense, destruction of lives and wealth, and fates of whole peoples."

Eisenhower kept Mamie informed of John's situation. He had some good news: the War Department had informed him that John had consented to leave the 71st and take another job in the European theater that would enable him to visit his father "at least occasionally." Eisenhower assured Mamie that he would be on the lookout to prevent any assignment that would injure John's self-respect and reputation. Eisenhower knew that leaving the 71st entailed sacrifice on John's part, but he was grateful ". . . that John sees a bit of my trouble and loneliness."

All week the Russian winter offensive, the largest of the war, involving an estimated two million troops, exposed the flimsy façade of German military strength in Poland. The early reports were sketchy, but as Eisenhower's messages reached Washington, it was clear that the Red Army was bidding for a decision in Poland on the scale of the tremendous center front offensive in July 1944.

Avoiding the frontal tactics of July, Russian columns by-passed all resistance and plunged deep behind German lines shattering cohesive resistance within a week. When the Warsaw garrison surrendered to Zhukov's First White Russian front on January 17, the city was already 70 miles behind Russian lines. Within sixteen days Russian armies streamed from the Vistula to Cracow, Upper Silesia and the upper Oder, 200 miles west, three main drives woven with five subsidiary concentric drives—the main one being a sustained attack in a long arc 80 miles northwest along the Baltic to break into the rear of East Prussian defenses and to pocket another German army group on the coast.

The spectacular advance severed land communications between the Army Group North and Germany and confined thirty German divisions huddled at Danzig–Königsberg in a slender bridgehead awaiting sea lift back to Germany. By the twenty-first, the Second White Russian Front reached Tannenberg, scene of Hindenburg's triumph over the czarist armies in August 1914. Hindenburg's remains were exhumed by German troops and taken to Berlin while the panicked German army formed behind the Oder River to stave off invasion. But it was also apparent that the Russian advance would not reach Berlin or the Oder, which Tedder confirmed on his return on the nineteenth. Large German pockets held out, and large numbers of retreating Germans slipped through Russian lines on foot to join new units assembling on the Oder, which pointed to one last great Russian-German battle on the Oder frontier later that spring.

Therefore, within hours of dispatching his January 15 message, Eisenhower had reason to believe that the Allies confronted the "best case" scenario, a fact that would give the Allies far more latitude than he had anticipated. This was welcome, but Eisenhower also knew that apparent freedom of action would inhibit support for his quest for "flexibility," his quest for French divisions and his ability to destroy German resistance west of the Rhine preliminary to Rhine crossings. Indeed, rising optimism all week meant that Eisenhower could no longer evade discussion of specific invasion objectives.

What were Allied objectives? Significantly, coinciding with the developing German collapse in Poland, SHAEF took steps to deal with the widely held speculation that the Nazis, facing defeat on both fronts, intended to relocate in the Alpine redoubt—fortifications in western Hungary, northern Italy, western Austria, the Black Forest and southern Germany bounded by the Alps. There, in almost impenetrable mountain terrain, the Nazis might hold out, establish a focal point for the Nazi movement and a base for guerrilla warfare, blocking a formal armistice and extending the war.

Years later, historians would ridicule SHAEF's sudden concern with the so-called redoubt in January 1945, but the controversy was not new. For months, Allied intelligence had tracked alleged German preparations hinted at in the Nazi press. Reports by January noted at least twenty defense sites under construction along a line from Munich in southern Germany to Lake Constance, Innsbruck–Landeck–Berghof and the Brenner Pass ringing Berchtesgaden. SS detachments were reportedly stockpiling weapons and food, and building underground factories, and by January several ministries, including the Foreign Ministry, were withdrawing to Austria. That the Germans intended a desperate last stand in the Alps seemed, in retrospect, to explain otherwise incomprehensible military decisions—the tenacious defense in Italy, a ready source of reinforcements should Kesselring withdraw beyond the Po, and the mid-January withdrawal of the Sixth Panzer Army from Belgium for the reported purpose of staging an offensive near Lake Balaton in Hungary. Aerial reconnaissance that month noted that the most advanced construction of Rhine defenses ran along Devers' 6th Army Group sector in the Black Forest.

Well before Malta, lines had been drawn in the Allied high command for the "Nazi redoubt" contingency. Brooke, who had long ago written off pursuit through the Ljubljana gap, choosing instead to bid for control of the decisive theater, discounted the Alpine-redoubt theory and adamantly opposed suggestions that Eisenhower's forces pursue southward. Brooke and the BCOS were determined to focus on essential British objectives, chiefly British control of the lowlands and northern Germany. Whether Brooke conceived of Berlin as a possibility is unknown, but Berlin was the logical extension of a 21st Army Group thrust through northern Germany to be aimed at the proposed British zone of occupation and the North Sea ports which would be jeopardized by a strategy that dispersed American forces into southern Germany.

Marshall had not spoken up on grand strategy, and so the prime factors governing U.S. strategy were unknown. On the one hand, the American Chief of Staff had to face the problem of ending the war quickly and commencing reinforcement of the Pacific. On the other hand, there was the problem of American prestige and the looming problem of Russia. The redoubt reports, if true, held out the prospect of indefinite Nazi resistance in the inaccessible reaches of the Alps, and Marshall would not dismiss strategies out of hand aimed at preempting this threat. But in view of rapidly changing perceptions of the Russians, Marshall could not dismiss the argument that Allied capture of Berlin and occupying all of Germany would enhance Allied prestige in Europe and, above all, strengthen the Allied position in negotiations over Russian compliance with agreements, especially on the all-important German issue. But a move on Berlin by either Montgomery or Bradley invited an outright break with the Russians, and unless such a move was justified for military reasons, it would say to the world that Allied-Soviet cooperation was not and perhaps had never been Allied policy.

Since August 1944 Eisenhower had been the main proponent of a southern strategy. After ANVIL, Eisenhower, Churchill and Ismay had first weighed the problem of the "redoubt as an objective for Alexander." Indeed, Allied planning with respect to the redoubt had originated in the talks surrounding Eisenhower's late-August pledge to Ismay that he would try not to weaken Alexander. At the time, Eisenhower's advocacy of Italy had been suspect in American eyes as a move on his part to support a Balkan strategy, even though the Balkans had been manifestly beyond Alexander's capacity. Significantly, during MARKET-GARDEN, Eisenhower had raised Linz–Nuremberg to Montgomery as an alternative to Berlin. Once again in

January, Eisenhower was apparently maneuvering to avoid an outright CCS order to concentrate on Berlin, yet it remained unclear whether he opposed Berlin in all circumstances or did so on anything except military grounds.

Did Eisenhower oppose Berlin? Eisenhower could not rule out the redoubt contingency, nor could he overlook the many military advantages of pursuit into the redoubt or the political troubles he might create by collisions with the Russians in Germany. A crucial factor in Eisenhower's thinking was that Germany was to be divided into occupation zones, which did not technically restrict military operations but implied (a) that the occupation of Germany was a uniquely sensitive issue, and (b) that the Allied policy of wartime and postwar cooperation with the Soviets would be jeopardized by bold unilateral moves to occupy Berlin and all of Germany. By contrast, the redoubt, situated in northern Italy, Austria, Yugoslavia, Hungary and Czechoslovakia, encompassed a zone not covered by Allied-Russian military understandings or EAC occupational agreements, which meant that occupation of the area held out the prospect of real Allied gains without risking a confrontation with the Soviet Union. According to the Moscow declaration, Austria was to be a "liberated" state, but subject to temporary four-power administration on terms to be worked out. In the EAC, negotiations on Austria languished, which left the matter in the hands of the predominant military force in Austria on V-E Day, at least as things stood. Churchill, the tireless proponent of Vienna, might welcome Austria even if Brooke no longer did. Churchill was mindful that Austria, technically a belligerent, like Rumania and Hungary, fell within a class of proven postwar threats to Soviet security.

All week Eisenhower kept the CCS at bay with a stream of messages mingling frankness about the difficulties ahead with optimistic reports of Bradley's ongoing attacks toward Houffalize. With linkup on the sixteenth and reversion of the First Army to Bradley, Eisenhower nudged the Chief of Staff to promote Bradley to four stars in recognition of the American achievement of withstanding two fully mobilized German armies, inflicting an estimated 120,000 serious casualties and destroying an estimated 600 tanks and assault guns and 500 aircraft. Bradley, in Eisenhower's opinion, deserved a Senate stamp of approval for conducting a battle likely to cause "widespread disillusionment" in German ranks over "the failure to seize any really important objective and the realization that this offensive, for which every effort had been brought to bear and on which such great hopes were pinned, has in no sense achieved anything decisive." When Marshall balked, Eisenhower added Spaatz and Patton to his promotion list.

A minor misunderstanding flared up over Tedder's mission. With word of Tedder's arrival in Moscow, Eisenhower composed a flowery telegram for Marshal Alexander Vasilevsky in which he hailed "the momentous news that the magnificent Red Army has surged forward," and pledged simultaneous attacks "with continued vigor until Nazi Germany is completely smashed." Marshall reluctantly approved, but not without advice to Eisenhower that a "simple Main Street Abilene style" was more appropriate, as the Russians appreciated "tough talk of which I give them a full measure."

Controversy also developed over public disclosure of Tedder's trip. Anxious to do so, Eisenhower wired Washington with a request to issue an announcement "revealing to friend and enemy that coordination at a military level . . . does exist." The BCOS adamantly objected to lifting censorship on the Tedder journey. Churchill intervened and protested that the American and British publics "would be alarmed to know that the Allies and Russians had not been in contact before." The CCS agreed, and endorsed censorship—too late. As Butcher wrote on the twenty-seventh, "the story of Ike's mission to Moscow, headed by Air Chief Marshal Tedder, and including Bull and G-2 Betts, was disclosed to the correspondents about three weeks ago by Beetle [Smith] with a severe injunction of secrecy. However, the inevitable happened and one of our correspondents returning from France to the United States has broken the story."

The source was the NBC correspondent Red Mueller, Eisenhower's friend and guest on the night of January 5 when Tedder wired from Naples to warn that inclement weather threatened his connecting trip to Cairo. In his final radio broadcast to America before leaving the theater, Mueller disclosed that "the Supreme Commander, Allied expeditionary force, has been in contact with the Soviet government," and that a "coordinated plan of action" was in effect, a story that generated interest as the presidential party steamed across the Atlantic aboard the U.S.S. *Quincy.*

This parting dispatch would eventually cause trouble for Mueller. SHAEF PRD Director General Frank Allen, incensed by the breach of censorship, initiated proceedings to suspend Mueller's accreditation. Back in Washington, to appease Mueller's angry colleagues, the War Department convened a hearing board to try him for a severe infraction of censorship and secrecy. Eisenhower would stand watch over the Mueller case. He personally drafted a SHAEF affidavit for Allen's signature for use in the Pentagon inquiry recommending leniency on the grounds of Mueller's "prior good record, and his long-standing reputation for discretion." After weeks of hearings, the board in mid-March would acquit Mueller. Afterward Mueller would write the Supreme Commander from the United States to invite him to his wedding, postponed by the War Department inquisition. "I hope you still regard me as a friend," Mueller wrote, assuring Eisenhower that his (Eisenhower's) "secrets were and still are safe with me."

"I remember with real pleasure the many pleasant hours we spent together and am glad you class me as your friend," Eisenhower replied. "I assure you the feeling is a mutual one."

As Malta approached, Eisenhower and Marshall corresponded over arrangements for the conference. The day after receiving the second part of

Eisenhower's 5,000-word war summary, Marshall passed to Eisenhower the news that the CCS was debating whether to ask Eisenhower and Alexander to attend the Malta conference, evidently for the purpose of pairing up the two and solemnizing a new command setup. Predictably, Eisenhower was not enthusiastic about attending the session at Malta. In his reply he told Marshall that he was not sure he would have time to break away from Paris, though he would be more than glad to receive Marshall in Paris beforehand to work things out face-to-face.

Was Berlin an issue between Eisenhower and Marshall? The historical record is murky, though it seems apparent that Marshall's personal confidence in Eisenhower was somewhat shaken. However, the Chief of Staff harbored little doubt of his ability to support Eisenhower's methodical and time-consuming strategy. Marshall, embroiled in debate with Congress over combat duty for eighteen-year-olds and increased draft quotas, was in the mood to hear out Brooke's ideas about a concentrated thrust over the north German plain. As things stood, Marshall found it impossible to judge the merits of allegations that Eisenhower had mismanaged the Ardennes, an inability perhaps heightened by the Strasbourg affair and Montgomery's January 7 press conference, which raised further questions about Eisenhower's ability to shield his command against partisan British and French pressures.

On the seventeenth Marshall informed Eisenhower that for "security reasons" he was unable to visit the Trianon. His advance staff was investigating a suitable spot closer to Malta, perhaps Toulon. Two days later Marshall denied Eisenhower's request to promote Bradley to four-star rank, a complication in Eisenhower's effort to reconcile Bradley to his post-Ardennes directive issued on the eighteenth in which he instructed Bradley to be prepared to pass "quickly to the defensive in the Ardennes sector" and to support Montgomery's resuming offensive in Holland.

Eisenhower's preliminary plan finally elicited a noncommittal reply from Marshall on the twentieth in which the Chief of Staff enclosed a description of the three-day schedule at Malta and word that the CCS after reflection had decided that Eisenhower's attendance at Malta would be "desirable" —which would make a meeting beforehand unnecessary. That afternoon Eisenhower replied that "due to uncertainties of air transportation in winter" he was doubtful he could travel "beyond the limits of motor and rail transport" in France. He expected to be preoccupied with problems at the front throughout the conference, but he offered to spare Smith and General Bull as his "responsible representatives" in Malta, with General Bull, his G-3, continuing on to the Crimea conference if necessary. "Aside from this program," Eisenhower continued, "it would be advisable for you and me to meet in southern France." Because of the tentative date set for Malta, Eisenhower assumed "that day or night of 28th would be logical for you" and told Marshall he had ordered confidential investigations "made to determine the most convenient place."

. . .

In his final directive before Malta, Eisenhower ordered all forces south of the Moselle River to erect "strong defenses" and form reserves. Thus Eisenhower decided against spelling out his intention to clear Alsace, hoping to avoid CCS debate over Alsace and thus achieve a fait accompli. In order to rush the Alsace project to completion, Eisenhower alerted Bradley to his plan to detach five divisions from Patton and Hodges, then placed the American VI Corps under Lattre de Tassigny's command in order to stiffen French determination to repel the Germans at Strasbourg and Colmar.

By the twentieth the French I Corps, now at four divisions, had failed to squeeze the German salient at Colmar. Leclerc's main attack east of the Belfort gap was stalled in a snowstorm, causing exasperation at SHAEF with Leclerc, which redoubled Eisenhower's determination to eliminate the Colmar pocket, which had "always been irritating." North of Colmar the battle of Strasbourg remained tense. Elements of Fifth Panzer Army armor withdrawn from the Ardennes appeared on the Haguenau sector, and as late as the twenty-second the French were losing ground near Strasbourg.

That morning, at a War Room conference at the Trianon, Eisenhower decreed that Strasbourg and reduction of the Colmar pocket were now *preconditions* for VERITABLE-GRENADE. Through Whiteley, Eisenhower passed a message to Devers "in no uncertain language" to get on with the offensive, and ordered a reorganization of the 6th Army Group. A new American XXI Corps would come on line between the two French corps with the mission of spearheading the assaults on the German salients.

But time was running out. Sensing that French determination was slipping away, Eisenhower invited Marshal Juin to Versailles for an eleventh-hour talk in hopes of spurring the French to greater exertions. The Juin meeting failed on every account. Eisenhower strenuously urged that "now is the time for the French to fight like fury." Juin countered that the French were "tired," that the British were "foolish" to plan attacks in the north, that the West was "exhausted," was capable of little more than fighting a defensive battle. Juin left Versailles and reported his conversation to De Gaulle, who quickly responded with a letter sternly protesting Eisenhower's implied disparagement of the valor and fighting quality of the French First Army.

With French support evaporating, Eisenhower decided that his one recourse was to bolster the attack with U.S. reinforcements, which meant a showdown with Bradley over the "hurry up" offensive. From the seventeenth to the twenty-fourth, the First and Third armies advanced from Houffalize, though "considerable reshuffling and regrouping of units was required as a result of the constriction of the front and the strengthening of the Allied line." Bradley staked all on a big attack over the Our River through the Ardennes with five corps of twenty-one divisions and 400,000 men spearheaded by elite First Infantry and 82nd Airborne to go off in stages on the twenty-eighth, twenty-ninth and thirtieth.

Eisenhower moved deliberately. On the night of the twenty-second Whiteley phoned Bradley to warn that Patton would be losing the 35th Division. In a memorandum, Bradley fumed that everything done now was "colored by our desire to keep our operations tactically sound and at the same time to meet nationalistic requirements. . . . There are many conflicts and, in my opinion, the command setup is definitely detrimental to efficiency." More was to come. The next day Whiteley visited Bradley to break the news that Eisenhower had firmly decided to draw five divisions from the Ardennes, which put a definite cap on Bradley's preparations for the "hurry up" offensive.

According to a witness, Bradley "lost his good humor" and warned Whiteley that more was at stake "than the mere moving of divisions and corps, and of a certain tactical plan." The reputation and the goodwill of the American Army were at stake, and if SHAEF was determined to break up the 12th Army Group, it was free to "take any goddam division and/or corps in the 12th Army Group, and do with them as you see fit" while he and his command sat it out "until hell freezes over."

According to SHAEF chronicles, everything seemed to converge on Eisenhower on the twenty-fifth, one of the longest days of the war. Rarely had a day gone by when the bonds unifying the Alliance seemed so fragile and precarious, or when spirits were so shaken about the future. Progress in Alsace was slow. The presidential party was on the high seas steaming toward Malta and discussions with Churchill arranged at the last minute and in acrimony over Roosevelt's stubborn refusal to coordinate with the British on an Allied position vis-à-vis Stalin. Churchill, as before, held out for a hardheaded negotiating position, which he felt was the only realistic approach, but he encountered a President who, after months of wavering, had resolved to bid for Stalin's goodwill and friendship. To quell troubles, the President had dispatched Hopkins to London and Paris for talks with Churchill and De Gaulle about "starting fresh." In Paris, Hopkins would visit Eisenhower for a firsthand look at the military and command situation and to sound out Eisenhower's availability for Malta.

Shortly before Hopkins' arrival, Eisenhower had hurriedly issued instructions imposing a January 28 deadline on Bradley's attack and ordered the release of five divisions to reinforce Devers in Alsace. Eisenhower confirmed these decisions at his morning conference in the Trianon shortly after rejecting Private Slovik's final appeal for clemency. Slovik's unit—the U.S. 28th Division—was among the units Eisenhower ordered south to Colmar that morning, so evidently the point in confirming the sentence was to spur the tired 28th Division to action.

That afternoon Eisenhower called on De Gaulle at the Elysée Palace in the hope that a direct appeal might succeed in goading the French First Army to action. He found De Gaulle neither cooperative nor uncooperative, offended by his exclusion from Yalta, skeptical of operations at Col-

mar, forgetful of Eisenhower's January 3 concession on Strasbourg and of
his more recent efforts to build up the French army. The minutes attest to
Eisenhower's patience, and his frustration.

Eisenhower began by attempting "to clarify what appeared to be a misunderstanding" about words Juin had attributed to him implying that
Leclerc was not fighting valiantly in the Colmar pocket. Juin had "misconstrued" their conversation, he said. Eisenhower "as Allied commander"
had "never criticized or minimized the effort of an army of a particular
nationality." Eisenhower told De Gaulle that he had spoken sternly to Juin
merely to "impress on him the necessity of impressing every single man
from the commanding general to the enlisted man with the critical significance of the offensive launched for cleaning up the Colmar pocket."

De Gaulle denied that there had been any thought of attributing criticism
to General Eisenhower, and denied that he personally had accused Eisenhower of such criticism. But was General Eisenhower "less than satisfied
with the drive of the French First Army?"

Eisenhower replied that he was anxious "to see the French First Army
carry on its present operations with the same punch that had characterized
its actions in Italy in the southern landings and in the Belfort drive."

De Gaulle noted that Leclerc's First Army was "tired" by virtue of the
aforesaid operations in Italy and southern France, and that Devers, not
Leclerc, was responsible for the "unfortunate" frontal tactics chosen for the
assault at Colmar, by which he implied that he sympathized with Leclerc's
reluctance to undertake such a frontal assault himself, and deplored American pressure that he should.

Eisenhower admitted that Leclerc "had been asked to do a great deal,"
but reminded De Gaulle that he, Eisenhower, had asked a lot of the Americans also. For instance, the U.S. 28th Division, also a "tired" unit, from the
Hürtgen and Ardennes, had been sent to reinforce General Milburn's XXI
Corps with barely any rest. Eisenhower urged De Gaulle as a soldier to
"instill the French forces with the will and drive that was essential to the
success of the operation."

De Gaulle pledged as a soldier to "take the matter in hand," then offered
his military analysis of the situation in Alsace as he saw it: first, Devers at
Colmar was understrength in infantry; second, the enemy was tenaciously
defending difficult terrain; third, artillery support was reportedly "incomplete," and in view of American preponderance in artillery this was a sign
of faulty tactics; fourth, air support was hampered by the weather, and the
enemy was "hard and resolved, and apparently disposed to fight it out."
Accordingly, De Gaulle foresaw only local operations by the First French
Army "at different spots and at various intervals" while the French government "constituted in the rear sufficient forces for a large scale operation in
the months ahead."

Indeed, De Gaulle hinted that the French would favor withdrawal behind the Vosges instead of persisting in Alsace. He doubted the accuracy of the modest American G-2 estimates of German strength in Alsace. De Gaulle repeated his complaints about air and artillery support, which Eisenhower agreed with "emphatically," and agreed too with General De Gaulle's earlier concern about "the shortage of Allied infantry." Eisenhower reminded De Gaulle that he was doing everything within his power to equip new French divisions.

De Gaulle knew this and he was grateful. But he was skeptical that a major offensive on the western front could be adequately supplied across French soil without additional locomotives and rolling stock. There were acute shortages of locomotives in France, and yet his Minister of Transport had just returned from America with word that an estimated 2,700 rail cars and a proportionate number of locomotives "seemed available for the European theater but that the impression appeared to exist in America that the Supreme Commander had not given his agreement to the early shipment of this rolling stock."

Eisenhower assured De Gaulle that SHAEF was "keenly aware of the logistical problems and the acute need for rolling stock in France and Belgium," and that he had urgently requested numbers far in excess of the 2,700 units. He would consult his staff on the source of this misunderstanding. De Gaulle was grateful, and the discussion ended.

Eisenhower left for the American embassy and a small dinner party for presidential emissary Harry Hopkins, hosted by Ambassador Caffery. Hopkins had phoned ahead to ask for a few moments alone with Eisenhower, and Eisenhower had deputized Butcher, experienced in dealing with fellow Iowan Hopkins, to join the party and to arrange a few moments of privacy. Butcher was thus on hand to provide an account of the tense evening, his first detailed notes on Eisenhower's activities since early September at Mont-St.-Michel.

Butcher recounted the anxious wait before Hopkins' arrival. Eisenhower, Butcher, Gault and Caffery sat in a semicircle in the first-floor living room of the embassy mansion mulling over the latest news from the front. Eisenhower, wary of Hopkins' arrival and shaken by his meeting with De Gaulle, was momentarily in despair over his inability to mobilize all commands for a last supreme effort against Germany.

Talk drifted to "the effect of the Democratic and Nazi systems on the development of hard fighting soldiers." According to Butcher, Eisenhower was "fearful that conditions in America and Britain had "inevitably instilled a pacific or non-fighting attitude in the troops." He seemed perplexed that the Nazis had been able to turn German youth psychologically and physically into fighters. One reason for the Ardennes setback had been the failure of Allied intelligence to take into account the fighting value of the Volkssturm units hastily scraped up from sixteen-year-olds and old men.

Colonel Gault, ever the diplomat, reminded Eisenhower that the latest dispatches indicated that the Germans were falling back in the Ardennes. Eisenhower agreed, but predicted that the Germans would escape a major defeat in the Ardennes and succeed in extricating armor for other fronts. Eisenhower cited the German struggle in Alsace against hopeless odds. With local superiority of 5 to 1, Devers would not move because his G-2 could not pinpoint the whereabouts of a single panzer division!

Butcher ventured to say that the Germans were fighting harder because "they can now see what they term as the 'sacred soil of the Fatherland' being invaded by their enemies," adding that the Americans would fight much harder "if they too saw an invader approaching their own soil." Eisenhower doubted the Americans would fight as fanatically for their home soil "because of different basic conditions in living habits, training and education."

Gault, sensitive to Eisenhower's anxiousness about Malta and perhaps aware of his denial that morning of the Slovik appeal, complimented the remarkable fighting determination of American troops in a war four thousand miles from home, fought for reasons that many if not most Americans felt were "none of their business." A slightly embarrassed Eisenhower subsided, adding that he would "sure like to have many more divisions like the U.S. 1st, 9th, 90th, 2nd Armored and 3rd Armored."

About then, Hopkins arrived. Eisenhower and Hopkins huddled for twenty minutes, then emerged, and the somber mood lifted somewhat at dinnertime. Butcher described how Hopkins regaled his guests with tidbits about his stormy weekend with Churchill at Chequers. The Prime Minister had been "volcanic" about recent State Department leaks that aroused Labourite opposition against Churchill's Greek policy. The Prime Minister was desolate over Roosevelt's refusal to visit London en route to Malta and furious about the choice of Yalta for the three-power summit. Finally, one night, after a long, wearying discussion, the Prime Minister had relaxed and in Hopkins' presence, had proceeded to give Eden a lesson on "the art of lecturing and arguing in the House of Commons."

"Churchill's first rule of oratory is never to peek slightly at notes," Hopkins recalled, but to study them, taking time, two to three minutes, if you need it, then "flagrantly" waving them in the eyes of the members. Another of Churchill's rules was that speakers must never lounge against "the box" (or the rostrum) in Commons, but should keep "well behind it" except for tapping it occasionally, since loud bangs distract attention. Then "the box should be solemnly banged with a fist at an appropriate moment, and a menacing scowl glowered at the audience that will give added theatrical effect." Hopkins added that the Prime Minister had been "fatherly" toward Eden, which meant "a feeling of kindness as well as consideration."

Hopkins' story had reminded Eisenhower of his own experience with Churchill during the ANVIL crisis in August, when the Prime Minister had "pulled out all the stops" and threatened to "lay down the mantle of his high office." Butcher wrote that he "got the impression Ike won his argument, and certainly the PM didn't quit as indeed he is too good a soldier to do so."

Afterward Eisenhower briefed Butcher on his private talk with Hopkins. First, Hopkins had related information on two critical subjects, manpower and Malta. The presidential emissary had revealed the intense Cabinet debate ignited by Eisenhower's manpower cables. Hopkins had intimated that he personally was on Eisenhower's side. Also, Marshall had decided to "back ETO to the hilt" by earmarking for Europe 80 percent of a planned 80,000-man call-up in February, though Marshall opposed activating divisions. Hopkins also told Eisenhower that he had learned at Chequers that the Prime Minister would soon cable Roosevelt to urge that Eisenhower and Alexander both be present in Malta by the twenty-ninth. The President needed to know Eisenhower's attitude about attending the Malta conference.

Eisenhower had told Hopkins that his hands were full, "not only with defensive actions to manage but with an impending offensive to get underway." He told Hopkins that he planned to see Marshall on the twenty-eighth, but then he would have to return to Brussels for a conference with Montgomery on the thirtieth, which he believed would rule out his attendance at Malta. Eisenhower had therefore proposed sending Smith in his stead. Hopkins replied that he would be glad to communicate Eisenhower's "desire not to attend," but because the U.S.S. *Quincy* was sailing in radio silence, there could be no reply until Roosevelt reached Gibraltar on the twenty-eighth.

The next day, Eisenhower's train left Paris for Marseilles by way of Vittel and conferences with Devers. With news of slow progress in the Colmar pocket, Eisenhower took drastic action and ordered the relief of the commander of the U.S. 75th Division. Eisenhower found Devers reluctant to push Leclerc and accordingly ordered him to assign Milburn's XXI Corps the main role in the Colmar offensive, which was set to resume not later than the twenty-ninth.

Eisenhower's meeting with Marshall on the afternoon of Sunday the twenty-eighth fell on the day historians identify as the official end of the Ardennes campaign. That day the Allied line stretched out from Holland to Basel, Switzerland, along the December 15 boundaries, with minor improvement in the Aachen sector. At four o'clock that morning, the 12th Army Group offensive opened in what the First Army diarist described as "the worst conditions of the war" against determined German defenses in the hills of the Eifel and bunkers of the West Wall.

The Eisenhower-Marshall meeting took place at the gloomy Château Valmonte, formerly the German naval headquarters in the area. The accounts emphasize Marshall's personal friendliness toward Eisenhower, but plainly, Eisenhower and Marshall were officially estranged, at least for the moment.

Eisenhower presented his list of needs; he asked Marshall's backing for his two-phase plan to force the Rhine preliminary to a two-prong invasion. He also asked Marshall to assist him in solving his command problem by quickly promoting Bradley. Marshall consented to back a promotion for Bradley provided Eisenhower also endorsed promotions for Devers, Clark, Eaker, and Patton. The Chief of Staff raised the possibility of the Alexander-Tedder proposal and asked for Eisenhower's views. Eisenhower intimated to Marshall that he himself had actually suggested that Alexander come to Paris, *provided* that everyone clearly understood that Alexander was to be a "deputy without portfolio." Eisenhower did not elaborate on what he meant by a deputy without portfolio, but he made it clear that in the absence of a CCS charter for Alexander setting forth his responsibilities, Eisenhower would define Alexander's responsibilities and they would resemble Tedder's current duties—manpower, civil relations with liberated governments, food relief, et cetera.

Manpower was Marshall's concern. He suggested that Eisenhower consider tapping Italy as a source of replacements. He revealed the 80,000-man call-up of additional infantry recruits set for February. Marshall turned down Eisenhower's specific request for the 10th Mountain Division currently in Italy, reminding him he had once turned it down as "not being trained for your area." Marshall seemed to like Eisenhower's plan and endorsed it especially insofar as it provided for a prominent American role and involved "the fewest number of divisions in attacks west of the Rhine possible."

Back in Versailles on the thirtieth, another tense day, according to Kay Summersby's chronicle, Eisenhower told his staff that Marshall had declared "that as long as he, Marshall, was Chief of Staff, he would not let the CIGS impose a ground commander"; however, in his memorandum for the record, dictated later that afternoon, he recounted Marshall's words in less ringing terms. Marshall had "spoken for himself." Eisenhower had gained the "definite impression" that Marshall would not agree to any proposal to set up a ground commander in chief, but this left the question of Alexander in the role of Eisenhower's deputy. Eisenhower noted Marshall's overriding concern that the "method of attack" chosen for defeating Germany west of the Rhine be the "least costly in the matter of replacements."

Eisenhower could not interpret Marshall precisely. Would Marshall's attitude at Malta turn exclusively on the replacement question? What were the President's views? Did Roosevelt favor "compromise" with the British? Had Marshall suddenly reached accord with Brooke on military strategy and did this represent Roosevelt's views? Or was Marshall simply maintaining an air of suspense to spur Eisenhower to maximum exertions to spare the CCS the task of making decisions? Eisenhower suspected the latter.

Interestingly, Eisenhower had borrowed his command technique largely from George C. Marshall, and many of his practices stemmed from meetings like the one at Château Valmonte, such as his later habit of confronting even the proposals he favored with skepticism or a sharp no. Years later I asked General Lucius Clay whether Eisenhower "confused a lot of people that way." Replied Clay, "He found he discovered a lot of weak men that way."

By the thirtieth the early returns from the Ardennes were unpromising. At the Trianon, Eisenhower decided to curtail Bradley's two-army offensive and to order Patton to reassume a posture of "aggressive defense" while VII and XVIII Corps, spearheads of the attack toward Prüm, moved back north toward the Roer in support of Simpson.

For Bradley, and the First Army, the curtailment came doubly hard. Word arrived late that day of Hitler's broadcast, heard widely throughout Europe, in which the Führer summoned every German man, woman and child to a supreme effort to stem the Bolshevik invasion. Hitler's counter-offensive, in which twenty-nine American and four British divisions had seen battle and sustained an estimated 75,000 casualties, was over, and with Von Rundstedt's depleted forces down to their last fuel reserves, Bradley's chances for avenging the Ardennes and developing a major U.S. offensive had never seemed better.

Hitler's broadcast also coincided with the opening sessions of the CCS in Malta, described in Pogue's account as a proceeding that "crackled with heat" as the improving battle news eroded the military basis for Eisenhower's two-phase, two-prong plea for flexibility. At Malta, the American and British Chiefs of Staff drew closer in support of concentration on the northern line of advance, the culmination of a trend first evident at Quebec. But Brooke and Marshall clashed over responsibility for the Ardennes, and by implication whether the main thrust would be led by the American 12th or British 21st Army Group, or whether the American and British thrusts north and south of the Ruhr would be of roughly equal strength, with Patton and Devers forming a reserve.

Marshall emerged as Eisenhower's defender against Brooke's charges of "undue reliance on Bradley," and ironclad motions to "cramp" Eisenhower's flexibility. Marshall complained to Brooke that Eisenhower had, if anything, lost sight of American interests in his eagerness to please the Prime Minister, who, he noted, habitually by-passed the CCS and communicated directly with SHAEF. Marshall also "lit out" against Montgomery as an "over-cautious" general who "wants everything," a headline seeker and a rude insubordinate who never visited Eisenhower at his headquarters and treated Americans with "open contempt."

In Roosevelt's absence, Churchill went through the motions of urging

Marshall that the Allies should "occupy as much of Austria as possible as it was undesirable that more of western Europe than necessary should be occupied by the Russians." But Churchill, having consented to reductions in Italy and Greece, deferred to Brooke, who assured Marshall that a Mediterranean advance was "illogical," and that "there was now no question of operations aimed at the Ljubljana Gap and, in any event, the advance of the Russian Army made such an operation no longer necessary."

This reduced the issue to northwest Europe, and in the absence of clear-cut American-British differences, the SHAEF plan provided the counterpoint. Smith assumed responsibility at the sessions for presenting the case for two thrusts, one at Düsseldorf and a second at Frankfurt, which he explained was preferable to a major 12th Army Group thrust at Cologne, which would be "too close to the main assault," thus simplifying the German problem of defense. He argued for a Rhineland campaign as Russian pressure tapered off, enabling the Germans to "concentrate safely for counterattack at our lines of communication." Thus, only after clearing the Germans west of the Rhine and securing the Rhine as a defensive barrier could the Allies "make a truly successful invasion with all forces available." Smith defended Eisenhower's estimates: 45 divisions needed in defensive roles without clearing the Moselle or Colmar; 35 divisions without Colmar; and only 25 divisions with the Germans driven behind the Rhine. Lastly, Smith could not specify objectives east of the Rhine beyond the possibility of a linkup between Montgomery's right flank and Bradley's left at Kassel, which would complete the encirclement of the Ruhr. Thereafter, pursuit north of the Ruhr offered "the greatest strategic rewards within a short distance," but again, the northern route to Berlin would be the area "most strongly held by the enemy," and the shortest distance toward linkup with the Red Army would be a center thrust toward Leipzig.

Smith insisted that Eisenhower's plan would provide ample support for Montgomery, but nothing satisfied Alan Brooke. In a celebrated incident, Smith and Brooke nearly came to blows in haggling over the definition of "main" and "subsidiary" offensives west of the Rhine. Brooke, in demanding a precise definition, explained to Smith that Eisenhower was "not strong enough," a man too liable to be "swayed by the last man he talked to," whereupon Smith demanded that the proceeding go off the record immediately and that both sides "have it out now."

According to Smith, Brooke proceeded to praise Eisenhower as a diplomat but "tolerant to a fault with subordinates including Montgomery," whereupon Smith told Brooke that since he had "less confidence in the Supreme Commander than the situation demanded it was his duty to report this to Eisenhower and ask the CCS either to affirm its confidence in Eisenhower, giving him freedom of action or remove him." Finally, Brooke denied that he lacked confidence in Eisenhower, and called removing Eisenhower "unthinkable."

. . .

Far away that night in the tiny village of Ste.-Marie-aux-Mines, near Colmar, General Frank "Shrimp" Milburn, commander of the newly formed XXI Corps, summoned his corps officers to his quarters. After two days of regrouping west of the Colmar Canal, the Allied assault, built up to five divisions, had resumed toward the Rhine.

In the group was Colonel Edward L.R. Elson, a chaplain, who after the war became minister of the National Presbyterian Church in Washington and Eisenhower's personal pastor and who later recounted the events at Ste.-Marie-aux-Mines to me personally.

At the end of the meeting, Milburn took Elson aside and told him about the Slovik case—sentence was set to be carried out the following morning. Twenty-two such cases were pending in XXI Corps, but none had reached this stage. Milburn believed the case would be "the only one of its kind," and accordingly asked Elson to serve as his personal representative with the duty of observing the event and ensuring that it was carried out according to regulations and with proper solemnity. Elson spent the night at a nearby château with several other officers whose career paths would intersect in unexpected ways. Lieutenant Colonel Henry Cabot Lodge was among the observers at Ste.-Marie-aux-Mines. Lodge had resigned his Senate seat to accept an Army commission two years before, and was destined to serve in the Eisenhower Cabinet.

Milburn would later question the revival of a practice dormant for a century, although he approved the sentence at the time. In view of the imminent end of the war, was the Slovik case really necessary to spur the 28th Division to action?

In defense of the judgment, Elson would later recall that Eisenhower had approved the sentence only after careful consideration of all the facts. Eisenhower faced a sudden steep rise in desertions and self-inflicted wounds at mid-month, due to the slow improvement in battle conditions. Elson recalled that "the purpose of an action of this kind is to save troops from themselves, from the constant temptation in a forward area in war to evade duty. Without a stiff reminder, unwitting soldiers might desert, eroding the effectiveness and morale of their units." Elson added that Slovik's actions were deliberate, and that the observers drawn from his unit he talked to that night were disappointed in Slovik for failing to do his duty not once but twice in time of crisis. In the judge advocate general's report issued that night, Eisenhower asserted that action was taken to provide for the security of the forces assigned him, and "to insure the accomplishment of the mission entrusted me."

On the western front, January 31, 1945, was a sullen, wintry day. At Ste.-Marie-aux-Mines, observers gathered in a château courtyard, surrounded by a high wall and a stream. Military police checked the rank and identification of the observers as they arrived. Elson later described a procession of two columns of two through the snow led by the provost marshal. An attending chaplain accompanied Slovik, who huddled under a blanket. The proceeding was quick. The provost marshal read the summary of the court findings and the attached endorsements. Slovik declined to make a statement, and was secured to the beam. The firing squad appeared, wheeled a right face and, after carrying out the sentence, remained for eight minutes at attention until the physicians pronounced Slovik dead.

General Norman D. Cota, commander of the 28th Division, would later affirm in the theater JAG report that "based upon personal observations and conversations, the present AWOL rate of the Division and reports from the unit commanders and other personnel of my command, that the execution did have in my division the deterrent effect visualized by the theater commander." According to the same report, spanning Eisenhower's tenure as ETO commander, of 386 capital cases involving 454 accused persons, 70 such sentences were carried out after June 6, 1944. Slovik was the only military offender. In a JAG poll of division and corps commanders, sixty agreed that the remedy for desertion was not essential to the accomplishment of their missions; forty-six stated that such a remedy was essential for a combat command and the security of military forces. Fifty-six commanders declared that execution for desertion was not a proper theater policy, while fifty-two "felt it was proper."

It seemed strange to some that an action ordered for its deterrent effect was not publicized outside the 28th Division. Many details of the case would be shrouded in mystery, and not revealed for thirty years until Slovik's widow petitioned for back payment of a federal pension as an Army dependent. One must assume that the action was tailored for the sole purpose of spurring the 28th Division to one final attack at Colmar. The Slovik case was exceptional. Informed on the morning of January 31 that sentence had been executed, Eisenhower pardoned two other offenders, who were never identified.

At the Trianon, the thirty-first was another long day. At a staff conference in the War Room, Eisenhower discussed developments at the Malta conference with Tedder, Spaatz, Whiteley and Strong. A message arrived from Smith, who reported that the portions of his January 18 directive dealing with operations south of the Moselle were unacceptable to the British. Marshall had urged Smith to ask Eisenhower to retrieve the situation by issuing, on his own initiative, an amendment to assure Brooke that post-VERITABLE operations west of the Rhine would be confined to forces posing "an obstacle to our subsequent Rhine crossing operations."

What this meant was that Marshall favored continuation of the "hurry up" offensive. On the bright side, Brooke's intransigence was a sign that the British were exceedingly wary of Bradley's offensive, making it un-

likely that Brooke and Marshall would unite on a single scheme of operation. Likewise, Eisenhower was encouraged that Marshall had kept Smith
informed throughout and had contributed timely suggestions to ward off
trouble. Eisenhower that day obliged Marshall with a "clarification"—
VERITABLE would go forward not later than the eighth, and GRENADE
not later than the tenth with the First Army edging northward to relieve
the Ninth Army at the Roer dams. The Ninth Army would be kept at a
minimum strength of three armored and seven infantry divisions, while
the 12th Army Group assumed "an aggressive defense forthwith on the
remainder of its front." Eisenhower pledged to exploit opportunities to
cross the Rhine before closing the river along its entire length "without
incurring unnecessary risks." Among Eisenhower's omissions, however,
were pledges to maintain the Ninth Army at full strength east of the
Rhine or that after VERITABLE-GRENADE the 12th Army Group attack
would resume in the Eifel reinforced by the units withdrawn for Colmar.
The latter omission spelled the formal demise of Bradley's "hurry up"
offensive.

Late that afternoon Bradley arrived at the Trianon for an emotional
showdown. For Eisenhower, breaking the news was distasteful. He was
empty-handed in his effort to promote Bradley to four stars and unable to
assure him that the Ninth Army would ever be returned, but he was
determined that Bradley not challenge the five-division transfer to Alsace.

In the give-and-take, Eisenhower and Bradley ignored protocol and argued heatedly in the presence of Morgan, Spaatz, Strong and Whiteley.
Bradley presented gains averaging six miles in the past forty-eight hours,
despite heavy snowfall and low temperatures, with large hauls of German
tanks, ammunition and prisoners, though he had not gained a breakthrough. Bradley warned Eisenhower that he was jeopardizing his efforts
to "retrieve the integrity of the U.S. command," and that "mail was pouring
into his headquarters from stateside demanding explanations for the mixed
command setup over a battle fought by American troops."

Eisenhower reminded Bradley that he, Bradley, had long agreed to the
logic of British command over an American army and had long accepted
Montgomery's priority. It was now "paramount to close the Rhine north
of Düsseldorf with all possible speed," and simultaneously to reduce the
Colmar pocket.

For good measure, Bradley told Eisenhower in the presence of Strong and
Whiteley, two British officers, that if Montgomery was promoted to overall
ground commander, Bradley would not continue to serve, "having forfeited
the confidence of his staff." Bradley was mystified that the Americans, who
"were doing the fighting and dying in Europe with 61 divisions in the field
next to 15 understrength British divisions," were forever obligated to give
and give.

Eisenhower reminded Bradley that he (Bradley) had been the first to devise the Frankfurt thrust, that he (Bradley) had supported the decision to place the Ninth Army under Montgomery at Maastricht on December 7. Moreover, Eisenhower reminded him that he (Bradley) had been the "one individual in Europe I can count on for anything I ask."

"I can't be responsible to the American people if you do this," Bradley snapped. "I wish to resign at once." According to Strong, who uncomfortably witnessed this exchange, Eisenhower turned pale, then red. "Brad," Eisenhower resumed, "I, not you, am responsible to the American people. Your resignation therefore means absolutely nothing."

After a long silence, Bradley backed down. He admitted that VERITABLE-GRENADE made "military sense," that he accepted the boundary shifts and troop transfers: he would give his loyal support. Bradley endorsed Eisenhower's revisions to the January 18 directive and pledged his best. As Bradley spoke, Eisenhower silently pledged to himself that he would find ways to reward Bradley, his finest field commander, before the war ended.

Shortly after Bradley left, Eisenhower instructed Whiteley to phone Montgomery, who was in London. Whiteley was to tell Montgomery that Eisenhower would be watching the 21st Army Group dispatches very carefully. One word denigrating Bradley or the American command, and Montgomery would find himself in command of a supporting offensive toward Düsseldorf under the overall command of Ground Commander in Chief Lieutenant General Omar Bradley, U.S.A.

The conference in Malta closed in the same spirit, one of uncertainty more than resolve. Years later Robert Sherwood noted that the "factual-sounding" minutes of the conference masked the most violent arguments of the war, but the arguments lacked focus. In his gloomy account, Brooke chronicled his compulsion to break away from the stifling discussions to walk alone in the cold, misty Maltese countryside. Real unity with Marshall and the Americans was elusive. Eisenhower escaped with vague instructions. Alexander's appointment was tentatively set but would not be finally agreed to until Yalta, two weeks later, which left Brooke feeling that "the meeting with the all-powerful Americans had seemed unsatisfactory."

The British position, which had wavered between pessimism and optimism, now weighed decisively in favor of an imminent German collapse with "no serious opposition likely to be encountered west of the Rhine," and that "the double attack might soon become a pursuit and as such fully justified." The CCS accepted Brooke's offer of five Canadian and British divisions from Italy to bolster the western front, an action significantly enhancing Montgomery's priority and Brooke's quest for Alexander to serve in Paris. But Brooke's effort to clarify the pattern of the northern thrust clashed with Marshall's. Eisenhower's "clarification" set no objectives east of the Rhine, which left the CCS with Eisenhower's estimates of

Allied capacity to supply divisions in Montgomery's sector and his estimates of German intentions, which were to defend the Ruhr and the Saar.
The CCS demurred on the size, place and timing of the secondary thrust,
which gave Brooke little choice but to rely on Eisenhower's goodwill and
Smith's personal pledge that he, Smith, "would use his influence to guide
him [Eisenhower]."

On the night of February 2, Roosevelt's party arrived in Malta. Aboard
the *Quincy* in Valletta harbor, the President met briefly with Churchill,
Brooke and Marshall to ratify the decisions of the CCS and to take up the
Alexander matter. According to Sherwood, Roosevelt was impressed by
the British concessions at Malta and anxious to accommodate Churchill's
evident wish to reward Alexander. But Roosevelt was also hesitant to
endorse an action that would reflect on Eisenhower's handling of the Ardennes. Roosevelt and Churchill tentatively agreed, with the effective date
of Alexander's transfer set six weeks hence, "to avoid the appearance of
any lack of confidence in Eisenhower." The subject would be reviewed at
Yalta.

"Wasn't the damage done at Teheran?" Churchill later asked his physician and confidant Lord Moran. In this spirit the American and British
staffs, numbering 700, boarded twenty American Skymasters and five British Yorks at midnight on the second. At ten-minute intervals the planes
took off for the three-and-a-half-hour flight due east, turned 90 degrees
north to avoid Cyprus in the final transit through German-controlled air-
space over Rumania and Bulgaria under cover of darkness.

YALTA

Critics would portray the events at Yalta in the next week as a shameless
capitulation to Soviet Communism, condemning half of Europe and much
of Asia to untold suffering. This attack, under way within weeks of the
conference, would be partly rebutted by Eisenhower and others, who attributed the Yalta understandings to the military situation on February 3
as the Anglo-American delegations left Malta.

As these rebuttals went, with the Red Army deployed from Stettin to
Trieste, Stalin was able to mobilize overwhelming power to impose his will
on eastern Europe regardless of Allied wishes. While Eisenhower's forces
restored the pre-Ardennes line west of the Rhine, Zhukov's armies closed
the Oder River on a broad front within sixty miles of Berlin. Konev's drive
reached the Neisse River, poised to seize the Silesian coal fields and Dresden, and triggered the panicked migration of millions of Germans westward
for sanctuary and the flight of German government officials from Berlin to
Austria.

But as Yalta opened, the Red Army, having advanced 300 miles, had

THE RUSSIAN DRIVE TO THE ODER, JANUARY–APRIL 1945

COURLAND

Riga
LATVIA

LITHUANIA

Baltic Sea

Königsberg

Danzig

EAST PRUSSIA

N

Rostock

Stettin

POMERANIA

Berlin

Vistula

Warsaw

Elbe

Oder

Neisse

SILESIA

POLAND

Bug

Leipzig

Dresden

Sandomierz

Cracow

Lvov

Prague

GERMANY

Brno

CARPATHIAN MTS

Danube

SLOVAKIA

Vienna

Bratislava

Tisza

OSTMARK (AUSTRIA)

ALPS

Budapest

HUNGARY

ITALY

Lake Balaton

Trieste

Zagreb

YUGOSLAVIA

Adriatic Sea

Belgrade

DINARIC ALPS

Kms.
0   100
0   100
Miles

© 1986 A·Karl/J·Kemp

FRONT LINES:

January 12, 1945

February 4, 1945

April 7, 1945

Soviet-controlled, April 7, 1945

German-held pockets

outrun supply lines, left sizable pockets at Breslau and at Königsberg, and attracted the bulk of German armor to the eastern front. Sizable numbers of Germans filtered back through Poland and re-formed behind the Oder–Neisse while the Sixth Panzer Army was en route to Lake Balaton, southwest of Budapest. With the Allied offensive opening on Montgomery's front mid-course in the conference, the military and political situation was gradually being recast in favor of the Allies. A long Soviet pause would coincide with diminishing German resistance in the west and resumption of the Allied offensive. This meant that for the first time since June 1944 the Allies had latitude in dealings with the Russians. The principals—Churchill and Roosevelt—would long be criticized for failing to heed voices in their own governments urging that the Allies were now in a position to avoid compromise with Soviet tyranny in Eastern Europe.

But the military situation was not as clear-cut as these critics implied; and even assuming that the Allies had significant latitude, it was not clear what they would gain by wielding it. In Roosevelt's judgment, to exploit Allied freedom of action openly might needlessly strengthen legions of skeptics who had long anticipated that the Allied-Soviet war effort would end with a collapse of the wartime alliance with the Russians. A rift was inevitable, but hindsight suggests that Roosevelt was determined to avoid actions that could imply that even such a proponent of the alliance as himself had had little faith in it, or that he considered the imminent victory over Germany only the prelude to hostilities with the Soviets. Churchill, though he questioned Roosevelt's methods, deferred to the American President, for he too had a stake in good relations with the Russians, and his policy, like Roosevelt's, had always aimed at a settlement that, as he had told Stalin at Teheran, would make the world "safe for at least fifty years."

But the main problem with the Yalta criticism is the implication that Roosevelt and Churchill journeyed to Yalta to decide fundamental issues not in effect resolved at Teheran. At Teheran, Churchill had formally reserved a position on important questions, such as ANVIL, Rome and Turkey, and he would attempt to do so again at Yalta on German unification and Poland. But, in retrospect, Churchill's purpose seems to have been to bargain for compliance with and clarification of agreements already reached rather than to seek advantage over Stalin, as such. By February 1945 it was apparent, again in retrospect, that the great design agreed upon at Teheran had unfolded with uncanny precision, though not without mutual distrust and looming unknowns, such as German actions in the next few months, the problem of coordinating an Allied advance into Germany that was about to begin just as the Russian winter offensive ended, and Allied—specifically American—public opinion.

Questions remained: formal approval of occupation zones; Allied-Soviet strategy in Germany; the effect of understandings worked out between Stalin and Churchill in October on the Balkans; understandings on open territory left in Scandinavia, Austria and Hungary. The status of France was murky, and political arrangements in Poland were an issue. Above all, Roosevelt, Churchill and Stalin met to decide what light to place on existing understandings, whether Allied-Soviet dealings were to be formal or tacit, wide-ranging or narrow. At Teheran the deliberations had been protected by wartime secrecy, and Roosevelt had been at his most effective as a Commander in Chief. In February 1945, as Allied capitals mulled over improving news from all battlefronts, parliamentary and congressional restraint loosened and debate resumed on long-dormant issues of war policy.

Once again, Churchill and Roosevelt found themselves at odds over the proper approach to take with Stalin. Churchill tirelessly argued to the end that the Soviets, securely in possession of Europe east of the Alps, were not capable of "collaboration" in the Western sense, that only clear-cut understandings duly ratified would hold up. Churchill, who doubted that the Allies and Russians, frozen in a virtual state of belligerency for four years, could suddenly be partners and opposed pretending otherwise. He hoped that Roosevelt, in his eagerness to handle his short-term problems with Congress, would not reject "a clear compromise" with Stalin, one disclaiming Allied responsibility for Soviet actions, but one that would, admittedly, result in a Russia being "satisfied and having no territorial or other ambitions."

To the end, Roosevelt ruled out such directness. Having wavered for months, he evaluated Stalin, and weighed his personal stake in the appearance of Russian cooperation to which he had linked his policy. He intended to suggest to Stalin the corresponding Russian stake in maintaining this image. Thus, Roosevelt had decided that Stalin was "gettable," but even if Stalin was not "gettable," that a change of course on his part would have confused his waning domestic support. But in any event, as Bohlen put it, Churchill's proposed "clear compromise" was an impractical policy in Eastern Europe, corrosive of the principles Roosevelt espoused, and a policy "not . . . possible in a democracy," or, at least, American democracy.

With the Allies outwardly drawing apart, the tone at Yalta was set by national factors: who was winning the most spectacular victories at the moment; who had sacrificed the most; who stood to contribute the most to reconstruction. Toting up the balance, American production in February 1945 was unmatched, indeed unmatched by any other society in history. The Allied intervention in 1944 was hastening the end of the war, and the second front had rounded out America's crucial wartime role. Britain had been in the war the longest and was vitally interested in the outcome, but had consumed her economic and political reserves. Soviet resources were potentially vast, but the Russian sacrifice in lives and her military contribution to the war had been decisive, and it was in this sense that Stalin dominated the conference.

Bohlen later described the somber arrival at Saki airport. After the review of the honor guard, and breakfast of vodka, caviar and cold cuts, the American and British delegations left on a six-hour, 85-mile drive to Yalta overland by auto through the mountains surrounding Simferopol. Since Yalta was accessible by air or rail, the trip by auto seemed unnecessary, as some complained. But the purpose of the conference was to acknowledge past decisions, and the sight of wasted villages, fields littered with tanks and transports, gutted factories—the remnants of the two campaigns fought through the area that had claimed two and a half million lives in the Crimea alone—was a reminder of the devastation of Russia, the basis of Stalin's demands in Eastern Europe. Roosevelt and Churchill were moved by the panorama of destruction, which, according to Stalin, was mild compared with what could be seen in the Ukraine, where German demolitions had been carried out with "method and calculation." The Allied delegation was impressed by the permanence of Stalin's hold, emphasized by the setting carefully chosen for the conference. The Livadia Palace, standing on a 150-foot bluff overlooking the Black Sea, had been built and used as a summer retreat by the Romanovs. The palace, though looted and wrecked by the retreating Germans, was made habitable with chairs, tables and bedding shipped from the Hotel Metropole in Moscow, and it conveyed the feel of an "extinct imperialism and nobility," as Churchill put it.

Several conferences unfolded simultaneously. In private, Roosevelt, Churchill and Stalin quickly disposed of sensitive questions not amenable to full discussion in formal plenary session. The three approved the EAC plan for occupation zones in Germany "without dissent or discussion." Stalin implied that he was worried about complications delaying Red Army occupation of the Russian zone encompassing Berlin. Stalin informed Churchill and Roosevelt privately that the Red Army, now encountering stiff resistance along the Oder, would pause to bring up supplies and liquidate vast German pockets in Courland and Latvia. He asked both Allied leaders about the Allied reaction in the event of a sudden collapse of resistance in the west. Stalin showed interest in Eisenhower's plans in the Saar and Alexander's plans in Italy, and in so doing indicated the supreme importance of Germany and Berlin in Russian thinking.

Churchill approved the occupation zones, but could not predict the military situation that would confront Eisenhower in six weeks. In turn, Churchill asked Stalin how the Red Army intended to respond should Hitler attempt to escape from Berlin, as rumored, and reorganize a government near Dresden or Berchtesgaden. "We shall follow him," Stalin replied, thereby inviting Churchill to do the same and to participate in the liberation of the nonbelligerents in the redoubt zone—Czechoslovakia and Austria— as well as in Denmark and Norway.

Roosevelt was less circumspect. In his first meeting with Stalin, he expressed the hope that MacArthur "would reach Manila as quickly as Zhukov reached Berlin." The President accepted and welcomed the inevitability that the Russians would take Berlin and occupy the zone before the Allies, a position followed up in the military committee discussions at which Antonov, Arnold and Portal drew bomb lines roughly along the EAC zonal boundaries in Germany, which, in retrospect, roughly corresponded to the actual demarcation line east and west and to what Churchill later called the Iron Curtain.

In the bomb-line talks, Antonov declined Portal's offer of direct tactical air support for Russian ground operations in Poland and revealed that the Soviets in January had flown 10,000 tactical sorties in support of the Warsaw attack. The three sides extended the bomb line southwest from Silesia through Vienna and Zagreb, a demarcation set to avoid entanglements between Allied and Soviet forces and as a reasonable estimate of where the Allied and Russian ground forces would meet.

Did bomb lines entail a commitment to restrain military advances beyond the agreed boundaries? The Antonov-Portal exchanges were reminiscent of the ANVIL discussions at Teheran, where talks had also focused on the conduct of a military pursuit aimed at achieving the quickest and most efficient destruction of German arms. The need for Allied-Soviet coordination was most pressing in the north, less so in the Balkans and Austria, where the stakes were secondary. Officially, the British viewed bomb-line commitments, as they had viewed ANVIL, as a pragmatic military bargain isolated from underlying political questions and subject to renegotiation in new strategic circumstances. But in 1945 between the statesmen of Communist Russia, Democratic America and Imperial England, military language was the only practical vehicle for discussion of all issues.

Military advisers predominated in the formal plenary sessions, as Harriman recalled, since "Stalin would talk more frankly about military matters if the number of civilians in the conference room was held to a minimum." There, "political problems" were put aside. Reminiscent of Teheran, Stalin in the first full plenary session quickly brought discussion to the crucial point by asking Churchill and Roosevelt, "How is Germany to be dismembered?" Would a divided Germany be jointly governed under military administration or separately governed? With German overtures inevitable in the next several weeks, how was an offer to surrender to one of the Allies to be dealt with?

Churchill called the partition of Germany "too complicated" to be settled quickly, and proposed a "searching history of historical and ethnographical and economic facts" to determine the future of Prussia, the Rhineland and the Saar, where the French would press claims. Roosevelt agreed, and according to witnesses, even Stalin seemed to admit that talk of dismemberment was "lip service to a dying ideal." Accordingly, in the articles of surrender being drafted by the EAC, Roosevelt and Stalin mildly favored references to "dismemberment," then deferred to Churchill's plea for time and deliberation, which Churchill later insisted kept the issue open but which in effect became the first step toward a policy of de facto instead of formal partition.

On it went. Churchill argued for an occupation economic policy interlinking the three EAC sectors. He emphasized the economic interdependence of the Saar, the Ruhr and Silesia, and warned that without a "coherent policy" Germany might be reduced to economic dependency; he ruled out, among other things, reparations. Stalin and Molotov responded with a demand for $20 billion of reparations "in kind," with 50 percent for the Soviet Union. To Churchill's protest that the $20 billion figure was well beyond German capacity, Molotov cited Ambassador Ivan Maisky's contention that "$20 billion was not a large sum." According to Soviet arithmetic, German prewar assets totaling $125 billion had been reduced by $75 billion by the war to $50 billion. But the German economy would quickly rebound. And, according to Maisky, the transfer of 33 percent of the wealth from a highly industrialized system was possible without undue hardship, and Germany was even now "highly industrialized." Second, the 50 percent Soviet claim was in line with the principle that reparations be drawn according to the "contribution to the winning of the war and the severity of their losses."

Molotov presented an either-or: either the pretense of a German-wide policy implying eventual unification, coupled with a reparations settlement implicating the Allies in a figure that would reduce a "unified" Germany to peonage, or no pretense of a single policy, leaving the Russians free to proceed with drawing $10 billion "in kind" as they saw fit, and the Western Allies free to build up the Allied zones as they chose. Like Churchill, Roosevelt believed the figure impractical and opposed reparations carried to the "point of creating mass starvation in Germany." But he did not deny the justice of the claim, and preferred a general formula. Also, reparations by now seemed linked to Harriman-sponsored talks about postwar U.S. credits for Russia. Allied stubbornness might convert the Soviet claims on Germany into a thinly disguised Soviet demand for Allied reparations, shattering the alliance. For Churchill and Roosevelt, the draconian Soviet position on reparations was troublesome—but as Raymond Moley wrote afterward, "the institutions of international capitalism were unsuitable to enforcing on Germany the judgment which the moral sense of the Allied nations requires . . . Stalin's method does promise the fulfillment of that judgement. Roosevelt and Churchill were sufficiently realistic to see this and agree."

Similarly, Roosevelt and Churchill joined Stalin in a pledge to repatriate the ten million displaced persons in Europe. Included in this were Allied prisoners of war in Russian hands and Russian nationals liberated by the

Allies. For a month, Deane and Burrows had discussed the problem in Moscow. Snags had developed over the return of thousands of American and British POWs held in Poland and liberated by the Red Army, pending the return of Soviet nationals of all categories held in western Germany, including military prisoners, technically criminals under Soviet law, and large numbers of Russian defectors who had fought with the German army on both fronts. In effect, Moscow demanded that hundreds of thousands of men be handed over by Allied authority to join the millions of German military prisoners never protected by the Geneva Convention on the eastern front to form a vast pool of labor for, according to *Newsweek,* "possibly long years of rebuilding cities destroyed in the heyday of Nazism," including plans to construct ninety new cities, "some the size of Pittsburgh and Detroit." According to estimates, between 70 and 90 percent of Russian iron, steel, and coal capacity had to be restored.

The Soviets were not alone, however. Defense Minister René Pleven of France was demanding "reparations in kind" in the form of 2.2 million German workers "to tend beet farms in France," the number selected being the number of Frenchmen detained in Germany as slave laborers. French claims were diminished somewhat because of the 1940 armistice and the small French forces in the field. But for France, Yalta represented an advance insofar as Stalin and Roosevelt set aside talk of stripping away the French empire. Eventually Churchill, with Roosevelt's indirect support, obtained an occupation zone for France, a major accomplishment secured in part by Roosevelt's casual prediction that the United States would not maintain a postwar U.S. ground presence exceeding one or two divisions in Europe. The suggestion could be interpreted many ways, but above all it confronted Stalin with the prospect of pacifying Germany with British support only. Thereafter Stalin endorsed a French seat in the UN Security Council, the inevitable French seat on the EAC and a French occupation zone carved out of the American and British zones while putting off plans for a corresponding Polish zone carved from the Soviet sector.

Roosevelt and Churchill accepted reparations and repatriation without enthusiasm. The decision compromised Western traditions of political sanctuary and justice on a scale conceivable only in 1945. The accords were a reason for backing an extended period of military occupation and rule. Only the military could carry out such a policy, a group toasted by Stalin at a banquet as "recognized only during a war and whose services after a war are quickly forgotten."

Proceeding, Churchill, Roosevelt and Stalin approved the EAC occupation zones in plenary session, then approved the fourth partition of Germany by approving the Curzon Line and granting Poland as compensation East Prussia and Silesia. They approved the fifth by consigning the Sudetenland to a new Czechoslovakia, a sixth in reaffirming Austrian independence, and a seventh by reserving the status of the Saar. The three leaders further resolved that Hitler and the Nazis would not be permitted to surrender even unconditionally, that Germany was to be invaded and rendered powerless to rearm or reorganize politically under the heel of indefinite military occupation, but they reserved a permanent solution to the German problem for future generations.

Poland, Asia and the UN dominated the talks afterward, and were to become the focal points of later controversy surrounding Yalta. Talks on Poland alone ran 18,000 words in the minutes. On Poland, Roosevelt and Churchill probed Russian intent. Roosevelt probed for a formula that would help ward off the political tornado looming in Washington over his policy as a whole. Churchill was faced with a similar tornado in Parliament, but he had other reasons as well. The issue of Poland, which he considered speculative, dramatized the "clear compromise" actually being struck in Eastern Europe, and it dramatized the hazards of imposing outside rule on places like Poland, as well as the folly of assuming that the Soviets would minimize their triumphs. In practical terms, Poland was an issue that bolstered the British position on France, Italy, Greece and Yugoslavia.

Four weeks before, Moscow had recognized Lublin, thereby presenting the Allies with a constituted provisional government in Poland. The leaders weighed the rival claims of the Lublin and London groups, election procedures, the composition of the provisional government to be entrusted to conduct elections, and settlement of Soviet-Polish and Polish-German issues. But the main issue was the status of the Lublin provisional government. Roosevelt and Churchill urged Stalin to accept territorial adjustments in lieu of insisting on Lublin. Stalin maintained that the boundary question was settled, and that the status of the Lublin Committee as the new provisional government of Poland was also settled.

In urging Stalin to reconsider, Churchill insisted that for Britain, Poland was "a question of honor," indeed "the sole reason why we had drawn the sword." Britain would insist Poland be the "mistress in her own house and the captain of her own soul" and never accept a settlement that would not leave Poland "free, independent and sovereign." Yet Churchill had long conceded to the Soviets the right to champion a friendly "Polish neighbor as a fundamental matter of security," thus accepting qualified Polish sovereignty in principle.

Roosevelt conceded that the American interest was more remote, but that postwar U.S. politics would be affected. Six million Poles in the United States watched on, and concessions "would make life easier on him at home ... if the Soviet Union could 'give something to Poland.' " Roosevelt asked for Lvov to remain Polish, and for an interim ruling council drawn from five Polish parties worthy of the support of all the great powers. Roosevelt repeatedly warned Stalin that "our people at home would look with a critical eye on ... a ... disagreement between us at this vital stage of the war. They in effect say that if we cannot get a meeting of minds now when our armies are converging on the common enemy, how can we get an understanding on even more vital things in the future?"

Again, Stalin gave his position: Poland was solved. Polish boundaries had been settled in 1939, restoring to Russia what had been taken in 1917. Since Poland was being liberated by the Russians, Moscow was entitled to full military and political cooperation. Legitimate political authority was established in Poland and, by Soviet reports, very popular. The political authority in place was also willing to conclude a defensive alliance with Moscow, which the Russians insisted on but in no way contravened Dumbarton Oaks or the Atlantic Charter. Churchill did not dispute that the anti-Communist Polish underground had waged a campaign of terror against the Lublin Committee. He had vainly taken the lead in urging Mikolajczyk to rid the London-based Polish Committee of anti-Russian radicals. He and Roosevelt solemnly discussed Stalin's agenda item entitled "Safeguarding the rear line of the Soviet Army," a discussion of measures to combat "insurrectionary activities" instigated by the London Poles. But in the end, it was Stalin's view that Poland, though a question of honor for Britain, was "for the Russians a question of life and death," that throughout history, Poland had been a corridor of attack against Russia from the west, and to close this corridor the Soviet Union for a while would have to insist on a "strong independent friendly Poland."

Several factors ruled out flexibility on Stalin's part. First, as Harriman indicated, the Soviet military occupation of eastern Poland had revealed the depths of anti-Russian feeling, fueled by Ukrainian nationalism. Second, Russian plans to occupy the Soviet zone in Germany would depend indefinitely on secure lines of communication through Poland. Third, Stalin and Molotov were unwilling to concede that a Communist government was not "popular" or "sovereign." Given the Russian obsession with Germany and the exigencies of Soviet ideology, Poland was not a negotiable issue. But because Poland had important political and symbolic significance to the West, the issue could not be settled completely.

Stalin entertained cosmetic concessions. He knew that he was called a "dictator, not a democrat," he said, but he was democratic enough to know that a Polish government could not be created without consulting the Poles. He suggested that the Lublin Committee might be "enlarged" to include "émigré elements." But Lublin would not disband. The Lublin Poles were committed to "eliminating the causes of Polish-Russian conflict," while Mikolajczyk refused even to concede on the Polish-Russian boundary question and spoke in terms of an ultimatum. Stalin claimed that the Lublin Committee was "popular and no less legitimate than De Gaulle's in Paris."

Lengthy discussion led to an agreement to "reorganize" the provisional Lublin Committee by enlarging it to include democratic Poles living abroad. The leaders agreed to set up an ambassadorial committee in Moscow to consult with Polish leaders on reorganizing the Lublin government, which was to conduct "free and unfettered" elections, and agreed as well to minor boundary concessions for Poland. In the communiqué, Molotov agreed to delete an objectionable reference to Polish "émigrés" and to accept the participation of democratic Poles living abroad, subject to ambassadorial-committee review. As to whether Mikolajczyk would be allowed to return to Poland, Molotov said that the question should "be left to the ambassadors," and cautioned the group against statements offending Lublin or the democratic sensibilities of the Polish people. Indeed, the Soviets would insist that they had retained a veto in the ambassadorial committee and would feel bound to exercise it in consultation with the Lublin Committee. Bohlen complained afterward that the terms were so vague that the "whole negotiation . . . completed at Yalta would have to be developed again from the ground up," having "established nothing more than the machinery for renegotiation." Roosevelt was troubled, but Harriman got the impression that "as long as he could put his own interpretation on the language, he didn't care what interpretation other people put on it." Toward the close of the conference, the group turned to the Far East. The factors bearing on Roosevelt's Asian "concessions" have often been cited: according to JCS military estimates, Russian aid against Japan was essential, and to be gained by diplomatic concessions if necessary.

By contrast with its bold stance on OVERLORD, the War Department called the planned invasion of Japan a task of "unprecedented military magnitude" in view of the immense shipping distances involved and the fanatical Japanese resistance encountered on Tarawa and Okinawa. An eighteen-month campaign against the Japanese mainland meant a million U.S. casualties, without solving the problem of subduing fifty Japanese divisions in Manchuria. Amid doubts that the atom bomb would work and the wisdom of using it, estimates concerning the Far East did not take into account this still-untested weapon. Estimates did, however, consider the potential benefits of "negotiating Soviet entry against Japan which was deemed inevitable anyway and timed to suit the convenience of the U.S.S.R. after the German collapse which would surely precede a Japanese collapse."

The Allied and Soviet positions in Asia were now reversed, for the similarity was striking between the Allied position in Asia and Stalin's position in Europe thirteen months before. Like the Russians in Europe a year earlier, the Allies were apparently capable of winning the Pacific war on their own by blockade or by invasion. And like the Russians a year earlier, the Americans, in planning the final stages of the Japanese war, confronted a rival power disposed to intervene with or without American endorsement, capable of unilateral moves to occupy substantial stretches of territory beyond the reach of American military power. The USSR was closer to China and Japan than America, and so the Soviet interest in the area was more direct, an important difference. Roosevelt could have de-

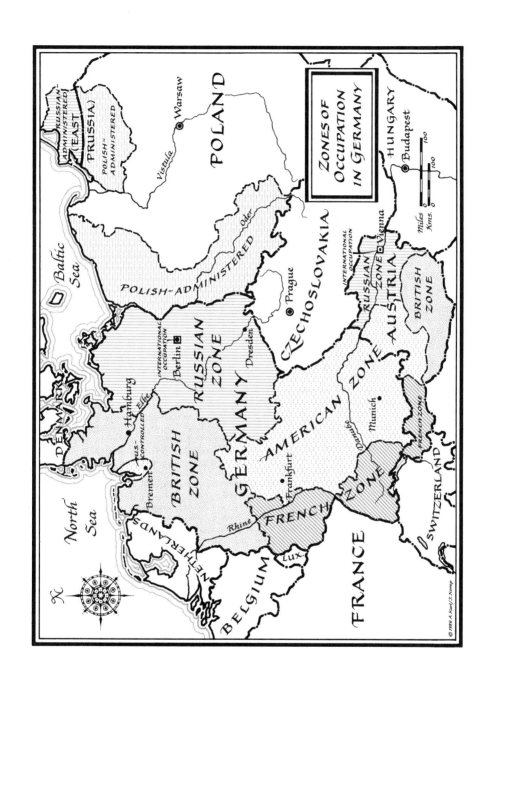

ZONES OF
OCCUPATION
IN GERMANY

POLAND

Warsaw

Vistula

Oder

RUSSIAN-
ADMINISTERED
(EAST)

PRUSSIA

POLISH-
ADMINISTERED

Baltic
Sea

POLISH-ADMINISTERED

CZECHOSLOVAKIA

Prague

INTERNATIONAL
OCCUPATION

RUSSIAN
ZONE

Vienna

AUSTRIA

RUSSIAN
ZONE

BRITISH
ZONE

HUNGARY

Budapest

Miles

100

Kms.

100

GERMANY

Dresden

Berlin

INTERNATIONAL
OCCUPATION

Hamburg

Elbe

DENMARK

BRITISH
ZONE

U.S.
CONTROLLED

Bremen

AMERICAN
ZONE

Munich

Danube

Frankfurt

FRENCH ZONE

FRENCH
ZONE

SWITZERLAND

North
Sea

NETHERLANDS

BELGIUM

Lux.

Rhine

FRANCE

© 1986 A Karl/J Kemp

cided not to solicit Russian entry, but perhaps mindful that Stalin might have done the same at Teheran with respect to Allied entry, he apparently decided to make a virtue of Russian intervention perhaps in the hope of shaping it, balancing accounts between Asia and Europe somewhat, and winning Stalin's trust. Accordingly, Roosevelt offered to recognize an old Czarist concession to operate the Manchurian railroads, title to Sakhalin and the Kuriles, lost in the 1905 war, Darien as a free port, and Port Arthur as a naval base, accompanied by acknowledgment that the "preeminent interests of the Soviet Union shall be safeguarded" at both ports.

Forebodings and disappointment were the theme of the backstage accounts. Discord on how to handle Stalin continued between the Americans and British, attributed partly to Roosevelt's faltering health. By Yalta, Roosevelt was "frail and ill" with a slender hold on life, lacking sustained interest in the business at hand, and overwhelmed by the formidable difficulties he faced in Washington. Lord Moran scrutinized Roosevelt and noted that the President, often short on facts in conference, had at one time been able to cover much by his shrewdness. Now the shrewdness was gone, and so there was "nothing left."

America remained a question mark. Would Congress, awakening to the dimensions of American power, accept the compromises Roosevelt had accepted long before to defeat Germany? At dinner in the Livadia Palace, Bohlen warned Vishinsky of likely troubles in Congress over Poland, and predicted that the American people would challenge any denial of fair play in the Polish elections. "The Soviet Union will never agree to the right of small nations to judge the acts of great powers," Vishinsky replied, adding that the American people "should be taught to obey their rulers." Bohlen laughed and suggested that Vishinsky "ought to go there and try telling the American people that." Vishinsky volunteered to do so, but did not dispute Bohlen's point that any settlement had to be flexible.

Accordingly, Churchill failed to firm up the problem of the nonbelligerents of central Europe, including Czechoslovakia and Austria. Nor did Churchill gain satisfactory assurances about the UN. Skeptical of a world congress that purported to resolve sensitive non-European questions, Churchill pressed for assurances that "the powers of the world organization would not be used against Britain if she was unconvinced and refused to agree." At a private conference with Stettinius, Churchill shouted his disgust and spoke so rapidly that he was barely understood to say that "the British Empire would not be run by a bunch of bunglers" and he would "refuse to countenance such folly." Similar Soviet misgivings led to the adoption of the Big Power veto safeguard in the Security Council. Stalin recalled the League of Nations' expulsion of Russia in 1939 over the Finnish war, which brought to mind the current "talk of a crusade against Russia." But Stalin noted prophetically that should China demand Hong Kong or the Egyptians demand the Suez Canal, neither would "be alone and would have friends and perhaps protectors in the Assembly or the council."

Stalin modified Molotov's proposal to seat all sixteen Soviet republics in the General Assembly to three—one each for the USSR, the Ukraine and Belorussia, to offset India and Canada, thus paving the way for U.S. Senate approval of U.S. participation in the United Nations. As insurance, Roosevelt asked for three U.S. seats if necessary for Senate ratification. Stalin agreed, and in the final conference approved the UN convocation set for April 25 in San Francisco, with a deadline of March 1 for declarations of war against the Axis by countries seeking membership.

In the end, even critics would look back and admit the logic of Roosevelt's bid for Soviet friendship. Roosevelt would be faulted for providing a "moral cloak" for aggressive Soviet designs in Eastern Europe, but could he have done otherwise? Soviet expansion had long been a foreseeable consequence of intervening in the war on the side of Russia. And so, in the circumstances, for Roosevelt to feign surprise over the consequences might have implied that he had never been wholehearted about his own policy, one that identified Germany as the mortal threat to Western civilization at mid-century—not Russia. Finally, despite the improving military situation in the west, military cooperation was still necessary to defeat Germany, though it is apparent that even if cooperation had not been necessary, Roosevelt's approach was to pursue it as an end in itself. For in the words of his fourth inaugural address, Roosevelt had arrived in Yalta convinced that "the only way to have a friend is to be a friend," and was determined to persuade Stalin of the advantages of restraint by the example of his own restraint. Harriman, a realist, would concede that "even with the advantage of hindsight" he did not believe that the Western Allies could have walked away from an attempt to reach understandings with Stalin.

But the question was, "What now?" With favorable war news flooding Washington and "sending optimism soaring like a balloon," Roosevelt bucked the tide. Congress was about to abandon inhibitions about probing secret agreements with the Russians, and British and European attitudes would also soon come into play. Discussion barely touched the ongoing world revolution against the colonial powers and United States influence in places like India and Egypt and in Southeast Asia, where Nazi and Japanese appeals had proven strong, and where Communist appeals would later prove still stronger. As the sessions wore on, Stalin spoke to Churchill and Roosevelt of his premonition that with the end of the fighting and the loss of "clear and understandable" objectives, the Alliance would lose "its character of intimacy and free expression of views."

Would the coalition survive? Roosevelt was exhausted, his powers spent. Churchill faced parliamentary elections and rising criticism in his own party, knowing the Conservative party had not been tested at the ballot box since 1938. Only Stalin was destined to remain in power, a fact sensed by the group and conveyed in the toasts at the many offstage banquets. On the night of February 10 Stalin praised both leaders generously, as though bidding them farewell. He raised his glass to Churchill, calling him a man born "once in a hundred years," one of the rare individuals whose personal qualities actually altered the course of history, a man who "when all Europe was ready to fall flat before Hitler said that Britain would stand and fight alone against Germany even without any Allies."

Churchill, in response, praised Stalin as a great conqueror and statesman. The Prime Minister cautioned against underestimating the difficulties ahead —history showed that even the strongest alliances tended to drift apart after victory. Churchill urged that it was their mutual responsibility to the "toiling millions of the world to avoid the errors of previous generations and of making a sure peace." He hoped the Americans and Russians would find ways to cooperate, and knew he could pledge that England would not be "behind-hand in her efforts in supporting their exertions." Churchill delivered a closing appeal for the smaller nations of Europe, a reminder that any accord struck would ultimately be unstable unless the larger powers respected the views of the smaller powers and that "the eagle should permit the small birds to sing and care not wherefore they sang."

According to the record of the toasts:

Marshall Stalin then proposed the health of the President of the United States. He said that he and Mr. Churchill in their respective countries had had relatively simple decisions. They had been fighting for their very existence against Hitlerite Germany, but there was a third man whose country had not been seriously threatened with invasion, but who had perhaps a broader conception of national interest and even though his country was not directly imperilled had been the chief forger of the instruments which had led to the mobilization of the world against Hitler . . .

[Roosevelt] felt the atmosphere at this dinner was that of a family, and it was in those words he liked to characterize the relations which existed between our three countries. He said that great changes had occurred in the world during the last three years, and even greater changes were to come. He said that each of the leaders represented here were working in their own way for the interests of their people. He said that fifty years ago there were vast areas of the world where people had little opportunity and no hope, but much had been accomplished. Although there were still great areas where people had little opportunity and little hope, their objectives here were to give to every man, woman and child on this earth the possibility of security and well being. . . .

In his narrative of the return voyage, Sherwood described feelings of relief in the presidential party, the talk of the progress made, of hopes for the future and the dawning of a new age secured in the closing days of the conference, imperfect but spared the perils of "unilateral action and exclusive alliances and spheres of influences and balances of power." Sherwood also noted the portents of trouble—De Gaulle's unavailability to meet Roosevelt in Cairo, Hopkins' abrupt departure at Oran after a never explained misunderstanding with the President, and Roosevelt's fitful concentration on his remarks to be delivered before Congress upon his return.

With the publication of the Declaration of Liberated Europe that week, the debate commenced. Roosevelt had his defenders. Just before Yalta, Raymond Moley had cautioned Americans about accepting the caricature of Stalin as the destroyer of little nations, Churchill as an opportunistic imperialist and Uncle Sam as a "sucker who is licking the shopworn candy of the Atlantic charter." Moley and others denied that Churchill and Stalin had "raped" Poland, noting that the Poland of Yalta was a stronger country than the prewar entity measured in terms of geography and ethnic composition. But Moley had forecast trouble if the arrangements denied the Poles freedom to choose their own government.

Adding and subtracting from Roosevelt's diminishing support had been Senator Arthur Vandenberg's speech in late January calling on the Republican party to accept a bipartisan foreign policy, and to end isolationism. Vandenberg urged a "hard and fast treaty" to disarm Germany and Japan, and other causes of trouble that tempted the Russians to move unilaterally. But he had urged a definite statement that the quicker the Axis agreed to unconditional surrender, the cheaper would be the cost of that surrender lest "we shall count the cost in mortal anguish even though we stumble onto a belated though inevitable victory," and had called for honest candor on Roosevelt's part to "restore full unity among the Allies and reassert the nation's faith in the objectives of an Allied victory."

Upon Roosevelt's return, problems arose over the White House refusal to disclose the details of the Yalta accords, a stance that excited suspicion of secret deals. Then came premature disclosure by the New York *Herald Tribune* of Roosevelt's approval of three Russian seats in the UN General Assembly. In his speech to Congress, Roosevelt appealed for reasoned acceptance of Yalta. He defensively recalled that for centuries no one had been able to decide what Poland was. He implied that with its tragic history of partition, Polish self-determination was at least temporarily a lost cause and a poor basis on which to provoke disagreements imperiling the structure of peace forged by the Big Three. But perhaps best remembered by the millions of radio listeners was Roosevelt's astonishing confession as he began to speak that he was too weary to stand, the President's first and last public acknowledgment of his physical paralysis.

9

Winter/Spring 1945

IN Versailles, Eisenhower had been biding his time. From afar, he anxiously monitored the conferences at Malta and Yalta and what was likely to be the last full policy review of the war. To his close staff he seemed confident that his outline plan would weather the storms of debate. But there were many unknowns, and the prospect of clear-cut CCS support quickly faded when Marshall sent his suggested amendments through Smith.

The signs from Malta had been mixed throughout. On the one hand, Marshall had seemed reluctant to question Eisenhower's plans and opposed to designating Alexander as a ground commander in chief. On the other, Smith's reports conveyed the mood of frustration and the urgency felt about getting on with the invasion of Germany, heightened by the Russian victories and the imminent Yalta conference. But there could be no consensus until the CCS could evaluate the results of the Russian offensive and Soviet attitudes at Yalta.

With this extension, Eisenhower—awaiting final word from Yalta—pushed hard to rush the Colmar battle to completion. A frontal assault by the U.S. 28th Division reached Colmar on the second, while eight French divisions attacked the northern and southern flanks of the pocket. But 50,000 defenders of the German Nineteenth Army fought an effective delaying action, which set the pattern for the slow German evacuation of Alsace.

Time was of the essence. All week Eisenhower peppered the 6th Army Group, "nagging Devers and finding fault with about every move he made," according to the historian Russell Weigley. To some, Eisenhower's impatience with Devers seemed obsessive, but the stakes riding on a quick victory at Colmar were high and mounted with each passing day.

It was now apparent that the war was entering its final phases. With the end of the Ardennes campaign, and as German strength flowed east, planning for an invasion of Germany, academic only weeks before, was no longer academic. The quick progress of Devers' hitherto obscure U.S. 6th Army Group had become a key factor in Eisenhower's quest to retain "flexibility" and to avoid an ironclad commitment to an invasion strategy that ruled out crossings south of the Moselle. Eisenhower had told Marshall at Marseilles that if German forces in the west continued to be a military threat, 6th Army Group operations would be essential to clear Alsace and the Palatinate in order to eliminate all threats to Allied communications before launching Rhine crossings. But even if German resistance dwindled away, it would be necessary to clear the Saar in order to deploy the 6th Army Group in crossings south of the Moselle, which would deploy all available Allied strength and gain flexibility.

Marshall had not disagreed, but an impatient CCS had already overruled Eisenhower, at least to the extent that he envisioned preparations stretching out for several months. Marshall's suggestions through Smith conveyed a clear meaning: the CCS was reluctant to interfere, but without quick results in Alsace, Marshall would be hard pressed to counter Brooke's line that the Allies lacked the resources to mobilize offensives north and south of the Moselle, and could no longer afford unsupervised competition among Eisenhower's three army groups. This was to say that it was Eisenhower's job to assure the CCS that his plan was not a formula for inaction, thereby avoiding the complications that would attend Alexander's appointment and a direct CCS order to cease operations south of the Moselle.

The complications would be serious. Alexander's appointment would undermine Eisenhower's authority and disrupt his command while a hurry-up directive would suspend Eisenhower's preparations west of the Rhine. The combined effect would be a premature invasion of Germany going off as a dangerous improvisation without settled command relations or settled procedures worked out with the Russians. Eisenhower knew that a number of factors could combine to bring this result about, but, above all, CCS approval of his broad-front plan would depend upon time—how long it would take to complete the preliminaries. The Colmar battle was an important preliminary, and Devers' attacks to clear the Colmar pocket had to succeed quickly so that Third Army–6th Army Group operations could begin to clear the Saar, permitting Eisenhower to muster strength for two offensives and prove that a broad-front invasion strategy was feasible as well as desirable. And so it was small wonder that "eliminating the Colmar pocket . . . an obvious and proper ingredient of Eisenhower's desire to close up the Rhine . . . had . . . become a virtual obsession."

On the third, Smith returned with details. He told Eisenhower of his emotional confrontation with Brooke over Eisenhower's tendency to "pay too much attention to the desires of his commanders." Marshall had been helpful throughout, but critical of the Prime Minister's influence at SHAEF.

In Malta, the CCS had weighed rejection of Eisenhower's strategy, but the situation was full of uncertainties. In the west the Germans were in retreat, but it was still too early to decide whether the Allies faced a long campaign against a determined enemy or whether the Allies were on the verge of gaining complete freedom of action, or something in between. The Russians were advancing in Poland, but already there were signs of a slowdown, which raised a host of questions about Soviet intentions. Eisenhower's broad-front strategy avoided the rigidities of a single thrust, and held out a wide range of military—and political—possibilities. But the premise of Eisenhower's military approach was effective cooperation with the Russians, and by dispersing Allied assets, a broad-front plan also entailed the risk of delay and of succeeding nowhere. Brooke's rival proposal for a single thrust toward Berlin was attractive in that a single thrust would tend to ensure that the Allies would overcome German resistance at some point *quickly*—maybe everywhere at once—but in curtailing flexibility, Brooke's plan practically foreclosed dealings with the Russians.

But did the Soviets intend to deal with the Western Allies? A question mark now surrounded Russian plans, particularly the timetable for extending the Red Army offensive beyond the Oder toward Berlin. Logically the Russians, after a brief pause on the Oder to bring up supplies and liquidate pockets by-passed in the January assault, would resume in order to secure Berlin and occupy the Russian EAC zone solemnized at Yalta. But another possibility, raised by Tedder's report, was that the Russian pause at the Oder would be an extended one. Stalin had cited plausible weather and supply difficulties, but his talk of starving the Germans out and of victory in late summer implied that the Russians had either reached the limit of their endurance or that they were thinking in other than military terms: that having established forces fifty miles from Berlin on the Oder, the Soviets intended to treat Berlin and their EAC zone as a sure thing, relegate Berlin to secondary forces and accelerate drives toward political objectives in Denmark, Czechoslovakia and Austria.

All of this raised a crucial point. At Yalta, Stalin, Churchill and Roosevelt were about to approve the EAC zones, and it was hard to quarrel with the idea that each side had thereby acquired an unqualified and exclusive right to occupy its respective zone, which in the Russian case encompassed Berlin. But there was a feeling—underscored by Churchill's reminders that the EAC zones were not binding on military operations—that such rights, if they existed, had to be exercised; that it would be untenable for the Allies, about to resume the offensive, to adopt Eisenhower's "military" approach, which directed Allied forces away from Berlin toward military objectives elsewhere just as the Russians began directing their main forces away from their military objective (Berlin) for the sake of pursuing political objectives everywhere else.

Berlin would vex the Alliance in the next several weeks. Though Allied forces were distant from Berlin, the timing of the Allied offensive actually stood to bring the objective within reach. The CCS could not overlook the fact that the prestige of capturing the city would be a measureless Allied asset in postwar Europe and that in theory even temporary Allied occupation of the Soviet EAC occupation zone would enhance Allied leverage on non-German questions such as a four-power ACC in Austria; Poland; Allied seats on control commissions in Rumania, Bulgaria and Hungary; and Allied access to areas Allied forces did not reach.

But nothing could be decided for a while. It was too early to rule out Soviet cooperation or to foreclose the possibilities offered by Eisenhower's plan. No one could say that Russian—or Allied—operations would not be necessary to preempt a German move into an Alpine redoubt. The feasibility of a Berlin strategy was unknown, and it was far from a given that the Russians would negotiate with the Allies over access to their EAC zone. The possibility of Allied-Soviet clashes for control of Berlin could not be ruled out, and the Allies had to assume that the Soviets would, at a minimum, respond to a Berlin strategy by attempting to counter the Allies elsewhere. Indeed, the risks were such that the British, ostensibly ready to mount a drive on Berlin, seemed uncertain in that their main concern appeared to be to ensure adequate resources for Montgomery's thrust to secure Denmark and the British zone—the British minimum—which raised a basic issue—how Berlin was to be taken and by whom. Only if Montgomery spearheaded the main drive toward Berlin could the British be sure of securing their EAC zone and reaching Denmark in the process. But the Ardennes counteroffensive had shifted the Allied center of gravity away from Montgomery while overall American preponderance, 2 to 1 in September 1944, had swollen to 4 to 1 by February 1945, meaning the power fueling a deep advance into Germany would be American.

But Berlin would become academic if the Russians pressed their current offensive beyond the Oder or resumed it after a short pause—by mid-March. What were Soviet intentions? At Yalta, Marshall and Brooke pressed Antonov hard for clues, without success. In talks with Antonov, Marshall spelled out the difficulties the Allies faced in crossing the Rhine and their need to know whether they could count on Russian activity on the vital Oder front. The Soviets promised operations "as weather permitted . . . to the limit of their ability." Similarly, the Soviets were elusive on bomb lines and other details of air coordination and showed enthusiasm for Allied air strikes to cut the flow of German forces moving east, but little enthusiasm for "specific liaison" between Allied and Russian commanders on ground and air operations, about which they provided few details except that they expected to join forces with the Allies along the Elbe. Several times

Marshall pointed out that the Allies had 14,000 operational aircraft in Europe and stood ready to see that "everything possible would be done ... to bring the greatest possible air assistance to the vital points of attack in the [Red Army] land offensive," but Antonov was noncommittal.

In this context, Alexander's appointment became more and more appealing in that Alexander would replace Tedder, the man identified in Soviet eyes as Eisenhower's spokesman at the height of the Ardennes. When Tedder had been allowed to go to Moscow, no one had foreseen the scale of the Russian offensive in Poland, which, in retrospect, made the Soviet pretense of coordinating plans with SHAEF on January 14 seem provocative. Stalin had drawn Tedder into talks about a summer campaign, and Tedder's continuing presence at SHAEF would indicate that Tedder's views were still fully endorsed by the Allied high command.

But Alexander's appointment had drawbacks. First, in the absence of a consensus on strategy, the appointment might generate confusion in Allied ranks and commit the CCS to supervising details of military operations. Second, the appointment might convey more to the suspicious Russians than the Allies really intended. Third, Brooke and Marshall, though close on grand strategy, still had differences, including differences about what the Alexander appointment would signify. Brooke had long favored Alexander's appointment in order to rectify past mistakes and to formalize priority for the 21st Army Group in the north. On the other hand, Marshall appeared to favor the appointment as a way of minimizing past differences and reconciling the British to the new major role he envisioned for Bradley's 12th Army Group. Finally, at Yalta, both sides had to reckon with the fact that for all of his open-mindedness, Eisenhower flatly opposed the appointment and had indicated in so many words that in the absence of a CCS charter for Alexander he, Eisenhower, would provide one.

And on it went. The tense Malta-Yalta interlude was depressing at all levels. At Versailles, the conferences sparked little of the anticipation of Cairo-Teheran thirteen months before, when the same parties had convened to settle the fate of the world. In Eisenhower's view, that fate had indeed been settled, leaving in suspense only the military means to the inevitable end. But troubles mounted in all quarters, and by February, though it was obvious that victory over the Germans could not be far off, relief was tempered by the agonizing process of the Allied recovery, the turmoil over command questions, and awareness that military success in the next few months would not solve the postwar problems overshadowing the conferences taking place that week.

The battles in the Eifel and at Colmar were slow going amid an early thaw, which converted roadbeds into quagmires and hampered air-ground support, enabling the Germans to withdraw from the Ardennes in good order. Simultaneously, Eisenhower was navigating a delicate passage in which he found himself at odds with the CCS, cordially estranged from Marshall, estranged from Bradley, and generally at odds with his American military colleagues, a potential threat to his grip on operations more serious than his long-ago troubles with the British.

As usual, the terms of Eisenhower's quarrel with the Americans were murky and ill-defined. At Marseilles, Marshall had not denied the logic of Eisenhower's plans, and had agreed that crossing the Rhine should be preceded by "a well-conducted campaign to help eliminate German forces west of the Rhine," *provided* the campaign was conducted by the fewest number of divisions, which would be less costly in the long run and ensure "well rested divisions when the time [came] for all out attack." Unlike Marshall, Bradley was not in favor of resting units, but, like Marshall, he saw the logic of Eisenhower's plans except as they undermined his ability to function as an army group commander. So far, all three had avoided the kind of hard-and-fast positions that had caused so much trouble in September 1944.

On the other hand, the Eisenhower-Bradley argument over the hurry-up offensive had exposed a conflict over objectives that would not go away. Bradley was determined to halt the attrition of the 12th Army Group units to other fronts and to avenge the Ardennes with a rebound offensive through the Cologne plain. Eisenhower was trying to build up a reserve and strengthen the 6th Army Group while observing CCS instructions to push VERITABLE-GRENADE. Presumably Bradley, when satisfied that 12th Army Group prestige had been restored, would render loyal support for Eisenhower's plans, which included a major 12th Army Group role in the Ruhr battle and a center thrust to Leipzig. But it remained to be seen what Bradley would consider enough to restore 12th Army Group prestige. He wanted to press the offensive toward Cologne without delay, arguing that otherwise he could not serve effectively. Moreover, Bradley indicated that he intended to extend the Cologne offensive over the Rhine heedless of German concentrations on his right flank in the Saar, though he was not specific about the long-range objectives he had in mind. On the night of the thirty-first, Bradley had backed down, but the reverberations of that conference would be felt for weeks.

Within a day of their talks at Versailles, the tug-of-war between Eisenhower and Bradley had resumed. Following up on his talks with Bradley, Eisenhower on the first sent private messages to him and Montgomery, in which he noted the Russian successes and the "paramount importance" of closing the Rhine north of Düsseldorf, and set VERITABLE for the eighth, GRENADE, the supporting operation, for the tenth, and ordered the First Army to seize the Roer dams and assume the role of "aggressive defensive . . . forthwith on the remainder of its front." The First Army diarist noted the "unsatisfactory" news of Eisenhower's order and Bradley's reluctance to mobilize support for it at a conference called at Spa the next day about "the shape of things to come."

At Spa, Bradley, Hodges, Patton and Simpson surveyed the results of Bradley's talks with Eisenhower, which included transfers of the crack 2nd and 3rd armored divisions and the 30th and 83rd infantry divisions from Hodges to Simpson, while Hodges suspended attacks in the Ardennes and took over the area held by XIX Corps. Patton criticized Eisenhower's directive "in the bitterest of possible terms," and damned the "political war" which for a third time thwarted a combined attack by the First and Third armies in midstream for Montgomery's sake, a "foolish and ignoble way for the Americans to end the war." Patton consoled Bradley by offering to lead a parade of resignations to force the issue against the British.

On the bright side, Patton and Bradley doubted that VERITABLE-GRENADE would come off on time. In the next few days they expected the withdrawing Germans to flood the Roer, forcing postponement of GRE-NADE, whereupon Montgomery was likely to go slow on VERITABLE in an effort to draw in First Army reinforcements, which Eisenhower would probably refuse. Eisenhower's orders left an opening for Bradley to extend the First Army attack in the Ardennes, provided casualties were not excessive. By now a modest improvement in the battle situation was evident. Ridgway's closing assaults along the Fifth Panzer–Fifteenth Army boundary had registered an eight-mile gain, and reports noted that German armor was regrouping, falling out of contact, and suffering a shortage of reserves in all sectors.

In short, Bradley intended to press on. With the time afforded by Montgomery's postponement, Hodges would deploy idle divisions of the First Army to support Patton over his Our River bridgeheads, while Patton advanced northeast on Prüm–Bitburg to start lines on the Kyll River for bigger attacks toward the Rhine. And with twenty-one American divisions still packed into the sector between Hürtgen and the Moselle, Bradley was confident that an American push "without a change in pace" would break the Siegfried Line and open a path to Bonn–Cologne which, despite the terrain, held out two advantages; first, pressing an ongoing offensive in the Eifel would save time it would otherwise take to organize a major Rhine offensive in Montgomery's sector; second, it would allow Hodges to by-pass the Hürtgen Forest and Roer dams and avoid yet a third battle for these objectives, which so far had defied the American Army. But even if all of this did not come to pass, gains in the next few weeks would set the stage for a large-scale extension of GRENADE southward to converge with an eventual First and Third Army offensive, which would secure Bradley's grip over all American forces north of the Moselle and a future role comparable to, if not greater than, Montgomery's.

All agreed, though not everyone agreed on every particular. Unlike Bradley, Patton questioned the apparent CCS decision to relegate the 6th Army

NETHERLANDS

Arnhem

Maas

Wesel

Münster

RUHR

Lippe

Hamm

Paderborn

Venlo

Duisburg

Krefeld

Düsseldorf

Kassel

1st Phase
OPERATION
VERITABLE

2nd Phase
OPERATION
GRENADE

Cologne

Liège

Aachen

Roer

BELGIUM

Meuse

Bonn

3rd Phase
OPERATION
LUMBERJACK

Giessen

Remagen

ARDENNES

EIFEL

Coblenz

Lahn

4th Phase
OPERATION
UNDERTONE

Bingen

Frankfurt

LUX.

Moselle

HUNSRÜCK

Mainz
Oppenheim

Neckar

Metz

Karlsruhe

FRANCE

GERMANY

Strasbourg

Rhine

THE RUNNING FUSE:
THE BATTLE OF
THE RHINELAND

Allied front as of
February 8, 1945

Assault crossings
of the Rhine by
Montgomery

Miles

0   50

0   50
Kms.

and Patton

© 1986 A. Karl / J. Kemp

Group to the defensive and to ignore the Saar. Likewise, Patton was reluctant to spare armor for Hodges that he needed for a planned XX Corps attack on his right flank toward the Moselle–Saar triangle, which would set the stage for a campaign into the Saar-Palatinate. For the moment, however, Patton, like Bradley, questioned Eisenhower's decision to form a reserve and agreed that extending the present attacks in the Ardennes would position the 12th Army Group to reach the Rhine more quickly than the 21st Army Group, which was to attack starting February 10 "if then."

But the hurry-up offensive was over—at least for a while. By the second, the Ninth Army had begun to return north to Düren for GRENADE; XVIII Corps, having broken off attacks in the Eifel, withdrew to refit for airborne operations in the Düsseldorf crossings, and V Corps pivoted northward with three divisions toward Schmidt and the Monschau forest, while Collins' as yet uncommitted VII Corps withdrew into First Army reserve behind Düren. And on the fifth Eisenhower, Bradley, Montgomery, Patton and Simpson gathered in Namur for a command conference convened to thrash out differences and firm up plans for the February offensives.

At Namur, American frustration was evident, heightened by a general improvement everywhere except at Schmidt, where V Corps, built up to five divisions, resumed the battle for control of the Monschau forest. Prisoner tallies were rising and armor was gradually falling out of contact in all sectors. German counterattacks were sluggish, and reserves were late in several threatened sectors near Schmidt, signs that the Germans were "hard put," as SHAEF intelligence put it, out of fuel, and immobile, with no improvement in sight as troops flowed east, and the overall enemy position deteriorated with the fall of Silesia and the round-the-clock bombing of rail lines and factories over the length and breadth of Germany.

Anglo-American relations were frosty. Still in command of fifteen American divisions, Montgomery was ill at ease and at his most imperious. Summersby, reflecting official SHAEF disapproval of Montgomery's January 7 press conference, asked to be seated at a distant table at the luncheon in Namur for fear she might "lose control and insult him." Few forgot that not long ago, as the senior Britisher in Europe, Montgomery had routinely exercised his prerogative to avoid similar gatherings where he might have to review his misfortunes.

By now the turnaround in roles was pronounced, with Montgomery as the conservative influence and Bradley cast in Montgomery's former role as the challenger. But the turnaround was more apparent than real. Montgomery's conservatism at Namur served the same purpose as had his earlier challenges; that of asserting British say over American forces and stemming the decline of his influence. Bradley, the foremost American ground commander in Europe, now had assigned forces almost twice the size of Montgomery's 21st Army Group less the Ninth Army, with the margin steadily expanding. Despite—or partly because of—the Ardennes, Bradley's position would thereafter be ascendant, a fact that only Bradley seemed not to recognize, and the real problem now was to define the growing role of the 12th Army Group and to reconcile it with Eisenhower's overall plans.

As before, Eisenhower at Namur weighed the merits of rival plans for resuming the offensive. Montgomery proceeded to present his well-known plan for a forty-division assault to be staged north of Düsseldorf, with the American Ninth Army in support and Hodges' First Army holding in reserve. Bradley unveiled the outlines of a First and Third Army thrust with Ninth Army support toward Cologne–Bonn (LUMBERJACK) to be followed up by Rhine crossings and envelopment of the Ruhr from the south. The two plans were consistent in that the Ruhr was the objective of both, and so Eisenhower did not have to choose one or the other and both men won concessions.

Montgomery agreed to accept reductions in Ninth Army strength from sixteen to twelve divisions and raised no objections to Patton's "probing attacks in progress," by which Montgomery appeared to concede the inevitability of 12th Army Group Rhine crossings, their extension as a southern pincer in the Ruhr campaign and, depending on events, their further extension into central Germany toward the Russian forces at Leipzig, which Eisenhower now saw as essential to insure the success of the drives toward Denmark and Austria. But this was some time off, and Montgomery, with Eisenhower's backing, was firm that 12th Army Group Rhine crossings be timed to support crossings by the 21st Army Group. Accordingly, Montgomery retained his power to "coordinate" Bradley's forces north of the Ardennes. Second, Bradley was to maintain a headquarters at Namur in order to ensure close coordination during VERITABLE-GRENADE. Third, Hodges was to "maintain readiness to employ the First Army in strength of not less than ten divisions" for exploitation of a 21st Army Group bridgehead north of the Ruhr, an open-ended provision which raised American suspicions that Eisenhower had reconverted to Montgomery's concept of a single thrust. But the provision was limited in effect. Its point was to ensure that VERITABLE-GRENADE succeeded; and that it succeed *before* Bradley's Cologne offensive, which was the crucial point. In the interval, Eisenhower intended to see to it that Patton and Devers completed the preliminaries for a Third and Seventh Army offensive into the Saar, drawing on First Army reserves for this operation as well—if needed. An offensive into the Saar was a crucial element of Eisenhower's strategy: it would clear Patton's flank and place Devers' forces in position to cross at Frankfurt and operate east of the Rhine. LUMBERJACK would take place, but only when all other preliminary operations were either accomplished or ready to start, which would ensure that the other preliminary operations occurred.

What emerged at Namur was, in sum, a plan of action for clearing the Rhine north of the Moselle. This was to proceed as a series of blunt concentric attacks from north to south, like a "running fuse," as Smith later put it, to push the dwindling German armored reserve from sector to sector until somewhere German reserves would arrive too late. Step one would be the seizure of the Roer dams by the First Army. Step two would be VERITA-BLE, beginning February 8, Crerar's massive attack from the Waal bridge-head toward Venlo consisting of XXX Corps and II Canadian Corps. Step three, GRENADE, would commence February 10. Three U.S. corps of the Ninth Army, assisted by Collins' VII Corps, would attack northwest from Düren to converge with the First Canadian Army and clear out German resistance north of the Erft River. Meanwhile, Patton would advance "with existing resources," which would position his forces to strike northeast or southeast toward Trier, a staging area for an invasion of the Saar in conjunc-tion with Devers, whose mission was not discussed. *After* steps one, two and three, Bradley's army group would "assume the offensive [LUMBERJACK] in the Eifel and, with the means then available . . . close the Rhine in his zone."

At Namur, Bradley resisted the restrictions imposed on the First Army, but approved. VERITABLE-GRENADE was three days off. That it would occur on time seemed doubtful, and so his position was "wait and see." Likewise, the group sidestepped the divisive problem of long-range objectives, and so the Namur talks did not resolve a basic question: How far would Bradley press his bid to restore his command and 12th Army Group prestige? Eisenhower had long made it a practice to avoid discussing long-range problems except when necessary, and it was plain that such problems could not be worked out by reasonable discussion for the moment. Apparently Bradley was in a position where he could not concede anything without conceding too much too soon, and Eisenhower could not concede much.

Eisenhower accompanied Bradley to Spa the night of the fifth for an overnight visit with Hodges. The trip was partly social. Confident that he and Bradley would work things out eventually, Eisenhower wanted Bradley to know that he completely approved of Bradley's efforts to maintain the effectiveness of the 12th Army Group, and to devise ways to employ it to the maximum. A standoff had developed, but the problem was not insoluble and Eisenhower was anxious to keep it from becoming so.

What was enough to restore the prestige and effectiveness of Bradley's command? So far, repulsing the German attack and expelling the Germans from the Ardennes had not been enough. Bradley had insisted on a prompt rebound offensive into the Cologne plain and now resisted the idea that LUMBERJACK should be secondary to any operation. Bradley intended to race Montgomery over the Rhine, thence beyond the Rhine into Germany. What then? To an extent, the competition between army groups was desir-able, but the Allies were on the German doorstep and sooner or later the competition would have to cease.

That night over dinner, Eisenhower assured Bradley that he had talked to Montgomery sternly about any repeat performance of his press conference on January 7. He had Montgomery's assurance that "nothing of the sort would happen again." Later, over a "desultory" game of bridge, Eisenhower raised a report he had received about the installation of a new 12th Army Group press facility at Namur. He cautioned Bradley about allowing 12th Army Group dispatches to undercut SHAEF control of information, though he assumed that this was "not what Bradley had in mind." Bradley assured Eisenhower that he was "anxious only to better report the war with a summary briefing each day at TAC,"* whereupon Eisenhower approved.

In the next few days, more concessions followed. From Namur, Eisenhower and Bradley continued to Third Army Headquarters at Bastogne to discuss Patton's ongoing Bitburg offensive and his plans to exploit a West Wall breakthrough with "2 possibly 3" armored divisions. They then proceeded to First Army Headquarters at Spa, thence on to V Corps Headquarters at Eupen to monitor the resuming five-division V Corps assault toward Schmidt.

LUMBERJACK took shape on the rainy, cloudy afternoon of February 6 at Eupen in a meeting between Eisenhower, Bradley, Simpson and Hodges. With his American colleagues, Bradley felt freer to press his position. He told Eisenhower that he was braced for a postponement of VERITABLE and foresaw a standstill on Montgomery's front lasting weeks, which would ground two American armies as things stood. Bradley did not want to stand idle, and to support his case for an early LUMBERJACK he could point to steady progress in the Third Army sector. By the sixth, VIII Corps had penetrated the West Wall near Prüm on an eleven-mile front north of XII Corps, which had gained several bridgeheads on the Our River, positioning Patton to drive northeast through the Ahr–Moselle corridor toward the Rhine at Andernach-Coblenz.

Eisenhower was not sure when LUMBERJACK would occur, but he was clear on one point; "in no circumstances" would Montgomery be given American forces for VERITABLE. He further assured Bradley that Collins' VII Corps, now operating on Simpson's right, would stay under Hodges. As for Patton, the Bitburg offensive involved shifting Third Army boundaries northeast. Eisenhower approved but cautioned that Patton's attacks were to be "strong enough to keep the enemy from shifting his strength to the Roer, but not so strong as to arouse the objections of Montgomery." Accordingly, he imposed a February 10 deadline on Patton, to be reviewed in the event GRENADE was postponed, as Bradley expected. Whether Bradley won Eisenhower's assurance that he would regain command of the Ninth Army after Montgomery's Rhine crossings is unknown, but after-

*Tactical Headquarters.

ward the group continued on to Ninth Army Headquarters at Maastricht for talks with Simpson, a gesture signifying Bradley's ongoing interest in Ninth Army affairs and the cohesion of the American command.

But the concessions were off the record. Indeed, Eisenhower would not approve the First Army portion of LUMBERJACK until March 3, one week after LUMBERJACK had started, and only then orally and upon a firm understanding that Patton, after seizing Trier, would swing major forces southeast over the Moselle. Not until March 13, six days after Bradley's seizure of a Rhine bridgehead at Remagen, would Eisenhower approve LUMBERJACK in writing. Bradley would hail Eisenhower's action as "one of the most significant orders of the war," a major shift in plan ordered without approval of the Combined Chiefs, though the record does not bear him out.

At each stage, Eisenhower meticulously operated within the confines of his CCS directive as he interpreted it. Significantly, his written approval of LUMBERJACK would come after an important meeting with Brooke and Churchill at which Eisenhower cleared LUMBERJACK with the British after assuring them that Bradley's offensive would be secondary to Montgomery's Rhine crossings and would not develop into a rival American offensive for Berlin. In hindsight, the return of the Ninth Army to Bradley's command was probably inevitable after the Düsseldorf crossings. The American Ninth Army properly belonged to the 12th Army Group, which even Montgomery probably understood. Moreover, with American, British and French forces across the Rhine, coherent German resistance was unlikely, and so Eisenhower's task would be to manage a chaotic and fluid situation. At that point he would want all American forces to be under the direct supervision of an American army group commander in order to eliminate confusion in the maneuvers necessary to expedite junction with Red Army forces at Leipzig, and to organize the large-scale maneuvers necessary to support Montgomery's 21st Army Group toward Denmark and Devers' 6th Army Group toward Austria. In the meantime, however, the Ninth Army was needed to support VERITABLE, which had to succeed quickly so that Eisenhower could turn his attention to the Saar and gain the secure flank and the active 6th Army Group front he needed to be sure he had flexibility in the coming invasion of Germany.

Eisenhower's need for flexibility was growing each day. By the first week of February it was obvious that only simultaneous Allied and Soviet offensives into Germany proper would avoid the military and diplomatic uncertainties looming in the next few months. Instead, all signs confirmed that the Allies would be resuming the offensive just as the Russians halted theirs. According to the First Army diary, a story circulated at Namur that Eisenhower was offering 3 to 1 that the "Russians would be in Berlin by the 31st of March," but this was a wish, not a prediction. In view of the earlier debates over Berlin, Eisenhower must have felt that nothing would be more divisive than further debate over Berlin and nothing less congenial than a CCS order to mobilize a Berlin offensive, which would probably finish the chances of Allied-Soviet cooperation. The easiest way out was not to have to face the problem at all—to have the Russians solve the problem by pressing on. But this was not to be, and by the sixth, Soviet communiqués confirmed that the tempo of Russian operations was lessening because of the weather, overstretched supply lines, and rearguard German resistance. Soviet prisoner claims were low, a sign that many by-passed units were holding out or reaching German lines. Soon Rokossovsky's northern thrust would veer north toward the Baltic to isolate pockets at Danzig and Pomerania, bearing out Tedder's report that the Russian objective was the Oder, and that the Soviets intended to devote several months to the task of regrouping and liquidating pockets before the dramatic finale at Berlin.

And so problems remained, though accounts of Eisenhower's early-February trip convey a feeling that the worst was over. Malta had come and gone. The Yalta meetings were continuing, but the Allies had weathered the German counteroffensive and Eisenhower's command was still intact. Sergeant Mickey McKeogh, who accompanied Eisenhower, recalled that his boss seemed less edgy than usual. The unhurried tour turned into a journey reminiscent of the trips through St.-Lô and Mortain in August, with time out for subdued inspection trips along the front lines.

Battle news was mixed. The American 78th Division waged a yard-by-yard struggle for Schmidt, forcing Hodges to deploy the 5th Armored, 9th Infantry and elements of Ridgway's XVIII Airborne Corps. At Maastricht, Eisenhower received the welcome news that the French I Corps and Milburn's XXI Corps had linked up, splitting the Colmar pocket. There he attended a conference on the quartering of German civilians in occupied zones, fraternization policy, currency problems, the denazification program, and the Messerschmitt-262 jet fighter, a symbol, in his opinion, of the misappropriated German war effort. In the years ahead Eisenhower would occasionally reflect back on the folly of the German V-weapon program, which had been a prestige weapon pushed at the expense of jet aircraft production. That week V-weapon attacks on Antwerp reached a peak, and yet millions of tons of supplies moved through the port practically without a hitch. Many, including Spaatz, felt that the Germans might have been in a position to fight the war to a stalemate as late as January had the ME-262 jet been in full production. But the ME-262 was not in full production, and so Germany's defeat was a matter of time.

Everywhere the group observed the wreckage exposed by the melting snow and the receding German tide. Houffalize, Bastogne and St.-Vith, sleepy villages before the war, were ghost towns littered with tanks, armored cars and firearms. The columns of sullen German prisoners trudging along the road attested to the stunning impact of the check in the

Ardennes Forest and the news from Poland, which dispelled German illusions of averting invasion.

The panorama made a deep impression on McKeogh, who described the trip in a short book published soon after the war. For McKeogh, the curtain on the western front had been lifted only occasionally when he accompanied the General on several trips to the field. From time to time, air raids had disrupted the routine at the St. Georges, the Villa dar el Ouad, the Dorchester and Telegraph Cottage, and the rumors of German assassination teams at Christmas had meant excitement at the Trianon. But like the thousands of arriving GIs that February, McKeogh was seeing the war in its most elemental terms that week: the desolate towns and villages in the raw February cold, abandoned vehicles, the shattered buildings and debris, the columns of prisoners crisscrossing the silent American columns moving up. The sights impressed him with "the destructiveness of war" and its remoteness from the kind of life he expected to resume back in the States that summer.

But much more destruction was in store. Postwar interrogations would suggest that the German retreat in the Ardennes marked the effective end of Hitler's real power and the strategy of prevailing everywhere over all enemies. By February, Hitler ruled Germany mostly in name at the sufferance of a population fearful of anarchy, slave revolt and the army, which had indirectly assumed supreme power. But despite the army's influence, a German "collapse" as part of a deal with the Allies was not imminent. Unlike the situation in July 1944, the Russians were on the German frontier, and so military and diplomatic strategies aimed at averting Russian invasion and partition were now pointless. Protecting Germans from capture by the Russians was the problem now, and this required time. Hence, the German army, much to Allied consternation, was determined to draw out the war for several more months, time enough to herd millions of refugees and soldiers into the western zones of occupation in what would be the last great migration of the war. In the interval, scenes like those at Houffalize and Bastogne would proliferate across the map of Europe until the Germans and Russians could tolerate the war no longer.

Meanwhile, Allied policy was to maintain maximum pressure. That week Eighth Air Force fighter-bombers struck Berlin on two successive nights in raids that neutral observers said were "like the end of the world." Two thousand bombers destroyed most of the surviving landmarks and heightened the chaos of refugees from the east choking the city. Essential services broke down, and at night, Nazi police systems temporarily collapsed, leaving the city in the control of gangs roaming the streets. By day, life in the German capital seemed orderly enough amid constant Nazi radio and newspaper exhortations playing on fears of invasion and slave uprisings by the estimated seven million Russian, Polish and French laborers working in Germany.

To the world at large, news of the Russian victories overshadowed everything. In world capitals, Russian successes, compared with the German triumphs of 1940, raised the question "How do they do it?" Observers noted that what made the Russian success even more remarkable was the fact that the Germans had expected the attack in Poland, and for weeks had published details of Russian concentrations and accurate forecasts of where the blows would fall. And yet within seventy-two hours the Russians had demolished German defenses on a 200-mile front and encircled Warsaw and Lodz, and in another seventy-two hours had advanced over 100 miles along the road to Berlin.

The press groped for explanations. American Lend-Lease had equipped the Red Army with trucks and clothing. The Allied strategic bombing campaign that winter was a direct factor in the Russian successes, and so was the German decision to wage a winter offensive in Belgium, abetted by the six-month Red Army pause on the Vistula. But the fact remained that the Red Army, written off in 1941 and 1942, had survived and gathered strength. Contradicting those who as late as the fall of 1944 had predicted that the Russians would be too exhausted to overcome determined resistance beyond the prewar frontier, an estimated 450 divisions advanced three hundred miles through western Poland, Bulgaria, western Rumania, Budapest and northern Yugoslavia, spreading destruction and terror on a vast front. The spectacle aroused misgivings about Soviet domination of Eastern Europe and even muffled pity for the Germans. But little could be done, and fatalism set in as word emerged of the German death camps uncovered by the Russians at Auschwitz and elsewhere, evidence of German crimes beyond imagination. The Red Army was bent on avenging twenty million Russian lives, and many quietly concluded that what the Russians did now was up to them. As Lincoln had said eighty years before: "Woe unto the world because of offenses, for it must needs be that offences come, but woe to that man by whom the offence cometh."

In February 1945 the American build-up was reaching peak strength with the arrival of the last of the sixty-one divisions mobilized for Europe. Soldiers arriving that month came too late to experience major fighting, but not too late to be indelibly impressed by the war and Europe's plight that winter. More than one and a half million Americans were destined to enter Germany, and, like McKeogh, to return home with stories. As would Second Lieutenant John S. D. Eisenhower, among the arrivals aboard H.M.S. *Queen Mary* before dawn on the morning of February 3 after an eleven-day transatlantic voyage with the 71st U.S. Army Division.

John Eisenhower's arrival in Europe was a slight letdown. In his months at Fort Benning, Lieutenant Eisenhower had readily adapted to command of his platoon. Like his contemporaries, he had experienced the first flush of pride in his newfound ability to lead men and the anticipation of being tested in combat. Then, shortly before he was shipped out, War Department officials informed him of his father's request that he leave the 71st Division for an unspecified headquarters assignment owing to the unacceptable risk of capture, a disappointment which painfully singled him out from his comrades, but which probably did not come as a real surprise.

John may have been braced for as much when Brigadier General Willard Wyman, an old family friend, returned from France in October to assume command of the 71st. Keeping his distance, John had gone about his business in training his platoon in small-unit tactics, mine warfare, hygiene, enemy habits and discipline. Wyman, meanwhile, had kept his distance too, all the while informing Eisenhower of their chance contacts and John's progress, which Wyman called "excellent." Then came the word from the War Department, and on the long transatlantic voyage aboard the *Queen Mary,* John said his good-byes.

Years later John would describe his predawn tug ride to Le Havre, which he had seen once before as a seven-year-old in 1929 on the return trip to America with his parents after their year in Paris. He remembered the year 1929 well, especially the Sunday outings with his father to tour St.-Mihiel, the Argonne and other battle sites of the Great War, places he looked forward to revisiting. As he stood at the railing General Wyman approached him. "John," he asked, "do you think your men are ready for long marches?"

"We can do anything we have to, sir," John replied, standing at attention.

"Twenty-five miles a day?"

"We have done it before, sir."

As he gazed out at the harbor, Wyman, a veteran of Normandy, told John that in his personal opinion the Germans were finished, and that after a brief campaign west of the Rhine he expected the war to turn into a series of swift marches through Germany.

"John," Wyman continued, "I know you are leaving. I have been proud to have you as a platoon leader in this division and would like to keep you. However, there are more important things in this war than your career and I want you to know there is not one person in this division who resents your going."

Thus began an odyssey, later described in a memoir, through battle zones and command posts, the French towns and villages emerging from the twilight of occupation, and through the fabled German towns and villages of his ancestors now entering the twilight. From Le Havre, John made his own way to Versailles, for a reunion with his father, where he noted the contrast to the electric atmosphere surrounding London and Portsmouth in the weeks after D-Day. Paris was war-weary and subdued, braced for left-wing violence and the dreary trials of Vichy officials.

Versailles was all business. The SHAEF staff seemed more professional and serious than the one John had left behind in Portsmouth. John had the impression that his father had grown in confidence after months of crushing responsibility, unalleviated by the ongoing German retreat. By February 1945 it was a truism that solving problems simply raised new problems, and much had happened since John's earlier visit just before the climactic phases of the Normandy battle. Since then, Eisenhower had directed the Allied liberation of France, the autumn battles along the German frontier, and the Ardennes battle, which had ended as the largest campaign in American history. Now Eisenhower was involved in an interminable wait, this time for news of VERITABLE-GRENADE, Colmar and Yalta.

Characteristically, Eisenhower was anxious to leave Paris. During John's visit he busily expedited the reopening of the forward headquarters at Reims that he had briefly occupied in November before the Ardennes battle. Eisenhower had chosen the drab red-brick schoolhouse along a noisy main First Army convoy route in the cathedral city as the scene for the enactment of the closing rituals in Europe, mainly for its proximity to the troops at the front so that he could devote as much time as possible to visits and conferences. Meanwhile, confined at Versailles, Eisenhower spent his hours at the office tending to routine business.

There were problems with the French, who had requested equipment to refit six divisions, one of De Gaulle's many eleventh-hour demands pressed in the wake of his exclusion from Yalta, where the Americans, British and Russians had met and presumed to decide questions of vital interest to France, including the terms of a French zone and an EAC seat. For all his sympathy with De Gaulle's attitude, Eisenhower could not overlook the slow progress at Colmar, and his relationship with De Gaulle suffered accordingly. But the Strasbourg affair had built up the 6th Army Group and thrust De Gaulle and a French occupation zone into the scales as a balancing factor in military planning, and so Eisenhower had to make do.

Complicating relations with the French, Comm-Z continued to defy Eisenhower's repeated edicts to keep a low profile in Paris. Comm-Z was now on everyone's blacklist. In her office diary, Summersby noted how Eisenhower's newly appointed manpower deputy, General Benjamin Lear, fenced with Major Lee over quotas for Lear's infantry-retraining centers set up in January. Lear, granted sweeping authority by Eisenhower to ferret out waste and duplication in the support and combat establishments, visited the Trianon several times to talk over the manpower problem and expedients to fill the quotas.

Lear had rounded up 23,000 recruits for air and service units, but the infantry was short 82,000 replacements. Estimates called for 90,000 replacements per month through June, or double what the War Department could provide. Efforts to fill out combat formations had fallen short; they included retraining, offers of pardon for court-martial offenders volunteering for the front, and cutbacks in officer training. Eisenhower, who had long spoken of an ever increasing Allied effort climaxing on the day of the German surrender, detected a morale problem.

In mid-February, Eisenhower authored several "top priority" reports on personnel problems, one for Lieutenant General Thomas Handy at the War Department and one for Marshall's background use in dealings with Congress in the debate over Selective Service quotas. In one, commenting on his firsthand observations at Schmidt, he noted that morale in recent weeks seemed to improve markedly the closer one got to the front. There, relations between officers and enlisted men in the combat zones seemed "satisfactory." He had taken "individual soldiers off by themselves seeking to uncover gripes and growls," and had heard very few. But morale in the rear areas was not as high, which he attributed to the War Department system of replacement depots, which instead of rotating units rotated individual soldiers through various units, and to procedures for handling "limited assignment" personnel and battle-fatigue cases. "The abrupt change from conditions troops have known in the States to the near combat situation upon arrival here accentuates their mental anxieties and possibly reduces their efficiency as soldiers," he observed. "The most important of these anxieties are . . . the soldier's lack of confidence in himself, his training, his weapons, physical condition and his natural fear of combat," the feeling no one in the long pipelines from home to the front was interested in him or his welfare, the feeling of being lost owing to the policy of recycling troops through various regiments from replacement pools and "the sense of being shunted around." Though it was too late to overhaul the replacement depot system, Eisenhower could think of stopgap measures that might help. In particular, he urged that the War Department start assigning trained education and information officers to serve aboard transport ships and conduct intensive indoctrination programs on the transatlantic voyage. In his opinion, a conspicuous problem was the limited attention officers in the European theater were paying to explaining basic war aims and Allied philosophy at the very time soldiers needed it most.

In Butcher's words, Eisenhower's "official and personal concern for morale" grew as February moved along, a concern that would keep growing. As U.S. Army Chief of Staff after the war, Eisenhower would push several Army studies on the subject. Later, as president of Columbia University, he would establish a manpower study project on all aspects of the American soldier in World War II, with emphasis on the problem of motivation and morale. Years later in retirement, Eisenhower would write on the subject. In his last book, *At Ease,* he would reflect back on his years of experience with the problem of morale in a modern army, and, in an appendix, reprint portions of a memorandum he had written to President Manuel Quezon in the thirties as the Philippines organized for independence, which he offered as his distilled wisdom on the subject.

In prefacing his memo, Eisenhower recalled Von Steuben's dictum from

Revolutionary War days that "the American soldier must know the reason why he must do thus and so." He noted that the truism applied with even greater force in the modern mass-conscript Army of the twentieth century, in which the individual soldier faced unprecedented problems of adjusting to new places and equipment, and particularly in the American Army, which served abroad in battles against enemies that did not directly menace American security. In excerpts from his earlier memo, Eisenhower listed the "constants" of morale in all armies in all times—loyalty, patriotism, discipline, unity and determination, qualities that often withstood disaster, but never withstood favoritism, neglect and injustice. Then Major Eisenhower had emphasized the duty of leadership in a modern Army to inculcate self-respect, and defended harsh methods at times, methods for which he would later be criticized in the Slovik case and the peremptory demotions of several division commanders for failure in combat in the Ardennes battle. "Coddling an Army does not promote efficiency," he had written—it merely condoned and encouraged inefficiency. The Army should be taught to respect itself and "to render a quality of service that will command respect throughout the nation so that the Army uniform would come to be seen as a badge of loyalty, duty and of efficiency."

During John's visit, father and son caught up on a few family matters untended to in the nine months since they had seen each other. They discussed John's assignment to a newly formed signal information and monitoring unit (SIAM) attached to Bradley's 12th Army Group Headquarters. John looked forward to several weeks of training in Bournemouth, England, then to an assignment with the 12th Army Group that would take him deep into central Germany, exposing him to occasional dangers and the unforgettable spectacle of Nazi Germany in twilight.

On the bright side, John learned that Butcher had rejoined the household at Versailles. Butcher still lived in the Raphael Hotel in downtown Paris, but with Eisenhower's entrenchment at the nearby Trianon Palace, he had become a regular visitor at mealtime to inject his Iowan calm and humor into the somber late-winter atmosphere.

The war raged on. At 10 A.M. on February 8, following the heaviest Allied artillery bombardment of the war, four assault divisions of Horrocks' XXX Corps attacked toward Cleve in the constricted neck between the Maas and the Rhine, joined on the left by Simonds' Canadian II Corps, which attacked toward Emmerich. Both attacks made slow progress. In the XXX Corps sector the German First Parachute Army took skillful advantage of dikes and improvised defense nets around Cleve. Heavy rains curtailed air support, and within two hours of the follow-on Canadian assault, the Germans demolished the sluice gates of the Spoy Canal, flooding the Cleve–Nijmegen highway. By the ninth, German reinforcements, including the 116th Panzer and Panzer Lehr, poured into the area from the Roer sector, and by dusk, XXX Corps, fighting up two roads, reached the northern suburbs of Cleve, opening a thirty-six-hour house-to-house battle.

Meanwhile, Huebner's V Corps, built up to five divisions, captured the town of Schmidt, and by the tenth, enemy resistance west of the Roer had ceased. Before Americans could capture the Schmidt dams, however, the retreating Germans, as expected, managed to destroy the power machinery and discharge valves of the Schmidt dams, letting off a steady flow of water. The river rose five feet, flooding the Roer basin. With high-water conditions expected to last two weeks, GRENADE was off, though Eisenhower decided to review the situation day to day in order to avoid the complications attending formal postponement.

With the neighboring American Ninth Army assault "on hold," Horrocks faced the brunt of enemy armor. As Bradley predicted at Eupen, Montgomery peppered Eisenhower with requests for Ninth and First Army reinforcements. As promised, Eisenhower declined and nudged Montgomery to draw on Dempsey's fourteen divisions refitting between Grave and Roermond, all the while keeping close watch on the First Army. On the tenth, as Patton's deadline expired, Eisenhower phoned Bradley and instructed him to transfer a corps headquarters from Patton to Hodges and to reinforce Collins' VII Corps with the 9th Armored Division. That day Patton suspended the Bitburg offensive, vowing in his diary to "be the first on the Rhine yet."

Meanwhile, word reached the Trianon that day that the Colmar battle had ended, "much to everyone's relief," as Summersby put it. But the relief was short-lived. The day-to-day postponements of GRENADE were frustrating for all, since no major operation could commence elsewhere until VERITABLE-GRENADE had succeeded, and every day spent waiting for that operation was another day spent in wondering whether anything would work. Summersby's diary chronicled the reports of fierce house-to-house struggle at Cleve, the Roer floods, De Gaulle's sudden decision to withdraw three of Leclerc's divisions for refitting after Colmar, the denunciation of Yalta by the London Polish Committee, the reports of starvation in neighboring Nazi-occupied west Holland, the reports of a political crisis in Belgium and General Bull's return from Yalta on February 11 with the startling news that Churchill, Roosevelt, Marshall and Brooke had agreed on Alexander's appointment, effective in six weeks.

Eisenhower spent several hours in conference with Bull on the Alexander matter. According to Bull, Churchill had agreed to transfer five Empire divisions from Italy to Holland in exchange for the Alexander-Tedder switch, and put it off six weeks to avoid the appearance of a connection with the Ardennes. Marshall had taken a "dim view" of the Alexander decision, and had warned Roosevelt that the British press would try "to put Alexander over as Eisenhower's Ground Commander," but he too had approved.

The CCS had taken no formal action yet, and so Bull's account raised questions. When did the CCS intend to proceed? Who had favored it? Was this decision final? Eisenhower found it hard to believe that the Prime Minister wanted to transfer five Empire divisions from Italy to Holland, and Roosevelt's support was baffling in view of Hopkins' visit in late January to convey the President's willingness to abide by Eisenhower's wishes that he not attend the Malta conference. This "decision," which Eisenhower did not think was final, was a sign of many things: of the fact that military talks with the Russians had not gone well; of the pressures on both Allied governments to reassess Allied-Soviet relations; of exhaustion. The hopeful aspect was that "six weeks" left an opening and suggested that the appointment was in effect a deadline for completing 21st Army Group preparations north of Düsseldorf. This interpretation was reinforced by the indirect method of notifying Eisenhower, but time would tell.

At Smith's insistence, Eisenhower returned to the Weiller compound to take the afternoon off. In a letter home, Eisenhower hinted at trouble. He chattily described John's visit and John's new assignment with the 12th Army Group. But he was

> more than tired of mud, rain, fog and generally bad weather. But maybe we'll have an early spring. The Russians are still making good progress after their earlier spectacular successes. Lord knows they can't go too fast and too well for me. More power to them. . . .
> So far as I can make out John thinks that both the Atlanta and New York girls are fine—but I think the N.Y. one really intrigues him. He doesn't say a lot about either.
> He's sleeping this morning, but told me he was hoping to write a bunch of letters soon. I suppose you'll get something from him soon.
>
> Always yours,
> Ike

The Alexander news spurred a brief round of late-winter negotiations, which provide yet another interesting glimpse of the Allied high command under stress. The situation was not unusual in that Eisenhower's struggle to strengthen and retain his authority had been unceasing since November 1943. Yet the policy implications were drastic, and this compelled Eisenhower, pending formal notification of the appointment and a CCS directive spelling out Alexander's responsibilities, to find ways of discouraging the appointment. Did the CCS desire the change? Eisenhower could not be sure, but what he did conclude was that Marshall was behind the proposal, reasoning that no such idea stood a chance of being accepted without the Chief of Staff's approval.

In personal terms, this was a disappointment. American Army officers of every stripe in February 1945 yearned for Marshall's approval, and

Eisenhower was no exception. Since Malta, he had managed to persuade himself that he had won Marshall's confidence and support for his plans. To suspect otherwise naturally led Eisenhower to question himself, then necessarily to question CCS—and Marshall's—equivocation about a straightforward military approach best calculated to defeat Germany in coordination with the Russians.

The plot thickened on the twelfth. A brief telegram arrived from Roosevelt inviting Eisenhower to join the presidential party docked in Alexandria, Egypt, "if you have anything you wish to see me about and the military situation permits." That morning Eisenhower, Bull and Smith huddled in a War Room to discuss the telegram, which, though it contained ambiguities, seemed timed to suggest that the President had decided to break the news about Alexander personally to Eisenhower.

Should Eisenhower go to Alexandria? On the one hand, a presidential invitation was, by custom, a command. On the other hand, Eisenhower was technically not Roosevelt's subordinate on CCS matters, and the President appeared to leave an "out" by phrasing his invitation so that Eisenhower could refuse it. Perhaps the President, lukewarm about the appointment, was probing Eisenhower's willingness to carry on. If so, failure to accept the President's "out" might convey that Eisenhower was tired, reconciled to the idea of Alexander, or reluctant to proceed in the weeks ahead without presidential guidance. Finally, deciding that a voluntary appearance in Alexandria would be fatal, Eisenhower approved a three-sentence reply in which he gratefully declined the President's offer, citing his need to consult his commanders about "some changes . . . that no one except myself can authorize." Forty-eight hours later, accompanied by John, Eisenhower was on his way to Namur and Hasselt for private talks with Bradley and Montgomery to present them with the news of Alexander's appointment, and to gauge their willingness to resist a move that would mean wholesale revisions of strategy and the demise of their efforts to recover from the Ardennes.

Years later, in describing his overnight visit at Namur, Bradley recalled that he had never seen Eisenhower so shaken or determined. He recalled Eisenhower as saying he found it hard to "understand Marshall's about-face at Yalta, and Marshall's failure to notify him of his reasons for his change of views." Convinced that the appointment meant trouble, Eisenhower found a ready listener in Bradley, who agreed that Alexander's appointment, in the circumstances, would reflect badly on the American command and be a confession of error in the Ardennes.

But a barrier remained between Eisenhower and Bradley. Eisenhower was still unable to say when LUMBERJACK could proceed, and was determined that Third Army–6th Army Group preliminaries in the Saar precede or coincide with 12th Army Group Rhine crossings. In turn, Bradley opposed more American help for VERITABLE-GRENADE and, apparently, resisted the idea of sparing elements of the Third Army for a campaign in the Saar–Palatinate. Significantly, while Eisenhower and Bradley mulled over the Alexander news in Namur, Patton was in Paris for a talk with Smith, which appears to have been a rare instance in which Eisenhower by-passed Bradley and dealt indirectly with Patton on a major strategy question.

On the fourteenth Patton, "on leave" in Paris, visited the Trianon to present plans he had worked up, "tenable on the assumption the Germans have not the power to hit back" for a Third Army–6th Army Group offensive to clear the Saar–Palatinate. Smith was receptive and gave Patton a rundown on the theater. Smith disclosed that SHAEF had set a 35-division limit on Montgomery's offensive at the Ruhr, which left 48 divisions by Smith's count which Eisenhower was anxious to deploy over the Rhine in the right sectors at the right time. Since the view at SHAEF was that it would be a waste to confine the Third Army and 6th Army Group to defensive tasks, Smith asked Patton if he was prepared to assume the offensive with XX Corps on his right flank toward Trier, gateway to the Saar, and if so, how many divisions would he need?

"I can make the attack with five," Patton replied.

Smith: "I think you should have twelve."

Smith told Patton that the 10th Armored was available to reinforce General Walton Walker's XX Corps "nibbling" attacks into the Saar–Moselle triangle, provided Walker's attacks gained a "clear breakthrough."

From Namur, Eisenhower proceeded on to Hasselt and talks with Montgomery, which were successful despite Montgomery's recent indiscretions and lack of affability, according to Major Hansen, an observer. Montgomery's inevitable cooperation on the Alexander matter came grudgingly.

At Hasselt, Eisenhower mixed concessions with warnings. In agreeing to reinforce GRENADE with two more American divisions, he emphasized the importance of keeping VERITABLE on the move to pin down German armor and to ease Simpson's Roer crossings. Second, he reminded Montgomery that First Army reinforcements for VERITABLE would not be possible in view of Dempsey's fourteen idle divisions in Holland. Third, in approving PLUNDER—Montgomery's plan for Rhine crossings north of Düsseldorf—Eisenhower set late March and urged him to be ready on time, alluding to JCS "bullying" over "being too British," epitomized by Marshall's sudden and unexplained approval of the Alexander-Tedder switch "to relieve me of my preoccupation with the land battle." Eisenhower assured Montgomery that, as always, he was opposed to an overall ground command as a matter of sound organization, and was worried that the shift would trigger a trial in the press over military policy, undoing their efforts to heal inter-Allied wounds since January.

Montgomery shared Eisenhower's concern over a "trial in the press" on military policy. In his words, American criticism would spark British countercriticism and "unnecessary strife," which the Allies could ill afford. As for organization, Montgomery understood Eisenhower to say that he (Eisenhower) "wished to handle the land battle and to divide the theater into two fronts with resources and geographical objectives allocated in line with his [Montgomery's] main effort," which he considered "satisfactory."

The meeting broke up and afterward Montgomery sent Brooke a full report in which he pronounced himself "delighted" to report that Eisenhower had "agreed with everything I was doing," that Eisenhower had decided to transfer two American infantry divisions to the U.S. Ninth Army for GRENADE, and had reaffirmed his intention to "concentrate all resources, Ground and Air, on doing one thing at a time," beginning with "21st Army Group to line up on the Rhine from Düsseldorf northwards and to get bridgeheads firmly established across the river." Eisenhower had spoken of his *intention* to leave the U.S. Ninth Army of twelve divisions in 21st Army Group for the rest of the war, which in Montgomery's mind made the whole idea of a land commander and switching of Tedder and Alexander unnecessary. "All of this is very good," he wrote, "and I do believe that we are at last all well set with a fair wind to help us into harbor. We have had a few storms, but the sky is now clear. . . ."

Eisenhower's poll of his commanders continued at Versailles on the fifteenth, where he received Devers for a conference on the French situation and to arrange the transfer of the U.S. 28th Division back to SHAEF reserve for GRENADE. The 6th Army Group, which had assumed new importance, faced problems. At the moment, Devers' forces, dispersed between Mulhouse and Thionville, still battled a small German pocket north of Strasbourg that had to be eliminated quickly in view of De Gaulle's abrupt recall of three French divisions.

Eisenhower and Devers discussed the outlines of UNDERTONE, a 6th Army Group plan to destroy the German Army Group G in the Saar–Palatinate which Eisenhower intended to start within four weeks as the 12th and 21st army groups arrived at the Rhine. General Patch's Seventh Army, built up to fourteen divisions, would attack through the West Wall defenses between Saarbrücken and Haguenau to engage the Germans and push to the base of the Saar–Palatinate triangle. This would coincide with the maneuver Smith and Patton had discussed the day before—a surprise Third Army attack east from Trier, then southeastward across the Moselle toward Mainz behind the German Army Group G facing Patch. UNDERTONE would eliminate a significant German force and position Patton and the 6th Army Group in the vicinity of a number of ideal Rhine crossing sites. But the key element would be Patch's ability to mobilize fourteen divisions effectively, and this would depend in part on the ability of the French First Army to garrison Alsace with reduced forces, which underscored the need to clear the Strasbourg pocket rapidly.

Finally, Eisenhower met with Tedder that afternoon, a principal in the debate who had not been informed about Alexander until late January. For months Tedder had borne the brunt of several inter-Allied controversies, and Eisenhower was reluctant to act before he was sure Tedder would not like to cap his war service by accepting the promotion to Supreme Command in the Mediterranean. At length Eisenhower explained to Tedder how the Alexander situation had developed in January, and why he himself had kept an open mind about the appointment. The Prime Minister seemed set on the idea, and the British had the unquestioned right to assign whomever they pleased as Eisenhower's deputy. What were Tedder's wishes?

According to Summersby, Tedder seemed unsure at first that Eisenhower wanted him to stay in Paris. When convinced, Tedder helped Eisenhower draft a message to Brooke, sent on the sixteenth with a copy to Marshall, in which Eisenhower, having polled his command, informed Brooke—and Marshall indirectly—that he knew of the Alexander proposal, that he opposed it, and that he would feel duty-bound to deploy all assets at his disposal, including public pressure, to minimize it unless the CCS came up with a charter spelling out Alexander's responsibilities.

In his message to Brooke, Eisenhower enumerated the major points as he saw them. First, Alexander was welcome at SHAEF, but if Tedder left, Eisenhower would need an Air officer at SHAEF—namely, Spaatz. Second, he flatly opposed the establishment of a separate ground headquarters. Third, he was concerned that nothing undermine American-British relations. Recalling the "lasting resentment" generated by Montgomery's January 7 press conference, Eisenhower was concerned that the press would interpret Alexander's appointment as a British victory over the Americans —thus, he would "find it immediately necessary to make a formal announcement setting forth the facts": that as deputy, Alexander would assume responsibility for items delegated to the senior British officer in his headquarters, including (a) liberated manpower, (b) civilian food relief and (c) civilian relations generally with emphasis on the problems of economic recovery in the liberated zones. Eisenhower added that in keeping with Alexander's stature and experience, he would "consult" his new deputy on ground operations, though his new deputy would not function as a land commander unless designated as one by the CCS. "I do not mean to protest arrangements my superiors might find necessary," he closed, "but one of my principal jobs is to see that nothing occurs that may tend to create misunderstandings within my own command or to mar the generally splendid British-American relationships that we try to promote. . . ."

BOCS reaction is unknown, but in the next week no formal British motion developed in the CCS. Roosevelt returned to Washington, and six days later, on the twenty-second, Churchill would reply on Brooke's behalf to express his surprise on learning that Tedder, Eisenhower's current deputy, was concerned with "military matters in an informal way" and observed that Alexander's transfer would "be a waste of Field Marshal Alexander's military gifts and experience." Churchill placed the matter on hold and asked Eisenhower to reserve time for a face-to-face talk. "The Prime Minister was sore," Summersby wrote, "but E. said that he [Churchill] would get over it. . . ."

The war raged on. Crerar's drive advanced slowly, twenty miles in fourteen days, through a narrow corridor between the Reichswald and the flood plains of the Rhineland; XXX Corps captured the key defensive position of Cleve on the eleventh, but the pursuit bogged down as elements of eleven German armored and parachute divisions massed against the attack along two roads in heavy rains and floods. For a while Crerar's advance became a hard struggle, one of the most bitterly fought actions of the entire war reminiscent of GOODWOOD and Walcheren Island. Finally, Montgomery deployed two divisions from Dempsey's Second Army reserve, and on the thirteenth the Canadians reached the Rhine at Emmerich, and Horrocks resumed south from Cleve toward the German communications hub at Goch. Meanwhile, inaction on the American front and the day-to-day postponements of GRENADE prompted articles in the American press that were critical of the "failure of the Allied high command to strike when German Western front defenses were disorganized earlier that month," amid predictions of much harder fighting ahead due to the respite Eisenhower had given the Germans by not pushing Bradley's Ardennes offensive hard enough.

When would the Germans quit? Brooke in London mulled over the JIC "weekly run around the world" for the War Cabinet on February 20, noting that "certainly a few small cracks [were] beginning to appear in the German fighting machine" but no indication of a general cracking up and it was "quite impossible to estimate how long it may last." Indeed, chastened by the Ardennes, intelligence estimates in mid-February were cautious to a fault, though gradually the scales were tipping against the thinned-out German formations in the west.

That week SHAEF marked down estimates of German divisions from 71 to 68, noting that many divisions were fighting at 20 percent effective strength. According to SHAEF intelligence, losses in the Ardennes left Germany with dwindling air reserves and approximately 33 percent of the estimated armor needed for prolonged defense of the western front. Of an estimated 1,700 new and repaired tanks produced by the Germans in February 1945, an estimated 1,650 were sent east to the Oder and Hungary, a shift in priority as dramatic as the shift from east to west in August 1944. With the departure of the Sixth Panzer Army, Von Rundstedt's entire reserve for the western front consisted of the veteran 17th SS, Panzer Lehr, the 15th and 116th Panzer, all currently deployed against VERITABLE. Elsewhere, Von Rundstedt lacked mobility, while American mobility was magnified by an unheard-of 5 to 1 Allied air superiority deployed around the clock against Ruhr industrial targets and communications. As GRENADE approached, intelligence estimated that Simpson's twelve divisions mustering at the edge of the Roer faced 30,000 defenders and 70 tanks on the far shore. Patton's Third Army between Prüm and Trier faced another 30,000 defenders, the remnants of Manteuffel's once proud Fifth Panzer Army and the Seventh Army.

Meanwhile Bradley and Hodges readied a plan for ending the reserve status of the U.S. First Army. As agreed at Namur, VII Corps was to attack on Simpson's right in the early stages of GRENADE. Then, once Simpson was across the Roer, Collins would drive along the Erft River toward Cologne. Bradley drew up a complicated "two phase" scheme of maneuver to exploit a VII Corps breakthrough by bringing Hodges' other three corps over the Roer into battle on the Cologne plain. In Phase I, III Corps would pass through VII Corps bridgeheads and "slip off to the right back into its zone of advance" which would "avoid the need for successive assault crossings." From the Erft River, III Corps would strike southward to roll up the Roer defense opposite Huebner's V Corps. Then, in Phase II with Simpson at the Rhine in the north, Hodges would unleash Collins' VII Corps south over the Erft and "strike with his whole Army to the southeast" toward Patton's columns moving up from Prüm–Bitburg into the Ahr Valley.

In a private and personal summary sent to Bradley on the twentieth, Eisenhower outlined his "three phase" plan for operations in the next several weeks which "enlarged" on Bradley's plan and differed from it in important respects. Phase I would be a "period of preparation" while Montgomery placed the 21st Army Group on the Rhine. Phase II would include "possible" 21st Army Group Rhine crossings, while Bradley's 12th Army Group proceeded with attacks onto the Cologne plain, and Devers' 6th Army Group attacked into the Saar with "existing resources." Phase III would consist of Third Army–6th Army Group attacks "with the remaining forces to complete the capture of the Saar area and advance to the Rhine" while all other forces, meaning the First Army, assumed "the defensive from the Rhine to the Moselle." Vague about timing, Eisenhower encouraged Bradley to look ahead and plan Phase III, which could entail either heavy Third Army commitments in the Saar or First Army reinforcements for Devers. As before, Eisenhower favored LUMBERJACK, but accorded it only a slightly higher priority than operations to clear the Saar, which would presumably precede 12th Army Group Rhine crossings, which he did not mention at all.

For all commands, the countdown toward GRENADE was agonizing and slow. German transfers to Crerar's front exposed gaps opposite Simpson and Patton, and the American command, sensing improvement, chafed at the inactivity. Patton found it "impossible to sit still" and despaired over his lack of armor pending the success of VERITABLE-GRENADE. "But," he wrote, "the brains are all set on another fool move which has never and will never succeed under Bernard Law Montgomery." On the eighteenth Patton quietly resumed attacks to envelop a German pocket west of the Prüm River, and then, as promised, began to reinforce Walker's XX Corps for the attack on Trier amid the noticeably stepped-up tempo of air operations, which fortified premonitions of an imminent breakthrough on all fronts. Like the preliminaries for GOODWOOD-COBRA, only on a grand scale, Allied bombers ranged at will over critical targets in Germany, devastating cities, industry and communications.

When would the Germans quit? For weeks, air operations had been the subject of a behind-the-scenes debate, vaguely reminiscent of the pre-OVERLORD debates. In January, Vandenberg's Ninth Air Force had drafted Plan BUGLE, a transport plan designed to support Montgomery's assault over the lower Rhine by a series of raids to isolate the Ruhr by destroying railheads, roads and the system of dikes and canals linking the Ruhr and Bremen. Portal, Spaatz and Arnold, anxious to deploy bombers strategically, had debated the pros and cons of CLARION, a similar concept but far more ambitious. CLARION objectives included destruction of the weakened German transport system as a whole, now burdened by refugee traffic and the military traffic flowing eastward. Additionally, CLARION would destroy the remaining refineries and factories in the Hungary-Czechoslovakia area and transportation targets near Russian lines to assist the Red Army advance.

The air debate differed from earlier ones in that resources existed for both CLARION and BUGLE, which reduced the issue to whether CLARION was necessary and desirable. Opinions differed, but Tedder would later recall his skepticism that CLARION served a useful military purpose in February 1945. In his memoir he would describe feelings at the Air Ministry that CLARION would be little more than a prestige project without prospect of significantly affecting the land battle or achieving the collapse of the German transport system. In this way Tedder would imply his doubt about unnecessary destruction, and perhaps too his misgivings about the drift of Allied-Soviet relations and the wisdom of provoking the Russians with air demonstrations under cover of "assisting the Red Army advance." In Moscow, Tedder had learned that the Russians were lukewarm about massive Allied air strikes near Red Army lines and considered the Soviet air forces self-sufficient. At Yalta the Soviets had shown interest in city raids, though bomb-line talks had become enmeshed in collateral questions such as Eisenhower's proposal for a SHAEF liaison mission in Moscow and, as Brooke put it, "the determination of the Russians to extend and preserve their special spheres of military and political influence." At Yalta the Soviets successfully held out for a wide separation of forces and an "arbitrary" bomb line running through Berlin, Leipzig, Vienna and Zagreb, in Brooke's words, "which did not suit us." But since the CCS had already issued final orders to implement CLARION, the consultations at Yalta on air policy had been a formality.

In the new POINTBLANK scheme, approved in mid-January and reaffirmed at Malta, oil and synthetic-oil plants retained first priority, with new emphasis placed on transportation centers, particularly those feeding the German positions facing the Red Army. POINTBLANK priorities were now (1) synthetic oil, (2) Berlin, (3) Leipzig and (4) Dresden, to be capped by the week-long CLARION, climaxing on Washington's birthday, February 22, featuring attacks throughout Germany to be staged simultaneously from England and Italy. CLARION was to be a rerun of BIG WEEK, but this time aimed not at engaging and defeating the now defeated Luftwaffe preliminary to land operations, but at overwhelming it and rendering a knockout blow, with sustained bombardment waged from widely dispersed bases against both industrial and morale targets, a harbinger of things to come.

Even as late as February 1945, only a handful were aware of the novelty of CLARION, and even fewer can have grasped the parallels between the questions it raised and the emerging debate in Washington over deployment of the atom bomb. In his diary Butcher had occasionally alluded to talk about the atom bomb, a device said to weigh thirteen pounds which when detonated would leave a crater two miles wide and, when detonated at night, would light the earth with the power of seven suns. As Churchill would later put it, American development of the bomb gave America "power to mould the world" and time to "fix things up" before the Russians got the bomb. But the first test drop was not due until summer, and so the brief CLARION controversy was merely a sketchy prelude to the debate over the use of the atom bomb against Japan.

The outlines of that fateful argument are well known. The advantages of atomic attack against Japan seemed straightforward. The use of the bomb was a possible way out of a costly land invasion of Japan, scheduled for November 1945, an undertaking estimated to entail eighteen months, one million American casualties, plus additional concessions to Moscow, possibly including an occupation zone in Japan. The use of the atom bomb against Japan would certify the bomb as a weapon of war, and in a single stroke signify that the Americans had devised a way to offset Russian conventional land forces in Europe and Asia after the war. Finally, proponents reasoned that the shock effect of the bomb would deter a third world war; they believed that unless the postwar settlement was backed by the power of something like the bomb, antagonisms would flare up again and the ongoing world war would resume until final destruction.

Skeptics questioned the decision to deploy the bomb on several grounds. First, there were doubts about its effectiveness in view of technical uncertainties and the limited number of bombs. Second, atom bombs would be of no use against the sizable Japanese forces in Manchuria, and so Soviet intervention would probably be necessary to force a Japanese surrender there anyway. Third, using the weapon might so provoke the Russians as to preclude postwar cooperation and chances of international control of the weapon, and there were many questions about the morality of using it and the corrosive effect on American democracy of such a ruthless decision.

Given the magnitude of the development, individual views were inconsistent. When polled by Stimson at the Potsdam conference in July 1945, Eisenhower would express the hope that the United States would not take the lead in introducing into war something as "horrible and destructive as this weapon was described to be," but he would later concede that his reaction was immediate, personal and not based on analysis of the subject. At Potsdam, Eisenhower was aware of Japanese surrender overtures, which may have led him to suspect that the use of the bomb was primarily aimed at the Russians, and to question, in his brother Milton's words, the "supreme provocation" of America's inaugurating the atomic era in August 1945. But at Potsdam the Japanese surrender overtures were overtures only, and by July 1945 the atomic era was a fact. In hindsight, Eisenhower would come to doubt that the use of the atom bomb had affected the course of the Allied-Soviet rift, and would grasp the deterrent effect of atomic weapons on would-be aggressors and custodians of the bomb alike. As for the moral implications, distinctions between the atom bomb and CLARION were blurry. The strategic-bombing technique developed by Spaatz and Arnold culminating in CLARION led logically to the still more devastating use of atomic weapons, and Spaatz himself would command the U.S. Twenty-ninth Air Force raids on Japan. In February, Eisenhower approved CLARION, weighing its corrosive long-range effects against the costs of allowing the war to drag on—as did Tedder.

On the heels of the devastating Berlin raids the February aerial offensive commenced in earnest. First came raids on Essen and Dortmund aimed at isolating the Ruhr. As the Yalta meetings ended, the tempo increased with attacks on Dresden the afternoon and night of February 13–14, recalled by historians and novelists as a portent of Hiroshima and Nagasaki. Officially, Dresden was chosen as an engineering-armaments center and communication hub linking armaments plants in Vienna, Prague, Brno and Pilsen to depots and communication zones behind German lines on the Oder-Neisse. There is debate whether STAVKA requested the attack, but the official histories concede that Dresden was of "minimal military significance," a center of German culture and art known for its medieval handiwork, museums and priceless architecture. The raid was designed to demoralize the Germans with a display of what to expect in the coming weeks if they did not quit, and perhaps also to impress the Russians who would eventually reach the city and become the first outsiders to observe the effectiveness of the concentrated aerial bombardment from widely dispersed bases of a select morale target.

The first RAF waves struck after dark and quickly exhausted flak defenses. The use of incendiaries forced the civilian population, including 600,000 refugees, out of bomb shelters into the open streets just as a second and more devastating raid struck, which enveloped Dresden in a strange phenomenon observed once before, in the firebombing in Hamburg in 1943. Fires raging uncontrollably throughout the city mixed with the chilly midwinter air and created the turbulence and winds at ground level typical of the junction of massive high- and low-pressure systems high above the earth. Hurricane winds swept the city, increasing the heat and building vacuum pressures, which intensified the winds. A "fire storm" swept the city, burning thousands caught outside their shelters and asphyxiating thousands trapped inside. Four hundred U.S. Air Force bombers followed early the next morning, and twenty-four hours later Summersby, in her journal, noted the Eighth Air Force reports that Dresden was "still burning from the night attacks."

In the wake of the Dresden raids the German high command weighed renouncing the Geneva Convention on the Western front. Allied intelligence learned of plans afoot to classify downed pilots as hostages and to begin executions with each successive raid. Word reached SHAEF from "clandestine sources" that the Germans were dismantling American and British POW camps in East Germany and transporting prisoners westward to camps in target areas.

Eisenhower wired the CCS proposing as "a matter of extreme emergency" a public statement reminding the German government that Article Nine of the Geneva Convention required that in circumstances where the transport of POWs was more hazardous than abandonment, POWs were to be abandoned "with adequate supplies." But snags developed. According to Article Nine, military forces retrieving prisoners were obligated to assure the retreating military force that repatriated prisoners would not be employed in military service for the duration of the war. The Red Army would be the retrieving force, and so the proposal would call on the Russians, not protected or bound by the Geneva Convention, to carry out the Geneva Convention to this limited extent on their front. Evidently, wary of accepting Western observers or of allowing the Wehrmacht to observe any article of the Geneva Convention on the eastern front lest they thereafter be expected to do so themselves, the Russians balked and no statement was issued.

Press reports of a new "terror raid policy" aroused behind-the-scenes misgivings in the Allied camp. As the story goes, photographs of devastated Dresden spurred Churchill to write a memo to Portal in which he questioned air policy and the Dresden mission in particular. But Churchill had personally authorized the Dresden mission and had long been a guiding force behind POINTBLANK. Portal threatened to resign unless Churchill struck his memo from the record, which Churchill finally did.

Similarly, in Washington, Stimson voiced his misgivings about the Dresden raids and about the whole idea of "precision bombing" and "legitimate military targets," which he had accepted uncritically in the past. As the leading second-front advocate, Stimson may have associated the terror bombing with the evolving hard line on Russia as well. In any event, his growing doubts about air policy may have been a factor in his selection to chair the Interim Committee, a panel of high-level scientists and government leaders assigned to draft a formal recommendation on the use of the atom bomb, a question that required Roosevelt to bind every shade of opinion in his government.

After Dresden came CLARION. By mid-February, bombers launched from England, France, Holland, Belgium and Italy ranged over two hundred industrial and communications targets, including Berlin, Vienna and Dresden, with pilots under special instructions not to "free-lance" and to concentrate exclusively on low-level pinpoint bombing of the German transport system and economic targets. In clearing winter skies, 9,000 Allied sorties encountered 360 German fighter sorties with Allied losses for the week set at 41 bombers and 40 fighters. The operation climaxed on February 22 as the U.S. Eighth, Ninth and Fifteenth air forces flew 6,000 sorties against marshaling yards and rail nets throughout Germany, a stunning blow that capped a weekly campaign that destroyed an estimated 3,000 rail cars, 500 rail engines, numerous rail centers and the bulk of tank production, and plunged Germany into chaos, heightened by the panicked retreat in Poland and the influx of refugees from the east.

In Poland and East Prussia, millions were abandoning their homes to flee with the remnants of Army Group Vistula. Men, women and children moved over snowbound roads by horse, cart and foot by the light of German cities burning in the maelstrom of the Allied bombardment. Thousands boarded fleets of tugs and passenger liners docked at Danzig and braved the Baltic. Refugees choked Berlin along with military units scheduled for the front that milled aimlessly through the city awaiting nonexistent transport. With food and fuel shortages, SS and Gestapo controls periodically broke down, and Hitler became "the forgotten man" of Berlin. But total collapse did not come, and the civilian population responded to eleventh-hour mobilization decrees and orders to erect barricades and fortifications for the defense of Berlin and the Oder.

When would the Germans quit? As CLARION proceeded, the Allied press speculated on the diminishing choices left to Hitler and the Army, choices ranging from doing nothing and "playing Samson," by standing fast on both fronts, to attempting to prolong the war by pivoting forces south into the so-called Alpine redoubt, an area that contained adequate petroleum and industrial resources to sustain a hundred divisions. A third choice would be to concentrate all military forces on the Oder front to stave off a Russian invasion for as long as possible and simultaneously to open the western front in hopes that the Allies would swiftly occupy the country.

The choices were not clear-cut, and Germany's ability to carry out any decision was limited. The German army was stretched on both fronts with major forces bottled up in remote areas such as the estimated 15 divisions in Norway, the 30 divisions in Pomerania, and 15 more in Yugoslavia covering the evacuation of the Balkans. Apparently the most talked-about choice, that of retiring into the Austrian redoubt, appealed mainly to an estimated 500,000 Nazi officials and war criminals with nothing to lose, who entertained illusions of a prolonged battle as they awaited the inevitable Allied-Soviet split. On the other hand, the redoubt encompassed non-German territory—and German territory was threatened. Moreover, portions of the redoubt were distant from Allied lines, so troops sent there would be exposed to Russian capture. From the German army point of view, the threat of a last stand had negotiating value in that withdrawals into a redoubt would enable the military to drag out the surrender process, but the redoubt was otherwise irrelevant to a strategy that would save Germans from capture by the Russians, the main objective of all military operations.

A strategy of sorts began to take shape in mid-February, spurred by recognition of the German high command that nothing could now prevent the loss of eastern Germany. Weeks before, the German high command had learned of the EAC occupation zones, which confirmed that Mecklenburg, Pomerania, Thuringia, Brandenburg and Germany east of the Oder were lost to the Russians. Additionally, the German high command could not assume that the Allies, having conceded these zones, would advance beyond the zonal boundaries. Thereafter, the first priority would be to hold the Oder River as long as possible so as to complete the evacuation of Germans from eastern Germany, Czechoslovakia and the Balkans. At the same time, it would be essential to position military forces to gain contact with the Allies in order to arrange surrenders, though what degree of contact with Allied forces would be necessary before the Allies accepted surrenders was unknown. Time was essential, and assuming that the Allies did not advance beyond the zonal boundaries, the Germans would have to hold portions of the Allied zones and avoid a precipitous collapse in the west.

Thus, with limited resources, the German high command would have to hold the Oder, hold some sectors in the Allied zones while yielding others, and then, at the last minute, rush everything west. Large distances were involved, and everything was complicated by the ongoing breakdown of transport, which meant that a German strategy for reaching the west would rely in part on diplomatic steps: first, to gain contact with the Allied high command and discuss terms; second, to sow discord between the Allies and the Soviets in hopes of gaining time. Four factors worked in favor of time: first, possession of the Oder and Rhine barriers; second, German possession of remote garrisons scattered throughout Europe, which might have to be rooted out one by one if the German high command did not formally surrender; third, Moscow's apparent willingness to string out the war in order to consolidate the Soviet grip, under cover of war measures, on Czechoslovakia, Poland, Hungary, Bulgaria and Rumania, a willingness likely to be fueled by Soviet fears of eleventh-hour Allied-German collaboration to deliver Germany to the Allies; fourth, Allied scruples about denying sanctuary to German civilians and soldiers.

Hence the Germans commenced the "secret surrender," an initiative that played on all four factors in favor of delay and at the same time established a mechanism for the surrender of German military units to the Allies in the course of a phased general capitulation. The episode would be recounted in detail by Allen Dulles in a postwar book, in which he described the round of talks involving Waffen SS General Karl Wolff, Kesselring's adjutant, who made contact with General Alexander through OSS in Berne, Switzerland, ostensibly to arrange surrender in Italy and, later, surrender on the western front. It began in late February, when an Italian industrialist, identified as Baron Luigi Parrilli, first contacted Dulles in Berne on behalf of Wolff to arrange a meeting between Wolff and Allied emissaries. The Parrilli overture would be reported to SHAEF, Washington and London on the twenty-seventh, though talks in Berne would not begin for a week, a delay that set the pattern of German evasions and feints in all subsequent talks.

Was the overture legitimate? Wolff's reputed connections with Himmler raised doubts and implied that the German army, an entity acceptable to the Allies and Russians in a general surrender, would stay at arm's length as long as possible. For the Allies, the question was whether to entertain the overture, which involved a trade-off of political and military factors. On the one hand, there was a chance the overture was the beginning of a process leading to a quick formal surrender or, barring this, it might be the first of a series of large-scale surrenders accomplishing the same thing and sparing the Allies and Russians a costly and dangerous campaign waged in close quarters to occupy all of Germany and to mop up dozens of outlying garrisons. Also, the Wolff overture offered the Allies diplomatic leverage over the Russians in that it emphasized the power the Allies were gaining over Germany and, correspondingly, that time was getting short if the Russians intended to occupy their EAC sector before the cessation of hostilities. On the other hand, the overture might be a ruse, and had to be handled carefully lest it fuel deep-seated Soviet suspicions and wreck what chances there were for Allied-Soviet cooperation. But on balance, the factors weighed in favor of Allied-German talks.

What were Soviet intentions? By the time of the Parrilli overture, the Russians, entrenching for an extended pause on the Oder, were methodically establishing the principle of "minority governments by force." Ten days after the fall of Budapest, Moscow had concluded a Hungarian armistice and installed a puppet provisional regime under General Bela Miklos. Within two weeks after Yalta, Andrei Vishinsky, amid a Rumanian political crisis instigated by the Communist left, flew to Bucharest to demand that King Michael oust the provisional coalition and appoint Communist Petru Groza as prime minister. Soon Moscow would refuse to renew the Soviet-Japanese nonaggression pact and, as it expired, cancel the Turkish treaty of friendship, raising concern about Soviet-Bulgarian pressures on the Dardanelles.

Closer to home, the ambassadorial committee on Poland broke down over procedural problems. In the first ambassadorial sessions in Moscow, Molotov told Kerr and Harriman that the Russians felt bound to consult Lublin on all British-American nominees for the Polish unity conference, and to respect Lublin's wishes. Simultaneously, Moscow expelled Allied air liaison officers, suspended shuttle bombings, and permitted snags to develop over the release of Allied prisoners of war liberated in the Russian offensive. Several hundred prisoners were transferred to Polish care in an effort to force the Allies to deal with Lublin directly, while others were detained in Odessa on various pretexts while Moscow sought assurances that the Allies would repatriate hundreds of thousands of Russian nationals in Allied hands classified under Soviet law as deserters.

So far, these blunt Russian actions, carried out with the ink barely dry on the Declaration of Liberated Europe, were not technical violations of Allied-Soviet agreements as such, but they violated the spirit of Yalta and boded ill for the future. In practical terms, they emphasized the gap between the suspense necessary for the Allies to deter flagrant Soviet political moves and the predictability needed for a coordinated military strategy. The gap reflected a mutual lack of confidence and the pressures building on the American, British and Russians to begin thinking in terms of securing postwar advantages. This was aggravated by what Churchill called the "deadly hiatus" in Washington, a period in Roosevelt's last days when American diplomacy became suspended between Roosevelt's refusal to acknowledge the fundamental change in the relations between the USSR and the Western democracies, and the growing need, sensed in both the Cabinet and Congress, for a new approach. Though threatened by Conservative party defections on the Polish issue and the breakup of the Conservative coalition as British elections approached, Churchill was in a position to act. Thereafter, it would fall to Churchill to confront the Polish questions and other Russian actions in Eastern Europe and to push for balanced measures to enhance military cooperation and Allied negotiating power in negotiations for a four-power ACC for Austria, a French zone, and other matters over which Churchill assumed authority in the closing days of the war. This involved a balancing act: moving the Americans to act on the Soviet danger on the one hand, but doing so without provoking a break with

Moscow on the other, a balancing act in which Churchill's effectiveness would depend in part on his access to Eisenhower and Eisenhower's complete authority over the front. Not surprisingly, as Allied-Soviet differences hardened after Yalta, Churchill lost interest in the Alexander appointment.

Meanwhile Eisenhower's military task would be to force surrenders, or to collect them where possible, to reduce German negotiating power while exploring ways of enlarging on Tedder's conversations in Moscow. When informed of the Parrilli overture, Eisenhower promptly cabled the CCS that he intended to monitor the SS-AFHQ contacts closely and would keep open all channels "recognized by the customs and usages of war" in anticipation of surrender talks. At about the same time, Eisenhower placed Bradley in contact with the Russians.

Years later Bradley would describe his late-February meeting with the Soviet ambassador to France, Alexander Bogomolov, who was an overnight visitor at the Château de Namur for talks and a briefing in Bradley's situation room. Bradley's mission was to update the Russians on Allied plans and the much improved situation on the western front in the hope of getting information about Soviet plans on the Oder. Bradley recalled that he rendered an "outline prospective strategy for completion of the Rhineland campaign," a sketch of the "running fuse" strategy aimed at eliminating the Germans north of the Moselle preparatory to the primary thrust at Düsseldorf and secondary thrusts elsewhere to envelop the Ruhr in an "iron ring." Bogomolov was impressed, but he had no brief to reveal Russian plans beyond the information reported in the press, which noted the early thaw that was hampering operations in Poland and the heavy sieges opening up behind Soviet lines at Kolberg, Danzig, Poznan and Breslau.

Bradley recalled that afterward the U.S. ambassador to the governments-in-exile, Anthony Biddle, took him aside to tell him how Bogomolov had spoken "delightedly of our guilelessness at the briefing and promised to report my hospitality to Marshal Stalin." Concerned about a news leak that Bogomolov had been admitted to a top-secret briefing room, Bradley took his PRO Les Allen aside to emphasize that he had "shown him [Bogomolov] less than met the eye."

"Don't worry about it, Brad," Allen quipped. "When the FBI comes around for a checkup, we won't let you down."

Eisenhower spent the third week of February restlessly confined in Versailles waiting for news. Battle reports were encouraging, but deadlines approached and much was riding on the success of the coming attacks. Butcher, a frequent visitor that week, described Eisenhower pacing his office and rubbing his lucky coins. He found Eisenhower preoccupied with breaking the Canadian army stalemate at Cleve and getting on with GRENADE, now set for the twenty-third. With favorable weather, luck and an aggressive attitude at all levels, Eisenhower told Butcher, closing the Rhine in all sectors was within reach.

Meanwhile, in letters home, Eisenhower complained about the "doldrums," how he disliked "periods of inactivity," and of his anxiety to be "getting along with things speedily." He described how lately he had been taking walks at night in the small courtyard adjoining the Weiller estate under the watchful eye of sentries. He described his travels and passed along news of John's recent visit before returning to the 71st Division to get his gear. John was always "lots of fun and we have a thoroughly good time when he is here," he wrote. But, to his father's chagrin, John was perpetually short of cash, forgetful of things like gloves and his Burberry coat. As usual, Eisenhower's mind wandered back to his all-consuming concern about the weather and his prayerful hopes for an early spring. "How glad I'll be when we can say 'all done,' " he wrote on the nineteenth. "Zowie! I hope to be on a plane within a week thereafter—probably it will take longer than that, though."

The following day the Alexander affair resumed. Brooke's deputy, General Ronald Weeks, visited the Trianon that day to query Eisenhower about the letter he had sent Brooke on the Alexander matter. "Weeks was interested to know how E. had found out ahead of time that Alexander was to be appointed E.'s deputy," Summersby noted. Eisenhower was very "noncommittal," and seemed startled when Smith, who was present, told Weeks that General Bull had brought the news back from Yalta.

Brooke's query through Weeks was a sign of divided counsels in London, which tended to confirm in Eisenhower's mind that approval of the appointment at Yalta had been tentative. Detecting a British softening, Eisenhower decided to fill Marshall in on his earlier letter to Brooke, a copy of which he had sent back to Washington.

In his letter to Marshall that day, Eisenhower explained that certain rumors had come to his attention about Alexander, which he minimized as "relatively unimportant." But mindful that public relations were a constant headache, he had decided to alert Brooke to them and to be sure that he (Brooke) "clearly understood what might occur" in the event rumors that Alexander replace Tedder were more than rumors.

Eisenhower proceeded to summarize recent operations. He explained that the current lull was due to German success in prolonging flood conditions by causing a gradual runoff from the Schmidt dams. He expected GRENADE on the twenty-third, and otherwise noted that the Germans had "thinned out substantially," opening the door to a "worthwhile attack" near Karlsruhe, considerably south of the points where the CCS envisioned the main attacks. Eisenhower commiserated with Marshall over the latest difficulties with De Gaulle on troops and supplies, ranking the French second only to the weather as his most constant source of trouble, though he was confident the French situation would eventually work out with "as little damage as possible."

In closing, Eisenhower assured Marshall that he retained his "fundamental optimism," then in passing returned to the subject of command and the pernicious effect of rumors. He expected to be seeing the Prime Minister soon and would take the occasion to point out to him (the Prime Minister) how "backdoor communications" were causing needless uncertainty. For instance, in recent weeks, he had met with Montgomery twice on the command situation. Both times, despite everything one was led to believe, Montgomery had been "emphatic" that everything was "developing soundly," and "especially vehement in protesting his complete loyalty and his belief in the efficiency of our command system." Eisenhower had urged Montgomery to inform the Prime Minister of his feelings so as "to avoid the creation of unease in our military superiors. . . ."

> Actually of course the vague rumors and statements that tend to create such uneasiness are largely froth—the fundamental soundness of this organization and readiness of all components to carry out my orders have been remarkable from the beginning. The trouble often is that to gain a particular end, people, even in high places, are sometimes not above using gossip and misinterpretation. All these things I ignore as long as they have no important effect upon this command.
>
> Sincerely, Ike

On the night of the twentieth, Eisenhower left Paris on a trip that he told Butcher was his last chance to make an extended inspection in rear areas, as henceforth his forward headquarters would be at Reims and his personal attention and presence "will be required with combat commanders up front." Eisenhower toured Cherbourg, Rouen and Le Havre. He reviewed the 71st and 56th divisions, visited Red Cross clubs and toured the 15th Reinforcement Depot to make observations for his report on morale. Along the way he visited an evacuation hospital and several battalions of limited-duty personnel composed of battle-fatigue and self-inflicted-wound patients, most of whom in his words "seemed thoroughly beaten and rarely smiled." Afterward Eisenhower told General Lear he was not satisfied with the type of instruction and rehabilitation given to limited-duty personnel and "wanted the problem solved immediately." Three days later, he returned to Versailles to await the news of Simpson's assault over the Roer and to hold his first press conference since late November.

In the field, excitement rose in the hours before GRENADE. On the twenty-first the First Army diarist noted the steady runoff of the lake waters behind the Schwammenauel dam, the eleventh-hour arrival of the U.S. 28th Division from Colmar and the U.S. 9th Armored from Prüm for "the show as planned—that is the morning of the 23rd." He noted the British slowdown at Goch to await the American attack, and talk around headquarters that all air had been "turned over to SHAEF [for] a saturation show in the front of the 9th Army . . . with all available heavies, mediums and fighter bombers."

Finally, in the early hours before dawn on February 23, the "going-home offensive" began. Simpson, evaluating the sluggish response of defenses on the far shore of the swollen Roer, decided to launch the crossings in darkness before the flood tides receded to normal levels. At three-thirty in the morning, after a forty-five-minute artillery barrage, four assault divisions attacked on a thirty-mile front from Düren to Roermond. Within sixty-five minutes, assault engineers and infantry of all four divisions were across the river and busy consolidating a bridgehead with heavy resistance confined to the VII Corps sector. This set the pattern for the twenty-third. By daylight, both Ninth Army infantry support bridges were in operation and heavy equipment was across the Roer; XIX Corps progress through the town of Jülich was swift, but in Collins' sector, the current tore boats loose and disrupted efforts to bridge the river and bring up heavy equipment.

Mixed reports greeted Eisenhower in Paris that evening. Casualties were moderate to heavy in the engineering groups, but otherwise light, and so Eisenhower was braced for difficulties with Bradley over his reluctance to authorize premature First Army crossings south of the Erft–Roer until Simpson's attacks had succeeded. But he was encouraged by a visit by presidential press secretary Stephen Early, a dinner guest that night at the Trianon, having left the presidential party at Alexandria and passed through Paris to "inspect PRD procedures" and to stand in for the ailing Hopkins as the President's personal emissary.

According to Butcher, Early's report on Yalta was not encouraging. He described the "sad voyage" home aboard the *Iowa,* heightened by the embarrassment of De Gaulle's public refusal of Roosevelt's invitation to meet in Algiers, another setback for U.S.-French relations. Early spoke of White House concern over congressional reaction to Yalta and the numerous quarrels that had cropped up with the Russians over such seemingly minor things as allowing Western press observers into Poland. Early lingered in Paris to coordinate arrangements for Eisenhower's oft-postponed press conference the next day, evidently called so that Eisenhower could inform the public of the significance of the resuming American offensive and to back his threat to go public on the Alexander matter.

On February 24, the Supreme Commander emerged to greet the press at the Scribe Hotel in Paris. In his opening statement, Eisenhower announced the resumption of a full-scale western-front offensive—in his words, the opening of "the stage of the war towards which all the Allies have laboriously struggled since the Teheran conference 14 months ago." In the give-and-take, he issued veiled calls for Allied-Soviet coordination. In confirming recent news reports that SHAEF-Russian military contacts had been established, Eisenhower complimented Russian willingness to provide all the information he needed *so far,* and "confirmed" reports that he had placed Tedder in charge of "coordinating Russian-Anglo-American operations." In the course of questions he sketched the background of the Roer operations and for the first time shed the barest light on the intense behind-the-scenes debate over the broad-front strategy. Eisenhower recalled the summer and fall campaigns and sketched his arguments in favor of the broad front, which had been mapped out as long ago as the spring of 1944 and adopted in August, and which continued to guide Allied operations. For instance, he expected that the Roer River attacks would develop as the first of attacks to defeat the German army west of the Rhine preliminary to Rhine crossings and the pursuit into Germany. Eisenhower's candor was unusual, and his disclosure of Tedder's role and the sketch he drew of the debates at the highest level left the sense with the reporters that it would be wrong to speculate that the Ardennes counteroffensive had materially affected Allied plans.

Early witnessed the conference. With Butcher afterward, he praised Eisenhower's "appearance of fitness" and the aplomb of his answers highlighted by his gritty aside that no one at SHAEF had been worried about the Ardennes situation until two weeks later, when the hometown newspapers arrived from Stateside. "It was the most magnificent performance of any man at a press conference that I have ever seen," Early told Butcher. "He knows his facts, he speaks freely and frankly, he has a sense of humor, he has poise, he has command."

Meanwhile, bulletins on the twenty-fourth told of "moderately satisfactory progress" in the drama unfolding in Collins' VII Corps sector. All morning, German artillery kept the crossing sites under constant fire while the Luftwaffe harassed attempts to erect bridges. Gradually the U.S. 104th Division cleared Düren, and by afternoon the engineers had placed five bridges including two treadways in operation. Then, after a tour of the VII sector, Hodges pronounced himself "well satisfied with the progress made" and decided the time was right to order III Corps across the Roer through Collins' bridgehead, commencing LUMBERJACK.

By late afternoon on the twenty-fourth, improvement was evident. German resistance in the Ninth Army sector was spotty and disorganized, centered in the small towns near road junctions, a sign that a German retreat was in progress. Collins steadily expanded the VII Corps bridgehead near Düren and decided to lay on a night attack in hopes of seizing the town by surprise. The VII Corps attack that night succeeded, and by the morning of the twenty-fifth VII Corps with nine bridges in operation held a three-mile bridgehead and moved on through "negligible" resistance to Düren. In the battle of the eastern periphery of Düren later that day, German defenses collapsed under heavy artillery bombardment, and reinforced by the U.S. 3rd Armored, Collins pursued the Germans ten miles toward the Erft River and the ruins of Cologne.

The First Army diarist noted the optimistic tenor of battle reports and the rising impatience felt at First Army Headquarters. As Simpson committed his armor and Collins secured Simpson's right flank, III Corps and V Corps idled amid reports of mass German surrenders and "startling" gains farther south in the Eifel, where Patton had resumed a full-scale offensive. In the Third Army sector, Walker's XX Corps approached the outskirts of Trier, while Middleton's VIII Corps and Eddy's XII Corps battled to reduce a large German pocket west of the Prüm River. That day the pocket collapsed and both corps pushed spearheads on a broad front toward Prüm and Bitburg. By nightfall, with news of Düren and a breakthrough reported near Prüm, the Allies were on the verge of splitting German defenses at two places north of the Moselle. Along the entire front north of the Moselle, three German armies were falling back on the Rhine, threatened on the flanks and faced with evacuation over the river through narrowing pockets combed by Allied air power. Was this a long-awaited break?

On the night of the twenty-fourth Bradley joined Eisenhower at Reims for urgent talks about LUMBERJACK. Confident that Simpson was on the verge of a major breakthrough, Bradley sought permission to push V Corps over the Roer and to wheel Collins and Millikin* south over the Erft toward Cologne, a plea anxiously monitored at First Army Headquarters, where Hodges waited, braced for word that Montgomery had reassumed command of the First Army.

That night, Eisenhower was hesitant about a First Army move southward before he could measure the extent of Simpson's progress toward the Canadians, but he went so far as to promise Bradley that after Simpson's success was "assured," the Ninth Army would extend its flank southward and provide two divisions for LUMBERJACK if necessary. In turn, Eisenhower wanted a few assurances from Bradley. As spelled out later in a private directive to Bradley and Devers, he wanted Bradley's support for extending Patton's Third Army attacks in the Eifel southeastward into the Saar. This was to occur before sustained First and Third Army operations east of the Rhine, which were to come after Devers and Patton had cleared the Saar–Moselle sector and "established bridgeheads in the Mainz–Mannheim sector."

And so the barrier remained. Bradley was insistent on LUMBERJACK practically to the exclusion of all other maneuvers, arguing in effect that he could not otherwise serve effectively. Eisenhower was meeting Bradley more than partway. He had approved the growing role assumed by the 12th Army Group, which would assume a major role in the envelopment of the Ruhr and the pursuit offensive. Sooner or later, however, Eisenhower would

---

*Major John Millikin, commander of III Corps.

insist on apportioning Bradley's forces to support offensives by Devers and Montgomery, and the success of these offensives depended on the success of the preliminary operations west of the Rhine in the next few weeks. Indeed nothing—not even 12th Army Group crossings—was certain until Montgomery had placed his 21st Army Group on the lower Rhine. Until then, Eisenhower could not categorically rule out 21st Army Group control of the First Army.

A major break was in the offing, however, and Eisenhower concluded that soon it would be unsound to insist that Bradley's army group stand idle in reserve for Montgomery and Devers. Thus, in the next twenty-four hours, as First Army forces advanced over the Roer on Simpson's right flank, Eisenhower moved to clarify the Alexander problem with Churchill, sensing that the intricate timetable for the "running fuse" strategy was about to be overtaken by events. On the night of the twenty-fourth, in a conciliatory reply to Churchill's petulant query about Alexander, Eisenhower encouraged the Prime Minister to visit him at his reopening Reims headquarters soon, and to bring Brooke.

Twenty-four hours later, Butcher and Early returned to Versailles for dinner. According to Butcher's account, Eisenhower briefed his two guests on the Alexander affair and told them about his recent correspondence with Churchill. He recited the main points of his latest letter, in which he had assured Churchill that he (Eisenhower) would "personally welcome" Alexander at SHAEF, and consult Alexander on all military questions. But he had gone on to point out that since Alexander's transfer would raise questions, it would require extensive explanation, and as he had told the Prime Minister, he did not want to place "him [Alexander] in a position that would make him unhappy or create . . . bad feelings." Eisenhower asked Butcher and Early what they thought. Butcher felt that Alexander's transfer would be a very unwise step. In his opinion, the British press would say "I told you so," and imply that "Ike had failed," whereupon "inferences would be counter-attacked in the American press and a merry war of words would ensue." Eisenhower agreed.

That night, reports continued to tell of the unfolding breakthrough along the Roer and the Moselle: XVI Corps, Simpson's left corps, crossed the Roer without opposition. Reports confirmed that two entire German regiments had surrendered to the American 104th Division—the beginning of a flood of prisoners that would soon swell Allied POW cages beyond capacity. According to the First Army diarist, even SS soldiers were flowing into POW cages glad to surrender and complaining about frostbite, the lack of food, and the pall cast over German troops by news of the Red Army surge through East Prussia, developments that confirmed premonitions of defeat.

The First Army diarist noted the ripple of excitement at Hodges' headquarters as Collins' VII Corps swept through the Elsdorf Forest and secured Erft crossings. Hodges readied Milliken's III Corps follow-up assault and after numerous efforts finally reached Bradley by phone to plead for permission to commence LUMBERJACK, sensing "that resistance is on the point of crumbling and . . . this time we are going to the Rhine without being slowed down."

Meanwhile, First and Ninth Army operations had begun to draw apart. Simpson, whose primary mission was to link with the Canadians, wheeled XIII Corps away from Collins' left flank toward München-Gladbach, commencing the dash for the Rhine town of Neuss and linkup with the Canadians. Within the next forty-eight hours it would be apparent that LUMBERJACK did not require Ninth Army support and that GRENADE did not require First Army support. By the twenty-seventh Hodges deployed three corps east of the Roer, and Simpson was embarked on a drive that would push out fifty-three miles from the Roer in ten days and achieve linkup with Crerar, and completion of VERITABLE-GRENADE.

This was progress, and on the twenty-seventh, for the first time in months, Summersby noted an optimistic mood around the new SHAEF offices at Reims. According to her journal, Eisenhower and his staff, having completed the move from Versailles, were busy setting up in the headquarters building. Smith was in and out of Eisenhower's new office all day with news: reports of fresh German identifications at Stettin and Breslau; reports of new units forming up in the Czech mountains, of rail movement from Norway and Italy east-bound; and positive identification of the 1st and 12th SS divisions near Lake Balaton, in Hungary, which meant that the Sixth SS Panzer Army had left the western front never to return, news that was corroborated by intercepts of diplomatic cables between Berlin and Tokyo. Eisenhower occasionally emerged from his office to chat with his staff and to compliment each on the fine job done in recent months.

By afternoon, Eisenhower had reports of Simpson's breakthrough at München-Gladbach, which confirmed that a decisive breakthrough north of the Moselle was in the offing. With the Prime Minister due in Reims for talks in four days, Eisenhower set a command conference at Montgomery's headquarters in Eindhoven to work out Ninth Army assistance for LUMBERJACK, to decide when and where to seize Rhine bridgeheads, and to work out the Third Army role in UNDERTONE, all of which now appeared to be attainable within the deadline set by Montgomery's preparations. "I have seen press reports . . . purporting to quote a War Department official to the effect that the Ardennes battle was the costliest in American history," Eisenhower cabled Marshall. "May I suggest it was also one of the most profitable? Simpson's advance today [the 27th] has been at the approximate rate of one mile per hour. . . ."

Before leaving for Eindhoven the next morning, Eisenhower worked at routine items in his new office. His photos of Mamie and the President were placed on his desk. A signal corps photographer entered the office to take pictures of the ceremonial flags set up in the facing corner. "General, when were you married?" the photographer asked.

"July 1, 1916," Eisenhower replied.

"Sir, did you and your bride have any premonition that someday a photographer would be in your office to take pictures of your personal flags for worldwide distribution?"

"I just gazed at him blankly," Eisenhower confessed in a letter to Mamie that night cautiously proclaiming the end of the winter crisis. "But later I realized I missed a chance to tell him I was thinking of something far more important—you. Beats the devil how one thinks of fine replies, an hour too late."

TUG-OF-WAR

Battles raged on three fronts, and by March 1, as Eisenhower, Montgomery, Simpson, Bradley and Hodges converged on Eindhoven, a breakthrough was unfolding on all fronts north of the Moselle, something unforeseen at Namur three weeks before, when the group had huddled to organize American support for VERITABLE and to discuss ways of appeasing CCS impatience. GRENADE was in the pursuit-and-mop-up phase, dramatized by the news that a single American regiment had captured the industrial city of München-Gladbach; VII Corps attacked southeast over the Erft and sliced through incoherent infantry resistance toward Cologne, now joined by III and V Corps, which had moved up on Collins' right flank and rounded up thousands of prisoners in the process. Meanwhile, Middleton and Eddy reached LUMBERJACK start points on the Kyll River, while Walker's XX Corps fought through the suburbs of Trier and start points for UNDERTONE. As usual, the breakthrough, in solving old problems, raised new ones in its wake. With German resistance north of the Moselle crumbling, little barred the way to UNDERTONE, but little seemed to stand in the way of Rhine crossings either, which might short-circuit UNDERTONE. Understandings on these points were essential, but hard to come by.

On the bright side, Montgomery was ready to make a virtue of necessity and to endorse LUMBERJACK, and he was surprisingly open-minded about the idea of Rhine bridgeheads in the First and Ninth Army sectors, which Bradley and Simpson insisted was possible with or without the capture of a Rhine bridge. Montgomery opposed Rhine crossings not coordinated with PLUNDER but, along with Eisenhower, showed "intense interest" in a *diversionary* First Army bridgehead in the Cologne–Bonn sector, which would ease 21st and 6th Army Group crossings.

Once again, the basic issue at Eindhoven involved the 12th Army Group: defining its role and ensuring that it did not go off on its own before

Montgomery was ready in the north and Devers in the south. With PLUN-
DER three weeks off, Bradley would have time for both LUMBERJACK and
follow-up operations. But where? Bradley was set on pressing forward with
a First and Third Army sweep beyond the Cologne plain in search of
bridgeheads. Eisenhower approved, though he was equally set on 12th Army
Group support for UNDERTONE, support that could be mobilized in one of
two ways: either diversionary Third Army supporting attacks from Trier,
coupled with major 12th Army Group reinforcements for Devers, or a major
Third Army offensive south over the Moselle, meaning that Bradley would
retain command of the 12th Army Group units committed to UNDERTONE.
Bradley was skeptical that a Saar offensive would gain enough to compensate for lost time, but he was sure that plans based on 6th Army Group
leadership would "go nowhere" and definitely preferred a Third Army
offensive to piecemeal reinforcement of Devers, which, though he "did not
advertise it," held out the possibility of Third Army crossings, a Third
Army–Seventh Army merger, and a "massive sweep to Frankfurt and
beyond." Thus, Bradley did not oppose UNDERTONE, but he was consumed
by the search for bridgeheads and not concentrating on UNDERTONE. To
this extent, the barrier remained and the simplest explanation for it was
Bradley's—that he was still not confident that he could bank on a 12th
Army Group role in the invasion, mindful that Eisenhower had still not
categorically promised him the Ninth Army back or, for that matter, that
the First Army would not be ordered back into reserve for Montgomery.
Bradley, with his forces still short of decisive objectives, and assured of
nothing in writing, would assume nothing, and so the Eisenhower-Bradley
tug-of-war resumed.

With Brooke and Churchill due in Reims on the fifth, Eisenhower and
Bradley continued on to Jülich for talks with Hodges and Collins and for
a tour of the Erft River battle. On the way back to Namur for the night,
they hammered out a summary of points to be sent the CCS, BCOS and
Devers, embodying a compromise that acknowledged the fact that Bradley's 12th Army Group offensive had begun. Eisenhower's update, dispatched that night, acknowledged that VERITABLE-GRENADE was "well
under way," that 12th Army Group attacks were making excellent progress,
and that Patton had advanced to start points for LUMBERJACK on the Kyll
River and had enveloped Trier. Meanwhile, the 6th Army Group had
"regrouped" for future operations in the Saar, where enemy forces, reduced
by losses and withdrawals had been "shown inadequate to contain simultaneous attacks on a broad front." Accordingly, Eisenhower had decided to
order LUMBERJACK and UNDERTONE, with emphasis on 12th Army Group
attacks toward Cologne "as quickly as possible after the early achievement
of VERITABLE and GRENADE" to eliminate threats to Montgomery's communications.

In the next twenty-four hours, LUMBERJACK continued to roll forward through the collapsing German front. By the second, VII Corps had moved into the Cologne suburbs, with III Corps moving up on Collins' right in pursuit of the German Fifteenth Army. Eisenhower was at Maastricht when meager information reached Simpson's headquarters confirming that the U.S. 83rd Division had succeeded in placing detachments at the Rhine south of Düsseldorf and had narrowly missed seizing a Rhine bridge. Eisenhower proceeded to 83rd Division Headquarters, then drove on to München-Gladbach to tour the ruins of the city and inspect the procedures for billeting the thousands of German civilians passing through Ninth Army lines.

After a luncheon at 3rd Armored Headquarters in Düren, Eisenhower decided to take a panoramic look at the battle, as he had done many months before in Normandy. To the consternation of his staff, he boarded an L-5 plane to fly up high over the Erft ridge into German-controlled territory to watch the VII Corps attacks in progress. Aloft, he again observed the striking calm of a modern battlefield. Occasional flashes of artillery fire disrupted an otherwise peaceful scene under a pale late-winter sun. And as the plane passed low over the ruined towns of Schmidt, Jülich and Düren, he gained a "remarkable picture of the destruction inflicted by our bombers during the past few months, as well as the progress we had made in desperate battles over that region in November." After the flight, Eisenhower motored back to Reims to host two days of conferences with Churchill, Brooke, Bradley, Spaatz and Tedder convened to resolve the command problem and to finalize strategy west of the Rhine.

Decisions approached, and as high-level deliberations resumed on invasion strategy, Phase I of Eisenhower's three-phase plan (VERITABLE-GRENADE) was history and Phase II (LUMBERJACK) was under way. No one—least of all, Brooke—had foreseen the speed of the American breakthrough over the Roer River, which posed urgent questions: whether to await Montgomery's elaborate preparations for PLUNDER before seeking Rhine crossings; or whether to exploit the developing opportunity on Patton's right flank to plunge east over the Moselle into the Saar–Palatinate, as Eisenhower had long proposed. The broader issue concerned the invasion: its objectives; how it would proceed, and whether the alliance would go forward with the command changes set for the end of March in new and fluid circumstances being ushered in by the American breakthrough.

Deliberations resumed on the second. Montgomery, Brooke and Churchill huddled at Hasselt. Time was growing short, and before their conference with Eisenhower, Churchill and Brooke had to work out the British position. Bradley's campaign was gaining momentum by the hour and seemed poised to cross the Rhine River in the Cologne–Bonn area, which had a significant bearing on British views. In the circumstances, the British had to weigh a range of possibilities, including the possibility that by continuing to oppose all operations south of the Moselle they stood to win a debate but lose control of a strategy they had promoted for months, but which would now probably be carried out by American forces and yield very different results from what the British intended—results that would jeopardize fundamental British interest at stake in their proposals at Malta and Yalta, which now had to be updated.

Accounts of the actual discussions are sketchy, but the situation faced by the British can be summarized as follows. British proposals for one major thrust north of the Moselle were becoming obsolete, in terms of both Allied strategy and the British interests underlying them. One hesitated to draw firm conclusions on the basis of operations less than two weeks old, as it was still too early to rule out the possibility that the Germans would succeed in extricating the bulk of their troops for a prolonged defense of the Rhine. But this did not seem likely, and the German collapse west of the Rhine appeared to be shaping up as the beginning of a general collapse of the western front, which raised opportunities and dilemmas. The apparent opportunity arose from the fact that German resistance was likely to be less than feared, which would place the Allies in a position from which they could select their objectives in the next phase of operations in the confidence that operations designed to reach these objectives would succeed. But this was not to say that the Allies were gaining freedom of action. On the contrary, the realization that the German resistance would be a diminishing constraint on the Allies heightened the constraining factor of the Russians and it exposed the lack of agreement between the British and the Americans about the next step, which from the British point of view was essential.

What were British objectives? In recent months the British had urged a single-thrust strategy as a way of guaranteeing the Allies' success over the Germans at some point *and* because the northern thrust—as proposed— would be the maneuver best tailored to attain minimum British aims. These aims included conquest of the British zone of occupation and control of the North Sea coast in an offensive that the British justified as the best method for reaching Berlin so as to (a) knock Germany out of the war, and (b) strengthen the overall Allied postwar position. How seriously the British took the possibility of Berlin is debatable, but British determination to take Denmark and their EAC zone was not, and the only real assurance they had of reaching their objectives "priority" was a 21st Army Group drive toward Berlin with American support. Could they count on it? What the British had on March 2 were tentative assurances from Eisenhower but none whatsoever from Marshall, and they confronted battle developments that made Montgomery's priority less and less tenable. Indeed, it was now likely that an invasion offensive staged north of the Moselle, instead of consisting of a major British attack and a secondary American attack, would go forward as two major attacks with the "secondary" American attack south of the Ruhr not only beginning before the British attack but likely to match Montgomery's strength regardless of formal constraints. Indeed, without operations south of the Ardennes, the "secondary" American attack would draw in reserve American strength and emerge as the much stronger of the two attacks, which might threaten attainment of Montgomery's objectives regardless of the objectives Bradley set for his advance.

This was certain to occur should Bradley cross the Rhine and choose to focus on Leipzig and points south, in which case American and British forces would draw apart. The other possibility—that Bradley's forces would spearhead an advance toward Berlin—was, if anything, worse from the British point of view. Such an offensive stood a chance of actually reaching Berlin, which was in itself desirable, but, like a British-led offensive, it would risk touching off Soviet efforts to preempt the Allies at Berlin and everywhere else. The problem this posed for the British was that unless they kept pace, Denmark was lost, but if the British did keep pace, Bradley's chances of reaching Berlin would improve, inviting the even greater risk of a determined Soviet effort to preempt the Allies elsewhere, and perhaps the loss of the British zone and Denmark anyway. Either way, Allied-Soviet clashes could not be ruled out and the collapse of Allied-Soviet cooperation would be a matter of time—results that were precisely those the British could offset in a 21st Army Group thrust, supervised by Alexander, that envisioned Berlin but *after* the Germans were defeated and *after* the British had secured their vital objectives in the north and could assess Soviet intentions.

What now? Again, the accounts of the second provide only the sketchiest details of what appears to have been a very significant British reappraisal that day. Montgomery's diary alludes to the intense discussions between himself, Churchill and Brooke on the Alexander matter and Eisenhower's current plans, which now had the virtue in British eyes of harnessing Bradley's current advance and the long-range advantage of ensuring 12th Army Group support for Montgomery. This did not assure British "priority" over the whole western front, but it offered Montgomery "priority" over the critical northern sector and gave the British say over the timing of an Allied offensive on Berlin. Implicit in this reassessment was British concern that the Americans, emerging from the trauma of the Ardennes and spurred by sudden distrust of the Russians, intended to shove Montgomery aside and mount an ill-considered drive on Berlin. The British had no reason to assume such American actions, but having sponsored Berlin for months, they had no tactful way of finding out. Again, it cannot be said for sure how the British saw their situation, but the dilemma posed by their sponsorship of Berlin and their uncertainty about Bradley would appear to explain a number of contradictory British actions in the next few weeks; why the British would persist in the weeks ahead as champions of an Allied offensive for Berlin, but would champion measures that undermined such a project in fact. For instance, the British would insist to the end that the Berlin idea was inseparable from a 21st

Army Group offensive, and that Montgomery retain the American Ninth Army even as that unit moved into position to spearhead a 12th Army Group dash for Berlin, which had an excellent chance of succeeding. Perhaps the clearest case in point was their imminent decision to set aside Alexander's appointment in order to avoid disrupting Eisenhower's control of the American army groups, this taken with their tacit approval of UNTERTONE; the next few weeks suggest that the British, proponents of Berlin when Berlin was unattainable, had in fact long since lost interest in that idea except as a device to bolster Montgomery's priority.

But the immediate question on the second concerned Alexander. In sum, were the British now better off going forward with Alexander's appointment, or better off acquiescing in Eisenhower's plans and dropping the matter quietly? In so many words, Churchill, Brooke and Montgomery had been arguing over just this point ever since November 1944. Montgomery had long questioned whether Alexander would enhance British influence with the Americans. Likewise, as of late, he had been urging that Eisenhower's plans were sound and that Eisenhower could be counted on to be true to his commitment to back a 21st Army Group drive to Denmark, an idea Eisenhower had broached as long ago as September 1944 in the MAR-KET-GARDEN controversy. Brooke, on the contrary, had argued that since Eisenhower had already proved he would not restrain Patton, the best approach was the direct one: a deal with Marshall on command and strategy. As things stood, Brooke had a deal on Alexander but lacked firm understandings on strategy. Moreover, Alexander's effectiveness had to be weighed in light of the ongoing American breakthrough, the attitude of the American Chief of Staff, who had approved Alexander but who was otherwise opposed to committing American forces to serve British ends, and Bradley's utterances to the effect that American forces could not stand idle while Montgomery raced for Berlin.

In the circumstances, Brooke had to consider that Eisenhower's plan was sound—and proceeding well, as shown by VERITABLE-GRENADE. In a more positive sense, Brooke had to consider that a single offensive was no longer mandatory but would in fact curtail Allied possibilities; that Eisenhower's proposals for two offensives purported to deploy maximum strength in Montgomery's sector, reserving extra strength for secondary but valuable objectives in Austria and southern Germany, objectives in keeping with the aim of minimal cooperation with the Soviets, which was to emerge as the key point.

Again, what were British objectives? As Churchill would argue endlessly in the days ahead, Berlin was the "prime" Allied military objective but not the only objective, and an objective, furthermore, that presupposed more basic ones—namely, the defeat of Germany, and a postwar settlement. It was true that Churchill favored a hard line on Russia and wanted to advance far eastward to gain leverage over the Soviets. But his avowed purpose was, as always, to bolster the Allied position in an eventual settlement, not to wreck the chances of one. Churchill believed that Roosevelt shared his aims, though years of pushing the Americans to back realistic efforts to work out a settlement in Europe had at times left him wondering. Now at long last, in 1945, Churchill had a settlement of sorts that featured a solution for Germany and ancillary agreements to which he had affixed certain provisos. In the process, he had succeeded in building up De Gaulle, in reestablishing the exile governments everywhere except in Poland, in establishing British predominance in Greece and a modus vivendi with Tito of Yugoslavia and restoring self-rule in Italy, all backed up by his personal relationship with Stalin and Roosevelt. Churchill was insisting on resolute steps to bolster the Allied position, but within bounds.

Forty-eight hours later Churchill, Brooke, Ismay, Bradley, Spaatz, Bull and Tedder converged in Reims for talks about LUMBERJACK, UNDERTONE, Austria, Czechoslovakia and Berlin, a session that again illustrated the complications attending each new phase of the war in Europe. Possibilities were opening up, but the mood was tense and reminiscent of many earlier meetings called to weigh the often troublesome question of military success. And, as so often before, the outcome was indicated by the site, Eisenhower's headquarters, and by the notable absentee, Montgomery, whose presence might have undermined reasonable discussion of Bradley's next step.

The issues on March 5 were twofold: first, Allied objectives in the coming invasion of Germany; second, the more immediate questions of the command arrangements to carry out the invasion and preliminary operations in the eighteen days between then and the beginning of Montgomery's 21st Army Group offensive. Apparently, discussion turned to Berlin as well, and Churchill proceeded to outline the British case for Berlin, consisting of the two points that he later recounted in *Triumph and Tragedy:* first, that Allied forces should not concede the city or overlook its intangible significance in European minds, arguments that also applied to Vienna, Prague and other unclaimed European capitals; second, that Berlin was a rallying point for German forces which, when seized, would quickly lead to the final demoralization of the German army and a quick cease-fire. Churchill also considered Berlin "the ultimate prize" and felt that the nation with military forces in Berlin on the day of the surrender would score a propaganda victory that would profoundly influence the mass of Europeans. But Churchill's intent in raising Berlin was to persuade Eisenhower, and failing this, he was willing to abide by Eisenhower's military judgment—as was Brooke.

Not surprisingly, Eisenhower disagreed that Berlin was a useful military objective in current operations. In support of this, Eisenhower could cite the evacuation of the German ministries and the threat of German forces withdrawing into redoubts in Norway and Austria, which diminished the importance of Berlin as a target. In early March the Allies were drawn up along the Rhine 250 miles away from Berlin while two million Russian troops massed 30 miles from Berlin on the Oder, making it illogical from a military point of view to concentrate Allied forces for the sake of remote objectives within Soviet reach at the expense of more attainable objectives elsewhere: first, seizure of the Ruhr; second, junction with Soviet forces at Leipzig; finally, pursuit in the north to Denmark and south through southern Germany into the Alpine-redoubt area made possible by UNDERTONE.

Apparently Brooke conceded the issue of UNDERTONE slowly and not without extensive questioning of Eisenhower about the objectives of the Frankfurt thrust. Brooke still viewed major American crossings anywhere as a "dispersion of effort" that would hold up seizure of the Ruhr, having remarked once that he wished the 12th Army Group were deployed north of the Ruhr with British forces in the center so that he could prove his sincerity. Eisenhower rejected the insinuation that he was concerned with American prestige, as he was "no more anxious to put Americans into the thick of the battle and get them killed" than he was to see the British take losses, and he denied ever planning operations "on the basis of what individual or what nation gets the glory"—his case for Frankfurt was a "military" one. Only thirty-five divisions would be sustained in Montgomery's sector, and so, "far from dispersing effort," a Frankfurt campaign would enable the Allies to deploy maximum strength and "bring such a concerted and tremendous power against him [the German] that his collapse would quickly follow." Moreover, southern crossings and control of the Frankfurt corridor would open the way to the Austrian redoubt and industrial targets in the Stuttgart area and the Leipzig–Dresden area.

As of March 5, Brooke's position was unrealistic. Fifty American and French divisions would not stand idle while Montgomery invaded Germany with thirty-five British and American divisions under British command. Soon the Allies would have ample strength for two major offensives and be in position to launch them. While Eisenhower's plans took this fact into account and endeavored to deploy all three army groups usefully, Brooke's did not. The need for accomplishing the preliminaries for an American offensive was dramatized that day by the news of Collins' conquest of Cologne, the fall of Venlo, the linkup of Canadian and American forces at Geldern, and Patton's rapid advance through the Ahr Valley while Walker's XX Corps mopped up pockets of resistance in Trier. The question was not whether there would be a major American offensive but when, and the relationship between Bradley who would spearhead it and the other army groups. Eisenhower would not halt Bradley but would adjust strategy in anticipation of Bradley's gains beginning with LUMBERJACK, then a Third Army–6th Army Group campaign in the Saar-Palatinate that could activate the 6th Army Group as an anchor for the Frankfurt thrust and a spearhead for later operations toward Austria to coincide with Montgomery's drive on Denmark. The discussions went on all day and, significantly, the effect of them was to commit Eisenhower—in Bradley's presence—all the more firmly.

This left the matter of Alexander's appointment, which still had advantages in British eyes: first, in jolting the Russians; second, in rewarding Alexander. But the Allied crossings of the Rhine would be a jolt sufficient in itself, and rewarding Alexander depended on Eisenhower's willingness to make use of him. As it turned out, Eisenhower opposed Alexander because of Tedder's importance and his concern that the appointment would reflect unjustly on the accomplishments of his command, whereupon Brooke subsided. In his diary, he remained highly critical of Eisenhower's "limited strategic vision," and deplored his relations with Montgomery as "insoluble." But, Brooke noted, things were "running smoothly for the present. But this cannot last, and I foresee trouble before too long. For all that, to insert Alex now is only likely to lead to immediate trouble for all I gather."

And so even as Eisenhower and the British groped toward a common approach, the British mood was anything but cheerful. In the circumstances, concessions, no matter how sensible, evoked wariness and regret. Setting aside Alexander's appointment was a major concession, and in Bradley's words, it was "the most emphatic demonstration yet that Ike had taken full command of the war on the continent."

Regret ran through the accounts of the meeting. Years later Bradley would recount the details of the luncheon conversation on March 5. Eisenhower, Brooke, Bradley, Spaatz, Tedder, and Ismay listened as the Prime Minister ruminated on subjects ranging from the forthcoming British elections to the dark implications of modern science and weaponry to the Prime Minister's difficulties with Washington over Greece, an old story and one that in Churchill's mind recalled Wilson's mistakes in 1919—mistakes that, in his opinion, had a lot to do with the troubles afflicting the world that month. At lunch the Prime Minister did not conceal his anger over recent criticism of his pro-monarchy policy in Greece in segments of the American press. He saw no harm in restoring ruling houses which, if kept in place twenty years before, might have barred the doors to the rise of tyrants like Hitler. Nor would Churchill apologize for British efforts to block the rise to power of small groups that now paraded as democrats, and defiantly vowed at one point that Britain would "never sit quietly by and allow an armed minority to force its will on a majority anywhere." Churchill dismissed his critics, and likened himself to a giant rhinoceros with a sharp tusk and a thick hide.

And on it went until Churchill's departure the next morning. Years later, in conversations with Alistair Cooke, Eisenhower too would recall the undercurrents of regret in the March 5–6 meetings, which would reverberate throughout the next several weeks and eventually find expression in American quarters eager to discredit Roosevelt's wartime leadership altogether. "We'd won the war and we'd gone much further than our own political bosses apparently thought we could and argued we would," he recalled. "Mr. Churchill always talked about this campaign before we launched it as requiring something on the order of two years. In eleven months, it was all done and ended. Why suddenly the belief that everything was a blunder? You'd think that we'd lost the war. I don't think we did."

But twenty years after the war, Eisenhower was thinking merely in military terms, whereas Churchill was anticipating the political and diplomatic complications arising from the military successes unfolding in the field, successes inseparable from Russian successes and the total defeat of Germany, which posed the looming postwar problem of Russian power in a Europe devoid of spirit and prospects. Churchill was urging his listeners to regard this problem carfully—and not for the last time. Indeed, exactly one year later, on March 5, 1946, he would address these subjects publicly in his historic Iron Curtain speech at Fulton, Missouri, a speech in which he would describe the closely guarded Soviet bloc that had formed in Eastern Europe, the implications of this development for Europe and the Free World, America's "awe-inspiring accountability to the future," and America's duty to persevere in the cause of a settlement ". . . of the problems which beset us on the morrow of our absolute victory in arms . . . to try to make sure . . . that what has been gained with so much sacrifice and suffering shall be preserved for the future glory and safety of mankind."

As Churchill and Brooke returned to London, a dramatic break was imminent. On the sixth, XX Corps took Trier as XII and VIII Corps rolled on through the Ahr Valley toward the Rhine town of Mayenne and Coblenz. Within seventy-two hours the U.S. 4th Armored Division would reach the Rhine at Andernach and stretch out to link up with Hodges near the Rhine town of Sinzig, bringing LUMBERJACK to an end.

For days Bradley and Simpson had anticipated gaining a Rhine bridgehead, but neither man had expected to seize a Rhine bridge intact. North of Cologne, the withdrawing Germans fought skillful delaying actions that week and systematically demolished spans in threatened sectors. But the American breakout into the Cologne plain quickly turned into a pursuit drive, and on March 7, the U.S. 9th Armored sped through the town of Euskirchen toward the junction of the Ahr and Rhine at the town of Remagen and the double-track Ludendorff railroad bridge. At one o'clock in the afternoon that day, lead infantry units spotted the bridge. By four o'clock, patrols of combat command B, the 9th Armored Division, crossed and seized the 1,300-foot span. After a brief skirmish Lieutenant Colonel Leonard Engeman pushed a tank and three infantry companies across, and held the bridgehead against a 100-man German engineer regiment, which unaccountably failed to destroy the span before the Americans captured it. By six o'clock, in line with Bradley's standing orders,

Hodges hastily ordered U.S. Navy landing craft and other units to the area to hold the bridge and adjusted V Corps–III Corps boundaries to enable General Milliken's III Corps to pour in reinforcements to consolidate the bridgehead.

This was a long-awaited event, one that would formalize the major strategy revisions in favor of Bradley, implicit at Reims on the fifth. Word of it reached Bradley on the night of the seventh, at the very moment that Bradley was locked in conference with General "Pinky" Bull, who had come to discuss a draft of Eisenhower's latest directive and to iron out the details of Patton's two-corps assault over the Moselle and/or to arrange for 12th Army Group replacements for Devers. As Bradley later put it, Bull wanted "the moon": an armored division, two infantry divisions, seven battalions of artillery and more, which, along with the still-standing SHAEF order to keep ten divisions in reserve for PLUNDER, amounted to a claim on the whole First Army. Bradley offered Bull several artillery battalions but otherwise balked. It was then, just before dinnertime, that Hodges phoned Bradley with the news of Remagen and his initiative in pushing III Corps units across. In Bull's presence, an exultant Bradley ordered Hodges to gather up every available unit in the surrounding area and exploit the bridgehead "with everything."

It is doubtful that news from Remagen came as a complete surprise, since Hodges had routed the 9th Armored into the area for the purpose of taking the bridge in line with SHAEF's standing orders. Nor was capturing a Rhine bridge considered essential to success in the battle of the Rhine. But a bridge would ease things, and Remagen, if held, would be a major military coup and cap a week of breaks that confirmed the drift of strategy in Bradley's favor.

On the night of the seventh, however, Bradley quickly found himself swimming upstream against cautious resistance in all quarters. Back in conference, Bradley listened as Bull reminded him that Remagen, if exploited, would conflict with Montgomery's Rhine crossings (PLUNDER) and disrupt the balanced plan that Eisenhower had painstakingly worked out, which was designed to keep the invasion of Germany from going off as a hasty and disorganized improvisation. Bradley was in no mood to hear any of this, and, declaring that he was ready to settle the issue on the spot, placed a call to Eisenhower.

It was seven o'clock. At the time, Eisenhower in Reims was hosting a dinner party for Generals Maxwell Taylor and James Gavin, who had flown in for talks about airborne operations in the American sector to gain a Rhine bridgehead. Eisenhower pronounced himself "delighted" with the news and quickly approved Hodges' decision to route local forces into the bridgehead. Eisenhower spoke of holding the bridgehead with four to five divisions but cautioned Bradley that widening the bridgehead would have to wait. By nightfall the Remagen build-up was on "hold," with Bull standing by in Namur as Eisenhower's man on the scene to relay instructions and to monitor the situation.

The tug-of-war resumed. According to Bradley, he and Bull pored over maps until one o'clock in the morning, discussing the possibilities opened up by the seizure of the bridge. Bradley had never seemed so determined, and intimated to Bull that his planners had foreseen something like this "six months ago," an allusion to September, when he and Montgomery had dueled over rival plans for a Berlin offensive. Was the Remagen sector a suitable base for the expansion of a bridgehead into a major offensive? Bradley conceded that the terrain surrounding Remagen was hilly, but he reminded Bull that six miles to the southeast there was a stretch of Frankfurt–Ruhr autobahn, and twenty-five miles east was the crossroad town of Giessen, a promising linkup point for the First Army and the Third Army —assuming Patton gained crossings in the Frankfurt–Coblenz area. From Giessen the First and Third armies might exploit the tank corridors toward Kassel and envelop the Ruhr from the south. Another possibility would be to pass the Third Army through the bridgehead and mobilize a major offensive thrust from it. In the next twenty-four hours Bradley pushed the build-up to the limit.

By the morning of the eighth, local resistance was still light and roads leading into the area were jammed with troops, guns and tanks of the U.S. 9th Armored and U.S. 9th Infantry. Through Bull, Eisenhower stood watch. On Eisenhower's direct orders, Hodges was to limit the advance from the bridgehead to a depth that could be "defended" by five divisions —no more—and Bradley was to await SHAEF approval before attempting any breakout. The restrictions were widely attributed then and later to Eisenhower's determination not to upstage Montgomery's elaborate preparations in the north. Whether upstaging Montgomery was a factor or not is debatable, but Eisenhower was determined to maintain order on the front and to ensure that Remagen developed as a diversionary attack. Pledges to the British were evidently a factor, but, more important, the limited build-up at Remagen that Eisenhower envisioned would divert German forces from both PLUNDER and UNDERTONE, which awaited the final outcome of Patton's ongoing armored attacks in the Lahn River Valley. On the eighth Eisenhower dispatched messages to Montgomery, Bradley and Devers setting PLUNDER for the twenty-fourth and redundantly ordering Bradley to complete LUMBERJACK quickly in order to support PLUNDER. Simultaneously he ordered Devers to "initiate operations in the Saar" with the objective of seizing bridgeheads in the Mainz–Mannheim sector and assisting 12th Army Group operations "southeast from the Moselle." Within forty-eight hours Churchill was in touch with Eisenhower to monitor his progress in carrying out the order.

March 8, the day of the Remagen bridgehead, was significant on all fronts. That day, word reached the outside world through the London Poles that the Red Army had arrested sixteen leaders of the Polish underground lured out of hiding by written guarantees of personal safety. Coinciding with a full-blown Polish crisis was the meeting between Allen Dulles, representing the American OSS, and SS General Wolff in Zurich. According to the account of this meeting received by Eisenhower several hours later, Wolff presented himself to Dulles as an emissary from Field Marshal Kesselring to discuss the terms of capitulation in Italy. Dulles was noncommittal and, correctly, told Wolff that the policy of unconditional surrender applied to large-scale military surrenders as well as political negotiations.

But Dulles would soon learn that on the eighth Kesselring had been in Berlin, where he found out that he was slated to leave Italy and to replace Von Rundstedt as OB West. Thereafter, Kesselring would have only indirect say over a cease-fire in Italy, but direct say over the western front in command of the armies facing Eisenhower. Was Wolff in fact suggesting that Kesselring was available for a deal on the western front?

There was no question of informing the Russians, since the Allies could assume that the German government had done so already. Once again, the question in Washington and London was whether to break off the talks. On the one hand, Wolff implied that he spoke on behalf of *both* front commanders in the west, and so the overture just might produce results. Likewise, discussion on this scale meant negotiating power in dealings with Moscow and might prompt Red Army action on the Oder front, fortified by a suspicion on the part of the Russians that Remagen was just one of the many windfalls about to occur in the West. On the other hand, the overture, by spurring Soviet suspicions, might succeed too well and lead to the utter breakdown of coordination between the two fronts.

In Washington a policy quickly developed on the Wolff situation: as before, the talks would continue. The State Department termed the overture "preliminary," "military" in nature and a local matter dealing with Italy. Hence, Allied emissaries would honor Wolff's conditions set for future contacts that only Allied representatives be included. On the twelfth Harriman so informed Molotov and invited Soviet comment. That day Molotov replied that Moscow would "not object" to the continuation of the talks, but for its part, the Soviet government wished "officers representing the Soviet Military Command to participate in those negotiations" and hoped the United States would arrange Swiss visas for three Soviet observers.

Meanwhile the Soviet halt at the Oder thirty-five miles east of Berlin wore on while the Red Army engaged large garrisons at Poznan, Danzig, Königsberg and Breslau and contained a massive 35-division German counteroffensive at Lake Balaton, southwest of Budapest. Along the Oder, the Russians were contained, hampered by supply, an early thaw and the arrival of German reserves. As each day passed, the Germans made frenzied preparations for the defense of Berlin and the Oder. Men, women and children, including refugees, were mobilized to construct trenches, anti-tank defenses and roadblocks along the outer perimeter of the city and along the natural defensive chain of lakes and rivers in Berlin's suburbs.

In view of the Remagen development, the Wolff overture and the prospect of an extended delay on the Oder front, the Allies could no longer put off making their plans final, a process that took seventy-two hours. On the tenth, Churchill spoke several times by phone with Eisenhower. The two men affirmed that Remagen would be subsidiary to PLUNDER but that it should be built up, as even Montgomery now agreed that the bridgehead would "draw enemy strength into it away from the business up north." But with the urgent question being how far Bradley would be allowed to commit the power of the Twelfth Army through the Remagen bridgehead, lingering British skepticism about Eisenhower's plans in the Saar dissolved.

By the tenth UNDERTONE was in readiness. The 6th Army Group had completed regrouping. Fourteen divisions of the U.S. Seventh Army were bunched up between Saarbrücken–Haguenau, posed for an advance through the Palatinate highlands to converge with Patton and trap the German Army Group G. On the assumption that UNDERTONE succeeded, Third Army crossings at Frankfurt would permit Sixth Army crossings into Baden–Württemberg, which would open up a wide range of possibilities, including pursuit into the Black Forest toward Austria on the right flank of a Third Army advance toward the Czech frontier.

As their pause at the Oder continued, the Russians advanced into the eastern portions of Czechoslovakia south of the Carpathians with the 2nd Ukrainian Front moving up from the south toward Bratislava and Vienna, and this raised questions about the military usefulness of Allied operations into Czechoslovakia. On the other hand, there were political reasons for the Allies to consider Czechoslovakia. Unlike Germany, Czechoslovakia was to be a liberated country, as was Austria, and not subject to indefinite Soviet occupation. Allied occupation of the area might affect the course of Czech politics, which was also true of Austria, though there the Allies had a solid military basis for intervention as well as to preempt the threat of the redoubt. As of March 10, the question of full Allied participation in an Austrian Allied Control Commission had been agreed upon "in principle," but the effect of this agreement might be jeopardized should the Russians overrun the country. Finally, the Allies would capture the Saar and 10 percent of remaining German iron and steel production and inflict a major defeat on the German army. An unforeseen military opportunity was shaping up because of a German decision to reinforce Army Group G defenses opposite Devers with forces drawn from Patton's sector in the belief that Patton, instead of attacking across the Moselle, would cross the Rhine through the Remagen bridgehead. This placed Patton in a position to cross the Moselle and to strike against the rear of the German First, Ninth and Seventh armies and cut the withdrawal of these forces into Bavaria.

All of these factors pointed to the Saar. The credence Eisenhower and Churchill gave to the prospects of a Bavarian redoubt will always be debatable, but one aspect of the Wolff overture could not be overlooked: Wolff spoke on behalf of Kesselring, who was about to assume command of the western front, which raised the possibility of a general surrender. Kesselring, who had spent twenty months in command of German forces in Italy, was also known as a "defensive specialist." The alternative to a phased surrender, by implication, was a withdrawal of German forces from the western front into an Austrian redoubt to link up with the German forces in Italy, enabling the Germans to hold out indefinitely. Hence, the redoubt contingency, long discounted in Allied thinking, suddenly became more plausible and a factor in Allied military strategy, as one must assume it did in Russian planning as well. A number of recent German decisions— otherwise illogical—seemed consistent with the possibility that Hitler, after losing Berlin and northern Germany, would relocate his government in the mountains of southern Germany with the idea of prolonging the fight there. The "strange" resistance at Budapest and at Lake Balaton and the prolonged German stand in Italy seemed "in harmony with such an intention," as Churchill put it that week. "But, of course, he [Hitler] is so foolishly obstinate about everything that there may be no meaning behind these moves. Nevertheless, possibilities should be examined. . . ."

On the tenth Churchill approved UNDERTONE, and Eisenhower flashed instructions to Devers ordering him to "proceed." That day Churchill also set aside the command issue for the duration of the war, telling Eisenhower that it had "now been decided to leave Tedder at SHAEF and Alexander in Italy," Summersby noted at the end of a busy day of conferences. "Everyone contented."

Meanwhile the Eisenhower-Bradley tug-of-war wore on. In the emotional hours surrounding the capture of the bridge at Remagen, Bradley struggled to consolidate the First Army prize, suspecting in his darkest moments that SHAEF would turn around and order Hodges' forces to fall back west of the Rhine. Bradley continued to push the build-up, all the while urging that Remagen was a decisive break, which if exploited would succeed in rolling up German defenses and concentrating American forces for a "massive push to Kassel and beyond."

Evidently, Bradley sensed the inevitable. Years later he would describe his feelings of elation in the days after the First Army seizure of the Remagen bridge, for Remagen marked an important turn in the fortunes of the war and ended all suspense about whether the Allies would breach the Rhine, the last great natural barrier on the German frontier. But as a practical matter, a German collapse was a matter of time, and so the true significance of Remagen was that it constituted a dramatic First Army gain, one that tended to make sure that the First Army would operate with

Patton in the Ruhr battle and the subsequent battle of pursuit. Otherwise, in mapping out plans to exploit Remagen (VOYAGE), Bradley had to weigh the dangers of unilateral action by a single army group against a wounded but still resisting German army, something that the lessons of all past campaigns warned against. Surprised by the success of Remagen, Bradley began to doubt the possibilities for tactical exploitation of Remagen as stout resistance developed late on the eighth, a sign that neighboring bridgeheads would be hard to come by. German resistance, a factor easy to discount in the electric hours surrounding news of Remagen, underscored the need for neighboring bridgeheads to the south, which was Patton's objective in UNDERTONE.

On the morning of the eighth, resistance at Remagen had been "light." But by midday the Luftwaffe made several attempts to bomb the bridge, and artillery moved up to shell the area. At dusk, columns of vehicles with headlights approaching from the north and south were observable from the hills overlooking the Remagen bridge, and on the ninth, German armor intervened. Indeed, in the forty-eight hours after the success at Remagen, German resistance markedly stiffened all along the Rhine. North of Remagen, Ninth Army attempts to gain bridgeheads in the Duisburg–Neuss area fell short, as three panzer divisions fought a successful delaying action before destroying the Wesel highway span. The Germans succeeded in destroying all spans in Middleton's sector, isolating the Remagen build-up, which went slower than expected because of traffic snarls, artillery fire and resistance along the bridgehead perimeter. By the ninth Bradley, like Patton, was alert to the fact that a major gap in German defenses had appeared between the Rhine and Trier behind the German Seventh Army, handing Patton a chance to roll up Army Group G and reach the Rhine simultaneously.

On the ninth, at a meeting with Simpson, Patton and Hodges in Namur, Bradley sketched his plan for a "right hook" toward Kassel (VOYAGE) and his "political strategy of gradually increasing the Remagen commitment until it would not be pulled back." But he emphasized "gradually" and conceded that exploitation eastward would have to await Third Army crossings at Mainz later on, lest the First Army "have no flank support on the right . . . go too far too fast and get chopped up for its pains." Afterward Bradley quietly took Patton aside and told him to "coordinate his plans with Patch." Patton resisted the idea of coordinating his plans with Patch, but he did not question the plan, having anticipated a dash into the Saar as long ago as February 2, when he had privately resolved in his diary that it would be the "height of folly both from a political and military angle" to end the war with the Third Army and 6th Army Group on the defensive. In the month since, Patton had set his sights on Trier and the Saar, an idea that had "popped" into his head "like Minerva."

In the next several days, bad fortune plagued the Remagen build-up, which confirmed Bradley's second thoughts about quick exploitation of the bridgehead. General Millikin's III Corps tanks and infantry poured across the river in what commanders on the scene testified was unusual confusion caused by transportation bottlenecks and cratered roads. Luftwaffe action intensified and by the tenth, Panzer Lehr and the 11th Panzer spearheaded German counterattacks by elements of twelve German divisions, staved off by Ninth Air Force attacks on German rail lines, hangars, dumps and the local autobahn.

The deliberate build-up at Remagen proceeded. By the eleventh, three heavy pontoon and treadway bridges were complete, and the 9th and 78th divisions were across with elements of others, including three infantry regiments, two armored infantry battalions and a tank battalion. German counterattacks failed to shake Millikin's hold, but the Germans contained the perimeter with infantry and set up blocking positions on the high ground between the bridge and the autobahn. Plans to push VII Corps and V Corps through the bridgehead were "on hold."

Thus Eisenhower's directive of March 13 was a formality and represented a tacit consensus among Eisenhower, Brooke, Churchill, Montgomery, Bradley and Devers insofar as UNDERTONE took precedence over efforts to develop the American bridgehead. In it he noted that LUMBERJACK had achieved "economical defensive lines north of the Moselle," and that Remagen had placed forces in a position "to assist both PLUNDER and UNDERTONE without detracting from either." Accordingly, the 12th Army Group was to *secure* the bridgehead for an eventual thrust toward Frankfurt upon completion of UNDERTONE, as well as to maintain ten divisions in readiness "for exploitation of the bridgehead north of the Ruhr."

Meanwhile UNDERTONE commenced, the product of Eisenhower's persistence and foresight. On the afternoon of the fourteenth, as Seventh Army assaults opened at Haguenau, Walker's XX Corps attack kicked off from Trier, and Eddy's XII Corps, consisting of the 5th and 90th divisions, crossed the Moselle unopposed at four points along the exposed right flank of the German Seventh Army. By the next morning the Third Army was operating deep against the flank of the disheveled remnants of the enemy's Seventh Army. "Visited Trier," Patton mused that night, "so did Ceasar whose Gallic wars I am now reading. It is interesting to view in imagination the Roman legions marching down that same road. . . ."

On it went, and by March 15 the German collapse west of the Rhine accelerated on a grand scale. Years later, Eisenhower would recall that in the western war, the German defeat in the Saar was exceeded in its completeness only by the mass surrender in Tunisia. The campaign lasted less than a week. In the south, fourteen divisions of Patch's army attacked the German First Army between Saarlautern and Haguenau on a broad front. In the north, XX Corps, built up to six divisions, pushed through the West

Wall near Trier while Eddy's XII Corps advanced into the rear of the German Seventh Army through the sector left exposed in the belief that Patton would advance over the Rhine at Remagen. By the sixteenth the front was "fluid." Spearheaded by Gaffey's 4th Armored, XII Corps plunged through the Hunsrück mountains into the Nahe River Valley toward the Rhine at Mainz and Worms, and the rout commenced.

In the next seventy-two hours Walker and Eddy enveloped the right wing of the German Seventh Army, and pressed south to cut German First Army communications opposite Patch, fending off the German withdrawal and a race for Rhine bridges that would net 50,000 prisoners and strip the Rhine of defenders between Mainz and Karlsruhe. For an interval, neighboring Allied forces enviously watched the textbook Third Army maneuver, which rolled up the flank and rear of two German armies and within ninety-six hours reached the Rhine at Coblenz, Worms and Bad Dürkheim. Patton in his diary made note of a rare compliment offered by Eisenhower, who flew in on the sixteenth for an inspection of the front lines near Trier. He quoted Eisenhower as generously praising him and telling him that the men of the Third Army were such veterans that they did not appreciate their own greatness and "should be more cocky and boastful. . . ."

In the next few days the American advance through the Saar triggered a burst of pride throughout the Army. Twelfth Army Group headquarters in Namur hummed with excitement over the salty congratulatory telegrams passing between Patton and Patch as Patton arrived at the Rhine with bridging equipment and tacit permission to push across before Montgomery's set-piece crossings north of Düsseldorf, set for the twenty-third. The diarist described the merriment, which included poking fun at SHAEF. In Namur, Bradley and Hodges bantered about SHAEF's lingering "hold" on a "major effort" east of the Rhine, and chuckled as they recounted 21st Army Group's long-ago requests for a "diversion" between Cologne–Bonn just before Hodges had taken Remagen. Descending from "the sublime to the ridiculous," according to the First Army diarist, everyone had a good laugh from the stories that SHAEF had been "disappointed" about the news of the Remagen bridge lest it interfere with Montgomery's preparations for PLUNDER.

Thereafter VII Corps moved into the Remagen bridgehead and pushed out six miles to the Frankfurt autobahn. By the seventeenth the five American divisions in the Remagen bridgehead stretched for twenty miles toward Bonn and Coblenz. Breakout attacks were still "on hold," though Bradley and Hodges were at work on a breakout offensive to bring V Corps through the bridgehead, push out on the right toward Giessen and link up with the Third Army for the assault on Kassel via the Frankfurt corridor.

Meanwhile Kesselring replaced Von Rundstedt as OB West, which excited Soviet suspicions of Allied-German dealings encompassing the entire western front. In Moscow, Stalin summoned Deane and drilled him with questions: Had Wolff spoken to Kesselring? Did the Wolff overture affect the plans presented by Tedder? Was the Remagen bridgehead a diversion? Or had Remagen become the main effort? Simultaneously, Harriman and British Ambassador Kerr met a "deadlock" in talks on Poland as the list of Allied-Soviet difficulties over Poland proliferated amid Moscow's intensified drive for recognition of the Lublin provisional government.

The sharp deterioration of Allied-Soviet relations produced one positive step. On March 19 General Ivan Susloparoff arrived in Reims as an observer at Allied Supreme Headquarters in surrender talks, and unofficially to serve as a point of contact between SHAEF and STAVKA. This was significant, and it bore out Harriman's encouraging assessment that week that the Soviets, recognizing that the Germans would insist on dealing with the Allies in the early stages of surrender talks, would not oppose SHAEF-Kesselring negotiations provided formal surrenders included the Soviets. But Susloparoff arrived with only vague information about the current Red Army campaign along the Baltic coast and no brief to reveal Soviet plans on the Oder.

Eager to develop the contact, Eisenhower met Susloparoff that morning for an hour and confronted him with the improving military situation, which made it likely that Allied forces would quickly succeed in gaining several major footholds east of the Rhine. Eisenhower raised the problem of coordinating a Soviet-Allied linkup, and emphasized that prearranged signals of recognition would not be good enough; firm understandings on lines of demarcation set in advance were necessary, along with a mechanism for coordinating military action. Susloparoff held out no hope of imminent resumption of Russian operations along the Oder, owing to an early spring thaw.

By the nineteenth, with PLUNDER ninety-six hours away, Eisenhower was ready to authorize breakout attacks at Remagen and Third Army Rhine crossings. The ongoing defeat of German Army Group G in the Palatinate was opening up a sixty-mile stretch of the Rhine. Soon Patton would be in a position to cross the Rhine at Coblenz and Mainz, where he could develop drives north to link up with Hodges and south to support Devers over the Rhine into the Karlsruhe area. Devers' relatively slow progress through the Siegfried Line at Haguenau was a complicating factor, but the defeat of the German Army Group G was a matter of days.

The night before, Bradley had flown in for talks about plans for the linkup between Hodges and Patton at Giessen and the First and Third Army offensive toward Kassel (VOYAGE). Eisenhower had authorized Huebner's V Corps to move into the Remagen bridgehead, and tentatively approved Hodges' plans setting the breakout attack from Remagen toward Giessen for the twenty-fifth. This raised the urgent question of long-range 12th Army Group objectives. To be sure that he and Bradley understood each other completely, Eisenhower had given Bradley a friendly order to accompany him and his staff on a brief trip to Cannes on the French Riviera for rest, relaxation and talks about Patton, Devers, the Ruhr, the Ninth Army and on the fateful topic of Berlin. On the afternoon of the nineteenth, the entourage was airborne.

BERLIN

By the nineteenth, Eisenhower was near exhaustion. For days Smith and Summersby had noted signs of extreme fatigue, building since mid-January after the Ardennes battle, which had taxed Eisenhower's mental and physical reserves without letup. Eisenhower, a man of seemingly inexhaustible energy, had been showing occasional lapses in concentration and finding it necessary to be away from the office more than usual. According to Summersby, Smith had taken it upon himself that week to confront Eisenhower with the fact that he was tired and needed a rest. "Look at you," Smith told him. "You have bags under your eyes. Your blood pressure is higher than it has ever been, and you can hardly walk across the room."

Summersby would later describe the brief Cannes interlude as Eisenhower's only real break in ten months. The group stayed at the Villa Sous le Vent, a spacious mansion near Cannes overlooking the Mediterranean, which had served as a hostel for American generals since September 1944. As the story goes, in the first forty-eight hours, Eisenhower was too tired to venture outside into the warming Riviera sunshine and too tired to concentrate at cards. He dressed and appeared at cocktail hour and meals, then skipped the movie and bridge and sauntered back to bed. Fourteen months of unceasing tension had left him old beyond his years, and yet, after two days of complete rest, he began to join in the card games and to look "somewhat human."

Cannes was a good setting for wide-ranging discussions between Eisenhower and Bradley. Eisenhower's idea was to get away for a talk far removed from the office so that the two of them could work out problems with a certain detachment. At Cannes he hoped to repair past misunderstandings and rekindle a bit of their camaraderie in the glow of the unfolding 12th Army Group pursuit campaign and Bradley's long-awaited promotion to four-star rank, approved earlier that week, which placed a Senate stamp of approval on his leadership. Eisenhower and Bradley got along, but to the others present it was apparent that a barrier remained.

Bradley had long borne the brunt of defending Eisenhower's policies to an American command that had become restless with what it felt were needless concessions to a seemingly ungrateful British ally. The list was a long one dating back to the earliest days of North Africa, and in the past fourteen months included 21st Army Group command over the invasion battle, the even-handed supply allocations in September 1944 that had sacrificed American position for the sake of MARKET-GARDEN, and the command transfer in December. All were questionable pro-British decisions in the eyes of men trained to think in terms of military professionalism, and not of inter-Allied problems, which were Eisenhower's concern.

But things had been going very well for the 12th Army Group, which at long last enabled Bradley to look beyond the problem of restoring the prestige and morale of the 12th Army Group and to rest assured about the eventual fate of the U.S. First and Third armies. In the weeks since the end of the German counteroffensive, Bradley had successfully launched a rebound offensive, expanded it first into the Cologne plain and then across the Rhine and the Moselle. And so the time was ripe to define Bradley's mission in the closing offensives.

What were Allied objectives? In the third week of March it was pointless to plan for every contingency. Bradley had two corps across the Rhine at Bonn instead of Frankfurt, which no one had foreseen two months before. PLUNDER was imminent, and in the Saar, Patton's forces had completed the capture of Coblenz and now drove southeast toward linkup with the Seventh Army and cross points at Oppenheim with bridging and amphibious equipment moving up close on the heels of the advancing infantry. Unknowns included how hard the Germans would fight and when the Russians would resume the offensive in full force. From the Allied point of view, however, this was the most favorable military situation imaginable, and it enabled the Allies to weigh many combinations of possible objectives in light of Eisenhower's overall mission of harnessing the combined strength of Allied and Russian forces for the purpose of achieving the total unconditional surrender of Germany. Exactly what this phrase meant had been debated for some time, but barring a formal German surrender, unconditional surrender meant the suppression of organized German resistance, rendering Germany powerless to oppose four-power occupation.

Toward this end, Eisenhower envisioned adjustments to exploit the possibilities created by the American breakthrough. His priority remained the seizure of the Ruhr, to be taken by envelopment from the north *and* south, which was now a settled feature of invasion strategy. Thereafter, Eisenhower's first priority—as Tedder had indicated to Stalin—would be the advance from the Ruhr toward the Russian lines in the center for the purpose of linking up Allied and Soviet forces and cutting Germany in two, which would pocket enemy forces and simplify the final task of suppressing German resistance. In this phase Eisenhower contemplated a change. The Ninth Army, currently assigned to Montgomery, would revert to Bradley's command in order to support the First Army drive on Leipzig. The British would probably object to this, since it would temporarily reduce Montgomery to a support role, but the transfer of the Ninth Army back to Bradley would have a number of advantages: first, as an American force, it appropriately belonged to the 12th Army Group; second, the shift would improve coordination in the Ruhr battle; third, it would centralize control of American ground forces under Bradley in the pursuit phase when tight control over all units would be at a premium to avoid clashes with the Russians and to carry out the complicated maneuvers entailed in linkup, and then to apportion units to support Montgomery and Devers in their drive to pre-empt German withdrawals into northern and southern redoubts. In short, the 12th Army Group now assumed a predominant role, but in pursuit of long-standing objectives set for the invasion: Denmark in the north, Leipzig in the center, Austria in the south.

Significantly, Eisenhower listed Berlin and western Czechoslovakia as low-priority Allied objectives. The omission of Berlin as a high priority was not surprising. Eisenhower's long-range intentions remained the very ones he had outlined for Montgomery as early as September 1944, when he had responded to the latter's proposed Berlin thrust with a plan calling for a major operation to seize the Ruhr, followed up by several thrusts towards Hamburg–Kiel, and a second toward Munich–Linz. Eisenhower's consistent support for this strategy suggests that he had long since ruled out Berlin, but even the firmest plans rested on one major contingency: that the Russians act in timely fashion to take Berlin.

Berlin's low priority had always been implicit in Eisenhower's thinking; what changed at Cannes was that it became explicit in the course of thorough discussions between Eisenhower and Bradley, who found themselves more or less in agreement. Years later, Bradley would recall to me the Cannes discussions about Berlin and Eisenhower's logic. Was Berlin attainable? Despite the distances separating Allied forces and Berlin, Bradley and Eisenhower concluded that Berlin was probably attainable, given the timing of the Allied offensive, the thinning out of forces in the west and the German build-up opposite the Russians. Berlin was not attainable cheaply, however. Operations that far east might outrun supply or bog down in the marshy western approaches to the city and be vulnerable to flanking attacks from Denmark and Austria, meaning that in the best of circumstances, Berlin would be a full-scale commitment of Allied resources. Indeed, assuming even light German resistance, Allied casualties might run as high as 100,000 —in Bradley's words, "a heavy price to pay for a prestige objective . . . especially when we've got to fall back and let the other fellow take over."

What was to be gained? In military terms, very little. In military terms the crucial fact was that along the critical center front between eastern Czechoslovakia and Stettin the Russians had massed overwhelming power. In the Oder sector alone an estimated 750,000 troops gathered within thirty-five miles of Berlin. In addition, Konev's First Ukrainian Army deployed five field and two tank armies in the Breslau–Dresden area with three Russian army groups advancing through Czechoslovakia. This meant that except in the case of an indefinite Soviet pause, Berlin was a logical Soviet target and that Allied operations into the area would be redundant at best.

There was the counterargument, advanced by Churchill, that with the fall of Berlin, German resistance would become incoherent and demoralized, but it was far from clear that an Allied seizure of Berlin would accomplish this. One factor that made Berlin a feasible project for the Allies was an apparent German decision to stand in the east in the hope that Allied forces would join up with German forces and spare them the fate of surrendering to the Russians. Hence, the Allied capture of Berlin in such circumstances might encourage the Germans to prolong the fighting indefinitely in areas that Allied troops did not reach, a prospect magnified by the respite afforded by-passed German units, which would probably try to withdraw into the redoubts. In short, Berlin would be a diversion at best, mainly if not solely justified in political terms—that is, by the idea that Allied seizure of the highly visible prestige objective and the surrounding Soviet EAC zone might provide postwar leverage via-à-vis the Soviet Union.

Officially, the merits and demerits of Berlin as a political objective did not directly concern Eisenhower in his capacity as a military commander. But military objectives were pointless unless they served political aims, and so, in formulating strategy, Eisenhower was interpreting policy. What was Allied policy? As embodied in Eisenhower's directives, Allied policy was the defeat of Germany in conjunction with the Soviets. Nowhere did his directive refer to long-range cooperation with the Soviets or deferring to Soviet conquests in Europe, but his directive did require him to consider the impact of his actions on Allied-Soviet military cooperation and to consider the specific aim of that cooperation—still unachieved: the unconditional surrender of German forces. In Eisenhower's view, unconditional surrender did not foreclose the pursuit of other objectives incidental to it, but objectives that undermined it were another matter. An Allied offensive at Berlin would require that other military objectives within the reach of his forces be by-passed for the sake of extending Allied conquests to distant areas within the immediate range of large Soviet forces. The consequences of such a move were speculative, but Eisenhower had reason to doubt that Allied-Soviet cooperation would survive an Allied drive on Berlin, and was mindful that his forces still lacked the power to accomplish the unconditional surrender of German forces without the cooperation of Russian forces, and that the phrase referred to an act of capitulation to the forces of all three powers. Moreover, Churchill had spoken of seizing portions of the Soviet EAC zone to enhance Allied bargaining power in negotiating Soviet compliance with agreements elsewhere. But Berlin was different, and the British, too, approached Berlin carefully in military terms, which implied that they recognized that a bargaining strategy based on the seizure of Berlin would probably be too provocative. Such a strategy could be effective only insofar as the Allies convinced the Russians that they were willing to hold on there and to subvert the EAC agreements. Confronted by a credible Allied threat to hold Berlin, the Soviets were as likely as not to conclude that the Allies had written off negotiations and the chances of even minimal cooperation.

On all of this, Eisenhower had no specific guidance. He relied on his personal judgment, reinforced by months of consultations and recent CCS silence about his updated plans, which implicitly accorded Berlin low priority. The lack of specific CCS guidance was not new. Eisenhower had not had CCS guidance in the Darlan affair, nor had he sought affirmative CCS approval of his decisions to order landings at Salerno and Normandy, or approval of a broad-front advance beyond the Seine, or to order the transfer of two American armies from Bradley to Montgomery at the height of the Ardennes battle, or to invade the Saar, which he had been neither encouraged nor forbidden to do. Eisenhower had often confronted such choices, which did not mean that war policy was ambiguous or that he was duty-bound to seek specific approval of his plans. Occasionally his duty had been to act without CCS approval, which (a) avoided involving the CCS in the details of theater policy, (b) avoided confusion stemming from prolonged debate, and (c) avoided compromising the ability of the CCS to disavow bad results.

Accordingly, Eisenhower and Bradley considered other objectives. They discussed "OSS reports" and cryptic ULTRA fragments indicating the possibility of German redoubts in Norway and Austria and evidence of a transfer under way of government ministries into the Erft–Leipzig area and to Berchtesgaden. The Allies had to reckon with the hundred-odd German divisions believed to be south of Frankfurt–Prague, and Bradley foresaw a potentially difficult struggle "rooting fanatical suicidal troops out of strongly fortified positions with heavy casualties to our side."

Bradley recalled that he and Eisenhower were in complete accord and quickly settled on the next steps: a Third and First Army advance from Frankfurt, encirclement of the Ruhr involving both armies and Simpson's Ninth Army at Kassel–Paderborn, reduction of the Ruhr pocket, return of the Ninth Army from Montgomery to Bradley, then pursuit from Kassel toward Leipzig. Having met the Soviets on the Elbe, the Allies would be in a position to push Simpson north to support Montgomery's effort to isolate Denmark while Patton and Devers drove south into the Austrian redoubt area. As for the technical problem of deciding on a demarcation line, Bradley suggested the Elbe–Mulde lines, which arched southeastward from Hamburg to Leipzig to Chemnitz.

Again, all of this was subject to a caveat: that the Russian forces move in timely fashion, for eventually the Allies would overrun their military objectives and be in position to assist the Soviets in reaching theirs. That time might come sooner than expected, and Eisenhower would soon be employing all public and official channels to prod the Soviets into action. But in practical terms Eisenhower's decision at Cannes in mid-March to orient Bradley on Leipzig with the idea of dividing up the 12th Army Group to support offensives into the north and south all but foreclosed the possibility that the Allies would take Berlin, and closed a long chapter in the wartime debates pending CCS ratification of his plans. Deciding on that policy had posed problems for Eisenhower; implementing that policy would bring further problems, but defending Berlin policy before a generation of American politicians and historians would present far greater ones.

Troubles were in the wind. No controversy involving Eisenhower would be more enduring, though in restrospect it would appear that the real source of disagreement between Eisenhower and future historians was Eisenhower's broad-front strategy decision in August 1944, which had all but ensured that Russian forces would be at the German frontier when the Allies invaded. Nevertheless, criticism would focus on Eisenhower's imminent actions in April 1945 and would parallel the arguments raised about Berlin in the closing weeks of the war.

Point one concerned British arguments that Eisenhower misjudged the "military" importance of Berlin. In the next several weeks Eisenhower would take the lead in propagating the idea that the Allied high command had written off the military importance of Berlin because of the bombings, the evacuation of German ministries elsewhere and so on, but this line obscured the main point: whatever its military significance, Berlin in Eisenhower's judgment was not an appropriate "military" target for Allied forces.

More enduring lines of criticism would focus on the appropriateness of Eisenhower's "military" approach in the spring of 1945. As the argument went, by March 1945 Eisenhower faced new circumstances. The German "military" threat had vanished, leaving only the Russian threat, and so one could argue that the goals of unconditional surrender had been fulfilled. This meant that Eisenhower's true military task—now that he had fulfilled the mission spelled out in his directive—was to position his forces in order to liberate as much European territory as possible and thus limit the reach of Soviet tyranny over Eastern Europe. In failing to do so, Eisenhower had blundered and signaled a failure of Allied will that subtly communicated itself throughout Europe and accounted, in part, for the ease with which the Soviets proceeded to install a system of satellites in Eastern Europe. Similarly, criticism would revive Churchill's argument that "military" and "political" objectives might have been combined at that late stage of the war, and that Allied control of the Soviet EAC zone would have enabled the Allies to negotiate Soviet "compliance" with a host of non-German agreements affecting Eastern Europe, Austria and so on. These arguments are essentially the same, for to combine "military" and "political" objectives would have meant combining policies as well, a policy of defeating Germany with a policy of blocking Russian gains. To an extent, the Allies had always had this dual objective, though the defeat of Germany had always taken overriding precedence, and even the British conceded the unique importance of the EAC zones as the thread linking the victorious powers.

In retrospect, it is doubtful that Eisenhower, in March 1945, foresaw the intensity of the debates ahead or realized how misunderstood Allied restraint on Berlin would be. But the alternative course was drastic, for it probably involved abandoning Allied-Soviet cooperation altogether with sizable German forces in the field and embarking on a challenge to vital Soviet interests in Germany that would have jeopardized and probably destroyed the emerging settlement of World War II. Criticism of Eisenhower's Berlin decision usually exaggerates Eisenhower's military freedom of action, but above all it minimizes the significance of unconditional surrender as an Allied war aim, the significance of the EAC zones and the importance of adhering to a military approach on all questions affecting Germany. These were not simply aspects of war policy and Allied-Soviet relations but the very essence of both—indeed it is tempting to say that the actual Russian conquest of Berlin had been preordained for months if not years.

Eisenhower's position on Berlin had long antecedents. The earlier COSSAC drafts of occupation sectors issued in July 1943, which on the eve of the Moscow-Teheran conferences had placed Berlin deep in the proposed Soviet occupation zone, were both an estimate of how far Russian forces would reach and a signal of Allied approval, though the zones reflected a decision to divide Germany equally in order to share the burden of occupation, and were not meant as stop lines for military action. At Teheran—the decisive moment—the three sides had resolved to set aside their quarrels for the sake of the unconditional surrender and three-power occupation of Germany. Allied commitments at Teheran, especially ANVIL, did not expressly entail the Soviet conquest of Eastern Europe or Berlin.

Thereafter, a Berlin policy had steadily evolved, however. In February 1944 the EAC opened shop and the CCS issued the SHAEF directive that called on Eisenhower to advance on the "heart" of Germany "in conjunction with" other Allied forces. By the spring of 1944 the Red Army was in Poland, and SHAEF planning had begun to focus on the Ruhr as an alternative to Berlin, since the Ruhr was within reach of Allied forces and a logical objective. The invasion followed, and Eisenhower's broad-front decision in August 1944 was carried out, which in Montgomery's mind settled Berlin for all time in that it made sure that Russian forces would be on the German frontiers when the Allied invasion of Germany commenced. But the broad-front decision was a defensive strategy as much as an invasion strategy, and that Eisenhower had made no final commitment to invasion strategy was borne out by Churchill's effort to clarify American views in March 1945.

But by March 1945 the Soviet conquest of Berlin was all but set, confirmed by the outcome of the German and Russian winter offensives, which left Allied forces distant from Berlin and Russian forces within reach of it as well as of the Russian EAC zone, duly ratified at Yalta. Since then the CCS had acquiesced in Eisenhower's preliminaries west of the Rhine, and had set aside plans for replacing Tedder with Alexander. Technically, Berlin remained a "military" question, an issue to be decided on a military basis, as the military circumstances obtained. But by late March, only unforeseen circumstances—for example, a Russian decision to forgo an offensive until summer—were likely to convince Eisenhower that Berlin was militarily wise.

Few were pleased by this, but few would oppose Eisenhower openly, and those who did had other objectives in mind. Churchill was depressed by the prospect of a Russian victory at Berlin, but resigned to it. He was concerned about the Russians, but an equal concern in March was the effect of the "deadly hiatus" in Washington, where that week a weary President Roosevelt ordered his personal office belongings shipped to Hyde Park, and left the White House for a desperately needed rest in Warm Springs. Marshall, who had gradually assumed caretaker leadership of the war effort, was weary too and known to be leaving the Pentagon by three o'clock daily. Thus, for the moment, the leadership in Washington lacked the energy to balance conciliation and firmness, which in British eyes left American policy dangerously suspended between the extremes of unqualified friendship toward Russia and all-out rivalry, which a Berlin offensive would have provoked.

Could the Allies have done otherwise? In an interview years later, Marshall would endorse Eisenhower's actions as understandable at the time, which implied regret. Montgomery would recite his many criticisms of the decision in his memoir, as would Brooke in his, but both blamed Eisenhower's broad-front strategy in August 1944 and neglected to explain why they failed to support the Berlin strategy, which might have succeeded in March 1945. Nor would Eisenhower in his memoir explain the decision in much detail. In *Crusade,* written in 1948 at the height of the Berlin airlift crisis, he would confine himself to the military arguments in favor of the redoubt strategy, which implied that he regretted the necessity of conceding Berlin to the Soviets in April 1945. But when wartime controversies failed to fade away, Eisenhower would embark on a political career implicitly devoted to defending his wartime decisions, which "hewed strictly to Roosevelt's political desires," as historian Forrest Pogue later put it. Difficulties lay ahead, but again, even had he foreseen them, Eisenhower presumably would not have mobilized an Allied offensive for Berlin.

Indeed, by March 20, Berlin was very straightforward, as Eisenhower and Bradley saw it. The Soviets were massed in the vicinity and Berlin was in the center of the Soviet EAC Zone. Allied forces were gaining strength, but the Allies had not reached their vital objectives in Denmark and

Austria. German forces at large numbered seven million and the universal desire was to end the fighting and impose order in Europe. Thus, the real question was not whether but how to proceed with the unfinished business of the invasion of Germany and ending the costliest war in history. And, as Pogue put it, "considered from the purely military viewpoint of the quickest way to end the war in Germany with the fewest number of casualties to our troops, leaving the maximum number available for rapid deployment to the Pacific, his [Eisenhower's] decision was certainly the proper one."

The final invasion of the war was in readiness. The Cannes interlude, which had finally brought Eisenhower and Bradley together after months of difficulties, came to an end amid news of fast-breaking developments. After sloughing off a German counterattack at Saarbrücken, the U.S. Seventh Army joined Patton in the pursuit. For several tense days, Third and Seventh Army pincers compressed the German withdrawal at Kaiserslautern into a six-mile corridor under merciless air and artillery bombardment in the Saar–Palatinate. In five days of perfect weather, the Ninth Air Force flew 2,300 sorties against rail links and roads in hopes of cutting the German retreat. On the twenty-first Eisenhower, in Cannes, phoned Patton and authorized him to push "vigorously with the object of establishing a firm bridgehead across the Rhine in the Frankfurt area from which an advance in strength can be made at a later date in the general direction of Kassel."

Twenty-four hours later, six battalions of General Irwin's 5th Division carried out night crossings at Oppenheim, where intelligence confirmed the wide gap in German defenses. By eleven o'clock that night the 5th Division was ashore at the cost of two casualties. By the morning of the twenty-third, engineers were constructing treadways and Irwin held a three-mile-square sector, with Allied intelligence reporting "scattered and ineffective resistance." Patton, with Eisenhower's permission, called a press conference that morning to announce the second American Rhine bridgehead, the climax of a ten-day U.S. Army campaign that netted 63,000 German prisoners.

PLUNDER, the culmination of four months of 21st Army Group planning and preparations, was set for that night. Dignitaries and press arriving to observe the assault witnessed scenes reminiscent of Portsmouth in May 1944. From Nijmegen to the Rhine town of Neuss, roadsides were piled high with ammunition and equipment brought in from railheads west of the Maas. Farms and meadowlands had been converted into a vast cantonment of trucks, assault craft, tanks, jeeps and gliders. But the preparations lacked the suspense and electricity surrounding OVERLORD, for the operation, with its origins in Montgomery's proposal for a bold war-ending offensive in September 1944, was overshadowed by the clamor of Patton's crossings, Patch's announcement on the twenty-fourth certifying that organized German resistance west of the Rhine had ceased, the stories of frenzied crowds rioting in Coblenz and Milan, the Hungarian surrender, the pro-Communist Rumanian coup, the opening of the UN conference in San Francisco, the news of the breakdown of the five-year British Conservative-Labour peace pact, the angry denunciations of Yalta by the London Polish government, and other tidings of turmoil in Europe.

British accounts of the day were subdued. At Venlo, Churchill toured Montgomery's command post, the nerve center for the thirty divisions and six armored brigades deployed on a 65-mile front poised to assault north and south of the Wesel. Churchill later wrote that he was favorably impressed by Montgomery's reliance on a system of officer-scouts who shuttled back and forth from the front with eyewitness reports, the so-called Phantom Service. Churchill nostalgically recalled Marlborough's similar system in the dynastic wars of the eighteenth century, when "battles were fought on a 5–6 mile front, ended in a day and settled the fortunes of generations."

That night, as the assault began, Montgomery and Churchill discussed history over dinner. Montgomery later recalled that he asked the Prime Minister if he knew the last time British troops had fought on German soil. Churchill instantly replied the Royal Brigade and Royal Horse Artillery, in the Battle of the Nations at Leipzig, 1813. The Prime Minister commented on the irony that Germans had fought on both sides of that battle.

At six in the evening near Xanten, 1,000 guns fired through the smoke screen laid to mask the naval preparations. Four battalions of the 51st Highland Division of El Alamein fame led the procession aboard the assault boats. The crossings began shortly after nine o'clock. Within seven minutes the first wave had landed safely, and by ten the Scots had gained a foothold with ease and a command brigade had crossed two miles west of the Wesel. That night 80,000 troops in four assault divisions crossed at ten points on a twenty-mile front.

Several miles away Eisenhower, somewhat restored from his sojourn at Cannes, arrived at Ninth Army Headquarters in Rheinberg to observe the night assault by the U.S. 30th and 79th divisions. He stayed up until four standing in a belfry watching the fire of 2,070 American artillery pieces light the night. At two o'clock the U.S. 30th Division crossed at the confluence of the Lippe and the Rhine against scattered and ineffective resistance. By midmorning on the twenty-fourth, the invasion force had moved an average of 500 yards inland along the fifteen-mile front against sporadic resistance. VARSITY followed, the largest airborne operation of the war. Applying lessons learned at Arnhem, 1,700 airplanes and 1,300 gliders dropped 22,000 troops and five million pounds of equipment close in on the assault formations to avoid a significant time lapse before linkup of the airborne and assault troops. By nightfall the Ninth Army had a bridgehead nine miles wide and three miles deep.

Meanwhile Eisenhower returned to Namur for meetings with Bradley.

There, he formally approved VOYAGE, relayed to the CCS a low-key message presenting the accomplished fact of American divisions across the Rhine at two bridgeheads capable of being expanded "very cheaply" and "consolidated and expanded rapidly to support a major thrust which will assist the northern operation more effectively and make our exploitation more effective." That night Eisenhower flew back to Rheinberg for meetings with Brooke and Churchill.

The morning of March 25 was dreary and overcast. Eisenhower, Churchill and Brooke discussed Moscow's latest protests over Wolff's meeting with Alexander's emissaries, about which Ambassador Kerr had kept Molotov closely informed. Several days earlier, Molotov had dispatched a rude telegram to Eden insinuating that separate-peace talks had started, demanding that all contacts be broken off and announcing his decision not to attend the UN meetings in San Francisco. According to Churchill, Eisenhower was deeply angered by Molotov's "unjust and unfounded" charges and demands. With Russian consent, "what could be settled by himself and Kesselring in an hour might be prolonged for three or four weeks." But Moscow was seemingly not ready for a quick cease-fire and content to stall for a while, which was a sign that an offensive on Berlin was still some time off.

And so a tense period, lasting three to four weeks, stretched out before Eisenhower that day. In the interval between PLUNDER and the formal German capitulation, assuming there was one, he would have to manage linkup between British, American and Russian forces, resolve the looming problem of Czechoslovakia, navigate the problem of Berlin and organize a dash to Austria and Denmark, all carried out without consultation with Moscow or clear-cut authority to work out arrangements with the Russians.

In approving VOYAGE, Churchill generously pronounced himself satisfied to rely on Eisenhower's discretion, adding that he did "not see why we should break our hearts, if, owing to mass surrender in the west, we get to the Elbe, or even farther, before Stalin." Churchill told Eisenhower he had doubts about dismembering Germany until his doubts about Russia's intentions had been cleared away. But Churchill had doubts, not suggestions.

Eisenhower, Churchill and Brooke ambled to a nearby house to observe the XVI Corps battle. From a porch, they watched the explosions and widely scattered flashes of answering artillery dimly visible in the fog. The scene emphasized the tranquillity of the Rhine, crossed by thousands of slow-gaited landing craft and small naval ships. The calm was startling. Montgomery would allude to it in a directive four days later in which he characterized enemy divisions east of the Rhine as "all very weak when the battles for the Rhineland began . . . getting no replacements and . . . mere skeletons . . . lacking fresh or complete divisions in reserve," which reduced the enemy to blocking "roads and approaches with personnel from schools, bath units, pigeon lofts, and so on."

The three men gazed at the crossing in awe. Brooke, the tireless advocate of concentration at Düsseldorf, was apparently the one least prepared for the spectacle of an assault so flawless, even effortless. Perhaps he thought back to 1940 and 1941, the years of defeat and isolation when the Germans had seemed to be so invincible. Was it conceivable that the war was over? "Thank God, Ike, you stuck by your plan," Brooke said at one point. "The German is now finished and I apologize if my fear of dispersed effort added to your burdens."

In the years ahead, Eisenhower would often recount the episode to illustrate that beneath the façade of differences, the Allied high command had always been closely united on basic aims. In 1948 Eisenhower would go on to publish the story in *Crusade,* and so it would stand for a decade. Then, perhaps inevitably, in January 1958, in the twilight of Eisenhower's presidency, and after the Suez trauma loosened inhibitions on both sides of the Atlantic, Brooke would publish his dairies, including *his* account of March 25, in which he quoted himself as having personally congratulated Eisenhower that day on the success of UNDERTONE, which to his mind exposed the weakness of German forces, a weakness that he had never permitted himself to assume in drawing up grand strategy. He would go on to explain that on March 25, 1945, he gave his formal consent to the American offensive because of this unforeseen collapse of German resistance, which enabled the Allies to contemplate plans on a broader scale than he had anticipated. Otherwise, Brooke denied that he had ever agreed with Eisenhower on strategy in Europe or on military matters. But truly, on the dull, overcast morning of March 25, the war in Europe, at the price of fifty million lives and untold demoralization and misery to be visited on many generations, was ending.

INVASION OF GERMANY

And so, by the night of the twenty-fifth, the Rhine front was pierced at two points with more to come. The Americans enlarged bridgeheads at Oppenheim and Remagen. The U.S. Seventh Army seized a third bridgehead at Worms on the twenty-sixth, soon followed by the French crossings at Mannheim. Meanwhile Hodges launched a three-corps break-out offensive at Remagen, and the Third Army was established at the town of Darmstadt, ninety-six hours away from linkup with the First Army at Giessen and a seventy-mile sweep to the Paderborn–Kassel area. In the 21st Army Group sector, Wesel quickly fell, and twelve Rhine bridges were operating within twenty-four hours of the assault. Anderson's XVI Corps of Simpson's Ninth Army pushed through scattered opposition toward Dortmund while XIX Corps moved over the Rhine. To the north, the Canadians broke out of the bridgeheads and secured Rees and Emmerich, launch points for operations into the north German plain. And by the twenty-eighth, seventy-two hours

THE ALLIED PLAN

Front lines as of
April 1, 1945

Proposed paths
for 12th, 21st and
6th Army Groups

Proposed British
demarcation line

Allied-controlled

N

NORWAY

DENMARK

SWEDEN

Baltic
Sea

North Sea

Lübeck

Stettin

Berlin

POLAND

NETH

Arnhem

BR.
21ST
ARMY
GROUP

RUHR

U.S. 12TH
ARMY
GROUP

Brussels

BELGIUM

Rhine

U.S. 6TH
ARMY
GROUP

Strasbourg

FRANCE

Nuremberg

Munich

OSTMARK
(AUSTRIA)

SWITZERLAND

Oder

Lodz

Breslau

Dresden

Leipzig

Elbe

Prague

GERMANY

Danube

Linz

Vienna

SLOVAKIA

Budapest

HUNGARY

Trieste

Zagreb

Genoa

Bologna

Adriatic
Sea

YUGOSLAVIA

ITALY

Miles
0   150
0   Kms. 150

after PLUNDER, Montgomery had deployed fifteen divisions east of the Rhine.

Evidently the pursuit offensive and the Ruhr battle were about to unfold as one, a development that raised new problems. Decisions approached as it became evident that Model's Army Group B, pressed back on both flanks, was falling back into the Ruhr. Six field corps with major elements of seventeen German divisions plus 100,000 flak corps troops gradually entrenched behind the Sieg and Hamm rivers, a maneuver that opened gaps north and south of the Ruhr and raised a new possibility—that of roping off and containing Model's forces with follow-up troops while the Ninth, Third and First armies advanced through the openings into the undefended reaches of central Germany.

At meetings on the twenty-sixth in Reims, Eisenhower was adamant that to "contain" a force the size of the German Army Group B would create an unacceptable hazard to Allied communications and unduly expose all units committed through the openings. This was a cautious assessment, which suggests that Eisenhower may have been motivated to fight a set-piece battle to compress a Ruhr pocket partly in hopes of buying time, which became all the more important with word once again on the twenty-seventh that the Russians still held out little prospect of resuming the offensive at the Oder.

That day, in a meeting with Ambassador Bogomolov and General Ivan Susloparoff at Reims, Eisenhower confronted them with new facts: German resistance in the west was incoherent. The Ninth Army, with first call on the Wesel bridges, would soon be advancing northeast toward linkup with the First Army, after which the Allied advance to the Elbe River would be limited only by maintenance. Allied forces could operate 150 miles from railheads with truck companies set up across the Rhine, and another 150 miles by airlift. Susloparoff again indicated that Red Army operations toward Berlin were still on hold because of ground conditions, fog and secondary operations to clear the German pockets at Danzig and Stettin.

Where were the Russians? The next morning, Eisenhower decided to present these facts at an "on the record" press conference in Paris, a veiled warning to all capitals that time was running short if the Allies and Russians were to proceed with a two-front strategy in the next few weeks. Tedder accompanied Eisenhower and spent the first fifteen minutes briefing reporters at the Scribe Hotel on the German losses since VERITABLE, which demonstrated the dimensions of the German defeat in recent weeks. On behalf of Allied forces since January 16, Tedder claimed 250,000 German troops killed or captured, the bulk of the Fifteenth, Seventh, First and Fifth panzer armies. Eisenhower followed Tedder to the podium.

In his opening statement, Eisenhower provided the most detailed outline yet of the strategy debates in recent months over ANVIL, the broad front, the Rhineland offensive, Remagen and Frankfurt. At length, he described how these debates had emanated from the two schools of Allied thought over what constituted the "heart" of Germany, which was a debate over the relative significance of the Ruhr and Berlin. Eisenhower sketched the development of Allied strategy to date aimed at the seizure of the Ruhr, the industrial heart of Germany as distinguished from Berlin, the political heart. He explained the considerations in his decision to clear out German forces west of the Rhine, a decision "opposed by some," which had set the stage for "defeats . . . he [the enemy] could not afford." Indeed, the Rhine crossings and the imminent encirclement of the Ruhr marked the end of a phase of operations, he said, and the Allies would soon be "entering upon another."

In the questioning, Eisenhower elaborated on the latter point, which emphasized that the time had come for all sides to unite around a plan for the next phase of operations. Asked whether the Germans were likely to establish "another coordinated defense line in view of what has happened," Eisenhower replied, "They need more strength than they have in the west now." Asked if he had changed his opinion of when "things would really crack," Eisenhower could not recall his earlier words, but called "the Germans, as a military force on the western front, and not considering anything else he might bring to bear, a whipped enemy." Eisenhower reminded the assembled reporters that few had foreseen that the Russians would hold in 1941, and so he could not rule out the possibility of a prolonged battle for the Ruhr but doubted it. He did "not mean to start waving flags and ringing bells," but German manpower was getting thinner and thinner, prisoners were flowing in and "if the German can bring no more to bear in the west, he can't make a front for long."

A reporter asked whether the Allies would win the race to Berlin. Eisenhower noted that the mileage factor favored the Russians. Allied spearheads were still operating more than 200 miles from Berlin, while the Russian main body massed on the Oder within 30 miles of Berlin. On the other hand, the Russians faced the bulk of German forces, and it was his understanding in talks with the Russians that poor roads and the deep frost rendered the terrain in Poland unsuitable for major thrusts for some weeks.

Accordingly, Eisenhower could not make any predictions. He entertained the theory that the Germans as a last resort might try to "hold" the Russians while letting the Allies through. He noted that the Germans, if they reasoned like human beings, "would realize the whole history of the United States and Great Britain is to be generous toward a defeated enemy," which was underscored by the fact that, unlike the Russians, the Allies observed the tenets of the Geneva Convention. And yet, the Germans in December had committed their reserves in Belgium knowing the Russians were preparing the major attack in Poland, and so Eisenhower confessed he did not know "who he [the German] considers his worst enemy in this war."

Eisenhower and Bradley met later that day to spell out in a directive pursuit plans discussed at Cannes. First, Simpson's Ninth Army would revert to Bradley's control after linkup with Hodges in the Kassel–Paderborn area. Eisenhower and Bradley decided to commit eighteen divisions of the First and Ninth armies to the task of liquidating the Ruhr pocket, an estimated concentration of 150,000 soldiers with the remainder attacking east from Paderborn toward Leipzig to "make junction with the Soviet forces in the area."

Military logic supported operations to reduce the Ruhr pocket, but Eisenhower and Bradley, in heeding military logic, would court controversy. Large forces would advance into the lifeless maze of factories and cities of the Ruhr where attackers would fight house-to-house battles without air support. As three army groups moved across the Rhine, it appeared that even if Model's Army Group B managed to convert the Ruhr into a fortress, ample strength would remain to contain Model while Bradley drove to the Elbe. Again, Eisenhower was determined to proceed methodically to encircle and defeat Army Group B, and was prepared to commit the bulk of three armies to accomplish this task, leaving only spearheads for the initial advance into central Germany. But Eisenhower was improvising, for in devising military plans with Bradley, several days before, he had not anticipated the ease of the Allied crossings or the dimensions of the German collapse along the Rhine.

How long would the Ruhr battle last? Probably not long, and so the time had come to draw out Russian views and to formalize a joint strategy. Word came late that afternoon from Washington, where news of the Rhine crossings had apparently provoked thought. Breaking silence after several weeks, Marshall dispatched a tentatively phrased cable in which he broached the problem of operations after the Ruhr. Had Eisenhower considered the possibility of an offensive toward Nuremberg–Linz or Karlsruhe–Munich to occupy the redoubt area? Marshall suggested "steps . . . initiated without delay to provide for the communications and liaison you will need with them [the Russians] during the period when your forces may be mopping up."

With this long-awaited opening, Eisenhower drafted an unprecedented "personal" message to Marshal Stalin of the Soviet Union, which he dispatched without consulting the CCS. The message was to be delivered via the military liaison office proposing "that we coordinate our action and make every effort to perfect liaison between advancing forces." In it Eisenhower outlined Allied plans for April 1945. First, Allied forces would encircle the Ruhr, which Eisenhower expected to be completed soon. Second, Allied forces would concentrate on liquidating the Ruhr pocket, an operation Eisenhower estimated would take until "late April." Thereafter, he formally proposed to concentrate on linking up with Soviet forces on an Erfurt–Leipzig–Dresden axis, whereupon his forces would advance through

Regensburg–Linz to preempt consolidation of the southern redoubt and join up with Allied-Soviet forces in central Austria. Eisenhower also proposed an immediate SHAEF-Soviet exchange of military liaison officers.

The next morning, Eisenhower followed up by sending an "amplifying" cable to Moscow in which he listed specifics on army group boundaries and missions in the next four weeks. In it he highlighted his decision to transfer the Ninth Army back to Bradley for the drive on Leipzig, which relegated Montgomery's army group to the mission of providing flank support for Bradley's 12th Army Group and foreclosed a British drive for Berlin. By revealing Montgomery's mission to the Soviets, Eisenhower apparently hoped to do two things at once: to bid for quick Soviet approval to seal the issue of Berlin; to display the scope of his authority over American and British forces so that the Soviets would refer all military queries to SHAEF. At this point, however, the CCS stepped in.

Ninety-six hours would elapse before the Allied military liaison office in Moscow delivered either message. Eisenhower's initiative spurred intense eleventh-hour debate in the CCS over two points: first, Allied plans and, second, the basis of Eisenhower's authority to deal with the Russians directly on grand strategy. What emerged was a consensus that Eisenhower was in charge, but not absolutely in charge, at least not until both the Americans and British were satisfied that the effect of Eisenhower's message would not be to lull the Russians into complacency, and until they could satisfy themselves that they understood the latent ambiguities in Eisenhower's message—specifically, what he meant by so brusquely downgrading Montgomery's role.

On the night of March 28, the BCOS chambers at Whitehall rang with indignation over Eisenhower's redundant demotion of Montgomery in the message and the surprise news of his plans to return to Bradley Simpson's Ninth Army, which he had "intended" to keep with Montgomery. In his diary Brooke chronicled the anger in the BCOS over Eisenhower's plan, which Brooke called "unintelligible," unauthorized, and a "clear breach of promise" in relegating Montgomery to a "static mission." The transfer of Simpson back to Bradley revived suspicions that, in the end, the Americans would muscle Montgomery to the sidelines, and even an American offensive for Berlin did not seem beyond the realm of possibility. On the twenty-ninth the BCOS promptly entered a motion in the CCS calling for a 21st Army Group offensive on Berlin and a second motion condemning Eisenhower's direct communication with Stalin.

The ensuing debate went on at two levels. At one, British and American representatives vented pent-up frustrations from which grew the criticism that Eisenhower had usurped his authority, and naïvely invited the Russians to enter Berlin, a criticism that ignored Eisenhower's months of consultations, his recent talks with Churchill at Rheinberg and Marshall's query on the twenty-eighth that had triggered Eisenhower's message to

Stalin. At a second level, Churchill aimed to clarify two points: first, that by foreclosing a 21st Army Group offensive for Berlin, Eisenhower had in fact foreclosed an Allied drive on Berlin; second, to remind the American JCS that Eisenhower's decision foreclosing Berlin would jeopardize attainment of crucial Allied aims along the North Sea. Churchill's reasons for raising the question of Eisenhower's right to deal with Stalin were murky, but it appears in hindsight that his purpose was as much to confront the JCS with the scope of Eisenhower's delegated powers for the purpose of maneuvering the JCS into endorsing them as it was to censure Eisenhower. The Allied front was in motion, and much would be jeopardized by planting doubts about Eisenhower's authority. According to Pogue, Churchill, who saw the weakness of the Allied case for Berlin very clearly, cautioned the BCOS that week that "this [Berlin] is a point on which the Supreme Commander must have the final word."

In hindsight, Eisenhower's message contained many ambiguities well calculated to draw the Russians into negotiations. In it he raised a wide range of possibilities for Allied and Soviet forces about which he invited Soviet comment and none of which he foreclosed for either side. First, he raised the question of Austria, a subject that Tedder had not discussed with Stalin in January. Second, he served notice that Allied forces soon to arrive en masse on the Weser River would not stand idle but would proceed to the Elbe and into what was to be the Soviet zone of occupation. Indeed, he anticipated that Allied forces would probably cross the Elbe in the north to establish a flank on the North Sea, and otherwise ruled nothing out, including Berlin, in that he committed himself to nothing beyond the proposed linkup at Leipzig and the definite Allied intention to campaign into Austria.

Had Eisenhower conceded Berlin? One might say that Eisenhower had effectively ruled out Berlin by according it a low priority, but the plan in its entirety rested on what must have appeared to the Russians a shaky assumption, given the fact that twenty-four hours earlier Eisenhower had publicly written off the German army in the west as a real military force. Likewise, Eisenhower was proposing to the Russians that Allied-Soviet forces link up along the Elbe, which meant that the Allies intended to occupy a hundred-mile sector of the Soviet EAC zone at a minimum, which might easily be extended northward to Berlin in the event the Soviets encountered unexpected delays. In short, Eisenhower proposed to present Stalin with a wide range of possible Allied moves and invited the Soviets to choose and act—quickly.

For several days, the submission of Eisenhower's two messages was on hold while messages flew back and forth between the Americans and British, who groped to clarify Eisenhower's meaning. In response to Montgomery's latest Berlin proposals, Eisenhower cabled Montgomery several times to be sure he understood that American troops would not be available in the foreseeable future to support a 21st Army Group drive for Berlin, which, he emphasized, was "largely destroyed and nothing but a geographical location." Montgomery bitterly complained to Brooke about the loss of Simpson's Ninth Army, which would confine the 21st Army Group to a holding action. Churchill addressed a stream of messages to Eisenhower and Roosevelt to protest Montgomery's demotion, and criticized for the record what he took to be Eisenhower's decision to foreclose Berlin as an Allied objective. Indeed, it is apparent that Churchill wanted no mistake about the fact that Eisenhower's plan, in weakening Montgomery, did in fact foreclose Berlin, a decision that he criticized for good measure as bound to strengthen Moscow's conviction "already apparent that they [the Russians] have done everything."

Then, on the thirtieth, the fury abated. In writing, Eisenhower pledged to Churchill that after Bradley and the Russians met at Leipzig, Simpson's Ninth Army would stand by to support Montgomery's thrust toward the Elbe and Denmark. In response to Marshall's queries, Eisenhower defended his message as a purely military one, sent in accordance with uncited "instructions to deal directly with the Russians concerning military coordination." As for the specific British charges that he had usurped political power, Eisenhower hotly insisted that destroying "enemy forces in conjunction with the Russians" by linkup at Kiel, Leipzig and Linz was a "military" problem, reminding Marshall of past British willingness to abandon the military approach at the drop of a hat. "I submit that these things are studied daily and hourly by me and my advisors," he wrote, "and that we are animated by one single thought, which is the early winning of the war." On the thirtieth, the British having subsided, the CCS ordered Eisenhower to withhold his amplifying message of March 29, thereby authorizing the submission of his first message to Stalin to probe Soviet intent.

On the night of March 31, Deane, Archer, Harriman and Kerr met Stalin and Molotov in the Kremlin. Harriman later filed a lengthy account of the conference. Stalin seemed "affable," unaffected by the recent exchanges on Poland and the Wolff affair, and appreciative of Deane's detailed brief on the western front. That night, First Army spearheads had reached the vicinity of Lippstadt, making junction with the U.S. Ninth Army, while the Third Army advanced north toward Kassel and Montgomery's armies advanced in a gradual slope northeastward toward Münster–Hannover.

Harriman "emphasized the urgency of obtaining Stalin's views" in order to coordinate plans properly, and invited attention to Eisenhower's proposal for an exchange of liaison officers.

> Stalin asked if Eisenhower had any knowledge of prepared positions toward the center of Germany to which we replied in the negative. Stalin then asked if we knew of German withdrawal of troops from Norway. We stated that Eisenhower had not given us any indication of this. Stalin asked whether the advance

of the secondary attack in the South would come from Italy or from the Western Front. We said that we understood it would come from the Western Front.

We then went over the present German order of the battle on the Western Front with Stalin as he indicated that he was interested in having us do so. Stalin asked if we could verify Soviet information that there were 60 German divisions on the Western Front. We replied that we had counted 61, but gave him the most recent changes that have been received from you. Stalin wished to know if the Germans had any additional reserves on the Western Front, and we replied that apparently they had not.

Stalin was much impressed with the number of prisoners that had been taken in the month of March and said certainly this will help finish the war very soon.

Harriman asked whether "previous estimates that operations on the Oder might be bogged down at the end of March still held good." Stalin called the situation "much better than anticipated," explaining that floods had come early, and the roads were now in the process of drying, giving Harriman the impression that the Russians were "*not* tied down because of the weather." Likewise, German pressure on the Baltic flanks was easing, though Stalin cautioned that the Germans still had sixteen divisions in Latvia, and "at best" the Germans could move out only three divisions without artillery and that would take a month. Stalin spoke of the determined German resistance along the Baltic, intimating that it had taken "about a week" to reduce Danzig—reports indicated that only about a third of the Germans really wanted to fight, but that SS troops were shooting down in the sight of the Red Army all Germans wishing to surrender.

As for Czechoslovakia–Austria, Stalin noted that the Germans were resisting strongly in the mountains of eastern Czechoslovakia, but that the resistance was of such character that it could be overcome. The Germans had committed ten armored divisions northeast of Lake Balaton, but "these had been defeated." He said that "the Germans were centering their resistance in the Bratislava Gap," but he "felt confident in overcoming it. . . ." According to Harriman:

> Stalin had apparently been considering Eisenhower's message all through the discussion, and at this point he reverted to it and said that the plan for Eisenhower's main effort was a good one in that it accomplished the most important objective of dividing Germany in half. He felt that the direction of the attack would also be favorable for a juncture with the Red Army. He felt that the Germans' last stand would probably be in the mountains of western Czechoslovakia and Bavaria. . . .

The next day, April 1, in his formal response to Eisenhower's proposals, Stalin made four points: first, Eisenhower's plan to cut the German forces by joining up at Leipzig "entirely coincides with the plan of the Soviet high command"; second, the Soviet high command considered that the main blow of the Soviet forces should also be delivered in that direction; third, the USSR agreed that Berlin had lost its former strategic importance, and, therefore, that only secondary Red Army forces should be allotted there; fourth, Stalin approved plans to link up Allied and Soviet forces in the area of Vienna–Linz–Regensburg. As for timing, Stalin predicted that the beginning of the main blow by the Soviet forces would come in mid-May, depending on the weather. The question of perfecting communications between troops was under study. Finally, regarding enemy troop strength on the eastern front, it had "been established their number is gradually being increased."

Stalin's reply gave Eisenhower the minimum. Its disingenuousness about the importance of Berlin was striking, which has often been cited as an instance of Stalin's trying to gull a naïve Allied high command. In fact, Allied reports confirmed that the bulk of the estimated two million Russian troops massed on the Oder River were poised to move southwest toward Leipzig and Czechoslovakia. But the estimated 750,000 troops that remained opposite Berlin would comprise the largest concentration of combat troops and supporting artillery of any battle in world history, and would proceed under the command of Marshal Georgi Zhukov, defender of Moscow, defender of Stalingrad, liberator of the Ukraine, Belorussia and Warsaw. Plainly, Berlin was a Soviet target, and a target of more than secondary importance—a point that required no elaboration.

The problem was timing, and on this point Stalin's message was ambiguous. Stalin did not say whether the "secondary" attack on Berlin would precede or follow the "main blow" into Czechoslovakia. But by calling Czechloslovakia the "main blow," Stalin appeared to contemplate major operations to liberate western Czechoslovakia even at the cost of delaying Berlin, which tended to confirm long-standing worries that the Russians would treat Berlin as a sure thing and postpone action there indefinitely as they campaigned elsewhere. Massive German forces were collecting in Czechoslovakia to protect the remaining industrial areas under German control and to cover the flight of refugees westward into the area, against which the Russians massed ever greater forces. In February two Red Army fronts in the western Carpathians had fought through heavy Hungarian and German resistance to open up major battles for Moravska Ostrava and Brno, and Konev's First Ukrainian Front on the Oder north of the Sudeten Mountains at Breslau bore down on Prague. The battle for western Czechoslovakia shaped up as a long one.

Despite the ambiguities, the exchange indicated progress. Stalin approved Leipzig without comment, meaning that the Soviets would not insist that the Allies stop short of the zonal boundary, though it was unclear whether or not the Russians would expect the Allies to vacate the Soviet zone on demand. Stalin had endorsed the Allied offensive to Linz–Regensburg—a sign that Moscow would not pose obstacles to an Allied zone of occupation in Austria or follow up the conquest of Vienna with a major effort there. Finally, Stalin, in supreme command of 450 divisions on the eastern front, had communicated directly with Eisenhower on a military matter, a precedent that in practical terms placed the stamp of Soviet "approval" on Eisenhower's plans and would soon bring the closing debates of the war to an abrupt end.

On the second Eisenhower followed up by submitting his detailed plans to the CCS. The British once again protested Eisenhower's decision to dissolve the northern thrust and foreclose an Allied march to Berlin. CCS approval of Eisenhower's plan came grudgingly. In messages to Roosevelt, Churchill held out for several days, opposed to any "final commitment" curtailing "latitude of discussion" before he could raise a host of political issues with the Russians. Finally, when assured by Roosevelt that the President considered Eisenhower's plans militarily sound, Churchill again subsided, adding, "Amantium irae amoris integratio est."

This was progress, but even as the three powers began to settle their problems on military strategy, Allied-Soviet diplomatic problems threatened to freeze cooperation in every sphere. April 1945, a month of victories and warming spring weather in north-central Europe was also to be the month most historians date as the true beginning of the Cold War.

By the second, Allied participation in control commissions in Bulgaria and Rumania had broken down. Czechoslovakian Communists had announced the formation of a National Front, a move sponsored by, but constituting a potential challenge to, pro-Western Czech President-in-Exile Eduard Beneš, who in March had left London for Moscow in order to be on hand for the liberation of his country. The wrangling over Poland was about to spill into the world press. Roosevelt, Churchill and Stalin appeared to be no closer on their interpretations of the Yalta accords on Poland with respect to such questions as the effect of a veto in the stillborn ambassadorial committee, Molotov's determination to consult the Lublin provisional government and to respect Lublin's views on Allied candidates for the Polish unity government, Lublin's status, and Lublin's right to "take legal or administrative action of a fundamental character affecting social, constitutional, economic or political conditions in Poland." On notice that Moscow intended to present Lublin's credentials before the UN in San Francisco, Churchill urgently pushed for a coordinated U.S.-British position and ways of handling the "discouraging lack of progress in the carrying out, which the world expects, of the political decisions which we reached at the conference [Yalta]." But Roosevelt hesitated to act on Poland.

Meanwhile the CCS placed a clamp on further SHAEF-STAVKA exchanges. This left Eisenhower in limbo, uncertain when the Soviet offensive on the Oder would resume, and up against the looming problem that Berlin would prove to be attainable *cheaply* after all. A related problem involved the extent to which the Allies should accept Stalin's opening to push Allied forces into the Russian EAC zone elsewhere. Stalin's casual attitude about the Russian EAC zone was striking, but Eisenhower informed Washington that he was frankly skeptical that the Soviets were in fact casual, and indeed, he was anxious to probe the limits of his discretion to hand over Allied-held portions of the Soviet EAC zone as the two forces came into contact.

How far to enter the Russian EAC zone and what to do once there quickly emerged as a key issue. Churchill felt that the Allies should accept Stalin's invitation to move major Allied forces into the Russian zones, but Roosevelt was noncommittal. Just then Antonov began to press the Allied military liaison team in Moscow for assurances that Eisenhower's plan to reach Leipzig would in no way affect the EAC agreement on zonal boundaries, which was a question Eisenhower also raised with the CCS.

On this Eisenhower found himself at odds with Churchill. In his mind the problem of entering the Russian EAC zone was similar to that of Berlin. The Soviets were entitled to occupy the area as they wished: whether the Allies should stay out of the Soviet EAC zone altogether was a technically different matter but essentially the same. Eisenhower endeavored to convince the CCS that if Allied forces entered the area, he should have authority to arrange for handovers of Soviet territory if the Soviets insisted on it, but the CCS balked at giving Eisenhower such authority.

Meanwhile the latest turn in the Wolff talks brought Allied-Soviet relations, at least outwardly, to a critical state. Wolff's return to Berne had been put off for two weeks because of "technical difficulties" he had experienced in shuttling between Kesselring and his successor in Italy, General von Vietinghoff, on a mission that involved "something broader than German forces in northern Italy. . . ." Then Parrilli arrived in Berne on April 2 with news of two developments: first, Wolff had returned to Army Group H Headquarters and "could not state precisely the day of his return [to Berne]," since talks with Kesselring had "taken on a greater scope than initially contemplated." But the Berne meeting with Parrilli coincided with news of the Third Army seizure of Kassel, XIX Corps crossings of the Weser River, and a German reorganization of the western front, apparently for the dual purpose of opening the way to the Allies in north-central Germany and closing it to the redoubts of southern Germany and Austria. Bearing this out, with the encirclement of Model's Army Group B, Field Marshal Busch had assumed command of the remnants of the 1st Parachute Army in Denmark while Blaskowitz assumed command of Army Group H in the Holland fortress, leaving Kesselring, at the point of Allied contact, with firm control over the German forces south of the Ruhr that defended the approaches to the redoubt zones.

Roosevelt and Churchill kept Moscow closely informed of the Wolff affair, which both emphasized the shortness of time before Allied forces would advance through Germany and the growing control the Allies were assuming over German affairs. Stalin pressed for breaking off contact with Wolff, and the resulting exchanges briefly threatened to engulf Allied-Soviet dealings in a sea of recriminations. On April 3, in messages to Roosevelt and Churchill, Stalin erupted with charges that the Germans had "ceased . . . war" in the west, and citing the reports of unnamed "informants," accused the Allies of conducting negotiations behind Russia's back "on the basis of which the German commander on the western front, Marshal Kesselring, has agreed to open the front and permit the Anglo-American troops to advance to the east." Stalin demanded that Soviet representatives be included at Berne, or that talks be broken off.

For several days Roosevelt and Churchill held out. Telegrams flashed back and forth between Washington, London and Moscow questioning the reliability of Stalin's informants. On the seventh, in a landmark message to Roosevelt, Stalin lashed out with a long train of accusations against the Allies, highlighted by his charge that General Marshall had given the Russians a false warning shortly after Yalta about alleged German plans to counterattack in Pomerania and Austria just as thirty-five German divisions, including eleven tank divisions, massed for an attack southwest of Budapest at Lake Balaton, which had nonetheless been held in check by the Red Army. Stalin insisted it was now "essential" where the enemy was "faced with inevitable surrender that all Allies be included in talks [and] absolutely essential if the Ally in question asks for such participation." The Russian point of view was "the only correct" one, and unless the Russians were included, he demanded that the Berne talks be broken off as a matter of "what is admissible and inadmissible as between one ally and another."

In practical terms, Stalin's personal charges against Marshall appeared to be a heavy-handed way of saying that Moscow proposed to by-pass the American and British liaison missions and reopen contacts with SHAEF. Another point was that Stalin would repudiate the results of current Allied-German talks, which pushed the prospect of a cease-fire into the indefinite future. Left unanswered was the question of when the Russians intended to resume on the Oder front.

In hindsight, the recriminations surrounding the Wolff affair highlighted what was becoming a permanent feature of Allied-Soviet relations. The hostility evident in Stalin's April 7 outburst was formidable, though Harriman, in Moscow, discounted the idea that Stalin suspected Allied-German collaboration or opposed the Wolff negotiations; in Harriman's opinion, the Soviets would favor any negotiations that resulted in disarming German units and would welcome surrender negotiations provided the Russians were "full participants in any major surrender." But this comforting assessment could not conceal a major fact: Moscow was stalling on steps toward a cease-fire presumably because its forces were not ready to resume the offensive, and only until the Russians had broken the Oder line could serious moves toward a cease-fire begin.

Then, suddenly, bearing out Harriman, Stalin came forward with an important concession on the Polish issue, and Allied-Soviet polemics ceased. On the seventh, the very day he criticized Marshall, Stalin agreed to consider including Mikolajczyk, the leader of the London Poles, in the Polish coalition, *provided* Mikolajczyk found a way to express his private support for the Yalta decisions publicly. In substance, Mikolajczyk's participation would not affect much, but the gesture was a sign that the Soviets would not use the forum of the UN meetings in San Francisco to shatter the Alliance.

Simultaneously, Churchill and Roosevelt decided to suspend the Wolff talks. On the eighth, General Lyman Lemnitzer of AFHQ returned to Berne with instructions to inform Parrilli that further talks were pointless until a German representative returned empowered to discuss unconditional surrender on all fronts. Ninety-six hours later, at Churchill's behest, Roosevelt, from Warm Springs, Georgia, thanked Stalin for his frankness about the Berne incident, "which now appears to have faded into the past without having accomplished any useful purpose." On the same day, the ailing President cabled Churchill and urged him to "minimize" the Soviet problem as much as possible now, "because these problems, in one form or another, seem to arise every day, and most of them straighten out, as in the case of the Berne meeting.

"We must be firm, however, and our course thus far is correct. . . ."

Day by day the German collapse in the west continued. In the first week of April, the U.S. First Army alone took over 200,000 prisoners east of the Rhine. Paralysis proceeded up and down the spine of the broken German front. In the Ruhr pocket the Germans mounted "stubborn resistance . . . wherever possible," according to a SHAEF intelligence report, but "this is insufficient because the power of adequate counteroffensive action is lacking completely." Simpson and Hodges repulsed counterattacks along the Lippe and Sieg rivers, and the battle of the Ruhr pocket evolved into a series of small-unit actions. Infantry and anti-aircraft artillery defended the northern rim of the pocket, but German units lacked small arms and heavy equipment, and soldiers began to toss down weapons and surrender —the beginning of the end.

Day by day the elements of strategy—time, space, logistics, concentration —became increasingly irrelevant, and Eisenhower was looking ahead. On the fifth he formally petitioned the CCS for authority to handle the delicate problem of the Allied-Soviet military linkup along the Elbe, including authority to negotiate Allied withdrawals back into the Allied EAC zones. In noting the absence of arrangements for linkup, he drew attention to his lack of guidance about how to respond to Soviet demands that Allied forces evacuate the Russian zone as the two forces came into contact. Citing several "minor incidents of air contact" between Soviet and Allied aircraft, he proposed that Tedder return to Moscow to hammer out arrangements for air-ground identification, as it would soon become impractical to restrict the Allied advance.

Eisenhower's request raised two issues: first, how deeply the Allies should venture into the Russian zone; second, whether they should precondition their withdrawal from stretches of the Soviet EAC zone on Soviet "compliance" with agreements elsewhere. His request for CCS guidance in effect suggested that he considered any attempt to advance into the Soviet sector dangerous without authority to withdraw from that area. How likely Eisenhower viewed the odds of outright Allied-Russian conflict is unknown, but his warnings, couched as a request for negotiating authority, did serve to strengthen his case for directing the mass of Allied forces toward Austria and Denmark and away from the main body of Russian forces—a step consistent with Eisenhower's broad-front approach, which had always, while emphasizing the quick defeat of the enemy, implicitly aimed at avoiding a collision with the Russians over objectives in central Europe, even if doing so meant forgoing such political prizes as Prague, Vienna and Berlin.

Was this CCS policy as well? Months of debate had not resolved the issue entirely, and the precise issues raised by Eisenhower's wire to Stalin had not been debated before. As expected, the British were unsure how liaison would "work out in practice," and promptly rejected the idea of Tedder's returning to Moscow, preferring instead that the Russians be informed ambiguously that "our respective armies will stand fast until they receive orders from their governments." But as Tedder returned to London for consultations with the BCOS, talk waned of a British move on Berlin, coinciding with Montgomery's vehement protests over his loss of the Ninth Army, which ruled out Berlin, a "terrible mistake," as he put it. Years later the historian Arthur Bryant described the anger in the BCOS over Simpson's transfer, even though "it mattered comparatively little what SHAEF and its Supreme Command now did, since, for all practical purposes, Germany was defeated."

All week, British suspicion persisted that the Americans would move on Berlin, a move which the British insisted that Eisenhower had ruled out. What were American objectives? Marshall was now on record suggesting that Eisenhower consider Stuttgart and Kiel, and the CCS had endorsed Eisenhower's April 2 directive. But each passing day seemed to bring new surprises, and yet as the Ruhr battle began to degenerate into mass surrenders and Ninth, Third and First Army spearheads headed toward the Elbe, signs of doubts cropped up in Washington about Eisenhower's commitment of eighteen divisions in the Ruhr battle which weakened Bradley's advance.

In the CCS, customary JCS support for delegating authority to the local command was qualified by significant gaps in the American position. The JCS was both noncommittal about how Eisenhower should handle the zonal problem and reluctant to allow SHAEF-STAVKA contacts, which was presumably a tactic to spur Russian actions. Yet American intelligence reports were now discounting the threat of a southern redoubt as "lacking substance," and confirmed hunches, as Pogue put it, that "the Supreme Commander was strengthening his case for not driving to Berlin."

Doubts concerning Eisenhower's intention to avoid Berlin were never expressed in so many words, though Eisenhower detected what he thought were hints of a reassessment in view of Bradley's breakthrough and Stalin's accusations in early April, which could have been read as a sign of Russian indecision about what to do next. On the fifth, Under Secretary of War John J. McCloy visited Reims for talks about military government, in the course of which he cautioned Eisenhower against unnecessary destruction in the Ruhr pocket battles at Essen, Hannover and Düsseldorf. Eisenhower assured McCloy that he intended no "useless or unnecessary damage for existing facilities," but the estimated 150,000 Germans in the pocket were fighting "tenaciously," and so attacks would proceed "to the point where it is cheaper to contain the pocket than to destroy it." Later that day Eisenhower sent Marshall a summary of his talks with McCloy, which he followed up a day later with a long progress report in which he justified operations in the Ruhr that would necessarily weaken Allied spearheads east of Kassel. Eisenhower warned Marshall that he could expect an extended pause at the Weser River to enable Simpson, Hodges and Patton to consolidate and bring up supplies.

In his reply, Marshall assured Eisenhower that McCloy's concern had to do with the ongoing debate between the "two schools of thought in high government circles here regarding a postwar pastoral Germany and a policy of leaving some industrial capability to benefit the related economy of other European countries," and not with Eisenhower's campaign, which he assumed was "proceeding in the manner best adapted to the security and rapidity of your thrusts." Parenthetically, Marshall solicited for his personal use a more detailed statement of Eisenhower's views on the current Ruhr battle. Marshall apologized if the request caused Eisenhower embarrassment, adding that in his personal view, the Ruhr battle was probably far enough along so that "whatever the political conclusions," it was "too late, too impractical" to stop the destruction.

Was Marshall criticizing Eisenhower's decision to concentrate on the Ruhr? In reply, Eisenhower defended his decision to commit eighteen American divisions against the Ruhr pocket. He pointed out that elements of the Ninth Army would soon stretch out 150 miles into Germany, making communications, and the security of rear areas, an "acute" problem, as he put it. Eisenhower intended no useless destruction in the Ruhr and assured Marshall that Ruhr assets would be preserved so that the UN leaders "could dispose of them as they see fit."

Several more exchanges between Eisenhower and Marshall crossed that day. In the first, Eisenhower again enumerated the reasons that he had decided to communicate directly with Stalin for Marshall's use in countering

BCOS charges. First, Eisenhower assured Marshall that there was no basis to British charges that he had not consulted Tedder before dispatching his messages to Moscow. In a second message that day, Eisenhower again raised the zonal problem and the need for some procedure "in the event our forces should meet the Russians in any part of Germany, each with an offensive mission." In a third message, Eisenhower sent Marshall a personal and confidential communication in which he summarized his views on Berlin. First, he had word that the German government was transferring all important ministries to southern Germany, and so Berlin had "diminished importance"; second, he was concerned that an advance on Berlin would divert forces from operations to sever the German front at Leipzig in conjunction with the Russians. Eisenhower reminded Marshall that linkup at Leipzig would be a necessary preliminary for later operations aimed at preempting a German attempt to organize redoubts in Norway and Austria. Toward these ends, Eisenhower intended to place a flank on the Danish coast to secure the British zone while mobilizing a thrust into the southern mountain areas, which again was his formula for preempting a move by the German army into areas where it might establish redoubts, and was consistent with his determination to avoid a collision with the Russians at all costs.

"I am the first to admit that a war is waged in pursuit of political aims," he closed, "and if the Combined Chiefs of Staff should decide that the Allied effort to take Berlin outweighs purely military considerations in the theater, I would cheerfully readjust my plans and my thinking so as to carry out such an operation. I urgently believe, however, that the capture of Berlin should be left as something that we would do if feasible and practical as we proceed on a general plan of (a) dividing the German forces by a thrust in the middle, (b) anchoring our left firmly in the Lübeck area, and (c) attempting to disrupt any German effort to establish a fortress in the southern mountains."

OVERRUNNING GERMANY

And so on this note, with the CCS left to debate these matters and Eisenhower left to act, the Allied march into Germany commenced. After months of consultation, Eisenhower could feel confident, but there were gaps in his authority, and the pace of Bradley's advance injected uncertainty. The Alliance was more dependent than ever on Eisenhower's control over the situation but reluctant to formalize it or to permit further exchanges between SHAEF and STAVKA. Eisenhower, in turn, was relying on the judgment of his commanders in the field, having conditioned them for months to think cautiously. Professionalism was the order of the day, a tone set by Bradley, who had returned from Cannes restored to command of the Ninth Army, which converged on Essen and Hagen and pushed beyond the Weser toward the Elbe and the undefended recesses of central Germany. Between April 6 and 9, the U.S. First, Third and Ninth armies advanced fifty miles a day and reached phase lines along the Leine River and Gotha. Attacks to begin the next phase, the hundred miles to Leipzig, Chemnitz and Magdeburg, were set for April 10, involving elements of seven corps and 22 divisions, a force strong enough to advance at will.

Meanwhile, having completed eight weeks of training in Bournemouth, England, John Eisenhower had returned for duty with the 3323rd SIAM Company, an innovation patterned on Montgomery's Phantom Service, which had so impressed Churchill at Venlo. The 3323rd SIAM consisted of a team of signal experts and line officers trained to shuttle between headquarters and the front as observers. Duty with the 3323rd would enable John Eisenhower to travel freely to witness the closing campaign at all levels, at Reims, at 12th Army Group Headquarters, and to join the procession as the Allied forces moved ahead, village by village, town by town, city by city, snuffing out sporadic pockets of resistance and imposing military government. First came the reunions. John spent several days at Reims with his father. Then he proceeded to 12th Army Group by way of Third Army Headquarters at Saarbrücken for a short stay with George Patton, an old family friend, whom he found embroiled in a controversy over the so-called Hammelburg affair.

Only days before, as XII Corps broke out of the Oppenheim bridgeheads, Patton had disregarded the advice of his staff and dispatched several combat teams thirty miles behind enemy lines to liberate a prisoner-of-war camp at Hammelburg—a foray that met with disaster. Some said Patton wanted to upstage MacArthur's dramatic liberation of prison camps in the Philippines that month. Then word slipped out that Patton's son-in-law, Lieutenant Colonel John K. Waters, was thought to be among the prisoners at Hammelburg.

Of 307 officers and men who set out at dawn on March 26, two survivors returned to tell how the assault battalions, after a dangerous trek, had reached the Hammelburg compound, overwhelmed the guards and released the prisoners, only to be ambushed outside the stockade. Nine were killed, thirty-two wounded and the rest captured. The ill-fated Hammelburg rescue attempt bolstered whispering campaigns that Patton, corrupted by his reputation, had become convinced he was beyond reproach. Criticism of Patton made little impact on John Eisenhower, however, who had known him since his days as a boy in Washington, and knew that Patton's flamboyance and disdain for convention was largely an affectation.

At Saarbrücken, Patton seemed unshaken by the Hammelburg controversy. In John's words, he was "absorbed in his favorite pastime of attack and pursuit." Patton's wartime immunity had several weeks to run, and so the warrior in twilight held court for a stream of visitors to Frankfurt, including McCloy and the financier Bernard Baruch, who, like McCloy, had flown to Europe to consult Eisenhower on occupation policy. "I have been told to hold up and let the rest catch up with me," Patton quipped to Baruch in young John's presence. "I am advancing 15 miles a day anyhow, though I'm not telling them. I don't want to give the Nazi bastards time to sow minefields." Turning to John, he winked. "Don't tell your Daddy!"

From Saarbrücken, John proceeded across the Rhine to First Army Headquarters at Marburg, and thence eastward by jeep to V Corps Headquarters at the Elbe town of Weissenfels, near Leipzig, deep in central Germany. With time on his hands, John took numerous detours to become acquainted with various First and Third Army units, and found himself moving with what journalists called "the greatest armored joy ride in history." First and Third Army columns rumbled along the large autobahns of central Germany against the westward flow of German prisoners and refugees. Occasionally, units dropped off to round up small pockets of anti-tank gunners or SS units. Passage through the towns and villages was mostly uneventful, since many villages were abandoned, while others limped along without the essential services of electricity and water. There were sanctuaries along the northern edges of the Black Forest, where GIs observed the relatively untouched castles, villages and gardens of the upper Rhine, but most of Bavaria had sunk into chaos, crisscrossed by American, French and German units.

In many places, GIs intermingled with displaced persons who aimlessly roamed the streets to loot and scavenge for food. Military police moved in and attempted to stop reprisals, but shootings and hangings were commonplace. In the larger towns, detachments dropped off to maintain order, but the main units were in a hurry and brushed off resistance as they pushed along. Casual cruelty was not uncommon—years later, General Bradley would recount the story of the Franconian city of Aschaffenburg. When troops entering the town came under sniper fire, the local commander decided against a house-to-house cleanup, withdrew and called in the Ninth Air Force to level the town. "And after the city's rubble had settled over the bodies of its defenders," Bradley wrote, "the Nazi commander, Major Von Lambert, walked meekly out of a bunker carrying a white flag."

By the tenth, three American armies skirted the Harz Mountains, and advanced 100 miles beyond Kassel toward Leipzig and the Elbe–Mulde, the advance position where they would gather to await junction with the Russians and orders to proceed north to Denmark, northeast to Berlin, east to Prague or south to Linz. Up the road, John found himself in a convoy of the 2nd Infantry Division returning from leave, which was made apparent by their "class A" uniforms and the wine bottles they were tossing about "in profusion." As the convoy passed the scene of a recent fire fight, John counted fifty or so German corpses strewn about and an equal number of Americans sitting among or *on* the corpses, eating K rations. Through the dust, John had difficulty telling the live Americans from the dead Germans, and yet his compatriots seemed "inured to the spirit of the battlefield." Back at V Corps Headquarters that night, John quickly groped into a dark farmhouse to roll down his bedding.

"You complain about lack of news from John," Eisenhower wrote Mamie. "I can't find anything concerning him myself except in a round-about way by telephoning to people who may have seen him 'day before yesterday.'

> However, in the next day or so I have a chance of meeting him at a station where I expect him to stop for at least one night. The only time he has written to me since arriving here he asked me for a camera—total length of letter, approximately six lines. But I keep remembering that he is a man with his own problems —daily life, etc. It is exceedingly hard for him to realize how important he is to us. But it is difficult to be philosophical. . . .

In letters home that week, Eisenhower exhibited his usual restlessness. Navigating his armies through unchartered terrain, he was braced for trouble. His objective as always was a speedy cease-fire, but the Russians were elusive, the British stalled, and the French also stalled. And with the Germans still fighting here and there and major battles forming on the eastern front, Eisenhower, in time, began to despair of a clear-cut end to hostilities and his ability to avoid clashes in the field.

A big factor now in hopes for a cease-fire was the German army. Allied dealings with Nazi officials had been ruled out, and so the German army held the key. As the Wolff affair demonstrated, the army had assets: hostage populations in Holland and Norway; garrisons in the Balkans and France; massive forces collecting opposite the Russians on the Oder and in Czecho-slovakia; and the ability to exacerbate Allied-Soviet tensions by withdraw-ing additional forces into the redoubt zones and drawing out the end. In dealing with the German army, Eisenhower held two trumps. First, his armies mustered great power and had the initiative. Second, the German objective was to seek sanctuary in the west, which Eisenhower was in a position to deny in a number of ways, including a refusal to accept German surrenders, closing off the front to refugee traffic and taking other steps when the time came. But Eisenhower's ability to play his trump depended on all sides being ready to proceed with a cease-fire, which was not likely until the Allies placed Allied forces at Lübeck and western Austria, and Russian operations resumed at the Oder.

For the moment, hammering out arrangements for the Allied-Soviet linkup was Eisenhower's first priority. The flash point ran along the 175-mile passage between Berlin and Prague along the Elbe–Mulde–Vltava rivers, where the Allied spearheads would soon encounter the main body of the Red Army. In his postwar account, Bradley disclosed that Eisenhower decided not to wait for the CCS to grant him formal authority to withdraw behind zonal boundaries. From the tenth on, as forward commanders grew uneasy about incidents, he wrote, Eisenhower authorized Army commanders to negotiate "directly" with their Soviet counterparts to work out Allied withdrawals if necessary.

"Let's put it this way," Bradley recalled telling Simpson later that week. "We would prefer to hold our present line until we can arrange an orderly changeover. But if the Russian insists on going forward to his line of occupation, we're not going to start any trouble. Work it out as best you can and allow him to." In the climate of Allied-Soviet tensions, Bradley was "not going to risk an explosion that might bring a sequel to the war and bring World War III."

Just how seriously Eisenhower and the Allied high command viewed the risk of military clashes with the Russians is a matter of debate, but Eisenhower carefully monitored the Allied-Soviet military balance along the central front, looking for clues to Russian intentions. The heavy Soviet margin in ground troops was, in theory, offset by Allied air superiority and mobility. But by all reports the Red Army did not rely on elaborate supply lines, so Allied air superiority, which provided a decisive margin over German forces, was less relevant. And by the second week of April, as operations began to draw away from the center front toward the flanks, Eisenhower, confronting the problem of arranging contact between his spearheads and the massive Russian forces along the Elbe, occasionally muttered that he "sure wished he had more in the center."

Meanwhile, as the American advance proceeded, Eisenhower and Montgomery found themselves in a tug-of-war over the slow progress of the 21st Army Group. Dempsey's twenty-division British-Canadian attacks toward Bremen–Hamburg moved only sixty miles in the twenty days after PLUNDER, partly because of German resistance, as the fragmented German command north of the Lippe River labored to hold isolated positions in Holland and sections of the British zone for evacuees. As always, the Americans were quick to attribute Montgomery's slowdown to his characteristic ultra-caution about British casualties, in the wake of the transfer of Simpson's army back to Bradley. Another effect of the British slowdown was to open a gap on Simpson's northern flank that would eventually exert a drag on Simpson's lead corps advancing on the Elbe at Magdeburg, which Bradley suspected was deliberate.

That Montgomery was stalling to slow down Bradley's progress seemed borne out by his contradictory actions all week. On the one hand, Montgomery kept up a steady drumfire of criticism of Eisenhower's Berlin decision. Yet he was pointedly unwilling to accept U.S. Ninth Army support for the British drive to the Elbe or to accelerate the British drive, which might have kept pace with the Ninth Army advance and accelerated it. Through the second week of April, Montgomery was suddenly grounded by weather and unavailable to meet with Eisenhower to discuss mutual 12th and 21st Army Group support. At a meeting with Bradley on the eighth, Montgomery, though critical of the Leipzig decision, was reluctant to accept Bradley's offer to move the Ninth Army support slightly north to assist Dempsey. Bradley left the meeting with "the feeling that Montgomery, denied the glory of taking Berlin, had lost all heart for the fight."

Whatever Montgomery's true reasons, the prospect of a prolonged British slowdown was troublesome, however. Evidently, the British were prepared to take their chances that North Sea objectives would be attainable either with eleventh-hour American support or no American support whatsoever. But Eisenhower was not so sure, and meanwhile a British slowdown would delay efforts to impose a cease-fire. Soon Eisenhower and Montgomery quarreled over the pace of British operations, especially as Simpson's spearheads reached the Elbe on the eleventh. Was Montgomery waiting for help? Eisenhower offered Montgomery the use of an American corps, but Montgomery continued to decline all aid; thus American spearheads began to collect on the Elbe fifty miles west of Berlin, where they would stand in place for seven tense days.

Similarly, on the southern flank, the French First Army began to go its own way under De Gaulle's orders to settle the problem of a French occupation zone de facto by establishing French positions in Württemberg. Anticipating U.S. interference, De Gaulle had ordered Lattre de Tassigny to cross the Rhine "even if the Americans do not agree and if you should cross it in rowing boats." By the fourth of April, 130,000 French solders had entered Karlsruhe, then turned and advanced toward Stuttgart under orders to set up a military government there regardless of 6th Army Group orders. By mid-April, Württemberg was a scene of confusion as American and French forces contended for control of key points in the region. For a time, Devers and Lattre de Tassigny were unable to agree on measures to reduce German First and Nineteenth Army pockets at Nuremberg and Stuttgart, which was necessary before Devers could mobilize the 6th Army Group thrust toward Salzburg.

Eisenhower's eleventh-hour difficulties with the French were reminiscent of Strasbourg. While the British backed the French, Washington apparently was skittish about allowing De Gaulle to inflame the French occupation zone issue on the eve of the San Francisco conference, where Polish credentials and a Polish zone in defeated Germany loomed as a major issue. Eventually, Eisenhower would find himself overlooking the French transgressions at Churchill's behest with one qualification: Stuttgart was forty-five miles from the town of Hechingen, the center of German atomic research and development, so until American forces occupied Hechingen and a team of American scientists (code name ALSOS) seized German data for American safekeeping, Eisenhower would stand in the way of French efforts to consolidate their hold on Württemberg.

·   ·   ·

Meanwhile, Allied-German negotiations resumed, this time in talks over the desperate situation in western Holland, talks that were a dress rehearsal for wider negotiations wherein the German army meant to step forward and capitulate on behalf of Germany. Conditions in western Holland were typical of the zones littered over the European map still under German control. All winter, German authorities had gradually starved out the population while the army busily converted the area into a military fortress to be held for the purpose of dragging out a formal termination of the war.

On April 13, preliminary talks opened between the Reich Commissar for the Netherlands, Arthur Seyss-Inquart, and Dutch authorities over food relief for western Holland. The Dutch authorities were anxious to arrange terms to stop wholesale inundations and political roundups as General Blaskowitz's Army Group H entrenched for a siege. The German high command demanded a guarantee that the Canadian First Army, which had entered Arnhem, would not advance beyond the Grebbe Line, whereupon Seyss-Inquart was purportedly ready to cease preparations for demolitions and inundations, transfer political prisoners to habitable quarters, stop executing Dutchmen for sabotage, and allow coal and food into Amsterdam to avert starvation. However, Seyss-Inquart insisted at the outset that there could be no capitulation in Holland until "Germany ceases to resist."

Like Wolff, Seyss-Inquart appeared to be a Nazi official injected into what was essentially a preliminary Allied-Wehrmacht discussion of a wider cease-fire. Eisenhower discounted Seyss-Inquart's threats to render Holland "uninhabitable" as bluff, since the Reich Commissar would not act independently of Army Group H, suspended between Seyss-Inquart's threats on its behalf to buy time for other fronts and the desire to seek sanctuary in the Allied zones. By rendering Holland "uninhabitable," the army would violate the laws of war and forfeit the protection of the Geneva Conventions. Indeed, Eisenhower saw a chance to make a test case of the situation, in which he might terminate hostilities in Holland by proclamation under threat of stripping German soldiers of belligerent status, a precedent that would be useful in efforts to disarm German soldiers on other fronts when the Russians and the British signaled their readiness to accept a cease-fire in place. Eisenhower made a special point of consulting Susloparoff on the situation in Holland. Susloparoff would not participate, but his sympathetic interest was a sign that the Russians might not object to Allied handling of wider talks growing out of Holland and a sign that a Russian offensive along the Oder was in the offing. When informed of Seyss-Inquart's threats, Churchill leaned to military action in Holland, prompted by Dutch warnings that all pumping installations, locks, sluices and dikes were being rigged with explosives. But fighting through the myriad canals and waterways could consume weeks, and British troops were not available both to march into western Holland and to sustain an offensive to Denmark.

Throughout, Eisenhower directed a stream of messages to Montgomery and Brooke to nudge Montgomery. As early as the eighth, within ninety-six hours of Simpson's transfer back to Bradley, Eisenhower had pronounced himself ready to lend American support for Montgomery's Denmark push. Eisenhower now informed Montgomery that he was quietly building up a SHAEF reserve in case Montgomery encountered an "unanticipated need," and that he had shifted supply priorities over the Wesel rail bridges to fuel the British dash for Lübeck. When Montgomery continued to procrastinate, Eisenhower dangled a push on to Berlin with sacrifices and honors equally shared if the German capital fell within the orbit of Allied successes—a move rejected all week by Montgomery as "useless" and "too late."

Would the Americans take Berlin? On the eleventh and twelfth Bradley conferred with Simpson, Allen, Patton, Hodges, Gerow and the corps commanders at his new headquarters in Wiesbaden to map out plans to wrap up the Ruhr campaign and to organize the final advance of the 12th Army Group. In the Ruhr, Anderson's XVI Corps on the north fought through the rubble of Essen and Dortmund toward III Corps, while Ridgway's reconstituted XVIII Corps moved through Remagen to Siegen on the left of III Corps. On the eleventh Essen fell, and contact was imminent between XVI Corps and III Corps near the industrial town of Hagen, which divided the remnants of Model's Army Group B two weeks ahead of plan.

To the east, Simpson pushed armored columns through the wide gaps north of the Harz Mountains, by-passing the makeshift German Eleventh Army at a rate of thirty miles per day. On the night of the eleventh, the 2nd Armored Division reached the Elbe at the towns of Magdeburg and Schönebeck, the 5th Armored crossed at Tangermünde and the 83rd Division at Barby. Three German divisions dispatched from Berlin intervened and forced the 2nd Armored to abandon the Magdeburg bridgehead. But the 83rd Division, after absorbing a counterattack, lost, then regained the bridgehead and expanded it to a depth of thirty miles to the outskirts of Potsdam, fifty miles from Berlin. Farther south, the Third Army advanced sixty miles through the Gebirge Mountains to the western border of Czechoslovakia and advance positions on the upper Mulde at Chemnitz.

After a 250-mile advance in eighteen days, the crack 2nd Armored Division paused at Magdeburg to consolidate. But the pause would be a short one, and with the British advancing slowly, Simpson's spearheads had no mission except to take and hold Elbe bridgeheads and to await the arrival of the 12th Army Group main body. Additionally, Gerow's newly formed U.S. Fifteenth Army would soon be in position to contain and mop up the Germans who still held out in the Ruhr pocket. Rail bridges at Weser and Mainz were on line, truck companies were operating, and airlift was available to sustain the Ninth Army spearheads.

On the twelfth, Eisenhower shuttled back and forth between First Army Headquarters at Marburg, 12th Army Group Headquarters at Wiesbaden, and Third Army Headquarters at Merkers in a round of meetings called to hammer out the details of a Third Army swing toward Austria and to spell out Simpson's mission. Inevitably, in Bradley's words, Berlin was under "active consideration." American and Russian forces were now equidistant from Berlin, though the American forces were still merely spearheads while the Russians massed two million troops along the Oder. Indeed, judging by the map, any consideration of Berlin seemed to be foreclosed by the balance of power so clearly in favor of the Russian forces in the Berlin area. But time was getting short.

Where were the Russians? For an interval, Eisenhower, having hoped that the Russians would solve the Berlin problem for him by taking it, would find himself in the uncomfortable role of actually having to restrain the Ninth Army, for despite the fact that the Allies were well short of their principal objectives, the temptation to move forward was strong. In his diary, Patton quoted Eisenhower as calling Berlin "tactically unwise," and saying he "hoped the politicans would not push him into it." Characteristically, Patton questioned a policy of self-imposed restraint and Eisenhower's argument that Berlin had lost its military significance, suspecting that the supply shortages cited by Eisenhower against a move on Berlin were "excuses for lack of any ideas as to what to do next."

On the other hand, Eisenhower's field commanders could not ignore two constraints: first, the slow progress in the 21st and 6th Army Group sectors, and, second, the reports that confirmed the colossal Russian-German battle shaping up on the lower Elbe. Between Stettin and Berlin, the Russians mustered in deep bridgeheads over the Oder River. Farther south, near Breslau, Konev's 1st Ukrainian Front, consisting of two tank armies and five field armies, was poised to attack west or swing south into northern Czechoslovakia to converge with the three other fronts battling the Army Group Center in central Czechoslovakia, which would soon muster a force of 900,000 men, 10,000 guns and 2,000 aircraft holding out in an area containing Germany's last airfields and factories, and covering the German evacuation of Yugoslavia. By contrast, Simpson's and Patton's forces were spearheads, lacking the power to sustain operations against any real German resistance. By the twelfth, three American armies stretched out from the Rhine to the Elbe 200 miles on a 400-mile front. While eighteen divisions mopped up the last of the resistance in the Ruhr pocket, VII Corps was engaged in the Harz Mountains, V Corps opened a battle for Leipzig, and isolated units pacified towns and processed the hordes of soldiers pouring into Allied prisoner-of-war cages. Indeed, German prisoners were about to become a source of problems with the Russians, as soon most of the units trying to surrender to the Allies would be in actual contact with the Russians. Eisenhower could not rule out the possibility that the Soviets might welcome any surrenders that disarmed German units on their front, but the Soviets had indicated that they wished to be included in all major surrenders. Even assuming that the Russians might acquiesce in piecemeal German surrenders to Allied forces, the Allies might find themselves confronted with a Soviet demand that eastern-front prisoners be turned over, which would oblige them to defy the Russians or to consign military prisoners to Russian capture. No one was eager for that, and so everything confirmed Eisenhower's view that Berlin posed grave military and political risks best avoided and that the best course was to proceed as planned.

Among the American field commanders, sentiment for Berlin, never strong, did not last very long. Fear of running headlong into Russian forces was the major factor. Another was the unforeseen problem of pacifying the sectors already overrun in central Germany, a task that quickly began to tax Allied resources to the breaking point. As Simpson's spearheads reached the Elbe, Bradley's armies elsewhere were involved in "the most gigantic life-saving enterprise of all time," routing food and medical care through a scene of destruction and ruin to millions of slave laborers and displaced persons, all the while administering distribution of bare-subsistence rations to 40 million German civilians and Geneva-mandated rations to 2.5 million military prisoners amid the breakdown of German transport. Occupied Germany was not ruled by anybody, which brought to mind the problem of hostage German garrisons strung out behind the Allied lines in Holland and the French ports of Lorient and St.-Nazaire, along with the big concentrations of troops in Norway, central Germany, Czechoslovakia, Austria, Yugoslavia and Hungary. The task of pacifying central Germany seemed huge even to Patton who complained of the overwhelming problem of DPs and the threat of disease bordering on plague. And, as the conferences recessed, the commanders took side trips and inspected conditions that forced a hardheaded appraisal of their task and reminded them that World War II, the most frightful war in history, was not destined to cease one morning in glory as former combatants embraced in no-man's-land, but would wind down as a police action to impose military government over the chaos of central Germany.

One might say that illusions of a glorious finish ended on April 12, 1945, a memorable day. Eisenhower did not know it, but he was on his last trip to a battlefield in Europe. Between conferences, he, Patton and Bradley made a side trip in the Third Army sector, which included stops to inspect a major find of Nazi loot near Gotha and a tour of a smallish work camp for political prisoners in the nearby village of Ohrdruf. The areas they visited were scenes of desolation. American columns were advancing from town to town at will, and reports confirmed that the Germans were not attempting to stabilize a line of resistance anywhere nearby or even to make a coordinated effort at delay, though sporadic fighting was evident in several places along the way. In the towns and villages, houses were boarded up, with curtains drawn, as the local population, fearing reprisals, took refuge.

Several days before, an American patrol, acting on a tip, had searched a salt mine on the outskirts of the town of Gotha and uncovered a vast cache of German government property, including art treasures and gold bullion thought to be the last gold reserves of the Third Reich. Eisenhower, Patton and Bradley inspected the mine, a monument to Nazi plunder. The group descended two thousand feet in an elevator and walked through the dingy rooms and tunnels containing an estimated $250 million in 25-pound gold bars and ornaments, and over 2,000 crates of art looted by Nazi officials from museums and homes throughout Europe. The find was already being inventoried by SHAEF G-5 officers and officials of the Guaranty Trust Company of New York before shipment to Frankfurt for safekeeping. Afterward, the group drove on for a tour of the "work camp" at Ohrdruf.

Ohrdruf was a small find compared with other camps soon to be overrun at Nordhausen, Buchenwald and Bergen-Belsen in the next forty-eight hours. Nor was its discovery a surprise. The Allies had come across similar camps in France and Belgium, and by now the world press was reporting news of the extermination camps overrun by the Red Army in Poland. But the impression Ohrdruf made on Eisenhower, Bradley and Patton was profound, and the visit, one of the first of many pilgrimages to the site, focused western attention on Nazi atrocities as never before.

For miles outside the compound, the smell of death was overpowering. Eisenhower, Bradley and Patton were apprehensive as they arrived, passed through the gates and disembarked to tour on foot. They pressed on, accompanied by Signal Corps photographers, Army sentries, and a group of inmates who guided them through a scene where, in Bradley's words, "death had become so fouled by degradation that it both stunned and numbed us."

The Ohrdruf-Nord installation was standard for German work camps, with facilities for torturing inmates and executing those too weak to work. The group visited the barracks areas, which housed one inmate per 35 cubic feet of space, and a nearby hospital where inmates, worn down by work and torture, were stacked shoulder to shoulder to await death. In a basement of an adjoining building the party toured a row of gallows where prisoners caught attempting to escape were hanged by piano wire slung low enough so that the toes of the condemned brushed the floor, a way of extending the agony. Outside, forty lice-infested corpses stacked up in a pile had been shot through the head at point-blank range by panic-stricken camp guards before fleeing. Patton refused to enter a toolshed where an equal number of corpses had been placed, awaiting burial in a pit found a mile away. In the surrounding fields, 3,200 corpses lay about in piles near a pyre of railway ties hastily erected in an effort to obliterate the evidence.

As the group walked on, what went through Eisenhower's mind is unknown. With access to all the information at Allied disposal, few had as yet been in closer touch than Eisenhower with the full extent of Europe's degradation in the grip of Nazism, so he knew Ohrdruf was just one of many such places. Eisenhower and his colleagues in the high command also knew that the mass killings and work-torture deaths had reached a peak in the winter of 1944–45. To an extent, the debates over strategy in the summer of 1944 had been debates ahead of time over the responsibility for prolonging these horrors, though postwar accounts of the principals—Eisenhower, Montgomery, Bradley, Churchill and Brooke—would grow vague or remain silent on the subject. Had enough been done? Was enough being done?

According to Third Army reports, citizens of Gotha denied any knowledge of what had gone on at Ohrdruf, and so Eisenhower issued orders that all men, women and children be turned out at bayonet point to parade through the camp and form work parties to bury the dead. Middleton and Walker had already ordered all soldiers in their command to visit the camp, which Eisenhower approved and made Army-wide. Witnesses recalled that as he left, Eisenhower suddenly turned to an unidentified GI sentry: "Still having trouble hating them?"

Bradley described the flight back to Marburg and the depressing dinner afterward at Patton's sparsely furnished field headquarters that night. No one had much to say. At one point Bradley teased Patton about his futile effort to censor reports of the gold find at Gotha so he could make off with the loot. Bradley asked him what he would have done with so much money, and Patton replied he would have "struck a lucky medallion for every SOB in the 3rd Army," or hid the money until after the war when Congress began cutbacks in Army appropriations. But the effort at good cheer contended with the rumblings of supply trucks outside Patton's field tent. Defensive about the censorship incident, Patton pronounced himself sure he was right about ordering the crackdown. "Well, I'll be damned," Eisenhower retorted. "Until you said that, maybe you were. But if you're that positive, I'm sure you're wrong."

Around two o'clock, bulletins reached Marburg reporting President Roosevelt's death in Warm Springs, Georgia, several hours before. Eisenhower, Bradley and Patton, who had retired early, gathered in their bathrobes and discussion continued late into the night. Like millions of others that night, the three talked about what FDR's death meant to the war, and, like millions, they had difficulty conceiving of Harry S. Truman as President of the United States.

Who was he? Fellow Missourian Omar Bradley had a favorable impression of Truman, but knew little except for what he had heard about Truman's role as the Senate watchdog over the Armed Forces. As someone chosen for his popularity in Congress, Truman did not seem to be the man to fill the position or be equal to the task of handling the tense situation in Europe. By repute, Truman venerated Marshall, which at least assured continuity in the closing weeks of the war.

McKeogh later recalled that as the group again retired, Eisenhower seemed unusually shaken. He chatted briefly with McKeogh about his regret that Roosevelt had not lived to see V-E Day, and his concern over the direction the nation would take now. McKeogh recalled that when he admitted that he had not voted in the last election, Eisenhower admonished him. "Mickey, you are a civilian," he said. "The vote is the most precious right you possess. You should exercise it."

McKeogh cherished the advice, though he doubted that Eisenhower had ever voted himself. McKeogh would later claim that the staff never knew what Eisenhower's political sympathies were, and merely assumed that Dwight Eisenhower, in thirty-five years of military service, had observed the military custom of abstention from all elections. Mickey knew about Eisenhower's Kansas Republican background, his experience with MacArthur's staff in Washington and Manila, and his impatience with politics and politicians. But Eisenhower's views were not doctrinaire, and as the commander of Allied forces in Europe and a committed interventionist, he had venerated Roosevelt's wartime leadership.

In the next several days, Roosevelt's death would dominate world attention. President for twelve years, longer than any other man, Roosevelt, buoyant and self-confident, had made Americans forget that he led the nation from a wheelchair. As President, Roosevelt had sustained the nation in the dark days of economic depression with the idea of mutual responsibility, and had gone on to link the generation of the Depression era to Europe's struggle against the Nazi terror. But whether all this would survive Roosevelt's passing was the question mark surrounding the observances for the fallen President, observances that would coincide with public Allied-Soviet bickering over Poland, the disclosures of the camps and other evidence of the German nightmare that seemed at once both to vindicate the American intervention in Europe and to undermine any policy built on faith in human goodness.

The thirteenth was a day most of those in Europe would remember. That morning, John Eisenhower, then on duty with V Corps at Weissenfels, was interrupted at breakfast with a summons to join his father at First Army Headquarters in Marburg. On the 120-mile flight aboard an L-5 liaison plane, John brooded over his summons and the news from home. Wondering why his father wanted to see him, John braced himself for word that the newly sworn-in President Truman had ordered his father back to Washington to serve in a new capacity.

That afternoon, First Army Headquarters at Marburg was a scene of busy confusion, typical of times of high drama. Eisenhower, Bradley and Hodges were away on a visit to XVIII Corps at Siegen, and so staff milled about the new First Army Headquarters complex, trading rumors about impending operations and plans for shipping out to the Pacific. By seven-thirty, the group was pronounced overdue, spurring thirty minutes of frantic phone calls and messages, before, finally, the motorcade arrived back around eight o'clock. Eisenhower seemed surprised to see John—as the story went, an overzealous staff officer had taken action on his casual query the night before about John's whereabouts and his desire to see his son if he happened to be nearby. John unpacked for the night, and dined alone with his father.

Hodges and Bradley joined them around ten, and the group sat up talking for a second night in a row about the state of the world. Talk drifted to Ohrdruf and larger camps overrun at Buchenwald and Nordhausen. "The only speck of optimism I can see is that I really don't think that the bulk of the Germans knew what was going on," Eisenhower said at one point, adding that Patton had told him the mayor of Gotha and his wife, after seeing Ohrdruf, had gone home and hanged themselves. "Maybe there is hope after all."

Back in Reims on the fourteenth, Eisenhower went to work to arrange for delegations of congressional leaders and newspaper editors to witness Buchenwald, a major slave-labor camp overrun near Weimar for Jews, political prisoners and Russians. Survivors being kept under care at Buchenwald had corroborated dark tales of torture beyond description, and those physically able directed visitors on tours through the camp. War correspondents sent there photographed a group of emaciated French prisoners grinning hysterically at the spectacle of mounds of bodies decomposing in an open field left by guards who before fleeing in panic two weeks before had attempted to slaughter all the inmates and incinerate the evidence. Most of the survivors, starved and abused, were beyond medical help.

With publication of the pictures and reports two questions arose. To what extent had the German people known? Who would be held accountable? By now the Allied War Crimes Commission and its Soviet counterpart were already wrestling with the legal aspects of the unprecedented questions raised by the discovery of the camps in mid-April 1945—attempting to define the crimes committed, standards of accountability and the judicial procedures appropriate for an international tribunal to try the perpetrators.

The tribunal had already encountered problems, such as how to define war crimes and crimes against the peace in a way that distinguished the criminal from the defeated. The defense of compliance with military orders would prove troublesome, though eventually it was disallowed. The less specific indictments under the heading of crimes against humanity, such as mass murder and the enslavement of labor, seemed clear-cut, but jurists would debate questions of standards of accountability and proper procedures. A basic question arose about the purpose of the proposed International Tribunal, whether it should seek to mete out individual justice or be concerned mainly with publicizing and documenting crimes. Misgivings would surface about the show-trial aspects of the proceedings eventually held at Nuremberg and the idea of lending Western jurists to a judicial proceeding that included Russians. Yet no tribunal could exclude the Russians and effectively document German crimes or purport to dispense justice on behalf of the victims, and the disclosures of mid-April meant, as historian Eugene Davidson would put it, that "even if the trial [Nuremberg] was imperfect and the representatives of the Soviet Union charged the Germans with crimes the Russians had committed, the trial had to be held in some form."

Beginning on the fourteenth, in towns and villages throughout Germany, sullen populations formed lines and trudged through the camps to observe and clean up under the gaze of armed sentries. Congressional delegations arrived, and soldiers of the American Army were ordered out to witness— among them was John Eisenhower, who, after leaving Marburg, commandeered a jeep and drove on to Weimar and Buchenwald.

By now the Army had moved in to distribute food, clothing and medicine to the estimated 55,000 survivors barely clinging to life. John, like his father, approached the camp wary of intruding on the privacy of the survivors and dead alike, but, like the other GIs, soon discovered that there were eager guides who wanted the world to be invited in to see everything. He would later recall that at the entrance of the camp, a bald-headed Belgian singled him out and offered to serve as his guide. The man seemed unembarrassed by his baggy striped clothing, pleased that John had a camera, and reproachful when John tried to tuck it away, afraid lest he "miss an inch of the scene which he wanted recorded and displayed forever."

With his Belgian guide, John toured the compound in awe. He observed the torture facilities, the execution rooms and the crematorium, which had blazed day and night for several years. Near the end of the tour, John and his guide passed a circle of emaciated prisoners taking turns kicking three uniformed German corpses with rope burns around their necks. "*Amerikanisch* officer," one shouted. When John instinctively hid the camera, his guide nudged him, "No, no, take more!" The prisoners in the circle paused and looked up, and John detected several faint smiles. As he stopped to watch, the group turned and resumed kicking.

"Allied troops saw only smooth German landscapes and clean little townhouses," erupted *Pravda,* leading the worldwide chorus of condemnation. "They now see concentration camps. What is Buchenwald? It is Maidenek, but in miniature. Our Allies had not seen what we had. Now that they too have seen, now that they share what we know, they will understand us better."

Meanwhile, Eisenhower and Bradley mapped out the details of the final Allied maneuvers of the war. First, after reaching the Elbe, Simpson's main body would divide up with two corps holding at the Elbe to process refugees and military prisoners while extending XIX Corps north to assist Montgomery; second, Hodges would transfer several divisions to Patton to strengthen a Third Army march south from Kassel–Chemnitz along the Danube on Devers' left flank. Eisenhower, Bradley and Patton then worked out a reshuffling of troops and commands: VIII Corps would return to the Ruhr, III Corps would transfer to the Third Army, to be built up to fourteen divisions for the attack southward. After linkup with Russian forces, V Corps would transfer to the Third Army and cross the Czech border in the Pilsen–Karlsbad line to stake a claim in western Czechoslovakia. But for the moment, the concern was still Berlin.

Where were the Russians? As late as the thirteenth, Berlin remained under "active consideration," since there was a limit to Allied patience, a limit hinted at in Simpson's mission, which was to hold the Ninth Army bridgeheads in order to "assist the Red Army advance." On that day Eisenhower again warned the CCS that he could not contemplate further operations in the First Army sector beyond the Elbe–Mulde rivers. At this natural line of demarcation he proposed to halt and consolidate his forces for the task of subduing resistance and pacification west of the Elbe, and then to concentrate his remaining energy on the two flanks. Eisenhower requested permission to send liaison officers to Moscow, and cautioned the CCS about the problems he anticipated in the event Allied forces found themselves occupying portions of the Soviet EAC sector in defiance of Russian wishes.

Elaborating on the fourteenth, Eisenhower warned the CCS that he now considered a German surrender "unlikely," and expected the Germans to prolong resistance "to the bitter end" by holding out in the Austrian redoubt, the North German ports, the Frisian Islands, western Holland, Norway, the Channel ports, and the Channel Islands. Eisenhower cautioned the CCS that a coordinated cease-fire proclamation issued by the three powers would be impractical and probably unwise until the three powers were certain that months of mopping-up resistance were unnecessary, further warning that the storming of Nazi citadels "may well call for acts of endurance and heroism on the part of the forces engaged comparable to the peak battles of the War."

Meanwhile Bradley and Simpson wrestled over the problem of what to do with the Elbe bridgeheads. Since the eleventh, Simpson had been eager to press on toward Potsdam and Berlin. Reluctant to give categorical orders forbidding Berlin, Bradley had discouraged the idea, reminding Simpson of Zhukov's favorable terrain on the eastern approaches to Berlin and the comparative strength of Russian forces in the area. With news of a 2nd Armored bridgehead south of Magdeburg, Bradley, who was with Simpson at the time, told him he frankly did not want more bridgeheads on the Elbe. Bradley authorized Simpson to place battalions on the far side, adding, "But let's hope the other fellow [the Germans] blows it up before you find yourself stuck with it."

On the fourteenth, American units advancing south of Magdeburg faced slight opposition. Follow-on units arrived, and with two divisions across the Elbe supplied by pontoon, airlift and a convoy of ten-ton trucks, Simpson later claimed that he could have broken through to Potsdam "within 24 hours," and could have followed it up with a corps by the afternoon of the seventeenth, and a second corps by noon the eighteenth. Confronted twenty-five years later with counterarguments by the historian Maclyn Burg, Simpson stated flatly that overextended communications were not a factor, that resistance had collapsed, and that he was "positive" he could have reached the city "if allowed."

Berlin remained under "active consideration" the night of the fourteenth as Eisenhower filed an update of his plans with the Combined Chiefs, but in his latest outline plan, Berlin appeared fourth on his list of priorities behind Leipzig, the Austrian redoubt and Denmark. His objective was the "defeat of the Germans in the shortest possible time," and so Berlin would remain a "low priority in point of time unless operations to clear our flanks proceed with unexpected rapidity." Eisenhower proposed to inform Stalin at once if the CCS agreed.

Once again, whether or not he expected quick CCS backing, Eisenhower's request served notice that whether or not Berlin was a practical operation, he considered it unsound militarily, and therefore outside the scope of his mission unless the CCS gave him authority to coordinate such an advance with the Russians at a minimum or gave him a direct order. None came and Eisenhower construed CCS silence as assent, which he backed up by a stream of cables spelling out the military basis for mobilizing attacks toward Denmark and Austria. Thus Eisenhower girded for the situation he had always hoped to avoid—an interval in which Allied forces arrived at the Elbe and gained bridgeheads with the way open to Berlin and nothing to do but stand in place while the Russians readied their attacks to start—whenever. Finally, amid CCS silence and with no word from the military missions in Moscow, Eisenhower, on the fifteenth, was compelled to issue a direct order suspending Simpson's advance.

The fateful order came on a warming spring afternoon at Reims, where Bradley had joined Eisenhower for a memorial observance for Roosevelt. After the service, the two men spent several hours in the War Room monitoring the situation at Magdeburg. As Simpson recalled, Bradley at midafternoon summoned him to an urgent conference at his headquarters in Heidelberg, where Bradley greeted him with the news: "You must stop on the Elbe and you may not go on to Berlin." Simpson protested, whereupon Bradley added, "On orders from General Eisenhower."

Bradley lingered for a conference to hammer out the wording of a quick directive formalizing the maneuvers he and Eisenhower had worked out at Wiesbaden. General Leonard Gerow's newly formed Fifteenth Army west of the Rhine moved up to assume responsibility for the Ruhr and 12th Army

Group communications. The Ninth Army was to extend flank support northward for Montgomery's lagging effort toward the Elbe while defending the Elbe bridgeheads. Patton's Third Army, arriving in stages at the Mulde River, would be built up to three corps and attack southward on a broad front in support of Devers' 6th Army Group, which was to consolidate the Black Forest before pushing into the western stretches of the Austrian redoubt at Salzburg and join with Alexander's forces north of the Brenner Pass.

After his conference with Bradley, Eisenhower dispatched three messages. In the first, he again pressed Marshall for authority to handle zonal problems on the scene, warning that he did not know how the linkup would work "except with firm prior understandings with the Soviet government." Eisenhower doubted that an "arbitrary demand" from Russian commands to vacate territories allocated the Russians by the ACC could be refused except on pain of "grave misunderstandings if not actual clashes." Then, without waiting for Marshall's approval, Eisenhower wired Deane in Moscow with a request that he propose to Antonov the "simplest possible" coordinating procedures at the Elbe "in order that we may devote our full energy to concerted action on other parts of the front until the enemy's resistance has completely dissolved." In the same message, Eisenhower asked Deane to convey assurances that the Allies had no thought that military movements would alter the EAC zones.

Once again, Eisenhower had taken the initiative on a sensitive problem which he assumed but could not know that the CCS wanted him to handle. In support of this action, he cabled Marshall and once more explained his views on Berlin; Linz and Lübeck were "vastly more important" targets in military terms and termed Berlin "foolish in view of the relative situation of the Russians and ourselves at this moment." He predicted the Allies would get "all coiled up for something that . . . would never come off," though he assured Marshall that he would maintain twenty-three divisions in the center sector, capable of pushing to Berlin *if* German resistance did not develop and *if* the Russians did not attack in the sector. Eisenhower again raised the problem of arranging local withdrawals into zones—he deplored the British "monkey wrench" on the subject, adding: "Frankly, if I should have forces in the Russian occupation zone and be faced with an order or 'request' to retire so that they may advance to the points they choose, I see no recourse except to comply. To do otherwise would probably provoke an incident with the logic of the situation all on the side of the Soviets." Eisenhower assured Marshall he would deal with the situation as it arose, but admitted he felt "a bit lost in trying to give sensible instructions to my various commanders in the field."

CCS debate resumed over Eisenhower's authority to approach Moscow, which left Eisenhower without guidance and apprehensive about the situation at Magdeburg. In a letter home on the night of the fifteenth, he seemed rushed and weary. He described his hectic pace in recent days. He re-counted John's overnight visit at Marburg, and passed along the cheerful news that John had found a challenging job with the 3323rd SIAM. In closing, he described Ohrdruf and confessed he had never dreamed "that such cruelty, bestiality and savagery could really exist in this world! It was horrible.

"Well—we're doing pretty well!

"If we all hang together tightly we ought to get this job done one of these days. How I hope!"

But relief was in the offing, and it came on the sixteenth, another hectic day of attending meetings and receiving visitors. Devers flew in to discuss a new wrinkle in the tug-of-war with Lattre de Tassigny. De Gaulle, deter-mined to firm up a deal for a French zone of occupation, had ordered Lattre de Tassigny to seize Stuttgart as a base for French military government over an expanded French zone in the state of Württemberg. Once again, the problem was Hechingen and ensuring that Patch's Seventh Army seize the town and German atomic data before the French arrived. Late that day, word came that twenty-two Russian divisions, backed by 11,000 artillery pieces under the tactical command of the illustrious General Chuikov, savior of Stalingrad, were attacking from the Oder bridgeheads north and south of Berlin, and the danger of Allied-Soviet clashes in central Germany passed.

Years later it would emerge that with the approach of the Allies, STAVKA, despite Zhukov's preference to clear the pockets in Pomerania and Danzig, had accelerated plans for an offensive along the Oder. Konev, in his memoir, would recall that after receiving Eisenhower's March 27 message, an exceedingly anxious Stalin decided to accelerate the attack on Berlin lest the Allies get there first. Other sources would suggest that Eisenhower's message convinced Stalin that the Allies would keep hands off Berlin, and that it was because of this that Stalin acted. In any event, Deane promptly cabled SHAEF with news of his meetings with Antonov, who confirmed that the Russians, confident of success, had launched a general offensive on the Oder front.

By the seventeenth, Chuikov's attack broadened into a general offensive, as Konev's 1st Ukrainian Front struck south from the Neisse bridgeheads to cut the Berlin–Dresden highway and to close the Sudeten mountains west of the Army Group Center in central Czechoslovakia. Simultaneously, the 4th Ukrainian Front pressed frontal attacks on the massive German concen-trations in the Moravska Ostrava area, joined from the south by the 2nd Ukrainian Front advancing from Bratislava, which appeared to be prelimi-naries for a massive drive toward Prague. With a major German-Russian battle shaping up for the control of western Czechoslovakia, Prague was one of the many problems Eisenhower needed to work out with Churchill, and by late afternoon Eisenhower was on a plane for London.

And so, by the night of April 17, the suspense had lifted somewhat. After a two-and-a-half-month pause, the Russians were attacking westward over the Oder. Allied forces were collecting at the Elbe and readying final drives into Austria and southern Germany. Questions remained—whether a German authority would step forward to surrender or whether the Allies and Russians would simply proclaim the "situation of victory" and impose military government by decree. But Allied and Russian forces had to reach their final positions first, and the timing of such a move was linked to the question of what was to be accomplished in the meanwhile, the subject of Eisenhower's talks with Churchill.

PRAGUE

At 10 Downing Street, Churchill and Eisenhower discussed the whole range of problems: an Allied-Soviet demarcation line north and south of the proposed link-up point on the Elbe–Mulde at Leipzig; the timing of Montgomery's dash for the Elbe; a policy toward De Gaulle's quest to occupy and firm up a French zone in Württemberg; Prague. Officially, Berlin remained under "active consideration" pending Red Army encirclement of the city, but the die was cast and within ninety-six hours Russian armored spearheads would enter the eastern city limits. Elsewhere, Russian forces entered Vienna, and Konev's assaults from the Neisse bridgeheads marked the opening of a Red Army drive toward Prague and what appeared to be a Soviet effort to climax the war by liberating every central European capital. Accordingly, Churchill was opposed to setting limits on Montgomery in the north, or on Patton's forces, which collected at Chemnitz near the Czech frontier with the way open to Prague. But the BCOS had carefully specified in their CCS memorandum of March 31 that the number one British priority was Denmark. Conceivably Denmark and Prague were not mutually exclusive, but conceivably they were. As much as Churchill may have disliked making the choice, the Allies might—for the sake of Denmark —have to give up Prague outright as a kind of quid pro quo.

But Allied resources were not limitless. Second, and this was the crucial point, with the Russians in motion, it was hard to imagine that the Berlin offensive would not turn into a general Russian offensive in the north of sufficient power to threaten Denmark, which meant that the simple solution of reinforcing Montgomery was not certain. On the contrary, negotiations looking to a Denmark–Prague trade-off seemed to offer a surer way, albeit one difficult to undertake politically. Inevitably, within ten days in communication with STAVKA, Eisenhower would find himself in effect bartering his approval of Russian plans to liberate Prague in exchange for Russian approval of Montgomery's plans to liberate Denmark over Churchill's persistent but informal objections.

In many ways the looming issue of Prague resembled Berlin: an opportunity—the last one—for the Allies to liberate a capital in central Europe at a small cost in casualties and time. Like Berlin, Prague would divert Allied forces from other objectives worked out long ago in favor of a political objective along the Allied-Soviet flash point where intervention would embroil Allied forces in a massive German-Russian battle with uncertain results. Like Berlin, Prague involved the growing dilemma of what to do about large eastern-front units attempting to surrender to Allied forces. Again, to refuse surrenders would be inhumane and prolong the fighting; yet to accept them would confront the Allies with the problem of choosing between defiance of Soviet demands for hand-overs of military prisoners or compliance with such demands. Under the Yalta accords, the Allies were already committed to "repatriate" displaced Russian and East European nationals, which would be hard enough.

But certain factors appeared to distinguish Prague from Berlin and weigh in favor of an Allied advance there. The main units of Schörner's Army Group Center were a hundred miles east of the Czech capital, which gave Patton an opportunity to sever Schörner's communications and shorten the campaign. Vital German communications links ran through the city, and Patton could not count on entering Prague without heavy casualties. Konev's forces were also in position to sever German communications at Prague, albeit more expensively. In political terms Czechoslovakia, unlike Germany, was to be a liberated state under a provisional government already recognized by both the Allies and the Russians, meaning that occupation sectors were not a factor, and intervention there would not be an overt challenge to vital Soviet interests. The diplomatic gains to be had there seemed more concrete: Allied forces in the area might bolster the pro-Western President Eduard Beneš in eventual negotiations for the evacuation of Soviet troops and in negotiations on questions that had suddenly arisen over the postwar status of the Czech province of Ruthenia, where "pro-Ukrainian partisans" agitated for union with the Ukraine and the USSR. The Soviet annexation of Ruthenia would mean a sizable loss of territory for Czechoslovakia and, more important, would create a new Soviet-Hungarian frontier along with the new Soviet-Czech frontier created by Soviet annexation of the Polish city of Lvov. Arguably, Prague involved the future independence of Hungary as well as Czechoslovakia.

And yet it was far from clear that the Allied occupation of Prague would actually bolster Beneš. A modest Allied foothold in western Czechoslovakia might well prove to be sufficient leverage to negotiate a mutual withdrawal of Allied and Soviet troops, while to bolster Beneš further was speculative, given the overriding Soviet interest in secure frontiers, an interest created by a Soviet Lvov and one that would endure long after Allied and Russian forces had mutually withdrawn in December 1945. And above all, Prague could not be decided in isolation. A move on Prague might lead to accelerated Soviet moves on western Austria from Vienna or on Denmark from Stettin with no assurance that Allied forces would prevail in either sector. At the time, there were only meager American resources on the Elbe and Bradley's push down the Danube was imminent, which meant that for the moment the Allies had to choose between Prague and other objectives, barring rapid progress on Montgomery's flank. Which of the objectives was more important?

On the night of the seventeenth, Churchill raised Prague as a major opportunity and a hedge against failure on Montgomery's front. But Churchill did not press his case hard. Nor would he turn his full attention to Prague until May 4, when Montgomery reached Lübeck, thus sealing the Danish peninsula, twelve hours before Rokossovsky's forces halted near Wismar in deference to Eisenhower's request. But then, final Allied-German negotiations would be under way for an overall cease-fire, making it incumbent on Eisenhower to avoid moves that would encourage German units in Czechoslovakia to hold out in hopes of gaining contact with Allied forces or of defying Moscow's declared military intentions. Eisenhower's Prague decision would raise yet another postwar controversy. Quid pro quo dealings with Russia over such questions as Denmark and Prague would quickly fall into disrepute, and in the absence of explanations by the principals—Eisenhower and Churchill—historians would be left to puzzle over Eisenhower's failure to exploit an open front in western Czechoslovakia to seize the Czech capital.

Turning to other matters, Churchill on the seventeenth decided to endorse Eisenhower's decision to by-pass Holland. Eisenhower in turn pledged Ninth Army support for Montgomery to advance to the Elbe at Hamburg–Bremen; though the timing of this move was unsettled for reasons unknown, it was presumably due to reluctance to rope off the British sector to refugee traffic. Eisenhower and Churchill discussed the problem of withdrawal from Russian EAC zones in Germany and arrangements for a French EAC. Churchill presented Eisenhower with a troublesome map outlining a new and expanded French zone, which encompassed the Saarland, and Württemberg. The zone cut across American communications to the Bremen enclave, a feature that created "impossible operating and maintenance problems" in Eisenhower's opinion, and ceded important airfields and facilities in the Frankfurt area. Adjustments were mandatory, but Churchill's point was not the zone as such but how to assure De Gaulle that the French would receive any zone at all.

Evidently, no assurances were adequate. With the French excluded from Yalta, voiceless in the CCS and relegated to a minor role at San Francisco, De Gaulle, with forces in the area, was not disposed to rely on assurances. Eisenhower and Churchill settled on the terms of a French zone of occupation, and apparently Eisenhower pledged not to interfere with De Gaulle's effort to occupy Württemberg when American forces reached Hechingen.

Another problem concerned procedures for linkup of American-Russian forces at Leipzig. Eisenhower wanted CCS authority to negotiate American withdrawal behind the zonal boundaries. Churchill opposed it, evidently convinced that the Russians were too tired to press the point of immediate occupation of their zone, and that the question of an Allied withdrawal could be safely bartered for Soviet "compliance" on agreements ranging from access to Berlin and Vienna to full Allied participation in an Austrian ACC. But the issue involved U.S. troops exclusively, which meant that Churchill would have to defer to Eisenhower's handling of the problem on the scene as it arose, and on this note, the saga of Eisenhower's wartime dealings with Churchill and the BCOS all but ended.

Questions remained, but as of the night of April 17, the major strategy questions were settled, and the fighting was winding down in the west. There was little elation in London as the end approached, however. The long-awaited Russian assault on Berlin was under way—a relief of sorts, though Churchill knew that the fall of Berlin would not be portrayed as a victory for the grand alliance; the Russians would see to that.

Churchill looked out on a troubled scene. The Prime Minister, who would be remembered in history as the man who may have single-handedly kept the British government from negotiating with Hitler in 1940, now confronted the price of having declared Hitler his enemy and Stalin his ally. The Russians, having conquered Budapest, had reached Vienna and approached the outskirts of Berlin. A three-prong offensive advanced on Prague, which would consolidate Russian sway over Czechoslovakia and Hungary. As yet no one was calling Eastern Europe a Soviet bloc, but Churchill intended to clarify matters soon. Churchill, in the twilight of his long career, was consumed by the future of France, Italy, Greece and other areas where British interests were vital, and he knew that American support would be needed to reconstruct a bastion from which future generations might restore Europe. But Churchill was unsure of such an undertaking, and as he would tell Stalin later that week, he took no comfort in looking to a future in which a Communist world dominated by Russia on one side confronted the English-speaking countries and their associates on the other, which was a formula for a quarrel that would "tear the world to pieces."

General elections in England could not be put off more than several weeks after V-E Day, and so the British were about to vote for the first time in ten years. Churchill occasionally spoke of his optimism about the outcome, which he saw shaping up as a long-overdue contest between Labourite visions of a brave new world and gratitude for his wartime leadership. Churchill was convinced that all Englishmen were grateful for his leadership but not convinced that all Englishmen were enthusiastic about a brave new world, or so he said.

But no event so clearly dramatized the passing of an era as the death of

Franklin Roosevelt. Earlier that day, in Parliament, the Prime Minister had moved in an address to the King to express the sympathy and sorrow of the House of Commons for the government and people of America. In his address, Churchill recalled the highlights of Roosevelt's efforts to save England and the Continent, as well as the history of his efforts to enlist American aid. He described his friendship with Roosevelt, which had evolved through their voluminous correspondence beginning in the fateful days of September 1939 and lasting through the gloom of two winters when British survival had been in the balance, then on through the "ups and downs of the world struggle" ending only with Roosevelt's last message to him on April 12. By Churchill's estimate, he and Roosevelt had exchanged 1,700 messages. They had participated in nine meetings covering 120 days at Argentia, Washington, Casablanca, Teheran, Quebec, Cairo and Yalta, at which he had conceived an admiration for Roosevelt as a statesman, a man of affairs and a war leader of skill and "a generous heart which was always stirred to anger and to action by spectacles of aggression and oppression by the strong against the weak."

"As the saying goes," Churchill said, "he died in harness, and we may well say in battle harness, like his soldiers, sailors and airmen who side by side with ours are carrying on their tasks to the end all over the world. . . ." He concluded:

> In the days of peace he had broadened and stabilized the foundation of American life and union. In war, he had raised the strength, might, and glory of the great Republic to a height never attained by any nation in history. . . . But all of this was no more than worldly power and grandeur, had it not been that the causes of human freedom and social justice, to which so much of his life had been given, added a luster which will long be discernible among men. He has left behind him a band of resolute and able men handling the numerous, interrelated parts of the vast American war machine. He has left a successor who comes forward with firm steps and sure conviction to carry on the task to its appointed end. . . . For us it remains to say that in Franklin Roosevelt there died the greatest American friend we have ever known, and the greatest champion of freedom who has ever brought help and comfort from the New World to the Old. . . .

Eisenhower and Butcher spent the night of the seventeenth at Telegraph Cottage. They stayed up past midnight catching up and reminiscing about Patton, North Africa and Widewing days. Eisenhower spoke of the splendid spirit of cooperation he detected in recent days at all levels, and of his deep pride in the American Army, which, having weathered the storms of 1944, had recovered and performed so magnificently. Eisenhower told Butcher that on recent trips he had noticed that his troops had developed a "veteran quality," adding that he doubted that any organization in the world could regroup on a large scale while sustaining offensive action more efficiently than Bradley's 12th Army Group. Butcher told Eisenhower that correspondents were suggesting that the time had come for another press conference. "I think I've talked enough," Eisenhower replied.

Eisenhower and Butcher returned to London the next morning for a brief round of talks before heading back to Paris. Butcher waited in the War Room, having presented the champagne Eisenhower had brought over for Churchill's staff for V-E Day when it came. Afterward Butcher noted that Churchill and Eisenhower emerged "homey as neighbors on adjoining Iowa farms." On the drive back to Telegraph Cottage, Eisenhower confessed to Butcher that he had grown very fond of Churchill, despite their occasional differences on military questions.

Thereafter, Eisenhower and Churchill would close ranks. In the next several days, as his problems with the French intensified, Eisenhower resolved the American-French duel for control of the Black Forest mostly in favor of the French. By the nineteenth, the Americans and the French raced for Stuttgart. Devers placed Stuttgart in the Seventh Army operational zone in order to secure VI Corps communications for the push into Bavaria, whereupon De Gaulle ordered Lattre de Tassigny to take Stuttgart and hold the city "until such time as the French occupation zone has been fixed in agreement between interested governments." On the nineteenth the French defied orders and plunged into the Seventh Army zone and, in the confusion, entered Stuttgart on the twentieth.

Apparently in line with his understanding with Churchill, Eisenhower declined to intercede against Lattre de Tassigny. Marshal Juin visited Versailles on the twenty-second with a revised occupation-zone proposal that would meet American objectives partway. Juin accepted a corridor linking the American zone and the port of Bremen, and endorsed U.S. retention of the Frankfurt airfields. The French would be "content" with Baden-Baden in the south, though Juin held out for a Rhine bridgehead in the Wiesbaden area. Eisenhower accepted the compromise, which reserved U.S. transit rights in Mannheim and Heidelberg. Since the new French zone linked the Saar to a proposed French zone in Austria, the French had an incentive to join in Devers' advance to the Austrian frontier. By the twenty-third, French and American forces advanced toward Munich and the Austrian frontier at Salzburg. Meanwhile Eisenhower wrote De Gaulle to deplore Lattre de Tassigny's ongoing defiance of Devers' orders, but told De Gaulle he would not recommend cutting supplies to Lattre de Tassigny because Eisenhower was personally "unwilling . . . to reduce the effectiveness of the military effort against Germany."

Churchill would later raise a storm over Berlin and Prague in *Triumph and Tragedy,* but his correspondence at the time confirmed his satisfaction with Eisenhower's balanced plans to push Devers' 6th Army Group into Austria and Montgomery's 21st Army Group to Denmark as Bradley divided his forces on the Elbe to support both. Eventually Churchill would cable Eden in San Francisco an excited description of Montgomery's arrival

FINAL ADVANCE,
APRIL 18–MAY 8, 1945

Baltic
Sea

Lübeck

Hamburg

Stettin

RUSSIAN
ARMIES

Bremen

NETH.

Berlin

POLAND

Poznan

21ST ARMY
GROUP

U.S.
NINTH
ARMY

Elbe

Oder

12TH ARMY
GROUP

U.S.
FIRST
ARMY

Torgau

GERMANY

Dresden

Bonn

Chemnitz

Rhine

Frankfurt

U.S.
THIRD
ARMY

Prague

Pilsen

6TH ARMY
GROUP

U.S.
SEVENTH
ARMY

Danube

FRANCE

Munich

Linz

Vienna

OSTMARK
(AUSTRIA)

SWITZERLAND

YUGOSLAVIA

Zagreb

Milan

Po

Venice

15TH ARMY
GROUP

ITALY

Kms.
0   60
0   60
Miles

Front lines,
April 18

American

British

Front lines,
May 8

Russian

French

Allied-controlled as of May 8

at Lübeck, the surrender of 2.5 million Germans in a week to British forces, and Eisenhower's "sportsmanship" and "dexterity" in providing Ridgway's corps, which provided the necessary margin to liberate Denmark. Meanwhile, in anticipation of this outcome, Churchill on the nineteenth had cabled Eden to brace him for the Russian seizure of Berlin, which he depicted as inevitable despite the improving military situation. "It would seem that the western Allies are not immediately in a position to force their way into Berlin," he wrote.

> The Russians have 2½ million troops on the sector of the front opposite that city. The Americans have only their spearheads, say 25 divisions, which are covering an immense front and are at many points engaged with the Germans.
>
> It is thought most important that Montgomery should take Lübeck as soon as possible and he has an additional American Corps to strengthen his movements if he requires it. Our arrival at Lübeck before our Russians friends from Stettin would save a lot of argument later on. There is no reason why Russia should occupy Denmark, which is a country to be liberated and to have its sovereignty restored. Our position at Lübeck, if we get it, would be decisive in this matter.
>
> Thereafter, but partly concurrent, it is thought well to push on to Linz to meet the Russians there, and also by an American enveloping movement to gain the region south of Stuttgart. In this region, there are German installations connected with their atomic research and we had better get hold of these in the interest of the special secrecy attaching to this topic.

Returning from London, Eisenhower stopped over in Brussels for a talk with Montgomery. Time was getting short, and Eisenhower was anxious that Montgomery accept support in order to accelerate Dempsey's advance to the Elbe and beyond. But Montgomery was still confident the 21st Army Group could reach Denmark on its own, though he had hoped Bradley would "extend his left" slightly. Eisenhower promptly extended Bradley's northern boundary, and placed Ridgway's XVIII Airborne Corps in SHAEF reserve.

That day the battle of the Ruhr pocket ended, formalized in Eisenhower's order of the day of April 20, in which he claimed the destruction of twenty-one German divisions, 317,000 prisoners taken and innumerable killed, a "fitting prelude to the final battles to crush the ragged remnants of Hitler's armies of the west." But how those final battles would be fought was still unsettled.

Montgomery's tempo picked up as the Soviets completed the encirclement of Berlin and the Russian advance commenced from Stettin. The vaunted German defense of Berlin fell short of expectations. In a matter of six days the Russians encircled Berlin, and by the twenty-fifth Russian forces were fighting block to block through the eastern suburbs. As German disintegration in Berlin proceeded, Dempsey, with his southernmost VIII Corps, having reached the Elbe on April 19, resumed toward Hamburg; XII

Corps in the center reached the Elbe at Hamburg on the twenty-third, followed by Horrocks' XXX Corps, which entered Bremen the next day, 120 miles southwest of Lübeck.

By the twenty-first, four days after the opening of the Russian offensive, Eisenhower still lacked formal authority to approach the Russians about linkup or authority to negotiate American withdrawals from the Russian sector. Eisenhower also lacked guidance on Czechoslovakia and three-power guidance on terms for an overall cease-fire, which hinged on three unknowns: first, Allied success in expediting the flank offensives; second, Hitler's whereabouts and the emergence of German authority able to conclude a cease-fire; third, the pace of Russian operations along a 375-mile front enveloping Czechoslovakia from Breslau to Brno. Finally, on the twenty-second, the BCOS conceded a major point by allowing Eisenhower to reopen direct SHAEF-Moscow communications, whereupon Eisenhower promptly dispatched a summary of his latest plans to Deane in hopes that Deane might learn of Soviet plans in the Leipzig–Prague region and to present his own for an advance toward Denmark.

Eisenhower informed Deane that Allied forces were "approaching the completion of that phase of our operations" outlined on the thirty-first of March. In his message, he went on to point out that Allied operations in the center could not be sustained without sacrificing efforts on the flanks against remaining enemy forces. The Allies would therefore halt all forces on the Elbe–Mulde "for the time being," but proceed on the left to Schleswig-Holstein, the North Sea ports and Denmark, and on the right along the Bayreuth–Salzburg axis and Würzburg–Munich. Third, Eisenhower asked Deane to convey this message to STAVKA, which served notice of Montgomery's plans to cross the Elbe and advance toward Denmark, coupled with the barest hint that Patton might extend his left flank toward Prague. Was this the quid pro quo?

But even as Eisenhower gained a CCS go-ahead to arrange a linkup, the CCS, not specifically asked to approve Eisenhower's plans, saw no reason to do so. The CCS would in fact remain silent over his plans for western Czechoslovakia for a few days and refuse to sanction Allied withdrawals from the Soviet EAC sector. Perhaps the CCS was waiting to see if a Soviet offensive toward Prague or Soviet demands to occupy its own EAC sector in fact materialized. In Washington the mood was tense as Molotov arrived in America for the UN conferences at San Francisco in the wake of Stalin's abrupt announcement of a new Soviet-Lublin treaty of mutual assistance. Plainly, the Soviets intended to force the Polish seating issue at San Francisco, an event that would crystallize American views and usher in a new and tougher American line in dealings with Moscow.

For weeks the State Department had been weighing a re-examination of Yalta in light of apparent Soviet violations. The War Department was evaluating the urgency of Russian entry in the war against Japan, and the odds that Moscow would demand participation in the Japanese occupation amid growing doubts about Soviet reliability, which focused on Poland and its implications for Western Europe, postwar cooperation and, above all, postwar U.S. politics.

Harriman, a key figure, had returned for Roosevelt's funeral "filled with foreboding over the increasingly difficult task of reconciling American and Soviet objectives." He warned of the "new barbarian invasion of Europe" under way through Soviet imposition of police states in Eastern Europe, which now had to be exposed and repudiated. Harriman found a new and invigorating realism about the Russians at the State Department and in the White House. In conferences with the new President, he quickly formed the impression of Truman as a decisive man, determined to "eliminate fear in dealing with the U.S.S.R.," opposed to courting Moscow's favor, and determined to confront Stalin with a united West. But it was not immediately clear that Truman's thinking had translated into a program of objectives and strategies to meet the Russian threat or that Truman had precisely defined that threat.

Were the Soviets a threat to the Allies and to Western Europe? Even by Harriman's estimate, the war would leave 90 percent of the surviving Russian people near poverty. Russian rail systems, industry and communications west of the Urals were destroyed. Moreover, Harriman was not the only figure in Washington who suggested that unilateral Soviet action in Poland might yet prove to be an exception and not the rule, on the theory that Poland's importance to the Soviets was as a supply link to eastern Germany, and that Soviet rigidity on Poland was linked to Russian anxiety on the German issue and not to desires to absorb Poland or to mount aggressive political challenges elsewhere. But such fine distinctions were getting less of a hearing by mid-April, and Harriman did nothing to restrain the American reassessment, which proceeded apace.

In Washington, opinion on the Russians was still divided. By now, some welcomed what appeared to be the inevitable break with the Soviets as a basis for extending urgently needed aid to Western Europe. Growing numbers believed that the United States must now assume the lead in a global ideological conflict with the Communist world and favored a political challenge in Eastern Europe. Others considered tensions inevitable but temporary, and called for a policy of patience and countervailing pressure, mainly economic. Still others opposed countering Russian ideology with a correspondingly rigid Western ideology or ruling out eventual conciliation as a goal. Diminishing numbers denied that an Allied-Soviet split was inevitable and urged steps to avoid a break with the Russians by applying Roosevelt's old formula of steady purpose and conciliatory actions toward a war-torn ally. But advocates of Roosevelt's position had to face the fact that the Soviets for their part appeared to agree that a split was inevitable because the reasons why one should be avoided were no longer as clear-cut as they had been months, even weeks, before.

On the twenty-second, Harriman, Eden, Kerr and Stettinius met with Molotov at the State Department for tense talks on Poland. Molotov defended the treaty and Moscow's policy of deferring to Lublin's views on the stillborn unity conference, which was a right the Soviets reserved at Yalta. Molotov urged a new interpretation of the Yalta formula as a coalition similar to the Tito-Subašić accords governing Yugoslavia, which recognized Tito's preeminence. Stettinius rejected the parallel, and Harriman informed Truman afterward that the two sides had reached "complete deadlock."

The following day, April 23, was to be a landmark in the history of the emerging Cold War. The Cabinet met amid a controversy surrounding columnist Drew Pearson's allegations that U.S. forces had reached Potsdam only to withdraw fifty miles behind the Elbe in accordance with a deal struck with Stalin at Yalta to hand over Berlin to the Russians. Denials by Hopkins of any so-called secret understandings on Berlin merely inflamed the controversy and, combined with the Polish issue, moved the Cabinet to a consensus in favor of a new, tougher line.

Truman told the Cabinet that in his considered opinion the Russians now viewed Yalta as a "one-way street." Truman had concluded that he could go no further in trying to ensure Molotov's attendance in San Francisco at the UN, and if the Soviets backed out, they could "go to hell."

According to Harriman, Cabinet discussion of Poland ensued, which exposed misgivings about approaching Moscow this firmly. Admiral Leahy expressed doubt that the Russians had actually violated the Yalta accords, which could be read "either way." He told the Cabinet he had gained the "definite impression" at Yalta that the Russians would never permit a free government in Poland, and cautioned that an Allied-Soviet break over Poland would be a "serious matter." Stimson observed that the United States was "sailing into dangerous waters" if Washington did not take the trouble to find out how seriously the Soviets took Poland as a security problem. He reminded Truman that the Soviets had always been "good on big-power matters," and warned against precipitate steps. Marshall raised the problem of Japan and the need for Russian aid in the Far East. Harriman, however, rephrased the issue; it was, in his words, "whether the United States was to be a party to the Soviet program for dominating Poland." The answer was no, and to this degree the tone of American dealings with Russia changed at that very moment, though Harriman would regret Truman's next move, which, in his opinion, handed Molotov a pretext to report to Stalin that Truman had repudiated Roosevelt's policy in toto.

Afterward Truman summoned Molotov to the White House for what was to be a celebrated confrontation over Poland. Truman came to his point quickly: that Washington viewed the "deadlock" in the Polish ambassadorial talks as a threat to the unity of the San Francisco conference; that the United States would demand the inclusion of non-Lublin Poles in the Moscow meetings; that Molotov was wrong in assuming that the United States would evade the issue any longer. "No American policy, foreign or domestic, can succeed unless it enjoys public confidence and support," he said. Congress would have to appropriate postwar aid, and so the United States had "gone as far as it could go," and would not recognize a government that failed to represent all the democratic elements in the country.

Molotov cautioned Truman against two parties of the wartime coalition ganging up on the third. He insisted that "equality" was the only acceptable basis for relations between the Big Three. Truman told Molotov that he was "merely trying to ensure Yalta was carried out." Molotov denied that the Soviets had violated Yalta. Truman professed a desire for friendship, but not on the basis of a "one-way street." Molotov remarked that he had "never been talked to like that." "Carry out your agreements," Truman replied, "and you won't get talked to like that."

What had the Soviets agreed to on Poland? On the twenty-fourth Truman joined Churchill in a joint protest disavowing Moscow's decision to consult Lublin on the inclusion of Mikolajczyk at the Polish Unity Conference in Moscow. In his curt reply, Stalin recited the Soviet position: he had understood the Yalta accord to call for reorganizing Lublin on a broader base, not dismissal of Lublin as a "faction," and since Lublin was a permanent government and ally, the Soviets felt duty-bound to consult its views about Mikolajczyk and other exile factions. Stalin emphasized that Mikolajczyk's recent grudging endorsements of the new Polish-Russian boundary based on the Curzon Line had not been sufficient, as Yalta had specified that Poland was to be strong, independent *and* friendly, which was a matter of "life and death" for Poland's neighbor Russia. The matter was at least as important to the USSR as Greece, France and Belgium were to Britain, countries where the British had, of course, "proceeded unilaterally without reference to the Soviet wishes."

Inevitably, the behind-the-scenes exchanges spilled over into the San Francisco conference later that week. San Francisco marked the first real public revelation of the downward spiral in Allied-Soviet relations, spurring criticism of the unwillingness of the American government to "call a spade a spade," now widely viewed as a key failure of the Roosevelt Administration. The seating issues in San Francisco developed into a long-postponed debate between Eden and Molotov that exposed the basis of Soviet-Western differences but at the same time revealed the outlines of the implicit consensus still intact about the system of world order being proclaimed in San Francisco.

At San Francisco, few disputed the professed objectives of the UN charter: the document committed all signatories to universal goals of human welfare, the illegality of fascism, the advancement of world citizenship and basic human rights. Both Eden and Molotov emphasized respect for diversity of philosophies and systems. Debate arose over what was meant by democratic rights and methods, the source of threats to human rights, and therefore how human rights were to be protected.

In speeches that week, Eden emphasized the rights of smaller nations, the principle of consent and the need for standards that small nations could apply to big-power conduct. In turn, Molotov addressed Eden's omissions: the practical problem of order and the question of who should resolve the problems Eden spelled out. Molotov cautioned against the use of "democratic watchwords and the arguments including the professed desire to protect the interests of small nations or of the principles of the equity and equality of nations" to frustrate the effectiveness of the UN design. Molotov emphasized the Russian view that no settlement was secure that ignored the vital interests of the major powers. Additionally, he emphasized the truism that the wartime lineup was to be the basis for membership in an inner directorate of responsible powers for some time to come. The USSR, the United States and Britain stood in the first rank of world powers; France and China stood in the second rank, being "great nations" that would strengthen the organization in the postwar world. The debates that week would be re-enacted many times in the years ahead, and Western-Soviet differences aired in the UN would often bring Western-Soviet relations to the breaking point, but without fundamentally altering them.

And as the debate commenced in San Francisco, the cease-fire in Germany began to take shape. On the twenty-second, Eisenhower informed Deane that he was satisfied with arrangements worked out to identify Russian and Allied forces, and had instructed all commands to report contact and halt as Allied and Soviet forces met. Crucial unanswered questions remained: Where would contact be established? And then what? Eisenhower proposed a linkup in the Dresden–Wittenberg area and the Elbe–Mulde line south of Dessau, chosen because of readily identifiable geographical features, and also suggested that Allied and Soviet army group commanders agree to meet and fix boundary lines as events dictated.

Seventy-two hours would elapse before Moscow's reply. In Washington, the Combined Chiefs of Staff questioned the implication in Eisenhower's message that the Allies would stand in place along the length of the Elbe, which appeared to rule out both Prague and Wismar. In Moscow the Russians peppered Deane with questions about the demarcation line Eisenhower proposed south of Dessau—would it extend along the upper Vltava and include Prague? The British still balked on formally permitting Eisenhower to withdraw his forces behind EAC boundaries as he saw fit, whereupon Eisenhower cabled Marshall to vent his exasperation.

Politely, Eisenhower suggested that the time had come for clarification of a few points. In his opinion, the situation he faced was potentially dangerous, though manageable, provided he or the CCS took in hand the matter of working out specific arrangements for the linkup of Allied and Soviet forces. Naturally, this involved questions of strategy, though in the course of weeks of debate he and the CCS had defined a more or less logical and acceptable plan of action, one that combined steps to pacify German resistance with ways of minimizing clashes with the Soviets. What was missing was a procedure governing the sensitive question of occupation zones in Germany. Eisenhower assured Marshall that he doubted the Russians would be arbitrary about it, but he added, for the record, that should the Russians prove arbitrary and serve notice of plans to push through to the limit of their zone, American forces would be "badly embarrassed." Eisenhower hastened to repeat that he did not expect this, and that he mentioned it in the hope of working something out "to protect my subordinate commanders from uncertainty and worry."

There matters stood as the scene shifted back to Holland and the exploratory talks under way with Seyss-Inquart and Blaskowitz. Eisenhower, on the twenty-third, informed the CCS of an expedient he had devised for rescuing Holland without military action. He acknowledged that foreign ministers' talks in San Francisco were dealing with the problem, but warned that something had to be done "at once." He proposed to inform Seyss-Inquart and Blaskowitz of plans to airlift food supplies, then to take the unprecedented step of a direct message to German Army Group Commander General Blaskowitz ordering him to cooperate with the airlift on pain of being declared in violation of the laws of war. Eisenhower summarized the message to be passed to Blaskowitz through the underground: that since the Army Group H position was indefensible, further military preparations, such as flooding, would constitute a crime and a "blot on [German] military honor which would never be effaced." Blaskowitz was to cease opening dikes, to assist the airlift in every way, and unless he did so, "each responsible member of his command will be considered by me as violators of the laws of war who must face the certain consequences of their acts."

The scheme had wide implications. In effect, Eisenhower proposed to terminate hostilities in Holland by a direct order issued by him to an enemy force not engaged by Allied troops. This was an obvious precedent for dealing with eastern-front units and German garrisons in Norway, the Channel Islands, Yugoslavia, northern Italy and southern Germany. With this step, Eisenhower would serve notice of his readiness to close the western front to German military traffic and to take other drastic steps to wring a cease-fire from the German army. Were the Russians ready to accept? Eisenhower had kept Susloparoff closely informed and Susloparoff did not object to the negotiations in Holland, another signal that Moscow would be content to follow the Allied-German lead in wider negotiations toward a cease-fire.

But British reluctance was still evident, perhaps owing to hesitation about entering wider talks on a general cease-fire before British forces were in complete control of the British zone and Lübeck. On the twenty-fifth, eight messages passed between Reims, Washington, London and Moscow, in which the Americans, Russians and finally the British approved the initiative. Then, on the night of the twenty-fifth, the divided German military authorities, angling for a field surrender, balked at guaranteeing the safety of the airlift. Word came back to Eisenhower that Seyss-Inquart "agreed in principle" with Eisenhower's order but opposed airdrops for "reasons of defense," a delaying tactic that coincided with word of a high-level Nazi feeler, a bizarre meeting the day before between Count Folke Bernadotte of the Swedish Red Cross and Heinrich Himmler at Lübeck. Exhausted and nervous, Himmler had "admitted to [Bernadotte] that Germany was finished," and claimed that Hitler was 'so desperately ill that he might be dead already." In the circumstances, Himmler asserted full authority to contact Eisenhower through the Swedish government to arrange meetings and capitulation on the western front. Allied reaction was swift and public. Truman and Churchill quickly affirmed unconditional surrender in a message to Stalin and decided to release the news of the overture evidently to close the door on further efforts by the German army to stall behind the façade of Nazi authority.

Meanwhile, on the twenty-fifth, Deane conveyed Antonov's long-awaited reply to Eisenhower's link-up plan sent on the twenty-second. Antonov indicated that Russian plans included "both the occupation of Berlin and also clearing of the German forces from the western shore of the Elbe River north and south of Berlin and the Vltava River Valley, where according to the information we have the Germans are concentrating considerable forces." The message was ambiguous: Moscow appeared to claim Prague, yet Antonov did not foreclose an Allied advance up to the west bank of the Vltava and appeared to invite it, which gave the Allies a plausible basis for proceeding beyond the upper Elbe into western Czechoslovakia, if not to the western suburbs of Prague itself.

The Antonov message sparked an eleventh-hour CCS debate on Prague. Still uncertain about Denmark, the BCOS proposed that the CCS direct Eisenhower to dispatch strong forces to western Czechoslovakia, which aroused a debate along now familiar lines. The BCOS noted the "remarkable political advantages derived from the liberation of Prague and as much as possible of Czechoslovakia by US-UK forces," and urged that Eisenhower be directed to take advantage of weakening German resistance in the area to advance into Czechoslovakia, *provided* that such action did not "hamper or delay final German defeat." In the course of the debate, Marshall cabled Eisenhower with word that he was "personally, and aside from all logistical tactical or strategic implications . . . loath to hazard American lives for purely political purposes," a suggestion that left the final steps to

Eisenhower, who noted from Antonov's message that Soviet forces in fact intended to liberate Prague, but that Antonov had not objected to Montgomery's plan to cross the Elbe from Lübeck.

In the vacuum of high-level understandings, the historic Allied-Russian linkup was unfolding along the Mulde–Elbe front south of Dessau. Aerial reconnaissance missions plotted the approach of Konev's forces. On the twenty-fourth, V Corps patrols had gained contact with Russian ground troops without incident, formalized at the town of Torgau on the twenty-sixth between elements of the U.S. 69th Division and the 58th Guards Armored Division, 1st Ukraine Front. In the early hours, no arbitrary Soviet demands developed, and as linkup occurred smoothly along the front, it became evident that the Soviets were content to maintain a safe distance between the two forces for the time being, and would not be immoderate. With the immediate threat of clashes passing, Eisenhower informed Marshall on the twenty-seventh of the linkup, and remarked in passing that his staff was at work on a victory-day speech. Personally, he wrote, "it is difficult for me, at this stage, to think of anything that I would want to say at such a moment or what anyone else would want to hear."

Gradually, things fell into place. That day Eisenhower and Bradley met to frame a directive to expedite Montgomery's assault toward Hamburg and to reinforce Patton's Third Army. Eisenhower ordered XVIII Corps, still at the Sieg River near the Ruhr, to pack up for a march toward Kiel and shifted V Corps to Patton's Third Army in order to bolster Third Army support for Devers' assault toward Munich–Salzburg. Simultaneously, Eisenhower cabled Brooke to make a record of the entire affair on the northern flank. Eisenhower reviewed the history of Montgomery's pursuit toward Hamburg, and recited the record of his efforts to reinforce Montgomery so that Brooke would know he had "done everything that is humanly possible for me to do and that I have not been merely giving lip service to an idea without doing anything to implement it." Eisenhower told Brooke that he had formed a reserve for Montgomery's use and in effect washed his hands of responsibility for any further delay. That day De Guingand, on behalf of the 21st Army Group, crossed the lines at Arnhem to meet the German and Dutch representatives to reopen the talks with Seyss-Inquart.

Another forty-eight hours passed before a conference took place between Smith, Seyss-Inquart and German army authorities in Susloparoff's presence at which the German delegation continued to hold out for delay. For hours, Smith labored to negotiate drop zones and the surrender of German forces in Holland. Seyss-Inquart denied that he had status as plenipotentiary. The military authorities refused to talk truce in Susloparoff's presence, since the army was still in contact with Berlin and lacked authority to speak with Russians. At length, Seyss-Inquart conceded that he acted autonomously and could surrender, but that as a loyal Nazi he would hold out until the end. Under Smith's threat to break off all talks, the delegations finally agreed on drop sites for an emergency airlift into western Holland between the daylight hours of 7 A.M. and 3 P.M., weather permitting, and truck convoys with a thousand tons of foodstuff daily to pass along a single road. Arrangements were made for sea convoys to enter through Rotterdam beginning on May 4.

10

Conclusion

SURRENDER

That week the fate of millions hung in the balance as the kaleidoscopic movements of armies and peoples neared a climax. In the center, Ninth and Twelfth German Army attacks failed to relieve the encirclement of Berlin, where 60,000 Germans died and 120,000 were captured in fourteen days of fighting through the rubble. In Saxony, Schörner maneuvered to check three Russian fronts that advanced on Prague from the northeast, east and southeast, while the Fourth Panzer Army moved erratically between the two battles, ordered first to Berlin, then ordered back to the Sudeten Mountains north of Prague, then back to Dresden. Meanwhile, Montgomery's 21st Army Group crossed the Elbe in a race with the Russians to the base of the Danish peninsula. In the south, the American Seventh and Third armies pushed south on a broad front toward Munich, Linz and linkup with Alexander's force working toward the Brenner Pass in the wake of the German surrender in Italy on April 29. Finally, Hitler's suicide on the thirtieth removed the main barrier to a formal surrender as a caretaker government under Grand Admiral Karl Dönitz assumed power at Flensburg on May 1 and pledged to "save Germany from destruction by the advancing Bolshevik enemy."

On May 1, the Germans finally dropped all pretense of defending Germany on two fronts and adopted an avowed policy of an open door for the Allies in the west. But it was late in the day, and according to postwar interrogations, the Flensburg government did so in hopes of gaining the ten days or so necessary to disengage the bulk of forces on the Baltic and the Oder and in Yugoslavia and evacuate them westward into the Allied zones or gain contact with Allied spearheads to surrender locally.

In the end, the Flensburg government would gain nine days, and along the way try to establish a basis for Allied leniency by linking the German cause to that of the Allies on the basis of feelings aroused by Soviet occupation of central Europe. But the strategy was transparent, and the benefits of a formal surrender diminished as German assets dwindled by the hour.

Soon the Allies would occupy the redoubt area, and a general Soviet offensive would break the German hold on central and western Czechoslovakia, leaving the Germans in control of scattered pockets here and there without industry or petroleum. Finally, as wider negotiations approached, Eisenhower held the trump because the German military was desperate for the protection of the Geneva accords that the Allies could provide or withhold. In Holland, Eisenhower had rehearsed the procedure for imposing a capitulation and had been hinting publicly and privately that he was on the verge of doing so to speed along a cease-fire and the imposition of order. But Eisenhower could not play his trump effectively until the Soviets were ready to join in, and so arranging Soviet participation absorbed most of Eisenhower's working hours for weeks, a hectic time when Eisenhower and his staff ate when hungry, slept when tired, without schedule or any sense of day or night.

Apparently, the holdup in Moscow was due to uncertainty about the success of the final offensive in Czechoslovakia. To prompt Russian action, Eisenhower offered Third Army help in subduing German resistance at Prague, but the Russians declined, and Eisenhower would find himself honoring Antonov's request not to advance into the Czech capital. It was to be Eisenhower's last major decision and one of his most controversial decisions, as, again, Eisenhower decided that he was bound by Soviet wishes provided the Red Army moved quickly and decisively.

To the end, Eisenhower's approach was military: defeating the German army and gaining an unconditional cease-fire. By the thirtieth, this dictated a strategy of pursuing, capturing and disarming organized German units where encountered, but otherwise depressing German hopes that anything was to be gained by delay, and of coordinating moves with the Russians to avoid clashes, to ensure that Allied movement did not interfere in areas where the Soviets were engaged, and to avoid overt unilateral action that might convince the Soviets that they had no recourse but to occupy every position of conceivable importance to them. With Allied forces advancing to the limit of stop lines in all sectors, Patton with large available reserves was in position to cut the communications of the German Army Group Center holding out east of Prague. But with four Russian fronts in position to converge on the Czech capital, Eisenhower found it essential that Allied movement not interfere with action in progress or prolong the Russian-German denouement by encouraging German forces east of the city to hope that they could resist in place and gain contact with Allied forces. This final consideration applied with special force in view of the fact that Field Marshal Schörner, commanding the Army Group Center, now functioned in the dual role of commander of the Army Group Center and Guderian's successor as OKH in charge of all the German land forces on the eastern front.

What were Soviet intentions? The continuing silence in the last few days of April suggested that the Soviet high command was wavering, an inference borne out by Antonov's reply, which appeared to invite Allied intervention in western Czechoslovakia. Then, following the BCOS motion and Marshall's cable, Eisenhower proceeded to dispatch a message to Antonov in which he solicited Soviet views. On the thirtieth, he informed STAVKA that the U.S. Third Army would cross the Elbe and advance to Karlsbad–Pilsen–Budejovice, where he proposed that link-up arrangements could be handled by "cooperative action of local commanders," a move that by implication suggested the Vltava as the next logical line of demarcation. The gist of Eisenhower's message was that the Soviets were free to take Prague, by which he intended to reinforce his earlier suggestion that the Soviets be guided by Allied wishes in Denmark. Likewise, the Third Army move east of the Elbe in the south was a reminder that major Allied forces would not stand idle indefinitely should the Soviets be unable or unwilling to sustain their drive in central Czechoslovakia or to approve a cease-fire. Five tense days would elapse before the arrival of Antonov's reply confirming that Konev intended to strike south through the Sudetens toward Prague to complete the encirclement of Schörner.

Meanwhile, on the thirtieth, resistance on the 21st Army Group front crumbled. Montgomery, reinforced by Ridgway's XVIII Airborne Corps, was in fast pursuit toward Lübeck. Dempsey dashed through Schleswig-Holstein at Wismar, and entered Lübeck the following morning before dawn, on the second, approximately twelve marching hours before the arrival of Rokossovsky's columns in pursuit of the bedraggled Army Group Vistula. Montgomery's arrival at Wismar two days later disposed of concern that unilateral American action at Prague would jeopardize Montgomery's success in the north, which reduced the problem to one of avoiding steps that would prolong the German-Russian battle in central Czechoslovakia. Elsewhere, the 6th Army Group and Patton's heavily reinforced Third Army advanced southward side by side on a 200-mile front into the Austrian redoubt. Patton's Third Army, built up to fifteen divisions, marched 150 miles down the Danube toward Vienna. On Patton's right, the Seventh Army, built up to two corps, advanced through Munich to Augsburg and linked up with Clark's Fifth Army winding its way northward through the Po Valley. On the fourth, as the Third Army entered Linz and Salzburg, Devers and Clark joined forces in the heart of Europe at the Brenner Pass. By the night of May 4, 1945, the Allied front from Lübeck to Trieste was stationary.

An eerie calm descended in all sectors, a calm John Eisenhower witnessed and later described. His 3323rd SIAM battalion had arrived in the Mulde–Elbe sector near Leipzig, the scene of Napoleon's triumph a hundred and thirty-one years before in the Battle of the Nations. There his brief adventure along the front ended in early-spring weather as he watched the historic panorama of the German army passing over the Mulde in flight before the Bolshevik armies of Zhukov and Konev.

War passion was spent, but as my father later recalled, months would pass before he could viscerally regard any German as a fellow human being. With detachment, he watched whole units of German soldiers appearing over the ridges of the Mulde with white flags. As a recent West Point graduate, he was professionally pleased by their presentable equipment and overcoats, but offended by the palpable relief of the arriving enemy soldiers availing themselves of a civilized code that they had not practiced in Russia. He and his fellow soldiers roamed through these units collecting P-38 pistols, sabers and other booty of war. He described passing through a forest near the Mulde River and at one point encountering a German officer in uniform. John drew a pistol, then carefully concealed his surprise as the officer clicked his heels to attention, rendered a Nazi salute, and declared, "I surrender."

Disapproving the Nazi salute as unsoldierly, John solemnly replied in pig German-French, "Sie saluten comme ça, do you get it." The officer, admonished that he was a prisoner of war, bowed slightly. John did an about-face and strode toward his jeep with the officer silently in tow. On May 2, 300,000 Germans passed through the stationary front on the Elbe, while 500,000 reached British lines near Lübeck.

On the third, twenty-four hours after Dempsey's arrival at Lübeck, Dönitz dispatched Admiral Friedeburg as an emissary to Montgomery's headquarters at Lüneburg empowered to offer capitulation of the three German army groups in the vicinity. The Germans wanted to sound out Montgomery on his plans. A British pause would be necessary for the Germans to move additional units into the British zone, and Friedeburg needed to know when Dempsey would resume his advance toward Rokossovky.

At II A.M. the party of four, consisting of Friedeburg, his chief of staff and two aides, arrived. Re-enacting a ritual devised by Wellington, Montgomery received the delegation under the Union Jack outside his trailer.

Montgomery: "Who are these men?"

The interpreter replied.

Montgomery: "What do they want?"

Friedeburg read a letter from Field Marshal Keitel offering to surrender the three German armies withdrawing between Berlin and Rostock.

Montgomery: "These armies should surrender to the Russians."

Friedeburg replied that it was "unthinkable" to surrender to the Russians because they were "savages," and all German soldiers doing so "would be sent straight off to work in Russia."

Montgomery: "The Germans should have thought of some of these things before they began the war, particularly before attacking the Russians in July 1941."

In conference in Montgomery's tent headquarters, Friedeburg, knowing the British would seek the surrender of the fleet and the Norwegian garrison, offered as a delaying tactic to surrender north Germany and Holland. Friedeburg also offered the surrender of Army Group Vistula and "invited special attention to the problem of refugees and troops in retreat on the eastern boundaries of the area occupied by the British."

Montgomery refused the army group surrender, though he added that he would accept the surrender of individual soldiers. Without prompt capitulation of the German fleet and Scandinavia, he would have no choice under his current directives but to resume the advance and close the front. In the course of the talks, Montgomery agreed to accept tactical surrenders by corps units and to care for civilians who reached Allied lines.

Over 21st Army Group communications, Friedeburg wired Flensburg to assure Dönitz that Montgomery was "no monster on the refugee problem" and had relented on individual surrenders. However, Montgomery's terms required Dönitz to cede the Navy, still evacuating Courland and East Prussia. After four inconclusive hours of talks, Friedeburg's party returned to Flensburg.

The end was near. The news failed to inspire joy at Versailles, where Eisenhower spent the night of the third. Negotiations lay ahead, and the somber accounts of the next seventy-two hours testify that looming postwar political and military problems overshadowed the ritual of capitulation.

Butcher noted the air of formality in the halls of the Trianon and the taut atmosphere in the staff offices. The mood was suspended between anticipation of the end, eagerness to announce the news to the world, and wariness about the local negotiations with the Germans and tensions with Russia. Eisenhower seemed subdued, perhaps sensing the controversies his recent decisions would generate and his heavy responsibility for defending them in the future.

Eisenhower's mind wandered to politics. He reflected on the troubles ahead and spoke of postwar challenges, particularly the great question mark of the Soviet Union. Butcher predicted that defense preparedness would be a major issue in Congress. Eisenhower agreed, and intimated that he occasionally thought of resigning his commission to "speak his mind freely" against the "same withering process as before" in military appropriations. What influence he had he would also use to oppose a repeat of the collapse of international cooperation that had occurred at the end of the Great War. Eisenhower would support universal military service, the cause of Anglo-American cooperation and a "decent modus vivendi" with the Russians.

Talk drifted to home. Butcher said that he was "not very sure the war had been understood" in America. He told Eisenhower of stories circulating at PRD that Truman planned to sponsor congressional visits to Germany and Japan to gain firsthand impressions of postwar problems and "to give our Congressmen and Senators a chance to look at the United States from distant shores and perhaps gain a better perspective of our country of destiny." Eisenhower approved.

The war saga ended in the red schoolhouse housing SHAEF forward headquarters in Reims. Eisenhower arrived there on the fourth to remain until the formal German capitulation he expected within twenty-four hours. Significantly, Moscow had ignored Soviet exclusion from the Montgomery-Friedeburg talks—confirmation that the Russians, on the verge of expanding the Czech offensive, would not oppose an armistice. How long should Eisenhower permit Flensburg to stall? Would the German military continue to balk, hoping for the opportunity to surrender to the West? The British had agreed to accept local surrenders, but could corps-level surrenders be kept "local" if the process was dragged out? Another problem was the lack of political guidance on the precise working of the instrument of capitulation. The EAC still had not worked out an agreed text, and talks had been complicated by admission of the French. Differences remained over technicalities such as the status of the surrendering government, and even whether the French would participate in the surrender. Several EAC working drafts of a surrender document had been sent to Reims, but there was no "agreed text."

According to an account written by John Keegan in 1966, on the morning of the fourth Bull summoned Lieutenant Colonel John Counsel, head of Post Hostilities section, to his office. "I understand you are the only officer here cognizant of the various documents pertaining to the surrender of Germany," Bull began.

"I am, sir," Counsel replied, but cautioned Bull that none of the documents was official and that basic differences over occupation policy and the like were as yet unresolved.

"That being the case," Bull said, "I would be grateful to know how I am to advise the Supreme Commander in the event Germany offers to surrender this afternoon."

"I would tell him to accept, sir," Counsel replied.

Eisenhower, that afternoon, told Bull he was "not interested in insurance forms and fine points when our object is to stop the fighting and killing." He placed Bull in charge of drafting a simple in-house document, kept brief and to the point, establishing a quick surrender on all fronts and four-power control over Flensburg. The existing policy was that relations between victor and vanquished would depend on national actions in the respective four occupation sectors. The four powers had agreed that any German central government would be powerless.

Because a number of minor unresolved points were not likely to be worked out, that afternoon the EAC drafts were officially "lost" and overlooked," a story repeated by Smith in his memoir perhaps to protect his chief against charges of by-passing civilian control. Counsel drew up a simple list of articles based on the text of the truce signed by Vietinghoff at Caserta, published in the May 2 issue of *Stars and Stripes.*

Anticipating British criticism, Smith took the precaution of informing John Winant, the American ambassador in London, of the text, who then informed Churchill. Winant phoned back with news that Churchill was "deeply disturbed" that SHAEF was proceeding with its own surrender document, and, in a delaying tactic, objected to the use of any document that the Russians did not already know about. Eisenhower expected Moscow to question an alien document and a ceremony conducted under SHAEF auspices, but doubted the Russians would oppose an accord that froze Allied movement and suspended action on all fronts. Late that afternoon, Eisenhower phoned back to tell Winant he believed the EAC instrument was "too long" and that he "preferred a shorter version." British objections dissolved, although Churchill eventually would suggest minor amendments, including a clause specifying that the surrender would be "superseded by any general instrument imposed by or on behalf of the United Nations and applicable to Germany and the German forces as a whole."

The British ceremony occurred that afternoon at 5 P.M. Friedeburg's delegation returned to Lüneburg to meet with Montgomery and offer the surrender of all German forces in Holland, Friesland (including Heligoland), Schleswig-Holstein and Denmark. Notably, he omitted Norway and the fleet. Montgomery construed the offer as a "local surrender" of forces facing the 21st Army Group, and convened a brief ceremony in a nearby pitched tent marking the end of the 21st Army Group campaign in Europe. The news reached Reims at 7 P.M. along with word that the German delegation was proceeding to Eisenhower's headquarters miles away to discuss a general capitulation.

Butcher, who was to supervise the taping of Eisenhower's victory broadcast and handle press relations for the ceremony, dined with Eisenhower that night. Eisenhower was tired and anxious, depressed that Friedeburg would undoubtedly stall and try to set conditions. To Butcher he vowed there would be no bargaining, and that he would not receive the delegation until terms were accepted on both fronts.

That night, fanatical German resistance blocked the Russian advance in central Czechoslovakia. As Schörner's forces began to fall back on Prague, uprisings broke out in the city. Patton, twenty-four hours away, agitated for permission to proceed, confronting Eisenhower with a situation similar to Simpson's proposed dash for Berlin two weeks before. Patton's V Corps faced a forty-mile open corridor to the Czech capital, and decisive action might enable American forces to intervene alongside the Czech resistance in order to block Schörner's communications. Amid silence from Moscow, Eisenhower weighed the appeals carefully and at one point gave Bradley permission to advance, which he quickly rescinded except for reconnaissance elements, which embarked that night and entered the western suburbs of Prague by dawn.

Meanwhile, Eisenhower cabled Deane twice, dealing separately with Prague and Dönitz. On Prague, he revealed that the Third Army now intended a thrust into Czechoslovakia along the line Budweis–Pilsen–Karlsbad, and "if the situation so dictates," proposed to clear the west bank of the Vltava and Elbe, thereby enveloping Prague. Eisenhower also asked Deane urgently to inform the Soviets that representatives from Dönitz were expected on the fifth and "that all remaining enemy forces desire to surrender." Eisenhower would confine the talks to his front only, or deal with both fronts simultaneously in the presence of a Russian representative "fully empowered to act" on his own as the Soviets wished. In practical terms, the message posed the difficulties Moscow could expect to arise if the Soviets were unable to agree to an armistice negotiated under Eisenhower's auspices. Confident that Moscow would approve, Eisenhower taped a brief statement for European newspapers and radio, a statement one step short of proclaiming the war over and declaring further resistance criminal. He recited the burgeoning list of German surrenders received that day and indicated "that further losses the Germans incur on this front" would be "due to their failure instantly to quit." Hesitation was "due either to their own stupidity or that of the German government." On land, sea and air, the Germans were "thoroughly whipped," and the only recourse was "surrender." The next day, Eisenhower, girding for cease-fire talks, declined to receive emissaries from Kesselring on grounds that he would not discuss the surrender on the western front unless the Germans sent representatives to his headquarters empowered to discuss the German Army Group Center, Army Groups E and G, and all outlying garrisons. But Soviet silence persisted.

Finally, to end the suspense on Prague, Eisenhower deputized Bradley to undertake the sensitive mission of sounding out his Soviet counterpart. On the fifth, at celebrations of the American-Russian linkup at Torgau, Bradley met with Konev with instructions to learn whether his forces intended to move into western Czechoslovakia. Years later, Bradley would describe his visit to the village adorned with bunting, red banners and huge posters of Roosevelt, Churchill and Stalin. After the ceremonies, he and Konev and their advisers met in a small villa well stocked with maps to formalize the linkup. Typically, the Soviets spoke and moved with an air of triumph, which Bradley responded to with courtesy and deference. Bradley presented Konev with a map with diagrams of the 12th

Army Group advance straight south into Austria. A line was drawn conspicuously along the Elbe–Mulde, thence through Pilsen–Karlsbad–Budejovice. Bradley asked Konev whether American forces could be of help in Czechoslovakia. Konev studied the map and asked, "How far do you intend do go?"

Bradley replied, "Pilsen," explaining that at Pilsen he would have to pause a while in order to protect Patton's flank on the Danube. With a trace of a smile Konev responded, "I hope you go no further."

Later that day Antonov responded. First, the Soviets endorsed the already completed Allied movement to Lübeck; second, they encouraged Eisenhower to accept the surrender of Norway; third, they declined Eisenhower's offer to clear the west bank of the Vltava in the vicinity of Prague, noting that the Soviets had the necessary forces in the area and had stopped at Wismar in deference to Eisenhower's wishes; fourth, the Soviet command did not object to dealings with Dönitz's emissaries, provided Dönitz accepted "simultaneous surrender to the Soviet forces of those German troops which faced them." Otherwise, Moscow suggested that talks be broken off. In view of the "shortness of time," Antonov authorized Susloparoff to take part.

Widespread revolt shook Prague that day. Throngs of partisans erected barricades throughout the city, seized the radio station, the train station, the power stations and other public buildings, and dispatched appeals for Allied aid by a wireless monitored at Patton's headquarters at Pilsen, where Eisenhower's fresh orders to stand fast were received with consternation and disbelief. By nightfall the revolt had enveloped the city and cut the westward retreat of Schörner's army group. Eisenhower repeated the order to Patton to remain at Pilsen and, ignoring Churchill's urgings on Prague by phone that night and responding to Antonov's rejection of Allied intervention, informed Deane and Archer that he had acted on the assumption that Soviet forces would "advance rapidly to clear up the situation in the center of the country."

"The halt line is mandatory," Patton fumed in his diary. "Eisenhower does not wish at this time to have any international complications. It seems to me that as great a nation as America should let the other people worry about the complications. Bradley also directed us to continue our advance east along the Danube . . . and let them [the Russians] make contact with us. . . . I doubt the wisdom of this. . . . "

At SHAEF forward, Butcher spent the afternoon converting the ground-floor G-3 offices into a message central for news dispatches and rigging the adjoining situation room with cameras and microphones for ceremonies expected that night. Reporters and staff permitted into the room found it strewn with radio and film equipment. Battle maps displayed the German pockets in Prague, Linz, Dresden and Breslau, and garrisons in Norway,

France, Czechoslovakia, Austria, Latvia and Yugoslavia, between the plots of Allied and Russian lines at noon, May 5, 1945.

With an escort of military police, the Friedeburg group arrived shortly after dusk at 7 P.M. Flanked by three aides, Friedeburg marched stiffly past the throng of staff and press and directly into conference in a second-floor office with Smith, Spaatz, Morgan, Bull, Air Marshal Robb and General Strong.

Strong later described Friedeburg as physically and morally spent, unable to do anything except present Flensburg's proposals for a "phased surrender" in the west, including seventy-two hours to permit the Germans complete freedom of movement. Friedeburg had no authority to discuss the eastern front.

On Eisenhower's behalf, Smith replied that SHAEF could not consider a phased surrender. The Germans had no alternative but unconditional surrender in place, meaning OKW must agree to implement Allied and Russian orders. Smith could offer no commitments about accepting troop surrenders or maintaining the flow of refugees. With formal surrender on all fronts, Germans would be treated "with the normal dictates of humanity." On the other hand, without prompt agreement, OKW might never be permitted to surrender. The Allies would implement an armistice, close the front to refugees and hold OKW responsible under the laws of war for needlessly prolonging hostilities.

The German delegation was crestfallen by the refusal to permit delay and the threat to close the front. Millions had as yet not escaped to safety; surrender to the Russians was "unthinkable." Smith conferred with Eisenhower several times. The Supreme Commander was unrelenting, and at the close Friedeburg informed Flensburg through SHAEF communications that Eisenhower was insisting Germany sign "at once." He requested authority to surrender, or, alternatively, for Flensburg to dispatch an officer empowered to discuss terms. Afterward, Smith walked into the War Room below to tell the assembled officials and technicians that "nothing was doing" that night, then Smith and Strong visited Eisenhower in his office one floor above. No one believed that the defeated Germans took the possibility of an Allied schism seriously, and so the request for separate terms appeared to be simply a matter of German officers asking for several more days to evacuate wives and children from Czechoslovakia, where they had been sent to escape the bombing of Germany.

An hour later, news arrived from Flensburg that General Alfred Jodl would join Friedeburg with full power to discuss the eastern front. Strong reminded Eisenhower of the importance of having prominent German military figures like Jodl sign the armistice. Relatively junior officials had signed the armistice document in 1918 before the whole process had been delegated to politicans, hence the myth that the German army had been betrayed by civilian politicians at the eleventh hour.

Eisenhower, fatigued and depressed, briefly lingered in his office. List-lessly he discussed with Butcher the staging of the ceremony. It was to be done in a way to impress the Germans with the fact of defeat lest the children of the world "be left an inheritance of World War III." Butcher reminded Eisenhower that as yet no arrangement had been made to include a French representative. Eisenhower assured him he would alert Smith, then left his offices for the night.

By the sixth, news reached Reims that Konev's 1st Ukrainian Front was attacking south through the Sudetens to envelop Prague from the west. Four Russian fronts now converged on Prague in a battle ranging along a 375-mile sector between Dresden and the Danube.

That morning Eisenhower arrived at the office late. Peering into the War Room on his way to his office, he observed the cameras and klieg lights, then mumbled his displeasure about the "Hollywood setting," a chance remark that set off a commotion for hours. Smith summoned Butcher to tell him the proceeding was "not going to be a Hollywood show," and that whoever was responsible for the staging "must get it out immediately." Butcher informed Smith that the staging had been arranged "through channels" with Bull. Smith did not care and ordered all cameras and sound equipment removed.

That afternoon Smith supervised the cleanup in the War Room. While Dönitz's emissaries bided their time in an adjoining villa, listening to the radio and playing cards, Eisenhower waited alone in his office for Moscow's reply to the draft terms sent through Deane that morning. Approval was in limbo, reportedly because the members of the Soviet General Staff had left Moscow and, according to Deane, "were said to be about in the country as a result of the Russian Easter weekend." Evidently, Moscow intended to acquiesce, but to reserve the right to find fault with any ceremony not arranged by the Soviets. Eisenhower expected the Russians to insist on a second ceremony arranged by themselves, perhaps in Berlin, which he hoped to attend.

Butcher, surmising that Smith's ulcers were bothering him, appealed to Eisenhower at lunch to reconsider Smith's order to remove the cameras. He found Eisenhower "pretty well whipped down from the tension of waiting," but sympathetic. Eisenhower explained that Smith did not want undue publicity "and that was the answer," though, personally, he favored press, radio and movie coverage for the public. "After all," he said, "it is their war." Uppermost on Eisenhower's mind was concern that the Russians would flamboyantly try to upstage Reims. Finally, at 5 P.M., Smith "com-promised" and permitted a single microphone and camera. Butcher heaved a sigh of relief and told Smith what a "sweat he had been in" over the world-press-pool arrangements.

"Your sweat," Smith snapped. "What do you think the rest of us are doing?"

Meanwhile, tensions accompanied the military steps toward cease-fire. Even as the Russian attacks opened, time remained for Patton to reach Prague, and in the next seventy-two hours Churchill committed his full weight to such a move, a maneuver that also bolstered Churchill's request to work out Austrian zones, "compliance" with Yalta and a proposed three-power summit conference to take up German problems. By now, responding to repeated press inquiries, Molotov in San Francisco "confirmed" that sixteen Polish leaders abducted in March were being held in Poland for trial on unspecified charges, which Stalin amplified on the fifth in a cable to Churchill, all but repudiating the principle of three-power supervision over Polish elections, and staking out his undeviating position in the negotiations ahead that the Soviet Union had a right and duty to resolve the Polish problem as she saw fit. But the Soviets posed no objections to a cease-fire, and Jodl's arrival at Reims was the long-awaited confirmation that the Germans were ready to surrender.

With the Americans, British, French and Soviets ready, Eisenhower for a brief interval found himself acting on behalf of the entire coalition, and so a formal cease-fire could not be far off. In his hectic diary account of the fourth and fifth, Brooke had described the agonizing wait for news from Czechoslovakia, the news from Eisenhower's headquarters, and the exhilaration of Montgomery's ceremony at Lüneburg Heath. He described Churchill's tearful expressions of thanks to his chiefs at the conclusion of a BCOS meeting on the night of the fifth for all they had done and the "endless work" that had brought them "from El Alamein to where we are now."

Like the Russians, the British were away from their offices that momentous weekend. On Sunday the sixth Brooke described a serene day spent in the countryside contemplating the work ahead: Czechoslovakia; clashes between Alexander and Tito over Trieste; Norway; the three-power meetings, Pacific strategy; and, finally, the military government of Germany, much of which he would probably bequeath to his successor—probably Montgomery. Occasionally his mind wandered back three years to the morning at Chequers when Churchill appointed him Chief of the Imperial Staff. Overcome after leaving Chequers, he had knelt in prayer to the "all-powerful God looking after the destiny of the world," whose existence now seemed confirmed again by the evidence of hope amid the suffering and agony, which he believed would educate mankind in the "fundamental law of charity and love." Only when that lesson was learned, would war cease to exist, the task of many centuries to come. And with those reflections, Brooke wrote, "I must leave behind me the German war."

At Chequers, Churchill, the historian, thought back in time to Appomattox and Grant's decision to permit Lee's soldiers to return home with swords and horses. "In the squalor of war," Churchill would later say, "what a magnificent act!" Churchill, the sentimentalist, lamented the absence of chivalry and grace in the harsh ritual being staged at Reims that night.

In Washington, Marshall prepared a congratulatory telegram to be dispatched with the first news of a surrender. In a rare tribute the Chief of Staff expressed his complete satisfaction with Eisenhower's work. He praised Eisenhower for having made "great history for the good of mankind," for completing his mission with "the greatest victory in the history of warfare," and for successfully disposing "of every conceivable difficulty incident to varied national interests and international political problems of unprecedented complications." Eisenhower had triumphed over "inconceivable logistical problems and military obstacles," and "through all of this, since the day of your arrival in England three years ago, you have been selfless in your actions, always sound and tolerant in your judgments and altogether admirable in the courage and wisdom of your military decisions."

Alone in his office, Eisenhower attempted to compose a letter to General Marshall, the man he still thought of as his mentor and guide and privately looked to as leader of the country. Marshall had always been an inhibiting figure, a man Eisenhower dealt with most comfortably as a subordinate, knowing where he stood and what the occasion demanded—something missing in the past four months. After floundering with a draft, Eisenhower set it aside and wrote Mamie.

"These are trying times," he wrote. "The enemy's armed forces are disintegrating, but in the tangled skein of European politics nothing can be done, except with utmost care and caution, where the interests of more than one country are involved." He would be glad when everything was finished, though some of the "worst headaches" would come after the shooting was over. He included a customary complaint about the quality of his bedside Westerns, which he could write better "left handed." As an aide arrived with a news summary, Eisenhower wrapped up. "Now I'll see what every office all over the world has to tell me," he closed, "in times such as these, everybody and his brother will have their say."

At moments past 5 P.M., an expressionless General Alfred Jodl and his adjutant, escorted by General de Guingand, arrived and proceeded into conference with Friedeburg in a small office. The group requested coffee and a map of Europe.

At 6:15, Strong led Jodl and Friedeburg to Smith's office for talks later described in detail by both Smith and Strong. While Friedeburg lapsed into incoherence, Jodl carried on impressively, pleading for time and an under-

standing from the Western powers not to cut the flow of refugees, numbering in the millions, especially in Czechoslovakia, where the uprisings in
Prague had cut Army Group Schörner's line of retreat and in Mecklenburg,
which was sure to be pillaged by the Red Army. At first, Jodl denied he
had authority to conclude an armistice, insisting that the Germans would
surrender to the Allies but never surrender to the Russians.

Smith had arranged his office to impress Jodl with the futility of negotiating Allied help. The walls were decorated with maps showing American,
British, French and Russian positions in red crayon, and lines of fictitious
attacks to compress German pockets and close the front.

At 7:20 Smith and Strong reported to Eisenhower in his office. Jodl's
request for delay had a tenuous basis: Allied radio intercepts confirmed
Flensburg's lack of control over German troop movements, particularly
near Prague. A cease-fire might be put off on grounds that it could not be
immediately implemented. Eisenhower instructed Smith and Strong to
grant Jodl twenty-four hours, meaning effectively several days for refugees
and army stragglers to cross Allied lines. But unless Dönitz promptly
empowered Jodl to sign, Eisenhower would order his troops to fire on all
units attempting to cross Allied lines from 0001 May 9 forward.

When Smith met with Jodl again, he backed the Allied pledge of humanitarian treatment with an appeal to the professional honor of the German
army, which, he argued, would be enhanced by assuming the initiative to
end the violence. Smith's appeal was also a reminder of the Geneva protec-
tions available—the turning point, in Strong's opinion, that induced Jodl to
wire Flensburg for authority.

Jodl informed Dönitz that Eisenhower was insistent. Unless Germany
signed, Allied lines would be closed even to persons attempting to surrender
individually and negotiations broken off. Seeing "no alternative other than
chaos or signature," Jodl requested "immediate radio confirmation whether
authorization for signing can be put into effect. Hostilities will then cease
on 9 May 0001 hours our time." Shortly after midnight, Dönitz empowered
Jodl to "sign in accordance with conditions as given."

By 2:15, the seventeen accredited correspondents and photographers in
Reims had turned on their lighting and sound equipment. Fifteen minutes
later, the Allied delegation led by General Smith took seats around a
doughnut-shaped conference table. Susloparoff and an aide represented the
Soviet Union. General Sir Frederick Morgan, Admiral Burrough, Air Marshals Robb and Tedder represented Great Britain. General François Sevez
represented France, and General Spaatz represented the United States.

At 2:35, Strong escorted Jodl and two aides through the entrance and
down the corridor into the blinding klieg lights. Jodl bowed stiffly before
taking his seat.

Strong set before Jodl the act of surrender, which proclaimed the cessation of hostilities at 2301 hours, May 8, 1945, and obligated the Wehrmacht to obey and transmit all orders issued by the Supreme Commander and by the Soviet high command. The German army was to remain in place and would be forbidden to scuttle or destroy equipment. A second document required the German high command to appear as ordered by the Allies and the Russians to execute a formal ratification of the proceedings that night. Strong remained on his feet, translating the brief exchanges as Jodl signed three copies of the Act of Military Surrender at 2:41.

Jodl stood and attempted to lend dignity to the German position with a brief statement. "With this signature," he said, "the German people and German armed forces are for better or worse delivered into the victors' hands. In this war which has lasted for more than five years they have achieved and suffered much more than any other people in the world. In this hour, I can only express the hope that the victors will treat them with generosity."

There was no reply. Only the whirring of cameras and sound equipment broke the silence. Observers present discerned neither compassion nor glee, only relief as Jodl sank back in his seat—having acknowledged that "the most terrible war in human history had finally come to an end." For as CBS correspondent Charles Collingwood put it, "the mad dog of Europe was put out of the way, the strange monstrosity that was Nazi Germany had been beaten into submission. To millions . . . the end of suffering . . . the best news the world ever had."

AFTERMATH

The ceremony concluded amid doubt about Flensburg's willingness and capacity to implement the cease-fire in the field. Throughout the night reports had been received from Czechoslovakia, where intense fighting continued. From Moscow there was only silence on the draft terms. Eisenhower and Churchill conferred eight times by phone that night on Prague and steps to maintain the clamp of censorship on Reims until it could be established that German forces were complying and Moscow endorsed the short terms drafted by SHAEF and signed by Jodl.

Afterward, Jodl asked for an opportunity to talk to Eisenhower. Accompanied by Smith and Strong, Jodl climbed the stairs to the second-floor office for a brief audience. Eisenhower, flanked by Air Marshal Tedder, stood behind his desk at attention in Army service dress uniform, without sword or pistol. He briefly warned Jodl that he and his colleagues in Flensburg would be held "officially and personally responsible for any violations of the surrender, including the provisions requiring the German commander to appear at subsequent ceremonies to accomplish formal ratification in the presence of the Soviets." Then he dismissed him.

Even after official notification to Washington and London, work went on during the night at Reims. At 4 A.M. AP reporter and bureau chief Edward Kennedy, defying the injunction of secrecy, wired his Paris station with the news that Germany had surrendered unconditionally. The press leak, igniting the greatest celebrations in history, coincided with a message from Deane forwarding Antonov's amendments to the draft, including a provision specifying nonrecognition of the Dönitz government. Deane conveyed Antonov's angry complaints that the war was not over, citing intercepts of radio Flensburg "calling upon the German troops to continue the war against Soviet forces on the one hand, and not to resist the Allied forces in the west on the other."

To allay questions, Eisenhower offered to attend the Berlin ceremony and, through Deane, reminded Antonov of his long record of cooperation even over CCS objections. At Churchill's insistence, Eisenhower, early the next morning, dropped plans to go to Berlin, thus relegating the proceeding to one staged mainly for the Russian press and people. Moscow's displeasure over Reims would have a grim sidelight. Late on the seventh Susloparoff left Reims for Moscow and a harsh reprimand for allegedly participating in the surrender ceremony without permission. According to Smith, all future inquiries about Susloparoff's fate would be met with embarrassed silence.

For the next thirty-six hours, Eisenhower remained at work on a cease-fire in central Czechoslovakia. Even as Spaatz and Tedder left Reims for the Soviet-sponsored ceremonies in Berlin, Army Group Schörner maneuvered desperately toward contact with the Allies. Schörner refused to acknowledge Flensburg messages, beamed warnings of "enemy propaganda" spreading false rumors of a German surrender, and vowed "that the war against the Soviet Union will continue."

As the American, French and British delegates arrived in Berlin, three Russian fronts pressed attacks in western Czechoslovakia, reinforced by Konev's army group, which, as it moved south through Dresden, overran Most and Teplice, thereby cutting off the last of Schörner's petrol reserve. On the afternoon of the eighth the fall of Dresden cut the escape routes between Prague and south Germany. Czech partisans meanwhile beamed radio appeals for Allied intervention, but to no avail.

In a cable to Marshall that afternoon, Eisenhower dispassionately noted the "very skillful" propaganda woven by people "terrified collectively and individually of Russian vengeance who desire to surrender to us instead of the Russians." He would not be deterred from closing the front that night and, if the Germans fought on, repudiating individual surrenders. He assured Marshall that despite the acrimony between his headquarters and the Russians, both sides acted "in complete understanding," and predicted that the Berlin ceremony would be "markedly cordial." Afterward, Eisenhower cabled Flensburg and warned that troops attempting to escape through Russian lines after midnight would be captured and returned to the Red Army as "violators of the military act of capitulation."

That afternoon, in Berlin, snags over a long-form surrender document were quickly resolved by the four-power delegates at the Wehrmacht Polytechnical School in Berlin. But the ceremony was a sidelight to the first Western glimpse of the city of Berlin in four years. The devastation evoked expressions of wonder, even sympathy. Harold King of AP filed dispatches likening Berlin to Carthage. "If Stalingrad, London, Guernica, Rotterdam and Coventry wanted avenging, they have had it, and make no mistake about it," he wrote. The center city was rubble. Destroyed were the prewar landmarks—the Kaiser's palace, the French, British, American and Japanese embassies, the Propaganda Ministry, the Opera House, and the Reichstag. Machine-gun fire could still be heard at points in the city as Soviet platoons combed out pockets of resistance. Except for Russian tanks and female Red Army MPs, business and residential districts were mostly deserted. The few Berliners seen that day were gaunt and dazed, devoid of spirit. No one knew what had become of Adolf Hitler, and as a reporter for *Stars and Stripes* wrote, no one seemed to care.

Field Marshal Keitel, carrying a silver marshal's baton adorned with swastikas, and wearing a gray-green Wehrmacht uniform bedecked with the Iron Cross and the gold emblem of the Nazi party, obliged the world press with a token display of Prussian arrogance. Like Jodl, Keitel was destined to hang as a war criminal, stripped of all military honors. At 2300 that night, three hours before Moscow's announcement of V-E Day, SHAEF ordered V Corps at Pilsen to fire on German soldiers attempting to cross through Russian lines.

For another twenty-four hours, isolated German pockets fought on. The remnants of Army Group North on the eastern front held out in East Prussia at the Frische Nehrung–Vistula line, as did garrisons at Breslau and the Army Group Schörner. Flensburg complained in a military communiqué that commanders of all three garrisons had failed to maintain contact with Flensburg—an alibi for continuing German resistance—and warned that a Czech rising was "taking place in the whole of Bohemia and Moravia and may threaten the execution of capitulation as well as communications in the area." On the ninth, accusing Flensburg of failing to implement the Reims cease-fire on time, Eisenhower ordered Dönitz, Keitel and Jodl arrested "forthwith," an action held up for several days by a flurry of British objections.

Late that day the Russian Fourth Guards Tank Army penetrated the southern suburbs of Prague as the Third Guards Tank Army seized the Elbe crossings east of the city. The 1st Ukrainian Front linked with Patton near Chemnitz and the 2nd Ukrainian reached Budejovice, occupying the remainder of Czechoslovakia northeast of Prague. Choosing forced labor and internment over death, 858,000 German soldiers, including 60 generals, surrendered to the Russians. Ragtag elements of the Army Group Center set out on foot for Austria. Allied units would round up an estimated 180,000 troops that they would hand over to the Russians, including the pitiful remnants of the Vlasov Army,* Russians captured by the Germans in earlier campaigns, who had volunteered to fight on the side of the Germans only to wind up fighting Germans and Russians on the side of Czech partisans in the final act at Prague.

By dawn, the eleventh of May 1945, all battlefronts were quiet.

THE FREEDOM OF LONDON

In the next four weeks Eisenhower retained control over American and British forces in Germany pending dissolution of SHAEF, which he persistently but unsuccessfully opposed. Meanwhile Eisenhower became military governor and the American representative on the four-power Allied Control Council, the activation of which was held up by the Soviets on numerous technical grounds until the American and British armies relinquished positions along the 100-mile strip of the Russian zone.

New tensions set in. As early as May 8, Truman ordered Lend-Lease shipments canceled, an action that affected the British and Russians but in actuality was one of the first of several get-tough gestures toward the Russians. In San Francisco, the UN Conference broke up momentarily over the Polish seating issue and Molotov's confirmation that the sixteen Polish underground leaders had been arrested. In late May, in a written response to press inquiries, Stalin would acknowledge the arrests of the Polish leaders for conducting "diversionary tactics in the rear of the Red Army." He denied reports that the arrested Poles had originally been invited by the Russians to carry on negotiations with the Soviet government, since "with violators of the law for safeguarding the rear of the Red Army, the Soviet authorities do not and will not conduct negotiations." Reconstruction of the Polish provisional government could be carried out only in accordance with

---

* The so-called Vlasov Army, formed and equipped by the Germans in late 1944, was a two-division army composed originally of Russian military prisoners in Germany who volunteered to fight alongside the German army on the eastern front. Since they felt the Vlasov Army could be relied on to fight to the death, the Germans permitted this unit to operate with considerable independence in the closing months of the war. Along the way, the Vlasov Army drew into its ranks an assortment of "Eastern workers" and refugees, Russians who, like Vlasov, considered themselves to be patriots fighting a war to liberate Russia from Bolshevism, Stalinism and collectivization. And though the Vlasov Army did not fight many battles, Vlasov's propaganda and organizing campaigns were effective enough to prompt Stalin's remark that Vlasov was "at the very least, a large obstacle on the road to victory over the German fascists." In August 1946 the Soviets announced that Vlasov, captured by the Americans and turned over to the Russians fifteen months before, had been executed for treason. See John Erickson, *The Road to Berlin* (Boulder, Colo.: Westview Press, 1983), p. 93.

the Crimean decisions, "analogously with the cause that had taken place in Yugoslavia, where the National Committee of Liberation was recognized as the basic nucleus of the United Yugoslav government." Stalin bluntly warned against efforts to revive the "cordon sanitaire" against the Soviet Union and demanded a Polish "policy of friendship with the Soviet Union."

In late May dangerous tensions flared in Yugoslavia, where the partisan forces of Josip Broz ("Tito") wrangled with Alexander over the Italian-Yugoslav ports of Fiume and Trieste. On the fifteenth Marshall and Eisenhower corresponded about Tito's "aggressive and contemptuous conduct." Eisenhower indicated that he believed Tito was acting on his own and he doubted that Moscow was deliberately using Tito as a pretext for intervention by her own forces. But he did weigh "the possibility that if we should get more awkwardly placed even than at present all along this tremendous front, the Yugoslav attitude might grow successively more bold and aggressive, and Russia might come into the open with even more impossible demands elsewhere." Eisenhower eventually dispatched five armored divisions of Patton's Third Army into the Enns Valley to link with British V Corps and moved Ninth Air Force units to the area. But realizing the depressing portents of the Yugoslav crisis, he continued in messages to Marshall to stress "the importance of adhering strictly to our existing general and local agreements with the Russians."

"The aggressive attitude assumed by Tito would indicate that he feels certain of strong backing," he cabled Marshall on May 17. "However, I simply cannot believe, in view of tremendous efforts made by the Russians during the past four years, that she would welcome any major trial of strength further to the west than the line she now occupies."

Indeed, the tensions in Yugoslavia would be short-lived, and events would show that the Soviets, in May 1945, were too exhausted to sustain a quarrel for very long. Perhaps this came as something of a surprise to Eisenhower and other military leaders who, having underestimated the Soviets in 1942–43, had come to overestimate them, particularly in the eighteen months in which Allied military strategy had necessarily revolved around the timetable of the Red Army. Now, in May 1945, as skeptics years before had speculated, the Red Army had reached a limit. Typically, Bradley would describe his personal impressions of the forces he observed at his meeting with Konev. He had been surprised by the spectacle of the dingy ill-clad Russian infantry and the horse-drawn carts and artillery caissons that so contrasted with the gleaming T-34 Stalin tanks and advanced fighters. Along the tense Allied-Soviet front, Soviet commanders seemed very wary of venturing forward and risking clashes. Indeed, Bradley would relate a story Collins told at Torgau about an earlier encounter with a Soviet Corps commander. Collins' counterpart had asked matter-of-factly whether American forces were "digging in." Collins had replied, "Why, of course not, we're Allies, you know," whereupon the Soviet general thanked him appreciatively and turned to his aide to tell him to pass an order to his own troops to cease digging in.

Other postwar accounts would describe the Soviets in similar terms, as tired but extremely wary of a showdown with Allied forces, which would seem to belie Allied concerns about a confrontation in late April and early May. Indeed, John Erikson's 1983 account of Stalin's Berlin decision based on Soviet sources maintained that Stalin, hesitant about Berlin, had ordered Zhukov to take the city only when assured by Eisenhower on March 31 that the Allies had ruled it out.

Whatever their accuracy, such stories convey the mood of mutual suspicion and the implicit rivalry between the Allied and Soviet sides, and imply that a more aggressive Allied posture in the spring of 1945 might have succeeded. On the other hand, it is hard to fault military men for respecting the abilities of a potential enemy, a mandatory feature of military thinking, especially when, only weeks before, even an exhausted Red Army had overcome the heaviest resistance the Germans could muster in gigantic battles on the Oder and the Vltava. Such second-guessing also presupposes that Allied efforts to block Soviet gains should have superseded a quick cease-fire and the unconditional surrender of German forces, which had been fundamental Allied policy since January 1943. Moreover, these criticisms overlook the possible role of Eisenhower's refusal to challenge the Russians at Berlin and Prague in maintaining peace in Europe, which has held for four decades.

Indeed, the endless debate on what the Allies might have done differently to block the Russians in eastern Europe then and later tends to obscure a deeper question: what the Allies might have done differently to check the Germans earlier and thus prevent the misery that Germany inflicted on Europe—how differently history might have turned out had Europe and America in the 1930s met the early threat of fascism, which, unlike communism, would in fact engulf much of western Europe and paralyze the rest of it. By the outbreak of World War II communism had been confined to the Soviet Union with no prospect of its expansion elsewhere except by force, despite avowed Soviet promises to expand Bolshevism worldwide. And yet, strangely, fascism had come to power in Germany, Italy, Spain, Poland, Hungary and Rumania, and had contributed to the demoralization of France while dividing England and America on the practicality or wisdom of doing anything to halt its spread. One could only speculate, but the feeling was that had Europe met the threat of fascism resolutely and had the United States backed Europe early on, there might have been no Munich, no war to rid Europe of Hitler and to recover the self-respect of the democracies, and no Soviet occupation of Warsaw, Berlin and Prague. But by May 1945 such thoughts were idle speculation, and attention was shifting to the problem of reconstructing a devastated Europe.

. . .

NORWAY

Oslo

SWED

North
Sea

DENMARK

Copenhac

Hamburg

Stetti

GREAT
BRITAIN

NETH

Berlin

London

Amsterdam

GERMANY

Brussels

BELGIUM

Cologne

Elbe

Lux

Rhine

Prag

Paris

Seine

Munich

FRANCE

SWITZERLAND

AUSTRI

Trieste

Venice

ITALY

POSTWAR
EUROPE

Miles

0   100   200

0   200

Kms.

FINLAND

Helsinki

ckholm

Tallinn

ESTONIA

LATVIA

Riga

Baltic
Sea

LITHUANIA

Kaunas

Minsk

Vistula

Warsaw

POLAND

Oder

Lvov

ECHOSLOVAKIA

RUTHENIA

Vienna

Budapest

HUNGARY

RUMANIA

Danube

Belgrade

Bucharest

YUGOSLAVIA

BULGARIA

Moscow

N

Frontiers as of late 1945
Frontiers as of mid-1938

OCCUPATION OF GERMANY
AND AUSTRIA, 1945

American zone
British zone
French zone
Russian zone
International zone

Kiev

U. S. S. R.

BESSARABIA

Black
Sea

© 1986 A Karl/J Kemp

As American troops began departing for home or the Pacific, SHAEF shifted focus to the problems in Germany, a story foreshadowed in Holland. At mid-month, Eisenhower flew to London for discussions with Churchill, the War Cabinet and BCOS to review the somber economic situation in the liberated and occupied zones in Allied hands, which was further complicated by the vast problem of displaced persons.

An estimated 8 million foreigners were in Germany, having worked as semi-slave laborers in factories and farms. Roughly half of these were in the eastern region, for which the Soviets took responsibility. In the British and American zones there were at least 400 Dutch and 700,000 Belgians, 1.25 million Frenchmen, 350,000 Italians, 100,000 Yugoslavs, 110,000 Greeks, 700,000 Czechs, 600,000 Poles, and small numbers of Hungarians, Rumanians, Bulgarians, Danes, Balts and Norwegians, along with 1.5 million Russians. Immediately after V-E Day, many DPs closest to the borders attempted to return home on their own, though the Army program discouraged mass migration and favored temporary collection at assembly centers for registration, medical exams, checks for military records, and transfer to their home governments.

The situation in Germany was grim. Eisenhower presented the facts: Food stocks were low. There was need for 175,000 tons of wheat and flour monthly. People in the liberated areas were being sustained on an average of 2,000 calories per day, while German civilians had been cut to a sustenance diet of between 1,000 and 1,500 calories. German military prisoners were a special case. Under the Geneva Convention, POWs were entitled to the same rations given depot troops and civilians and could be legally cut from the allotted 2,000 calories to 1,500 calories. Since the troops were performing heavy labor, in Eisenhower's opinion a ration of 1,500 calories per day was inadequate. Lack of coordination between the German occupation sectors was also a problem. Shipments of food were needed from the Soviet-held areas, long the granary for the Ruhr and the Saar, but chances for interzonal transfer of food and equipment were slim, since a policy of unified administration for Germany was unlikely. At the time, even the Allied Control Commission could not convene pending negotiations to arrange the Allied withdrawal from portions of the Soviet EAC zone, a problem now linked to negotiations for an Austrian ACC. Simultaneously a secret U.S.-British canvass of the 400- by 100-mile Russian strip was under way—a search for weapons laboratories, testing sites and storage depots. OSS Chief Allen Dulles later disclosed postsurrender OSS activity that included the removal of German atomic scientists and facilities. Using German operating personnel, the OSS conducted test firings of V-2 rockets at Nordhausen. The Nordhausen test firings, in Dulles' opinion, saved America years of research and development, and accelerated the move into new advanced weaponry on both sides of the Cold War, an acceleration foreshadowed by the V-weapons and to be dramatized that summer by the atom bomb.

As May wore on, Eisenhower unsuccessfully urged leaving SHAEF intact for the joint administration of the American and British zones. He spoke of SHAEF as a "testing ground" for the troubled United Nations and postwar cooperation. Roosevelt had discouraged the idea eighteen months before, and Churchill did so now. With British elections imminent, Churchill needed to emphasize British gains symbolized by British policy being carried out in a British zone. In this atmosphere, SHAEF quickly lost standing.

The London meetings were a foretaste of the concerns that would dominate Eisenhower's future—the slow rebuilding of Germany, the onset of a new and sinister arms race, covert Soviet-Allied competition, and also the honors and responsibilities. On the seventeenth, Eisenhower and his son, John, joined by Omar Bradley, James Gault, Lady Gault, Kay Summersby, her mother (Miss Toni Porter), and Sir Louis and Lady Grieg, spent the evening at Ciros and the theater. Crowds gathered outside the restaurant, and as the party left, throngs engulfed the entrance, and Eisenhower had to be escorted by police to his automobile.

The next day Eisenhower lunched privately with Churchill at 10 Downing Street. For several hours the two men set aside business. As he had resolved to do seven months earlier, Churchill asked Eisenhower to return in June for a ceremony conferring upon him the Freedom of London. Eisenhower requested a "ceremonial program" honoring a small but representative section of SHAEF "symbolic of the British-American team."

Politics crept into Butcher's closing entries. "The European war is over," Butcher wrote, "but Ike's troubles certainly aren't." Many complaints reached Reims about facilities maintained for American prisoners of war who had been released and were awaiting shipment back to the United States. The complaints were serious enough to warrant an inspection trip by Eisenhower to Camp Lucky Strike near Le Havre, in company with several visiting U.S. senators, including Burton Wheeler of Montana, Albert W. Hawkes of New Jersey and Homer Capehart of Indiana, prewar isolationists who were outspoken advocates of "finishing the job" in Europe, which meant confronting the Russians.

At the sprawling Lucky Strike complex the group toured the mess halls and bunkhouses with a throng of camp administrators and troops. Eisenhower carefully inspected the accommodations, sampled the food, and rigorously quizzed the camp personnel. He overlooked nothing and, before leaving, paused to address the soldiers of Camp Lucky Strike in his familiar stump style. He reminded the men about the plans for shipping them home aboard spacious, comfortable commercial liners. He offered them a choice.

They could go home as planned, or double-bunk day and night to "get home double time." Amid the tumultuous roar of cheers and applause, one of the senators turned to Butcher: "I hope that fellow never decides to run against me in my state. . . . He's got what it takes. I can see now why the GIs worship him. He speaks their language. He isn't high hat like you expect from the brass. He knows their problems, and they know it."

By June an Eisenhower for President coalition was forming among veterans groups, Republican newspapers and Midwestern Republicans, led by Eisenhower's old friend Senator Arthur Capper of Kansas. Eisenhower was puzzled by it. Never having addressed an American political rally, he knew nothing of campaigning, and his political views were unknown. At ETO, Eisenhower's contact with the press had always been closely controlled and in the line of business. Eisenhower had serious misgivings about his personal qualifications and only dimly grasped the depth of sentiment forming for him as a political figure.

Meanwhile, General Lucius Clay rejoined Eisenhower's staff that month after a tour as Byrnes' stern, exacting assistant in the Office of War Mobilization. Clay went to work on military government, and because of the political sensitivity his job required, soon became an indispensable counselor. German occupation policy, spelled out in JCS 1067, retained features of the Morgenthau Plan: thorough denazification, war crimes trials, return of displaced persons, and rehabilitation of industry sufficient only for reparations and averting starvation. Eisenhower's other tasks included withdrawal from the Russian zone and arranging Allied access to Berlin, undertakings that would shape his political future.

JCS 1067 primarily governed the treatment of Nazis and reeducation of the population, and took no account of the utter vacuum existing in Germany. The success of unconditional surrender in eradicating the outward forms of Nazism was striking. The SD and SS vanished, statues commemorating Nazi party and military heroes were torn down by Germans, and some eighty thousand suspected war criminals and high-level Nazis who fell into Allied hands aroused little sympathy. German war power was gone. There were shortages of coal and fuel, and industry was at a standstill. Total output of hard coal was 1.9 million tons monthly, as compared with 188 million tons in 1938. Monthly production of brown coal ran at 1.2 million tons, as compared with 237 million tons over the same period in 1938. Reports arriving at Eisenhower's headquarters revealed that there was little skilled labor, low output and poor motivation among the workers.

In time, few opposed financial and economic measures to restore basic industries in Germany and to prevent Europe from "being chained to a corpse," as Churchill put it. By autumn Eisenhower and Clay would be quietly implementing what they called Dragfoot, a suspension of reparations to the Soviet zone, which occasioned ritual Soviet protests in the ACC.

The Potsdam accords in July would instruct Eisenhower to carry out a "survey" of assets and productive capacity available for reparations. Reparations were tied to the excess of production over survival needs and to Russian deliveries. Tacitly, all sides suspended economic exchanges to reinforce the principle of separate administration over Germany. The Soviets were engaged in stripping the eastern zone of factories and equipment, and having converted German railways to the Russian gauge, quickly drew, in the words of *Newsweek*, "an economic barrier across Europe."

Allied-Soviet tensions soon were the main item of conversation, which Eisenhower hoped could be moderated despite divergent policies. By late May he occasionally spoke of sweeping gestures, such as offering the Russians a seat on the CCS, for beneath the political haggling, the wartime example of military cooperation loomed large. Petty quarrels might force the two sides apart, but cooperation, if developed at lower levels, could weather the political storms and, as Eisenhower put it, have "a happy and definite effect upon the whole question of whether communism and democracy could find a way to get along together in the same world."

In Paris after V-E Day, Eisenhower expressed this view to visitors, including Hopkins who was called out of retirement by Truman in mid-May to visit Moscow for discussions of Allied withdrawals, the four-power control council, UN occupation policy, Poland, and the clashes between Tito and Alexander. At a luncheon meeting on May 26, Eisenhower asked Hopkins and Harriman to sound out Stalin on granting wide latitude to his Soviet ACC counterpart, Marshal Zhukov, and about a personal visit by him to Russia.

Several days later, Butcher and Eisenhower had an "old-fashioned bull session" about Russia over dinner. Eisenhower remarked that Allied-Soviet relations were "at the same stage of arms-length dealing that marked the early Anglo-American contacts in 1940." He recalled that Anglo-American understanding had evolved slowly, but that after a while the Americans and British had become "allies in spirit as well as on paper." He hoped that wider contacts with the Russians would accomplish the same. He noted that the Soviets were "blunt and forthright," and that "evasiveness invariably aroused [their] suspicion."

Though Eisenhower spoke of Russia from the point of view of a military commander, he must have known that whatever he said thereafter would be evaluated politically. Perhaps he was realistic enough to suspect that genuine peacetime Allied-Soviet cooperation would not be possible, but nonetheless he was stirred by the possibility, which he saw as an extension of a successful war policy, and, in any event, he opposed the all-too-quick demonization of the Russians. More and more, Eisenhower spoke of "the betterment of the lot in life of the common man," and predicted more than once that "singleness of purpose on this theme would mean that peace is assured."

Butcher had misgivings about the whole situation. "I'm not too keen about staying here," he wrote.

> General Ike and his entire command are in for a rough time. Correspondents filing stories from Europe are bound to find keen competition for space with the exciting accounts of action in the Pacific. Consequently, only critical stories of General Ike and his policies in handling displaced persons, repatriated prisoners, and the occupation of Germany will find space. In other words, the open season is here—each of the Allies will tend to revert to his nationalistic interest and all our operations constitute game to be shot at by correspondents and Congressional committees.
>
> I hope General Ike doesn't have to stay too long. Governing his part of Germany will be very difficult, and although his military reputation will stand high in history, his standing in the near future is likely to slump.

On June 1, Eisenhower moved his permanent headquarters from Versailles into the cavernous I. G. Farben complex at Frankfurt, a site chosen as the permanent center for military government in the American zone. Summersby later described Frankfurt as a scene of ruin and despair. The local population had resumed work, but the once proud Germans were cowed and defeated. It was a sobering if appropriate backdrop as Eisenhower worked on his Guildhall address, his first significant public speech and his valedictory as Supreme Allied Commander.

Early in June, Eisenhower confessed to Marshall that he was "terrified" of addressing a formal body, and so he planned to speak "in the manner that I have spoken with troops and staff during the past three years." To his discomfort, Eisenhower also learned that according to the ritual of the Guildhall ceremony, he was expected to speak from memory. In the evenings at his villa in Bad Homburg, perhaps the first speech of his career took shape. As a former speech writer himself, Eisenhower was a meticulous draftsman, and after dinner he would retire to work over his text on a yellow pad in bed propped against pillows. Each morning he returned the endless revisions and corrections to secretaries, who had the new text ready for him at the end of the working day.

Eisenhower's Guildhall address would be notable in many respects. His statement on the war contrasted sharply with Lincoln's immortal second inaugural eighty years before, in which he had viewed the suffering visited on both North and South as a penance to purge the evil of slavery, and espoused reconciliation "with malice towards none." Eisenhower's Guildhall address proclaimed victory in a righteous cause, which had pitted decency against evil.

In retrospect, the two speeches reveal the differences between Lincoln and Eisenhower, their wars and their times. Lincoln faced a Civil War fought on American soil. Eisenhower dealt with a war fought far from

American shores, against an ideological as well as a military threat, and waged by total means, which magnified the stakes and eroded nineteenth-century constraints in its conduct. Whereas Lincoln had been in full command of the moral and material resources mobilized for the limited aim of subduing the Confederacy, Eisenhower was well aware that the Allies had sustained only a part of the colossal effort in Europe, and thus had had to compromise in a way that would extend the crisis that had afflicted them before the war began. The gains were precarious, and still dependent on accommodation with the devastated Russians, and Eisenhower saw his speech as a necessary affirmation amid the mood of unease and disillusionment of 1945. Eisenhower, like his contemporaries in government, did not anticipate Russian military aggression, but the inevitable Allied-Soviet tensions, if prolonged, would further erode the constraints of decency and fairness narrowly vindicated by the war in Europe. In his remarks, Eisenhower decided to emphasize the spiritual bond between the two Allies that had enabled America and Britain in the "deepest sense to be truly united." By this, he appeared to warn Moscow not to underestimate Anglo-American solidarity, and to ask the Russians in effect whether they counted themselves in or out, as friend or enemy.

Likewise, anticipating the controversies ahead, Eisenhower appeared to be urging that politicians and historians not be misled by the record of Anglo-American differences, that it would be a tragic mistake to overlook the unity on fundamental questions presupposed by those differences. As Eisenhower knew well, the record of the Anglo-American debates was a long one. Only time could tell the significance of those debates because many of the questions raised in them were still not settled. But he would suggest that all be weighed in light of the fact that the Allies had weathered great difficulties and had succeeded in their overriding aim: that of pooling their resources in the cause of defeating Germany. This was attributable in part to the unprecedented threat of Nazi Germany and the risks inherent in the military operations they had undertaken for the sake of assuming a major role in the fighting. In retrospect, however, the military operations undertaken would not have been possible were it not that two countries could see problems the same way. Seemingly, the aspirations that divided the Americans and British were not so dissimilar or irreconcilable, which he ventured to say were not dissimilar from the reasoned aspirations of peoples everywhere.

A week before the ceremony, newspaperman Frank Page was among the guests at a small dinner party. In the course of the evening he reminded Eisenhower that the Guildhall was a very solemn ceremony and urged that he "prepare carefully for it." Anxious for Page's opinion, Eisenhower excused himself from the room to get a copy of the draft. Unable to find it, he recited it from memory, stunning his guests.

Eisenhower began by expressing the high distinction he felt at the honor, mingled with his profound personal sadness at the circumstances that had required his appointment in the first place, the humility he felt in receiving acclaim earned by the blood of his fellow men, and his satisfaction in representing the "great human forces that have labored arduously and successfully for a righteous cause."

As he continued, he reviewed the success of the Alliance in prevailing over doubt, the persuasive fortitude of the British, which had dispelled American doubt in the early days and had drawn both sides closer together as "true partners in war." He spoke of the common future based on a kinship in values that are "the real treasures men possess." Especially moving were the passages describing the kinship between London and the remote hamlet of Abilene, Kansas, different superficially in size and grandeur but linked in freedom of worship, equality before the law, and liberty to speak and act as one saw fit; and the passages noting how unlikely it was that the ancient city of London would confer its honor of citizenship on a man with Eisenhower's background.

Eisenhower's tone was factual, his phrases rapid and fluent, and delivered with a formality and remoteness through which he seemed to recede into history in the presence of his guests. Breaking a long silence, Page commented, "Your remarks are adequate. In fact, I urge you not to change them."

In the ruins of Berlin on June 5, Eisenhower, Montgomery, Lattre de Tassigny and Zhukov, the appointed representatives to the Allied Control Council, attended a preliminary meeting to initial a declaration proclaiming Germany's defeat and the activation of the council as the supreme governing authority over Germany. Eisenhower hoped the ACC would be the crucial test of chances for the East-West "modus vivendi," a joint venture which, if permitted maximum latitude, might cement cooperation at the military level and provide a clearinghouse for the inevitable political storms about to break.

This meeting provided an important test of Soviet and British views. Significantly, the Soviets did not carry the dispute over Allied withdrawals from the Soviet zone to the point of walking out, though Eisenhower became convinced that day that the Allies could not delay their withdrawal any longer.

Eisenhower's State Department instructions included proposals to activate the council and to promulgate a unified policy in Germany, but "not to link withdrawal" with Allied positions on the Balkans, Germany and Poland. At close inspection, a unified policy of sorts already existed. EAC documents signed on June 5 committed all four powers to denazification, reparations, dismantling of the German war machine, and the partition of the country into occupation zones—the essence of the war aims formulated in Moscow eighteen months before, most of which had already been accomplished by military action. On the other hand, Montgomery's Foreign Office instructions specified "that the de facto occupation" by British and American armies of large parts of the Russian zone was an "important bargaining counter for obtaining satisfaction from the Soviet government on a number of outstanding questions." Tensions on this point marred the occasion.

Zhukov, whose instructions were to drive a wedge between the American and British delegations, rudely refused to meet privately with Montgomery, and a long delay developed over documents that had been inspected and approved beforehand. Zhukov would not discuss preliminary ACC organization until Allied withdrawals were under way. The Russians could transact no business until Soviet authorities were "acquainted first hand with problems in the Soviet zone," still occupied by Allied troops. Zhukov impressed Eisenhower and Montgomery with Soviet firmness on withdrawals. The Allies would not gain access to their zones in the city of Berlin until they had begun withdrawals elsewhere.

Eisenhower carefully evaluated Zhukov and probed his authority. The Soviet marshal's confident, direct manner in the presence of Vishinsky was impressive. He seemed secure in his position and capable of an independent line. Eisenhower later would describe Zhukov as having "scant patience with political men," meaning Vishinsky, and decided early on that Zhukov was a man to be watched and cultivated.

The Berlin meeting was the source of Robert Murphy's later complaint that Eisenhower quickly succumbed to Zhukov's spell, that he became naïvely convinced "that professional soldiers of all countries had much in common" and that he and Zhukov would "understand one another," though Eisenhower clearly had not been so charitable toward German soldiers. Murphy's criticism may have stemmed from Eisenhower's effort to shed his own diplomatic advisers. Like Vishinsky, Murphy had tried to supervise the proceeding, and, in Eisenhower's view, diplomacy, at least in the short run, would be divisive while military contacts remained essential, as Tedder's presence in Moscow had suggested in January. In time, Eisenhower would find himself defending his "give" on the withdrawal issue and charges of infatuation with Zhukov. Zhukov too would answer for his defiance of Vishinsky and his friendship with Eisenhower.

As the conference broke up, Eisenhower and Montgomery lingered for a lavish Russian banquet. They were encouraged by Zhukov's desire to pay return calls on both men for the purpose of conferring the rare Russian Order of Victory. Despite Zhukov's official insult, Montgomery volunteered to accept his decoration at Eisenhower's headquarters in Frankfurt.

June 6, the first anniversary of D-Day, passed virtually without notice. At Frankfurt, Eisenhower conferred with Smith and Clay over his reports to the American Chiefs of Staff on the outcome of the talks, reports in which he urged that withdrawal was essential "before any further discussion of control machinery with Zhukov will serve any purpose." He also revealed that the Soviets were unwilling to talk about preliminary matters of four-power policy, a sign that Moscow viewed the ACC as a "negotiating agency only and in no sense an overall government for Germany." Evidently, the Soviets planned to impose partition by force, and to block economic exchanges between the zones. Accordingly, Eisenhower urged "treatment of the American and British zones as an economic unit, with full realization of the implications involved."

Two days later, Hopkins passed through Frankfurt on his return journey to Washington. The presidential emissary was returning to Washington empty-handed on the issue of the Polish prisoners. Hopkins summarized his talks: Stalin had been indifferent to the congressional outcry over Poland and had denied wanting to communize Poland, but did insist on a weak Germany and that Poland, the Soviet land bridge to Germany, be friendly and not "stab the Red Army in the back." In talks ranging over Berlin, a summit, and ACC for Austria and Allied withdrawals, Stalin had been flexible. The Soviets would grant access to Berlin simultaneously with the Allied withdrawal from the Soviet zone with the latter to precede the former for appearance' sake. The sense Hopkins conveyed was that Austrian ACC zones could not be linked with the German problem, since the three powers had already agreed on the exact German zones, whereas Austria was an "agreement in principle." Finally, Stalin would not attend a summit before the Allies had left the Soviet zone.

Hopkins disclosed that Stalin had spoken of Russian admiration for Eisenhower and of his regret at not being able to receive him earlier in December. Hopkins conveyed Stalin's personal invitation to visit the Soviet Union in time for the planned victory celebrations in late June, or later as convenient.

From Frankfurt that day, Hopkins cabled Truman with word of Eisenhower's impressions of the Berlin conference, which, along with his own of Stalin, convinced him "that present indeterminate status of date for withdrawal of Allied troops from area assigned to the Russians is certain to be misunderstood by Russia as well as at home." Hopkins predicted Moscow would arrange unrestricted access to Berlin to coincide with the Allied withdrawal from the Soviet EAC sector.

The Hopkins cable triggered action. On the eleventh, Truman informed Churchill that he was "unable to delay the withdrawal of American troops from the Soviet zone in order to use pressure in the settlement of other problems." Churchill promptly conformed to Truman's decision, which he trusted "in the long run would make for a lasting peace in Europe."

On the night of June 4, Eisenhower composed a letter to Marshall with a request to look into the matter of allowing wives to join husbands in Europe who faced indefinite assignment there. He hoped Mamie would be able to join him because

> . . . the strain of the past three years has been very considerable as far as my wife is concerned, and because of the fact that she has had trouble with her general nervous system for many years I would feel far more comfortable about her if she could be with me.

Montgomery, on June 8, wrote Eisenhower that "with everyone about to go their own way," he wished to say "what a privilege and an honor it has been to serve under you."

> I owe much to your wise guidance and kindly forbearance. I know my own faults very well and I do not suppose I am an easy subordinate; I like to go my own way.
> But you have kept me on the rails in difficult and stormy times, and have taught me much.
> For this I am grateful. And I thank you for all you have done for me.

In his reply, Eisenhower thanked Montgomery and assured him: "Your own high place among the military leaders of your country is firmly fixed, and it has never been easy for me to disagree with what I know to be your own convictions." In closing, he hoped that "in whatever years are left to both of us, possibly we can occasionally meet, not only to reminisce, but to exemplify the spirit of comradeship that I trust will exist between our two countries for all time."

Victory celebrations followed. Zhukov's return trip to Frankfurt on the tenth was a happy occasion—in retrospect, the zenith of Allied-Soviet cordiality. Eisenhower hosted a luncheon held in a large outdoor gallery in late-spring weather. Seventeen hundred Eighth Air Force fighters and bombers passed in review overhead, an impressive sight as well as a reminder of residual U.S. strength in Europe.

Zhukov presented Montgomery and Eisenhower with the Soviet Order of Victory, the first time the decoration had been awarded to foreigners. Eisenhower admired the five-pointed red star set with rubies and diamonds, whose cost was later estimated at over $100,000. At lunch, Zhukov, Montgomery and Eisenhower watched a troupe of black entertainers, a cabaret show and an ensemble of swing music. Zhukov exhibited delight, and there were many encore performances followed by speeches and toasts, all looking toward a sunny future in which the lessons of wartime cooperation could be applied in peace.

In his toast, Zhukov expressed Soviet gratitude for the Allied invasion, and praised the "brilliant successes" of General Eisenhower, which the Soviet staff had closely studied. He looked forward to work on the Berlin council, confident "that the same cooperation that was shown before will show itself in peace."

Eisenhower, in reply, spoke for his millions of compatriots who had fought so that "the people might live a little better next year and the next," and of the hopes of "the common man of all the United Nations to have the opportunities we fought to preserve for him." Eisenhower called the European conflict "a holy war," an array of the forces of evil against those of righteousness, a conflict that "had to have its leaders and . . . had to be won, no matter what the sacrifices, no matter what the suffering to populations, to materials, to our wealth—oil, steel, industry—no matter what the cost the war had to be won. In Europe it has been won and to no man does the United Nations owe a greater debt than to Marshall Zhukov."

On the eleventh Eisenhower left Frankfurt for London and home, accompanied by Summersby, Gault, Butcher and McKeogh. They stayed at the Dorchester that night, Eisenhower's first residence in London in the hectic months of autumn 1942. Before him was the Guildhall address, and a private audience at Buckingham Palace with King George and Queen Elizabeth. There, King George would confer on him the Order of Merit, the only British decoration bestowed by the Crown without Cabinet approval and, by custom, held by twelve living men. Eisenhower became the first and only American soldier to receive a decoration that so few Britishers had ever seen that the proper Sir Alan Brooke would later ask for "a look." In the weeks to come, there would be more honors: an address before a joint session of Congress, a triumphant ticker-tape parade before four million onlookers in New York, a homecoming and reunion with his family in Abilene; then back to Europe and a visit to Paris, followed by tours of Warsaw, Moscow, Prague, Brussels and Dublin.

The next morning, on the day of the Guildhall address, there were anxious moments. Eisenhower impulsively left the hotel to walk alone through Hyde Park and rehearse his remarks in solitude. Instantly recognized in the park, he had to be extricated by police from the excited crowd. At ten-forty-five Air Marshal Tedder arrived at the Dorchester in the ceremonial horse-drawn open landau that would bear both men to the boundary of the City of London.

The lord mayor, Sir Frank Alexander, in his colorful gold and scarlet robes and holding a 600-year-old mace, greeted the coach and accompanied Eisenhower into the cathedral-like chamber filled with the entire officialdom of England. Eisenhower's sword, forged by the maker of the Stalingrad victory sword, was not ready, and in its place the lord mayor presented him with the gold-encrusted sword carried by Wellington at Waterloo. "If I were not so sure I was among friends, I do not know if I could make this speech," Eisenhower remarked in thanks. A low ripple of laughter echoed through the chamber, followed by silence.

In the opinion of those who heard him that morning, his delivery was flawless. Eisenhower stood ramrod-straight, and spoke in clipped, emphatic tones. The words were noble: his gratitude for the honor; the poignancy he felt for so many lives that had been lost; his ties to Kansas and his adopted ties to London; his devotion to the freedom restored and proclaimed in Europe; and the inspiration derived by all American soldiers in Europe from their association with the heroic British as brothers-in-arms. Eisenhower expressed the hope that history would show that the coalition had proved the doubters wrong, and that the ideal of unity in war could extend into a peace marked by "the same good-will, the same forbearance, the same objective attitude that the British and the Americans so amply demonstrated in the nearly three years of bitter campaigning."

Outside, in the glorious sunshine of mid-June, crowds gathered to render a tumultuous tribute unseen in London since Woodrow Wilson's visit in 1919. From Temple Bar, through Fleet Street, up Ludgate Hill, past St. Paul's to Mansion House, cheering hundreds of thousands pressed on the coach, and thousands remained to gather in the square below the balcony of Mansion House during the luncheon hosted in Eisenhower's honor by Churchill.

Several hours before, Churchill had consented to the Allied withdrawal back into zonal boundaries, effective by the end of the month to occur shortly before the Allied entry into Berlin, marking the fulfillment of Eisenhower's mission assigned to him by the CCS on February 13, 1944, and the true end of the war. Shortly, the CCS would dissolve SHAEF, bringing that historic chapter in diplomatic and military history to a close.

Churchill raised his glass to Eisenhower and, above the cheers outside, said, "I am quite sure that the influence he will wield in the world will be one of always bringing our countries together in the much more difficult task of peace in the same way he has brought them together in the grim and awful cataclysm of war." The Prime Minister, weary but glowing, reminisced about the terribleness of Eisenhower's decision of June 5, 1944. Churchill recalled his own nervousness that night, bringing laughter. Normandy had been "the mightiest decision of the war," he said. Nothing had compared with it, and "not only did he take the risk and arrive at the fence, but he cleared it in magnificent style."

Churchill guided Eisenhower to the balcony doors, then led him out by the arm. To the massive crowds stretching as far as the eye could see, the Prime Minister introduced Eisenhower as a friend, a "man who knows the power of words and can move the human heart." There is an unforgettable film clip of Churchill speaking, then stepping back, and of Eisenhower, coming forward to wave, joyously struggling for a chance to speak above the tumultuous cheering: "Whether you know it or not, I've got just as much right to be down there yelling as you do! . . . I'm a citizen of London now too!"

And he had become a citizen of the world.

Eisenhower's Guildhall Address, June 12, 1945

The high sense of distinction I feel in receiving this great honor from the City of London is inescapably mingled with feelings of profound sadness. All of us must always regret that your great country and mine were ever faced with the tragic situation that compelled the appointment of an Allied Commander-in-Chief, the capacity in which I have just been so extravagantly commended.

Humility must always be the portion of any man who receives acclaim earned in blood of his followers and sacrifices of his friends.

Conceivably a commander may have been professionally superior. He may have given everything of his heart and mind to meet the spiritual and physical needs of his comrades. He may have written a chapter that will glow forever in the pages of military history.

Still, even such a man—if he existed—would sadly face the facts that his honors cannot hide in his memories the crosses marking the resting places of the dead. They cannot soothe the anguish of the widow or the orphan whose husband or father will not return.

The only attitude in which a commander may with satisfaction receive the tributes of his friends is in the humble acknowledgement that no matter how unworthy he may be, his position is the symbol of great human forces that have labored arduously and successfully for a righteous cause. Unless he feels this symbolism and this rightness in what he had tried to do, then he is disregardful of courage, fortitude, and devotion of the vast multitudes he has been honored to command. If all Allied men and women that have served with me in this war can only know that it is they whom this august body is really honoring today, then indeed I will be content.

This feeling of humility cannot erase of course my great pride in being tendered the Freedom of London. I am not a native of this land. I come from the very heart of America. In the superficial aspects by which we ordinarily recognize family relationships, the town where I was born and the one where I was reared are far separated from this great city. Abilene, Kansas, and Denison, Texas, would together equal in size, possibly one five-hundredth of a part of great London.

By your standards those towns are young, without your aged tradition that carry the roots of London back into the uncertainties of unrecorded history. To those people I am proud to belong.

But I find myself today five thousand miles from that countryside, the honored guest of a city whose name stands for grandeur and size throughout the world. Hardly would it seem possible for the London Council to have gone further afield to find a man to honor with its priceless gift of token citizenship.

Yet kinship among nations is not determined in such measurements as proximity, size, and age. Rather we should turn to those inner things—call them what you will—I mean those intangibles that are the real treasures free men possess.

To preserve this freedom of worship, his equality before law, his liberty to speak and act as he sees fit, subject only to provisions that he trespass not upon similar rights of others—a Londoner will fight. So will a citizen of Abilene.

When we consider these things, then the valley of the Thames draws closer to the farms of Kansas and the plains of Texas.

To my mind it is clear that when two peoples will face the tragedies of war to defend the same spiritual values, the same treasured rights, then in the deepest sense those two are truly related. So even as I proclaim my undying Americanism, I am bold enough and exceedingly proud to claim the basis of kinship to you of London.

And what man who has followed the history of this war could fail to experience an inspiration from the example of this city?

When the British Empire stood—alone but unconquered, almost naked but unafraid—to defy the Hitler hordes, it was on this devoted city that the first terroristic blows were launched.

Five years and eight months of war, much of it on the actual battle-line, blitzes big and little, flying V-bombs—all of them you took in your stride. You worked, and from your needed efforts you would not be deterred. You carried on, and from your midst arose no cry for mercy, no wail of defeat. The Battle of Britain will take its place as another of your deathless traditions. And your faith and endurance have finally been rewarded.

You had been more than two years in war when Americans in numbers began swarming into your country. Most were mentally unprepared for the realities of war—especially as waged by the Nazis. Others believed that the tales of British sacrifice had been exaggerated. Still others failed to recognize the difficulties of the task ahead.

All such doubts, questions and complacencies could not endure a single casual tour through your scarred streets and avenues. With awe our men gazed upon the empty spaces where once had stood buildings erected by the toil and sweat of peaceful folk. Our eyes rounded as we saw your women, serving quietly and efficiently in almost every kind of war effort, even with flak batteries. We became accustomed to the warning sirens which seemed to compel from the native Londoner not even a single hurried step. Gradually we drew closer together until we became true partners in war.

In London my associates and I planned two great expeditions—that to invade the Mediterranean and later that to cross the Channel.

London's hospitality to the Americans, her good-humored acceptance of the added inconvenience we brought, her example of fortitude and quiet confidence in the final outcome—all these helped to make the Supreme Headquarters of the two Allied expeditions the smooth-working organizations they became.

They were composed of chosen representatives of two proud and independent peoples, each noted for its initiative and for its satisfaction with its own customs, manners, and methods. Many feared that those representatives could never combine together in an efficient fashion to solve the complex problems presented by modern war.

I hope you believe we proved the doubters wrong. And, moreover, I hold that we proved this point not only for war—we proved it can always be done by our two peoples, provided only that both show the same good-will, the same forbearance, the same objective attitude that the British and Americans so amply demonstrated in the nearly three years of bitter campaigning.

No man alone could have brought about this result. Had I possessed the military skill of a Marlborough, the wisdom of Solomon, the understanding of Lincoln, I still would have been helpless without the loyalty, vision, and generosity of thousands upon thousands of British and Americans.

Some of them were my companions in the High Command. Many were enlisted men and junior officers carrying the fierce brunt of battle, and many others were back in the United States and here in Great Britain and in London.

Moreover, back of us always were our great national war leaders and their civil and military staffs that supported and encouraged us through every trial, every test. The whole was one great team. I know that on this special occasion three million American men and women serving in the Allied Expeditionary Force would want me to pay a tribute of admiration, respect, and affection to their British comrades of this war.

My most cherished hope is that after Japan joins the Nazis in utter defeat, neither my country nor yours need ever again summon its sons and daughters from their peaceful pursuits to face the tragedies of battle. But—a fact important for both of us to remember—neither London nor Abilene, sisters under the skin, will sell her birthright for physical safety, her liberty for mere existence.

No petty differences in the world of trade, traditions, or national pride should ever blind us to our identities in priceless values.

If we keep our eyes on this guidepost, then no difficulties along our path of mutual cooperation can ever be insurmountable. Moreover, when this truth has permeated to the remotest hamlet and heart of all peoples, then indeed may we beat our swords into plowshares and all nations can enjoy the fruitfulness of the earth.

Principal Figures

Alexander, Field Marshal Sir Harold.   British commander, 18th Army Group, Tunisia; commander, 15th Army Group, Sicily, Italy; Supreme Allied Commander, Mediterranean Theater of Operations; later named Earl Alexander of Tunis.

Antonescu, Ion.   Rumanian minister of war; premier of Rumania. In 1940 he seized power and restored King Michael to the throne in place of Michael's father, Carol II.

Antonov, General Alexei.   Deputy chief of General Staff under Vasilevsky, 1942; chief of General Staff, 1945.

Arnold, General Henry H. ("Hap").   Appointed chief of Air Corps, 1938; deputy chief of staff (Air), 1940; in 1941 became chief, Army Air Forces; held seat on the Combined Chiefs of Staff; first five-star general of the Air Force.

Attlee, Clement Richard.   Leader, British Labour party 1935–55; deputy prime minister in War Cabinet 1940–45; prime minister 1945–51.

Barr, Major General David G.   Chief of staff, U.S. 6th Army Group, General Devers commanding.

Beaverbrook, 1st Baron.   Newspaper publisher; minister of aircraft production (British) 1940–41; minister of supply 1941–42; member of War Cabinet 1940–42; lord privy seal 1943–45.

Betts, Brigadier General Thomas J.   G-2 officer, War Department; intelligence officer, Mediterranean; deputy officer to General Strong, G-2, SHAEF.

Bevan, Aneurin.   Member of Parliament, Labour party, and constant critic of Churchill policies during World War II; editor of *Socialist Tribune* during the war; later a key figure in the Attlee government.

Blaskowitz, Colonel General Johannes von.   Commander, German Eighth Army, Poland; C-in-C East; commander, Ninth Army; military governor, northern France; commander, First Army; C-in-C, Army Group G; C-in-C, Army Group H.

Bogomolov, Alexander Y.   Soviet ambassador to France during the war; helped establish a line of communication between SHAEF and the Red Army.

Bohlen, Charles E.   State Department expert on Russian affairs and interpreter at the major wartime conferences; special liaison officer from the State Department to the White House; later ambassador to the Soviet Union.

Bradley, General Omar N.   Assistant secretary, General Staff, U.S. War Department, 1940; commander, Infantry School, Fort Benning; commander, 82nd Division; commander, 28th Division, June 1942; deputy commander, II Corps, 1943; commander, II Corps in North Africa; commander, U.S. First Army in France; commander, 12th Army Group; later General of the Army.

Brereton, Lieutenant General Lewis H.   Commander, U.S. Third Air Force; commander, Far East Air Force; commander, Fifth Air Force and deputy C-in-C, Allied Air Forces; commander, U.S. Army Forces in the Middle East; commander, Ninth Air Force; C-in-C, First Allied Airborne Army, August 1944.

Briggs, Ruth.   Secretary to Chief of Staff Walter Bedell Smith; later ran for governor of Rhode Island.

Brooke, Field Marshal Sir Alan.   Commander, II British Corps, France; commander, British Home Forces, 1940; chairman, British COS Committee; Chief of Imperial General Staff, 1941–45.

Browning, Lieutenant General Frederick.   Commander, 1st (British) Airborne Division (later expanded to Corps); deputy commander, Allied Airborne Army in MARKET-GARDEN; chief of staff to Mountbatten, Southeast Asia Command.

Bull, Major General Harold R.   Director, G-3 Division, U.S. War Department; deputy director, G-3, COSSAC; director, G-3, SHAEF.

Burrows, Lieutenant General Montagu Brocas.   British military attaché, Rome, Budapest, Tirana; director, British Military Mission to Moscow (later general officer C-in-C, West Africa Command).

Busch, Field Marshal Ernst.   Commander of the Sixteenth Army in the invasion of the Soviet Union; C-in-C, Northwest, March 1945.

Butcher, Captain Harry C.   Aide-de-camp (naval) to Eisenhower during the war; kept a detailed diary of war as seen by Eisenhower at headquarters.

Byrnes, James Francis.   Director, Office of Economic Stabilization; director, Office of War Mobilization; Secretary of State under Truman.

Caffery, Jefferson.   American representative to the French Committee for National Liberation (FCNL); ambassador to the French provisional government headed by De Gaulle.

Cherwell, Lord (Frederick A. Lindemann). Physicist and director of Clarendon Laboratory, England; during the war he acted as personal adviser to Churchill in science and technology, and was also paymaster general.

Clark, General Mark W. Commander, U.S. Fifth Army, Italy; commander, 15th Army Group, Italy.

Clay, General Lucius D. Director, First National Civil Airport Program; director, Army Procurement Program; base section commander, Normandy; deputy military governor, Germany; Eisenhower's successor as military governor.

Collins, Lieutenant General J. Lawton. Commander, U.S. 25th Division, Pacific Theater; commander, VII Corps, Europe.

Coningham, Air Marshal Sir Arthur. British Bomber Command, Eighth Army; formed 1st Allied Tactical Air Force, North Africa; commander, 2nd Tactical Air Force, Europe.

Conner, Major General Fox. On Pershing's staff in 1918 and Eisenhower's mentor during his duty in the Panama Canal Zone; impressed upon Eisenhower the idea of fighting in cooperation with allies, which he believed the next war would necessitate.

Corlett, Major General Charles H. Commander, U.S. 7th Infantry Division, Pacific theater; commander, U.S. XIX Corps, Europe.

Crerar, General Henry D. G. Chief of General Staff, Canada; commander, 2nd Canadian Division; commander, 1st Canadian Corps; commander, First Canadian Army.

Cunningham, Admiral Sir Andrew. Commander in chief, British Mediterranean Naval Forces; British naval representative to Joint Chiefs of Staff; naval C-in-C, Torch landings; First Sea Lord.

Darlan, Admiral Jean-François. Commander in chief, French navy; vice-premier, Vichy government; commander, Vichy French Forces in Algeria.

Davis, Brigadier General T. J. Adjutant general, Headquarters, ETOUSA, 1942; adjutant general, AFHQ; adjutant general, SHAEF, 1944; director, Public Relations Division, SHAEF, April 1944.

Deane, Major General John R. Secretary, War Department General Staff; American secretary, Combined Chiefs of Staff; director, U.S. Military Mission to Moscow.

De Guingand, Major General Sir Francis. Director of military intelligence, Middle East; COS, British Eighth Army; Chief of Staff, British 21st Army Group.

Dempsey, Lieutenant General Sir Miles. Commander, 13th Infantry Brigade, 1940; commander, British XIII Corps, Tunisia and Sicily; commander, British Second Army, Europe.

Devers, General Jacob L. C-in-C, European Theater of Operations, 1943; commanding general, North African Theater, 1943–44; Deputy C-in-C,

AFHQ; Deputy Supreme Allied Commander, Mediterranean; commander, 6th Army Group, 1945.

Dickson, Colonel Benjamin A. Assistant chief of staff for intelligence, U.S. II Corps; held same post for U.S. First Army in Europe.

Dietrich, General Josef ("Sepp"). Commander, I SS Panzer Corps, Normandy; commander, Sixth SS Panzer Army, Ardennes.

Dill, Sir John Greer. Commander, 1st British Corps; Chief of Imperial General Staff; director, British Joint Staff Mission in Washington.

Dönitz, Admiral Karl. Commander, German submarine fleet; supreme commander, German navy; Hitler's successor as chancellor of the Third Reich in May 1945.

Doolittle, General James Harold. Led bombing raid on Japan, 1942; commander, Anglo-American Strategic Air Force, Mediterranean, 1943; commander, Eighth Air Force, 1944–45.

Dulles, Allen. Director, Office of Strategic Services; on his mission to Berne, 1942–45, he gained intelligence on activities inside Germany.

Eaker, General Ira. American Air commander; led force of twelve B-17 bombers in the first bombing attack on western Europe; helped initiate daylight bombing raids; commander, AAF, during ANVIL.

Early, Stephen. Press secretary to President Roosevelt during most of his administration, including the war.

Forrestal, James Vincent. First Under Secretary of the Navy until he replaced Frank Knox as Navy Secretary in 1944, after the latter's death. Became first Secretary of Defense after the war.

Fredendall, Major General Lloyd R. Commander, U.S. II Corps, Tunisia; later replaced by General George Patton.

Friedeburg, General Admiral Hans von. Commanding admiral of submarines; C-in-C, German navy, in May 1945.

Gale, Lieutenant General Sir Humfrey Muddelton. Major general in charge of administration, Scottish Command, 1941; same position, British Home Forces; chief administrative officer, AFHQ, 1942–43; deputy chief of staff and chief administrative officer, SHAEF, 1944–45.

Gasser, Major General Lorenzo D. Deputy chief of staff, U.S. War Department, at the beginning of the war; headed a group of officers from War Department Manpower Board to study manpower problems, European theater.

Gault, Lieutenant Colonel James. Member of Scots Guard; British military assistant to Eisenhower, AFHQ and SHAEF.

Gavin, Major General James. Commander, U.S. 82nd Airborne Division.

Gerow, Lieutenant General Leonard T. Commander, U.S. 29th Division, 1942; commander, U.S. V Corps, Europe, 1943–44; commander, U.S. Fifteenth Army, Europe, February 1945.

Giraud, General Henri. Commander, French Ninth Army; C-in-C,

French forces in Algeria; co-president, FCNL; C-in-C, French armed forces until 1944.

Gromyko, Andrei A.   Appointed chief of U.S. Division, Peoples Commissariat on Foreign Affairs, 1939; counselor, Soviet embassy, Washington, 1940–43; ambassador to the United States, 1943–46. Later held many positions, including those of foreign minister and president of the Soviet Union.

Guderian, General Heinz.   Creator of German armored force Panzerwaffe; commanded armored units in invasions of Poland, Belgium, France and the USSR; inspector general of panzer troops, 1943; head of Army General Staff, 1944 through March 1945.

Haislip, Lieutenant General Wade H.   Commander, U.S. XV Corps, Europe.

Halifax, Edward Frederick Lindley Wood, 1st Earl.   British Foreign Secretary until 1940; British ambassador to the United States until 1945.

Handy, Brigadier General Thomas T.   Staff officer and assistant to Eisenhower, Operations Division, U.S. War Department; succeeded Eisenhower as assistant to Chief of Staff George C. Marshall, Operations Division.

Hansen, Major Chester B.   Aide to General Bradley throughout the war; later promoted to lieutenant colonel.

Harriman, W. Averell.   Roosevelt appointee to conduct Lend-Lease negotiations; ambassador to Moscow (1943–46).

Harris, Air Chief Marshal Arthur.   Commander, No. 5 Bomber Command, England, 1940; deputy chief of Air Staff; director, RAF mission to the United States, 1941; C-in-C, Bomber Command, 1942–45.

Hazlett, Captain Everett ("Swede").   Boyhood friend of Eisenhower's from Abilene; naval officer; kept up correspondence with Eisenhower throughout his lifetime.

Hodges, General Courtney Hicks.   Commander, U.S. X Corps, 1942; commander, Third Army, 1943; deputy commander, U.S. First Army in the invasion; commander, U.S. First Army, 1944–45.

Hopkins, Henry Lloyd.   President Roosevelt's closest personal adviser during the war; attended meetings of Combined Chiefs of Staff and the major wartime conferences.

Horrocks, General Sir Brian Gwynne.   Commander, British XIII Corps; commander, British X Corps; commander, British XXX Corps; in North Africa and Europe.

Horthy, Admiral Miklós.   Admiral and regent of Hungary during the war.

Huebner, Major General Clarence R.   Commander, 1st U.S. Infantry Division, Europe; commander, U.S. V Corps, Europe.

Hughes, General Everett S.   Assistant to Chief of Staff W. B. Smith at

SHAEF; personal friend of Eisenhower since their days together at Leavenworth.

Hull, Cordell.   Secretary of State (1933–44).

Hull, Major General John E.   Assistant to General George C. Marshall, Operations Division, U.S. War Department; represented Operations Division at Casablanca conference.

Ismay, General Sir Hastings Lionel.   Chief of staff to Churchill in his capacity as minister of defense on the Chief of Staffs Committee.

Jodl, General Alfred.   Director, Bureau of Operations, Oberkommando der Wehrmacht; director, Chiefs of Staff, of Dönitz government.

Juin, Marshal Alphonse.   Commander, French 15th Motorized Infantry Division; commander in chief, French forces in North Africa, 1943; commander, French Expeditionary Corps, 1943; director, COS for national defense, 1944–45.

Kállay, Miklós.   President of Hungarian Council; started secret negotiations with the Allies on behalf of Hungary.

Keitel, Field Marshal Wilhelm.   Director, Oberkommando der Wehrmacht; signed German surrender on behalf of the Wehrmacht.

Kennan, George F.   American counselor and chargé d'affaires, Moscow embassy, 1945; key figure in the formulation of postwar Soviet policy and, later, ambassador to Moscow.

Kesselring, Field Marshal Albert.   Commander in chief, South, until 1943; commander in chief, Southwest and Army Group C.

King, Fleet Admiral Ernest Joseph.   Chief of naval operations, commander in chief, U.S. Navy, 1941–45.

Kirk, Vice Admiral Alan G.   Chief of U.S. naval intelligence, Washington, 1941; chief of staff to Admiral Stark, London, 1942; commander, Amphibious Force, Atlantic Fleet; commander, naval force for invasion of Sicily; commander, U.S. naval force for cross-Channel attack; director, U.S. naval mission, SHAEF.

Kluge, Field Marshal Hans Günther von.   Commander, German Fourth Army, 1940; C-in-C, Army Group Center, eastern front, 1941; C-in-C, West, July–August 1944.

Knox, Frank.   Vice presidential candidate in 1936 election; appointed Secretary of the Navy, 1939.

Koenig, General Pierre.   Commander, 1st Free French Brigade; commander, FFI (armed French resistance group); governor of Paris.

Konev, Marshal Ivan S.   Commander in chief, West Front; commander in chief, Northwest Front; commander in chief, First and Second Ukrainian fronts.

Lattre de Tassigny, General Jean de.   Commander, 14th French Infantry Division, 1940; C-in-C, French First Army, April 1944.

Leahy, Fleet Admiral William Daniel.   Ambassador to Vichy government; chief of staff to President Roosevelt during the war.

Lear, Lieutenant General Benjamin. Commander, U.S. Second Army; commanding general, Army ground forces; deputy theater commander for all manpower affairs, SHAEF.

Leathers, Frederick, Viscount. Minister of war transport (1941–45).

Leclerc, Major General Jacques. Commander, 2nd Armored Division, French forces.

Lee, Major Ernest. Personal aide to Eisenhower during the war at AFHQ and SHAEF.

Lee, Lieutenant General J.C.H. Commander, U.S. Communications Zone, Europe.

Leigh-Mallory, Air Chief Marshal Sir Trafford. Commander, British 11th and 12th fighter groups, 1940–42; C-in-C, Fighter Command, 1942–43; C-in-C Allied Expeditionary Air Force, SHAEF, December 1943–September 1944.

Lucas, Major General John P. Assistant to Eisenhower, Mediterranean theater; conducted an investigation into the Patton slapping incident; later commander of U.S. VI Corps at Anzio.

Macmillan, Harold. Junior minister, 1940–42; minister resident, Algiers, 1942–45; later British prime minister, 1957–63.

Manteuffel, General Hasso von. Commander, 6th Lorried Infantry Regiment; commander, "Manteuffel Division," Tunisia; commander, 7th Panzer Division, Russia; commander, Panzer Grenadier Division; C-in-C, Fifth Panzer Army in the Ardennes battle; C-in-C, Third Panzer Army.

McAuliffe, General Anthony Clement. Artillery commander, 101st Airborne Division; acting commander, 101st Airborne during the Battle of the Bulge.

McCloy, John J. Assistant Secretary of War, United States.

McKeogh, Sergeant Mickey. Wartime orderly at SHAEF for Eisenhower; later wrote book on his relationship with Eisenhower entitled *Sgt. Mickey and General Ike.*

McNair, General Lesley James. As chief of Infantry, credited as the man who trained the U.S. Army for combat in World War II.

Middleton, Major General Troy H. Commander, U.S. 45th Division, Sicily; U.S. VIII Corps, Europe.

Milburn, Major General Frank W. Commander, U.S. XXI Corps in Alsace, January 1945.

Model, Field Marshal Walther. Commander, Army Group North, eastern front, January 1944; commander, C-in-C, West (August 1944) and C-in-C, Army Group B (August 1944–April 1945).

Molotov, Vyacheslav. Commissar of foreign affairs, Soviet Union, 1939–45; president, People's Council of Commissars; vice president, Committee for Defense of the State.

Montgomery, General Sir Bernard L. Commander, British II, V and XII

Corps; commander, Southeast Command; C-in-C, British Eighth Army, Tunisia and Sicily; commander in chief, British 21st Army Group, Europe; later named field marshal and Viscount Montgomery of Alamein.

Moran, Charles McMoran Wilson, 1st Baron.   Personal physician of Winston Churchill during the war; later published his extensive diary based on his experiences with Churchill.

Morgan, Lieutenant General Sir Frederick E.   Commander, British I Corps, 1942; chief of staff, COSSAC, 1943; deputy chief of staff, SHAEF, 1944–45.

Morgenthau, Henry.   Secretary of the Treasury, 1934–45; developed Morgenthau Plan for postwar treatment of Germany.

Moseley, General George Van Horn.   Eisenhower's immediate superior during Eisenhower's years in the U.S. War Department, 1929–34.

Mountbatten, Admiral Lord Louis.   Commander, 5th British Destroyer Flotilla; adviser on Combined Operations; chief of Combined Operations; supreme commander, Allied Forces, Southeast Asia.

Murphy, Robert Daniel.   U.S. consul to Algiers during TORCH landings; Eisenhower's political adviser in Algiers and Paris, 1943–44; U.S. political adviser for American zone of occupied Germany; political adviser, SHAEF.

Nelson, Donald.   Chairman of War Production Board in the United States.

Nimitz, Admiral Chester William.   C-in-C, U.S. Pacific Fleet; later fleet admiral.

Patch, Lieutenant General Alexander M.   Commander, U.S. Infantry Division, New Caledonia; commander, armed forces on Guadalcanal; commander, XIV Corps; commander, IV Corps; commander, Seventh Army; later commander of Fourth Army, Fort Sam Houston.

Patton, Lieutenant General George S., Jr.   Commander, ground elements, western task force; commander, U.S. II Corps, Tunisia; commander, U.S. Seventh Army, Sicily; commander, U.S. Third Army, Europe.

Pogue, Forrest.   Military historian and biographer of George C. Marshall; director, Dwight D. Eisenhower Institute for Historical Research, Smithsonian Institute; director, Research Center, Marshall Foundation.

Portal, Air Chief Marshal Sir Charles F.   Chief of Air Staff, 1940–45; member of Combined Chiefs of Staff.

Pyle, Ernie.   Famed World War II correspondent; after doing roving assignments for Scripps-Howard newspapers, he started a column that appeared in over two hundred newspapers; coverage of war campaigns earned him a Pulitzer Prize.

Quesada, Major General Elwood R.   Commander, U.S. Ninth Tactical Air Force Command.

Ramsay, Admiral Sir Bertram. Flag Officer Dover; commander, task force, Sicilian invasion; British naval commander, Mediterranean; Allied naval C-in-C, expeditionary force.

Ridgway, Lieutenant General Matthew B. Commander, 82nd U.S. Airborne Division, Sicily, Europe; commander, U.S. XVIII Airborne Corps, Europe.

Robb, Air Marshal James. Commander, Number Two Bomber Group, England; commander, Number Fifteen Fighter Group, England; deputy chief, Combined Operations HQ; commander, RAF North Africa; deputy COS, SHAEF; chief of air staff, SHAEF.

Robinson, William E. Businessman and personal friend of Eisenhower and golf/bridge partner in his postwar years; met Eisenhower once during the war and later to offer him a book proposal on his war years; urged him to seek the presidency.

Rommel, Field Marshal Erwin. Commander, 7th Panzer Division, France, 1940; commander, First Panzer Army, Africa; commander, Afrika Korps, 1941–43; commander, Army Group B, 1943–44.

Rundstedt, Field Marshal Karl Rudolf Gerd von. C-in-C, Army Group South, 1939; C-in-C, Army Corps A, western front, 1940; C-in-C, Army Group South, 1941, and West, 1942–44.

Seyss-Inquart, Arthur. Nazi high commissioner in Holland.

Simonds, Lieutenant General G. G. Commander, Canadian infantry division in Sicily and Canadian armored division in Italy; commander, Canadian II Corps.

Simpson, Lieutenant General William H. Commander, U.S. 30th Division; commander, XII Corps; commander, Fourth Army; commander, Ninth Army, 1944–45.

Smith, Major General Walter Bedell. Secretary, General Staff; U.S. secretary, CCS; chief of staff, European theater; chief of staff, AFHQ, Mediterranean; chief of staff, SHAEF.

Smuts, Jan Christiaan. Prime minister of South Africa, 1939–48, who brought his country into the war on the Allied side and was a confidant of Churchill.

Somervell, General Brehon. Supply and procurement director, U.S. War Department; in this capacity he was assistant to Chief of Staff George C. Marshall.

Spaatz, Major General Carl A. Chief of Army Air Forces Combat Command; commander, Eighth Air Force; commander, U.S. Army Air Forces, Europe; commander, Twelfth Air Force; commander, Northwest African Air Forces; commander, U.S. Strategic Air Forces, Europe.

Speidel, General Hans. Head of Chiefs of Staff of occupation troops in France; commanded an army corps on Russian front; Rommel's chief of staff during Normandy invasion.

Stagg, Group Captain John M. Director, Meteorologic Committee,

SHAEF; on his advice, the date for OVERLORD was postponed from June 5 to June 6 because of poor weather conditions.

Stark, Admiral Harold Raynsford.   Chief of naval operations, U.S., 1939–42; commander, naval forces in Europe and naval adviser to U.S. embassy, 1942.

Stettinius, Edward R., Jr.   Served on War Resources Board; Lend-Lease administrator; Under Secretary of State; Secretary of State; U.S. ambassador to United Nations.

Stimson, Henry Lewis.   Secretary of War under Roosevelt and briefly under Truman.

Strong, Major General K.W.D.   British intelligence officer, G-2 Division, SHAEF; assistant to General Eisenhower in this capacity.

Summersby, Kay.   Corresponding secretary and part-time driver for Eisenhower during the war.

Surles, Major General Alexander.   War Department chief public relations officer.

Susloparoff, Major General Ivan.   Represented the USSR at the German surrender negotiations in the Netherlands and at the final surrender in Reims.

Tedder, Air Chief Marshal Sir Arthur.   British air commander in the Middle East; C-in-C, Mediterranean Allied Air Forces; deputy supreme commander, SHAEF.

Tito (Josip Broz), Marshal.   Organized resistance movement in Yugoslavia, 1941; set up National Assembly, 1942; proclaimed marshal and president of Liberation Council, 1943; captured Belgrade, 1944.

Urquhart, General Robert.   Participated in North Africa campaign of 1941 and in Sicilian and Italian operations in 1942–43; commanded British 1st Airborne Division raid on Arnhem.

Vandenberg, Lieutenant General Hoyt S.   Chief of staff, U.S. Twelfth Air Force; deputy chief of air staff, Washington; deputy air commander, AEAF; commander, Ninth Air Force.

Voroshilov, Marshal Kliment E.   Commissar for defense, 1925–40; commander, northern front, 1941; member of Soviet State Committee for National Defense.

Walker, Lieutenant General Walton H.   Commander, U.S. XX Corps, Europe.

Wallace, Henry A.   Vice President of the United States, 1941–45, succeeded by Harry S. Truman.

Wedemeyer, General Albert.   Appointed to war-planning branch of War Department, 1941; deputy chief of staff to Admiral Mountbatten, 1943; commander, U.S. forces in China, 1944; chief of staff to Chiang Kai-shek.

White, Harry Dexter.   Assistant to Treasury Secretary Morgenthau; developed the idea of an International Stabilization Fund for the postwar world; member of several committees and delegations on postwar policy and economics; later accused of Communist party ties.

Whiteley, Major General J.F.M.   British adviser to Eisenhower in tactical and operational affairs; officer of G-2 Division, SHAEF.

Wilson, General Sir Henry Maitland.   Commander, British expedition to Greece; suppressed Iraqi revolt and assumed Persia-Iraq command; C-in-C, Middle East; supreme commander, Mediterranean; also held post as head of BCOS mission to the United States.

Wyman, Major General Willard G.   Commander, 71st U.S. Infantry Division, 1944-45.

Zeitzler, General Kurt.   Chief of Staff, First Panzer Group; chief of general staff of the land armies.

Zhukov, Marshal Georgi.   Chief of general staff, 1941; commander, western front, 1941; commander of four army groups at Battle of Stalingrad; commander, 1st Ukrainian and Belorussian fronts, 1944-45.

Zuckerman, Dr. Solly.   English professor of anatomy, who, after studying the effects of bombing in Rome, recommended that the Strategic Air Forces knock out key rail centers in France and the Netherlands before D-Day. His ideas were crucial to the formulation of the transportation plan.

Glossary of Terms and Acronyms

AEAF
: Allied Expeditionary Air Forces, air command arm of SHAEF.

ABC
: Code name, American-British global strategy conversations at the Washington Conference, January–March 1941. ABC-1 Staff Agreement called for the defeat of Germany first by a combined Anglo-American effort in which there would be "unity of command in all theaters" but integrity therein of the forces of each nation.

Abwehr
: The secret intelligence service of the German General Staff.

ACC
: Allied Control Commission, established in 1945 to govern Germany. Its membership consisted of the United States, USSR, Britain and France; Eisenhower served as the first American representative.

AEF
: American Expeditionary Force, World War I.

AFHQ
: Allied Force Headquarters, Allied command post for Mediterranean operations.

AKA
: Cargo ship, attack.

Allies
: The term refers to the countries belonging to the western-front military coalition against Germany in the two world wars. This is to be distinguished from the term "United Nations," which referred to all anti-Axis belligerents in World War II and included the USSR.

ALSOS
: Code name for Allied intelligence operation to secure information on German developments in nuclear fission.

ANVIL
: Code name, later changed to DRAGOON, for Allied invasion of southern France.

ARCADIA	Code name for U.S.-British staff conference held in Washington, December 1941–January 1942.
BCOS	British Chiefs of Staff.
BIGOT	Code name for documents containing information about NEPTUNE.
BODYGUARD	Code name for Allied cover and deception operations to mask Allied intentions in northeast Europe.
BOLERO	Code name for build-up of American forces in England in preparation for cross-Channel invasion of France.
BUGLE	Code name for overall strategic air force attacks in the Ruhr area—oil and communications targets in particular—March 1945.
C-47	Transport aircraft for cargo and personnel; twin engines.
CALIPH	Code name for the plan involving the invasion of the Bordeaux region of western France as an alternate site to landings in the south.
CCS	Combined Chiefs of Staff—highest authority in the war —combination of American and British officials.
C-in-C	Commander in Chief.
CIGS	Chief, Imperial General Staff—the highest position on the British side of Combined Chiefs, filled by Field Marshal Sir Alan Brooke for most of the war (preceding him for a short time was Sir John Greer Dill).
CLARION	Code name for overall air attacks on German communications systems, February 1945.
COBRA	Code name for the First U.S. Army operation, July 25, 1944, designed to break out of Normandy lodgement.
COCKADE	Code name for diversionary operations in 1943 designed to pin down German forces in the west.
Comm-Z	Communications Zone, senior U.S. logistical support echelon.
COSSAC	Chief of Staff to Supreme Allied Command; prior to the organization of SHAEF, the COSSAC staff served as the command center for the planning of OVERLORD.
CROSSBOW	Code name for the anticipated German pilotless aircraft offensive on England, 1944.
DD	Duplex Drive amphibious tank.
Division	The division has been described as the "building block" of an army in the way a ship is the building block of a fleet. And, like a "ship," a division comes in many sizes and shapes. Technically, a division is defined as the "largest identifiable unit" in the Army Table of Organization. Being

fixed in size and composition distinguishes the division from a corps (two or more divisions) or an army (two or more corps), both of which have permanently assigned artillery and auxiliary units but consist mainly of a headquarters to which divisions are attached. A division is a "combined arms" formation, which distinguishes the division from divisional components, which are smaller "fixed units" (brigades or regiments) but are all of a single branch (artillery or infantry). For instance, a typical American infantry in World War II consisted of three infantry regiments, divisional artillery, a headquarters company, reconnaisance troops, a combat engineer batallion, a medical batallion, a quartermaster company, a signal company and a MP platoon. In short, the division is the *largest* fixed unit in the Army Table of Organization but the smallest combined arms formation, which, as my father put it in explaining this to me, makes the division "a marvelous echelon of command."

But again, though *a given* division is generally fixed in size and composition, divisions are not identical and vary widely in combat strength and composition from army to army and often within an army. In World War I the U.S. Army fielded the so-called square division, which consisted of four regiments and two brigades, and usually numbered 22,000 as opposed to its "triangular" World War II counterpart, which consisted of three regiments and 20,000 men in 1941, but roughly 14,250 by 1945. Comparisons with other armies are apropos. A typical German infantry unit at the beginning of the war numbered 17,200 soldiers, but by June 1944 numbered 12,700. At the same time, the German panzer division was larger than a German infantry division and larger than its American counterpart, which sacrificed men and tanks for mobility. German panzer units entered the war ranging in size from 12,768 men to 21,386 men (1st SS Panzer). In June 1944 a panzer grenadier division, the equivalent of a motorized American infantry division, had 14,000 soldiers; Luftwaffe divisions had 16,000 troops, while the so-called static divisions were considerably smaller than either.

What is a division? This question assumed some significance in the war, for counting divisions became a common shorthand for measuring ground combat strength, and therefore measuring, the comparative size of the various fronts and, by extension, the comparative intensity of the American, British and Russian war efforts. By and large, American and British units were larger than their German counterparts and much larger than Russian divisions, though not so much larger than what Churchill suggested to Stalin at Teheran in response to Stalin's queries about the size of the proposed invasion. At Teheran, Churchill, applying a simple ratio of soldiers and divisions (which counted unattached service components), estimated that the Allied divisions about to land in France were 40,000 men strong. In fact frontline strength of the Allied divisions was even then around 15,000 men, though Allied divisions were kept up to strength.

Data on Russian units are hard to come by. According to Esposito, a Russian infantry division in 1941 had about 11,000 combat effectives; cavalry divisions had about 7,000; and armored divisions had more than both. The disparity between Allied and Russian divisions was therefore probably closer to 1.5 to 1 rather than the 4 to 1, as Churchill suggested.

Comparisons are inexact between the various fronts, however. Reportedly, the Soviets maintained 350 divisions deployed in late 1943. If a figure of 10,000 men each is accepted, then the Russians were deploying roughly three times more troops in 1943 than the 80 Allied divisions could deploy in the west by early 1945. Complicating matters, however, the Russians, unlike the Allies, were believed to maintain grossly understrength divisions in the field for propaganda value, which was not uncommon in World War II. Indeed, after the war Jodl would admit to his interrogators that not only did the Germans maintain understrength divisions in the field but that "Hitler wanted to copy the Russian and Chinese practice of giving a unit the next highest title, e.g., calling a company a battalion, a strong regiment a brigade." Jodl explained, "Over the long, long period this had an effect. You see divisions on the map and forget that they are not really divisions; it has a propaganda effect. The practice originated in the Russian revolution. Hitler liked giving smaller units titles prematurely." Jodl added that German soldiers were "sober," however, and did not like "inflated titles."

In summary, comparing the various fronts was a slippery business with one caveat: one army (German) fought on all fronts. After D-Day, nominal German strength on the eastern front was slightly more than double the nominal German strength in Italy plus France, or three times France and six times Italy, until November 1944, when nominal German strength in the west approached nominal strength in the east. Before D-Day, the Russians faced 75 percent of the German army, while only a fraction of the balance was actually engaged by Allied troops. By any measure, the Russians shouldered the main burden of the ground war.

DRAGOON   Later code name for ANVIL, Allied invasion of southern France.

EAC   European Advisory Commission, set up during the closing year of the war to formulate a postwar occupation policy for Germany and composed of representatives from the United States, USSR, and UK.

EAM   Greek initials for the National Liberation Front, a pro-Communist resistance group in Greece during the war, which after German withdrawal set up the Committee of National Liberation to push its political ideas.

ETO   European Theater of Operations.

ETOUSA   European Theater of Operations, U.S. Army.

FABIUS   Code name for amphibious landing exercises for OVERLORD, May 1944.

FCNL   French Committee of National Liberation.

FORTITUDE   Code name for cover operations to conceal NEPTUNE.

FRANTIC   Code name for England-to-Russia air shuttle bombing.

FUSAG   First U.S. Army Group, forerunner of U.S. 12th Army Group kept alive fictitiously as part of FORTITUDE.

G-1   Personnel division of a higher staff.

G-2   Intelligence division.

G-3   Operations division.

G-4   Supply division.

G-5   Civil Affairs division of SHAEF.

G-6   Public relations and psychological warfare division of SHAEF.

GOLD   Code name for Asnelles beach at Normandy landing site for OVERLORD.

GOODWOOD   Code name for British assault east of Caen in late July 1944, a preliminary to the U.S. operation COBRA.

GOOSEBERRY   Artificial harbors constructed off the coast of Normandy for OVERLORD invasion; part of MULBERRY system.

GRENADE   Code name for the Ninth U.S. Army crossing of the Roer and ensuing push northeastward to link up with VERITABLE First Canadian Army along the Rhine.

GYMNAST   Code name for 1941 North African invasion plan.

HALYCON   Code name for Y-Day which denoted when Allied invasion force was to be in readiness.

JAEL   Code name for Allied deception operations in 1943 designed to conceal Allied intentions in Europe. After Teheran the name was changed to BODYGUARD.

JAG   Judge Advocate General, the legal arm of the U.S. Army.

JCS   Joint Chiefs of Staff, the American high command in Washington and the President's "agency" to exercise strategic direction of U.S. forces.

JIC   Joint Intelligence Committee, the intelligence evaluation services based in London and Washington.

JUBILEE   Code name for the Combined Operations raid on Dieppe, France, in August 1942.

JUNO   Code name for Courseulles beach at Normandy landing site for OVERLORD.

LCI   Landing craft, infantry. Carries a payload of up to 200 troops or 75 tons of cargo.

LCS   Landing craft support.

LCVP   Landing craft, vehicle, personnel.

LST   Landing ship, tank. Used in transporting up to 1,900 tons of equipment.

LUCKY STRIKE   Code name for 21st Army Group plan, offered as an alternative to the plan to capture Brittany, calling for an eastward drive to capture the ports of the Seine, July 1944.

LUMBERJACK   Code name for simultaneous assaults by U.S. First and Third armies to destroy the German forces in the Eifel, February and March 1945.

MARKET   Allied airborne operation designed to seize the bridgehead at Arnhem, in the Netherlands, in conjunction with the land operation code-named GARDEN.

ME-109   Messerschmitt-109, tactical high-speed German fighter.

MI   British military intelligence units, designated by number, such as MI-6.

MP   Military Police.

MULBERRY   Code name for the two artificial harbors constructed off the coast of Normandy during the OVERLORD invasion.

NEPTUNE   Assault phase of OVERLORD. This code name was ap-
                 plied to all OVERLORD planning papers that referred to
                 the actual place and date of the operation.

OB   Oberbefehlshaber (commander in chief). Refers to
                 headquarters of German theater commanders—e.g.,
                 OB West.

OKH   Oberkommando des Heeres, high command of the Ger-
                 man army.

OKW   Oberkommando der Wehrmacht, German high com-
                 mand.

OMAHA   Code name for U.S. invasion beach in Normandy, on
                 the Calvados coast.

OPD   Operations and Planning Division, U.S. War Depart-
                 ment planning center in Washington for American op-
                 erations in World War II.

OSS   Office of Strategic Services; U.S. intelligence services,
                 forerunner of CIA.

OVERLORD   Code name for Allied strategic plans in northwest
                 Europe beginning with the cross–English Channel inva-
                 sion of Europe by Allied forces on June 6, 1944.

OWI   Office of War Information.

PLUNDER   Code name for the 21st Army Group's assault crossing
                 of the Rhine, March 1945.

POINTBLANK   Code name for American and British bomber offensives
                 launched from England against targets in Germany be-
                 fore D-Day.

POL   Petroleum, oil, and lubricants. An abbreviation used for
                 the supply of both air and ground units.

POW   Prisoner of war.

PRO   Public relations officer.

RAF   Royal Air Force, Great Britain.

RANKIN   Code name for Allied contingency plans in the event of
                 a German collapse.

RATTLE   Conference held in 1943 by combined operations head-
                 quarters to discuss the selection of beach sites and
                 deception operations in OVERLORD.

ROUNDHAMMER   Code name for modified ROUNDUP invasion proposed
                 for late 1943.

ROUNDUP   Before OVERLORD, the code name for the plan for a
                 cross-Channel invasion of France in 1943.

SHAEF   Supreme Headquarters, Allied Expeditionary Force.

SHINGLE   Code name for amphibious operation at Anzio, Italy.

SLEDGEHAMMER   Contingency plan for a cross-Channel invasion of
                 Europe in the fall of 1942 in the event that the threat-

ened collapse of Russia made it necessary to open a diversionary front in western Europe.

SOE   Special Operations Executive.

SS   Schutzstaffel, Nazi Elite Guard. The Waffen SS was the military arm.

STARKEY   Code name for deception operations against Pas-de-Calais, 1943.

STAVKA   General headquarters of the Soviet armed forces.

SWORD   Code name for Douvres beach at Normandy landing site for OVERLORD.

TINDALL   Code name for deception operations against Norway, 1943.

Todt   Paramilitary German labor organization, which built fortifications.

TORCH   Code name used in Allied North African campaign for landings on Mediterranean and Atlantic coasts in 1942.

ULTRA   Code name for information gleaned from decrypting German enciphered wireless traffic.

UNDERTONE   Code name for Seventh U.S. Army drive to break through the West Wall and establish a bridgehead over the Rhine in the vicinity of Worms–Mainz, March–April 1945.

UTAH   Code name for Normandy beach assaulted by troops of U.S. VII Corps on D-Day.

V-1   Vergeltungswaffe, vengeance weapon. The first-generation pilotless bomb or German rocket.

VARSITY   Code name for the first Allied airborne assault preceding PLUNDER.

VERITABLE   Code name for the 21st Army Group plan for attack by Canadian forces between the Maas and the Rhine, February 1945.

WADHAM   Code name for the Allied invasion threat against the Cotentin Peninsula in 1943.

WHALE   Code name for the roadway used in forming the piers for the MULBERRY artificial harbors.

Widewing   Code name for SHAEF headquarters, located at Bushy Park outside London.

ZEPPELIN   Code name for Allied deception plan that threatened an invasion of the Balkans to divert German divisions from Normandy before the D-Day invasion.

Select Bibliography

Abzug, Robert H. *Inside the Vicious Heart: Americans and the Liberation of Nazi Concentration Camps.* Oxford: Oxford University Press, 1985.

Allen, George E. *Presidents Who Have Known Me.* New York: Simon and Schuster, 1950.

Ambrose, Stephen. *Eisenhower and Berlin, 1945.* New York: W. W. Norton, 1967.

———. *The Supreme Commander: The War Years of General Dwight D. Eisenhower.* Garden City, N.Y.: Doubleday, 1970.

———. *Eisenhower: A Life.* Vol. I. New York: Simon and Schuster, 1983.

Arnold, Henry H. *Global Mission.* New York: Harper and Brothers, 1949.

Baldwin, Hanson W. *Battles Lost and Won: The Decisive Campaigns of World War II.* New York: Avon Books, 1966.

Berghahn, V. R. *Modern Germany: Society, Economy and Politics in the Twentieth Century.* Cambridge: Cambridge University Press, 1982.

Blumenson, Martin. *Breakout and Pursuit: United States Army in World War II: The European Theater of Operations.* Washington, D.C.: Office of the Chief of Military History, Department of the Army, 1961.

———. *Eisenhower.* New York: Ballantine Books, 1972.

———. *The Patton Papers 1940–1945.* 2 vols. Boston: Houghton Mifflin, 1972–1974.

Bohlen, Charles E. *Witness to History 1929–1969.* New York: W. W. Norton, 1973.

Bradley, Omar N. *A Soldier's Story.* New York: Henry Holt, 1951.

Bradley, Omar N., and Clay Blair. *A General's Life.* New York: Simon and Schuster, 1983.

Brown, Anthony Cave. *Bodyguard of Lies.* New York: Harper & Row, 1975.

Bryant, Arthur. *Triumph in the West: Based on the Diaries and Autobio-

graphical Notes of Field Marshal the Viscount Alanbrooke. London: William Collins Sons, 1959.

Burns, James MacGregor. *Roosevelt: The Soldier of Freedom.* New York: Harcourt Brace Jovanovich, 1970.

Butcher, Harry C. *My Three Years with Eisenhower.* New York: Simon and Schuster, 1946.

Chandler, Alfred D., Jr., and Stephen Ambrose, eds. *The Papers of Dwight David Eisenhower: The War Years.* Vols. I–V. Baltimore: Johns Hopkins University Press, 1970.

Chandler, Alfred D., Jr., and Louis Galambos, eds. *The Papers of Dwight David Eisenhower.* Vol. VI, *Occupation.* Baltimore: Johns Hopkins University Press, 1978.

Childs, Marquis. *Eisenhower: Captive Hero.* New York: Harcourt, Brace, 1958.

Churchill, Winston. *The Second World War.* Vol. III, *The Grand Alliance;* Vol. IV, *The Hinge of Fate;* Vol. V, *Closing the Ring;* Vol. VI, *Triumph and Tragedy.* Boston: Houghton Mifflin, 1948–1953; New York: Bantam Books, 1962. (Page numbers in the notes refer to the Bantam edition.)

Clay, Lucius D. *Decision in Germany.* Garden City, N.Y.: Doubleday, 1950.

Cline, Ray S. *Washington Command Post: The Operation Division.* Washington, D.C.: Office of the Chief of Military History, Department of the Army, 1951.

Craven, Wesley F., and James L. Cate. *The Army Air Forces in World War II.* Vol. III, *Europe from Argument to VE Day, June 1944 to May 1945.* Chicago: University of Chicago Press, 1951.

Crozier, Brian. *De Gaulle.* New York: Charles Scribner's Sons, 1973.

Davidson, Eugene. *The Trial of the Germans.* New York: Macmillan, 1966.

Davis, Kenneth S. *Soldier of Democracy.* Garden City, N.Y.: Doubleday, Doran, 1945.

Deane, John R. *The Strange Alliance.* New York: Viking Press, 1947.

de Guingand, Maj. Gen. Sir Francis. *Operation Victory.* London: Hodder & Stoughton, 1947.

———. *Generals at War.* London: Hodder & Stoughton, 1964.

Deutscher, Isaac. *Stalin.* 2nd ed. New York: Oxford University Press, 1966.

Divine, Robert A. *The Reluctant Belligerent: American Entry into World War II.* New York: John Wiley & Sons, 1967.

Dulles, Allen. *The Craft of Intelligence.* New York: Harper & Row, 1963.

———. *The Secret Surrender.* New York: Harper & Row, 1966.

Eden, Anthony. *The Eden Memoirs: The Reckoning.* London: Cassell, 1965.

Ehrman, John. *History of the Second World War.* Vol. V, *Grand Strategy* (August 1943 to September 1944). London: Her Majesty's Stationery Office, 1956.

Eisenhower, Dwight D. *Crusade in Europe.* Garden City, N.Y.: Garden City Books, 1948.

————. *At Ease: Stories I Tell to Friends.* Garden City, N.Y.: Doubleday, 1967.

————. *Letters to Mamie.* Edited by John S. D. Eisenhower. Garden City, N.Y.: Doubleday, 1978.

————. *The Eisenhower Diaries.* Edited with commentary by Robert Ferrell. New York: W. W. Norton, 1981.

Eisenhower, John S. D. *The Bitter Woods.* New York: G. P. Putnam's Sons, 1969.

————. *Strictly Personal.* Garden City, N.Y.: Doubleday, 1974.

————. *Allies: Pearl Harbor to D-Day.* Garden City, N.Y.: Doubleday, 1982.

Eisenhower, Milton. *The President Is Calling.* Garden City, N.Y.: Doubleday, 1974.

The Eisenhower Foundation. *D-Day: The Normandy Invasion in Retrospect.* Lawrence: University of Kansas Press, 1972.

Erickson, John. *The Road to Berlin.* Boulder, Colo.: Westview Press, 1983.

Farago, Ladislas. *Burn After Reading: The Espionage Story of World War II.* New York: Walker, 1961.

————. *Patton: Ordeal and Triumph.* New York: Ivan Obolensky, 1964.

————. *The Game of the Foxes.* New York: David McKay, 1971.

Feis, Herbert. *Churchill, Roosevelt, Stalin.* 2nd ed. Princeton: Princeton University Press, 1967.

Fergusson, Bernard. *The Watery Maze: The Story of Combined Operations.* New York: Holt, Rinehart & Winston, 1961.

Gaddis, John Lewis. *Strategies of Containment: A Critical Appraisal of Postwar American National Security Policy.* New York, Oxford: Oxford University Press, 1982.

Galambos, Louis, ed. *The Papers of Dwight David Eisenhower.* Vols. VII–IX. Baltimore: Johns Hopkins University Press, 1978.

Greenfield, Kent Roberts, ed. *The History of the European Theater of Operations.* Vol. IV. Washington, D.C.: Office of the Chief of Military History, Department of the Army, 1954.

————, ed. *Command Decisions.* New York: Harcourt, Brace, 1959.

Greenfield, Kent Roberts, Robert R. Palmer, and Bell I. Wiley. *The Organization of Ground Combat Troops: United States Army in World War II: The Technical Services.* Washington, D.C.: Office of the Chief of Military History, Department of the Army, 1955.

Grigg, John. *Nineteen Forty-three: The Victory That Never Was.* New York: Hill & Wang, 1980.

Groves, Leslie R. *Now It Can Be Told.* New York: Harper & Brothers, 1962.

Halle, Louis J. *The Cold War as History.* New York: Harper & Row, 1967.

Harriman, W. Averell, and Elie Abel. *Special Envoy to Churchill and Stalin 1941–1946.* New York: Random House, 1975.

Harrison, Gordon A. *Cross-Channel Attack: United States Army in World*

War II: European Theater of Operations. Washington, D.C.: Office of the Chief of Military History, Department of the Army, 1951.

Hastings, Max. *D-Day, June 6, 1944.* New York: Simon and Schuster, 1984.

Howarth, David A. *D-Day.* New York: McGraw-Hill, 1959.

Ingersoll, Ralph. *Top Secret.* New York: Harcourt, Brace, 1946.

Irving, David. *The War Between the Generals.* New York: Congdon & Lattes, 1981.

Ismay, Hastings. *The Memoirs of General Lord Ismay.* New York: Viking Press, 1960.

Jacobsen, H. A., and J. Rohwer, eds. *Decisive Battles of World War II: The German View.* New York: G. P. Putnam's Sons, 1965.

Keegan, John. *Six Armies in Normandy.* New York: Viking Press, 1982.

Kimball, Warren F. *Churchill and Roosevelt: The Complete Correspondence.* 3 vols. Princeton: Princeton University Press, 1984.

Kolko, Gabriel. *The Politics of War.* New York: Random House, 1968.

Kornitzer, Bela. *Great American Heritage: The Story of the Five Eisenhower Brothers.* New York: Farrar, Straus and Cudahy, 1955.

Krock, Arthur. *In the Nation: 1932–1966.* New York: McGraw-Hill, 1966.

Langer, Walter C. *The Mind of Adolf Hitler: The Secret Wartime Report.* New York: Basic Books, 1972.

Leahy, William D. *I Was There: The Personal Story of the Chief of Staff to Presidents Roosevelt and Truman Based on His Notes and Diaries Made at the Time.* New York: McGraw-Hill, 1950.

Leuchtenburg, William E. *Franklin D. Roosevelt and the New Deal.* New York: Harper & Row, 1963.

Lewin, Ronald. *Montgomery.* New York: Stein and Day, 1971.

Liddell Hart, B. H. *The German Generals Talk.* New York: William Morrow, 1948.

———. *History of the Second World War.* New York: G. P. Putnam's Sons, 1970.

———, ed. *The Rommel Papers.* New York: Harcourt, Brace, 1953.

———, ed. *History of the Second World War.* Published in 96 parts by Marshall Cavendish USA, 1973–1974. "Allies Invade Italy"; "Pre D-Day: Hitler's Fortress Europe"; "Pre D-Day: The Allied War Machine"; "Allies Smash Two German Armies"; "The Battle of the Bulge: The Allies Hit Back"; "Hitler Dead—Doenitz Appointed Führer."

Lyon, Peter. *Eisenhower: Portrait of the Hero.* Boston: Little, Brown, 1974.

McCann, Kevin. *Man From Abilene.* Garden City, N.Y.: Doubleday, 1952.

MacDonald, Charles B. *The Siegfried Line Campaign: United States Army in World War II: The European Theater of Operations.* Washington, D.C.: Office of the Chief of Military History, Department of the Army, 1963.

———. *The Mighty Endeavor.* New York: Oxford University Press, 1969.

————. *A Time for Trumpets: The Untold Story of the Bulge.* New York: Morrow, 1984.

McKeogh, Michael, and Richard Lockridge. *Sergeant Micky and General Ike.* New York: G. P. Putnam's Sons, 1946.

Manvell, Roger. *Conspirators.* New York: Ballantine Books, 1971.

Matloff, Maurice. *Strategic Planning for Coalition Warfare 1943–44.* Washington, D.C.: Office of the Chief of Military History, Department of the Army, 1959.

Matloff, Maurice, and Edwin M. Snell. *Strategic Planning for Coalition Warfare 1941–42.* Washington, D.C.: Office of the Chief of Military History, Department of the Army, 1953.

Mee, Charles L. *Meeting at Potsdam.* New York: M. Evans, 1975.

Montgomery, B. L. *The Memoirs of Field Marshal the Viscount Montgomery of Alamein, K.G.* Cleveland and New York: World Publishing Company, 1958.

Moran, Lord (Sir Charles Wilson). *Churchill: Taken from the Diaries of Lord Moran.* Boston: Houghton Mifflin, 1966.

Morgan, Lt. Gen. Sir Frederick, K.C.B. *Overture to OVERLORD.* Garden City, N.Y.: Doubleday, 1950.

Morgan, Kay Summersby. *Past Forgetting: My Love Affair With Dwight Eisenhower.* New York: Simon and Schuster, 1976.

Mosely, Leonard. *Marshall: Hero for Our Times.* New York: Hearst Books, 1982.

Murphy, Robert. *Diplomat Among Warriors.* New York: Pyramid Books, 1964.

Nelson, James, ed. *General Eisenhower on the Military Churchill: A Conversation with Alistair Cooke.* New York: W. W. Norton, 1970.

Pinkley, Virgil. *Eisenhower Declassified.* Old Tappan, N. J.: Fleming H. Revell, 1979.

Pogue, Forrest C. *The Supreme Command: United States Army in World War II: The European Theater of Operations.* Washington, D.C.: Office of the Chief of Military History, Department of the Army, 1954.

————. *George C. Marshall: Organizer of Victory, 1943–1945.* New York: Viking Press, 1973.

Pyle, Ernie. *Brave Men.* New York: Henry Holt, 1944.

Roosevelt, Elliott. *As He Saw It.* New York: Duell Sloan & Pearce, 1946.

Ryan, Cornelius. *The Last Battle.* New York: Simon and Schuster, 1966.

————. *A Bridge Too Far.* New York: Popular Library, 1977.

————. *The Longest Day.* New York: Popular Library, 1977.

Sainsbury, Keith. *The Turning Point.* New York: Oxford University Press, 1985.

Sherwood, Robert E. *Roosevelt and Hopkins: An Intimate History.* New York: Harper & Brothers, 1948.

Smith, Gaddis. *American Diplomacy During the Second World War, 1941–1945.* New York: John Wiley and Sons, 1967.

Smith, W. Bedell. *My Three Years in Moscow.* Philadelphia: Lippincott, 1950.

———. *Eisenhower's Six Great Decisions: Europe 1944–1945.* New York: Longmans, Green, 1956.

Snyder, Louis, ed. *Masterpieces of War Reporting.* New York: Julian Messner, 1962.

Speer, Albert. *Inside the Third Reich.* New York: Macmillan, 1970.

Stagg, Group Capt. J. M. *Forecast for OVERLORD.* New York: W. W. Norton, 1971.

Stamps, T. Dodson, and Vincent J. Esposito, eds. *A Military History of World War II.* Vol. I: *Operations in the European Theaters.* West Point, N.Y.: United States Military Academy, 1953.

Stimson, Henry L., and McGeorge Bundy. *On Active Service in Peace and War.* New York: Harper and Brothers, 1948.

Stoler, Mark Alan. *The Politics of the Second Front: American Military Planning and Diplomacy in Coalition Warfare, 1941–1943.* Westport, Conn.: Greenwood Press, 1977.

Strawson, John. *The Battle for Berlin.* New York: Charles Scribner's Sons, 1974.

Strong, Maj. Gen. Sir Kenneth. *Intelligence at the Top: The Recollections of a British Intelligence Officer.* Garden City, N.Y.: Doubleday, 1968.

———. *Men of Intelligence.* London: Cassell, 1970.

Sulzberger, C. L. *American Heritage Picture History of World War II.* New York: American Heritage, 1966.

———. *A Long Row of Candles.* New York: Macmillan, 1969.

Summersby, Kay. *Eisenhower Was My Boss.* New York: Prentice-Hall, 1948.

Tedder, Arthur. *With Prejudice.* Boston: Little, Brown, 1966.

Toland, John. *The Last Hundred Days.* New York: Random House, 1966.

Tute, Warren, John Costello, and Terry Hughes. *D-Day.* London: Sidgwick & Jackson, 1974.

Wedemeyer, Albert C. *Wedemeyer Reports.* New York: Henry Holt, 1958.

Weigley, Russell F. *The American Way of War* Bloomington, Ind.: Indiana University Press, 1977.

———. *Eisenhower's Lieutenants.* Bloomington, Ind.: Indiana University Press, 1981.

Wilmot, Chester. *The Struggle for Europe.* New York: Harper and Brothers, 1952.

Winterbotham, Frederick William. *The Ultra Secret.* New York: Harper and Row, 1974.

Wyman, David S. *The Abandonment of the Jews: America and the Holocaust.* New York: Pantheon Books, 1984.

OTHER SOURCES

(Papers, diaries, oral histories, and World War II documents can be found in the Eisenhower Library, Abilene, Kansas.)

Associated Press. "A D-Day Tale: How Code Word Showed Up in a Crossword Puzzle." *Philadelphia Inquirer,* May 22, 1984.

Barker, General Ray W., Deputy Chief of Staff, SHAEF, 1944; Assistant Chief of Staff, G-1, SHAEF, 1944–1945.

Papers, 1943–1945.

Oral History (OH-331).

Bull, General Harold R., Assistant Chief of Staff, G-3, SHAEF; Chief of Staff, USFET, 1945–1946.

Papers, 1943–1968.

Butcher, Harry C., personal aide to General Eisenhower.

Papers, 1910–1959.

Unedited Diary, 1942–1945.

Combined Chiefs of Staff. Conference Proceedings, 1941–1945.

Cota, General Norman D., Commanding General, 28th Infantry Division; ETO, 1944–1945.

Papers, 1912–1961.

Davis, General Thomas Jefferson, Adjutant General, SHAEF, 1944–1945.

Papers, 1916–1964.

Doud, Elivera M.

Collection of family memorabilia.

Eisenhower, Barbara Thompson.

Correspondence between Mamie Doud Eisenhower and Elivera Doud, 1917–1960.

Eisenhower, Dwight D.

"Memorandum for an Allied Command." DDE, Box 76, Mountbatten.

Report by the Supreme Commander to the Combined Chiefs of Staff on the Operations in Europe of the Allied Expeditionary Force, 6 June 1944–8 May 1945. Washington, D.C.: U.S. Government Printing Office, 1946.

"Supreme Commander's Dispatch for Operations in Northwest Europe." BSP, Collection of World War II Documents, Box 19, Report on Operations in Northwest Europe.

Diaries, 1935–1938, 1942, 1948–1953, 1966, 1968, 1969.

Diary (National Surety), 1942–1948, in author's possession.

Papers, Pre-Presidential, 1916–1952.

Eisenhower, J.S.D.

Oral History (OH-15).

Ellis, Edmund, U.S. Military Academy classmate.

Papers re U.S. Military Academy Class of 1915.

Gruber, William R., Army officer, friend of family.
    Papers, 1929, 1940, 1954.
Heaton, General Leonard D., Surgeon General, Department of the Army.
    Oral History (OH-337).
History of COSSAC. Prepared by the Historical Subsection, Office of Secre-
    tary, General Staff, SHAEF, May 1944. BSP, Collection of World War
    II Documents, Box 28.
Hobbs, General Leland, Commander, 30th Infantry Division, 1942–1945.
    Papers, 1918–1967.
Hodges, General Courtney, Commanding General, U.S. First Army.
    First Army Diary.
Hodgson, Paul A., U.S. Military Academy classmate, 1911–1915.
    Letters to family, 1911–1916.
Holmes, General Julius, Staff of JCS and CCS, 1942–1943; Deputy G-5
    Division, SHAEF, 1944.
    Papers, 1936–1948.
Interrogations conducted by the ETO staff *(Transcripts are in BSP, Collec-
    tion of World War II Documents, Box 40)*:
Jodl, Generaloberst Alfred
    July 25, 1945: On broad front strategy
    July 26, 1945: "Ardennes" (answers approved by G.F.M. Keitel)
    July 28, 1945: "Strategy Prior to Invasion"
    July 31, 1945: "Ardennes Counteroffensive"
    July 31, 1945: "Invasion and Normandy Campaign"
    August 2, 1945: Estimate of American operations and commanders
Keitel, General Feldmarschall Wilhelm (and Generaloberst Jodl)
    July 23, 1945: "Invasion"
    July 25, 1945: "Normandy"
Schwerin, General Gerhardt von. "Fragment of assigned report on 116
    Panzer Division from the Seine to Aachen"
Interviews conducted by the author:
    General Omar N. Bradley, Commander of the 12th Army Group
    Captain Harry C. Butcher, personal friend, aide, and diarist of the Euro-
        pean campaign
    General Craig Cannon, Assistant in the Occupation Army
    General Mark W. Clark, Commander, U.S. Fifth Army, Italy
    General Lucius D. Clay, Military Governor of Germany
    General J. Lawton Collins, Commander VII Corps, Europe
    Sergeant Leonard T. Dry, chauffeur and aide, Europe
    Barbara Thompson Eisenhower
    John Sheldon Doud Eisenhower
    Mamie Doud Eisenhower
    Milton S. Eisenhower

The Reverend Edward L. R. Elson, pastor, National Presbyterian Church

General Andrew J. Goodpastor, Staff Secretary in the White House years

Freeman Gosden, personal friend

General Alfred M. Gruenther, Chief of Staff, U.S. Fifth Army, Italy

Bryce N. Harlow, legislative aide to General Marshall, War Department

Averell Harriman, U.S. ambassador to the Soviet Union, 1943–1946

General Leonard D. Heaton, personal physician to Generals Eisenhower and Marshall

Kevin L. McCann, speech writer (1946–1961)

Sergeant Mickey McKeogh, personal aide

Sergeant John A. Moaney, personal aide

Ambassador Robert D. Murphy, political adviser

Jackson, C. D., executive, Time, Inc., Deputy Chief, Psychological Warfare Division, SHAEF, 1944–1945.

Papers, 1931–1967.

Kennan, George.

Intelligence Report, Navy Department, 11–45, "USSR—Estimation of Basic Policies Underlying Soviet Foreign Relations." BSP, Collection of World War II Documents, Box 37.

Laski, Harold J.

"Winston Churchill's War and Peace." *The Nation,* December 15, 1943.

Lucier, Ruby Norman, childhood friend.

Letters from DDE 1913–1967.

McCann, Kevin.

Oral History (OH-159).

Magazines:

Life: January 1942–July 1945

The Nation: January 1943–June 1945

Newsweek: January 1941–June 1945

Time: January 1941–June 1945

Moaney, John A., Jr., personal aide to DDE, 1942–1969.

Correspondence and memorabilia, 1942–1971.

Montgomery, Field Marshal B. L.

"Address Given by General Montgomery to the General Officers of Four Field Armies on 15 May 1944." DDE, Box 75, Montgomery (3).

"Brief Summary of Operation OVERLORD as affecting the Army," April 7, 1944. DDE, Box 75, Montgomery (3).

Moorehead, Alan.

"Montgomery's Quarrel with Eisenhower." *Collier's,* October 5, 1946.

Nevins, General Arthur S., Assistant to General Harold R. Bull, G-3, SHAEF, 1943–1945.

Manuscript, "Looking Back Over More Than Fifty Years of Friendship with General Eisenhower." (Later published as *Gettysburg's Five-Star Farmer.* New York: Carlton Press, 1977.)

Nixon, President Richard M.

Diaries, 1953–1961.

Robb, Sir James M., Chief of Air Staff and Deputy Chief of Staff, SHAEF, 1944–1945.

Narrative, "Higher Direction of War," and other memorabilia, 1944–1945.

Robinson, William E., personal friend of DDE.

Papers, 1935–1968.

Ryan, Cornelius.

"May 7, 1945: The 'Wrong' Peace Papers." *Des Moines Register,* May 7, 1972.

Schaeffer, J. Earl., U.S. Military Academy classmate.

Papers, 1913–1917.

Schramm, Professor P. E., former major and historian, OKW.

"The Preparation of the German Ardennes Counteroffensive (September–16 December 44)." BSP, Collection of World War II Documents, Box 40.

Simpson, General William H., Commanding General, U.S. Ninth Army, 1944–1945.

Oral History (OH-314).

Smith, Fred.

"The Rise and Fall of the Morgenthau Plan." *The United Nations World,* March 1947.

Smith, General Walter Bedell, Chief of Staff, SHAEF, 1944–1945.

Collection of World War II Documents, 1941–1945.

"Memorandum re: part played by Gen. Eisenhower in early days of OVERLORD." DDE, Box 154, Operation OVERLORD, Tab H of pamphlet entitled "Breakout."

Spaatz, General Carl.

"Strategic Air Power: Fulfillment of a Concept." *Foreign Affairs,* April 1946.

Summersby, Kay.

Desk Diary, June 1, 1944–March 10, 1945. DDE, Box 140.

Supreme Commander's Conferences. Minutes, January–May 1944. DDE, Box 136.

Supreme Headquarters, Allied Expeditionary Force. Selected Records, 1943–1945.

Teheran Conference Minutes. Combined Chiefs of Staff Proceedings, 1941–1945. BSP, Box 2.

Twenty-first Army Group Headquarters. "Report on German Atrocities" (against the civilian population in Belgium), December 1944. BSP, Collection of World War II Documents.

U.S. Strategic Bombing Survey, Volume I (published by Garland Publishing in 1976). "Summary Report" (European War), September 30, 1945; "The Effects of Strategic Bombing on the German War Economy," Overall Economic Effects Division, October 31, 1945.

U.S. War Department, Operations Division. Diary, 1941–1946.

War Room Daily Summaries. BSP, Collection of World War II Documents.

William, Ralph S.

"The Short Unhappy Life of the Messerschmidt-262." Memorandum for Captain Aurand. DDE Diary, 1960.

Wood, Brigadier General Eric F.

"Inspection of German concentration camp for political prisoners located at Buchenwald on the north edge of Weimar." BSP.

Notes

Key to frequently cited sources

DDE   Eisenhower's Pre-Presidential Papers, 1916–1952
BD   Butcher Diary (unedited)
BDP   Butcher Diary, published as *My Three Years with Eisenhower*
KSD   Kay Summersby (Morgan) Diary
EP   *The Papers of Dwight David Eisenhower: The War Years,* edited
           by Alfred D. Chandler, Jr., and Stephen Ambrose
FA   First Army Diary
BSP   W. Bedell Smith Papers

1   "What Is His Name?"

PAGE

4   "Accustomed to command": "Ike to His Friends," anonymous document in DDE, Box 15.

5   Nelson meeting. BDP, p. 427.

6   Letter is in BD, November 2, 1943.

7   Description of Eisenhower as a middle-grade officer is based on a personal interview with Harry C. Butcher in June 1978.

8   For discussion of the Salerno controversy and the factors hampering swift Allied pursuit of their victory in Sicily, see Liddell Hart, *History of the Second World War,* pp. 450–52. For criticism of Eisenhower's selection of Salerno, see *ibid.,* p. 473.

9   For Eisenhower's account of the air controversies and decision to

land at Salerno over the doubts of his subordinates, see *The Eisen-hower Diaries,* ed. Ferrell, p. 99.

10   "in headlong flight": BDP, p. 419.

10   "constitutional monarch": Interview with John Eisenhower.

11   "drastic change": EP, p. 1494.

11   "preclude" . . . "prohibitive": EP, p. 1495. Taken from Eisen-hower's summary of the meeting, contained in a summary sent to the CCS and BCOS.

13   "to us it is clear": *Ibid.*

13   "Eden gave up": J.S.D. Eisenhower, *Allies,* p. 376.

13   In response to BCOS complaints about the impact of the "rigidity" of decisions reached at Quebec, Churchill on the nineteenth di-rected the British Chiefs to reevaluate the possibilities for diver-sionary operations in the Mediterranean and the Balkans. Ehrman, *Grand Strategy,* pp. 105–18.

14   Description of destruction of Naples based on Raymond Moley, "Don't Call Them Vandals," *Newsweek,* October 25, 1943.

15   "inevitable phase": BD, October 30, 1943.

15   "frontiers of the Soviet Union": *Newsweek,* October 25, 1943.

16   "free, independent": *Time* magazine, August 30, 1943.

16   "piddling little things": Harriman and Abel, *Special Envoy,* p. 244.

16   "pulverizing" the German state: *Ibid.*

17   "no longer will there be need": Feis, *Churchill, Roosevelt, Stalin,* p. 238.

17   Estimates noted in Brown, *Bodyguard of Lies,* p. 383.

17   Churchill's detailed summary of Eden's talks with Stalin is in *Closing the Ring,* p. 249.

18   "must not be possible": Exactly which set of preconditions for the success of OVERLORD Deane presented to the Soviets is unclear. According to Deane, he and Ismay presented the three precondi-tions set forth in the text. Churchill claimed and won Soviet ap-proval for a fourth, that of overcoming the problem of "beach maintenance" by the construction of two effective synthetic har-bors. Eisenhower's records and the minutes of the subsequent Te-heran conferences do not bear out Churchill's assertion. See *Closing the Ring,* pp. 67 and 246, and Deane, *The Strange Alliance,* pp. 18–19.

18   "Yesterday's conference": Harriman and Abel, *Special Envoy,* p. 239.

19   "lawyer's bargain": The term "lawyer's bargain" first appears in Churchill's instructions to Eden at the Moscow conference, and recurs frequently thereafter. See *Closing the Ring,* p. 244.

19   "simpletons" questioned it: Churchill, *Closing the Ring,* p. 295.

19 The fear of a desperate German effort to defend France: "Hitherto we have prospered wonderfully," Churchill cabled Roosevelt on October 27, "but *now* I feel that the year 1944 is loaded with danger" (*Closing the Ring*, p. 268).

20 "In these changed conditions": Reprinted in Ehrman, *Grand Strategy*, p. 110.

21 "trained to anticipate": Sherwood, *Roosevelt and Hopkins*, p. 767.

21 Embick memo summarized in Brown, *Bodyguard of Lies*, p. 291.

22 "We are facing": Stimson and Bundy, *On Active Service*, pp. 436–38.

23 "the Russians want": Richard Leighton, in Greenfield, ed., *Command Decisions*, p. 190.

23 Staff conferences are described in Brown, *Bodyguard of Lies*, p. 380.

23 From the British point of view, Roosevelt's invitation to Chiang had the redeeming feature of making it impossible for Molotov to attend the preliminary conference. See Churchill, *Closing the Ring*, p. 272.

24 "Stalin would probably simplify": Leighton, in Greenfield, ed., *Command Decisions*, p. 197. At the second Cairo conference a week later, the CCS extended the LST deadline one month to January 15. See Leighton in Greenfield, ed., *Command Decisions*, p. 189.

24 These exchanges are recounted in Churchill, *Closing the Ring*, pp. 262–65, and elsewhere; "supreme importance" in Harriman and Abel, *Special Envoy*, p. 241.

24 "beleaguered, not by his enemies": J.S.D. Eisenhower, *Allies*, p. 392.

24ff. Except where indicated, quotes from the plenary and military committee sessions are from the Conference minutes on file in the W. Bedell Smith Papers at the Eisenhower Library under the heading: Combined Chiefs of Staff, Conference Proceedings 1941–1945, Eureka—Teheran.

25 "that Adriatic business": Sherwood, *Roosevelt and Hopkins*, p. 780.

27 "further project": Churchill, *Closing the Ring*, pp. 301–2.

29 "necessarily isolated": EP, p. 1539. Quote is from a message Eisenhower sent the CCS on October 29 in which he urged the CCS it would be "strategically unsound" to decide in the next several weeks that ANVIL would be "the best [strategic] contribution this theater can make at, or near, the time of OVERLORD." Eisenhower would change his views when briefed on Teheran and when, appointed Supreme Commander, he began to consider the problem of maintaining the flow of reinforcements to France.

33 "No more can be done": Moran, *Churchill: Taken from the Diaries of Lord Moran*, p. 148. See also J.S.D. Eisenhower, *Allies*, p. 415.

34   The informal discussions are recounted in Churchill, *Closing the Ring,* beginning on p. 308. Other versions include those of Charles Bohlen in *Witness to History* and Sherwood in *Roosevelt and Hopkins.*

35   The Curzon Line was a Soviet-Polish armistice line proposed in 1920 by the British Foreign Minister, Lord Curzon. Significantly, the southern portion had been intended to demarcate Poland and a Ukrainian state and not to delineate a Polish-Russian frontier; hence the ambiguity about what was meant by the phrase "Curzon Line" at Teheran and afterward. The dispute involved a strategic slice of territory encompassing Lwow, which if annexed by the USSR would create a Soviet-Czech frontier.

35   Roosevelt's seven-way partition consisted of five self-governing states and two U.N. mandates. Churchill, *Closing the Ring,* p. 343.

35   "Nothing is final": Churchill, *Closing the Ring,* p. 308.

36   "hottest one yet": BD, November 17, 1943.

36   British might "wash out": *Ibid.,* November 23, 1943.

37   "one third of every Army": BD, August 21, 1943.

38   "To sum up": EP, p. 1571.

39   Eisenhower's talk with Elliott Roosevelt is summarized in BD, December 4, 1943.

39   "unfortunately, the President": BD, October 19, 1943.

40   Letter to Milton is in EP, p. 1578.

40   "I have a hunch": EP, p. 1578.

40   For President's views on the historic credit due Marshall, see J.S.D. Eisenhower, *Allies,* p. 391.

40   Dinner is described sketchily in BD, December 5, 1943. The Marshall story, as told above, is drawn from Eisenhower, *At Ease,* p. 249.

41   "I miss you terribly": Eisenhower, *Letters to Mamie,* p. 158.

42   "treatment accorded neutrals": Feis, *Churchill, Roosevelt, Stalin,* p. 266.

42   In the talks at Cairo, Churchill and Eden pushed operation SATURN, a covert "fly-in" of British soldiers to secure Turkish airfields against German reprisals in anticipation of Turkish entry into the war. The Turks agreed to consult the Turkish parliament about it, and "there the matter rested." See Churchill, *Closing the Ring,* p. 357.

42   "fundamental and very grave error": Quoted in Pogue, *The Supreme Command,* p. 27.

42–43   Marshall's preparations for London are recounted by Pogue, among others. *Ibid.,* p. 761.

PAGE

43 Churchill, memo of November 25, 1943, is quoted in *Closing the Ring,* p. 288.

43 Churchill later claimed that he would have answered Marshall's appointment by appointing Alexander to Supreme Command of the Mediterranean.

44 "inspired by a spirit of unity": Wilmot, *The Struggle for Europe,* p. 115.

44 Marshall's response is quoted in Pogue, *The Supreme Command,* p. 32.

45 "I don't think I could sleep at night": Pogue, *George C. Marshall: Organizer of Victory,* p. 321. Pogue quotes Marshall as recalling that he felt at the time that this talk settled matters. Nothing was definite until the sixth, however.

45 Note is reprinted in J.S.D. Eisenhower, *Allies,* p. 422.

46 "Out of this meeting": *Newsweek,* December 13, 1943.

48–49 See Churchill, *Triumph and Tragedy,* p. 49.

49 "progressive destruction": Cited in Churchill's *Closing the Ring.* See also Wilmot, *The Struggle for Europe,* p. 207.

50 "date to be named later": Ehrman, *Grand Strategy,* p. 292.

51 Giraud's lapse is described by Crozier in *De Gaulle,* p. 233.

52 Landing-craft estimates: Churchill, *Closing the Ring,* p. 368.

52 Selecting of Anzio is described by Martin Blumenson in Greenfield, ed., *Command Decisions,* p. 247.

52 Risks of SHINGLE: Churchill, *Closing the Ring,* p. 368.

53 G-2 summary clashed with more optimistic American S2 Army summaries. *Ibid.,* p. 249.

53 "No chief of staff": BD, December 23, 1943.

54 Eisenhower's position is described by Blumenson in Greenfield, ed., *Command Decisions,* p. 247. Churchill's summary is in *Closing the Ring,* p. 373.

54 "love fest": BD, December 30, 1943.

54 Stimson's account is in Stimson and Bundy, *On Active Service,* p. 546–47.

54 "At last!": Crozier, *De Gaulle,* p. 277.

55 "atmosphere of doubt": Wilmot, *The Struggle for Europe,* p. 169.

55 "highly unsatisfactory": Butcher, *My Three Years With Eisenhower,* p. 465.

55 According to Leighton, the Americans and British informally settled on late May as the likely OVERLORD date as early as the second Cairo conference. Leighton, in Greenfield, ed., *Command Decisions,* p. 261.

56 "no victors": Hitler's proclamation was reprinted and analyzed by the London *Times,* January 1, 1944, p. 4.

56 "no-nonsense life": For description of trip, see Eisenhower, *Letters to Mamie,* pp. 161–62. Quote is from J.S.D. Eisenhower, *Strictly Personal,* p. 51.

57 Description of apartment obtained in personal interview with Mamie Doud Eisenhower.

57 Quotes are from undated letters from Mamie Eisenhower to her mother, Elivera Doud.

58 "dirges of sacrifice": Butcher, *My Three Years With Eisenhower,* p. 466.

58 "that Germany has irrevocably lost.": Barnet Nover, "Balkan Turmoil," *Washington Post,* January 6, 1944.

58 Arnold's article in *Washington Post,* January 5, 1944.

58 "proven conclusively": *Washington Post,* January 9, 1944.

59 "compromise" on the western frontier: *London Observer,* January 9, 1944, in an article by "a diplomatic correspondent."

59 "ominous" excursion: *Washington Post,* January 13, 1944.

59 On troop strength, see Russell Weigley, *Eisenhower's Lieutenants,* p. 13. The troop basis for Army ground forces had risen from 1,917,000 enlisted men at the end of 1942 to only 2,417,000 men organized in 88 divisions, and would rise only to 2,502,000 by March 31, 1945.

60 Quotes are from Ernest Lindley, "Relations with Russia," *Newsweek,* March 29, 1943. Lindley wrote extensively on the Russian problem thereafter.

60 Description of visit home obtained in personal interview with Mamie Eisenhower.

60 Eisenhower and Smith corresponded frequently that week. Messages in DDE, Box 101, Smith, WB (1).

61 "denouncing in the public press": Butcher, *My Three Years With Eisenhower,* p. 467.

61 Marshall's ANVIL views are summarized in Pogue, *Organizer of Victory,* p. 330.

62 "Ike still has the air problem": Butcher, *My Three Years With Eisenhower,* p. 467.

62 "have to fight": Eisenhower, *At Ease,* p. 195.

63 "savage press attacks": Butcher, *My Three Years With Eisenhower,* p. 225.

63 "I am a Lieutenant Colonel": EP, p. 965.

63–64 Description of meeting is in Eisenhower, *At Ease,* p. 268.

65 "funeral parlor": BDP, p. 6.

67 "take command of the British Army": BDP, p. 479.

67 That Eisenhower would directly command the ground forces upon

activation of an Army Group was "understood." Wilmot, *The Struggle for Europe,* p. 173.

68 "fearful and carefree": Brown, *Bodyguard of Lies,* p. 410.

68 Talk quoted in BD, January 20, 1944.

2 The "Bill" for OVERLORD

69 In a speech delivered on Labor Day, 1942, Roosevelt delivered a ringing defense of mobilization and anti-inflation actions, which he concluded by calling World War II "the toughest war of all time," testing Americans for "our fortitude, for our selfless devotion to our country and our cause." In reviewing the military situation, though vague on details, Roosevelt affirmed the American determination to assume the offensive against Germany and assured his audience that preparations were "being made here and in Britain toward this purpose," adding that the "power of Germany must be broken on the battlefields of Europe." Speech summarized in Sherwood, *Roosevelt and Hopkins,* p. 630–32.

69 On Churchill's speech to Commons on the importance of the 1940 American elections, see Sherwood, *Roosevelt and Hopkins,* p. 148.

70 "academic exercise": *History of COSSAC,* p. 1.

70 "Europe First": Matloff and Snell, *Strategic Planning for Coalition Warfare, 1941–42,* p. 27.

70 "*in the event*": See Sherwood, p. 273.

70 Lend Lease was the program, decided upon shortly after the 1940 elections and voted into law in early March of 1941, which authorized the President to lend and lease military supplies and equipment to "any country whose defense the President deems vital to the defense of the United States." It meant, as Sherwood points out, that the President gained the power to lend and lease equipment to the USSR, which was what the isolationists "feared most" (Sherwood, p. 264).

71 Britain's "hopeless" prospects: See Sherwood, p. 150. Sherwood calls Roosevelt's decision in the summer of 1940 to back the seemingly hopeless cause of Britain as his "first tremendous wartime decision," noting that never before or after did Roosevelt encounter so much opposition within his official family. His ambassadors —Bullitt in France and Kennedy in England—were "bleakly defeatist," especially Kennedy, who advised him "against 'holding the bag in a war in which the Allies expect to be beaten.'"

Who was an isolationist? Sherwood devotes a long chapter to defining the term and identifying opponents of U.S. intervention in Europe (see "The Phony War," pp. 123–139). In it, Sherwood estimates that before Dunkirk, the vast majority of the American people would have been glad to see the war end on "almost any inconclusive terms merely as a guarantee that the U.S. would not be drawn into it." He cites a Roper poll taken in September 1939 in which only 2.5 percent of the respondents supported immediate intervention, with 37.5 percent favoring a neutralist "cash and carry" trade policy with both sides, and 29.9 percent (the core group) favoring complete noninvolvement with the European belligerents. About these figures, Sherwood notes that isolationist sentiment, while less overtly pro-German than in 1917, was much broader in 1940–1941 than before. The new isolationists were "fortified with the experience that the previous generation . . . lacked, the experience of involvement in European war, and they wanted no more of it," except on two conditions: that the fighting had actually spread to the American hemisphere, and that U.S. involvement be kept pure "by having no allies whatsoever." By contrast, "the Roosevelt doctrine was that if we were to get into a war we should fight it as far from our own shores as possible and with the ideology that we could enlist, accepting whatever risks there might be of potential ingratitude, after the common enemies have been disposed of" (p. 126).

71   "ring": See Ambrose, *The Supreme Commander*, p. 24.

72   "postwar interests, commercial and military": Matloff and Snell, *Strategic Planning*, p. 29.

72   "providential occurrence": Stimson memo to Roosevelt (undated) in June 1941, quoted in Sherwood, p. 304.

73   The House vote on draft extension: According to Sherwood, the House vote was "one of the narrowest escapes of Roosevelt's wartime career." It occurred despite Marshall's warnings that failing to extend the draft would mean the "disintegration of the Army."

It should be noted that opposition to the Selective Service in 1940 and 1941 "crossed a wide spectrum," from conservatives like Senator Robert Taft of Ohio to progressives such as Senator George Norris of Nebraska and socialists like Norman Thomas, on various grounds, including the pacifists' and liberals' concern about the regimentation of American democracy in the name of opposing what they conceived as a purely hypothetical threat of actual German armed aggression. Leuchtenburg, *Franklin D. Roosevelt and the New Deal*, p. 308.

74   On rigidity: "Rocklike" or "rigid" stances on military and diplomatic questions were customary for Americans in their dealings with the British throughout the war. Wilmot, in *The Struggle for Europe,* devotes many critical passages to examining this attitude, which was evident in the planning for OVERLORD. "Early in 1942 Marshall had determined that France should be the decisive theatre and had approved Eisenhower's outline plan for a cross-channel assault," he writes. "Without Marshall's resolute and confident adherence to it, this plan might never have been brought to fruition, but his very single-mindedness had undoubted disadvantages. Eisenhower speaks with due admiration of his chief's ability to 'reach a rocklike decision,' but having done so, it seems that Marshall tended to close his mind to other possibilities created by the turn of events. He appears to have believed, as Eisenhower undoubtedly did, that 'the doctrine of opportunism, so often applicable in tactics, is a dangerous one to pursue in strategy.' Yet always to scorn 'opportunism' (in this sense) is often to spurn opportunity" (Wilmot, p. 453).

75   On bipartisan support for the European war, see Wilmot, pp. 128–29: "It was a considerable achievement on the part of Roosevelt and Marshall to maintain the 'Hitler First' strategy as resolutely as they did," Wilmot writes, "but the price of doing so was that they had to make some concessions to those who advocated priority for the war against Japan, and they had to be careful not to provide ammunition for the oft-repeated charge that they were employing American forces to advance British political purposes in Africa and Europe" (p. 128). See also Tute, Costello, and Hughes, *D-Day.* Tute gives Hopkins credit for constantly keeping this fact before British eyes. "If public opinion had its way," Hopkins told Brooke in July 1942, "the weight of the American war effort would be directed against Japan" (p. 23).

75   "the only possible method of approach": Stoler, *The Politics of the Second Front,* p. 13.

76   "of emphasis and priority": Wilmot, p. 99.

77   "faceless staff officers": Ambrose, *The Supreme Commander,* p. 13.

77   On nocturnal sessions: *Ibid.,* p. 28.

78   On the high stakes riding on OPD decisions, see Eisenhower, *Crusade in Europe,* "Command Post for Marshall," pp. 31–48. Of special interest in this chapter are Eisenhower's observations about Marshall's command technique, particularly his capacity to delegate: Marshall "had nothing but scorn for any man who attempted 'to do everything himself'—he believed that the man who

worried himself to tatters on minor details had no ability to handle the more vital issues of the war. Another type General Marshall disliked was the truculent personality . . . the man who combined firmness and strength with bad manners and deliberate discourtesy. He also avoided those with too great a love of the limelight" (p. 35).

78 "Eisenhower, . . . I received that intercept": Ambrose, *The Supreme Commander,* p. 9.

78 On competition over the OVERLORD idea: "Tom Handy and I stick to our idea that we must win in Europe," Eisenhower wrote on January 27. "Joe McNarney not only agrees—but was the first to state that the French coast *could* be successfully attacked. . . . It's going to be one h—— of a job—but so what?" (National Surety Diary, in author's possession).

78–79 On separate peace rumors, see Stoler, pp. 31–37.

79 On assessments of German strength: In the summer and fall of 1941, American assessments of German strength were pessimistic, changing only with the successful Soviet defense of Moscow in December 1941. In *Crusade in Europe,* recalling his early days at OPD, Eisenhower tells of a report rendered that month by the U.S. military attaché in Rumania, Colonel John P. Ratay, upon his return to Washington. "He [Ratay] was thoroughly convinced that the German military power had not yet been fully exerted and was so great that Russia and Great Britain would most certainly be defeated before the United States could intervene effectively. He believed that the Germans then had 40,000 combat planes in reserve, ready with trained crews to operate at any moment. . . . He also believed that Germany had sufficient numbers of reserve divisions, still uncommitted to action, to carry out a successful invasion of the British Isles."

Eisenhower noted that OPD "refused to give credence to Ratay's information concerning the 40,000 operational airplanes." Moreover, the German Army had "just been halted in front of Moscow and we were convinced that no army possessing a weapon of this overwhelming strength would have withheld it merely because of a future plan for its use, particularly when its employment would have insured the destruction and capture of such an important objective as Moscow" (*Crusade in Europe,* p. 33).

For the British, who were considerably less certain about Hitler's strength, the German check at Moscow came as less of a surprise. "Hitler's failure and losses in Russia are the prime fact in the war at this time," wrote Churchill on December 16, 1941, in a document entitled "The Atlantic Front," which he wrote in preparation for the ARCADIA talks. "We cannot tell how great the disaster to the German army and Nazi regime will be. This regime has hitherto lived upon easily and cheaply won successes. Instead of what was imagined to be a swift and easy victory, it has now to face the shock of a winter of slaughter and expenditure of fuel and equipment on the largest scale.

"Neither Great Britain nor the United States have any part to play in this event, except to make sure that we send, without fail and punctually, the supplies we have promised [to the Russians]. In this way alone shall we hold our influence over Stalin and be able to weave the mighty Russian effort into the general texture of the war" (Churchill, *The Grand Alliance,* p. 545).

79 On Russian long-range objectives, see Stoler, p. 51

80 "recognize its importance": EP, p. 151.

81 "vital tasks that must be performed": Vital tasks memo (undated) is in EP, pp. 145–48.

82 "the only way to get the initiative": Stimson and Bundy, p. 417.

82 "necessary" and "desirable" goals: EP, p. 150.

83 "strict economy in other theaters": Cline, *Washington Command Post,* p. 149.

83 "obsolete": *Ibid.,* p. 146.

83 "put an end to dispersion": Stoler, p. 32.

83 "under conditions of severe deterioration": Cline, p. 153. Eisenhower's task of reconciling the two proposals is summarized by Matloff and Snell, p. 180.

84 "a major portion": EP, p. 205.

84 "either-or": See Ambrose, *The Supreme Commander,* p. 32.

84–85 On Roosevelt's aims in the European war: According to Sherwood, before Pearl Harbor, Roosevelt's "greatest fear" was of a "negotiated peace, another Munich" dictated by the "same craven considerations that dictated the surrender at Munich—fear of Nazi might and fear that, if Nazi might were eliminated, Germany would no longer be a buffer state between Russia and the West" (Sherwood, p. 126). The effect, according to Sherwood, would have been to allow Hitler to consolidate his conquests before resuming his campaign of aggression elsewhere and to "push public sentiment in Britain and France [before Dunkirk]—and most important of all in the U.S.—back into peacetime isolationism ruts, and thereby retard if not nullify all efforts in the democracies to prepare for war."

85 "pulled to pieces": Stimson and Bundy, p. 417.

86 Concerning Marshall's intentions in proposing SLEDGEHAMMER, see EP, vol. VIII, pp. 1570–73. As Army Chief of Staff in March

1947, Eisenhower dictated a confidential memorandum for historian Forrest Pogue's use. In it, addressing the whole problem of SLEDGEHAMMER, Eisenhower disputed Mountbatten's assertion that the U.S. Army in fact expected to launch an invasion of France in 1942. "Much of what he [Mountbatten] says is true," Eisenhower wrote. "He does, however, give the impression that when I went to London in 1942 the Americans expected that we would attack across the channel very quickly. The fact is that General Marshall told me that the first real estimate they would want from us was the time that I figured the attack *could* take place. It is true that we were then hopeful that the attack *would not* have to be longer postponed than the spring of 1943."

87   "in principle": Burns, *Roosevelt, The Soldier of Freedom,* p. 231. Churchill's evasiveness was "uncharacteristic" and Burns speculates that "at this juncture he [Churchill] wanted neither to discourage his ally Stalin, who, after all, could make some kind of deal with Hitler, nor to thwart his friend Roosevelt, who might give in to popular clamor to concentrate in the Pacific and abandon Atlantic First."

88   Imposing North Africa on the military staffs: Ambrose, *The Supreme Commander,* p. 49.

88   Allies would "fight on": In *The Hinge of Fate* (pp 290–92), Churchill reprints a memorandum of his conference with Molotov in which Molotov urged Churchill to consider ways of drawing off "at least forty divisions from the USSR . . . where it seemed that at the present time the balance of advantage in armed strength lay with the Germans."

Churchill proceeded to explain the difficulties of mounting landings in France and he described the efforts being made to pin down German forces in the west, cautioning Molotov that "it would not further either the Russian cause or that of the Allies as a whole if, for the sake of action at any price, we embarked on some operation which ended in disaster. . . ." Asked by Molotov what the British would do in the event of a Russian collapse, Churchill replied that "if, contrary to expectation, they were defeated, and the worst came to worst, we should fight on and, with the help of the United States, hope to build up overwhelming air superiority, which, in the course of the next eighteen months or two years, would enable us to put down a devastating weight of air attack on the German cities and industries."

89   "full understanding": Burns, *Soldier of Freedom,* p. 234. Burns calls Roosevelt's pledge a "fateful" one. "Later there would be much controversy over just what he [Roosevelt] had promised—

what kind of second front, where and when—but all the discussions with Molotov clearly implied a cross-channel attack by all the ground and air power Britain and the United States could muster, in August or September of 1942" (p. 233). Burns further notes that "Marshall felt that the statement was too strong and urged that there be no reference to 1942, but Roosevelt wanted it kept in" (p. 234).

92   "daily being bought": *Life*, July 27, 1942, pp. 21–29.

92   "man above": *Ibid.*

93   London conference was over before it began: Burns, *Soldier of Freedom*, p. 236.

93   Churchill termed them "masterly": Churchill, *The Hinge of Fate*, p. 384. Churchill reprints the text of Marshall's instructions on pp. 384–86. Significantly, the War Department had submitted a set of proposed instructions for Roosevelt's approval which differed in many respects, but above all in the question of land operations in 1942. Both the War Department report and the approved instructions contemplated that SLEDGEHAMMER might prove to be "impossible of execution." "In that case," the War Department draft reads, "my [Roosevelt's] views as to our immediate and continued course of action are that we should continue our *planned* activities *and present* commitments in other areas. We should proceed at top speed with ROUNDUP operations . . . [to] be continued until it is evident that Russia cannot, any longer, contain appreciable German forces" (BD, pp. 51–52). By contrast, Marshall's actual instructions read that in the event SLEDGEHAMMER was judged impossible, he was to "consider the world situation as it exists at that time and determine upon another place for U.S. troops to fight in 1942" (Churchill, *The Hinge of Fate*, p. 385).

94   "we would be guilty": EP, p. 394. In this six-day period, Eisenhower drafted a number of memoranda which became the official American position at the conference. The main points, stressed over and over, were: that the defeat of Russia would "require profound changes in [the] Allied conduct of the war" (July 19); that a buildup in England, followed by diversionary landings in France as "the opening phase of ROUNDUP" (July 21) should proceed since it would (a) avoid dispersion, (b) infuse Allied and Russian morale, and (c) take advantage of German preoccupation in the east, which enhanced the prospects of tactical success (EP, pp. 408–9).

94   British estimates: EP, p. 405.

94   For summary of CCS-94, see Stoler, pp. 58–60.

95   "a waiting one": EP, p. 417.

95   "transatlantic essay contest": Ambrose, *The Supreme Commander,* p. 92.

96   "reconnaissance in force": Tute, Costello, and Hughes, *D-Day,* p. 26.

96   "and the consequent need": Harrison, *Cross-Channel Attack,* pp. 54–55.

97   Conner's letter: DDE, Conner (1).

97   "I have preached": EP, p. 485.

97   "strategic natural selection": Churchill, *The Hinge of Fate,* pp. 300–1.

98   "went over with him": EP, p. 572.

98   "frightful gap": In *The Hinge of Fate,* Churchill reprints two memos he sent to the BCOS in mid-November on 1943 operations. In the first, written on November 9, one day after TORCH, Churchill urged the BCOS not to consider that the interposition of TORCH was "an excuse for lying down during 1943, content in the descents on Sicily and Sardinia and a few more operations like Dieppe." Churchill urged stepped-up planning for pinning down the enemy in Northern France," an attack on Italy "or better still Southern France," along with operations to bring Turkey into the war and to operate overland in the Balkans with the Russians, asking was it "really to be supposed that the Russians will be content with our lying down like this during the whole of 1943, while Hitler has a third crack at them?"

    Nine days later, Churchill again reminded the BCOS that TORCH, an operation of 13 divisions, was no substitute for ROUNDUP with a "striking intent" of 48 divisions, which, by his count, meant that the Allies were "working on a basis of 35 divisions short of what was proposed. . . ."

    "I have no doubt myself that we and General Marshall overestimated our capacity," he wrote. "But there is a frightful gap between what the Chiefs of Staff contemplated as reasonable in the summer of 1942 for the campaign of 1943 and what they now say we can do in that campaign. I am not making criticisms, because I am in this myself to the full. But I feel we have got to get much closer to grips with the whole business. . . . I must repeat that 'TORCH' is no substitute for 'ROUNDUP.' We have, in fact, pulled in our horns to an extraordinary extent, and I cannot imagine what the Russians will say or do when they realize it. . . . I never meant the Anglo-American Army to be stuck in North Africa. It is a springboard and not a sofa" (p. 565).

98   On the impact of Stalingrad, Sherwood writes that "with one

battle . . . Russia assumed the position as a great world power to which she had long been entitled by the character as well as the numbers of her people. Roosevelt knew that he must now look beyond the military campaigns of 1943 to the actual shape of things to come in the post-war world" (Sherwood, *Roosevelt and Hopkins,* p. 699).

98   On mobilization of ground combat units: In overall numbers, ground combat troops totaled 1,917,000 at the end of 1942, which was only 124,000 fewer than the peak figure of 2,041,000 in March 1945. The number of divisions rose, but ground combat strength at no time exceeded U.S. mobilization for World War I by more than 25 percent, which, according to Robert Palmer, was attributable to (a) Russian land power; (b) U.S. naval superiority; (c) U.S. air superiority. See Greenfield, Palmer, and Wiley, *The Organization of Ground Combat Troops,* pp. 176–198.

The authors point out that the ceilings imposed on ground combat mobility represented "remarkably accurate planning of the maximum forces required for victory and a fairly narrow escape from disagreeable eventualities, in case general strategic plans had suffered a serious setback." In terms of divisions, the official ceiling never approached the 1941–1942 estimates of U.S. needs, which ranged as high as 334 divisions should the Russian Army collapse (p. 198). In October 1942, Roosevelt approved a 100-division ceiling, which in June 1944 was cut back to 91 divisions, with 89 kept "at full strength." To maintain this force, 4,400,000 American officers and men were trained for combat.

98–99 "Second front" emotions cooled: See Burns, p. 361, on "the rising controversy over Russia's western borders" in the spring of 1943, spearheaded by Michigan senator Arthur Vandenberg, who was "busy making various congressional declarations on postwar security and making clear his own sensitivity to the Polish question." Similarly, about then, Butcher in his diary began to note the trend in American opinion, which was "veering . . . both naturally and by campaign, to lick the Japs first, and let Hitler wait" (BDP, p. 290).

99   Churchill's approval of unconditional surrender: Churchill would later claim that he had been taken by surprise by the President's casual announcement of the policy at Casablanca, a policy which he had not fully approved. Indeed, after Casablanca, Roosevelt would intimate to Hopkins that his momentous announcement that the Allies would not offer Germany terms was made "on the spur of the moment." On the contrary, Wilmot asserts that the announcement had been carefully prepared. A week before, the

American Chiefs had approved the policy, which Roosevelt cleared with Churchill, including his intent to announce it. Churchill approved and, according to Wilmot, so informed the War Cabinet, which "endorsed the general proposal."

Wilmot questions the wisdom of the declaration, especially since it did not distinguish Germany from Italy or Japan. Wilmot writes that apparently "little consideration was given to the effect of this demand on enemy resistance . . . [or to] the effect upon post-war Europe" (Wilmot, *The Struggle for Europe*, pp. 122–23).

99 The Casablanca decisions: Apparently, the Allied decision to follow up North Africa with an invasion of Sicily caught the Russians by surprise. According to Burns, Stalin's replies to Churchill and Roosevelt on the subject were "frosty," and by mid-March he was alleging that because of Allied decisions, the Germans had moved 36 divisions to Russia, making good their losses that winter. Listing "broken promises of the second front," Burns notes, Stalin gave "emphatic warning, in the interest of our common cause, of the grave danger [unspecified] with which further delay in opening a second front in France is fraught" (Burns, *Soldier of Freedom*, pp. 325–27).

99 "won": See Stoler, p. 77.

99–100 "the progressive destruction": Harrison, *Cross-Channel Attack*, pp. 207–8.

100 "Well—there it is": *History of COSSAC*, p. 2.

100 "an elaborate camouflage": *Ibid.*, p. 3.

100 "in order to undermine the German will": From the military conclusions of the Casablanca conference, quoted in Brown, *Bodyguard of Lies*, p. 245.

100 "obsessed by the desire": *Ibid.*, p. 278.

101 The Washington Conference conclusions: J.S.D. Eisenhower, *Allies*, p. 298.

101 "map which starts at one end": *History of COSSAC*, p. 4.

101 "preoccupation of the British government": Tute, Costello, and Hughes, *D-Day*, p. 17.

102 "short-sighted": Harrison, *Cross-Channel Attack*, pp. 63–64.

102 "British arguments at the Washington conference": *Ibid.*, pp. 64–65.

102 "these planning figures": *Ibid.*, p. 66.

102 "feeling" of what an assault would require: *Ibid.*, p. 68.

104 Roosevelt's order suspending new landing-craft production: Leighton, in Greenfield, ed., *Command Decisions*, p. 199.

104 The Rattle conference: According to Morgan, the Rattle conference, chaired by Mountbatten and attended by twenty generals,

PAGE

eleven air marshals and air commanders, and eight admirals, with fifteen "high-ranking" Americans, and five Canadians observing, marked the beginning of Operation OVERLORD, for it was there that the British High Command found "not only unanimity but enthusiasm that a cross-channel operation could work" (Tute, p. 37).

105   Prerequisites for the landing site: Smith, *Eisenhower's Six Great Decisions,* pp. 21–24.

107   Description of MULBERRY: See J.S.D. Eisenhower, *Allies,* p. 455–51.

108   "truth deserves a bodyguard of lies": Brown, *Bodyguard of Lies,* p. 388.

109   "hated and distrusted the whole thing": Brown, p. 806.

109   Difficulty in looking beyond D plus 30: Wilmot, p. 213.

111   Informal arrangements: See J.S.D. Eisenhower, *Allies,* pp. 442–47. In *Allies,* John Eisenhower notes the closeness of Eisenhower's personal relationship with Spaatz, and the adequacy of informal arrangements in working out air priorities in earlier campaigns. But times had changed. ANVIL placed Eisenhower in an embarrassing situation, John Eisenhower writes, "but the stakes in the conflict in no way affected his own powers as Supreme Commander," which was "not so" in the case of OVERLORD. Among other things, by January 1944, "there was now a serious divergence on the question of air distributions and the strategic air force advocates were insisting on fighting their own war."

112   "neither necessary nor desirable": BD, November 23, 1943.

112   "puzzling" air-command formula: In a letter to General Ira Eaker, Commander of the U.S. Fifteenth Air Force, Eisenhower confessed that he was "puzzled" by Spaatz's assignment, "both as to purpose and position" (EP, p. 1616).

114   "small, mysterious man": Weigley, *Eisenhower's Lieutenants,* p. 138.

114   "railway dessert": Tedder, p. 512.

116   "strong views": BDP, p. 476.

116   *"had not rejected":* Taken from text of a letter Arnold sent to Eisenhower recalling their phone conversation on the subject of air command during Eisenhower's visit to Washington in January 1944. EP, p. 1677.

117   "chessman's talent": *London Observer,* January 2, 1944, p. 3.

117–118 "combined offensive": *History of COSSAC,* p. 35.

118   "first violins": Brown, *Bodyguard of Lies,* p. 480.

119   The German army: According to Weigley, even as late as January 1944, the German army could lay claim to being the greatest land

force in the world. "The panzer divisions no longer wielded the power of 1940, the Eastern Front demanded the Germany army's primary resources, and the wounds inflicted by the Russians had already drawn blood from the main arteries, but the German army in 1944 still could claim to be qualitatively the best army in the world. It had held the title in unbroken continuity since 1870. Its quality lay in firepower enhanced by professional skill among the officers and superior combat savvy and unexcelled courage among the ranks" (Weigley, *Eisenhower's Lieutenants,* p. 28).

119   "These conditions having been fulfilled": *History of COSSAC,* p. 29.

120   "essential for a decision": Blumenson, in Greenfield, ed., *Command Decisions,* p. 249.

121   "quick success": All quotes from this conference are taken from the "Minutes of Supreme Commander's Conference" (No. 1), January 21, 1944, in BD, February 2, 1944.

123   "bill" should include a "positive statement": "Minutes of Supreme Commander's Conference (No. 2), January 21, 1944, in BD, February 2, 1944.

123   "at the latest": EP, p. 1673.

124   "strong support": EP, p. 1677.

124   "directly useful" *Ibid.*

124   "an emergency to be met": Blumenson, in Greenfield, ed., *Command Decisions,* p. 252.

124   "with the same amateur": *Ibid.,* p. 255.

124   "lacked balance": *Ibid.,* p. 251.

125   "should be maintained without detriment": Copy of directive is in BD, February 14, 1944.

126   "the first war instrument": Spaatz, "Strategic Air Power," *Foreign Affairs,* April 1946, p. 9.

126   "not take orders": Tedder, *With Prejudice,* pp. 509–10.

126   "commit the irremediable error": *Ibid.,* p. 510.

127   "being realistic": BDP, p. 474.

127   "raiding AFHQ": BDP, p. 472.

127   "cautious": *The Eisenhower Diaries,* ed. Ferrell, p. 111.

128   "on impulse and not upon study and reflection": EP, pp. 938–39.

128   "meticulous planners": DDE, Box 84, Patton (2).

128   "master of flattery": BDP, p. 481.

128   "Ike, as you are now": *Ibid.*

128   "General Patton has just been in my office": *Ibid.,* p. 490.

129   "as planned is cancelled": COS(W) 1126, February 4, 1944, BSP.

131   "be disentangled in time": EP, p. 1707.

131   "be practically abandoned": Marshall to Eisenhower, February 6,

1944, DDE, Box 124, Cables, Official (GSN/DDE 7/29/43-2/19/44), #4.

132 "we can't close our eyes to that": *The Eisenhower Diaries,* ed. Ferrell, pp. 110–11.

132 "with everything. . . . To disabuse": EP, p. 1713.

132 "struggle . . . doctrine": EP, p. 1715.

133 "the only person whom the Americans": Fergusson, *The Watery Maze,* pp. 318–19.

133 "submit timely recommendations": The American and British proposals and counterproposals are juxtaposed in a chart drawn up by General Ray W. Barker. See Barker Papers, Box 1, "Papers Pertaining to COSSAC," October 1943–1944.

133 "from which further offensive action": For discussion of the debate over Eisenhower's directive, see Pogue, *The Supreme Command,* pp. 52–53. Directive is reprinted on p. 53.

3 Widewing

136 "great importance" of OVERLORD: Minutes of Special Meeting Held at Norfolk House, 14 February 1955. DDE, Box 136. Conferences January–June 1944.

138 "no single American in the theater": Eisenhower's summary of Alexander's message as relayed to Marshall on the sixteenth. EP, p. 1730.

139 "weighed lightly in the balance": Marshall message to Eisenhower, 3-25-44. BSP, Collection of World War II Documents, Box 19, Eyes only cables 1943–44, Incoming (2).

139 "we changed our minds too quickly": From Minutes of Meeting Held at Norfolk House, 2-26-44. DDE, Box 136, Conferences January–June 1944.

140 "[time had] come for a command decision": All quotes from meeting taken from Minutes of Meeting Held at Norfolk House, 2-18-44. DDE, Box 136, Conferences January–June 1944.

141 Nine-point memorandum is entitled "Assault Ships and Craft for OVERLORD" and is on file in DDE, Box 136, Conferences January–June 1944.

141 "other sources" . . . "successful conclusion": Minutes, BCOS (44), 52nd Meeting (o). DDE, Box 136, Conferences January–June 1944.

142 "all possible steps": BCOS memorandum. *Ibid.*

143 "generally . . . not too well situated": Montgomery to Eisenhower,

2-19-44. DDE, Box 75, Montgomery (1). Montgomery's abrupt turnaround is not explained, but evidently it was at Brooke's behest—"Luckily I had discovered last night from Monty that he and Bertie Ramsay had foolishly agreed to curtail the cross-channel operation to provide for a south of France operation," wrote Brooke on the nineteenth. "They should have realized that the situation in Italy now made such an operation impossible" (Bryant, p. 108).

143   Montgomery's second letter is dated 2-20-44. *Ibid.*

143   "events of the past week": Eisenhower to Montgomery, 21 February 1944. EP, p. 1743.

143   "we are committed": Message from Admiral Leahy to Eisenhower, February 21, 1944. DDE, Box 63, Leahy, William.

144   Minutes of Conference COS (44), 54th Meeting (o). DDE, Box 136, Conferences January–June 1944.

145   "near certainty": Minutes of Meeting, Norfolk House, 2-26-44. DDE, Box 136, Conferences January–June 1944.

145   Message announcing approval of the Eisenhower-Brooke accord on the campaign in Italy specified that Italy was to have "overriding priority over all existing and future operations in the Mediterranean . . . [with] first call on all resources, land, sea and air, in that theater." Subject to this, the Mediterranean Commander in Chief was to prepare "alternative plans" for amphibious operations "with the object of contributing to OVERLORD by containing and engaging the maximum number of enemy forces." The BCOS called ANVIL the "first" such alternative, which could be launched shortly after OVERLORD and maximize use of French forces. The CCS ordered the switch of capital ships subject to a review set for March 20. Message: CCS to SHAEF, 26 February. DDE Cables (CCS) October 1943–July 1945 (3).

145   "state of uncertainty": From JCS message to Eisenhower on February 21. "We agree that the present state of uncertainty should be terminated," the JCS wrote in response to the British proposal. "We disagree that ANVIL should be cancelled."

147   "lightning war": Deane, *The Strange Alliance,* p. 149. "The Russian advance progressed with unexpected rapidity," wrote Deane in 1947, "and I became fearful that it would outrun its communications sometime in the spring and that there would not be sufficient time to regroup, shorten its supply line, and be ready for the summer attack that was to help us across the channel." Deane's summary of his 2-27 cable to the CCS: *Ibid.,* p. 150.

148   Overtures are recounted in Brown, *Bodyguard of Lies,* pp. 449–50.

149 "skeptical" . . . "dissipating" . . . "jibe" . . . "probably work out alright": BDP, p. 476.

149 "not merely as a prerequisite" Craven and Cate, *Europe: From Argument to VE Day,* p. 76. Likewise, as Ehrman notes, "POINT-BLANK seemed to its supporters at the end of 1943 to be on the verge of success. . . . The conditions they had posited . . . had at last been provided. . . . Both British and American authorities were therefore confident that in the next six months they could justify their claims." Ehrman continues, "their confidence was not lessened, but indeed was rather *increased,* by the demands of OVER-LORD. For if, as they insisted, they could inflict decisive damage on the enemy within the next six months, they would have proven conclusively that strategic bombing could dictate not only the long-term issue of the war, but also the short-term issue of invasion" (Ehrman, *Grand Strategy,* p. 289).

150 "I am afraid that having started as a confirmed optimist": Tedder, *With Prejudice,* p. 508.

151 For the results of BIG WEEK, see Craven and Cate, p. 35.

151 "interest in the Transportation Plan was waning": Tedder, *With Prejudice,* pp. 509–10.

151–52 For accounts of the dinner at 10 Downing Street, see Eisenhower message to Marshall, 3-3-44, EP, pp. 1758–59; Tedder, pp. 510–12; BDP, pp. 498–99.

152 "have to pack and go home": BDP, p. 498.

153 "in this thing with both feet": Tedder, *With Prejudice,* p. 511.

154 "the feasibility of attack on rail centers": *Ibid.,* p. 513.

154 "Just when I think I have the air problem licked": BDP, p. 498.

154 "Reservations would exist in practice": Tedder, *With Prejudice,* p. 513.

154 Concerning the results of the February air offensive, the figures quoted are from the United States Strategic Bombing Survey: "The Effects of Strategic Bombing on the German War Economy," Overall Economic Effects Division, October 31, 1945 (p. 11). Fighter losses are from T. D. Stamps and V. J. Esposito, eds., *A Military History of World War II,* vol. I, p. 343. The authors go on to quote General Arnold's report on BIG WEEK, in which Arnold claimed "those five days [BIG WEEK] changed the history of the air war." German fighter losses meant that the Luftwaffe thereafter ceased to be an "effective" defensive air force. *Ibid.,* p. 343.

154 "The German fighter force will never be as strong again": Spaatz memorandum, 5 March 1944. BSP, Collection of World War II

Documents, Box 46: Documents of Air Force Units, Headquarters, USF&T: Plan for Combined Bomber Offensive.

155 "subject to intervention by the CCS": Tedder, *With Prejudice,* p. 514.

156 "that the time . . . has come": Quote from letter, Leigh-Mallory to Spaatz. DDE, Box 102, Spaatz (2).

157 "[go to Widewing] alone": BDP, p. 486.

157 Description of Widewing office: BDP, p. 500; Morgan, *Past Forgetting,* p. 181.

157 "watchman waiting to see": Strong, *Intelligence at the Top,* p. 115.

158 "a pious aspiration": *Ibid.,* p. 119.

159 "ill-informed": *Ibid.,* p. 114.

159 "Calling him an S.O.B.": Morgan, *Past Forgetting,* p. 71.

159 "colonel to whom you refer.": EP, p. 1723.

160 Letter to sixth-grade class in Roanoke, Virginia: *Ibid.,* pp. 1753–54.

160 "The introverted product": Weigley, *Eisenhower's Lieutenants,* p. 43.

161 "eager to cast aside conventions": Strong, *Intelligence at the Top,* p. 109.

161 "was less significant than it seemed": J.S.D. Eisenhower, ed., in *Letters to Mamie,* p. 30.

161 Strong's comparison of Moltke and Eisenhower is from Strong, *Men of Intelligence,* p. 24.

165 On the value of the resistance, see Pogue, *The Supreme Command,* pp. 152–57.

165 "Eisenhower's business": BDP, p. 503.

166 De Gaulle's declaration that no authority would be valid: Pogue, *The Supreme Command,* p. 146.

166 "keen and analytical": Public remarks by General Andrew Goodpaster, April 1977.

167 "imitate or interpret the performance": Brown, *Bodyguard of Lies,* p. 21.

167 On ULTRA procedures, see Winterbotham, *The Ultra Secret,* p. 89.

167 "resented" . . . "new tool": Winterbotham, pp. 122–24.

169 Rommel's respect for Allied fighting ability contrasted sharply with the views of Von Rundstedt and Von Schweppenburg. According to Liddell Hart, the latter two men were inclined to allow the Allies to land "so that their forces could then be destroyed and thrown back into the sea by a counter-offensive on the grand scale. . . . Moreover, they regarded the British and Americans as comparatively incompetent at mobile warfare" and believed they "could not possibly be any sort of match for the German Eastern

Front veterans." Rommel vehemently disagreed. "Here we are facing an enemy who applies all his native intelligence to the use of his many technical reserves," he remarked, "who spares no expenditure of material and whose every operation goes its course as though it had been the subject of repeated rehearsal" (Liddell Hart, ed., *The Rommel Papers,* pp. 466–67).

169 "[which he believed would be] decisive": Wilmot, p. 193.

170 On Rommel's choice of the Somme-Seine sector, see Wilmot, p. 180. Hitler's "hunch" about Normandy, inspired by the layout in England, spurred him to issue "repeated warnings about the possibility of a landing between Caen and Cherbourg" (Liddell Hart, *History of the Second World War,* p. 548).

170 German Command arrangements: Friedrich Ruge, "The Invasion of Normandy," in Jacobsen and Rohwer, eds., *Decisive Battles of World War II,* p. 326.

171 "serious crisis" . . . "stabilized.": CIS Appreciation #2, 17 March 1944, SHAEF/CIS/102/INT BSP.

171 "For the moment, it would seem": 21st Army Group Intelligence Review, April 2, 1944. Quoted in Wilmot, *The Struggle for Europe,* p. 196.

172 "super jitters": BDP, p. 503.

172 See Farago, *Burn After Reading.* Wrote Farago: "If the potentialities of the German unrest made any impression on him [Eisenhower], or if the historic opportunities were even perfunctorily recognized by the planners around Ike, it is not evident from either the documents of the era or from the past memoirs of the generals" (p. 258).

172 "moment of extraordinary opportunity": Brown, *Bodyguard of Lies,* p. 590.

174 "no doubt the 'greatest and most horrible crime' ": Churchill memorandum to Eden dated July 11, 1944. *Triumph and Tragedy,* p. 591.

174 "between high Nazi officials": Wyman, *The Abandonment of the Jews,* p. 243. Though conceding that the proposal for exchanging a million Jews for 10,000 trucks was "fantastic," Wyman questions the failure of the British Foreign Office to pursue the matter, since the German requirements were not "hard and fast." The Foreign Office did not do so partly because of doubts that the Himmler-Eichmann proposals were serious and partly because of the Soviets, who maintained that "it was absolutely impermissible 'to carry on any conversations whatever with the German government' on this question." In July, the Foreign Office decided to scuttle the

"entire, risky business" by leaking word of the Himmler overture to the press. *Ibid.,* p. 245.

174–75 Eisenhower's description of Chequers is in *The Eisenhower Diaries,* ed. Ferrell, p. 70.

175 "is fully as important to success in war": Eisenhower, *Crusade in Europe,* p. 60.

175–76 Hobart's career is recounted in Weigley, *Eisenhower's Lieutenants,* pp. 86–87. Weigley calls Hobart one of the "less famous figures" among the interwar prophets of armored warfare. In the late thirties, Hobart had organized the crack 7th Armored Division, which was about to see action in Normandy, only to be "retired early." Having been recalled by Churchill to develop armored techniques for the invasion, Hobart was to command the British 79th Armored Division in battle.

176 "should be carried into battle": Wilmot, *The Struggle for Europe,* p. 182.

176 The idea of requisitioning specialized British armor for the American forces came to very little. According to Weigley, Montgomery would offer Bradley approximately one-third of Hobart's "gadgets," but except for the D.D.s, "Bradley and his staff were not interested." Weigley attributes this "to the American attitude toward tanks as instruments of mobility rather than of breakthrough power" (Weigley, *Eisenhower's Lieutenants,* p. 87).

177 "[failed] to follow through": Cline, *Washington Command Post,* p. 78.

177 "never get over the feeling": EP, 985–86.

178–79 Text of Sandhurst Address is in DDE, Speeches.

179 Minutes of Meeting at Norfolk House, 3-13-44, Box 136, in DDE, Conferences January–June 1944.

179 Seventy-two hours after the Tedder-Portal accord, the BCOS informed the American chiefs that Tedder would now "supervise all air operations for OVERLORD." Right away, the Americans insisted that Eisenhower "command" the air forces: Lyon, *Eisenhower, Portrait of the Hero,* p. 287.

180 "clearly understood": EP, p. 1781.

181 Roberts memorandum is quoted by Matloff in "The ANVIL Decision: Crossroads of Strategy," in Greenfield, ed., *Command Decisions,* p. 293.

181–82 "the basis for a final decision": Marshall to Eisenhower, 3-17-44. Copy in BD, March 18, 1944.

182 "willing to live with shortages": EP, pp. 1776–77.

183 "nothing" . . . "since the Americans have rejected it so many times

PAGE

in the past": Quotes from Minutes of Meeting, COS (44), 95th Meeting, DDE, Box 136, Conferences, January–June 1944.

183 "excellent": Message from J.S.M., Washington, to W.C.O., London, 24 March 1944. BSP, Collection of World War II Documents, Box 20.

184 "to seize all air": Memo for the record reprinted in *The Eisenhower Diaries*, ed. Ferrell, pp. 111–13.

184 "cushion" . . . "railway desert": Spaatz memorandum entitled "Employment of Strategic Air Forces in the Support of OVERLORD." BSP, "Plans for Completion of Combined Bomber Offensive."

184–85 Tedder rebuttal is entitled "Employment of Allied Air Forces in Support of OVERLORD." DDE, Box 136.

185–90 Quotes from "Final Minutes of a Meeting Held on Saturday, March 25, to Discuss the Bombing Policy in the Period before OVERLORD." DDE, Box 136.

189 Personal interview with Freeman Gosden. Gosden told the story of an after-dinner talk in 1965 in which Eisenhower, asked to list the five greatest men he had ever known, wrote the cited names down on a small piece of paper.

190–91 Minutes of Meeting Held in Conference Room, Widewing, 27 March 1944. BSP, Collection of World War II Documents, Box 20, OVERLORD-ANVIL Papers.

191 "*no* repeat *no*": EP, pp. 1792–93.

192 "too great a price": Spaatz memo of 31 March 1944 in DDE, Box 102, Spaatz, Carl.

192 Estimates of casualties cited in Ehrman, *Grand Strategy*, p. 298.

192 "a rather grave and on the whole adverse view": Churchill, *Closing the Ring*, p. 451.

193 "[history would] never forgive them": Bryant, p. 134.

4 Invasion

PAGE

195 "decked out in my best": Eisenhower, *Letters to Mamie*, p. 164

196 "missing in action": *Ibid.*, p. 172.

196 "a man must develop": *Ibid.*

196 "The days are getting much longer": *Ibid.*, p. 173.

196 "their accuracy can be checked": "The Shape of Things," *The Nation*, April 29, 1944.

PAGE

197 "You could run faster": EP, p. 1815.

197 "all the signs point": Edgar Eisenhower letter in DDE, Box 178.

197 Harriman episode: Morgan, *Past Forgetting*, p. 49.

198 Eisenhower's early efforts as an artist are described by Summersby (*Ibid.*, p. 184).

198 "exclusive concern": Interview with author.

199 Butcher's comment that Eisenhower was afraid MacArthur would not notice: Interview with author.

201 "lived in the shadows of an early failure": DDE interview with Bela Kornitzer, DDE Diary, September 1954.

202 "I always thought": Morgan, *Past Forgetting*, p. 63.

202 "thoroughly united and fanatically prosecuting": BD, March 20, 1944.

203 The elevation of Darnard and Henriot, "arch-collaborationists," meant the end of "the last vestiges of Vichy independence" (Crozier, p. 263).

203 "become less ideological": Quoted in *The Nation*, June 3, 1944.

204 Wedemeyer visit: BDP, p. 519.

204 "would go down with tremendous prestige": BD, April 12, 1944.

204 "clarification" of the policy (summary of Anglo-American principles): From message Stettinius sent Hall after meeting; copy in BD.

205 "law, order and property rights": For one version of this talk, see Farago, *Burn After Reading*. For another, see BDP, in which Butcher describes the "feeling that, at Casablanca, the President and the Prime Minister . . . seized on Grant's famous term without realizing the full implication to the enemy," the consensus at SHAEF that the policy was strengthening German morale, and the growing support for a "clarification" of the policy, which would shorten the war. According to Butcher, Eisenhower "strongly" advocated such a view. Interestingly, the published version of Butcher's April 14 diary entry differs significantly from the original entry, and it attributes to Eisenhower far stronger views in favor of a modification of the policy. One cannot know, but it is possible that as he edited his diary for publication, Butcher decided to portray Eisenhower as a firm advocate of a modified policy either (a) not knowing Eisenhower's views fully or (b) knowing that Eisenhower later developed second thoughts about unconditional surrender. In any event, a close reading of the Stettinius cable reveals there were many unresolved points in the April 13 discussion: first, whether the proposed proclamation should occur at the time of the landings or much later as the Allies reached the German frontier; second, whether the Allies should

proceed with such declarations on their own, or await "prior coordination among the three governments which was a prerequisite," as Eisenhower put it (EP, p. 1872). Perusing the Stettinius cable, one gets the feeling Eisenhower and Smith were humoring the future Secretary of State and/or the SHAEF staffs since the effect of either putting off a declaration until victory in Normandy or submitting it to the Russians for their approval would, in either case, be to nullify Stettinius's apparent objective in seeking a "clarification" of the policy—to avoid a costly land battle in France.

205 "restore the devastated areas in Europe": The phrase is Eisenhower's and appears in a memo to Smith commenting on the President's reaction to the Stettinius proposals.

205 "nationals serving under compulsion": EP, p. 1871. Nationals serving under compulsion numbered 200,000 or more. The German army in the west included large numbers of Russians, Lithuanians, Ukraninians, Armenians, Georgians, Tartars, etc., who had chosen to volunteer for service in the German army rather than to serve out the war in labor camps. See Tute, Costello, and Hughes, *D-Day,* p. 51.

206 "as to the ability of the Allied High Command": EP, p. 1873.

206 "listless air of uncertainty": Wilmot, *The Struggle for Europe,* p. 218–19.

206 As for the ability of the Germans to deduce Allied intentions, Brown quotes Liddell Hart as telling Eisenhower that "it was possible to have made reasonably accurate deductions about Allied intentions between June 1943 and February 1944 simply by reading the main British and American newspapers" (Brown, *Bodyguard of Lies,* p. 529).

206 "The [British] people had hardened themselves": Wilmot, p. 218.

207 On Fredendall: Personal interview with John S. D. Eisenhower.

207 "Eisenhower is missed": BDP, p. 488.

207 "filled with optimism": BDP, pp. 505–6.

207 The *Tribune* assignment to scoop the invasion story: Tute, Costello and Hughes, *D-Day,* p. 85.

208 "such action as the fates have in store for me": Quoted by Brown in *Bodyguard of Lies,* p. 530.

208 "sitting as a judge": EP, p. 1848.

208 "Two agonizing hours passed": J.S.D. Eisenhower, *Allies,* p. 461.

208 *Daily Telegraph* incident: Brown, pp. 533–34.

209 "bound to say frankly": EP, p. 1814.

209 "the Soviets will never forgive us": BDP, p. 523.

PAGE

209　"with two or three days' margin": Deane, *The Strange Alliance,* p. 150.

210　"irrevocably, one war": Wilmot, *The Struggle for Europe,* p. 196.

212　"was always careful to search what the written record would show he promised in advance": Weigley, *Eisenhower's Lieutenants,* p. 117.

213　"certainly . . . was General Eisenhower's impression": *Ibid.*

213　British mobilization facts: *Ibid.,* p. 51.

215　"Pencil thrust" and "knifelike thrust" were terms coined by Eisenhower to describe Montgomery's post-Normandy strategy proposals. Montgomery would reject the idea that his single-offensive concept was "pencil-like" or "knifelike," insisting that his envisioned 40-division offensive was a front "so strong it need fear nothing."

216　"two hearts" of Germany: Smith, *Eisenhower's Six Great Decisions,* pp. 154–59. Likewise, this idea abruptly appears in Butcher's diary in an entry dated April 6: "Berlin is the political heart of Germany," he wrote, "but the industrial heart, which has always interested Ike, is the Ruhr Valley. A current study says that once the Ruhr Valley is taken by the Allies, Germany will lose sixty-five percent of her productive capacity for crude steel and fifty-six percent of her total coal production" (BDP, pp. 513–14).

　　　This entry is practically the only mention of such discussions in Eisenhower's papers, but it tends to bear out Eisenhower's claim that the basic approach toward long-range strategy in the west was decided upon early and that the "general plan, carefully outlined at staff meetings *before* D-Day, was never abandoned, even momentarily, throughout the campaign" (*Crusade in Europe,* p. 229).

218　"[attach] particular importance": Brown, *Bodyguard of Lies,* p. 619.

218　"Fifty-fifty": BDP, p. 538.

218　"Someone has to make the decision": Personal interview with Harry C. Butcher.

219　"infernal regions" . . . "evident destiny": Farago, *Patton: Ordeal and Triumph,* pp. 417–18.

219　"and the Russians": Irving, *The War Between the Generals,* p. 105.

219　Exercise TIGER had been "disappointing": For summary of Exercise TIGER, see J.S.D. Eisenhower, *Allies,* p. 458.

219　"sympathetic" underwater explosions: Wilmot, *The Struggle for Europe,* p. 195.

219–20　Gerow's misgivings and Tedder's suggestions are recounted in BDP, pp. 529–30.

PAGE

220 Effort to locate missing BIGOT officers: Brown, p. 547.

220 "stern disciplinary action": EP, p. 1837.

221 "I leave the [Patton] matter entirely to your decision": Marshall to Eisenhower, 4–30–44. DDE, Box 84 Patton (2).

221 "I feel like death": Farago, *Patton,* p. 422.

222 "When?": *Time,* May 1, 1944.

222 "tolerated as an eccentric genius": Farago, *Patton,* p. 420.

222 "I'd like to see the General": *Newsweek,* April 24, 1944.

223 "How far out until we can begin wading": My quote. See BDP, p. 519.

223 "runaround" he was getting: Harriman and Abel, *Special Envoy,* p. 290.

223 "hand-pick" a Polish government: *Ibid.,* p. 325.

224 "grown in stature": *Ibid.,* p. 310.

224 "The invasion had to succeed": Personal interview with Bradley.

224 "the layout of the war": Ehrman, *Grand Strategy,* p. 555. Quoted by Bryant, p. 150.

224 "General, it is good for commanders to be optimistic": Eisenhower, *At Ease,* pp. 274–75.

225 Angel of Mons episode: Brown, *Bodyguard of Lies,* p. 614.

225 "I must say": EP, p. 1847.

225 "God bless you, Ike": Hazlett to Eisenhower, 23 May 1944. DDE, Hazlett (5).

228 "like Iowa before a storm": Personal interview.

229 "smaller hazards of war": Ambrose, *The Supreme Commander,* p. 42.

229 "considerable misunderstanding": EP, p. 1843.

229 "I am in this with you to the end": BDP, p. 535.

230 "regrettable": Kimball, *Churchill and Roosevelt,* vol. III, p. 127.

230 "acute embarrassment": EP, p. 431.

230 Negotiations over De Gaulle's trip to London are recounted by Crozier in *De Gaulle* (pp. 278–80). As with the idea of accepting Churchill's invitation to be in London on D-Day, De Gaulle took his time deciding to go to Washington. De Gaulle would not accept Roosevelt's invitation until June 10, and then only after a visit by Smith "to plead with De Gaulle to visit President Roosevelt without further delay" (p. 285).

231 "the stark and elemental facts": EP, p. 1865.

232 "It seemed to most of us": Admiral Deyo, quoted in Tute, Costello, and Hughes, *D-Day,* p. 97.

232–34 Montgomery's remarks are taken from an outline of his address entitled "Address Given by General Montgomery to the General Officers of the Four Field Armies on 15 May 1944."

PAGE

234 "hardening towards this enterprise": Eisenhower, *At Ease,* p. 275.

234 "Your Majesty, there will be eleven thousand planes overhead": Ambrose, *The Supreme Commander,* p. 399.

235 "in complete chaos": Tedder, *With Prejudice,* p. 534.

236 "Being a son means nothing": BDP, p. 546.

236 "To his son, John": Eisenhower, *Letters to Mamie,* p. 183.

237 "It could have been like visiting a friend in Abilene": Paraphrased from BDP, p. 550.

237 "unpromising": Forrest C. Pogue, "D-Day, 1944," in Eisenhower Foundation: *D-Day, The Normandy Invasion in Retrospect,* p. 27.

239 "It is a tragic situation": Tute, Costello, and Hughes, *D-Day,* p. 110.

239 "Bet some big wig": Ryan, *The Longest Day,* p. 46.

239 According to Brown, news of the 352nd Infantry was withheld from the commanders of the 1st and 29th divisions "with Eisenhower's full knowledge and approval, in order not to increase the morale problem of the . . . divisions": Brown, *Bodyguard of Lies,* p. 616.

240 "fireside chat": Brown, p. 591.

240 "to be on hand": Brown, p. 624.

240 Minutes of Meeting Held in ANXF Conference Room at Southwick House, 29 May 1944.

241 Bradley's view on airborne drops: Bradley, *A Soldier's Story,* p. 235. "It's risky of course," Bradley told Eisenhower, "but not half so risky as a landing on UTAH beach without it."

241 "This bush is the center": Ryan, *The Longest Day,* p. 47.

241 "failing in my duty": Leigh Mallory to Eisenhower, 29 May 1944. DDE, Box 64, Leigh Mallory.

242 "Casper Milk-toast": BD, May 30, 1944.

242 Ronald French revealed the true story of the Dawe puzzle two weeks before the fortieth anniversary celebration of D-Day: "A D-Day Tale," *Philadelphia Inquirer,* May 22, 1984.

243 "For heaven's sake, Stagg": Brown, *Bodyguard of Lies,* p. 626.

243 "I will keep you informed": EP, p. 1902.

243 Cancellation of Churchill's trip: Churchill, *Closing the Ring,* pp. 534–35.

244 "sluggish and slow to show its hand": Wilmot, *The Struggle for Europe,* p. 221.

244 "[called the weather] untrustworthy": Brown, p. 626.

244 "For some days our experts": EP, p. 1904.

245 "differentiate one day from another": Wilmot, p. 222.

245 "Is there just a chance?": Stagg, *Forecast for OVERLORD,* p. 89.

245 "In all the charts": Stagg, p. 80.

PAGE

246 Task Force "U" incident: Brown, *Bodyguard of Lies*, p. 629.

247 "few people under fire": Churchill, *Closing the Ring*, p. 541.

247 "or, for that matter, Britain": Crozier, *De Gaulle*, p. 282.

247 "Ike did some too": BDP, p. 570.

248 "in these circumstances": Quotes are from Smith's memo to Eisenhower on his meeting with Koenig. DDE, Box 21, Churchill (2).

248 "The storm gathered in fury": Wilmot, p. 223.

248 On the factors weighing against postponement, see Bradley, *A Soldier's Story*, pp. 259–61.

249 "almost perfect visual bombing weather": Brown, p. 630.

250 "It's a helluva gamble": Wilmot, p. 225.

250 "I'm quite positive": *Ibid.*

250 "He alone is the one to say": KSD, June 4, 1944.

250 Eisenhower's faith in his hunches: Interview with John Eisenhower.

250 "in the direction of optimism": Brown, p. 632.

251 "clear responsibilities at every level": Ruge, "The Invasion of Normandy," in Jacobsen and Rohwer, eds., *Decisive Battles of World War II*, p. 331.

251 "as yet there is no immediate prospect": Brown, p. 838.

252 "too damn honorable": BDP, p. 562.

252 "a study in suppressed emotion": *Ibid.*

252 "our landings in the Cherbourg–Le Harve area": EP, p. 1908.

253 "Here then": Churchill, *Closing the Ring*, p. 544.

253 "It is very hard to believe": Bryant, p. 152.

254 "The hell with it": BDP, p. 566.

254 "Hamburg has left only about one hundred homes": "Entry for Journal," 5 June 1944. Barker Papers, Box 1.

256 "slowly, ponderously": Ryan, *The Longest Day*, p. 91.

256 "I think General Eisenhower's changes": Barker memo to Smith, 6 May, 1944. Barker Papers, Box 1.

5 Normandy

PAGE

260 "I am looking for four-leaf clovers": Tute, Costello, and Hughes, *D-Day*, p. 148.

261 "Does anyone think": *Ibid.*

261 "A kind of coma": Ruge in Jacobsen and Rohwer, eds., *Decisive Battles*, p. 333.

261   As for alerting the Seventh Army, Wilmot would claim that as early as 1:30 a "general alarm was raised throughout the Seventh Army area" (Wilmot, *The Struggle for Europe,* p. 246). It does not strike the author as very surprising that the German High Command took roughly three hours to sort out the significance of the various reports and alarms received from the Seventh Army area. The significance of this lapse, if any, is the premium placed on the prompt detection of the invasion and how this illustrates the overall weakness of the German position, stemming from Hitler's inability to reinforce France in May.

262   Krancke's cancellation of coastal reconnaissance patrols: Tute, Costello, and Hughes, p. 156.

263   "[landings] were to be expected at dawn": Brown, *Bodyguard of Lies,* p. 658.

263   "*if* this is actually a large-scale enemy operation": *Ibid.,* p. 659.

263   "not yet fully convinced that here and now": Tute, Costello, and Hughes, p. 221.

264   "was much on edge": On Churchill's vigil in the war room, see Tute, Costello, and Hughes, p. 152.

265   The fleet was proceeding according to plan: BDP, p. 567.

265   "air of unreality": Brown, p. 655.

265   "a soldier's battle": "Several of the senior officers who commanded the forces of invasion—Eisenhower among them—have commented the first assault was a 'soldier's battle,' and not a general's battle" (Howarth, *D-Day,* p. 13).

265   "At 08:00 there are still no reports": FA, June 6, 1944.

266   "tactical surprise": BDP, p. 568.

266   "I have as yet no information": EP, p. 1914.

267   "at 09:30, exactly as promised": FA, June 6, 1944.

267   Bradley's technical problems of communication with SHAEF on D-Day are recounted in his *A Soldier's Story,* pp. 280–81. Other accounts, including Bradley's memoir, published in 1983, imply that Bradley withheld information from Eisenhower in order to shield his command against unwanted interference when troubles developed. "Someday I'll tell General Eisenhower just how close it was those first few hours," Bradley remarked to his aide Chester Hansen that day.

267   "waiting for the reports to come in": KSD, June 6, 1944.

269   There are many accounts of the near disaster at OMAHA and the reasons therefor. Among others, see Howarth, *D-Day,* pp. 123–56, which emphasizes the loss of DUKW craft and the inability of the engineers in the first wave to blast gaps in the seawall to make openings for the tanks. Howarth credits the American recovery

starting around noontime to the slow effect of the increasing weight of American men and ships in the vicinity, noting that the 352nd had no reserve and no means of replacing batteries as they were destroyed. Nonetheless, even by nightfall, the American situation was still "critical": Allied communications were poor; beach obstacles were still intact, and American armor had not moved off the beaches.

270 "mostly confirmation of trouble": Weigley, *Eisenhower's Lieutenants,* p. 79.

270 "still critical": Ibid., p. 80.

270 "practically along its whole front": Bryant, p. 153.

271 Kraiss report at 13:35 on D-Day: Stamps and Esposito, p. 387.

271 "I could see from his questions": BDP, p. 570.

271 "By 1300 we can sight land": FA, June 6, 1944.

273 "have the enemy in the bridgehead annihilated": From "Extracts from Telephone Journal of Seventh Army," published by First Canadian Army, Intelligence Summary No. 59. BDP, pp. 662–63.

273 "regardless of reinforcements": *Ibid.,* p. 10.

273 "All that night": Wilmot, *The Struggle for Europe,* p. 287.

274 "tactical surprise": Tedder, *With Prejudice,* p. 549.

274 According to Wilmot, the exact number of German sorties flown was 319, roughly half of the expected number. Wilmot, p. 289.

275 "I have also to announce": Churchill, *Triumph and Tragedy,* p. 5.

275 Hottelet dispatch is in *Philadelphia Inquirer,* June 6, 1944.

275 "Well, I think this is a very happy conference today": Burns, *Soldier of Freedom,* p. 476.

276 Roosevelt's prayer is partially reprinted *ibid.*

277 "we will be there to stay": Eisenhower, *Strictly Personal,* p. 68.

277 "much love . . . as time has not permitted": Eisenhower, *Letters to Mamie,* p. 189.

277 "Well, Freddie, you started it": BDP, p. 568.

277 "it is sometimes difficult": The text of Leigh-Mallory's letter admitting he had been wrong about the air drops and congratulating Eisenhower on the "wisdom of [his] choice" is in DDE, Box 64, Leigh-Mallory.

278 Abolition of SHAEF rested on several factors, of which Leigh-Mallory's personality was only one. About Leigh-Mallory, Wilmot would write: "In directing operations, Leigh-Mallory was resolute and aggressive, but in planning he was inclined to take counsel of his fears. He had very strong opinions . . . and many of his original ideas were to be proved correct by events, but he was obstinate and blunt in presenting his views and extremely

PAGE

hot-tempered when crossed. He inspired great loyalty and confidence in his staff and his fighting squadrons, but he was not so successful in his dealings with other services or with the Americans, who resented his dogmatic manner" (*The Struggle for Europe*, p. 208).

278 "go down with the ship": Quotes are mine. Bradley in *A Soldier's Story* (p. 274) quotes an exchange with Gerow on the sixth when Bradley learned that Huebner was planning to shift his 1st Division headquarters ashore at OMAHA that night: " 'How about you, Gee?' I asked. 'When can you move V Corps Headquarters ashore?'

" 'Early in the morning, Brad. We'll have our communications by then.'

" 'To hell with your communications . . .'

"Gerow grinned. 'We'll set up on the beach tonight.' "

279 "choke points": Brown, *Bodyguard of Lies,* p. 683.

279 "kind" report: BDP, p. 573.

280 "zone of isolation": Liddell Hart, *History of the Second World War,* p. 547.

280 "one of the most brutal uses of aerial power": Brown, p. 684.

280 "Reports from the beaches": KSD, June 8, 1944.

281 "obvious" progress: EP, p. 1920.

281 "hardly knew what to say to them": BDP, p. 574.

281 "leading us into overoptimism": *Ibid.,* p. 575.

281 "Caen was to have been taken": *Ibid.*

282 "strong resistance along the whole front": SHAEF Daily Intelligence Summary, June 7, 1944.

282 "worry about a premature advance": Wilmot, p. 297.

282 "considerable night activity": SHAEF Daily Intelligence Summary, June 8, 1944.

283 Montgomery's letter to Brooke, dated the eleventh, is quoted in part by Wilmot, p. 312.

284 "speed along the long line": Actually, Stalin's message contained no such exact phrase and Eisenhower seemed slightly unsure of what the Russians were doing. See BDP, p. 576.

285 "to be followed by all the infantry divisions": The litany of Rommel's requests and OKW's refusals is given by Ruge in Jacobsen and Rohwer, eds., *Decisive Battles,* p. 337.

287 "then Joan Bright . . . knocked on the door": Brown, p. 687.

287 Hitler's contempt for democracy: Speer, *Inside the Third Reich,* pp. 365–66.

287 "If it becomes necessary to save time": Bradley, *A Soldier's Story,* p. 283.

PAGE

288 "fighter-bomber race course": Tute, Costello, and Hughes, p. 222.

289 "into a heap of ruins": ULTRA's interception of this message is quoted by Winterbotham in *The Ultra Secret*, p. 196.

289 "avert a complete catastrophe": Ruge, in Jacobsen and Rohwer, eds., *Decisive Battles*, p. 338.

289 "The Third Front had become a fact": *Ibid.*, p. 337.

290 "the outstanding feature": SHAEF Weekly Intelligence Summary No. 12.

290 "How strange that the Germans": Churchill, *Triumph and Tragedy*, p. 10.

291 JIC report is in BD, June 22, 1944.

291 "stabilization": "A stabilized battle implied a return to the old Western Front, the Somme and Passchendaele all over again. This stabilization was the grim prospect against which the ghosts of 1916 cried out so piercingly to Winston Churchill. It was the prospect, too, against which the planners labored to prepare a breakout from Normandy" (Weigley, *Eisenhower's Lieutenants*, p. 114).

291 "interesting": BD, June 22, 1944.

292 "We received frequent reports": Brown interview with Wingate, in *Bodyguard of Lies*, p. 597.

293 "[Marshall] worked Eden over": Irving, *The War Between the Generals*, p. 703.

293 "With the establishment of a firm lodgement": Editorial in *Life*, June 19, 1944.

294 *Saturday Evening Post*, April 1, 1944. The editorial was a rebuttal to articles by the journalist I. F. Stone, who warned that restoring the "cartel system" and a "capitalist Reich" would be repeating the errors of the past. Stone's views prompted the *Post* to accuse him of disseminating "propaganda not merely for destroying the military power of Germany but for using destruction of her military power as a pretext for destroying her industrial system . . . the kind of economic set-up we defend in America": All from I. F. Stone, reply to *Saturday Evening Post*, in *The Nation*, April 8, 1944, p. 410.

294 "a profoundly political war": Charles Bolte in *The Nation*, July 22, 1944.

294 "the joy to us all": Quoted in Churchill, *Triumph and Tragedy*, p. 6.

294 "But all this waits on the hazards of war": *Ibid.*, p. 7.

294 "the valiant British and American Armies": *Ibid.*

295 "the magnificent performance": EP, p. 1923.

PAGE

295   "As is evident": *Ibid.,* p. 8.

295   Marshall's openmindedness on CALIPH and the Adriatic: Bryant, pp. 156–57.

296   "It was interesting": *Ibid.,* p. 156. Similarly, the Americans were baffled by Brooke's sudden openmindedness on ANVIL and the fact that "after the heated controversy of February and March, southern France was back in the running apparently without acrimony" (Pogue, *Organizer of Victory,* p. 393).

296   "everyone experienced a thrilling and satisfying feeling": Gault, "General Eisenhower's Visit to France," in BD, June 12, 1944.

296   "D-Day cemented his personal confidence": Personal interview with Kevin McCann.

297   "finish forever his hope for arresting": Bradley, *A Soldier's Story,* pp. 298–99.

298   "workmanlike atmosphere": Gault, in BD, June 12, 1944.

298   "the cat's hold": BDP, p. 580.

298   "Why do you think we have been pushing you?": *Ibid.*

298   "contact such world figures": J.S.D. Eisenhower, Introduction to *Strictly Personal,* p. xi.

299   "military barrier": *Ibid.,* p. 63.

300   "first priority over everything": BDP, p. 588.

300   "write off" a German village: Bryant, p. 169.

301   "as both a terror weapon": Wilmot, *The Struggle for Europe,* p. 318.

301   V-1 incident: Irving, *The War Between the Generals,* p. 170.

301   "[Prospects were . . .] remote": Tedder, *With Prejudice,* pp. 552–53.

301   The British "air barons" were not the only Britishers critical of Dempsey's "excessive caution" in the early phases of Normandy. Years later, Liddell Hart would criticize Dempsey's failure in the first two days to push out west and southwest of Caen in the hours when German opposition was "negligible" behind the coast defenses, a delay he would blame for the prolongation of the battle of the bridgehead. In Liddell Hart's opinion, however, prolonging the battle of Normandy proved to be "the proverbial 'blessing in disguise' by grinding down the German infantry and panzers," thus "depriving the enemy of the mobile arm he needed when it came to fighting in the open country" (Liddell Hart, *History of the Second World War,* p. 546).

301   "severe setback": Tedder, *With Prejudice,* p. 552.

301   "by a set piece assault": Wilmot, p. 331.

302   "quickly called the airmen into a conference": J.S.D. Eisenhower, *Strictly Personal,* p. 61.

PAGE

303 "[attitude of the French people] sobering": J.S.D. Eisenhower, Unpublished manuscript (quoted in part by Irving, p. 168).

303 "we were bringing war and desolation to their country": Bryant, p. 159.

303 "Despite everything a soldier is led to believe": J.S.D. Eisenhower, *Strictly Personal,* pp. 71–72.

304 "taking the firm defensive at Caen": Derived from Eisenhower's description of Montgomery's strategy several weeks later in correspondence with the British general. EP, pp. 1982–83.

304 "excessive resistance at one point": Description of Montgomery's strategy derived from Bryant, p. 170.

305 "made himself responsible": *Ibid.,* p. 177.

305 "not started their offensives in other sectors": BD, June 11, 1944.

308 "we are at a strong point administratively": Montgomery directive in DDE, Montgomery Correspondence.

308 "to an ominous wind": Bradley, *A Soldier's Story,* p. 302.

309 "Thanks, and thank the Gods of war": EP, p. 1948. (Stagg memo is in BD, June 23, 1944.)

309 Storm damage: In wrecking MULBERRY A, the storm curtailed Allied port capacity for weeks, a situation that was not alleviated by the capture of Cherbourg. See Fergusson, *The Watery Maze,* pp. 346–50.

309 "that the Russians would not attack": Quoted by Gackenholz, in Jacobsen and Rohwer, eds., *Decisive Battles,* p. 363.

309 British reappraisal: Bryant, p. 180.

310 "savoring of spheres of influence": Churchill, *Triumph and Tragedy,* p. 63.

310 "coherent direction": *Ibid.,* p. 65.

310 "to bring order out of chaos": *Ibid.,* p. 66.

310 "exploitation through the Ljubljana gap": Wilmot, *The Struggle for Europe,* p. 450. See also Pogue, *Organizer of Victory,* p. 406.

311 "stir up all of Marshall's old suspicions": Bryant, p. 165.

312 "the comparative merits of the ANVIL assault": EP, p. 1930.

312 "fundamental issue of military policy": Text of message is in BD, June 20, 1944.

316 "Of course": Personal interview with General Lucius Clay, September 1976.

316 "new conditions": EP, p. 1937.

316 "AFHQ apparently fails": EP, p. 1938

317 "wanted ANVIL . . . Trieste": KSD, June 22, 1944.

317 "This is the worst weather I have ever seen": J.S.D. Eisenhower, *Strictly Personal,* p. 67.

318 "their friendship was all the more remarkable": *Ibid.,* p. 68.

318 "OVERLORD is the decisive campaign of 1944": EP, p. 1943.

318 "unacceptable": Informal JCS reply to BCOS, quoted in full in message from Marshall to Eisenhower dated 24 June 1944 in DDE.

319 "our situation is *not repeat not* as good": EP, p. 1941.

319 "withdrawal from present positions is punishable by death": Bradley, *A Soldier's Story,* p. 307.

320 American breakout: Several postwar accounts would claim that Eisenhower and Bradley on the twenty-fourth decided on a strategy of breakout in the American sector. This claim appears to be a matter of semantics in that such a strategy had been implicit in all Allied planning, though even the most carefully laid plans were subject to the dictate of events and German countermoves. At most, Eisenhower and Bradley that day could only predict—not decide upon—the likely outcome of the battle. One may assume that a "decision" to break out in the American sector served Eisenhower's purpose of emphasizing to Bradley the urgency of expediting the capture of Cherbourg.

320 Eisenhower was "moody": Bradley, *A General's Life,* p. 264.

320 "under strain": Wilmot, *The Struggle for Europe,* p. 319.

320 "which may not obtain too long": Quote from letter Eisenhower wrote Bradley on the twenty-fifth following up on their talks. EP, p. 1948.

320 "John, the people are now convinced": J.S.D. Eisenhower, *Strictly Personal,* p. 72.

321 "Soldier, how many experts": Bradley, *A Soldier's Story,* p. 311.

321 "There was no sight in the war": Eisenhower, *Crusade in Europe,* p. 261.

322 "no difficulty in the breakthrough to the Po": Smuts's report is quoted by Churchill in *Triumph and Tragedy,* p. 53.

322 "decisive" . . . "wisdom of General Eisenhower releasing landing craft": Quotes are from the text of the BCOS and JCS memos exchanged on the subject and forwarded to Eisenhower by Marshall on June 27. DDE, Marshall Correspondence.

323 "arbitrary" . . . "help Eisenhower": Kimball, *Churchill and Roosevelt,* vol. III, p. 212.

323 "History will not forgive": From BCOS reply of June 28, in Pogue, *Organizer of Victory,* p. 413.

323 "the bleak and sterile Toulon-Marseilles operation": Quotes are taken from the text of Churchill's lengthy message to Roosevelt, reprinted in full in Kimball, vol. III, pp. 214–21.

324 "All right, if you insist on being damned fools": Bryant, p. 168.

324 "the definite purpose": Phone call is noted in KSD, June 29, and

the quote is from Eisenhower's message to Marshall on the twenty-ninth. EP, p. 1598.

324 "For several natural and very human reasons": Kimball, vol. III, p. 222.

325 "done . . . in case the enemy": Churchill, *Triumph and Tragedy,* p. 57.

325 "bound to pay": Bryant, p. 120.

325 As for the German situation, Wilmot relates Jodl's interview in the German press in November 1943 in which Jodl is quoted as saying, "All the cowards are seeking a way out, or—as they call it—a political solution. They say that we must negotiate while there is something in hand. . . . They attack the people's instinct that in this war there can only be a fight to a finish. Capitulation is the end of the Nation, the end of Germany" (Wilmot, p. 165).

326 "directly fatal effect": Gackenholz, in Jacobsen and Rohwer, eds., *Decisive Battles,* p. 357.

326 "They are bound to wear themselves out": Quoted in Wilmot, p. 146.

326–27 On the subject of Hitler's relationship with his generals, see Wilmot, p. 161: "To a great extent Hitler's wide military reading and his extraordinary memory for detail made good his lack of professional training, and in one respect this deficiency was a decided advantage *as long as Germany held the initiative.* He possessed a radical approach to almost every problem and his military thinking was untrammeled by the conventional ideas, standing regulations and established procedures which cramped the mind and limited the imagination of the regular German officers."

327 For German division estimates, see Stamps and Esposito, p. 264.

327 On "strong points," see Gackenholz, in Jacobsen and Rohwer, *Decisive Battles,* p. 360. A strong point was a fortress position whose commander had given his personal oath that it would not be abandoned "without express permission, and that, failing such permission, they would hold out to the last." The purpose of such positions was to tie up strong enemy forces in the event of a breakthrough by threatening Russian supply lines and dissipating the driving force of the offensive.

328 "submit clear proofs": Gackenholz, *Ibid.,* p. 363.

328 "spirit of resignation": *Ibid.,* p. 364.

328–29 The numerous accounts of Hitler's visit to Soissons derive from three eyewitness accounts: (1) Speidel's in his memoir *We Defended Normandy;* (2) Rommel's in Liddell Hart's *The Rommel Papers;* (3) Blumentritt's interrogation, quoted in Liddell Hart's *The Other Side of the Hill.*

PAGE

329   "Do you believe this war can be won?": Exchange cited by Ruge, in Jacobsen and Rohwer, eds., *Decisive Battles,* pp. 340–41.

329   "in view of the great superiority": Winterbotham, *The Ultra Secret,* p. 196.

330   "What shall we do?": See, among other sources, Wilmot, *The Struggle for Europe,* p. 347.

331   Army Group's position was "critical": Gackenholz, in Jacobsen and Rohwer, eds., *Decisive Battles,* p. 368.

331   "pinched off": Liddell Hart, *History of the Second World War,* p. 579

331   "to be held at all costs": Gackenholz, in Jacobsen and Rohwer, eds., *Decisive Battles,* p. 369.

331   "veiled" withdrawals: Liddell Hart, *History of the Second World War,* p. 579.

334   "lack of insight": Gackenholz, in Jacobsen and Rohwer, eds., *Decisive Battles,* p. 369.

334   "new and far-reaching objectives": *Ibid.,* p. 372–73.

334   "their reduced forces were inadequate": Liddell Hart, *History of the Second World War,* p. 580.

335   "Allied forces have liberated Cherbourg": Stalin to Churchill, quoted in Churchill, *Triumph and Tragedy,* p. 19.

335   Harriman letter is in DDE, Box 50, Harriman Correspondence (I).

335   "professional envy": Personal interview.

335–36   On Germany strategy: Finally, General Kurt Dittmer, an official German military commentator, conceded publicly in early July that "the defense of the Reich" would now necessitate a "radical straightening of the whole [Russian] front," a concession that reads both as an effort to place the best light on things and a rationalization for actions already imposed on the German army by the Russian breakthrough. Dittmer's comments were a significant departure, however, in that for the first time an official German spokesman was conceding that the German strategy in Russia was essentially defensive. Thus, six months after the High Command had first advocated a "straightened front," the Nazi government was prepared to go along and, presumably, make a virtue of it. Noting Dittmer's statements, *The Nation* cautioned against drawing optimistic conclusions from the German disasters, writing: "The stage seems set not for an early peace but for a Wagnerian Götterdämmerung. Even if the nerves of the Führer should fail, there remains the danger that those of their troops, such as the SS, will not fail . . . fanatics who have at their command the technology which the last armies of fanatics, the Mahdi

PAGE

and the Chinese Boxers, did not possess" (*The Nation,* August 5, 1944).

336 "cannot . . . insure his unit": SHAEF Weekly Intelligence Summary No. 16.

336 Jodl interrogation on the impact of destroying 30 Allied divisions: 26 July 1945, "Re: Ardennes," p. 13.

336 "It is not clear whether Hitler proposes": Montgomery directive, 6-30-44; copy in BD, p. 1455.

336 "knowing what to expect": Smuts to Churchill, in Churchill, *Triumph and Tragedy,* p. 21.

336 "not entirely European": Bryant, p. 180.

337 "An intense impression must be made on the Americans": Churchill, *Triumph and Tragedy,* p. 589.

337 Farago, *Burn After Reading,* p. 259.

337 "mentioned the Spanish explanation": BD, July 10, 1944 (bulk of this conversation is reprinted in BDP).

338 "urgent need for the development of an aggressive spirit": Quote is from First Army after-action report on Normany, quoted in Weigley, *Eisenhower's Lieutenants,* p. 126.

339 "fought with a tenacity and a ferocity": Wilmot, p. 343.

339 "airmen who still believed": Bradley, *A General's Life,* p. 278.

340 Eisenhower leaned against it: Eisenhower, *Crusade in Europe,* p. 264.

340 "frittered away strength": SHAEF Weekly Intelligence Summary No. 16.

341 "always been to draw the main enemy force": All quotes from Montgomery's June 30 directive. BD, p. 1455.

342 "a general operation to exploit": Summary of LUCKY STRIKE: Weigley, *Eisenhower's Lieutenants,* p. 119. Weigley notes a similarity between the June 30 directive and LUCKY STRIKE in that both implied "the Americans must be next to move the ball" (*Ibid.,* p. 120).

342 "indefinitely": See Weigley, *Eisenhower's Lieutenants,* p. 120.

343 "resist . . . to my utmost": Bradley, *A General's Life,* p. 269. Bradley further notes that LUCKY STRIKE was a proposal, "in effect [to] *abandon* the OVERLORD plan and concentrate all our efforts on a drive on Pas de Calais" (*Ibid.,* p. 268).

343 "oppressive": Quote from Hansen diary, in Weigley, *Eisenhower's Lieutenants,* p. 120.

344 British manpower crisis: According to Irving, Montgomery was being warned by the British Adjutant General "that he could no longer rely on drafts from England to replace his casualties; there

simply were no more British reserves" (Irving, *The War Between the Generals,* p. 191).

345 "anything you might wish to discuss": Tedder, *With Prejudice,* pp. 554–55.

345 "shoulder to shoulder": Eisenhower's phrase. EP, p. 2019.

345 "I do not think that great and good man": Montgomery, *Memoirs,* p. 234.

346 "Montgomery is expecting a heavy counterattack": KSD, June 30, 1944.

346 "The first impression . . . was of rain": James Gault, "General Eisenhower's Visit to France." Copy is in BD.

346 "reminiscent to Ike of Tunisia": BDP, p. 604.

346 "This consideration . . . was always uppermost in Montgomery's mind": Personal interview, October 1976.

346 "a hole": Bradley, *A Soldier's Story,* p. 318.

347 "not only did its tall, bombed church": *Ibid.,* p. 294.

347 "Political considerations are obvious": Bradley, *A General's Life,* p. 268.

347 "This was the day": Gault, in BD, July 3, 1944.

347 "Isn't it facing New York?": *Ibid.*

348 "No surprise to us": FA, July 4, 1944.

348 "All right, Brad": Gault, in BD, July 4, 1944.

348 "loneliness": Eisenhower, *Crusade in Europe,* p. 314.

348 "Except for occasional flashes of enemy artillery": Gault, in BD, July 4, 1944.

348 "difficult time": Eisenhower, *Crusade in Europe,* p. 263.

349 "most of the people I know": BDP, p. 585.

349 V-1 data: Brown, *Bodyguard of Lies,* p. 727.

349 "the one important factor in which we enjoy tremendous superiority": EP, p. 1946.

349 Eisenhower memo to Tedder: EP, 1960.

350 "did not like them": Press conference quoted in BDP, pp. 608–9.

350 "What will be their application in our hands?": Tedder, *With Prejudice,* p. 583.

350 "a sort of grim jest": Hanson Baldwin, quoted by Charles Bolte, in "The War Fronts," *The Nation,* August 5, 1944.

350 "who knows whither": Churchill, *Triumph and Tragedy,* p. 69.

350 "that Germany is in a state of crisis": SHAEF Weekly Intelligence Summary No. 14, June 24, 1944.

351 "So far as His Majesty's Government are concerned": Atlee's address quoted in Brown, p. 740.

351 "leak" that Patton had been replaced: EP, p, 1991.

352 "demanded from the air": EP, pp. 1982–83.

PAGE

352 "I am myself quite happy about the situation": A copy of Montgomery's letter is in BD, July 10, 1944.

354 "While his troops are exhausted": SHAEF Weekly Intelligence Summary No. 19.

354 "operations of the Second Army": Copy of Montgomery directive in BD, July 11, 1944, p. 1489.

356 "Ike spoke to Beedle about using Bomber Command": BDP, p. 612.

357 "to keep in the closest possible touch": Tedder, *With Prejudice,* p. 554.

358 "stagnation" . . . "who could neither be removed nor moved to action": Tedder, p. 559.

359 "incurable defensive-mindedness": Wilmot, *The Struggle for Europe,* p. 338. Among other things, Wilmot attributes Morgan's attitude to antipathy felt for Montgomery owing to Montgomery's rejection of the revised SHAEF plan and the fact that Morgan considered himself the "expert on the operation."

359 "drive across the Orne from Caen": See Smith, memorandum for Chief, Historical Section, dated February 22, 1945, in BSP, Collection of World War II Documents, Box 27.

359 "quick exoneration": Bradley, *A Soldier's Story,* p. 335.

359 "undermining [Montgomery's] plan of command": Wilmot, p. 341.

359 "displaced strategists": Montgomery, *Memoirs,* pp. 230–35.

360 In recalling his visit, Stimson tells how he exchanged D-Day congratulations "with his friend and former adversary, the Prime Minister." "It is wonderful, a great triumph," said the PM, and Stimson did not see any need to quarrel when Mr. Churchill added, "But we never could have done it last year" (Stimson and Bundy, *On Active Service,* p. 445).

361 "A far larger Army than we now have. . . ." and "I am sure demands will be made": Churchill, *Triumph and Tragedy,* pp. 588–89, 593.

361–62 "evidence of a change in mind": Tedder, p. 561.

362 "would burst into flames": Montgomery's message of July 12, in DDE, Montgomery Correspondence (1).

362 Again, what were Montgomery's intentions? On this subject, see Liddell Hart, *History of the Second World War,* p. 553: "This miscarriage has long been enshrouded in mystery," he writes. "Eisenhower . . . spoke of an intended 'breakthrough' and a drive . . . exploiting in the direction of the Seine basin and Paris. But all the British histories written after the war declare that it had

PAGE

no such far-reaching aims, and that no breakthrough on this flank
was ever contemplated.

"They [the British accounts] follow Montgomery's own account, which insisted that this operation was merely a 'battle of
position,' designed to create a 'threat' in aid of the coming American breakout blow 'and secondly to secure ground on which major
forces could be poised ready to strike out to the south and southeast, when the American breakout forces thrust eastwards to meet
them.' "

362   "So pepped up": EP, p. 2002.

363   "negotiations with the British": BDP, p. 614.

363   "in order to bring personalities in the news": *Ibid.*, pp. 614–15.

363   "Beedle tells me": EP, pp. 2012–13.

364   "Undoubtedly he has some feeling . . . that he has always been
        carefully watched over": Eisenhower, *Letters to Mamie*, p. 191.

364   "humdrum existence": *Ibid.*, p. 194.

364   "maybe there is no such thing": *Ibid.*, p. 196.

364   "How glad I'll be when this is over": *Ibid.*

365   "a bastion on which the whole future": Wilmot, p. 354.

365   "[Eisenhower] just wants Montgomery to keep pressing": KSD,
        July 18, 1944.

366   "I am willing to lose 200–300 tanks": Wilmot; p. 356.

366   "draw up his administrative tail": BD, July 19, 1944.

366   "rejoiced on his gains": BDP, p. 617.

366   "fog which touched the ground": BD, July 19, 1944.

367   "satisfaction" . . . "battle of position": Liddell Hart, *History of the
        Second World War*, p. 556.

367   "anything Eisenhower wished to do": BDP, p. 617.

367   "limited the field of available replacements": BD, July 20, 1944.

367   "War Cabinet issue": BD, July 19, 1944.

367   "alone": KSD, July 19, 1944.

367   "tendency of the Prime Minister": Bryant, p. 175.

368   "blue as indigo": BDP, p. 618.

368   "Even if I have to swim": *Ibid.*

368   "full of confidence . . . single annihilating stroke": Wilmot, p. 362.

369   GOODWOOD losses: Tute, Costello, and Hughes, p. 248.

369   "Monty says it is up to Bradley to go ahead": KSD, July 20, 1944.

369   "How he will handle this situation": BDP, p. 619.

369   "If I speak to you today": *New York Times*, July 21, 1944.

370   "for the benefit and instruction of the reader": Churchill, *Tri-
        umph and Tragedy*, p. 23.

371   "simple invention": Eisenhower, *Crusade in Europe*, p. 259.

371   "in cats and dogs": FA, July 21, 1944.

PAGE

371 "excited about it": BDP, p. 620.

372 "German resistance, in other words, would stiffen?": *Ibid.* My quote. "In other words," Butcher wrote, paraphrasing Strong, "there might be a renascence of fighting spirit in Germany."

372 Many at the time questioned the authenticity of the July 20 plot. "Was there really a bomb or was the incident manufactured?" asked Walter Mehring in *The Nation*. Mehring suggested parallels between the episode and trumped-up incidents used to justify Hitler's purges in 1933–1934 and interpreted the affair as little more than part of the ongoing Nazi-Army struggle to transfer blame for the German disaster on the other. "Neither will succeed and both will go down together," he predicted, "for there is no group left in Germany which can be used as a scapegoat." Nehring, "The Last of the Scapegoats," *The Nation*, July 29, 1944.

372 "tying up tremendous air power": Irving, *The War Between the Generals*, p. 167.

372 OVERLORD buildup would "collapse": *Ibid.*, p. 559.

372 "good firm bridgehead": Montgomery directive is in BD.

373 "serious political questions": EP, p. 2018.

373 "any intention of stopping": DDE, Montgomery Correspondence (1).

373 "expressed in his own way": BDP, p. 621.

374 "Meeting—the War Room": KSD, July 23, 1944.

374 "historic opportunity": Tedder, *With Prejudice*, p. 565.

374 "the expression of my views": *Ibid.*, p. 569.

374 "doubts regarding this question": From Stalin's message to Churchill on July 15. Reprinted in Churchill, *Triumph and Tragedy*, p. 68.

375 "so conscious of Britain's ebbing manpower": BDP, p. 622.

376 "quite frightful": Montgomery to Eisenhower, dated July 24, 1944. The letter is a detailed outline of how Montgomery's "broad plan" contained in his latest directive was to work. In it, he described the resuming offensive, to begin with Bradley's "opening gambit" west of St.-Lô, which would turn into a "grand-scale operation." Montgomery proceeded to describe the favorable situation on the eastern flank. With the "bottleneck" of Caen behind Dempsey, the British Second Army was prepared to "draw enemy attention . . . to that side [eastern flank]" and to maintain a "definite and continuous threat" toward Falaise *while* the Third U.S. Army was swinging southward and eastward on the western flank. Since the U.S. Third Army was not scheduled for activation until after Hodges' breakout, Montgomery appeared to be saying that the British Second Army had discharged its obligation to

support the breakout attack and would await the results of Bradley's offensive before undertaking any more diversionary operations. Montgomery's left-right-left-right scenario, which followed, described the full-scale Second Army movement, which again would go forward in stages after Bradley's "opening gambit." In short, his concession was to consent to commence the preparations for what he described as practically an independent Second Army offensive earlier than planned. Document is in DDE, 2nd Army (1).

377   "My high hopes and best wishes": EP, p. 2027.

377   "Prime Minister, what do your people think?": BDP, p. 623.

378   "It is immaterial whether such a bomb": Letter quoted in Wilmot, p. 364.

378   "a likely member": FA, July 22, 1944.

379   "guileless": Bradley, *A Soldier's Story,* p. 336.

379   "a quick power drive": Stamps and Esposito, p. 412.

379   "sweep south . . ." and turn the corner: Bradley, *A Soldier's Story,* pp. 317, 330.

379   "his face set in a chilly stare": *Ibid.,* p. 334.

380   "Scads of aircraft overhead": BD, July 25, 1944.

380   "moon landscape": So described by General Fritz Bayerlein: "*Mondlandschaft*—a landscape on the moon, all craters and death" (Stamps and Esposito, p. 414).

381   "We're good soldiers, Courtney": FA, July 25, 1944.

381   "lost all faith in bombers": Bradley, *A Soldier's Story,* p. 349.

381   "The slow beginning": BDP, p. 625.

381   "day of suspense": Weigley, *Eisenhower's Lieutenants,* p. 155.

382   "tired of Montgomery's always stopping": Sherwood, *Roosevelt and Hopkins,* p. 811.

382   "we sensed that the initial crisis had passed": Bradley, *A Soldier's Story,* p. 358.

382   "My news this evening . . . is very sketchy": EP, p. 2028.

382   "Collins to throw everything in": FA, July 27, 1944.

382   "[worried] that the war would be over before he got in it": Blumenson, *The Patton Papers,* p. 482.

383   "I drew his attention to what your basic strategy had been": Bryant, p. 181.

383   "to step on the gas for Vire": Smith, Memo of 22 February 1945, p. 10. DDE, Box 154.

384   "This shows that while Ike has reasonably good teamwork": BDP, p. 627.

384   "to elucidate lessons learned": Tedder, p. 572.

384   "special situations" . . . "act as a drug": *Ibid.*

384 "had collapsed" . . . "ripped open": Wilmot, p. 395.

384 "quiet grunt of satisfaction": Winterbotham, *The Ultra Secret,* p. 146.

385 "[Eisenhower] slept late": KSD, July 30, 1944.

6 Pursuit

386 "August—the month when wars usually start": Bryant, p. 183.

389 "dangling loosely and in distress": Bradley, *A Soldier's Story,* p. 369.

389 "task of completing the destruction": Phrase taken from Eisenhower's message to Marshall, August 2, in EP, p. 2049.

389 "policy of taking up a firm defensive": EP, p. 2043.

390 "questioning and apparent dissension" . . . and "how it is to be achieved": Quotes from BDP, p. 639, and EP, p. 2074.

390 "Ike is impatient": BDP, p. 632.

390 "to hell and gone": BDP, pp. 630–31.

391 "the decision in the whole battle of France depends": Quoted in Brown, *Bodyguard of Lies,* p. 784.

391 "in view of the extreme importance": Winterbotham, *The Ultra Secret,* p. 149. Full text is quoted in Stamps and Esposito, *A Military History of World War II,* p. 423.

391 Bradley's claim that he received no word of the ULTRA exchanges until the sixth appears in Bradley, *A General's Life,* p. 291. Bradley goes on to question Winterbotham's specific "recollection" that in fact the Kluge-Hitler exchanges were intercepted. But Winterbotham's "recollection" is too specific to be doubted. Other sources, including the Patton diaries, Eisenhower's papers, and the First Army diary, contain evidence that the Allies were aware of LUTTICH several days in advance.

391 "to the best of my knowledge and conscience": Stamps and Esposito, p. 423.

391 "without taking into consideration": General Warlimont postwar interrogations, quoted in Stamps and Esposito, p. 424.

391 "contain the enemy": Item No. 3, "The Preparation of the German Ardennes Counteroffensive" (Sept.–16 Dec. 1944), p. 22. Document is Part I of a manuscript prepared by P. E. Schramm on the offensive. BSP, Box 40.

392 "not proven its superior skills": Jodl interrogation, August 2,

1945. BSP, Collection of World War II Documents, Box 40, Interviews with German Officers (2).

392   "the attack to split the American forces": Winterbotham, p. 150.

392   "war-winning drive": Bradley, *A General's Life,* p. 290.

392   Eisenhower had probably reached his decision to push spearheads eastward from Avranches the day before, as indicated by Eisenhower's message to Montgomery on the second in which he had suggested that German disintegration in the Avranches area would now permit "armored and mobile *columns . . .* to operate boldly against the enemy's flank," noting that "unlimited" capacity existed to supply spearheads by air. It appears likely that prompting the conference on the third was Montgomery's unwillingness or inability to order such a risky maneuver involving American forces on his own authority. See EP, p. 2048.

394   "looking very much like the newspapers": KSD, August 4, 1944.

395   "decisive battle": Churchill, *Triumph and Tragedy,* p. 57.

395   "backing up your suggestion": DDE, Box 21, Churchill (2).

396   "[what] ANVIL was meant for is already gained": Lifted from Churchill's message to Harry Hopkins one day later, in which the Prime Minister, for a final time, appealed for compromise. Churchill, *Triumph and Tragedy,* p. 58.

396   "finishing up Hitler this year": The accounts of this meeting are drawn from Butcher's diary; Eisenhower, *Crusade in Europe,* James Nelson, ed., *General Eisenhower on the Military Churchill;* and the messages surrounding it.

396   "Ike said no": BDP, p. 634.

397   Eisenhower-Cooke interview: Quoted from Nelson, *General Eisenhower on the Military Churchill,* pp. 40, 42–43.

397   "strongly opposed": "Who has been double crossing whom?" Brooke wrote. "In any case, we have certainly not improved our relations with the Americans": Bryant, p. 185.

397   "unwavering" support: "It is possible that the Prime Minister may have misconstrued or misunderstood my stated opinion on these matters," Eisenhower wrote Marshall, "but I have never wavered for a moment from the convictions [pro-ANVIL] above expressed" (EP, p. 2055–56).

398   "return to the subject": BDP, p. 635.

398   "the Prime Minister was rebuffed": *Ibid.*

398   "the Seine or further": Wilmot, p. 401.

398   "From the general trend": DDE, Montgomery Correspondence (1).

398   "now or never attempt": FA, August 9, 1944.

398   "more than four to eight weeks": Wilmot, p. 411. See also BDP,

PAGE

p. 637. Butcher quotes Crerar as saying "flatly" the war would end "in three weeks."

399 "decimating the Panzers": Irving, *The War Between the Generals,* p. 242.

399 "this kind of talk": BDP, p. 637.

399 "logistically untenable": Weigley, *Eisenhower's Lieutenants,* p. 199.

400 "the greatest tactical blunder": Bradley, *A General's Life,* p. 294.

400 Tactical and strategic envelopment. Months earlier, on February 19, Eisenhower had alluded to the merits and demerits of envelopment as a tactic and strategy in a cable to Marshall on the use of airborne troops on D-Day for this purpose. "The German has shown time and again that he does not particularly fear what we used to refer to as a 'strategic threat of envelopment,' " he wrote. "Any military man that might have been required to analyze, before this war, the situation that existed in Italy on about January 24, would have said that the only hope of the German was to begin the instant and rapid withdrawal of his troops in front of the Fifth Army" (EP, pp. 1737–38).

401 "solid shoulder": Bradley, *A Soldier's Story,* p. 377.

401 "seize the unforgiving minute": Blumenson, *The Patton Papers,* p. 523.

401 "great leader for exploiting a mobile situation": Eisenhower, *Crusade in Europe,* p. 275.

401 "Patton was an operational commander": EP, p. 2060, fn. 4.

401 "practically an open flank": EP, p. 2059.

402–3 Account of Eisenhower's meeting with Morgenthau is based on Eisenhower, *Crusade in Europe,* p. 287, and Lyon, *Eisenhower: Portrait of a Hero,* pp. 316–17.

403 Cannon memorandum on Morgenthau allegations: EP, vol. IX, p. 1877.

403 Patton's "coolness": Bradley, *A General's Life,* p. 294.

404 "with a nod": Smith, *Eisenhower's Six Great Decisions,* p. 60.

404 "far from comforting": Churchill, *Triumph and Tragedy,* p. 59.

404 "be in the negative": *Ibid.*

404 "actual and potential strength as a bludgeon": EP, p. 2065.

405 "essential to concentrate": Eisenhower's version of his talk with Churchill in BDP, p. 644.

405 "to get his agreement to change my orders": Nelson, *Eisenhower on the Military Churchill,* p. 42.

405 "any desire on the part of any responsible person": EP, p. 2065.

406 On the slender hope for a phased surrender, see Churchill's memo to Ismay dated August 23. In it, Churchill forwarded a suggestion

to publish "a list of war criminals . . . not . . . more than fifty to a hundred long"; these criminals were to be executed when captured, an action he hoped would "open a gulf between the persons named . . . and the rest of the population. It is very important to show the German people that they are not on the same footing as Hitler, Goering, Himmler and the other monsters, who will be infallibly destroyed" (Churchill, *Triumph and Tragedy,* p. 599).

407 Overture of August II: Brown, p. 792. Something like Kluge's alleged overture was anticipated. The CCS on the sixteenth went so far as to instruct Eisenhower on the policy he was to adopt in the event of "large-scale local capitulations by German forces surrendering in units through their commanders."

According to the CCS, such surrenders were to be accepted, but they were "in no way to 'prejudice' *fixed* terms of total surrender of Germany." All forces under the control of a surrendering general were to join in the capitulation, to agree to lay down arms and "obey all orders issued by UNITED NATIONS Commander as to their disposal." All surrenders were to be superceded by the general instructions "imposed" by the U.S., U.K., and U.S.S.R. and applied to Germany as a whole.

407 "one more battle": BDP, p. 642.

408 "Always be optimistic": Eisenhower, *Letters to Mamie,* pp. 204–5.

408 "refused to be trapped": FA, August 12, 1944.

409 Bradley writes in both his memoirs of his regret about not closing the ring at Chambois immediately. In both, Bradley attributes what he calls a "shattering disappointment" to British caution at Falaise and to Montgomery's refusal to alter the Argentan boundary, which he does not explain fully. Nor does Bradley fully explain why he and Eisenhower did not press Montgomery for a change in the boundaries or press Montgomery harder for aggressive action at Falaise to close the pocket. Again, it would seem that the simplest explanation for Montgomery's lack of aggressiveness and Bradley's neglect to push for more aggressive British actions was a tacit agreement between the two that an attempt to close the encirclement ring was not likely to work and was probably too risky in terms of Allied casualties.

411 "above all, a plan": Montgomery, *Memoirs,* p. 239.

412 "a solid mass of some 40 divisions": Churchill, *Triumph and Tragedy,* p. 239.

412 "*positioned*": *Ibid.*

413 "feelingly and earnestly": BDP, p. 645.

413 "the astonishing success": Paraphrased in BDP, p. 647.

PAGE

414   "to destroy representative government": The quote is from Eisenhower's recollection of these meetings four years later shortly after he learned of Forrestal's suicide. "There is no use trying, after his death, to decide exactly what I thought of Jim Forrestal," he wrote. "But one thing I shall always remember. He was the one man who, in the very midst of war, always counseled caution and alertness in dealing with the Soviets. He visited me in 1944 and in 1945 and I listened very carefully to his thesis—I never had cause to doubt the accuracy of his judgment on this point. He said, 'Be courteous and friendly in the effort to develop a satisfactory modus vivendi, but never believe we have changed [the Soviets'] basic purpose, which is to destroy representative government' " (*The Eisenhower Diaries,* ed. Ferrell, p. 160).

415   "destroy all bridges": Weigley, *Eisenhower's Lieutenants,* p. 250.

416   "stay put": FA, August 20, 1944.

416   "menace to the Allied flank": EP, p. 2088.

417   "for all practical purposes": Weigley, *Eisenhower's Lieutenants,* p. 268.

420   "linking up the whole front": Eisenhower, *Crusade in Europe,* p. 226.

420   "the existing system is undisturbed": EP, pp. 2090–1.

421   "firm and sound plan": Montgomery, *Memoirs,* p. 241.

421–22   All quotes in the account of this conference are from Montgomery, *Memoirs,* pp. 241–43.

423   "difference in urgency": *Ibid.,* p. 244.

423   "access to research centers": BDP, August 14, p. 643.

423–24   "enthusiastic" . . . "bend every effort": EP, pp. 2090–91.

424   "sufficient strength": EP, pp. 2092–94.

424   "complete disorder": Churchill's quote from Leclerc's letter to De Gaulle describing the event, in *Triumph and Tragedy,* pp. 30–31.

425   "proceed with cleaning up the city": FA, August 26, 1944.

427   "unruly elements": Ambrose, *The Supreme Commander,* p. 486.

430   "Winning the war": FA, August 15, 1944.

431   "a meaningful clue": Bradley, *A Soldier's Story,* p. 409.

431   "the enemy nevertheless": Quoted by Weigley, *Eisenhower's Lieutenants,* p. 257.

432   "grave split": Tedder, *With Prejudice,* p. 587.

432   "internal dissension": EP, pp. 2100–1.

433   "make the decisive choice": Bryant, pp. 195, 213.

434   "inevitable" . . . "add three to six months": *Ibid.,* p. 196.

434   Brooke's account of his meeting with Montgomery. See *Ibid.*

434   "every foot the Germans lost": BDP, p. 653.

435   "Inevitably, we will be checked": BDP, p. 655.

435 "little instances that seemed": EP, p. 2108.

436 "The action of the supreme command": From Jodl interrogations of July 25 and August 2, in BSP, Collection of World War II Documents, Interrogations (2).

437 "The best is to have such a position": *Ibid.,* August 2. Note: In his postwar interrogation, General Warlimont of OKW estimated it was on August 31 that the word "west wall" was used for the first time. This was two days after Model was forced to abandon the Seine line in disorder and it became apparent that holding the Somme line "was out of the question." Interrogator: "Who did finally mention it?" Warlimont: "I believe Jodl mentioned it [the west wall]. Jodl was able to do these things and had the courage to do it, and Hitler would permit him to get away with it."

437 "not many miles from the Belgium border": FA, September 1, 1944.

438 "extravagant supply requirements": Bradley, *A Soldier's Story,* p. 401.

438 "would have nothing left" . . . "pontifical": Blumenson, *The Patton Papers,* p. 537.

439 "curl up": FA, September 1, 1944.

440 "completely out of touch": Montgomery, *Memoirs,* p. 243.

440 "E. stays in bed": KSD, September 3, 1944.

440 "was scattered and incoherent": Wilmot, p. 474.

441 A word should be said here about when Eisenhower and Bradley learned about MARKET GARDEN. Bradley's first account of the whole episode, written in 1951, dates his first awareness of the plan as coming shortly after Eisenhower had approved it around the eleventh of September. Bradley's second account, in *A General's Life,* published in 1983, is slightly confusing on the point, but fixes Bradley's awareness of the plan as coming much earlier, and, indeed, claims that Bradley had an opportunity to thrash it out with Eisenhower *before* Eisenhower approved it. Bradley's second account is accepted by the author as the more accurate of the two, for it was written after several sources became available which indicate that the Americans were aware of the British planning afoot for airborne operations somewhere in Holland well before Eisenhower's meeting with Montgomery in Brussels on the tenth to discuss MARKET GARDEN. Significantly, MARKET GARDEN was not a mature plan when Eisenhower approved it on the tenth, and it was being planned simultaneously with COMET, a plan for a British offensive in Holland on the Venlo-Wesel axis, close in on Hodges' left flank. Dempsey preferred COMET, and so Montgomery's selection of MARKET GARDEN was a rejection of Dempsey's

(and Bradley's) advice that the 21st Army Group should not wander away from the U.S. First Army and open a gap between the two forces. Why did Montgomery choose MARKET GARDEN? General Kenneth Strong suggested one possible answer when, describing the affair, he wrote: "Eisenhower had not only to consider this wider strategy of campaign, but also to give due weight to the views of those immediately subordinate to him. Montgomery, now a Field Marshal, was the Chief British Commander and in close touch with Churchill and the British Chiefs of Staff. Montgomery's views were generally those of the British government and it was therefore extremely important not to turn down proposals out of hand . . . but in the end national considerations were subordinated to what were, in his view, the correct military solutions" (*Intelligence at the Top,* p. 203).

441 "certain as anything in war can be": See EP, p. 2092, fn. 1.

442 "attempt" to advance through Holland: Bradley, *A General's Life,* p. 327.

446 "equivalent" . . . "nominal": See SHAEF Weekly Intelligence Report No. 25, dated September 9. "The enemy's army has suffered a considerable deflation since the last publication of this summary," the report notes. "Some fifty further infantry divisions have been 'written off' . . . as being fluff only: the great bulk of these were on the eastern front, which had been even more inflated than the western. The total [of German Army divisions on all fronts] is brought down by these means to about 260 divisions, which of course is still very greatly in excess of real strength. . . . The number of enemy divisions in the west is put this week at a nominal forty-eight, including eleven Panzer divisions and three Panzer Grenadier divisions. . . . The *true* strength of these forty-eight divisions is estimated at twenty-four divisions . . . P2/PG Nominal (14) = Panzer (4), Infantry (Nominal) 34 = Infantry (20) > ." The report does not explain what criteria guided the G-2 staff in halving German strength in the west, but the potential for self-deception in such sweeping and summary evaluations seems to have been great.

447 "no hard or fast decision": FA, September 4, 1944.

447 "The general consensus": *Ibid.*

448 "reached a stage": Montgomery to Eisenhower, 2056, September 4, 1944. Text in BSP.

449 Memorandum for the record: *The Eisenhower Diaries,* ed. Ferrell, p. 127.

450 "The decision on the 79th division is final": FA, September 5, 1944.

PAGE

451 "though justified by events": Bryant, p. 200.

451 "frame up": *Ibid.,* p. 202.

451 "strong basis": Churchill, *Triumph and Tragedy,* p. 602.

451 On Churchill's view that the JIC report erred on the side of optimism, see Churchill, *Triumph and Tragedy,* p. 169. Note: According to Sherwood, Roosevelt agreed with Churchill, predicting at one point that the invasion of Germany would be a very difficult undertaking. As for the prospects of a "phased" German surrender in the next four weeks, Roosevelt was "less optimistic than most" (Sherwood, *Roosevelt and Hopkins,* p. 818).

452 "wonderful spirit of cooperation": Bryant, p. 207.

452 "sticky about their possessions in the Pacific": Sherwood, p. 716. Quote is from a memorandum of conversation between Eden and Roosevelt on Eden's visit to Washington in March 1943 to explore (a) American views on the postwar settlement and (b) methods for proceeding. A crucial point which these talks clarified was Roosevelt's view that he, the President, would be more effective in concluding postwar agreements acting in his constitutional capacity as Commander in Chief rather than as Chief Diplomat. This, in effect, told Eden that if agreements were to be reached with the Soviets, they had to be reached during, not after, the war and that, moreover, *formal* American approval for what the Soviets were bound to claim in Eastern Europe in the form of territory might never be possible.

452 "no sooner offered than accepted": Churchill, *Triumph and Tragedy,* p. 130.

452 "press on with all speed": *Ibid.,* p. 134.

453 "full collaboration in the military and commercial application": Sherwood, p. 703.

453 "in a blaze of friendship": Churchill, *Triumph and Tragedy,* p. 133.

455 "the tragedy is that the Americans": Bryant, p. 208.

455 "making Germans stand in soup lines": Burns, *Roosevelt, Soldier of Freedom,* p. 520. Note: Behind the scenes, Churchill was telling his entourage that he opposed the Morgenthau plan. According to Lord Moran, Churchill "did not seem happy about all this toughness" and muttered at one point that he agreed with Sir Edmund Burke: "You cannot indict a whole nation." Churchill's excuse for adopting the plan was Morgenthau's idea that the de-industrialization of Germany would secure Western Europe as a market for British industrial goods after the war. Moran, *Churchill,* pp. 190–91.

Note: Burns says that the statement on the treatment of postwar Germany approved at Quebec was dictated personally by Churchill. The statement drew attention to the fact that the "ease with which metallurgical, chemical and electrical industries in Germany can be converted from peace to war has been impressed upon us by bitter experience. It must also be remembered that the Germans have devastated a large portion of the industries in Russia and of neighboring Allies, and it is only in accordance with justice that these injured countries should be entitled to remove the machinery they require in order to regain the losses they have suffered. The industries referred to in the Ruhr and in the Saar would therefore be necessarily put out of action and closed down. . . .

"The program for eliminating the war-making industries in the Ruhr and in the Saar is looking forward to converting Germany into a country primarily agricultural and pastoral in its character."

Burns goes on to note that this statement provoked "testy quarrels" at Quebec between Churchill and Eden "while Roosevelt watched on." The so-called Morgenthau plan "had an aptitude for dividing people," Burns writes. "Stimson had hotly opposed it. Hull would soon turn against it, Churchill would eventually repudiate it, and Roosevelt would quietly back away" (Burns, pp. 520–21).

The Morgenthau controversy would emerge as an election issue.

455 "very doubtful" . . . "practical steps": Churchill, *Triumph and Tragedy,* p. 602.

456 "inch by inch": Schramm, "The Preparation of the German Ardennes Counteroffensive," p. 26.

457 "the old man set about his task": From 1st Canadian Army report quoted by Stamps and Esposito, p. 466.

457 "without fear of betrayal": Schwerin episode is based on "Item No. 7: Fragment of assigned report on 116 Panzer Division from the Seine to Aachen." Interrogation of General von Schwerin, BSP, Box 40, Interviews (1).

458 "merging imperceptibly": Blumenson, *Breakout and Pursuit,* p. 696.

458 "champagne atmosphere": BDP, p. 656.

459 "all-out drive to the Rhine": FA, September 7, 1944.

459 "itching for more territory to conquer": Characterization appears in FA, August 13, 1944.

459 "Remote objectives had always served the Third Army well": Weigley, *Eisenhower's Lieutenants,* p. 327.

459 "hard fight south of Nancy": Blumenson, *The Patton Papers,* p. 546.

461 "One of the duties of a general": BDP, p. 643.

462 "patient, grinding, probing action": Weigley, *Eisenhower's Lieutenants,* p. 283.

462 Bradley's determination: Blumenson, *The Patton Papers,* p. 532. "He [Bradley] said to me [Patton], with reference to the Brest operation, 'I would not say this to anyone but you, and have given different excuses to my staff and higher echelons, but we must take Brest in order to maintain the illusion of the fact that the U.S. Army cannot be beaten.' "

462 "stiffening somewhat": EP, p. 2125.

462 "rehearing all my objections": Bradley, *A Soldier's Story,* p. 328.

463 "unable to advance properly": Montgomery to Eisenhower, BD, September 8, 1944.

463 "disappointingly slow" progress: Weigley, *Eisenhower's Lieutenants,* p. 295.

464 "jerky and disjointed": Montgomery, *Memoirs,* p. 247.

464 "the last chance to end the war": Quotes in this account are taken from Wilmot, *The Struggle for Europe,* Ryan's *A Bridge Too Far,* Bradley's *A General's Life* and Montgomery's *Memoirs.*

465 "I not only approved": Remark to an editor of the Eisenhower papers, quoted in EP, p. 2135.

465 "an incident and extension": Quotation in Eisenhower's *Crusade in Europe,* p. 307.

465 "Ike is thinking": BDP, p. 661.

466 "the entire field": KSD, September 11, 1944.

466 "silenced": Bradley, *A Soldier's Story,* p. 418.

466 "wanted MARKET GARDEN on time": Bradley, *A General's Life,* p. 331.

466 "about the growing public relations problem": Irving, *The War Between the Generals,* p. 273.

466 "certain repercussions": *Ibid.*

467 "E. is sending Bedell": KSD, September 12, 1944.

467 "emergency in character": EP, p. 2133.

467 "all resources behind a single *knife-like and narrow thrust*": EP, pp. 2136–37.

468 "step on the northern route": Montgomery, *Memoirs,* p. 260–62.

468 barring rain: "Have seen Bradley and fixed up satisfactory arrangements with him," Montgomery wrote. "Am launching operation MARKET on 17th September though weather may cause delay but all hope it may not." Montgomery to Eisenhower, September 14, DDE, Montgomery (1).

468   "Clearly, Berlin is the main prize": EP, pp. 2148–49.

469   "unremitting advance against the heart of the enemy country": EP, pp. 2143–44.

469   "Monty does what he pleases": Blumenson, *The Patton Papers*, p. 548.

469   "or die in the attempt": *Newsweek*, October 2, 1944, p. 30.

469   Thumb-wrist analogy: See Schramm, p. 32. "A German thumb was pressing from the north against the clenched fist, which the Americans stretched out to the northeast. Consequently, the question arose, whether the American wrist would give way to the pressure of the German thumb, or whether the thumb would withdraw, because of the danger of being cut off."

470   "not long before the drop": Smith, *Eisenhower's Six Great Decisions*, pp. 218–19.

470   "with the greatest care": *Ibid.*, p. 219.

470   "in exact accordance": EP, p. 2152.

471   "that alone should be able to keep people": Letter dated September 14, EP, p. 2140.

471   "good knee": *Ibid.*, p. 2151.

471   "At one time": Davis, *Soldier of Democracy*, p. 140.

471   "hard, tough struggle": EP, p. 2140.

472   "how the people at home": Eisenhower, *Letters to Mamie*, p. 209.

472   "We were inordinately proud": Eisenhower, *Crusade in Europe*, p. 310.

472   "last slender chance": Wilmot, p. 497.

474   "policy of having a commandant": KSD, September 9, 1944. "I have issued orders that the main headquarters of L of C is *not* to be in Paris," Eisenhower wrote Lee on the sixteenth. ". . . I realize that due to the heavy shipment of your personnel and supplies to that area before I was aware of it, it is impossible to shift your first priority duties. Nevertheless, you will immediately stop the entry into Paris of every individual who is not needed at that spot for essential duty, and those essential duties will *not* include provision of additional facilities, services and recreation for L of C tours or Headquarters" (BD, September 16, p. 1723).

474   "crunched through the debris-littered streets": *Newsweek*, October 2, 1944.

475   "thought it best": Montgomery, *Memoirs*, p. 253.

475   "plead concentration on the battle": Personal interview. See also Bradley, *A Soldier's Story*, p. 442.

475   "not more": de Guingand, *Operation Victory*, p. 413. "If he [Eisenhower] had not taken the steps he did to link up at an early date with ANVIL and had held back Patton and had diverted adminis-

trative resources so released to the north, I think it possible that
we might have obtained a bridgehead over the Rhine before the
winter—but not more."

475   Bradley plan is in Bradley's letter to Eisenhower, September 21,
1944, DDE, Box 12.

476   Conference discussion is summarized by Wilmot, p. 535, and
Pogue, *The Supreme Command,* p. 294.

476   "excellent" conference: Pogue, *The Supreme Command,* p. 294.

476   "contained" . . . "nasty little Kasserine": EP, pp. 2185–86.

477   "As regards Arnhem": Churchill, *Triumph and Tragedy,* p. 174.

478   "more and more complicated": SHAEF Weekly Intelligence
Summary No. 28, p. 6.

478   "like Gamelin in 1940": Bryant, p. 216.

478   "a massive assault in the wrong direction": Bradley, *A General's
Life,* p. 333.

478   "torn the weak German front to pieces": Wilmot, p. 539. Similarly, Liddell Hart devotes a long passage to assessing the consequences of and reasons for the Allied failure to penetrate the
German frontier in September 1944, which he attributed to the
failure to prepare "mentally or materially to exploit it [a complete
collapse of the enemy in August]." Liddell Hart further criticizes
Eisenhower's attempt to compromise when confronted with "conflicting arguments." Hart goes on to remind his reader that "the
price that the Allied armies paid for the missed opportunity in
early September was very heavy": two-thirds of the Allied casualties sustained in Europe, millions of civilians dying in the bombings and concentration camps, and the Russian invasion of Eastern Europe. Liddell Hart, *History of the Second World War,* pp.
561–67.

479   "strategists may long debate these issues": Churchill, *Triumph
and Tragedy,* p. 167.

479   "an unapologetic advocate": Montgomery, *Memoirs,* p. 267.

479   "inclined one way, then the other": Bryant, p. 216.

480   "getting Comm-Z out of Paris ASAP": KSD, September 28, 1944.

480   "I could at least keep track of him": Eisenhower, *Letters to
Mamie,* p. 211.

480   "which would mean a lot to me": EP, p. 2179.

481   "succeeded in establishing a relatively stable . . . front": EP, p.
2199.

481   "fared better than might have been expected": SHAEF Weekly
Intelligence Summary No. 28, p. 7.

481   "steady intention of forming": *Ibid.,* p. 8.

7 Fall Campaign

483 "gross inhumanity": Bryant, p. 220.

483 "determined" to do "nothing": *Ibid.,* p. 221.

484 "ran the conference very well": *Ibid.,* p. 218.

485 "play things to a conclusion": Pogue, *Organizer of Victory,* p. 480.

485 Manpower statistics: See Stamps and Esposito, p. 490.

486 "too heavy": EP, p. 2212.

487 "where the emphasis lies": EP, p. 2215.

487 "wild statements": BD, p. 1771.

487 "I was careful to state in my telegram": EP, p. 2216.

488 "overwhelming egotism": Pogue, *Organizer of Victory,* p. 475.

488 "The questions you raise": EP, p. 2221.

488 "hear no more": DDE, 1916–52, Montgomery (1).

489 "Eisenhower has not visibly aged": *Time,* October 30, 1944.

489 "We wish to remain what we are": Bradley, *A Soldier's Story,* p. 433.

489 "rectify the line": Blumenson, *The Patton Papers,* p. 556.

490 "the western front is more stable": SHAEF Weekly Intelligence Report No. 33, November 5.

490 "lit up" at night: FA, October 12, 1944.

490 "the second great total effort": Partial text is in *Newsweek,* October 30, 1944.

493 "very responsible post for an English girl to hold": Air Marshal James, Robb, "Higher Direction of War," in DDE.

493 "but I'm comfortable enough": Eisenhower, *Letters to Mamie,* p. 215.

493 "high time": *Ibid.,* pp. 216–17.

494 "most unfortunate": In the article, political correspondent John H. Crider reported the growing consensus in administration circles that the hard peace terms promised by the Big Three for Germany were "most unfortunate in terms of hastening the end of the European phase of the war." *New York Times,* October 8, 1944.

494 "neglecting the problem of finishing the war": Bryant, p. 225.

494 "prepared to discuss plans now": Bryant, p. 231.

494 "sad tangle": Churchill, *Triumph and Tragedy,* p. 199.

495 "merits and drawbacks": Churchill, *Triumph and Tragedy,* p. 208.

495 "needed Allied help": Bryant, p. 228.

495 "interest and sentiments": Churchill, *Triumph and Tragedy,* p. 202.

495 "callous": From Churchill's letter to Stalin on Balkan problems, dated October 11, 1944. *Triumph and Tragedy,* p. 200.

PAGE

495   "You keep it": *Ibid.,* p. 197.

495   "Stalin will get what he wants": Moran, *Churchill,* p. 218.

496   "forces of disorder": For account of Eisenhower-Caffery meeting and Caffery's report back to Washington, see EP, p. 2227.

496   "whether or not we should conduct the war": Pogue, *Organizer of Victory,* p. 480. Pogue writes that Eisenhower's lukewarm response to this proposed doctrine was "not unexpected" in light of Eisenhower's (and Bradley's) views expressed during Marshall's trip in October.

497   "well into 1945": *Ibid.*

497   "hammering constantly at the enemy's oil": EP, p. 2247.

497   "behind" the front: Tedder, *With Prejudice,* p. 605.

498   "produce the desired break": EP, p. 2247.

498   "in this field": EP, p. 2254.

498   "Italy must now adapt": Pogue, *Organizer of Victory,* p. 474. Likewise, Pogue noted that Brooke had "dutifully" supported Churchill's proposals at Quebec for reinforcing Alexander for a December offensive.

498   "good progress" . . . "soft stuff": EP, p. 2244, fn. 5.

498   "I share your curiosity": EP, p. 2243.

498   Butcher's lengthy account of his trip to the front and visit with Eisenhower is in BDP, pp. 692–97.

499   "greatly desired to attack": EP, p. 2372.

499   "taking advantage of any opportunity": Directive is in EP, pp. 2257–60.

501   On the debate over the Morgenthau plan, see *Newsweek,* October 16, 1944. In several articles assessing the administration split, *Newsweek* vented criticism of hard peace talk, noting the contrast between Roosevelt's policy and Wilson's policy twenty-five years before, which had featured the fourteen points as a basis for peace terms.

502   "greater realism in postwar thinking": Pogue, *Organizer of Victory,* p. 460. Quote is taken from a memo from McCloy to Marshall recommending that Foreign Service officers be invited to attend the session of a proposed joint Army-Navy War College, a measure McCloy felt was necessary in view of the fact that probably no war in history "has more clearly shown the truth of Clausewitz's old dictum than this one. The political-military aspects of the war are so apparent that they do not need any enumeration" *(Ibid.).*

502   Quotes from Harriman's warnings to Hull and Hopkins shortly before his return to Washington: Harriman and Abel, *Special Envoy,* pp. 344–46. See also Stimson and Bundy, *On Active Service,* p. 606–7, where Stimson records cabinet discussions of ways to induce Stalin

PAGE

to accept liberal governments in Eastern Europe and even reforms in Russia, which "lies at the foundation of our successes."

504 "In the course of the public discussions": DDE, McCloy (1).

505 "Don't let anyone change you": See EP, p. 2212, and BD, July 14, in which Surles' trip is described.

505 "ideal for headlines": Personal interview with Harry C. Butcher.

507 "the best way to get out of trouble": Undated letter, Eisenhower to "Pupah" Doud, in Barbara Eisenhower collection.

507 "temporary socialization": *Ibid.*

508 "terrible systems in vogue": DDE, "Red Diary," October 29, 1933.

509 "This evening we have been listening": DDE, "The Philippine Diary" (1936–1940), September 3, 1939. In this entry, Eisenhower proceeded to speculate on Italy's course. Recalling his passing admiration for Mussolini in the mid-thirties, Eisenhower concluded that Mussolini was too shrewd to lend Italian support for a war that would result in either defeat or a German victory which would mean German domination of Italy along with the rest of Europe. Perhaps the most interesting feature of this entry is an omission: no reference whatsoever to the Nazi-Soviet pact signed only two weeks earlier. Evidently, Eisenhower perceived the pact as not surprising and as being a temporary expedient at most, agreeing with Churchill's assessment of it as "a legitimate expression of Soviet interests," and the military positions gained as a result of it as "clearly necessary for the safety of Russia against the Nazi menace" (Kimball, *Churchill and Roosevelt,* vol. III, p. 349).

509 "hoped and prayed": BDP, p. 701.

509 "make the German wish": *Ibid.* Eisenhower repeated the sentiment verbatim in a message to Marshall. See EP, p. 2297.

511 "Goebbels can claim": SHAEF Weekly Intelligence Report No. 33.

511 "left-wing" phase: Argus, "Hitler's Last Alibi," *The Nation,* September 9, 1944.

512 "war criminals": "Notes to Contemporary Germany and Austria from Allied Sources in Switzerland." Swiss report is summarized in SHAEF Weekly Intelligence Summary No. 43.

512 "handwriting on the military wall": SHAEF Weekly Intelligence Summary No. 31.

513 "forgetting Frederick's patient waiting game": Bryant, p. 268.

514 On the origin of the Ardennes concept, see Jodl interrogation, July 26, 1945.

514 "put his finger on the map": J.S.D. Eisenhower, *The Bitter Woods,* p. 115.

516   "shouting" . . . "inexperience": See Eisenhower's message to Marshall, March 30, 1945, EP, p. 2560.

516   "strange phase": Sherwood, p. 836.

517   "we would keep outside of the Russian sphere": Bohlen, *Witness to History*, p. 175.

517   "foreign policy not possible in a democracy": *Ibid.*, p. 176.

517   "all of its malice": Quote is borrowed from Churchill's appeal to Roosevelt in June 1944 for support of his effort to enter into an arrangement on the Balkans with Stalin. Churchill, *Triumph and Tragedy*, p. 64.

518   "self-glorification": EP, pp. 1993–97.

519   "organized thievery": Bradley, *A Soldier's Story*, p. 428.

519   "Unquestionably any soldier": EP, pp. 2289–90.

520   "his anxiety to paddle his own canoe": EP, p. 2304.

520   "Don't forget that I take a beating every day": Eisenhower, *Letters to Mamie*, pp. 219–20.

521   "It has rained every day": Blumenson, *The Patton Papers*, p. 574.

521   "that the enemy had chosen to commit": Bradley, *A Soldier's Story*, p. 441.

521   Comparisons between Eisenhower and Grant are almost commonplace in the histories consulted in the preparation of this book. Chester Wilmot was probably the first, perceiving similar military philosophies as well as the similarity of the fall campaign of 1944 and Grant's tactics in the wilderness. Of the Eisenhower-Montgomery dispute over strategy in Normandy, Wilmot wrote in 1951: "It is surprising that Eisenhower did not appreciate Montgomery's purpose, for he was planning to carry out deliberately the strategic maneuvers which had unconsciously brought about the Union victory in the American Civil War. He intended to do to the Germans what Sherman had done to the Confederate Army [indirect assault and rapid outmaneuvering] in his march through Georgia in 1864. Perhaps the explanation is that in American military thinking the view prevails that the decisive operation of the Civil War was fought not by Sherman but by Grant, the apostle of direct approach." This was in reference to Eisenhower's decision in Normandy to mount simultaneous all-out offensives on both flanks. Wilmot, p. 339.

522   German civilian morale in the occupied areas and the BBC episode are described by C. D. Jackson of SHAEF in "Impressions of a brief tour of Occupied Germany in the VII Corps area." Jackson Papers, DDE Library, Abilene, Kansas.

522   Breendonck: Details of the camp are described in the 21st Army Group Headquarters report entitled "Report on German Atrocities." Jackson Papers, Box 2.

PAGE

523 "interesting" document: BD, November 20, 1944.

524 "on no account": See Eisenhower, *Crusade in Europe,* p. 331.

524 "ceased to exist as a coherent tactical force": Weigley, *Eisenhower's Lieutenants,* p. 408.

524 "adverse impact on Allied operations": Stamps and Esposito, p. 489.

525 "the largest collection": BD, November 7, 1944, p. 1826.

525 "the subject of study": EP, p. 2316.

526 "unanticipated shortage of manpower": Kimball, vol. III, p. 357.

526 "extra punch for victory": Pogue, *Organizer of Victory,* p. 358.

526 "hand-to-mouth basis": Quote from letter from General Thomas Handy to Eisenhower dated December 5, 1944, EP, p. 2347.

526 "[morale] on this front shows no signs of cracking": EP, p. 2313.

527 "spend Christmas beyond the Rhine": All direct quotes in this conference are taken from the transcript of the press conferences in DDE, Box 156, Press Statements, 1944–46.

529 "clarifying" unconditional surrender proposals: Marshall's message enclosing transcript of American proposals clarifying unconditional surrender is in BD, November 22, 1944.

529 "occupation by the Russians": Churchill reply, BD, November 25, 1944.

530 "reassure the Germans as to their future": Churchill to Eisenhower, DDE, Box 21, Churchill (2).

530 "upon some operation that would be universally recognized": EP, p. 2319.

530 "wanted to stay out of European questions": Harriman, *Special Envoy,* p. 366.

530 On Stalin's willingness to see Eisenhower but no other member of his staff: KSD, November 26, 1944.

530 "it would be almost miraculous": EP, p. 2321.

531 "I consider that at the end of the winter campaign": Churchill, *Triumph and Tragedy,* p. 607.

532 "wide gulf between the wishes of the Supreme Command": Jodl interrogation, July 25, 1945, BSP, Collection of World War II Documents, Box 40.

532 "grand slam": J.S.D. Eisenhower, *The Bitter Woods,* p. 132.

532 "inalterable will": Luttichau, "The German Counteroffensive in the Ardennes," in Greenfield, ed., *Command Decisions,* p. 354.

533 "last possibilities": J.S.D. Eisenhower, *The Bitter Woods,* p. 134.

533 "It would be silly to wake these people up": *Ibid.,* p. 140.

534 "most logical way": SHAEF Weekly Intelligence Summary No. 36.

534 "spoiling attack of considerable power": See also Bradley, *A General's Life,* p. 351.

PAGE

534 "the necessity for alert OPs": SHAEF Weekly Intelligence Report No. 36.

535 "spoiling attack" . . , "air, armor and infantry": Bradley, *A Soldier's Story*, p. 448.

535 "Lacking the resources": Bradley, *A General's Life*, p. 354.

535 "calculated risk": Bradley, *A Soldier's Story*, p. 462.

536 "in synchronized attacks": *Newsweek*, January 29, 1945.

537 "Oh, things are okay": BDP, p. 714.

537 "the date and scale": Eisenhower to Marshall, December 5, 1944, EP, p. 2335.

538 "despondent" letter to Brooke: Bryant, p. 252.

538 "the set-up was bad": *Ibid.*, p. 244.

538 "wonderful telegram": *Ibid.*, p. 241.

540 "determined to show he is a great general": *Ibid.*, p. 254.

540 "I thoroughly appreciate": *Ibid.*, p. 253.

541 "Can you see Ike judging": *Ibid.*, p. 256.

541 "(a) to counter the pernicious American strategy": *Ibid.*

543 "evidently beginning to realize": *Ibid.*

543 "Ike is a good fellow": *Ibid.*, p. 262.

543 "far from good": Montgomery, *Memoirs*, p. 268.

544 "a grave mistake": Bryant, p. 258.

544 "definitely failed . . . we therefore": BD, November 27, 1944.

544 "Your letter does state your conceptions": EP, p. 2323.

546 "containing" the Metz fortress: From extract of letter reprinted in Montgomery, *Memoirs*, p. 269.

546 "to place before you the serious and disappointing war situation": Kimball, vol. III, p. 434.

547 "inflicting losses": *Ibid.*, pp. 446–47.

547 "on the problem confronting us": Quotes from meeting are from Montgomery's extensive summary of it in *Memoirs*, pp. 272–74.

548 "On the western front, the outward surface": SHAEF Weekly Intelligence Report No. 38.

549 "Let them come": Strong, *Intelligence at the Top*, p. 211.

549 "If he is ill": Bradley, *A General's Life*, p. 350.

549 "our replacement situation is exceedingly dark": EP, p. 2346.

550 "winter offensive should be launched": Harriman and Abel, *Special Envoy*, p. 379.

550 "and oh, Lordy, Lordy": Eisenhower, *Letters to Mamie*, p. 224.

550 "I do not pretend that my own feeling": Pyle, *Brave Men*, pp. 318–19.

551 "dispersion" of resources: Bryant, p. 266.

552 "grand visit" . . . "altogether enjoyable": EP, pp. 2350–51.

553 "This is just a short note": EP, p. 2351.

PAGE

555 "major": Bradley, *A Soldier's Story*, p. 460.
556 "for payment, I think": Irving, *The War Between the Generals*, p. 338.
556 "While it seems almost certain": EP, p. 2350.
556 "spoiling attacks": FA, December 16, 1944.
556 "all-out effort": *Ibid.*
557 "quiet sector": J.S.D. Eisenhower, *The Bitter Woods*, p. 140.
557 Fragmentary and contradictory reports: "The news was fragmentary and full of contradictions," Strong writes, "as it generally is before a battle develops fully and before the enemy's intentions can be clearly seen" (Strong, *Intelligence at the Top*, p. 213).
559 "on which the tide of the attack": Wilmot, p. 584.
559 "a no man's land": Stamps and Esposito, *A Military History of World War II*, p. 509.
560 "spoiling attack": Wilmot, p. 583.
562 "I hope he doesn't have to take it down": Bradley, *A Soldier's Story*, p. 466.
562 "never move backwards with a headquarters": Bradley, *A General's Life*, p. 357.
563 "launched a rather ambitious counterattack": EP, p. 2355.
563 "serious if not critical": FA, December 17, 1944.
563 "But what the hell": Bradley, *A Soldier's Story*, p. 469.
564 "guidance . . . regarding how the War Department": J.S.D. Eisenhower, *The Bitter Woods*, p. 33.
564 "The main point": SHAEF Weekly Intelligence Summary No. 39, December 17, 1944.
565 "the enemy line": FA, December 18, 1944.
565 "tragic tales": Quoted by Wilmot, p. 585.
566 "immediate action": EP, p. 2356.
567 "unable to leave his command": Strong, p. 220.
567 "Aw, come on": Bradley, *A General's Life*, p. 358.
567 "George, that's fine": Eisenhower, *Crusade in Europe*, p. 350.
568 "heaven-sent" opportunity: Strong, *Intelligence at The Top*, p. 220.
568 "accepted the intelligence forecast": *Ibid.*, p. 221.
568 "Forty-eight hours": *Ibid.*
569 "created a ripple of excitement": Stamps and Esposito, p. 519.
569 "methodical and sure": Eisenhower, *Crusade in Europe*, p. 351.
569 "plug holes": EP, pp. 2358–59.

PAGE

569   "not repeat not good": Bradley, *A General's Life*, p. 362.

570   "vital importance": EP, p. 2361.

570   "acute case of the shakes": Bradley, *A Soldier's Story*, p. 475.

570   "matter of routine": EP, p. 2361.

571   "considerable confusion and disorganization": Strong, *Intelligence at the Top*, p. 225.

571   "matching up to the situation": *Ibid.*, p. 224.

571   "Whenever there is any real trouble": *Ibid.*, p. 225.

571   "Dividing the front": Bradley, *A General's Life*, p. 363.

571   "Bedell, in that case": Bradley, *A Soldier's Story*, p. 476.

572   "Patton did not go off half-cocked": Bradley, *A General's Life*, p. 364.

572   "Well, Brad, those are my orders": Wilmot, p. 591.

572   "launch counteroffensives without delay": EP, pp. 2363–65.

573   "if anything had by chance happened": Strong, p. 236.

573–74 Was the transfer of command necessary? In a 1976 letter to General Bruce Clarke, Commander of the CCB of the U.S. 7th Armored Division, General Hasse Von Manteuffel would write that he fully agreed with both Clarke and historian Chester Wilmot that "the change of command . . .—a temporary one—came at the right moment." Von Manteuffel would explain that by mid-day of the twentieth, the northern rim of the Bulge "was very disorganized" and he would endorse Wilmot's contention that "the gravity of the situation was accentuated by the fact that Bradley had no reserves . . . except the division which he was belatedly withdrawing from the Roer" (Wilmot, p. 590). (Clarke provided his correspondence with Von Manteuffel to the author.)

574   "the most aggressive American Corps commander": FA, December 21, 1944.

576   "Christ come to cleanse the temple": Weigley, *Eisenhower's Lieutenants*, p. 505.

576   "thinking offensively": Bradley, *A General's Life*, p. 364.

576   "strong and patient handling": Wilmot, p. 610.

576   "tidy up" the northern rim: Bradley, *A General's Life*, p. 365.

576   "could be broken with relatively little strength": FA, December 21, 1944.

577   "certain the Germans would break through": Personal interview with the author.

577   "poor and timid decision": Bradley, *A General's Life*, p. 366.

577   "full of enthusiasm": Montgomery, *Memoirs*, p. 278.

577   "we can tell": FA, December 21, 1944.

PAGE
577–78 "It is impossible to tell": *Ibid.*

578 "close reserve" . . . "accepted in reserve": Wilmot, p. 595.

578 "did not entirely accept this view": *Ibid.*

579 "wild mixed fighting": FA, December 22, 1944.

580 "Aren't you packing?": Strong, *Intelligence at the Top,* p. 218.

580 "If he doesn't come back": Personal interview.

580 "awesome" . . . "odd sympathy": Personal interview.

581 "From the point of view": Tedder, *With Prejudice,* p. 610.

581 "unworried and unharassed": Robinson's memo describing the meeting is in Robinson Papers, Eisenhower Library.

583 All quotes from Eisenhower's conversation with Butcher are in BDP, pp. 727–30.

584 "several mighty Russian and Polish armies": *Newsweek,* January 15, 1945.

584 "Our military, not to say political, relations with Russia": Tedder, *With Prejudice,* p. 641.

584 "disturbed at Russian slowness": KSD, December 22, 1944.

584–85 Eisenhower's request for Russian views: EP, p. 2367.

585 "to discuss with you": BD, December 24, 1944.

585 Tedder's departure as weather permitted: "as soon as there is a break in the weather" (KSD, December 29, 1944).

585 "time has come": FA, December 22, 1944.

586 "continue to be a good soldier": From Report of the Theater Judge Advocate General, ETO, Barker Papers, Box 2.

587 "He [Bradley] must make absolutely certain": *The Eisenhower Diaries,* ed. Ferrell, p. 129.

587 "if anything, worse than before": FA, December 24, 1944.

587 "the German Panzers roughly handled the American divisions": Stamps and Esposito, p. 517.

588 "in fairly good condition": FA, December 23–25, 1944.

588 "best division he had ever seen": FA, December 23, 1944.

588 "Tonight it can be said": FA, December 25, 1944.

588 "You will understand from the papers": Eisenhower, *Letters to Mamie,* p. 228.

589 "the knowledge that Field Marshal Montgomery": Quoted in Strong, *Intelligence at the Top,* p. 229.

589 "lip service": Bryant, p. 267.

589 "useless" to pretend: From Montgomery's letter to Brooke describing the meeting, in Bryant, p. 278.

590 "let him have it with both barrels": Bradley, *A General's Life,* p. 370.

PAGE

593 "jumping the Rhine on the run": Bradley, *A General's Life*, pp. 372–73.

594 "in case of emergency": EP, pp. 2382–83.

596 "presence of . . . British XXX Corps": EP, pp. 2383–84.

596 "definite failure": Montgomery to Eisenhower, BD, December 29, 1944.

596 "long and trying journey": KSD, December 29, 1944.

597 "violating somewhat [his] own orders": Marshall message is quoted in full in Eisenhower, *Crusade in Europe*, p. 356.

597 Bradley's situation was becoming "intolerable": Quotes of this conference are from de Guingand's account in *Generals at War*, pp. 107–11.

598 "bad" . . . "perhaps gone a little far this time": *Ibid.*

598 "to the offensive": FA, December 31, 1944.

598 "Never has the world been plagued": Bradley, *A Soldier's Story*, p. 483.

599 "to the meaning of the Atlantic Charter itself": Sherwood, *Roosevelt and Hopkins*, p. 837.

600 "rise up and scare the daylights out of us": Charles A. Bolte in *The Nation*, January 1, 1945.

600 "concentration of force": J.F.C. Fuller, "Rundstedt's Counteroffensive and the Principles of War," *Newsweek*, January 1, 1945.

601 "carefully" . . . "priority": EP, pp. 2386–87.

602 "frank views": Montgomery to Eisenhower, BD, January 2, 1945.

602 "the German is pressing everywhere": KSD, January 2, 1945.

603 "at all costs": *Ibid.*

603 "socked him on the jaw": Ambrose, *The Supreme Commander*, p. 578.

603 "limited to what he can provide from the air": EP, p. 2392.

603 "extent of the withdrawal": Quotes are taken from De Gaulle's letter to Eisenhower delivered on the third. DDE, De Gaulle correspondence (1).

603 "Retreat in Alsace": Crozier, *De Gaulle*, p. 351.

604 "firmly": Eisenhower, *Crusade in Europe*, p. 363.

604 "control of the entire French situation": EP, p. 2400.

604 "You have done the wise and proper thing": Eisenhower, *Crusade in Europe*, p. 363.

605 "To me, it was a rather painful occasion": Strong, p. 231.

607 "His Majesty's government": Churchill, *Triumph and Tragedy*, p. 239.

607 "bad weather": Tedder, *With Prejudice*, p. 642.

607 "imperative" . . . "as soon as the weather improves": KSD, January 5, 1945.

PAGE

609 "a severe injunction of secrecy": Butcher, "Memorandum for Diary," January 27, 1945.

609 "knife turning in the wound": Wilmot, p. 607. "This thorn [Bastogne] thus became a knife, and, as Patton turned the knife in the wound, Hitler was forced to react more strongly than he intended."

610 On the performance of the Sixth Panzer Army, see Jodl interrogation, July 3, 1945. Asked about Dietrich's slow advance, Jodl denied that the Sixth Panzer had gone "too far north" and "too near Liège," noting that the embroilment of the Sixth Panzer at Elsenborn was a "development . . . forced on us by necessity." Jodl did add, however, that if the Sixth Army forces were in fact *aimed* at Liège, as his interrogator suggested, then Dietrich should have been "shot for disobeying orders."

610 "vast forces ready to attack": Wilmot, p. 620.

610 "area west of Houffalize": Wilmot, p. 608.

611 "large-scale operations against the Germans": Churchill, *Triumph and Tragedy,* p. 241.

611 Eisenhower's order to "proceed": Tedder, p. 642.

611 "ray" . . . "freezing bomb": KSD, January 5, 1945. The rumored "freezing bomb" was said to be a missile warhead designed "to produce extreme cold over a considerable area, resulting in the destruction of all animal and vegetable life." The rumors were discounted, since "no known material" was "capable of producing the results suggested" (BD, January 14, 1945).

611 "lose the war": KSD, January 7, 1945.

611 "no longer bleed ourselves": Pogue, *Organizer of Victory,* p. 497.

612 "by instant agreement of all concerned": Statement reprinted in Bradley, *A General's Life,* p. 381.

612 "whole Allied team": Text of press conference is reprinted in full in Montgomery, *Memoirs,* pp. 279–81.

613 "temporary": Bradley, *A General's Life,* p. 384.

613 "an undue share of credit": Text of speech quoted in Bradley, *A Soldier's Story,* p. 488.

614 "a most difficult situation": EP, p. 2407.

614 Companion message: EP, p. 2408.

614 "extraordinarily successful": Pogue, *Organizer of Victory,* p. 509.

614 "flatly opposed": *Ibid.,* pp. 492–93.

614 "filled a good-sized volume": Phrase is from Eisenhower's message to Marshall on the twelfth about the situation at Alsace. EP, p. 2424.

614 Portions of Roosevelt's text and Marshall's message are in BD, January 7, 1945. According to Sherwood, Marshall personally

drafted the military portions of Roosevelt's report. See Sherwood, p. 845.

614 "an authoritative interpretation": *Washington Post,* December 28, cited in Bradley, *A Soldier's Story,* p. 485.

615 "we now face a situation": BD, January 9, 1945.

615 "following the suppression of the present German offensive": BD, January 10, 1945.

615 "fine personality": EP, p. 2420.

616 "memorandum on strategy": BD, January 10, 1945.

616 "succeeded far beyond its capacity": Bryant, p. 267.

616 "the soundness of your estimate": BD, January 11, 1945.

617 "glad to get your reactions": EP, p. 2422.

617 "It is almost 8 o'clock": KSD, January 12, 1945.

618 "to shatter the entire German eastern front": *Newsweek,* January 22, 1945.

618 "the most powerful and mysterious world leader": George Kennan, "USSR—Estimation of Basic Policies Underlying Soviet Foreign Relations," May 7, 1945, BSP, Box 37, Navy Department Documents, p. 17.

618 "When do they go off?": Tedder, *With Prejudice,* p. 646.

618–19 Unless otherwise indicated, quotes from the Tedder-Stalin conversation are from "Memorandum of Conference with Marshal Stalin, 15 January 1945." DDE, Box 102, Stalin (1).

619 "As he [Stalin] disliked fulsome compliments": From text of Birse's message sent to Eisenhower via the BCOS on the nineteenth. DDE, Box 54, Ismay (1)

620 "courageous but wary": Kennan, p. 17.

620 "the Kremlin chimes": *Ibid.*

621 Ziegenberg meetings: BD, January 14, 1945.

622 "if you want something done quickly": Ambrose, *The Supreme Commander,* p. 611.

624 "considerable emphasis on the location": EP, p. 2429.

624 "quick decision in the west": Messages are in EP; Eisenhower's message to Marshall, pp. 2430–35; to the CCS, pp. 2444–49.

625 "The only thing to be added about plans": EP, p. 2430.

626 "opportunity of war": Weigley, *Eisenhower's Lieutenants,* p. 580. "Such a concentration for attack upon a relatively narrow front had been so infrequently achieved in the American campaign in Europe, and in its compacted force the concentration carried so much power and promise, that the mere existence of the concentration was indeed warrant enough for Bradley's desire to attack in the Eifel."

626 "continued for the sole reason": Bryant, p. 293.

PAGE

626 "These last few days": KSD, January 14, 1945.

627 "remiss" in not writing: Eisenhower, *Letters to Mamie,* p. 228.

627 "In some ways it seems like only yesterday": *Ibid.,* p. 231.

627 "at least occasionally": *Ibid.,* p. 233.

630 "widespread disillusionment": From Eisenhower's report to CCS on western front operations since June, dated January 20. EP, p. 2449.

630–31 "the momentous news": EP, p. 2428.

631 "simple Main Street Abilene style": Marshall to Eisenhower, January 17. BSP, Collection of World War II Documents.

631 "revealing to friend and enemy that coordination": EP, p. 2458.

631 "would be alarmed to know": *Ibid.*

631 "the story of Ike's mission": BDP, p. 751.

631 "I hope you still regard me": Mueller to Eisenhower, DDE, Mueller (1).

631 "I remember with real pleasure": EP, p. 2572.

632 "security reasons": KSD, January 18, 1945. Marshall's message that day in fact did not offer any explanation for why Marshall found a visit to Paris "inadvisable." Security reasons may have been Eisenhower's explanation to Summersby, or a War Department explanation to Smith by phone. In any event, Marshall made it plain that he desired Eisenhower to meet him at or near Malta.

632 "quickly to the defensive": EP, p. 2439.

632 "desirable": Marshall to Eisenhower, BD, January 20.

632 "due to uncertainties": EP, p. 2455.

633 "strong defenses": EP, p. 2439.

633 "always been irritating": Eisenhower, *Crusade in Europe,* p. 374.

633 "in no uncertain language": KSD, January 22, 1945.

633 "now is the time": *Ibid.,* January 23, 1945.

633 "considerable reshuffling": Stamps and Esposito, p. 534.

634 "colored by our desire": Bradley, *A General's Life,* p. 388.

634 "lost his good humor": *Ibid.*

634 "starting fresh": Crozier, p. 344.

634–36 Minutes of Eisenhower–De Gaulle conference: BD, January 26, 1945.

636 "the effect of the Democratic and Nazi systems": Butcher, "Memorandum for Diary," January 27, 1945.

637 "volcanic": Sherwood, p. 846.

637 "Churchill's first rule": Butcher, "Memorandum for Diary," January 27, 1945.

638 "not only with defensive actions": *Ibid.* See also BDP, p. 749.

638 "the worst conditions of the war": FA, January 30, 1945.

PAGE

639   "not being trained for your area": Pogue, *Organizer of Victory*, p. 512.

639   "the fewest number of divisions": From Eisenhower's memo of the conference, EP, p. 2461.

639   "that as long as he, Marshall": KSD, January 29, 1945.

640   "confused a lot of people": Personal interview.

640   "aggressive defense": Stamps and Esposito, p. 535.

640   "crackled with heat": Pogue, *Organizer of Victory*, p. 516.

640   "undue reliance . . . lit out": *Ibid.*

640   "at last . . . said flatly": *Ibid.*, p. 517.

641   "illogical . . . there was now no question": *Ibid.*, p. 515.

641   "not strong enough": KSD, January 31, 1945.

642   "the only one of its kind": Personal interview. See also the Reverend Edward L. R. Elson, Oral History, Columbia University, pp. 57–66.

642   "the purpose of an action of this kind": Personal interview.

642   "to insure the accomplishment": "Report of the Theater Judge Advocate General, ETO," p. 35, Barker Papers, Box 2.

643   "based upon personal observations and conversations": *Ibid.*

644   "an aggressive defense forthwith": EP, p. 2466.

644   "mail was pouring into his headquarters": Strong, *Intelligence at the Top*, p. 233.

644   "having forfeited the confidence of his staff": *Ibid.* Portions of this clash are taken from Bradley's *A Soldier's Story* (p. 488), the Summersby diary, and Tedder's *With Prejudice.* Interestingly, Strong states that this exchange occurred in mid-January. But, according to Eisenhower's desk diary, Strong was not present at Eisenhower's meeting with Bradley on the thirteenth, in which, Bradley writes, he was a "trifle constrained" (*A General's Life*, p. 386). Summersby's lengthy account of the meeting on the thirty-first, a conference that Strong attended, indicates that it was "quite stormy . . . at moments" and leaves no doubt that the quoted exchanges occurred on the night of the thirty-first. "Eisenhower has always to make the final decision," she writes, "and of course take full responsibility" (KSD, January 31, 1945).

645   "factual sounding": Sherwood, p. 848.

645   "the meeting with the all-powerful Americans": Bryant, p. 302.

645   "the double attack": *Ibid.*

646   "Wasn't the damage done at Teheran?": Moran, *Churchil,*, p. 247.

649   "satisfied and having no territorial or other ambitions": Pogue, *Organizer of Victory*, p. 525.

649   "not possible in a democracy": Bohlen, *Witness to History*, p. 175.

PAGE

650 "method and calculation": Harriman and Abel, *Special Envoy*, p. 393.

650 "extinct imperialism and nobility": Churchill, *Triumph and Tragedy*, p. 309.

650 "We shall follow him": Churchill, *Triumph and Tragedy*, p. 298.

651 "would reach Manila": Bohlen, p. 180.

651 "Stalin would talk more frankly about military matters": Harriman and Abel, p. 395.

651 "How is Germany to be dismembered?": Churchill, *Triumph and Tragedy*, p. 301.

651 "lip service to a dying ideal": Bohlen, p. 183.

652 "$20 billion was not a large sum": Harriman and Abel, p. 403.

652 "contribution to the winning of the war and the severity of their losses": *Ibid.*

652 "the institutions of international capitalism": Raymond Moley, "What Capitalism Learned at Yalta," *Newsweek*, February 26, 1945.

653 "possibly long years of rebuilding cities destroyed": *Newsweek*, May 14, 1945.

653 "recognized only during a war": Churchill, *Triumph and Tragedy*, p. 311.

654 "a question of honor": *Ibid.*, pp. 315–16.

654 "would make life easier on him at home": *Ibid.*, p. 314.

655 "dictator, not a democrat": Harriman and Abel, p. 407.

655 "popular and no less legitimate than De Gaulle's in Paris": *Ibid*, p. 411.

656 "whole negotiation . . . completed at Yalta": *Ibid.*, p. 412.

656 "as long as he could put his own interpretation": *Ibid.*, p. 399.

656 "unprecedented military magnitude": Pogue, *Organizer of Victory*, p. 527.

658 "preeminent interests": Harriman and Abel, p. 399.

658 "frail and ill": Moran, *Churchill*, p. 242.

658 "The Soviet Union will never agree": Bohlen, p. 181.

658 Churchill shouted his disgust: Morgan, p. 245.

658 "talk of a crusade against Russia": Churchill, *Triumph and Tragedy*, p. 306.

659 "be alone and would have friends": *Ibid.*, p. 305.

659 "the only way to have a friend is to be a friend": From Roosevelt's Fourth Inaugural Address, in Sherwood, p. 846.

659 "even with the advantage of hindsight": Personal interview.

659 "sending optimism soaring like a balloon": Pogue, *Organizer of Victory*, p. 496.

659 "clear and understandable": Quotes from toasts are from transcript of toasts printed in Sherwood, pp. 868-69.

660 "unilateral action": Wilmot, p. 635.

661 "sucker who is licking the shopworn candy": Raymond Moley, "The Polish Crisis," *Newsweek,* January 1, 1945.

661 "we shall count the cost in mortal anguish": Quotes from speech appear in *Newsweek,* January 22, 1945.

9 Winter/Spring 1945

662 "nagging Devers": Weigley, *Eisenhower's Lieutenants,* p. 580.

663 "eliminating the Colmar pocket": *Ibid.*

663–64 "pay too much attention": KSD, February 3, 1945.

664 For an account of British aims at Malta, see Pogue, *Organizer of Victory,* p. 515.

665 "as weather permitted": *Ibid.,* p. 540.

666 "everything possible": *Ibid.,* p. 541.

666 According to Weigley, "Marshall's belief [at Malta] that the British must be placated suggests the force of British pressure and concern" (Weigley, *Eisenhower's Lieutenants,* p. 578).

667 "a well-conducted campaign": KSD, January 29, 1945.

667 "paramount importance": EP, p. 2465.

667 "unsatisfactory" news: FA, February 1, 1945.

668 "in the bitterest of possible terms": Bradley, *A General's Life,* p. 392.

668 "without a change in pace": Bradley, *A Soldier's Story,* p. 495.

670 "hard put": SHAEF Weekly Intelligence Report No. 47, February 11, 1945.

670 "lose control": Bradley, *A General's Life,* p. 394.

671 "probing attacks in progress": Weigley, *Eisenhower's Lieutenants,* p. 583.

672 "running fuse": Smith, *Eisenhower's Six Great Decisions,* p. 128. As Smith put it, this strategy served a twofold purpose: (1) eliminating German threats west of the Rhine, and (2) handing the Allies the "capability of concentration" from behind the Rhine barrier and the ability to deploy all three Army groups for the invasion. *Ibid.,* pp. 122–23.

672 "with existing resources": From the text of a February 20 message from Eisenhower to Bradley recapitulating his position. EP, p. 2489.

PAGE

673   "nothing of the sort": Bradley, *A Soldier's Story,* p. 499. Simultaneously, Eisenhower informed Marshall of his talk with Montgomery, in which he had urged Montgomery to "use his entire influence to prevent this kind of thing from starting again" (EP, p. 2473).

673   "desultory": Bradley, *A Soldier's Story*, p. 498.

673   "2 possibly 3" armored divisions: Blumenson, *The Patton Papers,* p. 636.

673   "strong enough to keep the enemy from shifting his strength": Bradley, *A Soldier's Story,* p. 501.

674   "one of the most significant orders": Bradley, *A General's Life,* p. 409.

674   "Russians would be in Berlin": FA, February 5, 1945.

675   Concern persisted about the impact of the jet and, according to Weigley, "some Allied airmen feared that if the war lasted until June, the jets might yet restore control of the German skies to the Luftwaffe." On January 9, Spaatz accorded jet production plants equal priority with oil—jets did not appear in strength until March. Weigley, *Eisenhower's Lieutenants,* p. 573.

676   By February 11, SHAEF intelligence was noting that the Eastern Front was "comparatively quiet" and that "Russian advances towards Berlin . . . were [being] reported *only* by the Germans": SHAEF Weekly Intelligence Summary No. 47.

676   "the destructiveness of war": Personal interview with author.

676   "like the end of the world": *Newsweek,* February 19, 1945.

677   "How do they do it": See Ernest Lindley, "We Gave Red Army Its Speed," *Newsweek,* February 12, 1945.

678   "excellent": See EP, p. 2496, fn. 1

678   "John, I know you're leaving": J.S.D. Eisenhower, *Strictly Personal,* p. 79.

679   Manpower figures are cited by Weigley, *Eisenhower's Lieutenants,* p. 663.

680   "individual soldiers": Messages in EP, pp. 2488, 2492.

680   "official and personal concern": BDP, p. 761.

681   "constants" of morale: Excerpts from Eisenhower, *At Ease,* pp. 383–84, note 3.

682   "be the first": February 13, Blumenson, *The Patton Papers,* p. 638.

682   "much to everyone's relief": KSD, February 9, 1945.

682   "dim view": *Ibid.,* February 11, 1945.

683   "more than tired": Eisenhower, *Letters to Mamie,* pp. 234–35.

684   "if you have anything": EP, p. 2477.

684   "some changes": *Ibid.,* p. 2477.

684 "understand Marshall's about-face": Bradley, *A General's Life*, p. 397.

685 "I can make the attack": Blumenson, *The Patton Papers*, p. 643.

685 "bullying": Montgomery, *Memoirs*, p. 291.

686 "delighted": Bryant, p. 317.

687 "lasting resentment": EP, pp. 2480–81.

687 "military matters": DDE, Box 21.

688 "The Prime Minister was sore": KSD, February 24, 1945.

688 "failure of the Allied high command": *Newsweek*, February 26, 1945.

688 "weekly run around the world": Bryant, p. 316.

688 Estimates in SHAEF Weekly Intelligence Report No. 48.

689 Estimate of defenders opposite Simpson's Ninth Army and Patton's Third Army: Weigley, *Eisenhower's Lieutenants*, pp. 606 and 618.

689 "two phase" scheme described in Bradley, *A Soldier's Story*, pp. 505–6.

689 "Three phase" plan: EP, pp. 2489–90.

689 "impossible to sit still": Bradley, *A Soldier's Story*, p. 501.

690 See Tedder, pp. 664–68. The most intensive arguments arose over proposals to mount CLARION a second time. According to Craven and Cate, the British, while in favor of "area" raids on Dresden and Koltbus, were skeptical of including General Ira Eaker, commander of the Fifteenth Air Force, who at one point, noting the CLARION plan would involve attacks on many untouched smaller towns, wrote Spaatz, ". . . you and Bob Lovett are right and we should never allow the history of the war to convict us of throwing the strategic bomber at the man on the street" (Craven and Cate, p. 732).

690 "the determination of the Russians": Bryant, p. 309.

691 "power to mould the world": Lord Moran, *Churchill*, p. 309.

692 "horrible and destructive": Eisenhower, *Crusade in Europe*, p. 443. Eisenhower also recalled that he had the naïve hope that "if we never used the weapon . . . other nations might remain ignorant of the fact that the problem of nuclear fission had been solved" (*Ibid.*).

692 "supreme provocation": Milton Eisenhower, *The President Is Calling*, p. 220. See also Peter Lyon, *Eisenhower*. Did the atomic bomb attacks undermine postwar Allied-Soviet cooperation? "Before the atom bomb was used," Lyon quotes Eisenhower as saying in late 1945, "I would have said yes, I was sure we could keep the peace with Russia. Now, I don't know. . . . People are frightened

and disturbed all over. Everyone feels insecure again" (Lyon, p. 377).

692 "minimal military significance": Pogue, *Organizer of Victory*, p. 546. As is to be expected, authorship of the Dresden raids is very murky. Pogue attributes the decision to Churchill and SHAEF. Craven and Cate attribute it to Spaatz and SHAEF.

693 "still burning from the night attacks": KSD, February 15, 1945.

693 "clandestine sources": EP, p. 2485.

693 "terror raid policy": Pogue, *Organizer of Victory*, p. 545.

694 "military objectives": *Ibid.*

695 German High Command awareness of the EAC Zones: John Keegan, "The Surrender," in Liddell Hart, ed., *History of the Second World War*, p. 2420.

696 "minority governments by force": Harriman and Abel, p. 426.

697 "deadly hiatus": Churchill, *Triumph and Tragedy*, p. 390. "We can now see the deadly hiatus which existed between the fading of President Roosevelt's strength and the growth of President Truman's grip of the vast world problem," he wrote. "In this melancholy void one President could not act and the other could not know."

698 "recognized by the customs and usages of war": EP, p. 2500.

698 Account of Bogomolov meeting is in Bradley, *A Soldier's Story*, pp. 503–4.

698 "Don't worry about it, Brad": *Ibid.*, p. 504.

699 "doldrums": Excerpts from Eisenhower, *Letters to Mamie*, pp. 240–41.

699 "Weeks was interested": KSD, February 20, 1945.

699 "relatively unimportant": Eisenhower letter to Marshall, quoted in full in EP, pp. 2490–92. Eisenhower's reference to the possibility of "a very worthwhile attack between Karlsruhe and the Ardennes" was a hint that he was considering plans to clear the Saar-Palatinate.

700 "will be required": BDP, p. 761.

700 "wanted the problem solved immediately": *Ibid.*, p. 762.

700 "the show as planned": FA, February 21, 1945.

701 "going-home offensive": *Newsweek*, March 5, 1945.

701 Butcher's description of Early visit: BDP, pp. 763–63.

701 "the stage of the war": *Newsweek*, March 5, 1945.

702 "appearance of fitness": BDP, p. 763.

702 "moderately satisfactory progress": FA, February 24, 1945.

702 "well satisfied with progress made": *Ibid.*

703 "established bridgeheads in the Mainz–Mannheim sector": Directive is dated 3-8-45. EP, p. 2511.

PAGE

704 "personally welcome": BDP, p. 765.

705 "that resistance is on the point of crumbling": FA, February 25, 1945.

705 The intercepts indicated that the Germans would "(a) make a strong attack in the Balkans . . . (b) hold fast in the east and if forced, fall away in the west" (KSD, February 27, 1945).

705 "I have seen press reports": Eisenhower's two-paragraph message is in EP, p. 2499.

706 Entire episode described in Eisenhower's letter to Mamie dated February 28, 1945. Eisenhower, *Letters to Mamie,* p. 242.

706 "intense interest": Bradley, *A General's Life,* p. 400. Weigley notes that Montgomery was endeavoring to restrain Ninth Army attempts to seize crossings at Düsseldorf, which confirmed a "firm conviction at Bradley's and Patton's Headquarters, that the British intended to hog credit for defeating Germany" (Weigley, *Eisenhower's Lieutenants,* p. 615).

707 "go nowhere": Bradley, *A General's Life,* p. 403. On no other point are Bradley's memoirs so inconsistent as they are on UNDERTONE. At times Bradley implies that he practically devised the operation and that crossing the Rhine along its length was his idea. At other times, he disparages the operation—and especially the prospect that Devers would command it. Likewise, *The Patton Papers* (ed. Blumenson) shows Patton skirting around Bradley and dealing directly with General Bull at SHAEF on XX Corps and Trier and reveals that Bradley was reluctant to endorse *any* Third Army maneuver not coordinated with the First Army— even privately.

707 "well under way": EP, pp. 2504–5.

708 "remarkable picture": KSD, March 2, 1945.

709 Montgomery's account is on p. 292 of his *Memoirs,* and his views evidently persuaded Brooke that it would be wise to drop the Alexander matter. See Bryant, p. 324.

711 "prime" Allied military objective: Churchill, *Triumph and Tragedy,* p. 391. "The decisive, practical points of strategy" related to this objective were: "*First,* that Soviet Russia had become a mortal danger to the free world. *Secondly,* that a new front must be immediately created against her onward sweep. *Thirdly,* that their front in Europe should be as far east as possible. *Fourthly,* that Berlin was the prime and true objective of the Anglo-American Armies."

713 "no more anxious": Eisenhower, *Crusade in Europe,* pp. 370–71. Exactly when the quoted exchange took place is unknown. Eisenhower's *Crusade* dates it much earlier, but *Crusade* was dictated

from memory, and Eisenhower's appointment log shows that Eisenhower had not seen Brooke since early January when Eisenhower, Churchill, and Brooke huddled at the Trianon to discuss De Gaulle, manpower, and strategy for clearing the Ardennes salient. Thus it seems likely that this exchange took place on March 5, and that it was the opening shot of a three-week debate in which the British labored to clarify Eisenhower's intentions regarding the 12th Army Group and to salvage Montgomery's priority.

714   "limited strategic vision": Bryant, p. 324.

714   "the most emphatic demonstration yet": Bradley, *A General's Life*, p. 399.

714   "never sit quietly by": Bradley's description of this luncheon is in *A Soldier's Story*, p. 509.

715   "We'd won the war": Alistair Cooke, in Nelson, ed., *General Eisenhower on the Military Churchill*, pp. 56–57.

715   "awe-inspiring accountability": Excerpted from Copeland and Lamm, *The World's Great Speeches* (New York: Dover Publications, 1973), p. 614. "There is a deep sympathy and good will in Britain—and I doubt not here also—toward the people of all the Russias and a resolve to persevere through many differences and rebuffs in establishing lasting friendships."

716   Bull wanted "the moon": Bradley, *A General's Life*, p. 405.

716   "with everything": *Ibid.*

716   "delighted" with the news: See Eisenhower, *Crusade in Europe*, p. 380.

717   "six months ago": Bradley, *A Soldier's Story*, p. 512.

717   "Eisenhower did not want the Remagen bridgehead expanded beyond the ability of five divisions to *defend* it" (Weigley, *Eisenhower's Lieutenants* p. 629).

718   Summary of Kesselring-Wolff talks is in Allen Dulles, *The Secret Surrender*, pp. 89–92.

718   "preliminary" . . . "not object": Harriman and Abel, *Special Envoy*, p. 432.

719   "draw enemy strength": Bryant, p. 327.

720   "defensive specialist": "Kesselring generally gets credit for the extraordinarily skillful defense the Nazis put up in Italy," wrote *Newsweek* on April 2, noting his appointment. "It would be logical if he were given the job of pulling the remainder of the Wehrmacht in the west back into mountainous southern Germany where conditions would approximate those in Italy."

720   "strange" resistance at Budapest: Churchill, *Triumph and Tragedy*, p. 392.

PAGE

720   "now been decided": KSD, March 10, 1945.

720   "massive push to Kassel and beyond": Bradley, *A General's Life*, pp. 403–4.

720   "light" resistance at Remagen: FA, March 8, 1945.

721   "political strategy": Bradley, *A General's Life*, p. 408.

721   "height of folly": Blumenson, *The Patton Papers*, p. 634.

722   "economical defensive lines": EP, pp. 2520–27.

722   "Visited Trier": Blumenson, *The Patton Papers*, p. 655.

723   "fluid": Stamps and Esposito, p. 574.

723   "should be more cocky": Blumenson, *The Patton Papers*, p. 657.

723   "hold" . . . "major effort": FA, March 15, 1945.

724   "deadlock": Harriman and Abel, p. 429.

725   "Look at you": Morgan, *Past Forgetting*, p. 217.

725   "somewhat human": *Ibid.*, p. 218.

727   "a heavy price": In an interview with the author, Bradley recalled that he rendered this assessment at Cannes and stuck by it long after the tactical conditions in the west made it obsolete. See also Lyon, *Eisenhower*, p. 354.

729   "OSS reports": Bradley, *A General's Life*, p. 418.

732   "hewed strictly to Roosevelt's political desires": Pogue, *Organizer of Victory*, p. 578.

733   "considered from the purely military viewpoint": Pogue, "The Decision to Halt at the Elbe," in Greenfield, ed., *Command Decisions*, p. 387.

733   "vigorously with the object": EP, p. 2537.

733   "scattered and ineffective resistance": Stamps and Esposito, p. 583

734   According to Winterbotham, "Montgomery's build-up of forces for the Rhine crossing rivalled the invasion of Normandy itself" (*The Ultra Secret*, p. 185).

734   "battles were fought": Churchill, *Triumph and Tragedy*, p. 357.

735   "very cheaply": EP, p. 2539.

735   "unjust and unfounded": Churchill, *Triumph and Tragedy*, p. 380.

735   "not see why we should break our hearts": *Ibid.*, p. 381.

735   "all very weak": Montgomery to Eisenhower, 28 March 1945, DDE, Box 75.

736   "Thank God": Eisenhower, *Crusade in Europe*, p. 372.

736   "To the best of my memory, I congratulated him heartily on his success and said that, as matters turned out, his policy was now the correct one: that with the German in his defeated condition, no dangers existed in a dispersal of effort. I am quite certain I never said to him 'you were completely right,' as I am still convinced that he was 'completely wrong' " (Bryant, pp. 332–33).

PAGE

736 The situation Eisenhower would face within ninety-six hours is summarized by Wilmot: "The western front was now wide open," he writes, "for the encirclement of Model's armies . . . created a 200-mile breach which Kesselring had no chance of closing. . . . Between Eisenhower and Berlin, there were no prepared defenses, no field armies, no physical barriers that could not be quickly broken, nor any resistance that could not be brusquely swept aside by the 60 divisions available for his next offensive" (Wilmot, p. 685).

738 Weigley criticizes Eisenhower's decision to deploy eighteen divisions in the Ruhr area, emphasizing the Ruhr was a battleground "long shunned in SHAEF planning." Weigley, *Eisenhower's Lieutenants,* p. 678.

738 Transcript of press conference is reprinted in BDP, pp. 779–90.

740 "make junction with the Soviet forces": From April 2 directive, EP, p. 2576.

740 "steps . . . initiated without delay": Marshall to Eisenhower, 27 March 1945, in DDE.

740 "that we coordinate our action": EP, p. 2551.

741 "amplifying" cable: *Ibid.,* pp. 2557–58.

741 "unintelligible": Bryant, p. 336. "To start with, he had no business to address Stalin direct," Brooke wrote; ". . . secondly, he produced a telegram that was unintelligible, and . . . what was implied in it appeared to be entirely adrift and a change from all that had been previously agreed upon."

741 The BCOS motion is quoted by Marshall in a message to Eisenhower in DDE. The BCOS urged a main thrust across the open plains of northwest Germany with the object of capturing Berlin, "which would also '(A) . . . open German ports . . . , (B) . . . annul the U-boat war, (C) . . . move into Denmark, to open a line of communication with Sweden.' "

742 "This [Berlin] is a point": Pogue, *Organizer of Victory,* p. 556. Likewise, Brooke noted that the Prime Minister deplored the abandonment of Berlin "as yet another sacrifice, on the altar of American military prestige, of sound strategy and Britain's war aims. These included the early liberation of Holland, the occupation of the North German naval ports and the freeing of Denmark." The BCOS and Churchill subsided when Eisenhower assured them that "there is no very great change, except for the fact that he directs his main axis of advance on Leipzig instead of Berlin" (Bryant, pp. 338–39).

743 "largely destroyed": EP, p. 2568.

743   "already apparent": Churchill to Eisenhower, 31 March 1945. Churchill, *Triumph and Tragedy,* p. 397.

743   "instructions to deal directly with the Russians": EP, p. 2560.

743   Summary of talk is in message from Deane to Eisenhower on 3-31-45. BSP, Collection of World War II Documents.

744–45   Stalin's reply is summarized in Tedder, *With Prejudice,* p. 680.

746   "approval": An irony was apparent to Brooke, who chronicled the tense BCOS meetings in London at which Tedder was called on to explain Eisenhower's abrupt action. "I was astonished to find Ike found it necessary to call on Stalin in order to control Monty," he wrote. "Surely Stalin's help need not be called in such a transfer!" (Bryant, p. 340).

746   "Amantium irae amoris integratio est": Translated: Lover's quarrels are a part of love. Churchill to Roosevelt, April 5, quoted in Churchill, *Triumph and Tragedy,* p. 401.

746   "discouraging lack of progress": Kimball, *Churchill and Roosevelt,* vol. III, p. 595.

747   "something broader than German forces in northern Italy": Copy in BD, March 27, 1945, "Gamble to Cornfield."

748   "ceased . . . war": Churchill, *Triumph and Tragedy,* pp. 383–84.

748   "faced with inevitable surrender": *Ibid.,* p. 387.

749   "because these problems": Burns, *Soldier of Freedom,* p. 596.

749   "stubborn resistance": SHAEF Weekly Intelligence Summary No. 55. "In the west, the situation has never been so grave," the report noted. "Either he [the German] is completely misappreciating our strength and refusing to believe the Allies are capable of stalking into and beyond the center of Germany, or, he prefers to let the Western Allies into Germany."

749   "minor incidents of air contact": Warning to CCS on April 5 in EP, p. 2581.

750   "terrible mistake": Bryant, p. 340.

750   "it mattered comparatively little" Bryant, p. 341.

751   "lacking substance": Pogue, *Organizer of Victory,* p. 557.

751   "the Supreme Commander": *Ibid.,* p. 569. The SHAEF JIC had reached a similar conclusion and so, as Weigley notes, "Allied intelligence opinion was shifting away from fear of the Redoubt at the very time Eisenhower and Bradley were making their crucial decisions affecting Berlin" (Weigley, *Eisenhower's Lieutenants* p. 703). Likewise, the JCS in endorsing Eisenhower's plans on the thirty-first had noted that nothing, presumably including Berlin, seemed foreclosed by Eisenhower's message. The U.S. Chiefs were "confident that SHAEF's course of action will secure

the ports and everything else mentioned by the British more quickly and more decisively than the course of action urged by them" (Marshall to Eisenhower, 3-31-45, DDE).

751 "useless or unnecessary damage": EP, p. 2589.

751 "two schools of thought": Quoted in EP, p. 2589.

751 "could dispose of them as they see fit": *Ibid.*

752 "in the event our forces should meet": *Ibid.*, p. 2590.

752 "diminished importance": *Ibid.*, p. 2592.

753 Interview with J.S.D. Eisenhower.

753 "absorbed in his favorite pastime": J.S.D. Eisenhower, *Strictly Personal*, p. 84.

754 "I am advancing 15 miles a day": *Ibid.*

754 "the greatest armored joyride in history": Hal Boyle, AP, March 27, 1945, quoted in Snyder, *Masterpieces of War Reporting*, p. 414.

754 "And after the city's rubble had settled": Bradley, *A Soldier's Story*, p. 530.

754 "in profusion": J.S.D. Eisenhower, *Strictly Personal*, p. 85.

755 "You complain about lack of news from John": Eisenhower, *Letters to Mamie*, p. 246.

756 "[authorization to negotiate] directly": Bradley, *A Soldier's Story*, p. 544.

756 "sure wished he had more in the center": Personal interview with J.S.D. Eisenhower.

757 "the feeling that Montgomery": Bradley, *A General's Life*, p. 427.

757 "even if the Americans do not agree": Crozier, p. 352.

759 "unanticipated need": EP, p. 2617.

759 "useless" and "too late": Montgomery, *Memoirs*, p. 296. Montgomery later wrote that he believed the postwar balances in Europe would depend on "possession of certain political centers in Europe"—Berlin, Prague and Vienna. While he attributed the Allied failure to take Prague to last-minute decisions, Montgomery blamed the Russian seizure of Berlin on the Allied failure "to make a sound operational plan in August 1944 after the victory in Normandy." Thus, Montgomery neglected to explain why the Allies passed up their second opportunity to take Berlin, which arose despite the decisions of August 1944.

760 "active consideration": Bradley, *A General's Life*, p. 432.

760 "excuses for lack of any ideas": Blumenson, *The Patton Papers*, pp. 685–88.

761 "the most gigantic life-saving enterprise": Murphy, *Diplomat Among Warriors*, p. 283.

761 On the overwhelming problem of DPs: Blumenson, *The Patton Papers,* p. 682.

762 "death had become so fouled by degradation": Bradley, *A Soldier's Story,* p. 539.

762 Description of Ohrdruf is based on Blumenson, *The Patton Papers,* pp. 683–84.

763 "Still having trouble hating them?": Quoted by Robert Abzug in *Inside the Vicious Heart: Americans and the Liberation of Nazi Concentration Camps.*

763 "struck a lucky medallion": Bradley, *A Soldier's Story,* p. 541.

764 "Mickey, you are a civilian": Personal interview with author.

765 "The only speck of optimism": J.S.D. Eisenhower, *Strictly Personal,* pp. 86–87.

766 "even if the trial": Davidson, *The Trial of the Germans,* p. 36.

766 "miss an inch of the scene": Episode recounted in J.S.D. Eisenhower, *Strictly Personal,* p. 89.

766 *Pravda.* Quoted in *Time* magazine, April 30, 1945.

767 On Eisenhower's concern about effective link-up procedure: As Smith put it, "What we feared most was an encounter between armored divisions [American and Russian] and that, through lack of recognition, a fire fight might take place that would have the most serious implications" (Smith, *Eisenhower's Six Great Decisions,* p. 226).

767 "may well call for acts of endurance": EP, p. 2605.

767 "But let's hope the other fellow": Bradley, *A Soldier's Story,* p. 539.

768 "positive" . . . "if allowed": General William Simpson, Oral History (OH-314), p. 123, in Eisenhower Library.

768 "defeat of the Germans in the shortest possible time": EP, p. 2609.

768 "You must stop on the Elbe": Simpson, Oral History, p. 118.

769 "grave misunderstandings": EP, p. 2613.

769 "in order that we may devote our full energy": Follow-up message, EP, p. 2614.

769 "vastly more important": *Ibid.,* p. 2615.

770 "that such cruelty": Eisenhower, *Letters to Mamie,* p. 248.

773 "impossible operating and maintenance problems": Phrase used by Eisenhower in a cable to Marshall explaining the proposed changes n the French zone. EP, p. 2624.

774 "tear the world to pieces": Churchill, *Triumph and Tragedy,* p. 423.

775 "As the saying goes": Speech to the House of Commons, reprinted in *Triumph and Tragedy,* p. 409.

PAGE

775 "veteran quality": BDP, p. 803.

776 "I think I've talked enough" and "homey as neighbors": *Ibid.*, pp. 804–5.

776 "until such time": Crozier, p. 353.

776 "unwilling . . . to reduce the effectiveness": EP, p. 2657.

778 "sportsmanship" and "dexterity": Churchill to Eden, May 5, 1945, in Churchill, *Triumph and Tragedy*, p. 461.

778 "The Russians have 2½ million troops": Churchill to Eden, April 19, *ibid.*, p. 440.

778 "fitting prelude": EP, p. 2629.

779 "approaching the completion": *Ibid.*, p. 2632.

780 "filled with foreboding": Harriman and Abel, p. 446. Right away, Harriman noted the changed mood in Washington, the "growing strain of irritated feelings between our government and the Russians" and the "importance of firm dealing" (Pogue, *Organizer of Victory*, p. 561).

780 "new barbarian invasion of Europe": Harriman and Abel, pp. 448–49. Harriman's advice was to wield the leverage the United States had to prevent the Soviets from extending their control of bordering areas to "the next layer of adjacent countries" in Europe—presumably, Germany, Austria, and Yugoslavia. Harriman and Dean were by now advocating only a "quid pro quid" approach to the Soviets.

781 "complete deadlock": *Ibid.*, p. 451.

781 Pearson episode is recounted by Sherwood, p. 884.

781–82 "Accounts of Cabinet meetings and subsequent Truman meetings with Molotov are in Harriman and Abel, pp. 452–53.

782 Stalin-Churchill exchanges are quoted in Churchill, *Triumph and Tragedy*, pp. 421–22.

782 "call a spade a spade": Ernest Lindley, "How Good Is Russia's Word?," *Newsweek*, April 30, 1945.

783 "democratic watchwords": *Newsweek*, May 7, 1945.

784 "badly embarrassed": EP, p. 2641.

784 "at once": EP, pp. 2638–39.

784 "blot on [German] military honor": *Ibid.*, p. 2639.

785 "remarkable political advantages": BCOS message quoted in Marshall message to Eisenhower dated 28 April, in DDE.

786 "it is difficult": EP, p. 2653.

786 "done everything that is humanly possible": *Ibid.*, pp. 2650–51.

786 Minutes in DDE, Smith Correspondence (2).

10　Conclusion

788　As for the effect of Hitler's death, see Jodl interrogation dated August 2, 1945:

Q. After the collapse of the Ruhr ports, what . . . discussions did you have . . . regarding an overall surrender?
A. None . . .
Q. Did any individual speak of it?
A. Not so far as I know.
Q. When was surrender first suggested?
A. After Hitler's death, when Dönitz was in responsibility.

790　"cooperative action": EP, p. 2664.

791　"Sie saluten comme ça": Episode recounted in J.S.D. Eisenhower, *Strictly Personal,* p. 88.

791　"Who are these men?": Episode recounted in Montgomery, *Memoirs,* pp. 300–1.

792　"invited special attention": John Keegan, "The Surrender," in Liddell Hart, ed., *History of the Second World War,* pp. 2420–21.

792　"no monster": *Ibid.,* p. 2421.

792　"speak his mind freely": BDP, p. 820.

793　"to give our Congressmen": *Ibid.*

793　Counsel episode recounted in Cornelius Ryan, "May 7, 1945: The 'Wrong' Peace Papers," *Des Moines Register,* May 7, 1972.

793　"not interested in insurance forms": *Ibid.,* p. 28.

794　"deeply disturbed": *Ibid.*

794　"that all remaining enemy forces": EP, p. 2684.

796　"How far do you intend to go": Bradley, *A Soldier's Story,* p. 551.

796　"simultaneous surrender": Text quoted in message Eisenhower sent CCS on May 5. EP, p. 2687.

796　"The halt line is mandatory": Blumenson, *The Patton Papers,* p. 696.

797　"with the normal dictates of humanity": BDP, p. 826.

797　"at once": Keegan, in Liddell Hart, ed., *History of the Second World War,* p. 2422.

798　"be left an inheritance of World War III": BDP, p. 827.

798　"Hollywood setting": *Ibid.,* p. 828.

798　Russian absence described in Strong's *Intelligence at the Top,* p. 276.

798　Butcher's appeal to Eisenhower at lunch: BDP, p. 830.

PAGE

799 "endless work": Bryant, p. 346.

799 "all-powerful God": *Ibid.*, p. 347.

800 "In the squalor of war": From the unpublished diary of Richard Nixon, June 1954, description of a state dinner at the White House.

800 "great history for the good of mankind": Full text of message is in Pogue, *Organizer of Victory*, p. 583.

800 "The enemy's armed forces are disintegrating": Eisenhower, *Letters to Mamie*, p. 250.

800-1 In his account, Strong noted that Smith's appeal to German military honor probably struck Friedeburg as unmeant, for he had found Smith to be a "tough and uncompromising negotiator." Nonetheless, after a short recess in the talks, Jodl and von Friedeburg returned with a draft telegram for Dönitz in Jodl's hand "recommending capitulation" (Strong, *Intelligence at the Top*, pp. 278-79). Smith agreed (Smith, *Eisenhower's Six Great Decisions*, p. 206).

801 "no alternative other than chaos or signature": "Open Radio Gram," in BSP, Collection of World War II Documents.

802 "officially and personally responsible": Eisenhower, *Crusade in Europe*, p. 426.

803 "calling upon the German troops": EP, vol. VI, p. 4.

803 See Smith, *My Three Years in Moscow*, p. 22.

803 "enemy propaganda": Colonel Pavel Matronov, "The Last Act," in Liddell Hart, ed., *History of the Second World War*, p. 2429.

803 "very skillful": EP, vol. VI, p. 12.

804 Flensburg dispatch is quoted in EP, vol. VI, p. 23.

805 "diversionary tactics": Stalin, interview in *New York Times,* May 19, 1945.

806 "aggressive and contemptuous conduct": EP, vol. VI, p. 57.

806 "The aggressive attitude": *Ibid.*, p. 66.

806 "digging in": Bradley, *A Soldier's Story*, p. 550.

807 See John Erickson, *The Road to Berlin*, pp. 528-29.

810 Estimates of DPs, Berghahn, *Modern Germany*, p. 179.

810 Figures on Ford supplies are quoted in EP, vol. VI, p. 53.

811 Strong, commenting on the farewells after the breakup of SHAEF, noted that while the Americans were "generally optimistic" about the future, "few of the British, on the other hand, could see any reason to suggest the friendliness and comradeship of war were likely to continue in the years of peace" (Strong, *Intelligence at the Top*, p. 296).

811 "ceremonial program": From message Eisenhower sent to Churchill two days later confirming arrangements. EP, vol. VI, p. 69.

PAGE

811 "The European war is over": BDP, p. 853.

811 "finishing the job": Lyon, *Eisenhower,* p. 18.

812 "I hope that fellow never decides to run against me": BDP, p. 854. See also Eisenhower, *Crusade in Europe,* pp. 420–21.

812 Personal interview with Kevin McCann, former Eisenhower administration speech writer and president of Defiance College. Reference to "Dragfoot" appears in the privately published diaries of Ellis Slater in an entry about the time of Eisenhower's preparations for the 1955 Geneva conference. (See Slater, "The Ike I knew," a copy of which is available at the Eisenhower Library.) "Dragfoot" evidently referred to the limited measures Eisenhower and Clay implemented to slow up the flow of reparations from western zones to Russia in late 1945, when "everyone consulted conceded modifications [of Allied policy] were in order, but discussions . . . ran on and on" (Murphy, *Diplomat Among Warriers,* p. 320).

813 "an economic barrier": *Newsweek,* May 14, 1945.

813 "a happy and definite effect": BDP, p. 855.

813 "old-fashioned bull session": *Ibid.*

814 "I'm not too keen about staying here": BDP, p. 852.

814 "terrified" of addressing a formal body: EP, vol. VI, p. 157.

815 "prepare carefully for it": Eisenhower, *At Ease,* p. 298.

816 "your remarks are adequate": *Ibid.,* p. 299.

817 "that the de facto occupation": Instructions are summarized in Montgomery, *Memoirs,* p. 338.

817 "acquainted first hand": *Ibid.,* p. 339.

817 "scant patience with political men": Eisenhower, *At Ease,* p. 310. Murphy recalled Eisenhower's talk at this time of instituting a program of high-level military exchanges. Eisenhower's idea was "to give them [the Russians] a chance to get acquainted with our people and see how we run things . . . [and] none of your State Department quid pro quos! What I have in mind is a straightforward unconditional invitation." According to Murphy and Harriman, what Eisenhower did not appear to appreciate was the dominant position of the Soviet Communist party over the military and the fact that "Stalin was always thinking of how Napoleon had run away with the French Revolution" (Murphy, p. 292).

818 "negotiating agency only": EP, vol. VI, pp. 135–36.

818 "stab the Red Army in the back": Account of visit with Stalin in Sherwood, *Roosevelt and Hopkins,* pp. 893–95. Talks with Eisenhower in Frankfurt are on pp. 912–15.

818 "unable to delay": Quoted in Harriman and Abel, *Special Envoy,* p. 478.

819 "the strain of the past three years": EP, vol. VI, p. 134.

PAGE

819 "with everyone about to go their own way": DDE, Box 75.

819 "Your own high place": EP, vol. VI, pp. 148–49.

819 About this meeting, Eisenhower in 1948 wrote that "looking back
     on it, that day seems to have held nothing but bright promise for
     the establishment of cordial and close relations with the Russians.
     That promise, eventually lost in suspicion and recrimination, was
     never fulfilled" (*Crusade in Europe,* p. 438).

820 "the people might live a little better": BDP, p. 862.

820 "a look": Personal interview with John S.D. Eisenhower.

820 "If I were not so sure I was among friends": BDP, p. 863.

821 "the mightiest decision of the war": *Ibid.,* p. 864.

822 "Whether you know it or not": Eisenhower, *At Ease,* p. 300.

Index

About the Author

DAVID EISENHOWER is the grandson of Dwight Eisenhower and a son-in-law of former President Richard Nixon. He is a graduate of Amherst College and the George Washington University School of Law. Between 1970 and 1973, he served in the Navy as an officer aboard the U.S.S. *Albany,* a tour of duty that enabled him to visit some of the places covered in this book and rekindled his boyhood interest in military affairs. Since late 1976 he has been at work on a three-volume history of the Eisenhower years, of which *Eisenhower: At War 1943–1945* is the first. For the past three years he has been a lecturer in political science at the University of Pennsylvania. Mr. Eisenhower and his wife, Julie, and their three children make their home near Valley Forge, Pennsylvania.